Getting Started is as EASY as 1, 2, 3 . . . 4!

1. Sign Up

Instructors register with myBusinessCourse.com

2. Setup Your Course

Add your class details and additional materials.

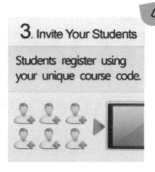

3. Invite Your Students

Students register using your unique course code.

4. Manage Your Course

Study, test, and grade assignments. It's simple!

Provide Instruction and Practice 24/7

◆ Assign homework from your Cambridge Business Publishers textbook and have myBusinessCourse grade it for you automatically.

◆ With our eLectures, your students can revisit accounting topics as often as they like or until they master the topic.

◆ Guided Examples show students how to solve select problems.

◆ Make homework due before class to ensure students enter your classroom prepared.

◆ Additional practice and exam preparation materials are available to help students achieve better grades and content mastery.

STUDENT SELF-STUDY OPTION

Not all instructors choose to incorporate **myBusinessCourse** into their course. In such cases, students can access the Self-Study option for MBC. The Self-Study option provides most of the learning tools available in the Instructor-Led courses, including:

◆ eLectures
◆ Guided Examples
◆ Practice Quizzes

The Self-Study option does not include homework assignments from the textbook. Only the Instructor-Led option includes homework assignments.

Want to learn more about myBusinessCourse?

Contact your sales representative or visit **www.mybusinesscourse.com**.

STUDENTS: Find your access code on the myBusinessCourse insert on the following pages. If you have a used copy of this textbook, you can purchase access online at **www.mybusinesscourse.com**.

my BusinessCourse

FREE WITH NEW COPIES OF THIS TEXTBOOK*

Start using myBusinessCourse Today: www.mybusinesscourse.com

myBusinessCourse is a web-based learning and assessment program intended to complement your textbook and faculty instruction.

Student Benefits

- **eLectures**: These videos review the key concepts of each Learning Objective in each chapter.
- **Guided examples**: These videos provide step-by-step solutions for select problems in each chapter.
- **Auto-graded assignments**: Provide students with immediate feedback on select assignments. **(with Instructor-Led course ONLY)**.
- **Quiz and Exam preparation**: myBusinessCourse provides students with additional practice and exam preparation materials to help students achieve better grades and content mastery.

You can access myBusinessCourse 24/7 from any web-enabled device, including iPads, smartphones, laptops, and tablets.

Interactive content that runs on any device.

Built for PCs, iPads, Laptops, Tablets, Smartphones

To my wife Ellie and our children, Grace and Christian
   —RFH

To Leslie and our children, Brian, Lisa, Maggie, and Will
   —PEH

Photo Credits
Chapter 1: © iStock Photo
Chapter 2: © iStock Photo
Chapter 3: © iStock Photo
Chapter 4: © iStock Photo
Chapter 5: © iStock Photo
Chapter 6: © iStock Photo
Chapter 7: © iStock Photo
Chapter 8: © iStock Photo
Chapter 9: © iStock Photo
Chapter 10: © iStock Photo
Chapter 11: © iStock Photo
Chapter 12: © iStock Photo
Chapter 13: © iStock Photo

ADVANCED ACCOUNTING, Third Edition, by Robert F. Halsey and Patrick E. Hopkins

COPYRIGHT © 2017 by Cambridge Business Publishers, LLC. Published by Cambridge Business Publishers, LLC. Exclusive rights by Cambridge Business Publishers, LLC for manufacture and export.

Student Edition ISBN: 978-1-61853-190-2

Bookstores & Faculty: to order this book, contact the company via email customerservice@cambridgepub.com or call 800-619-6473.

Students: to order this book, please visit the book's Website and order directly online.

Printed in the United States of America.
10 9 8 7 6 5 4 3

THIRD EDITION

Advanced Accounting

ROBERT F. HALSEY
Babson College

PATRICK E. HOPKINS
Kelley School of Business
Indiana University

Cambridge
BUSINESS PUBLISHERS

About the Authors

ROBERT F. HALSEY Robert F. Halsey is a professor at Babson College and has also served as Chair of the Division of Accounting & Law and the Associate Dean and Interim Dean of the undergraduate school. He received his MBA and PhD from the University of Wisconsin. Prior to obtaining his PhD he worked as the chief financial officer (CFO) of a privately held retailing and manufacturing company and as the vice president and manager of the commercial lending division of a large bank.

Professor Halsey teaches courses in financial and managerial accounting at both the graduate and undergraduate levels, including a popular course in financial statement analysis for second year MBA students. He has also taught numerous executive education courses for large multinational companies through Babson's school of Executive Education, as well as for a number of stock brokerage firms in the Boston area. He is regarded as an innovative teacher and has been recognized for outstanding teaching at both the University of Wisconsin and Babson College, where he earned Professor of the Year honors.

Professor Halsey co-authors *Financial Accounting for MBAs* and *Financial Statement Analysis & Valuation*, both published by Cambridge Business Publishers, as well as a forthcoming text in *Introductory Financial Accounting*. Professor Halsey's research interests are in the area of financial reporting, including firm valuation, financial statement analysis, and disclosure issues. He has publications in *Advances in Quantitative Analysis of Finance and Accounting, The Journal of the American Taxation Association, Issues in Accounting Education, The Portable MBA in Finance and Accounting*, the *CPA Journal, AICPA Professor/Practitioner Case Development Program*, and in other accounting and analysis journals.

PATRICK E. HOPKINS Patrick E. Hopkins, is the SungKyunKwan Professor and Chair of Accounting Graduate Programs at Indiana University's Kelley School of Business. Professor Hopkins received his B.S. and M.Acc. from the University of Florida and his Ph.D. from the University of Texas at Austin. Prior to entering the accounting doctoral program, Professor Hopkins served as a senior consultant with the Emerging Business Services practice of Deloitte, Haskins and Sells in Miami, Florida. Professor Hopkins has been at IU since 1995, where he teaches undergraduate and graduate courses on financial reporting for mergers, acquisitions and changes in corporate structure. He also served as a Visiting Professor at Stanford University's Graduate School of Business, where he taught courses on global financial reporting and on accounting for mergers, acquisitions and changes in corporate structure. During his career, Professor Hopkins won each of the top teaching awards in the Kelley School of Business, including the Trustees Teaching Award, the Schuyler F. Otteson Award, and the Sauvain Award. He also teaches in international and online executive MBA programs at Indiana University, and in the doctoral program at HHL University in Leipzig, Germany. Professor Hopkins is also a widely respected research scholar in the area of financial reporting, and investor and analyst judgment and decision making. His work has appeared in top accounting journals, including *The Accounting Review*, the *Journal of Accounting Research, Contemporary Accounting Research*, and *Accounting Organizations and Society*, and has been discussed in business press publications, including *Barron's, CFO*, and *The Deal*. He is the past winner of the American Accounting Association's Distinguished Contributions to Accounting Literature Award, the American Accounting Association's Financial Accounting and Reporting Section Best Research Paper Award, the Indiana University Outstanding Junior Faculty Award, and Kelley School of Business Outstanding Research Award. Professor Hopkins also served on the Financial Accounting Standards Advisory Council.

Preface

Welcome to the Third Edition of *Advanced Accounting*. Our goal in writing this book was to satisfy the needs of today's accounting students by providing the most contemporary, relevant, engaging, and student-oriented textbook available. We think that we have accomplished that objective by maintaining a conceptually rigorous discussion of the material in an intuitive and student-friendly style. Prior to writing this book, we both taught advanced financial accounting for many years, and we both felt that the structure and format of available textbooks contributed to the difficulties that our students have had in learning the material. Several examples come to mind:

1. **Too many issues discussed simultaneously.** Taken individually, consolidation issues can be difficult for students to grasp. The learning process is made all the more difficult when a particular topic (intercompany sales of assets, for example) is presented using alternative methods of pre-consolidation equity investment bookkeeping (e.g., equity, partial equity, and cost). Our experience—and the experience of many of our focus group participants—indicates that students are generally confused by the mixing of bookkeeping approaches in the main-chapter discussion of most textbooks. To address this issue, we present only two pre-consolidation bookkeeping approaches: equity method and cost method. In each consolidations-related chapter, we begin the consolidations-related discussion with the equity method because it provides the clearest and easiest-to-understand linkage between the parent's pre-consolidation financial statements and the consolidated financial statements. We then use a page-edge border to very clearly mark the pages in which we discuss cost-method consolidations procedures. By clearly distinguishing between the two approaches, we make it much easier for instructors and students to know exactly which approach we are covering. In addition, this makes tailoring the material much easier. For example, if an instructor wishes to only cover the equity method of pre-consolidation bookkeeping, the easy-to-follow chapter set-up makes this possible.

2. **Mechanics versus intuition.** After completing our courses and entering the working world, our former students have encountered many different consolidation approaches used by their employers and clients. Given the diversity of processes and procedures in practice, we adjusted our own teaching styles to emphasize an intuitive understanding of the concepts over the rote memorization of static journal-entry approaches. Unfortunately, the available textbooks were mostly written with a mechanical perspective. In writing this text, we incorporated our teaching-based observations. In each chapter, we initially focus on conceptual explanations and discuss mechanics only after we convey an intuitive perspective on each topic. In addition, to help students immediately identify each of the various consolidation entries, we consistently color-code the **C-E-A-D-I** consolidation entries throughout the chapter discussion, the consolidation-entry listings, and in the consolidation worksheets.

3. **Connection between fund-based statements and government-wide statements.** Most texts combine, in a single chapter, fund-based accounting and government-wide financial statements, and do not demonstrate how government-wide statements are generated from fund-based accounting. We address this issue by covering these topics in two separate chapters, and we focus on the adjustments necessary to create government-wide financial statements described in the reconciliations from fund statements to government-wide statements. We present this material within the context of an actual New England town. The town is large enough to demonstrate the accounting concepts, yet small enough to avoid obscuring the learning process with unnecessary complexity.

4. **Not written for students.** Many texts are written using overly technical language. Our text, while rigorous, is written in a student-friendly, conversational style that makes the material much easier for students to comprehend and apply.

This book is the product of extensive market research including focus groups, market surveys, class tests, manuscript reviews, and interviews with faculty from across the country. We are grateful for the feedback from faculty who reviewed, and students who studied, previous editions of our text.

TARGET AUDIENCE

Advanced Accounting is intended for use in undergraduate and graduate accounting programs that include a course in advanced accounting as part of the curriculum. This book is especially written for advanced accounting courses in which an intuitive understanding of the material, in addition to accounting mechanics, is emphasized. Feedback from students who used our text, and subsequently completed the Uniform CPA exam, has been extremely positive. They report that they felt well-prepared for the portions of the exam relating to advanced financial accounting topics.

> *"The examples in this textbook reinforced well the theoretical concepts discussed in the chapters. The understanding I gained after using this textbook helped prepare me well for some of the toughest material in the CPA Exam."*

> **Jon Slebodnick — Audit Associate, Deloitte**

EMPHASIS ON INTUITION

We introduce topics by discussing the intuition behind accounting standards before discussing the mechanics of the accounting process. In addition, we intentionally deemphasize memorization of journal entry mechanics. We believe that this approach allows students to better understand the material and to develop relevant transferrable knowledge.

> *"The advanced accounting textbook provided a clear and concise presentation of not only how certain accounting concepts are applied, but also why they are important and pertain to us directly."*

> **Dan Brown — Audit Associate, PriceWaterhouseCoopers**

EASY-TO-REMEMBER MNEMONIC

Although our text emphasizes the intuition underlying the consolidation process, we also introduce the **C-E-A-D-I** (pronounced "Seedy") consolidation journal entry sequence to assist students in learning the mechanics of consolidation. The sequence systematically eliminates the book value of subsidiary equity (**C, E**), establishes the fair value adjustments for subsidiary net assets (**A, D**), and eliminates intercompany transactions and balances (**I**). Over the years, we've observed that this easy-to-remember mnemonic improves students' understanding of consolidations and allows for easier recall of each step of the consolidation adjustment process.

FASB CODIFICATION THROUGHOUT

We wrote our text after implementation of the FASB's (and GASB's) Codification and we integrated the Codification throughout, including end-of-chapter problem assignments. Unlike many advanced accounting textbooks, we cite passages of the Codification frequently so that students can become familiar with the actual language of the standards, not just the authors' summary of the standards. This also allows students to easily find the relevant passages on their own. In addition, to familiarize students with the Codification search engine and to better develop their research skills, we also include numerous Codification-related research assignments in our end-of-chapter problem sets.

FASB ASC Research

CPA EXAM QUESTIONS

The primary purpose of the Advanced Accounting course at most universities it to prepare accounting majors for the CPA exam. To provide students with relevant practice, we have included a number of multiple choice questions in each chapter that have been adapted from past CPA exams. We are grateful to the AICPA for granting us permission to use former CPA exam questions for this purpose.

IFRS COVERAGE

Accounting students must become familiar with IFRS. Fortunately, the current accounting standards relating to the main topic of the book—business combinations and consolidation—were written jointly by the FASB and the IASB, and are 99% equivalent. In addition, other standards (e.g., segment reporting) are similar, but have key differences. In the text, we discuss the IFRS equivalent of accounting standards and highlight the differences between the two sets of accounting standards when they occur. These discussions are identified with the IFRS icon.

RELEVANCE AND ENGAGEMENT

Advanced accounting is a challenging topic. We have adopted a number of techniques in our book to make the material relevant and engaging to students. These techniques include:

Focus Companies for Each Chapter

Each chapter incorporates a "focus company" for special emphasis and demonstration. We chose companies that illustrate the topic of the chapter so that students can learn the material within context. In addition, our chapters on governmental accounting are written around a small New England town that is large enough to effectively communicate the concepts of governmental accounting, yet small enough not to obscure those concepts in unnecessary complexity.

The following are the focus companies we use to introduce our topics:

- Consolidation chapters—**AT&T, Coca-Cola, Cummins, Krispy Kreme, Alcoa, Walt Disney**
- Foreign currency, derivatives and consolidation of foreign subsidiaries—**Coca-Cola**
- Government and NFP—**Town of Acton, MA** and the **American Red Cross**
- Segments—**3M Company**
- Partnerships—**Boardwalk Pipeline Partners, LLP**

Real Company Data in Text and Assignments

We believe that an important part of the learning process involves the application of concepts to real-world data. We include references to actual footnotes in the body of our text and also include a number of end-of-chapter problems that are written around actual footnote disclosures. These problems allow students to think about accounting concepts more broadly (i.e., less mechanically) and from the perspective of the users of financial statements.

> *"This book was very engaging and simple to follow, which made for a more enjoyable class! The examples and exhibits do a great job supporting the text to better retain the information."*

Moises Numa— Audit Associate, Deloitte

The following is a typical example:

---

37. Acquisition accounting   LO4

On July 1, 2014, Actavis plc acquired 100 percent of the common stock of Forest Laboratories, Inc. for cash and stock consideration totaling $27,661.1 million. The following excerpt is from Actavis' December 31, 2014 SEC Form 10-K.

ACTAVIS PLC
FOREST
LABORATORIES, INC.

The following table summarizes the preliminary fair values of the assets acquired and liabilities assumed at the acquisition date (in millions):

	Preliminary Amounts as of September 30, 2014	Measurement Period Adjustments	Preliminary Amounts as of December 31, 2014
Cash and cash equivalents	$ 3,424.2	$ —	$ 3,424.2
Accounts receivable.	496.2	—	496.2
Inventories	1,455.8	—	1,455.8
Other current assets.	233.3	27.9	261.2
Current assets held for sale	87.1	—	87.1
Property, plant and equipment, net . . .	221.1	—	221.1
Other long-term assets	84.1	—	84.1
IPR&D intangible assets.	1,363.0	(1.0)	1,362.0
Intangible assets	11,405.5	110.0	11,515.5
Goodwill	16,706.1	(320.8)	16,385.3
Current liabilities.	(1,346.0)	23.9	(1,322.1)
Deferred tax liabilities, net	(2,449.7)	146.8	(2,302.9)
Other taxes payable	(661.5)	37.0	(624.5)
Other long-term liabilities	(96.2)	(23.8)	(120.0)
Outstanding indebtedness	(3,261.9)	—	(3,261.9)
	$27,661.1	$ 0.0	$27,661.1

a. Explain the meaning of the amounts relating to the acquired asset accounts.
b. Actavis assigns $1,363.0 million of fair value to an account called "IPR&D intangible assets." To what does this account relate? Briefly describe what will happen to this account in the years after the acquisition.
c. Briefly describe the manner in which the amount of $16,706.1 million relating to the Goodwill asset is determined.

Practice Insight Boxes

We provide a number of Practice Insight Boxes resulting from interviews with practicing accountants and financial managers. These boxes provide students with insight into issues that accountants face in the real world, and with a glimpse into the types of decisions that practicing accountants must make.

The following is a typical example:

PRACTICE INSIGHT

Impairment of Goodwill   Textbook examples of impairment testing for Goodwill usually provide information relating to the value of the subsidiary together with the fair value of its tangible and identifiable intangible assets and the fair value of its liabilities. In the real world, these values are difficult to estimate, especially for knowledge-based companies.

In the software industry, for example, technology has a relatively short life span and employees frequently move from company to company. It doesn't take long, therefore, for the technology and employees of an acquired software company to disappear. The acquired Goodwill, however, typically remains on the balance sheet long after the other acquired assets have disappeared.

Valuing the remaining Goodwill can be a messy process. Mr. Dana Russell, CFO of Novell, Inc., sheds some light on the practical aspects of the Goodwill impairment issue with the following description:

> As companies are acquired, the Goodwill is allocated to the segments of the acquiring company to which it pertains. The Goodwill loses its identity, so to speak. The cash flow analysis in future periods pertains to all of the products in that segment. That analysis is used to determine whether you have impairment. The impairment, if any, applies to all of the products in that segment, not necessarily to the particular Goodwill asset purchased in a single acquisition. For example, one of our segments is very profitable and its forecasted cash flows do not lead to an impairment conclusion. But, if you look at the specific Goodwill asset for a single acquisition, the specific products that were originally associated with that Goodwill might no longer exist, resulting in an impairment conclusion for that particular portion of the Goodwill asset. The Goodwill impairment test is just not that granular.

Mid-Chapter and Chapter-End Reviews

Advanced accounting concepts can be challenging. To reinforce concepts presented in each chapter and to ensure student comprehension, we include topic reviews that require students to recall and apply the financial accounting techniques and concepts described in each chapter.

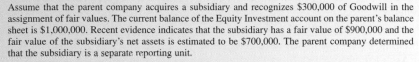

TOPIC REVIEW 4

Goodwill Impairment Test

Assume that the parent company acquires a subsidiary and recognizes $300,000 of Goodwill in the assignment of fair values. The current balance of the Equity Investment account on the parent's balance sheet is $1,000,000. Recent evidence indicates that the subsidiary has a fair value of $900,000 and the fair value of the subsidiary's net assets is estimated to be $700,000. The parent company determined that the subsidiary is a separate reporting unit.

Required

Assume that the company decided to forego the option to perform a qualitative assessment to determine whether it is more likely than not that the fair value of the reporting unit is less than the carrying value of the reporting unit. Perform the quantitative two-step Goodwill impairment test and make the required journal entry for impairment, if necessary.

The solution to this review problem can be found on page 178.

Readability

Our text is written with rigorous content, but in a student-friendly conversational style that facilitates the learning process. Previous textbooks by the authors have met with extremely positive reviews for writing quality, and students who have used our textbook comment on the relative ease with which they are able to assimilate the material.

NEW IN THE THIRD EDITION

■ **BusinessCourse (MBC):** The authors have revised and recorded the eLectures and Guided Examples in MBC. In addition, more assignments from the book are now available in MBC.

■ **Revised Chapters 3 through 6:** In recognition of the fact that, in practice, companies apply procedures that blend the cost and equity methods of pre consolidation bookkeeping, the authors have incorporated extensive new cost method coverage in the relevant chapters and assignment material. The 3rd edition continues to primarily focus on the full equity method in the consolidations chapters, but now the cost method is also extensively discussed and illustrated. To facilitate understanding, the chapters include clearly marked page borders when the text includes cost-method concepts.

■ All relevant **FASB Private Company Council** alternative accounting treatments have been incorporated into the text.

■ **Revised Chapter 7** has been largely rewritten to include an introduction to hedge accounting that will help ease students into this difficult material. This new section includes several basic examples to highlight the accounting for fair value and cash flow hedges and a new section relating to the accounting for hedges involving options. The authors have also added more references to ASC830, the guiding standard for foreign currency measurement and translation.

■ **Revised Chapter 8** has been substantially revised to incorporate more direct reference to ASC830 (including a much clearer discussion of the difference between measurement and translation), to improve the discussion of functional currency, to add a section relating to the analysis of F/X effects on financial statements, and to add a new section on the consolidation when the parent uses the cost method (all consolidation-related chapters now include cost method discussion).

- **Revised Chapter 9** includes a new emphasis on the reconciliations between government wide and fund-based financial statements to explain each reconciliation entry. This should help students better understand the objectives of these reconciliations and the information they contain.
- **Revised Chapter 10** incorporates reference to the proposed changes in the Not-For-Profit Financial Reporting Framework.
- Overall, **Chapters 8-10** have been revised to improve flow and readability and have added a number of additional references to relevant accounting standards. The authors have also added 10 new multiple choice questions for each chapter, revised the numbers for all existing problems, and added several new problems.
- **Real company examples and data:** All real-world examples in chapters and assignments have been updated and many new companies have been included.
- **End-of-chapter Assignments:** All real-world assignments and the majority of stylized assignments throughout the book have been refreshed with new scenarios, numbers, and solutions.

INSTRUCTOR SUPPLEMENTS

- **myBusinessCourse:** A web-based learning and assessment program intended to complement your textbook and classroom instruction. This easy-to-use course management system grades homework automatically and provide students with additional help when you are not available. In addition, detailed diagnostic tools assess class and individual performance. myBusinessCourse is ideal for online courses or traditional face-to-face courses for which you want to offer students more resources to succeed. Assignments with the in the margin are available in myBusinessCourse.
- **Solutions Manual:** we have a complete solutions manual for each chapter that has been developed by the authors.
- **PowerPoint:** we have instructional PowerPoint slides for each chapter that have been developed by the authors.
- **Test Bank:** The test bank includes multiple-choice items, exercises, and problems.
- **Excel Spreadsheets:** we have Excel solution spreadsheets available for all of the consolidation-related problems and for problems in our fund accounting and government-wide financial statements chapters. These spreadsheets support the preparation of consolidated financial statements, for the governmental accounting chapters, from a trial balance and related journal entries.
- **Website:** All instructor materials are accessible via the book's Website (password protected) along with other useful links and marketing information. www.cambridgepub.com

STUDENT SUPPLEMENTS

- **myBusinessCourse:** A web-based learning and assessment program intended to complement your textbook and faculty instruction. This easy-to-use program grades homework automatically and provides you with additional help when your instructor is not available. Assignments with the in the margin are available in myBusinessCourse. Access is free with new copies of this textbook (look for page containing the access code towards the front of the book). If you buy a used copy of the book, you can purchase access at **www.mybusinesscourse.com**.
- **Excel Spreadsheets:** We provide Excel spreadsheets for all of the end-of-chapter problems that require significant data input. These spreadsheets will save students' time in data entry and allow them to dedicate additional time to learning the material. The Excel spreadsheets are identified by the Excel icon.
- **Website:** Practice quizzes and other useful links are available to students free of charge on the book's Website.

ACKNOWLEDGMENTS

Out text book has benefited greatly from the valuable feedback of focus group attendees, reviewers, students, and colleagues. We are extremely grateful to them for their help in making this project a success.

John Abernathy, *Kennesaw State University*
Peter Aghimien, *Indiana University South Bend*
Marie Archambault, *Marshall University*
Andrea Astill, *Indiana University*
Paul Bahnson, *Boise State University*
Anne Beatty, *The Ohio State University*
Bill Belski, *Samford University*
Jason Bergner, *Baker University*
Mark Bezik, *Concordia University Wisconsin*
John Bildersee, *New York University*
Sam Bonsall, *The Ohio State University*
Quinton Booker, *Jackson State University*
Bruce Branson, *North Carolina State University*
Chester Brearey, *Siena College*
William Brown, *University of Massachusetts, Amherst*
Gene Bryson, *University of Alabama, Huntsville*
Tom Buchman, *University of Colorado*
Brian Burnett, *Indiana University*
Susan Cain, *Southern Oregon University*
Kate Campbell, *University of North Dakota*
Charles Carslaw, *University of Nevada, Reno*
Brian Carver, *Mississippi State University*
Lucy Chen, *Villanova University*
Niranjan Chipalkatti, *Seattle University*
Stanley Chu, *CUNY Baruch College*
Lynn Clements, *Florida Southern College*
Sarah Clinton, *University of Tennessee, Knoxville*
Jacklyn Collins, *University of Miami*
Cynthia Daily, *University of Arkansas, Little Rock*
Amanda Daugherty, *AIB College of Business*
Patricia Davis, *Keystone College*
James Desimpelare, *University of Michigan, Ann Arbor*
Timothy Dimond, *Northern Illinois University*
Cindy Durtschi, *DePaul University*
John Elfrink, *Western Illinois University*
Brooke Elliot, *University of Illinois*
Edwin Etter, *Eastern Michigan University*
Mark Evans, *Wake Forest University*
Charles Fazzi, *St. Vincent College*
Dorothy Feldmann, *Bentley University*
Linda Flaming, *Monmouth University*
Gary Freeman, *Northeastern State University, Broken Arrow*
Luis Garcia, *University of Warwick*
Sandra Gates, *Texas A&M University, Commerce*
John Gillett, *Bradley University*
Tom Giordano, *University of Maine at Augusta*
Earl Godfrey, *Gardner-Webb University*
Elizabeth Gordon, *Temple University*
Tony Greig, *University of Wisconsin*
Thomas Guarino, *Plymouth State University*
Linda Louise Hajec, *Penn State University, Erie*
Linda Hall, *SUNY Fredonia*
Coby Harmon, *University of California, Santa Barbara*

Ling Harris, *University of South Carolina*
Frank Heflin, *Florida State University*
Joshua Herbold, *University of Montana*
Natalie Hivert, *Bishop's University*
Joan Hollister, *SUNY at New Paltz*
Peter Hosker, *Southern New Hampshire University*
Jodi Hunter, *Lake Superior State University*
Angela Hwang, *Eastern Michigan University*
Arnold Jansen, *Harper College*
Marianne James, *California State University, L.A.*
Ching-Lih Jan, *California State University, Eastbay*
Nicole Jenkins, *Vanderbilt University*
Todd Jensen, *California State University, Sacramento*
Derek Johnston, *Colorado State University*
Patricia Johnson, *Canisius College*
David E. Jones, *Temple University*
Marinilka Kimbro, *Seattle University*
Philip Kintzele, *Central Michigan University*
Phillip Kohn, *Ferris State University*
Lisa Koonce, *University of Texas, Austin*
Stanley Kratchman, *Texas A & M University*
Sudha Krishnan, *California State University, Long Beach*
Ken Lambert, *University of Memphis*
Howard Lawrence, *University of Mississippi*
Charles Leflar, *University of Arkansas*
Craig Levin, *National American University*
Karen Jingrong Lin, *University of Massachusetts, Lowell*
Ayalew Lulseged, *University of North Carolina, Greensboro*
Sandra Mankins, *Gardner-Webb University*
Ron Mano, *Westminster College*
Cathy Margolin, *Brandman University*
Jim Martin, *Washburn University*
Nicholas Marudas, *Auburn University, Montgomery*
Maureen Mascha, *University of Wisconsin, Oshkosh*
Dawn Massey, *Fairfield University*
Betsy Matz, *University of Pittsburgh, Bradford*
Patrenia McAbee, *Southern New Hampshire University*
Dawn McKinley, *Harper College*
Allison McLeod, *University of North Texas*
Gregory Merrill, *Saint Mary's College of California*
Nebil Messabia, *Mount Allison University*
Bill Miller, *University of Wisconsin, Eau Claire*
Cathleen Miller, *University of Michigan, Flint*
Gerald J. Miller, *The College of New Jersey*
Anita Morgan, *Indiana University East*
Susan Muzorewa, *Delaware State University*
Curtis Nicholls, *Bucknell University*
Hugo Nurnberg, *CUNY Baruch College*
David O'Bryan, *Pittsburg State University*
Jeanie O'Laughlin, *Adams State College*
Gary Olsen, *Carroll University*
Stephen Owusu-Ansah, *University of Illinois, Springfield*

Susan Perry-Williams, *University of Virginia*
Julie Petherbridge, *Mercer University*
Mary Philips, *Middle Tennessee State University*
David Plumlee, *University of Utah*
Richard Price, *Utah State University*
Usha Ramachandran, *Emory University*
Donna Randolph, *National American University*
Paul Recupero, *Newbury College*
Sara Reiter, *Binghamton University (SUNY)*
Randall Rentfro, *University of Tampa*
Sandra Richtermeyer, *Xavier University*
John Robinson, *University of Texas, Austin*
Tom Rosengarth, *Bridgewater College*
John Rossi, *Moravian College*
Jiwoo Ryou, *University of Texas, Pan American*
Arjan Sadhwani, *South University*
Carol Sargent, *Middle Georgia State College*
Albert Schepanski, *University of Iowa*
Debbie Seifert, *Illinois State University*
Jamie Seitz, *University of Southern Indiana*
Kenneth Shaw, *University of Missouri*
Lewis Shaw, *Suffolk University*
Evan Shough, *Oklahoma City University*
Terrance Skantz, *University of Texas, Arlington*
Nathan Slavin, *Hofstra University*
Pam Smith, *Northern Illinois University*
Debbie Snyder, *Calvin College*
Mark Soczek, *Washington University in St. Louis*
Hakjoon Song, *University of Akron*
Liang Song, *Michigan Technological University*
Mary Stanford, *Texas Christian University*
Mary Stone, *University of Alabama*
Bill Stout, *University of Louisville*
Warren Strimling, *Harper College*
Ron Stunda, *Valdosta State University*
Aida Sy, *Marist College*
Peter Theuri, *Northern Kentucky University*
Mikel Tiller, *Indiana University*
Michael Tydlaska, *Mountain View College*
David Wallin, *The Ohio State University*
Bruce Wampler, *University of Tennessee at Chattanooga*
Jamie Wang, *University of Wisconsin Parkside*
Kimberly Webb, *Texas Wesleyan University*
Charlie Wellens, *Fitchburg State College*
John White, *University of Denver*
Donna Whitten, *Purdue University, North Central*
Jack Wilkerson, *Wake Forest University*
Latasha Williams, *Keiser University*
Jan L. Williams, *University of Baltimore*
Jia Wu, *University of Massachusetts, Dartmouth*
Alex Yen, *College of the Holy Cross*
Sung Wook Yoon, *California State University, Northridge*
Sandy Zelka, *Siena College*
Ling Zhou, *University of New Mexico*
Kathy Zolton, *University of Texas at Dallas*

We wish to thank Professor David Jones of Temple University and Professor Sam Bonsall of The Ohio State University for their support of our text and their helpful suggestions. Our book has also benefitted from the expert assistance of Steve Howe, Alecia Kauss and (especially) Kiley Wuellner. In addition, we are extremely grateful to George Werthman, Deborah McQuade, Terry McQuade, Jocelyn Mousel, Lorraine Gleeson, Beth Nodus, Pat Evett, Marnee Fieldman, Jill Sternard, and the entire team at Cambridge Business Publishers for their encouragement, enthusiasm, and guidance. Their market research, editorial development, and promotional efforts contributed greatly to the quality of our text and to market acceptance that we have enjoyed to date. We have had a very positive textbook authoring experience with this book thanks, in large part, to our publisher.

Bob and *Pat*
February, 2016

Brief Contents

Table of Contents

CHAPTER **3**
Consolidated Financial
Statements Subsequent to
the Date of Acquisition   108

CHAPTER **4**
Consolidated
Financial Statements
and Intercompany
Transactions   182

CHAPTER **7**

Accounting for Foreign Currency Transactions and Derivatives   456

CHAPTER **8**

Consolidation of Foreign Subsidiaries   510

CHAPTER **13**
Accounting for
Partnerships   **718**

Boardwalk Pipeline Partners, LP   719

LEARNING OBJECTIVES

1. Identify the types of business combinations and the accounting for each. (p. 5)

2. Explain the mechanics of the accounting for investments using the equity method of accounting. (p. 9)

3. Explain when the equity method should be used. (p. 12)

4. Explain the amortization of excess assets, and the deferral of unrealized income. (p. 14)

5. Explain the process for deferral of unrealized income. (p. 17)

6. Explain the equity method of accounting for less than 100% ownership. (p. 19)

7. Explain when the equity method should be discontinued. (p. 22)

8. Explain the accounting for changes to and from the equity method. (p. 23)

9. Explain the required disclosures for equity method investments. (p. 26)

10. Explain the criticisms of the equity method of accounting. (p. 26)

Accounting for Intercorporate Investments

*A **Focus Company** introduces each chapter and illustrates the relevance of accounting in everyday business.*

In 1982, AT&T Corporation ("Ma Bell"), the sole provider of local and long-distance phone service in the U.S., was declared to be a monopoly and was forced to divest and break up its local phone service operations into seven regional companies known as the "Baby Bells." In return, AT&T received the right to enter the computer business. During the next two decades, the market methodically recombined the Baby Bells into three surviving companies: AT&T (formed by the merger of Southwestern Bell, BellSouth, Ameritech, and Pacific Telesis), Verizon (formed by the merger of Nynex and Bell Atlantic), and Qwest (originally USWest).

AT&T

Prior to the merger of AT&T and BellSouth in 2006, these two companies formed a joint venture known as Cingular Wireless. Cingular, today known as AT&T Mobility LLC, is now the second largest wireless provider in the U.S., with over 120 million subscribers and revenues in excess of $74 billion. Prior to their merger, AT&T and BellSouth managed the Cingular Wireless joint venture equally, sharing voting rights and representatives on Cingular's board of directors. Each of these companies could exert "significant influence" over the operations of Cingular, but could not "control" the joint venture. As a result, both AT&T and BellSouth accounted for their respective investments in Cingular using the *equity method* of accounting.

Prior to their merger and under the equity method of accounting, AT&T and BellSouth recorded their investments in Cingular on their respective balance sheets as an asset. AT&T, for example, referred to this asset as "Investments in and Advances to Cingular Wireless," with a reported carrying amount of over $31 billion, representing over 20% of AT&T's total assets. The Equity Investment portion of this asset was equal to one-half of Cingular's Stockholders' Equity, the percentage owned by AT&T (the advances portion represents loans that AT&T made to the Cingular joint venture). And, as Cingular's Stockholders' Equity increased or decreased, so did the investment account on AT&T's balance sheet. That is the nature of the equity method of accounting for intercorporate investments. The basic idea is that each company reports as an asset the percentage of the Stockholders' Equity of the business that it owns, not its fair value, as is the case with passive investments, which you learned in your intermediate accounting class.

This chapter illustrates the equity method of accounting for intercorporate investments. Although a valuable topic in its own right, understanding the equity method of accounting is critical to an understanding of the consolidation process that comprises the next five chapters of this text. To give you a sneak peek, the consolidation process basically replaces this investment account with the assets and liabilities of the business represented by that investment (we make similar changes to the income statement). That is, instead of reporting the equity of the business, we report its assets and liabilities. We will tell you how this is done in Chapter 2. For now, just concentrate on learning the equity method of accounting thoroughly. The more time you spend on this chapter, the easier you will find the consolidation process that follows.

Sources: AT&T 10-K 2005–2014

CHAPTER ORGANIZATION

Accounting for Intercorporate Investments

Chapter Organization charts visually depict the key topics and their sequence within the chapter.

Types of Business Combinations	**Accounting for an Investment Using the Equity Method (Basics)**	**Accounting for an Investment Using the Equity Method (Advanced Issues)**
■ Net asset acquisition ■ Stock acquisition	■ Initial acquisition at book value ■ Accounting for the Equity Investment subsequent to its purchase (earnings and losses, dividends) ■ Accounting for the sale of the Equity Investment	■ When should the equity method be used? ■ Accounting for Equity Investments when the purchase price exceeds book value ■ Accounting for the effects on Equity Investments of intercompany sales of inventory ■ Equity method accounting when less than 100% of the investee is owned ■ Discontinuance of the equity method ■ Accounting for a change to and from the equity method ■ Required disclosures for equity method investments ■ Criticism of the equity method

Companies can invest in other companies just like you can, and they purchase these investments for a variety of reasons. Sometimes companies purchase an investment as an alternative to holding excess cash, and they earn a return on this equity investment in the form of dividends and appreciation in the value of the investment. Or, they may invest for strategic reasons, such as to solidify relations with suppliers or to gain entry into a new market. These investments are typically larger in amount and represent a significant percentage ownership in the other company.

The accounting for investments in the voting shares of other companies (i.e., equity investments) depends on the degree to which the company making the investment (the *investor*) can influence the operating activities of the company in which it is investing (the *investee*). The approaches for equity investments are illustrated in Exhibit 1.1.

EXHIBIT 1.1   Three Approaches to the Accounting for Equity Investments under GAAP

Infographics are used to convey difficult concepts and procedures.

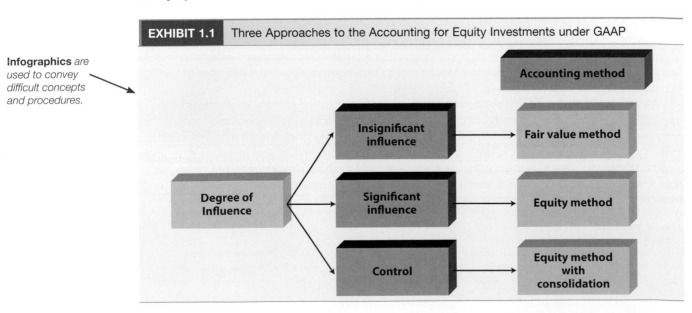

Insignificant influence (fair value method)—the investment account is reported on the balance sheet at its current fair value at each statement date. Dividends received are recognized as income, and increases in the fair value of the investment are reported in current income or other comprehensive income (OCI) depending on whether the investment is accounted for as a *trading* security or an *available-for-sale* security.[1] This method is required if the investment is passive in nature (i.e., the investor *cannot* exert significant influence over or control the investee company).[2]

Significant influence (equity method)—the investment account is not reported at fair value, but at an amount that is equal to the proportion of the stockholders' equity of the investee company that the investor owns (and typically also includes fair value adjustments which we discuss later in the chapter).

Control (consolidation)—after the investor company is deemed to "control" the investee, the financial statements of the two companies must be consolidated, that is, combined (we discuss the consolidation process beginning in Chapter 2).

The degree of influence or control that the investor company can exert over the investee company's operating activities determines the method that the investor must use to account for its equity investment.[3] Intermediate accounting textbooks typically include a discussion of the fair value method of accounting for passive investments and a brief introduction to the equity method and to the consolidation process. Our focus in this chapter is on investments involving significant influence and the equity method of accounting for these investments. In Chapter 2, we begin our discussion of the consolidation process relating to investments in which the investor has control over the investee.

Our experience suggests that you will be much better prepared to learn the consolidation process if you first understand well the accounting for investments using the equity method. Consolidation is just an expanded form of the equity method. So, if you invest the time now to thoroughly understand the equity method of accounting, you will find the consolidation process much easier to learn.

Let us now turn to a discussion of the ways in which one company can acquire another.

REVIEW OF ASSET ACQUISITION ACCOUNTING

In previous courses, you have learned that the accounting for the purchase of a single asset requires you to first determine the amount paid for the asset and, then, to assign that amount to the acquired asset. When a company acquires more than one asset in a single transaction, however, the appropriate accounting is determined by whether the group of assets qualifies as a *business*.[4] In addition, the acquired group of assets also includes any liabilities that are assumed in the acquisition (i.e., it applies to all of the "net assets," or assets minus liabilities, obtained).

---

[1] In early 2016, the FASB eliminated the separate *trading* and *available for sale* categories for passive investments in equity securities. Instead, all changes in fair value for passive equity investments (that have readily determinable fair values) will be immediately reflected in net income. These new rules will take effect for public business entities for fiscal years beginning after December 15, 2017 (e.g., in 2018 for a calendar-year public company), and for all other entities (e.g., private companies) for fiscal years beginning after December 15, 2018.

[2] If no readily determinable fair value exists for the securities owned, the investor accounts for the investment using the cost method as indicated by FASB ASC 325-20. Under the cost method, the investment is recorded at its cost (i.e., purchase price) and is not subsequently adjusted for changes in its fair value. Further, dividends received are recorded as income.

[3] Starting in 2008, FASB ASC 825-10-15 allows companies the option to make an irrevocable, investment-by-investment election to report *non-controlling investments* at fair value (i.e., "the fair value option"). Controlling equity investments must be consolidated, so they are not eligible for this election. When the fair value option is elected, companies basically report the investment as if it is a trading security (i.e., reported at fair value in each balance sheet with the change in fair value reported in net income). For example, at December 31, 2014, Note 8 of Goldman Sachs' annual report states that it reported over $230 billion of financial assets and $159 billion of financial liabilities reported at fair value under the fair value option. In addition, Note 13 states that $360 million of Goldman's equity investments are reported using the equity method, with $6.62 billion of equity investments reported under the fair value option.

[4] FASB ASC Master Glossary defines a **business** as follows: "an integrated set of activities and assets that is capable of being conducted and managed for the purpose of providing a return in the form of dividends, lower costs, or other economic benefits directly to investors or other owners, members, or participants. A business consists of inputs and processes applied to those inputs that have the ability to create outputs. Additional guidance on what a business consists of is presented in paragraphs [FASB ASC] 805-10-55-4 through 55-9."

Key Terms *are highlighted in bold, red font.*

eLecture *icons identify topics for which there are instructional videos in* **myBusinessCourse** *(MBC). See the Preface for more information on MBC.*

LO1 Identify the types of business combinations and the accounting for each.

Learning Objectives *are repeated at the start of the section covering that topic.*

If more than one net asset is purchased for a single lump-sum payment ("basket purchase") and the group of net assets does *not* qualify as a business, the purchaser should proportionately allocate the lump-sum payment to the individual acquired net assets on the basis of the *relative fair values* of the acquired net assets.[5] According to FASB ASC 805-50-30-1, amounts paid by the purchaser for transaction costs are also included in the lump sum amount allocated to the acquired net assets.

To illustrate, assume that an investor company acquires the following net assets of an investee company for a single lump sum cash payment of $810 to the seller and an additional $30 of transactions costs paid to a third-third party (e.g., appraiser or broker). Assume that the bundle of net assets does *not* meet the definition of a business in FASB ASC 805. The allocation of the $840 total cost (i.e., $810 to seller and $30 of transaction costs) to the individual net assets acquired is based on the relative fair values of the net assets as follows:

Debit (Credit)	Fair Value*	Fair Value Proportion	Allocated Cost
Equipment	$100	12.5%	$105
Building	300	37.5%	315
Intangible asset	600	75.0%	630
Accrued liability	(200)	(25.0%)	(210)
Total	$800	100.0%	$840

* It is important to note that the values assigned to the assets and liabilities are the investor's estimates of fair values in accordance with FASB ASC 820 ("Fair Value Measurement"). These fair values will be different from both the book values at which these assets are reported on the seller's balance sheet on the date of sale and, possibly, the seller's estimates of their fair values.

Given these allocated costs, the investor records the transaction as follows:

Equipment	105	
Building	315	
Intangible asset	630	
Accrued liability		210
Cash		840

The investor records the assets purchased and liabilities assumed at their *allocated costs* on the date of purchase, and cash is credited for the payment. A basket purchase of net assets that does *not* qualify as a business combination is accounted for just like the purchase of any other asset; each asset is recorded at the allocated cost that we compute in the table above.[6]

Types of Business Combinations

When the acquisition of net assets qualifies as the purchase of a "***business***," a specialized set of accounting principles, called the ***Acquisition Method***, applies. This method applies only to *business combinations*, which are most commonly executed via two general types of transaction structures: asset acquisitions and stock acquisitions. In a ***net asset acquisition***, the acquirer directly purchases

---

[5] As noted in FASB ASC 805-50-30-3, the cost of a group of net assets acquired in an asset acquisition is allocated to the individual net assets acquired or liabilities assumed based on their relative fair values and does *not* give rise to goodwill. This is one important difference between basket purchases of assets and the business combination transactions discussed in this chapter. As noted in Appendix A of the 2014 EY Financial Reporting Developments guide on Business Combinations, excess purchase cost over the accumulated fair value of the acquired net assets may be an indicator that (1) the acquired set of net assets is a business or (2) one or more intangible assets have not been identified. If purchase cost is greater than the accumulated fair value of the acquired net assets, care should be taken to ensure that all acquired net assets have been identified and that the acquired set of net assets does not meet the definition of a business.

[6] Appendix A of the 2014 EY Financial Reporting Developments guide on Business Combinations suggests that certain assets should not be recorded at amounts greater than their fair values if they will be realized at a loss in the next operating cycle (e.g., accounts receivable, inventories and assets to be disposed of by sale). In the present example, the net assets are recorded at amounts above their respective fair values, and the assets will need to be evaluated for impairment. Given the difficulty in triggering the undiscounted cash flow recoverability test (FASB ASC 360-10-35) in evaluating fixed assets for impairment, it is highly unlikely that an impairment will be recognized for noncurrent assets with allocated costs above their respective fair values. Fixed asset impairment analysis is typically covered in intermediate financial accounting.

the individual net assets that constitute a business.[7] In a ***stock acquisition***, the acquirer purchases the business by acquiring its voting shares. We discuss both of these acquisition structures in this section.

Net Asset Acquisition

In a net asset acquisition, the acquirer purchases some or all of the assets of the acquiree, and may assume selected liabilities, like a mortgage on a building it is acquiring. For the most part, this type of purchase is accounted for like any asset purchase: the net assets are recorded on the balance sheet with an offsetting reduction of cash and/or an increase in liabilities or common stock.

An important feature of ***business combinations*** is that the acquiring company must apply ***Acquisition Method*** accounting (as defined in FASB ASC 805) which requires that the acquired net assets are recorded on the balance sheet at ***fair value***, regardless of the amount paid by the acquirer. This means that the purchase price for the acquired net assets is *not allocated* to those net assets as in our previous example; instead, the assets are recorded at their respective fair values with any difference between the fair value of those net assets and the purchase price paid for them recorded as Goodwill.[8] Goodwill is an intangible asset that is only recorded in transactions that qualify as ***business combinations***. In addition, as we discuss more fully in Chapter 2, transaction costs related to acquiring a business are not capitalized in asset values; instead, when a business is acquired, all transaction costs are expensed in the period they are incurred.

To illustrate, let's return to the facts from the previous basket purchase example. Let's now assume that the asset acquisition qualifies as a business combination under FASB ASC 805. In this case, we will also modify the composition of the consideration paid in exchange for the net assets so that the acquirer pays the $810 purchase price with cash of $310 and by issuing 100 shares of $1 par value common stock with a fair value of $5 per share.[9] In addition, we still assume that the purchaser paid an additional $30 of transaction costs to a third party (e.g., appraiser or broker). The fair values of the net assets are the same amounts that we report in our previous example (note: we are using the fair values, not the allocated cost as we did previously), and the investor records the purchase of these assets as follows:

Equipment	100	
Building	300	
Intangible asset	600	
Goodwill	10	
Expenses (transaction costs)	30	
Cash		340
Accrued liability		200
Common stock (100 shares @ $1 par value)		100
Additional paid-in capital		400

The investor records the net assets purchased at their fair values on the date of purchase, and cash is credited for the payment. In the purchase of net assets that qualify as a business, transaction costs are expensed as incurred. The issuance of common stock is recorded by a credit to Common Stock for the par value of the shares issued, with the remainder recorded as an increase in Additional Paid-in Capital.

In many ways, the purchase of net assets that comprise a business is recorded much like the purchase of any asset. However, one important difference is that acquired net assets in a business combination are recorded at their *fair values*, not at the *allocated cost* of the acquired net assets as in our previous example. And, a second difference is that the acquisition may involve the recognition of a Goodwill asset at an amount that is equal to the difference between the amount paid for an acquisition and the fair value of the net assets acquired. We discuss the determination of Goodwill in Chapter 2. For now, you can view the Goodwill asset as the difference between the amount paid to the seller and the fair value of the net assets received in a business combination.

[7] The ***acquiree*** is defined as "the business or businesses that the acquirer obtains control of in a business combination." The ***acquirer*** is defined as "the entity that obtains control of the acquiree" (FASB ASC Master Glossary).

[8] In Chapter 2 we more fully discuss the Acquisition Method, accounting for Goodwill, including the case where Goodwill appears to be negative.

[9] If noncash assets (like land and building) are given as consideration, those assets are first adjusted to their fair values before removal from the investor's balance sheet. This adjustment results in a gain or loss that is reflected in the investor's income statement (FASB ASC 805-50-30-1).

Stock Acquisition   In our previous example, the investor purchased selected *net assets* of the investee with a value of $810, and that qualified as a business. Let us now assume that the investor purchases all of the investee's outstanding *common stock* from its shareholders, rather than specific assets, and the investee company qualifies as a business. The investor funds the purchase price of $810 by a cash payment of $310 and issuance of 100 shares of $1 par value common stock with a fair value of $500, like before. In addition, we still assume that the purchaser paid an additional $30 of transaction costs to a third party (e.g., appraiser or broker). The investor records the purchase of the investee's common stock as follows:

Equity investment.	810	
Expenses (transaction costs)	30	
Cash		340
Common stock (100 shares @ $1 par value)		100
Additional paid-in capital.		400

The Equity Investment account is an asset that is reported on the investor's balance sheet just like any other asset, and, our use of the term "investment" in this journal entry implies that the acquired company will remain in existence after the purchase.[10]

Notice that the Equity Investment account of $810 represents the *implied* Stockholders' Equity of the investee's business that the investor has acquired. In our previous example, the investor acquired specific assets (the equipment in the amount of $100, the building of $300, the intangible asset in the amount of $600, $10 of goodwill, less the accrued liability of $200). Now, we are acquiring the investee's common stock rather than its specific assets, and the Equity Investment account represents the investee's business in one account on our balance sheet at a reported amount of $810 that is equal to the fair value of the investee's Stockholders' Equity (assets of $100 + $300 + $600 + $10 − liabilities of $200 = Stockholders' Equity of $810) on the acquisition date.

In future years, under the Equity Method of investment accounting, the Equity Investment account on the investor's balance sheet will increase or decrease as the Stockholders' Equity of the investee's

Topic Review boxes reinforce the material just presented with self-study questions. To aid learning, solutions are provided at the end of the chapter

TOPIC REVIEW 1

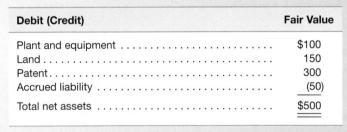

Guided Example icons denote the availability of a demonstration video in **myBusinessCourse** *(MBC). See the Preface for more on MBC.*

Accounting for Asset and Stock Purchases

Assume that an investor purchases an investee's net assets with a cash payment of $200 and issuance to the investee's shareholders of 52 shares of $1 par value common stock with a current fair value of $6 per share. In addition, we still assume that the purchaser paid an additional $8 of transaction costs to a third party (e.g., appraiser or broker). The investee has the following net assets:

Debit (Credit)	Fair Value
Plant and equipment	$100
Land	150
Patent	300
Accrued liability	(50)
Total net assets	$500

Required

a. Provide the journal entry on the investor's books for the purchase of the individual net assets of the investee. Assume the acquired net assets do not qualify as a business.

b. Provide the journal entry on the investor's books for the purchase of the individual net assets of the investee. Assume the acquired net assets qualify as a business.

c. Provide the journal entry on the investor's books for the purchase of the investee's business, assuming that the investor purchases the investee as a stock purchase.

The solution to this review problem can be found on pages 43-44.

---

[10] If the acquired company ceases to exist after the acquisition, we would record the assets purchased and liabilities assumed as in our asset purchase above. The dissolution of the acquired company following the sale is called a *statutory merger*.

business grows or shrinks. In the next section of this chapter, we discuss the mechanics by which the Equity Investment account increases and decreases following the acquisition.

ACCOUNTING FOR AN INVESTMENT USING THE EQUITY METHOD (BASICS)

In the previous section, the investor acquires the business of an investee by either purchasing its assets or purchasing its common stock, and recognizes the investee company on its balance sheet either as individual assets and liabilities (asset purchase) or with an account called Equity Investment (stock purchase). In this section, we focus only on the stock purchase and we discuss the accounting for this Equity Investment from its purchase through its ultimate sale.

LO2 Explain the mechanics of the accounting for investments using the equity method of accounting.

Accounting for the Purchase of an Equity Investment

This Equity Investment account represents the proportion of the equity of the acquired business that we own. To introduce the concept of equity-method accounting, we first assume that the fair values of the acquired company's net assets equal their reported amounts (i.e., their "book value") on the balance sheet (we will relax this assumption later). That is, the fair value of the company's business is initially assumed to be $800, rather than the $810 we used in the previous example, and this amount is equal to the Stockholders' Equity of the acquired company on the date of purchase. To simplify this discussion, we will also assume there are no transaction costs.

The investor records the Equity Investment as follows:

Equity investment.	800	
Cash		300
Common stock (100 shares @ $1).		100
Additional paid-in capital.		400

The purchase of the $800 Equity Investment is funded by a $300 decrease in Cash and a $500 increase in Stockholders' Equity. The investee's business is now represented on the investor's balance sheet as an asset (Equity Investment) that is equal to the Stockholders' Equity of the acquired company on the date of purchase.

Because, in this example, the investor owns 100% of the investee company and the fair value of the business is equal to its Stockholders' Equity, the investor's Equity Investment account in the amount of $800 is equal to the proportion of the investee's Stockholders' Equity that it owns, namely 100% of $800 = $800. Exhibit 1.2 depicts this relation.

EXHIBIT 1.2	Comparison of the Investor and Investee Balance Sheets Following the Purchase of the Equity Investment

Investee Company Balance Sheet				Investor Company Balance Sheet			
Equipment	$ 100	Accrued liability	$ 200	Cash	$ 300	Payables	$ 200
Building	300			Receivables	500	Accruals	300
Intangible asset	600			Inventories	900	L-T Debt	1,000
				PPE, net	2,500		
		Equity	800 ⟷	Investment	800	Equity	3,500
Total	$1,000	Total	$1,000	Total	$5,000	Total	$5,000

In this example, the investor acquires the Equity Investment at "book value," that is, in an amount equal to the book value of the investee's Stockholders' Equity. There will always be an important relation between the amount at which the Equity Investment is reported on the investor's balance sheet and the Stockholders' Equity of the investee company: **provided that the acquisition is made at book value, the balance reported in the Equity Investment account will always be equal to the proportion of** the investee company equity that we own.[11] And, as the investee's Stockholders' Equity increases or decreases, so does the Equity Investment on the investor's balance sheet. In our next section, we discuss the process by which these increases or decreases are recognized.

Accounting for the Equity Investment Subsequent to Its Purchase

We divide our discussion of the accounting treatment for an Equity Investment subsequent to purchase into two parts: accounting for changes in its reported amount during the holding period of the Equity Investment and accounting for its ultimate sale.

Accounting for Changes in the Reported Amount of the Equity Investment Subsequent to Its Purchase   Let us now assume that the investee earns a profit of $300 and pays a dividend of $100 to the investor. The investee's Stockholders' Equity has, therefore, increased by $200 ($300 profit − $100 dividend) to $1,000. To maintain the equivalence between the Equity Investment account on the investor's balance sheet and the investee's Stockholders' Equity, the Equity Investment must likewise increase by $200 to a balance of $1,000. This is accomplished by recording two changes to that account:

1. A $300 *increase* to recognize the investor's share of the increase in the investee's Stockholders' Equity resulting from the profit of $300,[12] and

2. A $100 *decrease* to recognize the investor's share of the decrease in the investee's Stockholders' Equity resulting from the payment of dividends (reduction of Retained Earnings) of $100.

The journal entries that an investor must make to accomplish these changes are as follows:

1.	Equity investment...	300	
	Equity income		300
	(to record the recognition of Equity Income)		
2.	Cash..	100	
	Equity investment		100
	(to record the receipt of dividends)		

A T-account for the investor's Equity Investment illustrates these changes:

Equity Investment			
Beginning balance	800		
Equity income	300	100	Dividends received
Ending balance	1,000		

As the investee earns a profit of $300, its Stockholders' Equity (Retained Earnings) increases by that amount and the Equity Investment account on the investor's balance sheet must increase accordingly. Likewise, the payment of dividends to the investor results in a decrease in the investee's Stockholder's Equity (Retained Earnings) and a consequent decrease in the Equity Investment on the investor's balance sheet. The equity method of accounting, then, results in an Equity Investment account that increases and decreases together with the Stockholders' Equity of the investee company.[13]

---

[11] Even when the investment is at an amount different from book value, there will be a similar relation to the Stockholders' Equity of the investee as we discuss later in the chapter.

[12] According to FASB ASC 323-10-45-2, "[t]he investor's share of accounting changes reported in the financial statements of the investee shall be classified separately." In addition, the investment account will change for all sources of recognized income, including "other comprehensive income." The investor also must segregate ordinary income from the individual sources of other comprehensive income (FASB ASC 323-10-35-18 and 323-10-45-3).

[13] FASB ASC 825-10-25 allows companies to *irrevocably* elect to measure Equity Investments at fair value, with changes in fair value reflected in income. Should a company elect to measure Equity Investments under this standard, the reported amount may differ from the Stockholders' Equity of the investee company that the investor owns. However, an Equity Investment that represents subsidiaries to be *consolidated* cannot be valued at fair value.

We conclude this section of our chapter with three observations relating to the investor's accounting for its Equity Investment under the equity method:

■ First, the investor does not report the receipt of dividends as income like it does under the fair value method of accounting for passive investments that you learned in previous financial accounting courses. Dividends are treated as a return of investment and the Equity Investment account is reduced accordingly. Instead, the investor reports income from the investment equal to the percentage of the investee's net income that it owns. In this case, the investor owns 100% of the investee. So, it reports 100% of the investee's net income as Equity Income in its own income statement.

■ Second, the investor only reports Equity Income commencing with the date on which it purchases the Equity Investment. For example, if the investor purchases the Equity Investment on March 1, it can only include in its income statement the percentage of the investee's profit that it earns subsequent to March 1.

■ And third, under the equity method, the investor does not adjust the Equity Investment account for changes in its fair value, as is the case with the fair value method of accounting for investments in which the investor cannot exert significant influence over the investee's operating activities. Consequently, there may be substantial unrealized gains that are not reported on the balance sheet, and the investor does not report these gains in its income statement. Instead, all unrealized gains are recognized in full when the investment is sold.

Accounting for the Sale of the Equity Investment

We account for the sale of an Equity Investment in the same way as we do for the sale of any other asset that we own:

■ Record the receipt of cash (or other assets, such as a note receivable).
■ Remove the Equity Investment from the balance sheet.
■ Recognize the difference between cash received and the reported amount (book value) of the Equity Investment as a gain or loss on the sale.

To illustrate, assume that the investor sells its Equity Investment (which it currently reports on its balance sheet at $1,000) for cash proceeds of $1,250. The journal entry to record this sale is as follows:

Cash	1,250	
Equity investment		1,000
Gain on sale		250
(to record the sale of the Equity Investment)		

The investor recognizes a gain on the sale of the Equity Investment because the proceeds ($1,250) exceed the reported amount (book value) of the investment ($1,000) on its balance sheet. Had it sold the Equity Investment for $700, however, it would record a loss as follows:

Cash	700	
Loss on sale	300	
Equity investment		1,000
(to record the sale of the Equity Investment)		

We provide a summary of the basic accounting for Equity Investments in Exhibit 1.3.

EXHIBIT 1.3	Summary of the Equity Method of Accounting

1. The Equity Investment is initially recorded at its purchase price.
2. Dividends received are treated as a recovery of the investment and, as a result, reduce the Equity Investment account.
3. The investor reports income equal to its percentage share of the investee's reported income.
4. As a result of #2 and #3, the Equity Investment account on the investor's balance sheet increases and decreases to reflect corresponding increases and decreases in the investee's Stockholders' Equity.
5. Changes in fair value of the Equity Investment are not reflected as adjustments to the reported amount of the Equity Investment and, thus, are not recognized in income until the Equity Investment is sold.

TOPIC REVIEW 2

Accounting for Equity Investments (Basic)

Assume that an investor purchases all of the stock of the investee (and, thus, its business) in a stock purchase for $500. The reported book values of the investee's net assets equal their fair values. The investee's balance sheet on the date of purchase is as follows:

Accounts receivable.	$ 50		Mortgage payable	$ 50
Inventories	100			
Building	400		Stockholders' equity	500
Total assets.	$550		Total liabilities and equity	$550

Now, assume that, subsequent to the purchase, the investee reports net income of $100 and pays $25 in dividends to the investor.

Required

a. At what amount will the investee's Stockholders' Equity be reported after income and dividends have been closed to Retained Earnings (assume no other changes to Stockholders' Equity)?

b. Provide the following journal entries:
   1. Record the recognition of Equity Income by the investor
   2. Record the receipt of the $25 dividend

c. At what amount is the Equity Investment reported on the investor's balance sheet? How does this compare to the investee's Stockholders' Equity?

The solution to this review problem can be found on page 44.

ACCOUNTING FOR AN INVESTMENT USING THE EQUITY METHOD (ADVANCED TOPICS)

LO3 Explain when the equity method should be used.

In the previous section, we discuss the purchase of the Equity Investment, the recognition of income and dividends subsequent to purchase, and the sale of the Equity Investment. These topics are the basics of the equity method of accounting. We now introduce a number of more advanced issues, such as the rules governing the use of the equity method, how we account for Equity Investments purchased at a price that exceeds book value, accounting issues that arise when the investor and investee companies sell assets to one another, the purchase of less than 100% ownership of the investee company equity, the circumstances under which we discontinue use of the equity method altogether, the reporting of changes to and from the equity method and other methods of accounting for intercorporate investments, and related disclosures to equity method investments. We begin with a discussion of when to use the equity method of accounting.

When Should the Equity Method Be Used?

GAAP prescribes that the equity method should be used to account for Equity Investments when the investor has the ability to exercise "significant influence" over operating and financial policies of an investee (FASB ASC 323).[14] According to FASB ASC 323-10-15-11, "[a]n investment (direct or indirect) of 20% or more of the voting stock of an investee shall lead to a presumption that in the absence of predominant evidence to the contrary an investor has the ability to exercise significant influence over an investee." However, this presumption is rebuttable (i.e., investments of 20% or more might not result in significant influence).

---

[14] FASB ASC 323 also requires the use of the equity method to account for investments in corporate *joint ventures*. A joint venture is a non-stock entity that is managed by more than one "owner." The AT&T and BellSouth Cingular Wireless joint venture is an example. Until their merger in 2006, both AT&T and BellSouth were required to account for the Cingular joint venture using the equity method of accounting for the Equity Investment since each company had an equal voice in the management of the business. We discuss the accounting implications of their merger in Chapter 2.

So, how should you decide if the investor has the ability to exercise significant influence over the investee's operating and financial policies? The ability to exercise significant influence may be indicated in a number of ways (FASB ASC 323-10-15-6):

■ Investor representation on the board of directors of the investee

■ Investor participation in policy making processes of the investee

■ The extent of ownership of investee voting shares by the investor in relation to the concentration of other shareholdings

■ Material intercompany transactions between the investor and the investee

■ Interchange of managerial personnel between the investor and the investee

■ Technological dependency of the investee on the investor

The first three criteria relate to the investor's participation in executive decision making bodies of the investee company and its ability to influence the board of directors and, thus, the operating policies of the investee. The last three criteria relate to direct involvement in the operating activities of the investee company. All of these criteria do not have to be met in order to conclude that the investor has the ability to exert significant influence. Any of them can provide sufficient evidence to conclude that the ability to exercise significant influence is present, even if the investor owns less than 20% of the outstanding voting stock of the investee.

The converse might also be true: the investor might not have significant influence even though it owns more than 20% of the outstanding voting stock of the investee. Examples of indications that an investor may be *unable* to exercise significant influence over the operating and financial policies of an investee include (FASB ASC 323-10-15-10):

■ The investee challenges the investor's ability to exercise significant influence, such as by litigation or complaints to governmental regulatory authorities.

■ The investor and investee sign an agreement under which the investor surrenders significant rights as a shareholder.

■ Majority ownership of the investee is concentrated among a small group of shareholders who operate the investee without regard to the views of the investor.

■ The investor needs or wants more financial information to apply the equity method than is available to the investee's other shareholders (for example, the investor wants quarterly financial information from an investee that publicly reports only annually), tries to obtain that information, and fails.

■ The investor tries and fails to obtain representation on the investee's board of directors.

When any of these conditions are present, the investor company may be justified in *not* employing the equity method in accounting for the investment despite ownership of more than 20% of the outstanding voting stock of the investee.

The investor must account for the Equity Investment using the equity method when it can exert significant influence over the investee company, and it can continue to account for this Equity Investment using the equity method even after it gains "control" over the activities of the investee (say, at ownership levels of 100% as in our example).[15] When the investor obtains control of the investee, however, it must *consolidate* the financial statements of both companies when reporting to *external* parties such as shareholders or the SEC. For *internal* reporting, however, the investor can use the equity method to account for its Equity Investment in the investee company.

We discuss the consolidation process beginning in Chapter 2. As you will see, consolidation is basically the replacement of the Equity Investment account with the assets and liabilities of the investee company to which that account relates. So, don't be surprised when we account for the parent company's investment in a wholly-owned subsidiary (investee) using the equity method. As long as the two companies are ultimately consolidated prior to issuance of the financial statements to shareholders and the SEC, that is perfectly acceptable.

---

[15] Control is often defined as legal control, that is, ownership of more than 50% of the outstanding voting stock of the investee company. As is the case with *significant influence*, however, accountants must look to all of the available evidence to determine when *control* is present. We discuss the determination of control in the next chapter and, in Chapter 6, we discuss circumstances where companies can own less than 50% of another entity but still control that entity.

Practice Insight boxes describe how accounting is used in real companies.

PRACTICE INSIGHT

What constitutes control of an equity investment? Prior to the merger of AT&T and Bell-South, Cingular Wireless (now known as AT&T Mobility) began as a joint venture between the two companies, which were also two of the original Baby Bells. A joint venture is an agreement between two or more companies to form a business. The joint venture agreement spells out how the company will be run and how the profits will be split. The Cingular joint venture agreement provided that AT&T had a 60% *economic interest* in Cingular, and BellSouth had a 40% economic interest. That meant that AT&T received 60% of the profit and BellSouth, 40%. How should AT&T have accounted for its investment in the Cingular joint venture given its 60% economic interest?

Following is a quote from the footnotes to AT&T's annual report that discusses this issue:

We account for our 60% economic interest in Cingular under the equity method of accounting in our consolidated financial statements since we share control equally (i.e., 50/50) with our 40% economic partner in the joint venture. We have equal voting rights and representation on the Board of Directors that controls Cingular.

AT&T contended that the equity method was appropriate since it shared voting control equally with its joint venture partner. As a result, it exerted significant influence over Cingular's operating activities, but did not *control* that company. Accounting for the Equity Investment using the equity method was, therefore, appropriate in this instance.

TOPIC REVIEW 3

Financial Reporting for an Equity Method Investment

According to its December 31, 2014 SEC Form 10-K, **Liberty Interactive Corporation** owns interests in subsidiaries and other companies that are primarily engaged in the video and online commerce industries. One of those interests is an equity investment in **Expedia, Inc.** According to Liberty's 10-K, "Liberty owns an approximate 18% equity interest and 58% voting interest in Expedia. Liberty has entered into governance arrangements pursuant to which Mr. Barry Diller, Chairman of the Board and Senior Executive Officer of Expedia, may vote its interests of Expedia, subject to certain limitations. Additionally, through our governance arrangements with Mr. Diller, we have the right to appoint and have appointed 20% of the members of Expedia's board of directors, which is currently comprised of 10 members." Expedia is a publicly traded company listed on the Nasdaq Global Select Market under the ticker symbol "EXPE." On December 31, 2014, Expedia had a closing stock price of $85.36, which suggests a total market capitalization of $9.6 billion.

Required

How should Liberty report its investment in Expedia in its December 31, 2014 financial statements? Specifically, should Liberty report Expedia as a controlled consolidated subsidiary, and equity method investment, or a passive investment reported at fair value? Explain your answer.

The solution to this review problem can be found on page 44.

Accounting for Equity Investments When the Purchase Price Exceeds Book Value

LO4 Explain the amortization of excess assets, and the deferral of unrealized income.

When we introduced the basics of equity-method accounting, the investor acquired all of the investee's outstanding stock for a purchase price of $800, equal to the investee's Stockholders' Equity on the date of acquisition. In this initial case, the purchase is said to be made at "book value."

Acquisitions are rarely made at book value, however. The reason is twofold: financial statements are prepared using historical costing and, for the most part, do not reflect current fair values (one exception is the investment in marketable securities accounted for using the fair value method); and, second, there may be unrecorded assets, such as an internally developed patent, for example, that will be factored into the purchase price but are not reported on the investee's balance sheet.

When the price of the Equity Investment exceeds the book value of the company acquired, the investor has, essentially, purchased two groups of assets: the net assets (assets less liabilities) that are reported on the balance sheet of the investee company (these net assets are equal to its reported Stockholders' Equity) *plus* some additional previously unrecorded assets. In order to account for these additional assets following the acquisition, the investor must first decide what they are. They could be tangible assets, such as PPE, or intangible assets, such as recorded Patent assets or the more general Goodwill asset. Once the investor determines the nature of these additional assets, it must subsequently account for these assets just like any other assets that it purchases. That is, tangible assets must be depreciated and definite-lived intangible assets (i.e., intangible assets other than Goodwill and other indefinite-lived intangibles) must be amortized over their useful lives.

To illustrate, assume that the investor purchases all of the stock of the investee for a purchase price of $1,100 (instead of $800), with a cash payment of $600 and issuance of 100 shares of $1 par value common stock with a fair value of $500 ($5 per share). Assume that the investor is willing to pay the increased purchase price because it feels that a building, reported on the investee's balance sheet at a net book value (cost less accumulated depreciation) of $600, has a current fair value of $900. The purchase price of $1,100, then, is comprised of two assets: the book value of the Stockholders' Equity of the investee company *plus* the portion of the building's value not reported on the investee's balance sheet:

Purchase Price		Assets Acquired
$1,100	$800	Book value of Stockholders' Equity of the investee company
	$300	Building value not reported on investee company's balance sheet

If the investor had purchased just the building for $900, the investor would depreciate it over its useful life. Acquiring the building as part of a stock purchase is no different. The investor and investee will still depreciate the full purchase price of the building. The only difference is that the depreciation will be done in two places:

1. The *investee* will continue to depreciate the $600 book value of the building it reports on its balance sheet, and

2. The *investor* will depreciate the additional $300 building asset that it purchased in the acquisition.

To illustrate, assume that the building has a remaining life of 20 years and is depreciated on a straight-line basis with no salvage value. The *total* depreciation expense is $45 per year ($900/20). The $45 depreciation expense, however, is recorded in two different income statements:

Total Depreciation Expense		Where Recorded
$45	$30 ($600/20)	Investee's income statement
	$15 ($300/20)	Investor's income statement

The investee continues to depreciate the book value of the building as it has been doing all along. This means that the $30 of depreciation expense that the investee (acquired) company recognizes will reduce its reported income (and this expense will ultimately affect the investor's income statement via the Equity Income adjustment under the equity method). In addition, the investor recognizes the additional $15 of depreciation expense in its own income statement. How? By reducing the Equity Income it is recognizing on its Equity Investment.

Let's see how this is accomplished. The investor's Equity Investment, reflecting the new purchase price, is recorded as follows:

Equity investment.	1,100	
Cash		600
Common stock (100 shares @ $1).		100
Additional paid-in capital		400

Let us continue to assume that the investee earns a profit (all in cash) of $300 and pays a dividend of $100 to the investor, just like before. The investee's Stockholders' Equity, therefore, increases by $200 to a balance of $1,000. Notice that the higher purchase price for the Equity Investment has not affected the investee at all. That additional investment is on the *investor's* balance sheet, not the investee's balance sheet.

The investor makes the following journal entries to recognize the Equity Income earned and dividends received as before:

1.	Equity investment..	300	
	Equity income		300
	(to record the recognition of Equity Income)		
2.	Cash	100	
	Equity investment		100
	(to record the receipt of dividends)		

These are the same journal entries that we recorded earlier. However, given the additional facts in the present example, one additional journal entry is required on the investor's books to record the depreciation of the new building asset. This is accomplished by the following journal entry:

Equity income...	15	
Equity investment		15
(to record the depreciation of the building asset)		

Equity Income is reduced by the depreciation of the additional building asset, and the Equity Investment account is reduced likewise.

As a result of these three journal entries, the investor reports a balance in the Equity Investment account on its balance sheet of $1,285, consisting of the beginning balance of $1,100, the recognition of equity income of $300, and a reduction of $115 relating to the $100 in dividends received and $15 depreciation of the additional building asset. The T-account for the Equity Investment illustrates these changes:

Equity Investment			
Beginning balance	1,100		
Equity income	300	100	Dividends received
		15	Depreciation of building asset
Ending balance	1,285		

Given that most acquisitions are made at a price that is greater than the investee's book value of Stockholders' Equity, we now need to modify the general rule about the relation between the Equity Investment account and the Stockholders' Equity of the investee company that we discussed earlier: **the balance reported in the Equity Investment account will always be equal to the proportion of the investee company Stockholders' Equity that the investor owns** *plus the book value of additional assets purchased.* In this case, the investor's Equity Investment of $1,285 is comprised of the following assets:

Equity Investment		Composition
$1,285	$1,000	Proportion of the book value of the investee company that we own (100% in this case)
	$ 285	Remaining book value of the additional building asset that we purchased ($300 − $15)

The additional assets purchased by the investor can relate to any of the reported assets (and even liabilities) of the investee and to a variety of unrecorded intangible assets. Each of these additional assets must be depreciated (*amortized* is the name we use to describe depreciation of intangible assets) over their respective useful lives. One exception to this relates to any Goodwill the investor recognizes in the purchase. We do not amortize Goodwill. Instead, we evaluate it annually for impairment and write it down if it is impaired. We discuss all intangible assets, including Goodwill and its impairment evaluation, in Chapters 2 and 3. For now, just appreciate the fact that these additional assets that are included in the Equity Investment account are real assets of the investor and should be accounted for just like any other assets that the investor owns.

To illustrate the additional assets (i.e., not reported on the books of the investee) implicit in equity-method investments, consider **Walgreen Co.**'s acquisition of a 45% investment in **Alliance Boots GmbH** on August 2, 2012. According to Walgreen's August 31, 2014 SEC Form 10-K, the Company purchased—for $6.1 billion in cash and Walgreen stock—a 45% interest in Alliance Boots. According to Walgreen's 10-K, "[t]he Company's initial investment in Alliance Boots exceeded its proportionate share of the net assets of Alliance Boots by $2.4 billion. This premium of $2.4 billion is recognized as part of the carrying value in the Company's equity investment in Alliance Boots. The difference is primarily related to the fair value of Alliance Boots indefinite-lived intangible assets and goodwill. The Company's equity method income from the investment in Alliance Boots is adjusted to reflect the amortization of fair value adjustments in certain definite-lived assets of Alliance Boots. The Company's incremental amortization expense associated with the Alliance Boots investment was approximately $42 million in fiscal 2014."[16]

We next consider intercompany sales of assets, such as inventories, and the ways in which these sales affect our accounting for the Equity Investment.

> **Real Companies** *and* **Institutions** *are highlighted in bold, blue font.*

TOPIC REVIEW 4

Accounting for the Equity Investment When Price Exceeds Book Value

Assume that an investor purchases all of the stock of the investee in a stock purchase for $600. The investee's balance sheet on the date of purchase is as follows:

Accounts receivable.	$ 50	Mortgage payable	$ 50
Inventories	100		
Building	400	Stockholders' equity	500
Total assets.	$550	Total liabilities and equity	$550

In this example, the amount paid (i.e., $600) is $100 greater than the book value of the net assets of the investee (i.e., $500). Assume that the additional $100 of purchase price relates to an unrecognized patent held by the investee that has a remaining useful life of 10 years on the acquisition date. We also assume that, subsequent to the purchase, the investee reports net income of $100 and pays $25 in dividends to the investor.

Required

a. Provide the journal entry to recognize the Equity Income by the investor.
b. Provide the journal entry to record the receipt of the $25 dividend.
c. Provide the journal entry to record the amortization of the patent asset.

The solution to this review problem can be found on page 44.

Accounting for the Effects on Equity Investments of Intercompany Sales of Inventory

Many companies acquire suppliers or customers in order to capture value in other portions of the supply chain (i.e., they are "vertically integrated"), and it is not uncommon for the investor and investee to sell products among themselves. A manufacturing investee company, for example, might sell completed or partially completed inventories to the investor who, subsequently, resells them to the end customer.

LO5 Explain the process for deferral of unrealized income.

---

[16] On December 31, 2014, Walgreens purchased the remaining 55% of Alliance Boots that it did not already own. Thus, on December 31, 2014 Alliance Boots was controlled by Walgreen and Walgreen would need to consolidate Alliance Boots instead of using the equity method. Pursuant to the acquisition, Walgreen formed a new holding company called **Walgreens Boots Alliance Inc.**, which combines 100% of both Walgreens' and Alliance Boots' businesses into a single consolidated entity.

To begin our discussion of accounting for the effects of intercompany sales of inventories between the investee and the investor, let's assume that the investee sells goods that cost $100 to the investor for $130 on account. When the intercompany (i.e., between investor and investee) sale occurs, the investee and investor companies make the following journal entries (assuming perpetual inventory costing) in their respective books:

Investee			**Investor**		
1. Accounts receivable.	130		Inventories	130	
Sales		130	Accounts payable		130
(to record the sale of product on account)			*(to record the purchase of inventory)*		
2. Cost of goods sold.	100				
Inventories.		100			
(to record the cost of goods sold)					

The investee records a gross profit on the sale of $30 ($130 − $100), and the investor records the inventory on its books at the purchase price of $130.

More importantly, the $30 gross profit has increased the investee's net income by $30, and that increase in profit results in a $30 increase in Equity Income that is reported by the investor (the investor owns 100% of the investee company and, thus, reports 100% of the investee's profit as Equity Income). Thus, *both* the investor and investee companies have reported the same $30 of profit. Now, if we think of the investor and investee companies as one organization, that organization has just written up its inventories by $30 and recorded the write-up as profit!

With very limited exceptions (e.g., trading securities under FASB ASC 320), GAAP does not permit the recognition of profit on appreciated assets until those assets are sold (i.e., when the profit is *realized*). And, because the investor has the ability to significantly influence the investee's operating activities (or possibly control those operations), GAAP views these two companies as one reporting group. If separate companies under one reporting group were allowed to recognize a profit on transfers of inventories within the reporting group, they could increase profit without limit without ever selling a good or service to an outside party. This would clearly be unacceptable. Consequently, **the gross profit on the intercompany sale must be** *deferred* **and cannot be recognized until those inventories are sold outside of the reporting group**. (By the way, it doesn't matter in which direction the sale occurs; we also would be required to defer the gross profit on the sale if the investor had sold inventory to the investee.)

The deferral of gross profit on intercompany inventory sales is accomplished by the following journal entry:[17]

Equity income.	30	
Equity investment		30
(to record the deferral of gross profit on inventory sale in the period of sale)		

Equity income has, thus, been reduced by the profit on the intercompany sale that we cannot recognize until the inventories are re-sold outside by the investor. The reduction in Equity Income has also reduced the Equity Investment account. And, in the subsequent year, when the investor sells the inventory to outside parties, we reverse the entry to recognize in the current period the deferred profit from the prior period:

Equity investment.	30	
Equity income		30
(to record the recognition of gross profit on inventory sale in the following period)		

The example we provide above assumes that *all* of the inventories sold by the investee to the investor remain on the investor's balance sheet at the end of the period. If some, but not all, of those inventories have been sold to independent companies by the end of the accounting period in the year of the inter-

---

[17] When we consolidate these two companies in Chapter 3, we will also need to eliminate the intercompany sale and Account Receivable of $130.

company sale, the gross profit on the sale relating to the inventories sold can be recognized in that year, and only the gross profit on the inventories that remain on the investor's balance sheet must be deferred.

To illustrate, suppose that 60% of the inventories have been re-sold by the investor and that 40% of the inventories still remain on the investor's balance sheet at the end of the year of the intercompany sale. In this case, only 40% of the $30 gross profit on the intercompany inventory sale must be deferred, and the deferral of gross profit on the intercompany inventory sale is accomplished by the following journal entry:

Equity income.	12	
Equity investment		12
(to record the deferral of 40% of the gross profit on inventory sale in the period of sale)		

TOPIC REVIEW 5

Accounting for the Effects on Equity Investments of Intercompany Sales of Inventory

Assume that an investor sells parts inventories, that originally cost the investor $50, to a 100% owned investee for a sale price of $75. Also assume that 60% of the parts inventories remain on the investee's balance sheet at the end of the period.

Required

Provide the journal entry to defer the recognition of gross profit on the inventories that remain on the investee's balance sheet.

The solution to this review problem can be found on page 45.

Equity Method Accounting When Less Than 100% of the Investee Is Owned

In our discussion thus far, the investor owns 100% of the investee. We now relax that assumption to consider ownership levels of less than 100%. We begin this section with a discussion of basic equity method mechanics when an investor owns less than 100% of the investee, and conclude with a further discussion of when the equity method can be used.

LO6 Explain the equity method of accounting for less than 100% ownership.

Equity Method Mechanics With Less Than 100% Ownership In this

discussion, we will slightly modify the facts of our previous example where the reported book values of the investee's net assets equal their fair values. In that example, the book value of the investee's Stockholders' Equity on the date of the acquisition is $800. Now, let's assume that, instead of purchasing 100% of the company for $800, the investor purchases a 30% interest in the investee for $240 ($800 × 30%), in cash, and has significant influence over the investee company. As before, assume that the investee earns a profit of $300 and pays a total dividend of $100, with $30 (30%) paid to the investor and the remainder paid to other shareholders. The investee's Stockholders' Equity at the end of the year increases by $200, as before, to a balance of $1,000.

Following are the required journal entries by the investor to record the initial investment and the subsequent recognition of equity income and dividends received:

1.	Equity investment.	240	
	Cash		240
	(to record the purchase of the Equity Investment)		
2.	Equity investment.	90	
	Equity income		90
	(to record the Equity Income — $30% of $300)		
3.	Cash.	30	
	Equity investment		30
	(to record the receipt of dividends of $30)		

We have multiplied all of the previous journal entry amounts by 30%, the proportion of the investee that the investor owns in this example. The investor initially records the Equity Investment at its purchase price of $240, and subsequently recognizes the dividends received of $30 as a reduction of that account. For the income recognition, when the investor owns less than 100% of the investee, it can only record equity income equal to the proportion of the investee's income that it owns. Since the investee is reporting $300 of income in this case, the investor recognizes 30% of that amount ($90) in its income statement as Equity Income.

The T-account for the Equity Investment illustrates these changes:

Equity Investment			
Beginning balance	240		
Equity income	90	30	Dividends received
Ending balance	300		

The relation between the Equity Investment account on the investor's balance sheet and the investee's Stockholders' Equity still holds. The investee reports Stockholders' Equity of $1,000 at the end of the year, and, since the 30% investment was acquired at book value, the investor reports an Equity Investment of $300, representing the 30% of the investee's Stockholders' Equity that it owns.

One final note: in the previous section we discuss the deferral of unrealized profit on intercompany inventory sales. In that example, the investee sold inventory with a gross profit of $30 that the investor deferred at the end of the year. The deferral of that profit *when the investor owns less than 100% of the investee* is handled in one of two ways:

1. **Investor *controls* the investee**—when the investor owns less than 100%, but still controls the investee (say, for ownership levels in excess of 51% of the outstanding common stock), the investor defers 100% of the intercompany profit for downstream sales (i.e., the intercompany inventory was sold by the parent to the subsidiary and it is still held by the subsidiary at the end of the period) or only the portion of the gross profit it owns for upstream sales (i.e., the intercompany inventory was sold by the subsidiary to the parent and it is still held by the parent at the end of the period). Note that Chapter 5 includes extensive discussion of the treatment of upstream versus downstream intercompany profits.

2. **Investor has a *significant influence* over the investee**—when the investor has a significant influence over the investee (say for ownership levels less than or equal to 50%), it defers only the proportion of the gross profit that it owns, regardless of whether the intercompany sale (and remaining period-end inventory) is upstream or downstream. For example, if the investor owns 30% of the investee, and the gross profit on the intercompany sale is $30, the investor defers $9 ($30 × 30%) in the following journal entry:[18]

Equity income.	9	
Equity investment		9
(to record the deferral of gross profit on inventory sale in the period of sale)		

To further illustrate case two, consider the deferral of intercompany profit at **Lion's Gate Entertainment Corp** (Lionsgate), an American entertainment company. In addition to sales of theatrical releases, other films, and television programs to third parties, Lionsgate generates $32.8 million in operating income licensing these products to **EPIX**, a 31.12% significant interest equity method investee. Similar to intercompany sales of inventory, Lionsgate defers, or eliminates, its propor-

---

[18] FASB ASC 323-10-35-9 through 35-11 indicates that proportionate elimination is only allowed if both of the following conditions are met: (1) the investor does not control the investee and (2) the intercompany transactions are considered arm's length. Otherwise, all of the intercompany transaction must be eliminated.

tionate share of the profits from these intercompany licenses by an adjustment to equity income. In the notes to its March 31, 2015 annual report, Lionsgate discloses "Eliminations of the Company's share of profits on licensing sales to EPIX" of $10.2 million (its 31.12% ownership interest in EPIX $\times$ $32.8 million in gross profit on sales to EPIX). The elimination, or deferral, of intercompany profit reduced both the equity income and investment accounts of Lionsgate by $10.2 million during the year ended March 31, 2015.

The reason we draw the distinction between the two cases above is this: for an entity that is controlled (and ultimately consolidated), the equity method of accounting should yield equity income for the investor equal to that which it would report if the investee is consolidated. We begin our discussion of the consolidation process in Chapter 2, and discuss intercompany asset sales more thoroughly in Chapter 4. Then, we will see that *all* intercompany sales are eliminated in the consolidation process. Thus, we draw a distinction between the first case above in which the two companies will be consolidated (and *all* intercompany sales will be eliminated), and the second case in which they will not (thus, the investor might only eliminate the investor's proportionate interest in the profit on the intercompany sale).

When Can the Equity Method be Used?

As we discuss earlier in this chapter, the equity method is required when the investor can exercise significant influence over the investee's operating activities. Further, at the point when the investor can "control" the operating activities of the investee, the investor is required to consolidate its financial statements with those of the investee company. In this section, we discuss what that means.

There are two important points to keep in mind. First, both the investor and investee companies are separate legal entities, each with their own financial statements. We need to account for the operations of both companies separately. That does not change even though one company owns another. And second, the investor will continue to report the investee on the investor's balance sheet using the same Equity Investment account that we have described throughout this chapter. This will be true whether the investor has significant influence over or controls the investee company.

The consolidation process that we describe in Chapter 2 involves a combining of the financial statements of the two companies for external reporting purposes. In its most basic form, consolidation involves replacing the Equity Investment account with the assets and liabilities of the investee company to which the Equity Investment relates. Likewise, we replace the Equity Income account in the income statement with the revenues and expenses of the investee company.[19]

Bottom line: the investor accounts for its Equity Investment using the equity method from the time it acquires significant influence and, for *internal* reporting purposes, can continue to account for the investee using the equity method even after it gains control. However, when the investor gains control over the investee, the investor must issue consolidated financial statements for *external* financial reporting purposes. We begin our discussion of the consolidation process in Chapter 2.

---

[19] As will become much clearer in Chapters 2 through 6, consolidation is a process of replacing the equity-investment-related accounts recorded on the parent's accounting records with the financial statements of the subsidiary investee. Because the parent company typically does not report the pre-consolidation equity-investment-related accounts, the parent company is free to use any investment accounting method for its pre-consolidation internal record keeping. However, even when issuing consolidated financial statements after control is reached, the parent is permitted to supplement its consolidated financial statements with "parent only" financial statements that reflect the subsidiary as an equity method investment (i.e., the parent must use the equity method in these publicly reported supplemental financial statements). The equity method provides the clearest linkage between the pre-consolidation financial statements of the parent company and the post-consolidation consolidated financial statements. This is why, in Chapters 2 through 6, we introduce consolidation topics assuming the parent company uses the equity method. However, in real-world applications, companies rarely use the equity method, and are more likely to use some hybrid method or the cost method. Therefore, in Chapters 2 through 6, we provide additional coverage assuming the parent company uses the cost method.

PRACTICE INSIGHT

Determining Degrees of Influence and Share of Profits   While this topic is covered in Chapter 6 on Variable Interest Entities, it deserves a bit of attention here so one understands the following assumptions used in this chapter do not always hold in the real world:

(1) control is determined by voting rights greater than 50%
(2) an investor can only recognize equity income in proportion to the investee that it owns.

In the modern business environment, various agreements govern control and economic interests. Financial statement preparers must review contractual arrangements and consider other factors in determining an entity's degree of influence and what income is attributable to investors. To illustrate, consider this disclosure from Merck's 2013 10-K about AstraZeneca LP (AZLP), a pharmaceutical joint venture of **Merck** and **AstraZeneca plc**, where control and income are determined by contractual rights.

> While maintaining a 1% limited partner interest in AZLP, Merck has consent and protective rights intended to preserve its business and economic interests, including restrictions on the power of the general partner to make certain distributions or dispositions. Furthermore, in limited events of default, additional rights will be granted to the Company, including powers to direct the actions of, or remove and replace, the Partnership's chief executive officer and chief financial officer. Merck earns ongoing revenue based on sales of KBI products and such revenue was $920 million, $915 million and $1.2 billion in 2013, 2012, and 2011, respectively, primarily relating to sales of Nexium, as well as Prilosec. In addition, Merck earns certain Partnership returns . . . Such returns include a priority return provided for in the Partnership Agreement, a preferential return representing Merck's share of undistributed AZLP GAAP earnings, and a variable return related to the Company's 1% limited partner interest
>
> Merck's partnership returns from AZLP are generally contractually determined as noted above and are not based on a percentage of income from AZLP, other than with respect to Merck's 1% limited partnership interest.
>
> Source: Merck 2013 10-K

TOPIC REVIEW 6

Accounting for the Effects on Equity Investments of Intercompany Sales of Inventory When Less Than 100% of the Investee Is Owned

Assume that an investor sells parts, that originally cost $50, to an investee for $75. Also assume that 60% of the parts inventories remain on the investee's balance sheet at the end of the period, and that the investor owns only 1/3 (33.3%) of the investee.

Required

Provide the journal entry to defer the recognition of gross profit on the inventories that remain on the investee's balance sheet.

The solution to this review problem can be found on page 45.

Discontinuance of the Equity Method

LO7 Explain when the equity method should be discontinued.

It is possible that the reported amount of the Equity Investment might be reduced to zero on the investor's balance sheet. This can occur because of any or all of the following:

1. Investee company losses
2. Payment of dividends by the investee to the investor in excess of the amount of cumulative Equity Income reported by the investor

3. Write-down of the Equity Investment by the investor as a result of its determination that the fair value of the investment has permanently declined.[20]

When the reported amount of the Equity Investment is reduced to zero, the investor ceases to use the equity method to account for its Equity Investment. Instead, the investment is carried on the investor's balance sheet at a zero amount until the investee earns sufficient profit such that the unrealized loss is eliminated.

To illustrate, assume that the investee company reports a number of years of losses followed by a number of profitable years as illustrated in the following graphic:

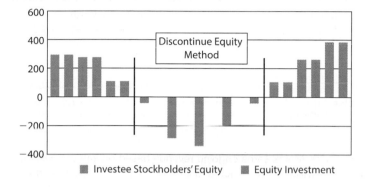

We assume that the investor owns 100% of the investee and that the Equity Investment was acquired at book value to simplify the example. The reported amount of the Equity Investment, therefore, equals the Stockholders' Equity of the investee. As the investee reports losses, the investor reduces the reported amount of its Equity Investment until the Stockholders' Equity of the investee company reaches zero. At that point, the investor ceases to recognize equity losses until the investee resumes profitability and the deficit Stockholders' Equity has been eliminated. At that point, the investor resumes accounting for its Equity Investment using the equity method.[21]

Accounting for a Change to and from the Equity Method

As we discuss in our introduction to this chapter, GAAP specifies different accounting methods for investments in securities that depend on the level of influence that the investor has over the investee. Sometimes, that level of influence can change over time, say, by the investor purchasing additional shares of the investee, the investee repurchasing its own shares from other parties, thereby increasing the percentage owned by the investor, or by other events, such as the investor gaining representation on the board of directors of the investee company or engaging in material intercompany transactions, and so forth. All of these events and transactions would suggest that the level of influence of the investor over the investee has increased.

LO8 Explain the accounting for changes to and from the equity method.

Prior to gaining significant influence, investments will have been accounted for by the fair value or cost methods. We first discuss the accounting procedures required for a change from both of these methods to the equity method, followed by a discussion of the change from the equity method to another method.

Change from the Fair Value Method to the Equity Method   If the investment had been accounted for by the fair value method, the investment account will consist of the original cost plus (minus) the fair value adjustment (the difference between fair value and cost). The adoption of equity method accounting for this investment involves two steps:

---

[20] Equity Investments are treated just like any other asset. If they decline in fair value, and that decline is deemed to be other than temporary, the investor must write down the reported amount of the Equity Investment to its lower fair value and report the write-down as a loss in the period it is recognized.

[21] An exception to this rule arises if the investor has guaranteed the debts of the investee company. In that case, the investor reports the negative balance of the Equity Investment as a liability.

1. Removing the Fair Value Adjustment from the investment account and the associated Unrealized Holding Gain (Loss) from the Accumulated Other Comprehensive Income (AOCI) account of Stockholders' Equity, and

2. Adjusting the Equity Investment account for the cumulative profit that the investor would have recorded had the equity method been in use, less the reduction for any dividends received. The offset to this adjustment is to the beginning balance of Retained Earnings (prior period adjustment).[22]

The objective of these adjustments is to adjust the Equity Investment account (and the investor's Retained Earnings) to what it would have been had the equity method been followed from the initial purchase of the investment.

To illustrate, assume that the investor has accounted for a $10,000 cost, 10% investment in the investee using the fair value method (available-for-sale designation). The following additional information is available:

Cumulative Dividends Received from Investee	10% of the Cumulative Profits Recorded by Investee	Cumulative Fair Value Adjustment for 10% Interest
$10,000	$30,000	$25,000

Now, assume that the investor acquires an additional 20% interest in the investee and concludes that it can now exert significant influence over the investee. We must now account for the investment using the equity method instead of the fair value method. The required journal entries to account for the change from the fair value method to the equity method for the original investment are as follows:

1.	Unrealized holding gain (AOCI)	25,000	
	Equity investment		25,000
	(to remove the unrealized gain from stockholders' equity and the fair value adjustment from the investment account)		
2.	Equity investment.	20,000	
	Retained earnings (prior period adjustment)		20,000
	(to adjust the Equity Investment to its correct amount at the beginning of the year and to increase the beginning of the year Retained Earnings for the cumulative equity income that would have been recognized)		

The Unrealized Holding Gain is reversed from both Stockholders' Equity and the investment account, and Retained Earnings is adjusted for the net effect of the equity income less the receipt of dividends ($30,000 − $10,000).

The effect of these adjusting entries is to report the Equity Investment at the balance that would have been reported as of the beginning of the year had the equity method been in use from the acquisition of the investment and to correct the beginning balance of Retained Earnings for the cumulative differences between the equity and fair value methods of accounting for this investment. In subsequent periods, then, the investor accounts for its Equity Investment using the equity method of accounting as we describe earlier in the chapter.

Change from the Cost Method to the Equity Method

The cost method is used for investments in which the investor cannot exercise significant influence and for which a readily determinable fair value does not exist. An example might be an investment in a privately held (non-public) company. The accounting for these investments is relatively simple: the investment is always reported on the balance sheet at its original cost and any dividends that the investor receives are treated as dividend income, thus increasing Retained Earnings.

---

[22] On November 19, 2015, the FASB unanimously voted to direct its staff to draft a new standard that eliminates "the requirement that entities retroactively adopt the equity method of accounting if an investment that was previously accounted for on other than the equity method becomes qualified for use of the equity method by an increase in the level of ownership interest or degree of influence" (FASB Meeting Minutes, November 19, 2015). When this text was printed, the FASB had not yet issued this final standard. If adopted, the new transition rule will require prospective (instead of retroactive) transition to the equity method, and, based on the June 5, 2015 Exposure Draft, will likely require an investor to add the pre-equity-method carrying value of an equity investment to the incremental cost of any additional investment (i.e., that results in the investor obtaining significant influence). This proposed change will greatly simplify the transition process.

As in our previous example, we assume that the investor has acquired additional shares of the investee company and concludes that it can now exert significant influence over the investee. Since the original investment is reported at its original cost of $10,000, to change from the cost method to the equity method for this investment, we need to increase the investment by the $20,000 difference between the cumulative profits and the dividends paid by the investee:

Equity investment.	20,000	
Retained earnings		20,000
(prior period adjustment)		

In subsequent periods, then, the investor accounts for its Equity Investment using the equity method of accounting as we describe earlier in the chapter.

Change from the Equity Method to the Fair Value or Cost Methods

When the level of influence changes, such that the investor can no longer exert significant influence over the investee company's operating activities, use of the equity method is no longer appropriate and either the fair value or cost method must be used. The change from the equity method to one of these two methods is simple: the amount at which the Equity Investment is reported (i.e., its book value) on the date of change becomes the cost of the security. The accounting for the security using either the cost or fair value methods proceeds as usual from that point forward.

To illustrate, assume that the investor reports an Equity Investment on its balance sheet in the amount of $20,000 and that it can no longer exert significant influence over the investee company (possibly due to the issuance of additional shares to outside parties, thus diluting the investor's ownership percentage). Assume that the investor will account for this investment using the fair value method (available-for-sale designation) and that the fair value of the shares owned has increased to $25,000 at the next reporting period. The investor will treat the investment as though it has a cost of $20,000 and a fair value of $25,000, and the required journal entry to record the increase in fair value is as follows:

Equity investment.	5,000	
Net unrealized holding gains and losses—OCI		5,000
(to record the increase in fair value of the AFS security)		

TOPIC REVIEW 7

Reporting a Change to the Equity Method

To illustrate, assume that the investor has accounted for a $20,000 cost, 10% investment in the investee using the fair value method (available-for-sale designation). The following additional information is available:

Cumulative Dividends Received from Investee	10% of the Cumulative Profits Recorded by Investee	Cumulative Fair Value Adjustment for 10% Interest
$20,000	$60,000	$50,000

Now, assume that the investor acquires an additional 20% interest in the investee and concludes that it can now exert significant influence over the investee. We must account for the original investment using the equity method instead of the fair value method.

Required

Provide the required journal entries to account for the change from the fair value method to the equity method for the original investment.

The solution to this review problem can be found on page 45.

LO9 Explain the required disclosures for equity method investments.

Required Disclosures for Equity Method Investments

FASB ASC 323-10-50 identifies required disclosures relating to investments accounted for under the equity method:

a. The name of each investee and percentage of ownership of common stock, the accounting policies of the investor with respect to investments in common stock, and the difference, if any, between the amount at which an investment is carried and the amount of underlying equity in net assets and the accounting treatment of the difference.

b. For those investments in common stock for which a quoted market price is available, the aggregate value of each identified investment based on the quoted market price usually should be disclosed. This disclosure is not required for investments in common stock of subsidiaries.

c. When investments in common stock of corporate joint ventures or other investments accounted for under the equity method are, in the aggregate, material in relation to the financial position or results of operations of an investor, it may be necessary for summarized information as to assets, liabilities, and results of operations of the investees to be presented in the notes or in separate statements, either individually or in groups, as appropriate.

d. Conversion of outstanding convertible securities, exercise of outstanding options and warrants and other contingent issuances of an investee may have a significant effect on an investor's share of reported earnings or losses. Accordingly, material effects of possible conversions, exercises or contingent issuances should be disclosed in notes to the financial statements of an investor.

LO10 Explain the criticisms of the equity method of accounting.

Criticism of the Equity Method

We make two final points about equity method accounting. First, there can be a substantial difference between the book value of an equity method investment and its fair value. An increase in value is not recognized until the investment is sold. If the fair value of the investment has permanently declined, however, the investment is deemed impaired and it is written down to that lower fair value. Second, if the investee company reports income, the investor company reports its share. Recognition of equity income by the investor, however, does not mean that it has received that income in *cash*. Cash is only received if the investee pays a dividend.[23]

The investor company reports equity method investments on the balance sheet at an amount equal to the percentage owned of the investee company's equity when that investment is acquired at book value. As we discussed previously, purchases of equity investments are rarely made at book value because (1) the investee's financial statements are prepared using historical costing and, for the most part, do not reflect current fair values and (2) there may be unrecorded assets, such as internally developed intangible assets. To illustrate, consider the case of **Simon Property Group**, a commercial real estate company based in Indianapolis, Indiana, and the largest real estate investment trust (REIT) in the United States. Simon describes its financial reporting for equity investments as follows:

Excerpts from recent financial statements and notes are used to illustrate and reinforce concepts.

> We consolidate properties that are wholly owned or properties where we own less than 100% but we control. Control of a property is demonstrated by, among other factors, our ability to refinance debt and sell the property without the consent of any other partner or owner and the inability of any other partner or owner to replace us.
>
> Investments in partnerships and joint ventures represent our noncontrolling ownership interests in properties. We account for these investments using the equity method of accounting. We initially record these investments at cost and we subsequently adjust for net equity in income or loss, which we allocate in accordance with the provisions of the applicable partnership or joint venture agreement, cash contributions and distributions, and foreign currency fluctuations, if applicable. The allocation provisions in the partnership or joint venture agreements are not always consistent with the legal ownership interests held by each general or limited partner or joint venture investee primarily due to partner preferences.

---

[23] To highlight this, the investor's statement of cash flows will include a reconciling item (a deduction from net income in computing operating cash flow) for its percentage share of the investee's net income. This is typically reported net of any cash dividends received.

> As of December 31, 2014, we consolidated 133 wholly-owned properties and 13 additional properties that are less than wholly-owned, but which we control or for which we are the primary beneficiary. We account for the remaining 82 properties, or the joint venture properties . . . using the equity method of accounting, as we have determined we have significant influence over their operations.

At the end of 2014, Simon's balance sheet included an equity-method net investment in unconsolidated entities equal to $1.2 billion. The presentation of this balance, in a single account, is why the equity method is called "one-line consolidation." If you think about it, this type of presentation suggests that the investment is a stand-alone asset that generates equity-method income. Indeed, Simon's income statement shows that the company reported income from equity method investments equal to $227 million.

A closer look, however, reveals how the equity method presentation can hide the real risks underlying the investment. Supplemental disclosures reveal that these unconsolidated joint ventures and partnerships have aggregate reported total assets equal to $12.5 billion and total liabilities equal to $14.8 billion. Yes, that means the book value of equity for these unconsolidated ventures is *negative* $2.3 billion! A logical question is, how does negative reported equity of $2.3 turn into a $1.2 billion positive equity method investment balance? Well, first of all, Simon owns less than half of these entities, so Simon's share of the accumulated deficit is only negative $0.7 billion. Second, Simon paid amounts higher than book value for the equity investments in these affiliates. The unamortized excess purchase price at December 31, 2014 is equal to $1.9 billion. This converts the negative $0.7 billion book value amount to a reported equity method investment balance of $1.2 billion. The one-line equity method presentation doesn't provide any information about the total assets included in these ventures, and, more importantly, completely ignores the negative equity caused by the high leverage of the affiliates.

The cooperative experience of **Dow Chemical Company** and **Corning, Incorporated** provides an illustration of the flexibility afforded by joint venture arrangements and the appropriateness of equity method accounting for those arrangements. The Dow Corning joint venture was formed in 1943 by Corning Glass Works (now Corning, Inc.) and Dow Chemical Company. The purpose of the joint venture is to develop silicone-based technologies and to pursue business opportunities related to those technologies. An extremely popular technology developed and sold by Dow Corning was silicone breast implants. Unfortunately, those implants caused serious health problems for thousands of consumers. According to Corning, Inc.'s December 31, 2014 SEC Form 10-K, "In May 1995, Dow Corning filed for bankruptcy protection to address pending and claimed liabilities arising from many thousands of breast implant product lawsuits. On June 1, 2004, Dow Corning emerged from Chapter 11 with a Plan of Reorganization (the Plan) which provided for the settlement or other resolution of implant claims. The Plan also includes releases for Corning and Dow Chemical as shareholders in exchange for contributions to the Plan." Dow Corning's history suggests that the joint venture arrangement allowed both Dow Chemical and Corning, Inc. to significantly reduce their potential liability related to the breast-implant lawsuits.

CHAPTER SUMMARY ← *Summaries review key points for each Learning Objective.*

The accounting for these investments depends on the degree to which the investor can influence the activities of the investee. Exhibit 1.4 summarizes the three levels of influence or control for publicly traded securities and the cost method for investments in companies for which readily determinable fair values for their stock does not exist (private companies, for example) and the prescribed accounting method for each:

EXHIBIT 1.4	Investment Type, Accounting Treatment, and Financial Statement Effects			
	Accounting	**Balance Sheet Effects**	**Income Statement Effects**	**Cash Flow Effects**
Passive	Fair value method	Investment account is reported at current fair value	Dividends and capital gains included in income Interim changes in fair value may or may not affect income depending on whether the investor actively trades the securities Sale of investment yields capital gain or loss	Dividends and sale proceeds are cash inflows Purchases are cash outflows
No readily determinable fair value	Cost	Investment account is reported at original cost (purchase price)	Dividends and capital gains included in income Interim changes in fair value not recognized	Dividends and sale proceeds are cash inflows Purchases are cash outflows
Significant influence	Equity method	Investment account equals percent owned of investee company's equity*	Dividends reduce investment account Investor reports income equal to percent owned of investee income Sale of investment yields capital gain or loss	Dividends and sale proceeds are cash inflows Purchases are cash outflows
Control	Consolidation	Balance sheets of investor and investee are combined	Income statements of investor and investee are combined (and sale of investee yields capital gain or loss)	Cash flows of investor and investee are combined (and sale/purchase of investee yields cash inflow/outflow)

*Investments are often acquired at purchase prices in excess of book value (on average, market prices are 1.5 times book value for public companies). In this case the investment account exceeds the proportionate ownership of the investee's equity by the amount of the unamortized excess. In addition, companies may take an irrevocable option to value each individual equity investment at fair value under ASC 825-10-25.

Use of the equity method is prescribed when the investor can exert significant influence over the investee company's operating activities. Significant influence is presumed when the investor owns in excess of 20% of the outstanding voting stock of the investee, but can arise with ownership levels less than that if it gains significant representation on the board of directors, participates actively in the investee's operating decisions, provides investee with significant technology, and so forth.

There are a number of important points relating to the use of the equity method:

1. The investor can only recognize equity income subsequent to the date it purchases the Equity Investment.

2. The investor can only recognize equity income equal to the proportion of the investee that it owns.

3. The investor must defer unrealized gains on intercompany sales.

4. The investor must discontinue the use of the equity method if the investee becomes insolvent (i.e., reports negative stockholders' equity) or if the investment is written down to a zero balance.

5. Reporting Equity Income does not imply that cash dividends have been received.

6. Reporting the Equity Investment potentially omits a significant amount of assets and liabilities from the investor's balance sheet and a significant amount of sales and expenses from the investor's income statement (this objection is overcome if the investee is consolidated with the investor).

7. The investor may have practical liability for the investee company's liabilities even if no actual liability exists.

COMPREHENSIVE REVIEW

Assume that in 2013 the investor purchases a 10% investment in the investee for $100,000 and accounts for that investment using the fair value method (available-for-sale designation). In 2016, the investor acquires an additional 25% of the outstanding common stock of the investee for $250,000. The following additional information is available on the date of purchase:

Cumulative Dividends Paid by Investee	Cumulative Profits Recorded by the Investee	Cumulative Fair Value Adjustment on Investor's Balance Sheet
$150,000	$400,000	$35,000

The investee's balance sheet on the date of the additional purchase is as follows:

Accounts receivable.	$100,000	Mortgage payable	$200,000
Inventories	200,000		
Building	400,000	Stockholders' equity	500,000
Total assets.	$700,000	Total liabilities and equity	$700,000

The investor is willing to pay $250,000 for 25% of the stock of the investee (implying a fair value of the investee of $250,000/25% = $1,000,000) because the investee has a patent that the investor estimates is worth $500,000. That patent will expire in 10 years.

Subsequent to the purchase, the investee reports net income of $200,000 and pays $90,000 in dividends. In addition, the investor sells inventories to the investee that cost $50,000 for a sale price of $80,000. At the end of the year, 60% of the parts inventories remain on the investee's balance sheet.

Required

Record each of the following adjustments subsequent to the purchase of the additional 25% interest.

a. Provide the journal entry to account for the change from the fair value method to the equity method for the original investment.
b. Provide the journal entry to recognize the Equity Income by the investor.
c. Provide the journal entry to record the receipt of the dividend.
d. Provide the journal entry to record the amortization of the Patent asset.
e. Provide the journal entry to record the deferral of gross profit on the intercompany inventory sale.

The solution to this review problem can be found on page 45.

QUESTIONS

1. Equity Investments are sometimes referred to as "one-line consolidations." That means that the balance sheets of the investor and investee companies are combined and that the Stockholders' Equity of the investor company is equal to that which would be obtained had the investor and the investee's balance sheets been combined. It also means that the investor's income statement reports the same net income as would have been reported by a combination of the income statements of the investor and investee companies.

   a. How is the reporting of an Equity Investment like a consolidation (i.e., yielding the same Stockholders' Equity for the Parent company that would result from a consolidation)? How is it different?

   b. How is the reporting of equity income in the investor's income statement a consolidation (i.e., yielding the same net income for the parent company that would result from a consolidation)? How is it different?

2. In applying the equity method of accounting for Equity Investments, dividends are treated as a reduction of the Equity Investment rather than as dividend income. Why?

3. Equity Income is recognized based on the net income of the investee company rather than from dividends. While this approach may have theoretical merit, what potential problems might this cause for your evaluation of the cash-flow-generating ability of the investor?

4. Prior to 2008, **CBS Corp.** owned approximately 18% of Westwood One, Inc. which managed the CBS Radio Network. CBS, in turn, managed Westwood under a management agreement. Further, one employee of CBS was a member of Westwood's board of directors. CBS did not control the board of directors, however. In this situation, how should CBS account for its investment in Westwood One?

5. According to Footnote 4 of **Time Warner Inc.**'s December 31, 2014 annual report:

> . . . [f]or the years ended December 31, 2014, 2013 and 2012, the Company incurred writedowns to reduce the carrying value of certain investments that experienced other-than-temporary impairments, as set forth below (millions):

	December 31		
	2014	**2013**	**2012**
Equity-method investments	$21	$ 5	$25
Cost-method investments	8	5	14
Available-for-sale securities	6	7	7
Total	$35	$17	$46

According to Time Warner, "the impairment of equity-method investments [were] primarily related to the shutdown of TNT television operations in Turkey." FASB ASC 323-10-35-32 provides the following guidance for other-than-temporary impairment of equity-method investments: "A loss in value of an investment that is other than a temporary decline shall be recognized. Evidence of a loss in value might include, but would not necessarily be limited to, absence of an ability to recover the carrying amount of the investment or inability of the investee to sustain an earnings capacity that would justify the carrying amount of the investment. A current fair value of an investment that is less than its carrying amount may indicate a loss in value of the investment. However, a decline in the quoted market price below the carrying amount or the existence of operating losses is not necessarily indicative of a loss in value that is other than temporary. All are factors that shall be evaluated."

   a. What must have Time Warner's managers concluded about the fair value of its investment in TNT to justify the write-down of this investment?

   b. How much judgment is involved in the decision to write down an investment and how might a company use that judgment to manage the level of net income that it reports?

6. In applying the equity method of accounting for an Equity Investment, profits on intercompany sales of assets are eliminated (FASB ASC 323-10-35-5). Why?

7. Consider the following scenario: an investor owns 10% of an investee company with publicly traded stock, and licenses technology to the investee for the production of its sole product. None of the investor's employees serve in the management of the investee company, nor sit on its board of directors. The license agreement prohibits the investee from certain business activities, such as entering into business arrangements with other companies without the investor's consent, using the technology to develop products except as authorized by the investor, and expanding the business into new lines of business without the investor's approval. How should the investor account for its investment in the investee company?

8. Consider the following scenario: an investor owns 30% of an investee company. The remaining 70% is owned by the investee's founder who has managed the company since its inception and takes no direction from "outsiders." How should the investor account for its investment?

9. FASB ASC 323-10-35-19 provides the following: "An investor's share of losses of an investee may equal or exceed the carrying amount of an investment accounted for by the equity method plus advances made by the investor. The investor ordinarily should discontinue applying the equity method when the investment (and net advances) is reduced to zero and should not provide for additional losses unless the investor has guaranteed obligations of the investee or is otherwise committed to provide further financial support for the investee. If the investee subsequently reports net income, the

investor should resume applying the equity method only after its share of that net income equals the share of net losses not recognized during the period the equity method was suspended."

a. **Enron**, the infamous energy company that failed in the early 2000s, disclosed that it invested in companies that reported substantial losses and were technically insolvent (i.e., deficit Stockholders' Equity). Enron used the equity method to account for these investments, had not made any advances to them, and did not guarantee their debts. How did the losses by its investee companies affect Enron's income statement?

b. What is meant by this phrase in FASB ASC 323-10-35-22: "only after its share of that net income equals the share of net losses not recognized during the period the equity method was suspended"?

10. What disclosures are required for equity method investments under FASB ASC 323?

Assignments with the logo in the margin are available in BusinessCourse.
See the Preface of the book for details.

MULTIPLE CHOICE

Use the following facts for Multiple Choice problems 11 through 14 (each question is independent of the others):

Assume that on January 1, 2016 an investor company paid $1,050 to an investee company in exchange for the following assets and liabilities transferred from the investee company:

Asset (Liability)	Estimated Fair Value
Production equipment	300
Factory	500
Licenses	350
Accrued liability	(150)

In addition, assume that the investor paid an additional $50 of transaction costs to a third party. The fair values are measured in accordance with FASB ASC 820: *Fair Value Measurement.*

Homework icons indicate which assignments are available in **myBusinessCourse** *(MBC). This feature is only available when the instructor incorporates MBC in the course.*

11. **Acquiring net assets that do not constitute a business**
Assume the net assets transferred from the investee do not qualify as a "business," as that term is defined in FASB ASC Master Glossary. At what amount will the Licenses be reported in the financial statements of the acquiring company on January 1, 2016?

LO1

a. $350
b. $368
c. $385
d. $400

12. **Acquiring net assets that do not constitute a business**
Assume the net assets transferred from the investee do not qualify as a "business," as that term is defined in FASB ASC Master Glossary. At what amount will Goodwill be reported in the financial statements of the acquiring company on January 1, 2016?

LO1

a. $100
b. $50
c. $0
d. $(50)

LOs link assignments to the Learning Objectives of each chapter.

13. **Acquiring net assets that constitute a business**
Assume the net assets transferred from the investee qualify as a "business," as that term is defined in FASB ASC Master Glossary. At what amount will the Licenses be reported in the financial statements of the acquiring company on January 1, 2016?

LO1

a. $350
b. $368
c. $385
d. $400

LO1 **14. Acquiring net assets that constitute a business**

Assume the net assets transferred from the investee qualify as a "business," as that term is defined in FASB ASC Master Glossary. At what amount will Goodwill be reported in the financial statements of the acquiring company on January 1, 2016?

   a. $100

   b. $50

   c. $0

   d. $(50)

Use the following facts for Multiple Choice problems 15 and 16:

Assume that on January 1, 2016, the investor company issued 7,000 new shares of the investor company's common stock in exchange for all of the individually identifiable assets and liabilities of the investee company. Fair value approximates book value for all of the investee's identifiable net assets. The following financial statement information is for an investor company and an investee company on January 1, 2016, prepared immediately before this transaction.

Multiple choice questions have been adapted from CPA exam questions to help students prepare for the exam.

	Book Values	
	Investor	Investee
Receivables & inventories	$ 80,000	$ 36,000
Land	160,000	80,000
Property & equipment	180,000	80,000
Total assets	$420,000	$196,000
Liabilities	$126,000	$ 63,000
Common stock ($1 par)	16,000	8,000
Additional paid-in capital	224,000	120,000
Retained earnings	54,000	5,000
Total liabilities & equity	$420,000	$196,000
Net assets	$294,000	$133,000

LO1 **15. Asset acquisition (fair value equals book value)**

If this transaction is to result in the investor recording no goodwill (or gain from "negative goodwill"), what is the per share fair value of the investor's common stock?

   a. $19/share

   b. $28/share

   c. $42/share

   d. $60/share

LO1 **16. Asset acquisition (fair value equals book value)**

Provide the investor company's balance (i.e., on the investor's books, before consolidation) for an "Investment in Investee" account immediately following the acquisition of the investee's net assets:

   a. $7,000

   b. $128,000

   c. $133,000

   d. $294,000

Use the following facts for Multiple Choice problems 17 and 18 (each question is independent of the other):

The following financial statement information is for an investor company and an investee company on January 1, 2016. On January 1, 2016, the investor company's common stock had a traded market value of $22 per share, and the investee company's common stock had a traded market value of $18 per share.

	Book Values		Fair Values	
	Investor	Investee	Investor	Investee
Receivables & inventories	$ 96,000	$ 48,000	$ 90,000	$ 43,200
Land.....................................	192,000	96,000	210,000	120,000
Property & equipment	216,000	96,000	240,000	124,800
Trademarks & patents	—	—	80,000	76,800
Total assets..........................	$504,000	$240,000	$620,000	$364,800
Liabilities............................	$144,000	$ 76,800	$160,000	$ 82,000
Common stock ($1 par)	20,000	16,000		
Additional paid-in capital	268,000	137,600		
Retained earnings	72,000	9,600		
Total liabilities & equity.................	$504,000	$240,000		
Net assets	$360,000	$163,200	$460,000	$282,800

17. **Asset acquisition (fair value is different from book value)**

Assume that the investor company issued 15,000 new shares of the investor company's common stock in exchange for all of the individually identifiable assets and liabilities of the investee company, in a transaction that qualifies as a business combination. The financial information presented, above, was prepared immediately before this transaction. Provide the Investor Company's balance (i.e., on the investor's books, before consolidation) for "Goodwill" immediately following the acquisition of the investee's net assets:

LO1

AICPA
Adapted

a. $166,800

b. $119,600

c. $47,200

d. $5,200

18. **Stock acquisition (fair value is different from book value)**

Assume that the investor company issued 15,000 new shares of the investor company's common stock in exchange for 100% of the common stock of the investee company, in a transaction that qualifies as a business combination. The financial information presented, above, was prepared immediately before this transaction. Provide the Investor Company's balance (i.e., on the investor's books, before consolidation) for "Investment in Investee" immediately following the acquisition of the investee's common stock:

LO1

AICPA
Adapted

a. $460,000

b. $330,000

c. $282,800

d. $270,000

Use the following facts for Multiple Choice problems 19 and 20 (each question is independent of the other):

On January 1, 2016, an investor purchases 18,000 common shares of an investee at $12 (cash) per share. The shares represent 25% ownership in the investee. The investee shares are not considered "marketable" because they do not trade on an active exchange. On January 1, 2016, the book value of the investee's assets and liabilities equals $650,000 and $170,000, respectively. On that date, the appraised fair values of the investee's identifiable net assets approximated the recorded book values. During the year ended December 31, 2016, the investee company reported net income equal to $32,500 and dividends equal to $12,000.

AICPA
Adapted

19. **Noncontrolling investment accounting (price equals book value)**

Assume the investor does not exert significant influence over the investee. Determine the balance in the "Investment in Investee" account at December 31, 2016.

LO2,3

AICPA
Adapted

a. $216,000

b. $20,500

c. $228,000

d. $221,125

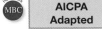

LO2, 3   20. **Noncontrolling investment accounting (price equals book value)**
Assume the investor can exert significant influence over the investee. Determine the balance in the "Investment in Investee" account at December 31, 2016.

a. $216,000

b. $20,500

c. $228,000

d. $221,125

Use the following facts for Multiple Choice problems 21 and 22 (each question is independent of the other):

On January 1, 2016, an investor purchases 16,000 common shares of an investee at $11 (cash) per share. The shares represent 22% ownership in the investee. The investee shares are not considered "marketable" because they do not trade on an active exchange. On January 1, 2016, the book value of the investee's assets and liabilities equals $850,000 and $300,000, respectively. On that date, the appraised fair values of the investee's identifiable net assets approximated the recorded book values, except for a customer list. On January 1, 2016, the customer list had a recorded book value of $0, an estimated fair value equal to $45,000 and a 5 year remaining useful life. During the year ended December 31, 2016, the investee company reported net income equal to $60,000 and dividends equal to $20,000.

LO2, 3, 4   21. **Noncontrolling investment accounting (price different from book value)**
Assume the investor does not exert significant influence over the investee. Determine the balance in the "Investment in Investee" account at December 31, 2016.

a. $216,000

b. $182,820

c. $184,800

d. $176,000

LO2, 3, 4   22. **Noncontrolling investment accounting (price different from book value)**
Assume the investor can exert significant influence over the investee. Determine the balance in the "Investment in Investee" account at December 31, 2016.

a. $216,000

b. $182,820

c. $184,800

d. $176,000

EXERCISES

LO1   23. **Effects of qualifying as a business on asset acquisitions**
Assume that on January 1, 2016 an investor company paid $2,900 to an investee company in exchange for the following assets and liabilities transferred from the investee company:

Asset (Liability)	Investee's Book Value	Estimated Fair Value
Production equipment	$ 300	$ 260
Factory	1,500	1,430
Land	100	390
Patents	0	650
Accrued liabilities	(120)	(130)

In addition, assume that the investor paid an additional $100 of transaction costs to a third party. The book values are from the investee's financial records immediately before the exchange. The fair values are measured in accordance with FASB ASC 820: *Fair Value Measurement*.

Parts a. and b. are independent of each other.

a. Provide the journal entry recorded by the investor company assuming that the net assets transferred from the investee do not qualify as a "business," as that term is defined in FASB ASC Master Glossary.

b.   Provide the journal entry recorded by the investor company assuming that the net assets transferred from the investee qualify as a "business," as that term is defined in FASB ASC Master Glossary.

24. **Asset acquisition vs. stock purchase (fair value equals book value)**   **LO1**
Assume that an investor purchases the business of an investee. The investee company reports the following balance sheet on the acquisition date:

Cash.............................	$ 1,400	Accounts payable..................	$ 2,800
Accounts receivable................	2,800	Accrued liabilities..................	4,200
Inventories	5,600		
Current assets	$ 9,800	Current liabilities..................	$ 7,000
		Long-term liabilities	5,600
PPE, net	14,000	Stockholders' equity	11,200
Total assets......................	$23,800	Total liabilities and equity............	$23,800

Parts a. and b. are independent of each other.

a.   Provide the journal entry if the investor pays cash and purchases the assets and assumes the liabilities of the investee company (assume that the fair value of the assets is equal to their book values).

b.   Provide the journal entry if the investor pays cash and purchases all of the stock of the investee's shareholders.

25. **Asset acquisition vs. stock purchase (fair value is greater than book value)**   **LO1**
Assume the investor purchases the same assets in #24, but now assume that the cash purchase price is $21,000. The investor is willing to purchase the investee's business for $21,000 because it appraises its PPE, net at $19,600, and because it values the investee's customer list at $4,200 (the fair values of all other assets and liabilities are equal to their book values).

Parts a. and b. are independent of each other.

a.   Provide the journal entry if the investor purchases the assets and assumes the liabilities of the investee company.

b.   Provide the journal entry if the investor purchases all of the stock of the investee's shareholders.

26. **Asset acquisition vs. stock acquisition (fair value is different from book value)**   **LO1**
The following financial statement information is for an investor company and an investee company on January 1, 2016. On January 1, 2016, the investor company's common stock had a traded market value of $35 per share, and the investee company's common stock had a traded market value of $31 per share.

	Book Values		Fair Values	
	Investor	Investee	Investor	Investee
Receivables & inventories	$150,000	$ 75,000	$ 135,000	$ 67,500
Land	300,000	150,000	450,000	225,000
Property & equipment	337,500	150,000	375,000	195,000
Trademarks & patents	—	—	225,000	120,000
Total assets.........................	$787,500	$375,000	$1,185,000	$607,500
Liabilities...........................	$225,000	$120,000	$ 270,000	$142,500
Common stock ($1 par)	30,000	15,000		
Additional paid-in capital	420,000	225,000		
Retained earnings	112,500	15,000		
Total liabilities & equity................	$787,500	$375,000		
Net assets	$562,500	$255,000	$ 915,000	$465,000

Parts a. and b. are independent of each other.

a. Assume that the investor company issued 14,250 new shares of the investor company's common stock in exchange for all of the individually identifiable assets and liabilities of the investee company. The financial information presented, above, was prepared immediately before this transaction. Provide the Investor Company's balances (i.e., on the investor's books, before consolidation) for the following accounts immediately following the acquisition of the investee's net assets:

- Receivables & Inventories
- Land
- Property & Equipment
- Trademarks & Patents
- Investment in Investee
- Goodwill
- Liabilities
- Common Stock ($1 par)
- Additional Paid-In Capital
- Retained Earnings

b. Assume that the investor company issued 14,250 new shares of the investor company's common stock in exchange for all of the investee company's common stock. The financial information presented, above, was prepared immediately before this transaction. Provide the Investor Company's balances (i.e., on the investor's books, before consolidation) for the following accounts immediately following the acquisition of the investee's net assets:

- Receivables & Inventories
- Land
- Property & Equipment
- Trademarks & Patents
- Investment in Investee
- Goodwill
- Liabilities
- Common Stock ($1 par)
- Additional Paid-In Capital
- Retained Earnings

LO2 **27. Equity method mechanics**

An investor owns 35% of the outstanding common stock of an investee company. The Equity Investment was reported at $400,000 as of the end of the previous year. During the year, the investee pays dividends of $40,000 to the investor. The investee reports the following income statement for the year:

Revenues	$1,600,000
Expenses	1,256,000
Net income	$ 344,000

a. How much equity income should the investor report in its current year income statement?

b. What amount should the investor report for the Equity Investment in its balance sheet at the end of the year?

c. Assume that the fair value of the investee company is $1.7 million at the end of the year (approximately five times reported earnings). How should the fair value of the investee company be reflected in the investor's financial statements?

LO2 **28. Equity method journal entries (price equals book value)**

Prepare journal entries for the transactions below relating to an Equity Investment accounted for using the equity method.

a. An investor purchases 14,400 common shares of an investee at $9 per share; the shares represent 25% ownership in the investee and the investor concludes that it can exert significant influence over the investee.

b. The investee reports net income of $96,000.

   c.   The investor receives a cash dividend of $1.50 per common share from the investee.

   d.   The investor sells all 14,400 common shares of the investee for $144,600.

29. Equity method journal entries with intercompany sales of inventory LO2, 5

Assume that an investor owns 35% of an investee, and accounts for its investment using the equity method. At the beginning of the year, the Equity Investment was reported on the investor's balance sheet at $360,000. During the year, the investee reported net income of $110,000 and paid dividends of $20,000 to the investor. In addition, the investor sold inventory to the investee, realizing a gross profit of $36,000 on the sale. At the end of the year, 15% of the inventory remained unsold by the investee.

   a.   How much equity income should the investor report for the year?

   b.   What is the balance of the Equity Investment at the end of the year?

   c.   Assume that the inventories are all sold in the following year, that the investee reports $160,000 of net income. How much equity income will the investor report for the following year?

30. Equity method deferred intercompany profits   LO5

Despite a 50% ownership interest, **Lions Gate Entertainment Corp.** (Lionsgate) accounts for its investment in **TVGN**, formerly known as the TV Guide Network, using the equity method of accounting. The company reports the following in its 2014 10-K:

LIONSGATE
TVGN

> *TVGN.* The Company's investment interest in TVGN consists of an equity investment in its common stock units and mandatorily redeemable preferred stock units. The Company has determined it is not the primary beneficiary of TVGN because pursuant to the amended and restated operating agreement of the entity, the power to direct the activities that most significantly impact the economic performance of TVGN is shared with the other 50% owner of TVGN. Accordingly, the Company's interest in TVGN is being accounted for under the equity method of accounting. During the year ended March 31, 2014, the Company contributed $6.5 million to TVGN. Additionally, the Company contributed $4.5 million to TVGN in April 2014.
>
> Transactions with TVGN:
> Lionsgate eliminates gross profit recognized by the Company on licensing sales to TVGN in proportion to the Company's ownership interest in TVGN. There were no revenues or gross profits for licensed product to TVGN recognized by Lionsgate for the year ended March 31, 2014. The table below sets forth the revenues and gross profits recognized by the Company and the calculation of the profit eliminated for the years ended March 31, 2013 and 2012:

Real financial data are used in the assignments to better prepare students for the work they will encounter as an accountant.

(amounts in thousands)	Year Ended March 31,	
	2013	**2012**
Revenue recognized on sales to TVGN	$2,925	$2,925
Gross profit on sales to TVGN	687	969
Ownership interest in TVGN..............................	50%	51%

   a   What amount of intercompany profits from TVGN does Lionsgate defer or eliminate for the year ended March 31, 2013?

   b.   How does the deferral or elimination of TVGN intercompany profits impact Lionsgate's equity income and investment accounts?

31. Equity method journal entries (price greater than book value) LO2, 4

An investor purchases a 30% interest in an investee company, and the investor concludes that it can exert significant influence over the investee. The book value of the investee's Stockholders' Equity on the acquisition date is $400,000, and the investor purchases its 30% interest for $156,000. The investor is willing to pay the purchase price because the investee owns an unrecorded (internally developed) patent that the investor estimates is worth $120,000. The patent has a remaining useful life of 10 years. Subsequent to the acquisition, the investee reports net income of $90,000, and pays a cash dividend to the investor of $13,000. At the end of the first year, the investor sells the Equity Investment for $195,000. Prepare all of the required journal entries to account for this Equity Investment during the year.

LO8 **32. Change from the fair value method to the equity method**

Assume that an investor has accounted for a $320,000 cost, 8% investment in the investee using the fair value method (available-for-sale designation). The following additional information is available:

Cumulative Dividends Received from Investee	8% of the Cumulative Profits Recorded by Investee	Cumulative Fair Value Adjustment for 8% Interest
$37,500	$98,300	$117,600

Now, assume that the investor acquires an additional 17% interest in the investee (bringing the total to 25%) and concludes that it can now exert significant influence over the investee.

a. Provide the required journal entries to account for the change from the fair value method to the equity method for the original investment.

b. Now, assume that the investor has accounted for its investment using the cost method. Provide the required journal entries to account for the change from the cost method to the equity method for the original investment.

LO2, 6 **33. Equity method computations from footnote**

DOW CHEMICAL

Dow Chemical reports Equity Investments of $3,487 million (5% of total assets) and equity income on those investments of $845 million (25% of net income) in its 2014 10-K report. In the footnotes, the company provides the following summary financial information relating to its equity investments:

Summarized Balance Sheet Information at December 31 (in millions)	2014
Current assets	$ 9,611
Noncurrent assets	27,025
Total assets.	$36,636
Current liabilities.	$ 6,321
Noncurrent liabilities.	21,047
Total liabilities	$27,368
Noncontrolling interests	$ 666

Summarized Income Statement Information (in millions)	2014
Sales.	$19,333
Gross profit.	$ 3,526
Net income.	$ 1,673

a. Approximately what percent of the investee companies does Dow Chemical own?

b. Do the investee total liabilities of $27,368 million appear on Dow Chemical's balance sheet? How might these liabilities affect Dow Chemical's cash flow?

LO2, 6 **34. Equity method computations from footnote**

ASTRAZENECA PLC

AstraZeneca PLC is bio-pharmaceutical company headquartered in London, United Kingdom. In Astra-Zeneca's December 31, 2014 Form 20-F filed with the United States Securities and Exchange Commission, the Company described the following joint venture arrangement:

On 30 April 2014, AstraZeneca entered into a joint venture agreement with Samsung Biologics Co. Ltd, to develop a biosimilar using the combined capabilities of the two parties. The agreement resulted in the formation of a joint venture entity based in the UK, Archigen Biotech Limited, with a branch in South Korea. AstraZeneca contributed $70m in cash to the joint venture entity and has a 50% interest in the joint venture. The investment is measured using the equity method. A summarised Statement of Financial Position for Archigen Biotech Limited is set out below.

(in millions)	31 December 2014
Noncurrent assets	$ 76
Current assets	58
Current liabilities.	(6)
Net assets	128
Share capital.	140
Retained earnings	(12)
Total equity	$128

AstraZeneca reported that its equity investment in Archigen Biotech Limited was equal to $64 million before currency translation adjustments.

a.   Confirm that the Equity Investment on AstraZeneca's balance sheet is the correct balance.

b.   AstraZeneca's investment balance on December 31, 2014 is less than its initial investment on April 30, 2014. What is the most likely cause of the decrease? How do you know?

35. **Equity method computations from footnote**

LO2, 6

CUMMINS, INC.

Cummins, Inc., a manufacturer of large engines and electric power generation systems, among other products, reports the following Equity Investments in the footnotes to the December 31, 2014 annual report:

Komatsu alliances	20%–50%	$160
Dongfeng Cummins Engine Company, Ltd.	50%	136
Beijing Foton Cummins Engine Company, Ltd	50%	117
Chongqing Cummins Engine Company, Ltd	50%	92
Cummins-Scania XPI Manufacturing, LLC.	50%	85
Tata Cummins, Ltd	50%	57
North American distributors	49%–50%	41
Other.	Various	293
Total		$981

In addition, Cummins provides the following information about these Equity Investments:

Net sales.	$7,426
Gross margin	1,539
Net earnings.	630
Cummins share of net earnings	$ 330

Current assets	$2,476
Noncurrent assets	1,667
Current liabilities.	(1,875)
Noncurrent liabilities.	(420)
Net assets	$1,848

Approximately what percentage of these investee companies did Cummins own, on average, during 2014?

PROBLEMS

LO2, 7

CORNING, INC.

36. Interpreting equity method footnote

In its December 31, 2014 annual report, **Corning Inc.** reports a $1,325 million balance related to its Equity Investment in **Dow Corning**. Corning owns 50% of Dow Corning (the other 50% is owned by **Dow Chemical**). Excerpts from its footnote relating to this Equity Investment follow:

Dow Corning's financial position and results of operations follow (in millions):

Statement of Operations	Year Ending December 31, 2014
Net sales.	$6,221
Gross profit.	1,543
Net income attributable to Dow Corning	513
Corning's equity in earnings of Dow Corning.	252
Related party transactions:	
Corning purchase from Dow Corning.	15
Dividends received from Dow Corning.	125

Balance Sheet	December 31, 2014
Current assets.	$4,712
Noncurrent assets.	6,433
Short-term borrowings, including current portion of long-term debt . . .	7
Other current liabilities	1,441
Long-term debt.	945
Other long-term liabilities	5,125
Noncontrolling liabilities	634

In May 1995, Dow Corning filed for bankruptcy protection to address pending and claimed liabilities arising from breast implant product lawsuits. In 1995, Corning fully impaired its investment in Dow Corning after it filed for bankruptcy protection. Corning did not recognize net equity earnings from the second quarter of 1995 through the end of 2002. Corning began recognizing equity earnings in the first quarter of 2003 when management concluded that Dow Corning's emergence from bankruptcy was probable. Corning considers the $171 million difference between the carrying value of its investment in Dow Corning and its 50% share of Dow Corning's equity to be permanent.

On June 1, 2004, Dow Corning emerged from Chapter 11 with a Plan of Reorganization (the "Plan") which provided for the settlement or other resolution of implant claims. The Plan also includes releases for Corning and Dow as shareholders in exchange for contributions to the Plan.

a. Does the amount that Corning reports as equity income seem consistent with its ownership percentage of the investee given the summary income statement data that Corning provides in this footnote?

b. Does the carrying amount of the Equity Investments appear to be consistent with the summary balance sheet information that Corning provides in this footnote?

c. Why did Corning discontinue the recognition of equity losses on this investment? Why did it resume the recognition of equity income?

d. What is the significance of the following statement in this footnote: "The Plan also includes releases for Corning and Dow Chemical as shareholders in exchange for contributions to the Plan."

LO2, 6

LIONSGATE

37. Interpreting the equity method footnote

Lions Gate Entertainment Corp. (Lionsgate) reports unconsolidated equity method investments at $181,941 thousand on its balance sheet and $24,724 thousand on its statement of operations. Additionally, the company presents the following material information about its unconsolidated equity method investments in the footnotes of its 2014 10-K annual report (the company has a March 31st year end):

The carrying amounts of significant equity method investments at March 31, 2014 and March 31, 2013 were as follows:

Equity Method Investee (amounts in thousands)	March 31, 2014 Ownership Percentage	March 31, 2014	March 31, 2013
EPIX	31.2%	$78,758	$ 66,697
TVGN	50%	86,298	91,408
Defy Media Group	20%	10,000	4,630
Roadside Attractions	43%	3,665	3,372
FEARnet	34.5%	3,220	3,343
		$181,941	$169,450

The Company also provided the following information about one of its equity method investees:

FEARnet. FEARnet is a multiplatform programming and content service provider of horror genre films. The Company licenses content to FEARnet for video-on-demand and broadband exhibition. The Company records its share of FEARnet's net income or loss on a one-quarter lag and, accordingly, during the years ended March 31, 2014, 2013, and 2012, the Company recorded its share of the income or loss generated by the entity for the year ended December 31, 2013, 2012 and 2011, respectively.

FEARnet Financial Information
The following table presents the summarized (100%) net income information for the years ended December 31, 2013, 2012, and 2011 for *FEARnet*:

(in thousands)	Year Ended December 31		
	2013	2012	2011
Net income (loss)	$(357)	$1,342	$206

a. By what amount does FEARnet's net loss for the year ended December 31, 2013 decrease the carrying amount of Lionsgate's equity method investment during the year ended March 31, 2014?
b. What do Lionsgate's share of losses and the change in FEARnet's carrying value suggest about any FEARnet dividend to Lionsgate during the year ended March 31, 2014?
c. Assuming the same ownership percentage and no dividends are paid, what was the approximate carrying value of Lionsgate's equity method investment in FEARnet on March 31, 2012?

38. **Interpreting equity method footnote**   LO2, 6
Prior to the merger of **AT&T** and **BellSouth** in 2006 (and the consolidation of **Cingular Wireless**), AT&T reported the following footnote to its 2005 10-K report (in millions).   AT&T, INC.

Equity Method Investments We account for our nationwide wireless joint venture, Cingular, and our investments in equity affiliates under the equity method of accounting. The following table is a reconciliation of our investments in and advances to Cingular as presented on our Consolidated Balance Sheets.

	2005	2004
Beginning of year	$33,687	$11,003
Contributions	—	21,688
Equity in net income	200	30
Other adjustments	(2,483)	966
End of year	$31,404	$33,687

continued

continued from previous page

Undistributed earnings from Cingular were $2,711 and $2,511 at December 31, 2005 and 2004. "Other adjustments" in 2005 included the net activity of $2,442 under our revolving credit agreement with Cingular, consisting of a reduction of $1,747 (reflecting Cingular's repayment of their shareholder loan during 2005) and a decrease of $695 (reflecting Cingular's net repayment of their revolving credit balance during 2005). During 2004, we made an equity contribution to Cingular in connection with its acquisition of AT&T Wireless. "Other adjustments" in 2004 included the net activity of $972 under our revolving credit agreement with Cingular, consisting of a reduction of $30 (reflecting Cingular's repayment of advances during 2004) and an increase of $1,002 (reflecting the December 31, 2004 balance of advances to Cingular under this revolving credit agreement).

We account for our 60% economic interest in Cingular under the equity method of accounting in our consolidated financial statements since we share control equally (i.e., 50/50) with our 40% economic partner in the joint venture. We have equal voting rights and representation on the Board of Directors that controls Cingular. The following table presents summarized financial information for Cingular at December 31, or for the year then ended.

	2005	2004	2003
Income Statements			
Operating revenues	$34,433	$19,565	$15,577
Operating income	1,824	1,528	2,254
Net income	333	201	977
Balance Sheets			
Current assets.	$ 6,049	$ 5,570	
Noncurrent assets.	73,270	76,668	
Current liabilities	10,008	7,983	
Noncurrent liabilities	24,333	29,719	

We have made a subordinated loan to Cingular that totaled $4,108 and $5,855 at December 31, 2005 and 2004, which matures in June 2008. This loan bears interest at an annual rate of 6.0%. During 2005, Cingular repaid $1,747 to reduce the balance of this loan in accordance with the terms of a revolving credit agreement. We earned interest income on this loan of $311 during 2005, $354 in 2004 and $397 in 2003. This interest income does not have a material impact on our net income as it is mostly offset when we record our share of equity income in Cingular.

a. At what amount is the equity investment in Cingular reported on AT&T's balance sheet? (*Hint:* The table in the footnote reports AT&T's equity investment plus its "advances" of $4,108 to Cingular plus $311 of interest accrued on the advances.) Confirm that this amount is equal to its proportionate share of Cingular's equity.

b. Did Cingular pay out any of its earnings as dividends in 2005? How do you know?

c. How much income did AT&T report in 2005 relating to this investment in Cingular?

d. Interpret the AT&T statement that "undistributed earnings from Cingular were $2,711 and $2,511 at December 31, 2005 and 2004."

LO2, 6, 10

GENERAL MILLS

39. Interpreting equity method footnote

In its May 25, 2014 balance sheet, **General Mills** reports a $1,146 million "Other assets" account, of which $506 million are equity method investments in joint ventures. (Note that General Mills' fiscal year end is the last Sunday in May [i.e., the exact date is variable and the fiscal year can be either 52 or 53 weeks in length]. Fiscal years 2014, 2013 and 2012 each consisted of 52 weeks.) The Company discusses its investments in joint ventures in the following footnote to its 2014 SEC Form 10-K:

We have a 50% equity interest in **Cereal Partners Worldwide** (CPW), which manufactures and markets ready-to-eat cereal products in more than 130 countries outside the United States and Canada. CPW also markets cereal bars in several European countries and manufactures private label cereals for customers in the United Kingdom. We have guaranteed a portion of CPW's debt and its pension obligation in the United Kingdom. We also have a 50% equity interest in **HäagenDazs Japan, Inc.** (HDJ). This joint venture manufactures and markets Häagen-Dazs ice cream products and frozen novelties.

Joint venture related financial information is as follows:

(in millions)	May 25, 2014	May 26, 2013
Cumulative investments.	$508	$479
Goodwill and other intangibles.	563	537
Aggregate advances.	332	392

(in millions)	Fiscal Year		
	2014	2013	2012
Total net sales.	$2,499	$2,553	2,582
Gross margin	1,030	1,057	1,084
Earnings before income taxes	219	260	250
Earnings after income taxes.	169	202	189

(in millions)	May 25, 2014	May 26, 2013
Current assets	$1,031	$ 977
Noncurrent assets	1,030	1,088
Current liabilities.	1,779	1,717
Noncurrent liabilities.	110	115

a. How does General Mills account for its investments in joint ventures? How are these investments reflected on General Mills' balance sheet, and how generally is income recognized on these investments?

b. Does the $506 million investment included in other assets on General Mills' balance sheet sufficiently reflect the assets and liabilities required to conduct these operations? Explain.

c. Do you believe that the liabilities of these joint venture entities represent actual obligations of General Mills? Explain.

d. What potential problem(s) does equity method accounting present for analysis purposes?

TOPIC REVIEW

Solution 1

	FV	FV%	Allocated Cost
Plant and equipment	$100	20.0%	$104
Land	150	30.0%	156
Patent	300	60.0%	312
Accrued liability	(50)	−10.0%	(52)
Total net assets	$500	100.0%	$520

a.

Plant and equipment	104	
Land	156	
Patent	312	
Accrued liability		52
Cash		208
Common stock		52
Additional paid-in capital		260

(to record the acquisition of the investee's net assets that do not qualify as a "business.")

b.

Plant and equipment	100	
Land	150	
Patent	300	
Goodwill	12	
Expenses (transaction cost)	8	
Accrued liability		50
Cash		208
Common stock		52
Additional paid-in capital		260
(To record the net asset acquisition of the investee that qualifies as a "business.")		

c.

Equity investment	512	
Expenses (transaction cost)	8	
Cash		208
Common stock		52
Additional paid-in capital		260
(To record the stock acquisition of the investee that qualifies as a "business.")		

Solution 2

a. The investee's stockholders' equity will be reported at $575 ($500 + $100 − $25).

b. 1.

Equity investment	100	
Equity income		100
(to record equity income of $100 representing 100% of the investee's net income)		

2.

Cash	25	
Equity investment		25
(to record the receipt of $25 dividend from the investee)		

c. The Equity investment account on the investor's balance sheet has a current balance of $575 ($500 + $100 − $25), the same as the investee's stockholders' equity. This is so because the investor owns 100% of the investee's equity.

Solution 3

This arrangement is interesting because it has various influence-related indicators that could lead to different conclusions about the level of influence of Liberty on Expedia. Based on the presumption that investments of less than 20% are "passive," the 18% equity interest could lead one to believe that the investment should be classified as a trading or available for sale equity investment (i.e., measured at fair value at every balance sheet date). However, this appears to be the level of financial interest, and not necessarily related to voting control. The 58% voting interest is more of an indicator of control, and is suggestive that Liberty should consolidate Expedia. However, Liberty has entered into a contractual arrangement with Expedia (and Barry Diller) whereby Barry Diller (Chairman of the Board and Senior Executive Officer of Expedia) may vote Liberty's interests of Expedia. This effectively relinquishes control to another party. Given that Liberty has the right to "appoint and have appointed 20% of the members of Expedia's board of directors," it is clearly more than a passive investment and, yet, is not a controlling investment. Therefore, Liberty most likely has significant influence over Expedia and should use the equity method to account for its investment.

Solution 4

a.

Equity investment	100	
Equity income		100
(to record equity income of $100 representing 100% of the investee's net income)		

b.

Cash	25	
Equity investment		25
(to record the receipt of $25 dividend from the investee)		

c.

Equity income	10	
Equity investment		10
(to record the amortization of the patent asset)		

Solution 5

Equity income.	15	
Equity investment		15
(to record the deferral of 60% of the $25 of gross profit on inventory sale in the period of sale)		

Solution 6

Equity income.	5	
Equity investment		5
(to record the deferral of 60% of the gross profit on inventory sale in the period of sale when the investor owns 1/3 of the investee − $25 × 60% × 1/3 = $5)		

Solution 7

a.

Unrealized holding gain (AOCI)	50,000	
Equity investment		50,000
(to remove the unrealized gain from stockholders' equity and the fair value adjustment from the investment account)		

b.

Equity investment.	40,000	
Retained earnings (prior period adjustment)		40,000
(to adjust the Equity Investment to its correct amount at the beginning of the year and to increase the beginning of the year retained earnings for the cumulative equity income that would have been recognized)		

COMPREHENSIVE REVIEW SOLUTION

a.

Unrealized holding gain (AOCI)	35,000	
Equity investment		35,000
(to remove the unrealized gain from stockholders' equity and the fair value adjustment from the investment account)		

Equity investment.	25,000	
Retained earnings (prior period adjustment)		25,000
(to increase the Equity Investment by $25,000 ([$400,000 − $150,000] × 10%) at the beginning of the year and to increase the beginning of the year retained earnings for the cumulative equity income that would have been recognized less cumulative dividends received)		

b.

Equity investment.	70,000	
Equity income		70,000
(to record equity income of $70,000 representing 35% of the investee's net income of $200,000)		

c.

Cash	31,500	
Equity investment		31,500
(to record the receipt of a $31,500 ($90,000 × 35%) dividend from the investee)		

d.

Equity income.	17,500	
Equity investment		17,500
(to record the amortization of the Patent asset of $17,500 ([$500,000/10] × 35%))		

e.

Equity income.	6,300	
Equity investment		6,300
(to record the deferral of 60% of the gross profit on inventory sale in the period of sale when the investor owns 35% of the investee ($80,000 − $50,000) × 60% × 35% = $6,300)		

Introduction to Business Combinations and the Consolidation Process

2

In this chapter, we introduce the topic of business combinations and consolidations by discussing **The Coca-Cola Company's** (Coca-Cola) acquisition, on October 2, 2010, of the North American operations of its largest bottling affiliate, **Coca-Cola Enterprises, Inc.** (CCE). To execute this transaction, Coca-Cola transferred total consideration of $6.8 billion to CCE's non-Coca-Cola shareholders. (We say "non-Coca-Cola" because Coca-Cola is a shareholder by virtue of its 34% investment in CCE.)

COCA-COLA

As we describe in Chapter 1, the equity method of accounting results in an investor reporting, as a net line item on its balance sheet, only the proportion of the investee's equity that the investor owns (adjusted for any unamortized excess amounts over the book value of the investee's equity).

Consequently, considerable amounts of assets and liabilities are netted into a single, summary asset line item. Because CCE suffered from poor performance in recent years, Coca-Cola reported in its December 31, 2008 annual report that its "investment in CCE was reduced to zero as of December 31, 2008." By December 31, 2009, the balance of the investment account increased to $25 million; however, CCE's total assets at that time were nearly $16.4 billion and its liabilities were approximately $15.5 billion, resulting in stockholders' equity of about $0.9 billion. (Coca-Cola notes that "our proportionate share of the net assets of CCE exceeded our investment by approximately $271 million," which is why the investment account is so far below its 34% interest in the book value of net assets of CCE.)

As we discuss later in this chapter, when a company owns a noncontrolling interest in a company, and then gains control, the company must revalue the noncontrolling interest to fair value immediately before acquiring the controlling interest. The related gain or loss on revaluation is recognized as part of net income. In the case of Coca-Cola's acquisition of CCE, we can see why equity method accounting can be a highly misleading indicator of an investee's value. Specifically, immediately prior to acquiring the remaining 66% of CCE it did not own (i.e., resulting in ownership of 100% of CCE's North American operations), Coca-Cola revalued its 34% investment in CCE to a fair value of $5 billion and recognized a gain in that amount in its net income for the year ending December 31, 2010. This caused an increase in Coca-Cola's reported net income of over 55% compared to the year ended December 31, 2009.

As a result of acquiring 100% of CCE's North American bottling operations, Coca-Cola includes 100% of those amounts in its consolidated financial statements. Conceptually, consolidation is a bringing together of the financial statements of the investor (usually called the parent company) and the investee (typically referred to as its subsidiary).

During the consolidation process, Coca-Cola removes the Equity Investment account (representing its holding of 100% of the common stock for CCE's North American bottling operations) and replaced it with CCE's North American bottling operations assets and liabilities. Further, in its consolidated income statement, Coca-Cola no longer reports Equity Income from CCE; rather, it includes CCE's North American bottling operations revenues and expenses together with its own.

We begin our discussion of the consolidation process in this chapter. To begin, we consider the consolidation of the parent and subsidiary as of the date of acquisition. In Chapter 3, we discuss consolidation of the parent and subsidiary in future periods.

Source: Coca-Cola 10-Ks, 2008-2010.

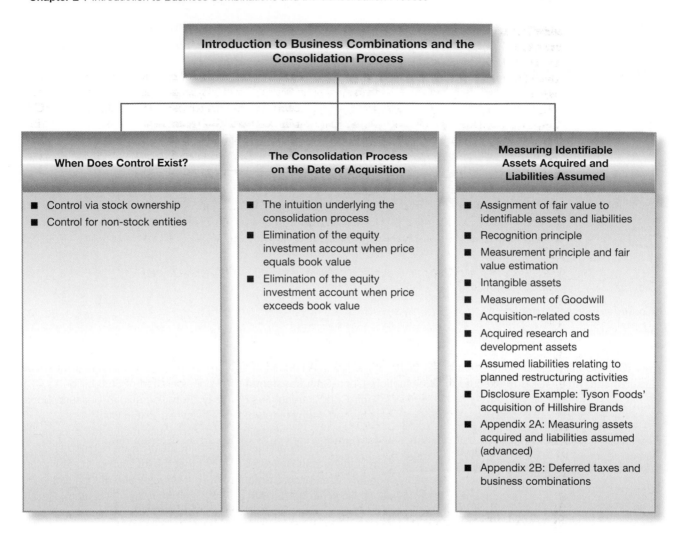

As we discuss in Chapter 1, the level of influence that the investor can exert over the investee determines the required accounting treatment for a company's investment in the voting shares of another company. Low levels of influence require accounting for the investment at fair value (or cost method if no readily determinable fair value exists for the equity securities of the investee). If an investor is able to exert significant influence over the investee, the investor is required to account for the investment using the equity method, and, <u>for internal reporting purposes,</u> can continue to account for its investment using the equity method even after it gains control over the investee company. However, generally accepted accounting principles (GAAP) require that, after control is reached, a parent (investor) company cannot publish financial statements to outside parties reporting its subsidiary (investee company) as an Equity Investment. Rather, it must consolidate its financial statements with those of the subsidiary.

In this chapter, we introduce you to the accounting concept of control and the mechanics of the consolidation process. The U.S. accounting standards for business combinations (FASB ASC 805) and consolidations (FASB ASC 810) are closely linked. The relation between accounting for business combinations and consolidations hinges on the concept of control, with (1) business combination recognition and measurement (i.e., *acquisition method* accounting) triggered when initial control of a business is obtained and (2) the requirement that consolidated financial statements include all entities controlled by an entity preparing financial statements.

The most recent changes in U.S. accounting for business combinations (FASB ASC 805) and consolidations (FASB ASC 810) occurred with the issuance of SFAS 141(R), "Business Combinations," and SFAS 160, "Noncontrolling Interests in Consolidated Financial Statements," in

2007.[1] These standards were developed as part of a joint standard-setting project with the International Accounting Standards Board (IASB) as part of an ongoing effort by the FASB and the IASB to harmonize U.S. and international accounting standards. The IASB issued its revised International Financial Reporting Standards No. 3 (IFRS 3), "Business Combinations," and International Accounting Standards No. 27 (IAS 27), "Consolidated and Separate Financial Statements" shortly after the release of SFAS 141(R) and SFAS 160, respectively.[2] Unless a difference is noted, IFRS 3 and IAS 27 are not materially different from SFAS 141(R) and SFAS 160, respectively.[3] These differences are few and will likely become fewer as the FASB and the IASB continue their efforts to harmonize U.S. and international accounting standards.

We now begin with a discussion of the factors indicating the existence of control, the threshold requiring consolidation. We, then, describe the assignment of fair values to the numerous assets acquired and liabilities assumed when one company obtains control of another business. And, our final section describes the mechanics of the consolidation process on the date of the acquisition (in Chapter 3, we extend the consolidation process to periods subsequent to the date of acquisition).

WHEN DOES "CONTROL" EXIST?

Control is a centrally important concept in financial reporting. For example, it is an explicit component of the definition of an asset.[4] In addition, control is implicit in the production of representationally faithful financial statements; that is, financial statements of a business enterprise are presumed to be a complete representation of the resources and obligations of the enterprise, and the financial flows into, out of, and within the enterprise (FASB SFAC No. 2, ¶76 & ¶79). Thus, control is a central element in determining the boundaries of every reporting entity. The concept of control also provides the basis for the material that we will discuss in the next few chapters of this book: the production of consolidated financial statements.

LO1 Explain the guidelines for determining the existence of "control."

More than half a century ago, accounting standard setters first codified the current decision rule for identifying the various entities that should be combined and reported in a single set of consolidated financial statements. Specifically, Accounting Research Bulletin No. 51 (ARB 51) states that the parent company should consolidate a subsidiary in which it has a "controlling financial interest." In the years since that time, the FASB has attempted to more clearly define that phrase, a task made extremely difficult by creative financial innovation and managers' incentives to keep certain financial arrangements off-balance-sheet (e.g., credit-card receivables) or activities off-income-statement (e.g., research and development).

---

[1] SFAS 141(R), "Business Combinations," was effective for *acquisitions consummated* during fiscal years beginning after December 15, 2008, and SFAS 160, "Noncontrolling Interests in Consolidated Financial Statements," was effective for *financial statements issued* for interim and annual periods beginning after December 15, 2008. "Prospective" application required in SFAS 141(R) means that acquisitions that occurred before the effective date include measurements determined using the accounting standard in effect when the acquisition occurred: either APB 16, *Business Combinations*, which permits the accounting for acquisitions using a book-value-based method called pooling-of-interest, or SFAS 141 (the standard preceding the most recent revision) which measures the net assets acquired using the *purchase method*. Although new acquisitions must be accounted for under SFAS 141(R), in practice you are likely to encounter business combinations that were consummated prior to December 15, 2008, and that continue to include measures determined under these prior standards. We provide summaries of these two previous acquisition standards in the Appendices to Chapters 3 and 5.

[2] The revised IFRS 3 is required to be applied prospectively to business combinations for which the acquisition date is on or after the beginning of the first annual reporting period beginning on or after July 1, 2009. Early application was permitted if the reporting entity also early adopted the revised IAS 27.

[3] The single biggest difference between U.S. GAAP and IFRS is that companies applying IFRS 3 are allowed to choose whether, in the case of acquiring control of a non-wholly owned subsidiary, the noncontrolling interest reflects (1) the noncontrolling interest's proportionate share of all of the subsidiary's net assets (which is what is required for all companies under U.S. GAAP) or (2) the noncontrolling interest's proportionate share of the fair value of the acquiree's identifiable net assets (i.e., exclusive of goodwill). Because this difference involves measurement of noncontrolling interest—a concept extensively covered in Chapter 5—we address this difference between U.S. GAAP and IFRS in the Appendix to Chapter 5.

[4] The FASB's Statements of Financial Accounting Concepts No. 6 defines assets as follows: "Assets are probable future economic benefits obtained or controlled by a particular entity as a result of past transactions or events" (¶25).

Notwithstanding the rather straightforward phrase, "controlling financial interest," the concept of control in consolidations-related GAAP is complex. The complexity stems from the fact that current U.S. GAAP includes two ways in which control can be achieved: (1) a *quantitative* majority of the *voting* equity interest and (2) a *qualitatively* determined power to direct an entity's activities and a majority of the entity's *economic* risks and rewards (i.e., the primary beneficiary of a variable interest entity), regardless of the level of equity ownership. The former definition of control has been the primary definition for many decades, while the latter was introduced into U.S. GAAP in 2003 in direct response to the non-consolidation of thousands of risky special purpose entities by Enron and other companies.

Because ownership of a majority voting interest is the most common triggering condition for consolidation, our discussion will primarily assume that consolidation is required because a parent company owns a majority of the voting equity securities of one or more subsidiaries. In addition, our discussion of business combination accounting will primarily assume that control is obtained when a parent company initially acquires a majority interest in the common stock of a subsidiary.[5] In practice, determining whether control exists for consolidation (i.e., FASB ASC 810) or application of acquisition accounting for a business combination (i.e., FASB ASC 805) is a judgment-intensive exercise in which all of the facts and circumstances must be evaluated (i.e., in addition to the percentage of the voting shares owned). Further, even if the investor owns more than 50% of the outstanding voting stock, control may not exist if the investee company is a variable interest entity, is in bankruptcy (it may be controlled by the courts), or has business activities that are controlled by a foreign government (see FASB ASC 810-10-15-10).[6]

PRACTICE INSIGHT

Is the Purchase of a Company's Assets an Asset Acquisition or a Business Combination? Many acquisitions that were previously accounted for as asset purchases are now considered business combinations, thus requiring consolidation of the financial statements of the investor and the investee companies. As we briefly discuss in Chapter 1, the FASB ASC Master Glossary defines a business as follows: "An integrated set of activities and assets that is capable of being conducted and managed for the purpose of providing a return in the form of dividends, lower costs, or other economic benefits directly to investors or other owners, members, or participants." It is not necessary that the investee company currently produce products or generate a positive return. According to FASB ASC 805-10-55-7, all that is necessary is that it:

a. has begun planned principal activities,
b. has employees, intellectual property, and other inputs and processes that could be applied to those inputs,
c. is pursuing a plan to produce outputs, and
d. will be able to obtain access to customers that will purchase the outputs.

Finally, there is a rebuttable presumption that acquired assets comprise a business if Goodwill is present in the acquisition. Contrary evidence would be needed to overcome this presumption (FASB ASC 805-10-55-9).

These provisions are likely to increase the number of transactions that qualify as business combinations. Technology companies, for example, will be particularly impacted as the acquisition of development-stage enterprises may now be considered business combinations since a business is no longer required to have outputs.

---

[5] FASB ASC 805-10-25-5 indicates that the definition of control that is included in the consolidations standards (i.e., FASB ASC 810-10) is also the definition of control that should be used to identify the acquiring entity in a business combination. Further, "if a business combination has occurred but applying that guidance does not clearly indicate which of the combining entities is the acquirer, the factors in paragraphs 805-10-55-11 through 55-15 shall be considered in making that determination." The Practice Insight, "Determining the Acquiring Company" includes these factors.

[6] For the next few chapters, we will assume that control is obtained through an investor's majority (i.e., > 50%) ownership of an investee's voting common stock. In Chapter 6, we will describe the qualitative analysis that is required for variable interest entities.

TOPIC REVIEW 1

Indications of Control

For each of the following independent scenarios, determine whether "control" exists that would require application of acquisition accounting (i.e., FASB ASC 805) and resulting consolidation of the financial statements of the two entities (i.e., FASB ASC 810):

Required

a. An investor owns a majority of the outstanding stock of the investee.
b. An investor owns a noncontrolling interest (i.e., less than 50%), and the majority of the investee's stock is owned by the investee's founder and original owner.
c. An investor owns a minority interest in the investee, and the remainder of the stock is widely disbursed such that shareholders cannot form coordinated voting blocks.
d. A company licenses technology to another company and does not own any of its stock. The license agreement allows the licensor to appoint a majority of the licensee's board of directors.

The solution to this review problem can be found on page 105.

PRACTICE INSIGHT

Determining the Acquiring Company   It may sound simple, but determining the acquiring company can sometimes be difficult, and that determination can have significant consequences for how we account for the acquisition. FASB ASC 805-10-55-11 and ASC 805-10-55-12 provide the following guidance:

- ■ **Cash purchase**—In a business combination effected primarily by transferring cash or other assets or by incurring liabilities, the investor usually is the entity that transfers the cash or other assets or incurs the liabilities.
- ■ **Stock purchase**—In a business combination effected primarily by exchanging equity interests, the investor usually is the entity that issues its equity interests. Nevertheless, we need to consider all of the following factors in determining the acquiring company:
    - ❏ *The relative voting rights in the combined entity after the business combination.* The investor usually is the combining entity whose owners as a group retain or receive the largest portion of the voting rights in the combined entity. In determining which group of owners retains or receives the largest portion of the voting rights, an entity shall consider the existence of any unusual or special voting arrangements and options, warrants, or convertible securities.
    - ❏ *The existence of a large minority voting interest in the combined entity if no other owner or organized group of owners has a significant voting interest.* The investor usually is the combining entity whose single owner or organized group of owners holds the largest minority voting interest in the combined entity.
    - ❏ *The composition of the governing body of the combined entity.* The investor usually is the combining entity whose owners have the ability to elect or appoint or to remove a majority of the members of the governing body of the combined entity.
    - ❏ *The composition of the senior management of the combined entity.* The investor usually is the combining entity whose former management dominates the management of the combined entity.
    - ❏ *The terms of the exchange of equity interest.* The investor usually is the combining entity that pays a premium over the pre-combination fair value of the equity interests of the other combining entity or entities.

CONSOLIDATION ON THE DATE OF ACQUISITION

We begin with a discussion of the intuition that underlies the consolidation process, followed by two examples of the consolidation process as of the date of acquisition: one when the purchase price *equals* the book value (of the net assets or Stockholders' Equity) of the investee company, and the other when the purchase price *exceeds* the book value of the investee company.

The Intuition Underlying the Consolidation Process

To facilitate our discussion of the intuition underlying the consolidation process, we will construct a fairly simple acquisition and ownership example. Assume that a parent company acquires a subsidiary by purchasing all of its common stock for a cash purchase price of $1,000. The parent records the purchase with a debit to the Equity Investment account (this is the same Equity Investment account that we discuss in Chapter 1) and a credit to Cash. For this example, we also assume that the purchase price of $1,000 is at book value, meaning that the purchase price is equal to the book value of the subsidiary's Stockholders' Equity. The (assumed) balance sheets of the parent and the subsidiary immediately following the acquisition follow:

	Parent	Subsidiary
Other assets.	$5,000	$1,500
Equity investment.	1,000	
Total assets.	$6,000	$1,500
Liabilities.	$2,000	$ 500
Stockholders' equity	4,000	1,000
Total liabilities and equity.	$6,000	$1,500

The parent reports the Equity Investment at the acquisition price of $1,000, equal to the book value of the subsidiary's Stockholders' Equity.

In Exhibit 2.1, we illustrate the two perspectives that relate the Equity Investment account to the subsidiary's financial statements. In Perspective A, we focus on the simple fact that the Equity Investment represents *legal ownership of the securities that comprise Stockholders' Equity*. Traditionally, these securities convey to the holder of the securities the ability to effectively control the subsidiary. Thus, the arrow linking the Equity Investment account on the parent's balance sheet with the Stockholders' Equity of the subsidiary illustrates the value of the residual claim embodied in the investment account to the future cash flows of the subsidiary. This linkage will come in handy when our primary concern is the mechanics of consolidation entries, but it does little good in helping to communicate the intuition underlying the consolidation process.

In contrast, Perspective B in Exhibit 2.1 provides a more intuitive representation of the relationship between the Equity Investment account and the claim to the future cash flows of the subsidiary. Specifically, the Equity Investment securities convey to the parent company the *right to control (and the ability to reap the future net residual rewards from) the net assets of the subsidiary*. Thus, conceptually, the Equity Investment asset is really a single-line representation of the various net assets held by the subsidiary. In this case, the Equity Investment account has a $1,000 balance, which is equal to the subsidiary's assets ($1,500) minus the subsidiary's liabilities ($500).

EXHIBIT 2.1	Two Perspectives on the Equity Investment			
	Perspective A		**Perspective B**	
	Parent	**Subsidiary**	**Parent**	**Subsidiary**
Other assets.	$5,000	$1,500	$5,000	**$1,500**
Equity investment.	1,000		1,000	
Total assets.	$6,000	$1,500	$6,000	$1,500
Liabilities.	$2,000	$ 500	$2,000	$ 500
Stockholders' equity	4,000	**1,000**	4,000	1,000
Total liabilities and equity.	$6,000	$1,500	$6,000	$1,500

Because the parent controls the subsidiary, there is a presumption under GAAP that the parent's financial statements are more informative if the subsidiary's individual net assets are reported by the parent instead of the single-line Equity Investment account. This process of *replacing* the parent's Equity Investment account with the subsidiary's assets and liabilities is called "consolidation." Exhibit 2.2 provides an illustration of the intuition underlying the consolidation process.

EXHIBIT 2.2	Intuition: Consolidation Is Really a Process of Replacement					
	Pre-Consolidation		**Replace Investment**			
	Parent	**Subsidiary**	**Parent**		**Subsidiary**	**Consolidated**
Other assets......................	$5,000	$1,500	$5,000	+	$1,500	$6,500
Equity investment..................	1,000		1,000			
Total assets......................	$6,000		$6,000			$6,500
Liabilities.......................	$2,000	$ 500	$2,000	+	$ 500	$2,500
Stockholders' equity	4,000		4,000			4,000
Total liabilities and equity...........	$6,000		$6,000			$6,500

In this example, the consolidation of the balance sheets of the parent and its subsidiary is accomplished by replacing the Equity Investment account with the assets and liabilities to which it relates. The Equity Investment account, therefore, is not reported on the consolidated balance sheet and the amounts that are reported for consolidated assets and liabilities include those of both the parent and its subsidiary.

It is important to note that the consolidation process, which we depict in Exhibit 2.2, is not simply one of adding together the financial statements of the parent and the financial statements of the subsidiary. To see why a simple addition would not present a true picture of the consolidated entity, compare the "Added" column in Exhibit 2.3 with the Consolidated column of Exhibit 2.2.

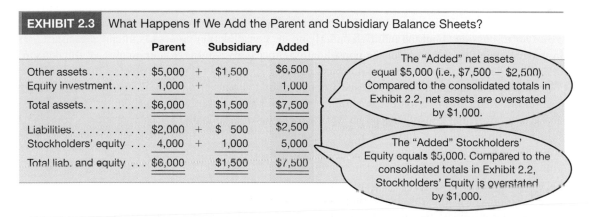

EXHIBIT 2.3	What Happens If We Add the Parent and Subsidiary Balance Sheets?		
	Parent	**Subsidiary**	**Added**
Other assets..........	$5,000 +	$1,500	$6,500
Equity investment......	1,000 +		1,000
Total assets..........	$6,000	$1,500	$7,500
Liabilities............	$2,000 +	$ 500	$2,500
Stockholders' equity ...	4,000 +	1,000	5,000
Total liab. and equity ...	$6,000	$1,500	$7,500

The "Added" net assets equal $5,000 (i.e., $7,500 − $2,500). Compared to the consolidated totals in Exhibit 2.2, net assets are overstated by $1,000.

The "Added" Stockholders' Equity equals $5,000. Compared to the consolidated totals in Exhibit 2.2, Stockholders' Equity is overstated by $1,000.

As is illustrated in Exhibit 2.3, if we simply add together the parent and subsidiary balance sheets, the resulting balance sheet would report Other Assets of $6,500 ($5,000 + $1,500), the Equity Investment of $1,000, Liabilities of $2,500 ($2,000 + $500) and Stockholders' Equity of $5,000. There are two problems with this simple addition of the parent and subsidiary balance sheet accounts: First, the net assets in the "Added" balance sheet double count the subsidiary's net assets. This double counting occurs because the parent's Equity Investment account is really just a one-line, net representation of the net assets (i.e., assets − liabilities) of the subsidiary (see Exhibit 2.1). As a result, the subsidiary's net assets are first included in the Equity Investment account and, then, included a second time in the Other Assets and Liabilities accounts.

The second source of error in Exhibit 2.3 is that the $5,000 "Added" balance for Stockholders' Equity includes $1,000 of the subsidiary's Stockholders' Equity. Compare this "Added" balance to the consolidated Stockholders' Equity in Exhibit 2.2; note that the consolidated Stockholders' Equity in

Exhibit 2.2 does not include the subsidiary's Stockholders' Equity. This is because the consolidated financial statements are still the *parent's* financial statements, but with additional detail about the net assets controlled by the parent. The subsidiary's Stockholders' Equity is not held by a party outside of the economic entity represented in the consolidated financial statements and, as a result, should not be included in the consolidated Stockholders' Equity.

Exhibit 2.4 illustrates the two separate legal entities (i.e., the parent and subsidiary ovals) and the single economic entity (i.e., represented by the single, large violet circle).

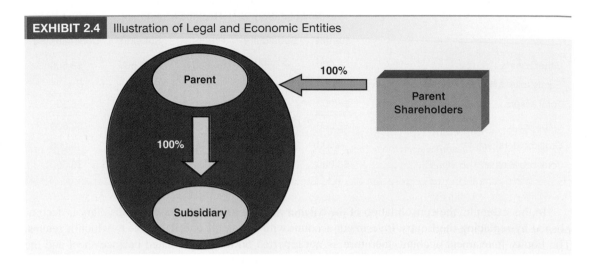

EXHIBIT 2.4 Illustration of Legal and Economic Entities

In Exhibit 2.4, the economic reporting entity is represented by the large violet circle. The primary objective of consolidation is to produce "as if" financial statements for the commonly controlled economic entity instead of the strictly defined separate legal entities. As you can see from the illustration, the only shareholders outside of the large violet circle are the parent company's shareholders. Thus, the Stockholders' Equity reported in the consolidated financial statements should be limited to the equity held by the *parent's* shareholders. This is why the consolidated Stockholders' Equity reported in Exhibit 2.2 is limited to the $4,000 Stockholders' Equity of the parent company.

Our discussion about the intuition underlying the consolidation process is intended to assist you in understanding the outcome of the consolidation process. We strongly suggest that you make sure that you understand the intuition behind consolidations before becoming too immersed in the mechanics of the consolidation process (e.g. specific consolidation entries and the like). All one must do is scan the myriad consolidation entry approaches included in other advanced accounting textbooks to quickly discover that consolidated financial statements can be prepared via numerous different consolidation entry sequences. Indeed, real-world companies take many different approaches to producing consolidated financial statements; therefore, your best chance for developing relevant, transferable knowledge is to have a firm grasp of the intuition behind the consolidation process.

In Exhibit 2.5, we present the acquisition-date balance sheets of the parent and its subsidiary (that have been provided to us by those companies before we began the consolidation process), the entry required to consolidate the two balance sheets that we now prepare, and the resulting consolidated balance sheet.

The net result of consolidation is that the parent's Equity Investment account should be replaced by the subsidiary's individual assets and liabilities and the consolidated Stockholders' Equity should be the same as the parent's Stockholders' Equity. While the intuitive process of consolidation results in "replacement" or substitution of the Equity Investment account with the individual assets and liabilities of the subsidiary, the *mechanics* of adding together the full balance sheet of the parent and subsidiary requires the "elimination" of the parent's Equity Investment account (with a credit since it is an asset) and the subsidiary's Stockholders' Equity accounts (with a debit since Stockholders' Equity has a credit balance). The last column is the consolidated balance sheet that you see in the company's annual report and its 10-K or 10-Q filings with the SEC, and it reflects the balance sheets of the parent and subsidiary with no double counting of the subsidiary's net assets.

| EXHIBIT 2.5 | Initial Consolidation Example | | | | | |

	Parent	Subsidiary	Consolidation Entries Dr.	Cr.	Consolidated
Other assets.	$5,000	$1,500			$6,500
Equity investment.	1,000			1,000	
Total assets.	$6,000	$1,500			$6,500
Liabilities.	$2,000	$ 500			$2,500
Stockholders' equity	4,000	1,000	1,000		4,000
Total liabilities and equity.	$6,000	$1,500	$1,000	$1,000	$6,500

Here is an important point: *the consolidation entries that we describe above are* not *actually recorded by either company in their respective general ledgers*. The entries are made only in our spreadsheet, and the consolidated balance sheet exists only in our spreadsheet. Thus, we have not changed the accounting records or the balance sheets of either the parent or the subsidiary.

Finally, we emphasize one more time the goals of the consolidation process. From an intuitive, conceptual perspective, the goal of the consolidation process is to replace the parent's Equity Investment account with the individual assets and liabilities of the subsidiary. We accomplish this by adding the individual assets and liabilities of the subsidiary to the individual net asset accounts of the parent, and by eliminating the parent's Equity Investment account and the reciprocal amount of subsidiary Stockholders' Equity. Given this introduction, we are now ready to delve a little more deeply into the consolidation entries.

Acquisition-Date Consolidation (Purchase Price Equals Book Value)

The consolidation process brings together the financial statements of the parent and the subsidiary by removing the Equity Investment account from the parent's balance sheet and replacing it with the assets and liabilities of the subsidiary company to which it relates. In this chapter, we are focusing on consolidation on the date of acquisition. As a result, neither the parent nor the subsidiary has yet recorded any revenues or expenses subsequent to the acquisition. In Chapter 3, we discuss the consolidation process *subsequent* to the date of acquisition. At that time, we will add the income statement to our spreadsheet.

LO2 Explain the consolidation process on the date of acquisition when price equals book.

Suppose that the parent acquires all of the subsidiary's outstanding shares by issuing 22,500 shares of its own $1 par value common stock with a fair value of $20 per share for a total purchase price of $450,000. We assume that this purchase price is equal to the book value of the subsidiary's Stockholder's Equity on the acquisition date (we relax this assumption in the next section). The journal entry that the parent makes to record the acquisition is as follows:

Equity investment.	450,000	
Common stock (22,500 shares @ $1)		22,500
Additional paid-in capital.		427,500

The (assumed) respective balance sheets of the parent and subsidiary, immediately after the purchase, are presented in Exhibit 2.6. Given that (1) the parent purchased 100% of the subsidiary's common stock and (2) the subsidiary's assets and liabilities have fair values equal to their book values, the Equity Investment account on the parent's balance sheet equals the sum of the individual net assets of its subsidiary (see Exhibit 2.6). Of course, given the accounting identity (i.e., Assets = Liabilities + Stockholders' Equity), the Equity Investment account also equals the Stockholders' Equity of its subsidiary.

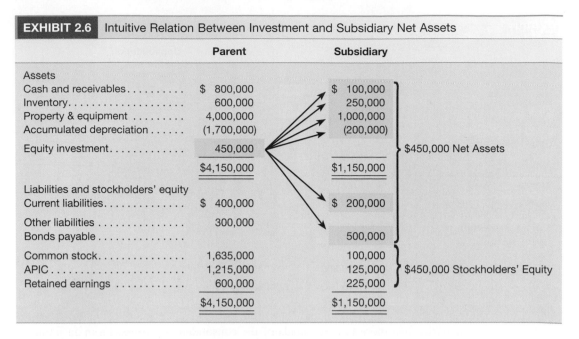

EXHIBIT 2.6 Intuitive Relation Between Investment and Subsidiary Net Assets

	Parent	Subsidiary	
Assets			
Cash and receivables..........	$ 800,000	$ 100,000	
Inventory....................	600,000	250,000	
Property & equipment	4,000,000	1,000,000	
Accumulated depreciation	(1,700,000)	(200,000)	
Equity investment............	450,000		} $450,000 Net Assets
	$4,150,000	$1,150,000	
Liabilities and stockholders' equity			
Current liabilities.............	$ 400,000	$ 200,000	
Other liabilities	300,000		
Bonds payable		500,000	
Common stock..............	1,635,000	100,000	}
APIC.....................	1,215,000	125,000	} $450,000 Stockholders' Equity
Retained earnings	600,000	225,000	}
	$4,150,000	$1,150,000	

As we illustrate in Exhibit 2.6, the Equity Investment account on the parent's balance sheet in the amount of $450,000 relates to the net assets of its subsidiary ($1,150,000 of assets less $700,000 of liabilities). Since we are reporting the subsidiary's assets and liabilities on the consolidated balance sheet, the Equity Investment account is redundant and should be eliminated, and the reduction of consolidated assets is matched by a corresponding elimination of the subsidiary's Stockholders' Equity. This elimination is accomplished by the following consolidation entry that debits the individual Stockholders' Equity accounts of the subsidiary (to reduce them since they have credit balances) and credits the parent's Equity Investment account (to reduce it since it has a debit balance).

[E]	Common stock (subsidiary)	100,000	
	APIC (subsidiary)	125,000	
	Retained earnings (subsidiary)....................	225,000	
	Equity investment (parent)..................		450,000
	(to eliminate the Equity Investment account and related		
	Stockholder's Equity of the subsidiary company)		

We will call this entry our **[E]** entry (relating to Stockholders' Equity).

If we insert this consolidation entry into the consolidation spreadsheet included in Exhibit 2.6, we obtain the consolidated balance sheet by adding across each row as presented in Exhibit 2.7.

After including the consolidation entry, the Equity Investment account balance in the "Consolidated" column is zero. Similarly, the account balances for the subsidiary's Stockholders' Equity (i.e., Common Stock, APIC, and Retained Earnings) are removed from the "Consolidated" column. The result is that the consolidated Stockholders' Equity equals the parent company's pre-consolidation Stockholders Equity. This will always be the case so long as the parent uses the equity method to account for its Equity Investment in the subsidiary.[7] After the consolidation entry, the "Consolidated" column reports the balance sheet that we will issue to shareholders and other external parties.

Although we already mentioned the following point, we cannot emphasize it enough: **none of the consolidation entries are actually made in the accounting records of either the parent or the subsidiary company.** They only exist on our consolidation worksheet. The consolidated financial statements are prepared only after the period-end adjustments have been made for the parent and subsidiary companies, and no further adjustments are made to the parent or subsidiary companies' accounting records after the consolidation process has begun.

---

[7] We assume that the investor accounts for the Equity Investment using the equity method throughout our text for this reason. In the appendix to Chapter 3, we illustrate how to perform the consolidation process when the investor uses the cost method or a hybrid equity method to account for its Equity Investment in the subsidiary.

EXHIBIT 2.7	Parent, Subsidiary, and Consolidated Balance Sheets				
			Consolidation Entries		
	Parent	**Subsidiary**	**Dr**	**Cr**	**Consolidated**
Assets					
Cash and receivables..........	$ 800,000	$ 100,000			$ 900,000
Inventory....................	600,000	250,000			850,000
Property & equipment	4,000,000	1,000,000			5,000,000
Accumulated depreciation......	(1,700,000)	(200,000)			(1,900,000)
Equity investment............	450,000			[E] $450,000	0
	$4,150,000	$1,150,000			$4,850,000
Liabilities and stockholders' equity					
Current liabilities..............	$ 400,000	$ 200,000			$ 600,000
Other liabilities	300,000				300,000
Bonds payable...............		500,000			500,000
Common stock..............	1,635,000	100,000	[E] $100,000		1,635,000
APIC.....................	1,215,000	125,000	[E] 125,000		1,215,000
Retained earnings	600,000	225,000	[E] 225,000		600,000
	$4,150,000	$1,150,000	$450,000	$450,000	$4,850,000

Acquisition-Date Consolidation
(Purchase Price Greater than Book Value)

Until now, we have made some fairly restrictive assumptions about the relation between the parent's Equity Investment account and the recorded values of the subsidiary's net assets. Now, we will relax our two most unrealistic assumptions. First, in real-world business combinations, the fair values of the subsidiary's individual net assets are usually *not* equal to their pre-combination recorded book values. Second, the acquiring company usually pays an amount that is higher than the fair value of the subsidiary's (reported) net assets.

In Exhibit 2.8, we present the subsidiary's net assets on the date of the acquisition. The first column contains the book values of the assets and liabilities (these are the same as those listed in the previous example and presented in the "Subsidiary" column in Exhibit 2.7). The second column reports the estimated fair values of the assets and liabilities.

In this example, appraisals that the parent conducted in conformity with the measurement requirements of Acquisition Accounting (FASB ASC 805-20-30-1) yielded estimated fair values that differed from net book value for two identifiable net assets: Property & Equipment and Patents. The fact that the subsidiary's preacquisition recorded net book values and estimated fair values differ is not unusual. GAAP rarely results in reported net asset values that equal fair values.

The preacquisition recorded net *book value* for Property & Equipment is equal to $800,000 (i.e., $1,000,000 gross value − $200,000 accumulated depreciation). The estimated *fair value* for Property & Equipment, however, is equal to $900,000. Under Acquisition Accounting, the estimated fair value will appear in the acquisition date balance sheet (with no accumulated depreciation). This is because Acquisition Accounting presents all acquired identifiable net assets of the subsidiary as if they were individually obtained at fair value on the acquisition date.

In addition to estimating the fair values of the *reported* assets and liabilities, Acquisition Accounting also requires companies to estimate the fair values of any *unreported* assets, such as intangible assets that the subsidiary company has created. An example is the development of patents. The development costs of patents consist of wages and other R&D costs that have been expensed, and the Patent asset does not appear on the subsidiary's balance sheet. Upon acquisition of the subsidiary, however, the Patent asset must be valued like other assets since it is an asset that is acquired in the purchase. In our example, the Patent asset is valued at $125,000.

LO3 Explain the consolidation process on the date of acquisition when price exceeds book.

EXHIBIT 2.8	Subsidiary Book and Fair Values		
		Subsidiary's Recorded Book Values	Subsidiary's Estimated Fair Values*
Assets			
Cash and receivables.		$ 100,000	$ 100,000
Inventory.		250,000	250,000
Property & equipment		1,000,000	900,000
Accumulated depreciation.		(200,000)	0
Patents.		0	125,000
Total identifiable assets.		$1,150,000	$1,375,000
Liabilities			
Current liabilities.		$ 200,000	$ 200,000
Other liabilities			
Bonds payable.		500,000	500,000
Total identifiable liabilities.		700,000	700,000
Identifiable net assets		$ 450,000	$ 675,000

* The FASB ASC Glossary defines fair value as "[t]he price that would be received to sell an asset or paid to transfer a liability in an orderly transaction between market participants at the measurement date." FASB ASC 805-20-30-10 through ASC 805-20-30-22 includes exceptions to this fair value measurement principle for income taxes, employee benefits, indemnification assets, reacquired rights, share based payment awards, and assets held for sale. Notwithstanding these technical exceptions from the general definition of fair value, we assume that items labeled, "fair value," throughout the textbook are measured in conformity with the requirements of Acquisition Accounting (FASB ASC 805-20-30-1).

In Exhibit 2.9, we summarize the difference between fair value and recorded net book value for the identifiable acquired net assets:

EXHIBIT 2.9	Subsidiary's Net Book Value and Fair Value		
	Subsidiary's Recorded Net Book Values	Subsidiary's Estimated Fair Values	Fair Value Minus Book Value
Property & equipment—net	$800,000	$900,000	$100,000
Patents.	0	125,000	125,000
Net difference: Fair value − Book value.			$225,000

Continuing with our example, we now additionally assume that the parent acquired all of the issued and outstanding common stock of the subsidiary by issuing $700,000 worth of the parent's common stock (i.e., 35,000 shares of the parent's $1 par value common stock that has a fair value of $20 per share). The journal entry that the parent makes to record the acquisition is as follows:

Equity investment.	700,000	
Common stock (35,000 shares @ $1)		35,000
Additional paid-in capital.		665,000

Note that the $700,000 given in payment for the 100% controlling interest in the subsidiary is $250,000 greater than the preacquisition recorded net book value of the subsidiary's net assets (i.e., $450,000). We will refer to this difference between the fair value of an acquired subsidiary (i.e., the purchase price of $700,000) and the preacquisiton recorded carrying value of the subsidiary's net assets (i.e., old subsidiary book value of $450,000)—whether this difference is positive or negative—as the **"Acquisition Accounting Premium" (AAP)**.

In our example, based on our analysis of the identifiable net assets of the subsidiary, the parent should be willing to pay $225,000 more than the recorded book value of the subsidiary's net assets based on the fair-value-minus-book-value differences for PP&E and Patents that it has identified. This leaves $25,000 (i.e., $250,000 − $225,000) of the fair-value-minus-book-value difference as unidentified. This unidentifiable positive difference between the fair value given up for a business and the fair value of the acquired identifiable business net assets is called *Goodwill*.

PRACTICE INSIGHT

Steps in the Acquisition Method

The **acquisition method** includes the following four steps:

a. Identifying the acquirer,

b. Determining the acquisition date,

c. Recognizing and measuring the identifiable assets acquired, the liabilities assumed, and any noncontrolling interest in the acquiree,

d. Recognizing and measuring goodwill or a gain from a bargain purchase.

(Source: FASB ASC 805-10-05-4)

We briefly discussed issues related to identifying the acquirer (i.e., step a.) in Chapter 1. In real-world business combinations, identification of the acquirer is most difficult in "stock for stock" transactions (i.e., one company exchanges its voting stock for the voting stock of one or more other companies).

At first glance, step b. seems to be fairly straightforward; however, there are situations in which an acquiring company purchases several noncontrolling blocks of a target company's voting common stock prior to gaining control of the target. Acquisition accounting is applied to 100 percent of the target company as soon as the acquiring company obtains control (e.g., 51 percent) of the target. Thus, the acquisition date for purposes of acquisition accounting is the date on which the parent first gains control of the subsidiary. Note that the recognition and measurement of the acquired net assets (i.e., step c.) occurs *before* the step in which the acquirer determines the amount paid by the acquirer for the acquired company (i.e., the value of the consideration paid first enters acquisition accounting in step d.).

This sequence reflects a subtle, but important, change in philosophy underlying business combination accounting. Prior to SFAS 141(R), business-combination accounting was a process of, first, determining the purchase price and then attempting to *allocate* the purchase price to the acquired net assets of the subsidiary. The allocated amounts often included measurement bases (e.g., net realizable value) that were not representative of the fair value measurement basis. Further, if the difference between purchase price and allocated net asset values made it look like a purchaser made a "bargain purchase" of the subsidiary, the allocated net asset values were adjusted to make the net recorded value of the acquired net assets equal the purchase price. In contrast, SFAS 141(R) gave primacy to recognizing and measuring the acquired identifiable net assets of the subsidiary at acquisition-date fair value (FASB ASC 805-20-30-1). This process of fair value *"assignment"* (in contrast to "allocation" required under pre-SFAS141(R) purchase accounting) implicitly assumes that fair value measurement of individual identifiable net assets is sufficiently reliable that identifiable net asset valuation is independent from the total amount paid for the subsidiary in the business combination.

We can summarize the explained and unexplained components of the AAP and the computation of Goodwill as follows: [8]

---

[8] FASB ASC 805-20-25-1 through 25-5 provide guidance for recognizing individual net assets acquired in a business combination. Although, the guidance is primarily "principles based" (i.e., FASB ASC 805-20-25-2 states that "identifiable assets acquired and liabilities assumed must meet the definitions of assets and liabilities in FASB Concepts Statement No. 6"), existing guidance includes certain exceptions for operating leases and other intangible assets. In addition, current GAAP specifically *precludes* recognition of an "assembled workforce" (FASB ASC 805-20-55-6), even though one could argue that an acquirer may attribute value to the assembled workforce and that it meets the definition of an asset in FASB Concepts Statement No. 6. (An assembled workforce is defined as "an existing collection of employees that permits the acquirer to continue to operate an acquired business from the acquisition date.") Because Acquisition Accounting does not allow assignment of recognized fair value to an assembled workforce, this value becomes part of the unexplained portion of the AAP (i.e., it is subsumed into goodwill).

Purchase price	$700,000
Book value of subsidiary	450,000 ❶
Acquisition Accounting Premium (AAP)	$250,000 ❷
AAP assigned to identifiable net assets:	
Undervalued property & equipment	100,000
Patent	125,000
Unidentifiable ("Plug") = Goodwill*	$ 25,000

* A positive excess unidentifiable residual (i.e., amount left after assigning the fair value/book value differences implied by the AAP to the identifiable net assets) is recognized as goodwill asset in the balance sheet (FASB ASC 805-30-30-1). Goodwill is an "indefinite lived" (not infinite!) intangible asset that is not amortized or depreciated, but that is evaluated annually for impairment (FASB 350-20-35-1). A negative excess unidentifiable residual is recognized as a "bargain purchase" gain in the parent company income statement in the year the business combination transaction is consummated (FASB ASC 805-30-25-2).

It is not unusual for business managers and financial analysts to attempt to explain or justify the existence of Goodwill recognized in a business combination. For example, we are often told that recognized Goodwill reflects "corporate synergies" between the parent and the subsidiary (such as the ability to: eliminate duplicate overhead, grow revenues through vertical integration and additional marketing power, or reduce costs via increased buying power with suppliers, etc.). Such explanations are sometimes no more than speculation about the reasons a parent company paid an unjustifiably high amount for a subsidiary. Further, these explanations have absolutely no bearing on Acquisition Accounting for the business combination. From a strictly practical accounting-recognition perspective, the notion of Goodwill is much simpler: it is a "plug" figure, the amount necessary to balance the excess of fair value given up for a subsidiary and the fair value of the subsidiary's identifiable net assets acquired.[9]

Of course, parent companies do not always pay an amount that exceeds the fair value of the subsidiary's identifiable net assets. Should the fair value of the consideration paid by the parent be *less* than the fair value of the subsidiary's acquired net assets, the parent company will continue to record the fair value of the acquired net assets as before, but will now recognize a "bargain purchase" *gain* equal to the amount by which the fair value of the identifiable net assets exceeds the amount paid by the acquiring entity. This is another example of a situation in which meeting the definition of a *Business Combination* is important: if the transaction fails to qualify as a Business Combination (as defined by FASB ASC 805-10-25-1 and as discussed in Chapter 1), then the acquired net assets would be recognized as allocated pieces of a "basket purchase," and no bargain purchase gain would be recognized.

Let's return to the original focus of our discussion in this section of the chapter: preparation of consolidated financial statements. Although Acquisition Accounting requires parent companies to recognize the fair value of acquired subsidiary net assets in the consolidated financial statements, the acquired subsidiary retains the preacquisition carrying values (i.e., book values) on its accounting records. If these preacquisition carrying-value-based statements are included as a starting point in the consolidated worksheet, then this means that the AAP must be recognized and assigned to individual net assets as part of the consolidation process. Taken from this perspective, the fair value of any individual subsidiary net asset account (labeled "$_i$") is comprised of two parts:

$$\text{Fair value of subsidiary account}_i = \text{Subsidiary } book\ value \text{ of account}_i + AAP \text{ of account}_i$$

These two components are labeled ❶ and ❷, in the Goodwill computation above and are illustrated in the following T-account for the Equity Investment immediately after the purchase:

---

[9] From the slightly more-nuanced perspective of accounting disclosure, companies' explanations for the source of goodwill are required disclosures in the notes to the financial statements. In particular, companies must provide "qualitative description of the factors that make up the goodwill recognized, such as expected synergies from combining operations of the acquiree and the acquirer, intangible assets that do not qualify for separate recognition, or other factors" (FASB ASC 805-30-50-1).

Equity Investment		
Beginning balance 700,000	

❶ Book value of subsidiary's stockholders' equity $450,000

❷ Acquisition accounting premium $250,000

Immediately after the acquisition of the subsidiary's outstanding common stock, the (assumed) respective balance sheets of the parent and the subsidiary are as presented in Exhibit 2.10:

EXHIBIT 2.10	Post-Acquisition Balance Sheets of Parent and Subsidiary		
		Parent	**Subsidiary**
Assets			
Cash and receivables.		$ 800,000	$ 100,000
Inventory.		600,000	250,000
Property & equipment, net.		2,300,000	800,000
Equity investment.		700,000	
		$4,400,000	$1,150,000
Liabilities and stockholders' equity			
Current liabilities.		$ 400,000	$ 200,000
Other liabilities.		300,000	
Bonds payable.			500,000
Common stock.		1,670,000	100,000
APIC.		1,430,000	125,000
Retained earnings		600,000	225,000
		$4,400,000	$1,150,000

The only differences from the parent and subsidiary pre-consolidation balance sheets included in the previous example (see Exhibit 2.7) are that the parent's Equity Investment is now $700,000 and the parent's Common Stock and Additional Paid-In Capital (APIC) have been increased by the value of the additional shares issued.

The consolidation process now involves *two* entries, because there are two components of the Equity Investment account: the parent's share of the book value of the subsidiary's net assets (i.e., ❶ component in the T-account above) and the AAP (i.e., ❷ component in the T-account above).[10] The first consolidation entry eliminates the component of the Equity Investment account relating to the subsidiary's Stockholders' Equity [E], as before:

[E]	Common stock (subsidiary)	100,000	
	APIC (subsidiary)	125,000	
	Retained earnings (subsidiary).	225,000	
	Equity investment (parent).		450,000
	(to eliminate the Equity Investment account and related Stockholders' Equity of the subsidiary company)		

The second entry eliminates the remainder of the Equity Investment account and assigns the AAP to (1) the individual identifiable net assets that had fair value that differed from their preacquisition

---

[10] GAAP includes no requirements dictating the number or format of individual consolidation entries. This is why different Advanced Accounting textbooks often include seemingly different consolidating entries. We choose to separate the elimination of the investment account into two components: the subsidiary net asset carrying values and the AAP. This allows us to retain the direct, intuitive bridge between the parent's Equity Investment account and the carrying value of the subsidiary's net assets. In addition, it isolates the effects of the AAP on the consolidated financial statements. As we will see in the next chapter, a substantial portion of the AAP will get amortized, so direct correspondence between the AAP amortization schedule and the consolidation entries can increase the understandability of the steps in the consolidation process.

recorded carrying values and (2) Goodwill. We will call the second entry our [A] entry (for *A*cquisition Accounting Premium): [11]

[A]	PPE, net	100,000	
	Patent.	125,000	
	Goodwill	25,000	
	Equity investment (parent).		250,000
	(to eliminate the remainder of the Equity Investment account		
	and assign the AAP to individual net assets and goodwill)		

We insert these two entries into the consolidation entries columns of our consolidation spreadsheet to yield the consolidated balance sheet in Exhibit 2.11:

EXHIBIT 2.11 Parent, Subsidiary, and Consolidated Balance Sheets When Purchase Price Exceeds the Book Value Subsidiary's Stockholders' Equity

	Parent	Subsidiary	Consolidation Entries Dr	Consolidation Entries Cr	Consolidated
Assets					
Cash and receivables.	$ 800,000	$ 100,000			$ 900,000
Inventory.	600,000	250,000			850,000
PPE.	2,300,000	800,000	[A] $100,000		3,200,000
Equity investment.	700,000			[E] $450,000	0
				[A] 250,000	
Patent.			[A] 125,000		125,000
Goodwill			[A] 25,000		25,000
	$4,400,000	$1,150,000			$5,100,000
Liabilities and stockholders' equity					
Current liabilities.	$ 400,000	$ 200,000			$ 600,000
Other liabilities	300,000				300,000
Bonds payable		500,000			500,000
Common stock.	1,670,000	100,000	[E] 100,000		1,670,000
APIC	1,430,000	125,000	[E] 125,000		1,430,000
Retained earnings	600,000	225,000	[E] 225,000		600,000
	$4,400,000	$1,150,000	$700,000	$700,000	$5,100,000

There are three important points about our second consolidated balance sheet:

1. The book value of Stockholders' Equity on the consolidated balance sheet is equal to the book value of Stockholders' Equity of the parent, just like before. Again, this will always be the case so long as the parent uses the equity method to account for its Equity Investment.

---

[11] In practice, companies will maintain separate accounts for the cost of the PPE asset and its Accumulated Depreciation, and the [A] consolidation entry must address both accounts as follows (book value amounts for the subsidiary's Property and Equipment (gross) and Accumulated Depreciation are included in Exhibit 2.7):

[A]	Accumulated depreciation	200,000	
	Patent.	125,000	
	Goodwill	25,000	
	Property & equipment		100,000
	Equity investment (parent)		250,000
	(to eliminate the remainder of the Equity Investment account and		
	assign the AAP to individual net assets and goodwill)		

This entry has the net effect of replacing the subsidiary's Property & Equipment at its original cost (i.e., $1,000,000) and Accumulated Depreciation (i.e., $200,000) at its balance on the date of acquisition with Property & Equipment cost of $900,000 and with no Accumulated Depreciation. This is accomplished by zeroing out Accumulated Depreciation (the "new" asset has yet to be depreciated) and reducing the cost of the PPE asset from $1,000,000 to $900,000. Thus, entry [A] causes the subsidiary's Property & Equipment to appear as if it had been newly acquired at its fair value of $900,000 on the acquisition date.

2. Total consolidated assets are $250,000 *more* than in the balance sheet in our previous consolidation example. This reflects the changes in the assumptions about the higher overall purchase price for the subsidiary and the fair values of Property & Equipment and Patents. The difference between acquisition-date fair values and preacquisition book values for Property & Equipment and Patents were $100,000 and $125,000, respectively. The remaining amount (i.e., $25,000) could not be explained by assignment to identifiable net assets, so it is assigned to Goodwill.

3. Our approach to the consolidation process involves elimination of two components of the Equity Investment account sequentially: the [E] entry to eliminate Stockholders' Equity of the subsidiary, and the [A] entry to eliminate the AAP. As a result of these entries, the Equity Investment account has been reduced to a zero balance on the consolidated balance sheet.

Before we conclude this section of the chapter, let's pause to think once more about the [A] entry for the AAP. The AAP represents the difference between the fair value and the book value of the subsidiary assets. Because the subsidiary records only the *book value* of its PPE, the fair values are incorporated into the consolidated acquisition-date financial statements by adding the difference between the *fair value* and the book value of those assets in our consolidation entry [A]. The reported amount for the PPE assets in the consolidated balance sheet is equal to:

Book value + (Fair value − Book value adjustment in the [A] entry) = Fair value

This is an important point. *All of the assets and liabilities of the subsidiary company are reflected in the acquisition-date consolidated balance sheet at their fair values on the date of the acquisition.* Please take a moment to look, once again, at the [A] consolidation entry in our consolidation worksheet to make sure you understand from where the fair values emerge on the consolidated balance sheet and the process by which they are broken out from the Equity Investment account into individual net asset accounts.

TOPIC REVIEW 2

Consolidation at Date of Acquisition

A parent acquires all of the outstanding common stock of a subsidiary for a cash purchase price of $250,000. One reason the parent agreed to pay more than book value for the subsidiary is because the net property, plant & equipment was undervalued by $50,000. On the date of acquisition, the parent and subsidiary report the following balance sheets:

	Parent	Subsidiary
Assets		
Cash	$ 150,000	$ 50,000
Receivables	250,000	100,000
Inventory	300,000	200,000
Property, plant & equipment (PPE), net	1,150,000	200,000
Equity investment	250,000	
	$2,100,000	$550,000
Liabilities and stockholders' equity		
Current liabilities	$ 100,000	$100,000
Bonds payable	250,000	250,000
Common stock	800,000	50,000
APIC	600,000	60,000
Retained earnings	350,000	90,000
	$2,100,000	$550,000

Required
Prepare the consolidated balance sheet on the date of acquisition.

The solution to this review problem can be found on page 105.

LO4 Explain the measurement of identifiable assets acquired, liabilities assumed and goodwill in business combinations.

RECOGNIZING AND MEASURING THE IDENTIFIABLE ASSETS ACQUIRED AND THE LIABILITIES ASSUMED

SFAS 141(R) introduced a subtle, but important, shift in the way the FASB writes accounting standards. In particular, SFAS 141(R) represents the first major FASB statement written in the "principles-oriented" format of IASB standards.[12] With respect to the assets acquired and the liabilities assumed in a business combination, current GAAP includes two fundamental principles:

> *Recognition Principle:* "As of the acquisition date, the acquirer shall recognize, separately from goodwill, the identifiable assets acquired, the liabilities assumed, and any noncontrolling interest in the acquiree" (FASB ASC 805-20-25-1)

> *Measurement Principle:* "The acquirer shall measure the identifiable assets acquired, the liabilities assumed, and any noncontrolling interest in the acquiree at their acquisition-date fair values" (FASB ASC 805-20-30-1)

We will discuss each of these principles in the following sections.

Recognition Principle

The recognition principle is comprised of two central requirements related to recognition of assets acquired and liabilities assumed:[13]

1. As of the acquisition date, they must meet the definition of assets or liabilities in FASB Concept Statement No. 6 (FASB ASC 805-20-25-2 and footnote #4), and

2. They must be part of the business combination and not the results of a separate transaction (FASB ASC 805-20-25-3).

As you can imagine, the latter requirement can be quite important given the operational complexity of real-world business combinations, and determining the boundaries of a business combination takes extensive professional judgment. Current GAAP includes additional guidance on determining the items to be included and excluded from the business combination transaction.

For purposes of our text, requirement #1 deserves a bit more attention. According to FASB Concepts Statement No. 6, assets and liabilities have the following definitions:

> *Assets*: Probable future economic benefits obtained or controlled by a particular entity as a result of past transactions or events (FASB Concepts Statement No. 6, ¶25)

> *Liabilities*: Probable future sacrifices of economic benefits arising from present obligations of a particular entity to transfer assets or provide services to other entities in the future as a result of past transactions or events (FASB Concepts Statement No. 6, ¶35)[14]

As illustrated in the immediately preceding example in this chapter, the measurement and reporting of identifiable net assets will often include assets and liabilities that are *not* reported in the preacquisition balance sheet of the subsidiary (e.g., in our example the subsidiary had previously unrecognized Patents). This is to be expected because current GAAP generally requires that companies expense (i.e., not capitalize) costs incurred to internally develop intangible assets. Thus, a company

---

[12] IASB standards traditionally include a set of parsimonious recognition, measurement, classification and/or disclosure principles printed in bold font, with the remaining standard providing background, explanation, embellishment and implementation guidance printed in regular font. The bold-face principle is regarded as the most important factor to be considered in the preparation of financial statements.

[13] FASB ASC 805-20-30-1 also requires that noncontrolling interest is recognized and measured at fair value. For now, we limit our discussion to acquisitions in which the parent company obtains 100% of the outstanding common equity of its subsidiaries (i.e., a situation in which there is no noncontrolling interest). We will discuss consolidation of non-wholly owned subsidiaries—and accounting for noncontrolling interest—in Chapter 5.

[14] The FASB is careful to note that the use of the word "probable" in the asset and liability definitions is nontechnical. That is, "[p]robable is used with its usual general meaning, rather than in a specific accounting or technical sense (such as that in FASB Statement No. 5, Accounting for Contingencies, par. 3), and refers to that which can reasonably be expected or believed on the basis of available evidence or logic but is neither certain nor proved. . .). Its inclusion in the definition is intended to acknowledge that business and other economic activities occur in an environment characterized by uncertainty in which few outcomes are certain" (FASB Concepts Statement No. 6, footnote 18).

may have expended significant resources to develop a valuable trade-related asset, but the company cannot capitalize those costs. Of course, if the company is acquired in a business combination, the trade-related assets would be recognized in the post-acquisition consolidated balance sheet.

These previously unrecognized assets and liabilities are identified by the purchasing company and implicitly included in the price it is willing to pay for the acquired subsidiary; thus, all of the previously *recorded and unrecorded* assets and liabilities of the subsidiary are *implicitly included* in the Equity Investment account. In the consolidation process, we remove the Equity Investment account from the consolidated balance sheet and replace it with the recorded and unrecorded assets and liabilities to which it relates. The assets and liabilities that were previously *implicitly* included in the Equity Investment account are, subsequently, *explicitly* recognized on the consolidated balance sheet.

Measurement Principle and Fair Value Estimation

With the introduction of the *Acquisition Method* in 2009, the measurement of identifiable assets and liabilities became much more consistent and conceptually driven. Prior to the effective date of SFAS 141(R), the *Purchase Method* included numerous exceptions to the fair value measurement attribute. These exceptions have now been mostly eliminated—the few remaining are briefly discussed below— and the measurement of acquired individually identifiable net assets must be carried out in conformity with the general fair value measurement guidance included in FASB ASC 820-10.[15]

Fair value is defined as "the price that would be received to sell an asset or paid to transfer a liability in an orderly transaction between market participants at the measurement date" (FASB ASC 820-10-20). The assumed exchange price is the price that *would be* received for an asset (or paid for settling a liability) in an orderly transaction between market participants to sell the asset or transfer the liability in the market in which the entity would ordinarily transact for the asset or liability. The market participants in this hypothetical market are assumed to be independent of the reporting entity, knowledgeable of the asset or liability, and able and willing to transact for the asset or liability (FASB ASC 820-10-20). "The transaction to sell the asset or transfer the liability is a hypothetical transaction at the measurement date, considered from the perspective of a market participant that holds the asset or owes the liability. Therefore, the objective of a fair value measurement is to determine the price that would be received to sell the asset or paid to transfer the liability at the measurement date (an exit price)" (FASB ASC 820-10-35-3).

In arriving at a fair value estimate, the accounting standards assume that the hypothetical transaction to sell the asset or transfer the liability either occurs in the principal market for the asset or liability or, in the absence of a principal market, the transaction or transfer occurs in the "most advantageous" market for the asset or liability (FASB ASC 820-10-35-5). In the context of assets, the most advantageous market is one that is related to the "highest and best use" of the asset in question.[16] Highest and best use is determined based on the use of the asset by market participants, even if the intended use of the asset by the reporting entity is different (FASB ASC 820-10-35-10).

Standard setters intentionally avoided prescribing specific approaches for estimating the fair values of individual net assets, instead allowing companies flexibility in determining the valuation technique that is appropriate for the circumstances. Companies are required to use the valuation techniques that are appropriate in the circumstances and for which sufficient data are available. In some cases, companies can use only one valuation technique (e.g., when valuing a bond investment for which there

---

[15] This general fair value measurement guidance is divided into two primary parts: initial fair value recognition (FASB ASC 820-10-30) and subsequent fair value measurement (FASB ASC 820-10-35). Because the guidance related to subsequent fair value measurement is mostly directed at hypothetical transactions for net asset accounts that were not individually bought or sold on the measurement date, the "subsequent measurement" guidance is more appropriately applied to the assignment of individual fair values obtained in a single business combination transaction.

[16] This requirement has interesting implications for the assignment of fair values to the assets obtained in business combinations. For example, assume that a company acquires the common stock of one of its competitors and, subsequent to the business combination, the acquirer intends to lock up (i.e., discontinue offering) one of the highly successful brands of the target company. This type of asset is called a **defensive intangible asset** (FASB ASC 805-20-20). In this example, the acquiring company is required to measure fair value from a perspective "that assumes the highest and best use of the asset by market participants, considering the use of the asset that is physically possible, legally permissible, and financially feasible at the measurement date." Thus, the parent company is required to recognize in the post-business-combination balance sheet the market-derived fair value of the highly successful brand that the parent does not intend to use. Of course, as the fair value of this unused brand diminishes in future periods, the parent company will need to recognize amortization over the period during which it will consume the expected benefits related to the **defensive intangible asset** (FASB ASC 350-30-35-5A).

are actively quoted market prices). However, in most cases valuing the myriad individual net assets acquired in a business combination, multiple valuation techniques will be appropriate (for example, as might be the case when valuing a factory). If multiple valuation techniques are used, then companies need to evaluate the ranges generated by application of the multiple methods. Of course, balance sheets only recognize one value from the range of potential values for a given net asset account; thus, the fair value measurement is required to be the point estimate (i.e., single amount) that is most representative of fair value in the circumstances (FASB ASC 820-10-35-24).

Current GAAP broadly defines three general valuation techniques that can be used to estimate fair values:

Market Approach: Includes valuation techniques that use prices and other relevant information generated by market transactions involving identical or comparable assets or liabilities (including entire companies or businesses). This approach includes the use of market multiples (and ranges of multiples) derived from a set of comparables (FASB ASC 820-10-35-29 through 35-31).

Income Approach: Uses valuation techniques to convert future amounts (e.g., cash flows or earnings) to a single, discounted present amount. The measurement includes current market expectations about future amounts. Techniques include present value, option-pricing models (e.g., Black-Scholes and/or binomial models), and "the multiperiod excess earnings method, which is used to measure the fair value of certain intangible assets" (FASB ASC 820-10-35-32 through 35-33).

Cost Approach: Valuation technique "based on the amount that currently would be required to replace the service capacity of an asset (often referred to as current replacement cost). From the perspective of a market participant (seller), the price that would be received for the asset is determined based on the cost to a market participant (buyer) to acquire or construct a substitute asset of comparable utility, adjusted for obsolescence" (FASB ASC 820-10-35-34 through 35-35).

In applying these approaches to arrive at fair value estimates, companies are required to "maximize the use of observable inputs and minimize the use of unobservable inputs." To assist with the description of observable and unobservable inputs in financial statement disclosures, the FASB devised a "fair value hierarchy," comprised of three input levels:

- **Level 1** fair value inputs are "quoted prices (unadjusted) in active markets for identical assets or liabilities that the reporting entity has the ability to access at the measurement date" (FASB ASC 820-10-35-40).

- **Level 2** fair value inputs are "inputs other than quoted prices included within Level 1 that are observable for the asset or liability, either directly or indirectly" (FASB ASC 820-10-35-47).

- **Level 3** fair value inputs are "unobservable inputs for assets or liabilities" (FASB ASC 820-10-35-52). Thus, companies are required to use Level 1 inputs whenever possible and resort to Level 2 (and then Level 3) only when necessary.

Finally, because of the complexity inherent in business combinations, it is not uncommon for the accounting to take some time to complete. FASB ASC 805-10-25-13 through 25-19 permits companies

PRACTICE INSIGHT

Oracle's Use of Provisional Amounts   In its May 31, 2015 SEC Form 10-K, **Oracle Corporation** provides the following footnote discussion relating to its use of provisional amounts in an acquisition:

> While we use our best estimates and assumptions to accurately value assets acquired and liabilities assumed at the acquisition date as well as contingent consideration, where applicable, our estimates are inherently uncertain and subject to refinement. As a result, during the measurement period, which may be up to one year from the acquisition date, we record adjustments to the assets acquired and liabilities assumed, with the corresponding offset to goodwill. Upon the conclusion of the measurement period or final determination of the values of assets acquired or liabilities assumed, whichever comes first, any subsequent adjustments are recorded to our consolidated statements of operations.

PRACTICE INSIGHT

Accounting for Changes in the Provisional Amount Assigned to an Acquired Asset   The following example of the accounting for a change in the provisional amount assigned to an acquired asset is provided in FASB ASC 805-10-55-27 through 55-29:

> A parent acquires a subsidiary on September 30, 20X7, recording Goodwill on the acquisition date. The parent seeks an independent appraisal for an item of property, plant, and equipment acquired in the combination, and the appraisal was not complete by the time the parent issued its financial statements for the year ending December 31, 20X7. In its 20X7 annual financial statements, the parent recognized a provisional fair value for the asset of $30,000. At the acquisition date, the item of property, plant, and equipment had a remaining useful life of five years. Six months after the acquisition date, the parent received the independent appraisal, which estimated the asset's acquisition-date fair value as $40,000.

In its interim financial statements for the quarter ending March 31, 20X8, the parent adjusts the provisional amounts recorded and the related effects on earnings as follows:

a. The carrying amount of property, plant, and equipment as of March 31, 20X8, is increased by $9,000. That adjustment is measured as the fair value adjustment at the acquisition date of $10,000 less the additional depreciation that would have been recognized had the asset's fair value at the acquisition date been recognized from that date (i.e., $1,000 for 6 months' depreciation).

b. The carrying amount of Goodwill as of March 31, 20X8, is decreased by $10,000.

c. Depreciation expense for the period ended March 31, 20X8, is increased by $1,000 to reflect the effect on earnings as a result of the change to the provisional amount recognized.

In addition, the parent discloses:

a. In its 20X7 financial statements, that the initial accounting for the business combination has not been completed because the appraisal of property, plant, and equipment has not yet been received.

b. In its 20X8 financial statements, the amounts and explanations of the adjustments to the provisional values recognized during the current reporting period. Therefore, the parent discloses that the increase to the fair value of the item of property, plant, and equipment was $10,000, with a corresponding decrease to Goodwill. Additionally, the change to the provisional amount resulted in an increase in depreciation expense and accumulated depreciation of $1,000, of which $500 relates to a previous reporting period.

to use "provisional" amounts, and to prospectively adjust those amounts when better information becomes available, provided that the final measurement of all assets and liabilities is completed within one year from the acquisition date.[17] Also, during the measurement period, the investor can recognize additional assets or liabilities if new information is obtained about facts and circumstances that existed as of the acquisition date that, if known, would have resulted in the recognition of those assets and liabilities as of that date.

In the remaining sections of this chapter, we discuss the special requirements for the recognition of intangible assets, the measurement of Goodwill, the accounting for direct acquisition-related costs, the treatment of in-process research and development assets, and the recognition of liabilities related to planned post-acquisition restructuring activities.

Intangible Assets   The existence of significant unrecorded intangible assets may be both a major reason why a given acquisition occurs and a major factor in determining the purchase price. Such intangibles include brand names, market position, customer loyalty, good locations, below-market lease

---

[17] Note that the FASB, in 2015, modified the accounting for adjustments of acquisition-related provisional amounts. Prior to 2015, the adjustments of provisional amounts required retroactive adjustment of financial statement information. The FASB changed to prospective adjustment of provisional amounts as part of its accounting-standards "simplification" initiative.

rights, valuable technology, and the like. Most of these intangibles are developed during the preacquisition life of the investee, and few of them are recorded as assets on the investee's books (for example, expenditures related to internally developed intangible assets are generally expensed as incurred as wage expense, advertising expense, R&D expense, etc.). As a result, we may (and frequently do) recognize intangible assets and liabilities on the consolidated balance sheet that the investee could not previously recognize as assets and liabilities on its own balance sheet (FASB ASC 805-20-25-4).

Prior to the passage of the original SFAS 141 in 1997 and its revision, SFAS 141(R) in 2007, little attempt was made to identify specific intangibles. Virtually all intangibles were combined under the generic title of Goodwill. This level of aggregation for intangible assets did not provide very useful information. An important change introduced in 2001 was to increase disaggregation and disclosure of separately identifiable intangible assets. *Current accounting standards require that acquired intangible assets be separately recognized if they can be identified.*

Intangible assets are considered to be **separately identifiable** if they meet either of the following criteria (FASB ASC 805-20-20):

- The intangible asset arises from **contractual or other legal rights**, or
- The intangible is **separable**, that is, it can be separated or divided from the acquired entity and sold, rented, licensed, or otherwise transferred.[18]

The category of intangibles arising from contractual or other legal rights is wide-ranging as many business activities are subject to contractual agreements. These contractual or legal intangibles should be separately recognized *whether (or not) they can be separated from the acquired entity.* FASB ASC 805-20-55-11 through 55-44 offers many examples, grouped into broad categories as follows:

- **Contract-based intangible assets**, such as lease agreements, franchise agreements, licensing agreements, construction contracts, employment contracts, and mineral rights.[19,20]

- **Marketing-related intangible assets**, such as brand names, trademarks, and Internet domain names.

- **Customer-related intangible assets**, such as customer contracts, relationships, and orders.

- **Technology-based intangible assets**, such as patent rights, computer software, and trade secrets.

- **Artistic-related intangible assets**, such as television programs, motion pictures and videos, recordings, books, photographs, and advertising jingles.

Other intangible assets that are not based in contractual or legal rights are recognized if they are **separable** from the acquired entity. Examples here are far fewer; they include customer lists, databases, and unpatented technology. Exhibit 2.12 provides a complete listing of intangible assets identified in FASB ASC 805 and whether they arise from the contractual or the separability criterion.

Once fair values are assigned to the assets acquired and to the liabilities assumed, any remaining, unassigned acquisition cost is classified as Goodwill. Investors must first determine whether any

---

[18] The determination of whether an intangible asset meets the separability criterion can be difficult. An investor must determine whether the asset is *capable* of being separated from the acquired business, regardless of the investor's intent with respect to that particular asset. For example, an acquired customer list is generally capable of being separated from the acquired business if the investor has the right to sell customer information and, therefore, would meet the separability criterion even if the investor does not plan to sell or license the customer list (FASB ASC 805-20-55-3 through 55-5).

[19] If the investee is the lessee in an operating lease, no asset or liability is recognized for the rights to use the leased asset and the related financial obligation (FASB ASC 805-20-25-11). However, if the terms of an investee's operating leases are favorable or unfavorable compared with the market terms of leases, the investor shall recognize an intangible asset if the terms of an operating lease are favorable relative to market terms and a liability if the terms are unfavorable relative to market terms (FASB ASC 805-20-25-12).

[20] One frequently encountered intangible asset that arises from contractual rights is an indemnification asset. The seller in a business combination may contractually indemnify the purchaser for the outcome of a contingency related to all or part of a specific asset or liability. For example, the seller may indemnify the purchaser against losses above a specified amount on a liability arising from a particular contingency, such as a pending lawsuit. As a result, the investor obtains an indemnification asset. The investor recognizes an indemnification asset at the same time that it recognizes the indemnified item (the contingent liability, for example). In addition, both the indemnification asset and the related liability are revalued subsequent to the acquisition. These revaluations should be offsetting, resulting in no net effect on income. The balance sheet will change, however, as these assets and liabilities increase or decrease (FASB ASC 805-20-25-27 through 25-28).

EXHIBIT 2.12	Listing of Intangible Assets under SFAS 141(R)

■ *Marketing-Related Intangible Assets*
- ○ Trademarks, trade names, service marks, collective marks, certification marks #
- ○ Trade dress (unique color, shape, package design) #
- ○ Newspaper mastheads #
- ○ Noncompetition agreements #
- ○ Internet domain names #

■ *Customer-Related Intangible Assets*
- ○ Customer lists *
- ○ Order or production backlog #
- ○ Customer contracts and related customer relationships #
- ○ Noncontractual customer relationships *

■ *Artistic-Related Intangible Assets*
- ○ Plays, operas, ballets #
- ○ Books, magazines, newspapers, other literary works #
- ○ Musical works such as compositions, song lyrics, advertising jingles #
- ○ Pictures, photographs #
- ○ Video and audiovisual material, including motion pictures or films, music videos, television programs #

■ *Contract-Based Intangible Assets*
- ○ Licensing, royalty, standstill agreements #
- ○ Advertising, construction, management, service or supply contracts #
- ○ Lease agreements (whether the investee is the lessee or the lessor) #
- ○ Construction permits #
- ○ Franchise agreements #
- ○ Operating and broadcast rights #
- ○ Servicing contracts such as mortgage servicing contracts #
- ○ Employment contracts #
- ○ Use rights such as drilling, water, air, timber cutting, and route authorities #

■ *Technology-Based Intangible Assets*
- ○ Patented technology #
- ○ Computer software and mask works #
- ○ Unpatented technology *
- ○ Databases, including title plants *
- ○ Trade secrets, such as secret formulas, processes, recipes #

Intangible assets that arise from contractual or other legal rights.
* Do not arise from contractual or other legal rights but are separable.
Source: FASB ASC 805-20-55-11 through 55-44

identifiable intangible assets exist (and value them) before they can assign any of the purchase price to Goodwill. We discuss the computation leading to the recognition of Goodwill in the next section.

In our Practice Insight box on page 71, we provide an example of the fair value assignment for **Actavis'** acquisition of **Allergan** in 2015. Please take a moment to review this disclosure as it provides a good example of how this is done in practice. Notice that Actavis assigns its $74.8 billion purchase price for Allergan (i.e., the implied fair value of the entire company) to the fair value of the assets and liabilities that Allergan reports on its balance sheet as well as to assets and liabilities that Allergan does not report on its balance sheet as of the acquisition date (primarily identifiable intangible assets and the Goodwill asset).

PRACTICE INSIGHT

Private Company Alternatives for Recognition and Measurement of Intangible Assets   In 2012, the Financial Accounting Foundation—the organization that oversees the FASB—created the Private Company Council (PCC). The PCC is an advisory body to the FASB and is charged with identifying and proposing simplifications to existing and proposed U.S. GAAP that should be available to private companies (i.e., entities that are not public business entities,[21] not-for-profit entities, or employee benefit plans). The PCC's specific simplification proposals are presented to the FASB for a vote of endorsement. If a PCC accounting-principles "carve out" is endorsed by the FASB, it becomes part of the FASB ASC and is available for adoption by private companies. Private companies need to be very careful in adopting these GAAP exceptions. If a private company attempts to transition to being a public business entity (e.g., by registering its common stock with the SEC and issuing the shares to investors via an Initial Public Offering), then the company will be required to retroactively restate its financial statements without the private-company exception included in the financial statements.

Two private company exceptions are particularly relevant to this chapter:

1. **Goodwill Amortization** (FASB ASC 350-20-35-62 through -82): As described in this chapter, ordinarily, if a company records goodwill pursuant to a business combination, the goodwill is not amortized; instead, it is annually tested for impairment. However, under the accounting alternative available to private companies, an acquirer has the option to amortize the goodwill "on a straight-line basis over 10 years, or less than 10 years if the entity demonstrates that another useful life is more appropriate." In addition, companies are not required to test goodwill for impairment on an annual basis; instead, goodwill is tested for impairment if an event occurs or circumstances change that indicate that the fair value of the entity may be below its carrying amount. This exception is effective for annual periods beginning after December 15, 2014, and interim periods within annual periods beginning after December 15, 2015.

2. **Identifiable Intangible Assets** (FASB ASC 805-20-25-29 through -33): As described in this chapter, ordinarily, a company must recognize and report an identifiable intangible asset if it meets either the separability criterion or the contractual-legal criterion. However, under the accounting alternative available to private companies, an acquirer has the option to not recognize separately from goodwill the following intangible assets: (a) customer-related intangible assets unless they are capable of being sold or licensed independently from other assets of a business and (b) noncompetition agreements. (Note that FASB ASC 805-20-15-3 requires private companies adopting this exception to also adopt the goodwill amortization exception described in (1), above.) This exception is effective for fiscal years beginning after December 15, 2015.

The FASB also endorsed PCC recommendations related to interest-rate-swaps-related hedging (FASB ASC 815) and variable interest entity assessments for common control lessors (FASB ASC 810). According to a survey published by PricewaterhouseCoopers LLP in June 2015, only 5% of responding private companies have adopted the goodwill amortization exception. In addition, when considering companies' future financial statements, only 32% of companies indicate that they have already adopted or plan, in future reporting periods, to adopt one or more of the currently available private-company exceptions.

Recent discussions at the FASB suggest that the Board is considering adopting some of the PCC exceptions for public companies; however, none of these exceptions are allowed for public company financial statements.

---

[21] According to the FASB ASC Master Glossary, a public business entity meets one of the following criteria: (a) It is required by the U.S. SEC to file or furnish financial statements, or does file or furnish financial statements (including voluntary filers), with the SEC, (b) it is required by the SEC Act of 1934 to file or furnish financial statements with a regulatory agency other than the SEC, (c) it is required to file or furnish financial statements with a foreign or domestic regulatory agency in preparation for the sale of or for purposes of issuing securities that are not subject to contractual restrictions on transfer, (d) it has issued, or is a conduit bond obligor for, securities that are traded, listed, or quoted on an exchange or an over-the-counter market or (e) it has one or more securities that are not subject to contractual restrictions on transfer, and it is required by law, contract, or regulation to prepare U.S. GAAP financial statements (including footnotes) and make them publicly available on a periodic basis. To meet requirement (e), an entity must meet both conditions to meet the criterion.

PRACTICE INSIGHT

On March 17, 2015, **Actavis plc** acquired **Allergan, Inc.** ("Allergan") for approximately $74.8 billion. The following excerpt from Actavis' March 31, 2015 SEC Form 10-Q lists the assignment of fair values to Allergan's various net asset accounts (in millions):

	Amounts
Cash and cash equivalents	$ 5,424.5
Accounts receivable	962.7
Inventories	1,223.2
Other current assets	318.8
Property, plant and equipment, net	1,202.5
Other long-term assets	189.3
IPR&D intangible assets	11,010.0
Intangible assets	45,050.5
Goodwill	26,368.5
Current liabilities	(1,212.2)
Contingent consideration	(379.1)
Deferred tax liabilities, net	(12,512.9)
Other taxes payable	(82.4)
Other long-term liabilities	(622.0)
Outstanding indebtedness	(2,183.5)
	$74,757.9

As part of the acquisition, Actavis recognized the fair value of Allergan's intangible assets, including approximately $11.0 billion of in-process research and development, $45.1 billion of identifiable intangible assets and $26.4 billion of goodwill. This means that the intangible assets recognized as part of the acquisition represents 110% of the net purchase price!

The in-process research and development and identifiable intangible assets primarily related to specific products owned by Allegan or categories in which Allergan was developing products. The following table identifies the summarized amounts recognized and the weighted average useful lives of intangible assets:

	Amount recognized as of the acquisition date	Weighted average useful lives (years)
Definite lived assets		
Restasis ®	3,970.0	4.0
Refresh® / Optive ®	2,720.0	7.6
Other Eye Care Products	6,690.0	4.2
Botox ®	22,570.0	8.0
Aczone ®	160.0	1.3
Other Skin Products	820.0	5.0
Other Aesthetics	6,370.0	6.0
Total CMP	43,300.0	6.7
Trade name	700.0	4.5
Customer relationships	1,050.5	3.4
Total definite lived intangible assets	45,050.5	6.6
In-process research and development		
Eye Care	6,460.0	
Botox ®	810.0	
Aesthetics	2,620.0	
Other	1,120.0	
	11,010.0	
Total Identifiable Intangible Assets	56,060.5	

Measurement of Goodwill   Companies often recognize Goodwill as one of the intangible assets acquired. The value assigned to Goodwill is not computed directly. Instead, it is computed as a residual amount (i.e., the amount left over after all other assets and liabilities have been identified and valued). Through Chapter 4, we focus exclusively on business combinations and consolidations procedures for parent company acquisitions of 100 percent of the subsidiary's common stock. However, for our discussion of the computation of Goodwill in this section, we will include the more general case of controlling interests of less than 100 percent.[22] Generally, Goodwill is defined as follows (FASB ASC 805-30-30-1):

	Fair value of the parent's post-acquisition controlling interest in the investee*
+	The fair value of any noncontrolling interest in the investee
=	Total value of the investee company
−	The acquisition-date amounts of the identifiable assets acquired and the liabilities assumed
=	Goodwill

* Business combination accounting is triggered when a parent company obtains a controlling interest in a subsidiary; thus, it is an all-or-nothing determination from a recognition and measurement perspective. In a purchase of a controlling interest in a subsidiary in a single transaction, the amount paid (i.e., total consideration transferred) for the controlling interest is presumed to be the fair value of the parent's post-acquisition interest in the investee. In an acquisition achieved in stages (or, "step acquisition") "the acquirer shall remeasure its previously held [i.e., noncontrolling] equity interest in the acquiree at its acquisition-date fair value and recognize the resulting gain or loss, if any, in earnings. In prior reporting periods, the acquirer may have recognized changes in the value of its equity interest in the acquiree in other comprehensive income (for example, because the investment was classified as available for sale). If so, the amount that was recognized in other comprehensive income shall be reclassified and included in the calculation of gain or loss as of the acquisition date." (FASB ASC 805-10-25-10)

The computation defines the total value of the investee company as the purchase price for the shares the investor purchased plus the value of the shares the investor does not own, if any (these are called *noncontrolling interest*).[23] That total fair value is, then, split up and assigned to all of the identifiable tangible and intangible assets acquired (net of the liabilities assumed). Finally, Goodwill is the difference between the value of the investee company and the value of its net tangible and intangible assets.

Over time, the FASB has sought to reduce the proportion of Goodwill that is recognized in an acquisition. The identification of intangible assets, such as those listed in Exhibit 2.12, results in the assignment of proportionately more fair value to this class of assets and a consequent reduction in the portion of fair value that is attributed to Goodwill. This is not by accident. As we will see in Chapter 3, Goodwill is not amortized like other intangible assets. Instead, it remains on the balance sheet until management deems it to be impaired, at which time it is written down. As a result of the fact that Goodwill is not amortized, companies might be inclined to assign more fair value to Goodwill. This reduces the fair value assigned to assets that are depreciated or amortized and, therefore, reduces the depreciation and/or amortization expense hitting their income statements following the acquisition. The SEC is particularly aware of this possibility and scrutinizes 10-Ks closely to identify excessively large amounts of fair value assigned to Goodwill.

TOPIC REVIEW 3

Measurement of Goodwill

The parent is purchasing a 100% interest in the subsidiary for $10,000,000. It estimates that the subsidiary's assets have a fair value of $8,000,000 on the acquisition date.

Required

a. How much Goodwill, if any, will the parent record in this acquisition?

b. Now, assume that the fair value of the identifiable assets is $11 million. How do you account for this new value?

The solution to this review problem can be found on page 105.

---

[22] We address issues related to consolidation of less-than-100-percent owned (i.e., non-wholly owned) subsidiaries in Chapter 5.

[23] The *per-share* fair value of the parent's controlling interest in the investee and the *per-share* fair value of the noncontrolling interest might differ. The main difference is likely to be the inclusion of a control premium in the per-share fair value of the investor's interest in the investee or, conversely, the inclusion of a discount for lack of control (also referred to as a minority interest discount) in the per-share fair value of the noncontrolling interest (FASB ASC 805-20-30-8).

PRACTICE INSIGHT

Allocating Fair Value and Determining Goodwill   NCR Corporation is an electronics company that sells self-service kiosks, automated teller machines, and check processing systems, among other products. In a 2011 expansion effort, the company completed its acquisition of Radiant Systems, a leading provider of management technology systems. Details of the transaction, including an assignment of the fair values to specifically identifiable net assets and goodwill, is provided in NCR's "Business Combinations and Investments" footnote to its 2011 annual report. Note that goodwill is determined as the excess consideration paid over the fair value of specifically identifiable tangible and intangible net assets.

Recording of Assets Acquired and Liabilities Assumed in Radiant Acquisition
The fair value of consideration transferred to acquire Radiant was allocated to the identifiable assets acquired and liabilities assumed based upon their fair values as of the date of the acquisition as set forth below. This allocation is final as of December 31, 2011.

(in millions)			
Purchase Consideration	Net Tangible Assets Acquired/ (Liabilities Assumed)	Purchased Intangible Assets	Goodwill
$1,206	$78	$319	$809

Acquisition-Related Costs   Acquisition-related costs for services provided by attorneys, accountants, and investment bankers, as well as indirect costs, such as office expenses of the investor company, are *expensed* in the income statement of the investor company in the period of the acquisition (FASB ASC 805-10-25-23).[24] These acquisition-related costs do not include costs relating to the issuance of securities in the acquisition. Stock issuance costs are treated as a reduction of the proceeds from the stock sale and typically reduce the amount of Additional Paid-In Capital recognized when the stock is issued.

TOPIC REVIEW 4

Acquisition-Related Costs

The parent is acquiring a subsidiary for $7 million. In addition to the purchase price, the parent's law firm is billing it $200,000 for preparation of the purchase documents, and its accounting firm is billing it $100,000 for analysis it performed in connection with the investigation of the subsidiary as a potential acquisition. How should the parent treat these acquisition costs?

The solution to this review problem can be found on pages 105–106.

Acquired Research and Development Assets   Investors frequently purchase investees for research projects currently in process and during their developmental states (i.e., before the research projects have reached technological feasibility). Identifiable assets resulting from research and development activities of the acquired enterprise might include, for example, patents received or applied for, blueprints, formulas, and specifications or designs for new products or processes, materials and supplies, equipment and facilities, and perhaps even a specific research project in process.

---

[24] This is in sharp contrast to prior accounting standards that treated these costs as includable in the purchase price and, thus, capitalized in the Equity Investment account on the balance sheet. Prior to 2009, these costs typically increased the amount of Goodwill recognized in consolidated financial statements pursuant to purchase-method acquisitions.

PRACTICE INSIGHT

Accounting for Acquired In-Process Research and Development Assets Acquisitions of knowledge-based companies (e.g., software, electronic device, pharmaceutical, and life science industries) usually entail the purchase of technology, both developed and under development. How is that technology valued in the assignment of fair values? **Novell, Inc.,** values the technology as the present value of expected cash flow to be derived from the technology. In addition to using the value it has estimated during the negotiation process, Novell, Inc., also retains an independent accounting firm to value the acquired technology a second time, this time for purposes of assignment of fair values. The firm it retains is not the firm that audits its financial statements. How much in-process technology is too much? Novell's CFO, Mr. Dana Russell, feels that in-process technology is good up to a point. Too much in-process technology, however, may indicate a long development cycle or an inability of management to bring projects to fruition.

In December 2013, the American Institute of Certified Public Accountants (AICPA) published its Accounting and Valuation Guide: *Assets Acquired to Be Used in Research and Development Activities*, replacing a practice aid it issued in 2001 for in-process research and development (IPRD). The original 2001 practice aid was issued to combat wide-spread abuse in the allocation of purchase price to IPRD. This was especially problematic because, prior to 2008, companies were required to expense 100% of acquired IPRD, which was a way for companies to "take a bath" through aggressive use of IPRD. Although IPRD is now required to be capitalized, the fair value assigned to IPRD in acquisitions still continues to be significant. For example, amounts allocated to IPRD have continued to be material. (For example, in the Actavis acquisition of Allergan discussed in a prior Practice Insight, $11 billion—or almost 15% of total purchase price—was assigned to IPRD and capitalized.) The new Accounting and Valuation Guide improves on the 2001 guide by integrating the fair value measurement guidance from FASB ASC 820, including best practices and examples related to valuation methods used to measure the fair value of IPRD, providing discussion of the differential accounting treatment of assets to be used in R&D activities that are acquired in a business combination vs. an asset acquisition, introducing the concept of "enabling technology," which replaces the previous concept of "core technology," and provides an expanded set of appropriate techniques for valuing IPRD, including the relief-from-royalty method and the cost approach. In a nutshell, the AICPA Accounting and Valuation Guide is an essential resource for practitioners, preparers, and valuation consultants when dealing with IPRD.

Under current GAAP, investors value and recognize research and development assets acquired in a business combination at their fair values just like any other assets acquired (FASB ASC 350-30-30-1; see discussion justifying this treatment in SFAS 141(R), ¶B149-B156).[25] After initial recognition, tangible research and development assets (like an R&D building and associated equipment, for example) are accounted for in accordance with their nature. Intangible research and development assets, on the other hand, should be considered indefinite-lived (i.e., not amortized) until the associated research and development activities are either completed (then, the intangible assets are amortized over their remaining useful lives) or abandoned (in which case they are written off in the year of abandonment). Acquired intangible research and development assets are included in the annual Goodwill impairment evaluation (FASB ASC 350-20-35-15).

Assumed Liabilities Relating to Planned Restructuring Activities

Often, the investor or the investee (or both) will adopt a restructuring plan to achieve expected synergies from the acquisition. These plans typically include the termination of employees as departments are merged, the divestiture of lines of businesses with related plant closing costs, and the relocation and training of employees.

In its assignment of fair values to acquired assets and liabilities, the investor must decide whether to record a planned restructuring obligation as a preexisting liability of the investee (and, thus, included

---

[25] Prior GAAP required an investor to immediately expense in-process research and development assets that had no alternative future use. An in-process research and development asset was recognized as an asset only if it had an alternative future use. Most acquired in-process research and development assets were expensed, resulting in large expenses in the year of acquisition for many companies.

in the fair value assignment) or as a post-acquisition obligation of the investor or investee company (and, thus, accrued and expensed subsequent to the acquisition). FASB ASC 805-20-25-2 provides the guidance relating to planned restructuring activities that is currently in effect: "costs the investor *expects but is not obligated to incur* in the future to affect its plan to exit an activity of an investee or to terminate the employment of or relocate an investee's employees are not liabilities at the acquisition date. Therefore, the investor does not recognize those costs as part of applying the acquisition method. Instead, the investor recognizes those costs in its post-combination financial statements in accordance with other applicable generally accepted accounting principles (emphasis added)."

PRACTICE INSIGHT

Oracle's Footnote Disclosure on Planned Restructuring Activities In its May 31, 2015 SEC Form 10-K, **Oracle Corporation** provides the following footnote disclosure relating to its accounting for anticipated restructuring activities in connection with an acquisition:

> In connection with a business combination or other strategic initiative, we may estimate costs associated with restructuring plans committed to by our management. Restructuring costs are typically comprised of employee severance costs, costs of consolidating duplicate facilities and contract termination costs. Restructuring expenses are based upon plans that have been committed to by our management, but may be refined in subsequent periods. We account for costs to exit or restructure certain activities of an acquired company separately from the business combination pursuant to ASC 420, *Exit or Disposal Cost Obligations*. A liability for costs associated with an exit or disposal activity is recognized and measured at its fair value in our consolidated statement of operations in the period in which the liability is incurred. When estimating the fair value of facility restructuring activities, assumptions are applied regarding estimated sub-lease payments to be received, which can differ materially from actual results. This may require us to revise our initial estimates which may materially affect our results of operations and financial position in the period the revision is made.

It is not sufficient that the investor and/or the investee *expect* to restructure their operations following the acquisition in order to record that obligation as an acquisition date liability. It is only when the investee has a restructuring plan already *in place* that the liability can be recognized. If not, the liability, and associated expense, must be recognized subsequent to the acquisition.

The implication of this is significant. Recording a restructuring liability on acquisition date allows the investor to debit future costs to the *liability* instead of to an *expense* account. As a result, post-acquisition profits are higher. The changes introduced via SFAS 141(R) ensure that these post-acquisition costs are recognized as a post-acquisition expense.[26]

DISCLOSURE EXAMPLE: TYSON FOODS' ACQUISITION OF HILLSHIRE BRANDS

We conclude this chapter by providing you with an excerpt from the acquisitions footnote included in **Tyson Foods, Inc.**'s September 27, 2014 annual report. (Note that Tyson's fiscal year end is the Saturday closest to September 30 [i.e., the exact date is variable and the fiscal year can be either 52 or 53 weeks in length]. Fiscal years 2014, 2013 and 2012 each consisted of 52 weeks.) This disclosure describes the company's acquisition of **The Hillshire Brands Company**. We highlighted several sections of this footnote, and provide you with discussion of these sections below.

---

[26] Furthermore, from an accounting standpoint, it makes no difference which facilities will be closed or whose employees will be severed (those of the acquired company or those of the buyer) to achieve the synergies expected from the transaction. All of these costs will be included in the post-acquisition consolidated income statement.

NOTE 3: ACQUISITIONS AND DISPOSITIONS

Acquisitions:

On August 28, 2014, we acquired all of the outstanding stock of The Hillshire Brands Company ("Hillshire Brands") as part of our strategic expansion initiative. The purchase price was equal to $63.00 per share for Hillshire Brands' outstanding common stock, or $8,081 million. In addition, we paid $163 million in cash for breakage costs incurred by Hillshire Brands related to a previously announced acquisition. We funded the acquisition with existing cash on hand, net proceeds from the issuance of new senior notes, Class A common stock (Class A stock), and tangible equity units as well as borrowings under a new term loan facility (refer to Note 7: Debt and Note 8: Equity). Hillshire Brands' results from operations subsequent to the acquisition closing are included in the Prepared Foods segment. The following table summarizes the preliminary fair values of the assets acquired and liabilities assumed at the acquisition date. Certain estimated values for the acquisition, including goodwill, intangible assets, plant property and equipment, and deferred taxes, are not yet finalized and the preliminary purchase price allocations are subject to change as we complete our analysis of the fair value at the date of acquisition.

	(in millions)
Cash and cash equivalents	$ 72
Accounts receivable	236
Inventories	421
Other current assets	344
Property, plant and equipment	1,306
Goodwill	4,804
Intangible assets	5,141
Other assets	45
Accounts payable	(347)
Other current liabilities	(324)
Long-term debt	(868)
Deferred income taxes	(2,069)
Other liabilities	(517)
Net asset acquired	$8,244

The fair value of identifiable intangible assets is as follows:

Intangible Asset Category	Type	Life in Years	(in millions) Fair Value
Brands & trademarks	Non-amortizable	Indefinite	$4,062
Brands & trademarks	Amortizable	20 years	532
Customer relationships	Amortizable	Weighted average life of 16 years	541
Non-compete agreements	Amortizable	1 year	6
Total identifiable intangible assets			$5,141

As a result of the acquisition, we recognized a total of $4,804 million of goodwill. The purchase price was assigned to assets acquired and liabilities assumed based on their estimated fair values as of the date of acquisition, and any excess was allocated to goodwill, as shown in the table above. Goodwill represents the value we expect to achieve through the implementation of operational synergies and growth opportunities primarily in our Prepared Foods segment. We do not expect the final fair value of goodwill to be deductible for U.S. income tax purposes.

We used various valuation techniques to determine fair value, with the primary techniques being discounted cash flow analysis, relief-from-royalty and excess earnings valuation approaches, which use significant unobservable inputs, or Level 3 inputs, as defined by the fair value hierarchy. Under these valuation approaches, we are required to make estimates and assumptions about sales, operating margins, growth rates, royalty rates and discount rates based on budgets, business plans, economic projections, anticipated future cash flows and marketplace data.

continued

The acquisition of Hillshire Brands was accounted for using the acquisition method of accounting, and consequently, the results of operations for Hillshire Brands are reported in our consolidated financial statements from the date of acquisition. Hillshire Brands' one month results were insignificant to our Consolidated Statements of Income.

The following unaudited pro forma information presents the combined results of operations as if the acquisition of Hillshire Brands had occurred at the beginning of fiscal 2013. Hillshire Brands' pre-acquisition results have been added to our historical results. The pro forma results contained in the table below include adjustments for amortization of acquired intangibles, depreciation expense, and interest expense related to the financing and related income taxes. Any potential cost savings or other operational efficiencies that could result from the acquisition are not included in these pro forma results.

The 2013 pro forma results include transaction related expenses incurred by Hillshire Brands prior to the acquisition of $168 million, including items such as consultant fees, accelerated stock compensation and other deal costs; transaction related expenses incurred by the Company of $115 million, including fees paid to third parties, financing costs and other deal costs; and $32 million expense related to the fair value inventory adjustment at the date of acquisition.

These pro forma results have been prepared for comparative purposes only and are not necessarily indicative of the results of operations as they would have been had the acquisitions occurred on the assumed dates, nor is it necessarily an indication of future operating results.

In millions (unaudited)	2014	2013
Pro forma sales	$41,311	$38,195
Pro forma net income from continuing operations attributable to Tyson....	1,047	655
Pro forma net income per diluted share from continuing operations		
attributable to Tyson.......................................	$ 2.50	$ 1.52

We emphasize a number of items included in the footnote (numbers correspond to the circled numbers in margin next to the footnote).

1. The acquisition date is August 28, 2014. Tyson paid $63.00 per share, in cash, to all holders of Hillshire Brands stock.

2. Prior to Tyson's bid to acquire Hillshire Brands, Hillshire Brands entered into an agreement to buy all of the common stock of Pinnacle Foods, Inc. Pinnacle is the owner of such brands as Birds Eye®, Vlasic®, Wish-Bone®, Mrs. Butterworth®, Log Cabin®, Duncan Hines®, Van de Kamp® and Lender's®. As part of their acquisition agreement, Hillshire Brands promised to pay Pinnacle $163 million (that's twice Pinnacle's 2013 net income!) if Hillshire's acquisition of Pinnacle was terminated. A condition of Tyson's acquisition of Hillshire was that Hillshire terminate the merger agreement with Pinnacle.

3. Tyson provides a table showing the assignment of fair values to the identifiable assets acquired and liabilities assumed. Notice that over 80% ([$4,804 + $5,141]/$12,369) of the total assets acquired are intangible assets. That is not unusual for a brand-name food producer in which most of the entity's value resides in brand names and trademarks. Prior to the transaction, some of Tyson's brands include Tyson®, Jimmy Dean®, Sara Lee® frozen bakery, Ball Park®, Wright®, Aidells® and State Fair®.

4. The significance of brand names is confirmed by the detail of acquired identifiable intangible assets. Brands and trademarks comprise almost 90% [($4,062 + $532)/$5,141] of the total of acquired identifiable intangible assets. Pinnacle is the owner of such brands as Hillshire Farm®, Birds Eye®, Vlasic®, Wish-Bone®, Mrs. Butterworth®, Log Cabin®, Duncan Hines®, Van de Kamp® and Lender's®. Note that this schedule also provides information on the expected amortization period for each class of acquired identifiable intangible assets. Note that most of the recognized intangible assets (including goodwill) have indefinite useful lives. That means that those intangible assets will not be amortized. Instead, they will be evaluated at least annually for impairment. We discuss the impairment test and the accounting for impairment in Chapter 3.

5. Tyson assigned a total of $4,804 million to goodwill. As we describe in this chapter, the identifiable net assets acquired we first recorded at fair value. At that point, if there is still excess purchase price,

the remainder is assigned to goodwill. As noted by Tyson, goodwill represents the value that Tyson expects to achieve through the implementation of operational synergies and growth opportunities primarily in our Prepared Foods segment. The fact that goodwill is assigned to the Prepared Foods segment will be important in the company's annual goodwill impairment assessment.

6. Tyson also provides a description of the techniques used to determine the fair value of Hillshire's net assets. This disclosure is required by FASB ASC Topic 820, Fair Value Measurement, and is intended to provide information about the potential for estimation error in reported fair value measures. In the case of the Hillshire acquisition, Tyson used discounted cash flow analysis, relief-from-royalty and excess earnings valuation approaches, which all incorporate significant unobservable inputs (i.e., management estimates).

7. Under the acquisition method, a subsidiary's income and its components are only recognized *after* the date of acquisition. Thus, the results of operations for Hillshire are only included in Tyson's income statement after August 28, 2014. As noted by Tyson, their year-end is September 27, 2014, and "Hillshire Brands' one month results were insignificant to our Consolidated Statements of Income." If Hillshire's revenues and expenses were considered material, then Tyson would be required to report the amount of revenue and expenses included in the income statement after the acquisition date.

8. According to FASB ASC 805-10-50-2(h), public business entities are required to provide pro-forma revenues and earnings information for the combined (i.e., post-merger) companies "as if" the merger occurred at the beginning of the period. If comparative financial statements are presented, then the revenue and earnings of the combined entity should be shown as though the business combination occurred as of the beginning of the comparable prior annual reporting period. Given the fact that income statement recognition is only allowed for the period after the acquisition (see #7, above), this pro-forma disclosure allows "apples-to-apples" comparisons of the company to itself (over time) and to its industry peers.

CHAPTER SUMMARY

Control is a central element in determining the boundaries of every reporting entity. Control in a legal entity can be achieved in two ways. The first and traditionally most-common triggering condition is by possessing majority voting equity interest in an entity. The second way of achieving control is—regardless of the percentage ownership of the voting equity of another entity—by possessing the power to direct the primary activities of another entity and also possessing a right to the majority of the entity's economic risk and rewards. When control of another entity is possessed by a reporting company, the reporting company must consolidate the entity.

The purpose of consolidation is to produce a single set of financial statements for an economic entity instead of separate financial statements for legally distinct entities that comprise an affiliated (commonly controlled) group of companies. The basic result of the consolidation is that the parent company's equity investment in its controlled subsidiaries should be replaced by the individual net assets of the subsidiaries. In the simplest case (i.e., a "book value" acquisition, where parent company acquires the subsidiary for the same amount as the subsidiary's recorded stockholders' equity and the fair values of the subsidiary's net assets equal their individual recorded book values), the mechanics of consolidation on the acquisition date can be achieved by simply adding together the balance sheets of the parent and the subsidiary, and then eliminating the subsidiary's stockholders equity accounts against the investment in subsidiary account on the parent's balance sheet. The consolidated financial statements are prepared only after the period end adjustments have been made for the parent and subsidiary companies, and no further adjustments are made to their accounting records after the consolidation process has begun.

Of course, acquisition-date consolidations are not usually as basic as the simplest case. FASB ASC 805 ("Business Combinations") requires that all of the assets and liabilities of controlled subsidiaries should be reflected in the acquisition-date consolidated balance sheet at their fair values. Because the subsidiary does not record the fair values recognized by the parent company in the consolidated financial statements, the parent company must keep track of all of the differences between fair values and book values of the subsidiary's net assets. We call this acquisition-date difference between the fair values and book values of the subsidiary's net assets the acquisition accounting premium (AAP). The AAP is a component of the investment account. When preparing an acquisition-date consolidated balance sheet in the presence of a non-zero AAP, the process proceeds in two steps. First, we again simply add together the balance sheets of the parent and the subsidiary, and then eliminate the subsidiary's stockholders equity accounts against the investment in subsidiary account on the parent's balance sheet. Because there is a non-zero AAP included in the investment account, this first step will not completely eliminate the investment account. The second step is to eliminate the AAP portion of the investment account and to establish the fair-value minus book-value differences in various individual net assets of the subsidiary. In cases where the parent and subsidiary have intercompany payables and receivables, this must also be eliminated in preparation of the acquisition-date consolidated balance sheet.

COMPREHENSIVE REVIEW

Consolidation at Date of Acquisition

Assume that a parent purchases all of the outstanding common stock of a subsidiary for a cash purchase price of $1,950,000. The parent agreed to pay more than book value for its subsidiary because it values a patent that the subsidiary owns (but is not reported on the subsidiary's balance sheet) at $300,000, and PPE assets have a fair value that is $500,000 in excess of their book value. The additional value is related to corporate synergies that the parent expects will add value to the consolidated entity. On the date of acquisition, the parent and the subsidiary report the following balance sheets:

Balance Sheet:	Parent	Subsidiary
Cash	$ 429,500	$ 226,000
Accounts receivable.	640,000	348,000
Inventory	970,000	447,000
Equity investment.	1,950,000	
Property, plant and equipment (PPE), net	4,666,000	827,000
	$8,655,500	$1,848,000
Liabilities and stockholders' equity		
Current liabilities.	$ 718,500	$ 348,000
Long-term liabilities	4,000,000	500,000
Common stock.	817,500	100,000
APIC	607,500	125,000
Retained earnings	2,512,000	775,000
	$8,655,500	$1,848,000

Required

Prepare the consolidated balance sheet on the date of acquisition.

The solution to this review problem can be found on page 106.

APPENDIX 2A: Measuring Assets Acquired and Liabilities Assumed (Advanced)

In this Appendix, we cover a number of more advanced issues relating to valuation of assets acquired and liabilities assumed. These include the treatment of discontinued operations, preacquisition contingencies, contingent consideration, and significant exceptions from the recognition and measurement principles included in current business-combination accounting. In Appendix 2B, we discuss the most common exception to the business combinations measurement principal: deferred taxes.

Discontinued Operations—Assets Held for Sale Occasionally, a parent company will acquire a subsidiary with the intention of subsequently disposing of a portion of the subsidiary's net assets. For example, the parent company could decide to eliminate subsidiary branch locations or manufacturing facilities that are geographically close to similar and redundant parent operations (i.e., a common occurrence in "horizontal" mergers and acquisitions). FASB ASC 805-20-30-22 requires that "[t]he acquirer shall measure an acquired long-lived asset (or disposal group) that is classified as held for sale at the acquisition. . . at fair value less cost to sell." This measurement basis is an exception to the fair value recognition principle for business combinations, but is consistent with the general financial accounting rules for assets held for sale as codified in FASB ASC 360-10-35.[27]

To qualify for the held-for-sale treatment, companies must comply with the "Initial Criteria for Classification as Held for Sale," as detailed in FASB ASC 360-10-45-9. These criteria include:

a. Management, having the authority to approve the action, commits to a plan to sell the asset (disposal group).

b. The asset (disposal group) is available for immediate sale in its present condition subject only to terms that are usual and customary for sales of such assets (disposal groups).

c. An active program to locate a buyer and other actions required to complete the plan to sell the asset (disposal group) have been initiated.

d. The sale of the asset (disposal group) is probable, and transfer of the asset (disposal group) is expected to qualify for recognition as a completed sale, within one year. The term probable refers to a future sale that is likely to occur.

e. The asset (disposal group) is being actively marketed for sale at a price that is reasonable in relation to its current fair value. The price at which a long-lived asset (disposal group) is being marketed is indicative of whether the entity currently has the intent and ability to sell the asset (disposal group). A market price that is reasonable in relation to fair value indicates that the asset (disposal group) is available for immediate sale, whereas a market price in excess of fair value indicates that the asset (disposal group) is not available for immediate sale.

f. Actions required to complete the plan indicate that it is unlikely that significant changes to the plan will be made or that the plan will be withdrawn.

According to FASB ASC 360-10-45-12, "[a] long-lived asset (disposal group) that is newly acquired and that will be sold rather than held and used shall be classified as held for sale at the acquisition date only if the one-year requirement in paragraph 360-10-45-9(d) is met . . . and any other criteria in paragraph 360-10-45-9 that are not met at that date are probable of being met within a short period following the acquisition (usually within three months)."

Preacquisition Contingencies If the acquisition-date fair value of the asset or liability arising from a contingency can be determined during the measurement period, that asset or liability is recognized at the acquisition date (FASB ASC 805-20-25-19).[28] Often in an acquisition, however, the actual values of certain contingent assets acquired and liabilities assumed are *not* known at the acquisition date. An example is a pending lawsuit. If the fair value of a contingent asset or liability cannot be determined, the acquirer does not recognize an asset or liability as of the acquisition date. In periods after the acquisition date, the acquirer accounts for an asset or a liability arising from a contingency in a subsequent period (FASB ASC 805-20-25-20B).

The FASB cites one contingent liability, however, that it expects to be recognized: the acquisition-date fair value of warranty obligations. The FASB's position is that the acquisition-date fair value of a warranty obligation often can be determined (FASB ASC 805-20-25-19). Therefore, if an acquisition target offers warranties, then one of the identifiable liabilities recognized on the date of acquisition is the fair value of the estimated "stand ready" obligation to service all future warranty claims.

---

[27] In an ordinary, non-business-combination setting, FASB ASC 360-10-35-43 requires that "[a] long-lived asset (disposal group) classified as held for sale shall be measured at the lower of its carrying amount or fair value less cost to sell. If the asset (disposal group) is newly acquired, the carrying amount of the asset (disposal group) shall be established based on its fair value less cost to sell at the acquisition date. A long-lived asset shall not be depreciated (amortized) while it is classified as held for sale. Interest and other expenses attributable to the liabilities of a disposal group classified as held for sale shall continue to be accrued."

[28] The FASB ASC Glossary defines a contingency as an existing condition, situation, or set of circumstances involving uncertainty as to possible gain or loss to an entity that will ultimately be resolved when one or more future events occur or fail to occur.

PRACTICE INSIGHT

Preacquisition Contingencies   Prior to the acquisition, a former employee filed suit against a company alleging violation of age discrimination laws. The parent company subsequently acquires that company as its subsidiary. As of the acquisition date, discovery proceedings related to the discrimination lawsuit were underway but were not yet complete. The subsidiary's management asserts that its hiring and promotion practices complied with all applicable laws and regulations.

   The parent *would not* recognize a liability as of the acquisition date if it concludes, based on the facts known as of the acquisition date, that it is not "probable" that its subsidiary had violated the age discrimination laws. In making that assessment, the parent would consider all relevant facts and circumstances, such as the results of discovery proceedings to date, advice from its lawyers about whether the subsidiary would be found liable based on the facts known at that date, and any other relevant information gathered through due diligence or other procedures. Contingencies that are not recognized in the balance sheet at the acquisition date must be disclosed in accordance with the disclosure requirements for contingencies that meet the "possible" and "remote" thresholds (FASB ASC 450-20-25).

TOPIC REVIEW 5

Preacquisition Contingencies

The following question is a direct quote from SEC guidance to accountants on the issue of preacquisition contingencies: "Assume that a [company] acquires a business enterprise . . . In connection with the acquisition, the acquiring company assumes certain contingent liabilities of the acquired company. How should the acquiring company account for and disclose contingent liabilities that have been assumed in a business combination?"

The solution to this review problem can be found on page 106.

Contingent Consideration   Acquisitions sometimes include a provision adjusting the purchase price of the subsidiary for future events. For example, the selling shareholders may feel that the true profitability of their company has not yet been revealed and are unwilling to accept a lower purchase price based on current profit levels. They, therefore, include a provision in the purchase agreement requiring an increase in the purchase price if future profits of the subsidiary improve during a specified period of time following the acquisition. Another example relates to a stock-for-stock exchange. If selling shareholders feel that the investor's stock is temporarily overvalued (or they feel that their stock is undervalued), they might include a provision increasing the number of investor shares they receive should the investor's share price decline (or their share price improve) prior to the acquisition.

   Acquisition Accounting requires recognition of contingent consideration at the acquisition date. This contingency will be recognized in the form of a liability that is measured at the acquisition date and is included in the computation of Goodwill as we discuss above.[29]

   To illustrate, assume that the parent acquires a subsidiary for $3 million by exchanging 100,000 shares of $1 par value common stock with a current fair value of $30 per share. The purchase and sale agreement contains a provision that:

1. The purchase price will increase by 10% of the excess over $500,000 of the subsidiary's net income during the first two years following the acquisition, and

2. The number of shares exchanged by the parent will increase proportionately for any decrease in the share price below $30 per share prior to the first anniversary date of the acquisition.

Assume that the parent values the purchase price contingency at $250,000 and the contingency related to share price at $50,000. The parent records the acquisition as follows:

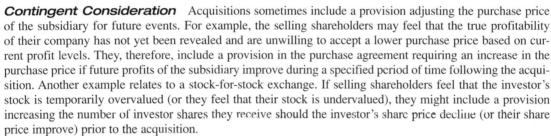

Equity investment.	3,300,000	
Common stock		100,000
Additional paid-in capital.		2,950,000
Contingent earnings liability		250,000
(to record the acquisition of the subsidiary)		

---

[29] Under *Purchase Method* accounting, neither an earnings nor a share price contingency was reported until it was settled. Further, an earnings contingency increased consideration paid, but a security price contingency did not.

The contingent earnings liability is reported on the parent's (and, thus, the consolidated) balance sheet as a liability and the contingent share obligation is reported in Stockholders' Equity.

PRACTICE INSIGHT

Contingent Consideration A company hired a candidate as its new CEO under a 10-year contract. The contract required the company to pay the candidate $5 million if the company is acquired before the contract expires. An investor acquires the company eight years later. The CEO was still employed at the acquisition date and will receive the additional payment under the existing contract.

This contractual provision is typically called an "earn-out," and is included in the terms of a transaction when a buyer and seller cannot agree on a cash and stock purchase price. It is also included if the selling company has unproven technology, products, and/or markets. In this example, the investee entered into the employment agreement before the negotiations of the combination began, and the purpose of the agreement was to obtain the services of CEO. Thus, there is no evidence that the agreement was arranged primarily to provide benefits to the investor or to the combined entity. Therefore, the $5 million liability is included in the identifiable liabilities incurred as part of the business combination.

In other circumstances, the investee might enter into a similar agreement with CEO at the suggestion of the investor during the negotiations for the business combination. If so, the primary purpose of the agreement might be to provide severance pay to CEO, and the agreement may primarily benefit the investor or the combined entity rather than the investee or its former owners. In that situation, the investor accounts for the liability to pay CEO in its post-combination financial statements separately from application of the acquisition method.

Subsequently, the two-year contingent earnings liability will be adjusted to its fair value on all future interim and year-end balance-sheet dates. If the fair value of the liability changes, that increase or decrease in the liability will be reflected in net income. In addition, on the contingency settlement date, any remaining gain or loss will be reflected in net income. In contrast, the contingent share obligation is not revalued and the difference between the original estimate and that ultimately realized is reflected in additional Paid-In Capital (FASB ASC 805-30-35-1).

Finally, assume that the subsidiary's profits exceed $500,000 and the parent is required to pay an additional $300,000 to the subsidiary's former shareholders. Also, assume that the parent's share price falls to $28, and the parent must issue 7,000 additional shares. The journal entries to record these additional payments are as follows:

Contingent earnings liability............................	250,000	
Loss related to contingent earnings liability............	50,000	
Cash		300,000
(to record the additional cash payment for the acquisition)		
Additional paid-in capital	7,000	
Common stock		7,000
(to record the additional shares issued for the acquisition)		

The underestimation of the contingent earnings liability has resulted in a loss of $50,000 as that liability is revalued. The additional shares issued only affect the equity section of the balance sheet and not the parent's profits; specifically, total stockholders' equity is unaffected, as the increase in Common Stock and decrease in APIC offset. This entry is required so that the Common Stock account reflects the par value of the total number of outstanding shares.

Note that the additional cash payment and the additional shares issued have not affected the Equity Investment (i.e., the cost of the acquisition). The value paid for the subsidiary that is reflected in the Equity Investment account is determined on the acquisition date and is not subsequently adjusted.

PRACTICE INSIGHT

Earn-outs in Practice   As noted in a recent article in *Financial Executives* magazine,[30] "[c]ontingent consideration, especially in the form of earn-outs, is an increasingly popular mechanism to address post-transaction performance uncertainties. It helps close the gap in expectations, shares future risk and rewards between the buyer and seller, and incentivizes the seller, to drive the ongoing success of the business. The 2011 *Private Target Mergers & Acquisitions Deal Points Study*, by the American Bar Association Business Law Section, shows that earn-outs were present in 19 percent, 29 percent, and 38 percent of public company acquisitions of private targets that closed in 2006, 2008, and 2010, respectively."

The article continues by describing a recent analysis conducted by the valuation firm, Duff & Phelps.[31] "Approximately one-quarter of the 120 transactions had earn-outs based on achieving technical, R&D or regulatory milestones. The likelihood of success for R&D or regulatory milestones can span a wide range. However, technical milestones, such as integrating the target's and buyer's technologies in a timely fashion, often have a high probability of success—exactly because the buyer believes they will do their job of incentivizing high levels of effort post-close."

The article's authors also offer caution: "Although earnings-based metrics may seem to align the interests of buyer and seller perfectly, unfortunately this can be a misleading illusion. Such metrics tend to encourage short-term performance rather than building the business for the long haul. In addition, these metrics may be more likely to lead to disputes down the road."

The December 31, 2014 SEC Form 10-K for **Merck & Co.**, Inc. provides an illustration of the use of contingent consideration in the M&A of R&D-intensive firms. Notice that the $316 million additional expense is caused by the successful transition of an acquired technology from the Food and Drug Administration category of "preclinical" to "Phase 1." Because of the success of the acquired technology, the company will pay more to the seller. The disclosure also illustrates the volatility that earn-outs can introduce into companies' post-M&A income statements:

Contingent Consideration
Summarized information about the changes in liabilities for contingent consideration is as follows:

($ millions)	2014	2013
Fair value January 1	$ 69	$49
Changes in fair value (recorded in Research and development expenses)	316	8
Additions	43	12
Fair value December 31	$428	$69

During 2014, the fair value of a liability for contingent consideration related to an acquisition that occurred in 2010 increased by $316 million resulting from the progression of the program from preclinical to Phase 1. The increase resulted from a higher fair value of future regulatory milestone and royalty payments due to an increased probability of success of the program given its progression into Phase 1. In addition, during 2014, the Company recognized a liability of $43 million for contingent consideration related to the acquisition of **OncoEthix** in 2014.

Exceptions from General Recognition and Measurement Principles   For a subset of net assets, current GAAP includes recognition and measurement approaches that diverge from the conceptually driven fair-value approach taken in Acquisition Accounting. For this subset of net assets,

[30] Weber, L., and G. Raichart. 2012. Lessons learned in valuing contingent consideration. *Financial Executive* (May): pp. 54-60.
[31] Duff & Phelps. 2012. *Contingent Consideration Study: Earn-out Structuring and Valuation.*

an acquirer should apply the accounting guidance of the topically appropriate U.S. accounting standard instead of the general business-combinations identifiable-net-assets recognition and/or measurement principles. Exceptions to the recognition principle include: assets and liabilities arising from contingencies, income taxes, employee benefits, and indemnification assets (see FASB ASC 805-20-25-17 through 25-28 for appropriate recognition criteria to apply for each of these exceptions). Exceptions to the measurement principle include income taxes, employee benefits, indemnification assets, reacquired rights, share-based payment awards (e.g., stock options), assets held for sale, and certain assets and liabilities arising from contingencies (see FASB ASC 805-20-30-13 through 30-23 for the appropriate measurement criteria to apply for each of these exceptions).

Another type of exception relates to the *classification* of certain net assets acquired in a business combination. The general classification principle in Acquisition Accounting is that the acquirer is required to classify identifiable assets acquired and liabilities assumed as necessary to subsequently apply appropriate post-acquisition GAAP for those individually recognized net assets. The classification should be made on the basis of the contractual terms, economic conditions, the acquirer's operating or accounting policies, and other conditions as they exist *at the acquisition date* (FASB ASC 805-20-25-6). For example, an acquirer would be required to make, on the acquisition date, an appropriate classification of investments in debt securities as trading, available for sale, or held to maturity in accordance with FASB ASC 320-10-25. Two exceptions to the acquisition-date criteria for classification are for (1) designating lease contracts as operating or capital and (2) designating written contracts as insurance, reinsurance or deposit-type contracts. In each of these exceptions, the acquirer is required to classify those contracts on the basis of the contractual terms and other factors at the *inception of the contract*; not the acquisition date (FASB ASC 805-20-25-8).

APPENDIX 2B: Deferred Taxes and Business Combinations

LO5 Explain when deferred taxes are recorded in business combinations and the effect of deferred taxes on the recognition of business combinations.

In Appendix 2A, we discussed significant exceptions from the recognition and measurement principal included in current business combination accounting. One important exception we did not discuss in that Appendix is accounting for the financial-reporting tax effects of business combinations. As noted in FASB ASC 805-740-05-1, when recording a business combination, deferred tax liabilities and deferred tax assets (and related asset valuation allowances) must be recognized for the deferred tax consequences of differences between the tax bases and the financial reporting values (i.e., "book bases") of assets acquired and liabilities assumed in a business combination.[32] In general, as the difference between tax bases and book bases of individually recognized net assets increases, the amount of deferred income taxes will increase. The amount of deferred tax recognized in a business combination counts as one of the identifiable net assets discussed previously in this chapter. Because this process results in recognizing an additional tax-related asset or liability during the business combination, the end result is that recognition of deferred taxes will mechanically affect the amount of goodwill that is recognized in a business combination. After reading this Appendix, you should better understand why this is true.

As a result of business combinations, temporary differences may arise due to differences between the tax bases of net assets acquired and liabilities assumed (determined by relevant tax laws) and the financial statement carrying values.[33] The single most important determinant of temporary differences in a business combination is the underlying "tax type" of the combination. Generally speaking, business combinations can be structured in two tax types: taxable or nontaxable. The descriptions "taxable" and "nontaxable" are from the perspective of the selling party in the business combination. (Specifically, did the seller pay taxes on the transaction?)

As a general principal under tax law, if a selling party pays taxes on the difference between the tax basis of an asset and the sales value of an asset, then the tax basis of the asset can be "stepped up" to its new sales value. If the selling party does not pay taxes on the gain in an asset transfer, then tax law usually requires

---

[32] Throughout this Appendix, we assume that readers have a basic understanding of deferred tax accounting required under FASB ASC 740. Readers who are unfamiliar with this area of accounting should first consult the relevant chapter of an intermediate textbook.

[33] ASC 805-740-25-2 also requires acquirers to recognize the tax effects of tax benefit carryforwards (e.g., Net Operating Losses) and income tax uncertainties of the acquiree that exist at the acquisition date. In our discussion of deferred taxes related to business combinations, we focus our attention on the deferred tax implications of temporary differences. Further, throughout the rest of the text (i.e., except for this Appendix and related homework problems), we generally ignore the tax effects of business combinations. If we wish for students to consider tax implications, we will provide information on the tax bases of acquired net assets and tax-rate information.

the asset's old tax basis to carry over from the selling party's tax books to the buying party's tax books. The logic underlying business combinations' tax status is the same.

In a "taxable" business combination, the selling party paid taxes on the difference between the old tax bases of the company's net assets and the purchase price paid by the acquirer. This means that the acquirer in a business combination will record the *new tax bases* for acquired assets and assumed liabilities at their fair values (as defined by the relevant tax regulations). In other words, the acquirer "steps up" the acquiree's historical tax bases in the assets acquired and liabilities assumed to their respective fair values. Because acquisition accounting also results in the recording of fair value in the financial accounting books, this means that taxable business combinations usually result in immaterially small amounts of temporary differences.

In a "nontaxable" business combination, the acquirer assumes the historical tax basis of the acquired assets and assumed liabilities.[34] This means that the acquirer retains the "historic" or "carryover" tax bases in the acquiree's assets and liabilities. For a target company that has a reasonably long operating history, this usually means that the tax bases of the company's net assets will be relatively low (i.e., because of accelerated tax depreciation). Thus, nontaxable business combinations usually result in significantly more (and higher magnitude) temporary differences than taxable business combinations.

Regardless of the tax-type of the business combination, the procedures for computing the amount of deferred taxes are the same:

1. Recognize the fair values of the *identifiable* net assets (i.e., not goodwill) according to FASB ASC 805. (Note: We describe this process in earlier sections of this chapter. This step is the same regardless of whether the transaction is taxable or nontaxable. The determination of deferred taxes occurs *before* goodwill is computed.[35])

2. Identify the tax bases of the identifiable net assets according to relevant tax laws and regulations. (Note: For taxable transactions, the tax bases usually will be stepped up to fair value. For nontaxable transactions, the tax bases will be carried over from the acquiree's tax books.)

3. Compute the difference between the financial reporting bases and the tax bases of the identifiable net assets. (Note: For the vast majority of identifiable net assets, these differences are the temporary differences.)

4. Recognize the deferred tax assets and/or deferred tax liabilities by multiplying the temporary differences by the appropriate tax rate.[36]

The resulting deferred tax assets and/or deferred tax liabilities are recognized with the identifiable net assets acquired pursuant to the business combination.[37] After deferred taxes are computed, the acquiring company will calculate the amount of goodwill recognized pursuant to the business combination. Except for the extra step of computing the amount of deferred taxes, this process is exactly the same as the goodwill-computation process described previously in this chapter. In fact, if we assume that the example on pages 57–63 is a taxable acquisition, the solution to that example would not change at all! That's because in a

---

[34] Qualifying for a nontaxable business combination usually requires the acquiring entity to exchange its common stock for the common stock of the acquiree (i.e., it qualifies as a "reorganization" under Section 368 of the Internal Revenue Code). However, not all stock-for-stock exchanges result in nontaxable combinations. Even if a stock for stock exchange is executed, an acquiring company can elect to have the exchange treated as a taxable asset purchase under Section 338 of the Internal Revenue Code. Of course, this means that taxes will have to be paid on any gains over the historic carrying values of the acquired net assets; however, the acquiring company will also have future benefits in the form of higher depreciation deductions on the stepped up net assets (i.e., for tax purposes).

[35] Another way of saying this is that deferred taxes are (almost) never computed for goodwill. The only exception to this rule is if tax-deductible goodwill is greater than goodwill for financial reporting purposes. Then, in only this case, FASB ASC 805-740-25-9 requires that *the excess* of tax-deductible goodwill over financial reporting goodwill should be treated as a temporary difference. FASB ASC 805-740-55-10 provides the following formula for determination of the resulting deferred tax asset: DTA = (Tax rate ÷ (1 − tax rate)) × preliminary temporary difference on excess goodwill.

[36] FASB ASC 740-10-30-8 requires companies to "measure a deferred tax liability or asset using the enacted tax rate(s) expected to apply to taxable income in the periods in which the deferred tax liability or asset is expected to be settled or realized." For purposes of this text, we will assume that current period tax rates also apply in future periods when the temporary difference is assumed to reverse and the associated deferred taxes are settled or realized.

[37] Note that the recognized deferred taxes are considered an exception to the general measurement principal in ASC 805 because deferred taxes are not measured using the fair value measurement attribute. Instead, deferred taxes are computed by scheduling out the expected reversals of timing differences, multiplied by currently enacted tax rates and aggregating the resulting amounts without discounting for the time value of money. At a minimum, a fair value estimate for deferred taxes would explicitly model the possibility of tax law changes and would discount future period reversals of temporary differences.

taxable acquisition the tax bases of net assets are stepped up to their fair values.[38] This means that the difference between the financial accounting basis and the tax basis of the net assets equals zero, so the resulting deferred taxes equal zero.

To illustrate, let's consider the same facts as the example on pages 57–63, but let's include the additional assumption that the transaction qualifies as a tax-free business combination. This means that the historic tax bases carryover from the subsidiary's tax books to the acquiring company's tax books. In Exhibit 2B.1, we modify the information originally presented in Exhibit 2.8 to also provide the tax bases of the subsidiary's net assets:

EXHIBIT 2B.1	Subsidiary Financial Reporting Book and Fair Values and Tax Bases		
	Subsidiary's Recorded Financial Reporting Book Values	Subsidiary's Estimated Financial Reporting Fair Values	Subsidiary's Tax Bases
Assets			
Cash and receivables.	$ 100,000	$ 100,000	$ 100,000
Inventory.	250,000	250,000	250,000
Property & equipment, net	1,000,000	900,000	1,000,000
Accumulated depreciation	(200,000)	0	(400,000)
Patents	0	125,000	0
Total Identifiable Assets.	$1,150,000	$1,375,000	$ 950,000
Liabilities			
Current liabilities.	$ 200,000	$ 200,000	$ 200,000
Other liabilities			
Bonds payable	500,000	500,000	500,000
Total Identifiable Liabilities	700,000	700,000	700,000
Identifiable Net Assets.	$ 450,000	$ 675,000	$ 250,000

In this modified example, we identified two assets for which the new ASC 805 reported fair values differ from the tax bases that will carryover from the acquiring company in a nontaxable acquisition: property & equipment, net and patents. The estimated fair value for property & equipment, net is equal to $900,000, while the net tax basis for the property & equipment, net is equal to $600,000 (i.e., $1,000,000 gross value − $400,000 accumulated tax depreciation). This means that property & equipment, net has a $300,000 temporary difference. In addition, estimated fair value for patents is equal to $125,000, while the net tax basis for the patents is equal to $0. This means that patents has a $125,000 temporary difference. Now that we have identified the temporary differences, we can compute the deferred tax liability by multiplying the temporary differences by the appropriate tax rate. In this example, we will assume a 40% tax rate. Exhibit 2B.2 summarizes the computation of deferred taxes for the identified temporary differences:[39]

EXHIBIT 2B.2	Computation of Deferred Taxes from Identified Temporary Differences				
Account – Dr (Cr)	Acquirer's Post-Acquisition Tax Basis	Recognized Financial Reporting Value	Temporary Difference	Tax Rate	Deferred Tax Asset (Liability)
Property & equipment, net	$600,000	$900,000	$(300,000)	40%	$(120,000)
Patents	0	125,000	(125,000)	40%	(50,000)
				Total	$(170,000)

[38] Fair values for tax accounting purposes are determined pursuant to relevant tax statutes, and these amounts can differ from the fair value amounts measured and recognized for financial reporting purposes pursuant to FASB ASC 805. In this chapter, we make the simplifying assumption that fair values for tax and financial reporting purposes are the same.

[39] We like to structure the table used to compute deferred taxes by subtracting the financial reporting fair values from the acquirer's post-acquisition tax basis. This setup causes the signs of any differences to result in positive numbers for deferred tax assets and negative numbers for deferred tax liabilities (i.e., this conforms to the traditional Dr. (Cr.) notation).

As illustrated in Exhibit 2B.2, the temporary difference for property & equipment, net is equal to $(300,000), which after multiplying times 40% results in a deferred tax liability equal to $120,000. In addition, the temporary difference for patents is equal to $(125,000), which after multiplying times 40% results in a deferred tax liability equal to $50,000. Adding together these two individual deferred tax liabilities leads to a total deferred tax liability equal to $170,000 on the acquisition date.

Recall that in Exhibit 2.9 (i.e., in the case of no temporary differences or deferred taxes), we summarized the difference between fair value and recorded net book value for the identifiable acquired net assets. We will do that, again; however, this time because we are now assuming that the parent engaged in a nontaxable acquisition of the subsidiary, we are now required to include the deferred taxes as one of the amounts recorded pursuant to FASB ASC 805. In Exhibit 2B.3 we summarize the difference between fair value and recorded net book value for the identifiable acquired net assets, including the deferred tax liability:

EXHIBIT 2B.3	Subsidiary's Net Book Value and Fair Value*		
Accounts – Debits (Credits)	Subsidiary's Recorded Net Book Values	Subsidiary's Estimated Fair Values	Fair Value Minus Book Value
Property & equipment, net	$800,000	$900,000	$100,000
Patents	0	125,000	125,000
Deferred tax liability	0	(170,000)	(170,000)
Net difference: Fair value – Book value			$ 55,000

* As we already mentioned, deferred taxes are an exception to the general measurement principal in FASB ASC 805. To make our descriptions in this discussion less cumbersome, we refer to all values computed pursuant to FASB ASC 805 as "fair values."

Notice what the introduction of deferred taxes did to the explained net difference between fair value and the subsidiary's old book values. In Exhibit 2.8 (i.e., the case with no temporary differences), the net difference between fair value and book value for the identifiable net assets was $225,000. As is illustrated in Exhibit 2B.3, the introduction of the deferred tax liability decreased the amount of the identified difference between fair value and book value to $55,000.

To allow the most informative comparison of the cases when we do not have temporary differences (i.e., a taxable transaction as illustrated in the main example in the chapter) and do have temporary differences (i.e., a nontaxable acquisition as illustrated in this Appendix), we will keep the purchase price of the subsidiary at the same amount: assume, again, that the parent paid $700,000 for a 100% interest in the issued and outstanding stock of the subsidiary.[40] In this case, when we attempt to determine the amount of goodwill that results from the nontaxable transaction, we have an additional liability that will reduce the amount of net assets acquired in the acquisition. Thus, holding all else equal, the existence of a deferred tax liability will dollar-for-dollar increase in the amount of goodwill recognized in a business combination. We can summarize the explained and unexplained components of the AAP and the computation of goodwill as follows:

Purchase price	$700,000
Book value of subsidiary	450,000 ❶
Acquisition Accounting Premium (AAP)	$250,000 ❷
AAP assigned to identifiable net assets [Dr. (Cr.)]:	
Undervalued property & equipment	100,000
Patent	125,000
Deferred tax liability	(170,000)
Unidentifiable ("Plug") = Goodwill	$195,000

As you can see, the only difference between the assumed taxable transaction (included in the main chapter) and the assumed nontaxable transaction (included in this Appendix) is the $170,000 deferred tax liability and the corresponding $170,000 increase in Goodwill (i.e., $195,000 − $25,000). Indeed, all of

---

[40] We are making this assumption to allow the clearest comparison of taxable and nontaxable acquisitions. Note that, in the real world, a selling shareholder who pays taxes in a taxable business combination will likely demand additional consideration. This is because the selling party knows that the buyer could have structured the transaction as a tax-free deal. Thus, in theory, a selling shareholder will attempt to set the price in a taxable transaction so that he/she is compensated for the taxes that will be paid as a result of the transaction.

the consolidation procedures documented on pages 61-63 remain identical, except for these two amounts. Exhibit 2B.4 summarizes the resulting consolidated financial statements for the taxable and nontaxable transactions:

EXHIBIT 2B.4	Comparison of Acquisition Date Consolidated Balance Sheets when the Business Combination is Taxable versus Nontaxable	
	Consolidated Balances for Assumed Taxable Transaction	Consolidated Balances for Assumed Nontaxable Transaction
Assets		
Cash and receivables...............................	$ 900,000	$ 900,000
Inventory	850,000	850,000
Property & equipment, net	3,200,000	3,200,000
Patents..	125,000	125,000
Goodwill	25,000	195,000
	$5,100,000	$5,270,000
Liabilities and stockholders' equity		
Current liabilities...................................	$ 600,000	$ 600,000
Other liabilities	300,000	300,000
Bonds payable.....................................	500,000	500,000
Deferred tax liability		170,000
Common stock.....................................	1,670,000	1,670,000
APIC..	1,430,000	1,430,000
Retained earnings	600,000	600,000
	$5,100,000	$5,270,000

Superscript ^A, (B) denotes assignments based on Appendix 2A (B).

QUESTIONS

FASB ASC Research

1. Companies often enter into joint ventures with other companies for research and development, marketing, and distribution of products. A joint venture is typically formed by two companies that own the joint venture equally. Do these joint ventures need to be consolidated? (*Hint*: Examine the Scope section of FASB ASC 805-10-15.)

2. Companies can recognize assets in a business combination that were not recognized by the company acquired. Provide examples of such assets.

FASB ASC Research

3. Investors sometimes transfer assets to the investee's shareholders other than cash and the investor's stock. How should these transferred assets be accounted for in the acquisition? (*Hint*: Examine FASB ASC 805-30-30-7 through 30-8.)

FASB ASC Research

4. The investor purchases all of the assets and liabilities of the investee, even if not recognized on the investee's balance sheet. One such example includes operating leases. Even though the acquiree has not recognized on its balance sheet either the leased asset nor the lease obligation relating to operating leases, the investor may recognize assets or liabilities relating to those leases in its assignment of fair values in a business combination. How? (*Hint*: Examine FASB ASC 805-20-25-11 through 25-13.)

FASB ASC Research

5. Assume that an investor places considerable value on the workforce of the investee as a result of comparatively low turnover and high morale. Can this workforce be recognized as a separately identifiable intangible asset? (*Hint*: Examine FASB ASC 805-20-55-6.)

FASB ASC Research

6. Assume that an investor places considerable value on a new contract that the investee is negotiating as of the acquisition date, but which has not been finalized. Can this potential contract be recognized as a separately identifiable intangible asset? (*Hint*: Examine FASB ASC 805-20-55-7.)

7. Assume that a parent acquires a subsidiary that has a five-year agreement to supply goods to a customer. Both the parent and the subsidiary believe that customer will renew the agreement at the end of the current contract. The agreement is not separable. Can the parent recognize an intangible asset related to the agreement? (*Hint*: Examine FASB ASC 805-20-55.)

> FASB ASC
> Research

8. Assume that a parent company acquires a subsidiary that does business with its customers solely through purchase and sales orders. On the acquisition date, the subsidiary has a backlog of customer purchase orders from 60 percent of its customers, all of whom are recurring customers. The other 40 percent of the subsidiary's customers also are recurring customers. However, as of the acquisition date, the subsidiary has no open purchase orders or other contracts with those customers. Can the customer backlog and ongoing customer relationship be recognized as an intangible asset? (*Hint*: Examine FASB ASC 805-20-55.)

> FASB ASC
> Research

9. Assume that a parent company acquires a subsidiary that has a portfolio of one-year auto insurance contracts that are cancelable by policyholders. Can the customer relationships be identified as an intangible asset? (*Hint*: Examine FASB ASC 805-20-55.)

> FASB ASC
> Research

10. Assume that a company hired a candidate as its new CEO under a 10-year contract. The contract required the company to pay the candidate $5 million if the company is acquired before the contract expires. A parent acquires the company eight years later. The CEO was still employed at the acquisition date and will receive the additional payment under the existing contract. Should the parent company include the employment contract liability in its assignment of fair values in a business combination? (*Hint*: Examine FASB ASC 805-10-55.)

> FASB ASC
> Research

11. Assume the same facts as in question #10, but, now, assume that the parent company asks the subsidiary to provide the severance to the CEO during the negotiations. Should the parent company include the employment contract liability in its assignment of fair values in a business combination? (*Hint*: Examine FASB ASC 805-10-55.)

> FASB ASC
> Research

12. Assume that an investor purchases a 20% interest in an investee company. In addition to the infusion of badly needed cash into the investee, the investor also agrees to license technology to the investee company. Since the technology is valuable, the investor includes in the terms of the license agreement that it has the right to appoint the majority of the Board of Directors, effective with the acquisition (existing directors can be removed on or after the acquisition date so that the investor can gain immediate control of the Board). Should the investee company be consolidated with the investor?

13. An investor company acquires the assets of an investee for $10.5 million. The investee is a start-up company that, until the current year, had devoted all of its energy to the development of patentable technology with commercial potential. Now, the development stage is finished, but commercial production of the technology has not yet commenced. The investee company has hired production and sales employees and has developed an operating plan for the upcoming year to produce and sell its products. As of the acquisition date, however, no production or sales had yet taken place. Should this acquisition be accounted for as an asset purchase or a business combination requiring consolidation?

14. Assume that, as part of recording a business combination, you were given the task of assigning fair values to the acquired identifiable net assets. The investee's balance sheet reports cash, accounts receivable, inventories, PPE, accounts payable, accruals, and long-term debt.
    a. Describe the approach you would use to value these assets and liabilities.
    b. Describe the approach you would use to determine if a portion of the purchase price should be assigned to the Goodwill asset.
    c. Describe the approach you would use to value any additional assets acquired.

15. Provide at least two examples of intangible assets that would be included in each of the following general categories: contract-based, marketing-related, customer-related, technology-based, and artistic-based.

16. What is an "indemnification asset"? How do we account for it?

17. Identify three intangible assets related to customers.

18. In business combinations, assigning fair values to liabilities has two implications: 1. the fair value of the identifiable net assets acquired decreases (because of the increase in liabilities), resulting in the assignment of more fair value to the Goodwill asset, and 2. Future cash payments are debited to this accrued liability rather than to expense, thus increasing post-acquisition profitability. Liabilities relating to restructuring plans are an example.
    a. Describe what the liability relating to a restructuring plan is.
    b. How does Acquisition Accounting prescribe how we should account for these liabilities?

19. What are "provisional" amounts recorded in business combinations? How do we account for them?

20.[A] Assume that, as part of recording a business combination, you were given the task of assigning fair values to the acquired identifiable net assets. In your investigation, you meet with the company's legal department. One of the lawyers tells you that the company has been sued for patent infringement. The company's lawyer says that the odds of an adverse judgment are slightly better than 50/50, and that, if the company loses the lawsuit, she expects a liability of about $10 million.

 a.   Are you justified in assigning fair value to this liability? If so, how much?

 b.   Assume that the company's lawyer also tells you that the investee has indemnified the company against any loss as a result of this lawsuit in the purchase and sale agreement. How do you handle this additional information in your assignment of fair values?

21.[A] Assume that your company has just signed an agreement relating to an acquisition, and you are charged with the task of recording the journal entry for the purchase. The terms of the purchase are as follows:

Acquisition date:	November 1
Price of acquiring company stock:	$21.00/share
Paid by:	Issuance of 900,000 shares of $1 par value common stock, and exchange of those shares for all of the voting shares owned by the investee's shareholders.

In addition, you are told that your company and the investee could not agree on the purchase price, and, as a result, your company consented to include a provision in the purchase and sale agreement providing for an additional payment of $5 million if the new subsidiary reports cumulative earnings in excess of $50 million within one year of the acquisition date. Your independent appraisal indicates that the fair value of this liability as of the acquisition date is $1.75 million.

 a.   Record the journal entry for the purchase.

 b.   Your company has a calendar year-end, and will issue financial statements as of December 31. As of that date, and based on its operating performance to date, you estimate that the fair value of the contingent consideration liability is now $2,150,000. Record any additional required journal entry to reflect this new information.

 c.   Now, assume that the subsidiary meets the earnings hurdle and that the additional $5 million must be paid. Record the journal entry for this payment.

22.[B] Assume that you have been charged with assigning fair values to the identifiable net assets acquired in a $6,000,000 "nontaxable" purchase of a subsidiary that qualifies as a business combination. All assets have a fair value equal to their book values ($4,500,000), except for a PPE asset that is undervalued by $900,000. Your tax rate is 34% and all assets have a tax basis equal to their pre-acquisition book value. Perform the computation to assign fair values to the acquired assets.

Assignments with the ⓶ logo in the margin are available in BusinessCourse.
See the Preface of the book for details.

MULTIPLE CHOICE

LO1   **23. Net asset acquisition qualifying as a business combination**

AICPA Adapted

Company A purchased from Company B a set of net assets. Which of the following conditions is not necessary for the transaction to qualify as a business combination?

 a.   Has a proven base of customers that has a history of purchasing the outputs

 b.   Has employees, intellectual property, and other inputs and processes that could be applied to those inputs

 c.   Is pursuing a plan to produce outputs

 d.   Has begun planned principal activities

LO1   **24. Accounting for a controlling financial interest**

AICPA Adapted

Company A, a manufacturing conglomerate, owns 85% of the voting interests of Company B, a financial services company. Company B owns 65% of the voting interests of Company C, an automobile leasing company. In Company A's consolidated financial statements, should consolidation accounting or equity method accounting be used for Company B and Company C?

 a.   Equity method used for both Company B and Company C

 b.   Equity method used for Company B and consolidation used for Company C

 c.   Consolidation used for both Company B and Company C

 d.   Consolidation used for Company B and equity method used for Company C

25. **Determining the acquirer for accounting purposes**

LO1

AICPA
Adapted

On January 1, 2016, Company A acquired 100% of the voting common stock of Company B from Company B's shareholders. Prior to the transaction, Company A had 11,440 shares of voting common stock outstanding and Company B had 5,000 shares of voting common stock outstanding. Which of the following terms or conditions of the transaction is an indicator that Company B is the acquiring entity for accounting purposes?

   a.   Immediately after the transaction, Company B's Chief Operating Officer became Company A's Chief Operating Officer. All other executive positions were held by Company A executives.

   b.   Company A changed its name to "Company B."

   c.   Company A issued 14,560 new shares of Company A common stock to execute the transaction.

   d.   The full slate of the Board of Directors is elected every two years. Company A Directors (from before the transaction) occupy 8 of the 12 seats on Company A's Board after the acquisition. Company B Directors (from before the transaction) occupy 4 of the 12 seats on Company A's Board after the acquisition.

26. **Accounting for a controlling financial interest**

LO2, 4

AICPA
Adapted

An acquiring company issues 600,000 shares of $2.50 par value common stock to acquire 100% of the voting common stock of an investee company in a transaction that qualifies as a business combination. The fair value of the acquiring company's common stock is $12.50 per share. Direct legal and consulting fees incurred pursuant to the combination are $175,000. Direct registration and issuance costs for the acquiring company's common stock are $60,000. The transaction did not result in goodwill recognition or bargain gain recognition. What is the total amount of net assets recognized as a result of this business combination?

   a. $7,675,000

   b. $7,500,000

   c. $7,615,000

   d. $1,500,000

Use the following facts for Multiple Choice problems 27 and 28 (each question is independent of the other):

AICPA
Adapted

On July 1, 2016, an acquiring company paid $1,275,000 for 100% of the outstanding common stock of an investee company in a transaction that qualifies as a business combination. Immediately preceding the transaction, the investee company had the following condensed balance sheet:

	Pre-acquisition amounts reported on investee's balance sheet
Current assets	$ 200,000
Property and equipment, net	1,500,000
Liabilities	800,000
Equity	900,000

The acquisition-date fair value of the property and equipment was $230,000 more than its carrying amount. For all other assets and liabilities, the pre-acquisition amounts reported on investee's balance sheet were equal to their respective fair values.

27. **Investment accounting by parent before consolidation**

LO3, 4

AICPA
Adapted

What amount of goodwill related to the acquisition of the investee must the acquiring company report in pre-consolidation parent-only balance sheet immediately following the acquisition of investee company common stock?

   a. $375,000

   b. $220,000

   c. $145,000

   d. $0

28. **Effects of consolidation on reported balance sheet amounts**

LO3, 4

AICPA
Adapted

What amount of goodwill related to the acquisition of the investee must the acquiring company report in its consolidated balance sheet immediately following the acquisition of investee company common stock?

   a. $375,000

   b. $220,000

   c. $145,000

   d. $0

Use the following facts for Multiple Choice problems 29 and 30:

Assume that on January 1, 2016, an investor company acquired 100% of the outstanding voting common stock of an investee company. The following financial statement information is for the investor company and the investee company on January 1, 2016, prepared immediately before this transaction.

	Book Values	
	Investor	**Investee**
Receivables & inventories	$125,000	$ 62,500
Land	250,000	125,000
Property & equipment, net	281,250	125,000
Total assets	656,250	312,500
Liabilities	$187,500	$100,000
Common stock ($2 par)	25,000	12,500
Additional paid-in capital	350,000	187,500
Retained earnings	93,750	12,500
Total liabilities & equity	$656,250	$312,500

29. **Compute the investment account (fair value equals book value)**

Assume that the fair values of the investee's net assets approximated the recorded book values of the investee's net assets, and the transaction resulted in no recorded goodwill or bargain purchase gain. What is the balance in the pre-consolidation "investment in investee" account on the investor company's books on January 1, 2016, immediately after the acquisition of the investee company voting common stock?

    a. $312,500

    b. $212,500

    c. $200,000

    d. Not enough information provided

30. **Compute the investment account (fair value differs from book value)**

Assume that the fair values of the investee's net assets approximated the recorded book values of the investee's net assets, except the fair value of receivables and inventories is $12,500 higher than book value, the fair value of land is $6,250 lower than book value, the fair value of property and equipment is $25,000 higher than book value and the fair value of liabilities is $8,750 lower than book value. In addition, the transaction resulted in goodwill in the amount of $31,250. What is the balance in the pre-consolidation "investment in investee" account on the investor company's books on January 1, 2016, immediately after the acquisition of the investee company voting common stock?

    a. $383,750

    b. $352,500

    c. $283,750

    d. Not enough information provided

31. **Consolidated financial statements**

Sun Co. is a wholly owned subsidiary of Star Co. Both companies have separate general ledgers, and prepare separate financial statements. Sun requires stand-alone financial statements. Which of the following statements is correct?

    a. Consolidated financial statements should be prepared for both Star and Sun.

    b. Consolidated financial statements should only be prepared by Star and not by Sun.

    c. After consolidation, the accounts of both Star and Sun should be changed to reflect the consolidated totals for future ease in reporting.

    d. After consolidation, the accounts of both Star and Sun should be combined together into one general-ledger accounting system for future ease in reporting.

32. **Consolidating entries (fair value differs from book value)**

Assume that on January 1, 2016, an investor company acquired 100% of the outstanding voting common stock of an investee company. The following financial statement information was prepared immediately after the acquisition and presents the acquisition-date balance sheet for the pre-consolidation investor company, the investee company and the consolidated financial statements for the investor and investee.

	Investor	Investee	Consolidated
Cash & receivables.	$1,500,000	$ 187,500	$1,687,500
Inventory.	1,125,000	468,750	1,593,750
Property & equipment, net	4,312,500	1,500,000	6,000,000
Investment in investee	1,312,500	—	—
Identifiable intangible assets	—	—	206,250
Goodwill	—	—	90,000
Total assets.	$8,250,000	$2,156,250	$9,577,500
Current liabilities.	$ 750,000	$ 375,000	$1,125,000
Accrued expenses	562,500	—	562,500
Bonds payable	—	937,500	952,500
Common stock.	3,131,250	187,500	3,131,250
Additional paid-in capital	2,681,250	234,375	2,681,250
Retained earnings	1,125,000	421,875	1,125,000
Total liabilities and equity	$8,250,000	$2,156,250	$9,577,500

In preparing the consolidated financial statements, what is the amount of the debit or credit made to the "investment in investee" account as part of the [A] consolidating entry? (Recall from the chapter that the [A] consolidating entry reclassifies the acquisition accounting premium from the investment account to the individual net assets that require adjustment from book value to fair value.)

a. $1,312,500

b. $483,750

c. $468,750

d. $90,000

33.[B] **Tax effects of business combinations (nontaxable, fair value differs from book value)**

Assume that on January 1, 2016, an investor company acquired 100% of the outstanding voting common stock of an investee company in exchange for $127,500 worth of investor company common stock. The transaction is a tax-free reorganization under the Internal Revenue Code. The following financial statement information is for the investor company and the investee company on January 1, 2016, prepared immediately before this transaction.

	Book Values	
	Investor	Investee
Current assets	$127,500	$ 68,000
Noncurrent assets	191,250	85,000
Total assets.	$318,750	$153,000
Liabilities.	$127,500	$ 68,000
Common stock ($1 par)	17,000	8,500
Additional paid-in capital	110,500	68,000
Retained earnings	63,750	8,500
Total liabilities & equity	$318,750	$153,000

Assume that the fair values of the investee's net assets approximated the recorded book values of the investee's net assets, except the fair value of the investee's identifiable noncurrent assets is $16,000 higher than book value. In addition, the investee's pre-transaction tax bases in its individual net assets approximate their reported book values. This difference relates entirely to tax-deductible items. Assume the marginal tax rate is 35% for the investor and investee. What amount of goodwill should be reported in the investor's consolidated balance sheet prepared immediately after this business combination?

a. $26,500

b. $32,100

c. $42,500

d. $127,500

LO5   34.[B] **Tax effects of business combinations (taxable, fair value differs from book value)**

Assume that on January 1, 2016, an investor company acquired 100% of the outstanding voting common stock of an investee company in exchange for $127,500. The transaction is a taxable asset acquisition under the Internal Revenue Code. The following financial statement information is for the investor company and the investee company on January 1, 2016, prepared immediately before this transaction.

	Book Values	
	Investor	Investee
Current assets	$127,500	$ 68,000
Noncurrent assets	191,250	85,000
Total assets	$318,750	$153,000
Liabilities	$127,500	$ 68,000
Common stock ($1 par)	17,000	8,500
Additional paid-in capital	110,500	68,000
Retained earnings	63,750	8,500
Total liabilities & equity	$318,750	$153,000

Assume that the fair values of the investee's net assets approximated the recorded book values of the investee's net assets, except the fair value of the investee's identifiable noncurrent assets is $16,000 higher than book value. In addition, the investee's pre-transaction tax bases in its individual net assets approximate their reported book values. This difference relates entirely to tax-deductible items. Assume the marginal tax rate is 35% for the investor and investee. What amount of goodwill should be reported in the investor's consolidated balance sheet prepared immediately after this business combination?

a. $26,500

b. $32,100

c. $42,500

d. $127,500

EXERCISES

LO4   35. **Computation of goodwill**

FACEBOOK, INC.
WHATSAPP, INC.

In October 2014, Facebook, Inc. acquired 100 percent of the common stock of WhatsApp, Inc. by paying $4,473 million of cash and issuing Facebook common stock with a fair value of $12,720 million. On the acquisition date, the total fair value assigned to tangible and intangible assets acquired (excluding goodwill) was $2,783 million, while the total fair value assigned to liabilities assumed was $932 million. What is the value of goodwill recognized in Facebook's consolidated financial statements as a result of the WhatsApp acquisition?

LO4   36. **Computation of goodwill**

Assume that an investor purchases 100% of an investee company for $22 million. The fair values of the identifiable net assets are as follows:

Tangible net assets:	Receivables, inventories, PPE, payables, and accruals	$ 8 million
Intangible assets:	Patents, customer lists, trade name, software, etc.	5 million
Research and development assets:	Research projects in process at the investee company	6 million
		$19 million

In addition to the purchase price, the investor also incurs acquisition-related costs amounting to $2 million for professional fees and the internal allocation of overhead relating to the purchase.

a. How much of the purchase price is assigned to Goodwill?

b. How do we account for Goodwill subsequent to the acquisition?

c. Given the accounting treatment for Goodwill subsequent to the acquisition, why might companies be motivated to increase the amount assigned to goodwill?

37. Acquisition accounting

LO4

ACTAVIS PLC
FOREST
LABORATORIES, INC.

On July 1, 2014, **Actavis plc** acquired 100 percent of the common stock of **Forest Laboratories, Inc.** for cash and stock consideration totaling $27,661.1 million. The following excerpt is from Actavis' December 31, 2014 SEC Form 10-K.

The following table summarizes the preliminary fair values of the assets acquired and liabilities assumed at the acquisition date (in millions):

	Preliminary Amounts as of September 30, 2014	Measurement Period Adjustments	Preliminary Amounts as of December 31, 2014
Cash and cash equivalents	$ 3,424.2	$ —	$ 3,424.2
Accounts receivable	496.2	—	496.2
Inventories	1,455.8	—	1,455.8
Other current assets	233.3	27.9	261.2
Current assets held for sale	87.1	—	87.1
Property, plant and equipment, net . . .	221.1	—	221.1
Other long-term assets	84.1	—	84.1
IPR&D intangible assets	1,363.0	(1.0)	1,362.0
Intangible assets	11,405.5	110.0	11,515.5
Goodwill	16,706.1	(320.8)	16,385.3
Current liabilities	(1,346.0)	23.9	(1,322.1)
Deferred tax liabilities, net	(2,449.7)	146.8	(2,302.9)
Other taxes payable	(661.5)	37.0	(624.5)
Other long-term liabilities	(96.2)	(23.8)	(120.0)
Outstanding indebtedness	(3,261.9)	—	(3,261.9)
	$27,661.1	$ 0.0	$27,661.1

a.   Explain the meaning of the amounts relating to the acquired asset accounts.

b.   Actavis assigns $1,363.0 million of fair value to an account called "IPR&D intangible assets." To what does this account relate? Briefly describe what will happen to this account in the years after the acquisition.

c.   Briefly describe the manner in which the amount of $16,706.1 million relating to the Goodwill asset is determined.

d.   Briefly describe why Actavis is making "Measurement Period Adjustments." Briefly describe how, under current GAAP, these adjustments will affect Actavis' quarterly financial statements for the three months ended December 31, 2014.

38. Who is the investor? Why does it matter?

LO1

Assume that we have an acquisition. But, we don't yet know who the investor is. Here are the facts:

Company A	Company B
Exchanged all of its stock for the stock issued by Company B	Issued stock valued at $4.3 billion
Can elect one-half of the Board of Directors	Can elect one-half of the Board of Directors
Its Chairman will become Chairman of the new entity for the first 3 years	Its Chairman will succeed the Chairman from Company A in 3 years
Its CFO will become CFO of the combined company	Its CEO will become CEO of the combined company

a.   Which company is the acquirer in your opinion?

b.   Now, assume the following facts about the financial profiles of these two companies.

Fair Values	If Company A is deemed to be the Subsidiary	If Company B is deemed to be the Subsidiary
Tangible net assets......................	$2.8 billion	$1.1 billion
Identifiable intangible assets	0.7 billion	1.8 billion
Total	$3.5 billion	$2.9 billion

Determine the fair values of the identifiable net assets (and goodwill, if any) assuming the transaction qualifies as a business combination and Company A is the accounting acquirer. Then, determine the fair values of the identifiable net assets (and goodwill, if any) assuming the transaction qualifies as a business combination and Company B is the accounting acquirer. Does it matter which company is the accounting acquirer? Why?

LO3 **39. Consolidation entries at date of acquisition (purchase price greater than book value)**
A parent company exchanges 12,000 shares of its $2 par value common stock, with a fair value of $9/share, for all of the shares owned by the subsidiary's shareholders. On the acquisition date, the subsidiary reported $30,000 of contributed capital (i.e., common stock) and $45,000 of Retained Earnings. An examination of the subsidiary's balance sheet revealed that book values were equal to fair values for all assets except for PPE (net), which has a book value of $40,000 and a fair value of $73,000.

a. Prepare the entry that the parent makes to record the investment.

b. Prepare the [E] and [A] consolidation entries.

LO3 **40. Consolidation entries at date of acquisition (purchase price greater than book value)**
A parent company acquires all of the outstanding common stock of its subsidiary for cash purchase price of $265,000. On the acquisition date, the subsidiary reported $60,000 for Common Stock and $45,000 for Retained Earnings. An examination of the subsidiary's balance sheet revealed that book values were equal to fair values for all assets, except for an unrecorded patent, which the parent values at $95,000.

a. Prepare the entry that the parent makes to record the investment.

b. Prepare the [E] and [A] consolidation entries.

LO3 **41. Composition of equity investment account**
Several years ago, a parent company acquired all of the outstanding common stock of its subsidiary for a purchase price of $275,000. On the acquisition date, this purchase price was $68,000 more than the subsidiary's book value of Stockholders' Equity. The AAP was entirely attributable to Goodwill. On the date of acquisition, the parent company management believes that the goodwill only has a 10-year useful life. Since the date of acquisition, the subsidiary has reported cumulative net income of $234,000 and paid $97,000 of dividends to its parent company.

a. Compute the balance of the Equity Investment account on the parent's balance sheet assuming that the Goodwill asset has not declined in value subsequent to the date of acquisition.

b. Briefly describe the nature of the assets that comprise the Equity Investment account.

LO3, 4 **42. Preparation of [A] entry from acquisition footnote**
PFIZER PHARMACIA
In 2003, Pfizer acquired Pharmacia for approximately $56 billion, and provides the following table in its footnote relating to the acquisition:

(millions of dollars)	
Estimated book value of net assets acquired	$ 8,795
Less: Existing goodwill and other intangible assets..................................	1,559
Tangible book value of net assets acquired.......................................	7,236
Remaining allocation:	
Increase inventory to fair value......................................	2,979
Increase long-term investments to fair value	40
Increase property, plant and equipment to fair value...............................	439
Record in-process research and development charge.........................	5,052
Record identifiable intangible assets	37,221
Increase long-term debt to fair value	(370)
Increase benefit plan liabilities to fair value	(1,471)
Increase other net assets to fair value	(431)
Restructuring costs incurred through December 31, 2003	(1,578)
Tax adjustments	(13,592)
Goodwill	20,447
Estimated purchase price...	$55,972

a. Using the information in the table above, prepare the consolidation entries as of the acquisition date.

b. Briefly describe the difference between the way in which Pfizer recorded the debit to In-Process R&D in 2003 and how that debit would be handled under current GAAP.

c. Briefly describe the difference between the way in which Pfizer recorded the credit to the Restructuring Cost Liability in 2003 and how that credit would be handled under current GAAP.

43. **Assignment of fair values and the [A] entry**

On April 2, 2012, **Express Scripts, Inc.** acquired, for $30,154.4 million, 100% of the voting common stock of **Medco Health Solutions, Inc.** Express Scripts' 2012 SEC Form 10-K summarized the assignment of fair values to net assets as follows (in millions):

LO3, 4

EXPRESS SCRIPTS, INC.

MEDCO HEALTH SOLUTIONS, INC.

FV of Acquired Net Assets:	
Current assets	$ 6,921.4
Property and equipment	1,390.6
Goodwill	23,978.3
Acquired intangible assets:	
Customer contracts	15,935.0
Trade names	273.0
Miscellaneous intangible assets	8.7
Other noncurrent assets	48.3
Current liabilities	(9,038.4)
Long-term debt	(3,008.3)
Deferred income taxes	(5,958.3)
Other noncurrent liabilities	(395.9)
	$30,154.4

a. Related to the Medco acquisition, are these the amounts that will appear in the [A] consolidation entry on the acquisition date?

b. Assume that none of the intangible assets were reported on Medco's pre-acquisition balance sheet. Prepare the [A] consolidation entry to recognize the intangible assets on the consolidated balance sheet.

c. According to Express Scripts' 2012 SEC Form 10-K, "[a] portion of the excess of purchase price over tangible net assets acquired has been allocated to intangible assets consisting of customer contracts in the amount of $15,935.0 million with an estimated weighted-average amortization period of 15.5 years. Additional intangible assets consist of trade names in the amount of $273.0 million with an estimated weighted-average amortization period of 10 years and miscellaneous intangible assets of $8.7 million with an estimated weighted-average amortization period of 5 years. The acquired intangible assets have been valued using an income approach and are being amortized on a basis that approximates the pattern of benefit." What is the accounting significance of assigning fair values to these amortizable intangible assets? Why didn't Express Scripts attribute that portion of fair value to Goodwill acquired in the Medco acquisition?

44.[A] **Valuation of acquired assets and assumed liabilities**

The following excerpt is from Note 4 of **Merck and Co., Inc.**'s financial statements included in the company's December 31, 2014 SEC Form 10-K.

LO4

MERCK AND CO., INC.

ONCOETHIX

Also in December 2014, Merck acquired **OncoEthix**, a privately held biotechnology company specializing in oncology drug development. Total purchase consideration in the transaction of $153 million included an upfront cash payment of $110 million and future additional milestone payments of up to $265 million that are contingent upon certain clinical and regulatory milestones being achieved, which the Company determined had a fair value of $43 million at the acquisition date. The transaction was accounted for as an acquisition of a business; accordingly, the assets acquired and liabilities assumed were recorded at their respective fair values as of the acquisition date. The determination of fair value requires management to make significant estimates and assumptions. Merck recognized an intangible asset for IPR&D of $143 million related to MK-8628 (formerly OTX015), an investigational, novel oral BET (bromodomain) inhibitor currently in Phase 2 studies for the treatment of hematological malignancies and advanced solid tumors, as well as a liability for contingent consideration of $43 million and other net assets and liabilities of $10 million. The fair value of the identifiable intangible asset related to IPR&D was determined using an income approach, through which fair value is estimated based upon the asset's probability adjusted future net cash flows, which reflects the stage of development of the project and the associated probability of successful completion. The net cash flows were then discounted to present value using a discount rate of 11.5%. The fair value of the contingent consideration was determined utilizing a probability weighted estimated cash flow stream adjusted for the expected timing of each payment also utilizing a discount rate of 11.5%. This transaction closed on December 18, 2014; accordingly, the results of operations of the acquired business have been included in the Company's results of operations beginning after that date.

a.   Describe the valuation approaches that Merck used for the OncoEthix acquisition and identify the assets to which each relates.

b.   How much subjectivity is involved in each valuation method? What kind of assumptions need to be made under each approach?

c.   What are the total possible contingent payments for achievement of "clinical and regulatory milestones" related to the OncoEthix acquisition? What is the acquisition-date fair value of these potential future payments? Why did the OncoEthix transaction include these contingent (future) payments instead of cash consideration equal to the contingent-payment acquisition-date fair value?

d.   Assume that, on July 1, 2017, Merck is required to make all contingent payments related to the OncoEthix acquisition (i.e., the contingency is resolved in favor of the seller). Propose the journal entry related to the contingent payments that Merck will make on July 1, 2017.

PROBLEMS

LO2 (45.) **Consolidation at date of acquisition (purchase price equals book value)**

A parent company acquires its subsidiary by exchanging 50,000 shares of its Common Stock, with a fair value on the acquisition date of $24 per share, for all of the outstanding voting shares of the investee.

a.   What is the total fair value of the subsidiary on the acquisition date?

b.   Prepare the consolidation entry or entries on the date of acquisition given the following balance sheets of the parent and subsidiary on the date of acquisition.

Balance Sheet	Parent	Subsidiary
Assets		
Cash	$ 480,000	$ 271,200
Accounts receivable	1,500,000	417,600
Inventory	2,300,000	536,400
Equity investment	1,200,000	—
Property, plant and equipment (PPE), net	11,150,000	992,400
	$16,630,000	$2,217,600
Liabilities and stockholders' equity		
Accounts payable	$ 750,000	$ 152,400
Accrued liabilities	880,000	265,200
Long-term liabilities	3,500,000	600,000
Common stock	1,600,000	120,000
APIC	3,800,000	150,000
Retained earnings	6,100,000	930,000
	$16,630,000	$2,217,600

c.   Prepare the consolidated balance sheet on the date of acquisition.

LO3 46. **Consolidation at date of acquisition (purchase price greater than book value)**

Assume that the parent company acquires its subsidiary by exchanging 103,000 shares of its Common Stock, with a fair value on the acquisition date of $26 per share, for all of the outstanding voting shares of the investee. In its analysis of the investee company, the parent values all of the subsidiary's assets and liabilities at an amount equaling their book values except for an unrecorded Patent owned by the subsidiary with a fair value of $290,000. Any further discrepancy between the purchase price and the book value of the subsidiary's Stockholders' Equity is attributed to expected synergies to be realized by the consolidated company as a result of the acquisition.

a.   What is the total fair value of the subsidiary on the acquisition date?

b.   Prepare the consolidation entry or entries on the date of acquisition given the following balance sheets of the parent and subsidiary on the date of acquisition.

Balance Sheet	Parent	Subsidiary
Assets		
Cash.	$ 4,600,000	$ 339,000
Accounts receivable.	1,900,000	522,000
Inventory	2,900,000	670,500
Equity investment.	2,678,000	—
Property, plant and equipment (PPE), net	14,000,000	1,240,500
	$26,078,000	$2,772,000
Liabilities and stockholders' equity		
Accounts payable.	$ 968,000	$ 190,500
Accrued liabilities	1,150,000	331,500
Long-term liabilities	4,460,000	750,000
Common stock.	3,600,000	150,000
APIC.	8,400,000	187,500
Retained earnings	7,500,000	1,162,500
	$26,078,000	$2,772,000

c.   Prepare the consolidated balance sheet on the date of acquisition.

d.   What additional assets have been recognized on the consolidated balance sheet that were not explicitly reported on the balance sheets of either the parent or the subsidiary? Where were they?

47. Determining ending balances of accounts on the consolidated balance sheet   **LO3**

Assume that the parent company acquires its subsidiary by exchanging 75,400 shares of its Common Stock, with a fair value on the acquisition date of $30 per share, for all of the outstanding voting shares of the investee. In its analysis of the investee company, the parent values all of the subsidiary's assets and liabilities at an amount equaling their book values except for a building that is undervalued by $480,000, an unrecorded License Agreement with a fair value of $230,000, and an unrecorded Customer List owned by the subsidiary with a fair value of $120,000. Any further discrepancy between the purchase price and the book value of the subsidiary's Stockholders' Equity is attributed to expected synergies to be realized by the consolidated company as a result of the acquisition.

a.   Given the following acquisition-date balance sheets of the parent and subsidiary, at what amounts will each of the following be reported on the consolidated balance sheet?

1.   Accounts Receivable
2.   Equity Investment
3.   PPE, net
4.   Goodwill
5.   Common Stock
6.   APIC
7.   Retained Earnings

Balance Sheet	Parent	Subsidiary
Assets		
Cash.....	$ 728,400	$ 181,440
Accounts receivable....	307,200	375,840
Inventory	465,600	482,760
Equity investment....	2,262,000	—
Property, plant and equipment (PPE), net	2,000,000	893,160
	$5,763,200	$1,933,200
Liabilities and stockholders' equity		
Accounts payable....	$ 150,480	$ 114,300
Accrued liabilities....	176,640	198,900
Long-term liabilities	1,062,320	540,000
Common stock....	176,000	108,000
APIC....	2,992,000	135,000
Retained earnings	1,205,760	837,000
	$5,763,200	$1,933,200

b.   What intangible assets will be reported on the consolidated balance sheet and at what amounts? Where were these assets on the parent or subsidiary's balance sheets?

LO3 **48.** **Consolidation at date of acquisition (purchase price greater than book value, acquisition journal entries)**

Assume that the parent company acquires its subsidiary by exchanging 84,000 shares of its $2 par value Common Stock, with a fair value on the acquisition date of $38 per share, for all of the outstanding voting shares of the investee. In its analysis of the investee company, the parent values all of the subsidiary's assets and liabilities at an amount equaling their book values except for an unrecorded Trademark with a fair value of $240,000, an unrecorded Video Library valued at $600,000, and Patented Technology with a fair value of $125,000.

a.   Prepare the journal entry that the parent makes to record the acquisition.

b.   Given the following acquisition-date balance sheets of the parent and the subsidiary, prepare the consolidation entries.

Balance Sheet	Parent	Subsidiary
Assets		
Cash.....	$ 514,020	$ 265,160
Accounts receivable....	450,300	633,360
Inventory	650,000	813,540
Equity investment....	3,192,000	—
Property, plant and equipment (PPE), net	10,600,000	1,505,140
	$15,406,320	$3,217,200
Liabilities and stockholders' equity		
Accounts payable....	$ 150,480	$ 177,800
Accrued liabilities....	176,640	309,400
Long-term liabilities	3,840,000	910,000
Common stock....	428,400	182,000
APIC....	3,276,000	227,500
Retained earnings	7,534,800	1,410,500
	$15,406,320	$3,217,200

c.   Prepare the consolidation spreadsheet.

d.   Where were the intangible assets on the parent or subsidiary's balance sheets?

49.[B] **Consolidation at date of acquisition (purchase price greater than book value, acquisition journal entries, deferred tax liability)**

Assume that the parent company acquires its subsidiary in a "nontaxable" transaction by exchanging 96,000 shares of its $5 par value Common Stock, with a fair value on the acquisition date of $42 per share, for all of the outstanding voting shares of the investee. In its analysis of the investee company, the fair value of each of the subsidiary's assets and liabilities equals their respective book values except for property, plant and equipment (PPE) assets that are undervalued by $760,000, an unrecorded Customer List with a fair value of $250,000, and an unrecorded Brand Name asset valued at $570,000. And, finally, assume that the tax bases of the subsidiary's pre-acquisition identifiable net assets equal their book values. The parent company's effective tax rate is 36%.

a.   Prepare the journal entry that the parent makes to record the acquisition.

b.   Given the following acquisition-date balance sheets for the parent and its subsidiary, prepare the consolidation spreadsheet.

Balance Sheet	Parent	Subsidiary
Assets		
Cash	$ 939,960	$ 149,760
Accounts receivable	460,800	1,002,240
Inventory	1,200,000	1,287,360
Equity investment	4,032,000	—
Property, plant and equipment (PPE), net	13,568,000	2,381,760
	$20,200,760	$4,821,120
Liabilities and stockholders' equity		
Accounts payable	$ 225,720	$ 182,880
Accrued liabilities	264,960	318,240
Long-term liabilities	2,400,000	1,440,000
Common stock	816,000	288,000
APIC	6,240,000	360,000
Retained earnings	10,254,080	2,232,000
	$20,200,760	$4,821,120

50.   Interpretation of footnote disclosure

On November 21, 2014, Scientific Games Corporation acquired Bally Technologies Inc. for $5.1 billion. The footnote relating to this acquisition, which Scientific Games included in its December 31, 2014 SEC Form 10-K, follows. Use this information to answer the following questions:

a.   Scientific Games describes its assignment of fair value as being "based on our preliminary estimates." Briefly describe the procedure under GAAP for companies to use provisional amounts and the process by which those estimates can be adjusted.

b.   Prepare the journal entry that Scientific Games made for the acquisition of Bally's common stock.

c.   Describe the process by which Scientific Games determined the assignment of fair value to Goodwill in the amount of $2,956.1 million.

d.   How much did Scientific Games assign to amortizable intangible assets? Briefly describe the valuation approaches used to determine the fair values of the individual intangible assets.

e.   Assuming no disposals, provisional adjustments or impairments, what is the amount that Scientific Games will amortize for Bally's acquired intangible assets during the year ending December 31, 2015?

f.   For the year ended December 31, 2014 Scientific Games reported consolidated revenues of $1,786.4 million and a net loss of $234.3 million. For what period of time is Bally's performance included in Scientific Games' revenues and expenses for the year ended December 31, 2014? How much did Bally contribute to Scientific Games' revenues and net losses for the year ended December 31, 2014?

g.   Assuming no intercompany transactions, what is Bally's approximate revenue for the full year ended December 31, 2014?

h.   Propose the entry that Scientific Games makes in the consolidation process to remove the Equity Investment account from the parent-company balance sheet in preparation of the consolidated balance sheet.

ACQUISITIONS

On November 21, 2014, the Company acquired all of the outstanding common stock of Bally for $5.1 billion (including the refinancing of approximately $1.9 billion of existing Bally indebtedness), creating one of the largest diversified global gaming suppliers.

We have recorded Bally's assets acquired and liabilities assumed based on our preliminary estimates of their fair values at the acquisition date. The determination of the fair values of the assets acquired and liabilities assumed (and the related determination of estimated lives of depreciable and amortizable tangible and identifiable intangible assets) requires significant judgment and estimates. The estimates and assumptions used include the projected timing and amount of future cash flows and discount rates reflecting risk inherent in the future cash flows. The estimated fair values of Bally's assets acquired and liabilities assumed and resulting goodwill are subject to adjustment as we finalize our fair value analysis. The significant items for which a final fair value has not been determined as of the filing of this Annual Report on Form 10-K include accrued liabilities, deferred income taxes and other long-term liabilities. We expect to complete our fair value determinations no later than the fourth quarter of 2015. We do not currently expect our fair value determinations to change; however, there may be differences compared to those amounts reflected in our consolidated financial statements at December 31, 2014 as we finalize our fair value analysis and such changes could be material.

Based on our preliminary estimates, the equity purchase price exceeded the aggregate estimated fair value of the acquired assets and assumed liabilities at the acquisition date by $2,956.1 million, which amount has been allocated and recognized as goodwill within our Gaming and Interactive business segments. We attribute this goodwill to our enhanced financial and operational scale, market diversification, opportunities for synergies, assembled workforce and other strategic benefits. None of the goodwill associated with the acquisition is deductible for income tax purposes and, as such, no deferred taxes have been recorded related to goodwill.

In connection with the Bally acquisition we incurred $76.6 million of acquisition-related costs which were recorded in SG&A in the Consolidated Statement of Operations and Comprehensive Loss for the year ended December 31, 2014.

The preliminary allocation of the purchase price to the estimated fair values of assets acquired and liabilities assumed is presented below:

At November 21, 2014

Cash and cash equivalents	$ 59.9
Restricted cash	16.0
Accounts receivable	217.1
Notes receivable	22.0
Inventories	134.0
Deferred income taxes, current portion	32.4
Prepaid expenses, deposits and other current assets	71.6
Property and equipment	335.3
Goodwill	2,956.1
Restricted long-term cash and investments	19.3
Intangible assets	1,800.3
Software	308.3
Other assets	61.8
Total assets	6,034.1
Long-term debt, including amounts due within one year	(1,882.9)
Accounts payable	(33.0)
Accrued liabilities	(133.7)
Deferred income taxes	(747.0)
Other long-term liabilities	(37.0)
Total liabilities	(2,833.6)
Total equity purchase price	$3,200.5

Our estimates of the fair values of depreciable tangible assets and identifiable intangible assets are presented below:

	Fair values at November 21, 2014	Remaining useful life range
Land and land improvements.	$ 18.1	Indefinite
Buildings and leasehold improvements	36.3	2—40 years
Furniture, fixtures, and other property, plant and equipment	33.6	2—15 years
Gaming equipment.	247.3	1—3 years
Total property and equipment	$ 335.3	

	Fair values at November 21, 2014	Weighted-average remaining useful life
Trade names.	$ 225.0	Indefinite
Brand names	90.7	9.2 years
Core technology and content.	734.7	7.2 years
Customer relationships	726.0	15.1 years
Long-term licenses.	23.9	3.0 years
Total intangible assets	$1,800.3	9.4 years

The fair value of acquired real property was determined primarily using a cost approach, in which we determined an estimated replacement cost for the assets. To determine the fair value of the land, we utilized the sales comparison approach, which compares the land to properties that have recently been sold in similar transactions. For gaming equipment and other personal property assets, we determined the fair value using cost approaches in which we determined an estimated reproduction or replacement cost, as applicable.

The estimated fair values of acquired finite and indefinite-lived trade names and finite-lived internally-developed intellectual property ("IP") were determined using the royalty savings method, which is a risk-adjusted discounted cash flow approach. Finite-lived intangible assets valued using the royalty savings method include gaming content and operating system software, casino management systems and game server software (all included within software above), certain product trade names and game cabinet design IP (included in core technology and content above). The royalty savings method values an intangible asset by estimating the royalties saved through ownership of the asset. The royalty savings method requires identifying the future revenue that would be impacted by the trade name or IP asset (or royalty-free rights to the assets), multiplying it by a royalty rate deemed to be avoided through ownership of the asset and discounting the projected royalty savings amounts back to the acquisition date. The royalty rate used in such valuation was based on a consideration of market rates for similar categories of assets. The indefinite-lived trade names include "Bally" and "SHFL." Game content and operating system software, casino management systems software and game server software is classified as capitalized software, net, on the Consolidated Balance Sheet as of December 31, 2014 and has a weighted average useful life of 4.4 years.

The estimated fair values of the acquired PTG IP and Utility products IP (both included in core technology and content above) and customer relationships were determined using the excess earnings method, which is a risk-adjusted discounted cash flow approach that determines the value of an intangible asset as the present value of the cash flows attributable to such asset after excluding the proportion of the cash flows that are attributable to other assets. The contribution to the cash flows that are made by other assets—such as fixed assets, working capital, workforce and other intangible assets, including trade names and game content and design IP—was estimated through contributory asset capital charges. The value of the acquired customer relationship asset is the present value of the attributed post-tax cash flows, net of the post-tax return on fair value attributed to the other assets.

The estimated fair value of accounts receivable includes consideration of the contractual amount of the receivables of $234.1 million and our estimate of the amount not expected to be collected of $17.0 million. The estimated fair value of notes receivable includes consideration of the contractual amount of the receivables of $68.2 million and our estimate of the amount not expected to be collected of $1.5 million.

continued

The estimated fair value of current and long-term deferred revenue was determined using the bottoms-up approach which involves the application of a normal profit margin to the direct and incremental costs required to fulfill the remaining performance obligation. The costs to fulfill are reflective of those that the Company will incur to fulfill the service and do not include costs such as selling, marketing and training. The estimated fair value of current and long-term deferred revenue is approximately $10.3 million.

The revenue and loss from continuing operations of Bally from the acquisition date through December 31, 2014 are presented below and included in our consolidated statements of operations. These amounts are not necessarily indicative of the results of operations that Bally would have realized if it had continued to operate as a stand-alone company during the period presented, primarily due to the elimination of certain headcount and administrative costs since the acquisition date resulting from integration activities or due to costs that are now reflected in our unallocated corporate costs and not allocated to Bally.

	From November 21, 2014 through December 31, 2014
Revenue	$151.6
Loss from continuing operations	$ (21.1)

As required by ASC 805, the following unaudited pro forma statements of operations for the years ended December 31, 2014 and 2013 give effect to the Bally acquisition as if it had been completed on January 1, 2013. The unaudited pro forma financial information is presented for illustrative purposes only and is not necessarily indicative of what the operating results actually would have been during the periods presented had the Bally acquisition been completed during the periods presented. In addition, the unaudited pro forma financial information does not purport to project future operating results. This information is preliminary in nature and subject to change based on final purchase price adjustments. The pro forma statements of operations do not reflect: (1) any anticipated synergies (or costs to achieve synergies) or (2) the impact of non-recurring items directly related to the Bally acquisition.

	Year Ended December 31,	
	2014	2013
Revenue from Consolidated Statements of Operations	$1,786.4	$1,090.9
Add: Bally revenue not reflected in Consolidated Statements of Operations	1,159.5	1,358.6
Unaudited pro forma revenue.	$2,945.9	$2,449.5

	Year Ended December 31,	
	2014	2013
Net loss from continuing operations from Consolidated Statements of Operations	$(234.3)	$(25.6)
Add: Bally net loss from continuing operations not reflected in Consolidated Statements of Operations plus pro forma adjustments	(195.4)	(349.1)
Unaudited pro forma net loss from continuing operations.	$(429.7)	$(374.7)

TOPIC REVIEW

Solution 1

The only scenario that does not result in control, and thus does not require consolidation, is (b). Scenario (a) gives the investor unilateral control to appoint the Board of Directors. Scenario (d) allows the investor to appoint the Board of Directors via contractual means, rather than from stock ownership. Finally, scenario (c) may allow the investor to exercise control because other shareholders cannot effectively vote in a block. This one is tricky, and will depend on your assessment of the ability of the other shareholders to mount a coordinated rebuff to the investor's attempts to control shareholder meetings.

Solution 2

	Parent	Subsidiary	Consolidation Entries Dr	Consolidation Entries Cr	Consolidated
Assets					
Cash	$ 150,000	$ 50,000			$ 200,000
Receivables	250,000	100,000			350,000
Inventory	300,000	200,000			500,000
Property, plant and equipment (PPE), net ...	1,150,000	200,000	[A] $ 50,000		1,400,000
Equity investment	250,000			[E] $200,000	0
				[A] $ 50,000	
	$2,100,000	$550,000			$2,450,000
Liabilities and stockholders' equity					
Current liabilities	$ 100,000	$ 100,000			$ 200,000
Bonds payable	250,000	250,000			500,000
Common stock	800,000	50,000	[E] 50,000		800,000
APIC	600,000	60,000	[E] 60,000		600,000
Retained earnings	350,000	90,000	[E] 90,000		350,000
	$2,100,000	$550,000	$250,000	$250,000	$2,450,000

Solution 3

a. Fair value of net identifiable assets = $8 million

$10,000,000	Total value of the subsidiary
− 8,000,000	Fair value of the identifiable assets
$ 2,000,000	Goodwill

b. Fair value of net identifiable assets = $11 million

$10,000,000	Total value of subsidiary
− 11,000,000	Fair value of the identifiable assets
$ (1,000,000)	Goodwill

The negative amount for Goodwill represents a "bargain purchase." The parent will continue to report the net assets of the subsidiary at their fair value of $11 million, and will recognize the bargain purchase as a gain in the acquisition year.

Solution 4

Under FASB ASC 805-10-25-23, acquisition-related costs are costs the investor incurs to effect a business combination. Those costs include finder's fees; advisory, legal, accounting, valuation, and other professional or consulting fees; and general administrative costs, including the costs of maintaining an internal acquisitions department. The parent should account for acquisition-related costs as *expenses* in the periods in which the costs are incurred and the services are received (the standard also provides, however, that costs to register the stock are netted against contributed capital).

Solution 5

"*Interpretive Response*: In accordance with Statement 141, the acquiring company should allocate the cost of an acquired company to the assets acquired and liabilities assumed based on their fair values at the date of acquisition. With respect to contingencies for which a fair value is *not* determinable at the date of acquisition, [accounting standards prescribe that the contingency should not be recorded]. If the registrant is awaiting additional information that it has arranged to obtain for the measurement of a contingency . . . the staff believes that the registrant should disclose that the purchase price allocation is preliminary. In that circumstance, the [company] should describe the nature of the contingency and furnish other available information that will enable a reader to understand its potential effects on the final allocation and on post-acquisition operating results. Management's Discussion and Analysis should include appropriate disclosure regarding any unrecognized preacquisition contingency and its reasonably likely effects on operating results, liquidity, and financial condition.

The staff believes that the allocation period should not extend beyond the minimum reasonable period necessary to gather the information that the [company] has arranged to obtain for purposes of the estimate. Since an allocation period usually should not exceed one year, registrants believing that they will require a longer period are encouraged to discuss their circumstances with the staff. If it is unlikely that the liability can be estimated on the basis of information known to be obtainable at the time of the initial purchase price allocation, the allocation period should not be extended with respect to that liability. An adjustment to the contingent liability after the expiration of the allocation period would be recognized as an element of net income."

(Source: www.sec.gov, Codification of Staff Accounting Bulletins, Topic 2: Business Combinations)

COMPREHENSIVE REVIEW SOLUTION

Balance Sheet	Parent	Subsidiary	Consolidation Entries Dr	Consolidation Entries Cr	Consolidated
Assets					
Cash	$ 429,500	$ 226,000			$ 655,500
Accounts receivable	640,000	348,000			988,000
Inventory	970,000	447,000			1,417,000
Equity investment	1,950,000			[E] $1,000,000	0
				[A] 950,000	
Property, plant and equipment (PPE), net	4,666,000	827,000	[A] $ 500,000		5,993,000
Patent			[A] 300,000		300,000
Goodwill			[A] 150,000		150,000
	$8,655,500	$1,848,000			$9,503,500
Liabilities and stockholders' equity					
Current liabilities	$ 718,500	$ 348,000			$1,066,500
Long-term liabilities	4,000,000	500,000			4,500,000
Common stock	817,500	100,000	[E] 100,000		817,500
APIC	607,500	125,000	[E] 125,000		607,500
Retained earnings	2,512,000	775,000	[E] 775,000		2,512,000
	$8,655,500	$1,848,000	$1,950,000	$1,950,000	$9,503,500

Notice that the Patent and Goodwill, which did not appear on the parent's or the subsidiary's pre-consolidation balance sheets, now appears on the consolidated balance sheet. These [A] assets were previously embedded in the Equity Investment account on the parent's balance sheet, and are now broken out separately as an asset on the consolidated balance sheet.

Consolidated Financial Statements Subsequent to the Date of Acquisition

3

According to its December 31, 2014 Securities and Exchange Commission (SEC) Form 10-K, **Cummins Inc.** is a global company that designs, manufactures, distributes, and services diesel and natural gas engines and engine-related component products, including filtration, aftertreatment, turbochargers, fuel systems, controls systems, air handling systems and electric power generation systems. Cummins sells its products to original equipment manufacturers (OEMs), distributors, and other customers worldwide; employs approximately 54,600 people worldwide; and serves its customers through a network of approximately 600 company-owned and independent distributor locations and approximately 7,200 dealer locations in more than 190 countries and territories.

CUMMINS INC.

Cummins is organized into four product-related business units, including:

- **Engines**—manufactures and markets a broad range of diesel and natural gas powered engines
- **Components**—supplies filtration products, turbochargers, aftertreatment systems, and fuel systems
- **Power Generation**—designs and manufactures engines, controls, alternators, transfer switches, and switchgear
- **Distribution**—consists of 23 company-owned and 18 joint venture distributors that service and distribute Cummins products and services to approximately 400 locations in approximately 80 distribution territories

Cummins reports $19.2 billion in sales and $15.8 billion in assets, and has more than 180 subsidiaries worldwide. Footnote 1 to Cummins' December 31, 2014 consolidated financial statements includes the following reference to the Company's consolidation policy:

> **Principles of Consolidation**
> Our *Consolidated Financial Statements* include the accounts of all wholly-owned and majority-owned domestic and foreign subsidiaries where our ownership is more than 50 percent of outstanding equity interests . . . Intercompany balances and transactions are eliminated in consolidation. . . .

This consolidation footnote sets the stage for the coming consolidations-related chapters in this textbook. In this chapter, we will tackle the problem of preparing consolidated balance sheets and performance statements for a parent company and its wholly owned subsidiaries. Next, in Chapter 4, we address the fact that consolidated financial statements always completely eliminate all intercompany transactions and balances among the affiliated consolidated companies. In Chapter 5, we address the issues that arise when companies consolidate less-than-wholly owned subsidiaries (i.e., cases where noncontrolling interests exist). Taken together, the Cummins' Principles of Consolidation statement means that the consolidated financial statements aggregate the statements of financial positions and statements of performance for the Cummins parent company and all of Cummins' controlled subsidiaries, regardless of the percentage ownership, and after eliminating 100 percent of the affiliated companies' transactions and balances.

Source: Cummins Inc. December 31, 2014 SEC Form 10-K

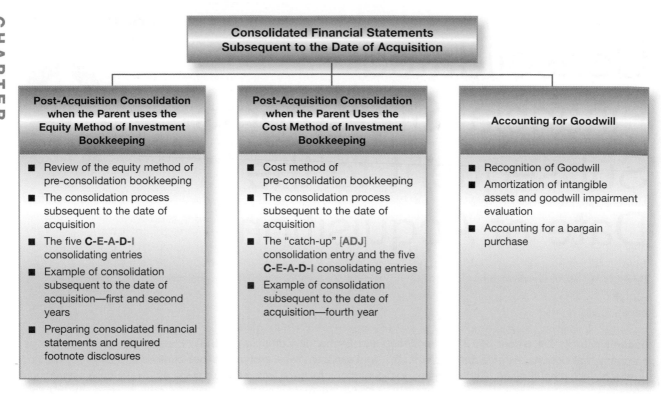

As we discuss in Chapter 2, the *acquisition-date* consolidation process replaces the Equity Investment account with the fair value of the assets and liabilities of the subsidiary. *After the acquisition date*, the subsidiary will engage in business activities (i.e., generating revenues, expenses, gains and/or losses), which will be recorded in the subsidiary's equity accounts and will also result in changes to the subsidiary's recorded amounts of assets and liabilities. These post-acquisition activities and changes in subsidiary net assets mean that the consolidation process is a bit more complicated than just replacing the parent's acquisition-date Equity Investment account with the fair value of the assets and liabilities of the subsidiary. This chapter introduces you to the post-acquisition consolidation process.

Parent companies are *always* required to prepare consolidated financial statements that include all *controlled* investee companies. Thus, the output of the consolidation process will always look the same. However, the starting point for the consolidation process (i.e., the parent's pre-consolidation financial statements) can appear quite different—even when comparing economically identical parent companies—because parent companies have a choice of how they account for the pre-consolidation Equity Investment account. This is a subtle, but important point: unless a parent company chooses to publish (completely optional) unconsolidated parent-company financial statements as a supplement to its required, GAAP-mandated consolidated financial statements—in which case the parent-only financial statements must reflect the full equity method—then the parent company is free to use *any* pre-consolidation Equity Investment bookkeeping method it chooses. Yes, *any*!

So, as a practical matter, in real-world consolidation settings, there are innumerable variations on the pure-form Equity Investment bookkeeping methods we discuss in this book. These variations occur because some company managers are highly concerned with repatriating foreign-subsidiary income in a tax-efficient manner, while other managers are more concerned with an accurate parent-level snapshot of periodic consolidated performance, and other managers are more concerned with achieving the highest level of efficiency during the consolidation process. The bottom line is that there are myriad motivations for structuring pre-consolidation Equity Investment bookkeeping in peculiar, idiosyncratic ways, and our survey of professional-service-firm partners and corporate managers suggests that there are endless variations on the basic Equity Investment accounting approaches we discuss in this text.

Despite this real-world variation, in this text, we will primarily discuss post-acquisition consolidation assuming the parent company uses one of two methods of Equity Investment bookkeeping for its subsidiaries:[1]

1. **Equity Method:** the parent company adjusts its pre-consolidation acquisition-date investment account for its proportionate share of the subsidiary's post-acquisition income, dividends, amortization of the acquisition accounting premium (AAP), and elimination of intercompany transactions. This is the same equity method for controlled companies that we discussed in Chapter 1.

2. **Cost Method:** the parent company does not adjust its pre-consolidation acquisition-date investment account for the subsidiary's post-acquisition activities. Of course, the parent company must record direct transactions with the subsidiary. For example, dividends declared by the subsidiary will be recorded as a debit to dividends receivable (or cash) and a credit to dividend income. From a pre-consolidation bookkeeping perspective, this is, by far, the easiest method to apply.

We focus on these two approaches because all pre-consolidation bookkeeping approaches observed in practice represent variations on these two basic methods (i.e., from adjusting the Equity Investment account for all subsidiary activity, AAP amortization and intercompany profit elimination through not adjusting the Equity Investment at all). Our hope is that students can grasp the basic intuition from each of these fundamental approaches, and then later adapt them to the specific approaches encountered in practice.

In each of the remaining consolidations chapters, we will introduce each consolidation topic assuming the parent company uses the equity method of pre-consolidation Equity Investment bookkeeping. As we will describe, we believe this is pedagogically superior because the resulting consolidated balances have a direct connection to important pre-consolidation parent company balances when the parent company uses the equity method. After we cover equity method consolidations, we will describe the steps to cost-method consolidation. Unfortunately, as we will describe in those cost-method sections, the resulting consolidated balances do not have an obvious, direct connection to pre-consolidation parent company balances. This is why students often find cost method consolidations to be more challenging than equity method consolidations.

POST-ACQUISITION CONSOLIDATION WHEN THE PARENT USES THE EQUITY METHOD OF INVESTMENT BOOKKEEPING

When the parent uses the equity method of pre-consolidation investment bookkeeping, the parent records an increase in its Equity Investment account on its balance sheet and an increase in Equity Income in its income statement relating to "Income from Subsidiary" that it earns. The parent also records an entry to reduce the Equity Investment account to reflect the dividends it receives from the subsidiary.[2] Thus, in addition to replacing the Equity Investment account on the balance sheet with the assets and liabilities to which it relates, as we discuss in Chapter 2, the post-acquisition consolidation process will now also need to replace the Income from Subsidiary account in the parent's pre-consolidation income statement with the disaggregated revenues and expenses of the subsidiary to which it relates. This means our consolidated financial statements will now include an income statement in addition to the balance sheet.

---

[1] Again, these are alternative, pre-consolidation bookkeeping procedures applied by the parent company for post-acquisition activity by controlled subsidiaries. If the parent does not control the investee, then the parent does not have a choice in accounting method. As we discussed in Chapter 1, if the noncontrolling investment is "passive" and the investee's securities are marketable, then the investor must use fair value for the noncontrolling investment. If the noncontrolling investment is "passive" and the investee's securities do not have a readily determinable fair value, then the investor must use the cost method for the noncontrolling investment. If the investor has "significant influence" over the noncontrolled investee, then the investor must use the equity method for the noncontrolling investment. Finally, for any individual noncontrolling equity investment (i.e., each case discussed in this footnote), an investor may make an irrevocable election to report the investment at fair value (i.e., including when there is "significant influence" over the investee) under the Fair Value Option allowed under FASB ASC 825.

[2] Under the equity method, "Income from Subsidiary" includes the parent company's share of the reported net income of the subsidiary adjusted for the parent company's share of amortization calculated on the Acquisition Accounting Premium (AAP). We discuss the AAP in Chapters 1 and 2 and the amortization process in this chapter. Of course, if Income from Subsidiary is negative (i.e., a net loss), then the Equity Investment account will decrease.

In this section, we briefly discuss the intuition behind this replacement process and provide detailed discussion of the post-acquisition consolidation mechanics when the parent uses the equity method of pre-consolidation investment bookkeeping. Throughout this chapter, we continue to assume that a parent company obtains control of the subsidiary by acquiring all of its voting shares (i.e., it is a wholly owned subsidiary).[3]

In general terms, under the equity method of pre-consolidation investment bookkeeping, the mechanics of the consolidation process subsequent to the acquisition involves six steps:[4]

1. Remove (eliminate) the *changes* in the parent company's financial statements caused by investment-related bookkeeping for the subsidiary. This has the effect of eliminating the equity method accounting applied by the parent *during* the year.

2. Remove (eliminate) the *beginning of year* (BOY) balance of the Equity Investment account from the consolidated balance sheet that relates to the beginning of the year book value of the Stockholders' Equity of the subsidiary. This step is the same as the procedure in Chapter 2 that we describe as our [E] consolidation entry.

3. Remove (eliminate) the *beginning of year* balance of the Equity Investment account from the consolidated balance sheet that relates to the AAP. This step is basically the same as the procedure in Chapter 2 that we describe in our [A] consolidation entry.[5]

4. Record the depreciation or amortization of the AAP for the year. This step is needed because the AAP is included in the *parent's* books as part of the Equity Investment account at the beginning of the year and the consolidated financial statements must reflect the depreciation or amortization of the AAP for the year.

5. Remove (eliminate) intercompany transactions and balances.

6. Add together the financial statements of the parent and subsidiary—together with the consolidation entries in (1), (2), (3), (4) and (5) above—to yield the consolidated financial statements.

We begin our discussion of the consolidation process subsequent to the date of acquisition with a review of the parent company application of the equity method of accounting.

LO1 Describe the equity method of accounting for the Equity Investment.

Review of the Equity Method of Pre-Consolidation Bookkeeping

Let's assume that on January 1, 2015, a parent purchases for $1,500,000 a subsidiary with a book value of Stockholders' Equity of $1,000,000. To finance the purchase, the parent issues 50,000 shares of its $1 par value common stock with a market value of $30 per share (total purchase price of $1,500,000) and exchanges those shares with the subsidiary's stockholders for all of the subsidiary's voting shares that they own. The acquired company is, therefore, a wholly (i.e., 100%) owned subsidiary of the parent.

The journal entry that the parent makes on January 1, 2015, to record the acquisition is as follows:

Equity investment.	1,500,000	
Common stock (50,000 shares @ $1)		50,000
Additional paid-in capital.		1,450,000
(to record the acquisition of the subsidiary)		

Assume that the parent is willing to purchase the subsidiary for $1,500,000 because the Property, Plant and Equipment (PPE) assets, reported on the subsidiary's balance sheet at $827,000, have a fair value equal to $1,027,000 (i.e., they are undervalued by $200,000). In addition, the subsidiary owns the

---

[3] We discuss consolidation of non-wholly owned subsidiaries (i.e., ownership percentage < 100%) in Chapter 5.

[4] Philosophically, the steps to consolidation are virtually identical under the equity and cost methods. To facilitate learning the consolidation process under the equity method, we will specifically tailor our discussion in this section to the equity method. We will describe the similarities and differences of consolidation under the two approaches when we discuss the cost method later in the chapter.

[5] The effect of the second and third steps on consolidation is that we will replace the beginning of the year Equity Investment account on the parent's balance sheet with the beginning of the year assets and liabilities of the subsidiary company to which it relates, including the book value of the assets and liabilities that are reported on the subsidiary's balance sheet and the unrecognized asset and liability values represented by the AAP.

rights to an *unrecorded* Patent with a fair value equal to $175,000.[6] Any remaining difference between the purchase price and identifiable tangible and intangible assets is attributed to corporate synergies that will result from the business combination. This unidentified intangible asset will be recorded as Goodwill.

The parent assigns fair values as follows:

		Useful life*	Deprec./Amort.*
Purchase price	$1,500,000		
Book value of subsidiary	1,000,000		
Acquisition Accounting Premium (AAP)	$ 500,000		
AAP Assigned to Identifiable Net Assets:		Useful life*	Deprec./Amort.*
Undervalued PPE	$ 200,000	20	$10,000
Patent	175,000	10	17,500
Goodwill (i.e., unidentifiable residual AAP)	$ 125,000	N/A	0
			$27,500

* assumed life with no salvage value

As we discuss in Chapter 2, the purchase price paid by the parent represents the fair value of the subsidiary's business. The difference between the *fair value* of the subsidiary (i.e., the purchase price) and the *net book value* of the subsidiary (i.e., the book value of its Stockholders' Equity) is the AAP. In this example, based on the parent's acquisition date appraisals, the AAP is comprised of two *identifiable* sources of fair-value-minus-book-value differences: (a) the subsidiary's recorded value for PPE is undervalued by $200,000 and (b) the *unrecorded* Patent asset held by the subsidiary has a fair value equal to $175,000. The $125,000 remainder of the AAP is an *unidentifiable* residual, and it is recorded as a Goodwill asset.

To recap, the Equity Investment on the acquisition date has two components:

1. $1,000,000 book value of the subsidiary's Stockholders' Equity, and
2. $500,000 of AAP (related to the undervalued PPE, the Patent asset and the Goodwill asset).

Based on an assessment by the parent of the expected remaining useful lives, the parent will depreciate the PPE asset over 20 years on a straight-line basis (with no salvage value) and amortize the Patent asset over 10 years.

To illustrate the post-acquisition accounting for the Equity Investment, we assume that during the year ended December 31, 2015 (the first year-end following the acquisition), the subsidiary reports sales of $1,500,000, earns a profit during the year of $210,000, and pays a dividend of $31,500 to the parent. At December 31, 2015, the parent makes the following journal entries to record its share (100% in this case) of the subsidiary's net income and to record the receipt of the dividends:

a.	Equity investment	210,000	
	Equity income		210,000
	(to record the recognition of equity earnings)		

b.	Cash	31,500	
	Equity investment		31,500
	(to record the receipt of dividends)		

The parent also records amortization related to depreciation of the PPE-related AAP and amortization of the Patent-related AAP (see the fair value assignment table above for the computations):

c.	Equity income	27,500	
	Equity investment		27,500
	(to record the $10,000 depreciation of the PPE asset and the $17,500 amortization of the Patent asset)		

---

[6] Under U.S. GAAP, the research and development costs of obtaining the Patent by the subsidiary were expensed when incurred, and the fair value of the Patent is not recorded on the subsidiary's balance sheet. This is typical of U.S. GAAP for internally generated intangible assets.

As a result of these three journal entries, the Equity Investment account on the parent's balance sheet at December 31, 2015, is $1,651,000, consisting of the beginning balance of $1,500,000, an increase relating to the recognition of net Equity Income of $182,500 ($210,000 − $27,500), and a reduction of $31,500 relating to the dividends received from the subsidiary. The T-account for the Equity Investment illustrates these entries:

	Equity Investment		
❶ Beginning balance	1,500,000		
❷ Equity income (BV)	182,500	31,500	Dividends
Ending balance	1,651,000		

There are two components to the Equity Investment account recorded on the parent's books at the end of the accounting period:

1. The *beginning balance* of the Equity Investment account on January 1, 2015. This is comprised of two pieces:
   a. The beginning-of-year book value of the subsidiary's Stockholders' Equity (equal to $1,000,000), and
   b. The beginning-of-year AAP (equal to $500,000—remember, this amount is not recorded on the subsidiary's books).
2. The *change* in the Equity Investment account recorded during the year ended December 31, 2015. This is comprised of two pieces:
   a. The net Equity Income recognized by the parent of $182,500 during 2015 (equal to the $210,000 net income of the subsidiary less the AAP amortized by the parent during 2015 equal to $27,500), and
   b. The dividends received from the subsidiary during 2015 (equal to $31,500).

Our consolidation entry approach starts with the elimination of each of these components. By eliminating the *change* in the investment account and the *beginning balance* of the investment account, we will eliminate the ending balance of the Equity Investment account.[7] We split the post-acquisition consolidation entry process into these two components because it facilitates preparation of the income statement and the balance sheet.

We discuss these consolidation entries in our next section of the chapter.

TOPIC REVIEW 1

Bookkeeping for an Equity Method Investment

Assume that a parent purchases all of the stock of its subsidiary for $800 on January 1, 2016. The subsidiary reports Stockholders' Equity of $600 on the date of purchase. The parent assigns the $200 excess purchase price to a Patent owned by the subsidiary. The Patent has a 10-year remaining life. Subsequent to the acquisition, the subsidiary reports $150 of net income and pays dividends of $50 during the year ended December 31, 2016.

Required

Provide the following journal entries:

a. Record the initial investment at January 1, 2016.
b. Record the recognition of Equity Income by the parent for the year ended December 31, 2016.
c. Record the receipt of the $50 dividend during 2016.

The solution to this review problem can be found on page 176.

---

[7] Of course, we use the word "eliminate" very loosely; the process of consolidation is really one of replacement, not elimination. In fact, because the AAP is not actually recorded on the subsidiary's books, the entries related to the AAP are actually reclassification entries. That's because the end result of all of the AAP-related consolidation entries effectively reclassifies the AAP out of the Equity Investment balance sheet and income statement accounts and distributes the AAP to the various net assets (and income/expense accounts) to which it relates.

The Consolidation Process Subsequent to the Date of Acquisition—Equity Method

The consolidation process combines the financial statements of the parent and its subsidiary by removing (eliminating) the Equity-Investment-related accounts from the parent's balance sheet and income statement and replacing that information with the assets, liabilities, revenues and expenses of the subsidiary company to which it relates.

LO2 Describe the consolidation process subsequent to the date of acquisition when the parent uses the equity method to account for its Equity Investment.

It is important to remember that **none of the consolidation entries are actually made in the books of either the parent or the subsidiary. They only exist on our consolidation spreadsheet or working paper. The consolidated financial statements are prepared <u>after</u> the financial statements have been prepared by the parent and subsidiary, and the consolidation entries exist only in our spreadsheet or working paper.**

We only needed two consolidation entries in Chapter 2 to eliminate the components of the acquisition-date balance in the Equity Investment account:

- [E] entry relating to the **elimination** of the book value of Stockholders' Equity, and the
- [A] entry to reclassify the **AAP** from the Equity Investment account to the individually identifiable net assets and unidentifiable Goodwill purchased by the parent in the acquisition.

We will, again, see these two consolidation entries in post-acquisition consolidations; however, this time we will use them to eliminate the beginning of period Equity Investment account balance.

In *post-acquisition consolidations*, however, we now have three more entries, which correspond to activities of the subsidiary during the period. These entries include the

- [C] entry to eliminate of the **changes** in the parent company's financial statements caused by investment-related bookkeeping for the subsidiary during the period (under the Equity Method, these are the equity method adjustments during the period),
- [D] entry to recognize the current-period AAP **depreciation** and amortization of the AAP in the consolidated income statement, and the
- [I] entry to eliminate **intercompany** transactions during the period and balances remaining at the end of the period.[8]

Each of these consolidation entries is denoted with a letter so that we can easily identify and remember them as **C-E-A-D-I**, or "seedy." Exhibit 3.1 presents a summary of these post-acquisition consolidation entries when the parent uses the equity method.

EXHIBIT 3.1	Post-acquisition Consolidation Entries—Equity Method
[C]	Eliminates all *changes* in the parent's books caused by investment bookkeeping during the year. When the parent uses the equity method to account for the pre-consolidation Equity Investment account it reverses all entries to the Equity Investment account during the consolidation period, leaving only the beginning balance.
[E]	Eliminates the portion of the investment account related to the book value of the subsidiary's Stockholders' Equity at the *beginning of the accounting period*. (After this entry, the investment account should equal the beginning of period unamortized AAP.)
[A]	Assigns the remaining Equity Investment account (i.e., unamortized beginning of period AAP) to appropriate asset & liability accounts as of the *beginning of the accounting period*.
[D]	Depreciates/amortizes AAP so that the income statement includes the activity and the balance sheet accounts include ending AAP assigned to the appropriate accounts.
[I]	Eliminates intercompany activity (e.g., sales between parent and subsidiary) and/or intercompany balances (e.g., account payable and account receivable between parent and subsidiary). (This will be covered in Chapter 4.)

---

[8] A parent and its subsidiaries may engage in many transactions between the entities; so, the consolidation process might involve many different [I] intercompany consolidation entries. We discuss one simple intercompany transaction in this chapter and more fully explore this topic in Chapter 4 with intercompany sales of inventory and PPE.

Exhibit 3.2 depicts the Equity Investment T-account and the journal entries that affect the account. Consolidation entry **[C]** will reverse out the two *changes* depicted in the Equity Investment T-account.[9] The first change is the parent company's recording of Equity Income. This item will include both the parent's share of Net Income reported by the subsidiary (assumed to be 100% in this chapter) along with the AAP amortization recorded under the Equity Method. (We describe the mechanics the parent uses to record equity method Equity Investment income and dividends in Chapter 1.)

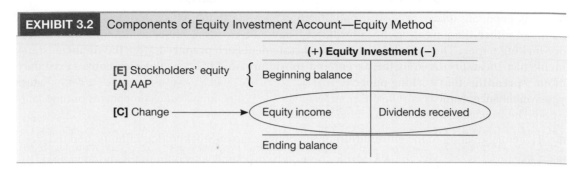

EXHIBIT 3.2 Components of Equity Investment Account—Equity Method

The next two consolidation entries, **[E]** and **[A]** are identical to the acquisition date adjustments we discussed in Chapter 2. One small exception is that entries **[E]** and **[A]** described in Chapter 2 were proposed on the *acquisition date*, whereas entries **[E]** and **[A]** included in this chapter (and in later chapters) are proposed for Equity Investment account information as of the *beginning of the period being consolidated*.

Ultimately, the process of consolidation requires us to eliminate the *ending* balance in the Equity Investment account, and because we also need to produce an income statement, we will also need to eliminate the *change* in the Equity Investment account. Thus, the way we end up eliminating the ending balance in the Equity Investment account is by separately eliminating the *beginning* balance and the *change* in the balance. This presents an easy way to remember the **[C]**, **[E]**, **[A]** part of the required consolidation entries:

1. eliminate the change to the Equity Investment account during the year (the **[C]** entry that leaves only the beginning balance of that account) and, then,

2. eliminate beginning balance of the Equity Investment account (the **[E]** and **[A]** entries).

After the **[C]**, **[E]**, **[A]** sequence of consolidation entries is made, the Equity Investment account is eliminated from the consolidated balance sheet. We still aren't quite done, however. The next step is to depreciate or amortize the individually identifiable net asset accounts embodied in the beginning of the year AAP balance. This is our **[D]** consolidating entry. Finally, in our last step, we will need a consolidating entry (or entries) to eliminate all intercompany transactions during the year as well as the ending balances of any intercompany receivables and payables. This is our **[I]** consolidation entry and it completes the consolidation process. We will discuss the **[I]** entry in Chapter 4.

In the next section, we will show you an example of the consolidation process subsequent to acquisition.

Example of Consolidation Subsequent to the Date of Acquisition—Equity Method

To illustrate the consolidation in the first year following acquisition (when the parent uses the equity method of pre-consolidation investment bookkeeping), we continue with the acquisition we introduced in the initial section of this chapter, "Review of the Equity Method of Accounting." Following is the T-account that represents the Equity Investment on the parent's balance sheet at December 31, 2015,

---

[9] Entry **[C]** will eliminate any other activity affecting the Equity Investment account. For example, if the subsidiary has "accumulated other comprehensive income" (AOCI) in its Stockholder Equity accounts, then under the Equity Method the Equity Investment account will change whenever the subsidiary records change in its AOCI. Thus, entry **[C]** can also be modified to incorporate other, specialized changes in the subsidiary's Stockholders' Equity.

in that example (i.e., the end of the first year following the acquisition of the subsidiary) along with the activity in the Equity Investment account:

	Equity Investment		
Beginning balance	1,500,000		
Equity income	182,500	31,500	Dividends
Ending balance	1,651,000		

We first illustrate the consolidation process at the end of the first year following the acquisition. Then, we describe the consolidation process at the end of the second year after the acquisition. Future years are handled similarly.

Consolidation at the End of the First Year Following the Acquisition—Equity Method

The consolidation process (when the parent uses the equity method of pre-consolidation investment bookkeeping) at the end of the first year following the acquisition proceeds by:

1. eliminating the changes in the Equity Investment account during the period **[C]**,
2. eliminating the beginning balance of the Equity Investment account **[E]** and **[A]**, and
3. recording the depreciation and/or amortization of the AAP **[D]**.

This is accomplished with the following entries that we post in our consolidation spreadsheet (BOY stands for beginning-of-year, EOY stands for end-of-year, (P) stands for parent, and (S) stands for subsidiary):

[C]	Equity income (P)	182,500	
	Dividends (S)		31,500
	Equity investment (P)		151,000
	(when the parent uses the equity method of pre-consolidation investment bookkeeping, eliminates all changes in the Equity Investment account, leaving only beginning balance in the account)		
[E]	Common stock (S) @ BOY	100,000	
	APIC (S) @ BOY	125,000	
	Retained earnings (S) @ BOY	775,000	
	Equity Investment (P) @ BOY		1,000,000
	(eliminates the portion of the investment account related to the book value of the subsidiary's Stockholders' Equity @ BOY)		
[A]	PPE, net (S) @ BOY	200,000	
	Patent (S) @ BOY	175,000	
	Goodwill (S) @ BOY	125,000	
	Equity investment (P) @ BOY		500,000
	(assigns the remaining Equity Investment account (i.e., unamortized BOY AAP) to appropriate asset & liability accounts)		
[D]	Operating expenses (S)	27,500	
	PPE, net (S)		10,000
	Patent (S)		17,500
	(depreciates/amortizes AAP so that income statement includes the activity and the balance sheet accounts include ending balances in appropriate accounts)		
[I]	No intercompany items until Chapter 4		

Exhibit 3.3 provides our consolidation spreadsheet at the end of the first year subsequent to the acquisition (the financial statements of the parent and subsidiary are assumed to be taken from their individual records at the end of the year and are given to us before we begin the consolidation process). We, then, insert the consolidation entries presented above and sum across each row to obtain the consolidated totals in the right-hand column.

EXHIBIT 3.3	Consolidation Spreadsheet at the End of the *First* Year Following Acquisition—Equity Method

	Parent	Subsidiary	Consolidation Entries		Consolidated
			Dr	**Cr**	
Income statement:					
Sales.	$10,000,000	$1,500,000			$11,500,000
Cost of goods sold.	(7,000,000)	(900,000)			(7,900,000)
Gross profit.	3,000,000	600,000			3,600,000
Equity income.	182,500		[C] $ 182,500		0
Operating expenses.	(1,900,000)	(390,000)	[D] 27,500		(2,317,500)
Net income.	$ 1,282,500	$ 210,000			$ 1,282,500
Statement of retained earnings:					
BOY retained earnings.	$ 5,024,000	$ 775,000	[E] 775,000		$ 5,024,000
Net income.	1,282,500	210,000			1,282,500
Dividends	(256,500)	(31,500)		[C] $ 31,500	(256,500)
Ending retained earnings	$ 6,050,000	$ 953,500			$ 6,050,000
Balance sheet:					
Assets.					
Cash.	$ 1,134,000	$ 404,500			$ 1,538,500
Accounts receivable.	1,280,000	348,000			1,628,000
Inventory.	1,940,000	447,000			2,387,000
Equity investment.	1,651,000			[C] 151,000	0
				[E] 1,000,000	
				[A] 500,000	
PPE, net	9,373,350	785,650	[A] 200,000	[D] 10,000	10,349,000
Patent.			[A] 175,000	[D] 17,500	157,500
Goodwill			[A] 125,000		125,000
	$15,378,350	$1,985,150			$16,185,000
Liabilities and stockholders' equity					
Current liabilities.	$ 1,478,350	$ 306,650			$ 1,785,000
Long-term liabilities	5,000,000	500,000			5,500,000
Common stock.	1,635,000	100,000	[E] 100,000		1,635,000
APIC.	1,215,000	125,000	[E] 125,000		1,215,000
Retained earnings	6,050,000	953,500			6,050,000
	$15,378,350	$1,985,150	$1,710,000	$1,710,000	$16,185,000

Remember, the consolidation entries are made only in our spreadsheet. They do not affect the accounting records of either the parent or the subsidiary. The parent still accounts for its Equity Investment in the subsidiary using the equity method, and both companies still prepare their own financial statements. However, because the parent controls the subsidiary, the parent cannot issue financial statements to the public without first consolidating its subsidiary.[10]

---

[10] As we mentioned at the beginning of the chapter, the parent is allowed to issue *supplemental* unconsolidated parent-only or subsidiary-only financial statements if (and only if) the parent also publishes consolidated financial statements in the same annual report. General Electric Co. is an example of a company that regularly publishes audited parent and subsidiary financial statements with its audited consolidated statements. You can download its financial statements from the SEC's website (http://www.sec.gov). The supplemental parent-only financial statements must apply the equity method for the unconsolidated subsidiary.

When the parent uses the equity method of pre-consolidation Equity Investment bookkeeping, the first four of our five **C-E-A-D-I** entries are designed to: (1) *eliminate* the subsidiary's reported net income and dividends from the Equity Investment/Equity Income accounts, (2) *eliminate* the book value of the subsidiary's Stockholder's Equity for the Equity Investment account, (3) *reclassify* the unamortized AAP from the Equity Investment account into the appropriate individual identifiable net asset accounts and Goodwill, and (4) *reclassify* the amortized AAP from the Equity Investment/Equity Income accounts into the appropriate income statement accounts (this example did not include the elimination of intercompany transactions and balances; we will include that wrinkle in Chapter 4).

As a result of these consolidation entries, the Equity Investment account (on the parent's balance sheet) and the Equity Income account (on the parent's income statement) are both reduced to a zero balance on the consolidated financial statements. In the completed spreadsheet, we show those accounts with zero balances to illustrate their elimination. In practice, they would not be reported at all. As you begin to learn the consolidation process, a good short-term goal is to remember that these two accounts always result in a zero balance at the end of the consolidation process.

Finally, notice that the consolidated Stockholders' Equity equals the Stockholders' Equity of the parent company. That will always be the case so long as the parent uses the equity method to account for its Equity Investment. That is because, when the parent uses the equity method to account for its Equity Investment in the subsidiary, it recognizes as part of its Stockholders' Equity all changes in the subsidiary's Stockholders Equity. The Stockholders' Equity of a wholly owned subsidiary is not considered equity of the consolidated entity. So, it is always eliminated in consolidation entry [E].

That's all there is to it. You've now completed your first consolidation spreadsheet subsequent to acquisition. Congratulations!

PRACTICE INSIGHT

The Consolidation Process in Practice   Textbooks utilize spreadsheets to demonstrate the consolidation process. Although spreadsheets can be utilized effectively for demonstration purposes, consolidation software is frequently employed in practice. This software performs the consolidation process in the same way we describe in the text, but the program integrates seamlessly with the company's IT system rather than as a stand-alone procedure.

One such software program is the **Hyperion** enterprise system. Hyperion was acquired by **Oracle** for $3.3 billion in 2007 and is now a part of the Oracle software suite for large and mid-sized companies. Intercompany transactions are coded as such when entered into the system by the parent and its subsidiary companies. At period-end, accountants at each subsidiary upload their company's income statement and balance sheet. Finally, the roll-up of subsidiaries' financial statements into the parent company proceeds seamlessly using the consolidation process we describe in the text to yield the consolidated income statements and balance sheets. The consolidated statement of cash flows is, then, prepared from these income statements and balance sheets just like you learned in intermediate accounting.

Mr. Chris Anderson, Corporate Controller for **Novell, Inc.**, reports that the initial consolidated numbers are available 3 days following the close of the accounting period. Further adjustments may take 3–5 more days, yielding consolidated financial statements within a week or so following the period-end close.

Consolidation at the End of the Second Year Following the Acquisition—Equity Method
Now, let's perform the consolidation for the second year following the acquisition. Both the parent and its subsidiary have accounted for their operating activities in their respective accounting records, and Exhibit 3.4 provides their financial statements for the year ended December 31, 2016, that have been given to us prior to the consolidation process.

EXHIBIT 3.4	Financial Statements of Parent and Subsidiary at the End of the *Second* Year Following the Acquisition—Equity Method		

		Parent	Subsidiary
Income statement:			
Sales.		$12,580,000	$1,887,000
Cost of goods sold.		(8,806,000)	(1,132,200)
Gross profit.		3,774,000	754,800
Equity income.		236,680	
Operating expenses		(2,390,200)	(490,620)
Net income		$ 1,620,480	$ 264,180
Statement of retained earnings:			
BOY retained earnings		$ 6,050,000	$ 953,500
Net income		1,620,480	264,180
Dividends		(324,096)	(39,627)
Ending retained earnings		$ 7,346,384	$1,178,053
Balance sheet:			
Assets			
Cash		$ 365,661	$ 429,361
Accounts receivable		1,610,240	437,784
Inventory.		2,440,520	562,326
Equity investment.		1,848,053	
Property, plant and equipment (PPE), net		11,739,656	1,040,366
		$18,004,130	$2,469,837
Liabilities and stockholders' equity			
Current liabilities.		$ 1,807,746	$ 437,784
Long-term liabilities		6,000,000	629,000
Common stock.		1,635,000	100,000
APIC		1,215,000	125,000
Retained earnings		7,346,384	1,178,053
		$18,004,130	$2,469,837

During 2016, the subsidiary reports net income of $264,180 and pays a dividend to the parent of $39,627.

The ending balance of the Equity Investment account on the parent's balance sheet is reported at $1,848,053 at December 31, 2016, calculated as follows:

BOY Equity Investment		$1,651,000
Subsidiary net income	$264,180	
Depreciation and amortization expense	(27,500)	
Equity income.	236,680	236,680
Dividends received		(39,627)
EOY Equity Investment		$1,848,053

The beginning balance of the Equity Investment account (i.e., at January 1, 2016) consists of the book value of the subsidiary's Stockholders' Equity plus the unamortized AAP at January 1, 2016:

BOY subsidiary Stockholders' Equity . . .	$1,178,500	($100,000 + $125,000 + $953,500)
BOY unamortized AAP for PPE	190,000	($200,000 − $10,000 depreciation for the 1st year)
BOY unamortized AAP for Patent	157,500	($175,000 − $17,500 amortization for the 1st year)
BOY unamortized AAP for Goodwill.	125,000	(not amortized)
BOY balance of Equity Investment	$1,651,000	

This BOY balance is equal to the EOY balance that we computed at the end of year 1 as we discuss above. Each year, the BOY balance of the Equity Investment account will be computed similarly as the AAP continues to be depreciated and amortized.

Exhibit 3.5 presents our consolidation spreadsheet for the year ending December 31, 2016, reflecting our **C-E-A-D-I** consolidation entries.

EXHIBIT 3.5 Consolidation Spreadsheet at the End of the *Second* Year Following Acquisition—Equity Method

	Parent	Subsidiary	Dr	Cr	Consolidated
Income statement:					
Sales.	$12,580,000	$1,887,000			$14,467,000
Cost of goods sold.	(8,806,000)	(1,132,200)			(9,938,200)
Gross profit.	3,774,000	754,800			4,528,800
Equity income.	236,680		[C] $ 236,680		0
Operating expenses	(2,390,200)	(490,620)	[D] 27,500		(2,908,320)
Net income.	$ 1,620,480	$ 264,180			$ 1,620,480
Statement of retained earnings:					
BOY retained earnings	$ 6,050,000	$ 953,500	[E] 953,500		$ 6,050,000
Net income.	1,620,480	264,180			1,620,480
Dividends	(324,096)	(39,627)		[C] $ 39,627	(324,096)
Ending retained earnings	$ 7,346,384	$1,178,053			$ 7,346,384
Balance sheet:					
Assets					
Cash	$ 365,661	$ 429,361			$ 795,022
Accounts receivable	1,610,240	437,784			2,048,024
Inventory	2,440,520	562,326			3,002,846
Equity investment	1,848,053			[C] 197,053	0
				[E] 1,178,500	
				[A] 472,500	
PPE, net	11,739,656	1,040,366	[A] 190,000	[D] 10,000	12,960,022
Patent			[A] 157,500	[D] 17,500	140,000
Goodwill			[A] 125,000		125,000
	$18,004,130	$2,469,837			$19,070,914
Liabilities and stockholders' equity					
Current liabilities	$ 1,807,746	$ 437,784			$ 2,245,530
Long-term liabilities	6,000,000	629,000			6,629,000
Common stock	1,635,000	100,000	[E] 100,000		1,635,000
APIC	1,215,000	125,000	[E] 125,000		1,215,000
Retained earnings	7,346,384	1,178,053			7,346,384
	$18,004,130	$2,469,837	$1,915,180	$1,915,180	$19,070,914

The individual components of the AAP have the following unamortized balances at the *beginning* of the *second* year (i.e., January 1, 2016):

$190,000	($200,000 − $10,000) for PPE
157,500	($175,000 − $17,500) for Patent
125,000	Goodwill
$472,500	

And, at the *end* of the *second* year (i.e., December 31, 2016), the individual components of the AAP will have the following unamortized balances:

$180,000	($200,000 − $20,000) for PPE
140,000	($175,000 − $35,000) for Patent
125,000	Goodwill
$445,000	

The depreciable components of the AAP will continue to be amortized until they have zero balances (i.e., we assumed no salvage value). Goodwill is *not* depreciated or amortized, so it will continue to have a balance of $125,000 unless it is determined to be impaired. We will discuss Goodwill determination and impairment in later sections of this chapter.

Notice that the **[A]** entry eliminates the beginning-of-year balance of the AAP assets in the amount of $472,500 (the balance at the end of the first year and the beginning of the second year). Next year (the *third* year), the **[A]** entry will eliminate the beginning-of-year balance of the AAP assets in the amount of $445,000 (the balance at the end of the second year and the beginning of the third year).

In our next section, we discuss our preparation of the financial statements that we will send to shareholders and to the SEC.

Consolidated Financial Statements

We can now prepare the consolidated income statement, consolidated statement of retained earnings, and consolidated balance sheet at the end of the second year from the spreadsheet that we developed in the previous section. The column labeled "consolidated" is the sum across each row, and provides the amounts we will use in our published financial statements.

Consolidated Income Statement   Based on the information in our spreadsheet for the year ended December 31, 2016, our consolidated income statement follows:

Consolidated Income Statement	
Sales.	$14,467,000
Cost of goods sold.	(9,938,200)
Gross profit.	4,528,800
Operating expenses.	(2,908,320)
Net income.	$ 1,620,480

This statement is computed as the income statement of the parent plus the income statement of the subsidiary, and less the amortization of the AAP related to the PPE and Patent assets.

Notice that consolidated net income is equal to the net income of the parent company. That will always be the case so long as the parent uses the equity method to account for its Equity Investment in the subsidiary. The reason is that the equity method requires the parent to recognize in its income its share of the subsidiary's net income and the depreciation and amortization of the AAP.

Consolidated Balance Sheet   The consolidated Retained Earnings are updated just like the Retained Earnings accounts for the parent and the subsidiary:

BOY consolidated retained earnings.	$6,050,000
Consolidated net income.	1,620,480
Dividends to parent's shareholders.	(324,096)
EOY consolidated retained earnings.	$7,346,384

Notice that the dividends reducing consolidated Retained Earnings are only those declared by the parent for payment to its shareholders. The intercompany dividends (i.e., subsidiary to parent) have been eliminated in the consolidation process.

Given our consolidated Retained Earnings, we can prepare our consolidated balance sheet as follows:

Consolidated Balance Sheet	
Cash.	$ 795,022
Accounts receivable.	2,048,024
Inventory.	3,002,846
Property, plant and equipment (PPE), net	12,960,022
Patent.	140,000
Goodwill	125,000
Total Assets	$19,070,914
Current liabilities.	$ 2,245,530
Long-term liabilities	6,629,000
Common stock.	1,635,000
APIC	1,215,000
Retained earnings	7,346,384
Total liabilities and stockholders' equity.	$19,070,914

Notice that the consolidated balance sheet does not include the Equity Investment account that appears on the parent's balance sheet. That account has been replaced by the assets and liabilities of the subsidiary company to which it relates. In addition, the book value of the PPE, Patent, and Goodwill assets that the parent purchased in its acquisition of the subsidiary is now included in the consolidated balance sheet.

Consolidated Statement of Cash Flows

The consolidated statement of cash flows is *not* the sum of the statements of cash flows of the individual companies in the consolidated group. Rather, it is prepared from the consolidated income statement and a comparative consolidated balance sheet in the same way that you learned in introductory and/or intermediate accounting. Consequently, all intercompany transactions have been eliminated and the additional depreciation/amortization expense relating to the AAP has been included.

There are some peculiarities relating to the consolidated statement of cash flows that are not present in a statement of cash flows for an individual company:

1. We need to add back the noncash expense relating to the depreciation and amortization of the AAP. This expense appears in the consolidated income statement, but is not reflected in the income statements of either the parent or its subsidiary.
2. In the year of acquisition,
   a. The *net* cash paid for an acquisition (cash paid less cash on the investee's balance sheet) is recorded in the investing section. To the extent that the acquisition is affected as a stock-for-stock exchange, however, no cash outflow is recognized since no cash has been paid.
   b. The changes in working capital accounts (current assets and liabilities) are computed based on amounts *excluding the effects of the acquisition*. For example, if accounts receivable increase by $100 year-over-year, but the parent acquired $30 of accounts receivable in its acquisition of a subsidiary, only $70 of that increase is included as an outflow in computing net cash flow from operating activities (the $30 is included in the investing section if the acquisition was paid for in cash, or excluded altogether if no cash was paid in the acquisition).

Required Footnote Disclosures   Companies are required to disclose details about their acquisitions in footnotes to their consolidated financial statements. A partial listing of these disclosures follows. We provide the complete listing of required disclosures in Appendix A.

a.   The name and a description of the acquiree.

b.   The acquisition date.

c.   The percentage of voting equity interests acquired.

d.   The primary reasons for the business combination and a description of how the acquirer obtained control of the acquiree.

e.   A qualitative description of the factors that make up the Goodwill recognized, such as expected synergies from combining operations of the acquiree and the acquirer, intangible assets that do not qualify for separate recognition, or other factors.

f.   The acquisition-date fair value of the total consideration transferred and the acquisition-date fair value of each major class of consideration.

g.   For contingent consideration arrangements and indemnification assets:
   1.   The amount recognized as of the acquisition date
   2.   A description of the arrangement and the basis for determining the amount of the payment
   3.   An estimate of the range of outcomes (undiscounted) or, if a range cannot be estimated, that fact and the reasons why a range cannot be estimated. If the maximum amount of the payment is unlimited, the acquirer shall disclose that fact.

PRACTICE INSIGHT

Limitations of consolidated financial statements   Consolidation of financial statements is meant to present a financial picture of the entire set of companies under the control of the parent. Because investors typically purchase stock of the parent company (and not the subsidiaries), consolidated statements are considered more relevant than the parent company merely reporting subsidiaries as equity investments in its balance sheet. Still, we must be aware of certain limitations that the consolidation process entails:

1.   Consolidated income does not imply that the parent company has received any or all of the subsidiaries' net income as cash. In general, the parent can only receive cash from subsidiaries via dividend payments. Conversely, the consolidated cash is not automatically available to the individual subsidiaries. Because of the potential for high taxes due on dividends received from foreign-domiciled subsidiaries, parent companies may leave cash parked off-shore in international subsidiaries for an indefinite period. Or, it is quite possible for an individual subsidiary to experience cash flow problems even though the consolidated group has strong cash flows. Likewise, unguaranteed debts of a subsidiary are not obligations of the consolidated group. Thus, even if the consolidated balance sheet is strong, creditors of a failing subsidiary are often unable to sue the parent or other subsidiaries to recoup losses.

2.   Consolidated balance sheets and income statements are a mix of the various subsidiaries, often from different industries. Comparisons across companies, even if in similar industries, are often complicated by the different mix of subsidiary companies.

3.   Segment disclosures on individual subsidiaries are affected by intercorporate transfer pricing policies relating to purchases of products or services that can artificially inflate the profitability of one segment at the expense of another. Companies also have considerable discretion in the allocation of corporate overhead to subsidiaries, which can markedly affect segment profitability. Because of the possibility of using transfer pricing policies to move profits into low tax-rate jurisdictions, national tax authorities (e.g., U.S. Department of the Treasury and the Internal Revenue Service) have extremely detailed and rigorous rules for intercompany transfer pricing.

4.   Segment disclosures are often too summarized for effective analysis, and may not be sufficient to discover if the results of poorly performing subsidiaries are being masked by positive results of others.

TOPIC REVIEW 2

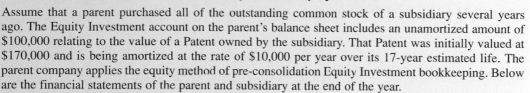

Consolidation Subsequent to Date of Acquisition—Equity Method

Assume that a parent purchased all of the outstanding common stock of a subsidiary several years ago. The Equity Investment account on the parent's balance sheet includes an unamortized amount of $100,000 relating to the value of a Patent owned by the subsidiary. That Patent was initially valued at $170,000 and is being amortized at the rate of $10,000 per year over its 17-year estimated life. The parent company applies the equity method of pre-consolidation Equity Investment bookkeeping. Below are the financial statements of the parent and subsidiary at the end of the year.

	Parent	Subsidiary
Income statement:		
Sales.	$10,000,000	$1,500,000
Cost of goods sold.	(7,000,000)	(900,000)
Gross profit.	3,000,000	600,000
Equity income.	200,000	
Operating expenses.	(1,900,000)	(390,000)
Net income.	$ 1,300,000	$ 210,000
Statement of retained earnings:		
BOY retained earnings.	$ 5,720,000	$ 630,000
Net income.	1,300,000	210,000
Dividends	(260,000)	(31,500)
Ending retained earnings	$ 6,760,000	$ 808,500
Balance sheet:		
Assets		
Cash.	$ 683,500	$ 259,500
Accounts receivable.	1,280,000	348,000
Inventory.	1,940,000	447,000
Equity investment.	1,123,500	
Building, net	9,332,000	827,000
	$14,359,000	$1,881,500
Liabilities and stockholders' equity		
Current liabilities.	$ 1,437,000	$ 348,000
Long-term liabilities	3,312,000	500,000
Common stock.	1,635,000	100,000
APIC.	1,215,000	125,000
Retained earnings	6,760,000	808,500
	$14,359,000	$1,881,500

Required

Prepare the consolidation spreadsheet.

The solution to this review problem can be found on page 177.

POST-ACQUISITION CONSOLIDATION WHEN THE PARENT USES THE COST METHOD OF INVESTMENT BOOKKEEPING

So far, we focused on consolidation when the parent company uses the equity method of pre-consolidation bookkeeping because it is the most intuitive condition under which to consolidate. To review, when the parent company uses the equity method, then (1) consolidated net income will equal the parent company's pre-consolidation net income and (2) consolidated owners' equity will equal the parent company's pre-consolidation owners' equity. This means that, when the parent company uses the equity method, consolidated return on equity (i.e., net income ÷ owners' equity) will equal the parent company's pre-consolidation return on equity!

LO3 Describe the consolidation process subsequent to the date of acquisition when the parent uses the cost method to account for its Equity Investment.

Cost Method

In real world settings, there are many reasons why companies will choose pre-consolidation Equity Investment bookkeeping methods other than the equity method (e.g., the cost method). Recall that investors and creditors rarely, if ever, see the parent's pre-consolidation financial statements, so the specific method the parent chooses is unobservable. Also, proposing all of the equity method adjustments can be highly complex for a company of any reasonable size, and especially so when one considers the topic of Chapter 4: elimination of intercompany transactions and balances. Because the consolidation process is mostly an exercise in reversing the Equity Investment bookkeeping applied by the parent company on its pre-consolidation books, many companies opt to not incorporate equity method bookkeeping in their pre-consolidation financial statements. While students often have a more difficult time understanding consolidations when the parent company uses the cost method for its pre-consolidation Equity Investment bookkeeping, in the real world, the bookkeeping and consolidation process can be quite a bit simpler using investment-bookkeeping methods other than the equity method.

Before we describe the cost method and discuss the consolidation process when the parent uses the cost method, we want to repeat an extremely important point: *the consolidated financial statements will look the same, regardless of the pre-consolidation method of Equity Investment bookkeeping applied by the parent company*. However, because parent company's pre-consolidation financial statements will be different under the cost method versus the equity method, the consolidation entries will (out of necessity) be slightly different. We will explore those differences in this section.

Cost Method of Pre-Consolidation Bookkeeping

As we already mentioned, companies use the cost method of pre-consolidation bookkeeping because it is much easier to apply than the equity method. Under the cost method, the Equity Investment balance always remains <u>unchanged</u> at its original acquisition-date amount,[11] and any dividends received by the parent are recorded as dividend income. Recall that under the equity method, the Equity Investment account would not be reported at its original cost, but, instead, would reflect an increase related to equity income, a decrease related to dividends received and a decrease related to the AAP amortization (or increase if the amortizable AAP is negative). Exhibit 3.6 illustrates these differences between the cost and equity methods.

EXHIBIT 3.6	Comparison of Cost and Equity Pre-Consolidation Bookkeeping Methods		
Cost Method		**Equity Method**	
(+) Equity Investment (−)		**(+) Equity Investment (−)**	
Beginning balance		Beginning balance Equity Income	Dividends received AAP amortization
Ending balance		Ending balance	

To illustrate, let's assume the following facts pertain to a parent company and its wholly owned subsidiary:

1. The parent purchases the subsidiary for $500,000 on January 1, 2016.
2. The subsidiary reports $100,000 of net income during 2016.
3. The subsidiary pays $20,000 of dividends to the parent during 2016.
4. The parent's investment in the subsidiary includes AAP. During 2016, AAP amortization is $5,000.

Assume that the parent accounts for its investment using the cost method for internal reporting purposes (i.e., pre-consolidation). The parent will make the following journal entries (on its pre-consolidation books) to record (1) the original investment under acquisition accounting and (2) the receipt of dividends under the cost method:

---

[11] This is a subtle point that deserves some emphasis. The acquisition date value for an Equity Investment in a controlled subsidiary is determined by applying the acquisition accounting procedures described in Chapter 2 (i.e., required under FASB ASC 805: Business Combinations). The equity method and cost method (and any other hybrid investment-bookkeeping procedure) are applied after the acquisition date and are independent of the determination of acquisition-date fair value. Thus, regardless of which investment-bookkeeping approach is selected by a company, the acquisition-date recorded value for the Equity Investment account will always be the same.

1.	Equity investment.	500,000	
	Cash		500,000
	(to record the acquisition of subsidiary)		
2.	Cash . . . . :	20,000	
	Dividend income		20,000
	(to record the receipt of dividends under cost method)		

A comparison of cost method and equity method investment accounts is presented in Exhibit 3.7:

EXHIBIT 3.7	Numerical Comparison of Cost and Equity Method Investment Accounts

Cost Method		Equity Method	
(+) Equity Investment (−)		**(+) Equity Investment (−)**	
500,000		500,000	
		100,000	20,000
			5,000
500,000		575,000	

Under the cost method, the Equity Investment is reported on the parent's December 31, 2016 pre-consolidation balance sheet at $500,000, and the parent reports dividend income of $20,000 in its pre-consolidation income statement for the year ended 2016. The subsidiary's dividends have, therefore, increased the parent's pre-consolidation net income by $20,000 during 2016 and have increased the parent's pre-consolidation ending retained earnings by $20,000 through December 31, 2016.

Exhibit 3.8 illustrates the parent-company pre-consolidation income and retained earnings effects of cost method versus equity method Equity Investment accounting.

EXHIBIT 3.8	Effect of Cost and Equity Methods on Parent Pre-Consolidation Net Income and Retained Earnings

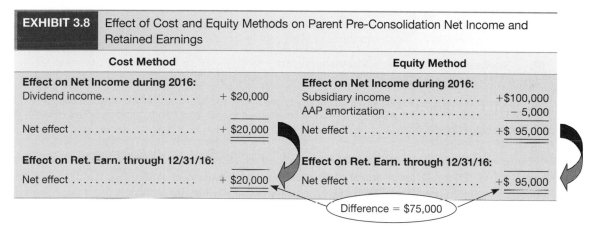

Cost Method		Equity Method	
Effect on Net Income during 2016:		**Effect on Net Income during 2016:**	
Dividend income.	+ $20,000	Subsidiary income	+$100,000
		AAP amortization	− 5,000
Net effect	+ $20,000	Net effect	+$ 95,000
Effect on Ret. Earn. through 12/31/16:		**Effect on Ret. Earn. through 12/31/16:**	
Net effect	+ $20,000	Net effect	+$ 95,000

Difference = $75,000

As we previously mentioned, one reason students prefer consolidating equity method Equity Investments is that the parent's pre-consolidation Net Income and pre-consolidation Stockholders' Equity under the equity method equals *consolidated* Net Income and *consolidated* Stockholders' Equity, respectively. Logically, one can infer that if the Equity Method allows the parent's Net Income and Stockholders' Equity to equal their consolidated totals, then the Cost Method does not provide correct consolidated balances for Net Income or Stockholders' Equity. Indeed, as illustrated in Exhibit 3.8, the difference in these totals is equal to the amount of *undistributed adjusted earnings of the Subsidiary*.

Upon closer scrutiny, you might notice that the $75,000 difference between the cost and the equity method Net Income and Stockholders' Equity (i.e., illustrated in Exhibit 3.8) is equal to the $75,000 difference between the cost and the equity method Equity Investment accounts (i.e., illustrated in Exhibit 3.7). That is, under the cost method, the Equity Investment account is reported on the parent's balance sheet at its original cost of $500,000. In contrast, had the parent used the equity method to account for its Equity Investment, it would report the Equity Investment at $575,000. While mechanically equal, the difference between the cost method and equity method affects consolidation not through the Equity Investment account (remember, the investment account is eliminated!), but through the fact that cost method/equity method differences will accumulate, over the years, in the Retained Earnings of the parent company. We will, however, use the mechanical equivalence we identified in the Equity Investment account to assist us in arriving at the correct consolidated balance for Retained Earnings.

Why does the cost method versus equity method difference in Retained Earnings accumulate over the years? Because our consolidating entries are not actually recorded by either company. Thus, even though our consolidated financial statements will reflect the correct Net Income and Retained Earnings totals (because of consolidation entries) and these totals are the same that the parent would report under the equity method, the parent's accounting records will continue to include cost method accounting reflected in the Equity Investment account and in the Stockholders' Equity account—*permanently*.

The Consolidation Process Subsequent to the Date of Acquisition—Cost Method

In consolidating a subsidiary for which the parent company has been applying cost method investment bookkeeping, we propose a slight modification to the **C-E-A-D-I** approach we used under the equity method. Exhibit 3.9 presents a summary of the post-acquisition consolidation entries when the parent uses the cost method:

EXHIBIT 3.9 Post-acquisition Consolidation Entries—Cost Method

[ADJ]	Changes the Equity Investment account and the parent company's retained earnings account to an "as-if-equity-method" basis as of the *beginning of the accounting period*.
[C]	Eliminates all *changes* in the parent's books caused by investment bookkeeping during the year. When the parent uses the cost method to account for the pre-consolidation Equity Investment account it eliminates dividend income.
[E]	Eliminates the portion of the investment account related to the book value of the subsidiary's Stockholders' Equity at the *beginning of the accounting period*. (After this entry, the investment account should equal the beginning of period unamortized AAP, on an "as-if-equity-method" basis.)
[A]	Assigns the remaining Equity Investment account (i.e., unamortized beginning of period AAP) to appropriate asset and liability accounts as of the *beginning of the accounting period*.
[D]	Depreciates/amortizes AAP so that the income statement includes the activity and the balance sheet accounts include ending AAP allocated to the appropriate accounts.
[I]	Eliminates intercompany activity (e.g., sales between parent and subsidiary) and/or intercompany balances (e.g., account payable and account receivable between parent and subsidiary). (This will be covered in Chapter 4.)

Under our slightly modified **C-E-A-D-I** approach for the cost method, the first thing to notice is that entries **[E]**, **[A]**, **[D]** and **[I]** are *identical* to the equity method consolidation entries (see Exhibit 3.1). This occurs because the consolidation entry **[ADJ]** causes the parent's Equity Investment account and Retained Earnings account to equal their beginning of period balances as if the parent company always used the equity method. A logical question is, "why would we want to adjust these balances to an as-if-equity-method basis?" It's because the resulting consolidated financial statements reflect a disaggregated form of the equity method. (Yes, consolidation is just a form of the equity method!) In particular, recall that consolidated net income and consolidated owners' equity are both the same as the parent company's net income and owners' equity when the parent company uses the equity method of pre-consolidation investment bookkeeping (i.e., ROE is identical for the consolidated financial statements and the equity-method pre-consolidation financial statements). So, despite the fact that the Equity Investment account will be completely eliminated after our modified **C-E-A-D-I** consolidation entries, the parent's owners' equity accounts will remain in the financial statements after consolidation and must be brought to an "as-if-equity-method" (i.e., consolidated) basis.

Conceptually, the process of bringing the cost-method Equity Investment account and parent-company retained earnings account to an "as-if-equity-method" (i.e., consolidated) basis is one of (1) backing out the *cumulative* cost-method activity that has been recorded in the parent's retained earnings account since acquisition and (2) inserting the *cumulative* retained earnings activity that would have been recorded if the parent company used the equity method.

We provide the following example to illustrate the required adjustment to convert from the cost method to an "as-if-equity-method" retained earnings balance. Assume that on January 1, 2011, a parent company purchased a subsidiary for $1,000,000. On the date of acquisition, the subsidiary reported book value of equity equal to $950,000, which was comprised of $450,000 of no-par common stock and $500,000 of retained earnings. Independent appraisals revealed that, on the date of acquisition, all of the subsidiary's reported book values of net assets equaled their individual fair values except for an asset that was undervalued by $40,000. This asset has an expected useful life of 10 years. To simplify computations, assume that *each year* between January 1, 2011 and December 31, 2015, the subsidiary reported net income of $20,000 and paid dividends of $10,000. Exhibit 3.10 illustrates the cumulative effect of cost-method and equity-method pre-consolidation investment bookkeeping on the parent's pre-consolidation net income and retained earnings.

EXHIBIT 3.10	Cumulative Effect of Cost and Equity Methods on Parent Pre-Consolidation Net Income and Retained Earnings

Cost Method		Equity Method	
Effect on Net Income Each Year:		**Effect on Net Income Each Year:**	
Dividend income.	+ $10,000	Subsidiary income	+ $20,000
		AAP amortization	− 4,000
Net effect each year	+ $10,000	Net effect each year	+ $16,000
Effect on Ret. Earn. through 12/31/15:		**Effect on Ret. Earn. through 12/31/15:**	
Net effect for 2011	+ $10,000	Net effect for 2011	+ $16,000
Net effect for 2012	+ $10,000	Net effect for 2012	+ $16,000
Net effect for 2013	+ $10,000	Net effect for 2013	+ $16,000
Net effect for 2014	+ $10,000	Net effect for 2014	+ $16,000
Net effect for 2015	+ $10,000	Net effect for 2015	+ $16,000
Cumulative effect through 12/31/2015. . .	+ $50,000	Cumulative effect through 12/31/2015. . .	+ $80,000

Cumulative Difference = $30,000

Obviously, tracking and adjusting for each year of the subsidiary's net income, dividends and the AAP amortization can be fairly arduous. Thus, we propose the following shortcut method for determining the adjustment to the parent's retained earnings on any date (assuming the parent owns 100% of the subsidiary):[12]

$$\text{RE(P) Adjustment from Cost to Equity Method} = \Delta \text{RE(S)}_{\text{Since Acquisition}} - \sum \text{AAP Amort}_{\text{Since Acquisition}}$$

Specifically, when the parent owns 100% of the subsidiary, the retained earnings adjustment for the parent company is equal to the change in the retained earnings balance for the subsidiary from the acquisition date to the date on which we want to calculate consolidated retained earnings minus the cumulative AAP amortization from the acquisition date to the date on which we want to calculate consolidated retained earnings. Let's use the preceding example to show that this approach works. Recall that the retained earnings of the subsidiary equaled $500,000 on the acquisition date. Each year the retained earnings balance will increase for the net income of the subsidiary and decrease for the dividends of the subsidiary, as follows:

		Retained Earnings (on Subsidiary books)	
		$500,000	January 1, 2011 balance
2011 subsidiary dividends	$10,000	20,000	2011 subsidiary net income
2012 subsidiary dividends	10,000	20,000	2012 subsidiary net income
2013 subsidiary dividends	10,000	20,000	2013 subsidiary net income
2014 subsidiary dividends	10,000	20,000	2014 subsidiary net income
2015 subsidiary dividends	10,000	20,000	2015 subsidiary net income
		$550,000	December 31, 2015 balance

---

[12] In Chapter 5, we will discuss the case where the parent owns less than 100% of the subsidiary. To provide a bit of foreshadowing, when the parent owns less than 100% of the subsidiary, the adjustment is determined by multiplying the ownership percentage times the change in the retained earnings of the subsidiary and the cumulative AAP adjustment.

In addition, under the equity method, the parent would have amortized $4,000 per year during January 1, 2011 through December 31, 2015. This amounts to five years of amortization, which equals $20,000 of cumulative "as if" amortization when converting from the cost method to the equity method. Thus the shortcut adjustment to the parent's retained earnings is computed as follows:

$$
\begin{aligned}
\text{RE(P) Adjustment from Cost to Equity Method} &= (\$550,000 - \$500,000) - (5 \times \$4,000) \\
&= \$50,000 - \$20,000 \\
&= \$30,000^{13}
\end{aligned}
$$

So, to adjust the parent company's retained earnings to an "as-if-equity-method" (i.e., consolidated) basis, the parent company would need to propose the following journal entry at December 31, 2015:

[ADJ]	Equity investment.	30,000	
	Retained earnings (parent).		30,000
	(to adjust the Equity Investment from cost to equity method)		

Although the Equity Investment account will be eliminated in consolidation (i.e., via consolidation entries [E], [A], [D] and [I]), the amount of the adjustment to the Equity Investment account can also be explained by the difference between what would have been recorded in the investment account under the equity method and what was recorded under the cost method. Specifically, under the cost method, the investment account did not change (i.e., it remained at its acquisition-date value of $500,000). In comparison, if the parent company would have used the equity method, the Equity Investment account would have increased by the $16,000 annual equity method income from the subsidiary (i.e., $20,000 net income − $4,000 AAP amortization), and would have decreased by the $10,000 annual dividend paid by the subsidiary. This is a net annual increase in the investment account of $6,000, which amounts to $30,000 over five years through December 31, 2015.

Finally, we reiterate a very important point: **the [ADJ] adjustment, just like the other C-E-A-D-I consolidation entries, is made only on our consolidation spreadsheet, not to the accounting records of the parent.** The parent will continue to use the cost method for its Equity Investment in its own pre-consolidation accounting records, which means that next year, the [ADJ] entry will have another year of accumulated net income, accumulated dividends and cumulative AAP amortization to incorporate into the adjustment.

Example of Consolidation Subsequent to the Date of Acquisition—Cost Method

To illustrate the consolidation process when the parent uses the cost method, we assume that the parent acquired its subsidiary on January 1, 2013. It is now December 31, 2016. Since the acquisition date, the parent used the cost method to account for its Equity Investment. Also, assume the following facts:

Original cost of Equity Investment on 1/1/2013.		$550,000
Subsidiary's common stock on 1/1/2013.	$100,000	
Subsidiary's APIC on 1/1/2013	125,000	
Subsidiary's retained earnings on 1/1/2013.	225,000	450,000
AAP on 1/1/2013		100,000
Unamortized AAP at 12/31/2015		40,000
Unamortized AAP at 12/31/2016		20,000
Annual depreciation of AAP		20,000
Subsidiary retained earnings on 12/31/2015 (i.e., BOY)		425,000
Dividend paid by subsidiary to parent during 2016 (recognized as income by parent). . .		10,000

---

[13] We believe students can benefit from considering why this shortcut adjustment approach works. The process of adjusting the parent's retained earnings from the cost method to the equity method (i.e., consolidation) is a process of removing cost method bookkeeping and inserting equity method bookkeeping. At its core, this is a process of removing the cumulative effect of the subsidiary's dividends from the retained earnings of the parent and inserting the cumulative effect of subsidiary's net income. Well, adding the cumulative sum of the net income of the subsidiary and subtracting the cumulative sum of the dividends of the subsidiary is the same as adding the change in retained earnings (i.e., Σ Net Income − Σ Dividends = Δ Retained Earnings). Because the cost method has no amortization of the AAP, the parent's retained earnings also needs to be adjusted for the cumulative amortization that would have been recognized if the parent company used the equity method since the acquisition date.

Because the parent used the cost method to account for its Equity Investment in the subsidiary, the Equity Investment account at both January 1, 2016 and December 31, 2016 equals the original cost of the investment: $550,000. If the parent, instead, used the equity method to account for the Equity Investment, the parent would have recorded the following cumulative changes to the parent company retained earnings (i.e., to make it appear "as-if-equity-method" which is the same as consolidated) and the Equity Investment account through December 31, 2015 (i.e., the <u>beginning</u> of the year of consolidation):

Change in subsidiary Retained Earnings 1/1/2013 through 12/31/2015 (i.e., $425,000 − $225,000)	$200,000
Cumulative AAP amortization (1/1/2013 through 12/31/2015).	(60,000)
Cumulative adjustment of Equity Investment (through 12/31/2015)	$140,000

Because most of our Equity Investment-related consolidation entries are at the beginning of year (BOY), we propose the following "catch up" adjustment in our consolidation working paper to (1) adjust the parent company retained earnings to equal its correct, consolidated (i.e., "as-if-equity-method") BOY balance, (2) allow us to eventually eliminate the book value of the BOY Equity Investment account against the BOY Stockholders Equity of the subsidiary in consolidating entry [E] and (3) allow us to eventually assign the BOY AAP to the appropriate net assets in consolidating entry [A].

	Equity investment (P) @ BOY	140,000	
[ADJ]	Retained earnings (P) @ BOY		140,000
	(to adjust the Equity Investment account and Retained Earnings from cost to equity method)		

Following are explanations for each of the remaining consolidation entries:

[C]	Dividend income (P)	10,000		Eliminates changes caused by parent's (cost) Investment bookkeeping during the year.
	Dividends (S)		10,000	
[E]	Retained earnings (S) @ BOY.	425,000		
	Common stock (S) @ BOY	100,000		Eliminate the BOY stockholders' equity of subsidiary.
	APIC (S) @ BOY	125,000		
	Equity investment (P) @ BOY		650,000	
[A]	Building, net (S) @ BOY	40,000		Record BOY AAP related to building:
	Equity investment (P) @ BOY		40,000	

Original amt.	$100,000
Depreciation to 12/31/15	(60,000)
BOY Book value.	$ 40,000

[D]	Depreciation expense (S).	20,000		Record 2016 depreciation related to AAP.
	Building, net (S)		20,000	
[I]	No intercompany items until Chapter 4			

After making the [ADJ] "catchup" adjustment, the only difference in the **C-E-A-D-I** entries from those we presented for the equity method is the change in the income account affected in the [C] entry under the cost method. Under the cost method, the parent records the dividends it receives as dividend income and does not report its proportionate share of the subsidiary's net income. Therefore, the [C] consolidation entry for the cost method is actually much easier than the equity method entry: it merely reverses the dividend income.

Exhibit 3.11 includes the completed consolidation spreadsheet, including the [ADJ] and **C-E-A-D-I** entries.

EXHIBIT 3.11 Consolidation When Parent Uses the Cost Method for the Pre-Consolidation Equity Investment

			Consolidation Entries				
Parent Uses Cost Method	**Parent**	**Subsidiary**		**Dr**		**Cr**	**Consolidated**
2016 Income Statement:							
Sales	$5,000,000	$ 960,000					$5,960,000
Cost of goods sold	(2,700,000)	(432,000)					(3,132,000)
Gross profit	2,300,000	528,000					2,828,000
Dividend income	10,000		[C]	$ 10,000			0
Operating expenses	(1,932,000)	(357,000)	[D]	20,000			(2,309,000)
Net income	$ 378,000	$ 171,000					$ 519,000
2016 Statement of retained earnings:							
BOY retained earnings	$1,424,000	$ 425,000	[E]	425,000	[ADJ]	$140,000	$1,564,000
Net income	378,000	171,000					519,000
Dividends	(50,000)	(10,000)			[C]	10,000	(50,000)
Ending retained earnings	$1,752,000	$ 586,000					$2,033,000
Balance sheet at 12/31/2016:							
Assets							
Cash	$ 88,000	$ 70,000					$ 158,000
Accounts receivable	487,000	210,000					697,000
Inventory	833,000	250,000					1,083,000
Building, net	2,709,000	1,000,000	[A]	40,000	[D]	20,000	3,729,000
Equity investment	550,000		[ADJ]	140,000	[E]	650,000	0
					[A]	40,000	
	$4,667,000	$1,530,000					$5,667,000
Liabilities and stockholders' equity							
Accounts payable	$ 477,000	$ 289,000					$ 766,000
Other current liabilities	264,000	230,000					494,000
Long-term liabilities	312,000	200,000					512,000
Common stock	1,238,000	100,000	[E]	100,000			1,238,000
APIC	624,000	125,000	[E]	125,000			624,000
Retained earnings	1,752,000	586,000					2,033,000
	$4,667,000	$1,530,000		$860,000		$860,000	$5,667,000

Cost Method

GuidedExamples MBC

TOPIC REVIEW 3

Consolidation Subsequent to Date of Acquisition—Cost Method

Assume that a parent company acquired, for $725,000, 100% of the outstanding voting common stock of a subsidiary on January 1, 2013. The purchase price was $75,000 in excess of the subsidiary's $650,000 book value of Stockholders' Equity on the acquisition date, and that excess was assigned to a portfolio of licenses that have $0 pre-acquisition book value and an average useful life of 10 years. On the acquisition date, the subsidiary's retained earnings account was equal to $312,500. The parent company applies the cost method of pre-consolidation Equity Investment bookkeeping. The parent and subsidiary financial statement information for the year ending December 31, 2016 follows:

	Parent	Subsidiary
Income statement:		
Sales.	$15,000,000	$2,100,000
Cost of goods sold.	(10,500,000)	(1,350,000)
Gross profit.	4,500,000	750,000
Dividend income.	47,250	
Operating expenses	(2,850,000)	(585,000)
Net income.	$ 1,697,250	$ 165,000
Statement of retained earnings:		
BOY retained earnings	$ 3,374,500	$ 850,000
Net income.	1,697,250	165,000
Dividends	(390,000)	(47,250)
Ending retained earnings	$ 4,681,750	967,750
Balance sheet:		
Assets		
Cash	$ 1,025,250	$ 389,250
Accounts receivable.	1,920,000	522,000
Inventory.	2,910,000	670,500
Equity investment.	725,000	
Building, net	9,500,000	875,000
	$16,080,250	$2,456,750
Liabilities and stockholders' equity		
Current liabilities.	$ 2,155,500	$ 472,500
Long-term liabilities	4,968,000	679,000
Common stock.	2,452,500	150,000
APIC	1,822,500	187,500
Retained earnings	4,681,750	967,750
	$16,080,250	$2,456,750

Required

Prepare the consolidation spreadsheet.

The solution to this review problem can be found on page 178.

ACCOUNTING FOR GOODWILL

Goodwill is an asset like other intangible assets that we purchase in an acquisition. Although the accounting is a bit different from other intangible assets, it must, nevertheless, meet the conceptual definition of an asset in order to be recognized on the balance sheet. That requires an affirmative answer to both of these questions:

LO4 Describe the accounting for Goodwill and Bargain Acquisition Gains.

1. Does the parent company *control* the Goodwill asset?
2. Will the Goodwill asset provide *future benefits*?

In a business combination that qualifies for the Acquisition Method, the answer to the first question is, "yes." The parent company obtained control of the Goodwill asset when it acquired the subsidiary. The second question, however, must be answered each year. That is, Goodwill must be evaluated annually for impairment (i.e., loss of future benefits), and, if it is found to be impaired, it must be written down just like any other asset. In this section, we discuss how Goodwill is initially recognized and is subsequently evaluated for impairment.

Recognition of Goodwill

Goodwill is included in the purchase price for the investee company, and is recognized as an asset in the consolidated balance sheet. The FASB ASC Glossary defines Goodwill as follows:

> **Goodwill** is an asset representing the future economic benefits arising from other assets acquired in a business combination that are not individually identified and separately recognized.

Goodwill is a *residual* asset, which means that it is the amount left over after we have first assigned the purchase price to all purchased identifiable tangible and intangible assets, and assumed liabilities:

	Total fair value of the investee company
−	The acquisition-date fair value of the identifiable assets acquired and the liabilities assumed
=	Goodwill

In the acquisition we describe in the previous section of this chapter, the parent company purchased all of the outstanding common stock of its subsidiary for $1,500,000 and assigned fair values as follows:

Purchase price	$1,500,000
Book value of subsidiary	1,000,000
Acquisition Accounting Premium (AAP)	$ 500,000
AAP assigned to identifiable net assets:	
Undervalued PPE	200,000
Patent	175,000
Goodwill	$ 125,000

Because the parent is acquiring all of the outstanding common stock of the subsidiary, there are no noncontrolling shareholders, and the value of the Goodwill asset purchased is equal to the purchase price for the subsidiary less the fair value of its identifiable net tangible and intangible assets.[14]

Determining the value assigned to Goodwill represents the culmination of a difficult, judgment-intensive process. Acquiring companies must first identify and measure each acquired identifiable tangible and intangible asset and each liability assumed (Exhibit 2.12 includes an extensive listing of common identifiable intangible assets). This process requires intensive involvement of all levels of management and typically involves hiring consultants and valuation specialists. The SEC scrutinizes reported acquisitions very carefully, making sure that companies value all tangible and intangible assets before assigning any of the acquisition price to Goodwill.

Goodwill appears on the consolidated balance sheet as an asset. And, like many other intangible assets, this Goodwill asset did not appear directly on the parent's pre-consolidation balance sheet. However, it was there—*implicitly*. As we describe in Chapter 1, Goodwill is included in the Equity Investment account, and that amount is separately reported in the consolidation balance sheet, just like any other post-acquisition asset or liability (e.g., Patent assets).

Amortization of Intangible Assets and Goodwill Impairment Evaluation

The amortization of Goodwill depends on two factors:

1. Whether the acquiring company qualifies as a "private company" (i.e., entities that are not public business entities, not-for-profit entities, or employee benefit plans) according to the definitions in the FASB ASC Master Glossary, and

2. Whether the acquiring company elects to adopt the Goodwill amortization exception available to private companies.

---

[14] We will revisit the computation of Goodwill again in Chapter 5 when we discuss noncontrolling shareholders and discuss then how we value those noncontrolling interests. However, the fundamental definition of Goodwill remains the same: it is the fair value of the entire *entity* (i.e., controlling and noncontrolling interests) minus the fair values of the identifiable assets and liabilities of the acquired entity. The case where a parent company acquires 100 percent of a subsidiary is a special case in which the fair value of the entire entity equals the Acquisition Method price for the subsidiary.

If the acquiring company satisfies both of these conditions, then the acquiring company is required to amortize the Goodwill "on a straight-line basis over 10 years, or less than 10 years if the entity demonstrates that another useful life is more appropriate." Although this seems like a fairly straightforward and simple alternative for private companies, private company managers need to be very careful in adopting this GAAP exception. If a private company attempts to transition to being a public business entity (e.g., by registering its common stock with the SEC and issuing the shares to investors via an Initial Public Offering), then the company will be required to retroactively restate its financial statements without the private-company exception included in the financial statements.

For companies that cannot (or do not) avail themselves of the private company exception (e.g., because they are public or aspire, someday, to be public), then Goodwill is not amortized like most identifiable intangible assets. This treatment was adopted by the IASB and the FASB because Goodwill is considered to have an "indefinite" (not *infinite*) life. As a practical matter, the life of Goodwill should be limited; we just don't know its useful life when we acquire it. As a result, Goodwill, like all other indefinite-lived assets, is not amortized (FASB ASC 350-30-35-1). Examples of other indefinite-lived intangible assets include trademarks, trade names and valuable renewable licenses.[15] Along with Goodwill, all indefinite-lived intangible assets must be evaluated, at least annually, for impairment.[16] Further, companies must conduct this annual evaluation during the same time of year (i.e., companies cannot "game" the impairment evaluation by conducting it in the first quarter one year and then the fourth quarter in the following year).

Some intangible assets, like our Patent assets, have a remaining *legal* life (e.g., 10 years in our previous example) that automatically limits their economic life. Other intangible assets, such as an acquired customer list, have *economic* lives that must be estimated in a manner similar to that used for tangible depreciable assets, like machinery. Regardless of an intangible asset's legal life, companies are required to consider the asset's expected economic life in determining the amortization period. For example, if a parent company acquires a Patent asset with a remaining 10-year legal life, but did not expect positive net cash flows from the Patent after six years, then the company must amortize the asset over no greater than six years (and quite possibly less than that).

According to the FASB ASC Master Glossary, "Impairment is the condition that exists when the carrying amount of a long-lived asset (asset group) exceeds its fair value." In your previous introductory and/or intermediate accounting courses, you learned about impairment accounting for long-lived tangible assets. Like those impairments, Goodwill impairment involves a qualitative assessment and a multi-stage test before it is measured and recognized in the financial statements. If we test Goodwill for impairment and find it to be impaired, we must write it down with a journal entry similar to the following (assuming the parent uses the equity method):[17]

Equity income.	xxx	
Equity investment*.		xxx
(to write down the book value of Goodwill)		

*The entry is to Equity-Investment-related accounts because the Goodwill asset is a component of the investment account. The Goodwill asset does not appear separately on the parent's pre-consolidation balance sheet. The consolidated financial statements will reflect a loss on Goodwill impairment and a reduction in the balance of consolidated Goodwill.

This entry reduces the book value of Goodwill and records the write-down as a loss in the income statement, thus reducing profit. After Goodwill is written down as impaired, it cannot be subsequently increased.

---

[15] The value of the licenses can far exceed the cost of license renewal. Therefore, despite the legal expiration date for a broadcast license, current GAAP requires companies to look at the most likely economic life of the asset. Because a rational manager would never allow the license to lapse, the license most likely has an indefinite life.

[16] As mentioned in Chapter 2, private companies that avail themselves of the Goodwill amortization exception are not required to test Goodwill for impairment on an annual basis; instead, Goodwill is tested for impairment if an event occurs or circumstances change that indicate that the fair value of the entity may be below its carrying amount. This impairment evaluation is similar to the Optional Qualitative Assessment illustrated in Exhibit 3.12 and described later in this chapter.

[17] If the parent company uses the cost method, then (most likely) no adjustment is made on the parent's pre-consolidation books. Instead, the Goodwill write off is tracked in the AAP amortization schedule and is recognized in the consolidated financial statements via consolidation entries.

PRACTICE INSIGHT

Determining the Useful Lives of Intangible Assets   According to FASB ASC 350-30-35-3, "[t]he estimate of the useful life of an intangible asset to an entity shall be based on an analysis of all pertinent factors, in particular, all of the following factors with no one factor being more presumptive than the other:

a. The expected use of the asset by the entity.

b. The expected useful life of another asset or a group of assets to which the useful life of the intangible asset may relate.

c. Any legal, regulatory, or contractual provisions that may limit the useful life. The cash flows and useful lives of intangible assets that are based on legal rights are constrained by the duration of those legal rights. Thus, the useful lives of such intangible assets cannot extend beyond the length of their legal rights and may be shorter.

d. The entity's own historical experience in renewing or extending similar arrangements, consistent with the intended use of the asset by the entity, regardless of whether those arrangements have explicit renewal or extension provisions...

e. The effects of obsolescence, demand, competition, and other economic factors (such as the stability of the industry, known technological advances, legislative action that results in an uncertain or changing regulatory environment, and expected changes in distribution channels).

f. The level of maintenance expenditures required to obtain the expected future cash flows from the asset (for example, a material level of required maintenance in relation to the carrying amount of the asset may suggest a very limited useful life). As in determining the useful life of depreciable tangible assets, regular maintenance may be assumed but enhancements may not.

Further, if an income approach is used to measure the fair value of an intangible asset, in determining the useful life of the intangible asset for amortization purposes, an entity shall consider the period of expected cash flows used to measure the fair value of the intangible asset adjusted as appropriate for the entity-specific factors in this paragraph."

If no legal, regulatory, contractual, competitive, economic, or other factors limit the useful life of an intangible asset to the reporting entity, the useful life of the asset shall be considered to be indefinite. The term *indefinite* does not mean infinite. Indefinite lived intangible assets must be tested at least annually for impairment.

Assigning Goodwill to Reporting Units

If a private company chooses to adopt the Goodwill amortization exception, then FASB ASC 350-20-35-65 requires the company to also make a policy election of whether to test Goodwill for impairment at the entire-company level or at the "reporting unit" level. For all public companies (and all private companies that do not adopt the Goodwill-amortization exception), all Goodwill impairment tests are performed at the reporting unit level (FASB ASC 350-20-35).[18] For the purpose of testing Goodwill for impairment, acquired assets and assumed liabilities must be assigned to individual reporting units as of the acquisition date if *both* (a) the asset will be employed in or the liability relates to the operations of a reporting unit, and (b) the asset or liability will be considered in determining the fair value of the reporting unit (FASB ASC 350-20-35-39). After the identifiable assets and liabilities are assigned to the reporting unit, then the acquiring company must calculate the amount of Goodwill assigned to each reporting unit.

---

[18] For now, we will make the simplifying assumption that reporting units are the same as companies' segments that are disclosed in the footnotes. This characterization of reporting units is an oversimplification. While companies' "operating segments" (as defined in FASB ASC Topic 280, and discussed in Chapter 11) are the starting point for defining reporting units, these units can actually be defined at a much more granular level than the operating segment or "reportable segment" level (i.e., the segments actually disclosed in the footnotes of the financial statements).

According to ASC 350-20-35-42 through 35-43, the amount of Goodwill that is assigned to a reporting unit is determined in a manner similar to the way in which the amount of Goodwill recognized in a business combination is determined. That is:[19]

a. An entity determines the fair value of the acquired business (or portion thereof) to be included in a reporting unit (the fair value of the individual assets acquired and liabilities assumed that are assigned to the reporting unit),

b. Any excess of the fair value of the acquired business (or portion thereof) over the fair value of the individual assets acquired and liabilities assumed that are assigned to the reporting unit is the amount of Goodwill assigned to that reporting unit.

As you can imagine, the assignment of Goodwill to reporting units is an extremely challenging activity that requires a considerable amount of professional judgment.

PRACTICE INSIGHT

Assignment of Goodwill to Reporting Units   After a subsidiary is acquired, Goodwill is recognized. The Goodwill impairment rules require that Goodwill must be assigned to the reporting units that realize its benefits. How is that assignment performed in practice? Mr. Dana Russell, CFO of Novell, Inc., provides some insight.

"We are organized by business units that are associated with particular product groupings. So, an acquisition will typically be assigned to a particular business unit based on its product groupings and the Goodwill associated with that acquisition is allocated to that business unit. Occasionally, the products acquired in an acquisition may pertain to more than one business unit. In that case, the Goodwill is likewise allocated across the business units to which it pertains."

The Annual Evaluation of Goodwill Impairment

Private companies that adopt the Goodwill amortization exception are not required to test Goodwill for impairment on an annual basis; instead, Goodwill is tested for impairment if an event occurs or circumstances change that indicate that the fair value of the entity may be below its carrying amount. In addition, Goodwill can be evaluated for impairment at the entity level or the reporting unit level, depending on what the company elected when acquiring the subsidiary.

In contrast, public companies and private companies that do not adopt the Goodwill amortization exception are required to annually evaluate Goodwill to determine if it is impaired. Recall that Goodwill is embedded in the Equity Investment account. That account also contains the book value of the net assets we purchased plus the AAP. Both of these components are assigned to individual reporting units as described in the previous subsection. These assigned amounts will constitute the carrying values of the reporting units. The Goodwill impairment tests are conducted on each of the reporting units.

Prior to 2012, all companies were required to perform the annual quantitative assessment that we describe below. Responding to negative feedback from companies about the cost of performing this annual quantitative assessment, in 2011 the FASB revised the requirements for annual Goodwill impairment testing to allow companies the annual option to assess *qualitative* factors to determine whether it is necessary to perform the quantitative two-step Goodwill impairment test (described below). The qualitative test allows a lower-cost means to determine whether it is more likely than not that the fair value of a reporting unit is less than its carrying amount.

---

[19] If Goodwill is to be assigned to a reporting unit that has not been assigned any of the assets acquired or liabilities assumed in that acquisition, the amount of Goodwill to be assigned to that unit can be determined by applying a "with-and-without" computation. That is, the difference between the fair value of that reporting unit *before* the acquisition and its fair value *after* the acquisition represents the amount of Goodwill to be assigned to that reporting unit.

According to FASB ASC 350-20-35-3C, in performing the qualitative assessment, companies should consider the totality of "relevant events and circumstances" that suggest it is more likely than not that the fair value of a reporting unit is less than its carrying amount.[20] Examples of these factors include:[21]

a. Macroeconomic conditions such as a deterioration in general economic conditions, limitations on accessing capital, fluctuations in foreign exchange rates, or other developments in equity and credit markets

b. Industry and market considerations such as a deterioration in the environment in which an entity operates, an increased competitive environment, a decline in market-dependent multiples or metrics (consider in both absolute terms and relative to peers), a change in the market for an entity's products or services, or a regulatory or political development

c. Cost factors such as increases in raw materials, labor, or other costs that have a negative effect on earnings and cash flows

d. Overall financial performance such as negative or declining cash flows or a decline in actual or planned revenue or earnings compared with actual and projected results of relevant prior periods

e. Other relevant entity-specific events such as changes in management, key personnel, strategy, or customers; contemplation of bankruptcy; or litigation

f. Events affecting a reporting unit such as a change in the composition or carrying amount of its net assets, a more-likely-than-not expectation of selling or disposing all, or a portion, of a reporting unit, the testing for recoverability of a significant asset group within a reporting unit, or recognition of a goodwill impairment loss in the financial statements of a subsidiary that is a component of a reporting unit

g. If applicable, a sustained decrease in share price (consider in both absolute terms and relative to peers).

If, after evaluating the "totality of the events and circumstances," a company determines that it is more likely than not that the fair value of a reporting unit is *greater* than its carrying amount, then no further evaluation is needed. The goodwill is not considered impaired. If, however, a company determines that it is more likely than not that the fair value of a reporting unit is *less* than its carrying amount, then the company is required to proceed through the two-step impairment test.

The first part of the two-step Goodwill impairment test is to examine whether a given *reporting unit* is impaired. If it is not, then the company can cease testing after the first step. If it is, then the second part of the test is designed to identify whether the impairment pertains to *the Goodwill asset that has been assigned to that reporting unit* or to its other components (i.e., the identifiable net tangible and intangible assets). Exhibit 3.12 illustrates the process by which this determination can be made.

The Goodwill impairment test has two steps:

1. **Is the fair value of the reporting unit less than its carrying value?** This part of the test is designed to screen potential impairments so that companies only record significantly large reductions in the value of Goodwill (i.e., so large that the decline in Goodwill value is not offset by increases in the value of other identifiable net assets). In this case, the value of the entire reporting unit would have to decline below its carrying value.

2. **Is the Goodwill *component* of the Equity Investment account impaired?** This step is only conducted if the reporting unit fails the first step (i.e., fair value < carrying value).[22] In step 2, the

---

[20] Companies have an unconditional option to bypass this qualitative assessment for any individual reporting unit in any period and proceed directly to the quantitative two-step Goodwill impairment test (described below). Companies can resume utilizing the qualitative assessment for any reporting unit in any subsequent period.

[21] The FASB is careful to point out that none of the following factors is more important than the others; they all need to be considered and weighed against each other.

[22] According to FASB ASC 350-20-35-8A, the second step of the quantitative Goodwill impairment test must also always be performed if the carrying amount of a reporting unit is zero or negative. In evaluating whether it is more likely than not that the goodwill of a reporting unit with a zero or negative carrying amount is impaired, an entity also should take into consideration whether there are significant differences between the carrying amount and the estimated fair value of its assets and liabilities, and the existence of significant unrecognized intangible assets.

EXHIBIT 3.12	Annual Goodwill Impairment Evaluation

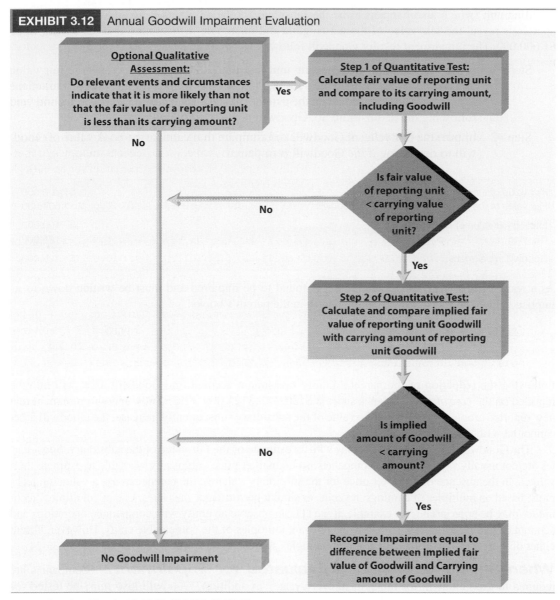

Source: Based on Flowchart in FASB ASC 350-20-55-25

company computes the current fair value of Goodwill assigned to the reporting unit in a manner similar to the way Goodwill was initially computed when the subsidiary was acquired. That is, fair values are estimated for all of the identifiable net assets in the reporting unit and the net sum of these fair values is deducted from the fair value of the reporting unit (i.e., as a stand-alone entity) to arrive at the implied fair value of Goodwill. The implied fair value of Goodwill is then compared to the carrying value of Goodwill assigned to the reporting unit.

An Example   We illustrate the two-step test by assuming that the subsidiary described in the two-year equity-method consolidation examples at the beginning of the chapter (i.e., Exhibits 3.3 through 3.5) is a separately identified reporting unit. In that example, under the equity method of pre-consolidation Equity Investment bookkeeping, the carrying value of the Equity Investment is $1,848,053 and the carrying value of Goodwill is $125,000 at the end of the second year following the acquisition of its subsidiary.[23] Let's assume for this example that we estimate the fair value of the

---

[23] If the parent company instead uses the cost method of pre-consolidation Equity Investment bookkeeping, then parent company would need to prepare and "as-if-equity-method" Equity Investment account on which to conduct the impairment evaluation. Of course, if the subsidiary is split up into numerous reporting units, then the equity method (i.e., consolidated) carrying value would need to be determined for each of the reporting units.

reporting unit (which also happens to be the subsidiary) to be $1,700,000. In addition, independent appraisals reveal the fair value of the net tangible and intangible assets, other than Goodwill, to be $1,600,000. The impairment test for Goodwill follows:

Step #1—Is the fair value of the reporting unit less than its book value? Yes—the fair value of $1,700,000 is less than the $1,848,053 book value (i.e., the carrying value) of the Equity Investment account on the parent's balance sheet at the end of the second year following the acquisition. So, Goodwill is *potentially* impaired.

Step #2—Impute the fair value of Goodwill and compare that value to the book value of Goodwill to determine if the Goodwill is impaired.

Fair value of the subsidiary.	$1,700,000
Fair value of the net assets exclusive of Goodwill	1,600,000
Implied fair value of Goodwill	$ 100,000
Carrying value of Goodwill	125,000
Goodwill impairment	$ (25,000)

As a result of this test, the Goodwill asset is found to be impaired and must be written down to its implied value with the following journal entry in the parent's books:

Equity income.	25,000	
Equity investment		25,000
(to write down the book value of Goodwill)		

Following the reduction of the parent's Equity Investment account, the Goodwill asset will now be reported on the *consolidated* balance sheet at $100,000 ($125,000 − $25,000), and will remain at that new reported amount (i.e., should the value of the subsidiary subsequently increase, the Goodwill asset cannot be written up).[24]

The Goodwill impairment test begins with an estimate of the fair value of the subsidiary. Subsidiaries are not usually publicly traded companies, so no market price is typically available to estimate their value.[25] In the absence of a market price for the subsidiary's shares, the parent can use a valuation technique based on multiples of earnings, revenue, or similar performance measures. Use of "multiples" techniques may be appropriate, for example, if we (1) can observe an entity with comparable operations and economic characteristics and (2) know the relevant multiples of the comparable entity. However, absent either of these two conditions, the use of a multiples approach is not appropriate (ASC 350-20-35-24).

When Should Goodwill Be Evaluated for Impairment?
Companies are required to test Goodwill for impairment every year.[26] In addition, Goodwill also must be tested for impairment between the annual evaluation dates "if an event occurs or circumstances change that would more likely than not reduce the fair value of a reporting unit below its carrying amount" (FASB ASC 350-20-35-30). Examples of these events and circumstances are the same examples that we previously described (e.g., macroeconomic factors, industry or market considerations, cost factors) in conjunction with the optional qualitative assessment associated with the annual Goodwill impairment test.

---

[24] Advanced accounting texts occasionally suggest that Goodwill impairments do not result in a reduction of the Equity Investment account recorded on the parent's books. Some of this confusion stems from misinterpretation of the equity method rules in FASB ASC 323-10-35, which state that "equity method Goodwill shall not be reviewed for impairment," but, that "equity method investments shall continue to be reviewed for impairment." These equity method guidelines apply to equity method investments that are not consolidated. In the case of a consolidated subsidiary, the Goodwill is actually included on the parent's books in the Equity Investment account. Thus, the only correct bookkeeping adjustment is for the parent to write off the Goodwill by crediting the account in which it is recorded (i.e., the Equity Investment account). Of course, this bookkeeping adjustment has no bearing on the reporting of the write-off in the consolidated financial statements.

[25] Even if a quoted market price exists for a subsidiary, "[a]n acquiring entity often is willing to pay more for equity securities that give it a controlling interest than an investor would pay for a number of equity securities representing less than a controlling interest. . . . The quoted market price of an individual equity security, therefore, need not be the sole measurement basis of the fair value of a reporting unit" (FASB ASC 350-20-35-23).

[26] "The annual Goodwill impairment test may be performed any time during the fiscal year provided the test is performed at the same time every year. Different reporting units may be tested for impairment at different times" (FASB ASC 350-20-35-28).

PRACTICE INSIGHT

Impairment of Goodwill   Textbook examples of impairment testing for Goodwill usually provide information relating to the value of the subsidiary together with the fair value of its tangible and identifiable intangible assets and the fair value of its liabilities. In the real world, these values are difficult to estimate, especially for knowledge-based companies.

In the software industry, for example, technology has a relatively short life span and employees frequently move from company to company. It doesn't take long, therefore, for the technology and employees of an acquired software company to disappear. The acquired Goodwill, however, typically remains on the balance sheet long after the other acquired assets have disappeared.

Valuing the remaining Goodwill can be a messy process. Mr. Dana Russell, CFO of Novell, Inc., sheds some light on the practical aspects of the Goodwill impairment issue with the following description:

> As companies are acquired, the Goodwill is allocated to the segments of the acquiring company to which it pertains. The Goodwill loses its identity, so to speak. The cash flow analysis in future periods pertains to all of the products in that segment. That analysis is used to determine whether you have impairment. The impairment, if any, applies to all of the products in that segment, not necessarily to the particular Goodwill asset purchased in a single acquisition. For example, one of our segments is very profitable and its forecasted cash flows do not lead to an impairment conclusion. But, if you look at the specific Goodwill asset for a single acquisition, the specific products that were originally associated with that Goodwill might no longer exist, resulting in an impairment conclusion for that particular portion of the Goodwill asset. The Goodwill impairment test is just not that granular.

TOPIC REVIEW 4

Goodwill Impairment Test

Assume that the parent company acquires a subsidiary and recognizes $300,000 of Goodwill in the assignment of fair values. The current balance of the Equity Investment account on the parent's balance sheet is $1,000,000. Recent evidence indicates that the subsidiary has a fair value of $900,000 and the fair value of the subsidiary's net assets is estimated to be $700,000. The parent company determined that the subsidiary is a separate reporting unit.

Required

Assume that the company decided to forego the option to perform a qualitative assessment to determine whether it is more likely than not that the fair value of the reporting unit is less than the carrying value of the reporting unit. Perform the quantitative two-step Goodwill impairment test and make the required journal entry for impairment, if necessary.

The solution to this review problem can be found on page 178.

Accounting for a Bargain Acquisition

As we discuss above, we compute Goodwill purchased in the acquisition of 100 percent of a company using the following formula:

	Total fair value of the investee company
−	The acquisition-date fair value of the identifiable assets acquired and the liabilities assumed
=	Goodwill

A **bargain acquisition** is said to occur if the total fair value of the investee company is *less* than the acquisition-date amounts of the identifiable assets acquired and the liabilities assumed (i.e., the amount computed for Goodwill is *negative*).[27] In that case, the investor recognizes the negative Goodwill as an ordinary **gain** in its income statement on the acquisition date.

To illustrate the computation and recognition of a bargain acquisition, assume that the parent company acquires a subsidiary, a private company, for $200. Because the former owners of the subsidiary need to dispose of their investment by a specified date, they do not have sufficient time to market the company to multiple potential buyers. On the acquisition date, the fair value of the subsidiary's identifiable net assets is $250, and the book value of the subsidiary's identifiable net assets is $100. Our computation of Goodwill acquired in the purchase of the subsidiary is as follows:

	$200	Purchase price of the subsidiary
−	250	Fair value of the subsidiary's identifiable net assets
=	$ (50)	Unexplained negative residual (i.e., Bargain Purchase Gain)

The acquisition date journal entry recorded by the parent company will equal the fair value of consideration exchanged for the subsidiary's shares, as follows:

Equity investment.	200	
Cash		200
(to record the purchase of the Equity Investment in the subsidiary)		

However, immediately upon purchase, the parent company will recognize the Bargain Acquisition Gain. This is basically just an immediate equity method amortization of the AAP for the amount of Bargain Acquisition Gain. Thus, on the acquisition date, the parent will make the following consolidating entries to consolidate the controlling Equity Investment in the subsidiary.

[E] Stockholders' equity accounts (S)	100	
Equity investment		100
(eliminates acquisition date stockholders' equity accounts against the investment account)		

[A] Net assets (broken out into individual asset and liability accounts)	150	
Equity investment		100
Bargain acquisition gain*		50
(eliminates the remaining Equity Investment account and reclassifies the AAP)		

* Given that this represents an income statement account (i.e., immediate amortization of the AAP), a case could be made that this adjustment should be made via the **[D]** consolidating entry. However, the bargain acquisition gain "amortization" has no valid asset or liability account to include in the **[D]** entry. Therefore, we include the immediate recognition of the bargain purchase gain in the **[A]** entry.

The net result is that the gain on the bargain acquisition is recognized in the consolidated income statement immediately upon acquisition.

CHAPTER SUMMARY

The consolidation process combines the financial statements of the parent and its subsidiary by removing the Equity-Investment-related accounts from the parent's financial statements and replacing that information with the assets, liabilities, revenues and expenses of the subsidiary company. It is important to remember that the consolidation process does not result in any real adjustments to the parent or subsidiary accounting records. Instead, the consolidated financial statements are prepared after the financial statements have been prepared by the parent and subsidiary, and the consolidated financial statements are prepared to reflect the commonly controlled economic entity.

---

[27] A bargain acquisition might happen, for example, if a business combination is a forced sale (i.e., the seller is acting under compulsion). A bargain purchase might also happen if significant unrecognized contingencies exist at the acquisition date.

In this chapter, we focus on the consolidation process subsequent to the date of acquisition. The sequence of consolidation entries we recommend first proceeds by eliminating the changes recorded by the parent company that relate to Equity Investment accounting that occurred during the period (i.e., the **[C]** consolidation entry). Under the equity method, this generally results in eliminating the income from subsidiary for the period and also eliminating the dividends received from the subsidiary. This will result in the investment in subsidiary account reflecting the beginning of year balance. At this point, we recommend eliminating the beginning stockholders' equity of the subsidiary and removing this amount from the investment account (i.e., the **[E]** consolidation entry). After this entry, the investment account will only contain the beginning of year unamortized balance for the acquisition accounting premium (AAP). The next consolidation entry removes the beginning of year unamortized AAP balance from the investment account and redistributes it to the underlying net assets of the subsidiary to which the AAP relates (i.e., the **[A]** consolidation entry). Now, the investment balance should equal zero. Because the financial statements are being prepared through the end of the year, the beginning of year AAP amounts reclassified in the **[A]** consolidation entry must be depreciated and amortized to their end of year balances (i.e., the **[D]** consolidation entry). Finally, the parent company must eliminate all intercompany transactions during the year, as well as the ending balance of any intercompany receivables and payables (i.e., the [I] consolidation entry). This completes the consolidation process, and will result in a consolidated income statement, consolidated statement of retained earnings and consolidated balance sheet.

When the parent company uses the cost method of pre-consolidation investment bookkeeping, the **C-E-A-D-I** consolidation entries are virtually identical to the entries required when the parent company uses the equity method. However, because, under the cost method, the parent company's pre-consolidation retained earnings does not equal consolidated retained earnings—recall consolidated retained earnings equals the parent company's pre-consolidation retained earnings when the parent uses the equity method—the parent company must start the consolidation process by adjusting the beginning balance of pre-consolidation retained earnings to an "as-if equity method" basis. This is the primary purpose of the **[ADJ]** consolidation entry. Next, the **[C]** consolidating journal entry eliminates the pre-consolidation investment bookkeeping performed by the parent during the year. Generally, this will be a reversal of the dividend income recorded by the parent. At this point, there is no difference between the cost and the equity methods for the remaining **E-A-D-I** consolidation entries.

We also discuss the accounting for goodwill. The first step after acquiring a subsidiary is to measure all identifiable assets acquired (i.e., both tangible and intangible) and liabilities assumed at fair value. Goodwill is the positive fair value of the entire subsidiary that is left over after we have assigned fair values to the identifiable net assets. Goodwill is not amortized or depreciated; instead, it is evaluated annually for impairment. The goodwill impairment evaluation can be extremely challenging and involves an extensive amount of professional judgment.

If the difference between the fair value of an entire subsidiary and the fair value of the subsidiary's identifiable net assets is negative, then the parent company recognizes a bargain acquisition gain when the acquisition transaction is consummated. Instead of recognizing this negative amount as negative goodwill, it is recognized as an ordinary gain in the determination of net income.

COMPREHENSIVE REVIEW—EQUITY METHOD

Consolidation Subsequent to the Date of Acquisition—Equity Method

Assume that on January 1, a parent company acquires 100 percent of the common stock of a subsidiary for $800,000. On the acquisition date, the subsidiary reports a book value of Stockholders' Equity equal to $320,000. The parent is willing to pay the purchase price because the subsidiary owns PPE assets that are worth $150,000 more than the amount at which they are reported on the subsidiary's books. In addition, the subsidiary owns a customer list that has a fair value equal to $50,000. Both of these identifiable assets are depreciated and/or amortized over a 10-year period with no salvage value. Any remaining excess purchase price is attributed to corporate synergies that the parent expects to realize following the combination of the two companies. The parent company applies the equity method of pre-consolidation Equity Investment bookkeeping. The parent and the subsidiary report the following financial statements at the end of the first year following the acquisition:

	Parent	Subsidiary
Income statement:		
Sales.	$5,700,000	$480,000
Cost of goods sold.	(3,990,000)	(288,000)
Gross profit.	1,710,000	192,000
Equity income.	47,200	
Operating expenses.	(1,083,000)	(124,800)
Net income.	$ 674,200	$ 67,200
Statement of retained earnings:		
BOY retained earnings.	$2,863,680	$248,000
Net income.	674,200	67,200
Dividends.	(134,840)	(10,080)
Ending retained earnings.	$3,403,040	$305,120
Balance sheet:		
Assets		
Cash.	$ 354,870	$129,440
Accounts receivable.	729,600	111,360
Inventory.	1,105,800	143,040
Equity investment.	837,120	
Property, plant and equipment (PPE), net	5,319,240	264,640
	$8,346,630	$648,480
Liabilities and stockholders' equity		
Current liabilities.	$ 819,090	$111,360
Long-term liabilities	2,500,000	160,000
Common stock.	931,950	32,000
APIC.	692,550	40,000
Retained earnings	3,403,040	305,120
	$8,346,630	$648,480

Required

Prepare the consolidated financial statements at the end of the first year following the acquisition.

The solution to this review problem can be found on page 179.

COMPREHENSIVE REVIEW—COST METHOD

Consolidation Subsequent to the Date of Acquisition—Cost Method

Assume that on January 1, 2014, a parent company acquires 100 percent of the common stock of a subsidiary for $473,000. On the acquisition date, the subsidiary reports a book value of Stockholders' Equity equal to $390,000, of which $187,500 was in the retained earnings account. On the acquisition date, the subsidiary owns the rights to a patent with a fair value equal to $45,000 and a recorded book value equal to $0. The patent had a six-year remaining economic useful life on the date of acquisition. Any remaining excess purchase price is attributed to corporate synergies that the parent expects to realize following the combination of the two companies. The parent company applies the cost method of pre-consolidation Equity Investment bookkeeping. The parent and the subsidiary report the following financial statements for the year ended December 31, 2016:

	Parent	Subsidiary
Income statement:		
Sales.	$9,000,000	$1,260,000
Cost of goods sold.	(6,300,000)	(810,000)
Gross profit.	2,700,000	450,000
Dividend income.	28,350	—
Operating expenses	(1,710,000)	(351,000)
Net income.	$1,018,350	$ 99,000
Statement of retained earnings:		
BOY retained earnings	$2,062,700	$ 510,000
Net income.	1,018,350	99,000
Dividends	(234,000)	(28,350)
Ending retained earnings	$2,847,050	$ 580,650
Balance sheet:		
Assets		
Cash	$ 615,150	$ 233,550
Accounts receivable.	1,152,000	313,200
Inventory.	1,746,000	402,300
Equity investment.	473,000	
Building, net	5,700,000	525,000
	$9,686,150	$1,474,050
Liabilities and stockholders' equity		
Current liabilities.	$1,293,300	$ 283,500
Long-term liabilities	2,980,800	407,400
Common stock.	1,471,500	90,000
APIC	1,093,500	112,500
Retained earnings	2,847,050	580,650
	$9,686,150	$1,474,050

Required

Prepare the consolidated financial statements for the year ended December 31, 2016.

The solution to this review problem can be found on page 180.

APPENDIX 3A: Complete Listing of Required Disclosures

Following is a complete listing of required disclosures that all acquiring companies must make in the footnotes to their financial statements following an acquisition:

FASB ASC 805-10-50-1: The acquirer shall disclose information that enables users of its financial statements to evaluate the nature and financial effect of a business combination that occurs either:

a. During the current reporting period

b. After the reporting date but before the financial statements are issued or are available to be issued (as discussed in Section 855-10-25).

FASB ASC 805-10-50-2: To meet the objective in the preceding paragraph, the acquirer shall disclose the following information for each business combination that occurs during the reporting period:

a. The name and a description of the acquiree

b. The acquisition date

    c. The percentage of voting equity interests acquired

    d. The primary reasons for the business combination and a description of how the acquirer obtained control of the acquiree

    e. For transactions that are recognized separately from the acquisition of assets and assumptions of liabilities in the business combination (see paragraph 805-10-25-20), all of the following:

      1. A description of each transaction

      2. How the acquirer accounted for each transaction

      3. The amounts recognized for each transaction and the line item in the financial statements in which each amount is recognized

      4. If the transaction is the effective settlement of a preexisting relationship, the method used to determine the settlement amount.

    f. The disclosure of separately recognized transactions required in (e) shall include the amount of acquisition-related costs, the amount recognized as an expense, and the line item or items in the income statement in which those expenses are recognized. The amount of any issuance costs not recognized as an expense and how they were recognized also shall be disclosed.

    g. In a business combination achieved in stages, both of the following:

      1. The acquisition-date fair value of the equity interest in the acquiree held by the acquirer immediately before the acquisition date

      2. The amount of any gain or loss recognized as a result of remeasuring to fair value the equity interest in the acquiree held by the acquirer before the business combination (see paragraph 805-10-25-10) and the line item in the income statement in which that gain or loss is recognized.

    h. If the acquirer is a public business entity, all of the following:

      1. The amounts of revenue and earnings of the acquiree since the acquisition date included in the consolidated income statement for the reporting period

      2. The revenue and earnings of the combined entity for the current reporting period as though the acquisition date for all business combinations that occurred during the year had been as of the beginning of the annual reporting period (supplemental pro forma information)

      3. If comparative financial statements are presented, the revenue and earnings of the combined entity for the comparable prior reporting period as though the acquisition date for all business combinations that occurred during the current year had occurred as of the beginning of the comparable prior annual reporting period (supplemental pro forma information).

If disclosure of any of the information required by (h) is impracticable, the acquirer shall disclose that fact and explain why the disclosure is impracticable. In this context, the term impracticable has the same meaning as in paragraph 250-10-45-9.

FASB ASC 805-10-50-3: For individually immaterial business combinations occurring during the reporting period that are material collectively, the acquirer shall disclose the information required by (e) through (h) in the preceding paragraph in the aggregate.

FASB ASC 805-10-50-4: If the acquisition date of a business combination is after the reporting date but before the financial statements are issued or are available to be issued (as discussed in Section 855-10-25), the acquirer shall disclose the information required by paragraph 805-10-50-2 unless the initial accounting for the business combination is incomplete at the time the financial statements are issued or are available to be issued. In that situation, the acquirer shall describe which disclosures could not be made and the reason why they could not be made.

LO5 Describe the accounting for common control business combinations and the pooling-of-interests method.

APPENDIX 3B: Common Control Business Combinations and the Pooling-of-Interests Method

As noted in FASB ASC 805-10-45-4(c), Acquisition Method accounting does not apply to combinations between entities or businesses under common control. FASB ASC 805-50-15-6 provides the following examples of common-control transactions:

    a. An entity charters a newly formed entity and then transfers some or all of its net assets to that newly chartered entity.

    b. A parent transfers the net assets of a wholly owned subsidiary into the parent and liquidates the subsidiary. That transaction is a change in legal organization but not a change in the reporting entity.

c. A parent transfers its controlling interest in several partially owned subsidiaries to a new wholly owned subsidiary. That also is a change in legal organization but not in the reporting entity.

d. A parent exchanges its ownership interests or the net assets of a wholly owned subsidiary for additional shares issued by the parent's less-than-wholly owned subsidiary, thereby increasing the parent's percentage of ownership in the less-than-wholly owned subsidiary but leaving all of the existing noncontrolling interest outstanding.

e. A parent's less-than-wholly owned subsidiary issues its shares in exchange for shares of another subsidiary previously owned by the same parent, and the noncontrolling shareholders are not party to the exchange. That is not a business combination from the perspective of the parent.

f. A limited liability company is formed by combining entities under common control.

FASB ASC 805-50-05-5 states that "some transfers of net assets or exchanges of shares between entities under common control result in a change in the reporting entity. In practice, the method that many entities have used to account for those transactions is similar to the pooling-of-interests method." Thus, although pooling-of-interests method was disallowed for Business Combinations recognized under SFAS No 141, "Business Combinations," and continues to be proscribed for Business Combinations within the scope of FASB ASC 805, pooling-of-interests method accounting is still applied for common control exchanges that result in a change of reporting entity.[28] In addition, the pooling-of-interests method is still applied to many business combinations that were finalized before the method was abolished for business combinations in 2001.

The pooling-of-interests method records the acquiree at its *book value* rather than its fair value. The implications of recording the acquiree at book value are these:

1. There is no AAP (i.e., no fair value recognition or Goodwill).

2. Because there is no AAP, there is no depreciation or amortization expense related to the AAP.

To illustrate accounting for an acquisition using the pooling-of-interests method, assume that the parent acquires its subsidiary for a purchase price of $700,000. To finance the purchase, it issues 20,000 shares of its $1 par value common stock (market value of $35 per share), and exchanges those shares for all of the subsidiary's voting shares that are owned by its shareholders.

Assume that the subsidiary reports the following balances in its Stockholders' Equity as of the *beginning of the year* in the year of acquisition:

Common stock.	$ 50,000
Additional paid-in capital	150,000
Retained earnings	300,000
Total stockholders' equity	$500,000

The parent is, therefore, purchasing a subsidiary with a book value of $500,000 for $700,000, and makes the following journal entry to record the acquisition under pooling-of-interests:

Equity investment.	500,000	
Common stock		20,000
Retained earnings (parent).		300,000
APIC.		180,000
(to record the acquisition of the subsidiary under pooling-of-interests)		

Several points are worthy of mention:

1. The Equity Investment is recorded at the *book value* of the subsidiary as of the beginning of the year, not at its fair value as would be the case under current GAAP.

2. The Retained Earnings of the *parent* are increased by the Retained Earnings of the subsidiary as of the beginning of the year. The effect of this part of the entry is to increase the parent's Retained Earnings by the cumulative increase in the subsidiary's Retained Earnings since it began operations, as though the subsidiary had always been a part of the parent.

---

[28] The International Accounting Standards Board (IASB) also disallowed application of pooling-of-interests method for transactions within the scope of International Financial Reporting Standard (IFRS) No. 3, "Business Combinations." However, like U.S. GAAP, IFRS No. 3 allows application of the pooling-of-interests method to common control exchanges that result in a change of reporting entity.

3. APIC is the plug figure to equate the increase in equity (Common Stock, APIC, and Retained Earnings) with the increase in the Equity Investment account.

Now, assume that the consolidation spreadsheet provided in Exhibit 3B.1 includes the parent and subsidiary information for the year ending December 31, 2016 (i.e., many years following the acquisition). The parent company uses the equity method of pre-consolidation investment bookkeeping.

EXHIBIT 3B.1 Consolidation Spreadsheet Under Pooling-of-Interests

	Parent	Subsidiary	Consolidation Entries Dr	Consolidation Entries Cr	Consolidated
Income statement:					
Sales	$ 7,000,000	$ 750,000			$ 7,750,000
Cost of goods sold	(4,900,000)	(450,000)			(5,350,000)
Gross profit	2,100,000	300,000			2,400,000
Equity income	105,000		[C] $ 105,000		0
Operating expenses	(1,330,000)	(195,000)			(1,525,000)
Net income	$ 875,000	$ 105,000			$ 875,000
Statement of retained earnings:					
BOY retained earnings	$ 3,516,800	$ 827,000	[E] 827,000		3,516,800
Net income	875,000	105,000			875,000
Dividends	(175,000)	(15,750)		[C] $ 15,750	(175,000)
Ending retained earnings	$ 4,216,800	$ 916,250			$ 4,216,800
Balance sheet:					
Assets					
Cash	$ 815,050	$ 329,250			$ 1,144,300
Accounts receivable	896,000	174,000			1,070,000
Inventory	1,358,000	223,500			1,581,500
Equity investment	1,116,250			[E] 1,027,000	0
				[C] 89,250	
Property, plant and equipment (PPE), net	6,532,400	813,500			7,345,900
	$10,717,700	$1,540,250			$11,141,700
Liabilities and Stockholders' Equity					
Current liabilities	$ 1,005,900	$ 174,000			$ 1,179,900
Long-term liabilities	3,500,000	250,000			3,750,000
Common stock	1,144,500	50,000	[E] 50,000		1,144,500
APIC	850,500	150,000	[E] 150,000		850,500
Retained earnings	4,216,800	916,250			4,216,800
	$10,717,700	$1,540,250	$1,132,000	$1,132,000	$11,141,700

Because there is no AAP, the consolidation process has no need for the consolidating entries [A] or [D]. Other than that omission, the consolidation spreadsheet is the same that we have used all along.

Comparison of Pooling-of-Interests with Acquisition Method

To further illustrate the difference between the pooling-of-interests method and the acquisition method under FASB ASC 805, assume that the acquisition occurred eight years ago and that the parent initially recorded its Equity Investment in the subsidiary at $700,000, including $150,000 relating to a Patent owned by the subsidiary with a 10-year life and $50,000 of Goodwill. Through the beginning of the year, the patent has been amortized for 7 years, and has a BOY book value of $45,000 ($150,000 − 7 × $15,000). The parent company uses the equity method of pre-consolidation investment bookkeeping.

On the acquisition date, the Acquisition Method entry recorded by the parent is as follows:

Equity investment.	700,000	
Common stock		20,000
APIC.		680,000
(to record the acquisition of the subsidiary under Acquisition Method)		

Note two differences between initially recording an acquisition under the FASB ASC 805 acquisition method versus pooling of interests: (1) the equity investment account is recorded at the fair value of the subsidiary under the acquisition method and at the book value of net assets under pooling of interests and (2) all of the excess over the par value of stock issued by the parent is recorded as additional paid-in capital under the acquisition method (i.e., none of the subsidiary's retained earnings is carried forward by the parent).

Based on the initial pre-consolidation balances included in the pooling of interests example illustrated in Exhibit 3B.1, we can compute the amounts that will be different in the December 31, 2016 consolidation worksheet assuming that the parent initially recorded acquisition under the acquisition method.[29]

1. Equity income: Under the acquisition method, the parent recorded the investment at fair value. Thus, the equity investment account includes the AAP for the Patent and Goodwill, and, each year, the parent amortizes $15,000 of AAP for the Patent. Thus, Equity Income = $105,000 − $15,000 = $90,000.

2. BOY retained earnings: Compared to pooling of interests, the parent recorded $300,000 less retained earnings upon initial acquisition. In addition, each year, through the beginning of the current year, the parent recognized $15,000 of AAP amortization when the initial acquisition was recorded under the acquisition method. Thus, under the acquisition method, BOY retained earnings = $3,516,800 − $300,000 − (7 × $15,000) = $3,111,800.

3. EOY equity investment: Under the equity method, the equity investment account always equals the stockholders' equity of the subsidiary at a given date plus the unamortized AAP at that same date. Under pooling of interests, there is no AAP, so the investment account equals the stockholders' equity of the subsidiary. Thus, under the acquisition method, we can take the pooling of interests investment account balance and add the unamortized AAP that exists under the acquisition method at the end of the year: $1,116,250 + [$200,000 − (8 × $15,000)] = $1,196,250.

4. Additional paid-in capital: Because, compared to pooling of interests, the acquisition method had $200,000 more recorded in the investment account and the entire excess over par value was recorded in additional paid-in capital, the acquisition method included $500,000 more recorded in additional paid-in capital: $850,500 + $500,000 = $1,350,500.

The consolidation spreadsheet under FASB ASC 805 Acquisition Accounting is provided in Exhibit 3B.2:

---

[29] Any amount not reconciled in this list can be inferred via basic arithmetic operations within the worksheet (e.g., EOY retained earnings = BOY retained earnings + net income - dividends)

EXHIBIT 3B.2	Consolidation Spreadsheet under FASB ASC 805

	Parent	Subsidiary	Consolidation Entries Dr	Consolidation Entries Cr	Consolidated
Income statement:					
Sales....................................	$ 7,000,000	$ 750,000			$ 7,750,000
Cost of goods sold.........................	(4,900,000)	(450,000)			(5,350,000)
Gross profit...............................	2,100,000	300,000			2,400,000
Equity income.............................	90,000		[C] $ 90,000		0
Operating expenses.........................	(1,330,000)	(195,000)	[D] 15,000		(1,540,000)
Net income................................	$ 860,000	$ 105,000			$ 860,000
Statement of retained earnings:					
BOY retained earnings......................	$ 3,111,800	$ 827,000	[E] 827,000		$ 3,111,800
Net income................................	860,000	105,000			860,000
Dividends.................................	(175,000)	(15,750)		[C] $ 15,750	(175,000)
Ending retained earnings....................	$ 3,796,800	$ 916,250			$ 3,796,800
Balance sheet:					
Assets					
Cash......................................	$ 815,050	$ 329,250			$ 1,144,300
Accounts receivable.........................	896,000	174,000			1,070,000
Inventory..................................	1,358,000	223,500			1,581,500
Equity investment..........................	1,196,250			[E] 1,027,000	0
				[A] 95,000	
				[C] 74,250	
Property, plant and equipment (PPE), net..........	6,532,400	813,500			7,345,900
Patent....................................			[A] 45,000	[D] 15,000	30,000
Goodwill..................................			[A] 50,000		50,000
	$10,797,700	$1,540,250			$11,221,700
Liabilities and stockholders' equity					
Current liabilities...........................	$ 1,005,900	$ 174,000			$ 1,179,900
Long-term liabilities.........................	3,500,000	250,000			3,750,000
Common stock.............................	1,144,500	50,000	[E] 50,000		1,144,500
APIC......................................	1,350,500	150,000	[E] 150,000		1,350,500
Retained earnings..........................	3,796,800	916,250			3,796,800
	$10,797,700	$1,540,250	$1,227,000	$1,227,000	$11,221,700

Under FASB ASC 805, we now record the unamortized [A] assets at the beginning of the year and their amortization with the [D] entry. The Equity Investment is, therefore, higher, and income is lower than under the pooling-of-interests method. One of the criticisms of the pooling-of-interests method, ultimately leading to its demise, was that balance sheets and income statements did not accurately reflect the true assets and profitability of the consolidated entity.

Superscript $^{A\ (B)}$ denotes assignments based on Appendix 3A (B).

QUESTIONS

1. Why is consolidated net income equal to the net income reported by the parent if the parent uses the equity method of accounting?

2. Under the equity method, why isn't the payment of dividends from the subsidiary to the parent included in the updating of consolidated Retained Earnings?

3. Explain how to convert a parent company's cost-method pre-consolidation net income to equity method pre-consolidation net income. What is the relation between the resulting parent company equity method pre-consolidation net income and consolidated net income?

4. Explain how to convert a parent company's cost-method pre-consolidation retained earnings to equity method pre-consolidation retained earnings. What is the relation between the resulting parent company equity method pre-consolidation retained earnings and consolidated retained earnings?

5. Why doesn't the Equity Investment account appear on the consolidated balance sheet?

6. Why do assets and liabilities appear on the consolidated balance sheet that did not appear on the balance sheet of either the parent or the subsidiary?

7. Why doesn't the consolidated statement of cash flows equal the sum of the statements of cash flows for the parent and the subsidiary?

8. Why is Goodwill referred to as a "residual" asset?

9. The quantitative two-step Goodwill impairment test begins with an estimate of the value of the reporting unit, typically a subsidiary, to determine if the value of the reporting unit is less than the reported balance of the Equity Investment account. Subsidiaries typically are not publicly traded companies. How can you perform a test using the value of a company that is not publicly traded?

10. Identify the events that can trigger an impairment test prior to the annual review.

11.[A] What are the required footnote disclosures relating to an acquisition?

12. What are the limitations of consolidated financial statements?

13. Determining the useful life of an intangible asset should generally be based on the lesser of management's estimate of the period of time over which it is expected to produce benefits (such as cash flows), legal, regulatory, or market-related factors (obsolescence, competition, etc.) that may limit its useful life. What useful life would you estimate for the following intangible assets?

   a. *An acquired customer list.* A direct-mail marketing company acquired the customer list and expects that it will be able to derive benefit from the information on the acquired customer list for at least one year but for no more than three years.

   b. *An acquired Patent that expires in 15 years.* The product protected by the patented technology is expected to be a source of cash flows for at least 15 years. The reporting entity has a commitment from a third party to purchase that Patent in 5 years for 60 percent of the fair value of the Patent at the date it was acquired, and the entity intends to sell the Patent in 5 years.

   c. *An acquired copyright that has a remaining legal life of 50 years.* An analysis of consumer habits and market trends provides evidence that the copyrighted material will generate cash flows for approximately 30 more years.

   d. *An acquired broadcast license that expires in five years.* The broadcast license is renewable every 10 years if the company provides at least an average level of service to its customers and complies with the applicable Federal Communications Commission (FCC) rules and policies and the FCC Communications Act of 1934. The license may be renewed indefinitely at little cost and was renewed twice prior to its recent acquisition. The acquiring entity intends to renew the license indefinitely, and evidence supports its ability to do so. Historically, there has been no compelling challenge to the license renewal. The technology used in broadcasting is not expected to be replaced by another technology any time in the foreseeable future. Therefore, the cash flows from that license are expected to continue indefinitely.

   e. *An acquired trademark that is used to identify and distinguish a leading consumer product that has been a market-share leader for the past eight years.* The trademark has a remaining legal life of 5 years but is renewable every 10 years at little cost. The acquiring entity intends to continuously renew the trademark, and evidence supports its ability to do so. An analysis of product life cycle studies; market, competitive, and environmental trends; and brand extension opportunities provides evidence that the trademarked product will generate cash flows for the acquiring entity for an indefinite period of time.

14. Intangible assets with an indefinite useful life are not amortized. Instead, they are tested at least annually for impairment and written down if found to be impaired. Consider the following scenario (FASB ASC 350-30-35-1 through 35-20): A trademark was acquired 10 years ago in an acquisition. When it was acquired, the trademark was assigned a value of $30 million, and was considered to have an indefinite useful life because the product to which it relates was expected to generate cash flows indefinitely. During the annual impairment test of the intangible asset, the company determines that unexpected competition has entered the market that will reduce future sales of the product. Management estimates that cash flows generated by that consumer product will be 20 percent less for the foreseeable future, and the present value of those expected cash flows is computed to be $10

> **FASB ASC Research**

million. However, management expects that the product will continue to generate cash flows indefinitely at those reduced amounts. Is the trademark impaired, thus requiring a write-down? If so, by what amount? If not completely written off, how would you treat the balance of the trademark that is not written off (do you amortize it or not)?

15. Many companies engage in restructuring activities following the acquisition of a subsidiary by the parent. The cost related to these restructurings is often significant and can substantially affect reported profit, possibly turning a profit into a loss for the year.

   a.   List the types of activities typically included under the general description of restructuring activities.

   b.   Describe the accounting for restructuring activities (hint: see FASB ASC 805-20-25-2 and FASB Concepts Statement No. 6, *Elements of Financial Statements*).

Assignments with the logo in the margin are available in BusinessCourse.
See the Preface of the book for details.

MULTIPLE CHOICE

LO1   16. **Review of investment accounting (noncontrolling investment in affiliate)**

AICPA Adapted

Assume an investor company purchased 20% of the outstanding voting common stock of an investee. Which of the following statements is false about the financial reporting of the investment in the investor's published financial statements? (Ignore any potential effects of intercompany transactions between the investor and the investee.)

   a.   The investor company can make an irrevocable election to report the Equity Investment at fair value, even if the investor has significant influence over the investee.

   b.   If the investor company has no influence over the investee and no readily determinable fair value exists for the investee's common stock, in all years the investor holds the investment it can report the investment at the original cost of the investment.

   c.   If the investor has significant influence, the balance of the investment in investee account will equal 20% of the investee's stockholders' equity, adjusted for 20% of the unamortized differences between the investee's net asset fair values and book values (i.e., for gross differences initially determined as of the date of investment in the investee).

   d.   If the investor company has no influence over the investee, changes in the market value of the investment in the investee are only recognized in other comprehensive income.

LO1   17. **Review of investment accounting (controlling investment in affiliate)**

AICPA Adapted

Assume an investor company purchased a controlling financial interest in 100% of the outstanding voting common stock of an investee. Which of the following statements is false about the investor's pre-consolidation bookkeeping and/or the post-consolidation financial reporting in the investor's published financial statements? (Ignore any potential effects of intercompany transactions between the investor and the investee.)

   a.   The investor company can make an irrevocable election to report the Equity Investment at fair value, even if the investor has control over the investee.

   b.   If the investor applies equity method, the balance of the pre-consolidation investment in investee account will equal 100% of the investee's stockholders' equity, adjusted for 100% of the unamortized differences between the investee's net asset fair values and book values (i.e., for gross differences initially determined as of the date of investment in the investee).

   c.   In its pre-consolidation accounting records, the investor can use any investment-accounting method it chooses.

   d.   In its published financial statements, the investor must consolidate the investee.

Use the following facts for multiple choice problems 18–25. Each of the problems is independent from the others.

AICPA Adapted

Assume an investee has the following financial statement information for the three years ending December 31, 2016:

(At December 31)	2016	2015	2014
Current assets	$228,376	$222,160	$165,600
Tangible fixed assets	529,384	459,440	450,400
Intangible assets	32,000	36,000	40,000
Total assets.	$789,760	$717,600	$656,000
Current liabilities.	$ 96,800	$ 88,000	$ 80,000
Noncurrent liabilities.	212,960	193,600	176,000
Common stock.	80,000	80,000	80,000
Additional paid-in capital	80,000	80,000	80,000
Retained earnings	320,000	276,000	240,000
Stockholders' equity	480,000	436,000	400,000
Total liabilities and equity	$789,760	$717,600	$656,000

(For the years ended December 31)	2016	2015	2014
Revenues	$776,000	$736,000	$680,000
Expenses	700,800	672,000	620,000
Net income.	$ 75,200	$ 64,000	$ 60,000
Dividends	$ 31,200	$ 28,000	$ 20,000

18. **Review of pre-consolidation equity method (controlling investment in affiliate, fair value equals book value)**

    Assume that on January 1, 2014, an investor company purchased 100% of the outstanding voting common stock of the investee. On the date of the acquisition, the investee's identifiable net assets had fair values that approximated their historical book values. In addition, the acquisition resulted in no goodwill or bargain purchase gain recognized in the consolidated financial statements of the investor company. Assuming that the investor company uses the equity method to account for its investment in the investee, what is the balance in the "investment in investee" account in the investor company's pre-consolidation balance sheet on December 31, 2016?

    a. $789,760
    b. $480,000
    c. $400,000
    d. $360,000

19. **Review of pre-consolidation equity method (controlling investment in affiliate, fair value equals book value)**

    Assume that on January 1, 2014, an investor company purchased 100% of the outstanding voting common stock of the investee. On the date of the acquisition, the investee's identifiable net assets had fair values that approximated their historical book values. In addition, the acquisition resulted in no goodwill or bargain purchase gain recognized in the consolidated financial statements of the investor company. Assuming that the investor company uses the equity method to account for its investment in the investee, what is the balance in the "income from investee" account in the investor company's pre-consolidation income statement for the year ended December 31, 2016?

    a. $75,200
    b. $60,000
    c. $44,000
    d. $31,200

20. **Review of pre-consolidation cost method (controlling investment in affiliate, fair value equals book value)**

    Assume that on January 1, 2014, an investor company purchased 100% of the outstanding voting common stock of the investee. On the date of the acquisition, the investee's identifiable net assets had fair values that approximated their historical book values. In addition, the acquisition resulted in no goodwill or bargain purchase gain recognized in the consolidated financial statements of the investor company. Assuming that the investor company uses the cost method to account for its investment in the investee, what is the balance in the "investment in investee" account in the investor company's pre-consolidation balance sheet on December 31, 2016?

    a. $789,760

    b. $480,000

    c. $400,000

    d. $360,000

 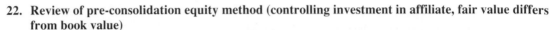

LO3

21. Review of pre-consolidation cost method (controlling investment in affiliate, fair value equals book value)

Assume that on January 1, 2014, an investor company purchased 100% of the outstanding voting common stock of the investee. On the date of the acquisition, the investee's identifiable net assets had fair values that approximated their historical book values. In addition, the acquisition resulted in no goodwill or bargain purchase gain recognized in the consolidated financial statements of the investor company. Assuming that the investor company uses the cost method to account for its investment in the investee, what is the balance in the "income from investee" account in the investor company's pre-consolidation income statement for the year ended December 31, 2016?

    a. $75,200

    b. $60,000

    c. $44,000

    d. $31,200

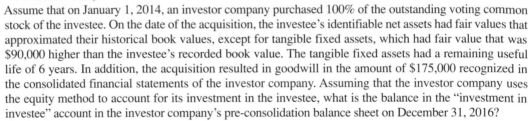

LO1

22. Review of pre-consolidation equity method (controlling investment in affiliate, fair value differs from book value)

Assume that on January 1, 2014, an investor company purchased 100% of the outstanding voting common stock of the investee. On the date of the acquisition, the investee's identifiable net assets had fair values that approximated their historical book values, except for tangible fixed assets, which had fair value that was $90,000 higher than the investee's recorded book value. The tangible fixed assets had a remaining useful life of 6 years. In addition, the acquisition resulted in goodwill in the amount of $175,000 recognized in the consolidated financial statements of the investor company. Assuming that the investor company uses the equity method to account for its investment in the investee, what is the balance in the "investment in investee" account in the investor company's pre-consolidation balance sheet on December 31, 2016?

    a. $480,000

    b. $625,000

    c. $700,000

    d. $789,760

LO1

23. Review of pre-consolidation equity method (controlling investment in affiliate, fair value differs from book value)

Assume that on January 1, 2014, an investor company purchased 100% of the outstanding voting common stock of the investee. On the date of the acquisition, the investee's identifiable net assets had fair values that approximated their historical book values, except for tangible fixed assets, which had fair value that was $90,000 higher than the investee's recorded book value. The tangible fixed assets had a remaining useful life of 6 years. In addition, the acquisition resulted in goodwill in the amount of $175,000 recognized in the consolidated financial statements of the investor company. Assuming that the investor company uses the equity method to account for its investment in the investee, what is the balance in the "income from investee" account in the investor company's pre-consolidation income statement for the year ended December 31, 2016?

    a. $75,200

    b. $60,200

    c. $44,000

    d. $29,000

LO3

24. Cost method consolidation entries (controlling investment in affiliate, fair value differs from book value)

Assume that on January 1, 2014, an investor company purchased 100% of the outstanding voting common stock of the investee. On the date of the acquisition, the investee's identifiable net assets had fair values that approximated their historical book values, except for tangible fixed assets, which had fair value that was $90,000 higher than the investee's recorded book value. The tangible fixed assets had a remaining useful life of 6 years. In addition, the acquisition resulted in goodwill in the amount of $175,000 recognized in the consolidated financial statements of the investor company. On January 1, 2014, the investee's retained earnings balance was $200,000. Assuming that the investor company uses the cost method to account for its investment in the investee, what is the amount of the [ADJ] entry necessary to prepare the consolidated financial statements for the year ended December 31, 2016?

a. $46,000

b. $75,000

c. $76,000

d. $120,000

25. **Cost method consolidation entries (controlling investment in affiliate, fair value differs from book value)**

LO3

AICPA
Adapted

Assume that on January 1, 2014, an investor company purchased 100% of the outstanding voting common stock of the investee. On the date of the acquisition, the investee's identifiable net assets had fair values that approximated their historical book values, except for tangible fixed assets, which had fair value that was $90,000 higher than the investee's recorded book value. The tangible fixed assets had a remaining useful life of 6 years. In addition, the acquisition resulted in goodwill in the amount of $175,000 recognized in the consolidated financial statements of the investor company. Assuming that the investor company uses the cost method to account for its investment in the investee, what is the amount of the debit in the [C] entry necessary to prepare the consolidated financial statements for the year ended December 31, 2016?

a. $31,200

b. $44,000

c. $60,200

d. $75,200

26. **Computing the amount of goodwill in an acquisition**

LO4

AICPA
Adapted

On July 1, 2016 an investor paid $3,500,000 for 100% of the voting common stock of an investee. The transaction qualifies as a business combination. At that time, investee had the following summarized balance sheet information:

	July 1, 2016
Current assets	$ 500,000
Plant and equipment, net	2,800,000
Liabilities	1,400,000
Equity	1,900,000

On July 1, 2016, the fair value of the plant and equipment was $700,000 more than its carrying amount. The acquisition-date fair values approximated their recorded book values for all of the remaining individual net assets of the investee. Related to this transaction, what amount of goodwill must the investor report in its post-acquisition consolidated balance sheet on July 1, 2016?

a. $2,300,000

b. $1,600,000

c. $900,000

d. $700,000

Use the following facts for Multiple Choice problems 27–30.

Assume that an investor acquired 100% of the voting common stock of an investee on January 1, 2009 in a transaction that qualifies as a business combination. As a result of the acquisition, the investor recognized no goodwill and no bargain purchase gain in the post-acquisition consolidated financial statements (i.e., all of the resulting Acquisition Accounting Premium relates to identifiable net assets). The investor uses the equity method to account for its pre-consolidation investment in the investee. In addition, there are no intercompany transactions between the investor and investee. The following summarized pre-consolidation financial statement information is for the year ending December 31, 2016:

AICPA
Adapted

Income Statement	Investor	Investee
Revenues	$1,920,000	$256,000
Income from Investee	120,000	0
Expenses	(1,280,000)	(128,000)
Consolidated net income	760,000	128,000
NCI		—
Net income	$ 760,000	$128,000

Statement of Retained Earnings

Retained earnings, January 1.	$ 601,600	$ 32,000
Net income.	760,000	128,000
Dividends declared.	(51,200)	(32,000)
Retained earnings, December 31.	$1,310,400	$128,000

Balance Sheet

Investment in Investee	$ 232,000	$ 0
All other assets.	3,830,400	320,000
Total assets.	$ 4,062,400	$320,000
Liabilities.	$2,112,000	$128,000
Common stock and additional paid-in capital	640,000	64,000
Retained earnings	1,310,400	128,000
Total liabilities and equity	$4,062,400	$320,000

LO2   27. **Understanding consolidated balances**

What amount of "expenses" will appear in the consolidated income statement for the year ending December 31, 2016?

AICPA Adapted

   a. $1,416,000

   b. $1,408,000

   c. $1,280,000

   d. $1,424,000

LO2   28. **Understanding consolidated balances**

What amount of "net income" will be reported in the consolidated income statement for the year ending December 31, 2016?

AICPA Adapted

   a. $120,000

   b. $128,000

   c. $752,000

   d. $760,000

LO2   29. **Understanding consolidated balances**

What amount of "retained earnings" will appear in the consolidated balance sheet at December 31, 2016?

AICPA Adapted

   a. $1,406,400

   b. $1,318,400

   c. $1,310,400

   d. $1,438,400

LO2   30. **Understanding consolidated balances**

What amount of "total assets" will appear in the consolidated balance sheet at December 31, 2016?

AICPA Adapted

   a. $4,382,400

   b. $3,830,400

   c. $4,062,400

   d. $4,190,400

EXERCISES

LO4   31. **Compute the amount of acquired Goodwill**

Assume that you are charged with assigning fair values related to a $1,375,000 acquisition. You assemble the following information relating to the acquiree's assets and liabilities:

Account	Book Value	Fair Value
Cash.	$ 75,000	$ 75,000
Accounts receivable.	150,000	142,500
Inventories	187,500	202,500
Property, plant and equipment (PPE).	600,000	750,000
Current liabilities.	(225,000)	(225,000)
Accrued liabilities	(262,500)	(262,500)
	$525,000	$ 682,500
Unrecorded asset:		
Patent.		395,000
		$1,077,500

How much Goodwill will you record in this acquisition, and how is the Goodwill accounted for subsequent to the acquisition?

32. **Compute the amount of acquired Goodwill, including contingent earnings and bargain purchase**   LO4
Assume that you are charged with assigning fair values related to a $3,765,000 acquisition. You determine that the fair value of the net identifiable tangible assets is $1,850,000. You also conclude that the purchase included a Customer List with a fair value at $337,000.

   a.   How much Goodwill will you record in this acquisition, and how is the Goodwill accounted for subsequent to the acquisition?

   b.   Continuing from *Part a*, now also assume that the purchase and sale agreement requires the payment of an additional $850,000 if the subsidiary achieves a certain level of earnings. You estimate the fair value of that contingent earnings clause in the agreement to be $216,500. How does this additional information affect your computation of Goodwill?

   c.   This part of the exercise is independent of *Parts a and b*. Assume that the purchase price is $3,765,000 and that fair value of the net identifiable tangible assets is $1,850,000. You also conclude that the purchase included a Customer List that you value at $638,000 and a Patent valued at $1,950,000. How much Goodwill will you record in this acquisition?

33. **Goodwill Impairment Test**   LO4
Assume that the equity method Equity Investment account relating to a subsidiary has a reported balance of $6,250,000, including $619,000 of Goodwill. You currently value that subsidiary at $5,625,000, and estimate that the fair value of the subsidiary's net assets is $5,375,000.

   a.   Should you perform a test for potential impairment of Goodwill?

   b.   If so, do you conclude that Goodwill is impaired?

   c.   Prepare the required journal entry if you find the Goodwill asset to be impaired.

34. **Interpreting footnote for restructuring accrual and affect on Goodwill computation**   LO4
In 2014, **Perrigo Company, plc** acquired **Elan Corporation, plc** for approximately $9.5 billion. As part of the acquisition, Perrigo assigned $41.2 million to a restructuring liability. The following footnote describes the restructuring liability:

PERRIGO COMPANY, PLC
ELAN CORPORATION, PLC

> During fiscal 2014, $41.2 million of the restructuring expense recorded was due to the Elan acquisition, and of this amount, $38.7 million was recorded in the Specialty Sciences segment. There were no other material restructuring programs in any of the years presented and the remaining liabilities did not materially impact any one reportable segment. Substantially all of the remaining liability for employee severance benefits will be paid within the next year, while cash expenditures related to the remaining liability for lease exit costs will be incurred over the remaining terms of the applicable leases.

   a.   What effect did this accrual have on the amount of the purchase price assigned to Goodwill?

   b.   How was this restructuring liability accounted for?

   c.   How will payments that Perrigo makes in connection with this restructuring activity affect its consolidated income statement subsequent to the acquisition?

35. **Determining post-acquisition accounting for AAP from footnote disclosure**   LO2
Pfizer acquired **Wyeth** in 2009 for approximately $68 billion. Its acquisition footnote reveals the following assignment of fair values:

PFIZER
WYETH

(in millions)	Amounts Recognized as of Acquisition Date
Working capital, excluding inventories.	$16,342
Inventories	8,388
Property, plant and equipment.	10,054
Identifiable intangible assets, excluding in-process research and development.	37,595
In-process research and development.	14,918
Other noncurrent assets.	2,394
Long-term debt	(11,187)
Benefit obligations	(3,211)
Net tax accounts	(24,773)
Other noncurrent liabilities	(1,908)
Total identifiable net assets	$48,612
Goodwill	19,954
Net assets acquired	$68,566

Describe the post-acquisition accounting for each of the accounts listed in the fair value assignment disclosure above.

LO2

ANHEUSER-BUSCH INBEV GRUPO MODELO

36. Interpreting acquisition footnote

Anheuser-Busch Inbev (AB Inbev), a publicly traded company based in Leuven, Belgium, acquired **Grupo Modelo S.A.B de CV** (Grupo Modelo) in 2013 for approximately $34 billion. The notes to AB Inbev's 2013 financial statements include the following fair value assignment disclosure for the Grupo Modelo acquisition:

(in millions U.S. dollars)	Before Purchase Price Allocation	Purchase Price Allocation	After Purchase Price Allocation
Non-current assets			
Property, plant and equipment.	$4,609	$ 99	$ 4,708
Goodwill	796	(796)	—
Intangible assets	458	4,454	4,912
Investment in associates	79	(4)	75
Investment in securities	19	—	19
Trade and other receivables	65	—	65
Current assets			
Inventories	630	(41)	589
Trade and other receivables	617	(11)	606
Income tax receivable	91	(91)	—
Assets held for sale	909	4,476	5,385
Cash and cash equivalent	2,610	—	2,610
Non-current liabilities			
Employee benefits	(256)	—	(256)
Provisions	(1)	(20)	(21)
Trade and other payables.	(77)	(489)	(566)
Deferred tax liabilities.	(418)	(714)	(1,132)
Current liabilities			
Interest-bearing loans and borrowings	(67)	—	(67)
Income tax payable	—	(1,468)	(1,468)
Trade and other payables.	(845)	(182)	(1,027)
Provisions	(16)	—	(16)
Net identified assets and liabilities	9,203	5,214	14,417
Goodwill on acquisition			19,592
Net assets acquired			34,008

Use the information in this table to answer the following questions about the Grupo Modelo acquisition:

a. Relating to "Property, plant and equipment" assets, describe what is meant by the three numbers across the three columns.

b.   Why is the $796 million "Goodwill" asset account (i.e., in the column headed "Before Purchase Price Allocation" reduced to zero (i.e., in the column headed "After Purchase Price Allocation")?

c.   How is the $19,592 million "Goodwill on acquisition" different from the Goodwill discussed in *Part b*?

d.   "Intangible assets" increased by $4,454 million as a result of the acquisition (an increase of almost 1,000%!). What is the most likely specific intangible asset to which this increase relates? Why?

e.   Describe why the "Deferred tax liabilities" account is increased by $714 million.

37. **Determining ending consolidated balances in the second year following the acquisition—Equity method**   LO2

Assume a parent company acquired a subsidiary on January 1, 2015. The purchase price was $745,000 in excess of the subsidiary's book value of Stockholders' Equity on the acquisition date, and that excess was assigned to the following [A] assets:

[A] Asset	Original Amount	Original Useful Life
Property, plant and equipment (PPE), net	$360,000	15 years
Goodwill	385,000	Indefinite
	$745,000	

The AAP asset relating to undervalued PPE with a 15-year useful life has been depreciated as part of the parent's equity method accounting. The financial statements of the parent and its subsidiary for the year ended December 31, 2016, are as follows:

	Parent	Subsidiary		Parent	Subsidiary
Income statement:			**Balance sheet:**		
Sales.....................	$6,875,000	$1,500,000	Assets		
Cost of goods sold..........	(4,950,000)	(900,000)	Cash................................	$ 1,295,313	$ 386,500
Gross profit...............	1,925,000	600,000	Accounts receivable...................	1,760,000	348,000
Equity income..............	186,000		Inventory............................	2,667,500	447,000
Operating expenses.........	(1,031,250)	(390,000)	Equity investment....................	1,875,500	
Net income................	$1,079,750	$ 210,000	Property, plant and equipment (PPE), net ...	14,206,500	827,000
				$21,804,813	$2,008,500
Statement of retained earnings:					
BOY retained earnings........	$4,639,750	$ 775,000	Liabilities and stockholders' equity		
Net income.................	1,079,750	210,000	Accounts payable.....................	$ 1,006,500	$ 143,000
Dividends..................	(217,000)	(31,500)	Accrued liabilities.....................	1,196,250	187,000
Ending retained earnings.....	$5,502,500	$ 953,500	Long-term liabilities	8,750,000	500,000
			Common stock.......................	640,563	100,000
			APIC...............................	4,709,000	125,000
			Retained earnings	5,502,500	953,500
				$21,804,813	$2,008,500

At what amount will the following accounts appear on the consolidated financial statements?

a.   Sales
b.   Equity income
c.   Operating expenses
d.   Accounts receivable
e.   Equity investment

f.   Property, plant and equipment (PPE), net
g.   Goodwill
h.   Common stock
i.   Retained earnings

38. **Determining ending consolidated balances in the third year following the acquisition—Equity method**   LO2

Assume that your company acquired a subsidiary on January 1, 2014. The purchase price was $969,000 in excess of the subsidiary's book value of Stockholders' Equity on the acquisition date, and that excess was assigned to the following [A] assets:

[A] Asset	Original Amount	Original Useful Life
Patent...	$615,000	10 years
Goodwill...	354,000	Indefinite
	$969,000	

The [A] assets with a useful life have been amortized as part of the parent's equity method accounting. The financial statements of the parent and its subsidiary for the year ended December 31, 2016, are as follows:

	Parent	Subsidiary		Parent	Subsidiary
Income statement:			**Balance sheet:**		
Sales..................	$3,125,000	$ 937,500	Assets		
Cost of goods sold.......	(2,250,000)	(562,500)	Cash..................................	$ 671,180	$ 241,570
Gross profit.............	875,000	375,000	Accounts receivable..................	800,000	217,500
Equity income...........	69,750		Inventory	1,212,500	279,375
Operating expenses......	(468,750)	(243,750)	Equity investment.....................	1,521,070	
Net income.............	$ 476,000	$ 131,250	Property, plant and equipment (PPE), net ...	6,457,500	516,875
				$10,662,250	$1,255,320
Statement of retained earnings:					
BOY retained earnings....	$4,020,000	$ 484,375	Liabilities and stockholders' equity		
Net income.............	476,000	131,250	Accounts payable.......................	$ 457,500	$ 89,375
Dividends	(95,000)	(19,680)	Accrued liabilities	543,750	116,875
Ending retained earnings ..	$4,401,000	$ 595,945	Long-term liabilities	625,000	312,500
			Common stock........................	555,000	62,500
			APIC................................	4,080,000	78,125
			Retained earnings	4,401,000	595,945
				$10,662,250	$1,255,320

At what amount will the following accounts appear in the consolidated financial statements for the year ended December 31, 2016?

a.   Cost of goods sold
b.   Equity income
c.   Operating expenses
d.   Cash
e.   Equity investment

f.   Property, plant and equipment (PPE), net
g.   Patent
h.   Goodwill
i.   Common stock
j.   Retained earnings

LO2   39. **Determining ending consolidated balances in the fourth year following the acquisition—Equity method**

Assume that your company acquired a subsidiary on January 1, 2013. The purchase price was $1,463,000 in excess of the subsidiary's book value of Stockholders' Equity on the acquisition date, and that excess was assigned to the following [A] assets:

[A] Asset	Original Amount	Original Useful Life
Property, plant and equipment (PPE), net	$ 612,000	12 years
Patent...	496,000	8 years
Goodwill...	355,000	Indefinite
	$ 1,463,000	

The [A] assets with a useful life have been amortized as part of the parent's equity method accounting. The financial statements of the parent and its subsidiary for the year ended December 31, 2016, are as follows:

	Parent	Subsidiary		Parent	Subsidiary
Income statement:			**Balance sheet:**		
Sales.	$6,200,000	$1,620,000	Assets		
Cost of goods sold.	(4,184,000)	(972,000)	Cash	$ 1,131,280	$ 417,420
Gross profit.	2,016,000	648,000	Accounts receivable.	1,843,200	375,840
Equity income.	113,800		Inventory	2,793,600	482,760
Operating expenses	(1,080,000)	(421,200)	Equity investment.	2,283,780	
Net income.	$1,049,800	$ 226,800	Property, plant and equipment (PPE), net . . .	14,878,080	893,160
				$22,929,940	$2,169,180
Statement of retained earnings:					
BOY retained earnings	$6,126,480	$ 837,000	Liabilities and stockholders' equity		
Net income.	1,049,800	226,800	Accounts payable.	$ 1,054,080	$ 154,440
Dividends	(216,960)	(34,020)	Accrued liabilities	1,252,800	201,960
Ending retained earnings . .	$6,959,320	$1,029,780	Long-term liabilities	6,600,000	540,000
			Common stock	845,820	110,000
			APIC	6,217,920	133,000
			Retained earnings	6,959,320	1,029,780
				$22,929,940	$2,169,180

At what amount will the following accounts appear on the consolidated financial statements?

a. Sales
b. Equity income
c. Operating expenses
d. Inventories
e. Equity investment

f. Property, plant and equipment (PPE), net
g. Patent
h. Common stock
i. Retained earnings

40. **Determining ending consolidated balances in the second year following the acquisition—Cost method**

Assume a parent company acquired a subsidiary on January 1, 2015, for $1,936,000. The purchase price was $816,200 in excess of the subsidiary's $1,119,800 book value of Stockholders' Equity on the acquisition date. Of this excess purchase price, $352,000 was assigned to Property, plant and equipment with a remaining economic useful life of 10 years, and $464,200 was assigned to Goodwill. On the acquisition date, the subsidiary reported retained earnings equal to $847,550. The parent uses the cost method of pre-consolidation Equity investment bookkeeping. The financial statements of the parent and its subsidiary for the year ended December 31, 2016, are as follows:

	Parent	Subsidiary		Parent	Subsidiary
Income statement:			**Balance sheet:**		
Sales.	$8,318,750	$1,815,000	Assets		
Cost of goods sold.	(5,989,500)	(1,089,000)	Cash	$ 1,567,280	$ 468,600
Gross profit.	2,029,250	726,000	Accounts receivable.	2,462,900	421,300
Investment income.	37,400		Inventory	3,226,850	540,650
Operating expenses	(1,247,840)	(471,900)	Equity investment.	1,936,000	
Net income.	$1,118,810	$ 254,100	Property, plant and equipment (PPE), net . . .	17,189,920	1,000,450
				$26,382,950	$2,431,000
Statement of retained earnings:					
BOY retained earnings	$5,801,070	$ 937,750	Liabilities and stockholders' equity		
Net income.	1,118,810	254,100	Accounts payable.	$ 1,217,920	$ 173,030
Dividends	(262,570)	(37,400)	Accrued liabilities	1,447,270	226,270
Ending retained earnings . .	$6,657,310	$1,154,450	Long-term liabilities	10,587,500	605,000
			Common stock	775,080	121,000
			APIC	5,697,890	151,250
			Retained earnings	6,657,310	1,154,450
				$26,382,950	$2,431,000

At what amount will the following accounts appear on the consolidated financial statements?

a. Sales

b. Investment income

c. Operating expenses

d. Inventories

e. Equity investment

f. Property, plant and equipment (PPE), net

g. Goodwill

h. Common stock

i. Retained earnings

LO3 **41. Determining ending consolidated balances in the third year following the acquisition—Cost method**

Assume a parent company acquired a subsidiary on January 1, 2014, for $2,112,000. The purchase price was $1,080,000 in excess of the subsidiary's $1,032,000 book value of Stockholders' Equity on the acquisition date. Of this excess purchase price, $600,000 was assigned to Property, plant and equipment with a remaining economic useful life of 8 years, and $480,000 was assigned to Goodwill. On the acquisition date, the subsidiary reported retained earnings equal to $735,000. The parent uses Investment cost method of pre-consolidation Equity investment bookkeeping. The financial statements of the parent and its subsidiary for the year ended December 31, 2016, are as follows:

	Parent	Subsidiary		Parent	Subsidiary
Income statement:			**Balance sheet:**		
Sales.................	$9,075,000	$1,980,000	Assets		
Cost of goods sold.......	(6,534,000)	(1,188,000)	Cash....................	$ 1,709,760	$ 511,200
Gross profit.............	2,541,000	792,000	Accounts receivable..............	2,686,800	459,600
Investment income.......	40,800		Inventory	3,520,200	589,800
Operating expenses......	(1,361,280)	(514,800)	Equity investment...........	2,112,000	
Net income............	$1,220,520	$ 277,200	Property, plant and equipment (PPE), net ...	18,752,640	1,091,400
				$28,781,400	$2,652,000
Statement of retained earnings:					
BOY retained earnings....	$6,328,440	$1,023,000	Liabilities and stockholders' equity		
Net income............	1,220,520	277,200	Accounts payable...........	$ 1,328,640	$ 188,760
Dividends	(286,440)	(40,800)	Accrued liabilities............	1,578,840	246,840
Ending retained earnings ..	$7,262,520	$1,259,400	Long-term liabilities	11,550,000	660,000
			Common stock	845,520	132,000
			APIC...................	6,215,880	165,000
			Retained earnings	7,262,520	1,259,400
				$28,781,400	$2,652,000

At what amount will the following accounts appear on the consolidated financial statements?

a. Sales

b. Investment income

c. Operating expenses

d. Inventories

e. Equity investment

f. Property, plant and equipment (PPE), net

g. Patent

h. Goodwill

i. Common stock

j. Retained earnings

LO3 **42. Determining ending consolidated balances in the fourth year following the acquisition—Cost method**

Assume a parent company acquired a subsidiary on January 1, 2013, for $1,760,000. The purchase price was $1,200,000 in excess of the subsidiary's $560,000 book value of Stockholders' Equity on the acquisition date. Of this excess purchase price, $500,000 was assigned to Property, plant and equipment with a remaining economic useful life of 16 years, $400,000 was assigned to an unrecorded patent with a remaining economic useful life of 8 years, and $300,000 was assigned to Goodwill. On the acquisition date, the subsidiary reported retained earnings equal to $312,500. The parent uses the cost method of pre-consolidation Equity investment bookkeeping. The financial statements of the parent and its subsidiary for the year ended December 31, 2016, are as follows:

	Parent	Subsidiary		Parent	Subsidiary
Income statement:			**Balance sheet:**		
Sales.................	$7,562,500	$1,650,000	Assets		
Cost of goods sold.......	(5,445,000)	(990,000)	Cash..................................	$ 1,424,800	$ 426,000
Gross profit.............	2,117,500	660,000	Accounts receivable...................	2,239,000	383,000
Investment income.......	34,000		Inventory	2,933,500	491,500
Operating expenses......	(1,134,400)	(429,000)	Equity investment.....................	1,760,000	
Net income.............	$1,017,100	$ 231,000	Property, plant and equipment (PPE), net ...	10,627,200	909,500
				$18,984,500	$2,210,000
Statement of retained earnings:					
BOY retained earnings....	$5,273,700	$ 852,500	Liabilities and stockholders' equity		
Net income.............	1,017,100	231,000	Accounts payable.....................	$ 1,107,200	$ 157,300
Dividends	(238,700)	(34,000)	Accrued liabilities....................	1,315,700	205,700
Ending retained earnings ..	$6,052,100	$1,049,500	Long-term liabilities	4,625,000	550,000
			Common stock	704,600	110,000
			APIC................................	5,179,900	137,500
			Retained earnings	6,052,100	1,049,500
				$18,984,500	$2,210,000

At what amount will the following accounts appear on the consolidated financial statements?

a. Sales
b. Investment income
c. Operating expenses
d. Inventories
e. Equity investment

f. Property, plant and equipment (PPE), net
g. Patent
h. Goodwill
i. Common stock
j. Retained earnings

PROBLEMS

43. **Consolidation at the end of the first year subsequent to date of acquisition—Equity method
(purchase price equals book value)**

Assume that a parent company acquires its subsidiary on January 1, 2016, by exchanging 40,000 shares
of its $1 par value Common Stock, with a market value on the acquisition date of $28 per share, for all
of the outstanding voting shares of the acquiree. You have been charged with preparing the consolidation of these two companies at the end of the first year.

On the acquisition date, all of the subsidiary's assets and liabilities had fair values equaling their
book values. Following are financial statements of the parent and its subsidiary for the year ended December 31, 2016.

	Parent	Subsidiary		Parent	Subsidiary
Income statement:			**Balance sheet:**		
Sales.	$2,960,000	$1,680,000	Assets		
Cost of goods sold.	(2,072,000)	(1,008,000)	Cash.	$ 701,920	$ 432,880
Gross profit.	888,000	672,000	Accounts receivable.	378,880	389,760
Equity income.	235,200		Inventory	574,240	500,640
Operating expenses.	(562,400)	(436,800)	Equity investment.	1,319,920	
Net income.	$ 560,800	$ 235,200	Property, plant and equipment (PPE), net . . .	2,170,240	926,240
				$5,145,200	$2,249,520
Statement of retained earnings:					
BOY retained earnings. . . .	$1,881,600	$ 868,000	Liabilities and stockholders' equity		
Net income.	560,800	235,200	Accounts payable.	$ 216,640	$ 160,160
Dividends	(112,160)	(35,280)	Accrued liabilities	257,520	209,440
Ending retained earnings . .	$2,330,240	$1,067,920	Long-term liabilities	—	560,000
			Common stock.	414,400	112,000
			APIC.	1,926,400	140,000
			Retained earnings	2,330,240	1,067,920
				$5,145,200	$2,249,520

a.   Prepare the journal entry to record the acquisition of the subsidiary.

b.   Show the computations to yield the Equity Investment reported by the parent in the amount of $1,319,920.

c.   Prepare the consolidation entries for the year ended December 31, 2016.

d.   Prepare the consolidated spreadsheet for the year ended December 31, 2016.

LO3   44. Consolidation at the end of the first year subsequent to date of acquisition—Cost method (purchase price equals book value)

Assume that the parent company acquires its subsidiary on January 1, 2016, by exchanging 31,500 shares of its $1 par value Common Stock, with a market value on the acquisition date of $40 per share, for all of the outstanding voting shares of the acquiree. You have been charged with preparing the consolidation of these two companies at the end of the first year.

On the acquisition date, all of the subsidiary's assets and liabilities had fair values equaling their book values. Following are financial statements of the parent and its subsidiary for the year ended December 31, 2016.

	Parent	Subsidiary		Parent	Subsidiary
Income statement:			**Balance sheet:**		
Sales.	$3,330,000	$1,890,000	Assets		
Cost of goods sold.	(2,331,000)	(1,134,000)	Cash.	$ 789,660	$ 486,990
Gross profit.	999,000	756,000	Accounts receivable.	426,240	438,480
Investment income.	39,690		Inventory	646,020	563,220
Operating expenses.	(632,700)	(491,400)	Equity investment.	1,260,000	
Net income.	$ 405,990	$ 264,600	Property, plant and equipment (PPE), net . . .	2,441,556	1,042,020
				$5,563,476	$2,530,710
Statement of retained earnings:					
BOY retained earnings. . . .	$2,116,800	$ 976,500	Liabilities and stockholders' equity		
Net income.	405,990	264,600	Accounts payable.	$ 243,756	$ 180,180
Dividends	(126,180)	(39,690)	Accrued liabilities	289,710	235,620
Ending retained earnings . .	$2,396,610	$1,201,410	Long-term liabilities	—	630,000
			Common stock.	466,200	126,000
			APIC.	2,167,200	157,500
			Retained earnings	2,396,610	1,201,410
				$5,563,476	$2,530,710

a.   Prepare the journal entry to record the acquisition of the subsidiary.

b.   Prepare the consolidation entries for the year ended December 31, 2016.

c. Prepare the consolidated spreadsheet for the year ended December 31, 2016.

d. Explain why the [ADJ] consolidating entry in *Part b* included the dollar amount that it did.

45. Consolidation at the end of the first year subsequent to date of acquisition—Equity method

LO2

Assume that the parent company acquires its subsidiary on January 1, 2016, by exchanging 41,500 shares of its $1 par value Common Stock, with a market value on the acquisition date of $36 per share, for all of the outstanding voting shares of the acquiree. You have been charged with preparing the consolidation of these two companies at the end of the first year.

On the acquisition date, all of the subsidiary's individual net assets had fair values that equaled their book values except for the following: PPE assets are undervalued by $81,000 (depreciation = $5,400 per year), and the subsidiary has an unrecorded Patent that has a fair value of $261,000 (amortization = $32,625 per year). Any remaining difference between the purchase price and the fair value of the identifiable assets results from expected synergies that are expected to be realized as a result of the business combination.

Following are financial statements of the parent and its subsidiary for the year ended December 31, 2016:

	Parent	Subsidiary		Parent	Subsidiary
Income statement:			**Balance sheet:**		
Sales...............	$4,950,000	$1,485,000	Assets		
Cost of goods sold.......	(3,465,000)	(891,000)	Cash.....................	$ 275,355	$ 382,635
Gross profit...........	1,485,000	594,000	Accounts receivable........	633,600	344,520
Equity income..........	169,875		Inventory	960,300	442,530
Operating expenses......	(940,500)	(386,100)	Equity investment.........	1,632,690	
Net income...........	$ 714,375	$ 207,900	Property, plant and equipment (PPE), net ...	3,629,340	818,730
				$7,131,285	$1,988,415
Statement of retained earnings:					
BOY retained earnings....	$2,570,400	$ 767,250	Liabilities and stockholders' equity		
Net income............	714,375	207,900	Accounts payable.........	$ 362,340	$ 141,570
Dividends	(144,180)	(31,185)	Accrued liabilities.........	430,650	185,130
Ending retained earnings ..	$3,140,595	$ 943,965	Long-term liabilities	—	495,000
			Common stock...........	566,100	99,000
			APIC...................	2,631,600	123,750
			Retained earnings	3,140,595	943,965
				$7,131,285	$1,988,415

a. Prepare the journal entry to record the acquisition of the subsidiary.

b. Show the computations to yield the equity income of $169,875 reported by the parent in its income statement.

c. Show the computations to yield the Equity Investment reported by the parent in the amount of $1,632,690.

d. Prepare the consolidation entries for the year ended December 31, 2016.

e. Prepare the consolidated spreadsheet for the year ended December 31, 2016.

f. What additional assets have been recognized on the consolidated balance sheet that were not explicitly reported on the balance sheets of either the parent or the subsidiary? Why were they not previously reported in pre-acquisition financial statements of the parent or the subsidiary?

46. Determining ending balances of accounts on the consolidated balance sheet at the end of the first year—Equity method

LO2

Assume that the parent company acquires its subsidiary on January 1, 2016, by exchanging 38,000 shares of its Common Stock, with a market value on the acquisition date of $48 per share, for all of the outstanding voting shares of the acquiree. On the acquisition date, all of the subsidiary's individual net assets had fair values that equaled their book values except for a building (included in PPE, net) that is undervalued by $248,000 (depreciation expense = $15,500 per year), an unrecorded License Agreement that has a fair value of $216,000 (amortization expense = $27,000 per year), and an unrecorded Customer List owned by the subsidiary that has a fair value of $144,000 (amortization expense = $16,000 per year). Any further discrepancy between the purchase price and the book value of the subsidiary's Stockholders' Equity is attributed to expected synergies to be realized by the consolidated company as a result of the acquisition.

The financial statements of the parent and its subsidiary for the year ended December 31, 2016, are as follows:

	Parent	Subsidiary		Parent	Subsidiary
Income statement:			**Balance sheet:**		
Sales................	$5,760,000	$1,560,000	Assets		
Cost of goods sold.......	(4,032,000)	(936,000)	Cash....................	$ 498,360	$ 401,960
Gross profit...........	1,728,000	624,000	Accounts receivable......	737,280	361,920
Equity income..........	159,900		Inventory	1,117,440	464,880
Operating expenses......	(1,094,400)	(405,600)	Equity investment........	1,951,140	
Net income...........	$ 793,500	$ 218,400	Property, plant and equipment (PPE), net ...	5,951,200	860,080
				$10,255,420	$2,088,840
Statement of retained earnings:					
BOY retained earnings....	$2,956,800	$ 806,000	Liabilities and stockholders' equity		
Net income...........	793,500	218,400	Accounts payable........	$ 421,600	$ 148,720
Dividends	(160,000)	(32,760)	Accrued liabilities	565,120	194,480
Ending retained earnings ..	$3,590,300	$ 991,640	Long-term liabilities	2,000,000	520,000
			Common stock.........	651,200	104,000
			APIC.................	3,027,200	130,000
			Retained earnings	3,590,300	991,640
				$10,255,420	$2,088,840

a. Prepare the journal entry to record the acquisition of the subsidiary.

b. Show the computation to yield the equity income of $159,900 reported by the parent in its income statement during 2016.

c. Show the computation to yield the Equity Investment balance of $1,951,140 reported by the parent on December 31, 2016.

d. Show the computation to determine whether any portion of the purchase price should be assigned to the Goodwill asset on January 1, 2016.

e. At what amounts will each of the following be reported in the consolidated financial statements for the year ended December 31, 2016?

 1. Consolidated net income

 2. Accounts receivable

 3. Equity investment

 4. Property, plant and equipment (PPE), net

 5. Goodwill

 6. Common stock

 7. APIC

 8. Retained earnings

f. What intangible assets will be reported on the consolidated balance sheet and at what amounts? Why were they not previously reported in pre-acquisition financial statements of the parent or the subsidiary?

LO2 47. **Consolidation several years subsequent to date of acquisition—Equity method**

Assume that a parent company acquired a subsidiary on January 1, 2014. The purchase price was $665,000 in excess of the subsidiary's book value of Stockholders' Equity on the acquisition date, and that excess was assigned to the following [A] assets:

[A] Asset	Original Amount	Original Useful Life
Property, plant and equipment (PPE), net	$140,000	16 years
Patent..	245,000	7 years
License...	105,000	10 years
Goodwill	175,000	Indefinite
	$665,000	

The **[A]** assets with definite useful lives have been depreciated or amortized as part of the parent's pre-consolidation equity method accounting. The Goodwill asset has been tested annually for impairment, and has not been found to be impaired.

The financial statements of the parent and its subsidiary for the year ended December 31, 2016, are as follows:

	Parent	Subsidiary		Parent	Subsidiary
Income statement:			**Balance sheet:**		
Sales..................	$4,802,000	$1,308,300	Assets		
Cost of goods sold.......	(3,457,300)	(784,700)	Cash....................................	$ 719,600	$ 337,400
Gross profit.............	1,344,700	523,600	Accounts receivable....................	1,229,200	303,800
Equity income...........	129,150		Inventory	1,624,000	389,900
Operating expenses......	(720,300)	(340,200)	Equity investment......................	1,530,550	
Net income.............	$ 753,550	$ 183,400	Property, plant and equipment (PPE), net ...	2,923,200	721,000
				$8,026,550	$1,752,100
Statement of retained earnings:					
BOY retained earnings....	$1,694,700	$ 676,200	Liabilities and stockholders' equity		
Net income.............	753,550	183,400	Accounts payable.....................	$ 702,800	$ 124,600
Dividends	(364,000)	(28,000)	Accrued liabilities	835,800	163,100
Ending retained earnings ..	$2,084,250	$ 831,600	Long-term liabilities	2,100,000	436,100
			Common stock........................	527,100	87,500
			APIC	1,776,600	109,200
			Retained earnings	2,084,250	831,600
				$8,026,550	$1,752,100

a. Compute the Equity Investment balance as of January 1, 2016.

b. Show the computation to yield the $129,150 equity income reported by the parent for the year ended December 31, 2016.

c. Show the computation to yield the $1,530,550 Equity Investment account balance reported by the parent at December 31, 2016.

d. Prepare the consolidation entries for the year ended December 31, 2016.

e. Prepare the consolidation spreadsheet for the year ended December 31, 2016.

48. **Inferring consolidation entries from consolidated financial statements—Equity method**   **LO2**

Assume that a parent company acquired a subsidiary on January 1, 2012. The purchase price was $396,000 in excess of the subsidiary's book value of Stockholders' Equity on the acquisition date, and that excess was assigned to the following **[A]** assets:

[A] Asset	Original Amount	Original Useful Life
Property, plant and equipment (PPE), net	$ 72,000	10 years
Customer list	108,000	6 years
Goodwill..	216,000	Indefinite
	$396,000	

The [A] assets with definite useful lives have been depreciated or amortized as part of the parent's pre-consolidation equity method accounting. The Goodwill asset has been tested annually for impairment, and has not been found to be impaired.

Selected accounts from the parent, subsidiary, and consolidated financial statements for the year ended December 31, 2016, are as follows:

	Parent	Subsidiary	Consolidated
Income statement:			
Sales.....................................	$1,950,000	$295,200	$2,245,200
Cost of goods sold...........................	(1,404,000)	(134,400)	(1,538,400)
Gross profit...............................	546,000	160,800	706,800
Equity income..............................	78,000		0
Operating expenses.........................	(292,800)	(57,600)	(375,600)
Net income................................	$ 331,200	$103,200	$ 331,200
Statement of retained earnings:			
BOY retained earnings......................	$1,332,000	$115,200	$1,332,000
Net income................................	331,200	103,200	331,200
Dividends	(52,800)	(4,800)	(52,800)
Ending retained earnings	$1,610,400	$213,600	$1,610,400
Balance sheet:			
Assets			
Cash......................................	$ 314,400	$189,600	$ 504,000
Accounts receivable........................	499,200	220,800	720,000
Inventory	757,200	198,000	955,200
Equity investment..........................	638,400		0
Property, plant and equipment (PPE), net	4,029,600	243,600	4,309,200
Customer list			18,000
Goodwill..................................			216,000
	$6,238,800	$852,000	$6,722,400
Liabilities and stockholders' equity			
Accounts payable...........................	$ 232,800	141,600	$ 374,400
Accrued liabilities..........................	340,800	147,600	488,400
Long-term liabilities	2,400,000	194,400	2,594,400
Common stock.............................	303,600	15,600	303,600
APIC......................................	1,351,200	139,200	1,351,200
Retained earnings	1,610,400	213,600	1,610,400
	$6,238,800	$852,000	$6,722,400

a. Show the computation to yield the equity income of $78,000 reported by the parent in its income statement during 2016.

b. Show the computation to yield the Equity Investment balance of $638,400 reported by the parent on December 31, 2016.

c. Show the computations that yield the ending balances of each of the following accounts at December 31, 2016.

   1. Property, plant and equipment (PPE), net

   2. Customer list

   3. Retained earnings

d. What is the relation between the parent's net income and consolidated net income?

e. Why aren't the Stockholders' Equity accounts of the subsidiary reflected in the consolidated balance sheet?

f. Provide the consolidation entries for the year ending December 31, 2016.

49. Inferring consolidation entries from consolidated financial statements—Cost method

Assume a parent company acquired a subsidiary on January 1, 2012. The purchase price was $1,242,000 in excess of the subsidiary's book value of Stockholders' Equity on the acquisition date, and that excess was assigned to the following [A] assets:

[A] Asset	Original Amount	Original Useful Life
Property, plant and equipment (PPE), net	$ 300,000	20 years
Patent	432,000	12 years
Goodwill	510,000	Indefinite
	$1,242,000	

The parent company uses the cost method of pre-consolidation Equity Investment bookkeeping. The Goodwill asset has been tested annually for impairment and has not been found to be impaired.

Selected accounts from the parent, subsidiary, and consolidated financial statements for the year ended December 31, 2016, are as follows:

	Parent	Subsidiary	Consolidated
Income statement:			
Sales	$ 9,075,000	$1,980,000	$11,055,000
Cost of goods sold	(6,534,000)	(1,188,000)	(7,722,000)
Gross profit	2,541,000	792,000	3,333,000
Investment income	40,800		0
Operating expenses	(1,361,280)	(514,800)	(1,927,080)
Net income	$ 1,220,520	$ 277,200	$ 1,405,920
Statement of retained earnings:			
BOY retained earnings	$ 6,328,440	$1,023,000	$ 6,574,440
Net income	1,220,520	277,200	1,405,920
Dividends	(286,440)	(40,800)	(286,440)
Ending retained earnings	$ 7,262,520	$1,259,400	$ 7,693,920
Balance sheet:			
Assets			
Cash	$ 1,709,760	$ 511,200	$ 2,220,960
Accounts receivable	2,686,800	459,600	3,146,400
Inventory	3,520,200	589,800	4,110,000
Equity investment	2,112,000		0
Property, plant and equipment (PPE), net	12,752,640	1,091,400	14,069,040
Patent list			252,000
Goodwill			510,000
	$22,781,400	$2,652,000	$24,308,400
Liabilities and stockholders' equity			
Accounts payable	$ 1,328,640	$ 188,760	$1,517,400
Accrued liabilities	1,578,840	246,840	1,825,680
Long-term liabilities	5,550,000	660,000	6,210,000
Common stock	845,520	132,000	845,520
APIC	6,215,880	165,000	6,215,880
Retained earnings	7,262,520	1,259,400	7,693,920
	$22,781,400	$2,652,000	$24,308,400

a. For the year ended December 31, 2016, explain how the parent's pre-consolidation investment income of $40,800 was determined.

b. Explain how the parent's December 31, 2016 pre-consolidation Equity Investment balance of $2,112,000 was determined.

c. For the year ended December 31, 2016, reconcile the parent company's pre-consolidation net income of $1,220,520 to the consolidated balance of $1,405,920.

 d. What was the subsidiary's retained earnings balance on the acquisition date? (*Hint:* You will need to use an account that does not change after the acquisition date.)

 e. Why aren't the Stockholders' Equity accounts of the subsidiary reflected in the consolidated balance sheet?

 f. Provide the consolidation entries for the year ending December 31, 2016.

LO2, 4

50. Consolidation several years subsequent to date of acquisition—Equity method (includes impairment of Goodwill)

Assume that a parent company acquired a subsidiary on January 1, 2013. The purchase price was $1.8 million in excess of the subsidiary's book value of Stockholders' Equity on the acquisition date, and that excess was assigned to the following [A] assets:

[A] Asset	Original Amount	Original Useful Life
Property, plant and equipment (PPE), net	$ 120,000	10 years
Customer list	480,000	8 years
Royalty agreement	360,000	12 years
Database	240,000	5 years
Goodwill	600,000	Indefinite
	$1,800,000	

The [A] assets with definite useful lives have been depreciated or amortized as part of the parent's pre-consolidation Equity Method accounting. The Goodwill asset has been tested annually for impairment, and has not been found to be impaired.

 The financial statements of the parent and its subsidiary for the year ended December 31, 2016, are as follows:

	Parent	Subsidiary		Parent	Subsidiary
Income statement:			**Balance sheet:**		
Sales	$5,022,000	$2,388,000	Assets		
Cost of goods sold	(3,615,600)	(1,432,800)	Cash	$ 758,400	$ 614,400
Gross profit	1,406,400	955,200	Accounts receivable	1,286,400	554,400
Equity income	183,600		Inventory	1,948,800	712,800
Operating expenses	(753,600)	(621,600)	Equity investment	3,074,400	
Net income	$ 836,400	$ 333,600	Property, plant and equipment (PPE), net	4,404,000	1,315,200
				$ 11,472,000	$3,196,800
Statement of retained earnings:					
BOY retained earnings	$ 4,574,400	$ 1,233,600	Liabilities and stockholders' equity		
Net income	836,400	333,600	Accounts payable	$ 736,800	$ 228,000
Dividends	(175,200)	(50,400)	Accrued liabilities	873,600	297,600
Ending retained earnings	$ 5,235,600	$ 1,516,800	Long-term liabilities	1,200,000	796,800
			Common stock	1,129,200	158,400
			APIC	2,296,800	199,200
			Retained earnings	5,235,600	1,516,800
				$11,472,000	$3,196,800

 a. Compute the Equity Investment balance as of January 1, 2016.

 b. Show the computation to yield the $183,600 of equity income reported by the parent for the year ended December 31, 2016.

 c. Show the computation to yield the $3,074,400 Equity Investment account balance reported by the parent on December 31, 2016.

 d. Prepare the consolidation entries for the year ended December 31, 2016.

 e. Prepare the consolidation spreadsheet for the year ended December 31, 2016.

 f. Now, assume that, prior to the issuance of your consolidated financial statements, you perform your annual test for potential impairment of Goodwill. You decide to forego the option to perform a qualitative assessment to determine whether it is more likely than not that the fair value of the reporting unit is less than the carrying value of the reporting unit. You estimate that the fair value of the subsidiary is $3.0 million and the fair value of the identifiable net assets (other than Goodwill) is $2.7 million. Conduct your test for potential impairment of Goodwill, and prepare any required journal entry as a result of that test.

g. Prepare the consolidated balance sheet on December 31, 2016 and the consolidated income statement and consolidated statement of retained earnings for the year then ended.

51. Consolidation several years subsequent to date of acquisition—Equity method (includes impairment of Goodwill)

LO2, 4

Assume that a parent company acquired a subsidiary on January 1, 2012. The purchase price was $540,000 in excess of the subsidiary's book value of Stockholders' Equity on the acquisition date, and that excess was assigned to the following [A] assets:

[A] Asset	Original Amount	Original Useful Life
Patent	$240,000	8 years
Goodwill	300,000	Indefinite
	$540,000	

The [A] assets with definite useful lives have been depreciated or amortized as part of the parent's pre-consolidation equity method accounting. The Goodwill asset has been tested annually for impairment, and has not been found to be impaired.

The financial statements of the parent and its subsidiary for the year ended December 31, 2016, are as follows:

	Parent	Subsidiary		Parent	Subsidiary
Income statement:			**Balance sheet:**		
Sales	$3,669,000	$1,840,800	Assets		
Cost of goods sold	(2,857,800)	(1,104,600)	Cash	$ 390,000	$ 474,000
Gross profit	811,200	736,200	Accounts receivable	715,800	427,200
Equity income	227,400		Inventory	1,540,200	548,400
Operating expenses	(595,200)	(478,800)	Equity investment	1,836,000	
Net income	$ 443,400	$ 257,400	Property, plant and equipment (PPE), net	2,802,000	1,015,200
				$7,284,000	$2,464,800
Statement of retained earnings:					
BOY retained earnings	$1,754,400	$ 951,000	Liabilities and stockholders' equity		
Net income	443,400	257,400	Accounts payable	$ 583,200	$ 175,200
Dividends	(150,000)	(38,400)	Accrued liabilities	690,000	229,200
Ending retained earnings	$2,047,800	$1,170,000	Long-term liabilities	1,800,000	614,400
			Common stock	618,000	122,400
			APIC	1,545,000	153,600
			Retained earnings	2,047,800	1,170,000
				$7,284,000	$2,464,800

a. Compute the Equity Investment balance as of January 1, 2016.

b. Show the computation to yield the $227,400 of Equity Income reported by the parent for the year ended December 31, 2016.

c. Show the computation to yield the $1,836,000 Equity Investment account balance reported by the parent at December 31, 2016.

d. Prepare the consolidation entries for the year ended December 31, 2016.

e. Prepare the consolidation spreadsheet for the year ended December 31, 2016.

f. Now, assume that, prior to the issuance of your consolidated financial statements, you perform your annual test for potential impairment of Goodwill. You decide to forego the option to perform a qualitative assessment to determine whether it is more likely than not that the fair value of the reporting unit is less than the carrying value of the reporting unit. You estimate that the fair value of the subsidiary is $1.8 million and the fair value of the identifiable net assets (other than

Goodwill) is $1.6 million. Conduct your test for potential impairment of Goodwill, and prepare any required journal entry as a result of that test.

g. Prepare the consolidated balance sheet on December 31, 2016, and the consolidated income statement and consolidated statement of retained earnings for the year then ended.

LO2, 4

52. **Consolidation several years subsequent to date of acquisition—Equity method (includes subsidiary loss and impairment of Licenses and Goodwill)**
Assume that a parent company acquired a subsidiary on January 1, 2012. The purchase price was $260,000 in excess of the subsidiary's book value of Stockholders' Equity on the acquisition date, and that excess was assigned to the following [A] assets:

[A] Asset	Original Amount	Original Useful Life
Licenses.	$160,000	10 year
Goodwill.	100,000	Indefinite
	$260,000	

The Licenses have been amortized as part of the parent's pre-consolidation equity method accounting. The Goodwill asset has been tested annually for impairment, and has not been found to be impaired.

The financial statements of the parent and its subsidiary for the year ended December 31, 2016, are as follows:

	Parent	Subsidiary		Parent	Subsidiary
Income statement:			**Balance sheet:**		
Sales.	$1,266,000	$493,200	Assets		
Cost of goods sold.	(911,600)	(296,000)	Cash.	$ 308,000	$ 8,800
Gross profit.	354,400	197,200	Accounts receivable.	324,000	114,400
Equity income (loss).	(74,800)		Inventory	491,200	146,800
Operating expenses.	(192,000)	(256,000)	Equity investment.	448,800	
Net income (loss)	$ 87,600	$ (58,800)	Property, plant and equipment (PPE), net . . .	1,056,000	272,000
				$2,628,000	$542,000
Statement of retained earnings:					
BOY retained earnings. . . .	$ 579,600	$254,800	Liabilities and stockholders' equity		
Net income.	87,600	(58,800)	Accounts payable.	$ 185,200	$ 47,200
Dividends	(17,200)	—	Accrued liabilities	220,000	61,600
Ending retained earnings . .	$ 650,000	$196,000	Long-term liabilities	800,000	164,400
			Common stock.	188,800	32,800
			APIC	584,000	40,000
			Retained earnings	650,000	196,000
				$2,628,000	$542,000

a. Compute the Equity Investment balance as of January 1, 2016.

b. Show the computation to yield the $(74,800) Equity Loss reported by the parent for the year ended December 31, 2016.

c. Show the computation to yield the $448,800 Equity Investment account balance reported by the parent at December 31, 2016.

d. Prepare the consolidation entries for the year ended December 31, 2016.

e. Prepare the consolidation spreadsheet for the year ended December 31, 2016.

f. Now, assume that, prior to the issuance of your consolidated financial statements, you perform your annual test for potential impairment of Goodwill. Since the subsidiary is losing money, it has suspended dividends. First, you conclude that the Licenses have lost all of their value and must be written off. Prepare the journal entry to write off the Licenses.

Then, you estimate that the fair value of the subsidiary is $340,000 and the fair value of the identifiable net assets (exclusive of the Licenses and Goodwill) is $320,000. Conduct your test for potential impairment of Goodwill, and prepare any required journal entry as a result of that test.

g. Prepare the consolidated balance sheet on December 31, 2016, and the consolidated income statement and consolidated statement of retained earnings for the year then ended.

53. Consolidation several years subsequent to date of acquisition—Cost method

Assume a parent company acquired a subsidiary on January 1, 2013. The purchase price was $1,035,000 in excess of the subsidiary's book value of Stockholders' Equity on the acquisition date, and that excess was assigned to the following [A] assets:

	Original Amount	Original Useful Life
Property, plant and equipment (PPE), net	$ 250,000	10 years
Patent	360,000	9 years
Goodwill	425,000	Indefinite
	$1,035,000	

The parent company uses the cost method of pre-consolidation Equity Investment bookkeeping. The Goodwill asset has been tested annually for impairment, and has not been found to be impaired.

Selected accounts from the parent, subsidiary, and consolidated financial statements for the year ended December 31, 2016, are as follows:

	Parent	Subsidiary		Parent	Subsidiary
Income statement:			**Balance sheet:**		
Sales	$7,562,000	$1,650,000	Assets		
Cost of goods sold	(5,445,000)	(990,000)	Cash	$ 1,425,000	$ 425,000
Gross profit	2,117,000	660,000	Accounts receivable	1,239,000	383,000
Investment income	34,000		Inventory	2,934,000	492,000
Operating expenses	(1,134,000)	(429,000)	Equity investment	1,760,000	
Net income	$1,017,000	$ 231,000	Property, plant and equipment (PPE), net	3,627,000	910,000
				$10,985,000	$2,210,000
Statement of retained earnings:					
BOY retained earnings	$3,273,700	$ 852,000	Liabilities and stockholders' equity		
Net income	1,017,000	231,000	Accounts payable	$ 907,000	$ 157,000
Dividends	(238,700)	(34,000)	Accrued liabilities	516,000	206,000
Ending retained earnings	$4,052,000	$1,049,000	Long-term liabilities	2,625,000	550,000
			Common stock	705,000	110,000
			APIC	2,180,000	138,000
			Retained earnings	4,052,000	1,049,000
				$10,985,000	$2,210,000

a. For the year ended December 31, 2016, explain how the parent's pre-consolidation investment income of $34,000 was determined.

b. Explain how the parent's December 31, 2016 pre-consolidation Equity Investment balance of $1,760,000 was determined.

c. What was the subsidiary's retained earnings balance on the acquisition date? You should assume that the Common Stock and APIC have not changed since the acquisition date. (*Hint:* You will need to use an account that does not change after the acquisition date.)

d. Compute the Equity Investment balance at December 31, 2016 assuming the parent company used the equity method of investment bookkeeping since the acquisition date.

e. Prepare the [ADJ] entry that is needed in order to bring the Equity Investment from its current balance (using cost method) to the required balance (using the equity method) on January 1, 2016. (*Hint:* You will use balance computed in *Part c.*) Explain the function of this consolidation entry.

f.   Provide the consolidation entries for the year ending December 31, 2016.

g.   Prepare the consolidation spreadsheet for the year ended December 31, 2016.

LO3   54. **Consolidation several years subsequent to date of acquisition—Cost method**

Assume a parent company acquired a subsidiary on January 1, 2013. The purchase price was $362,000 in excess of the subsidiary's book value of Stockholders' Equity on the acquisition date, and that excess was assigned to the following [A] assets:

	Original Amount	Original Useful Life
Property, plant and equipment (PPE), net	$ 48,000	10 years
Licenses	128,000	8 years
Customer list	16,000	4 years
Goodwill	170,000	Indefinite
	$362,000	

The parent company uses the cost method of pre-consolidation Equity Investment bookkeeping. The Goodwill asset has been tested annually for impairment, and has not been found to be impaired.

Selected accounts from the parent, subsidiary, and consolidated financial statements for the year ended December 31, 2016, are as follows:

	Parent	Subsidiary		Parent	Subsidiary
Income statement:			**Balance sheet:**		
Sales	$3,024,800	$660,000	Assets		
Cost of goods sold	(2,178,000)	(396,000)	Cash	$ 570,000	$170,000
Gross profit	846,800	264,000	Accounts receivable	495,600	153,200
Investment income	13,600		Inventory	1,173,600	196,800
Operating expenses	(453,600)	(171,600)	Equity investment	704,000	
Net income	$ 406,800	$ 92,400	Property, plant and equipment (PPE), net	1,450,800	364,000
				$4,394,000	$884,000
Statement of retained earnings:					
BOY retained earnings	$1,309,480	$340,800	Liabilities and stockholders' equity		
Net income	406,800	92,400	Accounts payable	$ 362,800	$ 62,800
Dividends	(95,480)	(13,600)	Accrued liabilities	206,400	82,400
Ending retained earnings	$1,620,800	$419,600	Long-term liabilities	1,050,000	220,000
			Common stock	282,000	44,000
			APIC	872,000	55,200
			Retained earnings	1,620,800	419,600
				$4,394,000	$884,000

a.   For the year ended December 31, 2016, explain how the parent's pre-consolidation investment income of $13,600 was determined.

b.   Explain how the parent's December 31, 2016 pre-consolidation Equity Investment balance of $704,000 was determined.

c.   What was the subsidiary's retained earnings balance on the acquisition date? You should assume that the Common Stock and APIC have not changed since the acquisition date. (*Hint:* You will need to use an account that does not change after the acquisition date.)

d.   Compute the Equity Investment balance at December 31, 2016 assuming the parent company used the equity method of investment bookkeeping since the acquisition date.

e.   Prepare the [ADJ] entry that is needed in order to bring the Equity Investment from its current balance (using cost method) to the required balance (using the equity method) on January 1, 2016. (*Hint:* You will use balance computed in *Part c*.) Explain the function of this consolidation entry.

f.   Provide the consolidation entries for the year ending December 31, 2016.

g.   Prepare the consolidation spreadsheet for the year ended December 31, 2016.

55.[B] **Consolidation subsequent to date of acquisition—Equity method (Pooling of interest on acquisition date)**   LO2, 5

Assume that on January 1, 2014, the parent company acquires a 100% interest in its subsidiary by issuing common stock with a fair value that is $600,000 over the book value of the subsidiary's Stockholders' Equity. All of the excess purchase price was attributable to the subsidiary's property, plant and equipment (PPE), which was undervalued by $600,000. The undervalued PPE has a remaining useful life of 10 years. Because it was a "common control" acquisition, the parent accounted for the acquisition under the pooling-of-interests method. (*Note:* Pooling of interests is no longer acceptable for new acquisitions, except in the case of "common control" acquisitions.)

The financial statements of the parent and its subsidiary for the year ended December 31, 2016, follow:

	Parent	Subsidiary		Parent	Subsidiary
Income statement:			**Balance sheet:**		
Sales..................	$5,520,000	$1,110,000	Assets		
Cost of goods sold.......	(2,964,000)	(670,000)	Cash.....................................	$ 945,000	$ 281,000
Gross profit.............	2,556,000	440,000	Accounts receivable...................	1,090,000	258,000
Equity income...........	150,000		Inventory	1,652,000	331,000
Operating expenses......	(1,618,000)	(290,000)	Equity investment......................	867,000	
Net income.............	$1,088,000	$ 150,000	Property, plant and equipment (PPE), net ...	3,246,000	761,000
				$7,800,000	$1,631,000
Statement of retained earnings:					
BOY retained earnings....	$1,280,000	$ 574,000	Liabilities and stockholders' equity		
Net income.............	1,088,000	150,000	Accounts payable......................	$ 724,000	$ 264,000
Dividends	(218,000)	(23,000)	Accrued liabilities	1,000,000	100,000
Ending retained earnings ..	$2,150,000	$ 701,000	Long-term liabilities	1,500,000	400,000
			Common stock........................	1,392,000	74,000
			APIC.................................	1,034,000	92,000
			Retained earnings	2,150,000	701,000
				$7,800,000	$1,631,000

a. Prepare the consolidation entries for the year ended December 31, 2016.

b. Prepare the consolidation spreadsheet for the year ended December 31, 2016.

56.[B] **Consolidation subsequent to date of acquisition—Cost method (Pooling of interest on acquisition date)**   LO3, 5

Assume that the parent company acquires a 100% interest in its subsidiary by issuing common stock with a fair value that is $500,000 over the book value of the subsidiary's Stockholders' Equity on January 1, 2009. On the acquisition date, the subsidiary's retained earnings was equal to $581,000. In addition, on the acquisition date, all of the excess purchase price was attributable to an unrecorded patent held by the subsidiary, which had a fair value of $500,000 and a remaining economic life of 10 years. Because it was a "common control" acquisition, the parent accounted for the acquisition under the pooling-of-interests method. (*Note:* Pooling of interests is no longer acceptable for new acquisitions, except in the case of "common control" acquisitions.)

The financial statements of the parent and its subsidiary for the year ended December 31, 2016, follow:

	Parent	Subsidiary		Parent	Subsidiary
Income statement:			**Balance sheet:**		
Sales.................	$3,700,000	$2,100,000	Assets		
Cost of goods sold.......	(2,590,000)	(1,260,000)	Cash....................................	$ 877,400	$ 541,100
Gross profit.............	1,110,000	840,000	Accounts receivable....................	473,600	487,200
Investment income.......	44,100		Inventory	717,800	625,800
Operating expenses......	(703,000)	(546,000)	Equity investment.....................	896,000	
Net income.............	$ 451,100	$ 294,000	Property, plant and equipment (PPE), net ...	2,712,840	1,157,800
				$5,677,640	$2,811,900
Statement of retained earnings:					
BOY retained earnings....	$1,848,000	$1,085,000	Liabilities and stockholders' equity		
Net income.............	451,100	294,000	Accounts payable......................	$ 270,840	$ 200,200
Dividends	(140,200)	(44,100)	Accrued liabilities	321,900	261,800
Ending retained earnings ..	$2,158,900	$1,334,900	Long-term liabilities		700,000
			Common stock........................	518,000	140,000
			APIC	2,408,000	175,000
			Retained earnings	2,158,900	1,334,900
				$5,677,640	$2,811,900

a. Prepare the consolidation entries for the year ended December 31, 2016.

b. Prepare the consolidation spreadsheet for the year ended December 31, 2016.

TOPIC REVIEW

Solution 1

a.

Equity investment...	800	
Cash		800
(to record Equity Investment)		

b.

Equity investment...	150	
Equity income		150
(to record Equity Income of $150 representing 100% of the subsidiary's net income)		

Equity income..	20	
Equity investment		20
(to record amortization of the $200 AAP over 10 years)		

c.

Cash	50	
Equity investment		50
(to record the receipt of $50 dividend from the subsidiary)		

Solution 2

	Parent	Subsidiary	Consolidation Entries		Consolidated
			Dr	Cr	
Income statement:					
Sales.	$10,000,000	$1,500,000			$11,500,000
Cost of goods sold.	(7,000,000)	(900,000)			(7,900,000)
Gross profit.	3,000,000	600,000			3,600,000
Equity income.	200,000		[C] $ 200,000		0
Operating expenses	(1,900,000)	(390,000)	[D] 10,000		(2,300,000)
Net income.	$ 1,300,000	$ 210,000			$ 1,300,000
Statement of retained earnings:					
BOY retained earnings.	$ 5,720,000	$ 630,000	[E] 630,000		$ 5,720,000
Net income.	1,300,000	210,000			1,300,000
Dividends	(260,000)	(31,500)		[C] $ 31,500	(260,000)
Ending retained earnings	$ 6,760,000	$ 808,500			$ 6,760,000
Balance sheet:					
Assets					
Cash	$ 683,500	$ 259,500			$ 943,000
Accounts receivable.	1,280,000	348,000			1,628,000
Inventory.	1,940,000	447,000			2,387,000
Equity investment.	1,123,500		[C] 168,500		0
			[E] 855,000		
			[A] 100,000		
Building, net	9,332,000	827,000			10,159,000
Patent.			[A] 100,000	[D] 10,000	90,000
	$14,359,000	$1,881,500			$15,207,000
Liabilities and stockholders' equity					
Current liabilities.	$ 1,437,000	$ 348,000			$ 1,785,000
Long-term liabilities	3,312,000	500,000			3,812,000
Common stock.	1,635,000	100,000	[E] 100,000		1,635,000
APIC	1,215,000	125,000	[E] 125,000		1,215,000
Retained earnings	6,760,000	808,500			6,760,000
	$14,359,000	$1,881,500	$1,165,000	$1,165,000	$15,207,000

Solution 3

	Parent	Subsidiary	Consolidation Entries Dr	Consolidation Entries Cr	Consolidated
Income statement:					
Sales.....................................	$15,000,000	$2,100,000			$17,100,000
Cost of goods sold.......................	(10,500,000)	(1,350,000)			(11,850,000)
Gross profit.............................	4,500,000	750,000			5,250,000
Dividend income..........................	47,250		[C] $ 47,250		0
Operating expenses.......................	(2,850,000)	(585,000)	[D] 7,500		(3,442,500)
Net income...............................	$ 1,697,250	$ 165,000			$ 1,807,500
Statement of retained earnings:					
BOY retained earnings.	$ 3,374,500	$ 850,000	[E] 850,000	[ADJ] $ 515,000	$ 3,889,500
Net income...............................	1,697,250	165,000			1,807,500
Dividends	(390,000)	(47,250)		[C] 47,250	(390,000)
Ending retained earnings	$ 4,681,750	$ 967,750			$ 5,307,000
Balance sheet:					
Assets					
Cash......................................	$ 1,025,250	$ 389,250			$ 1,414,500
Accounts receivable......................	1,920,000	522,000			2,442,000
Inventory.................................	2,910,000	670,500			3,580,500
Equity investment........................	725,000		[ADJ] 515,000	[E] 1,187,500	0
				[A] 52,500	
Building, net	9,500,000	875,000			10,375,000
Licenses			[A] 52,500	[D] 7,500	45,000
	$16,080,250	$2,456,750			$17,857,000
Liabilities and stockholders' equity					
Current liabilities........................	$ 2,155,500	$ 472,500			$ 2,628,000
Long-term liabilities	4,968,000	679,000			5,647,000
Common stock............................	2,452,500	150,000	[E] 150,000		2,452,500
APIC.....................................	1,822,500	187,500	[E] 187,500		1,822,500
Retained earnings	4,681,750	967,750			5,307,000
	$16,080,250	$2,456,750	$1,809,750	$1,809,750	$17,857,000

[ADJ] amount = ($850,000 − $312,500) − (3 × $7,500) = $515,000
[A] amount = $75,000 − (3 × $7,500) = $52,500

Solution 4

The $900,000 fair value of the subsidiary is less than the $1,000,000 book value of the Equity Investment (i.e., the carrying value of the reporting unit); therefore, Goodwill is potentially impaired.

Fair value of the subsidiary................................	$ 900,000
Fair value of the net assets exclusive of Goodwill..............	700,000
Implied fair value of Goodwill..............................	$ 200,000
Book value of Goodwill	300,000
Goodwill impairment	$(100,000)

Goodwill is found to be impaired and must, therefore, be written off in part with the following journal entry:

Equity income..	100,000	
Equity investment*.....................................		100,000
(to write down the book value of Goodwill)		

*In the consolidated financial statements, the debit to Equity Income will appear as a loss on write-down of Goodwill and the credit to the Equity Investment account will appear as a reduction in the balance of Goodwill.

COMPREHENSIVE REVIEW—EQUITY METHOD SOLUTION

	Parent	Subsidiary	Consolidation Entries Dr	Consolidation Entries Cr	Consolidated
Income statement:					
Sales...	$5,700,000	$480,000			$6,180,000
Cost of goods sold..............................	(3,990,000)	(288,000)			(4,278,000)
Gross profit....................................	1,710,000	192,000			1,902,000
Equity income..................................	47,200		[C] $ 47,200		0
Operating expenses.............................	(1,083,000)	(124,800)	[D] 20,000		(1,227,800)
Net income....................................	$ 674,200	$ 67,200			$ 674,200
Statement of retained earnings:					
BOY retained earnings...........................	$2,863,680	$248,000	[E] 248,000		$2,863,680
Net income....................................	674,200	67,200			674,200
Dividends	(134,840)	(10,080)		[C] $ 10,080	(134,840)
Ending retained earnings	$3,403,040	$305,120			$3,403,040
Balance sheet:					
Assets					
Cash...	$ 354,870	$129,440			$ 484,310
Accounts receivable.............................	729,600	111,360			840,960
Inventory......................................	1,105,800	143,040			1,248,840
Equity investment..............................	837,120			[C] 37,120	0
				[E] 320,000	
				[A] 480,000	
Property, plant and equipment (PPE), net	5,319,240	264,640	[A] 150,000	[D] 15,000	5,718,880
Customer list			[A] 50,000	[D] 5,000	45,000
Goodwill			[A] 280,000		280,000
	$8,346,630	$648,480			$8,617,990
Liabilities and stockholders' equity					
Current liabilities.................................	$ 819,090	$111,360			$ 930,450
Long-term liabilities	2,500,000	160,000			2,660,000
Common stock.................................	931,950	32,000	[E] 32,000		931,950
APIC...	692,550	40,000	[E] 40,000		692,550
Retained earnings	3,403,040	305,120			3,403,040
	$8,346,630	$648,480	$867,200	$867,200	$8,617,990

COMPREHENSIVE REVIEW—COST METHOD SOLUTION

	Parent	Subsidiary	Consolidation Entries Dr	Consolidation Entries Cr	Consolidated
Income statement:					
Sales.	$9,000,000	$1,260,000			$10,260,000
Cost of goods sold.	(6,300,000)	(810,000)			(7,110,000)
Gross profit.	2,700,000	450,000			3,150,000
Dividend income.	28,350		[C] $ 28,350		0
Operating expenses.	(1,710,000)	(351,000)	[D] 7,500		(2,068,500)
Net income.	$1,018,350	$ 99,000			$ 1,081,500
Statement of retained earnings:					
BOY retained earnings.	$2,062,700	$510,000	[E] 510,000	[ADJ] $ 307,500	$ 2,370,200
Net income.	1,018,350	99,000			1,081,500
Dividends	(234,000)	(28,350)		[C] 28,350	(234,000)
Ending retained earnings	$2,847,050	$580,650			$ 3,217,700
Balance sheet:					
Assets					
Cash.	$ 615,150	$ 233,550			$ 848,700
Accounts receivable.	1,152,000	313,200			1,465,200
Inventory.	1,746,000	402,300			2,148,300
Equity investment.	473,000		[ADJ] 307,500	[E] 712,500	0
				[A] 68,000	
Building, net	5,700,000	525,000			6,225,000
Patent.			[A] 30,000	[D] 7,500	22,500
Goodwill			[A] 38,000		38,000
	$9,686,150	$1,474,050			$10,747,700
Liabilities and stockholders' equity					
Current liabilities.	$1,293,300	$ 283,500			$ 1,576,800
Long-term liabilities	2,980,800	407,400			3,388,200
Common stock.	1,471,500	90,000	[E] 90,000		1,471,500
APIC	1,093,500	112,500	[E] 112,500		1,093,500
Retained earnings	2,847,050	580,650			3,217,700
	$9,686,150	$1,474,050	$1,123,850	$1,123,850	$10,747,700

[ADJ] amount = ($510,000 − $187,500) − (2 × $7,500) = $307,500
[A] Patent amount = $45,000 − (2 × $7,500) = $30,000

1. Describe the accounting for intercompany sales of inventory between the parent and the subsidiary when the parent uses the equity method of pre-consolidation investment bookkeeping. (p. 186)

2. Describe the accounting for intercompany sales of inventory between the parent and the subsidiary when the parent uses the cost method of pre-consolidation investment bookkeeping. (p. 198)

3. Describe the accounting for intercompany sales of non-depreciable noncurrent assets between the parent and the subsidiary when the parent uses the equity method of pre-consolidation investment bookkeeping. (p. 203)

4. Describe the accounting for intercompany sales of depreciable noncurrent assets between the parent and the subsidiary when the parent uses the equity method of pre-consolidation investment bookkeeping. (p. 207)

5. Describe the accounting for intercompany sales of non-depreciable noncurrent assets between the parent and the subsidiary when the parent uses the cost method of pre-consolidation investment bookkeeping. (p. 218)

6. Describe the accounting for intercompany sales of depreciable noncurrent assets between the parent and the subsidiary when the parent uses the cost method of pre-consolidation investment bookkeeping. (p. 221)

Consolidated Financial Statements and Intercompany Transactions

4

According to its February 1, 2015 Securities and Exchange Commission (SEC) Form 10-K, **Krispy Kreme Doughnuts, Inc.** (Krispy Kreme) "is a leading branded retailer and wholesaler of high-quality doughnuts, complementary beverages and treats and packaged sweets. The Company's principal business, which began in 1937, is owning and franchising Krispy Kreme stores, at which a wide variety of high-quality doughnuts, including the Company's Original Glazed® doughnut, are sold and distributed together with complementary products, and where a broad array of coffees and other beverages are offered. The Company generates revenues from four business segments: Company Stores, Domestic Franchise, International Franchise and KK Supply Chain."

KRISPY KREME DOUGHNUTS, INC.

The Company Stores segment is comprised of the doughnut shops operated by the Company. These shops sell doughnuts and complementary products through the on-premises and wholesale channels and come in two formats: factory stores and satellite shops. As of February 1, 2015, there were 167 domestic franchise stores in 32 states, consisting of 116 factory and 51 satellite stores.

The Domestic and International Franchise Segments derive revenue principally from initial development and franchise fees related to new stores and from royalties on sales by franchise stores. For franchise stores, direct operating expenses include costs incurred to recruit new domestic franchisees, to assist with domestic store openings, to assist in the development of domestic marketing and promotional programs, and to monitor and aid in the performance of domestic franchise stores, as well as direct general and administrative expenses and certain allocated corporate costs.

The KK Supply Chain segment produces doughnut mixes and manufactures doughnut-making equipment, which all factory stores, both Company and franchise, are required to purchase. In addition, KK Supply Chain sells other ingredients, packaging and supplies, principally to Company-owned and domestic franchise stores.

Because the company owns both the stores in the Company Stores segment and the KK Supply Chain segment, all of the sales of the doughnut ingredients and manufacturing equipment sold by KK Supply Chain to the company-owned stores must be eliminated in consolidation. (Krispy Kreme can't sell things to itself and recognize those sales or profits in the consolidated financial statements!) The segment information reported on Note 2 of the February 1, 2015 consolidated financial statements provides clues about the magnitude of these intra-company sales:

(in thousands)	Year Ended		
	February 1, 2015	February 2, 2014	February 3, 2013
Revenues:			
Company stores........................	$325,306	$306,825	$296,494
Domestic franchise......................	13,450	11,839	10,325
International franchise	28,598	25,607	24,941

(continued on next page)

(continued from previous page)

(in thousands)	Year Ended		
	February 1, 2015	February 2, 2014	February 3, 2013
KK Supply Chain:			
Total revenues........................	244,688	231,229	215,412
Less—Intersegment sales elimination	(121,708)	(115,169)	(111,329)
External KK Supply Chain revenues	122,980	116,060	104,083
Total revenues	$490,334	$460,331	$435,843

As reported in Note 2, the KK Supply Chain Segment recorded approximately $245 million of sales during the year ended February 1, 2015, but nearly $122 million of these sales were eliminated in consolidation because the sales were to Krispy Kreme-owned company stores. This is almost 50% of the total 2015 revenues of the KK Supply Chain Segment!

This brings us to the main point of this chapter:

In the preparation of consolidated financial statements, companies are required to eliminate all intercompany transactions and balances with and between commonly controlled affiliates.

This means that Krispy Kreme's income statement includes no sales or expenses that are based on transactions between the parent and any of its subsidiaries or among any of those subsidiaries. In addition, the balance sheets reported at the end of each period include no payables or receivables that are owed between the affiliated companies controlled by Krispy Kreme. The consolidation process is a bit more complex in the presence of intercompany transactions (e.g., eliminating intercompany profits in inventory), which is why we've devoted an entire chapter to the topic.

Source: Krispy Kreme Doughnuts, Inc. February 1, 2015 SEC Form 10-K

CHAPTER ORGANIZATION

Consolidated Financial Statements and Intercompany Transactions

Accounting for the Intercompany Sales of Inventory

- Intuition behind the elimination of intercompany sales and deferral of profit
- Deferral of profit in the initial period of sale and while inventories are held prior to resale
- Recognition of deferred profit when inventories are sold to an independent party
- Upstream vs. downstream sales for wholly owned subsidiaries
- Equity method and deferral of intercompany profit
- How much profit do we defer?
- Continuous sales of inventories
- Sequential coverage of equity-method and cost-method consolidation procedures for deferral of intercompany profit related to inventory

Accounting for the Intercompany Sale of Non-Depreciable Noncurrent Assets

- Intercompany sales of land
- Deferral of profit in the initial period of sale
- Deferral of profit during holding periods prior to resale of land to an independent party
- Recognition of deferred profit when land is sold to an independent party
- Sequential coverage of equity-method and cost-method consolidation procedures for deferral of intercompany profit related to non-depreciable noncurrent assets

Accounting for the Intercompany Sale of Depreciable Assets

- Consolidation entry in year of sale of a depreciable asset
- Consolidation entries during useful life of the depreciable asset
- Consolidation entry in period of sale of the depreciable asset to independent party
- Upstream vs. downstream sales of a depreciable asset
- Sequential coverage of equity-method and cost-method consolidation procedures for deferral of intercompany profit related to depreciable noncurrent assets

A common motive for business combinations is for companies to acquire suppliers or customers so that they can control a greater share of the overall value chain. As a result, parent and subsidiary companies often sell products and services among themselves. A manufacturing subsidiary might, for example, sell completed or partially completed inventories to the parent, which will subsequently sell the inventories to an unaffiliated end customer. Alternatively, the parent might sell property, plant and equipment (PPE) to the subsidiary, which might hold these assets until they are fully depreciated, sold to outside parties, or otherwise disposed.

For accounting purposes, the sale price of the asset for the seller becomes the recorded asset cost of that asset for the buyer. The asset sold is, thus, written up in value from its net book value on the seller's balance sheet to its fair value (purchase price) on the buyer's balance sheet at the time of sale.

To illustrate, consider the sale of inventory costing $140 for a cash sale price of $200. The following journal entries on the seller's and buyer's books (assuming perpetual inventory accounting) record the sale and purchase of the inventory:

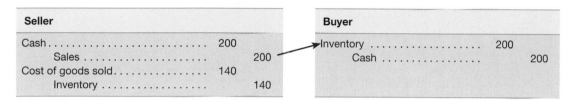

Under perpetual inventory accounting, the seller records the sale and the cash received and removes the cost of the inventory from its balance sheet, reflecting it as cost of goods sold. The cost of the inventory for the buyer is equal to the seller's book value for that inventory *plus* the gross profit recognized by the seller on the sale. As a result, inventory has been written up in this transaction from its (old) carrying value on the seller's books to its selling price, which is its new carrying value on the buyer's books.

For asset sales between two independent companies, the seller's recognition of the gain in an "arm's length" exchange is proper. In contrast, parent and subsidiary companies are not independent; these affiliated companies are viewed as one entity for accounting purposes, and they are required to issue one set of consolidated financial statements. These consolidated financial statements are not allowed to include gains and losses from the transfer of goods and services between affiliated parties. From the perspective of the consolidated company, this is like a single entity recording profit on transactions with itself.

If intercompany sales were recognized in the consolidated financial statements, sales and profit on the consolidated income statement would increase together with reported assets and equity (i.e., Retained Earnings) on the consolidated balance sheet. Affiliated companies in a consolidated group could, conceivably, grow their balance sheets and income statements via transactions among themselves. Because these companies are viewed as one consolidated entity for accounting purposes, this growth in the consolidated balance sheet and income statement does not represent "real" growth (i.e., as measured by transactions with independent, unaffiliated companies outside of the reporting group).

The important point is this: **in transactions among affiliated companies under common control, GAAP does not permit the recognition of intercompany sales transactions or any resulting profit or loss on those sales.** The sale can still occur (and is recognized in the separate, pre-consolidation accounting records of the affiliated companies)—we just can't recognize intercompany transactions in the *consolidated* financial statements, and the intercompany sales transactions must be eliminated from the consolidated income statement. The resulting profit is deferred until the asset is ultimately sold to unaffiliated (i.e., independent) parties.[1] We report the asset on the consolidated balance sheet at the pre-intercompany-transaction carrying value, and we accomplish this with the consolidation entries labeled [I] in our original group of the five core **C-E-A-D-I** entries.

---

[1] Technically, in the case of depreciable assets, like property and equipment, the deferred profit is ratably included in the consolidated financial statements as the asset is depreciated or amortized. We will discuss depreciable assets later in this chapter.

We discuss intercompany asset sales in this chapter, and describe the process by which the revenue on these sales is eliminated and the gain is deferred.[2] Recall, in Chapter 3, we discussed the fact that parent companies are always required to prepare consolidated financial statements that include all controlled investee companies. Thus, the output of the consolidation process will always look the same. However, the starting point for the consolidation process (i.e., the parent's pre-consolidation financial statements) can appear quite different—even when comparing economically identical parent companies—because parent companies have a choice of how they account for the pre-consolidation Equity Investment account. In real-world consolidation settings, there are innumerable variations on the pure-form Equity Investment bookkeeping methods we discuss in this book. Despite this real-world variation, in this text, we primarily discuss post-acquisition consolidation assuming the parent company uses one of two methods of pre-consolidation Equity Investment bookkeeping for its subsidiaries:

1. **Equity Method:** the parent company adjusts its pre-consolidation acquisition-date investment account for its proportionate share of the subsidiary's post-acquisition income, dividends, amortization of the acquisition accounting premium (AAP), and elimination of intercompany transactions.

2. **Cost Method:** the parent company does not adjust its pre-consolidation acquisition-date investment account for the subsidiary's post-acquisition activities. Of course, the parent company must record direct transactions with the subsidiary. For example, dividends declared by the subsidiary will be recorded as a debit to dividends receivable (or cash) and a credit to dividend income.

Despite the fact that parent companies can use different methods of pre-consolidation bookkeeping, the common thread throughout this chapter is focusing on the process by which profits (and losses) from intercompany asset sales are deferred in the preparation of consolidated financial statements. We begin by describing this process as it relates to intercompany sales of inventories, assuming that the parent company applies the equity method of pre-consolidation bookkeeping. We next turn to intercompany sales of inventory assuming that the parent uses the cost method of pre-consolidation bookkeeping. Inventory sales are distinctive because these assets are ultimately sold to outside (unaffiliated) parties within a relatively short period of time. We, then, discuss the intercompany sale of land and depreciable assets (PPE) assuming that the parent company uses the equity method of pre-consolidation bookkeeping. We conclude the chapter with a discussion of the intercompany sale of PPE assets assuming that the parent company uses the cost method of pre-consolidation bookkeeping. PPE assets will typically be kept by the buyer for a longer period of time before sale or disposition. In addition, unlike inventories, the carrying values of many of these noncurrent assets decline, through time, via depreciation and amortization (except for land, which is not depreciated or amortized).

ACCOUNTING FOR INTERCOMPANY SALES OF INVENTORY—EQUITY METHOD

LO1 Describe the accounting for intercompany sales of inventory between the parent and the subsidiary when the parent uses the equity method of pre-consolidation investment bookkeeping.

In this section, we describe the accounting for the intercompany sales of inventory, assuming that the parent applies the equity method of pre-consolidation bookkeeping. We initially discuss a two-period case in which one company in the consolidated group sells inventories to another in the first period. The inventories are then sold to an unaffiliated company in the following period. Next, we consider the continuous sales of inventories between companies within a consolidated group and their subsequent sale to unaffiliated companies.

When the sale is from the subsidiary to the parent it is called an **upstream sale**, and when the sale is from the parent to the subsidiary, it is called a **downstream sale**. This distinction is not as important

---

[2] Intercompany sales of **services** must also be eliminated. For example, the revenue (say, for consulting or legal services) for one company will likely exactly offset against a services-related expense recognized by the affiliate. In the consolidation process, both the service revenue and the related expense are eliminated just like Sales and Cost of Goods Sold in our discussion of intercompany inventory sales.

when subsidiaries are wholly owned (i.e., the assumption made throughout this chapter). However, the upstream-downstream distinction becomes extremely important in Chapter 5, where we introduce the concept of non-wholly owned subsidiaries and the resulting noncontrolling interest reported in consolidated financial statements.

Intuition Behind the Elimination of Intercompany Sales and Deferral of Profit—Equity Method

Assume that during the year ending December 31, 2015, a parent sells inventory that originally cost $100 to its subsidiary for $130 in cash.[3] To highlight the intercompany profit issue, let's also assume that neither the parent nor the subsidiary has any other transactions, assets, or liabilities except the inventory-related accounts and transactions through the year ended December 31, 2015. In addition, assume the parent uses the equity method. Exhibit 4.1 includes relevant inventory-related financial statement excerpts through December 31, 2015.

EXHIBIT 4.1	Year 1 Pre-Consolidation Financial Statement Effects of Intercompany Inventory Transactions—Equity Method		
Year Ended December 31, 2015		**Parent**	**Subsidiary**
Income statement (excerpt):			
Sales.		$130	$ 0
Cost of goods sold.		100	0
Net effect on gross profit		$ 30	$ 0
Income (loss) from subsidiary.		$ (30)	
Net effect on total profits		$ 0	$ 0
Balance sheet (excerpt):			
Inventory.		$ 0	$130
Equity investment.		$ (30)	
Cumulative effect on retained earnings		$ 0	$ 0

As we illustrate in Exhibit 4.1, the parent company will recognize $30 of (pre-consolidation) gross profit on the transaction with the subsidiary. Because the parent records the elimination of the intercompany profits under the equity method, the net effect on total profits is zero. The subsidiary will record the corresponding purchase of the inventory, and its (pre-consolidation) Inventory balance is $130. That balance includes the parent's original inventory cost (i.e., $100) *plus* the markup recognized by the parent in the intercompany inventory transaction (i.e., $30). Because the subsidiary still possesses the inventory at the end of the year, there are no other inventory-related transactions or balances.

In Exhibit 4.2, we illustrate the problem that emerges if the parent and subsidiary combine their financial statements by simply adding them together (without adjustment). If the parent attempts to consolidate its financial statements with those of its subsidiary without adjusting for the intercompany transaction, the resulting consolidated financial statements will include $130 of Sales, $100 of Cost of Goods Sold, $30 of Gross Profit, and $130 of Inventory (i.e., the inventory that was supposedly "sold").

---

[3] We assume cash consideration to highlight the effects of inventory transactions in this chapter. Of course, the sale could be made on account (i.e., Accounts Payable and Accounts Receivable). The form of consideration does not affect the intercompany inventory adjustments; however, any unpaid intercompany payables and receivables must be completely eliminated at the balance sheet date. We will illustrate this in a comprehensive example later in the chapter.

EXHIBIT 4.2	What Happens if We Simply Add the Parent and Subsidiary Inventory-Affected Accounts in Year 1 (Equity Method)?				
Year ended December 31, 2015		Parent	Subsidiary	(Incorrect) "Added"	(Correct) Consolidated
Income statement (excerpt):					
Sales..........................		$130	$ 0	$130	$ 0
Cost of goods sold..................		100	0	100	0
Net effect on gross profit		$ 30	$ 0	$ 30	$ 0
Income (loss) from subsidiary..........		$ (30)		$ (30)	0
Net effect on total profits		$ 0	$ 0	$ 0	$ 0
Balance sheet (excerpt):					
Inventory.........................		$ 0	$130	$130	$100
Equity investment..................		$ (30)		$ (30)	$ 0
Cumulative effect on retained earnings...		$ 0	$ 0	$ 0	$ 0

As we mention in previous chapters, the whole point of consolidation is to produce "as if" financial statements for the economic entity that is controlled by the parent. This means that, for consolidation purposes, we must eliminate all transactions and balances between the parent and its subsidiaries (or between subsidiaries) in the preparation of the consolidated financial statements.

Stated in slightly more technical language, because the intercompany sale is between members of an affiliated group controlled by the parent, GAAP requires elimination of the intercompany sale and the deferral of recognition of the intercompany profit until the inventories are sold to unaffiliated (i.e., independent) parties (FASB ASC 810-10-45-1).[4] In our consolidation spreadsheet, we will identify this intercompany profit as **deferred profit**.[5]

In this example, we eliminate the intercompany sale from the parent to its subsidiary, thereby deferring the $30 profit on that sale until the inventories are ultimately sold by the subsidiary to a company outside of the consolidated group. If we eliminate the intercompany sale, we are left with just the $100 purchase of inventory. The "Consolidated" column of Exhibit 4.2 provides this representation.

Now, let's assume that the intercompany inventory (held by the subsidiary at December 31, 2015) is sold by the subsidiary to an unaffiliated company for $180 during the year ended December 31, 2016. When this inventory passes to an unaffiliated (i.e., independent) entity, *all* of the profit will be recognized in the consolidated financial statements. Thus, following the sale of the inventory to independent parties during the year 2016, we recognize gross profit of $80, consisting of the $30 deferred profit (i.e., $130 − $100) on the intercompany sale and the $50 gross profit (i.e., $180 − $130) on the final sale. That is, from a consolidated perspective, the $30 profit on the intercompany sale is *first deferred* and, *then, recognized* in the consolidated financial statements. We depict this process in Exhibit 4.3:

EXHIBIT 4.3	Process of Deferring Intercompany Profit Until Sale to Non-Affiliate

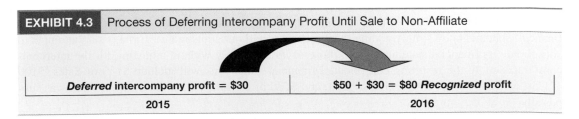

Deferred intercompany profit = $30	**$50 + $30 = $80 Recognized** profit
2015	2016

---

[4] For financial reporting purposes, the profit on the intercompany sale must always be deferred by the parent in the recognition of its Equity Income of the subsidiary (FASB ASC 323-10-35-7). If these intercompany profits are eliminated in the equity method bookkeeping applied by a parent company, then the pre-consolidation net income recognized by the parent is equal to consolidated net income.

[5] "Deferred profit" in our consolidation spreadsheet relates solely to these affiliate-related profits on intercompany sales and not to other, legitimate deferred revenues and profits commonly recognized by companies. We only use this phrase to refer to the amounts that must be shifted between periods during the consolidation process. Also, we generally refer to pre-consolidation profits and losses that appropriately belong in the consolidated financial statements as "confirmed" and profits and losses that are appropriately deferred as "unconfirmed."

In Exhibit 4.4, we provide a summary of the inventory-transaction-affected accounts for the year ended December 31, 2016 (Year 2). The purpose of Exhibit 4.4 is to illustrate the financial statement effects for the parent and its subsidiary in their accounting records for Year 2, the financial statements that will emerge if we simply "add together" the parent and subsidiary financial statements, and the correct consolidated financial statement amounts that should be reported for inventory-transaction-affected accounts.

As we illustrate in Exhibit 4.4, the financial statements that were just "added" do not reflect the economic transactions entered into (solely) with unaffiliated entities. That is, the inventory was originally purchased by the parent for $100 and sold by the subsidiary (to an unaffiliated party) for $180; thus the correct economic representation should include $180 of Sales, $100 of Cost of Goods Sold, and $80 of Gross Profit. These amounts are reflected in the "Consolidated" column.

EXHIBIT 4.4	What Happens if We Simply Add the Parent and Subsidiary Inventory-Affected Accounts in Year 2 (Equity Method)?			
Year ended December 31, 2016	**Parent**	**Subsidiary**	**(Incorrect) "Added"**	**(Correct) Consolidated**
Income statement (excerpt):				
Sales.	$ 0	$180	$180	$180
Cost of goods sold.	0	130	130	100
Net effect on gross profit	$ 0	$ 50	$ 50	$ 80
Income (loss) from subsidiary.	$80		$ 80	$ 0
Net effect on total profits	$80	$ 50	$130	$ 80
Balance sheet (excerpt):				
Inventory.	$ 0	$ 0	$ 0	$ 0
Equity investment.	$50		$ 50	$ 0
Cumulative effect on retained earnings.	$80	$ 50	$130	$ 80

Now that we've provided an intuitive description of the process of shifting of economic profits into the periods in which they are earned through transactions with unaffiliated entities, we turn our attention to the systematic elimination of intercompany transactions via consolidating entries.

Intercompany Inventory Transactions and Consolidating Entries—Equity Method

Here is an important point: *inventory transactions and balances always affect Cost of Goods Sold.* Thus, if we eliminate intercompany profits in ending Inventory, then Cost of Goods Sold is also affected by that elimination process.[6]

Recall the formula for Cost of Goods Sold from your introductory and intermediate accounting courses:

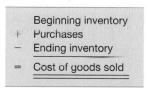

Considering each of the three components of the Cost of Goods Sold formula will allow for a systematic means to completely eliminate all of the effects of intercompany inventory transactions. In using the Cost of Goods Sold formula, you should first ask the following three questions:

---

[6] For strictly pedagogical purposes, in this and subsequent examples, we prefer to discuss intercompany inventory profit elimination by using the *periodic* approach to Inventory and Cost of Goods Sold computation. In a periodic inventory system, the purchasing company records the debit to a Purchases account instead of the Inventory account. The seller computes cost of goods sold and records the balance of ending inventories as a result of the end-of-period closing entry based on the final inventory count (i.e., Cost of Goods Sold = Beginning Inventory + Purchases − Ending Inventory). Of course, the elimination process also works for the perpetual system, too.

1. Did the parent and/or subsidiaries have profits in *beginning* Inventory that were the result of transactions with other companies in the affiliated group of companies?
2. Did the parent and/or subsidiaries engage in intercompany purchases *during the period* from other companies in the affiliated group of companies?
3. Did the parent and/or subsidiaries have profits in *ending* Inventory that were the result of transactions with other companies in the affiliated group of companies?

If we answer "yes" to questions #1 or #3, we will need to remove the deferred profit from these components of the Cost of Goods Sold equation. Note that the removal of profit from the beginning and ending Inventory balances will have **opposite** effects on Cost of Goods Sold. Specifically, the Cost of Goods Sold identity requires that removing deferred profit from *beginning* Inventory will *decrease* Cost of Goods Sold, while removing deferred profit from *ending* Inventory will *increase* Cost of Goods Sold (i.e., because Beginning Inventory is added while Ending Inventory is subtracted in the Cost of Goods Sold identity). Finally, answering "yes" to question #2 will result in removing the full amount of the intercompany sales transactions from Cost of Goods Sold.

The Period During Which Intercompany Sale Occurs Between Affiliated Companies (Prior to Resale to Outside Parties)—Equity Method

We can illustrate the deferral and recognition process that we discuss above using the amounts from our preceding example. Recall that during the year ending December 31, 2015, the parent company sold $130 of goods to the subsidiary and that the subsidiary's ending Inventory balance at December 31, 2015, included $30 of deferred profit (i.e., we answered "yes" to Cost of Goods Sold questions #2 and #3). As we describe in Chapter 1, a parent company applying the equity method will remove the deferred profit from the Equity Investment account and from the equity-method "Income (loss) from subsidiary" account until the period in which the inventory is sold to an unaffiliated entity. The equity-method journal entry recorded by the parent company in its pre-consolidation accounting records is as follows:

Income (loss) from subsidiary.	30	
Equity investment		30
(to eliminate deferred intercompany profit from Income (loss) from subsidiary and Equity Investment account in year of intercompany sale)		

Turning now to preparation of the consolidated financial statements, the adjustments necessary to arrive at the correct consolidated Cost of Goods Sold amounts for the year ended December 31, 2015, are determined as follows:

Beginning inventory	$ 0	Beginning Inventory includes no deferred profit at January 1, 2015
+ Purchases	130	2015 purchases includes a $130 intercompany sale
− Ending inventory	(30)	Ending Inventory includes all of the $30 of deferred profit at December 31, 2015, since none of the inventories have yet been resold to outside parties.
= Cost of goods sold	$100	Cost of Goods Sold is overstated by $100 ($130 − $30)

Notice that the consolidated amount of Cost of Goods Sold in Exhibit 4.2 is $100 less than simply adding together the parent and subsidiary balances for Cost of Goods Sold. This is accomplished by two separate adjustments in our consolidation worksheet: a reduction of the intercompany purchase by $130 and a reduction of ending inventory by $30.

In Exhibit 4.5, we present the two consolidating entries that are required in this example for the year ended December 31, 2015. We call this group of consolidation entries our [I] (for *Intercompany Transactions and Balances*) entries in our C-E-A-D-I sequence.[7] We also present the [C] consolidating entry necessary to reverse the incremental changes in the Equity Investment account recorded by the parent in applying the equity method.

---

[7] We will subscript the [I] entries throughout this chapter to help you identify the transaction to which they refer.

EXHIBIT 4.5	[I] Consolidation Entries in the Initial Period of Intercompany Sale of Inventories—Equity Method		
Consolidation entries to eliminate changes in the Equity Investment account during the year	**[C]**	Equity investment. . . . . Income (loss) from subsidiary . . . . *(to eliminate changes in the investment account during the year)*	30	 30
Consolidation entries to eliminate intercompany transactions and balances	[I_{sales}]	Sales. . . . . Cost of goods sold (purchase) . . . . *(to reverse the intercompany sale and related purchase)*	130	 130
	[I_{cogs}]	Cost of goods sold (EOY inventory). . . . . Inventories. . . . . *(to reverse the inventory write-up and defer the gross profit on the intercompany sale)*	30	 30

If we combine the two components of the [I] consolidation entries (above), the net effect reverses the intercompany sale (i.e., as though it had not occurred):

Sales	130	
Cost of goods sold		100
Inventories.		30
(to reverse the intercompany sale)		

Sales and Cost of Goods Sold for the intercompany sale are eliminated and the write-up of inventories as a result of the sale is reversed.[8] We show the effects of these consolidating entries in the excerpts from a consolidation spreadsheet (for the year ended December 31, 2015) presented in Exhibit 4.6. Notice that the effect of the consolidation process (when the parent uses the equity method) is that (1) the net effect on total profits remains at zero pre-consolidation and post-consolidation, and (2) the pre-consolidation $(30) reduction in income from the equity method accounting is redistributed among the post-consolidation sales and cost of sales accounts.

EXHIBIT 4.6	Excerpts of Inventory-Transaction-Affected Accounts in Consolidation Spreadsheet in the Initial Period of Intercompany Sale of Inventories—Equity Method					

			Consolidation Entries			
	Parent	**Subsidiary**	**Debits**		**Credits**	**Consolidated**
Income statement (excerpt):						
Sales.	$130	$ 0	[I_{sales}]	130		$ 0
Cost of goods sold.	100	0	[I_{cogs}]	30	[I_{sales}] 130	0
Net effect on gross profit	$ 30	$ 0		160	130	$ 0
Income (loss) from subsidiary.	$ (30)				**[C]** 30	0
Net effect on total profits	$ 0	$ 0		160	160	0
Balance sheet (excerpt):						
Inventory	$ 0	$130			[I_{cogs}] 30	$100
Equity investment.	$ (30)		**[C]**	30		$ 0

---

[8] We are only combining the two components to allow better understanding of the net effects of intercompany-transaction elimination. We strongly recommend that you record these as two separate consolidating entries. Doing so will make the transition to the topic of continuous intercompany sales of inventories, which we discuss later in the chapter, much easier.

The Period Following Intercompany Sale When Inventories Are Sold to an Independent (Unaffiliated) Company—Equity Method

We continue our discussion of the intercompany-profit deferral technique using the *second-year* amounts from our preceding example. Recall that during the year ending December 31, 2016, the subsidiary sold $180 of goods to an unaffiliated (i.e., independent) company. These goods were transferred to the subsidiary for $130 during 2015, and they originally cost the parent $100 (i.e., there was $30 of deferred profit in the subsidiary's inventory at December 31, 2015). When we consider the year ended December 31, 2016, we can only answer "yes" to Cost of Goods Sold question #1: there was $30 of deferred profit in the January 1, 2016, inventories, but there were no intercompany transactions during 2016 and there was no deferred profit in the ending inventories on December 31, 2016. A parent company applying the equity method will record the deferred profit in the Equity Investment account and recognize the deferred profit in the subsidiary income account in the period in which the inventory is sold to an unaffiliated entity. In addition, the parent will record its share of the subsidiary's $50 recognized net income on the sale of goods to the unaffiliated entity ($180 − $130 = $50). The combined (i.e., recognized subsidiary income of $50 plus deferred profit of $30 equals $80 total subsidiary income) equity-method journal entry recorded by the parent company in its pre-consolidation accounting records is as follows:

Equity investment...	80	
Income (loss) from subsidiary		80
(to recognize the deferred intercompany profit in the period of sale to an unaffiliated entity)		

Now, turning to the consolidated financial statements, the adjustment necessary to arrive at the correct Cost of Goods Sold amounts is determined as follows:

	Beginning inventory	$ 30	Beginning Inventory includes $30 of deferred profit at January 1, 2016
+	Purchases	0	There were no intercompany sales/purchases during 2016
−	Ending inventory	(0)	Ending Inventory includes no deferred profit on December 31, 2016
=	Cost of goods sold	$ 30	Cost of Goods Sold is overstated by $30

Notice that the consolidated amount of Cost of Goods Sold in Exhibit 4.4 is $30 less than simply adding together the parent and subsidiary balances for Cost of Goods Sold. That is, the amount of the overall consolidation adjustment is explained by one component: a reduction of the beginning Inventory component of Cost of Goods Sold by $30. Exhibit 4.7 presents the consolidating entry for the year ended December 31, 2016.

EXHIBIT 4.7	**[I] Consolidation Entries in the Subsequent Period the Intercompany Inventory is Sold to an Unaffiliated Entity—Equity Method**			
Consolidation entries to eliminate changes in the Equity Investment account during the year	**[C]**	Income (loss) from subsidiary.................... Equity investment .... *(to eliminate changes in the Equity Investment account during the year)*	80	80
Intercompany elimination entry to recognize deferred gross profit on the intercompany sale in the period the inventories are resold outside of the consolidated group	[I$_{pos}$]	BOY Equity investment (parent).................. Cost of goods sold (BOY inventory) .... *(to increase the Equity Investment account and recognize the deferred profit on the prior year's sale)*	30	30

The effect of this period of sale (POS) consolidating entry is to reduce the beginning-of-year Equity Investment balance for the deferred profit that has been deferred and, then, to recognize the deferred gain (by a reduction of Cost of Goods Sold with a credit) in the current year under the assumption that the inventories have now been sold.

We show the effects of these consolidating entries in the excerpts from a consolidation spreadsheet (for the year ended December 31, 2016) presented in Exhibit 4.8.

EXHIBIT 4.8	Excerpts of Inventory-Transaction-Affected Accounts in Consolidation Spreadsheet in the Period of Subsequent Sale of Inventories to Unaffiliated Entities—Equity Method

	Parent	Subsidiary	Consolidation Entries Debits		Consolidation Entries Credits		Consolidated
Income statement (excerpt):							
Sales..................................	$ 0	$180					$180
Cost of goods sold....................	0	130			[I_{pos}]	30	100
Net effect on gross profit	$ 0	$ 50				30	$ 80
Income (loss) from subsidiary...........	$80		[C]	80			0
Net effect on total profits	$80	$ 50		80		30	$ 80
Balance sheet (excerpt):							
Inventory...........................	$ 0	$ 0					$ 0
Equity investment...................	$50	$ 0	[I_{pos}]	30	[C]	80	$ 0

On a consolidated basis, the reported gross profit reflects the *original* cost of the inventories of $100, not the amount to which the inventories were written up in the intervening sale from the parent to the subsidiary. The [I_{pos}] consolidating entry removes the deferred profit from the beginning-of-year Equity Investment account and *reduces* Cost of Goods Sold and, thus, increases gross profit. The deferred profit on the intercompany inventory sale is now recognized in the consolidated income statement.

Upstream versus Downstream Transactions for Wholly Owned (i.e., 100%) Subsidiaries—Equity Method

The preceding example provides an illustration of the consolidation entries for a downstream intercompany inventory transaction. Interestingly, in the case of wholly owned subsidiaries, there is no difference in [I] consolidating entries for upstream versus downstream transactions. This is because all deferred profit must be removed from the combined financial statements, regardless of the direction of the transaction.[9]

If we consider the accounts affected and the amounts in the preceding example, all consolidating entries in Exhibit 4.5 and the account relationships and balances in Exhibit 4.6 are the same in the upstream case, except deferred profit will offset the regular equity method income recognized by the parent company. In our stylized example, because all of the sales by the subsidiary are intercompany sales, there is no need for consolidating entry [C] in either year. That's because, under the equity method of pre-consolidation Investment bookkeeping, the parent company would have made the following journal entry in the first year to record the parent's share of the subsidiary's income and to remove the deferred intercompany profits:[10]

Equity investment...	30	
Income (loss) from subsidiary		30
(to eliminate deferred intercompany profit from income and Equity Investment		
account in year of intercompany sale)		

---

[9] This statement is also true for a sale of inventory from one subsidiary to another subsidiary. These transactions among commonly controlled subsidiaries are also considered "upstream."

[10] Recall that we made some fairly big simplifying assumptions in this example. In particular, we assumed that there were no other transactions or balances, except for the inventory-related items. Thus, the subsidiary's only income would have been derived from the upstream sale. In typical consolidations, where the subsidiary also makes sales to unaffiliated parties, the [C] entry would eliminate all subsidiary net income resulting from sales to unaffiliated parties.

Thus, in the case of upstream sales, the equity method of accounting causes the parent's Equity-Investment-related accounts to reflect only transactions that involve unaffiliated entities.

How Much Gross Profit Do We Defer?

In our examples thus far, we have assumed that *none* of the inventories were resold in the initial period of intercompany sale. As a result, all of the profit on the intercompany sale ($30 in Exhibit 4.2) is deferred in the initial period of intercompany sale. In practice, some of the inventories will be resold by the buyer in the same period as the intercompany sale.

For those inventories that have been sold, it is completely appropriate to recognize the gross profit on the intercompany sale as those inventories have been sold to a buyer outside of the group of affiliated companies. Consequently, we need only defer the gross profit on the inventories that have *not* been resold during the period. The amount of profit to be deferred, then, is equal to the dollar amount of the gross profit on the intercompany sale multiplied by the percentage of inventories that are unsold at the end of the period:

$$\textbf{\$ Profit to defer} \ = \ \textbf{\$ Total deferred profit} \ \times \ \textbf{\% Unsold inventories}$$

For our previous numerical example, the parent sold to the subsidiary for $130 inventories that cost the parent $100. Assuming, as we did in our example, that all of those inventories remain unsold at December 31, 2015, we defer the full $30 of gross profit for the year ending December 31, 2015.

If we, instead, assume that 75% of those inventories were resold outside of the consolidated group at December 31, 2015, we need to defer only 25% of the deferred profit at December 31, 2015:

$$\textbf{\$7.50 of gross profit to defer} \ = \ \textbf{\$30 gross profit} \ \times \ \textbf{25\% of unsold inventories}$$

Considering this changed assumption, our second component of the [I] entries is as follows:

[I$_{cogs}$]	Cost of goods sold (EOY Inventory).............................	7.50	
	Inventories..		7.50
	(to reverse the inventory write-up and defer the gross profit on the intercompany sale)		

Continuous Sales of Inventories

In the previous section, we describe the required consolidation entries for *one* intercompany sale in one period and subsequent resale in the next. The usual case, however, is one where companies in a consolidated group will *continuously* sell inventories within the consolidated group. As we depict for Year 2 in Exhibit 4.9, the continuous sale of inventories means that, for each year, we have to make the following inventory-related adjustments:

❶ Recognize the profit we deferred in the previous year,

❷ Eliminate current-year intercompany sales/purchase transactions, and

❸ Defer the profit for the current year's sales of inventories.

This means that, for each year, companies will make all of the [I] consolidating entries illustrated in Exhibits 4.5 and 4.7, and, if the parent owns 100 percent of the subsidiary, there is only a slight difference in the consolidating entries for upstream versus downstream sales.[11] We will illustrate continuous sales of inventories in the next section.

---

[11] If the parent owns less than 100 percent of the subsidiary, the only change is that there is a slight difference in the deferred profit recognition entry included in Exhibit 4.7. We discuss the effects of noncontrolling interests in Chapter 5.

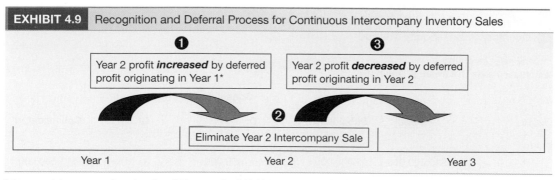

| EXHIBIT 4.9 | Recognition and Deferral Process for Continuous Intercompany Inventory Sales |

* Assumes intercompany Inventory is sold in year after initial intercompany sale. If it is not, then the profit is deferred until the year of subsequent sale.

Example of the Continuous Intercompany Sale and Resale of Inventories—Equity Method

To illustrate the consolidation process with *upstream and downstream* continuous intercompany inventory sales, assume the following facts relating to intercompany sales of inventories:

	2015	2016
Transfer price for upstream inventory sale.	$300,000	
Transfer price for downstream inventory sale		$400,000
Cost of goods sold.	230,000	320,000
Gross profit.	$ 70,000	$ 80,000
Percentage remaining in parent's inventory at 12/31/2015	25%	n/a
Percentage remaining in subsidiary's inventory at 12/31/2016	0%	35%
(Upstream) gross profit deferred at 12/31/2015.	$ 17,500	n/a
(Downstream) gross profit deferred at 12/31/2016	$ 0	$ 28,000
Intercompany receivable/payable at 12/31/2015.	$ 90,000	$ 0
Intercompany receivable/payable at 12/31/2016.	$ 0	$100,000

Also assume that on the date the parent acquired the subsidiary, the Acquisition Accounting Premium (AAP) was completely attributed to a building with an appraised value higher than its book value on the subsidiary's balance sheet. At December 31, 2015, the AAP has an unamortized balance of $90,000 depreciated/amortized at the rate of $9,000 per year.

The assumed financial statements of the parent and its subsidiary for the year ended December 31, 2016, are presented in the first two columns of the consolidation spreadsheet in Exhibit 4.10. The Income (loss) from subsidiary for 2016 and the balance in the Equity Investment account at December 31, 2016, are computed as follows:

2016 Equity Investment Income		12/31/2016 Equity Investment Balance	
Subsidiary net income	$200,000	BOY subsidiary retained earnings	$225,000
AAP depreciation/amortization.	(9,000)	BOY subsidiary common stock	100,000
12/31/15 Deferred profit recognized in 2016	17,500	BOY subsidiary APIC	125,000
12/31/16 Deferred profit deferred to 2017	(28,000)	BOY unamortized AAP	90,000
Income (loss) from subsidiary.	$180,500	BOY deferred profit (deferred at 12/31/15)	(17,500)
		Income (loss) from subsidiary.	180,500
		Dividends	(20,000)
		Equity investment.	$683,000

In Exhibit 4.10, we present the consolidation spreadsheet including **C-E-A-D-I** entries.

EXHIBIT 4.10	Consolidation Spreadsheet Reflecting Continuous Upstream and Downstream Intercompany Inventory Sales—Equity Method

Type of intercompany sale: **Inventory**
Direction of intercompany sale: **Upstream & Downstream**

			Consolidation Entries				
December 31, 2016	Parent	Subsidiary		Dr		Cr	Consolidated
Income statement:							
Sales.	$10,000,000	$2,000,000	[I$_{sales}$]	400,000			$11,600,000
Cost of goods sold.	(7,000,000)	(1,400,000)	[I$_{cogs}$]	28,000	[I$_{cogs}$]	17,500	(8,010,500)
					[I$_{sales}$]	400,000	
Gross profit.	3,000,000	600,000					3,589,500
Income (loss) from subsidiary. . . .	180,500		[C]	180,500			0
Operating expenses	(1,900,000)	(400,000)	[D]	9,000			(2,309,000)
Net income.	$ 1,280,500	$ 200,000					$ 1,280,500
Statement of retained earnings:							
BOY retained earnings	$ 582,500	$ 225,000	[E]	225,000			$ 582,500
Net income	1,280,500	200,000					1,280,500
Dividends	(400,000)	(20,000)			[C]	20,000	(400,000)
End retained earnings	$ 1,463,000	$ 405,000					$ 1,463,000
Balance sheet:							
Assets							
Cash	$ 329,000	$ 70,000					$ 399,000
Accounts receivable	900,000	210,000			[I$_{pay}$]	100,000	1,010,000
Inventory	940,000	250,000			[I$_{cogs}$]	28,000	1,162,000
Building, net	2,300,000	800,000	[A]	90,000	[D]	9,000	3,181,000
Equity investment	683,000		[I$_{cogs}$]	17,500	[C]	160,500	0
					[E]	450,000	
					[A]	90,000	
	$ 5,152,000	$1,330,000					$ 5,752,000
Liabilities and stockholders' equity							
Accounts payable	$ 388,000	$ 270,000	[I$_{pay}$]	100,000			$ 558,000
Other current liabilities	49,000	230,000					279,000
Long-term liabilities	312,000	200,000					512,000
Common stock	1,665,000	100,000	[E]	100,000			1,665,000
APIC	1,275,000	125,000	[E]	125,000			1,275,000
Retained earnings	1,463,000	405,000					1,463,000
	$ 5,152,000	$1,330,000		$1,275,000		$1,275,000	$ 5,752,000

Our consolidation entries are as follows:

[C]	Income (loss) from subsidiary.	180,500		Eliminate the changes in the parent's accounts caused by (equity method) investment accounting during 2016
	Dividends.		20,000	
	Equity investment		160,500	

[E]	Common stock (S) @ BOY	100,000		Eliminate the BOY stockholders' equity of subsidiary:
	APIC (S) @ BOY	125,000		BOY ret. earn $225,000
	Retained earnings (S) @ BOY	225,000		Common stock 100,000
	Equity investment @ BOY		450,000	APIC 125,000
				Total $450,000

| [A] | Building, net @ BOY . . . . | 90,000 | | Assign the remaining Equity Investment account |
| | Equity investment @ BOY . . . . | | 90,000 | (i.e., unamortized BOY AAP) building |

| [D] | Operating expenses . . . . | 9,000 | | Recognize current-year amortization of the AAP |
| | Building, net . . . . | | 9,000 | related to the building |

| [I_cogs] | Equity investment @ BOY . . . . | 17,500 | | Increases Equity Investment account and |
| | Cost of goods sold . . . . | | 17,500 | recognizes prior period deferred profit from inventories in current period |

| [I_sales] | Sales . . . . | 400,000 | | Eliminates current period intercompany sales and |
| | Cost of goods sold . . . . | | 400,000 | cost of goods sold |

| [I_cogs] | Cost of goods sold . . . . | 28,000 | | Defer current period deferred profit on |
| | Inventory . . . . | | 28,000 | intercompany sale of inventories |

| [I_pay] | Accounts payable . . . . | 100,000 | | Eliminates intercompany receivable and payable |
| | Accounts receivable . . . . | | 100,000 | |

TOPIC REVIEW 1

Accounting for the Intercompany Sale of Inventory—Equity Method

Assume that a parent company acquired its subsidiary on January 1, 2013, with an acquisition-date Acquisition Accounting Premium (AAP) equal to $437,500. The acquisition-date AAP was assigned to PPE assets ($172,500, depreciated at $7,500 per year), a Patent ($65,000, amortized at $5,000 per year), and Goodwill ($200,000). During the year ended December 31, 2016, the subsidiary sold $100,000 of inventory (on account) to its parent, all of which was unpaid at December 31, 2016. Deferred profit at December 31, 2015, equaled $18,525, with all of these inventories sold to unaffiliated companies in 2016. Deferred profit at December 31, 2016, equals $28,500. The parent uses the equity method to account for its Equity Investment. The parent and subsidiary financial statements for the year ended December 31, 2016, follow:

	Parent	Subsidiary			Parent	Subsidiary
Income statement:				**Balance sheet:**		
Sales	$10,000,000	$1,500,000		Assets		
Cost of goods sold	(7,000,000)	(900,000)		Cash	$ 708,694	$ 408,700
Gross profit	3,000,000	600,000		Accounts receivable	1,280,000	348,000
Income (loss) from subsidiary . .	187,525			Inventory	1,940,000	447,000
Operating expenses	(1,900,000)	(390,000)		Equity investment	1,541,700	
Net income	$ 1,287,525	$ 210,000		PPE, net	9,332,000	827,000
					$14,802,394	$2,030,700
Statement of retained earnings:						
BOY retained earnings	5,024,000	$ 775,000		**Liabilities and stockholders' equity**		
Net income	1,287,525	210,000		Current liabilities	$ 1,437,000	$ 348,000
Dividends	(296,131)	(27,300)		Long-term liabilities	4,500,000	500,000
EOY retained earnings	$ 6,015,394	$ 957,700		Common stock	1,635,000	100,000
				APIC	1,215,000	125,000
				Retained earnings	6,015,394	957,700
					$14,802,394	$2,030,700

Required

Prepare the consolidation spreadsheet for the year.

The solution to this review problem can be found on page 262.

LO2 Describe the accounting for intercompany sales of inventory between the parent and the subsidiary when the parent uses the cost method of pre-consolidation investment bookkeeping.

ACCOUNTING FOR INTERCOMPANY SALES OF INVENTORY—COST METHOD

In this section, we describe the accounting for the intercompany sales of inventory, assuming that the parent applies the cost method of pre-consolidation bookkeeping. Recall from Chapter 3 that companies are allowed to apply any method of pre-consolidation investment bookkeeping. The advantage of the equity method—especially from a pedagogical point of view—is that the parents' pre-consolidation net income and owners' equity accounts are the same balances pre- and post-consolidation. The advantage of the cost method is that it is easy to apply to the pre-consolidation parent company books and results in the most efficient consolidation process. (Recall that much of the consolidation process is comprised of steps which "undo" the pre-consolidation equity investment bookkeeping on the parent's books. The cost method has fewer of those pre-consolidation bookkeeping journal entries.) Exhibit 4.11 illustrates the differences between the cost and equity methods in the presence of deferred intercompany profits.

EXHIBIT 4.11	Comparison of Cost and Equity Pre-Consolidation Bookkeeping Methods, Including Deferred Intercompany Profits

Cost Method		Equity Method	
(+) Equity Investment (−)		**(+) Equity Investment (−)**	
Beginning balance		Beginning balance	
		Equity Income	Dividends received
			AAP amortization
		Intercompany profit deferred from prior period to current period	Intercompany profit deferred from current period to future period
Ending balance		Ending balance	

Before discussing the specifics of the elimination of intercompany inventory when the parent uses the cost method, we want to repeat an extremely important point from Chapter 3: *the consolidated financial statements will look the same, regardless of the pre-consolidation method of Equity Investment bookkeeping applied by the parent company.* Indeed, even the subsidiary's financial statements will be identical when the parent applies the cost method (i.e., because cost method versus equity method refers to bookkeeping applied by the parent, not the subsidiary). However, because parent company's pre-consolidation financial statements will be different under the cost method versus the equity method, the consolidation entries will (out of necessity) be slightly different.

To get a feel for the nature of the differences, let's consider the facts illustrated in the equity method example in Exhibit 4.1. Specifically, we assume that a parent company sold, during 2015, inventory that originally cost $100 to its subsidiary for $130 in cash. We also assume that the inventory is still held by the subsidiary on December 31, 2015. If, given these facts, the parent company, instead, applied the cost method of pre-consolidation bookkeeping, the pre-consolidation financial statement effects for the year ended December 31, 2015 are illustrated in Exhibit 4.12.

When comparing Exhibits 4.12 and 4.2, the first important thing to note is that there is no difference between the "Subsidiary" columns in the two exhibits. That's because the cost and equity methods are pre-consolidation bookkeeping approaches applied to the parent's books (i.e., not the subsidiary's books). In addition, as is illustrated in Exhibit 4.12, the $30 of pre-consolidation gross profit is not eliminated from the parent company's pre-consolidation profits under the cost method. If you compare this cost method treatment to the equity method treatment in Exhibit 4.2, you'll notice that the equity method's pre-consolidation deferred profit elimination caused the net effect on the parent company's pre-consolidation total profits to be zero. Under the cost method, this $30 of intercompany

EXHIBIT 4.12	Year 1 Pre-Consolidation Financial Statements Effects of Intercompany Inventory Transactions—Cost Method		

Year Ended December 31, 2015	Parent	Subsidiary
Income statement (excerpt):		
Sales.	$130	$ 0
Cost of goods sold.	100	0
Net effect on gross profit	$ 30	$ 0
Income (loss) from subsidiary.	$ 0	
Net effect on total profits	$ 30	$ 0
Balance sheet (excerpt):		
Inventory.	$ 0	$130
Equity investment.	$ 0	
Cumulative effect on retained earnings	(NI) $ 30	(NI) $ 0

profits becomes part of the parent company's pre-consolidation retained earnings (a balance sheet account) because each period's profits are closed out to retained earnings.[12] The differences between Exhibits 4.2 and 4.12 will result in differences between the equity and cost methods when we apply our consolidation entries. We will describe the differences, in detail, in the next section.

Before discussing the cost-method consolidation entries, we will complete the two-year sequence in our original example and assume the same "Year 2" assumptions illustrated in Exhibit 4.4. Specifically, we assume that the inventory is sold by the subsidiary in 2016 for $180. However, now we assume that the parent uses the cost method of pre-consolidation investment bookkeeping. The pre-consolidation financial statement effects for the year ended December 31, 2016 are illustrated in Exhibit 4.13.

EXHIBIT 4.13	Year 2 Pre-Consolidation Financial Statements Effects of Intercompany Inventory Transactions—Cost Method		

Year Ended December 31, 2016	Parent	Subsidiary
Income statement (excerpt):		
Sales.	$ 0	$180
Cost of goods sold.	0	130
Net effect on gross profit	$ 0	$ 50
Income (loss) from subsidiary.	$ 0	
Net effect on total profits	$ 0	$ 50
Balance sheet (excerpt):		
Inventory.	$ 0	$ 0
Equity investment.	$ 0	
Cumulative effect on retained earnings	$ 30	$ 50

---

[12] Closer study of Exhibits 4.2 and 4.12 can provide some clues about the mechanical difference in the consolidation entries necessary under the equity and cost methods. In Exhibit 4.2, there is a $30 credit balance in the parent's pre-consolidation Equity Investment account. In Exhibit 4.12, there is a $30 credit balance in the parent's pre-consolidation Retained Earnings account. Both of these accounts are $0 after consolidation, which means the consolidation entries debited the Equity Investment and Retained Earnings accounts under the equity and cost methods, respectively. (Note that the post-consolidation Equity Investment and Retained Earnings accounts are zero for different reasons. The Equity Investment account is always zero after consolidation, while the ending Retained Earnings account is zero because no deferred profit is allowed to be recognized in the consolidated financial statements until after the inventory is sold to non-affiliates.)

The differences between the cost and equity methods are best understood by comparing Exhibit 4.13 to the "Parent" and "Subsidiary" columns of Exhibit 4.4. Again, the first important thing to note is that there is no difference between the "Subsidiary" columns in the two exhibits. As we mentioned previously, this is because the cost and equity methods are pre-consolidation bookkeeping approaches applied to the parent's books (i.e., not the subsidiary's books). Another thing to notice is that the parent's pre-consolidation retained earnings is equal to $30 under the cost method, while parent's pre-consolidation retained earnings is equal to $80 under the equity method and consolidated retained earnings is also $80. The process of consolidation, and the specific consolidation entries, when the parent uses the cost method will yield consolidated financial statements that reflect the amounts in the "(Correct) Consolidated" columns in Exhibits 4.2 and 4.4 using the equity method.

Closely comparing Exhibit 4.2 to 4.12 and 4.4 to 4.13 will greatly facilitate understanding the difference between equity method consolidation entries and cost method consolidation entries. (Remember, the consolidated financial statements will look the same, regardless of the pre-consolidation method of Equity Investment bookkeeping applied by the parent company. However, if the pre-consolidation starting point is different, then the steps to consolidation must be slightly different.) However, for now, it is sufficient to notice there is a difference in the treatment of intercompany deferred profits between the two pre-consolidation bookkeeping methods. In the next section we continue our discussion of the consolidation process when there are continuous intercompany sales of inventory and the parent uses the cost method of pre-consolidation bookkeeping.

Example of the Continuous Intercompany Sale and Resale of Inventories—Cost Method

In this section, we illustrate the consolidation process when the parent uses the cost method of pre-consolidation Equity Investment bookkeeping, and there have been intercompany sales of inventories.[13] In this example, the parent acquired its subsidiary on January 1, 2013. We are preparing consolidated financial statements for the year ending December 31, 2016. Assume the following facts (all amounts in $):

Original cost of Equity investment	$550,000
Stockholders' equity of subsidiary at acquisition date	450,000
Increase in subsidiary retained earnings January 1, 2013, through December 31, 2015	200,000
Original AAP (building)	100,000
Unamortized AAP balance on January 1, 2016 (building)	40,000
Annual depreciation/amortization of the AAP	20,000

In addition, the subsidiary has sold inventories to its parent regularly since the acquisition. The intercompany sales and profit for the prior and current period are as follows:

---

[13] This discussion assumes that readers understand the [ADJ] consolidation entry proposed in the cost-method coverage in Chapter 3. In particular, readers should understand why the [ADJ] consolidation entry is necessary when the parent applies the cost method of pre-consolidation bookkeeping and why the adjustment is primarily based on the change in the subsidiary retained earnings since the acquisition date through the beginning of the current consolidation period. If readers do not have this understanding, then we <u>strongly</u> encourage those readers to review the cost method coverage in Chapter 3.

Year Ending	Dec. 31, 2015	Dec. 31, 2016
Transfer price for inventory sale.	$150,000	$200,000
Cost of goods sold.	102,000	150,000
Gross profit.	$ 48,000	$ 50,000
Percentage of inventory remaining.	25%	30%
Deferred intercompany profit (deferred profit) in ending inventory	$ 12,000	$ 15,000
Intercompany receivable/payable at end of period*.	$ 25,000	$ 30,000

* Paid at beginning of next period.

As we described in Chapter 3, when a parent company uses the cost method of pre-consolidation bookkeeping, it must propose a "catch up" [ADJ] consolidation entry to (1) adjust the parent company retained earnings to equal its correct, consolidated (i.e., "as-if-equity-method") BOY balance, (2) allow us to eventually eliminate the book value of the BOY Equity Investment account against the BOY Stockholders' Equity of the subsidiary in consolidating entry [E], and (3) allow us to eventually assign the BOY AAP to the appropriate net assets in consolidating entry [A]. In addition to these reasons, in the presence of deferred intercompany profits and losses on asset transfers, the [ADJ] entry should also capture all beginning-of-year unconfirmed intercompany profits and losses that deferred to the current and future periods. In the case of the present fact set, this leads to the following computation of the [ADJ] adjustment amount:

Increase in subsidiary retained earnings through BOY	$200,000
Cumulative depreciation of [A] assets through BOY	(60,000)
Deferred profit @ BOY	(12,000)
Cumulative understatement of Equity investment account @ BOY.	$128,000

Under the equity method, the beginning-of-year Equity Investment account would have increased by the parent's proportion (100% in this case) of the cumulative profit earned by the subsidiary since the acquisition, less the cumulative dividends paid to the parent, the cumulative depreciation of the AAP, and the deferred profit on the remaining unsold inventory from the intercompany sale. Thus, the consolidation process needs to include the following [ADJ] consolidation entry to adjust the beginning-of-year Equity Investment account to its equity-method balance with a corresponding adjustment to (the parent's) beginning-of-year Retained Earnings:

[ADJ]	Equity Investment @ BOY	128,000		Restate the Equity
	Retained earnings (P) @ BOY		128,000	Investment account
				from cost to equity
				method

Exhibit 4.14 provides the consolidation spreadsheet including our **C-E-A-D-I** entries. An important point to note is that, after we propose our [ADJ] "catch up" entry, the remaining **C-E-A-D-I** entries, with one exception, are identical to the **C-E-A-D-I** entries that would have been proposed under the equity method! The exception is the [C] entry: because the parent received dividend income from the subsidiary (i.e., and not equity-method income), the [C] entry must eliminate the dividends received from the subsidiary by the parent. After the cost-method [C] entry is proposed, the remaining **E-A-D-I** entries are exactly the same as they would have been under the equity method.

EXHIBIT 4.14 Consolidation Spreadsheet Reflecting Continuous Upstream and Downstream Intercompany Inventory Sales—Cost Method

	Parent	Subsidiary	Consolidation Entries Dr		Cr		Consolidated
Income statement:							
Sales..............................	$5,000,000	$ 960,000	[I$_{sales}$]	$ 200,000			$5,760,000
Cost of goods sold..................	(2,700,000)	(432,000)	[I$_{cogs}$]	15,000	[I$_{cogs}$]	$ 12,000	(2,935,000)
					[I$_{sales}$]	200,000	
Gross profit.......................	2,300,000	528,000					2,825,000
Dividend income....................	10,000		[C]	10,000			0
Operating expenses.................	(1,932,000)	(357,000)	[D]	20,000			(2,309,000)
Net income........................	$ 378,000	$ 171,000					$ 516,000
Statement of retained earnings:							
BOY retained earnings...............	$1,424,000	$ 425,000	[E]	425,000	[ADJ]	128,000	$1,552,000
Net income........................	378,000	171,000					516,000
Dividends	(50,000)	(10,000)			[C]	10,000	(50,000)
Ending retained earnings.............	$1,752,000	$ 586,000					$2,018,000
Balance sheet:							
Assets							
Cash.............................	$ 88,000	$ 70,000					$ 158,000
Accounts receivable.................	487,000	210,000			[I$_{pay}$]	30,000	667,000
Inventory..........................	833,000	250,000			[I$_{cogs}$]	15,000	1,068,000
Building, net.......................	2,709,000	1,000,000	[A]	40,000	[D]	20,000	3,729,000
Equity investment...................	550,000		[ADJ]	128,000	[E]	650,000	0
			[I$_{cogs}$]	12,000	[A]	40,000	
	$4,667,000	$1,530,000					$5,622,000
Liabilities and stockholders' equity							
Accounts payable...................	$ 477,000	$ 289,000	[I$_{pay}$]	30,000			$ 736,000
Other current liabilities	264,000	230,000					494,000
Long-term liabilities	312,000	200,000					512,000
Common stock.....................	1,238,000	100,000	[E]	100,000			1,238,000
APIC.............................	624,000	125,000	[E]	125,000			624,000
Retained earnings	1,752,000	586,000					2,018,000
	$4,667,000	$1,530,000	$1,105,000		$1,105,000		$5,622,000

Cost Method

TOPIC REVIEW 2

Accounting for the Intercompany Sale of Inventory—Cost Method

Assume that a parent company acquired its subsidiary on January 1, 2013, with an acquisition-date Acquisition Accounting Premium (AAP) equal to $437,500. The acquisition-date AAP was assigned to PPE assets ($172,500, depreciated at $7,500 per year), a Patent ($65,000, amortized at $5,000 per year), and Goodwill ($200,000). During the year ended December 31, 2016, the subsidiary sold $100,000 of inventory (on account) to its parent, of which $30,000 remains unpaid at December 31, 2016. Deferred profit at December 31, 2015, equaled $12,000, with all of these inventories sold to unaffiliated companies in 2016. Deferred profit at December 31, 2016, equals $22,400. The parent uses the cost method of pre-consolidation Equity Investment bookkeeping. The parent and subsidiary financial statements for the year ended December 31, 2016, follow:

	Parent	Subsidiary		Parent	Subsidiary
Income statement:			**Balance sheet:**		
Sales..................	$10,000,000	$1,500,000	Assets		
Cost of goods sold.........	(7,000,000)	(900,000)	Cash....................	$ 800,000	$ 406,000
Gross profit..............	3,000,000	600,000	Accounts receivable.........	1,280,000	348,000
Dividend income...........	30,000		Inventory.................	1,950,000	447,000
Operating expenses........	(1,900,000)	(390,000)	Equity investment..........	1,300,000	
Net income..............	$ 1,130,000	$ 210,000	PPE, net.................	4,000,000	827,000
				$9,330,000	$2,028,000
Statement of retained earnings:					
BOY retained earnings......	4,000,000	$ 775,000	Liabilities and stockholders' equity		
Net income..............	1,130,000	210,000	Current liabilities...........	$1,400,000	$ 348,000
Dividends...............	(300,000)	(30,000)	Long-term liabilities	1,500,000	500,000
Ending retained earnings	$ 4,830,000	$ 955,000	Common stock............	600,000	100,000
			APIC...................	1,000,000	125,000
			Retained earnings	4,830,000	955,000
				$9,330,000	$2,028,000

Required

Prepare the consolidation spreadsheet for the year.

The solution to this review problem can be found on page 263.

ACCOUNTING FOR THE INTERCOMPANY SALES OF NONCURRENT ASSETS BETWEEN THE INVESTOR AND THE INVESTEE(S)—EQUITY METHOD

Accounting for the deferred profit on sales of noncurrent assets among commonly controlled companies is similar, in concept, to the accounting for deferred profit on intercompany inventory sales: intercompany profits from non-depreciable asset transactions are deferred as long as the assets sold are held, and the deferred profit is recognized when the assets are resold to independent parties. Given this conceptual similarity, we will begin our discussion of intercompany sales of noncurrent assets with non-depreciable assets.[14]

Accounting for the Intercompany Sale of Non-Depreciable Assets—Equity Method

As with intercompany sales of inventories, intercompany sales of land result in a write-up of the asset to include the profit recognized by the seller upon sale.[15] From a consolidated perspective, the profit resulting from the intercompany sale of non-depreciable assets must be deferred until the period in which the asset is sold to an independent party. The most common non-depreciable asset is land. So, we will focus our attention on an intercompany land sale in our first example.

LO3 Describe the accounting for intercompany sales of non-depreciable noncurrent assets between the parent and the subsidiary when the parent uses the equity method of pre-consolidation investment bookkeeping.

---

[14] *Depreciable* noncurrent assets present additional challenges because the cost of these assets are realized into income over the useful lives of the assets (i.e., via depreciation). Recall that the consolidation problem posed by intercompany asset transactions is that the affiliated buyer's recorded asset values inappropriately include profits (losses) from the intercompany (i.e., affiliated) sale. Therefore, depreciable assets present the added complication that the depreciation expense of the intercompany asset must also be adjusted via the consolidation entries. Before tackling the challenges of depreciable assets, we will begin our discussion with transactions most similar to the inventory transactions that we discuss in the previous section of this chapter.

[15] Of course, assets can be sold for losses, too. We write in terms of asset-sale gains for expositional efficiency. In the case of deferred asset losses, the same general procedures will apply; however, journal entries will be modified accordingly.

Intercompany Sale of Land Assume that on January 1, 2014, a parent company sells land that originally cost $80 to its subsidiary for $100 in cash. On the date of the intercompany sale, the parent makes the following journal entry to record the sale:

Cash	100	
Land..		80
Gain on sale...		20
(to record the sale of land)		

On the same date, the subsidiary records the land purchase as follows:

Land	100	
Cash		100
(to record the purchase of land)		

Although both of these companies have correctly recorded the sale and purchase of land on their individual (i.e., pre-consolidation) books, without the required adjustments, the economic entity's net income is overstated by the gain, and the land account is overstated by the write-up of land during the sale (i.e., from $80 to $100).

Similar to the equity method accounting we applied in the case of intercompany inventory transactions, the parent company would adjust the Equity-Investment-related accounts to defer the gains (losses) on the intercompany sale of land. The following equity-method journal entry would be recorded on the pre-consolidation books of the parent:

Income (loss) from subsidiary.....................................	20	
Equity investment		20
(to defer, in the Equity-Investment-related accounts, the gain on the		
intercompany sale of land)		

The consolidation entries that we will make to correct for this overstatement is similar to the entry we made in the case of the inventory sale above: in entry **[C]** we eliminate the Equity Investment account changes during the year and in entry **[I]** we defer the gain on the sale and reduce the book value of the land to its pre-sale balance. Based on the facts in this simplified, stylized example, this leads to the following consolidation entries in the year of sale:

Consolidation entries to eliminate changes in the Equity Investment account during the year	**[C]**	Equity investment................................	20	
		Income (loss) from subsidiary		20
		(consolidation entry to eliminate changes caused by		
		equity method accounting)		
Intercompany elimination entry in the year of sale	**[I**$_\text{gain}$**]**	Gain on sale	20	
		Land......................................		20
		(to defer the gain on sale and to restate the Land account to		
		its pre-sale reported amount)		

As a result of the **[C]** entry, all changes in the Equity Investment account are eliminated. As a result of the **[I]** entry, the gain on sale has been removed from the consolidated income statement and the Land account, reported by the subsidiary at $100 following the purchase, is reduced to $80 on the consolidated balance sheet, the amount at which it was carried by the parent prior to the sale. We show the effects of these consolidating entries in the excerpts from a consolidation spreadsheet (for the year ended December 31, 2014) in Exhibit 4.15.

Notice that the effect of the consolidation process (when the parent uses the equity method) is that (1) the net effect on total profits remains at zero pre-consolidation and post-consolidation, and (2) the pre-consolidation $(20) reduction in income from the equity method accounting is reclassified to the gain on sale of land account. In addition, the $(20) reduction in the Equity Investment account is reclassified to the Land account. This is similar to the process we described for inventory, except non-depreciable noncurrent assets are typically held for much longer periods than the inventories transferred between affiliated companies.

EXHIBIT 4.15	Excerpts of Land-Transaction-Affected Accounts in Consolidation Spreadsheet in the Initial Period of Intercompany Sale of Land (i.e., 2014)—Equity Method

| | | | Consolidation Entries | | |
	Parent	Subsidiary	Debits	Credits	Consolidated
Income statement (excerpt):					
Gain on sale of land	$ 20	$ 0	[I$_{gain}$] 20		$ 0
Income (loss) from subsidiary.	(20)			[C] 20	0
Net effect on total profits	$ 0	$ 0	20	20	0
Balance sheet (excerpt):					
Land	$ 0	$100	[I$_{gain}$] 20		$ 80
Equity investment.	$(20)		[C] 20		$ 0
Accumulated in retained earnings	$ 0	$ 0	(NI) 20	(NI) 20	$ 0

To illustrate the process of intertemporal profit deferral, we extend the previous example to assume that the land transferred from parent to subsidiary was subsequently sold for $150 to an unaffiliated (i.e., independent) company on September 15, 2016. In this case, the deferred profit from the 2014 intercompany transaction will be deferred until the unaffiliated transaction takes place in 2016. The process of deferral is depicted in Exhibit 4.16.

EXHIBIT 4.16	Recognition and Deferral Process for Non-Depreciable Asset

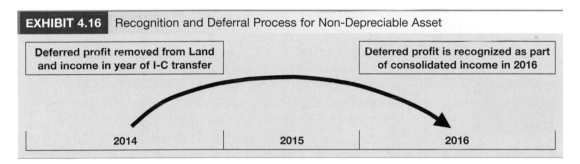

Although no transaction involving the land takes place in 2015, the effects of 2014 deferred profit-related consolidation entries *must be carried forward* to the consolidated financial statements in 2015. Specifically, the Land recorded on subsidiary's books will still be carried at $100 and the $20 deferral of the Gain on Sale of Land will still be in the parent's Equity Investment account.[16] To get these two balances to reflect the amounts presented to investors and creditors at the end of 2015, we will propose the following consolidating entry in 2015 (and every year in which the land remains unsold):

Intercompany elimination entry in the years after intercompany sale	[I$_{gain}$]	Equity Investment 20	
		Land.	20
		(to defer the gain on sale and to restate the Land account to its pre-sale reported amount)	

This [I$_{gain}$] entry is similar to that we present above, except that the debit is to the BOY Equity Investment balance (which includes the gain on the sale) rather than to the Gain on Sale income statement account.

Finally, when the land is ultimately sold to an independent party on September 15, 2016, the subsidiary will make the following journal entry in its books:

---

[16] Recall that consolidating entries aren't recorded by either company. This means that prior year net adjustments of long-term balance sheet accounts must be carried forward to future years. In 2015, the effect of 2014 equity method accounting (i.e., $(20) effect on the Equity Investment account) will still be in the Equity Investment account, despite our consolidating entry [C] in 2014. Therefore, in future years, when preparing consolidated financial statements, we must increase the Equity Investment account by this amount.

Cash	150	
Land.		100
Gain on sale.		50

(to record the sale of Land to an unaffiliated company)

In addition, the parent company will record the following equity-method-related journal entries in its pre-consolidation accounting records:

Equity investment.	50	
Income (loss) from subsidiary		50

(to record the equity method adjustment for income recognized by the subsidiary)

Equity investment.	20	
Income (loss) from subsidiary		20

(to recognize the deferred intercompany profit when the land is sold to an unaffiliated entity)

Given that the 2016 transaction is with an unaffiliated party, the entire gain from both land transactions (i.e., the intercompany transaction and the independent transaction) will be recognized in the consolidated income statement. This means that the deferred profit of $20 *and* the 2016 gain of $50 recognized by the subsidiary will be combined for a $70 gain recognized in the consolidated income statement. This is the same as taking the 2016 sales price (i.e., $150) and subtracting the original cost of the Land (i.e., $80); that is, it is like we are assuming the intercompany sale never took place. The effect of this transaction and the original sale (included in Retained Earnings by the parent) are reflected in the following excerpts from the consolidation worksheet in Exhibit 4.17:

EXHIBIT 4.17	Excerpts of Land-Transaction-Affected Accounts in Consolidation Spreadsheet in the Period in Which the Land Is Sold to an Unaffiliated Party (i.e., 2016)—Equity Method

	Parent	Subsidiary	Consolidation Entries Debits	Consolidation Entries Credits	Consolidated
Income statement (excerpt):					
Gain on sale of land	$ 0	$50		[I_{gain}] 20	$70
Income (loss) from subsidiary.	70	0	[C] 70		0
Net effect on total profits	$70	$50	70	20	$70
Balance sheet (excerpt):					
Land	$ 0	$ 0			$ 0
Equity investment.	$50		[I_{gain}] 20	[C] 70	$ 0
Accumulated in retained earnings	$70	$50	(NI) 70	(NI) 20	$70

As we illustrate in Exhibit 4.17, the following consolidating entries are necessary to bring forward the Equity Investment account and to recognize the full $70 of Gain on Sale of Land in 2016:

Consolidation entries to eliminate changes in the Equity Investment account during the year	[C]	Income (loss) from subsidiary.	70	
		Equity investment		70
		(consolidation entry to eliminate changes caused by equity method accounting)		

Intercompany elimination entry in the year of sale to unaffiliated party	[I_{gain}]	Equity investment.	20	
		Gain on sale of land.		20
		(to recognize deferred gain in year of sale to unaffiliated party)		

Upstream Intercompany Sale of Non-Depreciable Assets The preceding example provided an illustration of the consolidation entries for a downstream intercompany non-depreciable-asset sale transaction. In the case of *wholly owned subsidiaries*, there is no difference in the [I] consolidation entries for upstream versus downstream transactions involving intercompany (i.e., affiliated) transfers of non-depreciable assets among commonly controlled companies (assuming we hold constant the parent company's pre-consolidation bookkeeping for the Equity Investment account). This is because all deferred profit must be removed from the combined financial statements, regardless of the direction of the transaction.[17]

If we consider the accounts affected and the amounts in the preceding example, the account relationships, [I] consolidating entries, and consolidated balances in Exhibits 4.15 and 4.17 are the same in the upstream case. In our stylized example, because all of the income recognized by the subsidiary is related to the intercompany sale of non-depreciable assets, then there is no need for consolidating entry [C] in either year. That's because, under the equity method of pre-consolidation Investment bookkeeping, the parent company would have made the following journal entries in the first year to record the parent's share of the subsidiary's income and to remove the deferred intercompany asset-sale income:[18]

Equity investment.	20	
Income (loss) from subsidiary		20
(to record the equity method adjustment for income recognized by the subsidiary)		

Income (loss) from subsidiary.	20	
Equity investment		20
(to eliminate deferred intercompany profit from Income (loss) from subsidiary and		
Equity Investment accounts in year of upstream sale of land)		

Thus, in the case of upstream sales, the equity method of accounting causes the parent's Equity-Investment-related accounts to reflect only transactions that involve unaffiliated entities.

Accounting for the Intercompany Sale of Depreciable Assets— Equity Method

At first glance, the intercompany transfer of noncurrent depreciable assets, like buildings, seems like it should pose the same consolidation issues as the intercompany transfer of noncurrent non-depreciable assets, like land. Indeed, on the date of the sale between affiliated companies, the accounting implications are identical: defer *all* intercompany profit in the preparation of the consolidated balance sheet and income statement. However, *after* the date of the intercompany transfer, the accounting implications are quite different for depreciable and non-depreciable assets *because the purchasing company will depreciate the assets subsequent to acquisition based on the (higher) cost of the asset and, as a result, more depreciation expense will be recognized than would have been recognized had the asset not been sold.*[19] Thus, for depreciable assets, the consolidation procedures involve eliminating the remaining balance of the deferred profit from the balance sheet and the depreciated/amortized deferred profit from the income statement. The net results of the consolidation procedures are to report net asset and income statement balances that look as if the intercompany transaction never occurred. In the next section, we describe the intuition underlying these procedures.

LO4 Describe the accounting for intercompany sales of depreciable noncurrent assets between the parent and the subsidiary when the parent uses the equity method of pre-consolidation investment bookkeeping.

---

[17] This statement is also true for an "upstream" sale of non-depreciable assets from one subsidiary to another subsidiary.

[18] Once again, we made significant simplifying assumptions in this example. In particular, we assumed that there were no other transactions or balances, except for the land-related items. Thus, the subsidiary's only income would have been derived from the upstream sale of land. In typical consolidations, where the subsidiary also makes sales to unaffiliated parties, the [C] entry would eliminate all subsidiary net income resulting from transactions with unaffiliated parties.

[19] The increased annual depreciation expense on the books of the asset purchaser assumes that the asset was sold for a gain and the expected life of the asset for the purchaser is the same as the expected life on the books of the selling company. If the asset is sold for a loss (and if the expected life of the asset for the purchaser is the same as the expected life on the books of the selling company), then the annual depreciation expense on the books of the purchaser of the asset will be lower.

Example of Intercompany Sale of Equipment   Assume that on January 1, 2011, parent company sells equipment that originally cost $150 to its wholly owned subsidiary for a cash sale price of $135. The parent depreciated the equipment over a 10-year period, straight-line with no salvage value. At the time of sale, the parent's accounting records included $60 of Accumulated Depreciation related to the equipment. The parent makes the following journal entry to record the sale:

Cash..	135	
Accumulated depreciation..	60	
Equipment...		150
Gain on sale of equipment................................		45
(to record the sale of equipment)		

The subsidiary records the other side of the transaction as an equipment purchase:

Equipment	135	
Cash		135
(to record the purchase of equipment)		

Although both of these companies have correctly recorded the sale and purchase of equipment on their individual (i.e., pre-consolidation) books, consolidated financial statements cannot include transactions or balances that result from exchanges among the affiliated, commonly controlled companies. The easiest way to determine the overall effect of the intercompany transaction is to "net" the effects of these two journal entries on the combined financial statements of the commonly controlled companies. When we net the two entries we get the following combined journal entry.

Accumulated depreciation.......................................	60	
Equipment..		15
Gain on sale of equipment................................		45
(represents the net effect of the parent and subsidiary intercompany transaction entries taken together)		

This summary entry tells us that the intercompany equipment transaction had the net effect of reducing Accumulated Depreciation by $60, reducing the gross Equipment balance by $15, and increasing net income (via the Gain on Sale of Equipment) by $45. The process of consolidation for intercompany transactions and balances is basically one in which we reverse out the effects of the three items in the summary journal entry above. The effect of the consolidation entry is to produce financial statements that are "as if" the intercompany sale never happened. This leads to the following intercompany [I] consolidation entry *on the date of the intercompany transaction (i.e., January 1, 2011)*; the result is deferral of the gain and restoration of the Equipment account to its pre-sale reported amount:[20]

Intercompany elimination entry in the year of sale	[I_gain]	Gain on sale of equipment.........................	45	
		Equipment	15	
		Accumulated depreciation...................		60
		(to reverse the gain on sale recognized by the parent and adjust Accumulated Depreciation and gross Equipment to their pre-sale amounts)		

The net effects of the intercompany equipment sale have now been reversed in our consolidation worksheet:

■   The intercompany gain was completely eliminated.

■   The Equipment account, reported by the subsidiary at $135 following the purchase, was increased to $150, the amount at which it was carried by the parent prior to the sale.

---

[20] At this point, we are only concerned with developing the intuition behind the consolidating entry [I] necessary for the intercompany asset sale on the date of exchange. There are no equity-method-related entries recorded by the parent on the date of a downstream intercompany asset sale, thus we do not propose a [C] entry.

■   Finally, the original Accumulated Depreciation balance of $60 was restored.

For periods *after* the intercompany sale, we must now *also* consider the effects of equipment-related deferred profit that is included in the buyer's (in this case, the subsidiary's) recorded asset value and the resulting depreciation expense for the period. This fact makes the adjustments for depreciable assets following the date of sale a bit more complicated than those relating to non-depreciable assets, like intercompany inventories or the land sale we previously discussed.

In the case of our equipment example, the subsidiary will now depreciate its (higher) net book value for the equipment (i.e., $135 versus $90 [$150 − $60]), resulting in a higher depreciation expense per year as compared to the original amount recorded by the parent on its (lower) net book value for the equipment.

Let's assume that the subsidiary continues the depreciation policy of its parent and depreciates the equipment over the remaining 6 years of its original 10-year life. The depreciation expense that the parent *would have* recorded (i.e., assuming no intercompany transaction), and that the subsidiary *actually will* record (i.e., on its pre-consolidation accounting books), are computed as follows:

	("As If" No Intercompany Sale) Parent	(Actual) Subsidiary	Difference
Net book value	$90.0	$135.0	$45.0
Useful life	6	6	
Depreciation expense.	$15.0	$ 22.5	$ 7.5

Note that the subsidiary's depreciation expense is $7.5 per year *higher* than that which the parent would have recorded in its income statement had it not sold the equipment. That's because the deferred profit of $45 increases the carrying value of the equipment on the subsidiary's books and that higher book value will get depreciated over the remaining useful life of the equipment. As a result, the combined income of the two companies (before consolidation adjustments) is $7.5 lower for *each* year of the remaining useful life of the equipment.

In applying the equity method, the parent company makes an adjustment in its pre-consolidation books to record its proportionate share of the subsidiary's income, the elimination of intercompany gains and losses, and the confirmation of the $7.5 gain (i.e., from the reduction in depreciation expense). Because, in this highly simplified example, there are no other income statement accounts (e.g., revenues), this entry might seem a bit unusual. However, the important advantage of this example is that we are focusing only on the accounts and amounts affected by intercompany depreciable asset profits. In 2011, the equity method adjustment on the parent's books is a reduction of the investment account equal to $(60). This amount is comprised of $(22.5) share of subsidiary's depreciation expense, less the $(45.0) intercompany gain elimination, plus the $7.5 confirmation of gain for the year. This results in the following equity method adjustment actually recorded in the accounting records of the parent company:

Income (loss) from subsidiary.	60	
Equity investment		60

Our consolidation entries *after* the date of intercompany sale of the equipment must include an adjustment of depreciation-related accounts so that they reflect amounts that would have been reported "as if" the sale never took place. In the present example, this means that depreciation expense would be reduced by $7.5 each year that the equipment is still held by an affiliated company. This adjustment to depreciation expense will no longer be necessary at the end of the useful life of the equipment (i.e., after December 31, 2016), because the equipment will be fully depreciated on both the subsidiary's actual books and in the consolidated financial statements. For the year ended December 31, 2011, the consolidation adjustments are:

Consolidation entries to eliminate changes in the Equity Investment account during the year	**[C]**	Equity investment. . . . . Income (loss) from subsidiary . . . . *(Eliminate effects of equity method accounting during the year. The $60 adjustment = $(22.5) share of subsidiary's reported income, less the $(45.0) intercompany gain, plus the $7.5 gain confirmed during the year)*	60	60
Intercompany elimination entries at the end of the year of intercompany sale	**[I_gain]**	Gain on sale of equipment . . . . Equipment . . . . Accumulated depreciation. . . . . *(to adjust Gain, Equipment, and Accumulated Depreciation on the date of the intercompany transfer of equipment—given that the transaction occurred at the beginning of the year, usage of the equipment for the year must be reflected in a separate entry)*	45 15	60
	[I_dep]	Accumulated depreciation . . . . Depreciation expense . . . . *(to eliminate the excess depreciation expense recorded by the subsidiary, and to adjust accumulated depreciation from the BOY amount to the EOY amount)*	7.5	7.5

The **[C]** entry backs out all of the Equity Investment account activity recorded by the parent under the equity method. The $[I_{gain}]$ entry is the same entry that we discuss above. The $[I_{dep}]$ entry adjusts for the increase in depreciation expense.

We show the effects of these consolidating entries in the excerpts from a consolidation spreadsheet (for the year ended December 31, 2011) presented in Exhibit 4.18.

EXHIBIT 4.18	Excerpts of Equipment-Transaction-Affected Accounts in Consolidation Spreadsheet in the Initial Period of Intercompany Sale of Equipment (i.e., year ended December 31, 2011)—Equity Method

			Consolidation Entries		
	Parent	**Subsidiary**	**Debits**	**Credits**	**Consolidated**
Income statement (excerpt):					
Gain on sale of equipment	$ 45.0	$ 0	$[I_{gain}]$ 45.0		$ 0
Depreciation expense.	0	22.5		$[I_{dep}]$ 7.5	15.0
Income (loss) from subsidiary*	(60.0)			**[C]** 60.0	0
Net effect on total profits	$(15.0)	$ (22.5)	45.0	67.5	$ (15.0)
Balance sheet (excerpt):					
Equipment (gross)	$ 0	$135.0	$[I_{gain}]$ 15.0		$150.0
Accumulated depreciation	0	22.5	$[I_{dep}]$ 7.5	$[I_{gain}]$ 60.0	75.0
Equipment (net)	$ 0	$112.5	22.5	60.0	$ 75.0
Equity investment.	$(60.0)		**[C]** 60.0		$ 0
Accumulated in retained earnings	$(15.0)	$ (22.5)	**(NI)** 45.0	**(NI)** 67.5	$ (15.0)

* Income (loss) from subsidiary = $(22.5) share of subsidiary's depreciation expense, less the $(45.0) intercompany gain elimination, plus the $7.5 confirmation of gain for the year. We know this amount is correct because it makes the Net Effect on Total Profits for the Parent company's income $(15.0), which is the same as the Net Effect on Total Profits for the consolidated company.

The two **[I]** consolidation entries are necessary during 2011 to obtain the correct balances through December 31, 2011:

■ Entry $[I_{gain}]$ eliminates the gain on the date of the sale (i.e., January 1, 2011), and

■ Entry $[I_{dep}]$ eliminates the effect of "over-depreciation" that took place on the books of the subsidiary through the end of the year (i.e., December 31, 2011).

The end result is that the consolidated financial statements represent the income and financial position "as if" the intercompany sale of equipment never happened. Further, if we concentrate only on the two income statement adjustments during 2011, we also notice something interesting happening to the equipment-related deferred profit during the equipment's useful life. In particular, the original deferred profit of $45 that was disallowed at January 1, 2011 (i.e., the date of sale) is slowly being reversed and included in the determination of income during the period after the exchange date, at a rate of $7.5 per year. As we show in Exhibit 4.19, this process will continue throughout the useful life of the equipment, until the deferred profit is fully amortized into consolidated income by the end of 2016.

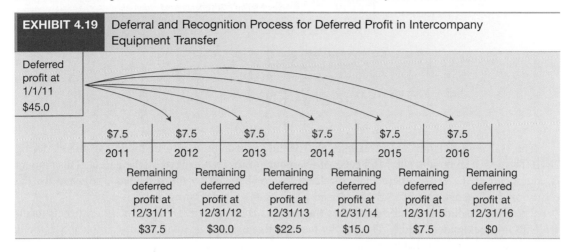

EXHIBIT 4.19 Deferral and Recognition Process for Deferred Profit in Intercompany Equipment Transfer

Deferred profit at 1/1/11 $45.0

$7.5	$7.5	$7.5	$7.5	$7.5	$7.5
2011	2012	2013	2014	2015	2016
Remaining deferred profit at 12/31/11	Remaining deferred profit at 12/31/12	Remaining deferred profit at 12/31/13	Remaining deferred profit at 12/31/14	Remaining deferred profit at 12/31/15	Remaining deferred profit at 12/31/16
$37.5	$30.0	$22.5	$15.0	$7.5	$0

As we express in Exhibit 4.19, the remaining portion of the deferred profit is slowly reduced during the life of the depreciable asset. This is a key difference between non depreciable assets, like inventory and land, and depreciable assets like equipment, buildings, and patents. In the case of non-depreciable assets, the costs of the assets are not realized in the income statement until they are sold, impaired, or otherwise eliminated from the balance sheet. In the case of depreciable assets, the costs of the assets are ratably realized in the income statement via periodic depreciation and/or amortization charges.

While the consolidation entry correctly eliminates the Gain on Sale of Equipment and adjusts the Equipment and Accumulated Depreciation accounts, the Equipment and Accumulated Depreciation accounts continue to reflect the effects of the intercompany sale on the subsidiary's unconsolidated balance sheet. Remember, the consolidating entries are not actually recorded in the accounting records of either the parent or the subsidiary. As a result, *in each year following the intercompany sale, we need to make consolidation adjustments (until the equipment is ultimately fully depreciated, otherwise impaired, or sold to an unaffiliated company).* These adjustments ensure that the balances reported in the consolidated financial statements at the end of one year agree with the consolidated balances reported at the beginning of the next year.

For example, the following consolidating entries will be necessary to prepare the annual financial statements for the year ended December 31, 2012:

Consolidation entries to eliminate changes in the Equity Investment account during the year	**[C]**	Equity investment.	15	
		Income (loss) from subsidiary		15
Eliminates the parent's BOY investment account against the subsidiary's BOY stockholders' equity	**[E]**	Equity investment.	22.5	
		• Retained Earnings (BOY)		22.5
		(eliminates the BOY accumulated depreciation on the intercompany asset held by the subsidiary and the corresponding amount in the parent company's investment account that was recorded through the equity method adjustments in Year 1)		

Intercompany	[I$_{gain}$]	Equity investment.	37.5	
elimination entries		Equipment	15.0	
in the first year		Accumulated depreciation.		52.5
following sale		*(to adjust BOY Equity Investment and Accumulated*		
		Depreciation for the consolidation adjustments made through		
		the end of the prior year (i.e., December 31, 2011) and to		
		restore the original (gross) cost of the Equipment)		
	[I$_{dep}$]	Accumulated depreciation	7.5	
		Depreciation expense		7.5
		(to eliminate the excess depreciation expense recorded by the		
		subsidiary, and to adjust accumulated depreciation from the		
		BOY amount to the EOY amount)		

The **[C]** consolidating entry reverses the parent company's equity-method investment during 2012. The $15.0 amount in entry **[C]** is equal to amount of loss recognized by the parent. This amount is comprised of the $(22.5) depreciation-related loss recognized by the subsidiary, adjusted for the equity-method recognition of $7.5 of deferred profit by the parent during 2012.

The **[E]** consolidating entry eliminates the parent's BOY investment account against the subsidiary's BOY stockholders' equity. Despite the fact that this example is intentionally simplified to focus only on the accounts affected by the intercompany transactions, the **[E]** entry is necessary because the subsidiary will record depreciation expense in its income statement (which becomes part of its retained earnings), and parent company will record its share of the income of the subsidiary in the Equity Investment account. The **[C]** entry, above, eliminated the depreciation expense recorded as part of the parent's equity method entries for the year ended December 31, 2012. This means the only amount remaining in the investment account is the accumulated depreciation recorded by the subsidiary during the year prior to December 31, 2012 (i.e., December 31, 2011).

In entry **[I$_{gain}$]**, the $37.5 debit to the parent's Equity Investment account at the beginning of 2012 is necessary because the entire unconfirmed gain of $45 was taken out of the Equity Investment account on the date of the intercompany sale during 2011, and $7.5 of this gain was confirmed via an equity-method adjustment during 2011 (i.e., the $37.5 is the remaining unconfirmed gain at the beginning of 2012). Because the consolidating entries during 2011 were not actually recorded on the books of either company, we must recognize their effects in the beginning balances the next year. This is also why consolidating entry **[I$_{gain}$]** for the year ended December 31, 2012, has a beginning-of-year adjustment of $52.5 to Accumulated Depreciation. This beginning-of-year 2012 adjustment is comprised of the $60.0 credit to Accumulated Depreciation in the 2011 adjustment **[I$_{gain}$]** and the $7.5 debit to Accumulated Depreciation in 2011 adjustment **[I$_{dep}$]**. The $15.0 debit to Equipment is necessary to increase its gross balance to $150.0 in the consolidated financial statements. The entry **[I$_{dep}$]** is necessary to show the confirmed gain as a reduction of depreciation expense during 2012. We show the effects of these consolidating entries in the excerpts from a consolidation spreadsheet (for the year ended December 31, 2012) presented in Exhibit 4.20.

If the subsidiary continues to hold the equipment through 2016, the parent's Equity Investment account will need to be adjusted *each* year until the equipment is fully depreciated (or otherwise impaired or disposed of).

For example, during the 2013 consolidation process, the consolidating entry **[I$_{gain}$]** will require a debit of $30.0 to the parent's Equity Investment account at the beginning of 2013 because the entire unconfirmed gain of $45 was taken out of the Equity Investment account on the date of the intercompany sale during 2011, and $7.5 of this gain was confirmed via an equity-method adjustment during each of the years 2011 and 2012 (i.e., the $30.0 is the remaining unconfirmed gain at the <u>beginning</u> of 2013). Likewise, in subsequent years, the parent's beginning-of-year Equity Investment in Subsidiary will require debits in the amounts of $22.5, $15.0, $7.5 and $0.0 during the consolidation process in 2014, 2015, 2016, and thereafter, respectively.

Accumulated Depreciation will experience a similarly declining "carry-forward" adjustment during the remaining life of the equipment. In particular, beginning-of-year Accumulated Depreciation will require credits in the amount of $45.0, $37.5, $30, $22.5, and $15.0 during the consolidation process in 2013, 2014, 2015, 2016, and thereafter, respectively. Note that the $15.0 credit to Accumulated

EXHIBIT 4.20	Excerpts of Equipment-Transaction-Affected Accounts in Consolidation Spreadsheet in Period (i.e., year ended December 31, 2012) Subsequent to the Period of the Intercompany Sale of Equipment—Equity Method

			Consolidation Entries		
	Parent	Subsidiary	Debits	Credits	Consolidated
Income statement (excerpt):					
Gain on sale of equipment	$ 0	$ 0			$ 0
Depreciation expense.	0	22.5		[I$_{dep}$] 7.5	15.0
Income (loss) from subsidiary.	(15.0)			**[C]** 15.0	0
Net effect on total profits	$(15.0)	$ (22.5)	0	22.5	$ (15.0)
Balance sheet (excerpt):					
Equipment (gross)	$ 0	$135.0	[I$_{gain}$] 15.0		$150.0
Accumulated depreciation	0	45.0	[I$_{dep}$] 7.5 [I$_{gain}$] 52.5		90.0
Equipment (net)	$ 0	$ 90.0	22.5	52.5	$ 60.0
Equity investment.	$(75.0)		**[C]** 15.0		$ 0
			[E] 22.5		
			[I$_{gain}$] 37.5		
Accumulated in retained earnings	$(30.0)	$(45.0)		**(NI)** 22.5	$ (30.0)
				[E] 22.5	

Depreciation after 2016 exactly offsets the continuing annual $15.0 consolidating debit to Equipment (gross). The fact that these exactly offset (i.e., they net to zero) at the end of the useful life is consistent with the equipment being fully depreciated after 2016.

Example of Sale of Equipment to Unaffiliated Party

Assume the same facts about the previously discussed intercompany sale of equipment from the parent to the subsidiary on January 1, 2011, except that the subsidiary sells the equipment to an unaffiliated (i.e., independent) company for a cash sale price of $140 on January 1, 2013. The subsidiary makes the following journal entry to record the sale:

Cash	140	
Accumulated depreciation*	45	
Equipment		135
Gain on sale of equipment.		50
(to record the sale of Equipment to an independent company)		

*$45 is 2 years of depreciation expense at $22.5 per year

The subsidiary computes its $50 Gain on Sale of equipment by subtracting from the $140 sale proceeds, the $90 net carrying value (i.e., $135 − $45) of the equipment. This net book value can be found in the "subsidiary" column of the financial statement excerpts in Exhibit 4.20. From a consolidated perspective, the subsidiary's accounting ignores $30 of remaining deferred profit from the January 1, 2011, intercompany equipment sale. This remaining unamortized deferred profit on December 31, 2012 is clearly identified in Exhibit 4.19, and is equal to the unconfirmed profit at December 31, 2012 (i.e., the $45.0 original unconfirmed profit on January 1, 2011, minus $7.5 deferred profit confirmed in each of the years 2011 and 2012).

From a consolidated perspective, the Gain on Sale of equipment at January 1, 2013, is *$80*, which is equal to the $50 recognized on the books of the subsidiary plus the $30 of unamortized deferred profit through January 1, 2013. There is another, more intuitive way to arrive at the same consolidated Gain on Sale of Equipment amount: simply subtract from the $140 sale proceeds, the $60 *consolidated* net carrying value (i.e., $150 − $90) of the Equipment that is listed in the "Consolidated" column of Exhibit 4.20.

The end result: now that the equipment has been sold to an independent company, the *entire remaining unamortized deferred profit can be fully recognized.*

When the parent company applies the equity method during 2013 (i.e., the year the subsidiary sells the equipment to an unaffiliated party), it will record the following two entries on its books to recognize (1) the gain recognized by the subsidiary on its books when it sells the equipment and (2) the remaining deferred profit through the date of sale to the unaffiliated party:

Equity investment.	50	
Income (loss) from subsidiary		50
(to record the equity method adjustment for equipment-gain-related income		
recognized by the subsidiary)		

Equity investment.	30	
Income (loss) from subsidiary		30
(to recognize the remaining deferred intercompany profit in income and remove		
the previously deferred profit from the Equity Investment account)		

When the parent uses the equity method, the consolidating **[C]** entry will eliminate the gain that corresponds to the income recognized in the subsidiary's income statement, the **[E]** entry eliminates the accumulated depreciation expenses recognized by the subsidiary prior to the date of sale, and the consolidating **[I]** entry will reclassify the $30 of Income from Subsidiary into the consolidated Gain on Sale of Equipment account. These consolidating entries for the year ended December 31, 2013 (i.e., the financial statements that include the January 1, 2013 date of sale) are as follows:

Consolidation entries to eliminate changes in the Equity Investment account during the year	**[C]**	Income (loss) from subsidiary. . . . . Equity investment	80	80
Eliminates the parent's BOY investment account against the subsidiary's BOY stockholders' equity	**[E]**	Equity investment. . . . . Retained Earnings (BOY) . . . . *(eliminates the BOY accumulated depreciation on the* *intercompany asset held by the subsidiary and the* *corresponding amount in the parent company's investment* *account that was recorded through the equity method* *adjustments in Year 1)*	45	45
Intercompany elimination entry in the year of sale to an unaffiliated company	**[I**gain**]**	Equity investment. . . . . Gain on sale of equipment. . . . . *(to increase the Equity Investment account for the remaining* *unconfirmed profit and recognize the deferred gain on the sale)*	30	30

Again, the total gain reported in the consolidated income statement is $80 (i.e., $50 by the subsidiary in its income statement and the recognition of the $30 deferred profit balance remaining on January 1, 2013). The consolidation worksheet is shown in Exhibit 4.21.

Upstream Intercompany Sale of Depreciable Assets

In the case of *wholly owned subsidiaries*, there is no difference in the **[I]** eliminating entries for upstream versus downstream transactions involving intercompany (i.e., affiliated) transfers of depreciable assets among commonly controlled companies (assuming we hold constant the parent company's pre-consolidation bookkeeping for the Equity Investment account). This is because all of the deferred profit must be removed from the combined financial statements, regardless of the direction of the transaction.

If we consider the accounts affected and the amounts in the preceding example, the account relationships, **[I]** consolidating entries, and consolidated balances in Exhibits 4.18 and 4.20 are the same in the upstream case. The only difference in the entries will relate to the **[C]** adjustment because in the case of the upstream sale, the subsidiary would have recorded the gain in its income statement. Thus the parent company would have recorded its equity method interest in the income of the subsidiary. In

EXHIBIT 4.21	Excerpts of Equipment-Transaction-Affected Accounts in Consolidation Spreadsheet in the Year of Sale to Unaffiliated Party (i.e., year ended December 31, 2013)—Equity Method

	Parent	Subsidiary	Consolidation Entries Debits	Consolidation Entries Credits	Consolidated
Income statement:					
Gain on sale of equipment	$ 0	$50		[I_gain] 30	$80
Depreciation expense.	0	0			0
Equity income (loss)	80	0	[C] 80		0
Net effect on total profits	$80	$50	80	30	$80
Balance sheet:					
Equipment (gross)	$ 0	$ 0			$ 0
Accumulated depreciation	0	0			0
Equipment (net)	0	0	0	0	0
Equity investment.	5	0	[I_gain] 30	[C] 80	0
			[E] 45		
Accumulated in retained earnings	$50	$ 5	(NI) 80	(NI) 30	$50
				[E] 45	

addition, the parent would make the same equity method adjustments to eliminate the deferred intercompany profits that result from the sale.[21] The following equity-method entries are recorded by the parent company assuming an upstream sale instead of a downstream sale:

Equity investment.	45	
Income (loss) from subsidiary		45
(to record the equity method adjustment for Subsidiary Income)		

Income (loss) from subsidiary.	37.5	
Equity investment		37.5
(to remove the unconfirmed profit of the subsidiary from the Subsidiary Income account and the Equity Investment account through the end of 2011)		

Just as it did in the downstream case illustrated in Exhibits 4.18 and 4.20, in the case of the upstream sale the beginning balance of the Equity Investment would still include the $37.5 reduction for elimination of the unamortized deferred profit at January 1, 2012 and $30.0 of unamortized deferred profit at January 1, 2013. That is because neither company records the consolidating entries in their accounting records. Therefore, the consolidating entry [I] adjustment to the beginning-of-year Equity Investment is also required in the upstream case for the year ended December 31, 2012 and any other year (through 2016) that the affiliated companies hold the Equipment.

Example of Upstream Intercompany Sale of Depreciable Assets— Equity Method
Assume that on January 1, 2015, a wholly owned subsidiary sells to its parent for $90,000, equipment that originally cost subsidiary $140,000. The subsidiary depreciated the equipment over a 10-year period, straight-line with no salvage value. At the time of the intercompany sale, the subsidiary recorded Accumulated Depreciation of $84,000 related to the equipment (i.e., six years after subsidiary's initial purchase of the equipment). The parent estimates that the equipment has a four-year remaining useful life on the date of the intercompany transaction.

---

[21] Again, we made some fairly big simplifying assumptions in this example. In particular, we assumed that there were no other transactions or balances, except for the equipment-related items. Thus, the subsidiary's only income would have been derived from the upstream sale.

On January 1, 2015, the subsidiary makes the following journal entry to record the sale of equipment to parent:

Cash	90,000	
Accumulated depreciation	84,000	
Equipment...		140,000
Gain on sale...		34,000
(to record the sale of equipment on subsidiary's books)		

On the same date, the parent records the purchase of equipment:

Equipment	90,000	
Cash		90,000
(to record the purchase of equipment on parent's books)		

On January 1, 2015, the deferred profit related to the intercompany equipment sale is equal to $34,000. Given that both companies use straight-line depreciation and assume the same (i.e., four-year) remaining useful life at the date of the intercompany sale, the deferred profit will be amortized and included in consolidated net income at the rate of $8,500 per year. The [I] consolidation entries for the year ended December 31, 2015, are:

Intercompany elimination entries for year ended December 31, 2015 (i.e., year of sale)	[I$_{gain}$]	Gain on sale of equipment........................	34,000	
		Equipment	50,000	
		Accumulated depreciation..................		84,000
		(to adjust Gain, Equipment, and Accumulated Depreciation on the date of the intercompany transfer of equipment—given that the transaction occurred at the beginning of the year, usage of the equipment for the year must be reflected in a separate entry)		
	[I$_{dep}$]	Accumulated depreciation........................	8,500	
		Depreciation expense		8,500
		(to eliminate the excess depreciation expense recorded by the subsidiary, and to adjust accumulated depreciation from the BOY amount to the EOY amount)		

Exhibit 4.22 provides the consolidation spreadsheet for the year ended December 31, 2016 (i.e., at the end of the year following the intercompany sale), with assumed financial statements of the parent and its subsidiary for the year ended December 31, 2016, presented in the first two columns of the consolidation spreadsheet and assuming that on January 1, 2016, the unamortized AAP related to the parent's acquisition of the subsidiary was $90,000 (depreciated/amortized $9,000 per year).

There is no intercompany gain recorded in the pre-consolidation income statements, and, because we assume the parent applies the equity method to account for its Equity Investment, the effects of the $34,000 intercompany gain are eliminated from the parent's Net Income and Retained Earnings accounts. We don't worry about correcting the subsidiary's Retained Earnings because the subsidiary's Stockholders' Equity is eliminated in consolidation. The [I] consolidation entries for the year ended December 31, 2016, are:

Intercompany elimination entries for year ended December 31, 2016	[I$_{gain}$]	Equity investment...............................	25,500	
		Equipment	50,000	
		Accumulated depreciation..................		75,500
		(to adjust Gain, Equipment, and Accumulated Depreciation on the date of the intercompany transfer of equipment—given that the transaction occurred at the beginning of the year, usage of the equipment for the year must be reflected in a separate entry)		
	[I$_{dep}$]	Accumulated depreciation........................	8,500	
		Depreciation expense		8,500
		(to eliminate the excess depreciation expense recorded by the subsidiary, and to adjust accumulated depreciation from the BOY amount to the EOY amount)		

| EXHIBIT 4.22 | Upstream Sale of Depreciable Assets in the Period Following Intercompany Sale—Equity Method |

			Consolidation Entries			
Upstream Sale of Depreciable Assets	Parent	Subsidiary	Dr		Cr	Consolidated
Income statement:						
Sales.	$10,000,000	$2,000,000				$12,000,000
Cost of goods sold.	(7,000,000)	(1,400,000)				(8,400,000)
Gross profit.	3,000,000	600,000				3,600,000
Income (loss) from subsidiary.	199,500		[C] $199,500			0
Operating expenses.	(1,900,000)	(400,000)	[D] 9,000	$[I_{dep}]$	$ 8,500	(2,300,500)
Net income.	$ 1,299,500	$ 200,000				$ 1,299,500
Statement of retained earnings:						
BOY retained earnings.	$ 574,500	$ 225,000	[E] 225,000			$ 574,500
Net income.	1,299,500	200,000				1,299,500
Dividends	(400,000)	(20,000)		[C]	20,000	(400,000)
Ending retained earnings	$ 1,474,000	$ 405,000				$ 1,474,000
Balance sheet:						
Assets						
Cash.	$ 329,000	$ 70,000				$ 399,000
Accounts receivable.	900,000	210,000				1,110,000
Inventory.	940,000	250,000				1,190,000
Land	700,000	300,000				1,000,000
Building, net.	1,300,000	350,000	[A] 90,000	[D]	9,000	1,731,000
Equipment, net.	300,000	150,000	$[I_{gain}]$ 50,000	$[I_{gain}]$	75,500	433,000
			$[I_{dep}]$ 8,500			
Equity investment.	694,000		$[I_{gain}]$ 25,500	[C]	179,500	0
				[E]	450,000	
				[A]	90,000	
	$ 5,163,000	$1,330,000				$ 5,863,000
Liabilities and stockholders' equity						
Accounts payable.	$ 388,000	$ 270,000				$ 658,000
Other current liabilities	49,000	230,000				279,000
Long-term liabilities	312,000	200,000				512,000
Common stock.	1,665,000	100,000	[E] 100,000			1,665,000
APIC.	1,275,000	125,000	[E] 125,000			1,275,000
Retained earnings	1,474,000	405,000				1,474,000
	$ 5,163,000	$1,330,000	$832,500		$832,500	$ 5,863,000

TOPIC REVIEW 3

Upstream Sale of Depreciable Assets (year of sale)—Equity Method

Assume that a parent company acquired a 100% interest in its subsidiary on January 1, 2014, at a price that equaled the book value of the net assets of the subsidiary. On January 1, 2016, the subsidiary sold equipment to the parent for a cash price of $80,000. The subsidiary acquired the equipment on January 1, 2013, at a cost of $100,000 and depreciated the equipment over its 10-year useful life using the straight-line method (no salvage value). On the date of sale, the parent retained the depreciation policy of the subsidiary and depreciated the equipment over its remaining 7-year useful life. Following are financial statements of the parent and its subsidiary for the year ended December 31, 2016. The parent uses the equity method for its investment in the subsidiary.

	Parent	Subsidiary		Parent	Subsidiary
Income statement:			**Balance sheet:**		
Sales............	$4,610,000	$1,330,500	Assets		
Cost of goods sold..	(3,319,200)	(798,300)	Cash.............	$ 408,331	$ 342,825
Gross profit........	1,290,800	532,200	Accounts		
			receivable.......	1,180,160	308,676
Gain on sale of			Inventory..........	1,788,680	396,489
equipment.......		10,000			
Income (loss) from			Equity investment...	1,036,758	
subsidiary.......	177,699				
Operating expenses.	(691,500)	(355,930)	PPE, net..........	6,760,104	733,549
Net income........	$ 776,999	$ 186,270		$11,174,033	$1,781,539
Statement of retained earnings:					
BOY ret. earnings...	$2,362,759	$ 687,425	Liabilities and stockholders' equity		
			Accounts payable...	$ 674,904	$ 126,841
Net income........	776,999	186,270	Accrued liabilities ...	802,140	165,869
Dividends.........	(157,114)	(27,941)	Long-term liabilities .	4,000,000	443,500
Ending ret. earnings .	$2,982,644	$ 845,754	Common stock.....	325,019	88,700
			APIC.............	2,389,326	110,875
			Retained earnings ..	2,982,644	845,754
				$11,174,033	$1,781,539

Required

Prepare the consolidation spreadsheet for the year.

The solution to this review problem can be found on page 264.

ACCOUNTING FOR THE INTERCOMPANY SALES OF NONCURRENT ASSETS BETWEEN THE INVESTOR AND THE INVESTEE(S)—COST METHOD

In this section, we describe the accounting for the intercompany sales of noncurrent assets, assuming that the parent applies the cost method of pre-consolidation bookkeeping. As we previously emphasized, the consolidated financial statements will look the same, regardless of the pre-consolidation method of Equity Investment bookkeeping applied by the parent company. In addition, the subsidiary's financial statements will be identical when the parent applies the cost method (i.e., because cost method versus equity method refers to bookkeeping applied by the parent, not the subsidiary). However, because parent company's pre-consolidation financial statements will be different under the cost method versus the equity method, the consolidation entries will (out of necessity) be slightly different. Just like our coverage of the equity method, we will begin our cost-method noncurrent-asset-transfer discussion with non-depreciable assets and then conclude with depreciable assets.

Accounting for the Intercompany Sale of Non-Depreciable Assets—Cost Method

To allow direct comparison of the cost method to the equity method, we illustrate the cost method with the same basic facts as our equity method discussion of non-depreciable assets. In this example, we assume that on January 1, 2014, a parent company sells to its subsidiary for $100 in cash, land that originally cost the parent $80. On the date of the intercompany sale, the parent makes the following journal entry to record the sale:

Cost Method

LO5 Describe the accounting for intercompany sales of non-depreciable noncurrent assets between the parent and the subsidiary when the parent uses the cost method of pre-consolidation investment bookkeeping.

Cash	100	
Land.		80
Gain on sale.		20
(to record the sale of land)		

On the same date, the subsidiary records the land purchase as follows:

Land	100	
Cash		100
(to record the purchase of land)		

In contrast to the equity method, where the parent company eliminates the intercompany profit in the Equity Investment account, under the cost method the parent company makes no investment-related bookkeeping adjustments on its pre-consolidation books. The fact that the parent recognized a $20 gain and the subsidiary's land accounting reflects the $20 gain will be "corrected" via the consolidation process. Because there was no equity-investment adjustment related to the last transfer, there is no [C] entry (related to intercompany profits) under the cost method. (Of course, in a fully fleshed-out scenario, a [C] entry would be required for any dividends paid by the subsidiary to the parent. In this example, we are only focusing on the intercompany-asset-transfer-related accounts.) Based on the facts in this simplified, stylized example, parent company would make the following consolidation entry in the year of sale:

Intercompany elimination entry in the year of sale	$[I_{gain}]$	Gain on sale	20	
		Land.		20
		(to defer the gain on sale and to restate the Land account to its pre-sale reported amount)		

As a result of the [I] entry, the gain on sale has been removed from the consolidated income statement and the Land account, reported by the subsidiary at $100 following the purchase, is reduced to $80 on the consolidated balance sheet, the amount at which it was carried by the parent prior to the sale. We show the effects of these consolidating entries in the excerpts from a consolidation spreadsheet (for the year ended December 31, 2014) in Exhibit 4.23.

Recall in Exhibit 4.15, under the equity method, the parent's pre-consolidation effect on total profits was the same as the consolidated effect on total profits. As we can see in Exhibit 4.23, under the cost method, the parent's total profits and ending retained earnings are both overstated by the $20 intercompany profits. This means that, unlike the equity method, under the cost method the parent's pre-consolidation profits and retained earnings do not equal the consolidated amounts. The $[I_{gain}]$ consolidation entry reduces the parent's net profits (and flows into retained earnings) to equal the consolidated amount. The $[I_{gain}]$ consolidation entry also reduces the value of land to equal its pre-intercompany transfer balance of $80.

EXHIBIT 4.23	Excerpts of Land-Transaction-Affected Accounts in Consolidation Spreadsheet in the Initial Period of Intercompany Sale of Land (i.e., 2014)—Cost Method

	Parent	Subsidiary	Consolidation Entries Debits	Consolidation Entries Credits	Consolidated
Income statement (excerpt):					
Gain on sale of land	$ 20	$ 0	$[I_{gain}]$ 20		$ 0
Income (loss) from subsidiary.	0				0
Net effect on total profits	$ 20	$ 0	20	0	$ 0
Balance sheet (excerpt):					
Land	$ 0	$100		$[I_{gain}]$ 20	$80
Equity investment.	0				0
Cumulative effect on retained earnings ...	$ 20	$ 0	(NI) 20	(NI) 0	$ 0

It is important to remember that the consolidating entries are not actually recorded by the parent. Thus, the effects of the $[I_{gain}]$ consolidation entry are not actually recorded in the books of the parent, which means, under the cost method, in periods after the year of the initial transaction, the retained earnings of the parent company will still have the $20 of intercompany profits included in it.

In the years after the intercompany transaction (and resulting gain or loss elimination), the parent will need to propose a "catch-up" [ADJ] consolidating entry to make the parent's investment and retained earnings account be on an "as if equity method" basis. For example, during 2015's consolidation procedures, the parent will propose the following [ADJ] entry:

Restate the Equity Investment account from cost to "as if" equity method	[ADJ]	Retained earnings @ BOY	20	
		Equity investment @ BOY		20

Again, this entry is necessary each year through the year in which the asset is sold to an unaffiliated third party. Again, this is because the parent's retained earnings is overstated at December 31, 2014. This ending balance becomes the beginning balance in the following year, and the $20 gain is included in that account. This [ADJ] entry removes the effects of the intercompany gain from the parent's retained earnings, which reflects the correct consolidated retained earnings. As we mentioned in the previous cost-method intercompany inventory discussion, after proposing the [ADJ] entry, the parent can propose the exact same **E-A-D-I** consolidation entries as would have been proposed under the equity method. This results in the following $[I_{gain}]$ entry in each period until the period before the land is sold to an unaffiliated party:

Intercompany elimination entry in the years after intercompany sale	$[I_{gain}]$	Equity investment...............................	20	
		Land.....................................		20
		(to defer the gain on sale and to restate the Land account to its pre-sale reported amount)		

Just as it was under the equity method, this $[I_{gain}]$ entry is similar to that we present above, except that the 2015 debit is to the BOY Equity Investment balance (which includes the gain on the sale) rather than the 2014 debit to the Gain on Sale income-statement account.[22]

As we did in the equity method case, we will assume that the land is ultimately sold to an independent party on September 15, 2016, for $150. On this date, the subsidiary will make the following journal entry in its books:

Cash	150	
Land..		100
Gain on sale...		50
(to record the sale of Land to an unaffiliated company)		

Unlike the equity method case, under the cost method there are no investment-related entries on the parent's books for the confirmation of the deferred profit.

---

[22] Given that the [ADJ] entry credits the equity investment and the $[I_{gain}]$ entry debits the equity investment, one might wonder if it is acceptable to net the two entries so that it results in a debit to BOY retained earnings and a credit to land. As we mentioned previously, there are many real-world variations on pre-consolidation equity investment bookkeeping and there are many variations on the consolidation entry sequence. Thus, really, "anything goes" as long as the process results in correct consolidated financial statements. We believe consistently applying the approach in this text will increase the likelihood that students will arrive at correct consolidated balances. Given the complexities that can be introduced into consolidations (e.g., subsidiary income, dividends, AAP, intercompany profits and noncontrolling interests), sticking to a single process—especially when first learning this material—will lead to the most consistently correct outcomes.

Cost Method

| | | EXHIBIT 4.24 — Excerpts of Land-Transaction-Affected Accounts in Consolidation Spreadsheet in the Period in Which the Land Is Sold to an Unaffiliated Party (i.e., 2016)—Cost Method |

EXHIBIT 4.24 — Excerpts of Land-Transaction-Affected Accounts in Consolidation Spreadsheet in the Period in Which the Land Is Sold to an Unaffiliated Party (i.e., 2016)—Cost Method

	Parent	Subsidiary	Consolidation Entries Debits	Consolidation Entries Credits	Consolidated
Income statement (excerpt):					
Gain on sale of land	$ 0	$50		[I$_{gain}$] 20	$70
Income (loss) from subsidiary.	0				0
Net effect on total profits	$ 0	$50		20	$70
Balance sheet (excerpt):					
Land	$ 0	$ 0			$ 0
Equity investment.	0		[I$_{gain}$] 20	[ADJ] 20	0
Cumulative effect on retained earnings . . .	$20	$50	[ADJ] 20	20	$70

As we illustrate in Exhibit 4.24, the following consolidating entries are necessary to bring forward the Equity Investment account, correct the beginning balance of the parent's retained earnings and to recognize the full $70 of Gain on Sale of Land in 2016:

Restate the Equity Investment account from cost to "as if" equity method	[ADJ]	Retained earnings @ BOY 20	
		Equity investment @ BOY	20
Intercompany elimination entry in the years after intercompany sale	[I$_{gain}$]	Equity investment. 20	
		Gain on sale of land.	20

After 2016, no further special consolidation adjustment is necessary for the deferred profits. The $20 of gain from the parent's sale to the subsidiary is part of the parent's retained earnings under the parent's cost method accounting. In future years, the $50 that became part of the subsidiary's retained earnings in 2016 (see the subsidiary column in Exhibit 4.24) will become part of the parent's retained earnings as part of the annual [ADJ] consolidation entry.[23]

Accounting for the Intercompany Sale of Depreciable Assets— Cost Method

Again, to allow direct comparison of the cost method to the equity method, we illustrate the cost method with the same basic facts as our equity method discussion of depreciable assets. As we did before, assume that on January 1, 2011, parent company sells equipment that originally cost $150 to its wholly owned subsidiary for a cash sale price of $135. The parent depreciated the equipment over a 10-year period, straight-line with no salvage value. At the time of sale, the parent's accounting records included $60 of Accumulated Depreciation related to the equipment. Refer back to the original discussion of these facts to see the equipment-sale and purchase-related journal entries originally recorded on the books of the parent and the subsidiary.

As we noted previously, the point of the consolidation process related to depreciable assets is to make the financial statements appear like the intercompany transaction never occurred. Again, the following table summarizes, on the date of intercompany sale, the "as-if" no sale occurred and the actual books where the balance of the equipment on the subsidiary's books includes the $45 of intercompany profits:

LO6 Describe the accounting for intercompany sales of depreciable noncurrent assets between the parent and the subsidiary when the parent uses the cost method of pre-consolidation investment bookkeeping.

Cost Method

---

[23] Recall from Chapter 3 that the [ADJ] consolidation entry records the parent's share of the change in the subsidiary's retained earnings from the acquisition date through the beginning of the period of consolidation. Thus, this $50 will be part of that subsidiary's retained earnings change included in the annual [ADJ] entry.

	("As-If" No Intercompany Sale) Parent	(Actual) Subsidiary	Difference
Net book value	$90.0	$135.0	$45.0
Useful life	6	6	
Depreciation expense	$15.0	$ 22.5	$ 7.5

As revealed by the table, the subsidiary's depreciation expense is $7.5 per year higher than that which the parent would have recorded in its income statement had it not sold the equipment. That's because the deferred profit of $45 increases the carrying value of the equipment on the subsidiary's books and that higher book value will get depreciated over the remaining useful life of the equipment. As a result, the combined income of the two companies (before consolidation adjustments) is $7.5 lower for each year of the remaining useful life of the equipment. For the year ended December 31, 2011, the consolidation adjustments are:

Intercompany elimination entries at the end of the year of intercompany sale	[I$_{gain}$]	Gain on sale of equipment	45	
		Equipment	15	
		Accumulated depreciation		60
		(to adjust Gain, Equipment, and Accumulated Depreciation on the date of the intercompany transfer of equipment—given that the transaction occurred at the beginning of the year, usage of the equipment for the year must be reflected in a separate entry)		
	[I$_{dep}$]	Accumulated depreciation	7.5	
		Depreciation expense		7.5
		(to eliminate the excess depreciation expense recorded by the subsidiary, and to adjust accumulated depreciation from the BOY amount to the EOY amount)		

Recall that in the equity-method consolidation illustrated in Exhibit 4.18, the parent's pre-consolidation effect on total profits was the same as the consolidated effect on total profits. As we can see in Exhibit 4.25, under the cost method, the parent's total profits and ending retained earnings are both

Cost Method

EXHIBIT 4.25   Excerpts of Equipment-Transaction-Affected Accounts in Consolidation Spreadsheet in the Initial Period of Intercompany Sale of Equipment (i.e., Year Ended December 31, 2011)—Cost Method

	Parent	Subsidiary	Consolidation Entries Debits	Consolidation Entries Credits	Consolidated
Income statement (excerpt):					
Gain on sale of equipment	$45.0	$ 0	[I$_{gain}$] 45.0		$ 0
Depreciation expense	0	22.5		[I$_{dep}$] 7.5	15.0
Income (loss) from subsidiary	0				0
Net effect on total profits	$45.0	$ (22.5)	45.0	7.5	$ (15.0)
Balance sheet (excerpt):					
Equipment (gross)	$ 0	$135.0	[I$_{gain}$] 15.0		$150.0
Accumulated depreciation	0	22.5	[I$_{dep}$] 7.5	[I$_{gain}$] 60.0	75.0
Equipment (net)	0	112.5	22.5	60.0	75.0
Equity investment	0				0
Cumulative effect on retained earnings	$45.0	$ (22.5)	**(NI)** 45.0	**(NI)** 7.5	$ (15.0)

overstated because of the intercompany gain on the equipment transfer and the failure to recognize depreciation expense for a depreciable asset held by the consolidated entity. This means that, unlike the equity method, under the cost method the parent's pre-consolidation profits and retained earnings do not equal the consolidated amounts. The $[I_{gain}]$ consolidation entry reduces the parent's net profits (and flows into retained earnings) to equal the consolidated amount. In addition, the $[I_{dep}]$ consolidation entry increases the parent's profits for the $7.5 of gain confirmed through the use of the equipment during the year (i.e., see Exhibit 4.19). The $[I_{gain}]$ and $[I_{dep}]$ consolidation entries also work together to arrive at the correct consolidated balances for Equipment (gross), Accumulated depreciation, and Equipment (net).

As in our previous cost method examples, it is important to remember that the consolidating entries are not actually recorded by the parent. Thus, the effects of the $[I_{gain}]$ and $[I_{dep}]$ consolidation entries are not recorded in the books of the parent, which means, under the cost method, in periods after the year of the initial transaction, the beginning retained earnings of the parent company will still have the unconfirmed intercompany profits included in it. To eliminate the unconfirmed beginning-of-year intercompany profits and to recognize the parent's share of the change in the retained earnings of the subsidiary, the parent company will need to propose an **[ADJ]** consolidating entry as part of the consolidation process. The amount of the **[ADJ]** adjustment will change during the depreciable life of the intercompany asset because (1) the amount of the unconfirmed profit changes each year and (2) the amount of the change in the subsidiary's retained earnings changes each year. In the case of this example (i.e., only focusing on amounts that directly relate to the transferred asset), this will lead to the following amounts included in the **[ADJ]** consolidating entry during fiscal years 2011 through 2016 as illustrated in Exhibit 4.26:

| **EXHIBIT 4.26** | Computation of the Annual **[ADJ]** Amount through December 31, 2016—Cost Method |

	2011	2012	2013	2014	2015	2016
Unconfirmed at 1/1 (BOY)	$(45.0)	$(37.5)	$(30.0)	$(22.5)	$ (15.0)	$ (7.5)
Confirmed during fiscal year	7.5	7.5	7.5	7.5	7.5	7.5
Unconfirmed at 12/31 (EOY)	(37.5)	(30.0)	(22.5)	(15.0)	(7.5)	—
Reported NI (S).	(22.5)	(22.5)	(22.5)	(22.5)	(22.5)	(22.5)
Cumulative in RE (S) (EOY).	(22.5)	(45.0)	(67.5)	(90.0)	(112.5)	(135.0)
Amount of **[ADJ]** (BOY)	$ n/a	$(60.0)	$(75.0)	$(90.0)	$(105.0)	$(120.0)

So, as part of the consolidation procedures in each year beginning in 2012, the parent company will need to propose a "catch-up" **[ADJ]** consolidating entry to make the parent's beginning of year investment and retained earnings accounts be on an "as if equity method" basis. For example, during 2012's consolidation procedures, the parent will propose the following **[ADJ]** entry to the beginning of year account balances:

Restate the Equity Investment account from cost to "as if" equity method	**[ADJ]**	Retained earnings @ BOY . . . . Equity investment @ BOY	60	60

In addition, the parent will propose the following **[E]** and **[I]** consolidation entries in 2012:

Eliminates the parent's BOY investment account against the subsidiary's BOY stockholders' equity	[E]	Equity investment. . . . . Retained Earnings (BOY) . . . . *(Eliminates the BOY accumulated depreciation on the intercompany asset held by the subsidiary and the corresponding amount in the parent company's investment account that was recorded through the equity method adjustments in Year 1)*	22.5	22.5

Intercompany elimination entry in the first year following sale	[I_{gain}]	Equity investment...	37.5
		Equipment	15.0
		Accumulated depreciation........................	52.5
		(to adjust BOY Equity Investment and Accumulated Depreciation for the consolidation adjustments made through the end of the prior year (i.e., December 31, 2011) and to restore the original (gross) cost of the Equipment)	
	[I_{dep}]	Accumulated depreciation................................	7.5
		Depreciation expense	7.5
		(to eliminate the excess depreciation expense recorded by the subsidiary, and to adjust accumulated depreciation from the BOY amount to the EOY amount)	

An important thing to note is that the **[ADJ]** adjustment basically adjusted the parent's pre-consolidation financial statements to an "as-if-equity-method" basis. This means that the **[I]** entries, above, are identical to the **[I]** consolidating entries proposed in the equity method example illustrated in Exhibit 4.20. In Exhibit 4.27, we include the above **[ADJ]** and **[I]** entries in the cost-method consolidation for the year ended December 31, 2012:

EXHIBIT 4.27   Excerpts of Equipment-Transaction-Affected Accounts in Consolidation Spreadsheet Consolidation (i.e., Year Ended December 31, 2012) Subsequent to the Period of the Intercompany Sale of Equipment—Cost Method

	Parent	Subsidiary	Consolidation Entries Debits	Consolidation Entries Credits	Consolidated
Income statement (excerpt):					
Gain on sale of equipment............	$ 0	$ 0			$ 0
Depreciation expense................	0	22.5		[I_{dep}] 7.5	15.0
Income (loss) from subsidiary.........	0				0
Net effect on total profits.............	$ 0	$ (22.5)		7.5	$ (15.0)
Balance sheet (excerpt):					
Equipment (gross)	$ 0	$135.0	[I_{gain}] 15.0		$150.0
Accumulated depreciation............	0	45.0	[I_{dep}] 7.5	[I_{gain}] 52.5	90.0
Equipment (net)	0	90.0	22.5	52.5	60.0
Equity investment...................	0		[I_{gain}] 37.5 [E] 22.5	[ADJ] 60.0	0
Cumulative effect on retained earnings...	$45.0	$ (45.0)	[ADJ] 60.0	(NI) 7.5 [E] 22.5	$ (30.0)

As is illustrated by the excerpted consolidation worksheet, the **[ADJ]** consolidation entry adjusts the equity investment account and the parent's retained earnings so that those balances reflect equity-method-basis amounts through the beginning of the year. Therefore, the **[E]** and **[I]** consolidation entries are identical to those included in the equity-method version of this fact set illustrated in Exhibit 4.20.

Example of Upstream Intercompany Sale of Depreciable Assets— Cost Method

Assume that on January 1, 2014, a wholly owned subsidiary sells to its parent for $80,000, property, plant and equipment (PPE) that originally cost subsidiary $60,000. The subsidiary depreciated the PPE over a 5-year period, straight-line with no salvage value. At the time of the intercompany sale, the subsidiary recorded accumulated depreciation of $12,000 related to the PPE (i.e., one year after subsidiary's initial purchase of the PPE). The parent estimates that the PPE has a four-year remaining useful life on the date of the intercompany transaction. While this is an example of an upstream transaction, it is important to note that, given that the parent company owns 100% of the subsidiary, none of the proposed consolidation entries would be different in the case of a downstream transaction.[24]

The parent originally purchased its 100% investment in the subsidiary on January 1, 2013 for $720,000. On that date, the subsidiary's owners' equity equaled $720,000 (i.e., there is no AAP), and the subsidiary's retained earnings equaled $540,000. The parent applies the cost method for its investment in the subsidiary.

In consolidating the parent and subsidiary financial statements for the year ended December 31, 2016, the parent must keep track of the confirmed and unconfirmed profits on the intercompany PPE sale (i.e., regardless of the method of pre-consolidation bookkeeping applied by the parent). In addition, the parent must know the amount that the subsidiary's retained earnings changed from the acquisition date through the beginning of the year of consolidation. With respect to the intercompany profits, the PPE had a carrying value of $48,000 on the date of the intercompany transfer. This means that the unconfirmed intercompany profit on January 1, 2014 was $32,000 (i.e., $80,000 − $48,000), and is getting confirmed at a rate of $8,000 per year (i.e., $32,000 ÷ 4) over the four-year remaining useful life. With respect to the change in the subsidiary's retained earnings, the balance at December 31, 2015 is $620,000, which means that the change since the acquisition date through the beginning of the consolidation year was $80,000 (i.e., $620,000 − $540,000). Exhibit 4.28 provides the consolidation spreadsheet and discussion of the consolidating entries follows the spreadsheet.

| EXHIBIT 4.28 | Upstream Sale of Depreciable Assets in the Period Following Intercompany Sale—Cost Method |

| | | | Consolidation Entries | | | | |
	Parent	Subsidiary	Dr		Cr		Consolidated
Income statement:							
Sales.	$8,000,000	$1,200,000					$9,200,000
Cost of goods sold.	(5,600,000)	(720,000)					(6,320,000)
Gross profit.	2,400,000	480,000					$2,880,000
Income (loss) from subsidiary.	24,000		[C]	$ 24,000			0
Depreciation expense.	(320,000)	(64,000)			[I$_{dep}$]	$ 8,000	$(376,000)
Operating expenses	(1,200,000)	(248,000)					(1,448,000)
Net income.	$ 904,000	$ 168,000					$1,056,000
Statement of retained earnings:							
BOY retained earnings	$2,880,000	$620,000	[E]	620,000	[ADJ]	64,000	$2,944,000
Net income.	904,000	168,000					1,056,000
Dividends	(240,000)	(24,000)			[C]	24,000	(240,000)
Ending retained earnings	$3,544,000	$ 764,000					$3,760,000
Balance sheet:							
Assets							
Cash	$ 640,000	$ 324,800					$ 964,800
Accounts receivable.	1,024,000	278,400					1,302,400
Inventory.	1,560,000	357,600					1,917,600
Equity investment.	720,000		[ADJ]	64,000	[E]	800,000	0
			[I$_{gain}$]	16,000			
PPE, net	3,200,000	661,600	[I$_{dep}$]	8,000	[I$_{gain}$]	16,000	3,853,600
	$7,144,000	$1,622,400					$8,038,400
Liabilities and stockholders' equity							
Current liabilities.	$1,120,000	$ 278,400					$1,398,400
Long-term liabilities	1,200,000	400,000					1,600,000
Common stock.	480,000	80,000	[E]	80,000			480,000
APIC	800,000	100,000	[E]	100,000			800,000
Retained earnings	3,544,000	764,000					3,760,000
	$7,144,000	$1,622,400		$912,000		$912,000	$8,038,400

---

[24] In Chapter 5, we will discuss the differences that emerge when a parent company owns less than 100% of a subsidiary.

Catch-up entry needed to place parent company on "as if equity method" basis at the beginning of the consolidation year	[ADJ]	Equity Investment @ BOY .... Retained Earnings (P) @ BOY	64,000	64,000
Removes dividend income from the income statement of the parent	[C]	Income (loss) from subsidiary.............. Dividends.........................	24,000	24,000
Eliminates the beginning of year investment balance against the beginning of year owners' equity accounts of the subsidiary	[E]	Common stock (S) @ BOY .... APIC (S) @ BOY .... Retained earnings (S) @ BOY.............. Equity investment @ BOY	80,000 100,000 620,000	800,000
Removes the unconfirmed intercompany profit from PPE, net at the beginning of the year	[I_{gain}]	Equity Investment @ BOY .... PPE, net @ BOY	16,000	16,000
Confirms one year of intercompany gain by reducing depreciation expense	[I_{dep}]	PPE, net .... Depreciation expense	8,000	8,000

The [ADJ] consolidation entry represents the "catch-up" adjustment that is necessary to place the parent's Equity Investment and retained earnings accounts on an "as-if-equity-method" basis through the beginning of the year. In this case, given that there is no AAP, the [ADJ] entry is comprised of only two items: the change in the subsidiary's retained earnings through the beginning of the year (i.e., $80,000) less the unconfirmed intercompany PPE profit at the beginning of the year (as of December 31, 2015) of $16,000 (i.e., $32,000 at January 1, 2014 − $8,000 confirmed in 2014 and − $8,000 confirmed in 2015). This makes the [ADJ] equal to $64,000 (i.e., $80,000 − $16,000).

The [C] reverses the dividend income recognized by the parent during 2016 and the [E] eliminates the beginning of year investment balance (after recording the catch-up equity-method effects in the [ADJ] entry) against the beginning of year owners' equity accounts of the subsidiary. Because there is no AAP, there is no need for the [A] or [D] entries.

The final consolidating entries are the intercompany profit entries. The [I_{gain}] consolidating entry removes the beginning of year unconfirmed intercompany profits from the PPE, net account. We need to do this because our consolidation process begins with the actual accounting records of the parent and subsidiary, and that intercompany gain became part of the recorded amount of the PPE. The [I_{dep}] consolidation entry confirms the gain for the year ended December 31, 2016 by reducing depreciation expense. At the end of 2016, there will be only one more year (i.e., $8,000) of unconfirmed gain in the pre-consolidation carrying value of the parent's PPE, net.

TOPIC REVIEW 4

Upstream Sale of Depreciable Assets (years after sale)—Cost Method

Assume that on January 1, 2015, a wholly owned subsidiary sells to its parent for $100,000, equipment that originally cost subsidiary $75,000. The subsidiary depreciated the equipment over a 5-year period, straight-line with no salvage value. At the time of the intercompany sale, the subsidiary recorded accumulated depreciation of $15,000 related to the equipment (i.e., one year after subsidiary's initial purchase of the equipment). The parent estimates that the equipment has a four-year remaining useful life on the date of the intercompany transaction.

The parent originally purchased its 100% investment in the subsidiary on January 1, 2014 for $900,000. On that date, the subsidiary's owners' equity equaled $900,000 (i.e., there is no AAP), and the subsidiary's retained earnings equaled $675,000. The parent applies the cost method for its investment in the subsidiary. Following are financial statements of the parent and its subsidiary for the year ended December 31, 2016.

	Parent	Subsidiary			Parent	Subsidiary
Income statement:				**Balance sheet:**		
Sales.	$10,000,000	$1,500,000		Assets		
Cost of goods sold.	(7,000,000)	(900,000)		Cash	$ 800,000	$ 406,000
Gross profit.	3,000,000	600,000		Accounts receivable. . .	1,280,000	348,000
Income (loss) from subsidiary. . .	30,000			Inventory.	1,950,000	447,000
Depreciation expense.	(400,000)	(80,000)		Equity investment.	900,000	
Operating expenses	(1,500,000)	(310,000)		PPE, net	4,000,000	827,000
Net income	$ 1,130,000	$ 210,000			$8,930,000	$2,028,000
Statement of retained earnings:						
BOY retained earnings	$3,600,000	$ 775,000		Liabilities and stockholders' equity		
				Current liabilities.	$1,400,000	$ 348,000
Net income	1,130,000	210,000		Long-term liabilities . . .	1,500,000	500,000
Dividends	(300,000)	(30,000)		Common stock.	600,000	100,000
Ending retained earnings	$4,430,000	$ 955,000		APIC	1,000,000	125,000
				Retained earnings	4,430,000	955,000
					$8,930,000	$2,028,000

Required

Prepare the consolidation spreadsheet for the year.

The solution to this review problem can be found on page 265.

CHAPTER SUMMARY

Commonly controlled affiliated companies often transfer assets among themselves. Any profits or losses recognized by the separate companies in these transactions among affiliates must be deferred in the consolidated financial statements because the transaction did not occur with an unaffiliated entity or individual. This profit or loss deferral is necessary because, after the intercompany transaction, the transferred asset is still held by the economic reporting entity. In the case of inventories or non-depreciable assets, the intercompany profit or loss is deferred until the asset is transferred to an unaffiliated entity, impaired, or otherwise disposed. For depreciable assets, the deferred gain or loss is ratably recognized in the consolidated financial statements as the asset is depreciated. For depreciable assets, the deferred gain or loss can also be immediately recognized if the asset is impaired or otherwise disposed.

Inventory transactions among affiliated companies are, by far, the most common type of intercompany asset transfer. In the year of the intercompany merchandise transaction, 100 percent of the intercompany sale must be eliminated from sales and cost of goods sold in the preparation of consolidated financial statements. This elimination will have no effect on consolidated gross profit because sales and cost of goods sold are adjusted for exactly the same amount. If any merchandise from an intercompany sale is included in beginning or ending inventory of any of the affiliated companies, then cost of goods sold must be adjusted, without an offsetting adjustment to sales. This means gross profit (and net income) of the consolidated company is affected by the elimination of profits in beginning and/or ending inventories. Perhaps the easiest way to understand the intuition behind the effect of cost of goods sold is to consider the formula for determining the amount:

```
  Beginning Inventory
+ Purchases
- Ending inventory
= Cost of goods sold
```

You will notice that any change in the amount of beginning or ending inventory will, by definition, change the bottom line amount of cost of goods sold. Thus, when we defer intercompany profits that are resident in beginning and/or ending inventory, we are also affecting cost of goods sold. Removing profits from beginning inventory decreases cost of goods sold (and increases gross profit and net income), while removing deferred profits from ending inventory increases cost of goods sold (and decreases gross profit and net income).

In the consolidated financial statements, accounting for the deferred profit on sales of non-depreciable assets among commonly controlled companies is similar to the accounting for deferred profit on intercompany inventory sales. The intercompany profits from non-depreciable asset transactions are deferred as long as the assets sold are held, and the deferred profit is recognized when the assets are resold to independent parties. The one difference is that the deferred gain or loss on non-depreciable asset transactions is recognized as an asset sale gain or loss (i.e., it is not recognized as an adjustment of cost of goods sold) in the year the asset is transferred to an unaffiliated party (or impaired or otherwise disposed).

Accounting for the intercompany sale of depreciable assets involves deferring all deferred profit in preparation of the consolidated balance sheet and income statement. However, after the date of the intercompany transfer, the purchasing company will depreciate the asset subsequent to acquisition based on the new (i.e., higher or lower) cost of the asset. As a result, depreciation expense will be higher or lower than would have been recognized had the asset not been sold. Therefore, the consolidation procedures involve eliminating the remaining balance of the deferred profit from the balance sheet and the depreciated deferred profit from the income statement. The net results of the consolidation procedures are to report net asset and income statement balances that look as if the intercompany transactions never occurred.

COMPREHENSIVE REVIEW—EQUITY METHOD

A parent company acquired 100 percent of the stock of a subsidiary company on January 1, 2012, for $555,000. On this date, the balances of the subsidiary's stockholders' equity accounts were Common Stock, $292,500, and Retained Earnings, $67,500.

On January 1, 2012, the subsidiary's recorded book values were equal to fair values for all items except four: (1) accounts receivable had a book value of $82,500 and a fair value of $72,000, (2) property, plant & equipment, net had a book value of $225,000 and a fair value of $252,000, (3) a previously unrecorded patent had a book value of $0 and a fair value of $45,000, and (4) notes payable had a book value of $45,000 and a fair value of $37,500. Both companies use the FIFO inventory method and sell all of their inventories at least once per year. The year-end net balance of accounts receivables are collected in the following year. On the acquisition date, the subsidiary's property, plant & equipment, net had a remaining useful life of 10 years, the patent had a remaining useful life of 4 years, and notes payable had a remaining term of 5 years.

On January 1, 2015, the parent sold a building to the subsidiary for $120,000. On this date, the building was carried on the parent's books (net of accumulated depreciation) at $82,500. Both companies estimated that the building has a remaining life of 10 years on the intercompany sale date, with no salvage value.

Each company routinely sells merchandise to the other company, with a profit margin of 40 percent of selling price (regardless of the direction of the sale). During 2016, intercompany sales amount to $75,000, of which $30,000 of merchandise remains in the ending inventory of the subsidiary. On December 31, 2016, $15,000 of these intercompany sales remained unpaid. Additionally, the parent's December 31, 2015 inventory includes $22,500 of merchandise purchased in the preceding year from the subsidiary. During 2015, intercompany sales amount to $60,000, and on December 31, 2015, $10,000 of these intercompany sales remained unpaid.

The parent accounts for its investment in the subsidiary using the equity method. Unconfirmed profits are allocated pro rata. The pre-closing trial balances (and additional information) for the two companies for the year ended December 31, 2016, are provided as follows:

	Parent	Subsidiary
Debits		
Cash.	$ 87,120	$ 63,750
Accounts receivable.	121,500	90,000
Inventories	292,500	137,250
Property, plant & equipment, net	283,500	202,500
Other assets.	128,250	225,000
Equity investment.	660,000	—
Cost of goods sold	648,000	243,000
Depreciation & amortization expense	27,000	21,600
Operating expenses.	339,000	81,150
Interest expense.	12,000	5,250
Dividends declared	135,000	31,500
Total debits.	$2,733,870	$1,101,000
Credits		
Accounts payable	$ 252,000	$ 52,500
Notes payable	121,470	45,000
Other liabilities	49,500	58,500
Common stock	540,000	292,500
Retained earnings (Jan. 1, 2016)	640,350	247,500
Sales	1,080,000	405,000
Income (loss) from subsidiary.	50,550	—
Total credits	$2,733,870	$1,101,000
Additional Information		
Retained earnings (Dec. 31, 2016).	$ 609,900	$ 270,000
Net income.	$ 104,550	$ 54,000

Required

a. Prepare a consolidation spreadsheet using the December 31, 2016 pre-closing trial balance information for the parent and subsidiary.*

b. Disaggregate and document the activity for the 100% Acquisition Accounting Premium (AAP).

c. Calculate and organize the profits and losses on intercompany transactions and balances.

d. Compute the pre-consolidation Equity Investment account beginning and ending balances starting
with the stockholders' equity of the subsidiary.

e. Reconstruct the activity in the parent's pre-consolidation Equity Investment T-account for the year
of consolidation.

f. Complete the consolidating entries according to the **C-E-A-D-I** sequence and complete the consolidation worksheet.

* We believe there is great pedagogical value in students creating their own functioning consolidation spreadsheets from
trial balance information. Programming the formulas that result in articulating consolidated financial statements can help
students better understand the basic relations in financial statements and the mechanics of consolidation. For students who
wish to skip this step, we provide, in *Part a* of the solution to this comprehensive review, the trial balance information
converted to financial statement format.

The solution to this review problem can be found on pages 266–270.

COMPREHENSIVE REVIEW—COST METHOD

A parent company acquired 100 percent of the stock of a subsidiary company on January 1, 2012, for $640,000. On this date, the balances of the subsidiary's stockholders' equity accounts were Common Stock, $300,000, and Retained Earnings, $143,000.

On January 1, 2012, the subsidiary's recorded book values were equal to fair values for all items except four: (1) accounts receivable had a book value of $73,000 and a fair value of $65,000, (2) property, plant & equipment, net had a book value of $200,000 and a fair value of $240,000, (3) a previously unrecorded patent had a book value of $0 and a fair value of $60,000, and (4) notes payable had a book value of $45,000 and a fair value of $40,000. Both companies use the FIFO inventory method and sell all of their inventories at least once per year. The year-end net balance of accounts receivables are collected in the following year. On the acquisition date, the subsidiary's property, plant & equipment, net had a remaining useful life of 8 years, the patent had a remaining useful life of 6 years, and notes payable had a remaining term of 5 years.

On January 1, 2014, the parent sold a building to the subsidiary for $100,000. On this date, the building was carried on the parent's books (net of accumulated depreciation) at $80,000. Both companies estimated that the building has a remaining life of 10 years on the intercompany sale date, with no salvage value.

Each company routinely sells merchandise to the other company, with a profit margin of 30 percent of selling price (regardless of the direction of the sale). During 2016, intercompany sales amount to $50,000, of which $30,000 of merchandise remains in the ending inventory of the subsidiary. On December 31, 2016, $16,000 of these intercompany sales remained unpaid. Additionally, the parent's December 31, 2015 inventory includes $20,000 of merchandise purchased in the preceding year from the subsidiary. During 2015, intercompany sales amount to $40,000, and on December 31, 2015, $12,000 of these intercompany sales remained unpaid.

The parent accounts for its investment in the subsidiary using the cost method. Unconfirmed profits are allocated pro rata. The pre-closing trial balances (and additional information) for the two companies for the year ended December 31, 2016, are provided below:

	Parent	Subsidiary
Debits		
Cash	$ 90,000	$ 60,000
Accounts receivable	120,000	90,000
Inventory	280,000	140,000
Equity investment	640,000	—
Property, plant & equipment, net	340,000	240,000
Other assets	130,000	220,000
Cost of goods sold	550,000	280,000
Depreciation & amortization expense	30,000	20,000
Operating expenses	300,000	80,000
Interest expense	15,000	5,000
Dividends	115,000	35,000
Total debits	$2,610,000	$1,170,000
Credits		
Accounts payable	$ 250,000	$ 54,000
Accrued liabilities	125,000	46,000
Notes payable	50,000	60,000
Common stock	600,000	300,000
Retained earnings (Jan. 1, 2016)	550,000	250,000
Sales	1,000,000	460,000
Income (loss) from subsidiary	35,000	—
Total credits	$2,610,000	$1,170,000
Additional Information		
Retained earnings (Dec. 31, 2016)	$ 575,000	$ 290,000
Net income	$ 140,000	$ 75,000

Required

a. Prepare a consolidation spreadsheet using the December 31, 2016 pre-closing trial balance information for the parent and subsidiary.*

b. Disaggregate and document the activity for the 100% Acquisition Accounting Premium (AAP).

c. Calculate and organize the profits and losses on intercompany transactions and balances.

d. Compute the amount of the beginning of year **[ADJ]** adjustment necessary for the consolidation of the financial statements for the year ended December 31, 2016.

e. Complete the consolidating entries according to the **C-E-A-D-I** sequence and complete the consolidation worksheet.

*Again, we believe there is great pedagogical value in students creating their own functioning consolidation spreadsheets from trial balance information. However, for students who wish to skip this step, we provide, in *Part a* of the solution to this comprehensive review, the trial balance information converted to financial statement format.

The solution to this review problem can be found on pages 271–274.

APPENDIX 4A: Consolidation When the Parent Uses the Partial Equity Method to Account for Its Equity Investment

As we mention throughout the chapter, companies have a choice of pre-consolidation bookkeeping approaches. We chose to focus on the cost and equity methods in the chapter because all methods used in practice represent a combination of these two approaches. In this Appendix, we will describe the consolidation process when the parent company applies a hybrid approach called the partial equity method. In our version of the partial equity method, the parent company will update the Equity Investment account for the net income and dividends of the subsidiary, and for the amortization of the AAP. However, the parent company will not run the intercompany transaction eliminations through the Equity Investment account.

In this example, the parent acquired its subsidiary on January 1, 2013. We are preparing consolidated financial statements for the year ending December 31, 2016. Assume the following facts (all amounts in $):

Original AAP (building)	$100,000
Unamortized AAP balance on January 1, 2016	40,000
Annual depreciation/amortization of the AAP	20,000

In addition, the subsidiary has sold inventories to its parent regularly since the acquisition. The intercompany sales and profit for the prior and current period are as follows:

Year Ending	Dec. 31, 2015	Dec. 31, 2016
Transfer price for inventory sale	$150,000	$200,000
Cost of goods sold	102,000	150,000
Gross profit	$ 48,000	$ 60,000
Percentage of inventory remaining	25%	30%
Deferred intercompany profit (deferred profit) in ending inventory	$ 12,000	$ 15,000
Intercompany receivable/payable at end of period*	$ 25,000	$ 30,000

* Paid at beginning of next period.

Exhibit 4A.1 presents the consolidation spreadsheet including the **C-E-A-D-I** entries.

Because the parent, in this example, uses the *partial* equity method to account for its investment in the subsidiary, the balance of the Equity Investment account at the end of the period is $831,000 as follows:

End of year stockholders' equity (S)	$811,000
Unamortized AAP at end of year	20,000
Cumulative understatement of Equity investment account	$831,000

EXHIBIT 4A.1	Consolidation When the Parent Uses the Partial Equity Method

	Parent	Subsidiary	Dr		Cr		Consolidated
				Consolidation Entries			
Income statement:							
Sales..................................	$5,000,000	$ 960,000	[I$_{sales}$]	$ 200,000			$5,760,000
Cost of goods sold........................	(2,700,000)	(432,000)	[I$_{cogs}$]	15,000	[I$_{cogs}$]	$ 12,000	(2,935,000)
					[I$_{sales}$]	200,000	
Gross profit............................	2,300,000	528,000					2,825,000
Income (loss) from subsidiary..............	151,000		[C]	151,000			0
Operating expenses.....................	(1,932,000)	(357,000)	[D]	20,000			(2,309,000)
Net income............................	$ 519,000	$ 171,000					$ 516,000
Statement of retained earnings:							
BOY retained earnings....................	$1,564,000	$ 425,000	[E]	425,000			$1,552,000
			[I$_{cogs}$]	12,000			
Net income............................	519,000	171,000					516,000
Dividends.............................	(50,000)	(10,000)			[C]	10,000	(50,000)
Ending retained earnings.................	$2,033,000	$ 586,000					$2,018,000
Balance sheet:							
Assets							
Cash.................................	$ 88,000	$ 70,000					$ 158,000
Accounts receivable.....................	487,000	210,000			[I$_{pay}$]	30,000	667,000
Inventory.............................	833,000	250,000			[I$_{cogs}$]	15,000	1,068,000
Building, net...........................	2,709,000	1,000,000	[A]	40,000	[D]	20,000	3,729,000
Equity investment.......................	831,000				[C]	141,000	0
					[E]	650,000	
					[A]	40,000	
	$4,948,000	$1,530,000					$5,622,000
Liabilities and stockholders' equity							
Accounts payable.......................	$ 477,000	$ 289,000	[I$_{pay}$]	30,000			$ 736,000
Other current liabilities...................	264,000	230,000					494,000
Long-term liabilities.....................	312,000	200,000					512,000
Common stock........................	1,238,000	100,000	[E]	100,000			1,238,000
APIC................................	624,000	125,000	[E]	125,000			624,000
Retained earnings	2,033,000	586,000					2,018,000
	$4,948,000	$1,530,000	$1,118,000		$1,118,000		$5,622,000

Under the *partial* equity method, the Equity Investment account increased by the parent's proportion of the cumulative profit earned by the subsidiary since the acquisition, less the cumulative dividends paid to the parent. (For convenience, we assume that the subsidiary's Retained Earnings are only affected by profit and dividends.) In addition, the parent depreciated/amortized the AAP.

The following are explanations for each of the consolidation entries:

[C]	Income (loss) from subsidiary..............	151,000	
	Dividends.........................		10,000
	Equity investment		141,000

Eliminate the Equity Income and intercompany dividends

[E]	Common stock (S) @ BOY...............	100,000	
	APIC (S) @ BOY	125,000	
	Retained earnings (S) @ BOY.............	425,000	
	Equity investment @ BOY		650,000

Eliminate the BOY stockholders' equity of subsidiary:

BOY Ret. earn.........................	$425,000
Common stock........................	100,000
APIC................................	125,000
Total	$650,000

[A]	Building, net @ BOY...........	40,000		Record BOY book value of **[A]** asset related to building:	
	Equity investment @ BOY...........		40,000	Original amt........................	$100,000
				Deprec. to date.......................	60,000
				BOY Book value......................	$ 40,000
[D]	Depreciation expense.................	20,000		Record depreciation expense related to AAP	
	Building, net......................		20,000		
[I$_{cogs}$]	Retained earnings (P) @ BOY.............	12,000		Reduces BOY Retained Earnings of subsidiary and	
	Cost of goods sold...............		12,000	recognizes deferred gain in current period	
[I$_{sales}$]	Sales	200,000		Eliminates current period intercompany Sales and Cost of	
	Cost of goods sold...............		200,000	Goods Sold	
[I$_{cogs}$]	Cost of goods sold...................	15,000		Defer current period profit on intercompany sale of	
	Inventory......................		15,000	inventories	
[I$_{pay}$]	Accounts payable....................	30,000		Eliminates intercompany receivable and payable	
	Accounts receivable.............		30,000		

QUESTIONS

1. Explain the process by which assets are written up (or down) on intercompany asset transfers and why GAAP prohibits the recognition of profit in the intercompany transfers of assets.

2. Guidance relating to the elimination of intercompany transactions in the consolidation process is provided in FASB ASC 810-10-45-1. Refer to that paragraph to answer the following questions:

    a. Which intercompany transactions should be eliminated?

    b. What is the underlying assumption of consolidated financial statements?

    c. Should *all* intercompany profit or loss be eliminated?

    FASB ASC Research

3. How much of deferred profit on inventory sales should be deferred?

4. How does the timing of the deferral and recognition of profit differ between sales of inventories and sales of land and depreciable assets?

5. How does the [I] consolidation entry differ for upstream and downstream intercompany sales of inventories?

6. For intercompany sales of inventories, the [I] consolidation entries [I$_{sales}$] and [I$_{cogs}$] are as follows:

[I$_{sales}$]	Sales	xxx	
	Cost of goods sold		xxx
[I$_{cogs}$]	Cost of goods sold........................	xxx	
	Inventories.............................		xxx

    Describe the effect of these two entries on the consolidated financial statements.

7. What is the purpose of the following entry that is made each period subsequent to an intercompany sale of land until the period in which the land is resold outside of the consolidated group?

[I$_{gain}$]	Equity investment..........................	xxx	
	Land....................................		xxx

8. What is the purpose of the following entry relating to intercompany sales of depreciable assets in the period of sale?

[I$_{gain}$]	Gain on sale	xxx	
	Equipment	xxx	
	Accumulated depreciation.................		xxx

9. What is the purpose of the following entry relating to intercompany sales of depreciable assets in periods subsequent to the sale?

> [I$_{dep}$] Accumulated depreciation xxx
>   Depreciation expense xxx

10. In your own words, describe the purpose of the **[ADJ]** consolidation entry when the parent company applies the cost method of pre-consolidation bookkeeping.

11. Describe how, despite the fact they include different accounts, conceptually, the **[C]** entry under the equity method of pre-consolidation bookkeeping is the same as the **[C]** entry under the cost method of pre-consolidation bookkeeping.

Assignments with the 🌐 logo in the margin are available in $\overset{my}{BusinessCourse}$.
See the Preface of the book for details.

MULTIPLE CHOICE

LO1

AICPA
Adapted

12. **Philosophy underlying elimination of intercompany transactions**
When preparing consolidated financial statements, what is the main reason we eliminate all intercompany transactions between and among a parent company and its subsidiaries?

   a. Intercompany transactions almost always result in gains, and the conservatism principle says that gains should be deferred, while losses should be recognized immediately

   b. The Sarbanes-Oxley Act of 2002 (i.e., U.S. Public Law 107-204) states that affiliated companies should not engage in transactions with each other

   c. Management theory suggests that it helps eliminate problems with adverse selection

   d. Commonly controlled affiliates represent a single economic entity, and an entity cannot engage in economically substantive transactions with itself

LO1

AICPA
Adapted

13. **Consolidation process for intercompany inventory sales**
Assume that a parent company sells $1 million of inventory to its wholly owned subsidiary during 2015. The parent's sales prices include a markup on cost equal to 33%. On December 31, 2015, the subsidiary still has $200,000 of merchandise that it purchased from the parent during 2015. This merchandise was completely sold by the subsidiary in 2016. In preparing the consolidated financial statements for the year ended December 31, 2015 the parent company makes consolidating entries to correct for the effects of the intercompany sales and to remove them from the consolidated financial statements. Why does the parent company, in preparing the consolidated financial statements for the year ended December 31, 2016, also make consolidating entries related to these intercompany inventory transactions from 2015?

   a. Vertically integrative business combinations usually have recurring transactions between affiliated companies.

   b. The subsidiary's ending inventory in 2015 is one of the factors that determines cost of sales in 2016.

   c. The subsidiary's sales in 2016 is also overstated by the amount of intercompany sales from 2015.

   d. The equity method mechanically "double counts" intercompany profits in ending inventory.

Use the following facts for Multiple Choice problems 14-15.

AICPA
Adapted

Assume that a parent company owns a 100% controlling interest in its long-held subsidiary. The following excerpts are from the parent's and subsidiary's pre-consolidation income statements for the year ending December 31, 2016:

	Parent	Subsidiary
Revenues	$2,520,000	$1,740,000
Cost of goods sold	(1,638,000)	(960,000)
Gross profit	$ 882,000	$ 780,000

On January 1, 2016, the subsidiary held no inventories purchased from the parent. During the year ending December 31, 2016, the parent company sold $480,000 of inventory to its subsidiary. All of the parent's sales to affiliates and non-affiliates have the same gross margin. The subsidiary sold to unaffiliated third-party customers all of the items of inventory purchased from the parent.

14. **Intercompany sales, no profits in ending inventory**
    What amount of revenues will be reported in the consolidated financial statements for the year ended December 31, 2016?
    a. $3,550,000
    b. $3,780,000
    c. $3,300,000
    d. $2,520,000

LO1

AICPA
Adapted

15. **Intercompany sales, no profits in ending inventory**
    What amount of gross profit will be reported in the consolidated financial statements for the year ended December 31, 2016?
    a. $1,662,000
    b. $1,638,000
    c. $1,494,000
    d. $882,000

LO1

AICPA
Adapted

Use the following facts for Multiple Choice problems 16–17.
Assume that a parent company owns a 100% controlling interest in its long-held subsidiary. The following excerpts are from the parent's and subsidiary's pre-consolidation income statements for the year ending December 31, 2016:

AICPA
Adapted

	Parent	Subsidiary
Revenues	$3,150,000	$2,175,000
Cost of goods sold	(1,890,000)	(1,200,000)
Gross profit	$1,260,000	$ 975,000

On January 1, 2016, the subsidiary held no inventories purchased from the parent. During the year ending December 31, 2016, the parent company sold $400,000 of inventory to its subsidiary. All of the parent's sales to affiliates and non-affiliates have the same gross margin. At December 31, 2016, the subsidiary still held in its inventory $120,000 of merchandise purchased from the parent. The remaining inventory was sold to unaffiliated third-party customers during the year ended December 31, 2016.

16. **Intercompany sales, profits in ending inventory**
    What amount of revenues will be reported in the consolidated financial statements for the year ended December 31, 2016?
    a. $5,325,000
    b. $5,205,000
    c. $4,925,000
    d. $3,150,000

LO1

AICPA
Adapted

17. **Intercompany sales, profits in ending inventory**
    What amount of gross profit will be reported in the consolidated financial statements for the year ended December 31, 2016?
    a. $2,235,000
    b. $2,225,000
    c. $2,197,000
    d. $2,187,000

LO1

AICPA
Adapted

Use the following facts for Multiple Choice problems 18–20. Each of the problems is independent of the other.
Assume that a parent company owns a 100% controlling interest in its long-held subsidiary. The following excerpts are from the parent's and subsidiary's "stand alone" pre-consolidation income statements for the year ending December 31, 2016, prior to any investment bookkeeping or intercompany adjustments:

AICPA
Adapted

	Parent	Subsidiary
Revenues	$3,360,000	$2,280,000
Cost of goods sold.	(2,184,000)	(1,368,000)
Gross profit.	1,176,000	912,000
Selling general & administrative expenses.	(780,000)	(606,000)
Net income.	$ 396,000	$ 306,000

On January 1, 2016, neither company held any inventories purchased from the other affiliate. All of the sales made by either company have the same gross margin regardless of whether they are made to affiliates or non-affiliates. The subsidiary declared and paid $240,000 of dividends during 2016.

LO1

AICPA
Adapted

18. **Pre-consolidation equity method accounting, downstream intercompany sales, profits in ending inventory—Equity method**
   Assume that during the year ended December 31, 2016, the parent sold to the subsidiary $300,000 of merchandise. At December 31, 2016, the subsidiary still held in its inventory 25% of the goods purchased from the parent during 2016. What is the amount of "income from subsidiary" recognized by the parent company if it applies the equity method of pre-consolidation investment bookkeeping?

   a. $396,000
   b. $332,250
   c. $306,000
   d. $279,750

LO1

AICPA
Adapted

19. **Pre-consolidation bookkeeping, upstream intercompany sales, profits in ending inventory—Equity method**
   Assume that during the year ended December 31, 2016, the subsidiary sold to the parent $300,000 of merchandise. At December 31, 2016, the parent still held in its inventory 25% of the goods purchased from the subsidiary during 2016. What is the amount of "income from subsidiary" recognized by the parent company if it applies the equity method of pre-consolidation investment bookkeeping?

   a. $279,750
   b. $276,000
   c. $231,000
   d. $186,000

LO2

AICPA
Adapted

20. **Pre-consolidation bookkeeping, upstream intercompany sales, profits in ending inventory—Cost method**
   Assume that during the year ended December 31, 2016, the subsidiary sold to the parent $300,000 of merchandise. At December 31, 2016, the parent still held in its inventory 25% of the goods purchased from the subsidiary during 2016. What is the amount of "income from subsidiary" recognized by the parent company if it applies the cost method of pre-consolidation investment bookkeeping?

   a. $279,750
   b. $276,000
   c. $240,000
   d. $210,000

LO1

AICPA
Adapted

21. **Continuous downstream intercompany inventory transactions**
   Assume that a parent company owns a 100% controlling interest in its long-held subsidiary. During the year ended December 31, 2016, the parent and subsidiary had "stand alone" (i.e., before any equity method adjustments) pre-consolidation income equal to $240,000 and $128,000, respectively. During the year ended December 31, 2015, the parent sold $50,000 of merchandise to the subsidiary. During the year ended December 31, 2016, the parent sold $40,000 of merchandise to the subsidiary. On December 31, 2015 and 2016, the subsidiary's ending inventory included $12,000 and $9,600, respectively, of merchandise purchased from the parent. The parent company realizes profits of 30% of selling price on intercompany transactions. What is the amount of the parent's consolidated net income for the year ending December 31, 2016?

   a. $370,400
   b. $368,720
   c. $368,000
   d. $367,280

Use the following facts for Multiple Choice problems 22–25.

Assume that a parent company owns a 100% controlling interest in its long-held subsidiary. The following excerpts are from the parent's and subsidiary's pre-consolidation financial statements and the consolidated financial statements for the year ending December 31, 2016:

	Parent	Subsidiary	Consolidated
Income Statement:			
Revenues	$3,360,000	$2,280,000	$4,920,000
Cost of goods sold.	(2,184,000)	(1,368,000)	(2,834,100)
Gross profit.	1,176,000	912,000	2,085,900
Income from subsidiary	183,900		—
Selling, general & administrative expenses	(960,000)	(726,000)	(1,686,000)
Net income.	$ 399,900	$ 186,000	$ 399,900
Statement of retained earnings:			
Retained earnings, January 1.	$ 240,000	$ 222,000	$ 240,000
Net income.	399,900	186,000	399,900
Dividends declared.	(72,000)	(54,000)	(72,000)
Retained earnings, December 31.	$ 567,900	$ 354,000	$ 567,900
Balance Sheet:			
Cash.	$ 72,000	$ 48,000	$ 120,000
Accounts receivable.	144,000	90,000	195,600
Inventories	156,000	108,000	245,100
Investment in Subsidiary	785,100		—
Property, plant & equipment.	1,020,000	744,000	1,764,000
Goodwill			60,000
Total assets.	$2,177,100	$ 990,000	$2,384,700
Accounts payable.	$ 96,000	$ 66,000	$ 123,600
All other liabilities	360,000	180,000	540,000
Common stock & APIC	1,153,200	390,000	1,153,200
Retained earnings	567,900	354,000	567,900
Total liabilities and equity	$2,177,100	$ 990,000	$2,384,700

The parent sold inventories to the subsidiary during both 2015 and 2016. For these sales to the subsidiary, the parent earns a gross profit of 35%.

22. **Intercompany inventory transactions**

    What is the amount of intercompany sales between the parent and subsidiary during the year ending December 31, 2016?

    a. $2,184,000

    b. $1,896,000

    c. $720,000

    d. $717,900

23. **Intercompany inventory transactions**

    What is the amount of parent-company profit from intercompany inventory transactions that was in the subsidiary's *ending* inventory on December 31, 2016?

    a. $54,600

    b. $37,800

    c. $18,900

    d. $16,800

24. **Intercompany inventory transactions**

    What is the amount of parent-company profit from intercompany inventory transactions that was in the subsidiary's *beginning* inventory on January 1, 2016?

    a. $37,800

    b. $18,900

    c. $16,800

    d. Not enough information

LO1

25. Intercompany inventory transactions

What is the amount of intercompany transactions between the parent and subsidiary that remained unpaid at December 31, 2016?

a. $38,400
b. $18,900
c. $16,800
d. $2,100

LO3

26. Intercompany transfers of non-depreciable noncurrent assets—Equity method

Assume that a parent company owns a 100% controlling interest in its long-held subsidiary. On January 1, 2015, a parent company sold land to the subsidiary for $530,000. The land originally cost the parent $380,000 when it was purchased on January 1, 2006. The parent company uses the equity method to account for its pre-consolidation investment in the subsidiary. Related to the transferred land, which of the following items is true regarding the preparation of the consolidated financial statements for the year ending December 31, 2016?

a. The consolidation entries will include a $150,000 debit to "Gain on Sale of Land."
b. The consolidation entries will include a $150,000 debit to "Investment in Subsidiary."
c. The consolidation entries will include a $380,000 debit to "Land."
d. The consolidation entries will include a $150,000 debit to "Land."

LO4

27. Gain on intercompany transfers of depreciable noncurrent assets

Assume that a parent company owns a 100% controlling interest in its long-held subsidiary. On January 1, 2016, a parent company sold equipment to the subsidiary for $210,600. The equipment originally cost the parent $234,000, and accumulated depreciation through December 31, 2015 was $58,500. The parent depreciated the equipment assuming a 12-year useful life under the straight-line method and no salvage value. After the transfer, the subsidiary will depreciate the equipment for 9 years with no salvage value. Related to the transferred equipment, what is the net balance that will be reported in the December 31, 2016 consolidated balance sheet?

a. $191,100
b. $152,100
c. $175,500
d. $156,000

LO4

28. Loss on intercompany transfers of depreciable noncurrent assets

Assume that a parent company owns a 100% controlling interest in its long-held subsidiary. On December 31, 2016, a parent company sold equipment to the subsidiary for $96,000. The equipment originally cost the parent $144,000, and accumulated depreciation through December 31, 2016 was $28,800. The parent depreciated the equipment for 10 years using the straight-line method and no salvage value. After the transfer, the subsidiary will depreciate the equipment for 8 years with no salvage value. Related to the transferred equipment, which of the following items is true regarding the preparation of the consolidated financial statements for the year ending December 31, 2016?

a. The consolidation entries will include a $19,200 credit to "Loss on Sale of Equipment."
b. The consolidation entries will include a $19,200 debit to "Loss on Sale of Equipment."
c. The consolidation entries will include a $48,000 credit to "Equipment (gross)."
d. The consolidation entries will include a $28,800 debit to "Accumulated depreciation."

EXERCISES

LO1

29. Computing the amount of investment income and preparing [I] consolidation entries—Equity method

Assume that a wholly owned subsidiary sells inventory to the parent company. The parent company, ultimately, sells the inventory to customers outside of the consolidated group. The parent company compiled the following data for the years ending 2015 and 2016:

	Subsidiary Net Income	Intercompany Inventory Sales	Gross Profit %	% Inventory Remaining at End of Year	Receivable (Payable)
2016	$750,000	$112,500	30%	12%	$37,500
2015	$600,000	$ 75,000	32%	10%	$30,000

Assume that inventory not remaining at the end of the year was sold outside of the consolidated group during the year. Assume the parent company uses the equity method to account for its subsidiary. The subsidiary paid $500,000 in dividends during 2016.

a.   How much Income (loss) from subsidiary should the parent report in its *pre-consolidation* income statement the year ending 2016 assuming that it uses the equity method of accounting for its Equity Investment?

b.   Prepare the required [I] consolidation entries for 2016.

30. Computing the amount of equity income and preparing [I] consolidation entries—Equity method

LO1

Assume that a parent company sells inventory to its wholly owned subsidiary. The subsidiary, ultimately, sells the inventory to customers outside of the consolidated group. You have compiled the following data for the years ending 2015 and 2016:

	Subsidiary Net Income	Intercompany Inventory Sales	Gross Profit on Unsold Inventories	Receivable (Payable)
2016	$150,000	$20,000	$7,000	$ 7,500
2015	$100,000	$25,000	$9,000	$14,000

Assume that inventory not remaining at the end of the year was sold outside of the consolidated group. The subsidiary paid $80,000 in dividends during 2016.

a.   How much Income (loss) from subsidiary should the parent report in its *pre-consolidation* income statement the year ending 2016 assuming that it uses the equity method of accounting for its Equity Investment?

b.   Prepare the required [I] consolidation entries for 2016.

31. Computing the amount of investment income and preparing [I] consolidation entries—Cost method

LO2

Assume that a wholly owned subsidiary sells inventory to the parent company. The parent company, ultimately, sells the inventory to customers outside of the consolidated group. You have compiled the following data for the years ending 2015 and 2016:

	Subsidiary Net Income	Intercompany Inventory Sales	Gross Profit %	% Inventory Remaining at End of Year	Receivable (Payable)
2016	$600,000	$90,000	34%	15%	$30,000
2015	$480,000	$60,000	30%	18%	$24,000

Assume that inventory not remaining at the end of the year was sold outside of the consolidated group during the year. The subsidiary paid $450,000 in dividends during 2016.

a.   How much Income (loss) from subsidiary should the parent report in its *pre-consolidation* income statement the year ending 2016 assuming that it uses the cost method of accounting for its Equity Investment?

b.   Prepare the required [I] consolidation entries for 2016.

32. Preparing the [I] consolidation entries for sale of land

LO3, 5

Assume that during 2012 a wholly owned subsidiary sells land that originally cost $225,000 to its parent for a sale price of $260,000. The parent holds the land until it sells the land to an unaffiliated company on December 31, 2016. The parent uses the equity method of pre-consolidation bookkeeping.

a.   Prepare the required [I] consolidation entry in 2012.

b.   Prepare the required [I] consolidation entry required at the end of each year 2013 through 2015.

c.   Assume that the parent re-sells the land outside of the consolidated group for $285,000 on December 31, 2016. Prepare the journal entry made by the parent to record the sale and the required [I] consolidation entry for 2016.

d.   What will be the amount of gain reported in the consolidated income statement in 2016?

e.   For this question only, assume the parent used the cost method of pre-consolidation investment bookkeeping. How would the preceding [I] entries differ?

LO3, 5   **33.   Preparing the [I] consolidation entries for sale of land**

Assume that on June 15, 2009 a parent company sells land that originally cost $95,000 to its wholly-owned subsidiary for a sale price of $120,000. The subsidiary holds the land until it sells the land to an unaffiliated company on November 12, 2016. The parent uses the equity method to account for its Equity Investment.

a.   Prepare the required [I] consolidation entry in 2009.

b.   Prepare the required [I] consolidation entry required at the end of each year 2010 through 2015.

c.   Assume that the subsidiary resells the land outside of the consolidated group for $155,000 on November 12, 2016. Prepare the journal entry made by the subsidiary to record the sale and the required [I] consolidation entry for 2016.

d.   What will be the amount of gain reported in the consolidated income statement in 2016?

e.   For this question only, assume the parent used the cost method of pre-consolidation investment bookkeeping. How would the preceding [I] entries differ?

LO4   **34.   Preparing the [I] consolidation entries for sale of depreciable assets—Equity method**

Assume that on January 1, 2014, a wholly owned subsidiary sells to its parent, for a sale price of $115,000, equipment that originally cost $150,000. The subsidiary originally purchased the equipment on January 1, 2010, and depreciated the equipment assuming a 12-year useful life (straight-line with no salvage value). The parent has adopted the subsidiary's depreciation policy and depreciates the equipment over the remaining useful life of 8 years. The parent uses the equity method to account for its Equity Investment.

a.   Compute the annual pre-consolidation depreciation expense for the subsidiary (pre-intercompany sale) and the parent (post-intercompany sale).

b.   Compute the pre-consolidation Gain on Sale recognized by the subsidiary during 2014.

c.   Prepare the required [I] consolidation entry in 2014 (assume a full year of depreciation).

d.   Now assume that you are preparing the year-end consolidation entries for the year ending December 31, 2016. Prepare the required [I] consolidation entries during the holding period.

e.   How long must we continue to make the [I] consolidation entries?

LO4   **35.   Preparing the [I] consolidation entries for sale of depreciable assets—Equity method**

Assume that on January 1, 2012, a parent sells to its wholly owned subsidiary, for a sale price of $157,500, equipment that originally cost $180,000. The parent originally purchased the equipment on January 1, 2009, and depreciated the equipment assuming a 10-year useful life (straight-line with no salvage value). The subsidiary has adopted the parent's depreciation policy and depreciates the equipment over the remaining useful life of 7 years. The parent uses the equity method to account for its Equity Investment.

a.   Compute the annual pre-consolidation depreciation expense for the subsidiary (post-intercompany sale) and the parent (pre-intercompany sale).

b.   Compute the pre-consolidation Gain on Sale recognized by the parent during 2012.

c.   Prepare the required [I] consolidation entry in 2012 (assume a full year of depreciation).

d.   Prepare the required [I] consolidation entry in 2016 (assuming the subsidiary is still holding the equipment).

e.   How long must we continue to make the [I] consolidation entries?

36. Preparing the [I] consolidation entries for sale of depreciable assets—Cost method   **LO6**

Assume that on January 1, 2013, a parent sells to its wholly owned subsidiary, for a sale price of $126,000, equipment that originally cost $144,000. The parent originally purchased the equipment on January 1, 2009, and depreciated the equipment assuming a 12-year useful life (straight-line with no salvage value). The subsidiary has adopted the parent's depreciation policy and depreciates the equipment over the remaining useful life of 8 years. The parent uses the cost method of pre-consolidation investment bookkeeping.

a. Compute the pre-consolidation annual depreciation expense for the subsidiary (post-intercompany sale) and the parent (pre-intercompany sale).

b. Compute the pre-consolidation Gain on Sale recognized by the parent during 2013.

c. Prepare the required [I] consolidation entry in 2013 (assume a full year of depreciation).

d. With respect to the deferred gain on intercompany sale, what effect (i.e., amount) will it have on the [ADJ] entry necessary to prepare the consolidated financial statements for the year ended December 31, 2016? In addition, specify the account that will be debited and the account that will be credited in the [ADJ] entry for the effect of the deferred gain on intercompany sale.

e. Prepare the required [I] consolidation entry in 2016 (assuming the subsidiary is still holding the equipment).

f. How long must we continue to make the [I] consolidation entries?

37. Interpreting footnote information   **LO1**

Caterpillar, Inc., provides a schedule to its 10-K entitled "Supplemental Data for Results of Operations"   **CATERPILLAR, INC.**
that we show on the following page. Use this information to answer the following questions for 2014:

a. Briefly interpret the statement in footnote #1 to the supplemental consolidating income statement.

b. CAT reports a consolidating adjustment of $344 related to Revenues of Financial Products. To what does this relate and why is this adjustment made?

c. Relating to the consolidating adjustment in *Part b*, what corresponding adjustment might we expect to see on the consolidating balance sheet?

d. Briefly explain the statement in footnote #6 to the supplemental consolidating income statement.

38. Interpreting footnote information   **LO1**

Harley-Davidson presents the following supplemental consolidating information to its 2014 10-K (in   **HARLEY-DAVIDSON**
thousands):

	Year Ended December 31, 2014			
	Motorcycles & Related Products Operations	Financial Services Operations	Eliminations	Consolidated
Revenue				
Motorcycle and related products ..	$5,577,697	$ —	$(10,016)	$5,567,681
Financial services	—	662,345	(1,518)	660,827
Total revenue.	$5,577,697	$662,345	$(11,534)	$6,228,508

a. Briefly explain the $1,518 elimination to arrive at consolidated financial services revenues of $660,827.

b. Relating to the consolidating adjustment in *Part a*, what corresponding adjustment might we expect to see on the consolidating balance sheet?

Supplemental Data for Results of Operations
For The Years Ended December 31

Supplemental Consolidating Data

($ millions)	Consolidated			Machinery, Energy & Transportation[1]			Financial Products			Consolidating Adjustments		
	2014	2013	2012	2014	2013	2012	2014	2013	2012	2014	2013	2012
Sales and revenues												
Sales of Machinery, Energy, & Transportation	$52,142	$52,694	$63,068	$52,142	$52,694	$63,068	$ —	$ —	$ —	$ —	$ —	$ —
Revenues of Financial Products	3,042	2,962	2,807	—	—	—	3,386	3,302	3,160	(344)[2]	(340)[2]	(353)[2]
Total sales and revenues	55,184	55,656	65,875	52,142	52,694	63,068	3,386	3,302	3,160	(344)	(340)	(353)
Operating costs												
Cost of goods sold	39,767	40,727	47,055	39,769	40,727	47,055	—	—	—	(2)[3]	—	—
Selling, general and administrative expenses	5,697	5,547	5,919	5,098	5,029	5,348	635	566	618	(36)[3]	(48)[3]	(47)[3]
Research and development expenses	2,135	2,046	2,466	2,135	2,046	2,466	—	—	—	—	—	—
Interest expense of Financial Products	624	727	797	—	—	—	631	734	801	(7)[4]	(7)[4]	(4)[4]
Goodwill impairment charge	—	—	580	—	—	580	—	—	—	—	—	—
Other operating (income) expenses	1,633	981	485	419	(23)	(495)	1,235	1,019	1,000	(21)[3]	(15)[3]	(20)[3]
Total operating costs	49,856	50,028	57,302	47,421	47,779	54,954	2,501	2,319	2,419	(66)	(70)	(71)
Operating profit	5,328	5,628	8,573	4,721	4,915	8,114	885	983	741	(278)	(270)	(282)
Interest expense excluding Financial Products	484	465	467	526	508	512	24	37	39	(42)[4]	(43)[4]	(45)[4]
Other income (expense)	239	(35)	130	(21)	(299)	(146)	24	37	39	236[5]	227[5]	237[5]
Consolidated profit before taxes	5,083	5,128	8,236	4,174	4,108	7,456	909	1,020	780	—	—	—
Provision (benefit) for income taxes	1,380	1,319	2,528	1,120	1,039	2,314	260	280	214	—	—	—
Profit of consolidated companies	3,703	3,809	5,708	3,054	3,069	5,142	649	740	566	—	—	—
Equity in profit (loss) of unconsolidated affiliated companies	8	(6)	14	8	(6)	14	—	—	—	—	—	—
Equity in profit of Financial Products' subsidiaries	—	—	—	640	726	555	—	—	—	(640)[6]	(726)[6]	(555)[6]
Profit of consolidated and affiliated companies	3,711	3,803	5,722	3,702	3,789	5,711	649	740	566	(640)	(726)	(555)
Less: Profit (loss) attributable to noncontrolling interests	16	14	41	7	—	30	9	14	11	—	—	—
Profit[7]	$ 3,695	$ 3,789	$ 5,681	$ 3,695	$ 3,789	$ 5,681	$ 640	$ 726	$ 555	$(640)	$(726)	$(555)

1 Represents Caterpillar Inc. and its subsidiaries with Financial Products accounted for on the equity basis.
2 Elimination of Financial Products' revenues earned from Machinery, Energy & Transportation.
3 Elimination of net expenses recorded by Machinery, Energy & Transportation paid to Financial Products.
4 Elimination of interest expense recorded between Financial Products and Machinery, Energy & Transportation.
5 Elimination of discount recorded by Machinery, Energy & Transportation on receivables sold to Financial Products and of interest earned between Machinery, Energy & Transportation and Financial Products.
6 Elimination of Financial Products' profit due to equity method of accounting.
7 Profit attributable to common stockholders.

PROBLEMS

39. Consolidation spreadsheet for continuous sale of inventory—Equity method

Assume that a parent company acquired a subsidiary on January 1, 2013. The purchase price was $500,000 in excess of the subsidiary's book value of Stockholders' Equity on the acquisition date, and that excess was assigned to the following AAP assets:

AAP Asset	Original Amount	Original Useful Life
Property, plant and equipment (PPE), net	$100,000	20 years
Customer list	175,000	10 years
Royalty agreement	125,000	10 years
Goodwill	100,000	Indefinite
	$500,000	

The AAP assets with a definite useful life have been amortized as part of the parent's equity method accounting. The Goodwill asset has been tested annually for impairment, and has not been found to be impaired.

Assume that the parent company sells inventory to its wholly owned subsidiary. The subsidiary, ultimately, sells the inventory to customers outside of the consolidated group. You have compiled the following data for the years ending 2015 and 2016:

	Inventory Sales	Gross Profit Remaining in Unsold Inventory	Receivable (Payable)
2016	$68,000	$19,380	$27,200
2015	$43,700	$12,597	$13,237

The inventory not remaining at the end of the year has been sold to unaffiliated entities outside of the consolidated group. The parent uses the equity method to account for its Equity Investment.

The financial statements of the parent and its subsidiary for the year ended December 31, 2016, follow:

	Parent	Subsidiary		Parent	Subsidiary
Income statement:			**Balance sheet:**		
Sales	$4,370,000	$783,000	Assets		
Cost of goods sold	(3,059,000)	(469,800)	Cash	$ 650,639	$ 253,087
Gross profit	1,311,000	313,200	Accounts receivable	559,360	181,656
Income (loss) from subsidiary	67,837		Inventory	847,780	233,334
Operating expenses	(830,300)	(203,580)	PPE, net	4,078,084	431,694
Net income	$ 548,537	$109,620	Equity investment	957,989	
				$7,093,852	$1,099,771
Statement of retained earnings:					
BOY retained earnings	$2,195,488	$404,550	Liabilities and stockholders' equity		
Net income	548,537	109,620	Accounts payable	$ 327,313	$ 93,459
Dividends	(126,164)	(14,251)	Other current liabilities	403,228	127,943
EOY retained earnings	$2,617,861	$499,919	Long term liabilities	2,500,000	261,000
			Common stock	714,495	52,200
			APIC	530,955	65,250
			Retained earnings	2,617,861	499,919
				$7,093,852	$1,099,771

a.   Show the computation to yield the pre-consolidation $67,837 Income (loss) from subsidiary reported by the parent during 2016.

b.   Show the computation to yield the Equity Investment balance of $957,989 reported by the parent at December 31, 2016.

c.   Prepare the consolidation entries for the year ended December 31, 2016.

d.   Prepare the consolidation spreadsheet for the year ended December 31, 2016.

LO1   **40. Prepare consolidation spreadsheet for continuous sale of inventory—Equity method**

Assume that a parent company acquired 100% of a subsidiary January 1, 2014. The purchase price was $175,000 in excess of the subsidiary's book value of Stockholders' Equity on the acquisition date, and that excess was assigned entirely to an unrecorded Patent owned by the subsidiary. The assumed economic useful life of the Patent is 10 years.

Assume that the wholly owned subsidiary sells inventory to the parent. The parent, ultimately, sells the inventory to customers outside of the consolidated group. You have compiled the following data for the years ending 2015 and 2016:

	Inventory Sales	Gross Profit Remaining in Unsold Inventory	Receivable (Payable)
2016	$103,300	$29,441	$41,320
2015	$ 87,900	$19,137	$27,986

The inventory not remaining at the end of the year has been sold to unaffiliated entities outside of the consolidated group. The parent uses the equity method to account for its Equity Investment.

The financial statements of the parent and its subsidiary for the year ended 2016 follows:

	Parent	Subsidiary		Parent	Subsidiary
Income statement:			**Balance sheet:**		
Sales.	$8,220,000	$1,549,500	Assets		
Cost of goods sold.	(5,754,000)	(929,700)	Cash	$ 555,910	$ 500,842
Gross profit.	2,466,000	619,800	Accounts receivable.	1,052,160	359,484
Income (loss) from subsidiary.	189,126		Inventory.	1,594,680	461,751
Operating expenses	(1,561,800)	(402,870)	Building, net	7,670,904	854,291
Net income	$1,093,326	$ 216,930	Equity investment.	1,314,788	
				$12,188,442	$2,176,368
Statement of retained earnings:					
BOY retained earnings	$4,129,728	$ 800,575	Liabilities and stockholders' equity		
Net income	1,093,326	216,930	Accounts payable.	$ 615,678	$ 184,948
Dividends	(251,465)	(28,201)	Other current liabilities	758,475	253,191
EOY retained earnings	$4,971,589	$ 989,304	Long-term liabilities	3,500,000	516,500
			Common stock.	1,343,970	103,300
			APIC	998,730	129,125
			Retained earnings	4,971,589	989,304
				$12,188,442	$2,176,368

a.   Show the computation to yield the pre-consolidation $189,126 Income (loss) from subsidiary reported by the parent during 2016.

b.   Show the computation to yield the $1,314,788 Equity Investment account balance reported by the parent at December 31, 2016.

c.   Prepare the consolidation entries for the year ended December 31, 2016.

d.   Prepare the consolidation spreadsheet for the year ended December 31, 2016.

41. Prepare consolidation spreadsheet for continuous sale of inventory—Equity method

LO1

Assume that a parent company acquired 100% of a subsidiary on January 1, 2012. The purchase price was $300,000 in excess of the subsidiary's book value of Stockholders' Equity on the acquisition date, and $200,000 of that excess was assigned to an unrecorded Patent owned by the subsidiary. On January 1, 2012, the Patent has a 10-year estimated remaining useful life. The remaining $100,000 was assigned to Goodwill.

Assume that the wholly owned subsidiary sells inventory to the parent. The parent, ultimately, sells the inventory to customers outside of the consolidated group. You have compiled the following data for the years ending 2015 and 2016:

	Inventory Sales	Gross Profit Remaining in Unsold Inventory	Receivable (Payable)
2016	$126,700	$36,110	$50,680
2015	$104,330	$23,472	$28,362

The inventory not remaining at the end of the year has been sold to unaffiliated entities outside of the consolidated group. The parent uses the equity method to account for its Equity Investment.

The financial statements of the parent and its subsidiary for the year ended December 31, 2016, follow:

	Parent	Subsidiary		Parent	Subsidiary
Income statement:			**Balance sheet:**		
Sales.	$5,000,000	$750,000	Assets		
Cost of goods sold.	(3,500,000)	(450,000)	Cash	$ 720,839	$ 242,421
Gross profit.	1,500,000	300,000	Accounts receivable.	640,000	174,000
Income (loss) from subsidiary.	72,362		Inventory.	970,000	223,500
Operating expenses	(950,000)	(195,000)	Building, net	4,666,000	413,500
Net income	$ 622,362	$105,000	Equity investment.	755,240	
				$7,752,079	$1,053,421
Statement of retained earnings:					
BOY retained earnings	$2,512,000	$387,500	Liabilities and stockholders' equity		
Net income	622,362	105,000	Accounts payable.	$ 374,500	$ 89,520
Dividends	(143,143)	(13,650)	Other current liabilities	461,360	122,551
EOY retained earnings	$2,991,219	$178,850	Long-term liabilities	2,500,000	250,000
			Common stock.	817,500	50,000
			APIC	607,500	62,500
			Retained earnings	2,991,219	478,850
				$7,752,079	$1,053,421

a. Show the computation to yield the pre-consolidation $72,362 Income (loss) from subsidiary reported by the parent for the year ended December 31, 2016.

b. Show the computation to yield the $755,240 pre-consolidation Equity Investment account balance reported by the parent at December 31, 2016.

c. Prepare the consolidation entries for the year ended December 31, 2016.

d. Prepare the consolidation spreadsheet for the year ended December 31, 2016.

LO1   42. **Prepare consolidation spreadsheet for continuous sale of inventory—Equity method**

Assume that a parent company acquired a subsidiary on January 1, 2012. The purchase price was $600,000 in excess of the subsidiary's book value of Stockholders' Equity on the acquisition date, and that excess was assigned to the following AAP assets:

AAP Asset	Original Amount	Original Useful Life
Property, plant and equipment (PPE), net	$100,000	20 years
Customer list	150,000	10 years
Royalty agreement	250,000	10 years
Goodwill	100,000	Indefinite
	$600,000	

The AAP assets with a definite useful life have been depreciated or amortized as part of the parent's equity method accounting. The Goodwill asset has been tested annually for impairment, and has not been found to be impaired.

Assume that the parent company sells inventory to its wholly owned subsidiary. The subsidiary, ultimately, sells the inventory to customers outside of the consolidated group. You have compiled the following data for the years ending 2015 and 2016:

	Inventory Sales	Gross Profit Remaining in Unsold Inventory	Receivable (Payable)
2016	$96,300	$27,446	$38,520
2015	$74,500	$17,840	$27,433

The inventory not remaining at the end of the year has been sold to unaffiliated entities outside of the consolidated group. The parent uses the equity method to account for its Equity Investment.

The financial statements of the parent and its subsidiary for the year ended December 31, 2016, follow:

	Parent	Subsidiary		Parent	Subsidiary
Income statement:			**Balance sheet:**		
Sales	$6,670,000	$1,350,000	Assets		
Cost of goods sold	(4,669,000)	(810,000)	Cash	$ 251,259	$ 436,358
Gross profit	2,001,000	540,000	Accounts receivable	853,760	313,200
Income (loss) from subsidiary	134,394		Inventory	1,293,980	402,300
Operating expenses	(1,267,300)	(351,000)	PPE, net	6,224,444	744,300
Net income	$ 868,094	$ 189,000	Equity Investment	1,411,984	
				$10,035,427	$1,896,158
Statement of retained earnings:					
BOY retained earnings	$3,351,008	$ 697,500	Liabilities and stockholders' equity		
Net income	868,094	189,000	Accounts payable	$ 499,583	$ 161,136
Dividends	(199,662)	(24,570)	Other current liabilities	615,454	220,592
EOY retained earnings	$4,019,440	$ 861,930	Long-term liabilities	3,000,000	450,000
			Common stock	1,090,545	90,000
			APIC	810,405	112,500
			Retained earnings	4,019,440	861,930
				$10,035,427	$1,896,158

a. Show the computation to yield the $134,394 Income (loss) from subsidiary reported by the parent during 2016.

b. Show the computation to yield the $1,411,984 Equity Investment account balance reported by the parent on December 31, 2016.

c. Prepare the consolidation entries for the year ended December 31, 2016.

d. Prepare the consolidation spreadsheet for the year ended December 31, 2016.

43. **Prepare consolidation spreadsheet for continuous sale of inventory—Cost method**   **LO2**
    A parent company acquired 100 percent of the stock of a subsidiary company on January 1, 2013, for
    $800,000. On this date, the balances of the subsidiary's stockholders' equity accounts were Common
    Stock, $50,000, Additional Paid-in Capital, $55,000, and Retained Earnings, $195,000. On the acquisi-
    tion date, the excess was assigned to the following AAP assets:

	Original Amount	Original Useful Life
Property, plant and equipment (PPE), net	$200,000	10 years
Customer list	100,000	8 years
Royalty agreement	80,000	8 years
Goodwill	120,000	Indefinite
	$500,000	

The Goodwill asset has been tested annually for impairment, and has not been found to be impaired.
    Assume that the parent company sells inventory to its wholly owned subsidiary. The subsidiary,
ultimately, sells the inventory to customers outside of the consolidated group. You have compiled the
following data for the years ending 2015 and 2016:

	Inventory Sales	Gross Profit Remaining in Unsold Inventory	Receivable (Payable)
2016	$40,000	$ 8,000	$28,000
2015	$60,000	$10,500	$15,000

The inventory not remaining at the end of a given year is sold to unaffiliated entities outside of the
consolidated group during the next year. The parent uses the cost method of pre-consolidation Equity
Investment bookkeeping. The financial statements of the parent and its subsidiary for the year ended
December 31, 2016, follow:

	Parent	Subsidiary		Parent	Subsidiary
Income statement:			**Balance sheet:**		
Sales	$4,350,000	$800,000	Assets		
Cost of goods sold	(3,050,000)	(480,000)	Cash	$ 650,000	$ 250,000
Gross profit	1,300,000	320,000	Accounts receivable	560,000	180,000
Operating expenses	(830,000)	(200,000)	Inventory	850,000	250,000
Income (loss) from subsidiary	15,000		Equity investment	800,000	
Net income	$ 485,000	$120,000	PPE, net	4,000,000	420,000
			Total assets	$6,860,000	$1,100,000
Statement of retained earnings:					
BOY retained earnings	$2,000,000	$405,000	Liabilities and stockholders' equity		
Net income	485,000	120,000	Accounts payable	$ 350,000	$ 100,000
Dividends	(125,000)	(15,000)	Other current liabilities	400,000	125,000
EOY retained earnings	$2,360,000	$510,000	Long-term liabilities	2,500,000	260,000
			Common stock	700,000	50,000
			APIC	550,000	55,000
			Retained earnings	2,360,000	510,000
			Total liabilities and equity	$6,860,000	$1,100,000

a. Disaggregate and document the activity for the 100% Acquisition Accounting Premium (AAP)
   through December 31, 2016.

b. Compute the amount of the beginning of year [**ADJ**] adjustment necessary for the consolidation
   of the financial statements for the year ended December 31, 2016.

c. Complete the consolidating entries according to the **C-E-A-D-I** sequence and complete the
   consolidation worksheet.

44. Prepare consolidation spreadsheet for continuous sale of inventory—Cost method

A parent company acquired 100 percent of the stock of a subsidiary company on January 1, 2012, for $1,700,000. On this date, the balances of the subsidiary's stockholders' equity accounts were Common Stock, $100,000, Additional Paid-in Capital, $125,000, and Retained Earnings, $1,225,000. On the acquisition date, the excess was assigned to the following AAP assets:

	Original Amount	Original Useful Life
Property, plant and equipment (PPE), net	$ 80,000	10 years
Customer list	50,000	8 years
Patent	120,000	12 years
	$250,000	

As indicated by the AAP schedule, there was no Goodwill included in the acquisition.

Assume that the wholly owned subsidiary company sells inventory to the parent. The parent, ultimately, sells the inventory to customers outside of the consolidated group. You have compiled the following data for the years ending 2015 and 2016:

	Inventory Sales	Gross Profit Remaining in Unsold Inventory	Receivable (Payable)
2016	$100,000	$14,000	$39,000
2015	$ 80,000	$12,000	$35,000

The inventory not remaining at the end of a given year is sold to unaffiliated entities outside of the consolidated group during the next year. The parent uses the cost method of pre-consolidation Equity Investment bookkeeping. The financial statements of the parent and its subsidiary for the year ended December 31, 2016, follow:

	Parent	Subsidiary		Parent	Subsidiary
Income statement:			**Balance sheet:**		
Sales	$9,600,000	$1,300,000	Assets		
Cost of goods sold	(6,700,000)	(800,000)	Cash	$ 700,000	$ 400,000
Gross profit	2,900,000	500,000	Accounts receivable	1,200,000	300,000
Operating expenses	(1,800,000)	(350,000)	Inventory	1,800,000	600,000
Income (loss) from subsidiary	50,000		Equity investment	1,700,000	
Net income	$1,150,000	$ 150,000	PPE, net	5,000,000	800,000
			Total assets	$10,400,000	$2,100,000
Statement of retained earnings:					
BOY retained earnings	$4,800,000	$1,425,000	Liabilities and stockholders' equity		
Net income	1,150,000	150,000	Accounts payable	$ 700,000	$ 150,000
Dividends	(250,000)	(50,000)	Other current liabilities	900,000	200,000
EOY retained earnings	$5,700,000	$1,525,000	Long-term liabilities	1,500,000	—
			Common stock	600,000	100,000
			APIC	1,000,000	125,000
			Retained earnings	5,700,000	1,525,000
			Total liabilities and equity	$10,400,000	$2,100,000

a. Disaggregate and document the activity for the 100% Acquisition Accounting Premium (AAP) through December 31, 2016.

b. Compute the amount of the beginning of year **[ADJ]** adjustment necessary for the consolidation of the financial statements for the year ended December 31, 2016.

c. Complete the consolidating entries according to the **C-E-A-D-I** sequence and complete the consolidation worksheet.

45. Prepare consolidation spreadsheet for continuous sale of inventory—Cost method

LO2

A parent company acquired 100 percent of the stock of a subsidiary company on January 1, 2014, for $960,000. On this date, the balances of the subsidiary's stockholders' equity accounts were Common Stock, $60,000, Additional Paid-in Capital, $66,000, and Retained Earnings, $234,000. On the acquisition date, the excess was assigned to the following AAP assets:

	Original Amount	Original Useful Life
Accounts receivable.	$ 24,000	
Property, plant and equipment (PPE), net	216,000	10 years
Licenses	144,000	8 years
Patent	72,000	8 years
Goodwill	144,000	Indefinite
	$600,000	

The Goodwill asset has been tested annually for impairment, and has not been found to be impaired.

Assume that the wholly owned subsidiary company sells inventory to the parent. The parent, ultimately, sells the inventory to customers outside of the consolidated group. You have compiled the following data for the years ending 2015 and 2016:

	Inventory Sales	Gross Profit Remaining in Unsold Inventory	Receivable (Payable)
2016	$48,000	$ 9,000	$33,600
2015	$72,000	$12,000	$18,000

The inventory not remaining at the end of a given year is sold to unaffiliated entities outside of the consolidated group during the next year. The parent uses the cost method of pre-consolidation Equity Investment bookkeeping. The financial statements of the parent and its subsidiary for the year ended December 31, 2016, follow:

	Parent	Subsidiary		Parent	Subsidiary
Income statement:			**Balance sheet:**		
Sales	$5,220,000	$960,000	Assets		
Cost of goods sold	(3,660,000)	(576,000)	Cash	$ 780,000	$ 300,000
Gross profit	1,560,000	384,000	Accounts receivable	672,000	216,000
Operating expenses	(996,000)	(240,000)	Inventory	1,020,000	300,000
Income (loss) from subsidiary	18,000		Equity investment	960,000	
Net income	$ 582,000	$144,000	PPE, net	4,800,000	504,000
			Total assets	$8,232,000	$1,320,000
Statement of retained earnings:					
BOY retained earnings	$2,400,000	$486,000	Liabilities and stockholders' equity		
Net income	582,000	144,000	Accounts payable	$ 420,000	$ 120,000
Dividends	(150,000)	(18,000)	Other current liabilities	480,000	150,000
EOY retained earnings	$2,832,000	$612,000	Long-term liabilities	3,000,000	312,000
			Common stock	840,000	60,000
			APIC	660,000	66,000
			Retained earnings	2,832,000	612,000
			Total liabilities and equity	$8,232,000	$1,320,000

a. Disaggregate and document the activity for the 100% Acquisition Accounting Premium (AAP) through December 31, 2016.

b. Compute the amount of the beginning of year [ADJ] adjustment necessary for the consolidation of the financial statements for the year ended December 31, 2016.

c. Complete the consolidating entries according to the C-E-A-D-I sequence and complete the consolidation worksheet.

LO3

46. Prepare consolidation spreadsheet for intercompany sale of land—Equity method

Assume that a parent company acquired its subsidiary on January 1, 2014, at a purchase price that was $300,000 in excess of the book value of the subsidiary's Stockholders' Equity on the acquisition date. Of that excess, $200,000 was assigned to an unrecorded Patent owned by the subsidiary that is being amortized over a 10-year period. The [A] Patent asset has been amortized as part of the parent's equity method accounting. The remaining $100,000 was assigned to Goodwill. In 2015, the wholly owned subsidiary sold Land to the parent for $100,000. The Land was reported on the subsidiary's balance sheet for $70,000 on the date of sale. The parent uses the equity method to account for its Equity Investment.

Following are financial statements of the parent and its subsidiary for the year ended December 31, 2016:

	Parent	Subsidiary		Parent	Subsidiary
Income statement:			**Balance sheet:**		
Sales...................	$3,000,000	$375,000	Assets		
Cost of goods sold...........	(2,100,000)	(225,000)	Cash.....................	$ 341,566	$121,211
Gross profit................	900,000	150,000	Accounts receivable...........	384,000	87,000
Income (loss) from subsidiary......	32,500		Inventory.................	582,000	111,750
Operating expenses...........	(570,000)	(97,500)	PPE, net.................	2,799,600	206,750
Net income.................	$ 362,500	$ 52,500	Equity investment...........	505,675	
				$4,612,841	$526,711
Statement of retained earnings:					
BOY retained earnings..........	$1,477,200	$193,750	Liabilities and stockholders' equity		
Net income.................	362,500	52,500	Accounts payable.............	$ 224,700	$ 44,760
Dividends.................	(83,375)	(6,825)	Other current liabilities.........	276,816	61,276
EOY retained earnings..........	$1,756,325	$239,425	Long-term liabilities...........	1,500,000	125,000
			Common stock...............	490,500	25,000
			APIC.....................	364,500	31,250
			Retained earnings	1,756,325	239,425
				$4,612,841	$526,711

a. Show the computation to yield the $32,500 of Income (loss) from subsidiary reported by the parent for the year ended December 31, 2016.

b. Show the computation to yield the $505,675 Equity Investment account balance reported by the parent on December 31, 2016.

c. Prepare the consolidation entries for the year ended December 31, 2016.

d. Prepare the consolidation spreadsheet for the year ended December 31, 2016.

LO3

47. Prepare consolidation spreadsheet for intercompany sale of land—Equity method

Assume that parent company acquired its subsidiary on January 1, 2013, at a purchase price that was $500,000 in excess of the book value of the subsidiary's Stockholders' Equity on the acquisition date. Of that excess, $300,000 was assigned to an unrecorded Royalty Agreement owned by the subsidiary that is being amortized over a 10-year period, and $200,000 was assigned to a Customer List that is also being amortized over a 10-year period. The Royalty Agreement and Customer List have been amortized as part of the parent's equity method accounting. In 2014, the wholly owned subsidiary sold Land to the parent for $150,000. The Land was reported on the subsidiary's balance sheet for $100,000 on the date of sale. The parent uses the equity method to account for its Equity Investment.

Following are financial statements of the parent and its subsidiary for the year ended December 31, 2016:

December 31, 2016	Parent	Subsidiary		Parent	Subsidiary
Income statement:			**Balance sheet:**		
Sales.	$4,600,000	$810,000	Assets		
Cost of goods sold	(3,220,000)	(486,000)	Cash	$ 616,891	$ 261,815
Gross profit.	1,380,000	324,000	Accounts receivable	588,800	187,920
Income (loss) from subsidiary	63,400		Inventory	892,400	241,380
Operating expenses	(874,000)	(210,600)	PPE, net	4,292,720	446,580
Net income	$ 569,400	$113,400	Equity investment	888,658	
				$7,279,469	$1,137,695
Statement of retained earnings:					
BOY retained earnings	$2,261,040	$418,500	Liabilities and stockholders' equity		
Net income	569,400	113,400	Accounts payable	$ 344,540	$ 96,682
Dividends	(130,962)	(14,742)	Other current liabilities	424,451	132,355
EOY retained earnings	$2,699,478	$517,158	Long-term liabilities	2,500,000	270,000
			Common stock	752,100	54,000
			APIC	558,900	67,500
			Retained earnings	2,699,478	517,158
				$7,279,469	$1,137,695

a. Show the computation to yield the $63,400 of Income (loss) from subsidiary reported by the parent during 2016.

b. Show the computation to yield the $888,658 Equity Investment account balance reported by the parent on December 31, 2016.

c. Prepare the consolidation entries for the year ended December 31, 2016.

d. Prepare the consolidation spreadsheet for the year ended December 31, 2016.

48. **Prepare consolidation spreadsheet for intercompany sale of land—Equity method**
Assume that a parent company acquired its subsidiary on January 1, 2013, at a purchase price that was $400,000 in excess of the book value of the subsidiary's Stockholders' Equity on the acquisition date. Of that excess, $300,000 was assigned to a Patent owned by the subsidiary that is being amortized over a 10-year period, and the remaining excess was assigned to Goodwill. The Patent has been amortized as part of the parent's equity method accounting. In 2015, the wholly owned subsidiary sold Land to the parent for $200,000. The Land was reported on the subsidiary's balance sheet for $160,000 on the date of sale. The parent uses the equity method to account for its Equity Investment.

Following are financial statements of the parent and its subsidiary for the year ended December 31, 2016:

	Parent	Subsidiary		Parent	Subsidiary
Income statement:			**Balance sheet:**		
Sales.	$6,000,000	$2,250,000	Assets		
Cost of goods sold	(4,200,000)	(1,350,000)	Cash	$ 369,831	$ 727,263
Gross profit.	1,800,000	900,000	Accounts receivable	768,000	522,000
Income (loss) from subsidiary	285,000		Inventory	1,164,000	670,500
Operating expenses	(1,140,000)	(585,000)	PPE, net	5,599,200	1,240,500
Net income	$ 945,000	$ 315,000	Equity investment	2,014,050	
				$9,915,081	$3,160,263
Statement of retained earnings:					
BOY retained earnings	$2,974,400	$1,162,500	Liabilities and stockholders' equity		
Net income	945,000	315,000	Accounts payable	$ 449,400	$ 268,560
Dividends	(217,350)	(40,950)	Other current liabilities	553,631	367,653
EOY retained earnings	$3,702,050	$1,436,550	Long-term liabilities	3,500,000	750,000
			Common stock	981,000	150,000
			APIC	729,000	187,500
			Retained earnings	3,702,050	1,436,550
				$9,915,081	$3,160,263

a. Show the computation to yield the $285,000 of Income (loss) from subsidiary reported by the parent for the year ended December 31, 2016.

b. Show the computation to yield the $2,014,050 Equity Investment account balance reported by the parent on December 31, 2016.

c. Prepare the consolidation entries for the year ended December 31, 2016.

d. Prepare the consolidation spreadsheet for the year ended December 31, 2016.

LO3   49. Prepare consolidation spreadsheet for intercompany sale of land—Equity method

Assume that a parent company acquired its subsidiary on January 1, 2012, at a purchase price that was $400,000 in excess of the book value of the subsidiary's Stockholders' Equity on the acquisition date. Of that excess, $200,000 was assigned to a Customer List owned by the subsidiary that is being amortized over a 10-year period, $100,000 was assigned to an unrecorded Patent that is being amortized over a 10-year period, and the remaining excess was assigned to Goodwill. The Customer List and Patent assets were amortized as part of the parent's equity method accounting. In 2015, the wholly owned subsidiary sold Land to the parent for $300,000. The Land was reported on the subsidiary's balance sheet for $220,000 on the date of sale. The parent uses the equity method to account for its Equity Investment.

Following are financial statements of the parent and its subsidiary for the year ended December 31, 2016:

	Parent	Subsidiary		Parent	Subsidiary
Income statement:			**Balance sheet:**		
Sales.	$8,000,000	$3,000,000	Assets		
Cost of goods sold.	(5,600,000)	(1,800,000)	Cash	$ 457,475	$ 469,684
Gross profit.	2,400,000	1,200,000	Accounts receivable.	1,024,000	696,000
Income (loss) from subsidiary.	390,000		Inventory.	1,552,000	894,000
Operating expenses	(1,520,000)	(780,000)	PPE, net	7,465,600	1,654,000
Net income	$1,270,000	$ 420,000	Equity investment.	2,535,400	
				$13,034,475	$3,713,684
Statement of retained earnings:			Liabilities and stockholders' equity		
BOY retained earnings	$3,939,200	$1,550,000			
Net income	1,270,000	420,000	Accounts payable.	$ 599,200	$ 358,080
Dividends	(292,100)	(54,600)	Other current liabilities . . .	738,175	490,204
EOY retained earnings	$4,917,100	$1,915,400	Long-term liabilities	4,500,000	500,000
			Common stock.	1,308,000	200,000
			APIC	972,000	250,000
			Retained earnings	4,917,100	1,915,400
				$13,034,475	$3,713,684

a. Show the computation to yield the $390,000 of Income (loss) from subsidiary reported by the parent for the year ended December 31, 2016.

b. Show the computation to yield the $2,535,400 Equity Investment account balance reported by the parent on December 31, 2016.

c. Prepare the consolidation entries for the year ended December 31, 2016.

d. Prepare the consolidation spreadsheet for the year ended December 31, 2016.

50. **Prepare consolidation spreadsheet for intercompany sale of equipment—Equity method**
    Assume that a parent company acquired its subsidiary on January 1, 2012, at a purchase price that was
    $300,000 in excess of the book value of the subsidiary's Stockholders' Equity on the acquisition date.
    Of that excess, $200,000 was assigned to a Customer List that is being amortized over a 10-year period.
    The remaining $100,000 was assigned to Goodwill.

    LO4

    In January of 2015, the wholly owned subsidiary sold Equipment to the parent for a cash price of
    $120,000. The subsidiary had acquired the equipment at a cost of $140,000 and depreciated the equip-
    ment over its 10-year useful life using the straight-line method (no salvage value). The subsidiary had
    depreciated the equipment for 4 years at the time of sale. The parent retained the depreciation policy of
    the subsidiary and depreciated the equipment over its remaining 6-year useful life.

    Following are financial statements of the parent and its subsidiary for the year ended December 31,
    2016. The parent uses the equity method to account for its Equity Investment. The Customer List was
    amortized as part of the parent's equity method accounting.

	Parent	Subsidiary		Parent	Subsidiary
Income statement:			**Balance sheet:**		
Sales.	$10,000,000	$1,000,000	Assets		
Cost of goods sold.	(7,200,000)	(600,000)	Cash	$ 1,058,100	$ 322,000
Gross profit.	2,800,000	400,000	Accounts receivable.	1,750,000	430,000
Income (loss) from subsidiary.	126,000		Inventory.	2,600,000	550,000
Operating expenses	(1,500,000)	(260,000)	PPE, net	10,060,000	1,030,000
Net income.	$ 1,426,000	$ 140,000	Equity investment.	800,000	
				$16,268,100	$2,332,000
Statement of retained earnings:					
BOY retained earnings	$ 5,814,300	$ 225,000	Liabilities and stockholders' equity		
Net income.	1,426,000	140,000	Accounts payable.	$ 1,010,000	$ 178,000
Dividends	(285,200)	(20,000)	Other current liabilities	1,190,000	230,000
EOY retained earnings	$ 6,955,100	$ 345,000	Long-term liabilities	2,500,000	1,300,000
			Common stock.	553,000	124,000
			APIC	4,060,000	155,000
			Retained earnings	6,955,100	345,000
				$16,268,100	$2,332,000

    a.   Prepare the journal entry that the subsidiary made to record the sale of the equipment to the
    parent, the journal entry that the parent made to record the purchase, and the [I] entries for the
    year of sale.

    b.   Compute the remaining portion of the deferred gain on January 1, 2016.

    c.   Show the computation to yield the $126,000 of Income (loss) from subsidiary reported by the
    parent for the year ended December 31, 2016.

    d.   Compute the Equity Investment balance of $800,000 on December 31, 2016.

    e.   Prepare the consolidation entries for the year ended December 31, 2016.

    f.   Prepare the consolidation spreadsheet for the year ended December 31, 2016.

LO4 **51. Prepare consolidation spreadsheet for intercompany sale of equipment—Equity method**

Assume that a parent company acquired its subsidiary on January 1, 2011, at a purchase price that was $490,000 in excess of the book value of the subsidiary's Stockholders' Equity on the acquisition date. Of that excess, $140,000 was assigned to a Royalty Agreement, and the remainder of $350,000 to an unrecorded Customer List owned by the subsidiary. Both the Royalty Agreement and the Customer List are being amortized over a 7-year period. Depreciation and amortization are computed on a straight-line basis with no salvage value.

In January 2013, the wholly owned subsidiary sold Equipment to the parent for a cash price of $250,000. The subsidiary had acquired the equipment at a cost of $480,000 and depreciated the equipment over its 10-year useful life using the straight-line method (no salvage value). The subsidiary had depreciated the equipment for 6 years at the time of sale. The parent retained the depreciation policy of the subsidiary and depreciated the equipment over its remaining 4-year useful life.

Following are financial statements of the parent and its subsidiary for the year ended December 31, 2016. The parent uses the equity method to account for its Equity Investment. The Customer List and Royalty Agreement assets were amortized as part of the parent's equity method accounting.

	Parent	Subsidiary		Parent	Subsidiary
Income statement:			**Balance sheet:**		
Sales.	$3,380,000	$876,000	Assets		
Cost of goods sold.	(2,433,600)	(525,600)	Cash.	$ 681,695	$ 243,272
Gross profit.	946,400	350,400	Accounts receivable.	591,500	376,680
Income (loss) from subsidiary.	67,140		Inventory.	878,800	481,800
Operating expenses.	(507,000)	(227,760)	PPE, net	3,400,280	902,280
Net income.	$ 506,540	$122,640	Equity investment.	616,624	
				$6,168,899	$2,004,032
Statement of retained earnings:					
BOY retained earnings.	$1,960,873	$197,100	Liabilities and stockholders' equity		
Net income.	506,540	122,640	Accounts payable.	$ 341,380	$ 155,928
Dividends	(101,308)	(17,520)	Other current liabilities	402,220	201,480
EOY retained earnings.	$2,366,105	$302,220	Long-term liabilities	1,500,000	1,100,000
			Common stock.	186,914	108,624
			APIC	1,372,280	135,780
			Retained earnings	2,366,105	302,220
				$6,168,899	$2,004,032

a. Prepare the journal entry that the subsidiary made to record the sale of the equipment to the parent, the journal entry that the parent made to record the purchase, and the [I] entries for the year of sale.

b. Compute the remaining portion of the deferred gain at January 1, 2016.

c. Show the computation to yield the $67,140 of Income (loss) from subsidiary reported by the parent for the year ended December 31, 2016.

d. Compute the Equity Investment balance of $616,624 at December 31, 2016.

e. Prepare the consolidation entries for the year ended December 31, 2016.

f. Prepare the consolidation spreadsheet for the year ended December 31, 2016.

52. **Prepare consolidation spreadsheet for intercompany sale of equipment—Equity method**   **LO4**
    Assume that a parent company acquired its subsidiary on January 1, 2013, at a purchase price that was
    $600,000 in excess of the book value of the subsidiary's Stockholders' Equity on the acquisition date.
    Of that excess, $100,000 was assigned to a Patent, and $200,000 to an unrecorded Customer List owned
    by the subsidiary. The Patent asset is being depreciated over its 10-year legal life and the Customer
    List is being amortized over a 5-year period. Amortization is computed on a straight-line basis with no
    salvage value. The remaining $300,000 of the purchase price was assigned to Goodwill.
        In January 2015, the parent sold Equipment to its wholly owned subsidiary for a cash price of
    $150,000. The parent had acquired the equipment at a cost of $175,000 and depreciated the equipment
    over its 10-year useful life using the straight-line method (no salvage value). The parent had depreci-
    ated the equipment for 5 years at the time of sale. The subsidiary retained the depreciation policy of the
    parent and depreciated the equipment over its remaining 5-year useful life.
        Following are financial statements of the parent and its subsidiary for the year ended December 31,
    2016. The parent uses the equity method to account for its Equity Investment. The Customer List and
    Patent assets were amortized as part of the parent's equity method accounting.

	Parent	Subsidiary		Parent	Subsidiary
Income statement:			**Balance sheet:**		
Sales.	$8,920,000	$2,548,000	Assets		
Cost of goods sold.	(6,422,400)	(1,528,800)	Cash	$ 167,196	$ 508,056
Gross profit.	2,497,600	1,019,200	Accounts receivable.	1,561,000	1,095,640
Income (loss) from subsidiary.	319,220		Inventory.	2,319,200	1,401,400
Operating expenses	(1,338,000)	(662,480)	PPE, net	8,973,520	2,624,440
Net income	$1,478,820	$ 356,720	Equity investment.	1,952,452	
				$14,973,368	$5,629,536
Statement of retained earnings:					
BOY retained earnings	$5,213,116	$ 573,300	Liabilities and stockholders' equity		
Net income	1,478,820	356,720	Accounts payable.	$ 900,920	$ 453,544
Dividends	(295,764)	(50,960)	Other current liabilities	1,061,480	586,040
EOY retained earnings	$6,396,172	$ 879,060	Long-term liabilities	2,500,000	3,000,000
			Common stock.	493,276	315,952
			APIC	3,621,520	394,940
			Retained earnings	6,396,172	879,060
				$14,973,368	$5,629,536

  a. Prepare the journal entry that the parent made to record the sale of the equipment to the
      subsidiary, the journal entry that the subsidiary made to record the purchase, and the [I] entries
      for the year of sale.
  b. Compute the remaining portion of the deferred gain at January 1, 2016.
  c. Show the computation to yield the $319,220 of Income (loss) from subsidiary reported by the
      parent for the year ended December 31, 2016.
  d. Compute the Equity Investment balance of $1,952,452 at December 31, 2016.
  e. Prepare the consolidation entries for the year ended December 31, 2016.
  f. Prepare the consolidation spreadsheet for the year ended December 31, 2016.

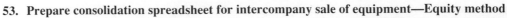

LO4   53. **Prepare consolidation spreadsheet for intercompany sale of equipment—Equity method**

Assume that a parent company acquired its subsidiary on January 1, 2010, at a purchase price that was $400,000 in excess of the book value of the subsidiary's Stockholders' Equity on the acquisition date. The excess was assigned entirely to an unrecorded License Agreement owned by the subsidiary. The License Agreement asset is being depreciated over its 10-year useful life on a straight-line basis with no salvage value.

In January 2013, the parent sold Equipment to its wholly owned subsidiary for a cash price of $70,000. The parent had acquired the equipment at a cost of $90,000 and depreciated the equipment over its 10-year useful life using the straight-line method (no salvage value). The parent had depreciated the equipment for 3 years at the time of sale. The subsidiary retained the depreciation policy of the parent and depreciated the equipment over its remaining 7-year useful life.

Following are financial statements of the parent and its subsidiary as of December 31, 2016. The parent uses the equity method to account for its Equity Investment.

	Parent	Subsidiary		Parent	Subsidiary
Income statement:			**Balance sheet:**		
Sales............................	$6,540,000	$3,011,000	Assets		
Cost of goods sold.................	(4,708,800)	(1,806,600)	Cash.......................	$ 344,062	$ 355,242
Gross profit.......................	1,831,200	1,204,400	Accounts receivable..........	1,144,500	1,294,730
Income (loss) from subsidiary.........	382,540		Inventory...................	1,700,400	1,656,050
Operating expenses...............	(981,000)	(782,860)	PPE, net	6,579,240	3,101,330
Net income.......................	$1,232,740	$ 421,540	Equity investment............	1,995,864	
				$11,764,066	$6,407,352
Statement of retained earnings:					
BOY retained earnings..............	$3,822,172	$ 677,475	Liabilities and stockholders' equity		
Net income.......................	1,232,740	421,540	Accounts payable............	$ 660,540	$ 535,958
Dividends	(246,548)	(60,220)	Other current liabilities	778,260	692,530
EOY retained earnings	$4,808,364	$1,038,795	Long-term liabilities	2,500,000	3,300,000
			Common stock..............	361,662	373,364
			APIC......................	2,655,240	466,705
			Retained earnings	4,808,364	1,038,795
				$11,764,066	$6,407,352

a. Prepare the journal entry that the parent made to record the sale of the equipment to the subsidiary, the journal entry that the subsidiary made to record the purchase, and the [I] entries for the year of sale.

b. Compute the remaining portion of the deferred gain at January 1, 2016.

c. Show the computation to yield the $382,540 of Income (loss) from subsidiary reported by the parent for the year ended December 31, 2016.

d. Compute the Equity Investment balance of $1,995,864 at December 31, 2016.

e. Prepare the consolidation entries for the year ended December 31, 2016.

f. Prepare the consolidation spreadsheet for the year ended December 31, 2016.

54. **Prepare consolidation spreadsheet for intercompany sale of equipment—Cost method**

    Assume that a parent company acquired a subsidiary on January 1, 2012 for $832,000. The purchase price was $299,000 in excess of the book value of the subsidiary's Stockholders' Equity on the acquisition date. On the acquisition date, the subsidiary's stockholders equity was comprised of $390,000 of no-par common stock and $143,000 of retained earnings. The Acquisition Accounting Premium (AAP) was assigned as follows: an increase of $13,000 in accounts receivable that were entirely collected during the year after acquisition, an increase of $65,000 for property, plant and equipment that has 10 years of remaining useful life, $104,000 for an unrecorded patent with an 8-year remaining life and $117,000 for goodwill. All amortizable components of the AAP are amortized using the straight-line method.

    On January 1, 2014, the parent sold Equipment to the subsidiary for a cash price of $128,700. The parent had acquired the equipment at a cost of $124,800 and depreciated the equipment over its 12-year useful life using the straight-line method (no salvage value). The parent had depreciated the equipment for 2 years at the time of sale. The subsidiary retained the depreciation policy of the parent and depreciates the equipment over its remaining 10-year useful life.

    Following are financial statements of the parent and its subsidiary as of December 31, 2016. The parent uses the cost method of pre-consolidation investment bookkeeping.

Income statement:	Parent	Subsidiary	Balance sheet:	Parent	Subsidiary
Sales..........................	$1,300,000	$598,000	Assets		
Cost of goods sold...............	(715,000)	(364,000)	Cash.........................	$ 117,000	$ 78,000
Gross profit.....................	585,000	234,000	Accounts receivable............	156,000	117,000
Deprec. & amort. expense	(39,000)	(26,000)	Inventory......................	364,000	182,000
Operating expenses..............	(390,000)	(104,000)	Equity investment..............	832,000	
Interest expense.................	(19,500)	(6,500)	PPE, net	442,000	312,000
Total expenses	(448,500)	(136,500)	Other assets...................	169,000	286,000
Income (loss) from subsidiary.......	45,500		Total assets...................	$2,080,000	$975,000
Net income.....................	$ 182,000	$ 97,500	Liabilities and stockholders' equity		
			Accounts payable..............	$ 325,000	$ 70,200
Statement of retained earnings:			Accrued liabilities	32,500	59,800
BOY retained earnings............	$ 715,000	$325,000	Notes payable	195,000	78,000
Net income.....................	182,000	97,500	Common stock.................	780,000	390,000
Dividends	(149,500)	(45,500)	Retained earnings	747,500	377,000
Ending retained earnings	$ 747,500	$377,000	Total liabilities and equity	$2,080,000	$975,000

a. Prepare the journal entry that the parent made to record the sale of the equipment to the subsidiary, the journal entry that the subsidiary made to record the purchase, and the [I] entries for the year of sale.

b. Compute the remaining portion of the deferred gain at January 1, 2016.

c. Prior to preparing consolidated financial statements, compute the amount of net income the parent would have reported for the year ended December 31, 2016 assuming the parent applied the equity method instead of the cost method of pre-consolidation bookkeeping.

d. Prior to preparing consolidated financial statements, compute the amount of Equity investment the parent would have reported on December 31, 2016 assuming the parent applied the equity method instead of the cost method of pre-consolidation bookkeeping.

e. Prepare the consolidation entries for the year ended December 31, 2016.

f. Prepare the consolidation spreadsheet for the year ended December 31, 2016.

LO6 **55. Prepare consolidation spreadsheet for intercompany sale of equipment—Cost method**

Assume that a parent company acquired a subsidiary on January 1, 2013 for $1,280,000. The purchase price was $540,000 in excess of the book value of the subsidiary's Stockholders' Equity on the acquisition date. On the acquisition date, the subsidiary's stockholders equity was comprised of $120,000 of common stock, $480,000 of additional paid-in capital and $140,000 of retained earnings. On the acquisition date, the Acquisition Accounting Premium (AAP) was assigned as follows: an increase of $120,000 for property, plant and equipment that has 8 years of remaining useful life, an increase of $180,000 for licenses with 5 years remaining life and $240,000 for goodwill. All amortizable components of the AAP are amortized using the straight-line method.

On January 1, 2014, the subsidiary sold Equipment to the parent for a cash price of $198,000. The subsidiary originally acquired the equipment at a cost of $200,000 and depreciated the equipment over its 10-year useful life using the straight-line method (no salvage value). The subsidiary had depreciated the equipment for 2 years at the time of sale. The parent retained the depreciation policy of the subsidiary and depreciates the equipment over its remaining 8-year useful life.

Following are financial statements of the parent and its subsidiary as of December 31, 2016. The parent uses the cost method of pre-consolidation investment bookkeeping.

	Parent	Subsidiary		Parent	Subsidiary
Income statement:			**Balance sheet:**		
Sales..........................	$2,400,000	$1,000,000	Assets		
Cost of goods sold..............	(1,400,000)	(600,000)	Cash.........................	$ 200,000	$ 100,000
Gross profit....................	1,000,000	400,000	Accounts receivable............	220,000	200,000
Deprec. & amort. expense.........	(60,000)	(40,000)	Inventory......................	600,000	300,000
Operating expenses..............	(600,000)	(160,000)	Equity investment..............	1,280,000	
Interest expense................	(30,000)	(10,000)	PPE, net......................	1,000,000	480,000
Total expenses.................	(690,000)	(210,000)	Other assets...................	200,000	370,000
Income (loss) from subsidiary.......	70,000		Licenses......................		50,000
Net income....................	$ 380,000	$ 190,000	Total assets...................	$3,500,000	$1,500,000
			Liabilities and stockholders' equity		
Statement of retained earnings:			Accounts payable..............	$ 500,000	$ 60,000
BOY retained earnings...........	$1,100,000	$ 500,000	Accrued liabilities..............	250,000	90,000
Net income....................	380,000	190,000	Notes payable	300,000	130,000
Dividends.....................	(230,000)	(70,000)	Common stock................	500,000	120,000
Ending retained earnings..........	$1,250,000	$ 620,000	APIC.........................	700,000	480,000
			Retained earnings	1,250,000	620,000
			Total liabilities and equity.......	$3,500,000	$1,500,000

a. Prepare the journal entry that the subsidiary made to record the sale of the equipment to the parent, the journal entry that the parent made to record the purchase, and the [I] entries for the year of sale.

b. Compute the remaining portion of the deferred gain at January 1, 2016.

c. Prior to preparing consolidated financial statements, compute the amount of equity income the parent would have reported for the year ended December 31, 2016 assuming the parent applied the equity method instead of the cost method of pre-consolidation bookkeeping.

d. Prior to preparing consolidated financial statements, compute the amount of Equity investment the parent would have reported on December 31, 2016 assuming the parent applied the equity method instead of the cost method of pre-consolidation bookkeeping.

e. Prepare the consolidation entries for the year ended December 31, 2016.

f. Prepare the consolidation spreadsheet for the year ended December 31, 2016.

56. **Prepare consolidation spreadsheet for intercompany sale of equipment—Cost method**

Assume that a parent company acquired a subsidiary on January 1, 2014 for $2,560,000. The purchase price was $816,000 in excess of the book value of the subsidiary's Stockholders' Equity on the acquisition date. On the acquisition date, the subsidiary's stockholders equity was comprised of $1,200,000 of no-par common stock and $544,000 of retained earnings. The Acquisition Accounting Premium (AAP) was assigned as follows: a $180,000 increase for property, plant and equipment that has 10 years of remaining useful life, $240,000 for an unrecorded patent with an 8-year remaining life, a $36,000 decrease in notes payable that have a 3-year remaining payback period, and $360,000 for goodwill. All amortizable components of the AAP are amortized using the straight-line method.

On January 1, 2015, the parent sold Equipment to the subsidiary for a cash price of $260,000. The parent had acquired the equipment at a cost of $300,000 and depreciated the equipment over its 9-year useful life using the straight-line method (no salvage value). The parent had depreciated the equipment for 3 years at the time of sale. The subsidiary retained the depreciation policy of the parent and depreciates the equipment over its remaining 6-year useful life.

Following are pre-consolidation financial statements of the parent and its subsidiary for the year ended December 31, 2016. The parent uses the cost method of pre-consolidation investment bookkeeping.

	Parent	Subsidiary		Parent	Subsidiary
Income statement:			**Balance sheet:**		
Sales.	$3,720,000	$1,840,000	Assets		
Cost of goods sold.	(2,000,000)	(1,120,000)	Cash.	$ 280,000	$ 260,000
Gross profit.	1,720,000	720,000	Accounts receivable.	520,000	340,000
Deprec. & amort. expense	(120,000)	(80,000)	Inventory.	1,200,000	720,000
Operating expenses.	(1,080,000)	(292,000)	Equity investment.	2,560,000	
Interest expense.	(60,000)	(20,000)	PPE, net	1,360,000	960,000
Total expenses	(1,260,000)	(392,000)	Other assets.	520,000	720,000
Income (loss) from subsidiary.	140,000		Total assets.	$6,440,000	$3,000,000
Net income.	$ 600,000	$ 328,000	Liabilities and stockholders' equity		
			Accounts payable.	$1,000,000	$ 164,000
Statement of retained earnings:			Accrued liabilities	100,000	248,000
BOY retained earnings.	$2,200,000	$1,000,000	Notes payable	600,000	200,000
Net income.	600,000	328,000	Common stock.	2,400,000	1,200,000
Dividends	(460,000)	(140,000)	Retained earnings	2,340,000	1,188,000
EOY retained earnings	$2,340,000	$1,188,000	Total liabilities and equity	$6,440,000	$3,000,000

a. Prepare the journal entry that the parent made to record the sale of the equipment to the subsidiary, the journal entry that the subsidiary made to record the purchase, and the [I] entries for the year of sale.

b. Compute the remaining portion of the deferred gain at January 1, 2016.

c. Prior to preparing consolidated financial statements, compute the amount of equity income the parent would have reported for the year ended December 31, 2016 assuming the parent applied the equity method instead of the cost method of pre-consolidation bookkeeping.

d. Prior to preparing consolidated financial statements, compute the amount of Equity investment the parent would have reported on December 31, 2016 assuming the parent applied the equity method instead of the cost method of pre-consolidation bookkeeping.

e. Prepare the consolidation journal entries for the year ended December 31, 2016.

f. Prepare the consolidation spreadsheet for the year ended December 31, 2016.

LO1, 4

57. **Comprehensive consolidation subsequent to date of acquisition, AAP computation, goodwill, upstream and downstream intercompany inventory profits, downstream intercompany depreciable asset gain—Equity method**

A parent company acquired 100 percent of the stock of a subsidiary company on January 1, 2012, for $690,000. On this date, the balances of the subsidiary's stockholders' equity accounts were Common Stock, $418,600, and Retained Earnings, $45,080.

On January 1, 2012, the subsidiary's recorded book values were equal to fair values for all items except four: (1) accounts receivable had a book value of $128,800 and a fair value of $115,920, (2) buildings and equipment, net had a book value of $112,700 and a fair value of $170,660, (3) the Customer List intangible asset had a book value of $32,200 and a fair value of $167,440, and (4) notes payable had a book value of $69,000 and a fair value of $64,400. Both companies use the FIFO inventory method and sell all of their inventories at least once per year. The net balance of accounts receivable are collected in the following year. On the acquisition date, the subsidiary's buildings and equipment, net had a remaining useful life of 6 years, the Customer List had a remaining useful life of 7 years, and notes payable had a remaining term of 4 years.

On January 1, 2015, the parent sold a building to the subsidiary for $209,300. On this date, the building was carried on the subsidiary's books (net of accumulated depreciation) at $161,000. Both companies estimated that the building has a remaining life of 6 years on the intercompany sale date, with no salvage value.

Each company routinely sells merchandise to the other company, with a profit margin of 25 percent of selling price (regardless of the direction of the sale). During 2016, intercompany sales amount to $48,300, of which $25,760 of merchandise remains in the ending inventory of the parent. On December 31, 2016, $12,880 of these intercompany sales remained unpaid. Additionally, the subsidiary's December 31, 2015 inventory includes $38,640 of merchandise purchased in the preceding year from the parent. During 2015, intercompany sales amount to $60,000, and on December 31, 2015, $7,000 of these intercompany sales remained unpaid. Following are pre-consolidation financial statements of the parent and its subsidiary for the year ended December 31, 2016. The parent uses the equity method of pre-consolidation investment bookkeeping.

	Parent	Subsidiary		Parent	Subsidiary
Income statement:			**Balance sheet:**		
Sales...........................	$1,564,000	$579,600	Assets		
Cost of goods sold..............	(791,200)	(347,760)	Cash........................	$ 109,940	$ 48,300
Gross profit....................	772,800	231,840	Accounts receivable...........	172,500	156,400
Deprec. & amort. expense	(38,640)	(30,820)	Inventories	418,600	149,500
Operating expenses..............	(502,320)	(123,740)	Buildings and equipment, net	404,800	289,800
Total expenses	(540,960)	(154,560)	Other assets..................	184,000	322,000
Income (loss) from subsidiary.......	59,570		Customer list		32,200
Net income.....................	$ 291,410	$ 77,280	Investment in subsidiary.........	856,060	
			Total assets..................	$2,145,900	$998,200
Statement of retained earnings:			Liabilities and stockholders' equity		
Beg. retained earnings............	$ 939,550	$354,200	Accounts payable..............	$ 103,500	$ 41,400
Net income.....................	291,410	77,280	Notes payable	161,000	69,000
Dividends	(193,200)	(45,080)	Other liabilities	70,840	82,800
Ending retained earnings	$1,037,760	$386,400	Common stock.................	772,800	418,600
			Retained earnings	1,037,760	386,400
			Total liabilities and equity.......	$2,145,900	$998,200

a. Disaggregate and document the activity for the 100% Acquisition Accounting Premium (AAP).

b. Calculate and organize the profits and losses on intercompany transactions and balances.

c. Compute the pre-consolidation Equity Investment account beginning and ending balances starting with the stockholders' equity of the subsidiary.

d. Reconstruct the activity in the parent's pre-consolidation Equity Investment T-account for the year of consolidation.

e. Complete the consolidating entries according to the **C-E-A-D-I** sequence and complete the consolidation worksheet.

58. Comprehensive consolidation subsequent to date of acquisition, AAP computation, goodwill, upstream and downstream intercompany inventory profits, downstream intercompany depreciable asset gain—Cost method

LO2, 6

A parent company acquired 100 percent of the stock of a subsidiary company on January 1, 2013, for $1,536,000. On this date, the balances of the subsidiary's stockholders' equity accounts were Common Stock, $144,000, additional paid-in capital, $576,000, and Retained Earnings, $282,000.

On January 1, 2013, the subsidiary's recorded book values were equal to fair values for all items except five: (1) accounts receivable had a book value of $192,000 and a fair value of $180,000, (2) property, plant & equipment, net had a book value of $432,000 and a fair value of $480,000, (3) licenses with a book value of $36,000 and a fair value of $132,000, (4) a previously unrecorded customer list had a book value of $0 and a fair value of $60,000, and (5) notes payable had a book value of $46,000 and a fair value of $40,000. Both companies use the FIFO inventory method and sell all of their inventories at least once per year. The year-end net balance of accounts receivable are collected in the following year. On the acquisition date, the subsidiary's property, plant & equipment, net had a remaining useful life of 16 years, the licenses had a remaining useful life of 10 years, the customer list had a remaining useful life of 5 years and notes payable had a remaining term of 5 years.

On January 1, 2014, the parent sold a building to the subsidiary for $240,000. On this date, the building was carried on the parent's books (net of accumulated depreciation) at $192,000. Both companies estimated that the building has a remaining life of 8 years on the intercompany sale date, with no salvage value.

Each company routinely sells merchandise to the other company, with a profit margin of 28 percent of selling price (regardless of the direction of the sale). During 2016, intercompany sales amount to $120,000, of which $72,000 of merchandise remains in the ending inventory of the subsidiary. On December 31, 2016, $38,400 of these intercompany sales remained unpaid. Additionally, the parent's December 31, 2015 inventory includes $48,000 of merchandise purchased in the preceding year from the subsidiary. During 2015, intercompany sales amount to $96,000, and on December 31, 2015, $28,800 of these intercompany sales remained unpaid.

The parent accounts for its investment in the subsidiary using the cost method. The pre-consolidation financial statement information for the two companies for the year ended December 31, 2016 are provided below:

	Parent	Subsidiary		Parent	Subsidiary
Income statement:			**Balance sheet:**		
Sales.	$2,376,000	$1,128,000	Assets		
Cost of goods sold.	(1,296,000)	(669,600)	Cash.	$ 216,000	$ 144,000
Gross profit.	1,080,000	458,400	Accounts receivable.	288,000	216,000
Deprec. & amort. expense	(72,000)	(48,000)	Inventory.	672,000	336,000
Operating expenses.	(720,000)	(192,000)	Equity investment.	1,536,000	
Interest expense.	(40,800)	(12,000)	PPE, net	816,000	600,000
Total Expenses.	(832,800)	(252,000)	Other assets.	312,000	504,000
Income (loss) from subsidiary.	86,400		Licenses		24,000
Net income.	$ 333,600	$ 206,400	Total assets.	$3,840,000	$1,824,000
			Liabilities and stockholders' equity		
Statement of retained earnings:			Accounts payable.	$ 420,000	$ 129,600
BOY retained earnings.	$1,320,000	$ 600,000	Accrued liabilities	240,000	110,400
Net income.	333,600	206,400	Notes payable	360,000	144,000
Dividends	(273,600)	(86,400)	Common stock.	432,000	144,000
Ending retained earnings	$1,380,000	$ 720,000	APIC.	1,008,000	576,000
			Retained earnings	1,380,000	720,000
			Total liabilities and equity	$3,840,000	$1,824,000

a. Disaggregate and document the activity for the 100% Acquisition Accounting Premium (AAP).

b. Calculate and organize the profits and losses on intercompany transactions and balances.

c. Compute the amount of the beginning of year [ADJ] adjustment necessary for the consolidation of the financial statements for the year ended December 31, 2016.

d. Complete the consolidating entries according to the [ADJ] and C-E-A-D-I sequence and complete the consolidation worksheet.

TOPIC REVIEW

Solution 1

Upstream Sale	Parent	Subsidiary	Consolidation Entries Dr		Consolidation Entries Cr		Consolidated
Income statement:							
Sales	$10,000,000	$1,500,000	[I_sales] $ 100,000				$11,400,000
Cost of goods sold	(7,000,000)	(900,000)	[I_cogs] 28,500		[I_cogs] $ 18,525		(7,809,975)
					[I_sales] 100,000		
Gross profit	3,000,000	600,000					3,590,025
Income (loss) from subsidiary	187,525		[C] 187,525				0
Operating expenses	(1,900,000)	(390,000)	[D] 12,500				(2,302,500)
Net income	$ 1,287,525	$ 210,000					$ 1,287,525
Statement of retained earnings:							
BOY retained earnings	$ 5,024,000	$ 775,000	[E] 775,000				$ 5,024,000
Net income	1,287,525	210,000					1,287,525
Dividends	(296,131)	(27,300)			[C] 27,300		(296,131)
Ending retained earnings	$ 6,015,394	$ 957,700					$ 6,015,394
Balance sheet:							
Assets							
Cash	$ 708,694	$ 408,700					$ 1,117,394
Accounts receivable	1,280,000	348,000			[I_pay] 100,000		1,528,000
Inventory	1,940,000	447,000			[I_cogs] 28,500		2,358,500
Equity investment	1,541,700		[I_cogs] 18,525		[C] 160,225		0
					[E] 1,000,000		
					[A] 400,000		
Property, plant and equipment (PPE), net	9,332,000	827,000	[A] 150,000		[D] 7,500		10,301,500
Patent			[A] 50,000		[D] 5,000		45,000
Goodwill			[A] 200,000				200,000
	$14,802,394	$2,030,700					$15,550,394
Liabilities and stockholders' equity							
Current liabilities	$ 1,437,000	$ 348,000	[I_pay] 100,000				$ 1,685,000
Long-term liabilities	4,500,000	500,000					5,000,000
Common stock	1,635,000	100,000	[E] 100,000				1,635,000
APIC	1,215,000	125,000	[E] 125,000				1,215,000
Retained earnings	6,015,394	957,700					6,015,394
	$14,802,394	$2,030,700	$1,847,050		$1,847,050		$15,550,394

Solution 2

	Parent	Subsidiary	Consolidation Entries Dr		Consolidation Entries Cr		Consolidated
Income statement:							
Sales....................................	$10,000,000	$1,500,000	[I$_{sales}$]	$ 100,000			$11,400,000
Cost of goods sold.....................	(7,000,000)	(900,000)	[I$_{cogs}$]	22,400	[I$_{cogs}$]	$ 12,000	(7,810,400)
					[I$_{sales}$]	100,000	
Gross profit..........................	3,000,000	600,000					3,589,600
Dividend income......................	30,000		[C]	30,000			0
Operating expenses....................	(1,900,000)	(390,000)	[D]	12,500			(2,302,500)
Net income...........................	$ 1,130,000	$ 210,000					$ 1,287,100
Statement of retained earnings:							
BOY retained earnings.................	$ 4,000,000	$ 775,000	[E]	775,000	[ADJ]	88,000	$ 4,088,000
Net income...........................	1,130,000	210,000					1,287,100
Dividends............................	(300,000)	(30,000)			[C]	30,000	(300,000)
Ending retained earnings..............	$ 4,830,000	$ 955,000					$ 5,075,100
Balance sheet:							
Assets							
Cash.................................	$ 800,000	$ 406,000					$ 1,206,000
Accounts receivable...................	1,280,000	348,000			[I$_{pay}$]	30,000	1,598,000
Inventory.............................	1,950,000	447,000			[I$_{cogs}$]	22,400	2,374,600
Equity investment....................	1,300,000		[ADJ]	88,000	[E]	1,000,000	0
			[I$_{cogs}$]	12,000	[A]	400,000	
Property, plant and equipment (PPE).......	4,000,000	827,000	[A]	150,000	[D]	7,500	4,969,500
Patent...............................			[A]	50,000	[D]	5,000	45,000
Goodwill.............................			[A]	200,000			200,000
	$ 9,330,000	$2,028,000					$10,393,100
Liabilities and stockholders' equity							
Current liabilities.....................	$ 1,400,000	$ 348,000	[I$_{pay}$]	30,000			$ 1,718,000
Long-term liabilities..................	1,500,000	500,000					2,000,000
Common stock......................	600,000	100,000	[E]	100,000			600,000
APIC................................	1,000,000	125,000	[E]	125,000			1,000,000
Retained earnings....................	4,830,000	955,000					5,075,100
	$ 9,330,000	$2,028,000		$1,694,900		$1,694,900	$10,393,100

[ADJ] = ($775,000 − $637,500) − ($12,500 × 3) − $12,000 = $88,000

Solution 3

	Parent	Subsidiary	Consolidation Entries Dr	Consolidation Entries Cr	Consolidated
Income statement:					
Sales.	$ 4,610,000	$1,330,500			$ 5,940,500
Cost of goods sold.	(3,319,200)	(798,300)			(4,117,500)
Gross profit.	1,290,800	532,200			1,823,000
Gain on sale of equipment		10,000	[I$_{gain}$] $ 10,000		0
Income (loss) from subsidiary.	177,699		[C] 177,699		0
Operating expenses.	(691,500)	(355,930)		[I$_{dep}$] $ 1,429	(1,046,001)
Net income.	$ 776,999	$ 186,270			$ 776,999
Statement of retained earnings:					
BOY retained earnings	$ 2,362,759	$ 687,425	[E] 687,425		$ 2,362,759
Net income.	776,999	186,270			776,999
Dividends	(157,114)	(27,941)		[C] 27,941	(157,114)
Ending retained earnings	$ 2,982,644	$ 845,754			$ 2,982,644
Balance sheet:					
Assets					
Cash.	$ 408,331	$ 342,825			$ 751,156
Accounts receivable.	1,180,160	308,676			1,488,836
Inventory.	1,788,680	396,489			2,185,169
Equity investment.	1,036,758			[E] 887,000	0
				[C] 149,758	
Property, plant and equipment (PPE), net . . .	6,760,104	733,549	[I$_{gain}$] 20,000	[I$_{gain}$] 30,000	7,485,082
			[I$_{dep}$] 1,429		
	$11,174,033	$1,781,539			$11,910,243
Liabilities and stockholders' equity					
Accounts payable.	$ 674,904	$ 126,841			$ 801,745
Accrued liabilities	802,140	165,869			968,009
Long-term liabilities	4,000,000	443,500			4,443,500
Common stock.	325,019	88,700	[E] 88,700		325,019
APIC	2,389,326	110,875	[E] 110,875		2,389,326
Retained earnings	2,982,644	845,754			2,982,644
	$11,174,033	$1,781,539	$1,096,128	$1,096,128	$11,910,243

Solution 4

	Parent	Subsidiary	Consolidation Entries Dr	Consolidation Entries Cr	Consolidated
Income statement:					
Sales.	$10,000,000	$1,500,000			$11,500,000
Cost of goods sold.	(7,000,000)	(900,000)			(7,900,000)
Gross profit.	3,000,000	600,000			3,600,000
Income (loss) from subsidiary.	30,000		[C] $ 30,000		0
Depreciation expense.	(400,000)	(80,000)		[I$_{dep}$] $ 10,000	(470,000)
Operating expenses	(1,500,000)	(310,000)			(1,810,000)
Net income.	$ 1,130,000	$ 210,000			$ 1,320,000
Statement of retained earnings:					
BOY retained earnings	$ 3,600,000	$ 775,000	[E] 775,000	[ADJ] 70,000	$ 3,670,000
Net income.	1,130,000	210,000			1,320,000
Dividends	(300,000)	(30,000)		[C] 30,000	(300,000)
Ending retained earnings	$ 4,430,000	$ 955,000			$ 4,690,000
Balance sheet:					
Assets					
Cash	$ 800,000	$ 406,000			$ 1,206,000
Accounts receivable.	1,280,000	348,000			1,628,000
Inventory.	1,950,000	447,000			2,397,000
Equity investment.	900,000		[ADJ] 70,000	[E] 1,000,000	0
			[I$_{gain}$] 30,000		
PPE, net	4,000,000	827,000	[I$_{dep}$] 10,000	[I$_{gain}$] 30,000	4,807,000
	$ 8,930,000	$2,028,000			$10,038,000
Liabilities and stockholders' equity					
Current liabilities.	$ 1,400,000	$ 348,000			1,748,000
Long-term liabilities	1,500,000	500,000			2,000,000
Common stock.	600,000	100,000	[E] 100,000		600,000
APIC	1,000,000	125,000	[E] 125,000		1,000,000
Retained earnings	4,430,000	955,000			4,690,000
	$ 8,930,000	$2,028,000	$1,140,000	$1,140,000	$10,038,000

[ADJ] = $100,000 ($775,000 − $675,000) − $30,000 (BOY unconfirmed gain)

COMPREHENSIVE REVIEW—EQUITY METHOD SOLUTION

a.   The trial balance information converted to financial statement format is presented, below. A completed
     consolidation spreadsheet is included in the solution to *Part f* of this comprehensive review.

Pre-Consolidation Financial Statements for the Year Ended December 31, 2016		
	Parent	**Subsidiary**
Income statement:		
Sales.	$1,080,000	$ 405,000
Cost of goods sold.	(648,000)	(243,000)
Gross profit.	432,000	162,000
Depreciation & amortization expense.	(27,000)	(21,600)
Operating expenses	(339,000)	(81,150)
Interest expense.	(12,000)	(5,250)
Total expenses	(378,000)	(108,000)
Income (loss) from subsidiary.	50,550	
Net income.	$ 104,550	$ 54,000
Statement of retained earnings:		
Beginning retained earnings.	$ 640,350	$247,500
Net income.	104,550	54,000
Dividends declared.	(135,000)	(31,500)
Ending retained earnings	$ 609,900	$270,000
Balance sheet:		
Cash	$ 87,120	$ 63,750
Accounts receivable.	121,500	90,000
Inventories	292,500	137,250
Property, plant & equipment, net	283,500	202,500
Other assets	128,250	225,000
Equity investment.	660,000	
Total assets.	$1,572,870	$718,500
Accounts payable.	$ 252,000	$ 52,500
Notes payable	121,470	45,000
Other liabilities	49,500	58,500
Common stock.	540,000	292,500
Retained earnings	609,900	270,000
Total liabilities and equity	$1,572,870	$718,500

b.   Given the five-year time horizon between the acquisition date and the consolidated financial statement
     date, the following schedules separately document the annual AAP amortization and the year-end
     unamortized AAP balance for each year, 2012 through 2016.

	Year Ended December 31,				
100% AAP Amortization – Dr (Cr)	**2012**	**2013**	**2014**	**2015**	**2016**
Accounts receivable........................	$(10,500)	$ —	$ —	$ —	$ —
Property, plant & equipment, net	2,700	2,700	2,700	2,700	2,700
Patent..................................	11,250	11,250	11,250	11,250	—
Notes payable	1,500	1,500	1,500	1,500	1,500
Net amortization.........................	$ 4,950	$15,450	$15,450	$15,450	$4,200

		December 31,				
100% Unamortized AAP – Dr (Cr)	**Jan. 1, 2012**	**2012**	**2013**	**2014**	**2015**	**2016**
Accounts receivable.............	$ (10,500)	$ —	$ —	$ —	$ —	$ —
Property, plant & equipment, net ...	27,000	24,300	21,600	18,900	16,200	13,500
Patent........................	45,000	33,750	22,500	11,250	—	—
Notes payable	7,500	6,000	4,500	3,000	1,500	—
Goodwill......................	126,000	126,000	126,000	126,000	126,000	126,000
Net unamortized................	$195,000	$190,050	$174,600	$159,150	$143,700	$139,500

c. **Intercompany depreciable asset sale**:
   One downstream asset sale.
   Intercompany profit recognized on January 1, 2015: $120,000 − $82,500 = $37,500, 10-year remaining life
   Profit confirmed each year: $37,500/10 = $3,750

	Downstream	**Upstream**
Net intercompany profit deferred at January 1, 2016	$33,750	$0
Less: Deferred intercompany profit recognized during 2016...............	3,750	0
Net intercompany profit deferred at December 31, 2016	$30,000	$0

   Intercompany inventory transactions:
   Intercompany inventory sales during 2016: $75,000

	Downstream (in Subsidiary's inventory)	**Upstream (in Parent's inventory)**
Intercompany profit in inventory on January 1, 2016....................	$0	$9,000
Intercompany profit in inventory on December 31, 2016...............	$12,000	$0

   Intercompany accounts receivables and payables at December 31, 2016: $15,000

d. The following is the general formula for computing the Equity Investment account (under the equity
   method) at any point in time *when the parent company owns 100% of a subsidiary*:

	(1) Book value of the net assets of the subsidiary
Plus:	(2) Unamortized AAP
Less:	(3) Downstream deferred intercompany profits
Less:	(4) Upstream deferred intercompany profits
	Equity method investment account

Equity Investment account balance at January 1, 2016:

	Jan. 1, 2016	
	$540,000	(1) $292,500 + $247,500
Plus:	143,700	(2) $143,700 (from *Part b*)
Less:	(33,750)	(3) $33,750 (from *Part c*)
Less:	(9,000)	(4) $9,000 (from *Part c*)
	$640,950	

Equity Investment account balance at December 31, 2016:

	Dec. 31, 2016	
	$562,500	(1) $292,500 + $270,000
Plus:	139,500	(2) $139,500 (from *Part b*)
Less:	(30,000)	(3) $30,000 (from *Part c*)
	(12,000)	(3) $12,000 (from *Part c*)
Less:	0	(4) none
	$660,000	

e. Equity method investment accounting includes the following routine adjustments during any given period: (1) recognition of p% of the subsidiary's income, (2) recognition of p% of the dividends declared by the subsidiary, (3) amortization of the p% AAP, (4) recognition of prior period deferred intercompany profits that have been confirmed through either transactions with unaffiliated parties or depreciation/amortization, and (5) deferral of intercompany profits newly originated during the current period. With respect to the deferred intercompany profits, when the parent company owns 100% of a subsidiary, then 100% of the profit is deferred for downstream and upstream transactions. Information for items (1) and (2) is available in the initial information, information for item (3) was summarized in *Part b*, and information for items (4) and (5) was summarized in *Part c*. These items are all reflected in the following completed T-account.

	Equity Investment		
January 1, 2016	640,950		
(1) p% × net income of Sub. = 100% × $54,000	54,000	31,500	(2) p% × dividends of Sub. = 100% × $31,500
(4) p% × BOY upstream inventory profits recognized during 2016 = 100% × $9,000	9,000	4,200	(3) p% AAP amortization (see *Part b*)
(4) 100% × downstream building profits recognized via depreciation during 2016	3,750	12,000	(5) 100% × EOY downstream inventory profits deferred until year of sale to unaffiliated party
December 31, 2016	660,000		

f.

[C]	Income (loss) from subsidiary	50,550	
	Dividends − subsidiary		31,500
	Equity investment		19,050

[E]	Common stock (S) @ BOY	292,500	
	Retained earnings (S) @ BOY	247,500	
	Equity investment @ BOY		540,000

[A]	Property, plant & equipment, net @ BOY	16,200	
	Note payable @ BOY	1,500	
	Goodwill	126,000	
	Equity investment @ BOY		143,700

[D]	Depreciation & amortization expense	2,700	
	Interest expense	1,500	
	Property, plant & equipment, net		2,700
	Notes payable		1,500

| [I_cogs] | Equity investment @ BOY | 9,000 | |
| | Cost of goods sold | | 9,000 |

| [I_sales] | Sales | 75,000 | |
| | Cost of goods sold | | 75,000 |

| [I_cogs] | Cost of goods sold | 12,000 | |
| | Inventories | | 12,000 |

| [I_pay] | Accounts payable | 15,000 | |
| | Accounts receivable | | 15,000 |

| [I_gain] | Equity investment @ BOY | 33,750 | |
| | Property, plant & equipment, net @ BOY | | 33,750 |

| [I_dep] | Property, plant & equipment, net | 3,750 | |
| | Depreciation expense | | 3,750 |

Consolidation Spreadsheet for the Year Ended December 31, 2016

	Parent	Subsidiary	Consolidation Entries Dr		Cr		Consolidated
Income statement:							
Sales	$1,080,000	$405,000	[I_sales]	$ 75,000			$1,410,000
Cost of goods sold	(648,000)	(243,000)	[I_cogs]	12,000	[I_cogs]	$ 9,000	(819,000)
					[I_sales]	75,000	
Gross profit.	432,000	162,000					591,000
Depreciation & amortization expense . . .	(27,000)	(21,600)	[D]	2,700	[I_dep]	3,750	(47,550)
Operating expenses	(339,000)	(81,150)					(420,150)
Interest expense	(12,000)	(5,250)	[D]	1,500			(18,750)
Total expenses	(378,000)	(108,000)					(486,450)
Income (loss) from subsidiary.	50,550	—	[C]	50,550			0
Consolidated net income	$ 104,550	$ 54,000					$ 104,550
Statement of retained earnings:							
BOY retained earnings	$ 640,350	$ 247,500	[E]	247,500			$ 640,350
Net income	104,550	54,000					104,550
	744,900	301,500					744,900
Dividends	(135,000)	(31,500)			[C]	31,500	(135,000)
Ending retained earnings	$ 609,900	$ 270,000					$ 609,900
Balance sheet:							
Cash	$ 87,120	$ 63,750					$150,870
Accounts receivable	121,500	90,000			[I_pay]	15,000	196,500
Inventories	292,500	137,250			[I_cogs]	12,000	417,750
Property, plant & equipment, net	283,500	202,500	[A]	16,200	[D]	2,700	469,500
			[I_dep]	3,750	[I_gain]	33,750	
Other assets	128,250	225,000					353,250
Patent							0
Equity investment	660,000		[I_cogs]	9,000	[C]	19,050	0
			[I_gain]	33,750	[E]	540,000	
					[A]	143,700	
Goodwill			[A]	126,000			126,000
Total assets.	$1,572,870	$718,500					$1,713,870
Accounts payable.	$ 252,000	$ 52,500	[I_pay]	15,000			$289,500
Notes payable	121,470	45,000	[A]	1,500	[D]	1,500	166,470
Other liabilities	49,500	58,500					108,000
Common stock.	540,000	292,500	[E]	292,500			540,000
Retained earnings	609,900	270,000					609,900
Total liabilities and equity	$1,572,870	$718,500		$886,950		$886,950	$1,713,870

COMPREHENSIVE REVIEW—COST METHOD SOLUTION

a. The trial balance information converted to financial statement format is presented, below. A completed consolidation spreadsheet is included in the solution to *Part f* of this comprehensive review.

Pre-Consolidation Financial Statements for the Year Ended December 31, 2016	Parent	Subsidiary
Income statement:		
Sales..	$1,000,000	$460,000
Cost of goods sold..	(550,000)	(280,000)
Gross profit..	450,000	180,000
Depreciation & amortization expense.......................	(30,000)	(20,000)
Operating expenses.......................................	(300,000)	(80,000)
Interest expense..	(15,000)	(5,000)
Total expenses..	(345,000)	(105,000)
Income (loss) from subsidiary.............................	35,000	
Net income..	$ 140,000	$ 75,000
Statement of retained earnings:		
BOY retained earnings.....................................	$ 550,000	$250,000
Net income..	140,000	75,000
Dividends...	(115,000)	(35,000)
Ending retained earnings..................................	$ 575,000	$290,000
Balance sheet:		
Assets		
Cash..	$ 90,000	$ 60,000
Accounts receivable.......................................	120,000	90,000
Inventory...	280,000	140,000
Equity investment...	640,000	
Property, plant & equipment, net..........................	340,000	240,000
Other assets..	130,000	220,000
Total assets..	$1,600,000	$750,000
Liabilities and stockholders' equity		
Accounts payable..	$ 250,000	$ 54,000
Accrued liabilities.......................................	125,000	46,000
Notes payable...	50,000	60,000
Common stock..	600,000	300,000
Retained earnings...	575,000	290,000
Total liabilities and equity.............................	$1,600,000	$750,000

b. Given the five-year time horizon between the acquisition date and the consolidated financial statement date, the following schedules separately document the annual AAP amortization and the year-end unamortized AAP balance for each year, 2012 through 2016.

		Year Ended December 31,			
100% AAP Amortization – Dr (Cr)	**2012**	**2013**	**2014**	**2015**	**2016**
Accounts receivable.	$ (8,000)	$ —	$ —	$ —	$ —
Property, plant & equipment (PPE), net	5,000	5,000	5,000	5,000	5,000
Patent.	10,000	10,000	10,000	10,000	10,000
Notes payable	1,000	1,000	1,000	1,000	1,000
Net amortization.	$ 8,000	$16,000	$16,000	$16,000	$16,000

			December 31,			
100% Unamortized AAP – Dr (Cr)	**Jan. 1, 2012**	**2012**	**2013**	**2014**	**2015**	**2016**
Accounts receivable.	$ (8,000)	$ —	$ —	$ —	$ —	$ —
Property, plant & equipment (PPE), net . . .	40,000	35,000	30,000	25,000	20,000	15,000
Patent.	60,000	50,000	40,000	30,000	20,000	10,000
Notes payable	5,000	4,000	3,000	2,000	1,000	—
Goodwill	100,000	100,000	100,000	100,000	100,000	100,000
Net amortization.	$197,000	$189,000	$173,000	$157,000	$141,000	$125,000

c. **Intercompany depreciable asset sale**:
One downstream asset sale.
Intercompany profit recognized on January 1, 2014: $100,000 − $80,000 = $20,000, 10-year remaining life
Profit confirmed each year: $20,000/10 = $2,000

	Downstream	**Upstream**
Net intercompany profit deferred at January 1, 2016	$16,000	$0
Less: Deferred intercompany profit recognized during 2016.	2,000	0
Net intercompany profit deferred at December 31, 2016	$14,000	$0

Intercompany inventory transactions:
Intercompany inventory sales during 2016: $50,000

	Downstream (in Subsidiary's inventory)	**Upstream (in Parent's inventory)**
Intercompany profit in inventory on January 1, 2016.	$0	$6,000
Intercompany profit in inventory on December 31, 2016.	$9,000	$0

Intercompany accounts receivables and payables at December 31, 2016: $16,000

d. **Amount of the beginning of year [ADJ] adjustment necessary for the consolidation of the financial statements for the year ended December 31, 2016:**

Change in retained earnings of subsidiary from acquisition date through BOY	$107,000
Cumulative AAP amortization from acquisition date through BOY	(56,000)
BOY downstream intercompany inventory profits.	—
BOY upstream intercompany inventory profits	(6,000)
BOY downstream unconfirmed asset gain.	(16,000)
BOY upstream unconfirmed asset gain	—
[ADJ] Amount	$29,000

e.

[ADJ]	BOY Equity Investment	29,000	
	BOY Retained Earnings (P)		29,000
[C]	Income (loss) from subsidiary.	35,000	
	Dividends.		35,000
[E]	BOY Common stock (S)	300,000	
	BOY Retained earnings (S).	250,000	
	Equity investment		550,000
[A]	Property, plant & equipment, net	20,000	
	Patent.	20,000	
	Goodwill	100,000	
	Notes payable	1,000	
	Equity investment		141,000
[D]	Depreciation & amortization expense.	15,000	
	Interest expense.	1,000	
	Property, plant & equipment, net.		5,000
	Patent		10,000
	Notes payable		1,000
[I_{cogs}]	Equity investment.	6,000	
	Cost of goods sold		6,000
[I_{sales}]	Sales	50,000	
	Cost of goods sold		50,000
[I_{cogs}]	Cost of goods sold.	9,000	
	Inventory		9,000
[I_{pay}]	Accounts payable.	16,000	
	Accounts receivable		16,000
[I_{gain}]	Equity investment.	16,000	
	Property, plant & equipment, net.		16,000
[I_{dep}]	Property, plant & equipment, net	2,000	
	Depreciation expense		2,000

Consolidation Spreadsheet for the Year Ended December 31, 2016

	Parent	Subsidiary	Consolidation entries Dr		Consolidation entries Cr		Consolidated
Income statement:							
Sales	$1,000,000	$460,000	[I_sales]	$ 50,000			$1,410,000
Cost of goods sold	(550,000)	(280,000)	[I_cogs]	9,000	[I_cogs]	$ 6,000	(783,000)
					[I_sales]	50,000	
Gross profit......................	450,000	180,000					627,000
Depreciation & amortization expense ...	(30,000)	(20,000)	[D]	15,000	[I_dep]	2,000	(63,000)
Operating expenses................	(300,000)	(80,000)					(380,000)
Interest expense..................	(15,000)	(5,000)	[D]	1,000			(21,000)
Total expenses	(345,000)	(105,000)					(464,000)
Income (loss) from subsidiary.........	35,000		[C]	35,000			0
Net income.......................	$ 140,000	$ 75,000					$ 163,000
Statement of retained earnings:							
BOY retained earnings..............	$ 550,000	$ 250,000	[E]	250,000	[ADJ]	29,000	$ 579,000
Net income.......................	140,000	75,000					163,000
Dividends	(115,000)	(35,000)			[C]	35,000	(115,000)
Ending retained earnings	$ 575,000	$290,000					$ 627,000
Balance sheet:							
Assets							
Cash..............................	$ 90,000	$ 60,000					$ 150,000
Accounts receivable...............	120,000	90,000			[I_pay]	16,000	194,000
Inventory	280,000	140,000			[I_cogs]	9,000	411,000
Equity investment	640,000		[ADJ]	29,000	[E]	550,000	0
			[I_cogs]	6,000	[A]	141,000	
			[I_gain]	16,000			
Property, plant & equipment, net	340,000	240,000	[A]	20,000	[D]	5,000	581,000
			[I_dep]	2,000	[I_gain]	16,000	
Other assets......................	130,000	220,000					350,000
Licenses			[A]	20,000	[D]	10,000	10,000
Goodwill			[A]	100,000			100,000
Total assets......................	$1,600,000	$750,000					$1,796,000
Liabilities and stockholders' equity							
Accounts payable..................	$ 250,000	$ 54,000	[I_pay]	16,000			$ 288,000
Accrued liabilities.................	125,000	46,000	[A]	1,000	[D]	1,000	171,000
Notes payable	50,000	60,000					110,000
Common stock....................	600,000	300,000	[E]	300,000			600,000
Retained earnings	575,000	290,000					627,000
Total liabilities and equity	$1,600,000	$750,000		$870,000		$870,000	$1,796,000

Consolidated Financial Statements with Less than 100% Ownership

5

According to **Alcoa, Inc.**'s December 31, 2014 Securities and Exchange Commission (SEC) Form 10-K, "Alcoa is a global leader in lightweight metals engineering and manufacturing. Alcoa's innovative, multi-material products, which include aluminum, titanium, and nickel, are used worldwide in aircraft, automobiles, commercial transportation, packaging, building and construction, oil and gas, defense, consumer electronics, and industrial applications. Alcoa is also the world leader in the production and management of primary aluminum, fabricated aluminum, and alumina combined, through its active participation in all major aspects of the industry: technology, mining, refining, smelting, fabricating, and recycling."

ALCOA, INC.

As noted by the company, "[a]luminum is one of the most plentiful elements in the earth's crust and is produced primarily from bauxite, an ore containing aluminum in the form of aluminum oxide, commonly referred to as alumina. Aluminum is made by extracting alumina from bauxite and then removing oxygen from the alumina. Alcoa processes most of the bauxite that it mines into alumina. The Company obtains bauxite from its own resources and from those belonging to **Alcoa World Alumina and Chemicals** (AWAC. . . During 2014, Alcoa consumed 40.8 million metric tons (mt) from AWAC and its own resources and 8.2 million mt from entities in which the Company has an equity interest. In addition, AWAC sold 1.6 million mt of bauxite to third parties."

According to Alcoa's 10-K and illustrated in the figure, below, AWAC is owned 60% by Alcoa and 40% by **Alumina Limited**.

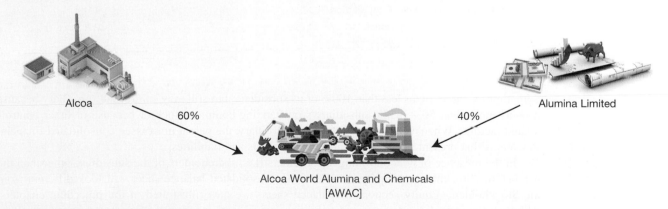

Alcoa 60% 40% Alumina Limited

Alcoa World Alumina and Chemicals
[AWAC]

Because Alcoa has a controlling interest in AWAC, Alcoa will consolidate 100% of the net assets of AWAC. However, because Alcoa only has a 60% economic interest in AWAC, Alcoa's consolidated balance sheet will also report a line item representing Alumina Limited's 40% equity in AWAC. Alumina Limited's interest is called a noncontrolling interest and is similar (in concept) to the equity interest of Alcoa's shareholders. The big difference is that Alcoa's Shareholders' Equity attributed to Alcoa's shareholders represents a 100% interest in all of Alcoa's non-AWAC net assets and a 60% interest in AWAC, while

(continued on next page)

(continued from previous page)

Alumina Limited's equity relates only to the 40% ownership interest in AWAC (none of Alumina Limited's interest is in the Alcoa parent company). Alcoa's 2014 SEC Form 10-K reflects the effects of this ownership structure, with noncontrolling interest increasing, totaling almost $2.5 billion, or almost 17% of Alcoa's total owners' equity.

Turning to Alcoa's income statement, a conceptually similar presentation format is evident. Because Alcoa owns a controlling interest in AWAC, 100% of AWAC's revenues and 100% of AWAC's expenses are presented in Alcoa's revenues and expenses line items. Of course, Alcoa, doesn't own 100% of AWAC, so Alcoa's income statement includes a line item "Net (loss) income attributable to noncontrolling interests," which represents Alumina Limited's 40% interest in the net income of AWAC. During the year ended December 31, 2014, the 40% interest in AWAC's net income yielded a $(91) million loss attributable to Alumina Limited. This means that AWAC's total loss must have been approximately $(227.5) million (i.e., $(91)/40% = $(227.5)). To complete the analysis, this also means that $(136.5) million of loss (i.e., $(227.5) × 60%) must be included in the bottom line "Net Income (Loss) Attributable to Alcoa." We will discuss the accounting for noncontrolling interests in this chapter.

Source: Alcoa Inc. December 31, 2014 SEC Form 10-K

CHAPTER ORGANIZATION

Consolidated Financial Statements with Less than 100% Ownership

Consolidation of Noncontrolling Interests

- Consolidation on the date of acquisition— majority-owned subsidiary
- Allocation of profit to controlling and noncontrolling interests and consolidation subsequent to acquisition—majority-owned subsidiary
- Consolidated income statement and balance sheet
- Consolidation subsequent to acquisition with intercompany inventory sales—Equity Method
- Consolidation subsequent to acquisition with intercompany depreciable asset sales—Equity Method
- Consolidation subsequent to acquisition with intercompany inventory sales and depreciable asset sales—Cost Method
- Suggested integrated approach for mastering complex consolidations

Additional Consolidation Topics

- Appendix 5A: Business Combinations and Alternative Measurements of Noncontrolling Interest (including IFRS)
- Appendix 5B: Consolidated Earnings Per Share
- Appendix 5C: Accounting for Changes in Ownership

Sometimes a parent owns less than 100% of its subsidiary, but still may *control* the subsidiary because it owns more than 50% of the subsidiary's outstanding common stock or because of other control-related factors.[1] Whenever a parent controls a subsidiary, the parent must issue consolidated financial statements that present 100% of the subsidiary's assets and liabilities.

In the presence of noncontrolling shareholders (i.e., shareholders of the subsidiary other than the parent), the Stockholders' Equity section of the consolidated balance sheet will look different from the Stockholders' Equity sections of balance sheets we have illustrated in the preceding chapters. Although the consolidated assets and liabilities remain unchanged in the presence of noncontrolling shareholders, the Stockholders' Equity section will clearly separate the interests of the two groups of shareholders:

---

[1] As we discuss in Chapter 2, "control" includes the percentage ownership of voting shares *and* other indicators such as representation on the board of directors, existence of licensing agreements and other contracts between the investor and investee companies, and the like.

- **Shareholders of the *parent company*** who have a claim on the net assets of the *total consolidated entity* by virtue of their ownership of the parent company, and

- **Noncontrolling shareholders of the *subsidiary*** who *only* have a claim on the net assets of the subsidiary (called **noncontrolling interests**, or NCI).[2]

To illustrate the concept of noncontrolling interests, assume that a parent company owns 80% of its subsidiary. The parent company shareholders own 100% of the parent company, which owns an 80% interest in the subsidiary. The noncontrolling interest holders own the remaining 20% of the subsidiary's common stock. The consolidated balance sheet reflects the ownership interests of the parent's shareholders through accounts that we have seen in the past: Common Stock, Additional Paid-In Capital, Retained Earnings, and Treasury Stock. The noncontrolling shareholders are also represented in the Stockholders' Equity section of the consolidated balance sheet with an account called Noncontrolling Interests.

Consolidated assets and liabilities remain the same in the presence of noncontrolling interests; only the Stockholders' Equity section changes. Similarly, consolidated revenues and expenses remain unchanged in the presence of noncontrolling shareholders. However, in the consolidated income statement, we need to allocate total consolidated net income into two subtotals:

- Consolidated net income that is *available to the parent's shareholders* and

- Consolidated net income *attributable to the noncontrolling shareholders.*

We provide guidelines for the reporting of noncontrolling interests in the balance sheet and the income statement in this chapter. We also explain the effects of noncontrolling interests on the elimination of deferred intercompany profits. Current GAAP requires all deferred intercompany profit to be completely eliminated during the consolidation process, but allows a choice of whether to allocate the deferred profit elimination to the noncontrolling interest (FASB ASC 810-10-45-18).

Accounting guidance relating to the initial measurement of noncontrolling interests is included in FASB ASC 805-20-30-7 and 805-20-30-8. Guidance related to presentation of consolidated financial statement information is included in FASB ASC 810-10.

Like the business combinations guidance included in FASB ASC 805, the consolidations guidance included in FASB ASC 810 is the product of a joint project between the FASB and the International Accounting Standards Board (IASB), which issued International Accounting Standard 27 (Revised 2007), *Consolidated and Separate Financial Statements* (IAS 27(R)). With limited exceptions, the principles in the FASB and IASB business combination and consolidation standards are the same. However, we describe one of the significant exceptions in an Appendix to this chapter.

BASICS OF CONSOLIDATING NONCONTROLLING INTERESTS

In this section, we illustrate the consolidation of a parent company and its subsidiary when the parent owns less than 100% of a subsidiary. We first review consolidation on the date of acquisition to show the adjustments necessary to account for the noncontrolling interest. Because the equity method and cost method are both pre-consolidation procedures applied to ***post-acquisition*** investment-related activity, on the acquisition date, there is no difference in the consolidation procedures if the parent decides to apply the equity method or the cost method. (Stated another way, on the acquisition date, there is no such thing as the equity method or cost method because they can only be applied to activity that occurs ***after*** the acquisition date.) Later in the chapter, we will separately discuss equity method and cost method consolidation procedures for ***post-acquisition*** consolidations.

---

[2] According to FASB ASC 810-10-45-16, the general principle is that noncontrolling interests are classified as equity in the consolidated financial statements. In our experience, this describes over 99 percent of the financial statements with which we are familiar. However, there are situations where the investment securities held by the noncontrolling interest have features that can cause the noncontrolling interest to be classified as a liability. According to the Securities and Exchange Commission *Accounting Series Release* (ASR) No. 268, *Presentation in Financial Statements of Redeemable Preferred Stocks*, "... equity instruments with redemption features that are not solely within the control of the issuer [must] be classified outside of permanent equity." Thus, noncontrolling interest in the consolidated balance sheet can be (albeit rarely) classified as a liability.

LO1 Explain consolidation on the date of acquisition for a non-wholly owned subsidiary.

Consolidation on Date of Acquisition—Parent Owns 80% of the Subsidiary

To illustrate the consolidation process in the presence of noncontrolling interests, let's begin by assuming that on January 1, 2016, a parent company acquires 80% of the outstanding common stock of its subsidiary for a purchase price of $1,570,000. On the acquisition date, the parent estimates that the 20% interest in the subsidiary that it does not own (the noncontrolling interest) has a market value of $380,000 (we discuss the valuation of the noncontrolling interest in the next section). The subsidiary, therefore, has a total market value on the date of acquisition of $1,950,000 ($1,570,000 + $380,000). Let us further assume that the book value of the subsidiary's Stockholders' Equity on the acquisition date is $1,000,000 and the parent determines that the fair value of the subsidiary's identifiable tangible and intangible assets is $1,800,000. Thus, the Acquisition Accounting Premium (AAP) is equal to $950,000 ($1,950,000 − $1,000,000). The parent estimates that the identifiable portion of the AAP is represented by the following two components:

	Identifiable AAP	Depreciation/ Amortization
1. Undervalued PPE, net	$500,000	$10,000
2. Unrecognized patent	300,000	30,000
Total	$800,000	$40,000

The subsidiary's Property, Plant and Equipment (PPE) balance is undervalued by $500,000. This is related to one of its buildings for which the appraised value is $500,000 more than the reported book value. The parent assigns a useful life of 50 years to this component of the AAP, resulting in annual (additional) depreciation expense of $10,000. The subsidiary also owns the rights to an unrecorded, internally developed patent that the parent values at $300,000. The parent assigns a useful life of 10 years to this patent, resulting in annual (additional) amortization expense of $30,000.

Given the AAP of $950,000 and the fair value of the identifiable portion of the AAP of $800,000, we know that the Goodwill asset in this example is $150,000. We are not quite done, however, as we must now apportion Goodwill between the parent's shareholders and the noncontrolling interests. This apportionment is necessary to properly allocate any future losses between the two groups should Goodwill become impaired.[3] In the next section, we discuss the process by which we apportion Goodwill.

Apportionment of Goodwill in the Presence of Noncontrolling Interests
Using the formula for the computation of Goodwill from Chapter 2, our computation of the Goodwill asset purchased requires an estimate of the fair value of the noncontrolling interest on the acquisition date (in this example, we are assuming this value to be $380,000).[4] The fair value of the noncontrolling interest can be determined in any reasonable manner, including the use of quoted market prices for the shares not owned if the subsidiary is a public company or using other valuation techniques such as discounted free cash flows, P/E multiples, etc. (FASB ASC 805-20-30-7).

FASB ASC 805-20-30-8 acknowledges that the per-share fair values of the parent's interest in the subsidiary and the noncontrolling interest might differ. The main difference is likely to be the inclusion of a *control premium* in the per-share fair value of the parent's interest in the subsidiary or, conversely, the inclusion of a *discount for lack of control* (sometimes called a noncontrolling interest discount) in the per-share fair value of the noncontrolling interest.[5]

[3] FASB ASC 350-20-35-57A requires the allocation of Goodwill impairment losses to the parent and the noncontrolling interests on a "rational basis," indicating that any impairment loss should be attributed to the parent and the noncontrolling interests using their relative interests *in the carrying value of the Goodwill*, not their relative ownership percentages in the subsidiary.

[4] In subsequent periods, the value of the noncontrolling interest is not remeasured. Instead, it is updated for the noncontrolling share of the profits earned less dividends received like the parent's Retained Earnings for the parent's controlling interest under the equity method.

[5] IFRS 3 (as revised in 2007) allows the investor a choice for each business combination to measure a noncontrolling interest either at its fair value or on the basis of its proportionate interest in the recognized amounts of the identifiable net assets of the investee company (IFRS 3, ¶19). We will discuss the implications of this difference in the Appendix to this chapter.

In Exhibit 5.1, we illustrate the allocation of the Goodwill asset, to the controlling and noncontrolling interests. An extremely important result in this exhibit is the fact that, given the purchase price assumptions in this example, *Goodwill was allocated to the controlling and noncontrolling interests in a proportion that does not equal an 80:20 split of the total Goodwill.* That is, if we were to multiply total Goodwill (i.e., $150,000) times the 80% controlling interest and the 20% noncontrolling interest, we would have calculated proportional Goodwill of $120,000 and $30,000, respectively. Instead, as we present in Exhibit 5.1, the actual amount of Goodwill allocated to the controlling interest is $130,000 and the allocation to the noncontrolling interest is $20,000. Bottom line: *the amount of Goodwill that is allocated to the controlling and noncontrolling interests is based on the separate fair values of each of those ownership interests that may not correspond with the proportion of the subsidiary's stock that they own.*[6]

Why does the allocated amount of Goodwill in Exhibit 5.1 deviate from a simple 80:20 (i.e., $120,000 for parent and $30,000 for subsidiary) split of the total amount of Goodwill? It's because, in our example, the fair value of the parent's investment includes a "control premium" equal to $50,000.[7,8] In this case, the parent paid a premium in order to obtain control, perhaps because it expected that increased competitive advantage or other synergies would result from the combination, to obtain entrance into an attractive market, to acquire valuable technology, or for any number of reasons typically cited in connection with acquisitions. Regardless of the motivation for the control premium paid, the implication is clear: should the parent pay a price that includes a control premium, it will also acquire a greater than proportional amount of the Goodwill asset.

EXHIBIT 5.1 Allocation of Goodwill to the Controlling and Noncontrolling Interests

100% of Subsidiary

①		$1,570,000	Fair value of controlling interest in subsidiary
②	+	380,000	The fair value of any noncontrolling interest in the subsidiary
	=	$1,950,000	Total fair value of the investee company
③	−	1,800,000	Fair value of the identifiable assets acquired and liabilities assumed
	=	$ 150,000	Goodwill (i.e., positive residual)

Allocation of Goodwill to Controlling Interest

Goodwill (Controlling Interest)
①   ③
= $1,570,000 − (80% × $1,800,000)
= $130,000

Allocation of Goodwill to Noncontrolling Interest

Goodwill (Noncontrolling Interest)
②   ③
= $380,000 − (20% × $1,800,000)
= $20,000

---

[6] Acquirers occasionally make "bargain purchases" in which the fair value of the total consideration transferred by the acquirer plus the fair value of the noncontrolling interest is less than the fair value of the identifiable net assets of the acquired entity. These bargain purchases can happen in cases where there is a forced sale or financial distress experienced by the acquired entity (e.g., this was not uncommon in the banking industry in the aftermath of the 2008 global credit crisis). As we noted in Chapter 3, in cases where our computations result in "negative goodwill," the acquirer recognizes the negative residual as an ordinary gain in its income statement on the acquisition date. In addition, FASB ASC 805-30-25-2 requires that 100% of the bargain purchase gain is attributed to the acquirer (i.e., controlling interest). Thus, this is an exception to the relative assignment of goodwill to the controlling and noncontrolling interests: the noncontrolling interest is allocated none of the bargain purchase gain.

[7] A **control premium** is an amount that a buyer is usually willing to pay over the current market price of a publicly traded company. This premium is usually justified by the expected synergies, such as the expected increase in cash flow resulting from cost savings and revenue enhancements achievable in the merger.

[8] Because the acquirer paid for control as an element of the overall cost of its 80% acquisition, the fair value of the control premium equals the total fair value of the controlling interest (i.e., $1,570,000) minus the 80% of the value of the subsidiary without the control premium. Using some basic algebra, we can solve for the control premium. Let's call the fair value of the control premium "x" and the fair value of the subsidiary without the control premium "y." We can then solve for x = $1,570,000 − .8y by substituting x + y = $1,950,000 (with a little rearrangement). In this case, we find that the control premium, or "x," equals $50,000 given the assumed value of $1,900,000 for y.

The Consolidation Process on the Date of Acquisition in the Presence of Noncontrolling Interests

The consolidation process is essentially the same as we have discussed previously, but the purchase of only 80% of the outstanding common stock adds one additional wrinkle to our consolidation: *we now need to account for the claim of the 20% noncontrolling shareholders in the subsidiary*. As we mentioned previously, there is no difference between equity method and cost method consolidation procedures on the acquisition date.

In Exhibit 5.2, we present our acquisition date consolidation spreadsheet using the apportionment of the AAP to the controlling and noncontrolling interests that we discuss above:

EXHIBIT 5.2 Acquisition Date Consolidation Spreadsheet in the Presence of Noncontrolling Interests

	Parent	Subsidiary	Consolidation Entries Dr	Consolidation Entries Cr	Consolidated
Balance sheet:					
Assets					
Cash..................................	$ 1,173,950	$ 311,250			$ 1,485,200
Accounts receivable..................	960,000	261,000			1,221,000
Inventory.............................	1,455,000	335,250			1,790,250
Equity investment....................	1,570,000			[E] $ 800,000	0
				[A] 770,000	
Property, plant and equipment (PPE), net	7,542,800	728,500	[A] $ 500,000		8,771,300
Patent................................			[A] 300,000		300,000
Goodwill			[A] 150,000		150,000
	$12,701,750	$1,636,000			$13,717,750
Liabilities and stockholders' equity					
Current liabilities.....................	$ 1,077,750	$ 261,000			$ 1,338,750
Long-term liabilities	3,750,000	375,000			4,125,000
Common stock........................	1,635,000	100,000	[E] 100,000		1,635,000
APIC.................................	1,215,000	125,000	[E] 125,000		1,215,000
Retained earnings	5,024,000	775,000	[E] 775,000		5,024,000
Noncontrolling interest................				[E] 200,000	380,000
				[A] 180,000	
	$12,701,750	$1,636,000	$1,950,000	$1,950,000	$13,717,750

Our [E] consolidation entry is as follows:

[E]	BOY retained earnings (S)	775,000	
	BOY common stock (S)	100,000	
	BOY APIC (S)	125,000	
	Equity investment ($1,000,000 × 80%)......................		800,000
	Noncontrolling interest ($1,000,000 × 20%)...................		200,000

(to eliminate the $1,000,000 BOY Stockholders' Equity of subsidiary, eliminate the 80% that the parent owns from its Equity Investment account and establish the BOY noncontrolling interest equity account for the 20% owned by noncontrolling interests)

The debit in the [E] entry removes 100% of the subsidiary's Stockholders' Equity, as we did in previous chapters. Now, however, only 80% of the subsidiary's $1,000,000 Stockholders' Equity is owned by the parent. Therefore, the credit to the Equity Investment account is $800,000 ($1,000,000 × 80%) because this account only represents the direct interest in the 80% controlled by the parent. The remaining $200,000 ($1,000,000 × 20%) corresponds to the 20% owned by the noncontrolling shareholders. *The credit to Noncontrolling Interest establishes a new account in the Stockholders' Equity section of the consolidated balance sheet, which represents the claim of the noncontrolling shareholders in the net assets of the subsidiary.*

Up until this point, the noncontrolling interest equity account only includes the noncontrolling share of the book value of the Stockholders' Equity of the subsidiary. The next entry will recognize the acquisition-date AAP assets and allocate the ownership interest in those assets to the controlling interests and the noncontrolling interests, respectively. The [A] entry is as follows:

[A]			
PPE, net	500,000	
Patent	300,000	
Goodwill	150,000	
Equity investment		770,000
Noncontrolling interest		180,000

(to recognize the BOY PPE, Goodwill, and Patent assets on the consolidated balance sheet, eliminate the portion owned by the parent from its Equity Investment account, and to credit the noncontrolling interest equity account for the portion of the [A] assets owned by the noncontrolling interests)

The AAP assigned to the PPE, Patent, and Goodwill assets is recorded as before. As we illustrate in Exhibit 5.2, only $770,000 ($800,000 identifiable AAP × 80% + $130,000 Goodwill allocated to the Parent), however, is included in the Equity Investment account on the parent's balance sheet.[9] The remaining credit of $180,000 is assigned to the noncontrolling interest equity account. Notice that the balance of the Noncontrolling Interest equity account is $380,000 ($200,000 from the [E] entry and $180,000 from the [A] entry). It is not a coincidence that this $380,000 is the parent's estimate of the acquisition date fair value of the noncontrolling ownership interest that we assumed at the outset of this example. In summary, the noncontrolling interest equity account appearing in consolidated Stockholders' Equity now reflects the interests of the noncontrolling shareholders in *both* the book value of the subsidiary's Stockholders' Equity and their 20% interest in the AAP assets that is not owned by the parent company.

Where is the $380,000 of noncontrolling interest reported in the Stockholders' Equity section of the consolidated balance sheet? FASB ASC 810-10-45-16 governs the presentation of noncontrolling interests in the equity section of the consolidated balance sheet: "The noncontrolling interest shall be reported in the consolidated statement of financial position within equity, separately from the parent's equity. That amount shall be clearly identified and labeled, for example, as *noncontrolling interest in subsidiaries* . . . An entity with noncontrolling interests in more than one subsidiary may present those interests in aggregate in the consolidated financial statements."[10]

POST-ACQUISITION CONSOLIDATION AND NONCONTROLLING INTERESTS—EQUITY METHOD

Recall from Chapters 3 and 4 that companies are allowed to apply any method of pre-consolidation investment bookkeeping. To recap, the advantage of the equity method—especially from a pedagogical point of view—is that the parent's pre-consolidation net income and owners' equity accounts are the same balances pre- and post-consolidation. The advantage of the cost method is that it is easy to apply to the pre-consolidation parent company books and results in the most efficient consolidation process. In this section, we discuss post-acquisition consolidation when the parent company uses the equity method of pre-consolidation investment bookkeeping. In the next section, we discuss post-acquisition consolidation when the parent company uses the cost method of pre-consolidation investment bookkeeping. It is important to keep in mind that, regardless of the post-acquisition, pre-consolidation

---

[9] Following is the calculation supporting the $770 versus $180 split:

	100% AAP	80% AAP	20% AAP
PPE	$500	$400 *	$100 **
Patent	300	240 *	60 **
Goodwill	150	130 ***	20 ***
	$950	$770	$180

* Equals 80% x 100% identifiable AAP value

** Equals 20% x 100% identifiable AAP value

*** The goodwill split is calculated in Exhibit 5.1

[10] As we note in Footnote 2, there are rare exceptions where noncontrolling interest is classified as a liability.

bookkeeping approach, the consolidated financial statements (i.e., the end product of consolidation) will always look identical to any other approach.

Allocation of Profit to Controlling and Noncontrolling Interests and Consolidation Subsequent to Acquisition—Parent Owns 80% of the Subsidiary—Equity Method

LO2 Explain allocation of profit to controlling and noncontrolling interests and consolidation subsequent to the date of acquisition for a non-wholly owned subsidiary.

We will continue with the preceding example to now examine the consolidation *subsequent* to the acquisition. Assume that, during the year ended December 31, 2016, the subsidiary reports net income of $210,000 and pays dividends of $21,000 (i.e., $16,800 or 80% to the parent and $4,200 or 20% to the noncontrolling shareholders). Finally, 80% ($32,000) of the $40,000 of annual depreciation/amortization expense relating to the identifiable AAP assets will be recognized by the parent (under the equity method) in its accounting for the Equity Investment and the remaining 20% ($8,000) of that expense will be chargeable to the noncontrolling interests (in the consolidated financial statements).

Based on these assumptions, under the equity method, the parent reports the following entries in its Equity Investment account:

Equity investment...	168,000	
Income (loss) from subsidiary		168,000
(to record the 80% proportionate share of Equity Income on subsidiary net income of $210,000)		
Cash	16,800	
Equity investment		16,800
(to record the intercompany dividend received from subsidiary)		
Income (loss) from subsidiary................................	32,000	
Equity investment		32,000
(to record the parent's 80% portion of the depreciation and amortization of the total AAP)		

At the end of the year, the Equity Investment account on the parent's balance sheet is reported at $1,689,200, and its T-account representation reflects the following components (all changes in the account are included in the preceding equity method entries):

Equity Investment			
Beg. Balance	1,570,000		
Income (loss) from subsidiary ($210,000 × 80%)	168,000	32,000	Amortization of AAP assets ($40,000 × 80%)
		16,800	Dividends received
End Balance	1,689,200		

Net Equity Income for the year ended December 31, 2016, equals $136,000 (i.e., $168,000 − $32,000). In a similar manner, we can update the balance of the Noncontrolling Interest equity in the company:

Noncontrolling Interest			
Beg. Balance		380,000	
Amortization of AAP assets ($40,000 × 20%)	8,000	42,000	Allocation of profit attributable to noncontrolling interests ($210,000 × 20%)
Dividends received	4,200		
End Balance		409,800	

The noncontrolling interest equity reports a balance of $380,000 at the beginning of the year. During the year, it increases by the allocation of profit attributable to the noncontrolling shareholders ($210,000 × 20% = $42,000), decreases by the amortization of the AAP assets attributable to the noncontrolling shareholders ($40,000 × 20% = $8,000), and decreases by the dividends declared and paid to the noncontrolling interests by the subsidiary ($4,200). The ending balance of Noncontrolling

Interests equity in the amount of $409,800 is reported separately in the Stockholders' Equity section of the consolidated balance sheet.

It is important to note that the noncontrolling shareholders have an interest only in the subsidiary company. As a result, the amount of profit that is attributable to them is equal to the proportion of the shares in the subsidiary that they own.[11] Since the subsidiary reports net income of $210,000 in this case, the profit attributable to the noncontrolling interests is equal to 20% of that amount, or $42,000. In a similar manner, the noncontrolling interests are also allocated 20% of the amortization expense related to the AAP assets, $8,000 ($40,000 × 20%) in this case.

As we discuss above, the $150,000 Goodwill asset was allocated $130,000 to the parent's interest and $20,000 to the noncontrolling interests. Neither the controlling nor the noncontrolling portions of Goodwill are amortized. Instead, Goodwill is tested annually for impairment, and is written down if found to be impaired. That charge, if realized, will be allocated to the parent's shareholders and the noncontrolling interests in proportion to the percentage of the Goodwill that has been allocated to them, not in proportion to their respective ownership interests.

In Exhibit 5.3, we present our consolidation spreadsheet at the end of the year in the presence of noncontrolling interests.

Our five basic **C-E-A-D-I** entries are a little more complex because of the noncontrolling interest. However, they are fundamentally the same:

[C]	Income (loss) from subsidiary	136,000		Eliminates all *changes* in the Equity Investment and Noncontrolling Interest accounts during the consolidation period. The NCI credit includes the net income attributable to the NCI less the dividends paid to the NCI.
	Consol. NI attributable to NCI	34,000		
	Dividends		21,000	
	Equity investment		119,200	
	Noncontrolling interest ($34,000 − $4,200)		29,800	
[E]	Common stock @ BOY	100,000		Eliminates subsidiary Stockholders' Equity @ BOY. The credit to the Equity Investment eliminates the BOY balance recognized in the parent's Equity Investment account. The credit to the Noncontrolling Interest equity account establishes its balance @ BOY.
	APIC @BOY	125,000		
	Retained earnings @ BOY	775,000		
	Equity investment − @ BOY ($1,000,000 × 80%)		800,000	
	Noncontrolling interest @ BOY ($1,000,000 × 20%)		200,000	
[A]	PPE, net − @ BOY (100% AAP)	500,000		The debits recognize the BOY AAP ($950,000 @ BOY) on the consolidated balance sheet. The credits eliminate the parent's share of the BOY AAP from its Equity Investment account and recognize the noncontrolling interests' share of the AAP in the NCI equity account. [Note that the allocation of the 100% AAP is equal to the split calculated in footnote 9.]
	Patent @ BOY (100% AAP)	300,000		
	Goodwill @ BOY (100% AAP)	150,000		
	Equity investment − @ BOY (see footnote 9.)		770,000	
	Noncontrolling interest (see footnote 9.)		180,000	
[D]	Operating expenses (AAP amort)	40,000		The debit to Operating Expenses recognizes depreciation/amortization expense relating to the identifiable AAP assets, and the credits to PPE, net and Patent, adjust the balances to reflect their correct end-of-year totals.
	PPE, net (for 100% AAP amort)		10,000	
	Patent (for 100% AAP amort)		30,000	
[I]	Not applicable in this example (we cover this topic later in the chapter)			

---

[11] If there are contractual arrangements that determine the attribution of earnings, such as a profit-sharing agreement, the attribution specified by the arrangement should be considered. If there are no such contractual arrangements, the relative ownership interests should be used if the parent's ownership and the NCI's ownership in the assets and liabilities are proportional. For example, if the controlling interest owns 80%, and the NCI owns 20%, then 80% of the subsidiary's earnings will be allocated to the controlling interest and 20% to the NCI. If, however, the parties have a contractual arrangement specifying a 50/50 split of the earnings, then 50% of the earnings would be allocated to the controlling interest and 50% to the noncontrolling interest, regardless of the ownership percentage.

EXHIBIT 5.3	Consolidation Spreadsheet at the End of the Year in the Presence of Noncontrolling Interests

	Parent	Subsidiary	Consolidation Entries Dr	Consolidation Entries Cr	Consolidated
Income statement:					
Sales.	$10,000,000	$1,500,000			$11,500,000
Cost of goods sold.	(7,000,000)	(900,000)			(7,900,000)
Gross profit.	3,000,000	600,000			3,600,000
Income (loss) from subsidiary.	136,000		[C] $ 136,000		0
Operating expenses.	(1,900,000)	(390,000)	[D] 40,000		(2,330,000)
Consolidated net income	1,236,000	210,000			1,270,000
Consolidated NI attributable to NCI.			[C] 34,000		(34,000)
Consolidated NI attributable to parent.	$ 1,236,000	$ 210,000			$ 1,236,000
Statement of retained earnings:					
BOY retained earnings.	$ 5,024,000	$ 775,000	[E] 775,000		$ 5,024,000
Consolidated NI attributable to parent.	1,236,000	210,000			1,236,000
Dividends	(247,200)	(21,000)		[C] $ 21,000	(247,200)
Ending retained earnings	$ 6,012,800	$ 964,000			$ 6,012,800
Balance sheet:					
Assets					
Cash.	$ 1,058,600	$ 415,000			$ 1,473,600
Accounts receivable.	1,280,000	348,000			1,628,000
Inventory.	1,940,000	447,000			2,387,000
Equity investment.	1,689,200			[C] 119,200	0
				[E] 800,000	
				[A] 770,000	
Property, plant and equipment (PPE), net	9,332,000	827,000	[A] 500,000	[D] 10,000	10,649,000
Patent.			[A] 300,000	[D] 30,000	270,000
Goodwill			[A] 150,000		150,000
	$15,299,800	$2,037,000			$16,557,600
Liabilities and stockholders' equity					
Current liabilities.	$ 1,437,000	$ 348,000			$ 1,785,000
Long-term liabilities	5,000,000	500,000			5,500,000
Common stock.	1,635,000	100,000	[E] 100,000		1,635,000
APIC	1,215,000	125,000	[E] 125,000		1,215,000
Retained earnings	6,012,800	964,000			6,012,800
Noncontrolling interest				[C] 29,800	409,800
				[E] 200,000	
				[A] 180,000	
	$15,299,800	$2,037,000	$2,160,000	$2,160,000	$16,557,600

Allocation of Losses to the Noncontrolling Interest

In our example above, the subsidiary is profitable and, as a result, the Equity Investment on the parent's balance sheet and the Noncontrolling Interest equity account on the consolidated balance sheet will likely increase. It is not always the case, however, that subsidiaries are profitable, and should the subsidiary report losses, it is conceivable that its Stockholders' Equity might become negative. We address this issue for the parent's Equity Investment account in Chapter 1. In this section, we address the impact of subsidiary losses on the accounting for noncontrolling interests.

FASB ASC 810-10-45-21 provides that we should continue to allocate losses to both the controlling and noncontrolling equity *even if such allocation results in a deficit equity balance.* This was one of the more controversial provisions of the FASB ASC rules introduced in SFAS 160. Many respondents to the draft of this standard commented that a deficit equity balance usually implies a continuing obligation to invest more equity capital into the business should earnings not improve, and the noncontrolling interests do not have the same compulsion to preserve the subsidiary that the parent does.

The FASB described its reasoning as follows (SFAS 160, ¶B42): "although it is true that the noncontrolling interest has no further obligation to contribute assets to the subsidiary, neither does the parent. A parent also can choose to abandon its investment in a subsidiary. The attribution of losses should not change because one party might be more likely to provide additional capital for the subsidiary to continue operations. Even if the parent is more likely to contribute capital to a less-than-wholly owned subsidiary, it is unlikely to do so without receiving anything in return. That is, if a parent contributes capital to a subsidiary, the parent would likely receive additional ownership interests in the subsidiary or something else in return for its additional investment. Both the parent and the noncontrolling interests will bear the costs of an underperforming subsidiary, and their respective equity balances would be proportionately affected."[12]

Consolidated Income Statement

FASB ASC 810-10-45-19 and -20 state the following: "Revenues, expenses, gains, losses, net income or loss, and other comprehensive income shall be reported in the consolidated financial statements at the consolidated amounts, which include the amounts attributable to the owners of the parent and the noncontrolling interest."

Using the information from our consolidation spreadsheet in Exhibit 5.3, the consolidated income statement that the parent will send to shareholders and the SEC looks like this:[13,14]

Consolidated Income Statement	
Sales.	$11,500,000
Cost of goods sold.	(7,900,000)
Gross profit.	3,600,000
Operating expenses.	(2,330,000)
Consolidated net income.	1,270,000
Consolidated net income attributable to noncontrolling interests.	(34,000)
Consolidated net income attributable to parent.	$ 1,236,000

Note that the consolidated net income attributable to parent (i.e., after attribution to noncontrolling shareholders) equals the net income of the parent. This will always be the case so long as the parent uses the equity method to account for its Equity Investment because Equity Income includes the parent's proportionate share of the subsidiary net income, including the depreciation and amortization of AAP assets and the deferral of gains (losses) on intercompany asset sales. In the consolidation process, the Equity Income account is replaced by the sales, expenses, and profit of the subsidiary to which it relates.

---

[12] You may have noticed an inconsistency between the attribution of losses to controlling and noncontrolling interests and our discussion of the equity method of accounting for Equity Investments in Chapter 1. In our discussion of the Equity Investment account, we observed that there is a relation between the Equity Investment balance and the balance of the investee company's Stockholders' Equity, and we commented that the Equity Investment balance cannot fall below zero. When the Stockholders' Equity of the investee company falls below zero, the accounting for the Equity Investment using the equity method must stop until the investee's Stockholders' Equity becomes positive.

Allowing for the attribution of losses to the controlling and noncontrolling interests may result in a negative Stockholders' Equity for the subsidiary, but the Equity Investment on the parent's and the noncontrolling interests' balance sheets cannot fall below zero. FASB's only comment was, "While the Board acknowledges the inconsistency, considering the investor's accounting for an investment in a nonconsolidated entity was outside the scope of this project" (SFAS 160, ¶B43).

[13] Prior to fiscal years beginning after December 31, 2008, net income attributable to the noncontrolling interest was reported as an *expense* in arriving at consolidated net income. In addition, the line item to which we currently refer as "Consolidated net income attributable to parent," was the bottom-line "consolidated net income" number in financial statements issued before fiscal years beginning after December 31, 2008. Thus, current GAAP includes more of an entity perspective in the determination of entity-wide net income, with an allocation of that income number to controlling and noncontrolling investors.

[14] We discuss the computation of consolidated earnings per share in Appendix B.

Here is an important point: *only the net income attributed to the parent is included in the updating of consolidated Retained Earnings* (the portion of net income attributed to noncontrolling interests is included in the determination of the consolidated Noncontrolling Interest equity account that we describe in the next section). Our reconciliation of consolidated Retained Earnings is as follows:

BOY retained earnings	$5,024,000
Consolidated net income attributable to parent. . .	1,236,000
Dividends	(247,200)
EOY retained earnings	$6,012,800

Notice that only the dividends declared and paid *by the parent to its shareholders* are included in the updating of consolidated Retained Earnings. The portion of the dividends declared and paid by the subsidiary to its parent is treated as a reduction of the Equity Investment account and is eliminated in the [C] consolidation entry. And, the portion of the dividends declared and paid by the subsidiary to the noncontrolling shareholders is treated as a reduction of the Noncontrolling Interest equity account.

Another extremely important point to recognize is that the consolidated Retained Earnings statement includes account balances and activities that are identical to the parent company's pre-consolidation balances and activities. This relation exists whenever the parent company applies the equity method to account for its Equity Investment in the subsidiary company.

Consolidated Balance Sheet

Using the information from our consolidation spreadsheet in Exhibit 5.3, the consolidated balance sheet that the parent will send to shareholders and the SEC looks like this:

Consolidated Balance Sheet				
Assets		Current liabilities	$ 1,785,000	
Cash	$ 1,473,600	Long-term liabilities	5,500,000	
Accounts receivable	1,628,000	Total liabilities	7,285,000	
Inventory	2,387,000	Common stock	1,635,000	
Property, plant and equipment (PPE), net . . .	10,649,000	APIC	1,215,000	
Patent	270,000	Retained earnings	6,012,800	
Goodwill	150,000	Noncontrolling interest	409,800	
		Total equity	9,272,600	
Total assets	$16,557,600	Total liabilities and equity	$16,557,600	

Our consolidated balance sheet now reflects an additional equity account, Noncontrolling Interest, with a balance of $409,800 that is computed as follows:

Noncontrolling Interest Equity "Account"		
	Beginning balance (fair value at acquisition date)	$380,000
+	Net income attributable to noncontrolling interests	34,000
−	Dividends declared and paid to noncontrolling shareholders	(4,200)
	Ending balance	$409,800

The Noncontrolling Interest equity account is reported on the consolidated balance sheet separately from the parent's equity, and should be clearly identified and labeled.[15]

---

[15] In fiscal years prior to years beginning after December 15, 2008, noncontrolling interest equity (sometimes called *minority interest*) was presented between liabilities and equity, in an area informally called "the *mezzanine*" section of the balance sheet (neither a liability nor equity). Current GAAP virtually always treats noncontrolling interest as an equity account.

TOPIC REVIEW 1

Consolidation subsequent to acquisition—Equity method, noncontrolling interest, and AAP

Assume that a parent company acquires an 80% interest in its subsidiary for a purchase price that was $300,000 over the book value of the subsidiary's Stockholders' Equity on January 1, 2013. On the acquisition date, the parent assigned the excess fair value to the following [A] assets:

AAP Item	Initial Fair Value	Useful Life
Property, plant and equipment (PPE)...................	$200,000	20 years
Patent..	100,000	10 years
	$300,000	

The parent and the subsidiary report the following financial statements for the year ended December 31, 2016:

	Parent	Subsidiary		Parent	Subsidiary
Income statement:			**Balance sheet:**		
Sales.....................	$7,330,000	$1,000,500	Assets		
Cost of goods sold...........	(5,131,000)	(600,300)	Cash..............	$1,007,384	$ 302,902
Gross profit................	2,199,000	400,200	Accounts receivable...	938,240	232,116
Income (loss) from subsidiary...	96,056		Inventory............	1,422,020	298,149
Operating expenses..........	(1,392,700)	(260,130)	Equity investment.....	804,848	
Net income.................	$ 902,356	$ 140,070	PPE, net	5,374,356	685,009
				$9,546,848	$1,518,176
Statement of retained earnings:					
BOY retained earnings........	$3,682,592	$ 516,925	Liabilities and stockholders' equity		
Net income.................	902,356	140,070	Current liabilities......	$1,053,321	$ 232,116
Dividends	(180,471)	(21,010)	Long-term liabilities ...	2,000,000	500,000
EOY retained earnings........	$4,404,477	$ 635,985	Common stock.......	1,198,455	66,700
			APIC..............	890,595	83,375
			Retained earnings	4,404,477	635,985
				$9,546,848	$1,518,176

Required

Prepare the consolidation spreadsheet for the year ended December 31, 2016.

The solution to this review problem can be found on page 372.

Intercompany Profit Elimination in Consolidated Financial Statements in the Presence of Noncontrolling Interests—Equity Method

We now turn our attention to the effect of noncontrolling interests on the elimination of intercompany profits and losses. As we discuss in Chapter 4, FASB ASC 810-10-45-18 states that "complete elimination of the intra-entity [i.e., intercompany] income or loss is consistent with the underlying assumption that consolidated financial statements represent the financial position and operating results of a single economic entity." This means that regardless of the direction of the sale, we are required to completely eliminate the Sales, Cost of Goods Sold or intercompany-asset-transaction gains or losses, and to defer any of the related profit on the intercompany sale until the assets have been resold outside of the consolidated group. (i.e., for inventory and land) or otherwise consumed via depreciation and amortization (i.e., for depreciable assets). This is the same approach we use in Chapter 4 in our discussion of intercompany asset sales, and the presence of noncontrolling interests does not change it.

LO3 Explain intercompany profit elimination in consolidated financial statements in the presence of noncontrolling interests when the parent uses the equity method of pre-consolidation investment bookkeeping.

FASB ASC 810-10-45-18 suggests that the "elimination of the intercompany income or loss may be allocated proportionately between the parent and noncontrolling interests."[16] In the presence of noncontrolling interests, *downstream* intercompany asset sales present no additional issues for the consolidation process when compared to wholly owned subsidiaries. *Upstream* sales do, however, as they affect subsidiary profit and, as a result, the allocation of recognized profit to the controlling and noncontrolling shareholders (remember, the noncontrolling shareholders have an equity interest in the subsidiary, not the parent). In summary, deferred profit on intercompany asset sales results in the following treatment in the consolidated financial statements:

1. *100% elimination of* **deferred profit** *and intercompany transactions.* This always occurs regardless of the direction of the intercompany sale (i.e., upstream versus downstream).

2. *Prorata allocation of* **deferred profit** *to the parent and noncontrolling interests.* Procedurally, prorata allocation will only result in allocation of deferred profit to the noncontrolling interest on *upstream* sales.[17]

Intercompany Profit Elimination for Upstream Inventory Sales—Equity Method

To illustrate the consolidation process with noncontrolling interests and *upstream* continuous intercompany inventory sales, we will continue with the post-acquisition consolidation example that we completed in Exhibit 5.3. In this example, we also assume the following additional facts relating to the *upstream* intercompany sales of inventories:

	Prior Period	Current Period
Transfer price for inventory sale	$300,000	$400,000
Cost of goods sold	230,000	320,000
Gross profit	$ 70,000	$ 80,000
Percentage of inventory remaining	25%	35%
Gross profit deferred	$ 17,500	$ 28,000
Intercompany receivable/payable at end of period (paid in beginning of next period)	$ 90,000	$100,000

The subsidiary has recorded the sale of inventory in the usual manner and its financial statements correctly reflect the profit on the sale. Since the entities are not independent, however, the profit must be deferred in the consolidation process and recognized only when the inventory has been sold to outside parties. As a result we must first adjust the subsidiary's reported profit to reflect this deferral and subsequent recognition so that we can properly allocate the subsidiary's profit to controlling and noncontrolling interests as follows:

Subsidiary net income (as reported)	$210,000	
Recognition of prior year gain	17,500	
Deferral of current period gain	(28,000)	
AAP depreciation/amortization	(40,000)	
Adjusted subsidiary net income	$159,500	
Allocation:		
Parent	$127,600	80%
Subsidiary	31,900	20%
Adjusted subsidiary net income	$159,500	

---

[16] Although current GAAP affords companies the choice of whether to allocate the elimination of deferred intercompany profit (DIP), we believe prorata allocation to the controlling and noncontrolling interests is conceptually superior. In particular, the entity approach to consolidations in current GAAP (i.e., noncontrolling interests are considered part of consolidated companies' equity) suggests that none of the entities (or interests therein) in the consolidated group should recognize profits on inter-affiliate transactions. Therefore, for the rest of this book, we will allocate DIP elimination to the parent and noncontrolling interests.

[17] Allocation of deferred profit to the noncontrolling interest only occurs on upstream sales because the noncontrolling interest owns a percentage of the *subsidiary* and owns 0% of the parent.

The adjusted subsidiary profit reflects the recognition of the prior year deferral of the profit relating to the intercompany upstream sale of inventory and its recognition in the current year under the assumption that the inventory has now been sold to outside parties. When we are finished with our consolidation, the amount of consolidated Net Income Attributable to the Noncontrolling Interest should be equal to $31,900. Exhibit 5.4 presents the consolidation spreadsheet including the C-E-A-D-I entries. The detailed consolidation entries are provided on the following page.

| EXHIBIT 5.4 | Consolidation Spreadsheet Reflecting Continuous Upstream Intercompany Inventory Sales in Presence of Noncontrolling Interest—Equity Method |

			Consolidation Entries		
	Parent	Subsidiary	Dr	Cr	Consolidated
Income statement:					
Sales.	$10,000,000	1,500,000	[I_{sales}] $ 400,000		$11,100,000
Cost of goods sold.	(7,000,000)	(900,000)	[I_{cogs}] 28,000	[I_{cogs}] $ 17,500	(7,510,500)
				[I_{sales}] 400,000	
Gross profit.	3,000,000	600,000			3,589,500
Income (loss) from subsidiary. . . .	127,600		[C] 127,600		0
Operating expenses.	(1,900,000)	(390,000)	[D] 40,000		(2,330,000)
Consolidated net income	1,227,600	210,000			1,259,500
Consolidated NI attributable to NCI. . . .			[C] 31,900		(31,900)
Consolidated NI attributable to parent. . . .	$ 1,227,600	$ 210,000			$ 1,227,600
Statement of retained earnings:					
BOY retained earnings*	$ 5,010,000	$ 775,000	[E] 775,000		$ 5,010,000
Consolidated NI attributable to parent. . . .	1,227,600	210,000			1,227,600
Dividends	(247,200)	(21,000)		[C] 21,000	(247,200)
Ending retained earnings	$ 5,990,400	$ 964,000			$ 5,990,400
Balance sheet:					
Assets					
Cash.	$ 1,058,600	$ 415,000			$ 1,473,600
Accounts receivable. . . .	1,280,000	348,000		[I_{pay}] 100,000	1,528,000
Inventory.	1,940,000	447,000		[I_{cogs}] 28,000	2,359,000
Equity investment. . . .	1,666,800		[I_{cogs}] 14,000 [C] 110,800		0
			[E] 800,000		
			[A] 770,000		
Property, plant and equipment (PPE), net	9,332,000	827,000	[A] 500,000 [D] 10,000		10,649,000
Patent.			[A] 300,000 [D] 30,000		270,000
Goodwill			[A] 150,000		150,000
	$15,277,400	$2,037,000			$16,429,600
Liabilities and stockholders' equity					
Current liabilities. . . .	$ 1,437,000	$ 348,000	[I_{pay}] 100,000		$ 1,685,000
Long-term liabilities	5,000,000	500,000			5,500,000
Common stock. . . .	1,635,000	100,000	[E] 100,000		1,635,000
APIC	1,215,000	125,000	[E] 125,000		1,215,000
Retained earnings	5,990,400	964,000			5,990,400
Noncontrolling interest. . . .			[I_{cogs}] 3,500 [C] 27,700		404,200
			[E] 200,000		
			[A] 180,000		
	$15,277,400	$2,037,000	$2,695,000	$2,695,000	$16,429,600

* The parent's Retained Earnings have been reduced by $14,000 to reflect its share of the deferred profit on the intercompany inventory sale ($17,500 × 80% = $14,000).

Our consolidation entries are as follows:

[C]	Income (loss) from subsidiary.....................	127,600		Eliminates all changes in the book value of the Equity Investment and establishes the changes in the book value of the noncontrolling interest accounts during the consolidation period
	Consol. NI attributable to NCI	31,900		
	Dividends.................................		21,000	
	Equity investment		110,800	
	Noncontrolling interest		27,700	
[E]	Common stock @ BOY	100,000		Eliminates subsidiary Stockholders' Equity @ BOY. The credit to the Equity Investment eliminates the BOY balance recognized in the parent's Equity Investment account. The credit to the Noncontrolling Interest equity account establishes its balance @ BOY.
	APIC @ BOY..................................	125,000		
	Retained earnings @ BOY	775,000		
	Equity investment @ BOY		800,000	
	Noncontrolling interest @ BOY		200,000	
[A]	PPE, net @ BOY (100% AAP)......................	500,000		The debits recognize the BOY AAP ($950,000 @ BOY) on the consolidated balance sheet. The credits eliminate the parent's share of the BOY AAP from its Equity Investment account and recognize the noncontrolling interests' share of the AAP in the NCI equity account. [Note that the allocation of the 100% AAP is equal to the split calculated in Exhibit 5.2.]
	Patent @ BOY (100% AAP)	300,000		
	Goodwill @ BOY (100% AAP).....................	150,000		
	Equity investment − @ BOY (80%)		770,000	
	Noncontrolling interest (20%)		180,000	
[D]	Operating expenses (for 100% AAP amort)............	40,000		The debit to Operating Expenses recognizes depreciation/amortization expense relating to the identifiable AAP assets, and the credits to PPE, net and Patent, adjust the balances to reflect their correct end-of-year totals.
	PPE, net (for 100% AAP amort)...............		10,000	
	Patent (for 100% AAP amort)		30,000	
[I$_{cogs}$]	Equity investment @ BOY	14,000		The deferred profit from the prior period is included in consolidated net income in the year in which the intercompany assets are sold to non-affiliates. As we describe in Chapter 4, for inventory transactions, deferred profit is ultimately included in consolidated net income via a reduction in cost of goods sold. The adjustments to BOY Equity Investment and BOY Noncontrolling Interest are necessary because last period's (1) Consolidated Net Income Attributable to the parent and (2) Consolidated Net Income Attributable to the Noncontrolling Interest were $14,000 and $3,500, respectively lower than the amounts based on the reported income of the subsidiary. Because these prior-year consolidation adjustments are not actually recorded, we need to adjust beginning balances of Equity Investment and Noncontrolling Interest so that they agree with last year's ending balances. This 80%/20% split between the parent and Noncontrolling Interest occurs because we allocate upstream deferred profit to the two sets of shareholders on a prorata basis.
	Noncontrolling interest @ BOY....................	3,500		
	Cost of goods sold		17,500	
[I$_{sales}$]	Sales	400,000		We always eliminate 100% of all intercompany transactions. Note: this entry has no effect on net income.
	Cost of goods sold		400,000	
[I$_{cogs}$]	Cost of goods sold............................	28,000		Consistent with the elimination of deferred profit which we describe in Chapter 4, we eliminate 100% of the deferred profit included on the balance sheet (i.e., this is the 100% elimination).
	Inventory		28,000	
[I$_{pay}$]	Accounts payable..............................	100,000		Elimination of intercompany receivable and payable.
	Accounts receivable		100,000	

The deferral and subsequent recognition of gains on intercompany asset sales affects the subsidiary net income that is attributable to controlling and noncontrolling interests. In the case of *upstream* intercompany transactions, the elimination and subsequent recognition of deferred profit is allocated to the noncontrolling interest in proportion to the percentage ownership. This allocation affects the net income attributable to the parent and subsidiary as we illustrate above. The only differences between this example and the example we illustrate in Exhibit 5.3 (no intercompany sale of inventory) are in the [C] and [I] entries.

We next consider the comparative effects of *downstream* transactions. In this case, the deferral of profit only affects the parent, not the noncontrolling interests.

Comparison of Upstream to Downstream Profit Elimination—Equity Method

In order to simplify the comparison of the downstream sale of inventory with the upstream case we discuss in the preceding section, we keep all of the assumptions the same except that we now reverse the direction of the intercompany sales, now assuming that they were *downstream* transactions. That is, we will not change the pre-consolidation amounts of sales and expenses for the parent and subsidiary (i.e., all *pre-consolidation* information is identical to the parent and subsidiary information presented in Exhibit 5.4).

Here's the important point: **since the parent is recording the intercompany sale, all of the profit relating to that sale is reflected in the parent's books, and the net income that is attributed to the noncontrolling interests is unaffected.** As a result, the adjusted subsidiary net income and the allocation of that net income to the parent's shareholders and the noncontrolling interests only reflects the amortization of the AAP as follows:

Subsidiary net income (as reported)	$210,000	
AAP depreciation/amortization	(40,000)	
Adjusted subsidiary net income	$170,000	
Allocation:		
Parent	$136,000	80%
Subsidiary	34,000	20%
Adjusted subsidiary net income	$170,000	

This schedule tells us that when we are finished with our consolidation, the amount of Consolidated Net Income Attributable to the Noncontrolling Interest should be equal to $34,000.

Exhibit 5.5 presents the consolidation spreadsheet including the **C-E-A-D-I** entries for the *downstream* case.

Our consolidation entries are as follows:

[C]	Income (loss) from subsidiary	125,500	
	Consol. NI attributable to NCI	34,000	
	Dividends		21,000
	Equity investment		108,700
	Noncontrolling interest		29,800

Eliminates all changes in the Equity Investment accounts and establishes the changes in the Noncontrolling Interest accounts during the consolidation period

[E]	Common stock @ BOY	100,000	
	APIC @ BOY	125,000	
	Retained earnings @ BOY	775,000	
	Equity investment – @ BOY		800,000
	Noncontrolling interest (@ BOY)		200,000

Eliminates subsidiary Stockholders' Equity @ BOY. The credit to the Equity Investment eliminates the BOY balance recognized in the parent's Equity investment account. The credit to the Noncontrolling Interest Equity account establishes its balance @ BOY.

[A]	PPE, net @ BOY	500,000	
	Patent @ BOY	300,000	
	Goodwill @ BOY	150,000	
	Equity investment @ BOY		770,000
	Noncontrolling interest		180,000

The debits recognize the BOY AAP ($950,000 @ BOY) on the consolidated balance sheet. The credits eliminate the parent's share of the BOY AAP from its Equity Investment account and recognize the noncontrolling interests' share of the AAP in the NCI equity account. [Note that the allocation of the 100% AAP is equal to the split calculated in Exhibit 5.2]

[D]	Operating expenses	40,000	
	PPE, net		10,000
	Patent		30,000

The debit to Operating Expenses recognizes depreciation/amortization expense relating to the identifiable AAP assets, and the credits to PPE, net and Patent, adjust the balances to reflect their correct end-of-year totals.

[I_cogs]	Equity investment @ BOY	17,500	
	Cost of goods sold		17,500

The deferred profit from the prior period is included in consolidated net income in the year in which the intercompany assets are sold to non-affiliates. As we describe in Chapter 4, for inventory transactions, deferred profit is ultimately included in consolidated net income via a reduction in cost of goods sold. For a downstream sale, all of the deferred profit is recognized in the parent's financial statements and there is no effect on the noncontrolling interest accounts.

[I_sales]	Sales	400,000	
	Cost of goods sold		400,000

We always eliminate 100% of all intercompany transactions. Note: this entry has no effect on net income.

[I_cogs]	Cost of goods sold...........................	28,000	
	Inventory		28,000

Consistent with the elimination of deferred profit which we describe in Chapter 4, we eliminate 100% of the deferred profit included on the balance sheet (i.e., this is the 100% elimination).

[I_pay]	Accounts payable............................	100,000	
	Accounts receivable		100,000

Elimination of intercompany receivable and payable

EXHIBIT 5.5	Consolidation Spreadsheet Reflecting Continuous Downstream Intercompany Inventory Sales in Presence of Noncontrolling Interest—Equity Method

			Consolidation Entries				
	Parent	**Subsidiary**		**Dr**		**Cr**	**Consolidated**
Income statement:							
Sales.................................	$10,000,000	$1,500,000	[I_sales]	$400,000			$11,100,000
Cost of goods sold.....................	(7,000,000)	(900,000)	[I_cogs]	28,000	[I_cogs]	$ 17,500	(7,510,500)
					[I_sales]	400,000	
Gross profit..........................	3,000,000	600,000					3,589,500
Income (loss) from subsidiary.............	125,500		[C]	125,500			0
Operating expenses....................	(1,900,000)	(390,000)	[D]	40,000			(2,330,000)
Consolidated net income................	1,225,500	210,000					1,259,500
Consolidated NI attributable to NCI........			[C]	34,000			(34,000)
Consolidated NI attributable to parent......	$ 1,225,500	$ 210,000					$ 1,225,500
Statement of retained earnings:							
BOY retained earnings..................	$ 5,006,500	$ 775,000	[E]	775,000			$ 5,006,500
Consolidated NI attributable to parent......	1,225,500	210,000					1,225,500
Dividends	(247,200)	(21,000)			[C]	21,000	(247,200)
Ending retained earnings	$ 5,984,800	$ 964,000					$ 5,984,800
Balance sheet:							
Assets							
Cash.................................	$ 1,058,600	$ 415,000					$ 1,473,600
Accounts receivable....................	1,280,000	348,000			[I_pay]	100,000	1,528,000
Inventory.............................	1,940,000	447,000			[I_cogs]	28,000	2,359,000
Equity investment.....................	1,661,200		[I_cogs]	17,500	[C]	108,700	0
					[E]	800,000	
					[A]	770,000	
Property, plant and equipment (PPE), net ...	9,332,000	827,000	[A]	500,000	[D]	10,000	10,649,000
Patent................................			[A]	300,000	[D]	30,000	270,000
Goodwill..............................			[A]	150,000			150,000
	$15,271,800	$2,037,000					$16,429,600

continued next page

EXHIBIT 5.5 cont.	Consolidation Spreadsheet Reflecting Continuous Downstream Intercompany Inventory Sales in Presence of Noncontrolling Interest—Equity Method

	Parent	Subsidiary	Consolidation Entries Dr		Cr	Consolidated
Liabilities and stockholders' equity						
Current liabilities....................	$ 1,437,000	$ 348,000	[I$_{pay}$]	100,000		$ 1,685,000
Long-term liabilities	5,000,000	500,000				5,500,000
Common stock.....................	1,635,000	100,000	[E]	100,000		1,635,000
APIC............................	1,215,000	125,000	[E]	125,000		1,215,000
Retained earnings	5,984,800	964,000				5,984,800
Noncontrolling interest..............			[C]	29,800		409,800
			[E]	200,000		
			[A]	180,000		
	$15,271,800	$2,037,000		$2,695,000	$2,695,000	$16,429,600

Now that we have assembled consolidated financial statements assuming (1) no intercompany transactions [i.e., Exhibit 5.3], (2) *upstream* intercompany transactions [i.e., Exhibit 5.4], and (3) *downstream* intercompany transactions [i.e., Exhibit 5.5], we can compare the effects of these three scenarios on the income statement and balance sheet. Exhibit 5.6 provides a summary comparison of the consolidated income statement, retained earnings statement, and balance sheet across the three exhibits. Note that because we are analyzing ***post-consolidation*** amounts in Exhibit 5.6, the related amounts and discussion apply equally to consolidations where the parent company uses the equity method and cost method of ***pre-consolidation*** bookkeeping.

Comparison of the three consolidated columns in Exhibit 5.6 reveals the differences in the effects of deferred profit, depending on whether it is completely ignored (i.e., Exhibit 5.3), the result of upstream transactions (i.e., Exhibit 5.4), or the result of downstream transactions (i.e., Exhibit 5.5). Beginning with Sales, the only difference is caused by the fact that both the upstream and downstream cases include elimination of the $400,000 of intercompany sales, compared with the no intercompany deferred profit example that did not require an adjustment to Sales.

Interestingly, this pattern of differences is the same for consolidated Cost of Goods Sold. In particular, both the upstream and the downstream Cost of Goods Sold balances are $389,500 lower than in our example with no intercompany transactions. This difference is comprised of a decrease in Cost of Goods Sold for the intercompany transaction (i.e., $400,000 that also adjusted Sales), a $17,500 decrease in Cost of Goods Sold for the prior year deferred profit that will be recognized in Net Income in the current year (i.e., the year of sale to a non-affiliate), a $28,000 increase in Cost of Goods Sold for the current year deferred profit that will be deferred until the inventory is sold to a non-affiliate. The fact that Upstream and Downstream treatment results in identical Sales and Cost of Goods Sold amounts demonstrates how we achieve "100% elimination" of intercompany transactions and intercompany profits.

Subtracting Cost of Goods Sold from Sales yields consolidated Gross Profit. Given the identical pattern of differences in Sales and Cost of Goods Sold, the Gross Profit in the upstream and downstream cases are identical and both are different from Gross Profit for the company with no deferred profit. However, careful analysis of the amount of the difference can reveal an important point about intercompany elimination of transactions and balances. Specifically, *the elimination of the $400,000 intercompany transaction has no effect on Consolidated Gross Profit or Consolidated Net Income.* Indeed, the entire $10,500 difference between the upstream/downstream cases and the example with no deferred profit (i.e., $3,600,000 − $3,589,500) is completely explained by the beginning inventory and ending inventory (i.e., $28,000 − $17,500 = $10,500).

Turning now to Consolidated Net Income Attributable to the Noncontrolling Interest, we see a new pattern of differences emerging. This pattern is one that demonstrates what we mean when we say that companies pro-rata allocate *upstream* deferred profit with elimination. In particular, the companies with no deferred profit and *downstream* deferred profit have identical (i.e., $34,000) amounts of Consolidated Net Income Attributable to the Noncontrolling Interest. These amounts must be the same because they both include the noncontrolling interests' proportion of the reported net income of the subsidiary and the allocated portion of the AAP amortization. However, neither was adjusted for deferred profit. In

EXHIBIT 5.6	Comparison of Consolidated Financial Statement Information in Presence of Noncontrolling Interest with Three Deferred Inventory Profit Conditions: None, Upstream, and Downstream

	Consolidated Balances for Year Ending December 31, 2016		
	Assuming *No* Inventory Deferred Profit (Exhibit 5.3)	Assuming *Upstream* Inventory Deferred Profit (Exhibit 5.4)	Assuming *Downstream* Inventory Deferred Profit (Exhibit 5.5)
Income statement:			
Sales.	$11,500,000	$11,100,000	$11,100,000
Cost of goods sold.	(7,900,000)	(7,510,500)	(7,510,500)
Gross profit.	3,600,000	3,589,500	3,589,500
Operating expenses	(2,330,000)	(2,330,000)	(2,330,000)
Consolidated net income	1,270,000	1,259,500	1,259,500
Consolidated NI attributable to NCI.	(34,000)	(31,900)	(34,000)
Consolidated NI attributable to parent.	$ 1,236,000	$ 1,227,600	$ 1,225,500
Statement of retained earnings:			
BOY retained earnings	$ 5,024,000	$ 5,010,000	$ 5,006,500
Consolidated NI attributable to parent.	1,236,000	1,227,600	1,225,500
Dividends	(247,200)	(247,200)	(247,200)
Ending retained earnings	$ 6,012,800	$ 5,990,400	$ 5,984,800
Balance sheet:			
Assets			
Cash	$ 1,473,600	$ 1,473,600	$ 1,473,600
Accounts receivable	1,628,000	1,528,000	1,528,000
Inventory.	2,387,000	2,359,000	2,359,000
Property, plant and equipment (PPE), net	10,649,000	10,649,000	10,649,000
Patent.	270,000	270,000	270,000
Goodwill	150,000	150,000	150,000
	$16,557,600	$16,429,600	$16,429,600
Liabilities and stockholders' equity			
Current liabilities.	$ 1,785,000	$ 1,685,000	$ 1,685,000
Long-term liabilities	5,500,000	5,500,000	5,500,000
Common stock.	1,635,000	1,635,000	1,635,000
APIC	1,215,000	1,215,000	1,215,000
Retained earnings	6,012,800	5,990,400	5,984,800
Noncontrolling interest	409,800	404,200	409,800
	$16,557,600	$16,429,600	$16,429,600

contrast, in our example with *upstream* intercompany sales of inventory, we allocated $10,500 (i.e., the same $28,000 − $17,500 described in the preceding paragraph) of income elimination to the subsidiary's income. The $2,100 difference in Consolidated Net Income Attributable to the Noncontrolling Interest is simply the noncontrolling interests' share of this elimination (i.e., 20% × $10,500).

Given the pattern of initial deferred profit recognition (i.e., $28,000 removed from Gross Profit) and subsequent reversal (i.e., $17,500 added to Gross Profit), the pattern of differences in Consolidated Net Income Attributable to the parent is predictable. The highest reported level of the parent's share of Net Income is for the example with no deferred profit. Because of the prorata allocation of deferred profit to the noncontrolling interest, the next highest level of Consolidated Net Income Attributable to the parent is in the *upstream* case. This is because pro-rata sharing of upstream profit deferral means that the parent's shareholders will only receive an 80% reduction in their allocated share of Net Income. The pattern of differences confirms this relationship: Consolidated Net Income Attributable to the parent is $8,400 lower in the upstream case (i.e., $1,236,000 − $1,227,600) which is equal to 80% of the net profit deferral and reversal (80% × $10,500 = $8,400). The case in which the companies engaged in downstream transactions has the lowest level of Consolidated Net Income Attributable to the parent (i.e., $1,225,500), which is $10,500 lower than the company for which we included no profit deferral. This difference is equal to 100% of the net profit deferral and reversal (i.e., deferred = $28,000 and reversed = $17,500).

Across Exhibits 5.3, 5.4, and 5.5, the beginning balance in consolidated Retained Earnings reflects a pattern of 100% deferred profit elimination for downstream intercompany sales and the parent's prorata deferred profit elimination for upstream intercompany sales. Specifically, the beginning balance in consolidated Retained Earnings for the downstream case is $17,500 lower (i.e., $5,024,000 − $5,006,500) than the case with no deferred profit (i.e., 100% of the beginning of year deferred profit), while the upstream case is $14,000 lower (i.e., $5,024,000 − $5,010,000) than the case with no deferred profit (i.e., 80% × $17,500). Again, this pattern illustrates the concept of 20% prorata allocation of upstream deferred profit to the noncontrolling interest, thereby only affecting beginning consolidated Retained Earnings by 80% (i.e., 100% − 20%).

The ending balance in consolidated Retained Earnings includes a similar pattern of deferred profit that exists at the end of the year. Specifically, the ending balance in consolidated Retained Earnings for the Downstream case is $28,000 lower (i.e., $6,012,800 − $5,984,800) than the case with no deferred profit (i.e., 100% of the end of year deferred profit), while the upstream case is $22,400 lower (i.e., $6,012,800 − $5,990,400) than the case with no deferred profit (i.e., 80% × $28,000). Similar to the beginning balance in consolidated Retained Earnings, this pattern illustrates the concept of 20% prorata allocation of upstream deferred profit to the noncontrolling interest, thereby only affecting ending consolidated Retained Earnings by 80% (i.e., 100% − 20%).

Given that we have already discussed ending Retained Earnings, this leaves only two balance sheet accounts that have different balances in Exhibits 5.3, 5.4, and 5.5: Inventory and Noncontrolling Interest. Given that both upstream and downstream intercompany transactions require 100% elimination of deferred profit, Inventory must have the same balance in the upstream and downstream cases (i.e., $2,359,000). This balance is $28,000 lower than the case with no deferred profit elimination (i.e., $2,387,000 − $2,359,000), which is 100% of the deferred profit at the end of the year.

The differences in balances in consolidated Noncontrolling Interest reflect the effects of prorata allocation of deferred profit in the upstream case. Specifically, Noncontrolling Interest has identical balances in the case with no deferred profit elimination and in the downstream case. This is because 0% of downstream deferred profit is allocated the noncontrolling interest. In comparison to the upstream case, consolidated Noncontrolling Interest is $5,600 lower (i.e., $409,800 − $404,200), which is equal to 20% of the year-end deferred profit (20% × $28,000 = $5,600).

TOPIC REVIEW 2

Consolidation subsequent to acquisition—Equity method, noncontrolling interest, and upstream and downstream intercompany inventory transactions

Assume that a parent company acquired 70% of the common stock of a subsidiary a few years ago. On the acquisition date, the fair value of the controlling interest and noncontrolling interest equaled the respective proportionate share of the subsidiary's reported book value of equity. In addition, the book values of the subsidiary's identifiable net assets approximated their fair values and there was no goodwill (i.e., there is no AAP).

Each company routinely sells merchandise to the other company, with a profit margin of 35 percent of selling price (regardless of the direction of the sale). During 2016, intercompany sales amount to $50,000, of which $20,000 of merchandise remains in the December 31, 2016 inventory of the subsidiary. On December 31, 2016, $16,000 of these intercompany sales remained unpaid. Additionally, the parent's December 31, 2015 inventory included $60,000 of merchandise purchased during 2015 from the subsidiary. During 2015, intercompany sales amount to $130,000, and on December 31, 2015, $20,000 of these intercompany sales remained unpaid.

The parent uses the equity method of pre-consolidation bookkeeping for its Equity Investment. The parent and the subsidiary report the following pre-consolidation financial statements for the year ended December 31, 2016:

	Parent	Subsidiary
Income statement:		
Sales.	$ 960,000	$360,000
Cost of goods sold.	(480,000)	(216,000)
Gross profit.	480,000	144,000
Depreciation & amortization expense.	(24,000)	(19,200)
Operating expenses	(300,000)	(72,600)
Interest expense.	(12,000)	(4,000)
Total expenses	(336,000)	(95,800)
Income (loss) from subsidiary.	41,440	—
Net income	$ 185,440	$ 48,200
Statement of retained earnings:		
BOY retained earnings	$ 404,000	$220,000
Net income	185,440	48,200
Dividends	(120,000)	(28,000)
EOY retained earnings	$ 469,440	$240,200
Balance sheet:		
Cash	$ 78,000	$ 30,000
Accounts receivable	108,000	96,000
Inventories	260,000	92,000
Buildings and equipment, net	252,000	180,000
Other assets	114,000	200,000
Licenses	—	20,000
Equity investment	343,140	—
Total assets	$1,155,140	$618,000
Accounts payable	$ 61,700	$ 23,800
Notes payable	100,000	42,000
Other liabilities	44,000	52,000
Common stock.	480,000	260,000
Retained earnings	469,440	240,200
Total liabilities and equity	$1,155,140	$618,000

Required

Prepare the consolidation spreadsheet for the year ended December 31, 2016.

The solution to this review problem can be found on page 373.

Intercompany Profit Elimination for Upstream Depreciable Asset Sales—Equity Method

To illustrate the consolidation process with noncontrolling interests and upstream intercompany sale of depreciable assets, we will provide a new set of facts. In the interest of clarity, we do not include AAP or intercompany inventory transactions in this example.[18] In our example, assume that a parent company acquired its 70% interest in its subsidiary on January 1, 2012. On the acquisition date, the total fair value of the controlling interest and the noncontrolling interest was equal to the book value of net assets of the subsidiary, and all of the subsidiary's net asset fair values approximated their recorded book values (i.e., there is no goodwill or individual net asset AAP differences).

---

[18] The Comprehensive Review at the end of the chapter will include simultaneous consideration of intercompany inventory transactions and intercompany depreciable asset transactions in the presence of noncontrolling interest.

On December 31, 2014, the subsidiary sold equipment to the parent for a cash price of $60,000. The subsidiary originally acquired the equipment at a cost of $125,000, estimated a 10-year useful life for the equipment, and used the straight-line method of depreciation (no salvage value). At the time of the intercompany sale, the subsidiary had depreciated the equipment for a full six years. The parent retained the depreciation policy of the subsidiary and depreciated the equipment over its remaining 4-year useful life. The parent uses the equity method of pre-consolidation bookkeeping for its Equity Investment. Exhibit 5.7 provides the pre-consolidation financial statements of the parent and its subsidiary for the year ended December 31, 2016.

EXHIBIT 5.7	Pre-Consolidation Financial Statements for the Year Ended December 31, 2016		
		Parent	**Subsidiary**
Income statement:			
Sales.		$480,000	$180,000
Cost of goods sold.		(240,000)	(108,000)
Gross profit.		240,000	72,000
Depreciation & amortization expense.		(12,000)	(9,600)
Operating expenses		(150,000)	(36,300)
Interest expense.		(6,000)	(2,000)
Total expenses		(168,000)	(47,900)
Income (loss) from subsidiary.		18,620	—
Net income.		$ 90,620	$ 24,100
Statement of retained earnings:			
Beginning retained earnings.		$202,000	$110,000
Income attributable to controlling interest		90,620	24,100
Dividends declared.		(60,000)	(14,000)
Ending retained earnings		$232,620	$120,100
Balance sheet:			
Cash		$ 39,000	$ 15,000
Accounts receivable.		54,000	48,000
Inventories		130,000	46,000
Buildings and equipment, net		126,000	90,000
Other assets.		57,000	100,000
Licenses		—	10,000
Investment in subsidiary.		171,570	—
Total assets.		$577,570	$309,000
Accounts payable.		$ 32,950	$ 11,900
Notes payable		50,000	21,000
Other liabilities		22,000	26,000
Common stock.		240,000	130,000
Retained earnings		232,620	120,100
Noncontrolling interest		—	—
Total liabilities and equity		$577,570	$309,000

Given that we assume no AAP and no intercompany inventory transactions, we can focus on the deferral and recognition of the profit on the intercompany equipment transfer. At the date of the intercompany sale on December 31, 2014, the equipment had a carrying value on the subsidiary's books equal to $50,000 (i.e., original cost of $125,000 less six years of depreciation at $12,500 per year, or $75,000 of total accumulated depreciation). This means that the intercompany transfer resulted in $10,000 of pre-consolidation profits recognized by the subsidiary on December 31, 2014. The consolidated entity is not allowed to recognize this profit on the date of the intercompany transaction. Instead, because the equipment is a depreciable asset, the $10,000 of deferred profit will be ratably recognized in the consolidated financial statements over the remaining 4-year useful life of the equipment. Exhibit 5.8 illustrates the process of deferral and subsequent recognition:

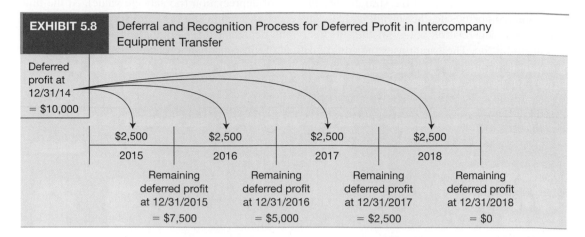

EXHIBIT 5.8   Deferral and Recognition Process for Deferred Profit in Intercompany Equipment Transfer

An important point to remember is that, regardless of whether the intercompany transfer is upstream or downstream, the intercompany deferred profit is always 100% eliminated from the consolidated financial statements at the date of intercompany transfer. Then, as the asset is depreciated during the periods after the intercompany sale, 100% of the deferred profit is ratably amortized and recognized in the consolidated financial statements as an adjustment of depreciation expense. For example, for the year ended December 31, 2015, the consolidated entity will confirm $2,500 of the deferred intercompany profit and recognize it as a reduction of consolidated depreciation expense. (The reduction of an expense has the same effect on net income as the recognition of a gain.)

With respect to the circumstances in our example, the parent company will record the equipment at its $60,000 pre-consolidation transfer price on December 31, 2014. Then, each year, the parent will depreciate the equipment in its pre-consolidation income statement for $15,000 for the equipment's remaining useful life of four years. In contrast, the consolidated balance sheet at December 31, 2014 will show the equipment at its pre-transfer carrying value of $50,000, and each consolidated income statement over the equipment's remaining useful life will reflect $12,500 of depreciation expense. The means through which the pre-consolidation depreciation expense of $15,000 becomes the post-consolidation balance of $12,500 is via the annual confirmation of $2,500 of deferred gain as illustrated in Exhibit 5.8. As we previously noted, the annual recognition of the $2,500 gain has the same effect on net income as the annual decrease of depreciation expense by $2,500.

Although we always defer and subsequently confirm 100% of deferred intercompany profits, the effect of this deferral on the controlling interest and the noncontrolling interest depends on whether the transaction is upstream or downstream. In this example, because the transaction is an *upstream* asset transfer, the deferral will affect the controlling and noncontrolling interests in proportion to their relative ownership percentages. As we will see later in this section, if the transfer were *downstream*, then the deferral would be 100% absorbed by the controlling interest with none assigned to the noncontrolling interest.

So, considering the facts in our present example, the equity method journal entry on the parent's pre-consolidation books on December 31, 2014 is as follows (note that this journal entry only considers the effect of the intercompany asset transfer—the other usual equity method entries would also need to be made):

Equity income.	7,000	
Equity investment		7,000
(to defer the $10,000 of intercompany gain on the date of the intercompany transfer—because the transaction is upstream, only 70% × $10,000 is absorbed by the controlling interest)		

Then, each year for the next four years, the parent company will confirm its proportionate share of the intercompany gain in its pre-consolidation books via its equity method adjustments. The annual journal entry that is made during the years ended December 31, 2015 through 2018 (again, this journal entry only considers the effect of confirming the gain from the intercompany asset transfer—the other usual equity method entries would also need to be made) is as follows:

Equity investment.	1,750	
Equity income		1,750

(to confirm the $2,500 of annual intercompany gain during the asset's useful life—because the transaction is upstream, only 70% × $2,500 is absorbed by the controlling interest each year)

If we combine the subsidiary's information in Exhibit 5.7 with the deferred profit information in Exhibit 5.8, we can compute the "Equity Income from Subsidiary" income statement account balance and the "Investment in Subsidiary" balance sheet account balance reported by the parent at December 31, 2016, as illustrated in Exhibit 5.9:[19]

EXHIBIT 5.9	Proof of Pre-Consolidation Investment Related Accounts for the Year Ended December 31, 2016

Equity Income from Subsidiary		Investment in Subsidiary	
70% × $24,100 net income of subsidiary	$16,870	70% × $250,100 stockholders' equity	$175,070
+ 70% × $2,500 upstream confirmed gain.	1,750	− 70% × $5,000 unconfirmed gain.	(3,500)
Equity Income from subsidiary.	$18,620	Investment in subsidiary.	$171,570

The fact that the subsidiary amounts are multiplied by 70% is how the parent's pre-consolidation books only reflects the portion of the subsidiary that it owns. Of course, after consolidation, the consolidated financial statements will reflect 100% of the subsidiary's assets, liabilities, revenues, expenses, AAP, and intercompany profit deferrals. The way that the consolidated financial statements reflect only the 70% owned by the parent is by creating the noncontrolling interest accounts and recording them in the consolidated financial statements as part of the consolidation procedures. Exhibit 5.10 provides the computation of the "Income Attributable to the Noncontrolling Interest" in the income statement and the "Noncontrolling Interest" balance sheet amount for the year ended December 31, 2016:

EXHIBIT 5.10	Proof of Consolidated Noncontrolling Interest Balances for the Year Ended December 31, 2016

Income Attributable to the Noncontrolling Interest		Noncontrolling Interest	
30% × $24,100 net income of subsidiary	$7,230	30% × $250,100 stockholders' equity	$75,030
+ 30% × $2,500 confirmed gain.	750	− 30% × $5,000 unconfirmed gain.	(1,500)
Income attributable to NCI.	$7,980	Noncontrolling interest	$73,530

Exhibit 5.11 presents the consolidation spreadsheet including the **C-E-A-D-I** entries for the upstream case. Our consolidation entries are as follows:

[C]	Equity income from subsidiary.	18,620		Eliminates all changes in the Equity Investment accounts and establishes the changes in the Noncontrolling Interest accounts during the consolidation period
	Income attributable to NCI.	7,980		
	Dividends—Subsidiary		14,000	
	Investment in subsidiary		8,820	
	Noncontrolling Interest		3,780	

[E]	Common stock (S) @ BOY.	130,000		Eliminates subsidiary Stockholders' Equity @ BOY. The credit to the Equity Investment eliminates the BOY balance recognized in the parent's Equity investment account. The credit to the Noncontrolling Interest Equity account establishes its book value balance @ BOY.
	Retained earnings (S) @ BOY.	110,000		
	Investment in subsidiary @ BOY		168,000	
	Noncontrolling interest (@ BOY)		72,000	

---

[19] Again, as we mention previously, we kept the number of adjusting items to a minimum to increase the power of our illustration of intercompany transfers of depreciable assets. The Comprehensive Review at the end of the chapter will include simultaneous consideration of AAP, intercompany inventory transactions and intercompany depreciable asset transactions in the presence of noncontrolling interest.

[I_gain]	Investment in subsidiary @ BOY	5,250	
	Noncontrolling interest @ BOY	2,250	
	Buildings & equipment, net @ BOY		7,500

Removes the BOY deferred profit from the buildings and equipment account and proportionately assigns it to eliminating the investment account and creating the noncontrolling interest that will be presented in the consolidated balance sheet.

[I_dep]	Buildings and equipment, net	2,500	
	Depreciation & amortization expense		2,500

Confirms the deferred gain that can be recognized in the consolidated financial statements for the current year.

EXHIBIT 5.11	Consolidation Spreadsheet Reflecting Upstream Intercompany Depreciable Asset Sale in Presence of Noncontrolling Interest—Equity Method

			Consolidated Entries		
	Parent	**Subsidiary**	**Dr**	**Cr**	**Consolidated**
Income statement:					
Sales.	$480,000	$180,000			$660,000
Cost of goods sold.	(240,000)	(108,000)			(348,000)
Gross profit.	240,000	72,000			312,000
Depreciation & amortization expense	(12,000)	(9,600)	[I_dep] 2,500		(19,100)
Operating expenses.	(150,000)	(36,300)			(186,300)
Interest expense.	(6,000)	(2,000)			(8,000)
Total expenses	(168,000)	(47,900)			(213,400)
Income (loss) from subsidiary.	18,620		[C] 18,620		0
Consolidated net income	90,620	24,100			98,600
Consolidated NI attributable to NCI			[C] 7,980		(7,980)
Consolidated NI attributable to parent.	$ 90,620	$ 24,100			$ 90,620
Statement of retained earnings:					
Beginning retained earnings.	$202,000	$110,000	[E] 110,000		$202,000
Consolidated NI attributable to parent.	90,620	24,100			90,620
Dividends declared.	(60,000)	(14,000)		[C] 14,000	(60,000)
Ending retained earnings	$232,620	$120,100			$232,620
Balance sheet:					
Cash.	$ 39,000	$ 15,000			$ 54,000
Accounts receivable.	54,000	48,000			102,000
Inventories	130,000	46,000			176,000
Buildings and equipment, net	126,000	90,000	[I_dep] 2,500	[I_gain] 7,500	211,000
Other assets.	57,000	100,000			157,000
Licenses		10,000			10,000
Equity investment.	171,570		[I_gain] 5,250	[C] 8,820	0
				[E] 168,000	
Total assets.	$577,570	$309,000			$710,000
Accounts payable.	$ 32,950	$ 11,900			$ 44,850
Notes payable	50,000	21,000			71,000
Other liabilities	22,000	26,000			48,000
Common stock.	240,000	130,000	[E] 130,000		240,000
Retained earnings	232,620	120,100			232,620
Noncontrolling interest			[I_gain] 2,250	[C] 3,780	73,530
				[E] 72,000	
Total liabilities and equity	$577,570	$309,000	$276,600	$276,600	$710,000

The end results of the consolidation is that the consolidated asset, liability, revenue and expense balances represent 100% of the parent's stand-alone financial statement information and 100% of the subsidiary's stand-alone financial statement information. Because the parent company doesn't own 100% of the subsidiary, the income statement and balance sheet need to include noncontrolling interest accounts that represent the portion of net income and net assets, respectively, that are not owned by the parent's shareholders. In this case, because the intercompany depreciable asset transfer was upstream, the deferral of profit is allocated to the noncontrolling interest accounts. In the next section, we will investigate the case where the intercompany transaction is downstream, instead of upstream.

Comparison of Upstream to Downstream Transfers of Depreciable Assets

In this example, we will assume the exact same facts as the preceding example, except the direction of the intercompany transfer is switched: it is now a downstream transaction. As we mention previously, regardless of whether the intercompany transfer is upstream or downstream, the intercompany deferred profit is always 100% eliminated from the consolidated financial statements at the date of intercompany transfer. Then, as the asset is depreciated during the periods after the intercompany sale, 100% of the deferred profit is ratably amortized and recognized in the consolidated financial statements as an adjustment of depreciation expense. Exhibit 5.8 illustrates the initial deferral and subsequent confirmation of the intercompany depreciable-asset profit in our example. Given that the asset transfer is now *downstream*, the deferral would be 100% absorbed by the controlling interest with none assigned to the noncontrolling interest. The equity method journal entry on the parent's pre-consolidation books on December 31, 2014 is as follows (note that this journal entry only considers the effect of the intercompany asset transfer—the other usual equity method entries would also need to be made):

Equity income..	10,000	
Equity investment		10,000

(to defer the $10,000 of intercompany gain on the date of the intercompany transfer—because the transaction is downstream, the full 100% × $10,000 is absorbed by the controlling interest)

Then, each year for the next four years, the parent company will confirm the intercompany gain in its pre-consolidation books via its equity method adjustments. The annual journal entry that is made during the years ended December 31, 2015 through 2018 (again, this journal entry only considers the effect of confirming the gain from the intercompany asset transfer—the other usual equity method entries would also need to be made) is as follows:

Equity investment...	2,500	
Equity income		2,500

(to confirm the $2,500 of annual intercompany gain during the asset's useful life—because the transaction is downstream, the whole 100% × $2,500 is absorbed by the controlling interest each year)

If we combine the subsidiary's information in Exhibit 5.7 with the deferred profit information in Exhibit 5.8, we can compute the "Equity Income from Subsidiary" income statement account balance and the "Investment in Subsidiary" balance sheet account balance reported by the parent at December 31, 2016 (you can find these balances in Exhibit 5.14):

EXHIBIT 5.12 Proof of Pre-Consolidation Investment Related Accounts for the Year Ended December 31, 2016

Equity Income from Subsidiary		Investment in Subsidiary	
70% × $24,100 net income of subsidiary........	$16,870	70% × $250,100 stockholders' equity	$175,070
+ 100% × $2,500 downstream confirmed gain ...	2,500	− 100% × $5,000 unconfirmed gain.........	(5,000)
Equity income from subsidiary................	$19,370	Investment in subsidiary...................	$170,070

With 100% of the intercompany deferred profit allocated to the parent company, none of the deferred profit will affect the noncontrolling interest. Exhibit 5.13 provides the computation of the "Income Attributable to the Noncontrolling Interest" in the income statement and the "Noncontrolling Interest" balance sheet amount for the year ended December 31, 2016:

| **EXHIBIT 5.13** | Proof of Consolidated Noncontrolling Interest Balances for the Year Ended December 31, 2016 |

Income Attributable to the Noncontrolling Interest		Noncontrolling Interest	
30% × $24,100 net income of subsidiary	$7,230	30% × $250,100 stockholders' equity	$75,030
+ 0% × $2,500 confirmed gain.	0	− 0% × $5,000 unconfirmed gain.	(0)
Income attributable to NCI.	$7,230	Noncontrolling interest.	$75,030

Exhibit 5.14 presents the consolidation spreadsheet including the **C-E-A-D-I** entries for the downstream case. Our consolidation entries are as follows:

[C]	Equity income from subsidiary.	19,370		Eliminates all changes in the Equity Investment accounts and establishes the changes in the Noncontrolling Interest accounts during the consolidation period. Removes changes in the investment account of the parent, eliminates declared dividends from the equity section of the subsidiary, establishes Income attributable to the noncontrolling interest (see computation above) and the change in the noncontrolling interest on the balance sheet during the year (i.e., $3,030 = $7,230 − [30% × $14,000]).
	Income attributable to NCI.	7,230	
	Dividends—Subsidiary		14,000
	Investment in subsidiary		9,570
	Noncontrolling interest		3,030
[E]	Common stock (S) @ BOY	130,000		Eliminates subsidiary Stockholders' Equity @ BOY. The credit to the Equity Investment eliminates the BOY balance recognized in the parent's Equity Investment account. The credit to the Noncontrolling Interest Equity account establishes its book-value balance @ BOY.
	Retained earnings (S) @ BOY.	110,000	
	Investment in subsidiary @ BOY		168,000
	Noncontrolling interest (@ BOY)		72,000
[I_gain]	Investment in subsidiary @ BOY	7,500		Removes the BOY deferred profit from the buildings and equipment account and proportionately assigns it to eliminating the investment account.
	Buildings & equipment, net @ BOY. . . .		7,500
[I_dep]	Buildings and equipment, net	2,500		Confirms the deferred gain that can be recognized in the consolidated financial statements for the current year.
	Depreciation & amortization expense . . .		2,500

| **EXHIBIT 5.14** | Consolidation Spreadsheet Reflecting Downstream Intercompany Depreciable Asset Sale in Presence of Noncontrolling Interest—Equity Method |

	Parent	Subsidiary	Consolidation Entries Dr		Cr	Consolidated
Income statement:						
Sales.	$480,000	$180,000				$660,000
Cost of goods sold.	(240,000)	(108,000)				(348,000)
Gross profit.	240,000	72,000				312,000
Depreciation & amortization expense	(12,000)	(9,600)		[I_dep]	2,500	(19,100)
Operating expenses.	(150,000)	(36,300)				(186,300)
Interest expense.	(6,000)	(2,000)				(8,000)
Total expenses	(168,000)	(47,900)				(213,400)
Income (loss) from subsidiary.	19,370		**[C]**	19,370		0
Consolidated net income	91,370	24,100				98,600
Consolidated NI attributable to NCI.			**[C]**	7,230		(7,230)
Consolidated NI attributable to parent.	$ 91,370	$ 24,100				$ 91,370

continued next page

EXHIBIT 5.14 cont.	Consolidation Spreadsheet Reflecting Downstream Intercompany Depreciable Asset Sale in Presence of Noncontrolling Interest—Equity Method

	Parent	Subsidiary	Dr		Cr		Consolidated
Statement of retained earnings:							
Beginning retained earnings.	$199,750	$110,000	[E]	110,000			$199,750
Consolidated NI attributable to parent.	91,370	24,100					91,370
Dividends declared.	(60,000)	(14,000)			[C]	14,000	(60,000)
Ending retained earnings	$231,120	$120,100					$231,120
Balance sheet:							
Cash	$ 39,000	$ 15,000					$ 54,000
Accounts receivable.	54,000	48,000					102,000
Inventories	130,000	46,000					176,000
Buildings and equipment, net	126,000	90,000	[I_dep]	2,500	[I_gain]	7,500	211,000
Other assets.	57,000	100,000					157,000
Licenses		10,000					10,000
Equity investment.	170,070		[I_gain]	7,500	[C]	9,570	0
					[E]	168,000	
Total assets.	$576,070	$309,000					$710,000
Accounts payable.	$ 32,950	$ 11,900					$ 44,850
Notes payable	50,000	21,000					71,000
Other liabilities	22,000	26,000					48,000
Common stock.	240,000	130,000	[E]	130,000			240,000
Retained earnings	231,120	120,100					231,120
Noncontrolling interest					[C]	3,030	75,030
					[E]	72,000	
Total liabilities and equity	$576,070	$309,000		$276,600		$276,600	$710,000

Now that we have assembled consolidated financial statements assuming (1) an upstream intercompany depreciable asset transaction [i.e., Exhibit 5.11], and (2) a downstream intercompany depreciable asset transaction [i.e., Exhibit 5.14], we can compare the effects of these two scenarios on the income statement and balance sheet. Exhibit 5.15 provides a summary side-by-side comparison of the consolidated income statement, retained earnings statement, and balance sheet across the two exhibits.

| EXHIBIT 5.15 | Comparison of Consolidated Financial Statement Information Between Upstream and Downstream Sales of Depreciable Assets in the Presence of Noncontrolling Interests |

	Consolidated Balances for Year Ending December 31, 2016		
	Assuming Deferred Profit from Upstream Depreciable Asset Sale (Exhibit 5.11)	Assuming Deferred Profit from Downstream Depreciable Asset Sale (Exhibit 5.14)	Difference Between Upstream and Downstream
Income statement:			
Sales.	$660,000	$660,000	
Cost of goods sold.	(348,000)	(348,000)	
Gross profit.	312,000	312,000	
Depreciation & amortization expense.	(19,100)	(19,100)	
Operating expenses.	(186,300)	(186,300)	
Interest expense.	(8,000)	(8,000)	
Total expenses	(213,400)	(213,400)	
Consolidated net income	98,600	98,600	
Consolidated NI attributable to NCI.	(7,980)	(7,230)	$ 750
Consolidated NI attributable to parent.	$ 90,620	$ 91,370	$ (750)
Statement of retained earnings:			
Beginning retained earnings.	$202,000	$199,750	$ 2,250
Consolidated NI attributable to parent.	90,620	91,370	(750)
Dividends declared.	(60,000)	(60,000)	
Ending retained earnings	$232,620	$231,120	$ 1,500
Balance sheet:			
Cash.	$ 54,000	$ 54,000	
Accounts receivable.	102,000	102,000	
Inventories	176,000	176,000	
Buildings and equipment, net	211,000	211,000	
Other assets.	157,000	157,000	
Licenses	10,000	10,000	
Total assets.	$710,000	$710,000	
Accounts payable.	$ 44,850	$ 44,850	
Notes payable	71,000	71,000	
Other liabilities	48,000	48,000	
Common stock.	240,000	240,000	
Retained earnings	232,620	231,120	$ 1,500
Noncontrolling interest.	73,530	75,030	(1,500)
Total liabilities and equity	$710,000	$710,000	$ 0

Before we compare the upstream and downstream cases in Exhibit 5.15, we want to emphasize that the lessons from these comparisons are valid regardless of the method or pre-consolidation bookkeeping applied by the parent company. That is, the fact that the parent company used the equity method, cost method, or some other method between these two extremes has no effect on the outcome: *the consolidated financial statements will always look the same.* So, the lessons learned from this comparison are just as valid when we discuss cost method consolidations in the next section.

A key advantage of this example is that we hold constant all information except the direction of the intercompany sale of depreciable equipment. You should note that the only difference is whether the deferred gain is allocated to the noncontrolling interest. Of course, if we change the amount assigned to the income attributable to the noncontrolling interest and the income attributable to controlling interest, it will have an effect on the retained earnings (i.e., where income attributable to the controlling interest is accumulated) and the noncontrolling interest (i.e., the place where income attributable to the noncontrolling interest is accumulated) balance sheet accounts.

Another important lesson to take from this comparison is the relation between the revenues and expenses (i.e., the determinants of consolidated net income) and the assets and liabilities (i.e., the determinants of consolidated stockholders equity): they are identical, regardless of whether the sale was upstream or downstream! This is an illustration of the concept that we always eliminate 100% of the intercompany profit on asset transfers regardless of transfer direction.

Now, we discuss the individual differences between the upstream and downstream cases. First, we focus on the $2,250 difference in beginning-of-year retained earnings between the upstream case and the downstream case. On the date of the transaction (i.e., December 31, 2014) in the upstream case, $3,000 of the intercompany gain allocated to the noncontrolling interest. This means the controlling interest income for the year ended December 31, 2014 was $3,000 higher in the upstream case, and this amount was closed to consolidated retained earnings. During the year ended December 31, 2015, $750 (i.e., 30% × $2,500) of the confirmed intercompany gain was assigned to the noncontrolling interest in only the upstream case. Thus, at the end of 2015 (i.e., which is the beginning balance for the 2016 consolidation), the upstream case had $2,250 (i.e., $3,000 − $750) higher retained earnings than the downstream case.

Next, the income attributable to the noncontrolling interest for the year ended December 31, 2016 is $750 higher in the upstream case because $750 of confirmed gain (i.e., $2500 × 30%) is assigned to the noncontrolling interest. This is also why income attributable to the controlling interest is $750 lower in the upstream case for the year ended December 31, 2016.

Finally, understanding the $1,500 differences for the ending retained earnings and ending noncontrolling interest requires the same logic as the difference for the beginning retained earnings balance discussed previously. In the case of the ending balance of retained earnings under the upstream case, because the $3,000 gain was eliminated from the noncontrolling interest in 2014, and $750 was confirmed for the noncontrolling interest in each of the years 2015 and 2016, this means the unconfirmed intercompany profit assigned to the noncontrolling interest (instead of the controlling interest) is $1,500 (i.e., $3,000 − $750 − $750) at December 31, 2016. Because it is assigned to the noncontrolling interest (in the upstream case) instead of the controlling interest this means that portion of the accumulated unconfirmed gain elimination is not in retained earnings (i.e., that is why the difference in retained earnings and noncontrolling interest offset—it is a mechanical relationship).

TOPIC REVIEW 3

Consolidation subsequent to acquisition—Equity method, noncontrolling interest, and upstream intercompany depreciable asset sale

Assume that a parent company acquired 70% of the common stock of a subsidiary a few years ago. On the acquisition date, the fair value of the controlling interest and noncontrolling interest equaled the respective proportionate share of the subsidiary's reported book value of equity. In addition, the book values of the subsidiary's identifiable net assets approximated their fair values and there was no goodwill (i.e., there is no AAP).

On December 31, 2014, the subsidiary sold equipment to the parent for a cash price of $90,000. The subsidiary originally acquired the equipment at a cost of $150,000, estimated a 10-year useful life for the equipment, and used the straight-line method of depreciation (no salvage value). At the time of the intercompany sale, the subsidiary had depreciated the equipment for a full 5 years. The parent retained the depreciation policy of the subsidiary and depreciated the equipment over its remaining 5-year useful life.

The parent uses the equity method of pre-consolidation bookkeeping for its Equity Investment. The parent and the subsidiary report the following pre-consolidation financial statements for the year ended December 31, 2016:

	Parent	Subsidiary		Parent	Subsidiary
Income statement:			**Balance sheet:**		
Sales.	$ 780,000	$ 285,000	Cash.	$ 58,500	$ 25,500
Cost of goods sold.	(420,000)	(177,000)	Accounts receivable.	81,000	72,000
Gross profit.	360,000	108,000	Inventories	195,000	69,000
Depreciation & amort. expense . . .	(18,000)	(14,400)	Buildings and equipment, net . . .	189,000	135,000
Operating expenses.	(225,000)	(54,450)	Other assets.	85,500	150,000
Interest expense.	(9,000)	(3,000)	Licenses		15,000
Total expenses	(252,000)	(71,850)	Equity investment.	258,405	
Income (loss) from subsidiary.	27,405		Total assets.	$867,405	$466,500
Net income.	$ 135,405	$ 36,150			
Statement of retained earnings:			Accounts payable.	$ 51,000	$ 17,850
BOY retained earnings	$ 303,000	$ 165,000	Notes payable	75,000	31,500
Net income.	135,405	36,150	Other liabilities	33,000	39,000
Dividends	(90,000)	(18,000)	Common stock.	360,000	195,000
EOY retained earnings	$ 348,405	$ 183,150	Retained earnings	348,405	183,150
			Total liabilities and equity	$867,405	$466,500

Required

Prepare the consolidation spreadsheet for the year ended December 31, 2016.

The solution to this review problem can be found on page 374.

POST-ACQUISITION CONSOLIDATION AND NONCONTROLLING INTERESTS—COST METHOD

LO4 Explain intercompany profit elimination in consolidated financial statements in the presence of noncontrolling interests when the parent uses the cost method of pre-consolidation investment bookkeeping.

In this section, we continue our discussion of post-acquisition consolidation in the presence of noncontrolling interests, but now focus on the case where the parent applies the cost method of pre-consolidation bookkeeping. As we previously emphasized, the consolidated financial statements will look the same, regardless of the pre-consolidation method of Equity Investment bookkeeping applied by the parent company. In addition, the subsidiary's financial statements will be identical when the parent applies the cost method (i.e., because cost method versus equity method refers to bookkeeping applied by the parent, not the subsidiary). However, because the parent company's pre-consolidation financial statements will be different under the cost method versus the equity method, the consolidation entries will (out of necessity) be slightly different.

We will discuss the cost-method consolidation procedures using an example that includes AAP, intercompany inventory transactions and an upstream intercompany sale of depreciable property. Assume that on January 1, 2012, a parent company acquires 80% of the common stock of a subsidiary for $234,000. On the acquisition date, the fair value of the 20% noncontrolling interest is equal to $52,500. On January 1, 2012, the subsidiary had recorded values for common stock equal to $195,000 and retained earnings equal to $21,000. This means that the 100% AAP on the acquisition date was equal to $70,500 (i.e., [$234,000 + $52,500] − [$195,000 + $21,000]).

On the acquisition date, the fair values of all of the net assets of the subsidiary equaled their reported book values except for buildings and equipment, which had a recorded net book value of $82,500 and a fair value of $105,000 (i.e., $22,500 of identifiable AAP). The buildings and equipment had a 6-year estimated remaining useful life, which resulted in 100% AAP amortization of $3,750 each year 2012 through 2017. In assigning the AAP to the identifiable net assets, the 80% portion of the acquisition-date AAP assigned to the buildings and equipment is $18,000 (i.e., 80% × $22,500) and the 20% portion attributable the noncontrolling interest is $4,500 (i.e., 20% × $22,500). The annual amortization for the controlling and noncontrolling interest is $3,000 per year and $750 per year, respectively.

On January 1, 2012, the 100% goodwill is equal to $48,000, which is calculated as the 100% fair value of the entity of $286,500 (i.e., fair value of the 80% interest equal to $234,000 plus the fair value of the noncontrolling interest equal to $52,500) minus the fair value of the identifiable net assets of $238,500 (i.e., the acquisition-date stockholders' equity of the subsidiary equal to $216,000 plus the identifiable AAP for the buildings and equipment equal to $22,500). The goodwill attributable to the controlling interest is equal to $43,200 (i.e., the fair value of the parent's 80% interest of $234,000 minus the parent's 80% proportionate share of the fair value of the identifiable net assets of $190,800, or 80% × $238,500). The goodwill attributable to the noncontrolling interest is equal to the residual that remains after assigning goodwill to the controlling interest.[20] This amount equals $4,800 (i.e., the 100% goodwill of $48,000 minus the controlling interest goodwill of $43,200).

During the year ended December 31, 2016, the parent and subsidiary recorded $33,000 of inter-company sales to each other. At December 31, 2016, $22,500 of the inventory remained on the pre-consolidation books of the parent company (i.e., sales were upstream) and $7,500 of the sales remained unpaid. At December 31, 2015, $15,000 of intercompany inventory remained on the books of the subsidiary (i.e., sales were downstream). The parent and subsidiary use the first-in, first-out inventory method, so all intercompany inventory holdings are sold to unaffiliated parties in the following year. All intercompany sales, regardless of direction, have a 35% profit margin.

On December 31, 2014, the subsidiary sold to the parent, for $63,000, buildings and equipment that had a depreciated carrying value of $54,000 (i.e., there was $9,000 of intercompany profit on the date of the transaction). On December 31, 2014, the equipment had a six-year remaining useful life, which means that $1,500 of intercompany gains are confirmed in the consolidated financial statements each year through December 31, 2020.

The parent applies the cost method of pre-consolidation investment bookkeeping. The parent and subsidiary pre-consolidation financial statements for the year ended December 31, 2016 are as follows:

	Parent	Subsidiary
Income statement:		
Sales.	$720,000	$300,000
Cost of goods sold.	(360,000)	(162,000)
Gross profit.	360,000	138,000
Depreciation & amortization expense.	(18,000)	(14,400)
Operating expenses	(225,000)	(54,450)
Interest expense.	(9,000)	(3,150)
Total expenses	(252,000)	(72,000)
Income (loss) from subsidiary.	16,800	
Net income.	$124,800	$ 66,000
Statement of retained earnings:		
Beginning retained earnings.	$284,550	$165,000
Income attributable to controlling interest	124,800	66,000
Dividends declared.	(90,000)	(21,000)
Ending retained earnings	$319,350	$210,000

continued

[20] As we discuss previously in this chapter, the amount assigned to the noncontrolling interest goodwill cannot be negative. If the computation results in a negative amount, it is absorbed by the controlling interest bargain purchase gain (FASB ASC 805-30-25-2).

continued previous page

	Parent	Subsidiary
Balance sheet:		
Cash.	$ 51,180	$ 22,500
Accounts receivable.	81,000	72,000
Inventories	195,000	69,000
Buildings and equipment, net	189,000	180,000
Other assets.	85,500	150,000
Investment in subsidiary.	234,000	
Total assets.	$835,680	$493,500
Accounts payable.	$ 48,330	$ 18,000
Notes payable	75,000	31,500
Other liabilities	33,000	39,000
Common stock.	360,000	195,000
Retained earnings	319,350	210,000
Total liabilities and equity	$835,680	$493,500

First, we can confirm that the parent company applied the cost method of pre-consolidation bookkeeping by analyzing the "Income (loss) from Subsidiary" and the "Equity Investment" accounts in the December 31, 2016 financial statement information. The Income (loss) from Subsidiary is equal to $16,800, which is 80% of the $21,000 in dividends declared by the subsidiary during 2016. In addition, despite the fact the financial statement information is dated December 31, 2016, the Equity Investment account equals the $234,000 amount paid on January 1, 2012, by the parent company for its 80% investment in the subsidiary. Because the parent company did not apply the equity method, it means that the parent company's pre-consolidation net income and stockholders' equity are not going to equal the consolidated totals for these accounts. Of course, as we mention in previous chapters, the difference is caused by the fact that the parent company, in each year since 2012, has not been recording its share of the equity method income of the subsidiary, and, instead, has been recording, as income, the dividends of the subsidiary.

As we mentioned in Chapters 3 and 4, conceptually, the best way to consolidate under these circumstances is to propose a "catch-up" **[ADJ]** consolidating entry to make the parent's beginning of year investment and Retained Earnings accounts be on an "as if equity method" basis. After that catch-up adjustment, except for some subtle differences in the **[C]** entry, the consolidation process is the same as the process we already discussed for the equity method.

As we discussed in previous chapters, the **[ADJ]** entry will be primarily based on the change in the subsidiary's Retained Earnings from the acquisition date to the beginning of the year of consolidation. The one difference is that, in the presence of a noncontrolling interest, the change in the subsidiary's retained earnings is multiplied by the parent's ownership percentage (i.e., 80% in the present example). In addition, the **[ADJ]** entry will include the accumulated 80% AAP amortization from the acquisition date through the beginning of the year of consolidation. This is because, under the equity method, the 80% AAP would have been annually amortized into net income (which gets accumulated in Retained Earnings) and out of the investment account. Finally, all beginning-of-year unconfirmed profits must be removed. As has been the case throughout the chapter, 100% of downstream, and 80% of upstream unconfirmed profits will be removed.

In the present case, the amount of the **[ADJ]** entry is computed as follows:

80% of change in subsidiary Retained Earnings from acquisition date through BOY (80% × [165,000 − 21,000]) . .	$115,200
Less: Cumulative 80% AAP amortization from acquisition date through BOY (4 × $3,000).	(12,000)
Less: 100% of the BOY downstream unconfirmed intercompany inventory profits	(5,250)
Less: 80% of the BOY upstream unconfirmed intercompany inventory profits.	N/A
Less: 100% of the BOY downstream unconfirmed intercompany depreciable asset profits	N/A
Less: 80% of the BOY upstream unconfirmed intercompany depreciable asset profits (80% × [9,000 − 1,500]). . . .	(6,000)
[ADJ] amount.	$ 91,950

The **[ADJ]** entry is proposed in the consolidation spreadsheet that follows. One other important difference from the equity method consolidations is the **[C]** entry. Specifically, because the parent company recognizes its share of declared dividends under the cost method of pre-consolidation bookkeeping, there is no equity method income to eliminate. However, like the equity method case, the [C] entry still eliminates 100% of the subsidiary's declared dividends, introduces the income attributable to the noncontrolling interest for the consolidation year, and establishes the change in the noncontrolling interest balance sheet account for the year (i.e., the difference between the income attributable to the noncontrolling interest and the noncontrolling interest's share of declared dividends for the year). The computation of the income attributable to the noncontrolling interest for 2016 is as follows:

NCI share of the subsidiary's reported net income for 2016 (20% × $66,000)................	$13,200
Less: 20% AAP amortization for 2016	(750)
Add: 20% of the BOY upstream intercompany inventory profits confirmed during 2016.........	N/A
Less: 20% of the EOY upstream intercompany inventory profits deferred from 2016	(1,575)
Add: 20% of the upstream confirmed intercompany depreciable asset profits (20% × 1,500)	300
Consolidated income attributable to the noncontrolling interest.........................	$11,175

Exhibit 5.16 presents the consolidation spreadsheet including the **ADJ** and **C-E-A-D-I** entries assuming a cost-method consolidation. Our consolidation entries are as follows:

[ADJ]	Investment in subsidiary..........................	91,950	
	Beg. retained earnings—Parent		91,950

Catch-up entry needed to place parent company on "as if equity method" basis at the beginning of the consolidation year. See computations above.

[C]	Income (loss) from subsidiary......................	16,800	
	Income attributable to NCI........................	11,175	
	Noncontrolling interest		6,975
	Dividends—Subsidiary		21,000

Removes dividend income from the income statement of the parent, and eliminates declared dividends from the equity section of the subsidiary. Establishes Income attributable to the noncontrolling interest (see computation above) and the change in the noncontrolling interest on the balance sheet during the year (i.e., $6,975 = $11,175 − [20% × $21,000]).

[E]	Common stock (S) @ BOY......................	195,000	
	Retained earnings (S) @ BOY..................	165,000	
	Investment in subsidiary @ BOY		288,000
	Noncontrolling interest (@ BOY)		72,000

Eliminates subsidiary Stockholders' Equity @ BOY. The credit to the Equity Investment eliminates the BOY balance recognized in the parent's Equity investment account. The credit to the Noncontrolling Interest Equity account establishes its balance @ BOY.

[A]	Buildings & equipment, net @ BOY	7,500	
	Goodwill...................................	48,000	
	Investment in subsidiary @ BOY..............		49,200
	Noncontrolling interest @ BOY		6,300

Establishes the BOY 100% unamortized AAP for the identifiable net assets and goodwill. The credit to the Equity Investment eliminates the remaining BOY balance (i.e., not eliminated in [E]). The credit to noncontrolling interest equity account establishes its BOY AAP.

[D]	Depreciation & amortization expense	3,750	
	Buildings and equipment, net		3,750

Amortizes the 100% AAP for the year

[I_cogs]	Investment in subsidiary @ BOY	5,250	
	Cost of goods sold		5,250

Recognizes the deferred downstream intercompany deferred inventory profit from the prior year.

[I_sales]	Sales	33,000	
	Cost of goods sold		33,000

Eliminates the intercompany inventory transactions for the year

[I_cogs]	Cost of goods sold............................	7,875	
	Inventories................................		7,875

Defers the upstream intercompany deferred inventory profit from the current year.

[I_pay]	Accounts payable.............................	7,500	
	Accounts receivable		7,500

Eliminates the intercompany payable and receivable at the end of the year

[I_gain]	Investment in subsidiary @ BOY	6,000	
	Noncontrolling Interest @ BOY...................	1,500	
	Buildings & equipment, net @ BOY............		7,500

Adjusts for the BOY unconfirmed profit from the upstream intercompany depreciable asset transaction

[I_dep]	Buildings & equipment, net	1,500	
	Depreciation & amortization expense		1,500

Confirms the current year of deferred profit from the upstream intercompany depreciable asset transaction

EXHIBIT 5.16	Consolidation Spreadsheet Reflecting Intercompany Transactions in the Presence of Noncontrolling Interest—Cost Method

Cost Method

	Parent	Subsidiary	Consolidation Entries Dr		Cr	Consolidated
Income statement:						
Sales	$720,000	$300,000	[I_sales] $ 33,000			$ 987,000
Cost of goods sold	(360,000)	(162,000)	[I_cogs] 7,875	[I_cogs]	$ 5,250	(491,625)
				[I_sales]	33,000	
Gross profit	360,000	138,000				495,375
Depreciation & amortization expense	(18,000)	(14,400)	[D] 3,750	[I_dep]	1,500	(34,650)
Operating expenses	(225,000)	(54,450)				(279,450)
Interest expense	(9,000)	(3,150)				(12,150)
Total expenses	(252,000)	(72,000)				(326,250)
Income (loss) from subsidiary	16,800		[C] 16,800			0
Consolidated net income	124,800	66,000				169,125
Income attributable to NCI			[C] 11,175			(11,175)
Income attributable to controlling interest	$124,800	$ 66,000				$ 157,950
Statement of retained earnings:						
Beginning retained earnings	$284,550	$165,000	[E] 165,000	[ADJ]	91,950	$ 376,500
Consolidated NI attributable to parent	124,800	66,000				157,950
Income attributable to controlling interest	409,350	231,000				534,450
Dividends declared	(90,000)	(21,000)		[C]	21,000	(90,000)
Ending retained earnings	$319,350	$210,000				$ 444,450
Balance sheet:						
Cash	$ 51,180	$ 22,500				$ 73,680
Accounts receivable	81,000	72,000		[I_pay]	7,500	145,500
Inventories	195,000	69,000		[I_cogs]	7,875	256,125
Buildings and equipment, net	189,000	180,000	[A] 7,500	[D]	3,750	366,750
			[I_dep] 1,500	[I_gain]	7,500	
Other assets	85,500	150,000				235,500
Investment in subsidiary	234,000		[ADJ] 91,950	[E]	288,000	0
			[I_cogs] 5,250	[A]	49,200	
			[I_gain] 6,000			
Goodwill			[A] 48,000			48,000
Total assets	$835,680	$493,500				$1,125,555
Accounts payable	$ 48,330	$ 18,000	[I_pay] 7,500			$ 58,830
Notes payable	75,000	31,500				106,500
Other liabilities	33,000	39,000				72,000
Common stock	360,000	195,000	[E] 195,000			360,000
Retained earnings	319,350	210,000				444,450
Noncontrolling interest			[I_gain] 1,500	[C]	6,975	83,775
				[E]	72,000	
				[A]	6,300	
Total liabilities and equity	$835,680	$493,500	$601,800		$601,800	$1,125,555

As we already noted, the cost-method consolidation is identical to the equity-method consolidation except for the **[ADJ]** entry and a slight modification of the **[C]** entry. However, because the parent company did not use the equity method of pre-consolidation bookkeeping, the parent company's pre-consolidation net income (i.e., $124,800) does not equal consolidated net income (i.e., $157,950), and the parent company's pre-consolidation retained earnings (i.e., $319,350) does not equal consolidated retained earnings (i.e., $444,450). (Note: if the parent used the equity method, these amounts would have been equivalent pre- and post-consolidation.)

By combining the consolidating journal entries related to the noncontrolling interest, we can trace how the consolidation process builds the balance using entries **[C]**, **[E]**, **[A]** and $[I_{gain}]$. We can also prove the $83,775 ending balance in noncontrolling interest by starting with the December 31, 2016 balance in stockholder's equity, as follows:

NCI share of the subsidiary's reported stcokholders' equity at December 31, 2016 (20% × $405,000)	$81,000
Add: unamortized 20% AAP at December 31, 2016 ([$4,500 + $4,800] − [5 years × $750])	5,550
Less: 20% of the EOY upstream intercompany inventory profits deferred from 2016	(1,575)
Less: 20% of the upstream unconfirmed intercompany depreciable asset profits (20% x [$9,000 − {2 × $1,500}]). . .	(1,200)
Consolidated noncontrolling interest	$83,775

The end of this chapter includes a cost method comprehensive review problem.

SUGGESTED INTEGRATED APPROACH FOR MASTERING COMPLEX CONSOLIDATIONS

Now that we have introduced the concepts of noncontrolling interests and intercompany transactions, it should be obvious why business combinations and consolidations are considered to be among the most challenging topics in accounting. The primary sources of difficulties encountered by even the most diligent students are (1) the volume and comprehensiveness of information that must be integrated and (2) the necessary mapping between the consolidation steps and the ongoing investment accounting included in the parent company's pre-consolidation financial statements. In this section of the chapter, we propose a systematic approach for mastering complex consolidations problems.[21]

We propose the following integrated procedure for organizing consolidation-relevant information and for generating consolidation entries:

1. Disaggregate and document the activity for the 100% Acquisition Accounting Premium (AAP), the controlling interest AAP and the noncontrolling interest AAP

2. Calculate and organize the profits and losses on intercompany transactions and balances

3. Compute the pre-consolidation Equity Investment account beginning and ending balances starting with the stockholders' equity of the subsidiary

4. Reconstruct the activity in the parent's pre-consolidation Equity Investment T-account for the year of consolidation

5. Independently compute the owners' equity attributable to the noncontrolling interest beginning and ending balances starting with the owners' equity of the subsidiary

6. Independently calculate consolidated net income, controlling interest net income and noncontrolling interest net income

7. Complete the consolidating entries according to the **C-E-A-D-I** sequence and complete the consolidation worksheet[22]

---

[21] The comprehensive consolidations problems at the end of this chapter will incorporate this approach.

[22] This example illustrates the integrated approach in the case where the parent company uses the equity method of pre-consolidation investment bookkeeping. However, this approach can be readily adapted to situations where the parent company uses the cost method. Although steps 3 and 4 are not necessary when dealing with a cost method situation, step 3 can be a useful exercise given that the [ADJ] entry produces an "as if equity method" Equity Investment account balance at the beginning of the year. Further, step 4 can be easily replaced in the cost case by independently producing the [ADJ] amount. We illustrate this suggested modified approach when solving the comprehensive cost-method example at the end of the chapter.

Cost Method

We will discuss each of these steps in context of the following comprehensive consolidation problem. To illustrate our systematic approach, let's assume that a parent company has been operating since 2009. Our task is to prepare consolidated financial statements for the parent and its subsidiary for the year ended December 31, 2016. The parent acquired 80% of the outstanding common stock of the subsidiary on January 1, 2014, for $1,400,000. On the acquisition date, the subsidiary reported owners' equity of $1,375,000. The fair value of the shares of the subsidiary not acquired by the parent (i.e., 20%) was $348,000. On the date of acquisition, the fair values of the subsidiary's net assets were equal to their book values, except for the following:

Account Dr (Cr)	Book Value	Fair Value
Inventories	$408,000	$368,000
Land	350,000	260,000
Patents	212,000	152,000
Notes payable	(90,000)	(100,000)

The subsidiary's notes payable are due in full on December 31, 2018, with any related premiums and discounts amortized using the straight-line method. The patents have a 10-year remaining useful life. Both the parent and subsidiary use the FIFO cost-flow assumption, and all inventories held by both companies at January 1, 2014 are sold during the year ended December 31, 2014.

On January 1, 2015, the subsidiary sold to the parent for $36,000 equipment with an original cost of $30,000 and accumulated depreciation of $15,000. On the date of intercompany transfer, both companies estimated that the equipment had a remaining useful life of three years. Both companies use the straight-line method of depreciation with zero salvage value.

During 2015, the subsidiary sold merchandise to the parent for $60,000, which included profit of $20,000. At December 31, 2015, half of this merchandise remained in the parent's inventory. During 2016, the subsidiary sold merchandise to the parent for $45,000, which included profit of $15,000. At December 31, 2016, $18,000 of this merchandise remained in the parent's inventory, and the parent still owes $10,000 of the purchase price.

The pre-consolidation financial statements for the year ended December 31, 2016 are presented in Exhibit 5.17.

Preparing consolidated financial statements—regardless of the method of pre-consolidation investment accounting applied by the parent company (e.g., equity, partial equity or cost methods)— requires the collection of information necessary to adjust the stated values reported in the parent and subsidiary pre-consolidation financial statements. This information falls into two general categories: (1) AAP information that is summarized in the parent company's pre-consolidation investment account and that must be disaggregated and reclassified in preparation of the consolidated financial statements, and (2) intercompany transactions and balances that are included in the pre-consolidation financial statements of the parent and subsidiary. The first two steps of our systematic approach focus on summarizing these two categories of information.

Step 1: Disaggregate and Document the Activity for the 100% AAP, the Controlling Interest AAP and the Noncontrolling Interest AAP

Our first step is focused on the AAP. Regardless of the percentage financial interest held by the parent company, the acquisition method requires consolidated financial statements to reflect 100% of the amortized acquisition date fair values of the subsidiary. Thus, when assembling AAP related information, our summary should always include the 100% AAP values. In addition, the 100% AAP should be allocated to the controlling and noncontrolling interests. The unamortized controlling-interest AAP

EXHIBIT 5.17	Pre-Consolidation Financial Statements for the Year Ended December 31, 2016		
		Parent	**Subsidiary**
Income statement:			
Sales.		$ 420,000	$ 175,000
Cost of goods sold.		(180,000)	(110,000)
Gross profit.		240,000	65,000
Depreciation & amortization expense.		(36,000)	(10,000)
Interest expense.		(54,000)	(8,000)
Other expenses		(60,000)	(30,000)
Total expenses		(150,000)	(48,000)
Income (loss) from subsidiary.		28,800	0
Net income.		$ 118,800	$ 17,000
Statement of retained earnings:			
Beginning retained earnings.		$ 272,800	$ 398,000
Net income.		118,800	17,000
Dividends declared.		(24,000)	(15,000)
Ending retained earnings		$ 367,600	$ 400,000
Balance sheet:			
Cash and short-term receivables.		$ 152,000	$ 245,000
Inventories		300,000	200,000
Buildings and equipment, net		714,000	677,000
Land		—	350,000
Patents		—	148,400
Equity investment.		1,460,800	—
Total assets.		$2,626,800	$1,620,400
Accounts payable.		$ 553,200	$ 124,400
Notes payable		1,500,000	96,000
Common stock.		206,000	1,000,000
Retained earnings		367,600	400,000
Total liabilities and equity		$2,626,800	$1,620,400

will be reflected in the <u>pre-consolidation</u> investment account, with amortization of the controlling-interest AAP included in the <u>pre-consolidation</u> investment income under the equity method. The unamortized noncontrolling-interest AAP will be reflected in the noncontrolling interest account in the consolidated balance sheet, with amortization of the noncontrolling-interest AAP included in the net income attributable to the noncontrolling interest in the consolidated income statement. This means there is a need to understand all three partitions of the AAP: 100%, the controlling interest portion, and the noncontrolling interest portion.

In our present example, the 100% AAP on January 1, 2014 was $373,000. The acquisition-date AAP is calculated by computing the fair value of 100% of the company (i.e., the controlling and noncontrolling interest fair values) and subtracting the book value of net assets on the subsidiary's books: ($1,400,000 fair value of 80% + $348,000 fair value of 20%) − $1,375,000 book value of the subsidiary's net assets = $1,748,000 − $1,375,000 − $373,000. This 100% AAP represents differences between fair values and recorded book values for the identifiable net assets of the subsidiary, with any residual difference assigned to goodwill. The identifiable differences between fair value and book value are summarized as follows:

Account Dr (Cr)*	January 1, 2014		
	Book Value	Fair Value	Assigned Identifiable 100% AAP (FV – BV)
Inventories	$408,000	$368,000	$ (40,000)
Land	350,000	260,000	(90,000)
Patents	212,000	152,000	(60,000)
Notes payable	(90,000)	(100,000)	(10,000)
Net	$880,000	$680,000	$(200,000)

* The debit (credit) notation in the AAP schedule is a useful tool that can help minimize mistakes when dealing with the AAP. The total AAP is an adjustment to the recorded book value of net assets of the subsidiary, so positive amounts will increase net assets and negative amounts will decrease net assets. In this case, the notes payable has a fair value (i.e., $100,000) that exceeds the book value (i.e., $90,000). By representing the notes payable as negative amount, the fair-value-minus-book-value difference automatically decreases the net AAP by $10,000. This is much easier than trying to remember the signs of AAP adjustments to individual asset and liability accounts.

Note that each of the identifiable components of the AAP represents a decrease to the net book value of the subsidiary's net assets. Specifically, inventories, land and patents are overvalued on the subsidiary's books by $40,000, $90,000 and $60,000, respectively, while the liability for notes payable is undervalued by $10,000. Taken together, these identifiable AAP components represent a net downward adjustment of recorded net assets equal to $200,000.

On the acquisition date, goodwill is the residual AAP that remains after assigning the AAP to the identifiable net assets. In this case, the net AAP adjustment writes down the subsidiary's net assets, resulting in goodwill that is larger than the total 100% AAP. Specifically, total goodwill is calculated as the total 100% AAP minus the net debit AAP assigned to the identifiable net assets: $373,000 − (−$200,000) = $573,000. (Because the AAP is a credit it has a negative sign.) On the acquisition date, all of the individual components of the $373,000 100% AAP—including both the identifiable and unidentifiable portions—are summarized as follows:

Account	Acquisition Date 100% AAP
Inventories	$ (40,000)
Land	(90,000)
Patents	(60,000)
Notes payable	(10,000)
Goodwill	573,000
Total AAP	$373,000

In the periods following the acquisition date, the 100% AAP assigned to inventories, patents and notes payable will be amortized over their respective useful lives/term in the consolidated financial statements. The AAP assigned to land is not amortized because land is not depreciated or amortized under current generally accepted accounting principles (GAAP). The AAP assigned to goodwill is not depreciated or amortized because goodwill is considered an indefinite-lived intangible that is subject to annual impairment review. (See Chapter 3 for discussion of goodwill accounting.)

Because the companies use the FIFO cost flow assumption and all inventories were sold during the year ended December 31, 2014, all $40,000 of the credit AAP assigned to inventories is amortized during the year ended December 31, 2014. Because the inventory-related AAP has a credit balance, its amortization will decrease cost of goods sold (i.e., increase consolidated net income) by $40,000 in the consolidated income statement for the year ended December 31, 2014. The patents have a 10-year remaining useful life, so the credit AAP assigned to patents will have $6,000 of amortization each year through December 31, 2023. Because the patent-related AAP has a credit balance, its amortization will decrease depreciation and amortization expense by $6,000 (i.e., increase consolidated net income) in the consolidated income statement each year through December 31, 2023. The notes payable have a 5-year remaining term, so the credit AAP assigned to notes payable will have $2,000 of amortization each year. Because the notes-payable-related AAP has a credit balance, its amortization will decrease interest expense by $2,000 (i.e., increase consolidated net income) in the consolidated income statement each year through December 31, 2018 (i.e., the due date of the last payment on the note).

The following table summarizes the balances and activity for the 100% AAP through December 31, 2016:

100% AAP – Dr (Cr)	Unamortized 100% AAP 1/1/2014	Fiscal Year 2014 Amortization	Unamortized 100% AAP 12/31/2014	Fiscal Year 2015 Amortization	Unamortized 100% AAP 12/31/2015	Fiscal Year 2016 Amortization	Unamortized 100% AAP 12/31/2016
Inventories	$(40,000)	$40,000	$ 0		$ 0		$ 0
Land	(90,000)		(90,000)		(90,000)		(90,000)
Patents	(60,000)	6,000	(54,000)	$6,000	(48,000)	$6,000	(42,000)
Notes payable	(10,000)	2,000	(8,000)	2,000	(6,000)	2,000	(4,000)
Goodwill	573,000		573,000		573,000		573,000
Net	$373,000	$48,000	$421,000	$8,000	$429,000	$8,000	$437,000

The 100% AAP is important to understand because it is necessary to determine account balances in the consolidated financial statements. Understanding the AAP allocated to the controlling and noncontrolling interests is also necessary because (1) the controlling interest AAP is included in the parent company's pre-consolidation investment account and (2) the noncontrolling-interest share of the AAP is reflected in the consolidated noncontrolling-interest-related accounts.

The controlling interest share of the AAP on January 1, 2014 equals $300,000, and is determined by taking the fair value of the controlling interest on the acquisition date and subtracting the controlling interest share of the book value of net assets of the subsidiary on that same date: $1,400,000 − (80% × $1,375,000) = $1,400,000 − $1,100,000 = $300,000. On the acquisition date, each of the identifiable net assets is assigned a controlling-interest share of their respective AAP amounts. The controlling-interest goodwill is then calculated as the residual controlling AAP that remains after factoring in the controlling portions of the AAP assigned to the all of the identifiable net assets. In addition, similar to the 100% AAP, the controlling interest AAP is amortized for any of the identifiable net assets subject to depreciation or amortization.

The following table summarizes the balances and activity for the controlling interest portion of the AAP from the acquisition date through December 31, 2016:

Controlling Interest AAP – Dr (Cr)	Unamortized 80% AAP 1/1/2014	Fiscal Year 2014 Amortization	Unamortized 80% AAP 12/31/2014	Fiscal Year 2015 Amortization	Unamortized 80% AAP 12/31/2015	Fiscal Year 2016 Amortization	Unamortized 80% AAP 12/31/2016
Inventories	$(32,000)	$32,000	$ 0		$ 0		$ 0
Land	(72,000)		(72,000)		(72,000)		(72,000)
Patents	(48,000)	4,800	(43,200)	$4,800	(38,400)	$4,800	(33,600)
Notes payable	(8,000)	1,600	(6,400)	1,600	(4,000)	1,600	(3,200)
Goodwill	460,000		460,000		460,000		460,000
Net	$300,000	$38,400	$338,400	$6,400	$344,800	$6,400	$351,200

The noncontrolling interest share of the AAP on January 1, 2014 equals $73,000, and is determined by taking the fair value of the noncontrolling interest on the acquisition date and subtracting the noncontrolling interest share of the book value of net assets of the subsidiary on that same date: $348,000 − (20% × $1,375,000) = $348,000 − $275,000 = $73,000. On the acquisition date, each of the identifiable net assets is assigned a noncontrolling-interest share of their respective AAP amounts. The noncontrolling-interest goodwill is then calculated as the residual noncontrolling AAP that remains after factoring in all of the noncontrolling portions of the AAP assigned to the identifiable net assets. In addition, similar to the 100% AAP and the controlling interest AAP, the noncontrolling interest AAP is amortized for any of the identifiable net assets subject to depreciation or amortization.

The following table summarizes the balances and activity for the noncontrolling interest portion of the AAP from the acquisition date through December 31, 2016:

Noncontrolling Interest AAP – Dr (Cr)	Unamortized 20% AAP 1/1/2014	Fiscal Year 2014 Amortization	Unamortized 20% AAP 12/31/2014	Fiscal Year 2015 Amortization	Unamortized 20% AAP 12/31/2015	Fiscal Year 2016 Amortization	Unamortized 20% AAP 12/31/2016
Inventories	$ (8,000)	$8,000	$ 0		$ 0		$ 0
Land	(18,000)		(18,000)		(18,000)		(18,000)
Patents	(12,000)	1,200	(10,800)	$1,200	(9,600)	$1,200	(8,400)
Notes payable	(2,000)	400	(1,600)	400	(1,200)	400	(800)
Goodwill	113,000		113,000		113,000		113,000
Net	$ 73,000	$9,600	$ 82,600	$1,600	$ 84,200	$1,600	$ 85,800

We will find that explicit documentation of the components and activity of the 100% AAP, controlling interest AAP and the noncontrolling interest AAP will make the rest of the consolidation process much easier to manage.

Step 2: Calculate and Organize the Profits and Losses on Intercompany Transactions and Balances

The second step involves gathering all information related to intercompany transactions and balances that affect the financial statements for the fiscal year of consolidation. As we discuss in Chapter 4, all intercompany transactions and balances are eliminated from the consolidated financial statements. In addition, under the equity method, intercompany transactions and balances are eliminated from the parent company's pre-consolidation Equity-Investment-related accounts.[23]

In the present example, the affiliated companies have two types of transactions that affect the consolidated financial statements for the year ended December 31, 2016. First, the companies engaged in an upstream intercompany sale of equipment on January 1, 2015. Second, the companies engaged in upstream intercompany sales of inventory, with intercompany profits in both the beginning-of-year and end-of-year inventories of the parent.

Turning first to the equipment, on January 1, 2015, the subsidiary sold to the parent for $36,000 equipment with an original cost of $30,000 and accumulated depreciation of $15,000. On the date of intercompany transfer, both companies estimated that the equipment had a remaining life of three years, and both companies use the straight-line method of depreciation with zero salvage value. As summarized in Exhibit 5.18, this means that the subsidiary recognized $21,000 of gain in its financial statements on January 1, 2015 that must be deferred and recognized in the consolidated financial statements over the remaining three-year useful life of the equipment. Because the companies use the straight-line method of depreciation and there is no salvage value, the deferred gain will get recognized in the consolidated financial statements in three equal $7,000 adjustments. Because the intercompany transaction occurred at the beginning of 2015, the net deferral will be $14,000 through the year ended

EXHIBIT 5.18	Initial Deferral and Subsequent Recognition of Gain on Upstream Intercompany Equipment Sale

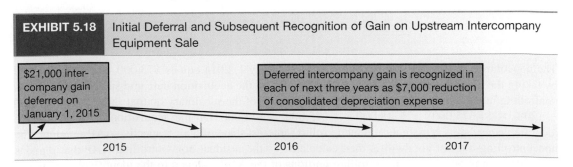

$21,000 intercompany gain deferred on January 1, 2015

Deferred intercompany gain is recognized in each of next three years as $7,000 reduction of consolidated depreciation expense

2015   2016   2017

---

[23] Under the partial equity method and the cost method, intercompany transactions and balances are not eliminated from the parent's pre-consolidation Equity Investment account. Regardless of the method of pre-consolidation Equity Investment accounting, intercompany transactions and balances are always eliminated from the consolidated financial statements.

December 31, 2015 (i.e., deferral of original intercompany gain of $21,000 at January 1, 2015 less $7,000 recognized through a reduction of depreciation expense for the year ended December 31, 2015).

When organizing intercompany-transaction-related information for completion of complex consolidations problems, we suggest that students completely summarize both upstream and downstream activity, even if there was no intercompany activity. For example, in the present problem, there is an upstream transaction involving depreciable fixed assets but no downstream transactions. So, in addition to summarizing the information for the upstream asset sale, we suggest explicitly indicating that there was zero downstream activity. This is important because the direction of the transaction affects pre-consolidation Equity Investment and Equity Income, and also affects the post consolidation non-controlling-interest-related accounts. By using a universal template that predictably categorizes and organizes information, we have a lower chance of making an error. The following table summarizes all relevant downstream and upstream amounts (for the year ending December 31, 2016) related to intercompany sales of noncurrent assets:

	Downstream	Upstream
Net intercompany profit deferred at January 1, 2016	$0	$14,000
Less: Deferred intercompany profit recognized during 2016	0	(7,000)
Net intercompany profit deferred at December 31, 2016	$0	$ 7,000

We now turn to the intercompany inventory transactions. Although it is important to eliminate all intercompany transactions and balances, we primarily focus on inventories sold between affiliated entities where one of the entities still holds the inventory at the beginning or end of the reporting period. These types of intercompany inventory holdings are particularly important because they impact pre-consolidation income and retained earnings for parent company (when the parent applies the equity method) and also affect consolidated income, retained earnings and noncontrolling interest.

In the present example, during 2015, the subsidiary sold merchandise to the parent for $60,000, which included profit of $20,000. At December 31, 2015, half of this merchandise remained in the parent's inventory. This means that $10,000 (i.e., $20,000 × 1/2) of upstream intercompany profits were in the parent's inventory on December 31, 2015, all of which were deferred. During 2016, the subsidiary sold merchandise to the parent for $45,000, which included profit of $15,000. At December 31, 2016, $18,000 of this merchandise remained in the parent's inventory. This means that $6,000 (i.e., $18,000 × ($15,000/$45,000)) of upstream intercompany profits were in the parent's inventory on December 31, 2016, all of which must be deferred. The companies engaged in no downstream inventory transactions. In addition to summarizing the information for the upstream inventory amounts, we also strongly recommend explicitly indicating that there are zero downstream amounts in beginning and ending inventories. The following table summarizes the intercompany profits included in the parent and subsidiary beginning and ending inventories:

	Downstream (in Subsidiary's Inventory)	Upstream (in Parent's Inventory)
Intercompany profit in inventory on January 1, 2016	$0	$10,000
Intercompany profit in inventory on December 31, 2016	$0	$ 6,000

The effects of these continuous intercompany inventory transactions are illustrated in Exhibit 5.19. Note that the full amount of the shifting of these intercompany profits is recognized in consolidated cost of goods sold and consolidated net income. Because they are upstream transactions, they will also be allocated to the noncontrolling interest. This means that their net effects on bottom-line controlling interest income will be only p% (i.e., 80%). If these were downstream inventory transactions, none of the inter-temporal shifting of profits would be allocated to the noncontrolling interest, meaning that 100% would affect the controlling interest.

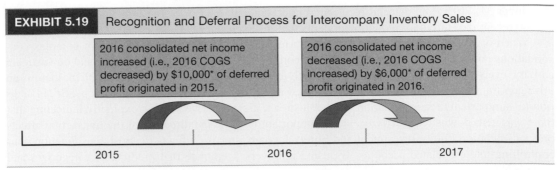

EXHIBIT 5.19 Recognition and Deferral Process for Intercompany Inventory Sales

* Because this is an upstream transaction, 20% will be allocated to the noncontrolling interest, resulting in an 80% allocation to the controlling interest. If this instead were a downstream transaction, none would be allocated to the noncontrolling interest, resulting in 100% allocation to the controlling interest.

Although they do not affect reported income or reported equity, we must also eliminate other amounts resulting from intercompany transactions. In this example, we also need to eliminate the intercompany sale of $45,000 that occurred during the year ending December 31, 2016. In addition, the parent still owes $10,000 on December 31, 2016, and this amount must be removed from accounts receivable and accounts payable in the consolidated financial statements.

Step 3: Compute the Pre-Consolidation Equity Investment Account Beginning and Ending Balances Starting with the Stockholders' Equity of the Subsidiary

In our experience, the most significant factor that contributes to difficulties in mastering consolidations is a fundamental lack of understanding of Equity Investment accounting on the pre-consolidation books of the parent company. This should not be a surprise if one considers the effects of the **C-E-A-D-I** consolidation entries: most of the entries "undo" the Equity Investment accounting recorded by the parent company. Thus, because of the importance of understanding Equity Investment accounting in consolidations, we believe it is important to independently calculate the beginning and ending Equity Investment balances, starting with the subsidiary's reported beginning and ending stockholders' equity balances, respectively.

At any point in time, the equity-method Equity Investment account can be derived from the net assets of the subsidiary, adjusted for unamortized AAP and any deferred intercompany profits that have not yet been confirmed through either third party transactions with unaffiliated parties or through depreciation and/or amortization. Specifically, on any given date, the equity method Equity Investment account can be computed as follows:

	(1) p% × book value of the net assets of the subsidiary
Plus:	(2) Unamortized p% AAP
Less:	(3) 100% × downstream deferred intercompany profits
Less:	(4) p% × upstream deferred intercompany profits
	Equity method Equity Investment account

Let's use this formula and apply it to the facts in the present example. First, we'll compute the beginning balance for the equity method Equity Investment account. Recall that January 1, 2016 stockholders' equity of the subsidiary is equal to $1,398,000. Our unamortized 80% AAP on January 1, 2016 (i.e., December 31, 2015) is equal to $344,800. On January 1, 2016, the companies had no downstream intercompany profits, but had two sources of upstream intercompany profits. First, the upstream intercompany equipment sale resulted in $14,000 of deferred intercompany profits on January 1, 2016. Second, the parent's inventory on January 1, 2016 included $10,000 of deferred upstream intercompany profits.

	Jan. 1, 2016	
	$1,118,400	(1) 80% × $1,398,000
Plus:	344,800	(2) $344,800 (from Step 1)
Less:	0	(3) 100% × $0 (from Step 2)
Less:	(11,200)	(4) 80% × $14,000 (from Step 2)
Less:	(8,000)	(4) 80% × $10,000 (from Step 2)
	$1,444,000	

Now, we'll compute the ending balance for the equity method Equity Investment account. Recall that December 31, 2016 stockholders' equity of the subsidiary is equal to $1,400,000. Our unamortized 80% AAP on December 31, 2016 is equal to $351,200. On December 31, 2016, the companies had no downstream intercompany profits, but had two sources of upstream intercompany profits. First, the upstream intercompany equipment sale resulted in $7,000 of deferred intercompany profits on December 31, 2016. Second, the parent's inventory on December 31, 2016 included $6,000 of deferred upstream intercompany profits.

	Dec. 31, 2016	
	$1,120,000	(1) 80% × $1,400,000
Plus:	351,200	(2) $351,200 (from Step 1)
Less:	0	(3) 100% × $0 (from Step 2)
Less:	(5,600)	(4) 80% × $7,000 (from Step 2)
Less:	(4,800)	(4) 80% × $6,000 (from Step 2)
	$1,460,800	

At this point it is useful to compare the December 31, 2016 Equity Investment account balance that we just computed to the Equity Investment account included in the pre-consolidation financial statements provided in Exhibit 5.17. They are exactly equal! By practicing the independent derivation of the Equity Investment account balance, students have a much better chance of understanding how the Equity Investment account is eliminated through the consolidation process.

Step 4: Reconstruct the Activity in the Parent's Pre-Consolidation Equity Investment T-Account for the Year of Consolidation

Now that we have the independently computed beginning and ending balances for the pre-consolidation Equity Investment, we will next focus on explaining the change in this balance during the year. We propose using a T-account format to document these changes.

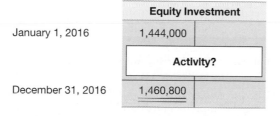

The equity method Equity Investment accounting includes the following routine adjustments during any given period: (a) recognition of p% of the subsidiary's income, (b) amortization of the p% AAP, (c) recognition of p% of the dividends declared by the subsidiary, (d) recognition of prior period deferred intercompany profits that have been confirmed through either transactions with unaffiliated parties or depreciation/amortization, and (e) deferral of intercompany profits newly originated during the current period. With respect to the deferred intercompany profits, the effect on the Equity Investment account is 100% for downstream transactions and p% for upstream transactions. Information for items (a) and (c) is available in Exhibit 5.17, information for item (b) was summarized in Step 1, and information for items (d) and (e) was summarized in Step 2. These items are all reflected in the following completed T-account.

Equity Investment			
January 1, 2016	1,444,000		
(a) p% × net income of Sub. = 80% × $17,000	13,600	12,000	(c) p% × dividends of Sub. = 80% × $15,000
(b) p% AAP amortization (see Step 1)	6,400	4,800	(e) p% × EOY upstream inventory profits deferred until year of sale to unaffiliated party = 80% × $6,000
(d) p% × BOY upstream inventory profits recognized during 2016 = 80% × $10,000	8,000		
(d) p% × upstream equipment profits recognized via depreciation during 2016 = 80% × $7,000	5,600		
December 31, 2016	1,460,800		

This T-account activity also provides insight into the determination of the $28,800 of Equity Income recognized in the parent's pre-consolidation income statement presented in Exhibit 5.17. Except for the dividends declared by the subsidiary, all of the above-listed changes in the Equity Investment account are included in arriving at equity method Equity Income.

This T-account includes two items that deserve further discussion. First, the amortization of the AAP (i.e., $6,400 debit) *increases* the Equity Investment account because the AAP adjustments subject to amortization represent write downs of the recorded net assets of the subsidiary (i.e., fair value was less than book value on the acquisition date). In the typical case, fair values exceed book values at the acquisition date, which would result in a reduction of the Equity Investment account when the AAP is amortized. Second, all of the deferred intercompany transaction adjustments are multiplied times 80% because all of the intercompany profits were the result of *upstream* transactions. If any of the intercompany profits were the result of downstream transactions, then those adjustments would have been multiplied times 100%.

Step 5: Independently Compute the Beginning and Ending Balances of Owners' Equity Attributable to the Noncontrolling Interest Starting with the Owners' Equity of the Subsidiary

Independently computing the equity attributable to the noncontrolling interest allows additional insight into the consolidation process, and also provides an important check figure that can be used to validate the consolidated financial statements that result from the C-E-A-D-I consolidation entries. Given that we start with the owners' equity of the subsidiary to arrive at noncontrolling interest, it should not be surprising that the noncontrolling-interest-related adjustments to owners' equity are quite similar to controlling-interest adjustments we made in Step 3. Indeed, on any given date, the value of the controlling interest (i.e., the equity method Equity Investment account balance) and the noncontrolling interest are complementary amounts that represent 100% of the consolidated net assets of the subsidiary! This is because the pre-consolidation Equity Investment account represents the portion of the subsidiary's net assets that *is owned* by the parent company, while the consolidated noncontrolling interest in the equity of the subsidiary represents the portion of the subsidiary's net assets that *is not owned* by the parent company (i.e., obviously, the percentage owned plus the percentage not owned equals 100%).

At any point in time, the noncontrolling interest in the owners' equity of the subsidiary can be derived from the net assets of the subsidiary, adjusted for unamortized AAP and any *upstream* deferred intercompany profits that have not yet been confirmed through either third party transactions with unaffiliated parties or through depreciation and/or amortization.[24] Specifically, on any given date, the noncontrolling interest in the owners' equity of the subsidiary can be computed as follows:

	(1) nci% × book value of the net assets of the subsidiary
Plus:	(2) Unamortized nci% AAP
Less:	(3) nci% × upstream deferred intercompany profits
	Noncontrolling Interest account

Let's use this formula and apply it to the facts in the present example. First, we'll compute the beginning balance for the Noncontrolling Interest account. Recall that January 1, 2016 stockholders' equity of the subsidiary is equal to $1,398,000. Our unamortized 20% AAP on January 1, 2016 (i.e., December 31, 2015) is equal to $84,200. On January 1, 2016, the companies had two sources of upstream intercompany profits. First, the upstream intercompany equipment sale resulted in $14,000 of deferred intercompany profits on January 1, 2016. Second, the parent's inventory on January 1, 2016 included $10,000 of deferred upstream intercompany profits.

	Jan. 1, 2016	
	$279,600	(1) 20% × $1,398,000
Plus:	84,200	(2) $84,200 (from Step 1)
Less:	(2,800)	(3) 20% × $14,000 (from Step 2)
Less:	(2,000)	(3) 20% × $10,000 (from Step 2)
	$359,000	

Now, we'll compute the ending balance for the Noncontrolling Interest account. Recall that December 31, 2016 stockholders' equity of the subsidiary is equal to $1,400,000. Our unamortized 20% AAP on December 31, 2016 is equal to $85,800. On December 31, 2016, the companies had two sources of upstream intercompany profits. First, the upstream intercompany equipment sale resulted in $7,000 of deferred intercompany profits on December 31, 2016. Second, the parent's inventory on December 31, 2016 included $6,000 of deferred upstream intercompany profits.

	Dec. 31, 2016	
	$280,000	(1) 20% × $1,400,000
Plus:	85,800	(2) $85,800 (from Step 1)
Less:	(1,400)	(3) 20% × $7,000 (from Step 2)
Less:	(1,200)	(3) 20% × $6,000 (from Step 2)
	$363,200	

Although not included as a separate step, we can also construct a T-account that documents the year's "activity" in the noncontrolling interest in the owners' equity of the subsidiary, as follows:[25]

---

[24] Given that 100% of downstream intercompany profits are attributable to the controlling interest, this means that 0% of downstream profits are attributable to the noncontrolling interest.

[25] Note that there are not actually general ledger accounts for, "noncontrolling interest," per se. The income statement and balance sheet accounts for noncontrolling interest are created during the consolidation process. Under our framework, these consolidated accounts are created through the C-E-A-D-I consolidation entries. (Recall that consolidation entries are not actually recorded in the accounting records of any of the consolidating companies.) Thus, any representation of a noncontrolling interest T-account is more symbolic than real.

	Noncontrolling interest in the owners' equity of the subsidiary		
		359,000	January 1, 2016
nci% × dividends of Sub. = 20% × $15,000	3,000	3,400	nci% × net income of Sub. = 20% × $17,000
nci% × EOY upstream inventory profits deferred until year of sale to unaffiliated party = 20% × $6,000	1,200	1,600	nci% AAP amortization (see Step 1)
		2,000	nci% × BOY upstream inventory profits recognized during 2016 = 20% × $10,000
		1,400	nci% × upstream equipment profits recognized via depreciation during 2016 = 20% × $7,000
		363,200	December 31, 2016

We can use this T-account activity to determine the amount of consolidated net income attributable to the noncontrolling interest. Except for the dividends declared by the subsidiary, all of the above-listed changes in consolidated noncontrolling interest equity account are included in arriving at $7,200 of consolidated net income attributable to the noncontrolling interest. We will provide additional discussion of the determination of this amount in Step 6.

Step 6: Independently Calculate Consolidated Net Income, Controlling Interest Net Income and Noncontrolling Interest Net Income Starting with the Pre-Investment-Accounting Incomes of the Parent and Subsidiary

In this step, we will use the "stand-alone" pre-consolidation incomes of the parent and the subsidiary to estimate consolidated net income, controlling interest net income and noncontrolling interest net income. The stand-alone income represents the income of each company without the including effects of Equity Investment accounting on the parent's books. Referring to Exhibit 5.17, this means that the pre-consolidation stand-alone income of the parent is $90,000 (i.e., $118,800 − $28,800) and the subsidiary is $17,000.

Consolidated net income represents the 100% combined income for the consolidated entity, before allocating the income to the controlling and noncontrolling interests. Thus, it is *mostly* explained by combining the pre-consolidation stand-alone net income of each of the two entities. We also must make adjustments for the 100% AAP amortization and 100% of the deferred intercompany profits. Because of the need to allocate consolidated income to the controlling and noncontrolling interests (and the differential proportional adjustment for upstream and downstream transactions), we separately deal with the parent's stand-alone income and the subsidiary's net income in the computation of consolidated net income in Exhibit 5.20.

Notice that consolidated net income is derived from the adjusted stand-alone net incomes of the parent and the subsidiary. We will also use these adjusted income amounts to derive the controlling interest portion of net income and the noncontrolling interest portion of net income. A quick and easy way to compute these two partitions is to recognize the fact that the controlling interest has a 100% financial interest in the adjusted stand-alone income of the parent (i.e., $90,000) plus the p% financial interest in the adjusted stand-alone income of the subsidiary (i.e., 80% × $36,000), which equals $118,800. Notice that this amount equals the parent's pre-consolidation net income in Exhibit 5.17. (Remember, consolidation is just a form of the equity method; thus, parent company income determined using the equity method must equal the controlling interest share of consolidated net income.) The remaining nci% (i.e., 1 − p%) interest in the adjusted stand-alone income of the subsidiary is equal to the net income attributable to the noncontrolling interest, which is $7,200 (i.e., 20% × $36,000).

EXHIBIT 5.20	Incremental Computation of Consolidated Net Income for the Year Ended December 31, 2016		
		Year ended Dec. 31, 2016	
Parent's stand-alone net income		$ 90,000	(see Exhibit 5.17)
Plus: 100% realized downstream deferred profits		0	(see Step 2)
Less: 100% unrealized downstream deferred profits		(0)	(see Step 2)
Parent's adjusted stand-alone net income		$ 90,000	
Subsidiary's stand-alone net income		$ 17,000	(see Exhibit 5.17)
Plus: 100% realized upstream deferred profits		10,000	(see Step 2)
		7,000	(see Step 2)
Less: 100% unrealized upstream deferred profits		(6,000)	(see Step 2)
Less: 100% AAP amortization		(−8,000)	(see Step 1)
Subsidiary's adjusted stand-alone net income		$ 36,000	
Consolidated net income		$126,000	

We can also incrementally compute the net incomes attributable to the controlling interest and noncontrolling interest, as is provided in Exhibits 5.21 and 5.22, respectively. Each of these independent computations helps to provide additional insight into the meaning of the reported consolidated amounts. In addition, they provide highly valuable check figures for the upcoming step in which we propose the **C-E-A-D-I** consolidating entries and complete our consolidation worksheet.

EXHIBIT 5.21	Incremental Computation of Consolidated Net Income Attributable to the Controlling Interest for the Year Ended December 31, 2016		
		Year ended Dec. 31, 2016	
100% × Parent's stand-alone net income		$ 90,000	(see Exhibit 5.17)
Plus: 100% realized downstream deferred profits		0	(see Step 2)
Less: 100% unrealized downstream deferred profits		(0)	(see Step 2)
100% of the Parent's adjusted stand-alone net income		$ 90,000	
80% × Subsidiary's stand-alone net income (80% × $17,000)		$ 13,600	(see Exhibit 5.17)
Plus: 80% realized upstream deferred profits (80% × $10,000)		8,000	(see Step 2)
(80% × $7,000)		5,600	(see Step 2)
Less: 80% unrealized upstream deferred profits (80% × $6,000)		(4,800)	(see Step 2)
Less: 80% AAP amortization (from schedule)		(−6,400)	(see Step 1)
80% of the Subsidiary's adjusted stand-alone net income		$ 28,800	
Consolidated net income attributable to the controlling interest		$118,800	

EXHIBIT 5.22	Incremental Computation of Consolidated Net Income Attributable to the Noncontrolling Interest for the Year Ended December 31, 2016		
		Year ended Dec. 31, 2016	
20% × Subsidiary's stand-alone net income (20% × $17,000)		$ 3,400	(see Exhibit 5.17)
Plus: 20% realized upstream deferred profits (20% × $10,000)		2,000	(see Step 2)
(20% × $7,000)		1,400	(see Step 2)
Less: 20% unrealized upstream deferred profits (20% × $6,000)		(1,200)	(see Step 2)
Less: 20% AAP amortization (from schedule)		(−1,600)	(see Step 1)
Consolidated net income attributable to the noncontrolling interest . .		$ 7,200	

Step 7: Complete the Consolidating Entries According to the C-E-A-D-I Sequence and Complete the Consolidation Worksheet

In this step, we prepare the consolidated financial statements using the information and check figures gathered in the preceding steps. Our consolidating entries are as follows:

[C]	Income (loss) from subsidiary...............	28,800		Eliminates all changes in the Equity Investment and establishes changes in Noncontrolling Interest accounts during the consolidation period
	Income attributable to NCI...................	7,200		
	Dividends – subsidiary...............		15,000	
	Equity investment		16,800	
	Noncontrolling interest		4,200	
[E]	Common stock @ BOY	1,000,000		Eliminates subsidiary BV of Stockholders' Equity @ BOY. The credit to the Equity Investment eliminates the BOY BV balance in the parent's Equity Investment account. The credit to the Noncontrolling Interest Equity account establishes BV balance @ BOY.
	Retained earnings @ BOY	398,000		
	Equity investment @ BOY		1,118,400	
	Noncontrolling interest @ BOY		279,600	
[A]	Goodwill @ BOY.........................	573,000		Recognizes the BOY AAP components on the consolidated balance sheet. Eliminates the parent's share of the BOY AAP from its Equity Investment account and recognizes the noncontrolling interests' share of the AAP in the NCI equity account. [Note that the allocation of the 100% AAP is equal to the split calculated in Step 1]
	Land @ BOY		90,000	
	Patents @ BOY		48,000	
	Notes payable @ BOY.................		6,000	
	Equity investment @ BOY		344,800	
	Noncontrolling interest @ BOY		84,200	
[D]	Patents....................	6,000		Recognizes depreciation/amortization expense and interest expense relating to the identifiable AAP net assets. Adjust the balance sheet accounts to reflect their correct end-of-year totals.
	Notes payable	2,000		
	Depreciation & amort. expense		6,000	
	Interest expense		2,000	
[I$_{cogs}$]	Equity investment @ BOY	8,000		The deferred profit from the prior period is included in consolidated net income in the year in which the intercompany assets are sold to non-affiliates. For an upstream sale, the deferred profit is split between the controlling and noncontrolling interests.
	Noncontrolling interest @ BOY...............	2,000		
	Cost of goods sold		10,000	
[I$_{sales}$]	Sales	45,000		We always eliminate 100% of all intercompany transactions. Note: this entry has no effect on net income.
	Cost of goods sold		45,000	
[I$_{cogs}$]	Cost of goods sold........................	6,000		We eliminate 100% of the deferred profit included on the balance sheet (i.e., this is the 100% elimination). It is pro-rata allocated to the noncontrolling interest because this is also included in entry [C] as an adjustment to the income attributable to the noncontrolling interest.
	Inventories.........................		6,000	
[I$_{pay}$]	Accounts payable.........................	10,000		We eliminate all intercompany payables and receivables.
	Cash and short-term receivables		10,000	
[I$_{gain}$]	Equity investment @ BOY	11,200		The deferred profit from the prior period equipment sale still on the books of the parent and must be removed as of the beginning of the year. For an upstream sale, the deferred profit is split between the controlling and noncontrolling interests.
	Noncontrolling interest @ BOY...............	2,800		
	Buildings and equipment, net		14,000	
[I$_{dep}$]	Buildings and equipment, net	7,000		A portion of the deferred profit from the prior period upstream equipment sale is confirmed as a depreciation adjustment. Because it is upstream, this effect is pro-rata allocated to the noncontrolling interest because this is also included in entry [C] as an adjustment to the income attributable to the noncontrolling interest
	Depreciation expense		7,000	

EXHIBIT 5.23	Consolidation Spreadsheet for the Year Ended December 31, 2016

	Parent	Subsidiary	Dr		Cr		Consolidated
Income statement:							
Sales........................	$ 420,000	$ 175,000	[I$_{sales}$]	$ 45,000			$ 550,000
Cost of goods sold..............	(180,000)	(110,000)	[I$_{cogs}$]	6,000	[I$_{cogs}$]	$ 10,000	(241,000)
					[I$_{sales}$]	45,000	
Gross profit...................	240,000	65,000					309,000
Depreciation & amort. expense	(36,000)	(10,000)			[D]	6,000	(33,000)
					[I$_{dep}$]	7,000	
Interest expense...............	(54,000)	(8,000)			[D]	2,000	(60,000)
Other expenses	(60,000)	(30,000)					(90,000)
Total expenses	(150,000)	(48,000)					(183,000)
Income (loss) from subsidiary.........	28,800		[C]	28,800			0
Consolidated net income	118,800	17,000					126,000
Consolidated NI attributable to NCI......			[C]	7,200			(7,200)
Consolidated NI attributable to parent....	$ 118,800	$ 17,000					$ 118,800
Statement of retained earnings:							
Beginning retained earnings...........	$ 272,800	$ 398,000	[E]	398,000			$ 272,800
Consolidated NI attributable to parent....	118,800	17,000					118,800
Dividends declared..............	(24,000)	(15,000)			[C]	15,000	(24,000)
Ending retained earnings	$367,600	$400,000					$ 367,600
Balance sheet:							
Cash and short-term receivables........	$ 152,000	$ 245,000			[I$_{pay}$]	10,000	$ 387,000
Inventories	300,000	200,000			[I$_{cogs}$]	6,000	494,000
Buildings and equipment, net	714,000	677,000	[I$_{dep}$]	7,000	[I$_{gain}$]	14,000	1,384,000
Land.......................		350,000			[A]	90,000	260,000
Patents.....................		148,400	[D]	6,000	[A]	48,000	106,400
Equity investment.................	1,460,800		[I$_{cogs}$]	8,000	[C]	16,800	0
			[I$_{gain}$]	11,200	[E]	1,118,400	
					[A]	344,800	
Goodwill.....................			[A]	573,000			573,000
Total assets..................	$2,626,800	$1,620,400					$3,204,400
Accounts payable	$ 553,200	$ 124,400	[I$_{pay}$]	10,000			$ 667,600
Notes payable	1,500,000	96,000	[D]	2,000	[A]	6,000	1,600,000
Common stock.................	206,000	1,000,000	[E]	1,000,000			206,000
Retained earnings	367,600	400,000					367,600
Noncontrolling interest................			[I$_{cogs}$]	2,000	[C]	4,200	363,200
			[I$_{gain}$]	2,800	[E]	279,600	
					[A]	84,200	
Total liabilities and equity.............	$2,626,800	$1,620,400		$2,107,000		$2,107,000	$3,204,400

CHAPTER SUMMARY

We discussed concepts related to circumstances where a parent company has a controlling interest in a subsidiary, but does not possess a 100% ownership interest in the subsidiary. Whenever a parent controls a subsidiary—even if the parent owns less than 100% of the subsidiary—the parent must issue consolidated financial statements that present 100% of the subsidiary's assets, liabilities, revenues and expenses. In the presence of noncontrolling shareholders (i.e., shareholders of the subsidiary other than the parent), GAAP requires the Stockholders' Equity section of the consolidated balance sheet to clearly separate the interests of two groups of shareholders: (1) shareholders of the parent company who have a claim on the net assets of the total consolidated entity by virtue of their ownership of the parent company, and (2) noncontrolling shareholders of the subsidiary who only have a claim on the net assets of the subsidiary. In addition, the consolidated income statement must allocate the 100% consolidated net income between the controlling and noncontrolling interests.

On the date of acquisition, the consolidated balance sheet will reflect 100% of the fair values of the subsidiary's net assets, including goodwill. This fair value of the subsidiary's net assets can be split into two pieces: (1) the recorded book value of net assets of the subsidiary, plus (2) the acquisition accounting premium (AAP). The AAP for all of the *identifiable* net assets (i.e., everything except for goodwill), is divided between the controlling and noncontrolling interests in proportion to the controlling and noncontrolling ownership percentages. Because of the possibility of a control premium or a bargain purchase, goodwill might not be divided according to the relative ownership interests of the controlling and noncontrolling interest. In the post-acquisition consolidated financial statements, the change in the AAP is allocated to the income attributable to the noncontrolling interests (along with its proportionate share of the subsidiary's net income), and the unamortized AAP is allocated to the noncontrolling interest equity account (along with its proportionate share of the subsidiary's book value of net assets).

As we discuss in Chapter 4, all profits and losses resulting from intercompany transactions must be eliminated from the consolidated financial statements. If the parent company owns 100% of its subsidiary, then downstream (i.e., transfers from parent to the subsidiary) and upstream transactions are treated the same. If the parent owns less than 100% of its subsidiary, then downstream and upstream transactions are treated differently from each other. In the presence of noncontrolling interests, downstream intercompany asset sales are completely eliminated with none of the elimination allocated to the noncontrolling interest. This is because the related gains and losses are recognized by the parent company in a downstream sale, and the noncontrolling interest owns 0% of the parent company. In the presence of noncontrolling interests, upstream sales require allocation of deferred and recognized profits and losses to the controlling and noncontrolling shareholders. This is because the related gains and losses are recognized by the subsidiary in an upstream sale; the parent company and noncontrolling shareholder(s) own p% and nci% (i.e., 1-p%), respectively, of the subsidiary.

We acknowledge that consolidations involving noncontrolling interests and intercompany profits and losses can be complex and difficult to complete. We recommend the following integrated approach to completing these complex problems:

1. Disaggregate and document the activity for the 100% Acquisition Accounting Premium (AAP), the controlling interest AAP and the noncontrolling interest AAP.

2. Calculate and organize the profits and losses on intercompany transactions and balances.

3. Compute the pre-consolidation Equity Investment account beginning and ending balances starting with the stockholders' equity of the subsidiary.

4. Reconstruct the activity in the parent's pre-consolidation Equity Investment T-account for the year of consolidation.

5. Independently compute the owners' equity attributable to the noncontrolling interest beginning and ending balances starting with the owners' equity of the subsidiary.

6. Independently calculate consolidated net income, controlling interest net income and noncontrolling interest net income.

7. Complete the consolidating entries according to the **C-E-A-D-I** sequence and complete the consolidation worksheet.

COMPREHENSIVE REVIEW—EQUITY METHOD

A parent company acquired 75 percent of the stock of a subsidiary company on January 1, 2012, for $280,000. On this date, the balances of the subsidiary's stockholders' equity accounts were Common Stock, $195,000, and Retained Earnings, $45,000. On January 1, 2012, the market value for the 25% of shares not purchased by the parent was $90,000.

On January 1, 2012, the subsidiary's recorded book values were equal to fair values for all items except four: (1) accounts receivable had a book value of $55,000 and a fair value of $48,000, (2) property, plant & equipment, net had a book value of $150,000 and a fair value of $168,000, (3) a previously unrecorded customer list intangible asset had a book value of $0 and a fair value of $30,000, and (4) notes payable had a book value of $30,000 and a fair value of $25,000. Both companies use the FIFO inventory method and sell all of their inventories at least once per year. The year-end net balance of accounts receivables are collected in the following year. On the acquisition date, the subsidiary's property, plant & equipment, net had a remaining useful life of 10 years, the customer list had a remaining useful life of 4 years, and notes payable had a remaining term of 5 years.

On January 1, 2015, the parent sold a building to the subsidiary for $80,000. On this date, the building was carried on the parent's books (net of accumulated depreciation) at $55,000. Both companies estimated that the building has a remaining life of 10 years on the intercompany sale date, with no salvage value.

Each company routinely sells merchandise to the other company, with a profit margin of 40 percent of selling price (regardless of the direction of the sale). During 2016, intercompany sales amount to $50,000, of which $20,000 of merchandise remains in the ending inventory of the subsidiary. On December 31, 2016, $10,000 of these intercompany sales remained unpaid. Additionally, the parent's December 31, 2015 inventory includes $15,000 of merchandise purchased in the preceding year from the subsidiary. During 2015, intercompany sales amount to $40,000, and on December 31, 2015, $8,000 of these intercompany sales remained unpaid.

The parent accounts for its Equity Investment in the subsidiary using the equity method. Unconfirmed profits are allocated pro rata.

The pre-closing trial balances (and additional information) for the two companies for the year ended December 31, 2016, are provided below:

	Parent	Subsidiary
Debits		
Cash.	$ 58,080	$ 42,500
Accounts receivable.	81,000	60,000
Inventories	195,000	91,500
Property, plant & equipment, net	189,000	135,000
Other assets.	85,500	150,000
Equity Investment.	325,500	—
Cost of goods sold.	432,000	162,000
Depreciation & amortization expense.	18,000	14,400
Operating expenses.	226,000	54,100
Interest expense.	8,000	3,500
Dividends declared.	90,000	21,000
Total debits.	$1,708,080	$734,000
Credits		
Accounts payable.	$ 168,000	$ 35,000
Notes payable	80,980	30,000
Other liabilities	33,000	39,000
Common stock.	360,000	195,000
Retained earnings (Jan. 1, 2016)	322,200	165,000
Sales.	720,000	270,000
Income (loss) from subsidiary.	23,900	—
Total credits	$1,708,080	$734,000
Additional Information		
Retained earnings (Dec. 31, 2016).	$ 292,100	$180,000
Net income.	$ 59,900	$ 36,000

Required

a. Prepare a consolidation spreadsheet using the December 31, 2016 pre-closing trial balance information for the parent and subsidiary.[26]

b. Disaggregate and document the activity for the 100% Acquisition Accounting Premium (AAP), the controlling interest AAP and the noncontrolling interest AAP.

c. Calculate and organize the profits and losses on intercompany transactions and balances.

d. Compute the pre-consolidation Equity Investment account beginning and ending balances starting with the stockholders' equity of the subsidiary.

e. Reconstruct the activity in the parent's pre-consolidation Equity Investment T-account for the year of consolidation.

f. Independently compute the owners' equity attributable to the noncontrolling interest beginning and ending balances starting with the owners' equity of the subsidiary.

g. Independently calculate consolidated net income, controlling interest net income and noncontrolling interest net income.

h. Complete the consolidating entries according to the **C-E-A-D-I** sequence and complete the consolidation worksheet.

The solution to this review problem can be found on pages 375–381.

COMPREHENSIVE REVIEW—COST METHOD

A parent company acquired 80 percent of the stock of a subsidiary company on January 1, 2012, for $360,000. On this date, the balances of the subsidiary's stockholders' equity accounts were Common Stock, $260,000, and Retained Earnings, $28,000. On January 1, 2012, the market value for the 20% of shares not purchased by the parent was $88,000.

On January 1, 2012, the subsidiary's recorded book values were equal to fair values for all items except four: (1) accounts receivable had a book value of $60,000 and a fair value of $52,000, (2) property, plant & equipment, net had a book value of $100,000 and a fair value of $136,000, (3) patents had a book value of $70,000 and a fair value of $154,000, and (4) notes payable had a book value of $40,000 and a fair value of $28,000. Both companies use the FIFO inventory method and sell all of their inventories at least once per year. The year-end net balance of accounts receivables is collected in the following year. On the acquisition date, the subsidiary's property, plant & equipment, net had a remaining useful life of 5 years, the patents had a remaining useful life of 7 years, and notes payable had a remaining term of 4 years.

On December 31, 2014, the parent sold a building to the subsidiary for $130,000. On this date, the building was carried on the parent's books (net of accumulated depreciation) at $100,000. Both companies estimated that the building has a remaining life of 5 years on the intercompany sale date, with no salvage value. Each company routinely sells merchandise to the other company, with a profit margin of 30 percent of selling price (regardless of the direction of the sale). During 2016, intercompany sales amount to $48,000, of which $28,000 of merchandise remains in the ending inventory of the subsidiary. On December 31, 2016, $16,000 of these intercompany sales remained unpaid. Additionally, the parent's December 31, 2015 inventory includes $22,000 of merchandise purchased in the preceding year from the subsidiary. During 2015, intercompany sales amount to $40,000, and on December 31, 2015, $13,500 of these intercompany sales remained unpaid.

The parent accounts for its Equity Investment in the subsidiary using the cost method. Unconfirmed profits are allocated pro rata.

The pre-closing trial balances (and additional information) for the two companies for the year ended December 31, 2016, are provided as follows:

---

[26] As we mention as part of the comprehensive review in chapter 4, we believe there is great pedagogical value in students creating their own functioning consolidation spreadsheets from trial balance information. Programming the formulas that result in articulating consolidated financial statements can help students better understand the basic relations in financial statements and the mechanics of consolidation. In part a. of the solution to this comprehensive review, we provide the trial balance information converted to financial statement format.

	Parent	Subsidiary
Debits		
Cash...	$ 77,440	$ 30,000
Accounts receivable....................................	108,000	96,000
Inventories	260,000	92,000
PPE, net	252,000	220,000
Other assets...	114,000	200,000
Patents..	—	20,000
Investment in subsidiary.............................	360,000	—
Cost of goods sold....................................	480,000	236,000
Depreciation & amortization expense............	24,000	19,200
Operating expenses...................................	260,000	52,600
Interest expense.......................................	12,000	4,200
Dividends declared....................................	120,000	28,000
Total debits..	$2,067,440	$998,000
Credits		
Accounts payable......................................	$ 64,440	$ 24,000
Notes payable	100,000	42,000
Other liabilities	44,000	52,000
Common stock..	480,000	260,000
Retained earnings (Jan. 1, 2016)	436,600	220,000
Sales...	920,000	400,000
Income (loss) from subsidiary......................	22,400	—
Total credits	$2,067,440	$998,000
Additional information		
Retained earnings (Dec. 31, 2016)...............	$ 483,000	$280,000
Net income...	$ 166,400	$ 88,000

Required

a. Prepare a consolidation spreadsheet using the December 31, 2016 pre-closing trial balance information for the parent and subsidiary.[27]

b. Disaggregate and document the activity for the 100% Acquisition Accounting Premium (AAP), the controlling interest AAP and the noncontrolling interest AAP.

c. Calculate and organize the profits and losses on intercompany transactions and balances.

d. Compute the pre-consolidation Equity Investment account beginning and ending balances assuming that the parent company used the equity method instead of the cost method. For each of these computations, start with the stockholders' equity of the subsidiary.

e. Compute the amount of the [ADJ] consolidating entry.

f. Independently compute the owners' equity attributable to the noncontrolling interest beginning and ending balances starting with the owners' equity of the subsidiary.

g. Independently calculate consolidated net income, controlling interest net income, and noncontrolling interest net income.

h. Complete the consolidating entries according to the **C-E-A-D-I** sequence and complete the consolidation worksheet.

The solution to this review problem can be found on pages 382–388.

---

[27] For students who do not wish to program their own consolidation spreadsheets, in *Part a.* of the solution to this comprehensive review, we provide the trial balance information converted to financial statement format.

LO5 Explain differences in measurement of noncontrolling interest under current U.S. GAAP, former U.S. GAAP, and the proportionate alternative allowed under International Financial Reporting Standards.

APPENDIX 5A: Business Combinations and Alternative Measurements of Noncontrolling Interest

In this appendix, we describe two alternative measurements of noncontrolling interest: one required by U.S. GAAP prior to the issuance of SFAS 141(R)[28] in 2007, and one that is an alternative currently allowed under International Financial Reporting Standards (IFRS).

Measurement of Noncontrolling Interest in the United States Prior to SFAS 141(R) and ASC 805

Prior to the effective date of SFAS 141(R) in 2009, business combinations in the United States were accounted for under a method called "Purchase Accounting."[29] In comparison to "Acquisition Accounting" currently mandated by U.S. GAAP, Purchase Accounting had many differences in the recognition and measurement of business combinations. In Exhibit 5A.1 we summarize the most significant differences between Acquisition Accounting currently included in FASB ASC 805 and Purchase Accounting applied to business combinations in fiscal years beginning before December 15, 2008. We highlight current GAAP in light beige.

| **EXHIBIT 5A.1** | Comparison of Acquisition Method in FASB ASC 805 and Purchase Method in FASB SFAS No. 141 |

Area	FASB SFAS No. 141 (prior to 2009)	FASB ASC 805 (current GAAP)
1. Definition of a Business	Excluded development-stage enterprises and entities without existing markets for outputs.	Definition is expanded to include entities that are "capable of" generating a revenue stream.
2. Equity Instruments Issued as Consideration	Equity instruments issued by the acquirer measured at fair value a few days before and after the parties agreed to the acquisition (i.e., usually also the initial announcement date).	Equity instruments issued by the acquirer are measured at fair value on the acquisition date (i.e., deal closing).
3. Acquisition-Related Costs	The purchase price includes the direct costs of the business combination (e.g., investment banking fees, legal fees, etc.).	If costs are unrelated to issuance of debt or equity securities, the costs are generally expensed in the period incurred.
4. Earnings-Based Contingent Consideration	Recognized as an adjustment to the purchase price when the contingency is resolved and consideration is issued or issuable.	Recognized and measured at fair value on the acquisition date, with subsequent changes in fair value of liability-classified contingent consideration recognized in earnings.
5. Recognizing and Measuring Assets Acquired, Liabilities Assumed, and Noncontrolling Interests	The assets acquired and liabilities assumed are adjusted only for the acquirer's share (i.e., p%) of their fair values. Noncontrolling interests are based on the noncontrolling share (i.e., nci%) of the book value of net assets of acquiree.	Whether the acquirer acquires all or a partial interest in the acquiree, the full fair value (i.e., 100%) of the assets acquired, liabilities assumed, and noncontrolling interests is recognized.
6. Step Acquisitions	Each tranche of ownership interests obtained by the acquirer includes separate adjustments to fair value.	The carrying amounts of previously acquired tranches are adjusted to fair value at the date control is obtained, and the acquirer recognizes the differences as a gain or loss in income at the acquisition date.
7. In-Process Research and Development (IPR&D)	The fair value of intangible assets to be used in IPR&D projects that have no alternative future use is charged to expense at the acquisition date.	The acquiree's IPR&D projects are recognized as an intangible asset and measured at fair value. The IPR&D asset is treated as an indefinite-lived intangible asset, and therefore is capitalized, but it is not subject to amortization until the project is completed or abandoned.
8. Restructuring Costs	Restructuring costs for plans to be implemented subsequent to the acquisition are recognized as a liability in Purchase Accounting if certain criteria are met within a short period of time after the acquisition date.	Restructuring costs are not recognized as a liability in Acquisition Accounting unless the criteria in FASB ASC 420 are met at the acquisition date.

---

[28] SFAS No. 141(R) was issued in 2007 as a replacement of SFAS No. 141, which the FASB issued in June 2001.

[29] Purchase Method accounting was mandated under SFAS No. 141 and Accounting Principles Board (APB) Opinion No. 16. APB Opinion No. 16 also required an alternative method of accounting, called "Pooling of Interests" if 12 conditions were met. SFAS No. 141 abolished Pooling of Interests, but business combinations completed prior to 2002 might still include recognition and measurement determined under Pooling procedures. Thus, given the length of time many companies hold onto their subsidiaries, you will continue to encounter acquisitions accounted for using these two previous methods for many years. We provide an overview of Pooling of Interests in the Appendix to Chapter 3.

We highlight the differences in Exhibit 5A.1 because they are likely to affect consolidated financial statements for many years to come. These differences will impede the ability of analysts and investors to make valid comparisons across companies that engaged in acquisitions pre- versus post-2009. In this section, we emphasize the difference described in Item #5 in Exhibit 5A.1 (i.e., "Recognizing and Measuring Assets Acquired, Liabilities Assumed, and Noncontrolling Interests") that results in different measurement of noncontrolling interest, recognized net assets, and goodwill. Specifically, under the purchase method, companies were not allowed to recognize noncontrolling interest at fair value, as is required under SFAS 141(R) and currently codified in FASB ASC 805. Instead, noncontrolling interest was recognized at the subsidiary's pre-acquisition carrying value of its net assets.

To illustrate the measurement and reporting differences caused by purchase-accounting treatment, we provide the following basic example. First, we will illustrate the accounting that is required by ASC 805, and then we will illustrate the accounting that would results under application of the purchase method that was required in the U.S. prior to 2009. Assume that a parent company purchased its 70% interest in a subsidiary on January 1, 2016 with a combination of cash and stock valued at $1,340. The parent paid a premium to gain control of the subsidiary; thus, the value of the 30% noncontrolling interest is $560. The total acquisition-date fair value of the entire subsidiary is summarized, as follows:

Fair value of the controlling interest (70%)..	$1,340
Fair value of the noncontrolling interest (30%).......................................	560
Fair value of the entire subsidiary..	$1,900

In addition, assume that the subsidiary reports the following book values and fair values for its assets and liabilities:

	Book Value	Fair Value
Current assets	$300	$ 300
PPE, net	900	1,500
Current liabilities..	(150)	(150)
Long-term liabilities	(300)	(300)
Net assets	$750	$1,350

The PPE assets have a market value that is $600 (i.e., $1,500 − $900) in excess of the reported book value. The fair value of the subsidiary's identifiable net assets is $1,350 (i.e., $300 + $1,500 − $150 − $300). FASB ASC 805 is a fair-value-based standard; the $550 of reported goodwill is equal to the difference between the $1,900 fair value of the entire subsidiary and $1,350 fair value of the subsidiary's identifiable net assets. The goodwill is assigned to the controlling and noncontrolling interests, as follows:

Controlling interest goodwill: $1,340 − (70% × $1,350)...	$395
Noncontrolling interest goodwill: $560 − (30% × $1,350)	155
Total goodwill: $1,900 − $1,350..	$550

In contrast, the old purchase accounting method did not allow the noncontrolling interest to have any fair value adjustments; that is, it was always equal to the noncontrolling interest percentage ownership times the book value of the net assets of the subsidiary. In addition, under purchase accounting, the identifiable net assets could only be adjusted for the controlling interest share of the AAP. Using the same facts as our previous illustration, purchase accounting would yield the following amounts for the controlling and noncontrolling interest portions:

Fair value of the controlling interest (70% = equity investment in S)	$1,340
Book value of the noncontrolling interest (30% × $750 book value of net asset of S)...........	225
Recorded value of the entire subsidiary..	$1,565

This means that the resulting net assets all had recognized values that were a blend of 70% of the net assets' acquisition-date fair values and 30% of the net assets' acquisition date recorded book values. In our example, the only asset for which this is an issue is the PPE, net, because it has a difference between fair value and book value. Interestingly, pursuant to the old purchase accounting method, the recognized value of the PPE would be $1,320 (i.e., 70 % × $1,500 fair value plus 30% × $900 book value). Further, the following is a breakdown of the goodwill recognized in the U.S. (prior to 2009) under the purchase method:

Controlling interest goodwill: $1,340 − (70% × $1,350)	$395
Noncontrolling interest goodwill	0
Total goodwill	$395

Exhibit 5A.2 provides an illustration of the different amounts recognized currently under FASB ASC 805 and the amounts recognized under the old purchase method of accounting for business combinations:

EXHIBIT 5A.2	Comparison of Current U.S. GAAP (Acquisition Accounting) to Previous U.S. GAAP (Purchase Accounting) for Non-Wholly Owned Subsidiaries	

Consolidated (excluding the parent)	Current U.S. GAAP (ASC 805) Acquisition Accounting	Previous U.S. GAAP (APB 16 & SFAS 141) Purchase Accounting
Current assets	$ 300	$ 300
PPE, net	1,500	1,320
Goodwill	550	395
Total assets	$2,350	$2,015
Current liabilities	$ 150	$ 150
Long-term liabilities	300	300
Noncontrolling interest	560	225
Controlling interest in subsidiary	$1,340	$1,340

An extremely important point to note is that, *regardless of valuation of the Noncontrolling Interest or Goodwill, the total for "Controlling interest in subsidiary" is equal to $1,340.* Further, this amount is equal to the $1,340 paid by the parent for the subsidiary (i.e., it is equal to the Equity Investment account on the parent's books). This is an excellent demonstration that regardless of consolidation approach and noncontrolling interest measurement, the net effects of the subsidiary on the consolidated financial statements must always equal the balance of the investment account.

Measurement of Noncontrolling Interest Under International Financial Reporting Standards

The accounting adopted in SFAS 141(R) (and currently codified in FASB ASC 805) is the result of a joint standard-setting project undertaken by the FASB and the International Accounting Standards Board (IASB), which is based in London, England. Because of the close working relationship between the FASB and IASB in developing the new accounting standard for business combinations, the IASB issued a virtually identical standard—*IFRS No. 3(R)*—in January 2008.[30]

We describe the FASB and IASB versions of business combinations accounting as "virtually identical" because the recognition, measurement, and classification guidance related to business combinations is almost word-for-word the same across the two standards. However, there is one important difference: *in less-than-100% acquired subsidiaries, U.S. GAAP in ASC 805 mandates 100% Goodwill recognition along with the resulting initial fair-value recognition of the noncontrolling interest, while IFRS No. 3 allows a choice—on a business-combination-by-business-combination basis—between the 100% Goodwill approach used in the U.S. and a proportional approach in which the noncontrolling interest is recognized at its proportionate share of the fair value of the identifiable net assets of the subsidiary.* When compared to the amounts recognized under ASC 805, this alternative treatment will result in different recognized amounts for noncontrolling interest and goodwill for business combination in which a parent company buys a less-than-100% controlling interest in a subsidiary.[31]

---

[30] IFRS No. 3(R) was issued as a replacement of IFRS No. 3, which the IASB issued in March 2004.

[31] To ease exposition, we will refer to the approach that is consistent with ASC 805 acquisition accounting as the "full fair value approach," and the IFRS alternative that is inconsistent with U.S. GAAP as the "proportionate share alternative."

To illustrate the difference, we continue with the same facts we discussed in the preceding section. Specifically, we assume that a parent company purchased its 70% interest in a subsidiary on January 1, 2016 with a combination of cash and stock valued at $1,340. On the acquisition date, the subsidiary reports the following book values and fair values for its assets and liabilities:

	Book Value	Fair Value
Current assets	$300	$ 300
PPE, net	900	1,500
Current liabilities	(150)	(150)
Long-term liabilities	(300)	(300)
Net Assets	$750	$1,350

Despite the fact that our original facts indicated that the noncontrolling interest has a fair value equal to $560, we ignore this amount and estimate the recorded value of noncontrolling interest based on the fair value of the identifiable net assets of the subsidiary. This leads to the following total recognized amount that will appear in the post-acquisition financial statements under the proportionate share alternative allowed under IFRS:

Fair value of the controlling interest (70% = equity investment in S)	$1,340
Recognized value of the noncontrolling interest (30% × $1,350)	405
Recorded value of the entire subsidiary	$1,745

Interestingly, this results in recognized goodwill that is identical to the purchase accounting method that was required under U.S. GAAP prior to 2009. This is because, under both purchase accounting and the proportionate share alternative allowed under IFRS, the only goodwill that is recognized is based on the 70% controlling interest acquired by the parent company. Goodwill under the IFRS proportionate share alternative is computed as follows:

Controlling interest goodwill: $1,340 − (70% × $1,350)	$395
Noncontrolling interest goodwill: $405 − (30% × $1,350)	0
Total goodwill: $1,745 − $1,350	$395

Although the goodwill amount is the same as purchase accounting, the recognized identifiable net assets are measured on a conceptually superior, full fair value basis. In the present example, the recognized post-acquisition value for the PPE, net will be the full 100% fair value of $1,500. Exhibit 5A.3 provides a comparison of the full fair value alternative allowed under IFRS (i.e., the approach identical to acquisition accounting in current U.S. GAAP), the proportionate share alternative allowed under IFRS, and the purchase method that was required under U.S. GAAP before 2009:

EXHIBIT 5A.3	Comparison of Two IFRS Alternatives (i.e., Full Fair Value and Proportionate Share) to Previous U.S. GAAP (Purchase Accounting) for Non-Wholly Owned Subsidiaries

Consolidated (excluding the parent)	IFRS Full Fair Value Alternative (same as ASC 805 Acquisition Accounting)	IFRS Proportionate Share Alternative	Previous U.S. GAAP (APB 16 & SFAS 141)—Purchase Accounting
Current assets	$ 300	$ 300	$ 300
PPE, net	1,500	1,500	1,020
Goodwill	550	395	395
Total assets	$2,350	$2,195	$2,015
Current liabilities	$ (150)	$ (150)	$ (150)
Long-term liabilities	(300)	(300)	(300)
Noncontrolling Interest	(560)	(405)	(225)
Controlling interest in subsidiary	$1,340	$1,340	$1,340

An interesting feature of Exhibit 5A.3 is that it reveals the IFRS proportionate share alternative to be a blend between the full fair value alternative allowed under IFRS (and required under U.S. GAAP) and the old purchase method recognition required in the U.S. prior to 2009. In particular, both the full fair value approach and proportionate share approach recognized all identifiable net assets at their 100% fair values. However, the goodwill in the IFRS proportionate share alternative is identical to the amount recognized under U.S. GAAP prior to 2009.

In closing, we repeat an important property of the three different approaches for measurement of Noncontrolling Interest or Goodwill: each of the totals for "Controlling interest in subsidiary" is equal to $1,340. As we mentioned previously, this amount is equal to the $1,340 fair value of the parent's investment in the subsidiary (i.e., it is equal to the Equity Investment account on the parent's books). Again, regardless of consolidation approach and noncontrolling interest measurement, the net effects of the subsidiary on the consolidated financial statements must always equal the balance of the investment account.

APPENDIX 5B: Consolidated Earnings Per Share (EPS)

LO6 Explain the computation of earnings per share for consolidated companies.

In this appendix, we describe the computation of consolidated Earnings Per Share (EPS). Basic EPS is unaffected by the presence of subsidiary companies and noncontrolling interests. Basic EPS is computed according to the following formula:

$$\text{Basic EPS} = \frac{\text{Consolidated net income} - \text{Preferred dividends}}{\text{Weighted average number of common share outstanding}}$$

Note that the preferred dividends in the numerator refer to the dividends of the parent company and the weighted average number of common shares outstanding in the denominator refers to the parent's common shares outstanding.

Diluted EPS adds the effects of conversion of all convertible securities and exercise of all options at their earliest possible opportunity (assuming, of course, that the convertible securities and options are not anti-dilutive) for both the parent and its subsidiary:

$$\text{Diluted EPS} = \frac{\begin{pmatrix} \text{Net income} \\ \text{of parent} \end{pmatrix} - \begin{pmatrix} \text{Preferred} \\ \text{dividends} \end{pmatrix} + \begin{pmatrix} \text{Adjustment for} \\ \text{parent securities} \end{pmatrix} + \begin{pmatrix} \text{Shares} \\ \text{held} \end{pmatrix} \times \begin{pmatrix} \text{Subsidiary diluted} \\ \text{EPS} \end{pmatrix}}{\begin{pmatrix} \text{Weighted average number of} \\ \text{common shares outstanding} \end{pmatrix} + \begin{pmatrix} \text{Additional shares outstanding} \\ \text{from dilution} \end{pmatrix}}$$

To illustrate, assume the following facts:

	Parent	Subsidiary
1. Net income	$100,000	$40,000
2. Common shares outstanding	30,000	20,000 (16,000 = 80% owned by parent)
3. Convertible preferred stock	Dividends = $10,000 Convertible into 5,000 shares of common stock	
4. Convertible bonds		Interest expense after tax = $6,000 Convertible into 3,000 shares of common stock

$$\text{Consolidated basic EPS} = \frac{\$100,000 - \$10,000 + (\$40,000 \times 0.8)}{30,000} = \frac{\$122,000}{30,000} = \$4.07$$

Consolidated diluted EPS
    Step 1: Compute diluted EPS of subsidiary:

$$\text{Diluted EPS of subsidiary} = \frac{\$40,000 + \$6,000}{20,000 + 3,000} = \frac{\$46,000}{23,000} = \$2.00$$

Step 2: Compute consolidated diluted EPS:[32]

$$\text{Consolidated diluted EPS} = \frac{\$100,000 - \$0 + (16,000 \times \$2.00)}{30,000 + 5,000} = \frac{\$132,000}{35,000} = \$3.77$$

APPENDIX 5C: Accounting for Changes in Ownership

Companies often change their level of ownership in subsidiaries over time. It is not uncommon for an investor to purchase a relatively small interest in the investee initially, and to increase its Equity Investment by successive purchases over time. These investments may, therefore, be accounted for as passive investments (fair value method) when the investor has no influence over the investee, and, then, as Equity Investments (equity method) once the investor can exert significant influence over the investee. Finally, at some point, the investor owns enough of the outstanding common stock to give it control over the investee (legal control exists at an amount greater than 50% of the outstanding voting common stock). The acquisition of a controlling interest triggers several accounting-related events, including the requirement to consolidate the financial statements of the investor and the investee.

LO7 Explain the effects on consolidated financial statements of changes in the ownership percentage of a subsidiary.

A company may also reduce its Equity Investment in a subsidiary over time. This reduction can result from the sale of shares by the investor company or by the issuance of shares of newly issued stock by the investee company to outside parties. Reductions of the level of Equity Investment in the subsidiary also trigger accounting-related events, eventually resulting in deconsolidation of the subsidiary.

We discuss the accounting-related effects of both increases and decreases in the level of Equity Investment in this appendix.

Accounting for an Acquisition Achieved in Stages (Step Acquisitions)

Some acquisitions occur over a period of time, with the investor acquiring successive blocks of the outstanding common stock of the investee. We discuss the accounting for acquisitions achieved in stages (called step acquisitions) in two parts: the accounting for an acquisition on the date when control is achieved, and accounting for an additional purchase of stock subsequent to the date when control is achieved.

Accounting for an Acquisition on the Date When Control Is Achieved   The date on which the investor gains control of the investee is the **acquisition date**. It is on that date when the amount of Goodwill to be recognized, if any, is determined by the following formula:

	Fair value of controlling interest in subsidiary
+	Fair value of any noncontrolling interest in the subsidiary
=	Total fair value of the investee company
−	Fair value of the identifiable assets acquired and liabilities assumed
=	Goodwill (i.e., positive residual)

Both of the following occur on the acquisition date:

1. *All of the Equity Investments made by the investor in the investee must be revalued, and any gain or loss as a result of the revaluation should be recognized currently in income.*[33]
2. Goodwill is measured (this only occurs on the date that the parent obtains control of the investee).

The revaluation gain or loss in the first item represents the transition from the accounting for the investment securities using the fair value or equity method to the accounting for the investment as a *controlling* interest in the investee on the acquisition date. At the point when the investor gains the ability to control the operating activities of the investee, the value of its prior ownership interest changes from a noncontrolling investment to an investment with control. The parent must determine the fair value of its Equity Investment immediately prior to gaining control and then adjust the Equity Investment balance to the post-control fair value. *Any holding gain or loss on the parent's pre-control Equity Investment must be recognized in earnings in the period in which control of the investee is obtained.*

---

[32] The $0 in the numerator is due to the fact that the Preferred Stock is assumed to be converted at the beginning of the year. Thus, no preferred dividends are paid.

[33] Also, if the investment was previously accounted for as an available for sale security under FASB ASC 320-10, the amount reflected in Other Comprehensive Income (OCI) relating to that investment must be reclassified and included in the calculation of gain or loss as of the acquisition date (FASB ASC 805-10-25-10).

To illustrate, assume that a parent's acquisition of its 80% interest in subsidiary occurred over several purchases:

Purchase	Percentage Purchased	Purchase Price
1	5%	$ 20,000
2	30%	150,000
3	45%	315,000
Total	80%	

Immediately prior to the third acquisition, assume that the parent's Equity Investment account includes the following activity:

Equity Investment			
Purchase #1	20,000		
Equity income	2,000	500	Dividend
Balance	21,500		
Purchase #2	150,000		
Equity income	17,000	4,000	Dividend
Balance	184,500		

Immediately prior to obtaining control of the investee, the 35% (5% + 30%) interest in subsidiary has a book value of $184,500. Based on accepted valuation practices, the parent determined that its 35% pre-control Equity Investment has a fair value of $245,000. The Equity Investment must now be written up to its fair value with the following journal entry:

Equity investment.	60,500	
Gain on revaluation of subsidiary		60,500
(to record the write-up of the Equity Investment account to its fair value)		

The revaluation gain of $60,500 is recognized by the parent in its income statement during the period in which the controlling interest in the subsidiary is obtained. In addition, the parent must make the following disclosures in the footnotes to the consolidated financial statements:

■ The acquisition-date fair value of the equity interest in the investee held by the investor immediately before the acquisition date

■ The amount of any gain or loss recognized as a result of remeasuring to fair value the equity interest in the investee held by the acquirer before the business combination and the line item in the income statement in which that gain or loss is recognized.

Assume that the parent determines that its 80% controlling Equity Investment has a fair value of $560,000.[34] In addition, the parent estimates that the noncontrolling interest has a fair value of $140,000. Further assume that the fair value of the identifiable net assets is $540,000. The computation of Goodwill on the acquisition date is as follows:

	$560,000	Fair value of parent's controlling interest in subsidiary
+	140,000	The fair value of any noncontrolling interest in the subsidiary
=	700,000	Total fair value of the investee company
−	540,000	Fair value of the identifiable assets acquired and liabilities assumed
=	$160,000	Goodwill (i.e., positive residual)

Note that this computation of Goodwill is the same whether control of the subsidiary is obtained in stages or whether it is obtained in a single transaction.

---

[34] FASB ASC 805-30-30-1 states that the fair value of the controlling interest obtained in stages equals the sum of (1) the consideration transferred for the incremental investment that triggers control, as measured in accordance with FASB ASC 805, (i.e., $315,000 for the 45% interest) and (2) the fair value of the Equity Investment immediately before control is obtained (i.e., $245,000 for the 35% interest).

Inclusion of Subsidiary's Income Statement Following the Acquisition of a Controlling Interest   When a subsidiary is initially consolidated, the consolidated financial statements include the subsidiary's revenues, expenses, gains, and losses *only from the date the subsidiary is initially consolidated* (FASB ASC 810-10-45-4).[35] This is consistent with the accounting for the Equity Investment on the parent's balance sheet, which recognizes Equity Income only subsequent to the date of acquisition.

Companies are required to present income statements for the current year and the previous two years for comparison in annual reports and 10-K filings. Inclusion of the sales, expenses, and profits of the subsidiary only from the date of acquisition means that,

1. The current-year revenues, expenses, and profit may not reflect the true current annualized revenue, expenses, and profit for the combined entity, and
2. The current-year income statement is not comparable to those of the previous two years.

To provide readers of financial statements with more meaningful information relating to the acquired subsidiary, FASB ASC 805-10-50-2h requires the following disclosures relating to consolidated income statements:

1. The amounts of revenue and earnings of the acquiree since the acquisition date included in the consolidated income statement for the reporting period
2. The revenue and earnings of the combined entity for the current reporting period as though the acquisition date for all business combinations that occurred during the year had been as of the beginning of the annual reporting period (*supplemental pro forma information*)
3. If comparative financial statements are presented, the revenue and earnings of the combined entity for the comparable prior reporting period as though the acquisition date for all business combinations that occurred during the current year had occurred as of the beginning of the comparable prior annual reporting period (*supplemental pro forma information*).

As a result of these disclosures, readers are provided with a history (albeit condensed) of the consolidated operating activities for the current and previous two years to serve as a baseline for comparison with future operating performance.

Accounting for an Additional Purchase of Stock Subsequent to the Date on Which Control Is Achieved   If the parent owns less than 100% of the outstanding stock of the subsidiary, and if the parent subsequently purchases additional shares from the noncontrolling shareholders, the purchase of those additional shares is recorded by a reduction of the noncontrolling interest and an increase or decrease in Additional Paid-In Capital for the difference between the book value of the noncontrolling interest purchased and the cash payment. The book value of the noncontrolling interest is based on the values determined on the date the parent first gained control of the subsidiary.

For example, let's consider the case where we modify the facts in Exhibit 5.3 to reflect that, on December 31, 2016, the parent purchases an additional 10% interest in its subsidiary from the noncontrolling shareholders (one-half of the outstanding noncontrolling interest shares) for a purchase price of $225,000. On that date, the 20% noncontrolling interest is equal to $409,800 (see Exhibit 5.3). Thus, the parent purchased $\frac{1}{2}$ of this outstanding interest.

For purposes of measurement in business combinations, FASB ASC 805 clearly indicates that the date on which control is obtained is the only measurement date on which the identifiable net assets and Goodwill are measured (i.e., there is no remeasurement for subsequent acquisitions or disposals as long as control is retained). Therefore, the carrying value of consolidated noncontrolling interest determines the value of the incremental (i.e., 10%) portion of the controlling interest acquired by the parent. This means that the parent's Equity Investment account will increase by $204,900 (i.e., $409,800/2). The remaining portion of the purchase price for the 10% interest (i.e., $225,000 − $204,900) is presented as an adjustment of the parent's contributed capital (i.e., Additional Paid-In Capital). The parent makes the following journal entry in its books:

Equity investment.	204,900	
APIC	20,100	
Cash		225,000
(to record the purchase of an additional 10% interest in subsidiary from the noncontrolling shareholders)		

The consolidation process and **C-E-A-D-I** entries will now reflect the 90% ownership interest of the parent and the 10% noncontrolling interest.

---

[35] Before SFAS 160 was ratified and included in FASB ASC 810, a company could include the subsidiary in its consolidated financial statements as though it were purchased at the beginning of the year, with a deduction recorded at the bottom of the income statement for the subsidiary's pre-acquisition earnings. This presentation alternative is no longer allowed.

One final point: just like the subsidiary's net income, the subsidiary's *comprehensive* income or loss is allocated to the controlling interest and the noncontrolling interest each reporting period. Upon a change in a parent's ownership interest, the carrying amount of Accumulated Other Comprehensive Income (AOCI) is adjusted to reflect the change in the ownership interest in the subsidiary through a corresponding charge or credit to equity, attributable to the parent (FASB ASC 810-10-45-24). The AOCI is reallocated proportionately between the controlling interest and the noncontrolling interest. For financial statement purposes, the line item titled, "Accumulated Other Comprehensive Income," will be attributed entirely to the controlling interests. The AOCI related to the noncontrolling interest is included in the noncontrolling interest balance.

Reductions of the Investor's Ownership Interest in the Investee

Reductions in the investor's ownership percentage of the investee generally arise in two ways: either the investor sells shares in the investee that it owns to outside parties, or the investee sells additional common stock to outside parties, thus diluting the ownership interest of the investor. We begin with a discussion of the sale of shares that the investor owns in the investee company.

Sale of the Equity Investment by the Investor We consider two cases involving the sale by a parent company of the shares it owns in the subsidiary: the sale of the entire subsidiary (100% of its outstanding common stock), and the sale of a portion of the subsidiary with the parent still retaining control of the subsidiary following the sale (we consider the sale of a block of stock in the subsidiary, such that the parent loses control, later in this section of the chapter).

Sale of All of the Equity Investment by the Investor If the parent sells the subsidiary, the sale is treated like the sale of any other asset: we record the increase in cash (debit) and remove the book value of the asset sold (credit). The net debit or credit that we need to balance the journal entry represents the gain (if a credit) or loss (if a debit) on the sale.

To illustrate, assume that a parent sells all of its Equity Investment in its subsidiary for $800,000 at the end of the year. Further assume that the book value of the Equity Investment account on the parent's balance sheet is $656,800 on the date of sale. The sale results in a recognized gain of $143,200, and the journal entry that the parent makes to record the gain on sale is as follows:

Cash	800,000	
Equity investment		656,800
Gain on sale		143,200
(to record the sale of 100% of the Equity Investment)		

If we, instead, assume that the parent sells all of its Equity Investment for $600,000, the parent will record a loss on the sale as follows:

Cash	600,000	
Loss on sale	56,800	
Equity investment		656,800
(to record the sale of 100% of the Equity Investment)		

In addition, depending on the significance of this subsidiary to the overall operations of the parent, this disposal could qualify for treatment as a Discontinued Operation (i.e., net of tax presentation at the bottom of the income statement).[36] If the disposal does not qualify as a Discontinued Operation, the gain or loss should be presented as part of Income from Continuing Operations.

Sale of Less than All of the Equity Investment by the Parent—Parent Retains Control over the Subsidiary If the parent sells a portion of the subsidiary stock that it owns, but *retains control* over the subsidiary, the sale is viewed as a transaction among owners (parent and noncontrolling shareholders). As a result, *no gain or loss is recognized* in the consolidated income statement.

For example, assume that the parent sells 10% of the stock that it owns in its wholly owned subsidiary for $60,000, thus reducing its ownership interest to 90%. Assume that the subsidiary reports a balance of stockholders' equity of $530,000 on the date of sale, and that the Equity Investment was originally acquired at book value. Since the parent still controls its subsidiary, it must continue to consolidate the financial statements of the subsidiary with its own financial statements. The journal entry to record the sale is as follows:

---

[36] Accounting for discontinued operations is traditionally covered, in detail, in Intermediate Accounting texts. In addition, FASB ASC 205-20 provides detailed guidance on reporting discontinued operations.

Cash	60,000	
Equity investment		53,000
APIC (parent)..		7,000
(to record the parent's sale of 10% of the stock owned in the subsidiary)		

In the consolidation process, only 90% of the subsidiary's Stockholders' Equity will be attributable to the parent, with 10% now attributable to the noncontrolling interest. A noncontrolling interest equity account will, thus, be established in the [**E**] consolidation entry. The noncontrolling interest will have a beginning balance of $53,000, 10% of the subsidiary's BOY Stockholders' Equity.

FASB ASC 810-10-45-23 provides the following guidance for the recognition of a $7,000 increase in APIC rather than a gain on sale: "Changes in a parent's ownership interest while the parent retains its controlling financial interest in its subsidiary shall be accounted for as equity transactions (investments by owners and distributions to owners acting in their capacity as owners). Therefore, no gain or loss shall be recognized in consolidated net income or comprehensive income. The carrying amount of the noncontrolling interest shall be adjusted to reflect the change in its ownership interest in the subsidiary. Any difference between the fair value of the consideration received or paid and the amount by which the noncontrolling interest is adjusted shall be recognized in equity attributable to the parent."

Sale of Common Stock by the Subsidiary to Outside Parties
Sometimes, subsidiaries sell newly issued shares to outside parties. If the market value per share of the subsidiary's shares is greater than the market value per share of the parent's shares, raising equity capital in this manner may be a better option than the parent selling its own shares and infusing the cash proceeds into the subsidiary.[37] As a result of the sale, the parent now owns a smaller percentage of the subsidiary's common stock than it did before the sale.

As we discuss the accounting related to reductions in the parent's ownership interest, it will help you to keep in mind the relation between the Equity Investment account on the parent's balance sheet and the Stockholders' Equity of the subsidiary company: the Equity Investment account will always be equal to the proportion of the subsidiary's Stockholder's Equity that the parent owns plus the book value of unamortized AAP assets that the parent owns, if any. The implication is this: *any increase (decrease) in Stockholders' Equity of the subsidiary resulting from the sale of additional shares must result in a corresponding increase (decrease) in the Equity Investment account on the parent's balance sheet.*

We illustrate the accounting for sale of stock by a subsidiary to outside parties with a simple example. Assume that a parent owns a wholly owned (100% ownership) subsidiary that reports a Stockholders' Equity of $1,000,000 and 40,000 shares of $1 par value common stock outstanding. Assume, further, that the parent acquired this subsidiary at book value. The Equity Investment account on the parent's balance sheet is, therefore, reported at $1,000,000, its proportionate (100%) share of subsidiary's Stockholders' Equity.

Next, we assume that the subsidiary sells 10,000 shares (a 20% interest) to outsiders for $30 per share, or $300,000. The subsidiary makes the following journal entry to record the sale:

Cash	300,000	
Common stock		10,000
APIC..		290,000
(to record the sale of 10,000 shares of $1 par value common stock for $300,000)		

The subsidiary's Stockholders' Equity is now $1,300,000, and the parent owns 80% $\left(\frac{40,000}{50,000}\right)$ of the outstanding common stock (noncontrolling shareholders now own 20% of the subsidiary).

The parent's Equity Investment account must now be reported at $1,040,000 (80% of $1,300,000) following the sale of stock. The parent, therefore, makes the following journal entry in its records to reflect the required increase in its Equity Investment account:

Equity investment...	40,000	
APIC..		40,000
(to record the increase in the Equity Investment account resulting from the subsidiary's sale of 10,000 shares of common stock above book value)		

---

[37] The sale of stock by a subsidiary in an IPO, also called an "equity carve out," is often cited as a means for the parent to unlock the value it has in its ownership of the subsidiary for the benefit of its shareholders. In addition, the dividend exclusion rules under the Federal Tax Code allow the IPO proceeds obtained by the subsidiary to be transferred to the parent in a tax-free dividend transaction. This is why it is not uncommon to see subsidiaries "carve out" a portion of equity in an IPO followed by a subsequent tax-free spin-off of the non-IPO shares of the subsidiary.

The parent now owns a smaller (80%) percentage of a larger book value ($1,300,000) company, and its Equity Investment account increases to reflect the increased dollar equivalent of the book value that it owns. The offsetting credit is to Additional Paid-In Capital.[38,39] Finally, our **[E]** consolidation entry to eliminate the Stockholders' Equity of the subsidiary will now include a credit to noncontrolling interest equal to $260,000 ($1,300,000 × 20%).

Deconsolidation of the Subsidiary If the parent loses control of the subsidiary, it ceases to consolidate the financial statements of the subsidiary with its own financial statements (the subsidiary is deconsolidated). This may occur for a variety of reasons (FASB ASC 810-10-55-4A):

a. A parent sells all or part of its ownership interest in its subsidiary, and, as a result, the parent no longer has a controlling financial interest in the subsidiary.

b. The subsidiary issues shares, which reduces the parent's ownership interest in the subsidiary so that the parent no longer has a controlling financial interest in the subsidiary.

c. The expiration of a contractual agreement that gave control of the subsidiary to the parent.

d. The subsidiary becomes subject to the control of a government, court, administrator, or regulator.

The first two of these events are discussed above in this section. The second two deal with the loss of control as a result of legal or regulatory issues. In either case, once the parent loses control and deconsolidates the subsidiary, and the parent *recognizes a gain or loss on the deconsolidation*. This gain or loss is computed as follows (FASB ASC 810-10-40-5):

	The fair value of any consideration received
+	The fair value of any retained noncontrolling investment in the former subsidiary at the date the subsidiary is deconsolidated
+	The carrying amount of any noncontrolling interest in the former subsidiary at the date the subsidiary is deconsolidated
−	The carrying amount of the former subsidiary's assets and liabilities
=	Gain or loss on the deconsolidation of a subsidiary

TOPIC REVIEW 4

Sale of common stock by the subsidiary to outside parties

Assume that a parent has a wholly owned subsidiary that reports a Stockholders' Equity of $500,000 and 10,000 shares of $1 par value common stock outstanding. Assume, further, that the parent acquired this subsidiary at book value. The Equity Investment account on the parent's balance sheet is, therefore, reported at $500,000, its proportionate (100%) share of subsidiary's Stockholders' Equity. Assume that the subsidiary sells 2,000 shares to outsiders for $60 per share, or $120,000.

Required

Prepare the journal entry that the parent makes upon the sale of stock by its subsidiary.

The solution to this review problem can be found on page 375.

---

[38] Before SFAS 160 was introduced in the FASB ASC, companies had an option to treat this credit as a gain (in the income statement) rather than an increase in APIC (in the balance sheet). This option was provided in Staff Accounting Bulletin 51 (SAB51) and these gains were called "SAB51 gains." FASB ASC 810-10-45-23 no longer allows this treatment while the parent retains control of the subsidiary. However, if the investor does not have control of the investee, these gains and losses must be recognized as part of Income from Continuing Operations.

[39] The Equity Investment account increased in this example because the sale price of the newly issued shares ($30) exceeds the $25 ($1,000,000/40,000 shares) book value per share of the subsidiary's Stockholders' Equity prior to the sale. If the sale price of the shares issued was $150,000, however, the Equity Investment account would be reduced, since the parent would own 80% of a subsidiary with a Stockholders' Equity of $1,150,000 ($1,000,000 + $150,000) following the sale. The parent's Equity Investment account, therefore, should be reported at $920,000 (80% × $1,150,000), a reduction of $80,000, and the parent would make the following journal entry to reflect the sale of stock by its subsidiary at a market price below book value:

APIC	80,000	
Equity Investment		80,000
(to record the decrease in the Equity Investment account resulting from the subsidiary's sale of 10,000 shares of common stock below book value)		

Required Disclosures

FASB ASC 810-10-50-1A lists a number of required disclosures relating to noncontrolling interests. A parent must disclose for each reporting period:

1. Separately, on the face of the consolidated financial statements, the amounts of consolidated net income and consolidated comprehensive income and the related amounts of each attributable to the parent and the noncontrolling interest.

2. Either in the notes or on the face of the consolidated income statement, amounts attributable to the parent for the following, if reported in the consolidated financial statements:
   a. Income from continuing operations
   b. Discontinued operations

3. Either in the consolidated statement of changes in equity, if presented, or in the notes to consolidated financial statements, a reconciliation at the beginning and the end of the period of the carrying amount of total equity (net assets), equity (net assets) attributable to the parent, and equity (net assets) attributable to the noncontrolling interest. That reconciliation shall separately disclose:
   a. Net income
   b. Transactions with owners acting in their capacity as owners, showing separately contributions from and distributions to owners
   c. Each component of other comprehensive income.

4. In notes to the consolidated financial statements, a separate schedule that shows the effects of any changes in a parent's ownership interest in a subsidiary on the equity attributable to the parent.

Finally, if a subsidiary is deconsolidated, the parent is required to disclose the following in the footnotes to its financial statements (FASB ASC 810-10-50-1B):

a. The amount of any gain or loss recognized

b. The portion of any gain or loss related to the remeasurement of any retained investment in the former subsidiary or group of assets to its fair value

c. The caption in the income statement in which the gain or loss is recognized unless separately presented on the face of the income statement

d. A description of the valuation technique(s) used to measure the fair value of any direct or indirect retained investment in the former subsidiary or group of assets

e. Information that enables users of the parent's financial statements to assess the inputs used to develop the fair value in item (d)

f. The nature of continuing involvement with the subsidiary or entity acquiring the group of assets after it has been deconsolidated or derecognized

g. Whether the transaction that resulted in the deconsolidation or derecognition was with a related party

h. Whether the former subsidiary or entity acquiring a group of assets will be a related party after deconsolidation.

Superscript ^A, (B, C) denotes assignments based on Appendix 5A (B, C).

QUESTIONS

1. What is a noncontrolling interest?

2. FASB ASC 810-10-10-1 defines the objective of consolidated financial statements. What is that objective and who is the primary audience of consolidated financial statements?

3. FASB ASC 810-10-45-12 discusses the appropriate procedure to follow when a subsidiary has a different fiscal year-end from that of its parent. What is that procedure?   `FASB ASC Research`

4. Companies are required to value noncontrolling interests on the acquisition date. What approaches might a company take to value noncontrolling interests? (*Hint:* See FASB ASC 805-20-30-7.)   `FASB ASC Research`

5. Where in the consolidated balance sheet should noncontrolling interests be reported? (*Hint:* See FASB ASC 810-10-45-16.)   `FASB ASC Research`

6. What is the appropriate procedure to follow if losses attributable to a noncontrolling interest exceed its equity balance (i.e., would result in a negative balance for noncontrolling interest equity)? (*Hint:* See FASB ASC 810-10-45-21.)   `FASB ASC Research`

7. Describe the different effects on consolidated financial statements when a parent and subsidiary engage in upstream versus downstream intercompany sales of depreciable fixed assets.

8. Describe the reason why the [ADJ] consolidating entry is necessary when preparing consolidated financial statements for a parent company that applies the cost method of pre-consolidation bookkeeping.

9. Describe the similarities and differences in the [C] consolidating entry when a parent company uses equity method versus the cost method of pre-consolidation bookkeeping.

10.^A Describe the difference between consolidated goodwill and noncontrolling interest when a parent company chooses the IFRS alternatives of "full fair value" recognition versus "proportionate share" recognition.

11.^C Describe the accounting for acquisitions that are achieved in stages (i.e., step acquisitions).

12.^C Describe the accounting for the deconsolidation of a subsidiary.

13. Assume that a wholly owned subsidiary company reports sales of $500,000 and net income of $100,000 for the year in which it is acquired on July 1. What amount of sales and net income are includable in consolidated income statement in the year of acquisition assuming that sales and net income are earned evenly over the year?

Assignments with the 🌐 logo in the margin are available in BusinessCourse.
See the Preface of the book for details.

MULTIPLE CHOICE

LO1

AICPA Adapted

14. **Consolidation of noncontrolling interest**
    Assume that a parent company owns less than 100% of a long-controlled subsidiary. Which of the following statements is false?
    a. Balance sheet presentation of noncontrolling interest is necessary because consolidated balances always reflect 100% of the net assets of the subsidiary.
    b. Goodwill is always assigned to the controlling and noncontrolling interests in the relative proportion of their ownership interests.
    c. Noncontrolling interest represents the portion of the subsidiary's net assets that is not owned by the parent.
    d. Noncontrolling interest is classified as an owners' equity account.

LO1

AICPA Adapted

15. **Assigning goodwill to controlling and noncontrolling interests**
    Assume that a parent company purchased less than 100% of the voting common stock when it acquired a controlling interest in a subsidiary on August 15, 2016. The parent uses the equity method to account for the subsidiary on its pre-consolidation books. Both companies have a December 31, 2016 fiscal year end. Which of the following statements is correct?
    a. The amount of total assets reported in the consolidated balance sheet is usually less than total assets in the parent company's pre-consolidation balance sheet.
    b. In the balance sheet prepared immediately after the acquisition, the parent company's pre-consolidation retained earnings will always equal consolidated retained earnings.
    c. Noncontrolling interest reported in the consolidated balance sheet always equals the percentage of shares held by the noncontrolling shareholders multiplied times the pre-acquisition reported net assets of the subsidiary.
    d. Consolidated net income for the year ended December 31, 2016 will include 100% of the subsidiary's income for the entire year.

LO1

AICPA Adapted

16. **Assigning goodwill to controlling and noncontrolling interests**
    Assume that on July 1, 2016, a parent company paid $2,821,500 to purchase a 75% interest in a subsidiary's voting common stock. On that date, the fair value of the 25% interest not purchased by the parent company is $937,500. The acquisition-date fair value of the identifiable net assets of the subsidiary is $3,600,000. What is the amount of goodwill assigned to the controlling and noncontrolling interests, respectively, on the acquisition date?
    a. $121,500 and $37,500
    b. $120,000 and $39,000
    c. $119,250 and $39,750
    d. $112,500 and $37,500

17. **Assigning bargain purchase gain (i.e., "negative goodwill") to controlling and noncontrolling interests**

Assume that on July 1, 2016, a parent company paid $2,760,000 to purchase a 80% interest in a subsidiary's voting common stock. On that date, the fair value of the 20% interest not purchased by the parent company is $690,000. The acquisition-date fair value of the identifiable net assets of the subsidiary is $3,600,000. What is the amount of goodwill (or bargain purchase gain) assigned to the controlling and noncontrolling interests, respectively, on the acquisition date?

a. $75,000 bargain purchase gain assigned to the controlling interest and $75,000 bargain purchase gain assigned to the noncontrolling interest

b. $120,000 goodwill assigned to the controlling interest and $30,000 goodwill assigned to the noncontrolling interest

c. $120,000 bargain purchase gain assigned to the controlling interest and $30,000 bargain purchase gain assigned to the noncontrolling interest

d. $150,000 bargain purchase gain assigned to the controlling interest and zero assigned to the noncontrolling interest

18. **Consolidated net income and net income attributable to the noncontrolling interest**

Assume that on January 1, 2015, a parent company acquired an 80% interest in a subsidiary's voting common stock. On the date of acquisition, the fair-value of the subsidiary's net assets equaled their reported book values except for machinery and equipment, which had a fair value of $300,000 and a reported book value of $150,000. The machinery and equipment had a 5-year remaining useful life and no salvage value. The following are the highly summarized pre-consolidation income statements of the parent and subsidiary for the year ended December 31, 2016:

Income Statement	Parent	Subsidiary
Revenues	$1,296,000	$172,800
Equity income	45,120	—
Expenses	(864,000)	(86,400)
Net income	$ 477,120	$ 86,400

For the year ended December 31, 2016, what amounts will be reported for (1) consolidated net income and (2) net income attributable to the noncontrolling interest, respectively, in the parent's consolidated financial statements?

	Consolidated NI	NCI NI
a.	563,520	17,280
b.	494,400	17,280
c.	488,400	11,280
d.	477,120	11,280

19. **Deferred intercompany inventory profits**

Assume that on May 15, 2013, a parent company purchased a 65% interest in a subsidiary's voting common stock. During the year ended December 31, 2016, the subsidiary sold merchandise to the parent for $600,000. Before consolidation, the parent and subsidiary earn the same profits on intercompany sales as they earn on sales to unaffiliated customers. The parent's gross profit percentage is 30% and the subsidiary's is 35%. On December 31, 2016, 25% of this merchandise was in the parent's ending inventory. What amount of intercompany profit in ending inventory that must be deferred in preparation of the December 31, 2016 consolidated financial statements?

a. $31,500
b. $52,500
c. $45,000
d. $150,000

20. **Upstream versus downstream inventory profits and net income attributable to the noncontrolling interest**

Assume that on January 1, 2015, a parent company acquired a 70% interest in a subsidiary's voting common stock. On the date of acquisition, the fair value of the subsidiary's net assets equaled their reported book values. There were no intercompany sales during 2015. During the year ended December 31, 2016, the companies made $200,000 of intercompany sales. All intercompany sales include profits of 25% of selling price. At December 31, 2016, there was $50,000 of intercompany merchandise (i.e., inventory purchased via intercompany transactions) in ending inventory. The following are the highly summarized "stand alone" pre-consolidation income statements of the parent and subsidiary for the year ended December 31, 2016 (i.e., they do not include the effects of pre-consolidation investment accounting, like the equity method):

Income Statement	Parent "Stand Alone"	Subsidiary
Revenues	$1,350,000	$630,000
Expenses	(900,000)	(450,000)
Net income.	$ 450,000	$180,000

For the year ended December 31, 2016, what amounts will be reported for net income attributable to the noncontrolling interest in the parent's consolidated income statement assuming either (1) all of the intercompany inventory is held by the parent or (2) all of the intercompany inventory is held by the subsidiary at December 31, 2016?

a. $54,000 or $54,000, respectively

b. $50,250 or $50,250, respectively

c. $50,250 or $54,000, respectively

d. $54,000 or $50,250, respectively

Use the following facts for Multiple Choice problems 21-27.

Assume that a parent company acquired 75% of the outstanding voting common stock of a subsidiary on January 1, 2015. On the acquisition date, the identifiable net assets of the subsidiary had fair values that approximated their recorded book values except for a patent, which had a fair value of $60,000 and no recorded book value. On the date of acquisition, the patent had five years of remaining useful life and the parent company amortizes its intangible assets using straight line amortization. During the year ended December 31, 2016, the subsidiary recorded sales to the parent in the amount of $72,000. On these sales, the subsidiary recorded pre-consolidation gross profits equal to 30%. Approximately 40% of this merchandise remains in the parent's inventory at December 31, 2016. The following summarized pre-consolidation financial statements are for the parent and the subsidiary for the year ended December 31, 2016:

	Investor	Investee
Income statement:		
Revenues	$1,440,000	$240,000
Income from Investee.	56,520	0
Expenses	(960,000)	(144,000)
Net income.	$ 536,520	$ 96,000
Statement of retained earnings:		
BOY retained earnings	$ 446,400	$ 24,000
Net income.	536,520	96,000
Dividends declared.	(38,400)	(24,000)
EOY retained earnings	$ 944,520	$ 96,000
Balance sheet:		
Current assets	$ 480,000	$ 60,000
Investment in subsidiary.	128,520	—
Noncurrent assets	2,400,000	180,000
Total assets.	$3,008,520	$240,000
Liabilities.	$1,584,000	$ 96,000
Common stock & APIC	480,000	48,000
Retained earnings	944,520	96,000
Total liabilities & stockholders' equity	$3,008,520	$240,000

Based on this information, determine the balances for the accounts listed in questions 21–27:

21. **Intercompany inventory transactions**
    Consolidated Revenues:
    a. $1,680,000
    b. $1,440,000
    c. $1,752,000
    d. $1,608,000

22. **Intercompany inventory transactions and Acquisition Accounting Premium**
    Consolidated Expenses:
    a. $1,052,640
    b. $1,124,640
    c. $960,000
    d. $1,104,000

23. **Noncontrolling interest, upstream deferred intercompany inventory profits and Acquisition Accounting Premium**
    Consolidated net income attributable to noncontrolling interest:
    a. $21,840
    b. $18,840
    c. $24,000
    d. $21,000

24. **Intercompany inventory transactions**
    Current Assets:
    a. $540,000
    b. $518,400
    c. $548,640
    d. $531,360

25. **Acquisition Accounting Premium**
    Noncurrent Assets:
    a. $2,580,000
    b. $2,628,000
    c. $2,616,000
    d. $2,568,000

26. **Equity method and consolidations**
    Retained Earnings:
    a. $944,520
    b. $1,040,520
    c. $1,064,520
    d. $1,088,520

27. **Noncontrolling interest, upstream deferred intercompany inventory profits and Acquisition Accounting Premium**
    Noncontrolling Interest:
    a. $24,000
    b. $42,840
    c. $12,840
    d. $18,000

Use the following facts for Multiple Choice problems 28-32.

Assume that on January 1, 2012, a parent company acquired a 80% interest in a subsidiary's voting common stock. On the date of acquisition, the fair value of the subsidiary's net assets equaled their reported book values. On January 1, 2014, the subsidiary purchased a building for $336,000. The building has a useful life of 8 years and is depreciated on a straight-line basis with no salvage value. On January 1, 2016, the subsidiary sold the building to the parent for $294,000. The parent estimated that the building had a six year remaining useful life and no salvage value. The parent also uses the straight-line method of amortization. For the year ending December 31, 2016, the parent's "stand-alone" income (i.e., net income before recording any adjustments related to pre-consolidation investment accounting) is $350,000. The subsidiary's recorded net income is $70,000.

Based on this information, determine the balances for the accounts listed in questions 28-32:

LO3 **28. Equity investment accounting**

Income from investment in subsidiary (on parent's pre-consolidations books preceding consolidation):

a. $21,000
b. $28,000
c. $56,000
d. $63,000

LO3 **29. Intercompany sale of depreciable assets**

Consolidated building (net of accumulated depreciation):

a. $210,000
b. $245,000
c. $294,000
d. $336,000

LO3 **30. Intercompany sale of depreciable assets**

Consolidated depreciation expense:

a. $25,200
b. $29,400
c. $42,000
d. $49,000

LO2, 3 **31. Intercompany sale of depreciable assets**

Consolidated net income attributable to the controlling interest:

a. $371,000
b. $378,000
c. $406,000
d. $413,000

LO2, 3 **32. Noncontrolling interest and intercompany sale of depreciable assets**

Consolidated income attributable to noncontrolling interest:

a. $15,400
b. $14,000
c. $7,000
d. $5,600

EXERCISES

LO2 **33. Preparing a consolidated income statement—With noncontrolling interest, but no AAP or intercompany profits**

A parent company purchased an 70% interest in its subsidiary several years ago with no AAP (i.e., purchased at book value). Each reports the following income statement for the current year:

	Parent	Subsidiary
Income statement:		
Sales.	$6,000,000	$900,000
Cost of goods sold.	(4,200,000)	(540,000)
Gross profit.	1,800,000	360,000
Income (loss) from subsidiary.	88,200	0
Operating expenses.	(1,140,000)	(234,000)
Net income.	$ 748,200	$126,000

a. Compute the Income (loss) from subsidiary of $88,200 reported by the parent company.

b. Prepare the consolidated income statement for the current year.

34. **Preparing a consolidated income statement—Equity method with noncontrolling interest and AAP** LO2

    A parent company purchased a 65% controlling interest in its subsidiary several years ago. The aggregate fair value of the controlling and noncontrolling interest was $250,000 in excess of the subsidiary's Stockholders' Equity on the acquisition date. This excess was assigned to a building that was estimated to be undervalued by $150,000 and to an unrecorded patent valued at $100,000. The building asset is being depreciated over a 20-year period and the patent is being amortized over a 10-year period, both on the straight-line basis with no salvage value. During the current year, the subsidiary declared and paid $40,000 of dividends. The parent company uses the equity method of pre-consolidation investment bookkeeping. Each company reports the following income statement for the current year:

	Parent	Subsidiary
Income statement:		
Sales.	$6,000,000	$600,000
Cost of goods sold.	(4,200,000)	(360,000)
Gross profit.	1,800,000	240,000
Income (loss) from subsidiary.	43,225	0
Operating expenses.	(1,140,000)	(156,000)
Net income.	$ 703,225	$ 84,000

    a. Compute the Income (loss) from subsidiary of $43,225 reported by the parent company in its pre-consolidation income statement.

    b. Prepare the consolidated income statement for the current year.

35. **Preparing a consolidated income statement—Equity method with noncontrolling interest, AAP and** LO2, 3
    upstream and downstream intercompany inventory profits

    A parent company purchased a 70% controlling interest in its subsidiary several years ago. The aggregate fair value of the controlling and noncontrolling interest was $350,000 in excess of the subsidiary's Stockholders' Equity on the acquisition date. This excess was assigned to a building that was estimated to be undervalued by $200,000 and to an unrecorded patent valued at $150,000. The building asset is being depreciated over a 16-year period and the patent is being amortized over an 8-year period, both on the straight-line basis with no salvage value. During the current year, the parent and subsidiary reported a total of $600,000 of intercompany sales. At the beginning of the current year, there were $40,000 of upstream intercompany profits in the parent's inventory. At the end of the current year, there were $60,000 of downstream intercompany profits in the subsidiary's inventory. During the current year, the subsidiary declared and paid $80,000 of dividends. The parent company uses the equity method of pre-consolidation investment bookkeeping. Each company reports the following income statement for the current year:

	Parent	Subsidiary
Income statement:		
Sales.	$10,000,000	$1,000,000
Cost of goods sold.	(6,800,000)	(600,000)
Gross profit.	3,200,000	400,000
Income (loss) from subsidiary.	37,125	0
Operating expenses.	(1,800,000)	(270,000)
Net income.	$ 1,437,125	$ 130,000

    a. Compute the Income (loss) from subsidiary of $37,125 reported by the parent company in its pre-consolidation income statement.

    b. Prepare the consolidated income statement for the current year.

36. **Preparing a consolidated income statement—Equity method with noncontrolling interest, AAP and** LO2, 3
    upstream intercompany depreciable asset profits

    A parent company purchased an 80% controlling interest in its subsidiary several years ago. The aggregate fair value of the controlling and noncontrolling interest was $230,000 in excess of the subsidiary's Stockholders' Equity on the acquisition date. This excess was assigned to a building that was estimated to be undervalued by $150,000 and to an unrecorded Customer List valued at $80,000. The building asset is being depreciated over a 12-year period and the Customer List is being amortized over a 5-year period, both on the straight-line basis with no salvage value. During a previous year, the subsidiary sold to the parent company a piece of depreciable property. The unconfirmed upstream gain on this intercompany transaction was $60,000 at the beginning of the current year. The upstream gain confirmed each year is $15,000. During the current year, the subsidiary declared and paid $90,000 of dividends. The parent company uses the equity method of pre-consolidation investment bookkeeping. Each company reports the following income statement for the current year:

	Parent	Subsidiary
Income statement:		
Sales.	$12,000,000	$1,200,000
Cost of goods sold.	(8,400,000)	(720,000)
Gross profit.	3,600,000	480,000
Income (loss) from subsidiary.	123,600	0
Operating expenses.	(2,280,000)	(312,000)
Net income.	$ 1,443,600	$ 168,000

a. Compute the Income (loss) from subsidiary of $123,600 reported by the parent company in its pre-consolidation income statement.

b. Prepare the consolidated income statement for the current year.

LO2, 4   **37. Preparing a consolidated income statement—Cost method with noncontrolling interest and AAP**
A parent company purchased a 75% controlling interest in its subsidiary several years ago. The aggregate fair value of the controlling and noncontrolling interest was $324,000 in excess of the subsidiary's Stockholders' Equity on the acquisition date. This excess was assigned to a building that was estimated to be undervalued by $180,000 and to an unrecorded Customer List valued at $144,000. The building asset is being depreciated over a 15-year period and the Customer List is being amortized over a 4-year period, both on the straight-line basis with no salvage value. During the current year, the subsidiary declared and paid $80,000 of dividends. The parent company uses the cost method of pre-consolidation investment bookkeeping. Each company reports the following income statement for the current year:

	Parent	Subsidiary
Income statement:		
Sales.	$9,600,000	$1,040,000
Cost of goods sold.	(6,720,000)	(576,000)
Gross profit.	2,880,000	464,000
Income (loss) from subsidiary.	60,000	0
Operating expenses.	(1,824,000)	(281,600)
Net income.	$1,116,000	$ 182,400

a. Starting with the parent's current-year pre-consolidation net income of $1,116,000, compute the amount of current-year net income attributable to the parent that will be reported in the consolidated financial statements.

b. Prepare the consolidated income statement for the current year.

LO2, 4   **38. Preparing a consolidated income statement—Cost method with noncontrolling interest, AAP and upstream and downstream intercompany inventory profits**
A parent company purchased a 60% controlling interest in its subsidiary several years ago. The aggregate fair value of the controlling and noncontrolling interest was $140,000 in excess of the subsidiary's Stockholders' Equity on the acquisition date. This excess was assigned to a building that was estimated to be undervalued by $90,000 and to an unrecorded Trademark valued at $50,000. The building asset is being depreciated over a 10-year period and the Trademark is being amortized over a 5-year period, both on the straight-line basis with no salvage value. During the current year, the parent and subsidiary reported a total of $250,000 of intercompany sales. At the beginning of the current year, there were $25,000 of upstream intercompany profits in the parent's inventory. At the end of the current year, there were $20,000 of downstream intercompany profits in the subsidiary's inventory. During the current year, the subsidiary declared and paid $45,000 of dividends. The parent company uses the cost method

of pre-consolidation investment bookkeeping. Each company reports the following income statement for the current year:

	Parent	Subsidiary
Income statement:		
Sales.	$5,000,000	$500,000
Cost of goods sold.	(3,400,000)	(300,000)
Gross profit.	1,600,000	200,000
Income (loss) from subsidiary.	27,000	0
Operating expenses.	(900,000)	(135,000)
Net income.	$ 727,000	$ 65,000

a. Starting with the parent's current-year pre-consolidation net income of $727,000, compute the amount of current-year net income attributable to the parent that will be reported in the consolidated financial statements.

b. Prepare the consolidated income statement for the current year.

39. **Preparing a consolidated income statement—Cost method with noncontrolling interest, AAP and upstream intercompany depreciable asset profits**   LO2, 4

A parent company purchased a 90% controlling interest in its subsidiary several years ago. The aggregate fair value of the controlling and noncontrolling interest was $92,000 in excess of the subsidiary's Stockholders' Equity on the acquisition date. This excess was assigned to a building that was estimated to be undervalued by $60,000 and to an unrecorded patent valued at $32,000. The building asset is being depreciated over a 12-year period and the patent is being amortized over an 8-year period, both on the straight-line basis with no salvage value. During a previous year, the subsidiary sold to the parent company a piece of depreciable property. The unconfirmed upstream gain on this intercompany transaction was $40,000 at the beginning of the current year. The upstream gain confirmed each year is $8,000. During the current year, the subsidiary declared and paid $30,000 of dividends. The parent company uses the cost method of pre-consolidation investment bookkeeping. Each company reports the following income statement for the current year:

	Parent	Subsidiary
Income statement:		
Sales.	$4,600,000	$500,000
Cost of goods sold.	(3,280,000)	(308,000)
Gross profit.	1,320,000	192,000
Income (loss) from subsidiary.	27,000	0
Operating expenses.	(960,000)	(128,000)
Net income.	$ 387,000	$ 64,000

a. Starting with the parent's current-year pre-consolidation net income of $387,000, compute the amount of current-year net income attributable to the parent that will be reported in the consolidated financial statements.

b. Prepare the consolidated income statement for the current year.

40. **Computing the noncontrolling interests equity balance**   LO2

Assume the following facts relating to an 75% owned subsidiary company:

BOY stockholders' equity.	$880,000
BOY AAP assets.	96,000
Net income of subsidiary (not including [A] asset depreciation and amortization)	200,000
AAP assets depreciation and amortization expense	32,000
Dividends declared and paid by subsidiary.	16,000

a. Compute the net income attributable to noncontrolling interests for the year.

b. Compute the amount reported as noncontrolling equity at the end of the year.

LO6   41.^B Computing consolidated earnings per share (EPS)

Assume the following facts about a parent and its 80% owned subsidiary company:

	Parent	Subsidiary
Net income.................	$200,000	$50,000
Common shares outstanding....	40,000	20,000 (16,000 = 80% owned by parent)
Convertible preferred stock	Dividends = $20,000 Convertible into 10,000 shares of common stock	
Convertible bonds		Interest expense after tax = $8,000 Convertible into 5,000 shares of common stock

a.   Compute basic earnings per share

b.   Compute diluted earnings per share

LO7   42.^C Acquisitions achieved in stages (step acquisitions)

Assume that a parent company gains control over its subsidiary with the purchase of a 45% interest for $216,000. The Equity Investment account reports a balance of $120,000 on the acquisition date and represents a 35% interest in the subsidiary. The total value of the subsidiary on the acquisition date is $480,000 (assume no premium for control). Prepare the journal entries to record the acquisition.

LO7   43.^C Acquisitions of additional shares of a subsidiary once control has been achieved

Assume that a parent company increases its ownership in a subsidiary from 60% to 75% by the purchase of additional shares of the subsidiary's outstanding stock from noncontrolling shareholders for a purchase price of $120,000. Assume that the noncontrolling interest reports a balance of $1,080,000 on that date. Prepare the journal entry by the parent to record the purchase.

LO7   44.^C Sale of subsidiary stock by parent

Assume that a parent company sells 25% of the shares it owns in its wholly owned subsidiary for $600,000. The Equity Investment is $1,440,000 on the date of sale. Prepare the pre-consolidation journal entry to record the sale assuming that the parent maintains control over the subsidiary.

LO7   45.^C Sale of stock by the subsidiary to outside parties

Assume that a parent has a wholly owned subsidiary that reports a Stockholders' Equity of $600,000. The Equity investment was acquired at book value (i.e., no [A] assets). Further assume that the subsidiary sells a 20% interest to outsiders for $216,000. Record the entry that the parent makes as a result of the sale of stock by its subsidiary.

LO1, 2, 7   46.^C Interpretation of Noncontrolling Interest information in financial statements

VERIZON
VODAFONE

Verizon reports the following information in its December 31 annual reports:

Years Ended December 31 (*in millions*)	2014	2013	2012
Noncontrolling Interest			
Balance at beginning of year	$56,580	$52,376	$49,938
Acquisition of noncontrolling interest (Note 2)................	(55,960)	—	—
Net income attributable to noncontrolling interest..............	2,331	12,050	9,682
Other comprehensive income (loss).........................	(23)	(15)	10
Total comprehensive income (loss)	2,308	12,035	9,692
Distributions and other.....................................	(1,550)	(7,831)	(7,254)
Balance at end of year	$ 1,378	$56,580	$52,376

According to the footnotes in Verizon's 2014 annual report, on February 21, 2014, Verizon acquired from **Vodafone** for $130 billion the 45% interest in Verizon Wireless that Verizon did not already own. Note 6 to Verizon's 2014 financial statements includes the following detail of its noncontrolling interest (*in millions*):

At December 31,	2014	2013
Verizon Wireless...	$ —	$55,465
Wireless partnerships and other.........................	1,378	1,115
	$1,378	$56,580

a. Prepare the journal entry related to the $2,331 million Net Income Attributable to Noncontrolling Interest. Is this journal entry recorded in the books of the parent or subsidiary? Is this amount equal to the subsidiary net income multiplied by the proportionate ownership of the noncontrolling interest?

b. To what do the $(1,550) million Distributions relate? By what amount did this affect the Net Income Attributable to Noncontrolling Interest?

c. Pursuant to the acquisition of the 45% noncontrolling interest from Vodafone, were Verizon Wireless' net assets revalued and was a gain or loss recognized by Verizon? Explain your answer. If your answer is "no," explain what would need to happen for Verizon Wireless' net assets to be revalued and for a gain or loss to be recognized by Verizon.

d. Where is the ending balance of $1,378 million reported in Verizon's financial statements?

47. **Interpretation of Noncontrolling Interest information in financial statements**
Alcoa, Inc. reports the following Stockholders' Equity and Noncontrolling Interests footnote in its 2014 SEC Form 10-K (*in millions*):

LO1, 2, 7

ALCOA, INC.

December 31,	2014	2013
Equity		
Alcoa shareholders' equity:		
Preferred stock.....................................	$ 55	$ 55
Mandatory convertible preferred stock................	3	—
Common stock.....................................	1,304	1,178
Additional capital	9,284	7,509
Retained earnings..................................	9,379	9,272
Treasury stock, at cost	(3,042)	(3,762)
Accumulated other comprehensive loss	(4,677)	(3,659)
Total Alcoa shareholders' equity....................	12,306	10,593
Noncontrolling interests	2,488	2,929
Total equity	$14,794	$13,522

In its 2014 SEC Form 10-K, Alcoa also reports the following detailed information for noncontrolling shareholders' interests in the equity of certain Alcoa majority-owned consolidated subsidiaries (*in millions*):

December 31,	2009	2008
Alcoa World Alumina and Chemicals.......................	$2,474	$2,896
Other...	14	33
	$2,488	$2,929

a. Alcoa reports its Noncontrolling Interest equity account as an addition to "Total Alcoa shareholders' equity" in arriving at "Total equity." What is Alcoa trying to convey by this presentation format?

b. Alcoa's footnote to the NCI table reveals that it received "contributions" from the noncontrolling shareholder (Alumina Limited) of Alcoa World Alumina and Chemicals in the amount of $43 million in 2014. Prepare the journal entry for this transaction. What effect did the transaction have on the consolidated balance sheet and income statement?

48. Interpretation of Noncontrolling Interest information in financial statements

According to its 2014 SEC Form 10-K, "**HCA Holdings, Inc.** (HCA) is one of the leading health care services companies in the United States. At December 31, 2014, we operated 166 hospitals, comprised of 162 general, acute care hospitals; three psychiatric hospitals; and one rehabilitation hospital." The following is an excerpt from HCA's consolidated balance sheet at December 31, 2014:

Liabilities and Stockholders' Deficit (December 31, dollars in millions)	2014	2013
Current liabilities:		
Accounts payable....................................	$ 2,035	$ 1,803
Accrued salaries.....................................	1,370	1,193
Other accrued expenses..............................	1,737	1,913
Long-term debt due within one year	338	786
	5,480	5,695
Long-term debt	29,307	27,590
Professional liability risks...........................	1,078	949
Income taxes and other liabilities.....................	1,832	1,525
Stockholders' deficit:		
Common stock $0.01 par; authorized 1,800,000,000 shares; outstanding 420,477,900 shares — 2014 and 439,604,000 shares — 2013	4	4
Capital in excess of par value........................	—	1,386
Accumulated other comprehensive loss	(323)	(257)
Retained deficit.....................................	(7,575)	(9,403)
Stockholders' deficit attributable to HCA Holdings, Inc.....................	(7,894)	(8,270)
Noncontrolling interests	1,396	1,342
	(6,498)	(6,928)
	$31,199	$28,831

According to HCA's 2014 annual report footnotes, the noncontrolling interest relates to non-wholly owned consolidated partnerships.

HCA reports a shareholders' deficit of $(6,498) million and noncontrolling interest of $1,396 million at December 31, 2014. What does this say about the relative health of its wholly owned operations and its non-wholly owned operations? Explain.

PROBLEMS

49. Consolidation on date of acquisition—Equity method with noncontrolling interest and AAP

Assume that a parent company acquires an 70% interest in its subsidiary for a purchase price of $1,078,000. The excess of the total fair value of the controlling and noncontrolling interests over the book value of the subsidiary's Stockholders' Equity is assigned to a building (in PPE, net) that is worth $100,000 more than its book value, an unrecorded patent that the parent valued at $200,000, and Goodwill of $300,000. There is no control premium, so goodwill is assigned proportionally to the controlling and noncontrolling interests.

The parent and the subsidiary report the following pre-consolidation balance sheets on the acquisition date:

	Parent	Subsidiary		Parent	Subsidiary
Cash.................................	$ 920,000	$ 215,000	Current liabilities............	$ 810,000	$ 330,000
Accounts receivable...................	782,000	330,000	Long-term liabilities	4,000,000	500,000
Inventory.............................	1,100,000	425,000	Common stock.............	920,000	90,000
Equity investment.....................	1,078,000		APIC.....................	700,000	120,000
Property, plant and equipment (PPE), net ...	5,400,000	800,000	Retained earnings	2,850,000	730,000
Total assets..........................	$9,280,000	$1,770,000	Total liabilities and equity	$9,280,000	$1,770,000

a. Prepare the consolidation entries on the acquisition date.

b. Prepare the consolidation spreadsheet on the acquisition date.

50. Consolidation on date of acquisition—Equity method with noncontrolling interest and AAP LO1

Assume that a parent company acquires a 75% interest in its subsidiary for a purchase price of $855,000. The total fair value of the controlling and noncontrolling interests in the subsidiary is $1,140,000 on the acquisition date. The excess of the purchase price over the book value of the subsidiary's Stockholders' Equity is assigned to an unrecorded Customer List that the parent values at $300,000 and the remainder to Goodwill in the amount of $200,000.

The parent and the subsidiary report the following pre-consolidation balance sheets on the acquisition date:

	Parent	Subsidiary		Parent	Subsidiary
Cash	$ 445,000	$ 100,000	Current liabilities	$ 400,000	$ 200,000
Accounts receivable	800,000	200,000	Long-term liabilities	1,500,000	360,000
Inventory	900,000	300,000	Common stock	500,000	60,000
Equity investment	855,000		APIC	1,000,000	80,000
Property, plant and equipment (PPE), net	2,000,000	600,000	Retained earnings	1,600,000	500,000
Total assets	$5,000,000	$1,200,000	Total liabilities and equity	$5,000,000	$1,200,000

    a. Prepare the consolidation entries on the acquisition date.

    b. Prepare the consolidation spreadsheet on the acquisition date.

51. Consolidation on date of acquisition—Equity method with noncontrolling interest and AAP LO1

Assume that a parent company acquires a 90% interest in its subsidiary for a purchase price of $1,584,000. The total fair value of the controlling and noncontrolling interests in the subsidiary is $1,760,000 on the acquisition date. The excess of the purchase price over the book value of the subsidiary's Stockholders' Equity is assigned to an unrecorded Royalty Agreement with a fair value of $350,000, an unrecorded Customer List with a fair value of $250,000, and Goodwill in the amount of $160,000.

The parent and the subsidiary report the following pre-consolidation balance sheets on the acquisition date:

	Parent	Subsidiary		Parent	Subsidiary
Assets			Liabilities and stockholders' equity		
Cash	$ 250,000	$ 200,000	Current liabilities	$ 674,000	$ 400,000
Accounts receivable	640,000	400,000	Long-term liabilities	2,400,000	800,000
Inventory	1,000,000	600,000	Common stock	800,000	100,000
Equity investment	1,584,000		APIC	600,000	150,000
Property, plant and equipment (PPE), net	3,000,000	1,000,000	Retained earnings	2,000,000	750,000
Total assets	$6,474,000	$2,200,000	Total liabilities and equity	$6,474,000	$2,200,000

    a. Prepare the consolidation entries on the acquisition date.

    b. Prepare the consolidation spreadsheet on the acquisition date.

52. Consolidation subsequent to date of acquisition—Equity method with noncontrolling interest and AAP LO2

Assume that, on January 1, 2013, a parent company acquired a 90% interest in its subsidiary. The total fair value of the controlling and noncontrolling interests was $480,000 over the book value of the subsidiary's Stockholders' Equity on the acquisition date. The parent assigned the excess fair value to the following [A] assets:

[A] Asset	Initial Fair Value	Useful Life
Property, plant and equipment (PPE)	$160,000	20 years
Patent	80,000	10 years
Customer list	40,000	10 years
Goodwill	200,000	Indefinite
	$480,000	

90% of the Goodwill is allocated to the parent.

The parent and the subsidiary report the following pre-consolidation financial statements December 31, 2016:

	Parent	Subsidiary		Parent	Subsidiary
Income statement:			**Balance sheet:**		
Sales....................	$6,800,000	$880,000	Cash.................................	$ 320,000	$ 228,000
Cost of goods sold..........	(5,200,000)	(528,000)	Accounts receivable...................	480,000	200,000
Gross profit...............	1,600,000	352,000	Inventory............................	720,000	264,000
Income (loss) from subsidiary ..	82,800		Equity investment....................	982,800	
Operating expenses.........	(1,280,000)	(240,000)	Property, plant and equipment (PPE), net ...	1,600,000	600,000
Net income...............	$ 402,800	$112,000		$4,102,800	$1,292,000
Statement of retained earnings:					
BOY retained earnings.......	$ 580,000	$468,000	Current liabilities.....................	$ 720,000	$ 200,000
Net income...............	402,800	112,000	Long-term liabilities	1,600,000	400,000
Dividends................	(160,000)	(16,000)	Common stock.......................	320,000	56,000
EOY retained earnings.......	$ 822,800	$564,000	APIC...............................	640,000	72,000
			Retained earnings	822,800	564,000
				$4,102,800	$1,292,000

a. Disaggregate and document the activity for the 100% Acquisition Accounting Premium (AAP), the controlling interest AAP and the noncontrolling interest AAP.

b. Calculate and organize the profits and losses on intercompany transactions and balances.

c. Compute the pre-consolidation Equity Investment account beginning and ending balances starting with the stockholders' equity of the subsidiary.

d. Reconstruct the activity in the parent's pre-consolidation Equity Investment T-account for the year of consolidation.

e. Independently compute the owners' equity attributable to the noncontrolling interest beginning and ending balances starting with the owners' equity of the subsidiary.

f. Independently calculate consolidated net income, controlling interest net income and noncontrolling interest net income.

g. Complete the consolidating entries according to the **C-E-A-D-I** sequence and complete the consolidation worksheet.

LO2   53. **Consolidation subsequent to date of acquisition—Equity method with noncontrolling interest and AAP**

Assume that, on January 1, 2012, a parent company acquired an 75% interest in its subsidiary. The total fair value of the controlling and noncontrolling interests was $530,000 over the book value of the subsidiary's Stockholders' Equity on the acquisition date. The parent assigned the excess to the following [A] assets:

[A] Asset	Initial Fair Value	Useful Life
Property, plant and equipment (PPE), net	$180,000	12 years
Customer list	100,000	5 years
Goodwill..	250,000	Indefinite
	$530,000	

75% of the Goodwill is allocated to the parent. The parent and the subsidiary report the following pre-consolidation financial statements at December 31, 2016:

	Parent	Subsidiary		Parent	Subsidiary
Income statement:			**Balance sheet:**		
Sales.	$7,300,000	$1,800,000	Cash.	$ 520,000	$ 130,000
Cost of goods sold.	(5,100,000)	(1,100,000)	Accounts receivable.	940,000	250,000
Gross profit.	2,200,000	700,000	Inventory.	1,200,000	550,000
Income (loss) from subsidiary . . .	123,750		Equity investment.	963,750	
Operating expenses.	(1,400,000)	(500,000)	Property, plant and equipment (PPE), net . . .	2,800,000	900,000
Net income.	$ 923,750	$ 200,000		$6,423,750	$1,830,000
Statement of retained earnings:					
BOY retained earnings.	$1,600,000	$ 500,000	Current liabilities.	$1,000,000	$ 400,000
Net income.	923,750	200,000	Long-term liabilities	2,000,000	500,000
Dividends	(200,000)	(50,000)	Common stock.	200,000	120,000
EOY retained earnings.	$2,323,750	$ 650,000	APIC.	900,000	160,000
			Retained earnings	2,323,750	650,000
				$6,423,750	$1,830,000

a. Disaggregate and document the activity for the 100% Acquisition Accounting Premium (AAP), the controlling interest AAP and the noncontrolling interest AAP.

b. Calculate and organize the profits and losses on intercompany transactions and balances.

c. Compute the pre-consolidation Equity Investment account beginning and ending balances starting with the stockholders' equity of the subsidiary.

d. Reconstruct the activity in the parent's pre-consolidation Equity Investment T-account for the year of consolidation.

e. Independently compute the owners' equity attributable to the noncontrolling interest beginning and ending balances starting with the owners' equity of the subsidiary.

f. Independently calculate consolidated net income, controlling interest net income and noncontrolling interest net income.

g. Complete the consolidating entries according to the **C-E-A-D-I** sequence and complete the consolidation worksheet.

54. **Consolidation subsequent to date of acquisition—Equity method with noncontrolling interest and AAP**

LO2

Assume that, on January 1, 2010, a parent company acquires a 70% interest in its subsidiary. The total fair value of the controlling and noncontrolling interests was $480,000 over the book value of the subsidiary's Stockholders' Equity on the acquisition date. The parent assigned the excess to the following [A] assets:

[A] Asset	Initial Fair Value	Useful Life
Patent.	$320,000	8 years
Goodwill	160,000	Indefinite
	$480,000	

70% of the Goodwill is allocated to the parent. The parent and the subsidiary report the following pre-consolidation financial statements at December 31, 2016.

	Parent	Subsidiary		Parent	Subsidiary
Income statement:			**Balance sheet:**		
Sales.	$6,000,000	$2,000,000	Cash.	$ 200,000	$ 120,000
Cost of goods sold.	(4,000,000)	(1,200,000)	Accounts receivable.	600,000	400,000
Gross profit.	2,000,000	800,000	Inventory.	800,000	880,000
Income (loss) from subsidiary . .	112,000		Equity investment.	1,400,000	
Operating expenses.	(1,500,000)	(600,000)	Property, plant and equipment (PPE), net . . .	2,000,000	1,200,000
Net income.	$ 612,000	$ 200,000		$5,000,000	$2,600,000
Statement of retained earnings:					
BOY retained earnings.	$1,978,000	$970,000	Current liabilities.	$ 500,000	$ 200,000
Net income.	612,000	200,000	Long-term liabilities	1,100,000	600,000
Dividends	(190,000)	(100,000)	Common stock.	600,000	280,000
EOY retained earnings	$2,400,000	$1,070,000	APIC.	400,000	450,000
			Retained earnings	2,400,000	1,070,000
				$5,000,000	$2,600,000

a.   Disaggregate and document the activity for the 100% Acquisition Accounting Premium (AAP), the controlling interest AAP and the noncontrolling interest AAP.

b.   Calculate and organize the profits and losses on intercompany transactions and balances.

c.   Compute the pre-consolidation Equity Investment account beginning and ending balances starting with the stockholders' equity of the subsidiary.

d.   Reconstruct the activity in the parent's pre-consolidation Equity Investment T-account for the year of consolidation.

e.   Independently compute the owners' equity attributable to the noncontrolling interest beginning and ending balances starting with the owners' equity of the subsidiary.

f.   Independently calculate consolidated net income, controlling interest net income and noncontrolling interest net income.

g.   Complete the consolidating entries according to the **C-E-A-D-I** sequence and complete the consolidation worksheet.

LO2, 3   **55.** **Consolidation subsequent to date of acquisition—Equity method with noncontrolling interest, AAP, and upstream intercompany inventory sale**

Assume that, on January 1, 2013, a parent company acquired an 80% interest in its subsidiary. The total fair value of the controlling and noncontrolling interests was $430,000 over the book value of the subsidiary's Stockholders' Equity on the acquisition date. The parent assigned the excess to the following **[A]** assets:

[A] Asset	Initial Fair Value	Useful Life
Property, plant and equipment (PPE), net	$180,000	15 years
Patent.	250,000	10 years
	$430,000	

This acquisition resulted in no recognized goodwill. Assume that the subsidiary sells inventory to the parent (upstream) which includes that inventory in products that it ultimately sells to customers outside of the controlled group. You have compiled the following data for the years ending 2015 and 2016:

	2015	2016
Transfer price for inventory sale.	$200,000	$300,000
Cost of goods sold.	(140,000)	(200,000)
Gross profit.	$ 60,000	$100,000
% Inventory remaining	25%	35%
Gross profit deferred	$ 15,000	$ 35,000
EOY receivable/payable.	$ 80,000	$ 90,000

The inventory not remaining at the end of the year has been sold outside of the controlled group. The parent uses the equity method of pre-consolidation investment bookkeeping. The parent and the subsidiary report the following pre-consolidation financial statements at December 31, 2016:

	Parent	Subsidiary		Parent	Subsidiary
Income statement:			**Balance sheet:**		
Sales....................	$6,500,000	$1,200,000	Cash................................	$ 450,000	$ 50,000
Cost of goods sold..........	(4,500,000)	(750,000)	Accounts receivable.................	250,000	300,000
Gross profit...............	2,000,000	450,000	Inventory...........................	650,000	400,000
Income (loss) from subsidiary ..	74,400		Equity investment..................	1,021,600	
Operating expenses.........	(1,200,000)	(300,000)	Property, plant and equipment (PPE), net ..	5,000,000	650,000
Net income................	$ 874,400	$ 150,000		$7,371,600	$1,400,000
Statement of retained earnings:					
BOY retained earnings.......	$3,000,000	$ 600,000	Current liabilities.....................	$ 600,000	$ 70,000
Net income................	874,400	150,000	Long-term liabilities	1,559,200	300,000
Dividends	(250,000)	(20,000)	Common stock.......................	800,000	100,000
EOY retained earnings.......	$3,624,400	$ 730,000	APIC................................	788,000	200,000
			Retained earnings	3,624,400	730,000
				$7,371,600	$1,400,000

a. Disaggregate and document the activity for the 100% Acquisition Accounting Premium (AAP), the controlling interest AAP and the noncontrolling interest AAP.

b. Calculate and organize the profits and losses on intercompany transactions and balances.

c. Compute the pre-consolidation Equity Investment account beginning and ending balances starting with the stockholders' equity of the subsidiary.

d. Reconstruct the activity in the parent's pre-consolidation Equity Investment T-account for the year of consolidation.

e. Independently compute the owners' equity attributable to the noncontrolling interest beginning and ending balances starting with the owners' equity of the subsidiary.

f. Independently calculate consolidated net income, controlling interest net income and noncontrolling interest net income.

g. Complete the consolidating entries according to the **C-E-A-D-I** sequence and complete the consolidation worksheet.

56. **Consolidation subsequent to date of acquisition—Equity method with noncontrolling interest, AAP, and upstream intercompany inventory sale**

LO2, 3

Assume that, on January 1, 2010, a parent company acquired a 75% interest in its subsidiary. The total fair value of the controlling and noncontrolling interests was $550,000 over the book value of the subsidiary's Stockholders' Equity on the acquisition date. The parent assigned the excess to the following [A] assets:

[A] Asset	Initial Fair Value	Useful Life
Patent..	$200,000	10 years
Goodwill.......................................	350,000	Indefinite
	$550,000	

75% of the Goodwill is allocated to the parent. Assume that the subsidiary sells inventory to the parent (upstream) which includes that inventory in products that it ultimately sells to customers outside of the controlled group. You have compiled the following data as of 2015 and 2016:

	2015	2016
Transfer price for inventory sale	$600,000	$700,000
Cost of goods sold	(500,000)	(580,000)
Gross profit	$100,000	$120,000
% Inventory remaining	25%	35%
Gross profit deferred	$ 25,000	$ 42,000
EOY receivable/payable	$ 70,000	$120,000

The inventory not remaining at the end of the year has been sold outside of the controlled group. The parent uses the equity method of pre-consolidation investment bookkeeping. The parent and the subsidiary report the following pre-consolidation financial statements at December 31, 2016:

	Parent	Subsidiary		Parent	Subsidiary
Income statement:			**Balance sheet:**		
Sales	$6,700,000	$2,500,000	Cash	$ 600,000	$ 400,000
Cost of goods sold	(4,500,000)	(1,500,000)	Accounts receivable	800,000	600,000
Gross profit	2,200,000	1,000,000	Inventory	1,000,000	800,000
Income (loss) from subsidiary	122,250		Equity investment	1,401,000	
Operating expenses	(2,000,000)	(800,000)	Property, plant and equipment (PPE), net	3,700,000	1,000,000
Net income	$ 322,250	$ 200,000		$7,501,000	$2,800,000
Statement of retained earnings:					
BOY retained earnings	$2,000,000	$1,000,000	Current liabilities	$ 878,750	$ 500,000
Net income	322,250	200,000	Long-term liabilities	3,000,000	800,000
Dividends	(200,000)	(40,000)	Common stock	500,000	140,000
EOY retained earnings	$2,122,250	$1,160,000	APIC	1,000,000	200,000
			Retained earnings	2,122,250	1,160,000
				$7,501,000	$2,800,000

a. Disaggregate and document the activity for the 100% Acquisition Accounting Premium (AAP), the controlling interest AAP and the noncontrolling interest AAP.

b. Calculate and organize the profits and losses on intercompany transactions and balances.

c. Compute the pre-consolidation Equity Investment account beginning and ending balances starting with the stockholders' equity of the subsidiary.

d. Reconstruct the activity in the parent's pre-consolidation Equity Investment T-account for the year of consolidation.

e. Independently compute the owners' equity attributable to the noncontrolling interest beginning and ending balances starting with the owners' equity of the subsidiary.

f. Independently calculate consolidated net income, controlling interest net income and noncontrolling interest net income.

g. Complete the consolidating entries according to the **C-E-A-D-I** sequence and complete the consolidation worksheet.

LO2, 3

57. **Consolidation subsequent to date of acquisition—Equity method with noncontrolling interest, AAP, and downstream intercompany inventory sale**
Assume that, on January 1, 2013, a parent company acquired a 90% interest in its subsidiary. The total fair value of the controlling and noncontrolling interests was $200,000 over the book value of the subsidiary's Stockholders' Equity on the acquisition date. The parent assigned the excess to the following [A] asset:

[A] Asset	Initial Fair Value	Useful Life
PPE, net	$200,000	10 years

This acquisition resulted in no recognized goodwill. Assume that the parent sells inventory to the subsidiary (downstream) which includes that inventory in products that it ultimately sells to customers outside of the controlled group. You have compiled the following data as of 2015 and 2016:

	2015	2016
Transfer price for inventory sale.	$200,000	$250,000
Cost of goods sold.	(150,000)	(180,000)
Gross profit.	$ 50,000	$ 70,000
% Inventory remaining	30%	25%
Gross profit deferred	$ 15,000	$ 17,500
EOY receivable/payable.	$ 40,000	$ 25,000

The inventory not remaining at the end of the year has been sold outside of the controlled group. The parent uses the equity method of pre-consolidation investment bookkeeping. The parent and the subsidiary report the following pre-consolidation financial statements at December 31, 2016:

	Parent	Subsidiary		Parent	Subsidiary
Income statement:			**Balance sheet:**		
Sales.	$5,400,000	$1,200,000	Cash.	$ 500,000	$ 100,000
Cost of goods sold.	(4,000,000)	(800,000)	Accounts receivable.	700,000	200,000
Gross profit.	1,400,000	400,000	Inventory.	900,000	300,000
Income (loss) from subsidiary	114,500		Equity investment.	788,000	
Operating expenses.	(1,200,000)	(250,000)	Property, plant and equipment (PPE), net	3,000,000	600,000
Net income.	$ 314,500	$ 150,000		$5,888,000	$1,200,000
Statement of retained earnings:					
BOY retained earnings.	$1,500,000	$ 500,000	Current liabilities.	$ 503,500	$ 125,000
Net income.	314,500	150,000	Long-term liabilities	2,300,000	300,000
Dividends.	(130,000)	(15,000)	Common stock.	800,000	60,000
EOY retained earnings.	$1,684,500	$ 635,000	APIC.	600,000	80,000
			Retained earnings	1,684,500	635,000
				$5,888,000	$1,200,000

a. Disaggregate and document the activity for the 100% Acquisition Accounting Premium (AAP), the controlling interest AAP and the noncontrolling interest AAP.

b. Calculate and organize the profits and losses on intercompany transactions and balances.

c. Compute the pre-consolidation Equity Investment account beginning and ending balances starting with the stockholders' equity of the subsidiary.

d. Reconstruct the activity in the parent's pre-consolidation Equity Investment T-account for the year of consolidation.

e. Independently compute the owners' equity attributable to the noncontrolling interest beginning and ending balances starting with the owners' equity of the subsidiary.

f. Independently calculate consolidated net income, controlling interest net income and noncontrolling interest net income.

g. Complete the consolidating entries according to the **C-E-A-D-I** sequence and complete the consolidation worksheet.

58. **Consolidation subsequent to date of acquisition—Equity method with noncontrolling interest, AAP, and downstream intercompany inventory sale**   LO2, 3

Assume that, on January 1, 2009, a parent company acquired an 80% interest in its subsidiary. The total fair value of the controlling and noncontrolling interests was $900,000 over the book value of the subsidiary's Stockholders' Equity on the acquisition date. The parent assigned the excess to the following [A] assets:

[A] Asset	Initial Fair Value	Useful Life
Property, plant and equipment (PPE), net	$300,000	15 years
Patent.	200,000	10 years
Goodwill.	400,000	
	$900,000	

Based on the relative acquisition-date fair values of the controlling and noncontrolling interests, Good-will was allocated to the parent and subsidiary in an 80:20 split, respectively. Assume that the parent sells inventory to the subsidiary (downstream) which includes that inventory in products that it ulti-mately sells to customers outside of the controlled group. You have compiled the following data as of 2015 and 2016:

	2015	2016
Transfer price for inventory sale.	$500,000	$400,000
Cost of goods sold.	(350,000)	(300,000)
Gross profit.	$150,000	$100,000
% Inventory remaining	25%	30%
Gross profit deferred	$ 37,500	$ 30,000
EOY receivable/payable.	$ 75,000	$ 50,000

The inventory not remaining at the end of the year has been sold outside of the controlled group. The parent uses the equity method of pre-consolidation investment bookkeeping. The parent and the subsid-iary report the following pre-consolidation financial statements at December 31, 2016:

	Parent	Subsidiary		Parent	Subsidiary
Income statement:			**Balance sheet:**		
Sales.	$6,000,000	$1,000,000	Cash.	$ 500,000	$ 50,000
Cost of goods sold.	(4,500,000)	(600,000)	Accounts receivable.	750,000	300,000
Gross profit.	1,500,000	400,000	Inventory.	1,000,000	400,000
Income (loss) from subsidiary	55,500		Equity investment.	1,354,000	
Operating expenses.	(900,000)	(300,000)	Property, plant and equipment (PPE), net	3,000,000	1,000,000
Net income.	$ 655,500	$ 100,000		$6,604,000	$1,750,000
Statement of retained earnings:					
BOY retained earnings.	$2,000,000	$ 600,000	Current liabilities.	$ 648,500	$ 100,000
Net income.	655,500	100,000	Long-term liabilities	2,000,000	500,000
Dividends.	(200,000)	(80,000)	Common stock.	500,000	100,000
EOY retained earnings.	$2,455,500	$ 620,000	APIC.	1,000,000	430,000
			Retained earnings	2,455,500	620,000
				$6,604,000	$1,750,000

a. Disaggregate and document the activity for the 100% Acquisition Accounting Premium (AAP), the controlling interest AAP and the noncontrolling interest AAP.

b. Calculate and organize the profits and losses on intercompany transactions and balances.

c. Compute the pre-consolidation Equity Investment account beginning and ending balances starting with the stockholders' equity of the subsidiary.

d. Reconstruct the activity in the parent's pre-consolidation Equity Investment T-account for the year of consolidation.

e. Independently compute the owners' equity attributable to the noncontrolling interest beginning and ending balances starting with the owners' equity of the subsidiary.

f. Independently calculate consolidated net income, controlling interest net income and noncontrolling interest net income.

g. Complete the consolidating entries according to the **C-E-A-D-I** sequence and complete the consolidation worksheet.

LO2, 4 59. **Consolidation subsequent to date of acquisition—Cost method with noncontrolling interest, AAP, and upstream intercompany inventory sale**
Assume that, on January 1, 2010, a parent company acquired an 80% interest in a subsidiary for $889,600 in cash. The total fair value of the controlling and noncontrolling interests on the acquisition date was $1,112,000, which is $440,000 over the book value of the subsidiary's Stockholders' Equity on the acquisition date. The parent assigned the excess to the following [A] assets:

[A] Asset	Initial Fair Value	Useful Life
Patent.	160,000	10 years
Goodwill	280,000	
	$440,000	

On the acquisition date, the retained earnings of the subsidiary was $400,000. The acquisition-date Goodwill is allocated to the parent and subsidiary in an 80:20 proportion, respectively. Assume that the subsidiary sells inventory to the parent (upstream) which includes that inventory in products that it ultimately sells to customers outside of the controlled group. You have compiled the following data as of 2015 and 2016:

	2015	2016
Transfer price for inventory sale	$480,000	$560,000
Cost of goods sold.	(400,000)	(464,000)
Gross profit.	$80,000	$96,000
% Inventory remaining	25%	35%
Gross profit deferred	$ 20,000	$ 33,600
EOY receivable/payable.	$ 56,000	$ 96,000

The inventory not remaining at the end of the year has been sold outside of the controlled group. The parent uses the cost method of pre-consolidation investment bookkeeping. The parent and the subsidiary report the following pre-consolidation financial statements at December 31, 2016:

	Parent	Subsidiary		Parent	Subsidiary
Income statement:			**Balance sheet:**		
Sales.	$5,360,000	$2,000,000	Cash	$ 480,000	$ 320,000
Cost of goods sold.	(3,600,000)	(1,200,000)	Accounts receivable.	640,000	480,000
Gross profit.	1,760,000	800,000	Inventory.	800,000	640,000
Income (loss) from subsidiary . . .	25,600		Equity investment.	889,600	
Operating expenses	(1,600,000)	(640,000)	Property, plant and equipment (PPE), net . . .	2,960,000	800,000
Net income.	$ 185,600	$ 160,000		$5,769,600	$2,240,000
Statement of retained earnings:					
BOY retained earnings	$1,441,000	$ 800,000	Current liabilities.	$ 703,000	$ 400,000
Net income.	185,600	160,000	Long-term liabilities	2,400,000	640,000
Dividends	(160,000)	(32,000)	Common stock.	400,000	112,000
EOY retained earnings	$1,446,600	$ 928,000	APIC	800,000	160,000
			Retained earnings	1,466,600	928,000
				$5,769,600	$2,240,000

a. Disaggregate and document the activity for the 100% Acquisition Accounting Premium (AAP), the controlling interest AAP, and the noncontrolling interest AAP.

b. Calculate and organize the profits and losses on intercompany transactions and balances.

c. Compute the pre-consolidation Equity Investment account beginning and ending balances assuming that the parent company used the equity method instead of the cost method. For each of these computations, start with the stockholders' equity of the subsidiary.

d. Compute the amount of the [ADJ] consolidating entry.

e. Independently compute the owners' equity attributable to the noncontrolling interest beginning and ending balances starting with the owners' equity of the subsidiary.

f. Independently calculate consolidated net income, controlling interest net income and noncontrolling interest net income.

g. Complete the consolidating entries according to the C-E-A-D-I sequence and complete the consolidation worksheet.

60. Consolidation subsequent to date of acquisition—Equity method with noncontrolling interest, AAP, and gain on downstream intercompany equipment sale

A parent company acquired its 90% interest in its subsidiary on January 1, 2012. The total fair value of the controlling interest and the noncontrolling interest on that date was $180,000 in excess of the book value of the subsidiary's Stockholders' Equity on the acquisition date. $120,000 of that excess was assigned to a Customer List that is being amortized over a 10 year period. The remaining $60,000 was assigned to Goodwill. The Goodwill is allocated to the parent and subsidiary in a 90:10 split, respectively.

On January 1, 2015, the parent sold Equipment to the subsidiary for a cash price of $75,000. The parent originally acquired the equipment at a cost of $90,000 and depreciated the equipment over its 15-year useful life using the straight-line method (no salvage value). At the time of the intercompany sale, the parent depreciated the equipment for 5 full years. The subsidiary retained the depreciation policy of the parent (i.e., it depreciated the equipment over its remaining 10-year useful life).

The parent uses the equity method of pre-consolidation investment bookkeeping. Following are pre-consolidation financial statements of the parent and its subsidiary for the year ended December 31, 2016.

	Parent	Subsidiary		Parent	Subsidiary
Income statement:			**Balance sheet:**		
Sales.	$6,000,000	$600,000	Cash	$ 635,040	$ 193,200
Cost of goods sold	(4,320,000)	(360,000)	Accounts receivable	1,050,000	258,000
Gross profit	1,680,000	240,000	Inventories	1,560,000	330,000
Income (loss) from subsidiary . . .	66,300		PPE, net	6,036,000	618,000
Operating expenses	(900,000)	(156,000)	Equity investment	432,960	
Net income	$ 846,300	$84,000	Total assets	$9,714,000	$1,399,200
Statement of retained earnings:					
BOY retained earnings	$3,450,300	$135,000	Accounts payable	$ 606,000	$ 106,800
Net income	846,300	84,000	Other current liabilities	714,000	138,000
Dividends	(170,400)	(12,000)	Long-term liabilities	1,500,000	780,000
EOY retained earnings	$4,126,200	$207,000	Common stock	331,800	74,400
			APIC	2,436,000	93,000
			Retained earnings	4,126,200	207,000
			Total liabilities and equity	$9,714,000	$1,399,200

a. Disaggregate and document the activity for the 100% Acquisition Accounting Premium (AAP), the controlling interest AAP and the noncontrolling interest AAP.

b. Calculate and organize the profits and losses on intercompany transactions and balances.

c. Compute the pre-consolidation Equity Investment account beginning and ending balances starting with the stockholders' equity of the subsidiary.

d. Reconstruct the activity in the parent's pre-consolidation Equity Investment T-account for the year of consolidation.

e. Independently compute the owners' equity attributable to the noncontrolling interest beginning and ending balances starting with the owners' equity of the subsidiary.

f. Independently calculate consolidated net income, controlling interest net income and noncontrolling interest net income.

g. Complete the consolidating entries according to the **C-E-A-D-I** sequence and complete the consolidation worksheet.

61. Consolidation subsequent to date of acquisition—Equity method with noncontrolling interest, AAP, and gain on downstream intercompany equipment sale

(Note: The facts in Problems 61 and 62 are identical, except for the direction of the intercompany sale of equipment.) A parent company acquired its 75% interest in its subsidiary on January 1, 2011. On the acquisition date, the total fair value of the controlling interest and the noncontrolling interest was $350,000 in excess of the book value of the subsidiary's Stockholders' Equity. All of that excess was allocated to a Royalty Agreement, which had a zero book value in the subsidiary's financial statements (i.e., there is no Goodwill). The Royalty Agreement has a 7 year estimated remaining economic life on the acquisition date. Both companies use straight line depreciation and amortization, with no salvage value.

In January 2014, the parent sold Equipment to the subsidiary for a cash price of $250,000. The parent acquired the equipment at a cost of $480,000 and depreciated the equipment over its 10-year useful life using the straight-line method (no salvage value). The parent had depreciated the equipment for 6 years at the time of sale. The subsidiary retained the depreciation policy of the parent and depreciated the equipment over its remaining 4 year useful life.

Following are pre-consolidation financial statements of the parent and its subsidiary for the year ended December 31, 2016. The parent uses the equity method to account for its Equity Investment.

	Parent	Subsidiary		Parent	Subsidiary
Income statement:			**Balance sheet:**		
Sales.	$3,400,000	$900,000	Cash	$ 619,500	$ 250,000
Cost of goods sold.	(2,400,000)	(500,000)	Accounts receivable.	530,000	420,000
Gross profit.	1,000,000	400,000	Inventory.	900,000	550,000
Income (loss) from subsidiary . . .	89,500		PPE, net	3,500,000	1,000,000
Operating expenses	(522,000)	(250,000)	Equity investment.	450,500	
Net income.	$ 567,500	$150,000	Total assets.	$6,000,000	$2,220,000
Statement of retained earnings:					
BOY retained earnings	$1,792,500	$200,000	Accounts payable.	$ 340,000	$ 250,000
Net income.	567,500	150,000	Other current liabilities	400,000	300,000
Dividends	(100,000)	(30,000)	Long-term liabilities	1,500,000	1,100,000
EOY retained earnings	$2,260,000	$320,000	Common stock.	200,000	100,000
			APIC	1,300,000	150,000
			Retained earnings	2,260,000	320,000
			Total liabilities and equity	$6,000,000	$2,220,000

a. Disaggregate and document the activity for the 100% Acquisition Accounting Premium (AAP), the controlling interest AAP and the noncontrolling interest AAP.

b. Calculate and organize the profits and losses on intercompany transactions and balances.

c. Compute the pre-consolidation Equity Investment account beginning and ending balances starting with the stockholders' equity of the subsidiary.

d. Reconstruct the activity in the parent's pre-consolidation Equity Investment T-account for the year of consolidation.

e. Independently compute the owners' equity attributable to the noncontrolling interest beginning and ending balances starting with the owners' equity of the subsidiary.

f. Independently calculate consolidated net income, controlling interest net income and noncontrolling interest net income.

g. Complete the consolidating entries according to the **C-E-A-D-I** sequence and complete the consolidation worksheet.

62. **Consolidation subsequent to date of acquisition—Equity method with noncontrolling interest, AAP, and gain on upstream intercompany equipment sale**

LO2, 3

(Note: The facts in Problems 61 and 62 are identical, except for the direction of the intercompany sale of equipment.) A parent company acquired its 75% interest in its subsidiary on January 1, 2011. On the acquisition date, the total fair value of the controlling interest and the noncontrolling interest was $350,000 in excess of the book value of the subsidiary's Stockholders' Equity. All of that excess was allocated to a Royalty Agreement, which had a zero book value in the subsidiary's financial statements (i.e., there is no Goodwill). The Royalty Agreement has a 7 year estimated remaining economic life on the acquisition date. Both companies use straight line depreciation and amortization, with no salvage value.

In January 2014, the subsidiary sold Equipment to the parent for a cash price of $250,000. The subsidiary acquired the equipment at a cost of $480,000 and depreciated the equipment over its 10-year useful life using the straight-line method (no salvage value). The subsidiary had depreciated the equipment for 6 years at the time of sale. The parent retained the depreciation policy of the subsidiary and depreciated the equipment over its remaining 4 year useful life.

Following are pre-consolidation financial statements of the parent and its subsidiary for the year ended December 31, 2016. The parent uses the equity method to account for its Equity Investment.

	Parent	Subsidiary		Parent	Subsidiary
Income statement:			**Balance sheet:**		
Sales............................	$3,400,000	$900,000	Cash............................	$ 619,500	$ 250,000
Cost of goods sold..............	(2,400,000)	(500,000)	Accounts receivable..............	530,000	420,000
Gross profit.....................	1,000,000	400,000	Inventory........................	900,000	550,000
Income (loss) from subsidiary.......	85,875		PPE, net	3,500,000	1,000,000
Operating expenses..............	(522,000)	(250,000)	Equity investment.................	454,125	
Net income.....................	$ 563,875	$150,000	Total assets.....................	$6,003,625	$2,220,000
Statement of retained earnings:					
BOY retained earnings............	$1,799,750	$200,000	Accounts payable.................	$ 340,000	$ 250,000
Net income.....................	563,875	150,000	Other current liabilities	400,000	300,000
Dividends declared..............	(100,000)	(30,000)	Long-term liabilities	1,500,000	1,100,000
EOY retained earnings	$2,263,625	$320,000	Common stock...................	200,000	100,000
			APIC...........................	1,300,000	150,000
			Retained earnings	2,263,625	320,000
			Total liabilities and equity	$6,003,625	$2,220,000

    a.   Disaggregate and document the activity for the 100% Acquisition Accounting Premium (AAP), the controlling interest AAP and the noncontrolling interest AAP.

    b.   Calculate and organize the profits and losses on intercompany transactions and balances.

    c.   Compute the pre-consolidation Equity Investment account beginning and ending balances starting with the stockholders' equity of the subsidiary.

    d.   Reconstruct the activity in the parent's pre-consolidation Equity Investment T-account for the year of consolidation.

    e.   Independently compute the owners' equity attributable to the noncontrolling interest beginning and ending balances starting with the owners' equity of the subsidiary.

    f.   Independently calculate consolidated net income, controlling interest net income and noncontrolling interest net income.

    g.   Complete the consolidating entries according to the **C-E-A-D-I** sequence and complete the consolidation worksheet.

LO2, 3   **63. Consolidation subsequent to date of acquisition—Reconciling effects of downstream versus upstream intercompany equipment sales**
Compare Problems 61 and 62. Reconcile the following:

    a.   The parent's pre-consolidation net income in Problem 61 to the parent's pre-consolidation net income in Problem 62.

    b.   The parent's pre-consolidation retained earnings in Problem 61 to the parent's pre-consolidation retained earnings in Problem 62.

    c.   The parent's pre-consolidation equity investment account in Problem 61 to the parent's pre-consolidation equity investment account in Problem 62.

    d.   The amount of income attributable to the noncontrolling interest calculated in Problem 61 to the amount of income attributable to the noncontrolling interest calculated in Problem 62.

    e.   The amount of noncontrolling interest calculated in Problem 61 to the amount of noncontrolling interest you calculated in Problem 62.

In each case, clearly explain what is causing the differences. Except for totals (e.g., total assets), are there any other differences in the pre-consolidation or consolidated financial statements?

LO2, 3   **64. Consolidation subsequent to date of acquisition—Equity method with noncontrolling interest, AAP, and loss on upstream intercompany equipment sale**

A parent company acquired its 80% interest in its subsidiary on January 1, 2013. On the acquisition date, the total fair value of the controlling interest and the noncontrolling interest was $500,000 in excess of the book value of the subsidiary's Stockholders' Equity. $280,000 of that excess was assigned to a patent. The patent has a zero recorded book value in the subsidiary's financial statements, and has a 10 year remaining economic life on the date of acquisition. Amortization is computed on a straight-line basis. The remaining $220,000 of the purchase price was assigned to Goodwill. The Goodwill is allocated to the parent and subsidiary in a 80:20 split, respectively.

On January 1, 2014, the subsidiary sold Equipment to the parent for a cash price of $84,000. The subsidiary acquired the equipment at a cost of $180,000 and depreciated the equipment over its 10-year useful life using the straight-line method (no salvage value). The subsidiary had depreciated the equipment for 3 years at the time of sale. The parent retained the depreciation policy of the subsidiary and depreciated the equipment over its remaining 7 year useful life.

Following are pre-consolidation financial statements of the parent and its subsidiary for the year ended December 31, 2016. The parent uses the equity method to account for its Equity Investment.

	Parent	Subsidiary		Parent	Subsidiary
Income statement:			**Balance sheet:**		
Sales.	$9,000,000	$2,500,000	Cash. . . . . $	443,200	$ 500,000
Cost of goods sold.	(7,000,000)	(1,500,000)	Accounts receivable.	800,000	700,000
Gross profit.	2,000,000	1,000,000	Inventory.	1,400,000	1,000,000
Income (loss) from subsidiary.	252,800	—	Equity invetment.	1,609,600	
Operating expenses.	(1,400,000)	(650,000)	PPE, net	3,500,000	2,000,000
Net income.	$ 852,800	$ 350,000	Total assets.	$7,752,800	$4,200,000
Statement of retained earnings:					
BOY retained earnings.	$2,500,000	$ 570,000	Accounts payable. . . . . $	600,000	$ 450,000
Net income.	852,800	350,000	Other current liabilities	800,000	650,000
Dividends	(500,000)	(50,000)	Long-term liabilities	2,000,000	1,500,000
EOY retained earnings	$2,852,800	$ 870,000	Common stock.	500,000	200,000
			APIC	1,000,000	530,000
			Retained earnings	2,852,800	870,000
			Total liabilities and equity	$7,752,800	$4,200,000

a. Disaggregate and document the activity for the 100% Acquisition Accounting Premium (AAP), the controlling interest AAP and the noncontrolling interest AAP.

b. Calculate and organize the profits and losses on intercompany transactions and balances.

c. Compute the pre-consolidation Equity Investment account beginning and ending balances starting with the stockholders' equity of the subsidiary.

d. Reconstruct the activity in the parent's pre-consolidation Equity Investment T-account for the year of consolidation.

e. Independently compute the owners' equity attributable to the noncontrolling interest beginning and ending balances starting with the owners' equity of the subsidiary.

f. Independently calculate consolidated net income, controlling interest net income and noncontrolling interest net income.

g. Complete the consolidating entries according to the **C-E-A-D-I** sequence and complete the consolidation worksheet.

65. **Consolidation subsequent to date of acquisition—Cost method with noncontrolling interest, AAP, and gain on downstream intercompany equipment sale**

LO2, 4

A parent company acquired its 90% interest in its subsidiary on January 1, 2012. The total fair value of the controlling interest and the noncontrolling interest on that date was $300,000 in excess of the book value of the subsidiary's Stockholders' Equity on the acquisition date. $200,000 of that excess was assigned to a Customer List that is being amortized over a 10-year period. The remaining $100,000 was assigned to Goodwill. The Goodwill is allocated to the parent and subsidiary in a 90:10 split, respectively.

On January 1, 2015, the parent sold equipment to the subsidiary for a cash price of $125,000. The parent originally acquired the equipment at a cost of $150,000 and depreciated the equipment over its 15-year useful life using the straight-line method (no salvage value). At the time of the intercompany sale, the parent depreciated the equipment for 5 full years. The subsidiary retained the depreciation policy of the parent (i.e., it depreciated the equipment over its remaining 10-year useful life).

The parent uses the cost method of pre-consolidation investment bookkeeping. Following are pre-consolidation financial statements of the parent and its subsidiary for the year ended December 31, 2016.

	Parent	Subsidiary		Parent	Subsidiary
Income statement:			**Balance sheet:**		
Sales.	$10,000,000	$1,000,000	Cash.	$ 800,000	$ 385,000
Cost of goods sold.	(7,600,000)	(600,000)	Accounts receivable.	1,000,000	460,000
Gross profit.	2,400,000	400,000	Inventories	1,500,000	570,000
Income (loss) from subsidiary.	18,000		PPE, net	6,000,000	1,150,000
Operating expenses.	(1,500,000)	(300,000)	Equity investment.	765,000	
Net income.	$ 918,000	$ 100,000	Total assets.	$10,065,000	$2,565,000
Statement of retained earnings:					
BOY retained earnings.	$3,000,000	$ 500,000	Accounts payable.	$ 400,000	$ 80,000
Net income.	918,000	100,000	Other current liabilities	1,147,000	230,000
Dividends	(400,000)	(20,000)	Long-term liabilities	2,500,000	1,300,000
EOY retained earnings	$3,518,000	$ 580,000	Common stock.	500,000	125,000
			APIC.	2,000,000	250,000
			Retained earnings	3,518,000	580,000
			Total liabilities and equity	$10,065,000	$2,565,000

a. Disaggregate and document the activity for the 100% Acquisition Accounting Premium (AAP), the controlling interest AAP and the noncontrolling interest AAP.

b. Calculate and organize the profits and losses on intercompany transactions and balances.

c. Compute the pre-consolidation Equity Investment account beginning and ending balances assuming that the parent company used the equity method instead of the cost method. For each of these computations, start with the stockholders' equity of the subsidiary.

d. Compute the amount of the **[ADJ]** consolidating entry.

e. Independently compute the owners' equity attributable to the noncontrolling interest beginning and ending balances starting with the owners' equity of the subsidiary.

f. Independently calculate consolidated net income, controlling interest net income, and noncontrolling interest net income.

g. Complete the consolidating entries according to the **C-E-A-D-I** sequence and complete the consolidation worksheet.

LO2, 3

66. **Comprehensive consolidation subsequent to date of acquisition—Equity method, noncontrolling interest, AAP computation, goodwill, upstream and downstream intercompany inventory profits, downstream intercompany depreciable asset gain**

A parent company acquired 70 percent of the stock of a subsidiary company on January 1, 2012, for $120,000. On this date, the balances of the subsidiary's stockholders' equity accounts were Common Stock, $104,000, and Retained Earnings, $11,200. On January 1, 2012, the market value for the 30% of shares not purchased by the parent was $51,040.

On January 1, 2012, the subsidiary's recorded book values were equal to fair values for all items except four: (1) accounts receivable had a book value of $24,000 and a fair value of $20,800, (2) buildings and equipment, net had a book value of $40,000 and a fair value of $54,400, (3) the licenses intangible asset had a book value of $28,000 and a fair value of $61,600, and (4) notes payable had a book value of $16,000 and a fair value of $11,200. Both companies use the FIFO inventory method and sell all of their inventories at least once per year. The net balance of accounts receivables are collected in the following year. On the acquisition date, the subsidiary's buildings and equipment, net had a remaining useful life of 6 years, licenses had a remaining useful life of 7 years, and notes payable had a remaining term of 4 years.

On January 1, 2015, the parent sold a building to the subsidiary for $52,000. On this date, the building was carried on the parent's books (net of accumulated depreciation) at $40,000. Both companies estimated that the building has a remaining life of 6 years on the intercompany sale date, with no salvage value.

Each company routinely sells merchandise to the other company, with a profit margin of 25 percent of selling price (regardless of the direction of the sale). During 2016, intercompany sales amount to $12,000, of which $6,400 of merchandise remains in the ending inventory of the parent. On December 31, 2016, $3,200 of these intercompany sales remained unpaid. Additionally, the subsidiary's December 31, 2015 inventory includes $9,600 of merchandise purchased in the preceding year from the parent. During 2015, intercompany sales amount to $16,000, and on December 31, 2015, $4,800 of these intercompany sales remained unpaid.

The parent accounts for its Equity Investment in the subsidiary using the equity method. Unconfirmed profits are allocated pro rata. The pre-consolidation financial statements for the two companies for the year ended December 31, 2016, are provided below:

	Parent	Subsidiary		Parent	Subsidiary
Income statement:			**Balance sheet:**		
Sales........................	$384,000	$144,000	Cash...........................	$ 31,520	$ 12,000
Cost of goods sold..............	(192,000)	(86,400)	Accounts receivable..............	43,200	38,400
Gross profit....................	192,000	57,600	Inventory......................	104,000	36,800
Depreciation & amort. expense	(9,600)	(8,000)	Buildings and equipment, net	100,800	72,000
Operating expenses..............	(120,000)	(28,800)	Other accts......................	45,600	80,000
Interest expense................	(4,800)	(1,600)	Licenses.......................	—	8,000
Total expenses	(134,400)	(38,400)	Investment in subsidiary............	143,360	
Equity income from subsidiary......	11,680	—	Total assets....................	$468,480	$247,200
Net income....................	$ 69,280	$ 19,200			
Statement of retained earnings:					
BOY retained earnings............	$172,000	$ 88,000	Accounts payable.................	$ 25,600	$ 9,600
Net income....................	69,280	19,200	Notes payable	40,000	17,600
Dividends	(48,000)	(12,000)	Other liabilities	17,600	20,800
EOY retained earnings...........	$193,280	$ 95,200	Common stock....................	192,000	104,000
			Retained earnings	193,280	95,200
			Total liabilities and equity...........	$468,480	$247,200

a. Disaggregate and document the activity for the 100% Acquisition Accounting Premium (AAP), the controlling interest AAP, and the noncontrolling interest AAP.

b. Calculate and organize the profits and losses on intercompany transactions and balances.

c. Compute the pre-consolidation Equity Investment account beginning and ending balances starting with the stockholders' equity of the subsidiary.

d. Reconstruct the activity in the parent's pre-consolidation Equity Investment T-account for the year of consolidation.

e. Independently compute the owners' equity attributable to the noncontrolling interest beginning and ending balances starting with the owners' equity of the subsidiary.

f. Independently calculate consolidated net income, controlling interest net income, and noncontrolling interest net income.

g. Complete the consolidating entries according to the **C-E-A-D-I** sequence and complete the consolidation worksheet.

67. **Comprehensive consolidation subsequent to date of acquisition—Equity method, noncontrolling interest, AAP computation, bargain purchase gain, downstream intercompany inventory profits, upstream intercompany depreciable asset gain**

LO2, 3

A parent company acquired 90 percent of the stock of a subsidiary company on January 1, 2014, for $196,250. On this date, the balances of the subsidiary's stockholders' equity accounts were Capital Stock, $125,000, and Retained Earnings, $25,000. On January 1, 2014, the market price for the 10% noncontrolling interest was $22,500.

An examination of the subsidiary's assets and liabilities on January 1, 2014 revealed that book values were equal to fair values for all items except two: (1) merchandise, which had a book value of $30,000 and a fair value of $42,500, and (2) intangible assets which had a fair value of $75,000 and a book value of zero. Both companies use the FIFO inventory method and sell all of their inventories at least once per year. The intangible assets had a useful life of 10 years.

On January 1, 2015, the subsidiary sold a building to the parent for $125,000. On this date, the building was carried on the subsidiary's books (net of accumulated depreciation) at $100,000. Both companies estimated that the building has a remaining life of 10 years on the intercompany sale date, with no salvage value.

The parent regularly sells merchandise to the subsidiary with a profit margin of 35 percent of selling price. During 2016, intercompany sales amount to $50,000, of which $15,000 of merchandise remains in the ending inventory of the subsidiary. On December 31, 2016, $12,500 of these intercompany sales remained unpaid. Additionally, the subsidiary's December 31, 2015 inventory includes $7,500 of merchandise purchased in the preceding year from the parent.

The parent accounts for its Equity Investment in the subsidiary using the equity method. Unconfirmed profits are allocated pro rata. The pre-consolidation financial statements for the two companies for the year ended December 31, 2016, are provided below:

	Parent	Subsidiary		Parent	Subsidiary
Income statement:			**Balance sheet:**		
Sales.	$500,000	$187,500	Cash	$ 19,500	$ 25,000
Cost of goods sold.	(250,000)	(112,500)	Accounts receivable.	25,000	50,000
Gross profit.	250,000	75,000	Inventories	125,000	37,500
Depreciation & amort. expense	(12,500)	(10,000)	Buildings and equipment, net	100,000	75,000
Operating expenses.	(162,500)	(40,000)	Other assets	59,375	125,000
Total expenses	(175,000)	(50,000)	Investment in subsidiary.	260,250	
Income (loss) from subsidiary.	15,375	—	Total assets.	$589,125	$312,500
Net income	$ 90,375	$ 25,000			
Statement of retained earnings:					
BOY retained earnings	$223,750	$125,000	Accounts payable.	$ 25,000	$ 12,500
Net income.	90,375	25,000	Other liabilities	75,000	37,500
Dividends	(75,000)	(12,500)	Common stock.	250,000	125,000
EOY retained earnings	$239,125	$137,500	Retained earnings	239,125	137,500
			Total liabilities and equity	$589,125	$312,500

a. Disaggregate and document the activity for the 100% Acquisition Accounting Premium (AAP), the controlling interest AAP, and the noncontrolling interest AAP.

b. Calculate and organize the profits and losses on intercompany transactions and balances.

c. Compute the pre-consolidation Equity Investment account beginning and ending balances starting with the stockholders' equity of the subsidiary.

d. Reconstruct the activity in the parent's pre-consolidation Equity Investment T-account for the year of consolidation.

e. Independently compute the owners' equity attributable to the noncontrolling interest beginning and ending balances starting with the owners' equity of the subsidiary.

f. Independently calculate consolidated net income, controlling interest net income and noncontrolling interest net income.

g. Complete the consolidating entries according to the **C-E-A-D-I** sequence and complete the consolidation worksheet.

LO2, 4

68. **Comprehensive consolidation subsequent to date of acquisition—Cost method, noncontrolling interest, AAP computation, goodwill, upstream and downstream intercompany inventory profits, downstream intercompany depreciable asset gain**
A parent company acquired 80 percent of the stock of a subsidiary company on January 1, 2012, for $144,000. On this date, the balances of the subsidiary's stockholders' equity accounts were Common Stock, $104,000, and Retained Earnings, $11,200. On January 1, 2012, the market value for the 20% of shares not purchased by the parent was $35,200.

On January 1, 2012, the subsidiary's recorded book values were equal to fair values for all items except four: (1) accounts receivable had a book value of $24,000 and a fair value of $20,000, (2) property, plant & equipment, net had a book value of $40,000 and a fair value of $68,000, (3) patents had a book value of $28,000 and a fair value of $52,000, and (4) notes payable had a book value of $16,000 and a fair value of $11,200. Both companies use the FIFO inventory method and sell all of their inventories at least once per year. The year-end net balance of accounts receivables are collected in the following year. On the acquisition date, the subsidiary's property, plant & equipment, net had a remaining useful life of 10 years, the patents had a remaining useful life of 6 years, and notes payable had a remaining term of 4 years.

On December 31, 2014, the parent sold a building to the subsidiary for $56,000. On this date, the building was carried on the subsidiary's books (net of accumulated depreciation) at $40,000. Both companies estimated that the building has a remaining life of 5 years on the intercompany sale date, with no salvage value. Each company routinely sells merchandise to the other company, with a profit margin of 35 percent of selling price (regardless of the direction of the sale). During 2016, intercompany sales amount to $19,200, of which $12,800 of merchandise remains in the ending inventory of the subsidiary. On December 31, 2016, $6,400 of these intercompany sales remained unpaid. Additionally, the parent's December 31, 2015 inventory includes $9,600 of merchandise purchased in the preceding year from the subsidiary. During 2015, intercompany sales amount to $16,000, and on December 31, 2015, $2,560 of these intercompany sales remained unpaid.

The parent accounts for its Equity Investment in the subsidiary using the cost method. Unconfirmed profits are allocated pro rata.

The pre-consolidation financial statements for the two companies for the year ended December 31, 2016, are provided below:

	Parent	Subsidiary		Parent	Subsidiary
Income statement:			**Balance sheet:**		
Sales..........................	$368,000	$160,000	Cash............................	$ 34,640	$ 12,000
Cost of goods sold...............	(192,000)	(94,400)	Accounts receivable...............	43,200	38,400
Gross profit.....................	176,000	65,600	Inventories	104,000	36,800
Depreciation & amort. expense	(9,600)	(7,680)	PPE, net	100,800	88,000
Operating expenses..............	(104,000)	(21,040)	Other assets....................	45,600	80,000
Interest expense.................	(4,800)	(1,680)	Patents.........................	—	8,000
Total expenses	(118,400)	(30,400)	Investment in subsidiary............	144,000	
Income (loss) from subsidiary.......	12,800	—	Total assets......................	$472,240	$263,200
Net income....................	$ 70,400	$ 35,200			
Statement of retained earnings:					
BOY retained earnings............	$174,640	$ 88,000	Accounts payable.................	$ 25,600	$ 14,400
Net income....................	70,400	35,200	Notes payable	40,000	16,800
Dividends	(48,000)	(16,000)	Other liabilities	17,600	20,800
EOY retained earnings............	$197,040	$107,200	Common stock....................	192,000	104,000
			Retained earnings	197,040	107,200
			Total liabilities and equity...........	$472,240	$263,200

a. Disaggregate and document the activity for the 100% Acquisition Accounting Premium (AAP), the controlling interest AAP, and the noncontrolling interest AAP.

b. Calculate and organize the profits and losses on intercompany transactions and balances.

c. Compute the pre-consolidation Equity Investment account beginning and ending balances assuming that the parent company used the equity method instead of the cost method. For each of these computations, start with the stockholders' equity of the subsidiary.

d. Compute the amount of the [ADJ] consolidating entry.

e. Independently compute the owners' equity attributable to the noncontrolling interest beginning and ending balances starting with the owners' equity of the subsidiary.

f. Independently calculate consolidated net income, controlling interest net income and noncontrolling interest net income.

g. Complete the consolidating entries according to the **C-E-A-D-I** sequence and complete the consolidation worksheet.

TOPIC REVIEW

Solution 1

	Parent	Subsidiary	Consolidation Entries Dr	Cr	Consolidated
Income statement:					
Sales	$7,330,000	$1,000,500			$ 8,330,500
Cost of goods sold	(5,131,000)	(600,300)			(5,731,300)
Gross profit	2,199,000	400,200			2,599,200
Income (loss) from subsidiary	96,056		[C] $ 96,056		0
Operating expenses	(1,392,700)	(260,130)	[D] 20,000		(1,672,830)
Consolidated net income	902,356	140,070			926,370
Consolidated NI attributable to NCI			[C] 24,014		(24,014)
Consolidated NI attributable to parent	$ 902,356	$ 140,070			$ 902,356
Statement of retained earnings:					
BOY retained earnings	$3,682,592	$ 516,925	[E] 516,925		$ 3,682,592
Consolidated NI attributable to parent	902,356	140,070			902,356
Dividends	(180,471)	(21,010)		[C] $ 21,010	(180,471)
Ending retained earnings	$4,404,477	$ 635,985			$ 4,404,477
Balance sheet:					
Assets					
Cash	$1,007,384	$ 302,902			$ 1,310,286
Accounts receivable	938,240	232,116			1,170,356
Inventory	1,422,020	298,149			1,720,169
Equity investment	804,848			[C] 79,248	0
				[E] 533,600	
				[A] 192,000	
Property, plant and equipment (PPE), net	5,374,356	685,009	[A] 170,000	[D] 10,000	6,219,365
Patent			[A] 70,000	[D] 10,000	60,000
Goodwill			[A] 0		0
	$9,546,848	$1,518,176			$10,480,176
Liabilities and stockholders' equity					
Current liabilities	$1,053,321	$ 232,116			$ 1,285,437
Long-term liabilities	2,000,000	500,000			2,500,000
Common stock	1,198,455	66,700	[E] 66,700		1,198,455
APIC	890,595	83,375	[E] 83,375		890,595
Retained earnings	4,404,477	635,985			4,404,477
Noncontrolling interest				[C] 19,812	201,212
				[E] 133,400	
				[A] 48,000	
	$9,546,848	$1,518,176	$1,047,070	$1,047,070	$10,480,176

Solution 2

	Parent	Subsidiary	Consolidation Entries Dr		Consolidation Entries Cr		Consolidated
Income statement:							
Sales......................................	$ 960,000	$360,000	[I$_{sales}$]	$ 50,000			$1,270,000
Cost of goods sold.........................	(480,000)	(216,000)	[I$_{cogs}$]	7,000	[I$_{cogs}$]	$ 21,000	(632,000)
					[I$_{sales}$]	50,000	
Gross profit................................	480,000	144,000					638,000
Depreciation & amortization expense	(24,000)	(19,200)					(43,200)
Operating expenses.........................	(300,000)	(72,600)					(372,600)
Interest expense...........................	(12,000)	(4,000)					(16,000)
Total expenses	(336,000)	(95,800)					(431,800)
Income (loss) from subsidiary.................	41,440	—	[C]	41,440			0
Consolidated net income....................	185,440	48,200					206,200
Income attributable to NCI..................	—	—	[C]	20,760			(20,760)
Income attributable to controlling interest	$ 185,440	$ 48,200					$ 185,440
Statement of retained earnings:							
Beginning retained earnings..................	$ 404,000	$220,000	[E]	220,000			$ 404,000
Income attributable to controlling interest	185,440	48,200					185,440
Dividends declared.........................	(120,000)	(28,000)			[C]	28,000	(120,000)
Ending retained earnings	$ 469,440	$240,200					$ 469,440
Balance sheet:							
Cash......................................	$ 78,000	$ 30,000					$ 108,000
Accounts receivable........................	108,000	96,000			[I$_{pay}$]	16,000	188,000
Inventory..................................	260,000	92,000			[I$_{cogs}$]	7,000	345,000
Buildings and equipment, net	252,000	180,000					432,000
Other assets...............................	114,000	200,000					314,000
Licenses	—	20,000					20,000
Equity investment..........................	343,140		[I$_{cogs}$]	14,700	[C]	21,840	0
					[E]	336,000	
Total assets...............................	$1,155,140	$618,000					$1,407,000
Accounts payable	$ 61,700	$ 23,800	[I$_{pay}$]	16,000			$ 69,500
Notes payable	100,000	42,000					142,000
Other liabilities	44,000	52,000					96,000
Common stock.............................	480,000	260,000	[E]	260,000			480,000
Retained earnings	469,440	240,200					469,440
Noncontrolling interest......................			[I$_{cogs}$]	6,300	[C]	12,360	150,060
					[E]	144,000	
Total liabilities and equity....................	$1,155,140	$618,000		$636,200		$636,200	$1,407,000

Solution 3

	Parent	Subsidiary	Consolidation Entries		Consolidated
			Dr	**Cr**	
Income statement:					
Sales.	$780,000	$285,000			$1,065,000
Cost of goods sold.	(420,000)	(177,000)			(597,000)
Gross profit.	360,000	108,000			468,000
Depreciation & amortization expense	(18,000)	(14,400)		[I$_{dep}$] $ 3,000	(29,400)
Operating expenses.	(225,000)	(54,450)			(279,450)
Interest expense.	(9,000)	(3,000)			(12,000)
Total expenses	(252,000)	(71,850)			(320,850)
Income (loss) from subsidiary.	27,405	—	[C] $ 27,405		—
Consolidated net income	135,405	36,150			147,150
Income attributable to NCI.	—	—	[C] 11,745		(11,745)
Income attributable to controlling interest	$135,405	$ 36,150			$135,405
Statement of retained earnings:					
Beginning retained earnings.	$303,000	$165,000	[E] 165,000		$303,000
Income attributable to controlling interest	135,405	36,150			135,405
Dividends declared.	(90,000)	(18,000)		[C] 18,000	(90,000)
Ending retained earnings	$348,405	$183,150			$348,405
Balance sheet:					
Cash.	$ 58,500	$ 25,500			$84,000
Accounts receivable.	81,000	72,000			153,000
Inventory.	195,000	69,000			264,000
Buildings and equipment, net	189,000	135,000	[I$_{dep}$] 3,000	[I$_{gain}$] 12,000	315,000
Other assets.	85,500	150,000			235,500
Licenses	—	15,000			15,000
Equity investment.	258,405		[I$_{gain}$] 8,400	[C] 14,805	0
				[E] 252,000	
Total assets.	$867,405	$466,500			$1,066,500
Accounts payable	$ 51,000	$ 17,850			$68,850
Notes payable	75,000	31,500			106,500
Other liabilities	33,000	39,000			72,000
Common stock.	360,000	195,000	[E] 195,000		360,000
Retained earnings	348,405	183,150			348,405
Noncontrolling interest.	—	—	[I$_{gain}$] 3,600	[C] 6,345	110,745
				[E] 108,000	
Total liabilities and equity	$867,405	$466,500	$414,150	$414,150	$1,066,500

Solution 4

The subsidiary's Stockholders' Equity is now $620,000, and the parent owns 83% $\left(\frac{10,000}{12,000}\right)$ of the outstanding common stock (noncontrolling shareholders now own 17% of the subsidiary). The parent's Equity Investment account must now be reported at $514,600 (83% of $620,000) following the sale of stock. The parent, therefore, makes the following journal entry in its records to reflect the required increase in its Equity Investment account:

Equity investment.	14,600	
APIC.		14,600

(to record the increase in the Equity Investment account resulting from the subsidiary's sale of 2,000 shares of common stock above book value)

COMPREHENSIVE REVIEW SOLUTION—EQUITY METHOD

a. The trial balance information converted to financial statement format is presented, below. A completed consolidation spreadsheet is included in the solution to part h of this comprehensive review.

Pre-Consolidation Financial Statements for the Year Ended December 31, 2016		
	Parent	**Subsidiary**
Income statement:		
Sales.	$720,000	$270,000
Cost of goods sold.	(432,000)	(162,000)
Gross profit.	288,000	108,000
Depreciation & amortization expense.	(18,000)	(14,400)
Operating expenses.	(226,000)	(54,100)
Interest expense.	(8,000)	(3,500)
Total expenses	(252,000)	(72,000)
Income (loss) from subsidiary.	23,900	
Net income.	$ 59,900	$ 36,000
Statement of retained earnings:		
Beginning retained earnings.	$322,200	$165,000
Net income.	59,900	36,000
Dividends declared.	(90,000)	(21,000)
Ending retained earnings	$292,100	$180,000
Balance sheet:		
Cash.	$ 58,080	$ 42,500
Accounts receivable.	81,000	60,000
Inventories	195,000	91,500
Property, plant & equipment, net	189,000	135,000
Other assets.	85,500	150,000
Equity investment.	325,500	
Total assets.	$934,080	$479,000
Accounts payable.	$168,000	$ 35,000
Notes payable	80,980	30,000
Other liabilities	33,000	39,000
Common stock.	360,000	195,000
Retained earnings	292,100	180,000
Total liabilities and equity	$934,080	$479,000

b. Given the five-year time horizon between the acquisition date and the consolidated financial statement date, the following schedules separately document the annual AAP amortization and the year end unamortized AAP balance for each year, 2012 through 2016.

100% AAP:

	Year Ended December 31,				
100% AAP Amortization – Dr (Cr)	**2012**	**2013**	**2014**	**2015**	**2016**
Accounts receivable.....................	$(7,000)	$ —	$ —	$ —	$ —
Property, plant & equipment, net...........	1,800	1,800	1,800	1,800	1,800
Customer list	7,500	7,500	7,500	7,500	—
Notes payable	1,000	1,000	1,000	1,000	1,000
Net amortization......................	$ 3,300	$10,300	$10,300	$10,300	$2,800

		December 31,				
100% Unamortized AAP – Dr (Cr)	**Jan. 1, 2012**	**2012**	**2013**	**2014**	**2015**	**2016**
Accounts receivable.............	$ (7,000)	$ —	$ —	$ —	$ —	$ —
Property, plant & equipment, net ...	18,000	16,200	14,400	12,600	10,800	9,000
Customer list	30,000	22,500	15,000	7,500	—	—
Notes payable	5,000	4,000	3,000	2,000	1,000	—
Goodwill......................	84,000	84,000	84,000	84,000	84,000	84,000
Unamortized balance...........	$130,000	$126,700	$116,400	$106,100	$95,800	$93,000

75% AAP:

	Year Ended December 31,				
75% AAP Amortization – Dr (Cr)	**2012**	**2013**	**2014**	**2015**	**2016**
Accounts receivable.....................	$(5,250)	$ —	$ —	$ —	$ —
Property, plant & equipment, net...........	1,350	1,350	1,350	1,350	1,350
Customer list	5,625	5,625	5,625	5,625	—
Notes payable	750	750	750	750	750
Net amortization......................	$ 2,475	$7,725	$7,725	$7,725	$2,100

		December 31,				
75% Unamortized AAP – Dr (Cr)	**Jan. 1, 2012**	**2012**	**2013**	**2014**	**2015**	**2016**
Accounts receivable.............	$ (5,250)	$ —	$ —	$ —	$ —	$ —
Property, plant & equipment, net ...	13,500	12,150	10,800	9,450	8,100	6,750
Customer list	22,500	16,875	11,250	5,625	—	—
Notes payable	3,750	3,000	2,250	1,500	750	—
Goodwill*	65,500	65,500	65,500	65,500	65,500	65,500
Unamortized balance...........	$100,000	$97,525	$89,800	$82,075	$74,350	$72,250

*$280,000 − (75% × $286,000) = $65,500

25% AAP:

	Year Ended December 31,				
25% AAP Amortization – Dr (Cr)	**2012**	**2013**	**2014**	**2015**	**2016**
Accounts receivable.....................	$(1,750)	$ —	$ —	$ —	$ —
Property, plant & equipment, net	450	450	450	450	450
Customer list	1,875	1,875	1,875	1,875	—
Notes payable	250	250	250	250	250
Net amortization......................	$ 825	$2,575	$2,575	$2,575	$700

		December 31,				
25% Unamortized AAP – Dr (Cr)	**Jan. 1, 2012**	**2012**	**2013**	**2014**	**2015**	**2016**
Accounts receivable.............	$ (1,750)	$ —	$ —	$ —	$ —	$ —
Property, plant & equipment, net ...	4,500	4,050	3,600	3,150	2,700	2,250
Customer list	7,500	5,625	3,750	1,875	—	—
Notes payable	1,250	1,000	750	500	250	—
Goodwill*	18,500	18,500	18,500	18,500	18,500	18,500
Unamortized balance...........	$30,000	$29,175	$26,600	$24,025	$21,450	$20,750

* $90,000 − (25% × $286,000) = $18,500

c. **Intercompany depreciable asset sale:**
One downstream asset sale.
Intercompany profit recognized on January 1, 2015: $80,000 − $55,000 = $25,000, 10-year remaining life
Profit confirmed each year: $25,000/10 = $2,500

	Downstream	**Upstream**
Net intercompany profit deferred at January 1, 2016	$22,500	$0
Less: Deferred intercompany profit recognized during 2016...........	2,500	0
Net intercompany profit deferred at December 31, 2016	$20,000	$0

Intercompany inventory transactions:
Intercompany inventory sales during 2016: $50,000

	Downstream (in Subsidiary's Inventory)	**Upstream (in Parent's Inventory)**
Intercompany profit in inventory on January 1, 2016...............	$ 0	$6,000
Intercompany profit in inventory on December 31, 2016............	$8,000	$ 0

Intercompany accounts receivables and payables at December 31, 2016: $10,000

d. The following is the general formula for computing the Equity Investment account (under the equity method) at any point in time:

	(1) p% × book value of the net assets of the subsidiary
Plus:	(2) Unamortized p% AAP
Less:	(3) 100% × downstream deferred intercompany profits
Less:	(4) p% × upstream deferred intercompany profits
	Equity method Equity Investment account

Equity Investment account balance at January 1, 2016:

	Jan. 1, 2016	
	$270,000	(1) 75% × ($195,000 + $165,000)
Plus:	74,350	(2) $74,350 (from *Part b*)
Less:	(22,500)	(3) 100% × $22,500 (from *Part c*)
Less:	(4,500)	(4) 75% × $6,000 (from *Part c*)
	$317,350	

Equity Investment account balance at December 31, 2016:

	Dec. 31, 2016	
	$281,250	(1) 75% × ($195,000 + $180,000)
Plus:	72,250	(2) $72,250 (from *Part b*)
Less:	(20,000)	(3) 100% × $20,000 (from *Part c*)
	(8,000)	(4) 100% × $8,000 (from *Part c*)
Less:	0	(4) none
	$325,500	

e. The equity method Equity Investment accounting includes the following routine adjustments during any given period: (1) recognition of p% of the subsidiary's income, (2) recognition of p% of the dividends declared by the subsidiary, (3) amortization of the p% AAP, (4) recognition of prior period deferred intercompany profits that have been confirmed though either transactions with unaffiliated parties or depreciation/amortization, and (5) deferral of intercompany profits newly originated during the current period. With respect to the deferred intercompany profits, the effect on the Equity Investment account is 100% for downstream transactions and p% for upstream transactions. Information for items (1) and (2) is available in the initial information, information for item (3) was summarized in part b, and information for items (4) and (5) was summarized in part c. These items are all reflected in the following completed T-account.

	Equity Investment		
January 1, 2016	317,350		
(1) p% × net income of Sub. = 75% × $36,000	27,000	15,750	(2) p% × dividends of Sub. = 75% × $21,000
(4) p% × BOY upstream inventory profits recognized during 2016 = 75% × $6,000	4,500	2,100	(3) p% AAP amortization (see *Part b*)
(4) 100% × downstream equipment profits recognized via depreciation during 2016	2,500	8,000	(5) 100% × EOY downstream inventory profits deferred until year of sale to unaffiliated party
December 31, 2016	325,500		

f. The following is the general formula for computing the noncontrolling interest in consolidated equity at any point in time:

	(1) nci% × book value of the net assets of the subsidiary
Plus:	(2) Unamortized nci% AAP
Less:	(3) nci% × upstream deferred intercompany profits
	Noncontrolling Interest

The balance of noncontrolling interest in consolidated equity at January 1, 2016:

Jan. 1, 2016		
	$ 90,000	(1) 25% × ($195,000 + $165,000)
Plus:	21,450	(2) $21,450 (from *Part b*)
Less:	(1,500)	(3) 25% × $6,000 (from *Part c*)
	$109,950	

The balance of noncontrolling interest in consolidated equity at December 31, 2016:

Dec. 31, 2016		
	$ 93,750	(1) 25% × ($195,000 + $180,000)
Plus:	20,750	(2) $20,750 (from *Part b*)
Less:	0	(3) none at December 31, 2016 (from *Part c*)
	$114,500	

g.

Incremental Computation of Consolidated Net Income for the Year Ended December 31, 2016

Parent's stand-alone net income	$36,000	($59,900 − $23,900)
Plus: 100% realized downstream deferred profits	2,500	(see *Part c*)
Less: 100% unrealized downstream deferred profits	(8,000)	(see *Part c*)
Parent's adjusted stand-alone net income	$30,500	
Subsidiary's stand-alone net income	$36,000	(see facts)
Plus: 100% realized upstream deferred profits	6,000	(see *Part c*)
Less: 100% unrealized upstream deferred profits	0	(see *Part c*)
Less: 100% AAP amortization	(2,800)	(see *Part b*)
Subsidiary's adjusted stand-alone net income	$39,200	
Consolidated net income	$69,700	

Incremental Computation of Consolidated Net Income Attributable to the Controlling Interest for the Year Ended December 31, 2016

Parent's stand-alone net income	$36,000	($59,900 − $23,900)
Plus: 100% realized downstream deferred profits	2,500	(see *Part c*)
Less: 100% unrealized downstream deferred profits	(8,000)	(see *Part c*)
Parent's adjusted stand-alone net income	$30,500	
75% × subsidiary's stand-alone net income (75% × $36,000)	$27,000	(see facts)
Plus: 75% realized upstream deferred profits (75% × $6,000)	4,500	(see *Part c*)
Less: 75% AAP amortization (from schedule)	(2,100)	(see *Part b*)
75% of the Subsidiary's adjusted stand-alone net income	$29,400	
Consolidated net income attributable to the controlling interest	$59,900	

Incremental Computation of Consolidated Net Income Attributable to the Noncontrolling Interest for the Year Ended December 31, 2016

25% × subsidiary's stand-alone net income (25% × $36,000)	$9,000	(see facts)
Plus: 25% realized upstream deferred profits (25% × $6,000)	1,500	(see *Part c*)
Less: 25% AAP amortization (from schedule)	(700)	(see *Part b*)
Consolidated net income attributable to the noncontrolling interest	$9,800	

h.

[C]	Income (loss) from subsidiary..................		23,900	
	Income attributable to NCI.....................		9,800	
	Dividends—subsidiary...................			21,000
	Equity investment			8,150
	Noncontrolling interest			4,550
[E]	Common stock @ BOY		195,000	
	Retained earnings (S) @ BOY...................		165,000	
	Equity investment @ BOY			270,000
	Noncontrolling interest @ BOY			90,000
[A]	Property, plant & equipment @ BOY		10,800	
	Notes payable @ BOY		1,000	
	Goodwill		84,000	
	Equity investment @ BOY			74,350
	Noncontrolling interest @ BOY			21,450
[D]	Depreciation & amortization expense............		1,800	
	Interest expense............................		1,000	
	Property, plant & equipment, net			1,800
	Notes payable			1,000
[I$_{cogs}$]	Equity investment @ BOY		4,500	
	Noncontrolling interest @ BOY..................		1,500	
	Cost of goods sold			6,000 ✓
[I$_{sales}$]	Sales		50,000	
	Cost of goods sold			50,000 ✓
[I$_{cogs}$]	Cost of goods sold..........................		8,000	
	Inventories...........................			8,000
[I$_{pay}$]	Accounts payable...........................		10,000	
	Accounts receivable			10,000 ✓
[I$_{gain}$]	Equity investment @ BOY		22,500	
	Property, plant & equipment, net @ BOY ...			22,500 ✓
[I$_{dep}$]	Property, plant & equipment, net		2,500	
	Depreciation expense			2,500 ✓

Consolidation Spreadsheet for the Year Ended December 31, 2016

	Parent	Subsidiary	Consolidation Entries Dr		Cr		Consolidated
Income statement:							
Sales	$720,000	$270,000	[I$_{sales}$]	$ 50,000			$ 940,000
Cost of goods sold	(432,000)	(162,000)	[I$_{cogs}$]	8,000	[I$_{cogs}$]	$ 6,000	(546,000)
					[I$_{sales}$]	50,000	
Gross profit	288,000	108,000					394,000
Depreciation & amortization expense	(18,000)	(14,400)	[D]	1,800	[I$_{dep}$]	2,500	(31,700)
Operating expenses	(226,000)	(54,100)					(280,100)
Interest expense	(8,000)	(3,500)	[D]	1,000			(12,500)
Total expenses	(252,000)	(72,000)					(324,300)
Income (loss) from subsidiary	23,900	—	[C]	23,900			0
Consolidated net income	59,900	36,000					69,700
Consolidated NI attributable to NCI	—	—	[C]	9,800			(9,800)
Consolidated NI attributable to parent	$ 59,900	$ 36,000					$59,900
Statement of retained earnings:							
Beginning retained earnings	$322,200	$165,000	[E]	165,000			$322,200
Consolidated NI attributable to parent	59,900	36,000					59,900
Dividends declared	(90,000)	(21,000)			[C]	21,000	(90,000)
Ending retained earnings	$292,100	$180,000					$292,100
Balance sheet:							
Cash	$ 58,080	$ 42,500					$100,580
Accounts receivable	81,000	60,000			[I$_{pay}$]	10,000	131,000
Inventories	195,000	91,500			[I$_{cogs}$]	8,000	278,500
Property, plant & equipment, net	189,000	135,000	[A]	10,800	[D]	1,800	313,000
			[I$_{dep}$]	2,500	[I$_{gain}$]	22,500	
Other assets	85,500	150,000					235,500
Equity investment	325,500		[I$_{cogs}$]	4,500	[C]	8,150	0
			[I$_{gain}$]	22,500	[E]	270,000	
					[A]	74,350	
Goodwill			[A]	84,000			84,000
Total assets	$934,080	$479,000					$1,142,580
Accounts payable	$168,000	$ 35,000	[I$_{pay}$]	10,000			$193,000
Notes payable	80,980	30,000	[A]	1,000	[D]	1,000	110,980
Other liabilities	33,000	39,000					72,000
Common stock	360,000	195,000	[E]	195,000			360,000
Retained earnings	292,100	180,000					292,100
Noncontrolling interest			[I$_{cogs}$]	1,500	[C]	4,550	114,500
					[E]	90,000	
					[A]	21,450	
Total liabilities and equity	$934,080	$479,000		$591,300		$591,300	$1,142,580

COMPREHENSIVE REVIEW SOLUTION—COST METHOD

a. The trial balance information converted to financial statement format is presented, below. A completed consolidation spreadsheet is included in the solution to *Part h* of this comprehensive review.

Pre-Consolidation Financial Statements for the Year Ended December 31, 2016	Parent	Subsidiary
Income statement:		
Sales.	$ 920,000	$400,000
Cost of goods sold.	(480,000)	(236,000)
Gross profit.	440,000	164,000
Depreciation & amortization expense.	(24,000)	(19,200)
Operating expenses.	(260,000)	(52,600)
Interest expense.	(12,000)	(4,200)
Total expenses	(296,000)	(76,000)
Income (loss) from subsidiary.	22,400	
Net income.	$ 166,400	$ 88,000
Statement of retained earnings:		
Beginning retained earnings.	$ 436,600	$220,000
Income attributable to controlling interest	166,400	88,000
Dividends declared.	(120,000)	(28,000)
Ending retained earnings	$ 483,000	$280,000
Balance sheet:		
Cash.	$ 77,440	$ 30,000
Accounts receivable.	108,000	96,000
Inventories	260,000	92,000
PPE, net	252,000	220,000
Other assets.	114,000	200,000
Patents.		20,000
Investment in subsidiary.	360,000	
Total assets.	$1,171,440	$658,000
Accounts payable.	$ 64,440	$ 24,000
Notes payable	100,000	42,000
Other liabilities	44,000	52,000
Common stock.	480,000	260,000
Retained earnings	483,000	280,000
Total liabilities and equity	$1,171,440	$658,000

b. Given the five-year time horizon between the acquisition date and the consolidated financial statement date, the following schedules separately document the annual AAP amortization and the year-end unamortized AAP balance for each year, 2012 through 2016.

100% AAP:

100% AAP Amortization – Dr (Cr)	Year Ended December 31,				
	2012	2013	2014	2015	2016
Accounts receivable....................	$ (8,000)	$ —	$ —	$ —	$ —
Property, plant & equipment, net...........	7,200	7,200	7,200	7,200	7,200
Patents...............................	12,000	12,000	12,000	12,000	12,000
Notes payable	3,000	3,000	3,000	3,000	—
Net amortization......................	$14,200	$22,200	$22,200	$22,200	$19,200

100% Unamortized AAP – Dr (Cr)	Jan. 1, 2012	December 31,				
		2012	2013	2014	2015	2016
Accounts receivable.............	$ (8,000)	$ —	$ —	$ —	$ —	$ —
PPE, net......................	36,000	28,800	21,600	14,400	7,200	—
Patents.......................	84,000	72,000	60,000	48,000	36,000	24,000
Notes payable	12,000	9,000	6,000	3,000	—	—
Goodwill......................	36,000	36,000	36,000	36,000	36,000	36,000
Unamortized balance...........	$160,000	$145,800	$123,600	$101,400	$79,200	$60,000

80% AAP:

80% AAP Amortization – Dr (Cr)	Year Ended December 31,				
	2012	2013	2014	2015	2016
Accounts receivable....................	$(6,400)	$ —	$ —	$ —	$ —
Property, plant & equipment, net...........	5,760	5,760	5,760	5,760	5,760
Patents...............................	9,600	9,600	9,600	9,600	9,600
Notes payable	2,400	2,400	2,400	2,400	—
Net amortization......................	$11,360	$17,760	$17,760	$17,760	$15,360

80% Unamortized AAP – Dr (Cr)	Jan. 1, 2012	December 31,				
		2012	2013	2014	2015	2016
Accounts receivable.............	$ (6,400)	$ —	$ —	$ —	$ —	$ —
PPE, net......................	28,800	23,040	17,280	11,520	5,760	—
Patents.......................	67,200	57,600	48,000	38,400	28,800	19,200
Notes payable	9,600	7,200	4,800	2,400	—	—
Goodwill*.....................	30,400	30,400	30,400	30,400	30,400	30,400
Unamortized balance...........	$129,600	$118,240	$100,480	$82,720	$64,960	$49,600

*$360,000 − (80% × [288,000 − 8,000 + 36,000 + 84,000 + 12,000]) = $30,400

20% AAP:

20% AAP Amortization – Dr (Cr)	Year Ended December 31,				
	2012	2013	2014	2015	2016
Accounts receivable..................	$(1,600)	$ —	$ —	$ —	$ —
Property, plant & equipment, net...........	1,440	1,440	1,440	1,440	1,440
Patents................................	2,400	2,400	2,400	2,400	2,400
Notes payable	600	600	600	600	—
Net amortization.....................	$ 2,840	$4,440	$4,440	$4,440	$3,840

20% Unamortized AAP – Dr (Cr)	Jan. 1, 2012	December 31,				
		2012	2013	2014	2015	2016
Accounts receivable.............	$ (1,600)	$ —	$ —	$ —	$ —	$ —
PPE, net	7,200	5,760	4,320	2,880	1,440	—
Patents.......................	16,800	14,400	12,000	9,600	7,200	4,800
Notes payable	2,400	1,800	1,200	600	—	—
Goodwill*	5,600	5,600	5,600	5,600	5,600	5,600
Unamortized balance...........	$30,400	$27,560	$23,120	$18,680	$14,240	$10,400

* $88,000 − (20% × [288,000 − 8,000 + 36,000 + 84,000 + 12,000]) = 5,600

c. **Intercompany depreciable asset sale:**
One downstream asset sale.
Intercompany profit recognized on December 31, 2014: $130,000 − $100,000 = $30,000, 5-year remaining life
Profit confirmed each year: $30,000/5 = $6,000

	Downstream	Upstream
Net intercompany profit deferred at January 1, 2016	$24,000	
Less: Deferred intercompany profit recognized during 2016...........	6,000	
Net intercompany profit deferred at December 31, 2016	$18,000	

Intercompany inventory transactions:
Intercompany inventory sales during 2016: $48,000

	Downstream (in Subsidiary's Inventory)	Upstream (in Parent's Inventory)
Intercompany profit in inventory on January 1, 2016..............	$ 0	$6,600
Intercompany profit in inventory on December 31, 2016............	$8,400	$ 0

Intercompany accounts receivables and payables at December 31, 2016: $16,000

d. The following is the general formula for computing the Equity Investment account (under the equity method) at any point in time:

	(1) p% × book value of the net assets of the subsidiary
Plus:	(2) Unamortized p% AAP
Less:	(3) 100% × downstream deferred intercompany profits
Less:	(4) p% × upstream deferred intercompany profits
	Equity method Equity Investment account

Equity Investment account balance at January 1, 2016:

	Jan. 1, 2016	
	$384,000	(1) 80% × ($260,000 + $220,000)
Plus:	64,960	(2) $64,960 (from *Part b*)
Less:	(24,000)	(3) 100% × $24,000 (from *Part c*)
Less:	(5,280)	(4) 80% × $6,600 (from *Part c*)
	$419,680	

Equity Investment account balance at December 31, 2016:

	Dec. 31, 2016	
	$432,000	(1) 80% × ($260,000 + $280,000)
Plus:	49,600	(2) $49,600 (from *Part b*)
Less:	(18,000)	(3) 100% × $18,000 (from *Part c*)
Less:	(8,400)	(4) 100% × $8,400 (from *Part c*)
	$455,200	

e. In the present case, the amount of the **[ADJ]** entry is computed as follows:

80% of change in subsidiary retained earnings from acquisition date through BOY = (80% × [$220,000 − $28,000])	$153,600
Less: Cumulative 80% AAP amortization from acquisition date through BOY = $11,360 + (3 × $17,760).	(64,640)
Less: 100% of the BOY downstream unconfirmed intercompany inventory profits	N/A
Less: 80% of the BOY upstream unconfirmed intercompany inventory profits (80% × $6,600)	(5,280)
Less: 100% of the BOY downstream unconfirmed intercompany depreciable asset profits	(24,000)
Less: 80% of the BOY upstream unconfirmed intercompany depreciable asset profits.	N/A
[ADJ] amount at BOY	$ 59,680

f. The following is the general formula for computing the noncontrolling interest in consolidated equity at any point in time:

	(1) nci% × book value of the net assets of the subsidiary
Plus:	(2) Unamortized nci% AAP
Less:	(3) nci% × upstream deferred intercompany profits
	Noncontrolling Interest

The balance of noncontrolling interest in consolidated equity at January 1, 2016:

	Jan. 1, 2016	
	$ 96,000	(1) 20% × ($260,000 + $220,000)
Plus:	14,240	(2) $14,240 (from *Part b*)
Less:	(1,320)	(3) 20% × $6,600 (from *Part c*)
	$108,920	

The balance of noncontrolling interest in consolidated equity at December 31, 2016:

	Dec. 31, 2016	
	$108,000	(1) 20% × ($260,000 + $280,000)
Plus:	10,400	(2) $10,400 (from *Part b*)
Less:	N/A	(3) 20% × upstream deferred intercompany profits
	$118,400	

g. Independently calculate consolidated net income, controlling interest net income and noncontrolling interest net income.

Incremental Computation of Consolidated Net Income for the Year Ended December 31, 2016

Parent's stand-alone net income	$144,000	($166,400 − $22,400)
Plus: 100% realized downstream deferred profits	6,000	(see *Part c*)
Less: 100% unrealized downstream deferred profits	(8,400)	(see *Part c*)
Parent's adjusted stand-alone net income	$141,600	
Subsidiary's stand-alone net income	$ 88,000	(see facts)
Plus: 100% realized upstream deferred profits	6,600	(see *Part c*)
Less: 100% unrealized upstream deferred profits	0	(see *Part c*)
Less: 100% AAP amortization	(19,200)	(see *Part b*)
Subsidiary's adjusted stand-alone net income	$ 75,400	
Consolidated net income	$217,000	

Incremental Computation of Consolidated Net Income Attributable to the Controlling Interest for the Year Ended December 31, 2016

Parent's stand-alone net income	$144,000	($166,400 − $22,400)
Plus: 100% realized downstream deferred profits	6,000	(see *Part c*)
Less: 100% unrealized downstream deferred profits	(8,400)	(see *Part c*)
Parent's adjusted stand-alone net income	$141,600	
80% × subsidiary's stand-alone net income (80% × $88,000)	$70,400	(see facts)
Plus: 80% realized upstream deferred profits (80% × $6,600)	5,280	(see *Part c*)
Less: 80% unrealized upstream deferred profits	—	
Less: 80% AAP amortization (from schedule)	(15,360)	(see *Part b*)
80% of the Subsidiary's adjusted stand-alone net income	$60,320	
Consolidated net income attributable to the controlling interest	$201,920	

Incremental Computation of Consolidated Net Income Attributable to the Noncontrolling Interest for the Year Ended December 31, 2016

20% × subsidiary's stand-alone net income (20% × $88,000)	$17,600	(see facts)
Plus: 20% realized upstream deferred profits (20% × $6,600)	1,320	(see *Part c*)
Less: 20% unrealized upstream deferred profits (none)	—	(see *Part c*)
Less: 20% AAP amortization (from schedule)	(3,840)	(see *Part b*)
Consolidated net income attributable to the noncontrolling interest	$15,080	

h.

[ADJ]	Investment in subsidiary.	59,680	
	Beg. retained earnings—Parent		59,680
[C]	Income (loss) from subsidiary.	22,400	
	Income attributable to NCI.	15,080	
	Noncontrolling interest		9,480
	Dividends—Subsidiary		28,000
[E]	Common stock (S) @ BOY	260,000	
	Retained earnings (S) @ BOY.	220,000	
	Investment in subsidiary @ BOY		384,000
	Noncontrolling interest @ BOY		96,000
[A]	PPE @ BOY	7,200	
	Customer list @ BOY	36,000	
	Goodwill	36,000	
	Investment in subsidiary @ BOY		64,960
	Noncontrolling interest @ BOY		14,240
[D]	Depreciation & amortization expense.	19,200	
	PPE, net		7,200
	Patents		12,000
[I_cogs]	Investment in subsidiary @ BOY	5,280	
	Noncontrolling interest @ BOY.	1,320	
	Cost of goods sold		6,600
[I_sales]	Sales	48,000	
	Cost of goods sold		48,000
[I_cogs]	Cost of goods sold.	8,400	
	Inventories.		8,400
[I_pay]	Accounts payable.	16,000	
	Accounts receivable		16,000
[I_gain]	Investment in subsidiary @ BOY	24,000	
	PPE, net @ BOY		24,000
[I_dep]	PPE, net	6,000	
	Depreciation expense		6,000

Consolidation Spreadsheet for the Year Ended December 31, 2016

	Parent	Subsidiary	Consolidation Entries Dr		Cr		Consolidated
Income statement:							
Sales	$ 920,000	$400,000	[I$_{sales}$]	$ 48,000			$1,272,000
Cost of goods sold	(480,000)	(236,000)	[I$_{cogs}$]	8,400	[I$_{cogs}$]	$ 6,600	(669,800)
					[I$_{sales}$]	48,000	
Gross profit	440,000	164,000					602,200
Depreciation & amortization expense	(24,000)	(19,200)	[D]	19,200	[I$_{dep}$]	6,000	(56,400)
Operating expenses	(260,000)	(52,600)					(312,600)
Interest expense	(12,000)	(4,200)					(16,200)
Total expenses	(296,000)	(76,000)					(385,200)
Income (loss) from subsidiary	22,400	—	[C]	22,400			0
Consolidated net income	166,400	88,000					217,000
Income attributable to NCI	—	—	[C]	15,080			(15,080)
Income attributable to controlling interest	$ 166,400	$ 88,000					$ 201,920
Statement of retained earnings:							
Beginning retained earnings	$ 436,600	$220,000	[E]	220,000	[ADJ]	59,680	$ 496,280
Income attributable to controlling interest	166,400	88,000					201,920
	603,000	308,000					698,200
Dividends declared							
Parent	(120,000)						(120,000)
Subsidiary		(28,000)			[C]	28,000	—
Ending retained earnings	$ 483,000	$280,000					$ 578,200
Balance sheet:							
Cash	$ 77,440	$ 30,000					$ 107,440
Accounts receivable	108,000	96,000			[I$_{pay}$]	16,000	188,000
Inventories	260,000	92,000			[I$_{cogs}$]	8,400	343,600
PPE, net	252,000	220,000	[A]	7,200	[D]	7,200	454,000
			[I$_{dep}$]	6,000	[I$_{gain}$]	24,000	
Other assets	114,000	200,000					314,000
Patents		20,000	[A]	36,000	[D]	12,000	44,000
Investment in subsidiary	360,000		[ADJ]	59,680	[E]	384,000	0
			[I$_{cogs}$]	5,280	[A]	64,960	
			[I$_{gain}$]	24,000			
Goodwill			[A]	36,000			36,000
Total assets	$1,171,440	$658,000					$1,487,040
Accounts payable	$ 64,440	$ 24,000	[I$_{pay}$]	16,000			$ 72,440
Notes payable	100,000	42,000					142,000
Other liabilities	44,000	52,000					96,000
Common stock	480,000	260,000	[E]	260,000			480,000
Retained earnings	483,000	280,000					578,200
Noncontrolling interest			[I$_{cogs}$]	1,320	[C]	9,480	118,400
					[E]	96,000	
					[A]	14,240	
Total liabilities and equity	$1,171,440	$658,000		$784,560		$784,560	$1,487,040

1. Describe why companies use special purpose entities. (p. 393)

2. Describe and apply the comprehensive consolidation model in United States generally accepted accounting principles, including the concepts of variable interests and voting interests, and the issues related to consolidation of variable interest entities. (p. 396)

3. Describe and apply the consolidation procedures necessary when affiliated companies acquire each other's debt, including immediate recognition of gain or loss on constructive retirement of the debt and subsequent recognition of the gain or loss via discount and/or premium amortization in the separate pre-consolidation financial statements of the affiliated companies. (p. 410)

4. Describe the consolidation procedures necessary when subsidiary companies have outstanding preferred stock. (p. 420)

Consolidation of Variable Interest Entities and Other Intercompany Investments

According to The Walt Disney Company's (Disney's) September 27, 2014 Securities and Exchange Commission (SEC) Form 10-K, Disney "is a diversified worldwide entertainment company with operations in five business segments: Media Networks, Parks and Resorts, Studio Entertainment, Consumer Products, and Interactive." Disney's 2014 segment disclosures reveal that the Parks and Resorts segment has $23,335 million of identifiable assets, which is 28 percent of the company's total consolidated assets.

THE WALT DISNEY COMPANY

At September 27, 2014, approximately 21 percent of the identifiable assets of the Parks and Resorts Segment were comprised of fixed assets at Disneyland Paris (51 percent owned by Disney), Hong Kong Disneyland Resort (48 percent owned by Disney), and Shanghai Disney Resort (43% owned by Disney). According to Note 6 of Disney's September 27, 2014 SEC Form 10-K, these non-wholly-owned international theme-park companies are consolidated with Disney because they are "Variable Interest Entities" (VIE) and because Disney is their "Primary Beneficiary."

Prior to March 31, 2004, Disney did not consolidate these international theme park companies. Indeed, according to Disney's September 30, 2003 SEC Form 10-K, Disney's 39 percent interest in Disneyland Paris and its 43 percent interest in Hong Kong Disneyland were both reported using the Equity Method. On March 31, 2004, Disney began applying a new Financial Accounting Standards Board (FASB) Interpretation that expanded the notion of a "controlling financial interest" well beyond the traditional majority-voting-interest model that existed before then.[1] As a result, Disney's September 30, 2004 SEC Form 10-K presented Disneyland Paris and Hong Kong Disney as consolidated subsidiaries instead of line-item equity method investments. The following consolidating schedule from Note 4 of Disney's 2004 10-K shows the effects of initially consolidating Disneyland Paris (i.e., Euro Disney), Hong Kong Disneyland, and Shanghai Disney Resort (labelled "International Theme Parks" in the disclosure.)

(continued on next page)

[1] The specific source of the change was FASB Interpretation No. 46 (revised December 2003), "Consolidation of Variable Interest Entities, and interpretation of ARB No. 51." The still-effective provisions of FIN 46(R) are currently codified in FASB ASC 810.

(continued from previous page)

	As of September 27, 1014		
	Before International Theme Parks Consolidation	International Theme Parks and Adjustments	Total
Cash and cash equivalents	$ 2,645	$ 776	$ 3,421
Other current assets.	11,452	303	11,755
Total current assets.	14,097	1,079	15,176
Investments/Advances.	6,627	(3,931)	2,696
Parks, resorts and other property	17,081	6,251	23,332
Other assets.	42,958	24	42,982
Total assets.	$80,763	$ 3,423	$84,186
Current portion of borrowings	$ 2,164	$ —	$ 2,164
Other current liabilities	10,318	810	11,128
Total current liabilities	12,482	810	13,292
Borrowings.	12,423	253	12,676
Deferred income taxes and other long-term liabilities . . .	9,859	181	10,040
Equity.	45,999	2,179	48,178
Total liabilities and equity	$80,763	$ 3,423	$84,186

There are two interesting items to note in this reconciliation. First, we can see the replacement process that occurs when we consolidate. In particular, note that the investment account decreased by $3,931 million while all of the other accounts either increased or stayed the same. As we learned in the prior consolidation chapters, this is because the equity investment account is getting replaced with the subsidiaries' detailed financial statement accounts. The second item we wish to emphasize is the effect of consolidating these minority-owned subsidiaries on reported fixed assets. Specifically, fixed assets increased from $17.1 billion to $23.3 billion, an increase of over $6 billion (i.e., 36 percent).

In this chapter, we will discuss accounting for variable interest entities, and the role of variable interest entity analysis in the comprehensive consolidation model included in FASB ASC 810.

Source: The Walt Disney Company 2003, 2004 and 2014 10-Ks.

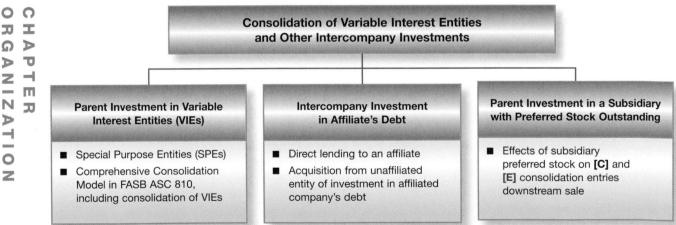

CHAPTER ORGANIZATION

Consolidation of Variable Interest Entities and Other Intercompany Investments

Parent Investment in Variable Interest Entities (VIEs)
- Special Purpose Entities (SPEs)
- Comprehensive Consolidation Model in FASB ASC 810, including consolidation of VIEs

Intercompany Investment in Affiliate's Debt
- Direct lending to an affiliate
- Acquisition from unaffiliated entity of investment in affiliated company's debt

Parent Investment in a Subsidiary with Preferred Stock Outstanding
- Effects of subsidiary preferred stock on [C] and [E] consolidation entries downstream sale

According to FASB ASC 810-10-10-1, "[t]he purpose of consolidated financial statements is to present, primarily for the benefit of the owners and creditors of the parent, the results of operations and the financial position of a parent and all its subsidiaries as if the consolidated group were a single economic entity. There is a presumption that consolidated financial statements are more meaningful than separate financial statements and that they are usually necessary for a fair presentation when one of the entities in the consolidated group directly or indirectly has a controlling financial interest in the other entities." Interestingly, these two sentences are virtually identical to the first paragraph of Accounting Research

Bulletin (ARB) No. 51, *Consolidated Financial Statements*, which was issued by the American Institute of Certified Public Accountants' (AICPA's) Committee on Accounting Procedure (CAP) in 1959. Thus, the triggering condition for consolidation in the U.S. has remained largely unchanged for more than half a century. Specifically, a reporting company consolidates another entity when the reporting company has a "controlling financial interest" in that other entity.

Because the AICPA's CAP did not specifically define what is meant by "controlling financial interest," subsequent consolidations-related standard setting has been primarily focused on interpreting this phrase. Specifically, the Financial Accounting Standards Board (FASB) has issued three major consolidations-related standards since its inception in 1973:

- **Statement of Financial Accounting Standards (SFAS) No. 94**, *Consolidation of All Majority-owned Subsidiaries—an amendment of ARB No. 51, with related amendments of APB Opinion No. 18 and ARB No. 43, Chapter 12* (1987): This standard amended ARB No. 51 to eliminate the exception that allowed certain majority-owned subsidiaries to remain unconsolidated.

- **FASB Interpretation No. (FIN) 46 and FIN 46 (Revised)**, *Consolidation of Variable Interest Entities—an interpretation of ARB No. 51* (2003): Established the concept that a reporting company can control another entity through means other than voting common stock (i.e., through "variable interests"). The analyses in FIN 46 and FIN 46(R) were highly quantitative.

- **SFAS No. 167**, *Amendments to FASB Interpretation No. 46(R)* (2009): This standard relaxed much of the quantitative analysis in FIN 46(R), and made the determination of a controlling financial interest based on a qualitative assessment of the power to direct the primary activities of another entity.

The original guidance in ARB 51 and these subsequent FASB standards and interpretation are all codified in FASB ASC 810. In this chapter, we will provide an overview of the comprehensive consolidation model that was established by the original majority-interest-in-voting-common-stock model and the relatively new variable-interest-entity model. Again, each of these models was intended to operationalize the same underlying triggering condition: "controlling financial interest." Before we discuss the comprehensive consolidation model, we will discuss special purpose entities (SPEs). These are the entities that were at the heart of the consolidations controversy in the early 2000s, and were the primary reason the FASB developed the variable interest entity concept for consolidation.

This chapter also includes coverage of consolidations issues that arise when consolidated affiliates hold each other's debt instruments.

PARENT INVESTMENT IN VARIABLE INTEREST ENTITIES (VIES)

Special Purpose Entities (SPEs)

In the aftermath of the 2001 **Enron** scandal, the term **Special Purpose Entity** (SPE) became synonymous with aggressive and dishonest accounting practices. While Enron did create over 3,000 off-balance-sheet (i.e., unconsolidated) SPEs that allowed the company to overstate its financial performance and significantly understate its leverage and risk, Enron's problems were not caused by the SPE structures, *per se*. Instead, the scandal was caused by willful fraud and market manipulation perpetrated by Enron's managers. These managers merely used the SPE structures as vehicles to perpetrate the fraud, and aggressively interpreted the then-existing generally accepted accounting principles (GAAP) on SPEs to avoid consolidating these entities.

Notwithstanding the bad press received by SPEs during the last decade and a half, they actually have a legitimate and extremely important role in modern corporate finance: they help to reduce the cost of capital for operating companies. When extending credit to operating companies, creditors face uncertainty with respect to repayment of principal and interest. What will the operating company do with the borrowed money? Will the operating company take actions that decrease its future ability to pay back its debts? Will the operating company pay other creditors, first? Because operating companies' cash and other resources are fungible, it is extremely difficult for an operating company's creditors to reduce uncertainty related to repayment of principal and interest. And, if the operating company goes bankrupt, then the creditor will have to "get in line" with other creditors and share a

LO1 Describe why companies use special purpose entities.

(usually small) percentage of what is owed. Of course, creditors don't bear this risk for free; they get compensated for taking this risk by charging a higher interest rate. Thus, in the end, it is really the borrowing company that pays for the uncertainty regarding its business and its ability to repay its debts.

How can SPEs help alleviate this problem? Well, if the operating company can take a subset of its assets that generate predictable cash flows (e.g., accounts receivable) and transfer those assets to a "bankruptcy remote" entity, like a trust, then the creditors can lend money to the trust in exchange for the right to the future cash flows from assets held by the trust.[2] Because the transferred assets are legally isolated from the operating company, the creditor no longer worries about prospects of the operating company or the actions of its managers. This reduction in the creditor's concerns about moral hazard leads the creditor to charge a lower rate of interest and this saving is passed on to the operating company and its investors.

The type of transaction described in the preceding paragraph is basically the same structure as an asset **securitization**.[3] Exhibit 6.1 illustrates a simple securitization scenario that involves an SPE. This general structure is typical of many arrangements that use SPEs, even if they are not asset securitizations.[4] In the case of securitizations, here are some characteristics of the SPEs:

■ The SPE is legally distinct from the sponsoring company (i.e., the operating company in the Exhibit) and is bankruptcy remote. Having these features is really important because they ensure that assets transferred to the SPE will be available to repay the investors, no matter what happens to the operating company. So, even if the operating company files for bankruptcy, the general creditors of the operating company will have no way to make a claim against the assets in the SPE.

■ The SPE is only allowed to engage in a highly restricted set of activities. These activities are usually defined in the SPE's organizational charter, and are limited to things like holding the SPE assets, collecting cash flows from the SPE assets and distributing the contractually required cash flows to the investors (i.e., securities holders). This is from where the phrase "special purpose" emanates: these entities are not businesses, and their activities are restricted to the particular, precisely defined purpose for which they are formed. In essence, SPEs are highly preprogrammed "robot-like" organizations that have no distinct physical location, have no independent management or employees, and make no strategic business decisions.

■ Cash flows from the assets held by the SPE are used by the SPE to repay the securities holders. For example, if accounts receivable were held by the SPE, then the securitization investors would be repaid when the receivables are collected.

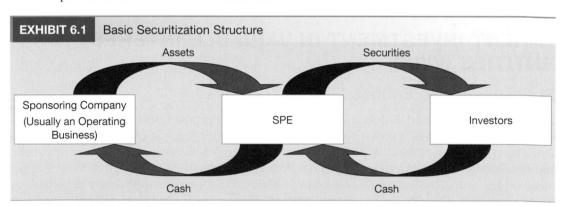

EXHIBIT 6.1 Basic Securitization Structure

---

[2] Generally speaking, an SPE is "bankruptcy remote" if a sponsoring company (i.e., the company that sets up the SPE and transfers assets to the SPE) or its creditors are unable to reacquire the transferred assets even in the case where the sponsoring company goes bankrupt. This is considered to be a fairly strong test of whether the assets are legally isolated from the sponsoring company.

[3] The main difference is that the preceding paragraph described the SPE borrowing from a single creditor. In an asset securitization, the SPE offers debt securities to outside investors (e.g., institutional investors, like pension funds). The fact that the SPE offers *securities* backed by the transferred asset is why we say the asset became "securitized."

[4] Of course, diagrams of the structure of many real-world SPE-related transactions appear to be much more complex than the representation in Exhibit 6.1. These complexities usually relate to the number of parties involved in the transactions and the roles played by those parties (e.g., guarantors, servicers, etc.). However, if we reduce the arrangement to its fundamental economic structure, you will usually find that the SPE holds an undivided right to some asset or intellectual property, and parties other than the SPE's sponsoring company will provide financing to that SPE.

In the case of securitizations, the sponsoring company and its owners benefit from improved liquidity and operating cash flows, and from lower net borrowing costs. Because the SPE is not burdened with the myriad business risks that can affect an operating company, its investors do not need to be compensated for additional risk. In addition, prior to 2009, sponsoring companies also usually benefitted because they were able to easily qualify for "sale accounting" treatment when transferring the assets to the SPE. These benefits derived from having assets, and their related debt, moved "off-balance-sheet." In the case of sale accounting, the sponsoring company enjoys an improved asset turnover ratio (assets are less in the denominator of the turnover ratio) and an improved financial leverage ratio (liabilities are less in the numerator of the liabilities-to-equity ratio). While companies can still qualify for sale-accounting treatment when transferring financial assets to unaffiliated parties, in 2009 the FASB made sale-accounting treatment much more difficult for companies to obtain.[5]

Indeed, even after the FASB tightened up the consolidation rules related to SPEs during the 2000s, resulting in the consolidation of many of these structures, companies still use SPEs to obtain lower-cost financing. For example **Ford Motor Credit LLC**, a wholly owned subsidiary of **Ford Motor Company**, routinely transfers its finance receivables and net investments in operating leases to SPEs (see Practice Insight—SPEs and Asset Securitization). These SPEs then sell to outside investors securities that are backed by these financial assets (i.e., the assets are "securitized" by the SPE). The following excerpt comes from Ford Motor Credit's 2014 annual report:

> *Our securitization transactions involve sales to consolidated entities or we maintain control over the assets. As a result, the securitized assets and related debt remain on our balance sheet and affect our financial condition.*

So, even though Ford Motor Credit does not achieve the often-preferred off-balance-sheet sale-accounting treatment for the securitization of their financial assets, they still transfer these assets to an SPE and borrow against these SPE holdings. This suggests that SPEs provide real economic benefits beyond the financial reporting shell game played by Enron and other companies.

Securitizations are not just limited to financial assets held by companies like Ford. We can securitize almost any asset or intellectual-property right that is expected to generate future cash flows. For example, in 1997, the rock star, David Bowie, famously securitized the future royalties from his entire pre-1990 song catalog (i.e., 287 songs in 25 albums). This transaction yielded a $55 million lump sum payment to David Bowie in 1997, while the investor (Prudential Insurance Company of America) was repaid based on the sales of these 287 songs over the next 10 years. Other examples include film rights, taxi medallions, tax liens, toll roads, death benefits, etc.

Although we have focused mainly on the role of SPEs in securitizations, SPEs are also used to facilitate the financing of many other business ventures. For example, SPEs are commonly used in the life sciences industry to share the risks and costs of their highly uncertain research and development activities. In addition, SPEs are often used to hold commercial real estate. A significant financial reporting issue is whether these SPEs are consolidated by any of the sponsoring entities. Non-consolidation of SPEs allows assets and liabilities related to the business to be reported "off-balance-sheet." This improves the sponsoring company's asset turnover (Sales/Assets), which in turn improves its return on assets (ROA), an important metric of financial performance.[6] In addition, many SPEs are highly levered (i.e., have an extremely high proportion of debt). Thus, if an SPE is not consolidated, it can also greatly improve a sponsoring company's leverage ratios. In the next section, we discuss the issue of consolidating these nontraditional entities.

---

[5] U.S. GAAP relating to transfers of financial assets is included in FASB ASC 860, "Transfers and Servicing." The accounting principles governing the transfers of financial assets in securitizations are the same accounting principles that apply to factoring of accounts receivable (i.e., a topic typically covered in the first intermediate accounting class).

[6] ROA is improved so long as the increase in asset turnover (NOAT) is not offset by a reduction in operating profit margin due to the increased cost of using the SPE structure (such as from purchasing goods in a finished state from wholesalers rather than manufacturing those goods, selling receivables at a discount, or leasing property from outside investors). This is a reasonable assumption; because, otherwise, the sponsoring company would likely not have created the SPE and transferred assets.

eLectures
MBC

LO2 Describe and apply the comprehensive consolidation model in United States generally accepted accounting principles, including the concepts of variable interests and voting interests, and the issues related to consolidation of variable interest entities.

Comprehensive Consolidation Model in FASB ASC 810, Including Consolidation of VIEs

SPEs pose a particularly thorny problem when viewed through the lens of this traditional majority-interest consolidation model. The problem stems from the fact that the sponsoring entity rarely retains a significant percentage ownership in a given SPE; thus, the continuing financial interest of the sponsor might be relatively small. However, the sponsoring entity might have latent rights to the assets held by the SPE, or might be explicitly or implicitly obligated to fund the operations of the SPE if the SPE experiences financial hardship. Thus, technically, the sponsoring company might own a minority of the voting shares of the SPE but might excessively participate in the risks and rewards of the SPE.

Because of these features, the FASB promulgated a comprehensive consolidation model that supplements the traditional majority interest model. The new model, first introduced in 2003, is often called the **Variable Interest Entity** (VIE) approach to consolidations. Many people mistakenly believe that the VIE approach is separate and distinct from the traditional majority-interest approach that has formally been part of U.S. GAAP for more than half a century. As we illustrate in Exhibit 6.2 (and as is required by FASB ASC 810-10-15-3), the VIE evaluation is integrated with the majority-voting-interest approach as part of a comprehensive evaluation of an entity for potential consolidation. In fact, if you look at Exhibit 6.2, you'll notice that the bottom-left corner of the illustration includes the majority-voting-interest criterion for consolidation (i.e., the box that states, "Does the company own (either directly or indirectly) more than 50% of the voting shares of the entity?"). However, you should also notice that the evaluation of consolidation based on **variable interests** is actually done before the parent company applies the majority interest criteria when evaluating a consolidation candidate.[7]

Before we will discuss the comprehensive consolidation model illustrated in Exhibit 6.2, we will discuss the concept of a variable interest.

What is a Variable Interest?   Variable interests are contractual, ownership, or other financial interests in a legal entity that change in value as a result of changes in the fair value of the net assets of the legal entity.[8] Although this terminology might seem a little unusual, it actually describes

---

[7] In other words, in all of the consolidation discussion, examples and exercises we discuss in Chapters 2 through 5, we implicitly applied this full model and decided that the consolidation target was not a VIE. We then decided to consolidate because the parent companies owned greater than 50% of the voting common stock of their subsidiaries. (When subsidiaries are evaluated for consolidation on the basis of the parent's ownership percentage of the subsidiary's voting common stock, these subsidiaries are commonly referred to as "voting interest entities.")

[8] To ease exposition throughout this section, we refer to the company performing the consolidation evaluation as "the company," and we refer to the target of the consolidation evaluation as "the legal entity."

EXHIBIT 6.2	Comprehensive Consolidation Model in FASB ASC 810

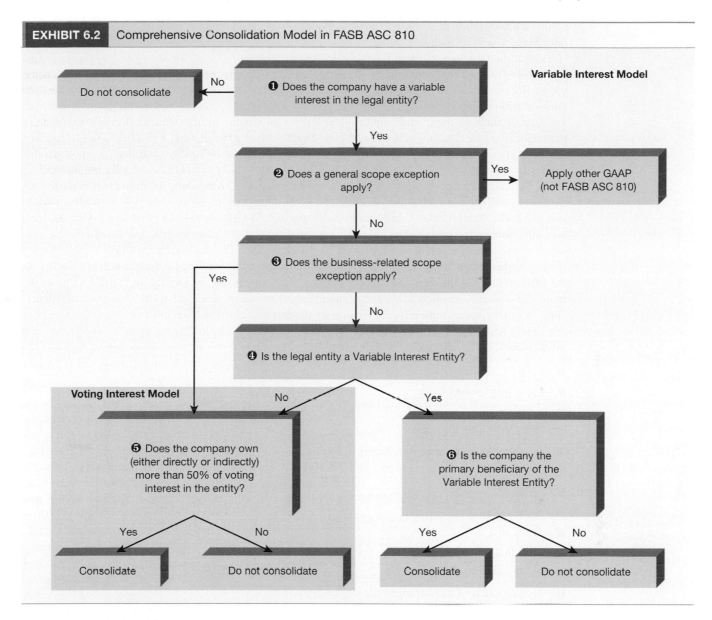

the behavior of a financial instrument with which you are quite familiar: voting common stock. For an ordinary legal entity that is capitalized with voting common stock, the legal entity's assets *create* variability in the legal entity's overall fair value that is *absorbed* by the voting common stock. The idea is that as a legal entity's assets and operations increase or decrease in value, these changes in value are received by (i.e., absorbed by) the providers of the entity's equity capital.

To illustrate this concept, assume that on January 1, 2016 Entity Z is legally incorporated by Investor A. At the formation of Entity Z, Investor A contributed assets with a $200 fair value and Investor A received 100% of the voting common stock of Entity Z. To make this example a little easier to follow, let's assume that the asset values perfectly capture the economic value of the legal entity (i.e., there are no unrecognized intangible assets) and there are no taxes or transaction costs. Thus, the value of the voting common stock of Entity Z is equal to $200 because Entity Z holds assets worth $200. That is, the voting common stock does not cause Entity Z to be worth $200; instead its voting common stock reflects the value of the assets held by Entity Z.

Next, let's assume that on December 31, 2016 the value of Entity Z's assets changed and now have a fair value of $250. Given our assumptions, what is the fair value on December 31, 2016 of the voting common stock held by Investor A? Hopefully, it is clear to you that the fair value of the voting common stock equals $250 on December 31, 2016. Not only that, we know that the $50 change in the fair value of the Entity Z's voting common stock is caused by the changes in the fair value of the net assets held by Entity Z. The cause of the change in value is important, because variable interests can only *absorb* variability in fair values, they *can't cause* variability. In our example, the voting common stock absorbed the variability in the fair value of the assets.

Aside from voting common stock, many other financial interests in legal entities absorb the variability of the fair values of those entities. It is really these other variable interests that the VIE consolidation model is intended to capture. That's because for typical SPEs, the voting equity interests are a small share of the overall capital of SPEs and the voting equity interests do not participate in the majority of the risks and rewards of SPEs. As indicated by FASB ASC 810-10-25-26, "[t]ypically, assets and operations of the legal entity create the legal entity's variability (and thus, are not variable interests), and liabilities and equity interests absorb that variability (and thus, are variable interests)."

A difficult concept for most students to understand is that many debt instruments represent variable interests because their value is affected by the fair value of the borrower. The easiest way to understand this concept is to think about what happens to the likelihood of a borrower paying its debts when the borrower encounters significant financial difficulty. As a borrower's cash flows become constrained, the lender has a lower probability of getting repaid. The decline in cash flows and solvency of the borrower results in a downgrade of the borrower's credit rating and a consequent decline in the market value of the debt. This means that the debt absorbs the variability on the fair value of the borrower's assets and operations. The bottom line is that many of a legal entity's contractual, ownership, or other financial interests can change as the fair value of the legal entity's assets change.[9] For example, FASB ASC 810-10-55-16 through 55-41 includes the following financial arrangements that might meet the definition of a variable interest:

- ■ Equity Securities
- ■ Debt Instruments
- ■ Guarantees
- ■ Put and Call Options
- ■ Management Contracts
- ■ Franchise Agreements
- ■ Leases
- ■ Service Contracts
- ■ Derivatives
- ■ Residual Value Guarantees
- ■ Technology Licenses
- ■ Collaborative R&D Arrangements

Applying the Comprehensive Consolidation Model in FASB ASC 810

As suggested by Step ❶ in Exhibit 6.2, the consolidation model in ASC 810 only applies to legal entities. FASB ASC 810-10-20 defines a legal entity as "[a]ny legal structure used to conduct activities or to hold assets. Some examples of such structures are corporations, partnerships, limited liability companies, grantor trusts, and other trusts." Thus, ASC 810 is not applied to divisions, departments, branches, and pools of assets.[10] Further, it is applied to majority-owned subsidiaries of other reporting entities that are legal entities separate from their parents.

Step ❶ also suggests that the consolidation model in ASC 810 (and that we discuss in preceding chapters) is only applied if the reporting company holds a variable interest in the legal entity. This

---

[9] Identifying variable interests can be extremely challenging. As noted by FASB ASC 810-10-55-10, "[t]he identification of variable interests involves determining which assets, liabilities, or contracts create the legal entity's variability and which assets, liabilities, equity, and other contracts absorb or receive that variability. The latter are the entity's variable interests. The labeling of an item as an asset, liability, equity, or as a contractual arrangement does not determine whether that item is a variable interest. It is the role of the item—to absorb or receive the entity's variability—that distinguishes a variable interest. That role, in turn, often depends on the design of the legal entity."

[10] One possible exception to this general restriction relates to "silos" within VIEs. FASB ASC 810-10-25-57 and -58 describe a silo as specified assets of a VIE that are essentially the only source of payment for specified liabilities or specified other interests. In certain cases, silos can be separately evaluated as VIEs. Note that this really isn't an exception to the whole-legal-entity requirement because silos are only separately evaluated as VIEs if the overall legal entity holding the "siloed" asset has been determined to be, in its entirety, a VIE.

step explicitly includes voting common stock as a variable interest. If we look ahead to Step ❺, you'll notice that the voting common stock variable interest can actually result in evaluation for consolidation via the evaluation of majority voting interest.

General Scope Exceptions to the Comprehensive Consolidation Model in FASB ASC 810

As soon as we know we are evaluating a legal entity for consolidation on the basis of its variable interests, we proceed to Step ❷ in which FASB ASC 810 provides numerous scope exceptions that might preclude application of its consolidation guidance. For example, the following entities/arrangements are considered outside the scope of FASB ASC 810:

- Employee benefit plans subject to FASB ASC 712 (Compensation—Nonretirement Postemployment Benefits) or FASB ASC 715 (Compensation—Retirement Benefits)
- Investments accounted for at fair value in accordance with the specialized guidance in FASB ASC 946 (Financial Services—Investment Companies)
- Not-for-profit entities
- Governmental organizations
- Registered money market funds

In each of these cases where the legal entity is outside of the scope of FASB ASC 810, the company would apply GAAP from other codification sections. For example, if the legal entity holds and manages the company's employee pension plan, then the company would apply FASB ASC 715, *Compensation—Retirement Benefits*, which is generally covered in Intermediate Financial Accounting courses. If the legal entity does not qualify for a general scope exception, then the legal entity must be evaluated for consolidation under FASB ASC 810.

Business-Related Shortcut to the Voting Interests Test

Step ❸, does allow one shortcut opportunity to skip straight to the "voting interest model" represented in Step ❺, thereby bypassing the complex VIE evaluation of the legal entity. This shortcut is usually allowed if the legal entity is a "business," as that term is defined in FASB ASC 805.[11] This exception is based on the presumption that legitimate business enterprises usually distribute their risks and rewards in proportion to voting control of the enterprise. However, there are four instances in which the business-related shortcut does not apply to legal entities:

- The reporting entity, its related parties or both, participated significantly in the design or redesign of the legal entity. Note that this condition does not apply if the legal entity is an operating joint venture under *joint* control of the reporting entity and one or more independent parties.
- The legal entity is designed so that substantially all of its activities either involve or are conducted on behalf of the reporting entity and its related parties.
- The reporting entity and its related parties provide more than half of the total of the equity, subordinated debt, and other forms of subordinated financial support to the legal entity based on an analysis of the fair values of the interests in the legal entity.
- The activities of the legal entity are primarily related to securitizations or other forms of asset-backed financings or single-lessee leasing arrangements.

In other words, the legal entity may very well be a legitimate business enterprise, but if any of these conditions apply, then the reporting entity must still apply the VIE provisions of FASB ASC 810. If the legal entity qualifies as a business under FASB ASC 805 and if none of these four restrictions exist, then the reporting entity does not need to apply the VIE provisions of FASB ASC 810. Instead, the reporting entity can skip straight down to the voting interest model in Step ❺ and evaluate whether it has a majority of the voting shares of the legal entity.

---

[11] Recall from Chapters 1 and 2 that ASC 805 Acquisition Method accounting is only applied when an acquired company qualifies as a business. A business is an integrated set of activities and assets that is capable of being conducted and managed for the purpose of providing a return in the form of dividends, lower costs, or other economic benefits directly to investors or other owners, members, or participants. A business consists of inputs and processes applied to those inputs that have the ability to create outputs." Additional guidance on what a business consists of is presented in FASB ASC 805-10-55-4 through 55-9

Is the Legal Entity a Variable Interest Entity?   If the legal entity does not qualify for the business-related scope exception, then we proceed to Step ❹. In this step, the reporting entity is required to evaluate whether the legal entity is a VIE. VIEs can take any organizational form, including partnerships, trusts, joint ventures, and corporations. In a nutshell, Step ❹ attempts to determine whether the legal entity is controlled through its voting common equity (i.e., it is a "voting interest" entity), or whether conditions exist that suggest that it is controlled by means other than voting common equity (i.e., it is a VIE).[12] According to FASB ASC 810-10-15-14, a legal entity is a VIE if, by design, any of the following conditions exist:

a. The total equity investment at risk is not sufficient to permit the legal entity to finance its activities without additional subordinated financial support provided by any parties, including equity holders.

b. As a group the holders of the equity investment at risk <u>lack</u> any one of the following three characteristics:
   1. The power, through voting rights or similar rights, to direct the activities of a legal entity that most significantly impact the entity's economic performance.
   2. The obligation to absorb the expected losses of the legal entity.
   3. The right to receive the expected residual returns of the legal entity.

These conditions include terminology that is defined in the VIE subchapters of FASB ASC 810. We will attempt to clarify some of the more important terms. With respect to condition (a) in Step ❹, "total equity investment at risk" is basically defined as the equity investment that constitutes the *reported* owners' equity of the legal entity. Specifically, it is the legal entity's owners' equity as that term is operationalized by GAAP. To be considered "equity investment at risk," it should also participate significantly in the profits and losses of the entity, even if those equity investments do not carry voting rights. In addition, the equity investment should be "arm's length," meaning that it cannot be provided by, or financed by, the legal entity or other parties involved with the legal entity.

Another term that is central to the concept of a VIE is "subordinated financial support." According to FASB ASC 810-10-20, subordinated financial support is comprised of variable interests that will absorb some or all of a VIE's expected losses. The idea is that the party that has the most exposure to the risks and rewards of an enterprise is the one that will bear the losses of the enterprise. For a typical operating business that is financed with traditional voting common equity, it would be the common equity shareholders that would bear the risk of loss. For VIEs, the equity holders provide a small fraction of the overall capital for the legal entity and typically bear very little of the residual risk of loss.

TOPIC REVIEW 1

Balance Sheet Classification and Equity at Risk

Assume a legal entity's capital structure consists of reported equity at risk of $50 and subordinated debt, loaned by the equity holder, of $30. Thus, the total capital is $80, and all comes from the same party.

Required

a. Assume the expected losses are predicted to be $50 or less. Is the equity investment at risk sufficient to permit the legal entity to finance its activities without additional subordinated financial support provided by any parties, including equity holders?

b. Assume the expected losses are greater than $50. Is the equity investment at risk sufficient to permit the legal entity to finance its activities without additional subordinated financial support provided by any parties, including equity holders?

The solution to this review problem can be found on page 442.

---

[12] Terminology is especially important in this chapter. The distinction between a "voting interest entity" and a VIE determines whether a Legal Entity will be evaluated for consolidation based on the majority interest in its voting equity (i.e., this is exactly what we did in Chapters 2 through 5) or whether a legal entity will be evaluated for consolidation based on financial interests other than voting interests (i.e., it is a VIE).

FASB ASC 810-10-25-45 does include a suggested quantitative threshold to help assess whether total equity investment at risk is sufficient to permit the legal entity to finance its activities without additional subordinated financial support. In particular, "[a]n equity investment at risk of less than 10 percent of the legal entity's total assets shall not be considered sufficient to permit the legal entity to finance its activities without subordinated financial support." However, this 10 percent threshold is rebuttable. Reporting companies have the opportunity to demonstrate that equity investment less than 10 percent of the legal entity's total assets is sufficient. In addition, FASB ASC 810 explicitly states that equity in excess of 10 percent of the legal entity's total assets might not be sufficient. Thus, effectively, reporting companies have to test for sufficiency regardless of the relation to the 10 percent threshold of the legal entity's equity at risk. According to the FASB, the preferred ways to satisfy the 10 percent presumption are to demonstrate that the legal entity can either obtain financing without additional subordinated financial support, or to refer to the equity invested in another similar entity with similar assets, liabilities and other interests that has financed itself without additional subordinated financial support. If these qualitative assessments fail to provide sufficient evidence, then the reporting company should conduct a quantitative assessment of whether the "amount of equity invested in the legal entity exceeds the estimate of the legal entity's expected losses based on reasonable quantitative evidence."

TOPIC REVIEW 2

Evaluating Equity Investment Provided by Parties Involved with the Entity

Shamco forms a limited partnership with Moneyco, a third-party company. The purpose of the partnership is to acquire and lease construction equipment. Shamco contributes $8 million to the partnership in exchange for a 10% general partnership interest. Moneyco contributes $72 million in exchange for a 90% limited partnership interest. At its inception, the partnership acquires construction equipment for $72 million. Additionally, as compensation for identification and acquisition of the construction equipment, and structuring of the partnership, Moneyco pays an $8 million fee to Shamco. What is the amount of equity investment at risk for Shamco?

The solution to this review problem can be found on page 442.

Although condition (a) is focused on the sufficiency of the legal entity's owners' equity, it does not require that the owners' equity, by itself, be sufficient to finance all of the legal entity's future activities. A legal entity can satisfy this requirement if it can obtain debt financing that is sufficient to finance its future activities. Taken together, condition (a) basically says that it is sufficient to categorize a legal entity as a VIE if its reported owners' equity (that is obtained in an arm's length fashion) is not sufficient to finance its expected future activities without seeking additional financing that is likely to bear some of the expected future losses. If the legal entity is not classified as a VIE via condition (a), then it is sufficient to categorize a legal entity as a VIE if it satisfies the criteria listed under condition (b).

Condition (b) in Step ❹ is intended to evaluate whether the equity investors possess the rights and responsibilities usually possessed by traditional voting-equity shareholders; specifically, power over the operations of the legal entity and the right to receive the residual proceeds generated by the legal entity. Before we discuss the details of condition (b), we need to define a few terms used in the evaluation of potential VIEs:

Expected Losses: the expected *negative* variability in the fair value of a legal entity's net assets. This determination is exclusive of variable interests in other legal entities, and is *not* the anticipated amount or variability of the net income or loss.

Expected Residual Returns: the expected *positive* variability in the fair value of a legal entity's net assets. Again, this determination is exclusive of variable interests, and not the anticipated amount or variability of the net income or loss.

Expected Variability: the sum of the absolute values of the expected residual return and the expected loss.

As indicated in Step ❹, Part (b)(1), for an entity *not* to be a VIE, the holders of the equity investment at risk, as a group, must have the power to direct the activities of an entity that most significantly impact the entity's economic performance. This decision making authority must be substantive, giving the holders of the equity at risk the ability to make decisions to enter or exit lines of business, sell significant assets, borrow money, and affect the economic performance of the legal entity (e.g., revenues, expenses, gains and losses). Further, the power to direct activities must derive from the equity interests themselves; the power cannot be the result of some separate agreement provided to parties that happen to also hold the equity interests. The requirement in Part (b) (1) is logical because, as the decision-making power of the equity holders becomes relatively less significant, a model that bases consolidation on ownership of voting interests (e.g., voting common stock) becomes less appropriate.

TOPIC REVIEW 3

At-Risk Equity: Test for Equity Sufficiency Versus Test for Power to Direct

A biotechnology company forms a limited partnership for the development of a new molecule for the treatment of Alzheimer's disease. A group of independent investors contribute at-risk equity equal to 93% of the entity's capitalization in exchange for limited partnership interests. The biotechnology company contributes equity equal to 7% of the entity's capitalization in exchange for the general partnership interest. Thus, the limited partnership has no liabilities. At formation of the limited partnership, the biotechnology company is paid a management fee equal to 8% of the entity's total capitalization. The biotechnology company, as general partner, makes all substantive decisions for the partnership. As we describe in our discussion of Step ❹, part (a), because the fee is not "arm's length" (i.e., it is provided by other parties involved with the legal entity), the fee is netted against the biotechnology company's equity investment, reducing it to zero for purposes of determining the equity investment at risk. Accordingly, the biotechnology company does not have an equity investment at risk. However, the expected losses for the limited partnership are only expected to be 20 percent of the total capitalization of the limited partnership. Given that the 93 percent of total capitalization contributed by the group of independent investors is considered to be at risk, the limited partnership has more than enough equity at risk to permit the legal entity to finance its activities without additional subordinated financial support. Thus, the limited partnership is not a VIE on the basis of the equity sufficiency test in Part (a) of Step ❹. Turning now to the test in Step ❹, Part (b)(1), do the holders of the equity investment at risk lack the power, through voting rights or similar rights, to direct the activities of a legal entity that most significantly impact the entity's economic performance?

The solution to this review problem can be found on page 442.

Parts (b)(2) and (b)(3) of Step ❹ require the evaluation of whether the holders of the equity investment at risk lack the obligation to absorb the expected losses or the right to receive the expected residual returns, respectively, of the legal entity. Again, the whole point of determining whether a legal entity is a VIE is to identify situations in which the equity investors do not control the legal entity. As we discussed previously, for most operating companies, voting common stock is the means through which control is exercised. That is, for most companies, the voting common equity provides the power to direct activities and also means through which the entity distributes the excess profits and losses of the entity to the equity investors. For VIEs, either the power to direct activities or the right to receive the excess profits and losses is not possessed by the equity investors.

Turning to Part (b)(2) of Step ❹, to be considered a voting interest entity, the equity owners of the legal entity, as a group, must have the obligation to absorb the expected losses of the entity through the equity investments they hold. This provision exists to identify situations in which the equity holders are protected from fair-value losses incurred by the legal entity. This means that the holders of the equity investment at risk cannot be protected from the risk of loss on any portion of their investment, either by the entity itself or by others involved with the entity. Common ways to protect the value of the equity holders' investment is to provide the equity holders with financial guarantees or put options that allow them to sell their equity investments back to the entity (or to a related counterparty) at an amount that results in no losses to the equity investors.[13] For example, assume a partnership was financed with $100 of debt and $20 of equity. The partnership uses the proceeds to purchase a risky asset that is worth $120. To protect the partnership against a possible decline in value of the risky asset, the partnership purchased a put option that gives the partnership the right to sell, for $120, the risky asset to the writer of the option. In this scenario, the equity holders are not at risk of loss because if the value of the risky asset declines below $120, the partnership will exercise the option and sell the asset to the writer of the option for $120. Because the equity investors are protected against incurring expected losses, the legal entity would fail the expected losses test in Step ❹, Part (b)(2). Thus, the entity is a VIE.

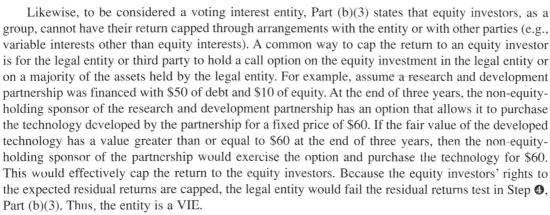

TOPIC REVIEW 4

Obligation to Absorb the Expected Losses of the Legal Entity

Investor A owns 100 percent of the equity issued by Legal Entity X. All of Legal Entity X's equity is considered equity at risk. Company Y (an unrelated company) enters into a contract to purchase finished goods from the Legal Entity X at a price equal to the actual costs of production (including raw materials, labor, overhead, etc.) plus a 1.5 percent fixed margin. The purchase agreement is structured so that Company Y absorbs all variability associated with the production of the finished product. This contract represents a variable interest in Entity X. There are no other variable interest holders in the entity. What is the effect of this contract on Investor A's obligation to absorb the expected losses of Legal Entity X?

The solution to this review problem can be found on page 443.

Likewise, to be considered a voting interest entity, Part (b)(3) states that equity investors, as a group, cannot have their return capped through arrangements with the entity or with other parties (e.g., variable interests other than equity interests). A common way to cap the return to an equity investor is for the legal entity or third party to hold a call option on the equity investment in the legal entity or on a majority of the assets held by the legal entity. For example, assume a research and development partnership was financed with $50 of debt and $10 of equity. At the end of three years, the non-equity-holding sponsor of the research and development partnership has an option that allows it to purchase the technology developed by the partnership for a fixed price of $60. If the fair value of the developed technology has a value greater than or equal to $60 at the end of three years, then the non-equity-holding sponsor of the partnership would exercise the option and purchase the technology for $60. This would effectively cap the return to the equity investors. Because the equity investors' rights to the expected residual returns are capped, the legal entity would fail the residual returns test in Step ❹, Part (b)(3). Thus, the entity is a VIE.

Because all of the analyses in Step ❹, Part (b) are conducted on holders of the equity investment at risk, *as a group*, it would be possible for a sponsor to satisfy the specific requirements of Part (b) (i.e., the legal entity is not a VIE based on group-level analyses) and to then avoid consolidation as a voting interest entity by providing nonsubstantive voting rights to another equity investor. To mitigate the potential for this type of behavior, the FASB includes the following "anti-abuse provision" in FASB ASC 810-10-15-14: the equity investors as a group also are considered to lack the characteristic in Step ❹ (b)(1) if *both* of the following conditions are present: (1) the voting rights of some investors are not proportional to their obligations to absorb the expected losses of the legal entity, their rights to receive the expected residual returns of the legal entity, or both, *and* (2) substantially all of the legal entity's activities (for example, providing financing or buying assets) either involve or are conducted on behalf

---

[13] We will discuss the accounting for put options and call options in Chapter 7. For now, the important point to understand is that put options give the holder of the option the right to *sell* at an agreed upon price and by an agreed upon date the asset on which the option is written. The holder of a call option has the right to purchase at an agreed upon price and by an agreed upon date the asset on which the option is written. Thus, put options provide the option holder with protection against decreases in the value of the asset on which the option is written, while call options provide the holder with the ability to profit from increases in the value of the asset on which the option is written.

of an investor that has disproportionately few voting rights.[14] In other words, regardless of the determinations made about the holders of the equity investments at risk, *as a group*, if disproportionately few voting rights are held by an investor for whose benefit the legal entity primarily operates, then this condition provides de facto evidence that the equity investor has the power to direct the activities of the legal entity that most significantly affect the entity's economic performance.

For example, assume that Reporting Company X contributed 70 percent of the equity financing for Partnership A and Reporting Company Y contributed the remaining 30 percent equity financing. Reporting Companies X and Y share in the profits and losses of Partnership A in a 7:3 ratio, respectively. However, the governing documents for Partnership A stipulate that Reporting Company X and Reporting Company Y each have 50 percent voting power for all operating, financing and investing decisions for Partnership A. Further, Reporting Company X and Partnership A have a contract committing Partnership A to sell 90 percent of its production output to Reporting Company X. Reporting Company X's voting rights (i.e., 50 percent) are disproportionately low in relation to its exposure to the risks (i.e., 70 percent); thus, the first anti-abuse criterion is met. Further, given that 90 percent of the output of Partnership A is sold to Reporting Company X, this means that substantially all of the legal entity's activities are conducted on behalf of Reporting Company X; thus, the second anti-abuse criterion is met. This means that Partnership A is a VIE.

If the Legal Entity is not a Variable Interest Entity then Evaluate Control Based on Voting Interests

If, in Step ❹, we determine that the legal entity *is not* a VIE, then we proceed to the evaluation of voting control in Step ❺. Basically, this is exactly the procedure we performed in the consolidations material covered in Chapters 2 through 5. An extremely important point to understand is that we must always perform the analyses in Steps 1 through 5 before applying the voting interests test for control. That is, the voting interest evaluation is only allowed after we determine that the variable interest entity-related sections of FASB ASC 810 do not apply.

If the Legal Entity is a Variable Interest Entity then Determine if Reporting Entity is the Primary Beneficiary

If, in Step ❹, we determine that the legal entity *is* a VIE, then we proceed to the Step ❻ evaluation of whether the Reporting Entity is the **Primary Beneficiary**.[15] As we discussed previously, reporting companies are required to consolidate legal entities in which the reporting company has a controlling financial interest. Thus, for VIEs, the Primary Beneficiary is a reporting company that has a controlling financial interest in a VIE. According to FASB ASC 810-10-25-38A, "[a] reporting entity shall be deemed to have a controlling financial interest in a VIE if it has both of the following characteristics:

a. The power to direct the activities of a VIE that most significantly impact the VIE's economic performance, and

b. The obligation to absorb losses of the VIE that could potentially be significant to the VIE or the right to receive benefits from the VIE that could potentially be significant to the VIE."

Note that these Step ❻ conditions mirror the Step ❹ conditions for determining whether a legal entity is a VIE. The focus in Step 4 was whether the at-risk equity investors have power or will receive the expected losses and residual returns of the legal entity. In Step 6, we are considering the case in which the equity investors do not have these attributes (i.e., the legal entity is a VIE), so we are now determining whether other holders of (non-equity-at-risk) variable interest have both (1) the power to direct the legal entity's activities, and (2) the obligation to absorb the expected losses or the right to receive the expected residual returns.

---

[14] The intent of this provision was best summed up by Securities and Exchange Commission (SEC) Staff Member, Eric Schuppenhauer, at the 2003 American Institute of Certified Public Accountants National Conference on Current SEC Developments: "The intent of this provision is to move the consolidation analysis from the voting interests model to the variable interests model in those instances where it is clear that the voting arrangements have been skewed such that the investor with disproportionately few voting rights, as compared to its economic interest, derives substantially all of the benefits of the activities of the entity. In other words, it is an abuse-prevention mechanism intended to identify instances where there is something occurring in the relationship that indicates the voting arrangements are not useful in identifying who truly controls the entity."

[15] Technically, according to FASB ASC 810-10-20, the Primary Beneficiary is "[a]n entity that consolidates a variable interest entity (VIE)." Of course, this definition is not all that helpful, so we will focus on the indicators that determine whether a legal entity should be consolidated by a reporting company under the VIE guidance in FASB ASC 810.

In evaluating the "power" criterion, the reporting entity is supposed to consider the "purpose and design" of the VIE and the risks the VIE was designed to create and pass to its variable interest holders. In evaluating purpose and design, a reporting company should evaluate the nature of the legal entity's activities. This evaluation should consider the terms of the contracts the legal entity has entered into, the variable interests in the legal entity, and how investments in the legal entity were marketed to potential investors. Clues about the legal entity's purpose and design could come from a review of the legal entity's governing documents, marketing materials and contractual arrangements, and this material should be closely reviewed. The risks that the VIE was designed to create and pass to its variable interest holders may include credit risk, operations risk, interest rate risk, foreign currency exchange risk, commodity price risk, and others.

For example, consider a legal entity that was formed to hold and securitize residential mortgages. A reporting company determined that it has a variable interest in the legal entity and that the legal entity is a VIE. In the reporting company's evaluation of whether it is the primary beneficiary of the legal entity, the reporting entity must determine the purpose and design of the legal entity, including identification of the risks the legal entity was designed to create and pass through to the variable interest holders. If the reporting company determines that credit risk most affects the economic performance of the legal entity, then the variable interest holder with the power to direct activities related to delinquent and defaulted mortgages is the party that has the power described in the first criterion. This is not to say that interest rate risk is unimportant for pools of mortgages; however, in this case, the determination was made that credit risk was more important.

With respect to the "losses and benefits" criterion, FASB ASC 810-10-25-38A specifically states that "[t]he quantitative approach described in the definitions of the terms expected losses, expected residual returns, and expected variability is not required and shall not be the sole determinant as to whether a reporting entity has these obligations or rights." It is important to note that the FASB *did not* require the losses and gains to be the legal entity's most significant criterion in identifying the primary beneficiary. The losses and gains just need to be potentially significant to the VIE. The interpretive guidance issued by the largest international public accounting firms suggests that most variable interests in VIEs are potentially significant; thus, losses and benefits criterion is often assumed to be satisfied when a variable interest holder has the power to direct a VIE's economic activities.

Although FASB ASC 810-10-25-38A indicates that it is inappropriate for more than one reporting company to consolidate the same VIE, given the independent analyses conducted by each reporting company and the significant professional judgments included in those analyses, it is possible for more than one reporting company to conclude that it should consolidate the same VIE. For example, a reporting company might determine that a legal entity is a voting interest entity because the reporting company determined that the legal entity is sufficiently capitalized with at-risk equity. As a result of its majority ownership of the legal entity, the reporting company consolidates the legal entity. Because of the significant judgments involved in concluding whether a legal entity is a VIE, a second unrelated reporting company with a variable interest in the legal entity could determine that the legal entity is a VIE and consolidate that same legal entity under the VIE sections of FASB ASC 810. Although this circumstance is unusual and undesirable, it is possible because of the many judgments necessary under the comprehensive consolidation model illustrated in Exhibit 6.2.

Consolidation of a Variable Interest Entity   If a reporting company is identified as the primary beneficiary of a VIE, then the reporting company has a controlling financial interest in the VIE and must consolidate the VIE. At this point, the primary beneficiary must determine whether the VIE is a business, as that term is defined in FASB ASC 805.[16] When initially consolidating a VIE, the primary beneficiary should recognize goodwill *only if* the VIE satisfies the FASB ASC 805 definition of a business.

Initial Measurement if the VIE is a Business   When a reporting entity becomes the primary beneficiary of a VIE that is a business, then the reporting entity should apply the same ASC 805 **Acquisition Method** recognition and measurement principles we describe in Chapter 2. If the fair

---

[16] It is also the same definition of business that was used in Step ❸ of the comprehensive consolidation model illustrated in Exhibit 6.2.

value of the VIE is greater than the sum of the individual fair values of the identifiable net assets inside the VIE, then the primary beneficiary will recognize goodwill in the consolidated financial statements. If the fair value of the VIE is less than the sum of the individual fair values of the identifiable net assets inside the VIE, then the primary beneficiary will recognize a bargain purchase gain. The amount of goodwill (if positive) or gain (if negative) recognized upon initial consolidation is determined in the same manner we described in Chapter 2:

> Fair value of the consideration paid for the VIE
> + Fair value of any previously held interests[17]
> + The fair value of any noncontrolling interest in the VIE
> ___
> = Total fair value of the VIE
> − The initial consolidation-date fair value of the VIE's identifiable net assets[18]
> ___
> = Goodwill (if positive) or Bargain Acquisition Gain (if negative)

For example, assume that prior to June 15, 2016, a Reporting Company owned a 15 percent interest in a Legal Entity. The Reporting Company acquired its 15 percent ownership interest in the Legal Entity on April 20, 2001 for $10,000, and correctly accounted for this investment under the cost method (i.e., it was a passive investment and it was not marketable). On June 15, 2016, the Reporting Company purchased an additional 25 percent interest in the Legal Entity for $100,000. As a result of an evaluation of the facts and circumstances on June 15, 2016, the Reporting Entity determined that the Legal Entity is a VIE and that the Reporting Company is the primary beneficiary. The Reporting Company also determined that, on June 15, 2016, the fair value of the previously held 15 percent interest is $60,000. In addition, independent appraisals revealed that the fair value of the noncontrolling interest (i.e., the 60 percent not owned by the Reporting Company) is $240,000. On June 15, 2016, the Legal Entity has reported book values for its identifiable net assets equal to $200,000 and fair values for its identifiable net assets equal to $320,000. Assume that the Legal Entity is a business, as that term is defined in FASB ASC 805.

In this example, because the VIE is a business, all of the ownership interests are measured at fair value. This results in an overall value for the VIE equal to $400,000 (i.e., the 15 percent interest at $60,000, plus the 25 percent interest at $100,000, plus the 60 percent noncontrolling interest at $240,000). Because the fair value of the identifiable net assets of the VIE is equal to $320,000, this results in goodwill equal to $80,000 (i.e., $400,000 − $320,000).

Initial Measurement if the VIE is not a Business

"When a reporting entity becomes the primary beneficiary of a VIE that is not a business, then no goodwill shall be recognized" (FASB ASC 810-10-30-3). In addition, upon becoming a primary beneficiary, the reporting entity should recognize an initial gain or loss determined as follows:

> Fair value of the consideration paid for the VIE
> + Historical carrying value of any previously held interests
> + The fair value of any noncontrolling interest in the VIE
> ___
> = Total reported value of the VIE
> − The initial consolidation-date fair value of the VIE's identifiable net assets
> ___
> = Loss (if positive) or Gain (if negative) on Initial Consolidation of VIE

---

[17] Just as we describe in Chapter 2, if the primary beneficiary already had a recognized investment in the VIE prior to achieving primary beneficiary status, then the primary beneficiary "shall remeasure its previously held [i.e., noncontrolling] equity interest in the [VIE] at its acquisition-date fair value and recognize the resulting gain or loss, if any, in earnings. In prior reporting periods, the [primary beneficiary] may have recognized changes in the value of its equity interest in the [VIE] in other comprehensive income (for example, because the investment was classified as available for sale). If so, the amount that was recognized in other comprehensive income shall be reclassified and included in the calculation of gain or loss as of the acquisition date" (FASB ASC 805-10-25-10).

[18] If the reporting entity transferred any assets or loaned any amounts to the VIE "at, after, or shortly before the date that the reporting entity became the primary beneficiary", those assets and liabilities are measured at their book values on the date of transfer, that is, no write-up to fair value is permitted and no gain or loss shall be recognized because of such transfers (FASB ASC 810-10-30-4).

For example, assume the same fact pattern as the preceding illustration, except now we will assume that the VIE is *not* a business, as that term is defined in FASB ASC 805. In this case, in determining the overall value of the VIE, we must incorporate the historical carrying value of the 15 percent previously held interest in the Legal Entity. This results in an overall value for the VIE equal to $350,000 (i.e., the 15 percent interest at its pre-VIE carrying value of $10,000, plus the 25 percent interest at $100,000, plus the 60 percent noncontrolling interest at $240,000). Because the fair value of the identifiable net assets of the VIE is equal to $320,000, this results in a loss on consolidation of the VIE equal to $30,000 (i.e., $350,000 - $320,000).

Financial Reporting After Initial Measurement   Finally, after the initial consolidation of the VIE has been prepared, the assets, liabilities, and noncontrolling interests of a consolidated VIE are accounted for in the consolidated financial statements as if the entity were consolidated based on voting interests, including elimination of all intercompany transactions between the primary beneficiary and the VIE. One caveat is that FASB ASC 810-10-35-3 requires 100 percent of the elimination of "[f]ees or other sources of income or expense between a primary beneficiary and a consolidated VIE" be attributed to the primary beneficiary. In other words, regardless of the direction of payment between the primary beneficiary and the VIE, these intercompany payments are always treated as downstream intercompany transactions (i.e., none of the intercompany elimination is attributed to the noncontrolling interest).[19] The FASB put in this restriction to address situations where the primary beneficiary may not have an equity interest in the VIE. In such a situation, if allocation between the controlling and noncontrolling interests was allowed, the primary beneficiary would not record any income from fees earned from the VIE!

To illustrate, let's assume that on January 1, 2016, a Reporting Company acquires a 50 percent interest in a Legal Entity for $1,000,000 cash. The fair value of the 50 percent interest not acquired by the Reporting Company is $1,000,000. The fair value and book value of the identifiable net assets of the Legal Entity equals $2,000,000. The Reporting Company has a right to 50 percent of the reported income (loss) of the Legal Entity.[20] The Legal Entity is determined to be a VIE, and the Reporting Company is determined to be primary beneficiary. For year ended December 31, 2016, the Reporting Company and the VIE reported the following pre-consolidation income statements assuming that the Reporting Company applies the equity method:

	Reporting Company	VIE
Sales.	$2,200,000	$600,000
Cost of goods sold.	(1,320,000)	(400,000)
Gross profit.	880,000	200,000
Operating expenses.	(352,000)	(60,000)
Equity method income (loss) from VIE	(10,000)	
Net income.	$ 518,000	$140,000

Assume that the Legal Entity's income statement for the year ended December 31, 2016 includes sales to the Reporting Company in the amount of $200,000. On intercompany sales, the Legal Entity earns a gross profit equal to 40 percent of sales price. Assume that all of these intercompany items are in the ending inventory of the Reporting Company on December 31, 2016. As we describe in Chapter 5, the theoretically preferred way to treat upstream profit elimination for traditional

---

[19] In Chapter 5, we discuss the elimination of intercompany asset-transfer profits and losses in the presence of noncontrolling interests for companies that we characterize in this chapter as "voting interest entities." We note that the theoretically preferred approach to eliminating intercompany profits in upstream asset transactions (for voting interest entities) is to allocate the deferred (and reversing) profit proportionally to the controlling and noncontrolling interests. The income effects of downstream asset transactions are 100 percent allocated to the controlling interests.

[20] Because VIEs are typically entities that are often structured to distribute the risks and rewards of the VIE to various variable interest holders, the VIE's governing agreement should be carefully analyzed to determine the appropriate assignment of the VIE's net income or loss to the primary beneficiary and the equity investors.

voting-interest entities is to completely eliminate the deferred intercompany profit from the determination of consolidated net income, and to pro-rata allocate the noncontrolling interest percentage of the upstream deferred profit to the consolidated income attributable to the noncontrolling interest. However, FASB ASC 810-10-35-3 prohibits pro-rata allocation for upstream transactions from a VIE, instead requiring that 100 percent of the elimination be attributed to the controlling interest. In other words, for VIEs, all profit deferrals from intercompany asset transfers are treated like downstream transactions. In our example, this is how we arrived at the pre-consolidation "Equity method income (loss) from VIE" equal to $(10,000) (i.e., [50% × $140,000] − 100 percent of upstream deferred intercompany profit of $80,000).

Given the facts, our **C-E-A-D-I** consolidation entries will be as follows:

[C]	Investment in VIE	10,000	
	Income attributable to noncontrolling interest	70,000	
	Equity method income (loss) from VIE		10,000
	Noncontrolling Interest		70,000
[E]	Owners' Equity of VIE @ BOY	2,000,000	
	Investment in VIE @ BOY		1,000,000
	Noncontrolling Interest @ BOY		1,000,000
[I$_{sales}$]	Sales	200,000	
	Cost of goods sold		200,000
[I$_{cogs}$]	Cost of goods sold	80,000	
	Inventories		80,000

With respect to the income statement (only), these entries will result in the following consolidated balances.

	Consolidated
Sales	$2,600,000
Cost of goods sold	(1,600,000)
Gross profit	1,000,000
Operating expenses	(412,000)
Equity method income (loss) from VIE	0
Consolidated net income	588,000
(Income) Loss attributable to noncontrolling interest	(70,000)
Income attributable to controlling interest	$ 518,000

In this example, consolidated net income reflects the full elimination of all of the $80,000 deferred intercompany profit. None of this deferred inventory profit was eliminated from the "Income attributable to noncontrolling interest" (i.e., 50 percent × $140,000 = $70,000). This means that 100 percent of the upstream deferred inventory profit was assigned to the controlling interest.[21]

Required Disclosures Relating to VIEs FASB ASC 810 includes significant reporting and disclosure requirements for VIEs, regardless of whether the reporting entity is determined to be the primary beneficiary. These requirements include the following:

[21] If the Legal Entity qualified as a "voting interest entity" under FASB ASC 810, then the theoretically preferred accounting is to assign the profit elimination proportionally between the controlling and noncontrolling interests. (In terms of the comprehensive consolidation model introduced in this chapter, all of the consolidated subsidiaries included in Chapters 2-5 are considered "voting interest entities.") Thus, consolidated net income would remain the same (i.e., $588,000), but the Income attributable to the noncontrolling interest would change to $30,000 (i.e., 50 percent × ($140,000 − $80,000)) and the income attributable to the controlling interest would change to $558,000 (i.e., $588,000 − $30,000).

1. On the face of the consolidated statement of financial position for the primary beneficiary (See "Practice Insight—GE's Balance Sheet Reporting of VIEs" for an example of the disclosures required on the face of the balance sheet on page 410):

    a. Assets of a consolidated variable interest entity (VIE) that can be used only to settle obligations of the consolidated VIE.

    b. Liabilities of a consolidated VIE for which creditors (or beneficial interest holders) do not have recourse to the general credit of the primary beneficiary. (FASB ASC 810-10-45-25)

2. For *all* entities within the scope of the FASB ASC 810 VIE model (i.e., whether a primary beneficiary or a non-consolidating variable interest holder):

    a. The significant judgments and assumptions made by a reporting entity in determining whether it must do any of the following:

        i. Consolidate the VIE

        ii. Disclose information about its involvement in a VIE

    b. The nature of restrictions on a consolidated VIE's assets reported by a reporting entity in its statement of financial position, including the carrying amounts of such assets and liabilities

    c. The nature of, and changes in, the risks associated with a reporting entity's involvement with the VIE.

    d. How a reporting entity's involvement with the VIE affects the reporting entity's financial position, financial performance, and cash flows.

    e. Companies are allowed to disclose the foregoing information in multiple notes to the financial statements. If the disclosures are provided in more than one note to the financial statements, the reporting entity is required to provide a cross reference to the other notes to the financial statements that provide the required disclosures. (FASB ASC 810-10-50-2AA through -2AC)

3. The primary beneficiary of a VIE that is a business is required to provide disclosures required by other FASB ASC subsections (e.g., the Acquisition Method disclosures in FASB ASC 805). The primary beneficiary of a VIE that is not a business is required to disclose the amount of gain or loss recognized on the initial consolidation of the VIE. The primary beneficiary of a VIE is also required to disclose all of the following (note that these disclosures are not required for a primary beneficiary that also holds a majority voting interest):

    a. The carrying amounts and classification of the VIE's assets and liabilities in the statement of financial position that are consolidated in accordance with the VIE subsections of FASB ASC 810, including qualitative information about the relationship(s) between those assets and liabilities. For example, if the VIE's assets can be used only to settle obligations of the VIE, the reporting entity shall disclose qualitative information about the nature of the restrictions on those assets.

    b. Lack of recourse if creditors (or beneficial interest holders) of a consolidated VIE have no recourse to the general credit of the primary beneficiary.

    c. Terms of arrangements, giving consideration to both explicit arrangements and implicit variable interests that could require the reporting entity to provide financial support (for example, liquidity arrangements and obligations to purchase assets) to the VIE, including events or circumstances that could expose the reporting entity to a loss. (FASB ASC 810-10-50-3)

4. For the "nonprimary" beneficiary holder of a variable interest in a VIE, the following disclosures are required

    a. The carrying amounts and classification of the assets and liabilities in the reporting entity's statement of financial position that relate to the reporting entity's variable interest in the VIE.

    b. The reporting entity's maximum exposure to loss as a result of its involvement with the VIE, including how the maximum exposure is determined and the significant sources of the reporting entity's exposure to the VIE. If the reporting entity's maximum exposure to loss as a result of its involvement with the VIE cannot be quantified, that fact shall be disclosed.

    c. A tabular comparison of the carrying amounts of the assets and liabilities, as required by (a) above, and the reporting entity's maximum exposure to loss, as required by (b) above.

A reporting entity shall provide qualitative and quantitative information to allow financial statement users to understand the differences between the two amounts. That discussion shall include, but is not limited to, the terms of arrangements, giving consideration to both explicit arrangements and implicit variable interests, that could require the reporting entity to provide financial support (for example, liquidity arrangements and obligations to purchase assets) to the VIE, including events or circumstances that could expose the reporting entity to a loss.

d. Information about any liquidity arrangements, guarantees, and/or other commitments by third parties that may affect the fair value or risk of the reporting entity's variable interest in the VIE is encouraged.

e. If applicable, significant factors considered and judgments made in determining that the power to direct the activities of a VIE that most significantly impact the VIE's economic performance is shared. (FASB ASC 810-10-50-4)

PRACTICE INSIGHT

General Electric's Balance Sheet Reporting of VIEs   The face of **General Electric**'s (GE's) consolidated balance sheet at December 31, 2014 provides the following mandated disclosure related to assets and liabilities that are reported as a result of GE's status as primary beneficiary in consolidated VIEs:

(a) Our consolidated assets at December 31, 2014 include total assets of $50,453 million of certain variable interest entities (VIEs) that can only be used to settle the liabilities of those VIEs. These assets include net financing receivables of $43,620 million and investment securities of $3,374 million. Our consolidated liabilities at December 31, 2014 include liabilities of certain VIEs for which the VIE creditors do not have recourse to GE. These liabilities include non-recourse borrowings of consolidated securitization entities (CSEs) of $28,664 million.

INTERCOMPANY INVESTMENT IN AFFILIATES' DEBT

Direct Lending to an Affiliate

LO3 Describe and apply the consolidation procedures necessary when affiliated companies acquire each other's debt, including immediate recognition of gain or loss on constructive retirement of the debt and subsequent recognition of the gain or loss via discount and/or premium amortization in the separate pre-consolidation financial statements of the affiliated companies.

Parent companies can lend money directly to their subsidiaries, either via loans or the purchase of subsidiary bonds. Parent companies can also become creditors of their subsidiaries by purchasing subsidiary bonds in the open market. In this section, we discuss the direct lending between a parent company and a subsidiary (e.g., via direct issue of notes and/or bonds by the subsidiary to the parent). In the next section, we explore the accounting implications of the parent's secondary purchase of subsidiary bonds in the open market. As you will see, in both cases the intercompany debt must be eliminated in the consolidated financial statements.

In a direct purchase of subsidiary notes and/or bonds by a parent company, the journal entries made by the parent mirrors those made by the subsidiary. Because of this fact, the required consolidation entry is merely a reversal of these initial entries by the two companies. To illustrate, assume that on December 31, 2013, a subsidiary issues to a parent company a $2,000,000 face amount of 4% (interest payable annually), 5-year bond at a discount to yield 5%. The proceeds received by the Subsidiary equal $1,913,410. Exhibit 6.3 provides the bond amortization schedule assuming annual compounding and straight-line amortization of the bond discount.[22]

---

[22] The sale price is equal to ($2,000,000 x 0.783526) + ($2,000,000 x 4% x 4.329477) = $1,913,410. Straight-line amortization of the bond discount is permitted so long as the difference between the straight-line and effective interest methods is not material. We assume straight-line to simplify the example so that you can focus on the consolidation issues.

EXHIBIT 6.3	Bond Amortization Schedule			
Year	Cash Payment	Amortization of Discount	Interest Expense	Carrying Amount
Dec. 31, 2013				$1,913,410
Dec. 31, 2014	$80,000	$17,318	$97,318	$1,930,728
Dec. 31, 2015	$80,000	$17,318	$97,318	$1,948,046
Dec. 31, 2016	$80,000	$17,318	$97,318	$1,965,364
Dec. 31, 2017	$80,000	$17,318	$97,318	$1,982,682
Dec. 31, 2018	$80,000	$17,318	$97,318	$2,000,000

Exhibit 6.4 provides the journal entries made by the subsidiary and the parent at December 31, 2014.

EXHIBIT 6.4	Journal Entries Made by the Subsidiary and Parent through December 31, 2014		
	Cash.	1,913,410	
	Discount on bonds payable	86,590	
	Bonds payable.		2,000,000
On the books of the Subsidiary	*(to record issuance of bonds on December 31, 2013)*		
	Interest expense.	97,318	
	Discount on bonds payable.		17,318
	Cash		80,000
	(to record interest expense, amortization of discount and payment of cash for the year ended December 31, 2014)		
	Bond investment	1,913,410	
	Cash		1,913,410
On the books of the Parent	*(to record purchase of bond investment on December 31, 2013)*		
	Cash.	80,000	
	Bond investment	17,318	
	Interest income		97,318
	(to record cash receipt, increase in bond investment, and interest income for the year ended December 31, 2014)		

The required consolidation entries eliminate all of these intercompany transactions and balances. We call this group of consolidation entries our $[I_{bond}]$ entries, for intercompany bond transactions. Exhibit 6.5 provides the $[I_{bond}]$ entries at December 31, 2014.[23]

EXHIBIT 6.5	$[I_{bond}]$ Consolidation Entries at December 31, 2014		
	a. Bonds payable	2,000,000	
$[I_{bond}]$ Consolidation entries for intercompany bond transactions	Investment in bonds		1,930,728
	Discount on bonds payable.		69,272
	(to eliminate intercompany bond holdings)		
	b. Interest income	97,318	
	Interest expense		97,318
	(to eliminate the intercompany interest income and expense)		

In each succeeding year, the $[I_{bond}]$ consolidation journal entries will be the same as above, but with different amounts for the bond discount and bond investment to reflect the change in the carrying value of the bonds. For example, Exhibit 6.6 presents the $[I_{bond}]$ consolidation journal entries at December 31, 2015.

---

[23] If the interest is not paid in cash, the consolidation entries must also eliminate the intercompany interest receivable and payable balances. This elimination entry is the same as that for the intercompany receivable and payable relating to inventory transactions we discuss in Chapter 4.

EXHIBIT 6.6	[I_bond] Consolidation Entries at December 31, 2015		
[I_bond] Consolidation entries for intercompany bond transactions	a. Bonds payable	2,000,000	
	Investment in bonds		1,948,046
	Discount on bonds payable.		51,954
	(to eliminate intercompany bond holdings)		
	b. Interest income.	97,318	
	Interest expense		97,318
	(to eliminate the intercompany interest income and expense)		

Acquisition from Unaffiliated Entity of Investment in Affiliated Company's Debt—Equity Method

As illustrated in the previous section, when parents and subsidiaries provide direct financing to each other, the consolidation process is relatively straightforward. This is because the lending company's intercompany-borrowing-related accounts mirror the reciprocal accounts on the borrowing affiliate's books (i.e., the discount and premium accounts exactly offset on the two companies' books). Alternatively, when a consolidated affiliate purchases from an unaffiliated party the indebtedness of another consolidated affiliate, the consolidation issues can be a bit more complex. For example, a subsidiary could issue bonds to an independent third party on July 15, 2014 and on September 20, 2017 the parent company could purchase those same bonds. In this example, because the market interest rates likely shift between initial issuance of the bonds (i.e., July 15, 2014) and the subsequent purchase of the bonds by the affiliated entity (i.e., September 20, 2017), the discount/premium accounts of the affiliated bond issuer and affiliated bond holder will likely not equal. We will still need to eliminate the intercompany indebtedness, just like we did in the last section. However, because of the likely asymmetry in the bond discounts/premiums for the affiliated companies, the initial elimination will likely result in a gain or loss on constructive retirement of the intercompany debt. In this section, we will explain the intuition behind this accounting result and provide an illustration.

Before we discuss the specific procedures when one affiliate purchases another affiliate's debt from an unaffiliated entity, it is important to make sure we understand what happens when a company purchases (i.e., retires) its own debt before maturity. This simple one-company case provides the intuition for the accounting that results for consolidated affiliates. In our one-company example, assume that on June 30, 2013 Company X issues $1,000,000 principal, 5 year, annual, 6% bonds when the market rate is 5%. Assuming no transaction costs, the proceeds from the bond on June 30, 2013 are $1,043,295. Now, assume that market rates increase during the next two years, such that the market rate of interest is 6% at June 30, 2015. Given the increase in rates to 6%, this means the value of the bonds on June 30, 2015 is $1,000,000 (i.e., market rate equals the nominal rate, which means there is no discount or premium). If we assume straight line amortization of the originally issued bond premium, then the carrying value of the bonds, on Company X's books, is $1,025,977. Thus, Company X is able to pay $1,000,000 to repurchase its own bonds and retire its bond liability which has a carrying value of $1,025,977. This will result in a gain on retirement of debt equal to $25,977.

Now let's consider the case where one consolidated affiliate purchases the bonds (or other debt instrument) of another of its consolidated affiliates. Because consolidated affiliates represent a single economic entity, this case is economically identical to the one-company case. Let's slightly modify the previous one-company case to illustrate the intuition. In this example, let's assume that on June 30, 2013 a parent company issues $1,000,000 principal, 5 year, annual, 6% bonds when the market rate is 5%. As before, if we assume no transaction costs, the proceeds from the bond on June 30, 2013 are $1,043,295. Again, assume that market rates increase during the next two years, such that the market rate of interest is 6% at June 30, 2015. Given the increase in rates to 6%, this means the market value of the bonds on June 30, 2015 is, again, $1,000,000. Using straight line amortization of the originally issued bond premium, then the carrying value of the bonds, on the parent company's books, is $1,025,977. However, in this case, let's assume that *the subsidiary* purchases the parent's bonds in the open market. Although, on their separate pre-consolidation accounting books, the parent company has a bond payable in the amount of $1,025,977 and the subsidiary has a bond investment in the amount of $1,000,000, from an economic perspective, the consolidated economic entity repurchased its own debt.

Thus, from a consolidated perspective, the economic entity is able to pay $1,000,000 to repurchase its own bonds and retire its bond liability which has a carrying value of $1,025,977. Although it is not recognized in the individual company's accounting records, the consolidated financial statements will show a gain on retirement of debt equal to $25,977.

Note that the consolidation process for constructive retirement of intercompany debt is quite different from the consolidation process for intercompany assets sales (e.g., inventory, fixed assets) that we discuss in Chapter 4. For intercompany asset transfers, the individual companies recognize gains and losses in their separate pre-consolidation accounting books and the consolidation process removes those gains and losses until they are confirmed via a transaction with an unaffiliated party. In the case where one affiliate purchases another affiliate's debt, the resulting gains and losses on constructive retirement are confirmed in the consolidated financial statements, but are recognized in the individual pre-consolidation accounting books of the separate companies later.[24]

To illustrate the purchase of an affiliated company's debt from an unaffiliated entity, let's modify the previous example we used to illustrate direct lending between affiliates. This time, assume that on December 31, 2013, a subsidiary issues to an unaffiliated entity a $2,000,000 face amount of 4% (interest payable annually), 5-year bond at a discount to yield 5%. The proceeds received by the subsidiary equal $1,913,410. As before, Exhibit 6.3 provides the bond amortization schedule at the issuance date assuming annual compounding and straight-line amortization of the bond discount. After this bond is issued to the unaffiliated entity, it is an obligation of the consolidated company. Thus, unlike the direct-affiliate-financing case, it does not need to be eliminated in the consolidation process for as long as the bond is held by an unaffiliated company. That is, the bond is an obligation of the consolidated entity and should be reported like any other liability.

Now, assume that we are at December 31, 2015. The subsidiary still has the bond outstanding and reports the bond on its balance sheet at $1,948,046 ($2,000,000 face amount less the unamortized discount of $51,954). Let's assume that interest rates have risen to 6% on December 31, 2015 from 5% on the date the bond was initially issued (i.e., December 31, 2013). The bond still has a coupon rate of 4%, as before, and has a remaining life of 3 years. The parent purchases the bond from the unaffiliated entity at the current market price of $1,893,080.[25]

Exhibit 6.7 presents the bond amortization schedules for the parent and the subsidiary following the purchase of the bonds by the parent.

| EXHIBIT 6.7 | Bond Amortization Schedules for Parent and Subsidiary |

Parent:

Year	Cash Payment	Amortization of Discount	Interest Expense	Carrying Amount
Dec. 31, 2015				$1,893,080
Dec. 31, 2016	$80,000	$35,640	$115,640	$1,928,720
Dec. 31, 2017	$80,000	$35,640	$115,640	$1,964,360
Dec. 31, 2018	$80,000	$35,640	$115,640	$2,000,000

Subsidiary (as before):

Year	Cash Payment	Amortization of Discount	Interest Expense	Carrying Amount
Dec. 31, 2015				$1,948,046
Dec. 31, 2016	$80,000	$17,318	$97,318	$1,965,364
Dec. 31, 2017	$80,000	$17,318	$97,318	$1,982,682
Dec. 31, 2018	$80,000	$17,318	$97,318	$2,000,000

From a consolidated standpoint, the bond issue has been economically retired (i.e., no holders of the bond is outside of the controlled group), and the consolidated company should recognize a

[24] The gains and losses on constructive retirement of intercompany debt are recognized in the separate pre-consolidation financial statements of the companies as the related discount(s) and/or premium(s) on the intercompany debt are amortized.

[25] The purchase price is equal to ($2,000,000 x 0.839619) + ($2,000,000 x 4% x 2.673012) = $1,893,080.

gain on the repurchase in the amount of the difference between the price the parent pays for the bond ($1,893,080) and its carrying amount on the subsidiary's balance sheet ($1,948,046), or $54,966. While this difference between the carrying amount of the bond and the price paid for the bond is the reason why we will recognize a retirement gain in the year of constructive repurchase of the bond, it is important to mechanically consider how the carrying value and the repurchase amounts differ. Given that the maturity value of the bond is the same for both the parent and the subsidiary (i.e., $2,000,000), then it is the discount on the bond that is causing the difference in the current carrying value of the bond for each party. For the subsidiary, the discount is equal to $51,954 (i.e., $2,000,000 − $1,948,046, while for the parent, the discount is equal to $106,920 (i.e., $2,000,000 − $1,893,080). Thus, the gain on retirement of the bond equal to $54,966 is the difference between the discount on the parent's books and the discount on the subsidiary's books (i.e., $106,920 − $51,954).

The parent and subsidiary are individual companies, however, each with their own pre-consolidation accounting records. Thus, the parent, on its separate books, records the bond investment of $1,893,080, and the subsidiary, on its separate books, continues to record the bond payable on its balance sheet at a current amount of $1,948,046 (i.e., gross amount of $2,000,000 minus the unamortized discount of $51,954). In the year of the repurchase of the bond by the parent, the $[I_{bond}]$ consolidation entry to eliminate the intercompany receivable and payable and to record the gain on the repurchase on December 31, 2015 is provided in Exhibit 6.8:

EXHIBIT 6.8	$[I_{bond}]$ Consolidation Entries at December 31, 2015		
$[I_{bond}]$ Consolidation entries for intercompany bond transactions	Bonds payable	2,000,000	
	Discount on bond payable		51,954
	Investment in bond		1,893,080
	Gain on bond repurchase		54,966
	(to eliminate intercompany bond holdings and to record the gain on the repurchase)		

After the date the bond was purchased by the parent, the subsidiary will continue to make cash payments and record interest expense, and the parent will receive cash payments and will record interest income. To arrive at the appropriate interest amounts, each company will amortize the bond discounts presented in Exhibit 6.7. This means that by the time the bond matures on December 31, 2018, the discount will be fully amortized to a zero balance. As a result of the normal amortization actually recorded by each of the companies on their separate books, the $54,966 gain recognized in the consolidated income statement via constructive retirement (i.e., the $[I_{bond}]$ adjustment in Exhibit 6.8) will actually be recognized across the two companies' separate pre-consolidation income statements through December 31, 2018. Another way to look at this, if the parent company fails to record any consolidation adjustments for the constructive retirement of the bond (e.g., the consolidation entry in Exhibit 6.8), the effect of the gain will eventually run through the income statement via the discount amortizations recorded in the pre-consolidation income statements of the parent and subsidiary. Thus, the effect of the consolidation adjustment to recognize constructive retirement of the bond is to accelerate the future income-statement effects of the bond discounts and recognize them in the year of the bond repurchase by the economic entity.

In addition, if we assume that the parent company uses the equity method of accounting for the investment in the subsidiary, then we also need to make equity-method adjustments to the Investment in Subsidiary account on the parent's pre-consolidation financial statements. That's because, as we describe in Chapter 4, under the equity method, we also adjust the parent's books for intercompany-profit "elimination."[26] Therefore, the net income statement effect of the foregoing $[I_{bond}]$ consolidation entry must also get recorded in the parent company's separate books as part of its equity method

---

[26] We refer to them as "eliminations" (i.e., in quotation marks) because bond-related consolidation adjustments are actually recognizing gains and losses that are not part of the separate pre-consolidation financial statements of the parent and the subsidiary. Thus, it might seem a little strange to call them elimination adjustments. However, the consolidation process actually does eliminate all of the bond-related accounts in the consolidated balance sheet and income statement. Therefore, while bond-related adjustments result in different patterns of gain/loss recognition from asset-related adjustments, there is still an element of elimination to both sets of entries.

accounting for its investment in the subsidiary. Exhibit 6.9 includes the equity method entry for the year ended December 31, 2015:

EXHIBIT 6.9	Bond Related Adjustment of the Parent's Books Under the Equity Method During the Year Ended December 31, 2015
On the books of the Parent	Investment in subsidiary. . . . . 54,966 Income (Loss) from subsidiary. . . . . 54,966 *(to recognize equity method effects of constructive retirement of bond in 2015)*

In the years following the bond repurchase, the subsidiary makes its annual cash payment of interest (now, to its parent) and records interest expense, which includes amortization of the bond discount. The parent receives cash from the subsidiary and reports interest income, which also includes amortization of the bond discount. From a consolidated standpoint, however, none of the accounts related to the bond should appear in the income statement or balance sheet. Our $[I_{bond}]$ consolidation entry on December 31, 2016 is provided in Exhibit 6.10:

EXHIBIT 6.10	$[I_{bond}]$ Consolidation Entries at December 31, 2016

$[I_{bond}]$ Consolidation entries for intercompany bond transactions	Bond payable. 2,000,000
	Interest income. 115,640
	      Discount on bond payable 34,636
	      Investment in bond 1,928,720
	      Interest expense 97,318
	      BOY Investment in subsidiary 54,966
	(to eliminate intercompany bond holdings, the intercompany interest income and expense, and to record the BOY elimination of the prior period bond gain from the investment account)

The components of this journal entry are as follows:

1. The carrying value of the bond payable on the subsidiary's pre-consolidation books (i.e., $2,000,000 face amount – $34,636 unamortized discount = $1,965,364) is removed from the consolidated balance sheet.

2. The carrying value of the bond investment on the parent's pre-consolidation books (i.e., $1,928,720) is removed from the consolidated balance sheet.

3. The parent's reported pre-consolidation interest income (i.e., $115,640) and the subsidiary's pre-consolidation interest expense (i.e., $97,318) are removed from the consolidated income statement. The net effect of eliminating these two accounts is a reduction to consolidated income equal to $18,322 (i.e., $115,640 - $97,318). Because the cash interest paid between the companies is identical (i.e., $80,000), this means the $18,322 income statement effect is equal to the difference in the bond discount amortization on the parent and subsidiary books (i.e., $35,640 - $17,318 in Exhibit 6.7).

4. The pre-consolidation BOY Investment in Subsidiary account is decreased by the amount of gain that was confirmed in the consolidated financial statements through the end of the preceding year (i.e., $54,966 at December 31, 2015). (Recall that one purpose of consolidation entries is to "undo" the investment accounting that is actually recorded on the parent's pre-consolidation books.) The gain from constructive retirement of the bond was actually recorded in the investment account, so this journal entry reverses that effect.

During the year ended December 31, 2016, the parent company also must record the equity method adjustment for the amortization of the discounts on the pre-consolidation parent and subsidiary financial statements. For most students, this is probably the most difficult equity method adjustment to understand. Ultimately, proper application of the equity method means that the parent's pre-consolidation net income equals the parent's (post-consolidation) consolidated net income attributable to the controlling interest, and the parent's pre-consolidation retained earnings equals the parent's (post-consolidation) consolidated retained earnings. Arithmetically, because this equivalence occurs via equity investment accounting, we must record the net income-statement effect for the year ended December 31, 2016 (i.e., discussed in point

#3, above) in the parent's pre-consolidation "Investment in Subsidiary" account with the corresponding income statement effect recognized in the parent's pre-consolidation "Income (Loss) from Subsidiary." Exhibit 6.11 includes the equity method entry for the year ended December 31, 2016:

EXHIBIT 6.11	Bond Related Adjustment of the Parent's Books Under the Equity Method During the Year ended December 31, 2016		
On the books of the Parent	Income (Loss) from subsidiary . . . . Investment in subsidiary . . . . *(to recognize equity method effects of recognition of the previously confirmed gain related to amortization of the bond discounts)*	18,322	18,322

Thus, cumulatively, through the end of December 31, 2016, the net effect on the investment account of the bond-related equity-method adjustments is a net increase of $36,644 (i.e., a $54,966 debit in Exhibit 6.9 and an $18,322 credit in Exhibit 6.11).[27] We'll see this net amount eliminated as the BOY adjustment to the investment in the consolidation entry for the year ended December 31, 2017 in Exhibit 6.12:

EXHIBIT 6.12	[I_bond] Consolidation Entries at December 31, 2017		
[I_bond] Consolidation entries for intercompany bond transactions	Bond payable. . . . . Interest income. . . . . Discount on bond payable . . . . Investment in bond . . . . Interest expense . . . . BOY Investment in subsidiary . . . . *(to eliminate intercompany bond holdings, the intercompany interest income and expense, and to record the BOY elimination of the prior period bond gain and subsequent discount amortization from the investment account)*	2,000,000 115,640	17,318 1,964,360 97,318 36,644

Just as it did before, the parent company also needs to adjust the "Investment in Subsidiary" and the "Income (Loss) from Subsidiary" accounts for the equity method for the year ended December 31, 2017. Exhibit 6.13 includes this adjustment:

EXHIBIT 6.13	Bond Related Adjustment of the Parent's Books Under the Equity Method During the Year Ended December 31, 2017		
On the books of the Parent	Income (Loss) from subsidiary . . . . Investment in subsidiary . . . . *(to recognize equity method effects of recognition of the previously confirmed gain related to amortization of the bond discounts)*	18,322	18,322

Thus, cumulatively, through the end of December 31, 2017, the net effect on the investment account of the bond-related equity-method adjustments is a net increase of $18,322 (i.e., a $54,966 debit in Exhibit 6.9, an $18,322 credit in Exhibit 6.11, and an $18,322 credit in Exhibit 6.13). We'll see this net amount eliminated as the BOY adjustment to the investment in the consolidation entry for the year ended December 31, 2018 in Exhibit 6.14. Notice that this entry only deals with the

[27] FASB ASC 810 does not mandate any specific proportion of elimination to the parent or the subsidiary. Therefore, even if the parent company owns less than 100 percent of the subsidiary and regardless of whether the purchasing party is the parent or the subsidiary, we assign 100 percent of the intercompany bond elimination to the parent's interest in the subsidiary. This is consistent with the parent company being in control, and therefore responsible for the constructive retirement of the debt, even in cases where the subsidiary purchases the parent's bonds on the open market.

discount-related accounts and the investment because the bond payable was settled at its face amount of $2,000,000 (i.e., during 2018 the discounts were completely amortized and on December 31, 2018 the subsidiary paid the parent $2,000,000):

EXHIBIT 6.14	[I_bond] Consolidation Entries at December 31, 2018		
[I_bond] Consolidation entries for intercompany bond transactions	Interest income.	115,640	
	Interest expense		97,318
	BOY Investment in subsidiary		18,322
	(to eliminate the intercompany interest income and expense, and to record the BOY elimination of the prior period bond gain and subsequent discount amortization from the investment account)		

As we noted in prior years, proper application of the equity method means that the parent's pre-consolidation net income equals the parent's (post-consolidation) consolidated net income attributable to the controlling interest, and the parent's pre-consolidation retained earnings equals the parent's (post-consolidation) consolidated retained earnings. The only way this can happen is if the income-statement effects included in the consolidation adjustment in Exhibit 6.14 are also recorded in the parent's pre-consolidation financial statements via the equity method. Thus, Exhibit 6.15 includes the equity method entry for the year ended December 31, 2018:

EXHIBIT 6.15	Bond Related Adjustment of the Parent's Books Under the Equity Method During the Year Ended December 31, 2018	
On the books of the Parent	Income (loss) from subsidiary.	18,322
	Investment in subsidiary	18,322
	(to recognize equity method effects of recognition of the previously confirmed gain related to amortization of the bond discounts)	

After December 31, 2018, the deferred gain will have been fully amortized and the face amount of the bond is paid off. Indeed, cumulatively, through the end of December 31, 2018, the net effect on the investment account of the bond-related equity-method adjustments is a net increase of $0 (i.e., a $54,966 debit in Exhibit 6.9, an $18,322 credit in Exhibit 6.11, an $18,322 credit in Exhibit 6.13, and an $18,322 credit in Exhibit 6.15). This means there is no bond-related effects in the investment account to eliminate in future years. Therefore, in future years there are no additional [I_bond] consolidation entries required.

TOPIC REVIEW 5

Constructive Retirement of Intercompany Debt—Equity Method

Assume that a parent company acquires a 90% interest in its subsidiary on January 1, 2012. On the date of acquisition, the fair value of the 90 percent controlling interest was $495,000 and the fair value of the 10 percent noncontrolling interest was $55,000. On January 1, 2012, the book value of net assets equaled $550,000 and the fair value of the identifiable net assets equaled the book value of identifiable net assets (i.e., there was no AAP or Goodwill).

On December 31, 2013, the parent company issued $1,000,000 (face) 6 percent, five-year bonds to an unaffiliated company for $1,043,295 (i.e., the bonds had an effective yield of 5 percent). The bonds pay interest annually on December 31, and the bond premium is amortized using the straight-line method. This results in annual bond-payable premium amortization equal to $8,659 per year.

On December 31, 2015, the subsidiary paid $948,458 to purchase all of the outstanding parent company bonds (i.e., the bonds had an effective yield of 8 percent). The bond discount is amortized using the straight-line method, which results in annual bond-investment discount amortization equal to $17,181 per year.

The parent uses the equity method of pre-consolidation investment bookkeeping. The parent and the Subsidiary report the following financial statements for the year ended December 31, 2016:

	Parent	Subsidiary		Parent	Subsidiary
Income statement:			**Balance sheet:**		
Sales.	$10,000,000	$1,000,000	Assets		
Cost of goods sold.	(7,200,000)	(600,000)	Cash	$ 925,258	$ 323,250
Gross profit.	2,800,000	400,000	Accounts receivable.	1,750,000	430,000
Income from subsidiary	169,623		Inventory.	2,600,000	550,000
Bond interest income		77,181	PPE, net	10,060,000	1,030,000
Bond interest expense	(51,341)		Equity investment.	705,242	
Operating & other expenses. . . .	(1,500,000)	(260,000)	Investment in bonds.		965,639
Net income	$1,418,282	$ 217,181		$16,040,500	$3,298,889
Statement of retained earnings:			Liabilities and stockholders' equity		
BOY retained earnings	$5,741,500	$ 225,000	Accounts payable.	$ 844,400	$ 478,000
Net income	1,418,282	217,181	Current liabilities.	1,190,000	500,000
Dividends	(284,000)	(20,000)	Bonds payable	1,017,318	
EOY retained earnings	$6,875,782	$ 422,181	Long-term liabilities	1,500,000	1,594,708
			Common stock.	553,000	149,000
			APIC	4,060,000	155,000
			Retained earnings	6,875,782	422,181
				$16,040,500	$3,298,889

Required

Provide the consolidation entries and prepare a consolidation worksheet for the year ended December 31, 2016.

The solution to this review problem can be found on pages 443–444.

Acquisition from Unaffiliated Entity of Investment in Affiliated Company's Debt—Cost Method

Based on our discussion in Chapters 3 through 5, you should recognize that the consolidation procedures necessary when the parent company uses the cost method of pre-consolidation bookkeeping is very similar to the consolidation procedures necessary when the parent company uses the equity method of pre-consolidation bookkeeping. To review, conceptually, the best way to consolidate under these circumstances is to propose a "catch-up" [ADJ] consolidating entry to make the parent's beginning of year investment and Retained Earnings accounts be on an "as if equity method" basis. After that catch-up adjustment, except for some subtle differences in the [C] entry, the consolidation process is the same as the process we already discussed for the equity method.

As we discussed in previous chapters, the [ADJ] entry will be primarily based on the change in the subsidiary's Retained Earnings from the acquisition date to the beginning of the year of consolidation multiplied by the parent's ownership percentage. In addition, under the equity method, the p% AAP would have been annually amortized into net income (which gets accumulated in Retained Earnings) and out of the investment account. Thus, the [ADJ] entry also captures the accumulated amortization of the AAP from the acquisition date to the beginning of the period of consolidation. As we stated in Chapters 4 and 5, all beginning-of-year unconfirmed asset profits must be removed. With respect to the present chapter, all confirmed intercompany-debt gains and losses must also be included in the [ADJ] entry.

We can illustrate the computation of the [ADJ] amount if we add a few facts to the intercompany bond example discussed in the previous section. In that example, we assumed that a parent company purchased, on December 31, 2015, a subsidiary's bond from an unaffiliated entity at the current market price of $1,893,080. Immediately following the purchase by the parent, the subsidiary still has the bond outstanding and reports the bond on its pre-consolidation balance sheet at $1,948,046 ($2,000,000 face amount less the unamortized discount of $51,954). Exhibit 6.7 presents the bond amortization schedules for the parent and the subsidiary following the purchase of the bonds by the parent.

For purposes of illustrating the cost-method modification of the example, assume that the subsidiary's Retained Earnings was $1,000,000 on the date the parent acquired its controlling 100% interest in the subsidiary. The beginning of year (i.e., January 1, 2016) balance of Retained Earnings for the subsidiary equals $1,500,000. In addition, assume that, on the date the parent acquired control of the subsidiary, the AAP was equal to $900,000. The unamortized AAP at the beginning of the year of consolidation is equal to $600,000. Given these facts, the amount of the **[ADJ]** entry is computed as follows:

p% of change in RE(S) from acquisition date through BOY	$500,000
Less: Cumulative p% AAP amortization from acquisition date through BOY	(300,000)
Plus: 100% of the BOY confirmed (but unrecognized) intercompany debt retirement gain	54,966
[ADJ] amount.	$254,966

Exhibit 6.16 provides the **[ADJ]** entry that converts the pre-consolidation beginning-of-year investment account and retained earnings of the parent company to an "as if equity method" basis.

EXHIBIT 6.16	**[ADJ]** Consolidation for Fiscal Year End December 31, 2016

[ADJ] Catch-up adjustment for cost-method consolidation	Investment in subsidiary. . . . . 254,966 Retained earnings of parent at BOY . . . . 254,966 *(to convert the pre-consolidation beginning-of-year investment account and retained earnings of the parent company to an "as if equity method" basis)*

As we illustrated in Chapters 3 through 5, all of the remaining **C-E-A-D-I** entries are identical to the equity-method consolidation, except the **[C]** entry will eliminate the dividend income instead of the equity-method income from the subsidiary. The cost-method Topic Review 6 more fully illustrates this important point.

TOPIC REVIEW 6

Constructive Retirement of Intercompany Debt—Cost Method

Assume that a parent company acquires a 90% interest in its subsidiary on January 1, 2012. On the date of acquisition, the fair value of the 90 percent controlling interest was $742,500 and the fair value of the 10 percent noncontrolling interest was $82,500. On January 1, 2012, the book value of net assets equaled $825,000 and the fair value of the identifiable net assets equaled the book value of identifiable net assets (i.e., there was no AAP or Goodwill). On January 1, 2012, the Retained Earnings of the subsidiary was $369,000.

On December 31, 2013, the parent company issued $1,500,000 (face) 6 percent, five-year bonds to an unaffiliated company for $1,564,942 (i.e., the bonds had an effective yield of 5 percent). The bonds pay interest annually on December 31, and the bond premium is amortized using the straight-line method. This results in annual bond-payable premium amortization equal to $12,988 per year.

On December 31, 2015, the subsidiary paid $1,422,687 to purchase all of the outstanding parent company bonds (i.e., the bonds had an effective yield of 8 percent). The bond discount is amortized using the straight-line method, which results in annual bond-investment discount amortization equal to $25,771 per year.

Cost Method

The parent uses the cost method of pre-consolidation investment bookkeeping. The parent and the subsidiary report the following financial statements for the year ended December 31, 2016:

	Parent	Subsidiary		Parent	Subsidiary
Income statement:			**Balance sheet:**		
Sales.	$13,500,000	$1,650,000	Cash.	$ 1,350,000	$ 484,875
Cost of goods sold.	(9,300,000)	(1,050,000)	Accounts receivable.	2,625,000	645,000
Gross profit.	4,200,000	600,000	Inventories	3,900,000	825,000
Income from subsidiary	27,000	—	PPE, net	7,500,000	1,545,000
Bond interest income.		115,771	Investment in subsidiary.	742,500	
Bond interest expense	(77,012)		Investment in bond (net).		1,448,458
Operating & other expenses. . . .	(2,250,000)	(390,000)	Total assets.	$16,117,500	$4,948,333
Net income.	$1,899,988	$ 325,771			
Statement of retained earnings:					
BOY retained earnings	$2,524,322	$ 337,500	Accounts payable.	$ 913,713	$ 717,000
Net income.	1,899,988	325,771	Other current liabilities	1,350,000	750,000
Dividends declared.	(426,000)	(30,000)	Bond payable (net)	1,525,977	
EOY retained earnings	$3,998,310	$ 633,271	Other long-term liabilities	3,000,000	2,392,062
			Common stock.	829,500	223,500
			APIC	4,500,000	232,500
			Retained earnings	3,988,310	633,271
			Total liabilities and equity	$16,117,500	$4,948,333

Required

Provide the consolidation entries and prepare a consolidation worksheet for the year ended December 31, 2016.

The solution to this review problem can be found on pages 445–446.

LO4 Describe the consolidation procedures necessary when subsidiary companies have outstanding preferred stock.

PARENT INVESTMENT IN A SUBSIDIARY WITH PREFERRED STOCK OUTSTANDING

The existence of preferred stock in the subsidiary does not present any new conceptual issues. If the parent owns some or all of the preferred stock, it must be eliminated against the Equity Investment account like our elimination of common stock. And, the portion of the preferred stock not owned by the parent is included in the noncontrolling interest equity on the balance sheet. Further, any dividends accrued on preferred stock are attributed to noncontrolling interests in the consolidated income statement.

We discuss the consolidation issues relating to subsidiary preferred stock in this section. We begin with an example in which the parent does not own any of the preferred stock, then consider the case in which the parent owns all of the preferred stock, and conclude with an example when a portion of the preferred stock is owned by both the parent and the noncontrolling interests.

Effects of Subsidiary Preferred Stock on [C] and [E] Consolidation Entries

Preferred stock has a preference as to dividends over common shareholders, meaning that dividends are first paid to preferred shareholders before any dividends are paid to common shareholders. As a result, any dividends declared on preferred stock should be deducted from the subsidiary's net income before attributing the remainder to controlling and noncontrolling common shareholders.

In each of the examples below, we assume that the parent owns 80% of a subsidiary that has 4% preferred stock outstanding with a reported par value of $1,000,000. Aside from the preferred dividends, no other dividends are paid (i.e., no dividends are paid to the common shareholders). We also assume that the subsidiary reports net income of $100,000. Subsidiary net income is, therefore, attributed to controlling and noncontrolling shareholders as follows:

Subsidiary net income	$100,000
Preferred dividends	(40,000)
Income accruing to common shareholders	$60,000
Income attributable to noncontrolling interest (20%)	12,000
Income attributable to the controlling interest (80%)	$48,000

<u>None</u> of the Preferred Stock is Owned by the Parent

The [C] and [E] entries of our **C-E-A-D-I** consolidation-entry sequence are affected by preferred stock holdings. If none of the preferred stock is owned by the parent company, all of the preferred stock equity account is assigned to the noncontrolling interests.

Our **[C]** entry is as follows:

[C]			
	Income (loss) from subsidiary	48,000	
	Net income attributable to noncontrolling shareholders	12,000	
	Noncontrolling interest ($40,000 − $12,000)	28,000	
	Preferred dividends		40,000
	Investment in subsidiary		48,000
	(to eliminate the equity income that the parent recognizes, reallocate the noncontrolling shareholders' share of net income to the noncontrolling interest equity account, and eliminate the preferred dividends)		

This entry eliminates the $48,000 of equity income that the parent recorded on its 80% Equity Investment in the Subsidiary. The second part of the entry reallocates $12,000 (20%) of the $60,000 of consolidated net income available to common shareholders to noncontrolling interests and attributes that profit to the noncontrolling interest equity account. This entry also eliminates all of the preferred dividends and records them as a reduction of the noncontrolling shareholders equity account. (Again, we assume here that none of the preferred stock is owned by the parent company.) In addition, if the subsidiary also declares common dividends, they are treated in the usual manner (e.g., the Chapter 5 [C] consolidation entries).

Our **[E]** entry relating to the preferred stock is as follows:[28]

[E]			
	Preferred stock	1,000,000	
	Noncontrolling interest		1,000,000
	(to eliminate the preferred stock equity account and reallocate to the noncontrolling interest equity account)		

<u>All</u> of the Preferred Stock is Owned by the Parent

If all of the preferred stock is owned by the parent company, then all of the preferred stock equity account is eliminated against the Investment in Subsidiary account on the parent's balance sheet. Our **[C]** entry is as follows:

[C]			
	Income (loss) from subsidiary	48,000	
	Net income attributable to noncontrolling shareholders	12,000	
	Preferred dividends		40,000
	Investment in subsidiary ($48,000 − $40,000)		8,000
	Noncontrolling interest		12,000
	(to eliminate the equity income that the parent recognizes, reallocate the noncontrolling shareholders' share of net income to the noncontrolling interest equity account, and eliminate the preferred dividends)		

[28] Note that the remainder of the [E] entry relating to common stock and retained earnings is not affected, so those accounts are excluded. We also exclude the common stock and retained earnings account in the remaining case where all of the preferred stock is owned by the parent and the case where 30% of the preferred stock is owned by the parent.

Our [E] entry relating to the preferred stock is as follows:

[E]	Preferred stock..	1,000,000	
	Investment in subsidiary		1,000,000
	(to eliminate the preferred stock equity account and the portion attributable to the controlling interest equity)		

30% of the Preferred Stock is Owned by the Parent
If 30% of the preferred stock is owned by the parent company, 30% of the preferred stock equity account is eliminated against the Equity Investment account on the parent's balance sheet and 70% is allocated to the noncontrolling interests equity account. Our [C] entry is as follows:

[C]	Income (loss) from subsidiary..	48,000	
	Net income attributable to noncontrolling shareholders	12,000	
	Noncontrolling interest (70% × $440,000) − $12,000....................	16,000	
	Preferred dividends......................................		40,000
	Investment in subsidiary [$48,000 − (30% × $40,000)]		36,000
	(to eliminate the equity income that the parent recognizes, reallocate the noncontrolling shareholders' share of net income to the noncontrolling interest equity account, and eliminate the preferred dividends)		

Our [E] entry relating to the preferred stock is as follows:

[E]	Preferred stock...	1,000,000	
	Investment in subsidiary (30% × $1,000,000)		300,000
	Noncontrolling interest (70% × $1,000,000).....................		700,000
	(to eliminate the preferred stock equity account and reallocate to the noncontrolling interest and controlling interest accounts)		

CHAPTER SUMMARY

In this chapter, we discussed a loosely-related set of advanced issues related to consolidations. Most importantly, we provided a comprehensive description of the integrated consolidation model currently promulgated in FASB ASC 810. For at least the last 50 years, United States GAAP has required parent companies to consolidate any entities in which the parent company has a "controlling financial interest." During the last half-century, the definition of a controlling financial interest has evolved with the increasing sophistication of off-balance-sheet arrangements. Currently, depending on the circumstances, companies might make the determination of a controlling financial interest based on a "variable interest entity" (VIE) evaluation or a (majority) "voting interest entity" evaluation. The VIE evaluation is relatively new to GAAP, and was motivated by the widespread use (and abuse) of off-balance-sheet special purpose entities (SPEs). As the name implies, SPEs are entities that are formed to satisfy some special purpose, like holding financial assets and processing related cash flows. There are many legitimate uses for SPEs, and properly using SPEs can lead to reduced borrowing costs for the companies that sponsor the SPEs. An important point to understand about the structure of U.S. GAAP is that the VIE evaluation must be made *before* an entity is considered a candidate for consolidation via the traditional assessment of voting interests.

The concept of a VIE is *much* broader than the concept of an SPE. VIEs can take any organizational form, including partnerships, trusts, joint ventures, and corporations. VIEs often have such small amounts of equity capital at risk that they cannot finance their activities or execute their operations without an infusion of additional subordinated funding to absorb some of the VIE's expected future losses. Because of this, the equity holders are not usually in control of the entity. Instead, some other holder of a non-equity variable interest is in control of the VIE. This is why the traditional (majority) voting-interest consolidation model is not the best way to determine which party is in control of a VIE.

If a reporting company determines that it has a variable interest in a VIE, then the reporting company must determine if it is the primary beneficiary of the VIE. The primary beneficiary is the variable interest holder deemed to have a "controlling financial interest" (i.e., must consolidate the VIE). The criteria to determine the primary beneficiary requires both the power to direct the most significant activities of the VIE and also the obligation to absorb the losses/gains of the VIE. Even if a holder of a variable interest in a VIE is not the primary beneficiary, the holder of a variable interest has significant disclosure requirements related to the VIE.

When a primary beneficiary first consolidates a VIE, the primary beneficiary must determine whether the VIE is a "business," as that term is defined in FASB ASC 805. If the consolidated VIE is a business, then all ownership interests are measured at fair value at the initial consolidation date and goodwill (or bargain acquisition gain) is determined by subtracting the fair value of the identifiable net assets from the overall entity-wide fair value. If the consolidated VIE is not a business, then goodwill cannot be recognized.

Another issue we discuss is the holding of affiliates' debt within a consolidated group of companies. As we discuss in previous chapters, intercompany payables and receivables must be eliminated during preparation of consolidated financial statements (i.e., a single economic entity cannot owe itself money). If one affiliate (e.g., a parent company) directly borrows from another affiliate (e.g., a subsidiary), then the consolidation entry is pretty simple because the amounts of the payable and receivable will usually exactly offset. It is much more complex if one affiliate acquires another affiliate's long-term debt from an unaffiliated third party because the effective interest rate implicit in the debt likely changed after original issuance. This means the carrying amount of the debt on the affiliated borrower's books likely will not equal the amount for which the affiliated holder of the debt paid to acquire the intercompany obligation.

The affiliated companies will continue to recognize interest expense and interest income on their separate pre-consolidation accounting books. These intercompany income and expense amounts, for the periods after acquisition of the intercompany debt, must be eliminated in preparation of the consolidated financial statements. In addition, the balance sheet accounts related to the intercompany debt must be eliminated. These consolidation adjustments must be made each year until the intercompany obligation is settled (or, alternatively, until it is transferred to an unaffiliated company). In addition, under the equity method, the parent company must include any income-statement (net) effects in the determination of equity-method Income from Subsidiary and in the determination of the Investment in Subsidiary balance sheet account.

Finally, we discussed the implications on consolidations of subsidiaries having outstanding preferred stock. Because preferred stock is part of a subsidiary's owners' equity, it will not appear in the consolidated balance sheet. (Recall that the **C-E-A-D-I** entries completely remove subsidiary stockholders' equity.) If the parent company owns none of the preferred stock, then the preferred stock carrying amount is reclassified into noncontrolling interest during consolidation. If the parent company owns all of the preferred stock, then it is reflected in the investment account and is completely eliminated in consolidation and implicitly reflected in the controlling interest. If the parent company owns between zero and 100 percent of the preferred stock, then the preferred stock is completely eliminated, with the noncontrolling interest adjusted for the proportion of the preferred stock value not owned by the parent company.

COMPREHENSIVE REVIEW

(This comprehensive review problem includes business combinations and consolidations concepts discussed in Chapters 1 through 5 and the intercompany bond material from the current chapter.)

A parent company acquired 90 percent of the stock of a subsidiary company on January 1, 2012, for $765,000. On this date, the balances of the subsidiary's stockholders' equity accounts were Common Stock, $119,200; Additional Paid-in Capital, 124,000; and Retained Earnings, $306,800. On January 1, 2012, the market value for the 10% of shares not purchased by the parent was $85,000.

On January 1, 2012, the subsidiary's recorded book values were equal to fair values for all items except one: a previously unrecorded patent asset had a book value of $0 and a fair value of $200,000. Both companies use the FIFO inventory method and sell all of their inventories at least once per year. On the acquisition date, the patent had a remaining economic useful life of 10 years.

On January 1, 2015, the parent sold a building to the subsidiary for $150,000. On this date, the building was carried on the parent's books (net of accumulated depreciation) at $96,000. Both companies estimated that the building has a remaining life of 10 years on the intercompany sale date, with no salvage value.

Each company routinely sells merchandise to the other company, with a profit margin of 40 percent of selling price (regardless of the direction of the sale). During 2016, intercompany sales amount to $60,000, of which $25,000 of merchandise remains in the ending inventory of the parent. On December 31, 2016, $20,000 of these intercompany sales remained unpaid. Additionally, the parent's December 31, 2015 inventory includes $15,000 of merchandise purchased in the preceding year from the subsidiary. During 2015, intercompany sales amount to $50,000, and on December 31, 2015, $10,000 of these intercompany sales remained unpaid.

On December 31, 2013, the subsidiary company issued a $500,000 (face) 5 percent, five-year bond to an unaffiliated company for $522,259 (i.e., the bond had an effective yield of 4 percent). The bond pays interest annually on December 31, and the bond premium is amortized using the straight-line method. This results in annual bond-payable premium amortization equal to approximately $4,452 per year.

On December 31, 2015, the parent paid $486,635 to purchase the outstanding subsidiary company bond (i.e., the bond had an effective yield of 6 percent). The bond discount is amortized using the straight-line method, which results in annual bond-investment discount amortization equal to $4,455 per year.

The parent accounts for its investment in the subsidiary using the equity method. Unconfirmed profits are allocated pro rata, except for intercompany bond profits which are allocated 100 percent to the parent company.

The pre-closing trial balances (and additional information) for the two companies for the year ended December 31, 2016, are as follows:

Pre-Closing Trial Balance	Parent	Subsidiary
Debits		
Cash.	$ 900,013	$ 400,000
Accounts receivable.	1,113,100	480,000
Inventories	1,840,000	623,749
Property, plant and equipment, net	8,048,000	824,000
Investment in bond (net).	491,090	—
Investment in subsidiary.	594,401	—
Cost of goods sold.	5,760,000	480,000
Depreciation and amortization expense.	700,000	58,000
Operating & other expenses.	500,000	150,000
Bond interest expense	—	20,548
Dividends declared.	227,200	16,000
Total debits.	$20,173,804	$3,052,297
Credits		
Accounts payable.	$ 808,000	$ 240,000
Other current liabilities	995,548	480,193
Bond payable (net).	—	508,904
Other long-term liabilities	2,000,000	600,000
Common stock.	442,400	119,200
APIC	3,248,000	124,000
Retained earnings (Jan. 1, 2016)	4,593,201	180,000
Sales.	8,000,000	800,000
Bond interest income	29,455	—
Equity income from subsidiary.	57,200	—
Total credits	$20,173,804	$3,052,297
Additional information		
Retained earnings (Dec. 31, 2016).	$ 5,492,656	$ 255,452
Net income.	$ 1,126,655	$ 91,452

a. Prepare a consolidation spreadsheet using the December 31, 2016 pre-closing trial balance information for the parent and subsidiary.[29]

b. Disaggregate and document the activity for the 100% Acquisition Accounting Premium (AAP), the controlling interest AAP and the noncontrolling interest AAP.

c. Calculate and organize the profits and losses on intercompany transactions and balances.

d. Compute the pre-consolidation equity investment account beginning and ending balances starting with the stockholders' equity of the subsidiary.

e. Reconstruct the activity in the parent's pre-consolidation equity investment T-account for the year of consolidation.

f. Independently compute the owners' equity attributable to the noncontrolling interest beginning and ending balances starting with the owners' equity of the subsidiary.

g. Independently calculate consolidated net income, controlling interest net income and noncontrolling interest net income.

h. Complete the consolidating entries according to the **C-E-A-D-I** sequence and complete the consolidation worksheet.

The solution to this review problem can be found on pages 447–454.

QUESTIONS

1. What is a special purpose entity?

2. What is meant when a special purpose entity is called bankruptcy remote?

3. What is the primary benefit most likely obtained by the sponsor of a special purpose entity when the sponsor transfers assets to a special purpose entity?

4. One motive for transferring assets to a special purpose entity is to move assets "off-balance-sheet." What are the primary benefits for operating companies in obtaining off-balance-sheet treatment for assets?

5. Refer to our discussion of Ford Motor Credit LLC (FMC) in the Special Purpose Entity section of the chapter. Why does FMC's use of special purpose entities suggest that there are legitimate financing benefits to transferring assets to special purpose entities?

6. What is a variable interest entity?

7. What is a voting interest entity?

8. Describe how FASB ASC 810 ("Consolidation") integrates to analysis of variable interest entities and voting interest entities into a single, comprehensive consolidation model.

9. What is a variable interest?

10. What is the purpose of the business-related scope exception in FASB ASC 810 ("Consolidation")?

11. If a legal entity does not qualify for the business-related scope exception in FASB ASC 810 ("Consolidation"), what are the criteria that determine whether a legal entity is a VIE?

12. What are expected losses and expected residual returns?

13. What is a primary beneficiary?

14. What conditions determine whether a reporting entity is the primary beneficiary of a variable interest entity?

15. If an operating company is the primary beneficiary of a variable interest entity under FASB ASC 810 ("Consolidation"), why do we need to know whether the variable interest entity meets the definition of a business under FASB ASC 805 ("Business Combinations")?

---

[29] As we mention as part of the comprehensive review problems in Chapters 4 and 5, we believe there is great pedagogical value in students creating their own functioning consolidation spreadsheets from trial balance information. Programming the formulas that result in articulating consolidated financial statements can help students better understand the basic relations in financial statements and the mechanics of consolidation. However, this is not necessary, and, in part a. of the solution to this comprehensive review, we provide the trial balance information converted to financial statement format.

16. Assume a Parent company acquires bonds directly from a Subsidiary that issued the bonds. Describe in plain language the consolidation adjustments the Parent must make in preparing its consolidated financial statements in the year of the purchase of the Subsidiary's bonds. Describe in plain language the consolidation adjustments the Parent must make in preparing its consolidated financial statements in the years after the purchase of the Subsidiary's bonds.

17. Would your answer to question 16 change if, instead, a Subsidiary acquires bonds directly from a Parent company that issued the bonds?

18. Assume a Parent company acquires from an unaffiliated third party bonds that were issued by one of its subsidiaries (i.e., they are bonds payable by the Subsidiary). Describe in plain language the consolidation adjustments the Parent must make in preparing its consolidated financial statements in the year of the purchase of the Subsidiary's bonds. Describe in plain language the consolidation adjustments the Parent must make in preparing its consolidated financial statements in the years after the purchase of the Subsidiary's bonds.

19. Would your answer to question 18 change if, instead, a Subsidiary acquires from an unaffiliated third party bonds that were issued by the Parent company?

20. When a Parent company acquires from an unaffiliated third party a Subsidiary's debt instruments (or vice versa), how is the consolidated gain or loss on constructive retirement of the debt calculated? In what period should the gain or loss be recognized in the consolidated financial statements?

21. When a Parent company acquires from an unaffiliated third party a Subsidiary's debt instruments (or vice versa), the consolidated financial statements should recognize gain or loss on constructive retirement of the debt. On the date of the affiliated-company bond purchase, how does this gain or loss relate to the discount and/or premium accounts recognized on the separate pre-consolidation financial statements of the Parent and Subsidiary companies?

22. When a Parent company acquires from an unaffiliated third party a Subsidiary's debt instruments (or vice versa), the consolidated financial statements should recognize gain or loss on constructive retirement of the debt. Over the remaining life of the bonds, how does this gain or loss get recognized in the separate pre-consolidation financial statements of the Parent and Subsidiary companies?

23. When a Parent company acquires from an unaffiliated third party a Subsidiary's debt instruments (or vice versa), the consolidated financial statements should recognize gain or loss on constructive retirement of the debt. Thereafter, the $[\mathrm{I}_{bond}]$ consolidation entry is required to correct the beginning balance of the Investment in Subsidiary account. Why is this adjustment required? Why does the amount of this gradually decline over the remaining life of the bonds?

24. A Parent company acquires from an unaffiliated third party the outstanding bonds of its Subsidiary. In the consolidated financial statements, this transaction resulted in a loss on constructive retirement of debt equal to $100,000. How should this loss be allocated to the controlling and noncontrolling interests? Why?

25. A Parent company owns a 70 percent controlling interest in the voting common stock of its Subsidiary. The Subsidiary also has outstanding 10,000 shares of 3% cumulative preferred stock outstanding with par value equal to $5,000,000. If the parent company owns none of the preferred stock, how should the preferred stock be accounted for in the consolidated financial statements?

26. How would your answer to question 25 change if the parent company owned 100 percent of the preferred stock?

27. How would your answer to question 25 change if the parent company owned 35 percent of the preferred stock?

Assignments with the 🔵 logo in the margin are available in BusinessCourse.
See the Preface of the book for details.

MULTIPLE CHOICE

LO1   28. **Attributes of Special Purpose Entities**

Special-purpose entities

a.   Are usually used in fraudulent business transactions

b.   Are usually "robot-like" entities that have no distinct physical location, have no independent management or employees, and make no strategic business decisions

c.   Usually have most of their operations financed by equity investors

d.   Are usually only used to obtain "off balance sheet" treatment of risky assets

29. Attributes of Special Purpose Entities

Which of the following characteristics does not usually exist for a special purpose entity (SPE) that is used in a securitization transaction?

a. The SPE is usually legally distinct from the sponsoring company that forms the SPE and is bankruptcy remote

b. If the SPE is formed to securitize accounts receivable, then the SPE's security holders are only repaid if the securitized accounts receivable are collected

c. The SPE is expected to seek strategic business opportunities that maximize returns to the SPE's equity investors

d. All of the above

30. Examples of variable interests

Which of the following is not a variable interest?

a. Common stock

b. Guarantee of indebtedness

c. Corporate bond rated BBB- by Standard & Poors

d. U.S. treasury bond

31. Scope of FASB ASC 810 ("Consolidations")

Which of the following is not automatically exempt from the consolidation guidance included in FASB ASC 810 ("Consolidations")

a. Legal entities that meet the definition of "businesses" as defined by FASB ASC 805 ("Business Combinations")

b. Legal entities that are not-for profit

c. Legal entities that administer employee benefit plans subject to FASB ASC 712 ("Compensation—Nonretirement Postemployment Benefits")

d. Legal entities that qualify as investments accounted for at fair value in accordance with the specialized guidance in FASB ASC 946 ("Financial Services—Investment Companies")

32. Shortcut to voting interest entity consolidation evaluation

If a legal entity is within the scope of FASB ASC 810 ("Consolidations"), when can a reporting company completely skip an evaluation of whether the legal entity is a variable interest entity (i.e., the "variable interest entity model") and solely determine consolidation based on whether the reporting company owns a majority of the voting common stock of the legal entity (i.e., the "voting interest entity model")?

a. The legal entity is only capitalized with a bank loan and voting common stock

b. The legal entity satisfies one of the four conditions for the business-related scope exception

c. The reporting company does not have the power to direct the activities that most significantly impact the legal entity's business activities

d. The reporting company does not have the obligation to absorb the losses of the legal entity that could potentially be significant to the legal entity

33. Determination of primary beneficiary

FASB ASC 810 ("Consolidations") states that a Primary Beneficiary is the company that consolidates a variable interest entity (VIE). What is the triggering condition for a reporting entity to be deemed the Primary Beneficiary of a VIE in which the reporting entity has a variable interest?

a. The reporting entity owns a majority of the voting common stock of the VIE

b. The reporting entity has the power to direct the activities of a VIE that most significantly impact the VIE's economic performance

c. The reporting entity has the obligation to absorb losses of the VIE that could potentially be significant to the VIE or the right to receive benefits from the VIE that could potentially be significant to the VIE.

d. The reporting entity has both b and c, above

34. Initial recognition of consolidated legal entity by primary beneficiary

When a Primary Beneficiary initially consolidates a variable interest entity (VIE), the primary beneficiary must determine whether the VIE is a "business" as defined by FASB ASC 805 ("Business Combinations") because

a. FASB ASC 805 only applies to acquisitions of "businesses," so the Primary Beneficiary can avoid consolidation if the VIE is not a business

b. Goodwill is only recognized by the Primary Beneficiary when a consolidated VIE is a "business"

c. The initial consolidation-date fair value of the VIE's identifiable net assets will depend on whether the VIE is a "business"

d. If the VIE is not a "business," then a gain or loss is always recognized upon initial consolidation by a Primary Beneficiary

LO3

35. Effects on consolidated financial statements of acquisition of affiliate's debt from non-affiliate

On January 1, 2016, a Parent company has a debt outstanding that was originally issued at a discount and was purchased, on issuance, by an unaffiliated party. On January 1, 2016, a Subsidiary of the Parent purchased the debt from the unaffiliated party. The debt was purchased by the Subsidiary at a slight premium. The Parent is a calendar year company. Which one of the following statements is true?

a. The consolidated balance sheet at December 31, 2016 will report the debt, and the consolidated income statement for the year ended December 31, 2016 will not report any interest expense from the debt

b. The consolidated balance sheet at December 31, 2016 will report none of the debt, and the consolidated income statement for the year ended December 31, 2016 will report a gain or loss from constructive retirement of the debt and will not report any interest expense from the debt

c. The consolidated balance sheet at December 31, 2016 will report the debt, and the consolidated income statement for the year ended December 31, 2016 will report a gain or loss from constructive retirement of the debt and will not report any interest expense from the debt

d. The consolidated balance sheet at December 31, 2016 will report none of the debt, and the consolidated income statement for the year ended December 31, 2016 will report a gain or loss from constructive retirement of the debt and will report interest expense from the debt

LO3

36. Effects on consolidated financial statements of acquisition of affiliate's debt from non-affiliate

On January 1, 2016, a Parent company has a debt outstanding that was originally issued at a discount and was purchased, on issuance, by an unaffiliated party. On July 1, 2016, a Subsidiary of the Parent purchased the debt from the unaffiliated party. The debt was purchased by the Subsidiary at a slight premium. The Parent is a calendar year company. Which one of the following statements is true?

a. The consolidated balance sheet at December 31, 2016 will report none of the debt, and the consolidated income statement for the year ended December 31, 2016 will not report any interest expense from the debt

b. The consolidated balance sheet at December 31, 2016 will report none of the debt, and the consolidated income statement for the year ended December 31, 2016 will report a gain or loss from constructive retirement of the debt and will not report any interest expense from the debt

c. The consolidated balance sheet at December 31, 2016 will report the debt, and the consolidated income statement for the year ended December 31, 2016 will report a gain or loss from constructive retirement of the debt and will not report any interest expense from the debt

d. The consolidated balance sheet at December 31, 2016 will report none of the debt, and the consolidated income statement for the year ended December 31, 2016 will report a gain or loss from constructive retirement of the debt and will report some interest expense from the debt

LO3

37. Effect on consolidated net income of acquisition of affiliate's debt from non-affiliate

A Parent Company owns 100 percent of its Subsidiary. During 2015, the Parent company reports net income (by itself, without any investment income from its Subsidiary) of $500,000 and the subsidiary reports net income of $200,000. The parent had a bond payable outstanding on January 1, 2015, with a carry value equal to $420,000. The Subsidiary acquired the bond on January 1, 2015 for $395,000. During 2015, the Parent reported interest expense (related to the bond) of $35,000, while the Subsidiary reported interest income (related to the bond) of $32,000. What is consolidated net income for the year ended December 31, 2015?

a. $700,000

b. $703,000

c. $725,000

d. $728,000

38. Effect on consolidated net income of acquisition of affiliate's debt from non-affiliate

A Parent Company owns 100 percent of its Subsidiary. During 2016, the Parent company reports net income (by itself, without any investment income from its Subsidiary) of $500,000 and the subsidiary reports net income of $200,000. The parent had a bond payable outstanding on January 1,

2015, with a carry value equal to $420,000. The Subsidiary acquired the bond on January 1, 2015 for $395,000. During 2016, the Parent reported interest expense (related to the bond) of $35,000 while the Subsidiary reported interest income (related to the bond) of $32,000. What is consolidated net income for the year ended December 31, 2016?

    a. $700,000

    b. $703,000

    c. $725,000

    d. $728,000

39. **Effect on consolidated net income of acquisition of affiliate's debt from non-affiliate**

    A Parent Company owns 100 percent of its Subsidiary. During 2015, the Parent company reports net income (by itself, without any investment income from its Subsidiary) of $500,000 and the subsidiary reports net income of $200,000. The parent had a bond payable outstanding on December 31, 2015, with a carry value equal to $420,000. The Subsidiary acquired the bond on December 31, 2015 for $395,000. During 2015, the Parent reported interest expense (related to the bond) of $35,000 while the Subsidiary reported no interest income (related to the bond). What is consolidated net income for the year ended December 31, 2015?

    LO3

    AICPA Adapted

        a. $700,000

        b. $725,000

        c. $735,000

        d. $760,000

40. **Effect on consolidated net income of acquisition of affiliate's debt from non-affiliate**

    A Parent Company owns 80 percent of its Subsidiary. During 2016, the Parent company reports net income (by itself, without any investment income from its Subsidiary) of $750,000 and the subsidiary reports net income of $350,000. The Subsidiary had a bond payable outstanding on January 1 2016, with a carry value equal to $550,000. The face amount of this bond is $500,000. The Parent acquired the bond on January 1, 2016 for $565,000. During 2016, the Parent reported interest income (related to the bond) of $55,000 while the Subsidiary reported interest expense (related to the bond) of $52,000. What is consolidated net income attributable to the controlling interest for the year ended December 31, 2016?

    LO3

    AICPA Adapted

        a. $1,012,000

        b. $1,023,000

        c. $1,030,000

        d. $1,100,000

41. **Effect on consolidated net income attributable to noncontrolling interest of affiliate's debt acquired from non-affiliate**

    Refer to the facts in Multiple Choice #40, above. What is consolidated net income attributable to the noncontrolling interest for the year ended December 31, 2016?

    LO3

    AICPA Adapted

        a. $59,000

        b. $67,000

        c. $70,000

        d. $80,400

EXERCISES

42. **Application of variable interest entity provisions of FASB ASC 810 ("Consolidations")**

    A Reporting Company is evaluating for consolidation a Legal Entity in which the Reporting Company has a variable interest. The Reporting Company is currently attempting to determine if it qualifies for the business-related scope exception in FASB ASC 810 ("Consolidations"). The Reporting Company has determined that the Legal Entity is a "business" as that term is defined in FASB ASC 805 ("Business Combinations"). Unless otherwise indicated, each of the following parts of this question is independent.

    LO2

        a.   What incentive does the Reporting Company have to qualify, with respect to its variable interest in the Legal Entity, for the business-related scope exception in FASB ASC 810?

b. Assume that the chairman of the board of directors of the Reporting Company worked with an investment bank to structure the Legal Entity. Does the Reporting Company qualify for the business-related scope exception? Why?

c. Does your answer to (b) change if the Legal Entity is a joint venture? Why?

LO2 43. Business-related scope exception to consolidation under variable interest entity provisions of FASB ASC 810 ("Consolidations")

A Reporting Company is evaluating for consolidation a Legal Entity in which the Reporting Company has a variable interest. The Reporting Company is currently attempting to determine if it qualifies for the business-related scope exception in FASB ASC 810 ("Consolidations"). The Reporting Company has determined that the Legal Entity is a "business" as that term is defined in FASB ASC 805 ("Business Combinations"). Unless otherwise indicated, each of the following parts of this question is independent:

a. Assume that the sole purpose of the Legal Entity is to own and lease a building. The sole lessee of the building is the Reporting Company. Does the Reporting Company qualify for the business-related scope exception? Why?

b. Does your answer to (a) change if the Reporting Entity leases 30 percent of the building and an unaffiliated company leases the remaining 70 percent of the building? Why?

c. Does your answer to (a) change if the sole purpose of the Legal Entity is to administer the pension and postretirement plans for the Reporting Entity? Why?

LO2 44. Business-related scope exception to consolidation under variable interest entity provisions of FASB ASC 810 ("Consolidations")

A Reporting Company is evaluating for consolidation a Legal Entity in which the Reporting Company has a variable interest. The Reporting Company is currently attempting to determine if it qualifies for the business-related scope exception in FASB ASC 810 ("Consolidations"). The Reporting Company has determined that the Legal Entity is a "business" as that term is defined in FASB ASC 805 ("Business Combinations"). Unless otherwise indicated, each of the following parts of this question is independent:

a. Assume that the Legal Entity is a joint venture. The Reporting Company provides 50 percent of the equity at risk to the Legal Entity, and an unaffiliated company provides the remaining 50 percent. The Reporting Company also provides the subordinated loan to the Legal Entity. Does the Reporting Company qualify for the business-related scope exception? Why?

b. Does your answer to (a) change if, instead of the Reporting Company, the unaffiliated company provides the subordinated loan to the Legal Entity? Why?

c. Assume that the Legal Entity is a joint venture. The Reporting Company provides 50 percent of the equity at risk to the Legal Entity, and an unaffiliated company provides the remaining 50 percent. Also assume that the activities of the legal entity are primarily related to securitization of unaffiliated companies' accounts receivable. Does the Reporting Company qualify for the business-related scope exception? Why?

LO2 45. Determination of whether a legal entity is a variable interest entity

Assume a Legal Entity's capital structure consists of the following accounts:

Short-term note payable	$ 50,000
Long-term note payable	200,000
Mandatorily redeemable preferred stock	75,000
Common stock	20,000
Additional paid-in capital	50,000
Retained earnings	10,000
Total liabilities and equity	$405,000

Note that FASB ASC 480 ("Distinguishing Liabilities from Equity") requires mandatorily redeemable preferred stock to be classified as a liability for financial reporting purposes. Unless otherwise indicated, each of the following parts of this question is independent:

a. What is the maximum amount of expected losses that the Legal Entity can expect to sustain without being considered a variable interest entity (VIE)? Why?

b. How does your answer to (a) change if the lender of the long term note payable is the sole shareholder of the Legal Entity? Why?

    c.   How does your answer to (*a*) change if the long term note payable is convertible to common equity at the option of the holder of the note? Why? [Note that FASB ASC 470-20 ("Debt with Conversion and Other Features") requires convertible debt to be classified as a liability for financial reporting purposes.]

46. Determination of whether a legal entity is a variable interest entity   LO2
Assume a Legal Entity's capital structure consists of the following accounts:

Short-term note payable	$ 25,000
Bond payable	150,000
Common stock	40,000
Additional paid-in capital	100,000
Retained earnings	0
Total liabilities and equity	$315,000

Reporting Company A contributed $84,000 for a 60 percent interest in the Legal Entity and Reporting Company B contributed $56,000 for a 40 percent interest in the Legal Entity. Unless otherwise indicated, each of the following parts of this question is independent:

    a.   Assume that Reporting Company B borrowed from an unaffiliated bank $40,000 of its $56,000 capital contribution. What is the maximum amount of expected losses that the Legal Entity can expect to sustain without being considered a variable interest entity (VIE)? Why?

    b.   Assume that the Chairman of the Board of Directors of Reporting Entity A paid $40,000 to Reporting Company B for consulting services. What is the maximum amount of expected losses that the Legal Entity can expect to sustain without being considered a variable interest entity (VIE)? Why?

47. Determination of whether a legal entity is a variable interest entity   LO2
Assume a Legal Entity's capital structure consists of the following accounts:

General partner capital	$ 40,000
Limited partner capital	360,000
Total capital	$400,000

A Reporting Company is the sole general partner of the Legal Entity. The limited partnership capital was contributed by unaffiliated individual investors recruited by a regional boutique investment bank. The Reporting Company is paid a $30,000 management fee. The limited partners expect the partnership to be highly successful over the next five years. The investment bank estimated that the distribution of income to these investors should be at least $50,000 during that time period. What is the maximum amount of expected losses that the Legal Entity can expect to sustain without being considered a variable interest entity (VIE)? Why?

48. Determination of whether a legal entity is a variable interest entity   LO2
Assume that a limited partnership is formed to perform research and development. The general partner acquires a 1% interest in the limited partnership, and its investment is considered an equity investment at risk. The 99% limited partner interests are also considered substantive at-risk equity. As is customary in a limited partnership, the general partner makes day-to-day decisions about the activities of the limited partnership that most significantly impact the entity's economic performance. The limited partners have only protective rights, and do not have the ability to make decisions about the activities of an entity that most significantly impact the entity's economic performance. There are no other variable interest holders in the partnership (e.g., a lender) that have participating rights. Assume that the equity at risk is sufficient to absorb all expected future losses. Is the limited partnership a variable interest entity (VIE) on the basis of the power test? Explain your answer.

49. Determination of whether a legal entity is a variable interest entity   LO2
Assume that a Legal Entity owns and operates a real estate development and property management company. The decisions that significantly impact the performance of the Legal Entity include making capital investments, such as incurring capital expenditure for new developments to continue to attract tenants. The Legal Entity typically funds its capital investments via a mix of equity and debt financing. However, all capital investment decisions involving new property developments need the lender's approval (one party). There are no other variable interest holders in the Legal Entity (e.g.,

a lender) that have participating rights. Assume that the equity at risk is sufficient to absorb all expected future losses of the partnership. Is the limited partnership a variable interest entity (VIE) on the basis of the power test? Explain your answer.

LO2 **50. Determination of whether a legal entity is a variable interest entity**
Assume that a limited partnership is formed to perform research and development. None of the partnership interests have voting rights, but one partner, a pharmaceutical company, makes all significant decisions for the partnership under the terms of a service agreement entered into at inception of the entity. The pharmaceutical company is not required to have a substantive equity investment at risk as long as it provides services pursuant to the service agreement. Assume the service agreement is a variable interest. There are no other variable interest holders in the partnership (e.g., a lender) that have participating rights. Assume that the equity at risk is sufficient to absorb all expected future losses of the partnership. Is the limited partnership a variable interest entity (VIE) on the basis of the power test? Explain your answer.

LO2 **51. Recognition upon initial consolidation of a variable interest entity (VIE) when VIE is a business**
Assume that prior to January 1, 2016, a Reporting Company owned a 10 percent interest in a Legal Entity. The Reporting Company acquired its 10 percent ownership interest in the Legal Entity on June 15, 1995 for $20,000, and correctly accounted for this investment under the cost method (i.e., it was a passive investment and it was not marketable). On January 1, 2016, the Reporting Company purchased an additional 30 percent interest in the Legal Entity for $150,000. As a result of an evaluation of the facts and circumstances on January 1, 2016, the Reporting Entity determined that the Legal Entity is a variable interest entity (VIE) and that the Reporting Company is the primary beneficiary of the VIE. The Reporting Company also determined that, on January 1, 2016, the fair value of the previously held 10 percent interest is $50,000. In addition, independent appraisals revealed that the fair value of the noncontrolling interest (i.e., the 60 percent not owned by the Reporting Company) is $300,000. On January 1, 2016, the Legal Entity has reported book values for its identifiable net assets equal to $350,000 and fair values for its identifiable net assets equal to $450,000. Assume that the Legal Entity is a "business," as that term is defined in FASB ASC 805 ("Business Combinations"). Related to the initial consolidation of the Legal Entity on January 1, 2016, determine the following amounts:

a. Goodwill

b. Gain or Loss on initial consolidation of the Legal Entity

LO2 **52. Recognition upon initial consolidation of a variable interest entity (VIE) when VIE is not a business**
Assume that prior to January 1, 2016, a Reporting Company owned a 10 percent interest in a Legal Entity. The Reporting Company acquired its 10 percent ownership interest in the Legal Entity on June 15, 1995 for $20,000, and correctly accounted for this investment under the cost method (i.e., it was a passive investment and it was not marketable). On January 1, 2016, the Reporting Company purchased an additional 30 percent interest in the Legal Entity for $150,000. As a result of an evaluation of the facts and circumstances on January 1, 2016, the Reporting Entity determined that the Legal Entity is a variable interest entity (VIE) and that the Reporting Company is the primary beneficiary of the VIE. The Reporting Company also determined that, on January 1, 2016, the fair value of the previously held 10 percent interest is $50,000. In addition, independent appraisals revealed that the fair value of the noncontrolling interest (i.e., the 60 percent not owned by the Reporting Company) is $300,000. On January 1, 2016, the Legal Entity has reported book values for its identifiable net assets equal to $350,000 and fair values for its identifiable net assets equal to $450,000. Assume that the Legal Entity is not a "business," as that term is defined in FASB ASC 805 ("Business Combinations"). Related to the initial consolidation of the Legal Entity on January 1, 2016, determine the following amounts:

a. Goodwill

b. Gain or Loss on initial consolidation of the Legal Entity

LO2 **53. Elimination of intercompany profits for variable interest entities (VIEs) and voting interest entities**
Assume that on January 1, 2016, a Reporting Company acquires a 40 percent interest in a Legal Entity for $400,000 cash. The fair value of the 60 percent interest not acquired by the Reporting Company is $600,000. The fair value and book value of the identifiable net assets of the Legal Entity equals $1,000,000. The Reporting Company has a right to 40 percent of the reported income (loss) of the Legal Entity. The Legal Entity is determined to be a VIE, and the Reporting Company is determined to be primary beneficiary. For year ended December 31, 2016, the Reporting Company

and the VIE reported the following pre-consolidation income statements assuming that the Reporting Company applies the equity method:

	Reporting Company	VIE
Sales.	$1,100,000	$300,000
Cost of goods sold.	(660,000)	(200,000)
Gross profit.	440,000	100,000
Operating expenses.	(176,000)	(30,000)
Equity method income (loss) from VIE.	(24,500)	
Net income.	$ 239,500	$ 70,000

Assume that the Legal Entity's income statement for the year ended December 31, 2016 includes sales to the Reporting Company in the amount of $150,000. On intercompany sales, the Legal Entity earns a gross profit equal to 35 percent of sales price. Assume that all of these intercompany items are in the ending inventory of the Reporting Company on December 31, 2016.

a. Show how the Equity method income (loss) from VIE is computed.

b. Compute the amount of consolidated net income

c. Compute the amount of consolidated net income attributable to the noncontrolling interest

d. Compute the amount of consolidated net income attributable to the controlling interest

e. How would your answers to items (b) through (d) change if the Legal Entity is a "voting interest entity?"

54. **Consolidated gain or loss on constructive retirement of debt**   LO3
Assume that a Parent Company owns 100 percent of its Subsidiary. Each of the following independent scenarios describes an intercompany bond transaction between the Parent and the Subsidiary. For each independent case, determine the amount of gain or loss on constructive retirement of the bond reported in the consolidated income statement. Assume straight-line amortization.

a. P issues directly to S bonds that have a par value of $100,000. S paid $95,000 for the bonds. The term of the bonds is 10 years and they have an 8 percent stated interest rate. Interest is paid annually on December 31.

b. P issues to an unaffiliated company bonds that have a par value of $100,000. The unaffiliated company paid par value for the bonds. Four years later, S paid $60,000 for 60 percent of the outstanding bonds. The bond term is 10 years and they have an 8 percent stated interest rate. Interest is paid annually on December 31.

c. P issues to an unaffiliated company bonds that have a par value of $100,000. The unaffiliated company paid 105 percent of par value for the bonds. Four years later, S paid $96,000 for all of the outstanding bonds. The bond term is 10 years and they have an 8 percent stated interest rate. Interest is paid annually on December 31.

d. S issues to an unaffiliated company bonds that have a par value of $100,000. The unaffiliated company paid 95 percent of par value for the bonds. Four years later, P paid $82,000 for 80 percent of the outstanding bonds. The bond term is 10 years and they have an 8 percent stated interest rate. Interest is paid annually on December 31.

e. How would your answers to parts (a) through (d) change if the Parent company owned 90 percent of the Subsidiary instead of 100 percent?

55. **Consolidated amounts when affiliate's debt is acquired from non-affiliate**   LO3
Assume that a Parent company owns 100 percent of its Subsidiary. On January 1, 2016, the Parent company had a $400,000 (face) bond payable outstanding with a carrying value of $420,000. The bond was originally issued to an unaffiliated company. On that same date, the Subsidiary acquired the bond for $396,000. During 2016, the Parent company reported $180,000 of (pre-consolidation) income from its own operations (i.e., prior to any equity method adjustments by the Parent company) and after recording interest expense. The Subsidiary reported $100,000 of (pre-consolidation) income from its own operations after recording interest income. Related to the bond during 2016, the parent reported interest expense of $45,000 while the subsidiary reported interest income of $41,000. Determine the following amounts that will appear in the 2016 consolidated income statement:

a. Interest income from bond investment

b. Interest expense on bond payable

   c.   Gain (loss) on constructive retirement of bond payable

   d.   Consolidated net income

LO3   **56.** **Consolidated amounts when affiliate's debt is acquired from non-affiliate**

Assume that a Parent company owns 100 percent of its Subsidiary. On December 31, 2016, the Parent company had a $400,000 (face) bond payable outstanding with a carrying value of $420,000. The bond was originally issued to an unaffiliated company. On that same date, the Subsidiary acquired the bond for $396,000. During 2016, the Parent company reported $180,000 of (pre-consolidation) income from its own operations (i.e., prior to any equity method adjustments by the Parent company) and after re-cording interest expense. The Subsidiary reported $100,000 of (pre-consolidation) income from its own operations. Related to the bond during 2016, the parent reported interest expense of $45,000. The unaf-filiated company that held the bond prior to December 31, 2016 recorded interest income of $45,000. Determine the following amounts that will appear in the 2016 consolidated income statement:

   a.   Interest income from bond investment

   b.   Interest expense on bond payable

   c.   Gain (loss) on constructive retirement of bond payable

   d.   Consolidated net income

LO3   **57.** **Consolidated amounts when affiliate's debt is acquired from non-affiliate**

Assume that a Parent company owns 75 percent of its Subsidiary. On January 1, 2016, the Parent company had a $100,000 (face) 8 percent bond payable outstanding with a carrying value of $96,600. Several years ago, the bond was originally issued to an unaffiliated company for 92 percent of par value. On January 1, 2016, the Subsidiary acquired the bond for $92,000. During 2016, the Parent company reported $400,000 of (pre-consolidation) income from its own operations (i.e., prior to any equity method adjustments by the Parent company) and after recording interest expense. The Subsid-iary reported $120,000 of (pre-consolidation) income from its own operations after recording interest income. Related to the bond during 2016, the parent reported interest expense of $8,500 while the subsidiary reported interest income of $9,200. Determine the following amounts that will appear in the 2016 consolidated income statement:

   a.   Interest income from bond investment

   b.   Interest expense on bond payable

   c.   Gain (loss) on constructive retirement of bond payable

   d.   Controlling interest in consolidated net income

   e.   Noncontrolling interest in consolidated net income

LO3   **58.** **Consolidation adjustment necessary when affiliate's debt is acquired from non-affiliate**

Assume that a Parent company owns 80 percent of its Subsidiary. The parent company uses the equity method to account for its Investment in Subsidiary. On January 1, 2012, the Parent company issued to an unaffiliated company $1,000,000 (face) 10 year, 10 percent bonds payable for a $61,000 premium. The bonds pay interest in December 31 of each year. On January 1, 2015, the Subsidiary acquired 40 percent of the bonds for $386,000. Both companies use straight-line amortization. In preparing the con-solidated financial statements for the year ended December 31, 2016, what consolidating entry adjust-ment is necessary for the beginning-of-year Investment in Subsidiary account balance?

LO4   **59.** **Income attributable to controlling and noncontrolling interests in the presence of subsidiary preferred stock**

Assume that a Parent owns 70% of a Subsidiary that has 5% preferred stock outstanding with a reported par value of $800,000. Aside from the preferred dividends, no other dividends are paid (i.e., no divi-dends are paid to the common shareholders). The Parent owns none of the preferred stock. Assume that the Subsidiary reports net income of $120,000. During the year, the Parent company reported $300,000 of (pre-consolidation) income from its own operations (i.e., prior to any equity method adjustments by the Parent company). Compute the amount of consolidated net income attributable to the noncontrol-ling interest and the amount of net income attributable to the controlling interest.

LO4   **60.** **Income attributable to controlling and noncontrolling interests in the presence of subsidiary preferred stock**

Assume that a Parent owns 90% of a Subsidiary that has 4% preferred stock outstanding with a re-ported par value of $500,000. Aside from the preferred dividends, no other dividends are paid (i.e., no dividends are paid to the common shareholders). The Parent Company owns 40 percent of the preferred stock. Assume that the Subsidiary reports net income of $140,000. During the year, the Parent company reported $200,000 of (pre-consolidation) income from its own operations (i.e., prior to any equity method adjustments by the Parent company). Compute the amount of consolidated net income attributable to the noncontrolling interest and the amount of net income attributable to the controlling interest.

PROBLEMS

61. **Consolidation procedures for constructive retirement of affiliate debt acquired from non-affiliate—Equity method**   LO3

   Assume that on January 1, 2011, a Parent company issued to an unaffiliated party $200,000 (face) of 10-year, 8 percent bonds at 105 percent of par value. Interest is payable annually on January 1. On January 1, 2016, a 90 percent owned Subsidiary acquired 50 percent of these bonds for 102 percent of par value. Assume straight-line amortization of all premiums and discounts. In addition, on January 1, 2016, the Subsidiary had common stock of $60,000 and retained earnings of $40,000. There is no acquisition accounting premium (AAP) associated with the Parent's investment in the Subsidiary. The Parent company reported $50,000 of (pre-consolidation) income from its own operations (i.e., prior to any equity method adjustments by the Parent company) and after recording interest expense. The Subsidiary reported $30,000 of (pre-consolidation) income from its own operations after recording interest income. Neither company paid dividends. The parent uses the equity method of pre-consolidation investment bookkeeping.

   a. Compute the amount of gain or loss that must be recognized in the consolidated financial statements for the constructive retirement of debt. In what year is this gain or loss recognized?

   b. Prepare the bond-related journal entries recorded in the pre-consolidation financial statements by each company for the year ended December 31, 2016.

   c. For the year ended December 31, 2016, compute the controlling interest in consolidated net income and the noncontrolling interest in consolidated net income.

   d. Prepare the complete set of consolidation entries for the year ended December 31, 2016.

62. **Consolidation procedures for constructive retirement of affiliate debt acquired from non-affiliate—Equity method**   LO3

   Assume that on January 1, 2014, a Parent company issued to an unaffiliated company a 7-year, 10 percent bond with a par value of $500,000 for $450,000. Interest is paid annually on December 31. On December 31, 2015, an affiliated Subsidiary purchased $400,000 (face) of the bonds for $410,000. In addition, on January 1, 2016, the Subsidiary had common stock of $100,000 and retained earnings of $70,000. The Parent owns 90 percent of the Subsidiary, and it is consolidated by the parent as a voting interest entity. There is no acquisition accounting premium (AAP) associated with the Parent's investment in the Subsidiary. Both companies use the straight-line amortization of bond premiums and discounts. The Parent and Subsidiary reported the following (pre-consolidation) income from their own operations (i.e., prior to any equity method adjustments by the Parent company), but after recording interest income and interest expense:

	NI Parent	NI Subsidiary
2015	140,000	80,000
2016	160,000	100,000

   The Subsidiary also declared and paid a $25,000 cash dividend in each year, 2015 and 2016. The parent uses the equity method of pre-consolidation investment bookkeeping.

   a. Compute the amount of gain or loss that must be recognized in the consolidated financial statements for the constructive retirement of debt. In what year is this gain or loss recognized?

   b. Prepare the bond-related journal entries recorded in the pre-consolidation financial statements by each company for the year ended December 31, 2016.

   c. For the year ended December 31, 2016, compute the controlling interest in consolidated net income and the noncontrolling interest in consolidated net income.

   d. Prepare the consolidation entries for the year ended December 31, 2016.

63. Consolidation worksheet for gain on constructive retirement of parent's debt with no AAP—Equity method

Assume that a Parent company acquires an 80% interest in its Subsidiary on January 1, 2012. On the date of acquisition, the fair value of the 80 percent controlling interest was $416,000 and the fair value of the 20 percent noncontrolling interest was $104,000. On January 1, 2012, the book value of net assets equaled $520,000 and the fair value of the identifiable net assets equaled the book value of identifiable net assets (i.e., there was no AAP or Goodwill).

On December 31, 2013, the Parent company issued $400,000 (face) 6 percent, five-year bonds to an unaffiliated company for $426,340 (i.e., the bonds had an effective yield of 4.5 percent). The bonds pay interest annually on December 31, and the bond premium is amortized using the straight-line method. This results in annual bond-payable premium amortization equal to $5,268 per year.

On December 31, 2015, the Subsidiary paid $389,503 to purchase all of the outstanding Parent company bonds (i.e., the bonds had an effective yield of 7 percent). The bond discount is amortized using the straight-line method, which results in annual bond-investment discount amortization equal to $3,499 per year.

The Parent and the Subsidiary report the following financial statements for the year ended December 31, 2016:

	Parent	Subsidiary		Parent	Subsidiary
Income statement:			**Balance sheet:**		
Sales.	$8,000,000	$850,000	Assets		
Cost of goods sold.	(6,000,000)	(530,000)	Cash.	$ 800,000	$ 350,000
			Accounts receivable.	1,500,000	450,000
Gross profit.	2,000,000	320,000	Inventory.	2,000,000	550,000
Equity income.	109,232		PPE, net	8,240,000	950,000
Bond interest income.		27,499	Equity investment.	555,533	
Bond interest expense	(18,732)		Investment in bonds.		393,002
Operating & other expenses.	(1,200,000)	(200,000)			
				$13,095,533	$2,693,002
Net income.	$ 890,500	$147,499			
			Liabilities and stockholders' equity		
Statement of retained earnings:			Accounts payable.	$ 700,000	$ 478,000
BOY retained earnings	$5,741,500	$225,000	Current liabilities.	850,000	500,000
Net income.	890,500	147,499	Bonds payable	410,536	
Dividends	(284,000)	(20,000)	Long-term liabilities	836,997	1,042,503
			Common stock.	450,000	150,000
EOY retained earnings	$6,348,000	$352,499	APIC	3,500,000	170,000
			Retained earnings	6,348,000	352,499
				$13,095,533	$2,693,002

The parent uses the equity method of pre-consolidation investment bookkeeping. Provide the consolidation entries and prepare a consolidation worksheet for the year ended December 31, 2016.

64. **Consolidation worksheet for gain on constructive retirement of subsidiary's debt with no AAP—Equity method**　**LO3**

Assume that a Parent company acquires a 90% interest in its Subsidiary on January 1, 2012. On the date of acquisition, the fair value of the 90 percent controlling interest was $720,000 and the fair value of the 10 percent noncontrolling interest was $80,000. On January 1, 2012, the book value of net assets equaled $800,000 and the fair value of the identifiable net assets equaled the book value of identifiable net assets (i.e., there was no AAP or Goodwill).

On December 31, 2013, the Subsidiary company issued $750,000 (face) 7 percent, five-year bonds to an unaffiliated company for $814,942 (i.e., the bonds had an effective yield of 5 percent). The bonds pay interest annually on December 31, and the bond premium is amortized using the straight-line method. This results in annual bond-payable premium amortization equal to $12,988 per year.

On December 31, 2015, the Parent paid $730,672 to purchase all of the outstanding Subsidiary company bonds (i.e., the bonds had an effective yield of 8 percent). The bond discount is amortized using the straight-line method, which results in annual bond-investment discount amortization equal to $6,443 per year.

The Parent and the Subsidiary report the following financial statements for the year ended December 31, 2016:

	Parent	Subsidiary		Parent	Subsidiary
Income statement:			**Balance sheet:**		
Sales....................	$6,500,000	$800,000	Assets		
Cost of goods sold...........	(4,750,000)	(520,000)	Cash......................	$ 775,000	$ 500,000
Gross profit.................	1,750,000	280,000	Accounts receivable...........	1,125,000	650,000
Equity income...............	35,008		Inventory....................	1,150,000	843,465
Bond interest income..........	58,943		PPE, net....................	6,813,500	1,250,000
Bond interest expense.........		(39,512)	Equity investment.............	884,402	
Operating & other expenses.....	(1,150,000)	(180,000)	Investment in bonds...........	737,114	
Net income.................	$ 693,951	$ 60,488		$11,485,016	$3,243,465
			Liabilities and stockholders' equity		
Statement of retained earnings:			Accounts payable.............	$ 750,000	$ 478,000
BOY retained earnings.........	$3,500,000	$225,000	Current liabilities..............	1,000,000	600,000
Net income.................	693,951	60,488	Bonds payable		775,977
Dividends..................	(185,000)	(20,000)	Long-term liabilities	1,113,065	450,000
EOY retained earnings.........	$4,008,951	$265,488	Common stock...............	1,053,000	149,000
			APIC......................	3,560,000	525,000
			Retained earnings	4,008,951	265,488
				$11,485,016	$3,243,465

The parent uses the equity method of pre-consolidation investment bookkeeping. Provide the consolidation entries and prepare a consolidation worksheet for the year ended December 31, 2016.

LO3 65. **Consolidation worksheet for loss on constructive retirement of parent's debt with no AAP—Equity method**

Assume that a Parent company acquires an 80 percent interest in its Subsidiary on January 1, 2012. On the date of acquisition, the fair value of the 80 percent controlling interest was $544,000 and the fair value of the 20 percent noncontrolling interest was $136,000. On January 1, 2012, the book value of net assets equaled $680,000 and the fair value of the identifiable net assets equaled the book value of identifiable net assets (i.e., there was no AAP or Goodwill).

On December 31, 2013, the Parent company issued $1,000,000 (face) 5 percent, five-year bonds to an unaffiliated company for $957,876 (i.e., the bonds had an effective yield of 6 percent). The bonds pay interest annually on December 31, and the bond discount is amortized using the straight-line method. The following schedule provides the bond amortization schedule from the initial issuance date.

Date	Cash Payment	Amortization of Discount	Interest Expense	Carrying Amount
Dec. 31, 2013.				$ 957,876
Dec. 31, 2014.	$50,000	$8,425	$58,425	966,301
Dec. 31, 2015.	50,000	8,425	58,425	974,726
Dec. 31, 2016.	50,000	8,425	58,425	983,151
Dec. 31, 2017.	50,000	8,425	58,425	991,575
Dec. 31, 2018.	50,000	8,425	58,425	1,000,000

On December 31, 2015, the Subsidiary paid $1,027,751 to purchase all of the outstanding Parent company bonds (i.e., the bonds had an effective yield of 4 percent). The bond premium is amortized using the straight-line method. The following schedule provides the bond amortization schedule for the Subsidiary's bond investment.

Date	Cash Payment	Amortization of Premium	Interest Income	Carrying Amount
Dec. 31, 2015.				$1,027,751
Dec. 31, 2016.	$ 50,000	$(9,250)	$ 40,750	1,018,501
Dec. 31, 2017.	50,000	(9,250)	40,750	1,009,250
Dec. 31, 2018.	50,000	(9,250)	40,750	1,000,000

The parent uses the equity method of pre-consolidation investment bookkeeping. The Parent and the Subsidiary report the following financial statements for the year ended December 31, 2016:

	Parent	Subsidiary		Parent	Subsidiary
Income statement:			**Balance sheet:**		
Sales.	$9,500,000	$900,000	Assets		
Cost of goods sold.	(6,800,000)	(550,000)	Cash	$ 883,551	$ 275,957
			Accounts receivable	1,500,000	400,000
Gross profit.	2,700,000	350,000	Inventory.	2,500,000	600,000
Equity income.	142,275		PPE, net	9,000,000	1,030,000
Bond interest income		40,750	Equity investment.	588,450	
Bond interest expense	(58,425)		Investment in bonds.		1,018,501
Operating & other expenses.	(1,650,000)	(235,000)			
				$14,472,001	$3,324,458
Net income.	$1,133,850	$155,750			
			Liabilities and stockholders' equity		
Statement of retained earnings:			Accounts payable.	$ 850,000	$ 450,000
BOY retained earnings	$4,955,000	$350,000	Current liabilities.	1,000,000	500,000
Net income.	1,133,850	155,750	Bonds payable	983,151	
Dividends	(800,000)	(26,000)	Long-term liabilities	1,400,000	1,594,708
			Common stock.	850,000	100,000
Ending retained earnings	$5,288,850	$479,750	APIC	4,100,000	200,000
			Retained earnings	5,288,850	479,750
				$14,472,001	$3,324,458

Provide the consolidation entries and prepare a consolidation worksheet for the year ended December 31, 2016.

66. **Consolidation worksheet for loss on constructive retirement of subsidiary's debt with no AAP—Equity method**

LO3

Assume that a Parent company acquires a 75 percent interest in its Subsidiary on January 1, 2012. On the date of acquisition, the fair value of the 75 percent controlling interest was $600,000 and the fair value of the 25 percent noncontrolling interest was $200,000. On January 1, 2012, the book value of net assets equaled $800,000 and the fair value of the identifiable net assets equaled the book value of identifiable net assets (i.e., there was no AAP or Goodwill).

On December 31, 2013, the Subsidiary company issued $500,000 (face) 6 percent, five-year bonds to an unaffiliated company for $460,075 (i.e., the bonds had an effective yield of approximately 8 percent). The bonds pay interest annually on December 31, and the bond discount is amortized using the straight-line method. The following schedule provides the bond amortization schedule from the initial issuance date.

Date	Cash Payment	Amortization of Discount	Interest Expense	Carrying Amount
Dec. 31, 2013.				$460,075
Dec. 31, 2014.	$30,000	$7,985	$37,985	468,060
Dec. 31, 2015.	30,000	7,985	37,985	476,045
Dec. 31, 2016.	30,000	7,985	37,985	484,030
Dec. 31, 2017.	30,000	7,985	37,985	492,015
Dec. 31, 2018.	30,000	7,985	37,985	500,000

On December 31, 2015, the Parent paid $513,614 to purchase all of the outstanding Subsidiary company bonds (i.e., the bonds had an effective yield of approximately 5 percent). The bond premium is amortized using the straight-line method. The following schedule provides the bond amortization schedule for the Parent's bond investment.

Date	Cash Payment	Amortization of Premium	Interest Income	Carrying Amount
Dec. 31, 2015.				$513,614
Dec. 31, 2016.	$30,000	$(4,538)	$25,462	509,076
Dec. 31, 2017.	30,000	(4,538)	25,462	504,538
Dec. 31, 2018.	30,000	(4,538)	25,462	500,000

The parent uses the equity method of pre-consolidation investment bookkeeping. The Parent and the Subsidiary report the following financial statements for the year ended December 31, 2016:

	Parent	Subsidiary		Parent	Subsidiary
Income statement:			**Balance sheet:**		
Sales..........................	$5,700,000	$540,000	Assets		
Cost of goods sold.............	(4,080,000)	(330,000)	Cash.........................	$ 528,955	$ 269,045
			Accounts receivable............	900,000	440,000
Gross profit..................	1,620,000	210,000	Inventory......................	1,400,000	560,000
Equity income................	35,784		PPE, net	4,450,000	900,000
Bond interest income...........	25,462		Equity investment..............	586,215	
Bond interest expense..........		(37,985)	Investment in bonds...........	509,076	
Operating & other expenses......	(990,000)	(141,000)			
				$8,374,246	$2,169,045
Net income....................	$ 691,246	$ 31,015			
			Liabilities and stockholders' equity		
Statement of retained earnings:			Accounts payable..............	$ 850,000	$ 270,000
BOY retained earnings..........	$2,973,000	$550,000	Current liabilities................	750,000	300,000
Net income....................	691,246	31,015	Bonds payable		484,030
Dividends	(800,000)	(26,000)	Long-term liabilities	940,000	300,000
			Common stock.................	510,000	60,000
Ending retained earnings	$2,864,246	$555,015	APIC.........................	2,460,000	200,000
			Retained earnings	2,864,246	555,015
				$8,374,246	$2,169,045

Provide the consolidation entries and prepare a consolidation worksheet for the year ended December 31, 2016.

LO3 67. **Consolidation worksheet for gain on constructive retirement of subsidiary's debt with no AAP—Cost method**

Assume that a Parent company acquires a 90% interest in its Subsidiary on January 1, 2012. On the date of acquisition, the fair value of the 90 percent controlling interest was $1,080,000 and the fair value of the 10 percent noncontrolling interest was $120,000. On January 1, 2012, the book value of net assets equaled $1,200,000 and the fair value of the identifiable net assets equaled the book value of identifiable net assets (i.e., there was no AAP or Goodwill). On January 1, 2012, the retained earnings of the subsidiary was $189,000.

On December 31, 2013, the Subsidiary company issued $1,125,000 (face) 7 percent, five-year bonds to an unaffiliated company for $1,222,413 (i.e., the bonds had an effective yield of 5 percent). The bonds pay interest annually on December 31, and the bond premium is amortized using the straight-line method. This results in annual bond-payable premium amortization equal to $19,483 per year. The following schedule provides the bond-amortization schedule from the initial issuance date.

Year	Cash Payment	Amortization of (Prem) Disc	Interest Expense	Carrying Amount
Dec. 31, 2013.............				$1,222,413
Dec. 31, 2014.............	$78,750	$(19,483)	$59,267	1,202,931
Dec. 31, 2015.............	78,750	(19,483)	59,267	1,183,448
Dec. 31, 2016.............	78,750	(19,483)	59,267	1,163,965
Dec. 31, 2017.............	78,750	(19,483)	59,267	1,144,483
Dec. 31, 2018.............	78,750	(19,483)	59,267	1,125,000

On December 31, 2015, the Parent paid $1,096,008 to purchase all of the outstanding Subsidiary company bonds (i.e., the bonds had an effective yield of 8 percent). The bond discount is amortized using the straight-line method, which results in annual bond-investment discount amortization equal to $9,664 per year. The following schedule provides the bond-amortization schedule for the Parent's bond investment.

Year	Cash Payment	Amortization of (Prem) Disc	Interest Income	Carrying Amount
Dec. 31, 2015.............				$1,096,008
Dec. 31, 2016.............	$78,750	$9,664	$88,414	1,105,672
Dec. 31, 2017.............	78,750	9,664	88,414	1,115,336
Dec. 31, 2018.............	78,750	9,664	88,414	1,125,000

The parent uses the cost method of pre-consolidation investment bookkeeping. The Parent and the Subsidiary report the following financial statements for the year ended December 31, 2016:

	Parent	Subsidiary
Income statement:		
Sales........................	$9,750,000	$1,200,000
Cost of goods sold............	(7,125,000)	(780,000)
Gross profit..................	2,625,000	420,000
Operating & other expenses......	(1,725,000)	(270,000)
Bond interest income...........	88,414	
Bond interest expense..........		(59,267)
Total expenses	(1,636,586)	(329,267)
Income from subsidiary	27,000	—
Net income...................	$1,015,414	$ 90,733
Statement of retained earnings:		
BOY retained earnings..........	$5,028,911	$ 337,500
Net income...................	1,015,414	90,733
Dividends declared............	(277,500)	(30,000)
EOY retained earnings..........	$5,766,825	$ 398,233

	Parent	Subsidiary
Balance sheet:		
Cash........................	$ 1,162,500	$ 750,000
Accounts receivable...........	1,687,500	975,000
Inventories	1,725,000	1,265,198
Property, plant & equipment, net ..	10,220,250	1,875,000
Investment in subsidiary.........	1,080,000	
Investment in bond (net)........	1,105,672	
Total assets..................	$16,980,922	$4,865,198
Accounts payable..............	$ 1,125,000	$ 717,000
Other current liabilities	1,500,000	900,000
Bond payable (net)............		1,163,965
Other long-term liabilities........	1,669,597	675,000
Common stock.................	1,579,500	223,500
APIC........................	5,340,000	787,500
Retained earnings	5,766,825	398,233
Total liabilities and equity	$16,980,922	$4,865,198

Provide the consolidation entries and prepare a consolidation worksheet for the year ended December 31, 2016.

68. **Consolidation worksheet for loss on constructive retirement of subsidiary's debt with no AAP— LO3 Cost method**

Assume that a Parent company acquires an 80 percent interest in its Subsidiary on January 1, 2012. On the date of acquisition, the fair value of the 80 percent controlling interest was $652,800 and the fair value of the 20 percent noncontrolling interest was $163,200. On January 1, 2012, the book value of net assets equaled $816,000 and the fair value of the identifiable net assets equaled the book value of identifiable net assets (i.e., there was no AAP or Goodwill).

On December 31, 2013, the Parent company issued $1,200,000 (face) 5 percent, five-year bonds to an unaffiliated company for $1,149,452 (i.e., the bonds had an effective yield of 6 percent). The bonds pay interest annually on December 31, and the bond discount is amortized using the straight-line method. The following schedule provides the bond-amortization schedule from the initial issuance date.

Year	Cash Payment	Amortization of (Prem) Disc	Interest Expense	Carrying Amount
Dec. 31, 2013.........				$1,149,452
Dec. 31, 2014.........	$60,000	$10,110	$70,110	1,159,561
Dec. 31, 2015.........	60,000	10,110	70,110	1,169,671
Dec. 31, 2016.........	60,000	10,110	70,110	1,179,781
Dec. 31, 2017.........	60,000	10,110	70,110	1,189,890
Dec. 31, 2018.........	60,000	10,110	70,110	1,200,000

On December 31, 2015, the Subsidiary paid $1,233,301 to purchase all of the outstanding parent company bonds (i.e., the bonds had an effective yield of 4 percent). The bond premium is amortized using the straight-line method. The following schedule provides the bond-amortization schedule for the Subsidiary's bond investment.

Year	Cash Payment	Amortization of (Prem) Disc	Interest Income	Carrying Amount
Dec. 31, 2015.				$1,233,301
Dec. 31, 2016.	$60,000	$(11,100)	$48,900	1,222,201
Dec. 31, 2017.	60,000	(11,100)	48,900	1,211,100
Dec. 31, 2018.	60,000	(11,100)	48,900	1,200,000

The parent uses the cost method of pre-consolidation investment bookkeeping. The Parent and the Subsidiary report the following financial statements for the year ended December 31, 2016:

	Parent	Subsidiary		Parent	Subsidiary
Income statement:			**Balance sheet:**		
Sales.	$11,400,000	$1,080,000	Cash.	$ 1,060,261	$ 331,149
Cost of goods sold.	(8,160,000)	(660,000)	Accounts receivable.	1,800,000	480,000
Gross profit.	3,240,000	420,000	Inventories	3,000,000	720,000
			Property, plant & equipment, net . . .	10,800,000	1,236,000
Operating & other expenses.	(1,980,000)	(282,000)	Investment in subsidiary.	652,800	
Bond interest income.		48,900	Investment in bond (net).		1,222,201
Bond interest expense	(70,110)				
Total expenses	(2,050,110)	(233,100)	Total assets.	$17,313,061	$3,989,350
Income from subsidiary	24,960		Accounts payable.	$ 1,020,000	$ 540,000
Net income.	$ 1,214,850	$ 186,900	Other current liabilities	1,200,000	600,000
			Bond payable (net)	1,179,781	
Statement of retained earnings:			Other long-term liabilities	1,680,000	1,913,650
BOY retained earnings	$ 6,038,430	$ 420,000	Common stock.	1,020,000	120,000
Net income.	1,214,850	186,900	APIC.	4,920,000	240,000
Dividends declared.	(960,000)	(31,200)	Retained earnings	6,293,280	575,700
EOY retained earnings	$ 6,293,280	$ 575,700	Total liabilities and equity	$17,313,061	$3,989,350

Provide the consolidation entries and prepare a consolidation worksheet for the year ended December 31, 2016.

TOPIC REVIEW

Solution 1

a. If the expected losses were predicted to be $50 or less, then the equity at risk would be considered sufficient.

b. If the expected losses were greater than $50, then the equity investment at risk is not sufficient. The important point is that the equity investment at risk can only include interests reported as equity in the legal entity's GAAP financial statements, regardless of the source of that equity.

Solution 2

Shamco has zero equity investment at risk in the partnership because the fees received from Moneyco (a party also participating in the partnership) are not "arm's length" and must be deducted from Shamco's investment in the partnership.

Solution 3

As indicated in the facts, the general partner makes all substantive decisions for the partnership, and the general partner does not have an equity investment at risk. The entity is a VIE because the holders of the equity investment at risk (i.e., the group of outside investors serving as limited partners) lack the power to direct the activities of the entity that most significantly impact the entity's economic performance. This violates Step ❹, Part (b). Accordingly, the research and development partnership is a VIE.

Solution 4

In this example, because Company Y absorbs all of the variability related to the manufacturing of the products under the purchase agreement, Investor A's equity at risk is protected from some portion of expected losses of Legal Entity X. Therefore, the equity at risk lacks the obligation to absorb the expected losses of the legal entity (i.e., Step ❹, Part (b)(2)) and the entity would be considered a VIE. Note that if we instead assumed that the contract was a fixed-price purchase contract, then (1) the contract would likely not be considered a variable interest and (2) equity at risk in Legal Entity X would also have the obligation to absorb the expected losses of Legal Entity X.

Solution 5

Bond amortization tables provided to help with computations:

	Original Issue by Parent			
Year	Cash Payment	Amortization of (Prem) Disc	Interest Expense	Carrying Amount
Dec. 31, 2013................				$1,043,295
Dec. 31, 2014................	$60,000	$(8,659)	$51,341	1,034,636
Dec. 31, 2015................	60,000	(8,659)	51,341	1,025,977
Dec. 31, 2016................	60,000	(8,659)	51,341	1,017,318
Dec. 31, 2017................	60,000	(8,659)	51,341	1,008,659
Dec. 31, 2018................	60,000	(8,659)	51,341	1,000,000

	Subsequent Purchase by Subsidiary			
Year	Cash Payment	Amortization of (Prem) Disc	Interest Income	Carrying Amount
Dec. 31, 2015................				$ 948,458
Dec. 31, 2016................	$60,000	$17,181	$77,181	965,639
Dec. 31, 2017................	60,000	17,181	77,181	982,819
Dec. 31, 2018................	60,000	17,181	77,181	1,000,000

Consolidation Entries:

		Debit	Credit
[C]	Equity Income from subsidiary..	169,623	
	Income attributable to NCI...	21,718	
	Dividends – subsidiary.......................................		20,000
	Investment in subsidiary.....................................		151,623
	Noncontrolling interest		19,718
[E]	Common stock (S) @ BOY..	149,000	
	APIC..	155,000	
	Retained earnings (S) @ BOY..	225,000	
	Investment in subsidiary @ BOY..............................		476,100
	Noncontrolling interest @ BOY		52,900
[I_bond]	Bond payable (net)...	1,017,318	
	Interest income..	77,181	
	Investment in bonds (net)		965,639
	Interest expense		51,341
	BOY Investment in subsidiary................................		77,519

Consolidation Worksheet:

	Parent	Subsidiary	Consolidation Entries Dr		Consolidation Entries Cr		Consolidated
Income statement:							
Sales..........................	$10,000,000	$1,000,000					$11,000,000
Cost of goods sold...............	(7,200,000)	(600,000)					(7,800,000)
Gross profit.....................	2,800,000	400,000					3,200,000
Operating and other expenses.......	(1,500,000)	(260,000)					(1,760,000)
Bond interest income..............		77,181	[I$_{bond}$]	$ 77,181			0
Bond interest expense............	(51,341)				[I$_{bond}$]	$ 51,341	0
Total expenses...................	(1,551,341)	(182,819)					(1,760,000)
Equity Income from subsidiary.......	169,623	—	[C]	169,623			0
Consolidated net income...........	1,418,282	217,181					1,440,000
Income attributable to NCI..........			[C]	21,718			(21,718)
Income attrib. to controlling int	$ 1,418,282	$ 217,181					$ 1,418,282
Statement of retained earnings:							
Beginning retained earnings.........	$ 5,741,500	$ 225,000	[E]	225,000			$ 5,741,500
Income attrib. to controlling int	1,418,282	217,181					1,418,282
Dividends declared................	(284,000)	(20,000)			[C]	20,000	(284,000)
Ending retained earnings...........	$ 6,875,782	$ 422,181					$ 6,875,782
Balance sheet:							
Cash..........................	$ 925,258	$ 323,250					$ 1,248,508
Accounts receivable..............	1,750,000	430,000					2,180,000
Inventories	2,600,000	550,000					3,150,000
Property, plant and equipment, net ...	10,060,000	1,030,000					11,090,000
Investment in subsidiary............	705,242				[C]	151,623	0
					[E]	476,100	
					[I$_{bond}$]	77,519	
Investment in bond (net)............		965,639			[I$_{bond}$]	965,639	0
Total assets.....................	$16,040,500	$3,298,889					$17,668,508
Accounts payable.................	$ 844,400	$ 478,000					$ 1,322,400
Other current liabilities	1,190,000	500,000					1,690,000
Bond payable (net)................	1,017,318		[I$_{bond}$]	1,017,318			0
Other long-term liabilities..........	1,500,000	1,594,708					3,094,708
Common stock...................	553,000	149,000	[E]	149,000			553,000
APIC..........................	4,060,000	155,000	[E]	155,000			4,060,000
Retained earnings	6,875,782	422,181					6,875,782
Noncontrolling interest.............					[C]	19,718	72,618
					[E]	52,900	
Total liabilities and equity...........	$16,040,500	$3,298,889		$1,814,840		$1,814,840	$17,668,508

Solution 6

Bond amortization tables provided to help with computations:

		Original Issue by Parent		
Year	Cash Payment	Amortization of (Prem) Disc	Interest Expense	Carrying Amount
Dec. 31, 2013				$1,564,942
Dec. 31, 2014	$90,000	$(12,988)	$77,012	1,551,954
Dec. 31, 2015	90,000	(12,988)	77,012	1,538,965
Dec. 31, 2016	90,000	(12,988)	77,012	1,525,977
Dec. 31, 2017	90,000	(12,988)	77,012	1,512,988
Dec. 31, 2018	90,000	(12,988)	77,012	1,500,000

		Subsequent Purchase by Subsidiary		
Year	Cash Payment	Amortization of (Prem) Disc	Interest Income	Carrying Amount
Dec. 31, 2015				$1,422,687
Dec. 31, 2016	$90,000	$25,771	$115,771	1,448,458
Dec. 31, 2017	90,000	25,771	115,771	1,474,229
Dec. 31, 2018	90,000	25,771	115,771	1,500,000

Consolidation Entries:

[ADJ]	Investment in subsidiary @ BOY	87,928	
	Retained earnings (P) @ BOY		87,928

[C]	Income from subsidiary	27,000	
	Income attributable to NCI	32,577	
	Dividends—subsidiary		30,000
	Noncontrolling Interest		29,577

[E]	Common stock (S) @ BOY	223,500	
	APIC	232,500	
	Retained earnings (S) @ BOY	337,500	
	Investment in subsidiary @ BOY		714,150
	Noncontrolling interest @ BOY		79,350

[I$_{bond}$]	Bond payable (net)	1,525,977	
	Interest income	115,771	
	Investment in bonds (net)		1,448,458
	Interest expense		77,012
	BOY Investment in subsidiary		116,278

[ADJ] = (90% × [$337,500 − $369,000]) + ($1,538,965 − $1,422,687) = $87,928

Consolidation Worksheet:

	Parent	Subsidiary	Consolidation Entries Dr		Consolidation Entries Cr		Consolidated
Income statement:							
Sales...................	$13,500,000	$1,650,000					$15,150,000
Cost of goods sold...........	(9,300,000)	(1,050,000)					(10,350,000)
Gross profit...............	4,200,000	600,000					4,800,000
Operating & other expenses.......	(2,250,000)	(390,000)					(2,640,000)
Bond interest income...........		115,771	[I_bond]	$ 115,771			0
Bond interest expense..........	(77,012)				[I_bond]	$ 77,012	0
Total expenses.............	(2,327,012)	(274,229)					(2,640,000)
Income from subsidiary.........	27,000		[C]	27,000			0
Consolidated net income........	1,899,988	325,771					2,160,000
Income attributable to NCI.......	—	—	[C]	32,577			(32,577)
Income attrib. to controlling int.....	$ 1,899,988	$ 325,771					$ 2,127,423
Statement of retained earnings:							
Beginning retained earings........	$ 2,524,322	$ 337,500	[E]	337,500	[ADJ]	87,928	$ 2,612,250
Income attrib. to controlling int.....	1,899,988	325,771					2,127,423
Dividends declared.............	(426,000)	(30,000)			[C]	30,000	(426,000)
Ending retained earnings.........	$ 3,998,310	$ 633,271					$ 4,313,673
Balance sheet:							
Cash....................	$ 1,350,000	$ 484,875					$ 1,834,875
Accounts receivable...........	2,625,000	645,000					3,270,000
Inventories................	3,900,000	825,000					4,725,000
PPE, net.................	7,500,000	1,545,000					9,045,000
Investment in subsidiary.........	742,500		[ADJ]	87,928	[E]	714,150	0
					[I_bond]	116,278	
Investment in bond (net)..........		1,448,458			[I_bond]	1,448,458	0
Total assets................	$16,117,500	$4,948,333					$18,874,875
Accounts payable.............	$ 913,713	$ 717,000					$ 1,630,713
Other current liabilities..........	1,350,000	750,000					2,100,000
Bond payable (net)............	1,525,977		[I_bond]	1,525,977			0
Other long-term liabilities.........	3,000,000	2,392,062					5,392,062
Common stock...............	829,500	223,500	[E]	223,500			829,500
APIC....................	4,500,000	232,500	[E]	232,500			4,500,000
Retained earnings.............	3,998,310	633,271					4,313,673
Noncontrolling interest...........					[C]	29,577	108,927
					[E]	79,350	
Total liabilities and equity.........	$16,117,500	$4,948,333		$2,582,753		$2,582,753	$18,874,875

COMPREHENSIVE REVIEW SOLUTION

a. The trial balance information converted to financial statement format is presented, below. A completed consolidation spreadsheet is included in the solution to part h of this comprehensive review.

Pre-Consolidation Financial Statements for the Year Ended December 31, 2016	Parent	Subsidiary
Income statement:		
Sales.	$ 8,000,000	$ 800,000
Cost of goods sold.	(5,760,000)	(480,000)
Gross profit.	2,240,000	320,000
Depreciation and amortization expense.	(700,000)	(58,000)
Operating and other expenses.	(500,000)	(150,000)
Bond interest income	29,455	
Bond interest expense		(20,548)
Total expenses	(1,170,545)	(228,548)
Equity income from subsidiary.	57,200	
Net income	$ 1,126,655	$ 91,452
Statement of retained earnings:		
Beginning retained earnings.	$ 4,593,201	$ 180,000
Net income.	1,126,655	91,452
Dividends declared.	(227,200)	(16,000)
Ending retained earnings	$ 5,492,656	$ 255,452
Balance sheet:		
Cash	$ 900,013	$ 400,000
Accounts receivable	1,113,100	480,000
Inventories	1,840,000	623,749
Property, plant & equipment, net	8,048,000	824,000
Investment in subsidiary.	594,401	
Investment in bond (net).	491,090	
Total assets.	$12,986,604	$2,327,749
Accounts payable.	$ 808,000	$ 240,000
Other current liabilities	995,548	480,193
Bond payable (net)		508,904
Other long-term liabilities.	2,000,000	600,000
Common stock.	442,400	119,200
APIC	3,248,000	124,000
Retained earnings	5,492,656	255,452
Total liabilities and equity	$12,986,604	$2,327,749

b. Given the five-year time horizon between the acquisition date and the consolidated financial statement date, the following schedules separately document the annual AAP amortization and the year-end unamortized AAP balance for each year, 2012 through 2016.

100% AAP:

100% AAP Amortization – Dr (Cr)	Year Ended December 31,				
	2012	2013	2014	2015	2016
Patent...............................	$20,000	$20,000	$20,000	$20,000	$20,000
Net amortization...........................	$20,000	$20,000	$20,000	$20,000	$20,000

100% Unamortized AAP – Dr (Cr)	Jan. 1, 2012	December 31,				
		2012	2013	2014	2015	2016
Patent........................	$200,000	$180,000	$160,000	$140,000	$120,000	$100,000
Goodwill......................	100,000	100,000	100,000	100,000	100,000	100,000
Unamortized balance............	$300,000	$280,000	$260,000	$240,000	$220,000	$200,000

90% AAP:

90% AAP Amortization – Dr (Cr)	Year Ended December 31,				
	2012	2013	2014	2015	2016
Patent...............................	$18,000	$18,000	$18,000	$18,000	$18,000
Net amortization...........................	$18,000	$18,000	$18,000	$18,000	$18,000

90% Unamortized AAP – Dr (Cr)	Jan. 1, 2012	December 31,				
		2012	2013	2014	2015	2016
Patent........................	$180,000	$162,000	$144,000	$126,000	$108,000	$90,000
Goodwill......................	90,000	90,000	90,000	90,000	90,000	90,000
Unamortized balance............	$270,000	$252,000	$234,000	$216,000	$198,000	$180,000

10% AAP:

10% AAP Amortization – Dr (Cr)	Year Ended December 31,				
	2012	2013	2014	2015	2016
Patent...............................	$2,000	$2,000	$2,000	$2,000	$2,000
Net amortization...........................	$2,000	$2,000	$2,000	$2,000	$2,000

10% Unamortized AAP – Dr (Cr)	Jan. 1, 2012	December 31,				
		2012	2013	2014	2015	2016
Patent........................	$20,000	$18,000	$16,000	$14,000	$12,000	$10,000
Goodwill......................	10,000	10,000	10,000	10,000	10,000	10,000
Unamortized balance............	$30,000	$28,000	$26,000	$24,000	$22,000	$20,000

c. **Intercompany depreciable asset sale:**
There was one downstream asset sale.
Intercompany profit recognized on January 1, 2015: $150,000 − $96,000 = $54,000, 10-year remaining life
Profit confirmed each year: $54,000/10 = $5,400

	Downstream	Upstream
Net intercompany profit deferred at January 1, 2016	$48,600	$0
Less: Deferred intercompany profit recognized during 2016............	5,400	0
Net intercompany profit deferred at December 31, 2016	$43,200	$0

Intercompany inventory transactions:
Intercompany inventory sales during 2016: $60,000

	Downstream (in Subsidiary's Inventory)	Upstream (in Parent's Inventory)
Intercompany profit in inventory on January 1, 2016..................	$0	$ 6,000
Intercompany profit in inventory on December 31, 2016...............	$0	$10,000

Intercompany accounts receivables and payables at December 31, 2016: $20,000

Constructive retirement of debt upon purchase by affiliate:
On December 31, 2015, the Parent Company paid $486,635 to purchase from an unaffiliated company the Subsidiary's outstanding bond payable. On the date of the intercompany transaction, the bond had a carrying value (on the Subsidiary's books) of $513,356. This results in a constructive gain on the retirement of debt during the year ended December 31, 2015 equal to $26,721 (i.e., $513,356 − $486,635). This amount is also equal to the sum of the unamortized premium on the bond payable (i.e., $513,356 − $500,000 = $13,356) plus the discount on the bond investment (i.e., $500,000 − $486,635 = $13,365) on the date of the intercompany bond purchase.

On the date of the intercompany transaction, this constructive retirement gain is completely confirmed in the consolidated financial statements. However, it is gradually recognized in the separate pre-consolidation financial statements as the bond discount and premium are amortized by the Parent company and the Subsidiary, respectively. As the discount and premium accounts are amortized, this amount will be 100 percent allocated to the parent's controlling interest. (We discuss our reasoning for this allocation scheme in the chapter discussion.) The companies use straight-line amortization, so the annual amount that will become recognized in the separate pre-consolidation financial statements is the same each year, and equals the sum of the annual amount of bond-payable premium amortization and the annual amount of bond-investment discount amortization. (Note that if there was a bond-payable discount and a bond-investment premium, there would have been a loss on constructive retirement.) The following table summarizes how the bond gain (loss) enters the separate pre-consolidation financial statements of the affiliated companies.

	Bond Payable		Bond Investment		Net	
	Unamortized (Premium) Discount	Amortization of (Premium) Discount	Unamortizated (Premium) Discount	Amortization of (Premium) Discount	Gain (Loss) Recognized Each Year in Pre-Consolidated Income Statements	Remaining Gain (Loss) Confirmed but not in Pre-Consolidated Statements
Dec. 31, 2015...	$(13,356)		$13,365			$26,721
Dec. 31, 2016...	(8,904)	$(4,452)	8,910	$4,455	$8,907	17,814
Dec. 31, 2017...	(4,452)	(4,452)	4,455	4,455	8,907	8,907
Dec. 31, 2018...	0	(4,452)	0	4,455	8,907	0

d. The following is the general formula for computing the equity investment account (under the equity method) at any point in time:

	(1) p% × book value of the net assets of the subsidiary
Plus:	(2) Unamortized p% AAP
Less:	(3) 100% × downstream deferred intercompany asset profits
Less:	(4) p% × upstream deferred intercompany asset profits
Plus:	(5) 100% of upstream and downstream gains (losses) on constructive retirement of intercompany debt that have not yet been recognized in pre-consolidation income of affiliated companies
	Equity method investment account

Note: Item (5) was introduced in this chapter. Items (1) through (4) were included in the comprehensive review problem in Chapter 5.

Equity investment account balance at January 1, 2016:

Jan. 1, 2016		
	$380,880	(1) 90% × ($119,200 + $124,000 + $180,000)
Plus:	198,000	(2) $198,000 (from *Part b*)
Less:	(48,600)	(3) 100% × $48,600 (from *Part c*)
Less:	(5,400)	(4) 90% × $6,000 (from *Part c*)
Plus:	26,721	(5) 100% × $26,721 (from *Part c*)
	$551,601	

Equity investment account balance at December 31, 2016:

Dec. 31, 2016		
	$448,787	(1) 90% × ($119,200 + $124,000 + $255,452)
Plus:	180,000	(2) $180,000 (from *Part b*)
Less:	(43,200)	(3) 100% × $43,200 (from *Part c*)
Less:	(9,000)	(4) 90% × $10,000 (from *Part c*)
Plus:	17,814	(5) 100% × $17,814 (from *Part c*)
	$594,401	

e. Equity method investment accounting includes the following routine adjustments during any given period: (1) recognition of p% of the subsidiary's income, (2) recognition of p% of the dividends declared by the subsidiary, (3) amortization of the p% AAP, (4) recognition of prior period deferred intercompany profits that have been confirmed though either transactions with unaffiliated parties or depreciation/amortization, (5) deferral of intercompany profits newly originated during the current period, and (6) adjustment for bond gain recognized during the year in the separate pre-consolidation income statements of separate affiliates via amortization of premium & discount. With respect to the deferred intercompany asset profits, the effect on the equity investment account is 100% for downstream transactions and p% for upstream transactions. With respect to the intercompany bond gains (losses), the effect on the equity investment account is 100% for downstream and upstream transactions. Information for items (1) and (3) is available in the initial information, information in item (2) was summarized in part b, and information for items (4) through (6) was summarized in part c. These items are all reflected in the following completed T-account.

Equity Investment

January 1, 2016	551,601		
(1) p% × net income of Sub. = 90% × $91,452	82,307	14,400	(2) p% × dividends of Sub. = 90% × $16,000
(4) p% x BOY upstream inventory profits recognized during 2016 = 90% × $6,000 (see part c)	5,400	18,000	(3) p% AAP amortization (see part b.)
(4) 100% × downstream equipment profits recognized via depreciation during 2016 (see part c)	5,400	9,000	(5) p% × EOY upstream inventory profits deferred until year of sale to unaffiliated party = 90% × 10,000 (see part c)
		8,907	(6) 100% of intercompany bond gain recognized in separate pre-consolidation income statements of separate affiliates via amortization of premium & discount (see part c)
December 31, 2016	594,401		

f. The following is the general formula for computing the noncontrolling interest in consolidated equity at any point in time:

	(1) nci% × book value of the net assets of the subsidiary
Plus:	(2) Unamortized nci% AAP
Less:	(3) nci% × upstream deferred intercompany profits
	Noncontrolling interest

The balance of noncontrolling interest in consolidated equity at January 1, 2016:

	Jan. 1, 2016	
	$42,320	(1) 10% × ($119,200 + $124,000 + $180,000)
Plus:	22,000	(2) $22,000 (from Part b)
Less:	(600)	(3) 10% × $6,000 (from Part c)
	$63,720	

The balance of noncontrolling interest in consolidated equity at December 31, 2016:

	Dec. 31, 2016	
	$49,865	(1) 10% × ($119,200 + $124,000 + $255,452)
Plus:	20,000	(2) $20,000 (from Part b)
Less:	(1,000)	(3) 10% × $10,000 (from Part c)
	$68,865	

g.

Incremental Computation of Consolidated Net Income for the Year Ended December 31, 2016	Year Ended Dec. 31, 2016	
Parent's stand-alone net income	$1,069,455	($1,126,655 − $57,200)
Plus: 100% realized downstream deferred asset profits	5,400	(see part c)
Less: 100% unrealized downstream deferred asset profits	—	(none)
Less: 100% of prev debt gain recognized in current pre-consol I/S	(8,907)	(see part c)
Parent's adjusted stand-alone net income	1,065,948	
Subsidiary's stand-alone net income	91,452	(see facts)
Plus: 100% realized upstream deferred asset profits	6,000	(see part c)
Less: 100% unrealized upstream deferred asset profits	(10,000)	(see part c)
Less: 100% AAP amortization	(20,000)	(see part b)
Subsidiary's adjusted stand-alone net income	67,452	
Consolidated net income	$1,133,400	

Incremental Computation of Consolidated Net Income Attributable to the Controlling Interest for the Year Ended December 31, 2016	Year Ended Dec. 31, 2016	
Parent's stand-alone net income	$1,069,455	($1,126,655 − $57,200)
Plus: 100% realized downstream deferred asset profits	5,400	(see part c)
Less: 100% unrealized downstream deferred asset profits	—	(none)
Less: 100% of prev debt gain recognized in current pre-consol I/S	(8,907)	(see part c)
Parent's adjusted stand-alone net income	1,065,948	
p% x Subsidiary's stand-alone net income	82,307	(see facts)
Plus: p% realized upstream deferred asset profits	5,400	(see part c)
Less: p% unrealized upstream deferred asset profits	(9,000)	(see part c)
Less: p% AAP amortization	(18,000)	(see part b)
P% share of Subsidiary's adjusted stand-alone net income	60,707	
Consolidated net income attributable to the controlling interest	$1,126,655	

Incremental Computation of Consolidated Net Income Attributable to the Noncontrolling Interest for the Year Ended December 31, 2016	Year Ended Dec. 31, 2016	
nci% x subsidiary's stand-alone net income	$9,145	(see facts)
Plus: nci% realized upstream deferred asset profits	600	(see part c)
Less: nci% unrealized upstream deferred asset profits	(1,000)	(see part c)
Less: nci% AAP amortization	(2,000)	(see part b)
Consolidated net income attributable to the noncontrolling interest	$6,745	

h.

[C]	Equity Income from subsidiary	57,200	
	Income attributable to NCI	6,745	
	Dividends – subsidiary		16,000
	Investment in subsidiary		42,800
	Noncontrolling interest		5,145
[E]	Common stock (S) @ BOY	119,200	
	APIC	124,000	
	Retained earnings (S) @ BOY	180,000	
	Investment in subsidiary @ BOY		380,880
	Noncontrolling interest @ BOY		42,320
[A]	Patent	120,000	
	Goodwill	100,000	
	Investment in subsidiary @ BOY		198,000
	Noncontrolling interest @ BOY		22,000
[D]	Depreciation & amortization expense	20,000	
	Patent		20,000
[I_cogs]	Investment in subsidiary @ BOY	5,400	
	Noncontrolling interest @ BOY	600	
	Cost of goods sold		6,000
[I_sales]	Sales	60,000	
	Cost of goods sold		60,000
[I_cogs]	Cost of goods sold	10,000	
	Inventories		10,000
[I_pay]	Accounts payable	20,000	
	Accounts receivable		20,000
[I_gain]	Investment in subsidiary @ BOY	48,600	
	Property, plant & equipment, net @ BOY		48,600
[I_dep]	Property, plant & equipment, net	5,400	
	Operating expenses		5,400
[I_bond]	Bond payable (net)	508,904	
	Interest income	29,455	
	Investment in bonds (net)		491,090
	Interest expense		20,548
	BOY Investment in subsidiary		26,721

Consolidation Spreadsheet for the year ended December 31, 2016

	Parent	Subsidiary	Consolidation Entries Dr		Consolidation Entries Cr		Consolidated
Income statement:							
Sales.........................	$ 8,000,000	$ 800,000	[I~sales~]	$ 60,000			$ 8,740,000
Cost of goods sold..................	(5,760,000)	(480,000)	[I~cogs~]	10,000	[I~cogs~]	$ 6,000	(6,184,000)
					[I~sales~]	60,000	
Gross profit........................	2,240,000	320,000					2,556,000
Depreciation & amortization expense....	(700,000)	(58,000)	[D]	20,000	[I~dep~]	5,400	(772,600)
Operating & other expenses..........	(500,000)	(150,000)					(650,000)
Bond interest income...............	29,455		[I~bond~]	29,455			0
Bond interest expense..............		(20,548)			[I~bond~]	20,548	0
Total expenses...................	(1,170,545)	(228,548)					(1,422,600)
Equity income from subsidiary........	57,200		[C]	57,200			0
Consolidated net income.............	1,126,655	91,452					1,133,400
Income attributable to NCI...........			[C]	6,745			(6,745)
Income attributable to controlling int	$ 1,126,655	$ 91,452					$ 1,126,655
Statement of retained earnings:							
Beginning retained earnings...........	$ 4,593,201	$ 180,000	[E]	180,000			$ 4,593,201
Income attributable to controlling int	1,126,655	91,452					1,126,655
Dividends declared..................	(227,200)	(16,000)			[C]	16,000	(227,200)
Ending retained earnings.............	$ 5,492,656	$ 255,452					$ 5,492,656
Balance sheet:							
Cash.............................	$ 900,013	$ 400,000					$ 1,300,013
Accounts receivable.................	1,113,100	480,000			[I~pay~]	20,000	1,573,100
Inventories	1,840,000	623,749			[I~cogs~]	10,000	2,453,749
Property, plant & equipment, net	8,048,000	824,000	[I~dep~]	5,400	[I~asset~]	48,600	8,828,800
Patent...........................			[A]	120,000	[D]	20,000	100,000
Investment in subsidiary.............	594,401		[I~gain~]	48,600	[C]	42,800	0
			[I~dep~]	5,400	[E]	380,880	
					[A]	198,000	
					[I~bond~]	26,721	
Investment in bond (net).............	491,090				[I~bond~]	491,090	0
Goodwill			[A]	100,000			100,000
Total assets.......................	$12,986,604	$2,327,749					$14,355,662
Accounts payable..................	$ 808,000	$ 240,000	[I~pay~]	20,000			$ 1,028,000
Other current liabilities	995,548	480,193					1,475,741
Bond payable (net).................		508,904	[I~bond~]	508,904			0
Other long-term liabilities.............	2,000,000	600,000					2,600,000
Common stock.....................	442,400	119,200	[E]	119,200			442,400
APIC	3,248,000	124,000	[E]	124,000			3,248,000
Retained earnings	5,492,656	255,452					5,492,656
Noncontrolling interest..............			[I~cogs~]	600	[C]	5,145	68,865
					[E]	42,320	
					[A]	22,000	
Total liabilities and equity.............	$12,986,604	$2,327,749		$1,415,504		$1,415,504	$14,355,662

Accounting for Foreign Currency Transactions and Derivatives

The Coca-Cola Company (Coca-Cola) transacts its business in many different currencies through its nearly 200 subsidiaries as it buys and sells products around the world. Since it must report its financial statements in $US, foreign currency-denominated transactions must be translated into $US. This translation may result in gains or losses as the $US fluctuates in value vis-à-vis other world currencies, adding unwanted variability in reported earnings. These fluctuations in the relative value of the $US can be significant as seen in the following graph of the $US vis-à-vis the Euro over the past decade:

COCA-COLA

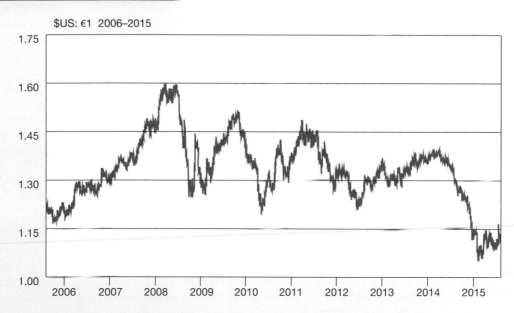

$US: €1 2006–2015

Since 2006, the $US value of the Euro (€) has ranged from a high of $1.59:€1 to a low of $1.05:€1 and has exhibited considerable volatility over the past decade as the $US weakened and strengthened vis-à-vis the Euro.

To mitigate this risk, Coca-Cola, like all other large companies, purchases financial securities (called "derivative financial instruments") which have unique characteristics: some derivatives allow the purchaser to lock in the future foreign currency exchange rates, thus relieving uncertainty about future exchange rates; others fluctuate in value in the opposite direction from the relative value of the $US, thus cancelling out most of the fluctuations. As a result, foreign currency-related losses that Coca-Cola might incur on a foreign-currency transaction can be offset by gains on the financial derivatives, and vice versa. The purchase of

continued

(continued from previous page)

these derivative financial instruments to mitigate foreign currency risk is called hedging, and these financial derivative instruments serve a valuable economic function to transfer risk from the party seeking to avoid it to the party willing to accept it for a price.

Companies often hedge a variety of risks, including foreign currency risks and commodity price risks, and the accounting for the investment in these securities is the subject of this chapter. We first discuss the nature of these risks and illustrate the case in which these risks are not hedged. We, then, add the purchase of derivative financial instruments and illustrate the accounting for these securities when the transaction is hedged.

The basic idea is relatively straight-forward: under hedge accounting, the derivative financial instrument and the asset or liability that the company is hedging are reported at fair value on the statement date and fluctuations in their fair values are ultimately reported in income. To the extent that the hedge is effective, then, volatility in reported income is reduced.

In this Chapter, we discuss the accounting for foreign currency gains and losses and for derivative financial instruments.

Source: Coca-Cola 2014 10-K report.

CHAPTER ORGANIZATION

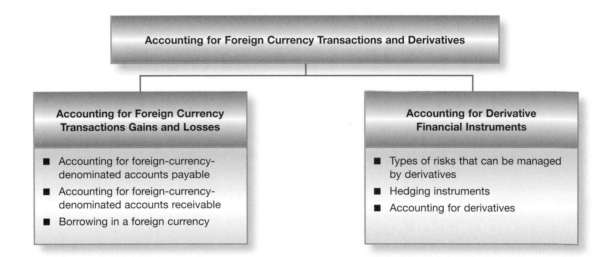

Companies are required to disclose, in the MD&A section of their 10-K reports, various risk factors that affect their businesses. For example, **Coca-Cola** (Coke) provides the following discussion of risk relating to fluctuations in foreign currency exchange rates in its 2014 10-K:

> We earn revenues, pay expenses, own assets and incur liabilities in countries using currencies other than the U.S. dollar, including the Euro, the Japanese yen, the Brazilian real and the Mexican peso. In 2014, we used 70 functional currencies in addition to the U.S. dollar and derived $26.2 billion of net operating revenues from operations outside the United States. Because our consolidated financial statements are presented in U.S. dollars, we must translate revenues, income and expenses, as well as assets and liabilities, into U.S. dollars at exchange rates in effect during or at the end of each reporting period. Therefore, increases or decreases in the value of the U.S. dollar against other major currencies affect our net operating revenues, operating income and the value of balance sheet items denominated in foreign currencies.

Increases and decreases in the value of the $US relative to other world currencies affect the reported dollar amount of Coke's income statement and balance sheet accounts, as well as the amount of cash it receives from foreign currency-denominated transactions. As a result, Coke's profitability and cash flow are both affected as the value of the $US weakens and strengthens relative to other world currencies. We discuss the accounting for foreign-currency-denominated transactions in this chapter.

Coca-Cola reports that it employs derivative financial instruments ("*derivatives*") to reduce its exposure to these currency-related risks. Companies also use derivatives to mitigate risks associated with fluctuating commodity prices and interest rates. Derivatives can act like an insurance policy to transfer risk from Coca-Cola to another party that understands how to manage these risks and how to price them.[1] This other party (called the *counterparty*) accepts that risk for a fee, and Coca-Cola treats the fee as a cost of doing business. We also discuss the accounting for *derivatives* in this chapter.

---

[1] Of course, as we learned during the world financial crisis beginning in 2007, companies and individuals can also increase their risk by entering into derivatives contracts for a speculative or unhedged position.

We begin with a general overview of fluctuations in the value of the $US vis-à-vis other world currencies and how these fluctuations affect financial statements. We then proceed to a more general discussion of the use of derivatives to mitigate risk and how to account for derivative financial instruments.

EFFECT OF EXCHANGE RATES ON THE INCOME STATEMENT AND THE BALANCE SHEET

If one of **Coca-Cola**'s U.S.-based companies purchases product from a vendor located in Ireland, that vendor may write the purchase invoice to be payable in Euros (€), the currency of the European Economic Union. To make payment, Coca-Cola will sell $US to purchase Euros. Similarly, if Coca-Cola's U.S.-based company sells products with an invoice denominated in Japanese Yen (¥), upon payment by its customer, Coke will sell Yen and purchase $US if it desires to hold $US rather than Yen.[2]

Currency is really just a commodity. It is bought and sold in foreign exchange markets in the same way that copper and orange juice are purchased and sold in commodities markets. And like other commodities, as the demand for $US increases, the price of $US increases, and as demand falls, so does the price. Demand for $US increases as the United States exports more of its products (foreign customers must purchase $US to make payment). Demand also increases as the U.S. stock and bond markets increase since foreign investors will need to purchase $US in order to make investments in these markets. Conversely, demand for $US falls as the United States imports more goods and services and as interest rates and stock returns decline. $US also become less desirable as the inflation rate in the United States increases because the $US lose their purchasing power.

As we graphically illustrate in our opening vignette, in recent years, the value of the $US has strengthened with respect to many world currencies as a result of the factors cited above. Since its height in 2008 (i.e., highest amount of $US to purchase €1), the value of the $US has strengthened from an exchange ratio of $1.59:€1 in 2008 to $1.05:€1 in 2015. As a result, it cost less $US to purchase one Euro in 2015 than it did in 2008.[3] Although the $US has strengthened vis-à-vis other world currencies in recent years, the $US was relatively weak during the financial crisis of 2008, thus making imports more expensive.

So, what does this mean for the financial statements of large, U.S.-based multinational companies? Because much of their business is conducted outside of the United States, these companies likely generate receivables and payables that are denominated in currencies other than the $US. And because U.S. companies report to their shareholders and to the SEC in $US, they are required to remeasure their foreign-currency-denominated accounts receivable and payable into $US as they prepare their financial statements.

We begin our discussion with the accounting for foreign-currency-denominated assets and liabilities and illustrate the manner in which fluctuations in currency exchange rates affect reported profit. We, then, discuss the ways in which companies can reduce these fluctuations in earnings by the use of financial instruments (derivatives) and how we account for these securities.

ACCOUNTING FOR FOREIGN CURRENCY TRANSACTIONS GAINS AND LOSSES

U.S. companies may transact business in foreign currencies and their subsidiaries may be headquartered in foreign countries, conducting business in multiple currencies as well. Further, these subsidiary companies typically maintain their accounting records in currencies other than the $US *and produce financial statements that are denominated in those foreign currencies.* Ultimately, however, the U.S.

LO1 Describe the accounting for foreign currency transactions gains and losses.

---

[2] In all of our examples, we assume that the U.S.-based reporting entity (i.e., the company issuing financial statements) uses the $US as its reporting currency. As noted in FASB ASC 830-10-15-4, "a currency other than the U.S. dollar may be the reporting currency in financial statements that are prepared in conformity with U.S. generally accepted accounting principles (GAAP). For example, a foreign entity may report in its local currency in conformity with U.S. GAAP." If so, then the requirements described in this chapter also apply to those foreign-currency-denominated financial statements.

[3] Our discussion thus far has focused on exchange rates of the $US relative to one unit of the foreign currency. Sometimes exchange ratios are expressed in terms of the value of $1. For example, an exchange rate of $1.48:€1 can also be expressed as $1:€0.68. Expressing the exchange ratio as $1.48:€1 implies a cost of €0.68 to purchase $1. Both ratio forms are published in the financial press.

parent company must produce consolidated financial statements that are expressed in $US. So, all of these foreign currency-denominated transactions and financial statements must first be converted into $US before the consolidation process can begin.

The process by which this conversion is accomplished is codified in ASC 830, *Foreign Currency Matters*, which articulates the following two distinct processes to express all of a reporting entity's foreign currency-denominated transactions and financial statements in a single reporting currency:

■ **Foreign currency measurement**—This is the process by which a company expresses *transactions*, whose terms are denominated in a foreign currency, in its functional currency (the primary currency in which the company conducts its business).[4] Changes in functional currency amounts that result from fluctuations in exchange rates are called *transaction gains or losses* and transaction gains and losses are included in net income (these are the transaction gains and losses that companies may seek to hedge by the use of derivative financial instruments which we discuss in this chapter).

■ **Foreign currency translation**—This is the process of expressing a subsidiary's foreign currency-denominated *financial statements* in $US so that those financial statements can be consolidated with those of the parent company. Changes in reporting currency amounts that result from the translation process are called *translation adjustments*. Translation adjustments are included in the Cumulative Translation Adjustment (CTA) account, which is a component of Other Comprehensive Income (we describe the translation process in Chapter 8).

In this chapter, we discuss foreign currency measurement of *transactions* (i.e., the impact of exchange rate fluctuations on profitability) and the ways in which companies can mitigate earnings volatility through the use of financial derivatives. Then, in Chapter 8, we continue to focus on foreign currency issues, but direct our attention to the consolidation of subsidiaries for which financial statement information is denominated in foreign currencies.

We begin with three examples of the accounting for foreign-currency-denominated accounts payable and accounts receivable and the accounting for borrowing in a foreign currency. These examples will highlight the effects of foreign exchange rates on profitability and provide the motivation for our discussion of derivative financial instruments that follows in the last section of this chapter.

Accounting for Foreign-Currency-Denominated Accounts Payable

Assume that, on November 17, 2014, we purchase product from a manufacturer located in Italy. Further assume that the manufacturer requires payment in Euros (€). Our company purchases 10,000 units of product at a sales price of €15 per unit, and the assumed exchange rate on the date of sale is $1.30:€1. The invoice terms are 90 days and the due date for payment is February 15, 2015.

When the inventories are received, our company records the inventories and an account payable as follows (assuming perpetual inventory accounting):

Inventories	195,000	
Accounts payable (€150,000)		195,000
(to record the purchase of inventories for €150,000 when the exchange rate is		
$1.30:€1)		

The inventories are recorded at their $US equivalent of $195,000 (10,000 units × €15/unit × $1.30/€). The payable is also recorded at the $US equivalent of $195,000; however, it is important to understand that this $US recorded value is only an approximation of the $US amount we expect to pay to settle the €150,000 account payable. The account payable never actually becomes a payable denominated in $US; it's just that our accounting system can only record transactions in one currency (i.e., in this case, $US).

The fundamental principle underlying foreign-currency-denominated transactions (i.e. FASB ASC 830-20-35) is that any foreign-currency-denominated receivables or payables must be remeasured to the current spot rate (the exchange rate at the present time) on each balance sheet date and on the settlement date. On December 31, 2014, our company issues its financial statements, and the assumed exchange rate is now $1.40:€1. If we were to make payment on that date, our company would have to sell $210,000 (€150,000 × $1.40/€) to purchase the €150,000 required for payment. As a result our

---

[4] We discuss functional currency in Chapter 8.

company's cash flow would be reduced by $15,000 ($210,000 − $195,000) at current exchange rates. We are required to accrue this estimated transaction loss of $15,000 on the December 31, 2014, balance sheet date.[5] This is accomplished with the following journal entry:

Foreign currency transaction loss	15,000	
Accounts payable (€150,000)		15,000
(to record the increase in accounts payable due to a decline in the $US from		
$1.30:€1 to $1.40:€1)		

The account payable is now correctly reported on our balance sheet at its current $US-equivalent value of $210,000 and the increase in the recorded liability is reflected as a foreign currency transaction loss in our income statement for the period ended December 31, 2014.

Now, assume that on February 15, 2015 (i.e., the date payment is made), the $US further declines in value to $1.45:€1. The journal entry to record the payment is as follows:

Accounts payable (€150,000)	210,000	
Foreign currency transaction loss	7,500	
Cash		217,500[6]
(to record the payment of €150,000 when the exchange rate is $1.45:€1)		

To settle its €150,000 liability, our company must sell $217,500 to purchase Euros. Because the account payable is reported at $210,000 on the payment date, we must recognize the additional liability as a foreign exchange transaction loss.

From the inception of the payable to its ultimate payment, our company's cash flow has been reduced by $22,500 ($15,000 + $7,500) as a result of the weakening $US, and that cash flow decline is reflected in our income statement as a loss of $22,500 ($15,000 recognized in the period ending December 31, 2014, and $7,500 recognized in the period including settlement on February 15, 2015).

To illustrate the opposite case of a gain, let us now assume that, instead of weakening further between December 31, 2014, and February 15, 2015, the $US *strengthens* to an exchange rate of $1.35:€1. The €150,000 account payable can now be settled for $202,500 on February 15, 2015. Because the account payable is reported at a balance of $210,000, our entry to record the payment now results in a gain as follows:

Accounts payable (€150,000)	210,000	
Foreign currency transaction gain.		7,500
Cash		202,500
(to record the payment of €150,000 when the exchange rate is $1.35:€1)		

As a result of the strengthening $US, the dollar equivalent of our €150,000 account payable has decreased, and the reduction of the liability is recognized as a foreign currency transaction gain in our income statement.

---

[5] FASB ASC 830-20-25-1 prescribes that "At the date a foreign currency transaction is recognized, each asset, liability, revenue, expense, gain, or loss arising from the transaction shall be recorded in the functional currency of the recording entity." And FASB ASC 830-25-35-1 recognizes a subsequent change from the initial recognized amount in income: "A change in exchange rates between the functional currency and the currency in which a transaction is denominated increases or decreases the expected amount of functional currency cash flows upon settlement of the transaction. That increase or decrease in expected functional currency cash flows is a foreign currency transaction gain or loss that generally shall be included in determining net income for the period in which the exchange rate changes."

[6] To simplify exposition we credit the cash account. In practice, we would first have the intermediate step to acquire the Euros:

Investment in Euros	217,500	
Cash.		217,500

and, then, record the settlement of the payable:

Accounts payable (€150,000)	210,000	
Foreign currency transaction loss	7,500	
Investment in Euros		217,500

Accounting for Foreign-Currency-Denominated Accounts Receivable

Assume that, on December 3, 2014, our company sells ¥12,500,000 of goods to a customer located in Japan (i.e., the invoice is written in Japanese Yen [¥]). When the goods are shipped, the exchange rate is $0.008:¥1 and the receivable is due in 90 days, on March 3, 2015. The $US equivalent value of ¥12,500,000 on the date of sale is $100,000 (i.e., ¥12,500,000 × $0.008/¥). On the collection date, we will sell the ¥12,500,000 we collect from our customer and will purchase $US at the prevailing exchange rate on that date.

Because our accounting system is denominated in $US, the sale is recorded as follows:

Accounts receivable (¥12,500,000)	100,000	
Sales		100,000
(to record the sale of ¥12,500,000 of goods on account when the exchange rate is $0.008:¥1)		

Assume that, on December 31, 2014, the dollar weakens to an exchange rate of $0.0085:¥1. The ¥12,500,000 account receivable, therefore, is worth $106,250 (¥12,500,000 × $0.0085:¥1) as of December 31, 2014. The dollar's decline in value vis-à-vis the Yen means that the Yen our company will receive are worth more $US, and the $US equivalent of the ¥12,500,000 our company will receive has increased, resulting in a gain of $6,250 (¥12,500,000 × [$0.0085:¥1 − $0.008:¥1]).

The increase in the $US value of the Yen-denominated receivable and the resulting gain is reported as follows:

Accounts receivable (¥12,500,000)	6,250	
Foreign currency transaction gain		6,250
(to record the increase in accounts receivable due to a decline in the $US to $0.0085:¥1)		

Now, assume that the $US further declines to $0.009:¥1 on March 3, 2015. Our company receives ¥12,500,000 from its customer and sells the Yen to receive $112,500. This transaction is recorded as follows:

Cash	112,500	
Accounts receivable (¥12,500,000)		106,250
Foreign currency transaction gain		6,250
(to record the receipt of ¥12,500,000 at an exchange rate of $0.009:¥1)		

Over the life of the receivable, our company has recognized a foreign currency transaction gain of $12,500 (¥12,500,000 × [$0.009/¥ − $0.008/¥]), $6,250 during the period ending December 31, 2014, and the remainder upon collection of the receivable and conversion of Yen into $US during the period including settlement on March 3, 2015.

If, instead, the $US had strengthened to $0.00825:¥1 on March 3, 2015, the $US equivalent of the ¥12,500,000 received would have been $103,125, resulting in the following journal entry:

Cash	103,125	
Foreign currency transaction loss	3,125	
Accounts receivable (¥12,500,000)		106,250
(to record the receipt of ¥12,500,000 at an exchange rate of $0.00825:¥1)		

Foreign Currency Transaction Gains and Losses—Summary

Our discussion of gains and losses in foreign-currency-denominated assets and liabilities can be summarized as follows:

- A strengthening or weakening $US means that the $US buys more (less) of the foreign currency. It also means we receive less (more) $US for the foreign currency owed to us.

■ If we have a receivable or payable denominated in a foreign currency and the $US strengthens or weakens, since we will either receive or pay a fixed amount of the foreign currency and it is now worth more or less $US, we have experienced a gain or loss due to the fluctuation in the relative value of the $US vis-à-vis the foreign currency. These gains or losses arising from transactions denominated in a foreign currency are foreign currency transaction gains or losses.

■ The following chart illustrates the relationship between fluctuations in exchange rates and exchange gains and losses:

	Accounts Receivable Denominated in Foreign Currency	Accounts Payable Denominated in Foreign Currency
$US **Weakens**	Exchange gain	Exchange loss
$US **Strengthens**.	Exchange loss	Exchange gain

When the $US weakens, foreign-currency-denominated assets and liabilities are worth *more* $US. As the $US-value of assets increases, we recognize a gain, and as the $US-value of liabilities increases, we recognize a loss. Conversely, when the $US strengthens, assets and liabilities are worth *less* $US. As the $US-value of assets decreases, we recognize a loss, and as the $US value of liabilities decreases, we recognize a gain.

The easiest way to remember the recognition of gains and losses is to think of the accounting equation: Assets = Liabilities + Equity. As assets and liabilities increase and decrease, equity must change in order to maintain the equality. An increase in equity is recognized as a gain and a decrease is recognized as a loss.

TOPIC REVIEW

Accounting for Foreign-Currency-Denominated Receivable and Payable

Assume that on November 2, 2014, we purchase product from a manufacturer located in Ireland and that the manufacturer requires payment in Euros (€). Our company purchases 6,000 units of product at a sales price of €10 per unit, and the assumed exchange rate on the date of sale is $1.20:€1. The invoice terms are 90 days and the due date for payment is January 31, 2015. Assume that the exchange rate rises to $1.25:€1 on December 31 and to $1.30:€1 on January 31, 2015.

Required

a. Prepare the journal entries for the date of purchase, December 31, and the date of payment.

b. Prepare the journal entries for the date of purchase, December 31, and the date of payment assuming that we are selling the inventory instead of purchasing it.

The solution to this review problem can be found on page 507.

Borrowing in a Foreign Currency

Many companies borrow money from banks outside of the U.S. or sell bonds in global capital markets. While this debt is often denominated in other world currencies, it is, otherwise, structured like any other borrowing (e.g., includes contractual terms, like scheduled payments of interest and principal). And, just like the foreign-currency-denominated account payable in our example above, foreign-currency-denominated debt must be translated into $US during the reporting process.

To illustrate, assume our company borrows €5 million at 5% interest on July 1, 2014, with interest payments due semiannually and the principal due in 5 years. Also assume the following exchange rates:

July 1, 2014	$1.20: €1
September 30, 2014.	$1.25: €1
December 31, 2014	$1.30: €1

The journal entries that our company will record related to this borrowing are as follows:

July 1, 2014	Cash...	6,000,000	
	Debt (€5,000,000)................................		6,000,000
	(to record debt at €5,000,000 × $1.20/€ = $6,000,000)		
September 30, 2014	Interest expense...................................	78,125	
	Interest payable................................		78,125
	(to accrue interest (July 1–Sept. 30, 2014) of *€5,000,000 × 5%/4 = €62,500 × $1.25/€ = $78,125)*		
	Foreign currency transaction loss	250,000	
	Debt (€5,000,000)................................		250,000
	(to recognize the increase in the $US value of the debt of *€5,000,000 × ($1.25 − $1.20) /€ = $250,000)*		
December 31, 2014	Interest expense...................................	81,250	
	Interest payable................................		81,250
	(to accrue interest (Oct.1–Dec.31, 2014) of *€5,000,000 × 5%/4 = €62,500 × $1.30/€)*		
	Foreign currency transaction loss	253,125	
	Interest payable................................		3,125
	Debt (€5,000,000)................................		250,000
	(to recognize the increase in the $US value of the debt of €5,000,000 × *($1.30 − $1.25)/€ = $250,000 and an increase in the $US value of the* *interest payable of €5,000,000 × .05/4 × ($1.30 − $1.25)/€ = $3,125)*		
January 1, 2015	Interest payable	162,500	
	Cash		162,500
	(to record semiannual payment of interest of €5,000,000 × 5%/2= *€125,000 × $1.30/€)*		

Following are explanations for the journal entries presented above:

■ July 1, 2014—record the debt at the current exchange rate of $1.20:€1 for a $US equivalent of €5,000,000 × $1.20/€ = $6,000,000.

■ September 30, 2014—accrue interest expense of and interest payable of $78,125 at the current exchange rate (€5,000,000 × 5%/4 = €62,500 × $1.25/€ = $78,125).

■ September 30, 2014—accrue a foreign exchange loss of $250,000 to revalue the debt at the current exchange rate of $1.25:€1 [€5,000,000 × ($1.25 − $1.20)/€ = $250,000].

■ December 31, 2014—accrue interest of $81,250 at the current exchange rate of $1.30:€1 (€5,000,000 × 5%/4 × $1.30/€ = $81,250).

■ December 31, 2014—accrue a foreign exchange loss of $253,125 relating to the increase in the $US value of both the debt and the interest payable that was accrued at September 30, 2014 (all of our liabilities must be revalued to the new exchange rate). The interest payable is now reported at $162,500 (€5,000,000 × 0.05/2 × $1.30/€ = $162,500), and that is the amount that is paid on January 1, 2015, for the first semiannual interest payment.

■ January 1, 2015—record payment of the interest payable of $162,500.

Through January 1, 2015, our company suffered a cash transaction loss of $12,500.[7] This loss is reported as additional Interest Expense of $9,375 ($78,125 + $81,250 − $150,000),[8] with the remainder of $3,125 reported as part of the Foreign Exchange Loss to adjust the Interest Payable on December 31 to arrive at the $162,500 of interest required to be paid. We have also accrued a noncash loss of $500,000 (€5,000,000 × [($1.30 − $1.20)]/€ = $500,000) to recognize that the payment of the debt will likely require more $US as a result of the weakening dollar.

We now turn our attention to the ways in which a company can mitigate the above-discussed risks from international currency fluctuations.

---

[7] (€5,000,000 × 5%/2 = €125,000 × ($1.30 − $1.20)/€ = $12,500)

[8] (€5,000,000 × 5%/2 = €125,000 × $1.20/€ = $150,000)

DERIVATIVE FINANCIAL INSTRUMENTS

In the previous section, we discuss three scenarios in which the current settlement value of a U.S. company's account receivable, account payable, and debt obligations change as a result of changes in the value of the $US vis-à-vis other world currencies. And, these changes are recognized as gains and losses in net income to reflect the associated changes in their estimated cash flows.

LO2 Describe the accounting for derivative financial instruments.

The variability in cash flows resulting from foreign-currency exchange-rate fluctuations can create headaches for companies' cash management and treasury functions. In addition, these fluctuations can cause volatility in reported earnings. One way that a company can mitigate this risk is to hold an asset denominated in a foreign currency and a liability denominated in an equal amount of that same currency. Then, any movement in currency exchange rates will exactly offset in currency-exchange gains and losses. This practice might not be optimal, however, from an operational, strategic or financial perspective. As an alternative, financial intermediaries (e.g., foreign-currency brokers) offer ways in which companies can contractually create desired offsetting positions in foreign currencies. These intermediaries agree to make payment to offset any loss should the fair value of our account receivable decrease or our account payable and debt obligations increase, but they will require *us* to make payment in a like amount should the opposite occur (i.e., the value of the receivable increases or the payable and debt obligations decrease). Thus, for a fee, our company can insulate itself against loss, but we also give up the prospect of a gain should exchange rates move favorably.

This is the concept behind **derivative financial instruments ("derivatives")**. As we describe in the Practice Insight boxes on pages 468 and 481, these are generally legal contracts or exchange-traded securities that are designed to transfer risk for a price. In concept, derivatives involve three parties: the company seeking to reduce a particular risk (our company in this case), a company willing to assume that risk (for a fee), and an intermediary that brings the two companies together and receives a fee for doing so. If done properly, this is a win-win-win situation. In practice, companies deal only with the derivatives broker who serves as the counterparty on our derivative contract and whose business it is to find offsetting positions to counterbalance the risk embodied in our derivative.

We begin with a discussion of the types of risks that can be managed by derivatives and, then, proceed to a discussion of the accounting for derivatives.

Types of Risks that Can Be Managed by Derivatives

Companies routinely face risk exposures that can significantly affect their balance sheets, earnings and cash flows. Accounting standards group these exposures into the following two broad categories:[9]

a. **Fair value risk.** Exposure to changes in the *fair value* of a recognized asset or liability (such as an account receivable or payable) or the fair value of an unrecognized firm *commitment* (such as a noncancelable purchase order or sales invoice)

b. **Cash flow risk.** Exposure to variation in *cash flows* relating to a recognized asset or liability or a *forecasted* transaction (such as the planned purchase of raw materials by a manufacturing company).

Companies often use derivatives to hedge their exposure to changes in the fair values of recognized assets and liabilities, generally seeking to protect against an exposure to loss of value of their receivables, investments (e.g., debt and equity securities or loans receivable), and inventories, or an increase in the fair value of their liabilities (accounts payable and debt-related obligations). Cash flow hedges generally relate to the management of cash flow-related risk exposure with respect to recognized assets and liabilities, such as exposures to changes in variable-rate investment income and payments on variable-rate debt obligations, and to cash flow-related risks with respect to forecasted purchases or sales of recognized assets or liabilities, such as the forecasted purchase of a commodity or the forecasted sale of inventory.

Hedging Instruments

Companies hedge foreign exchange, commodity price and interest rate risks by employing a wide variety of financial instruments. All of these instruments can be purchased in the financial markets or from

[9] It is not uncommon for finance and accounting professionals to characterize risk along additional dimensions, like interest rate risk or foreign currency risk. These alternative descriptions of risk generally refer to the contextual origins of risk that ultimately affect fair value or cash flow realizations. For example, variable-interest-rate financial instruments are often characterized as creating increased risk related to future cash flows derived from interest payments while fixed-interest-rate financial instruments are often characterized as creating increased risk related to future financial instrument fair values.

a derivatives broker. Derivatives are generally of three types: forward and futures contracts, option contracts, and swap contracts. We present a brief glossary of terms in the table below and describe each of these instruments in greater detail in Appendix 7B.

Glossary of Terms Related to Derivatives and Hedging	
Forward contract	Agreement to purchase or sell something at a later date at a price agreed upon today. (This is an *obligation* not a *right* as in an option described below). Forward contracts are typically made with dealers of foreign exchange and can be tailored to particular needs.
Futures contract	Similar to forward contracts except futures have standardized contract terms, are traded on organized exchanges, and changes in value must be realized on each and every trading day.
Spot rate	The number of units of a currency that would be exchanged for one unit of another currency on a given date.
Forward rate	The number of units of one currency that would be exchanged for units of another currency at a specified future point in time.
Option contract	A **call option** gives the option holder the right (not the obligation) to buy something at a set price at some future time. A **put option** gives the option holder the right (not the obligation) to sell something at a set price at some future time. The option writer is obligated if the option holder exercises their right to buy or sell.
Exercise (Strike) Price	The price specified in an option contract at which the optioned asset can be purchased.
Interest Rate Swap	Exchange of interest rates between borrowers, typically relating to a borrower with fixed-rate debt exchanging interest payments with a borrower with variable-rate debt.

Examples of the Use of Derivatives to Hedge Exposures

The following are common examples of the ways in which companies hedge fair value, cash flow, and foreign currency exposures with the hedging instruments we discussed in the previous section:

- Fair Value Exposures
  - The use of *futures contracts* to hedge the fair value of inventory (e.g., copper and other types of commodities)
  - The use of *purchased options* to hedge available-for-sale securities
  - The use of a *forward contract* to hedge a firm commitment to buy or sell inventory
  - The use of an *interest rate swap* to convert the fixed-rate debt into variable-rate debt

- Cash Flow Exposures
  - The hedge of a forecasted sale or purchase of a commodity with *forward, futures,* or *option contracts*
  - The hedge of a forecasted foreign-currency-denominated sale or purchase through the use of *foreign-currency forward contracts*
  - The hedge of variable debt interest payments through the use of an *interest rate swap* that converts the variable payments into fixed payments or receipts

- Foreign Currency Exposures
  - The use of a *forward contract* as a foreign currency fair value hedge of an unrecognized foreign-currency-denominated commitment to purchase inventory
  - The use of a *fixed-to-fixed cross-currency swap* to hedge the fair value of recognized foreign-currency-denominated debt and to fix the exchange rate at which the interest is calculated and the interest expensed throughout the life of the debt
  - The use of a *forward-exchange contract* to hedge the foreign currency risk related to an available-for-sale security denominated in a non-U.S. currency

Accounting for Derivatives

The accounting for derivatives is codified in FASB ASC 815, and is largely based on an accounting model introduced in Statement of Financial Accounting Standards No. 133: *Accounting for Derivative Instruments and Hedging Activities*. The fundamental requirement in ASC 815 is simple: **All derivatives must always be measured and reported in the balance sheet at fair value at every interim and annual financial statement date**. There are no exceptions to this principle.

Current GAAP allows companies to designate derivative financial instruments as hedges of either (1) future changes in the fair value of an exposure (i.e., a "fair value" hedge) or (2) future changes in cash flows from an exposure (i.e., a "cash flow" hedge).

- **Fair Value hedge**—If a derivative instrument qualifies as a fair value hedge, both the derivative and the asset or liability to which it relates are reported at fair value at each statement date. Gains or losses on the hedged assets or liabilities are offset (in whole or in part) by losses or gains in the derivative financial instrument. Consequently, the company's income statement is less volatile.

- **Cash flow hedge**—If a derivative instrument qualifies as a cash flow hedge, the after-tax gain or loss on fair value remeasurement of the derivative is included as a component of Other Comprehensive Income (OCI). This means that these gains and losses are deferred until the transaction to which the derivative relates occurs and affects net income. Then, these deferred gains or losses are reclassified from Accumulated Other Comprehensive Income (AOCI) into current net income to offset (in whole or in part) the hedged transaction's effect on reported profit.

Hedge Accounting

The basic idea behind hedge accounting is this. Let's say that a company is concerned about the possible increase in the $US value of a €150,000 Euro-denominated account payable like we illustrate at the beginning of this chapter (recall from our initial example that the $US value of the payable increased from $195,000 to $217,500 as the $US weakened, resulting in a cash loss of $22,500). In order to hedge (mitigate) this risk, let's assume that, on the day the payable arises (when the exchange rate is $1.30:€1), the company purchases a forward contract which allows it to buy Euros at an assumed fixed price of $1.35:€1 (the forward rate) on the day that the payable is due. By the purchase of this forward contract, the company has committed to pay $202,500 to purchase €150,000 to settle the account payable on its due date ([$1.35:€1] × €150,000 = $202,500). It is willing to commit to pay $202,500 to settle this liability because it is concerned that the exchange rate may rise *above* $1.35:€1, resulting in a potentially *larger* cash loss if the $US weakens significantly.

Using our example at the beginning of this chapter, this hedge would have worked to the benefit of the company because the $US ultimately weakened significantly to $1.45:€1 and, had the company not hedged its exposure to exchange rate fluctuations, the company would have been required to spend $217,500 ([$1.45:€1] × €150,000) to settle the payable. However, by the use of a forward contract to hedge that risk, the company has reduced its cash outlay by $15,000 to $7,500. The company has, thus, locked in a cost of $7,500 in order to avoid the risk of a much larger loss and you could think of the $7,500 expense as the cost of buying insurance.[10]

So, how do we recognize the effects of the fluctuations in foreign exchange rates and the purchase of the forward contract in the company's balance sheet and income statement? Earlier in the chapter, we discuss the accounting for the Euro-denominated account payable in which changes in the carrying value of the payable are reflected currently in earnings. Now, in this section, we discuss the accounting for the other half of this transaction, the derivative financial instrument (the forward contract in this case).

Derivatives are accounted for like securities. They are reported at their fair market value (marked-to-market) on the statement date as either assets or liabilities depending on whether the contract confers benefits or obligations on the company that purchases them. In our illustration above, the forward contract is reported as an asset. Why? Because we have the ability to purchase Euros at $1.35:€1 on the date that the contract is settled when the actual exchange rate (the "spot rate") is $1.45:€1. Since the company owns the forward contract and it provides a benefit to the company that can be reliably measured, it meets the test of an asset.

---

[10] The $7,500 cost is the difference between the forward rate of $1.35:€1 and spot rate of $1.30:€1 on the day the forward contract is purchased multiplied by the €150,000 contract amount.

In this case, the forward contact asset serves as an offset to the account payable liability. And, as the $US weakens and the $US value of the €150,000 Euro-denominated account payable increases, the value of the forward contract also increases (because it is giving the company the ability to buy Euros at a lower cost than would have been required given the current spot rate). The foreign currency transaction loss from the increase in $US value of the payable that we illustrate in our first example of this chapter is now partially offset by the gain on the forward contract (leaving only a $7,500 difference). The effect of the exchange rate fluctuation on net income is, therefore, reduced. And, the increase of the reported amount of the Euro-denominated account payable on the balance sheet is partially offset by the increase in the reported amount of the forward contract asset, thus reducing the effect of the exchange rate fluctuation on Stockholders' equity.

PRACTICE INSIGHT

Definition of a Derivative Financial Instrument As the term is used in general business and finance, a ***derivative financial instrument*** ("derivative") is a contract among two or more parties in which the future settlement value of the contract is determined by the price or value of some referenced asset, index, commodity or event. For example, weather derivatives are contracts that pay the holder of the derivative if some meteorological conditions (e.g., rain or snow) occur within a predefined geographic region for specified dates, duration, and intensity. Derivatives can serve as insurance (e.g., for sporting events, in the case of weather derivatives) or can be held for speculative purposes (i.e., they are little more than bets on some future occurrence).

FASB ASC 815-10-15-83 provides the following formal definition of derivatives for accounting purposes:

A derivative instrument is a financial instrument or other contract with all of the following characteristics:

a. The contract has both of the following terms, which determine the amount of the settlement or settlements, and, in some cases, whether or not a settlement is required:
  1. One or more **underlyings**
  2. One or more **notional amounts** or payment provisions or both.
b. The contract requires **no initial net investment** or an initial net investment that is smaller than would be required for other types of contracts that would be expected to have a similar response to changes in market factors.
c. The contract can be settled net by any of the following means:
  1. Its terms implicitly or explicitly require or permit **net settlement**,
  2. It can readily be settled net by a means outside the contract
  3. It provides for delivery of an asset that puts the recipient in a position not substantially different from net settlement.

An **underlying** is a variable that, along with either a notional amount or a payment provision, determines the settlement of a derivative instrument. It can be a specified interest rate, security price, commodity price, foreign exchange rate, index of prices or rates, or other variable. An underlying may be a price or rate of an asset or liability but is not the asset or liability itself (FASB ASC 815-10-15-88).

A **notional amount** is a number of currency units, shares, bushels, pounds, or other units specified in the contract. The settlement of a derivative instrument with a notional amount is determined by interaction of that notional amount with the underlying. The interaction may be simple multiplication, or it may involve a formula with leverage factors or other constants. A payment provision specifies a fixed or determinable settlement to be made if the underlying behaves in a specified manner (FASB ASC 815-10-15-92).

Net settlement means that neither party is required to deliver an asset (FASB ASC 815-10-15-100). An example is forward contract on the price of wheat that does not require either party to deliver bushels of wheat at the settlement of the contract. Net settlement can be made in cash or by delivery of any other assets, say by selling the derivative contract or entering into an offsetting contract. Many derivative instruments are actively traded and can be closed or settled before the contract's expiration or maturity by net settlement in active markets.

These income statement and balance sheet effects can be summarized as follows (we have simplified the accounting in this example to illustrate the net effects on the income statement and balance sheet):

Transaction	Assets	Liabilities
At inception	No entry for purchase of forward contract	Inventories . . . . 195,000 Accounts payable (€150,000) . . . 195,000 *(to record the purchase of inventories for €150,000 when the exchange rate is $1.30:€1)*

At maturity	Forward contract 15,000
	    Foreign currency transaction gain . . . 15,000[11]
	(to record the increase in the value of the forward contract: [$1.45:€1 − $1.35:€1] × €150,000 = $15,000)
	
	Cash 15,000
	    Forward contract 15,000
	(to record the net settlement of the forward contract)
		Foreign currency transaction loss . . . 22,500
		    Accounts payable (€150,000) . . . 22,500
		(to record the increase in the $US value of the €150,000 when the exchange rate is $1.45:€1)
		
		Accounts payable (€150,000) 217,500
		    Cash 217,500
		(to record the payment of €150,000 when the exchange rate is $1.45:€1)

This example highlights the impacts on the income statement and the balance sheet of the use of the forward contract to hedge the risk of foreign exchange rate fluctuations:

- The negative impact on profit from the increase in the $US value of the Euro-denominated account payable has been reduced by $15,000 as the gain on the forward contract has partially offset the loss on the upward revaluation of the payable,

- The increase in the $US value of the Euro-denominated account payable has been partially offset by the increase in value of the forward contract asset, thus mitigating the negative effect on Stockholders' equity.

And, in addition to the accounting effects, the negative impact on cash flow of the weakening $US has also been reduced as the increase in cash *outflow* to settle the Euro-denominated account payable is partially offset by the cash *inflow* from the forward contract (this positive cash flow effect would be realized regardless of our accounting for the transaction).

The matching of the accounting for the derivative security with the asset or liability to which it relates is critical to the mitigation of the adverse effects on profit and Stockholders' equity that would be recognized in the absence of an effective hedging program. This matching is called *hedge accounting* and it allows us to link the accounting for the derivative and the asset or liability to which it relates so that income and expense are recognized in the same accounting period (thus lessening the effect on net income) and assets and liabilities increase and decrease in the same accounting period (thus lessening the effect on Stockholders' equity). So, in order to achieve the beneficial *accounting* effects of the use of derivatives to hedge business exposures, companies must take great care to satisfy the qualifications to be able to use hedge accounting that we discuss later in this chapter.

Once a financial derivative is qualified for hedge accounting, the general principles of hedge accounting are applied (FASB ASC 815-20-25, 30, and 35) as follows:

1. The derivative is reported on the balance sheet at fair value on the statement date.[12]
2. Changes in the fair value of the derivative and the asset or liability to which it relates will be recognized in earnings as follows:
   a. **Fair Value Hedge:** both the change in the fair value of the derivative and the change in the fair value of the hedged item are recognized currently in earnings.[13]
   b. **Cash Flow Hedge:** the change in the fair value of the *effective portion* of the derivative is recognized, net of tax, in other comprehensive income (OCI) and, later, is reclassified to

---

[11] As we illustrate later in the chapter, if the hedge is classified as a cash flow hedge, the credit is to other comprehensive income until the transaction occurs, at which time it is reclassified into current earnings.

[12] The derivative is generally classified as current or noncurrent depending on its expected settlement within or after one year, respectively (FASB ASC 210-10-45). Derivatives may be separated into both current and noncurrent components like other assets and liabilities.

[13] ASC815 Overrides Previous Accounting when hedge is designated:

  - When the hedged item is the *fair value* of an AFS security the unrealized gains and losses are *included in net income and NOT AOCI*. Note that this treatment is consistent with the accounting for fair value hedges.

  - When the hedged item is the *cash flows* of an AFS security the unrealized gains and losses are *included in AOCI*. Note that this treatment is consistent with the accounting for cash flow hedges.

earnings when the hedged item impacts earnings.[14,15] The *ineffective* portion of the cash flow hedge is reported currently in earnings.[16]

We now look more closely at the accounting for fair value and cash flow hedges.

Fair Value Hedge

Fair value hedges protect existing assets, liabilities and *firm* commitments against changes in fair value. Some examples of fair value hedges include,

1. The use of a futures contract to hedge against fluctuations in the fair value of inventory, such as commodities like copper,
2. The use of a forward contract to hedge against fluctuations in the amount that a company will need to pay under a *firm* commitment to purchase inventory or the amount that it will receive under a firm commitment to sell inventory where the purchase or sale price may be at the prevailing future market price,
3. The use of options to hedge against fluctuations in the fair value of available-for-sale securities,
4. The use of an interest rate swap to change nonprepayable fixed-rate debt into variable-rate debt.

In this case, the asset or liability whose value we are trying to protect is already on the balance sheet. Then, at each reporting period subsequent to the purchase of the derivative security, both the derivative and the asset or liability to which it relates are reported on the balance sheet at fair value and changes in the fair values of *both* the derivative security *and* the asset or liability to which it relates are recognized currently in earnings.

PRACTICE INSIGHT

Definition of a Firm Commitment   FASB ASC Master Glossary defines a *firm commitment* as follows:

An agreement with an unrelated party, binding on both parties and usually legally enforceable, with the following characteristics:

a. The agreement specifies all significant terms, including the quantity to be exchanged, the fixed price, and the timing of the transaction. The fixed price may be expressed as a specified amount of an entity's functional currency or of a foreign currency. It also may be expressed as a specified interest rate or specified effective yield.

b. The agreement includes a disincentive for nonperformance that is sufficiently large to make performance probable.

It is important to note that the accounting for the asset or liability to which the derivative security relates under ASC 815 *overrides* its traditional accounting. For example, in our example #2 above, if a company hedges against fluctuations in the fair value of available-for-sale securities by the purchase of a forward contract, the available-for-sale security is reported at fair value at each statement date with changes in fair value reported *in current earnings*, not in other comprehensive income (OCI) as would be the case had hedge accounting not been employed. Also, Inventory that is normally carried at the

---

[14] FASB ASC 815-3-45-1 governs the placement of unrealized gains and losses on cash flow hedges in Other Comprehensive Income: "An entity shall display as a separate classification within other comprehensive income the net gain or loss on derivative instruments designated and qualifying as cash flow hedging instruments that are reported in comprehensive income."

[15] Beyond this general guidance, FASB ASC 815 does not specify the line item in the income statement in which changes in fair value of derivative instruments that are designated as hedges should be presented (FASB ASC 815-10-45-8). Customary practice is to reflect the changes in the fair value of derivative instruments in the same financial statement line item as that of the hedged item. (For example, Southwest Airlines includes the reclassification adjustments related to the effective portion of its fuel hedges in the "Fuel and Oil" line item in the operating-expenses section of its income statement.) Further, FASB ASC 230 and ASC 815 provide guidance on the statement of cash flows presentation of cash receipts and payments related to derivative instruments. Generally, the cash receipts or payments from a derivative should be classified according to the nature of the derivative and not with regard to the item being hedged. For example, purchase or sale of a futures contract is an investing activity even though the contract might be intended as a hedge of a firm commitment to purchase inventory.

[16] Change in the fair value of the ineffective portion of the hedge is reported currently in earnings. We discuss the effective and ineffective portion of a hedge later in the chapter.

lower of cost or market on the balance sheet when it is not hedged, will be reported at fair value under hedge accounting, with changes in fair value reflected in current earnings. Accounting for changes in the fair value of hedged assets and liabilities in current earnings does not result in increased earnings volatility to the extent that the hedge is effective, however, as the inventory gains (losses) are offset by losses (gains) in the derivative security.

Foreign Currency Fair Value Hedge Example

Hedge accounting can be used to reduce the effects of changes in fair values of recognized assets and liabilities. In this example, we illustrate the accounting for a foreign currency fair value hedge of an available-for-sale security with a purchase price of €100,000 that a company purchases on September 30 and intends to sell in 3 months. Assume that current exchange rate ("spot rate") on the date the security is purchased is $1.50:€1 and the company is concerned about the prospect of a weakening $US that will reduce the $US fair value of the security. To hedge this risk, the company purchases a forward contract to sell €100,000 for $1.49:€1 (the current forward rate) on December 31. On December 31, the spot rate for the Euro is $1.30 as summarized in the following table:

Date	Spot Rate	Forward Exchange Rate to 12/31/01	Fair Value of Forward Contract
September 30............	$1.50:€1	$1.49:€1	$ —
December 31	$1.30:€1	$1.30:€1	19,000
			([$1.49:€1 − $1.30:€1] × €100,000 = $19,000)

We summarize the accounting for the available-for-sale security and the derivative security (the forward contract) as follows:[17]

Transaction	AFS Security	Forward Contract
At inception	Investment in AFS security........ 150,000 Cash .... 150,000 *(to record the purchase of the AFS security for €100,000 when the exchange rate is $1.50:€1)*	No entry

At maturity	Loss on hedge activity........... 20,000
	  Investment in AFS security ... 20,000
	(to record the decrease in the value of the AFS security [$1.30:€1 − $1.50:€1] × €100,000 = $20,000)
		Forward contact receivable 19,000
		  Gain on hedge activity....... 19,000
		(to record the increase in fair value of the forward contract [$1.49:€1 − $1.30:€1] × €100,000 = $19,000)
		
		Cash......................... 149,000
		  Forward contract receivable .. 149,000
		(to record the settlement of the forward contract [$1.49:€1 × €100,000 = $149,000])

Notice that, under a fair value hedge, both the hedge (the forward contract) and the asset to which it relates (the AFS security) are reported at fair value on the balance sheet and that changes to their respective fair values are recognized in current earnings. In this case, the increase in the $US value of the forward contract offsets the decrease in the $US value of the AFS security and the net cost to the company (recognized in earnings) is the $1,000 difference between the spot and forward rates at the inception of the forward contract. This is the "cost" of the hedge that the company locked in at inception in order to avoid the prospect of a greater loss in the future.

The net effect is that the fluctuation in Stockholders' equity has also been minimized as the decline in the $US value of one asset (AFS security) is offset by the increase in the $US value of the other (forward contract). In addition, the fluctuation in net income arising from changes in foreign exchange rates is minimized as the changes in fair values of the two assets are both reflected in current earnings, leaving only the $1,000 cost of the hedge as an expense in the company's income statement. And, finally, the effect on cash flow is minimized as the cash inflow from the forward contract nearly offsets the reduced cash flow from the sale of the AFS security when the €100,000 is converted into $US.

---

[17] In order to focus on the accounting for derivative securities in this example, we are only hedging the exposure to changes in fair value of the AFS security arising from fluctuations in foreign exchange rates. AFS securities can also fluctuate in value because of fluctuations in stock prices, and we are holding the stock price constant in this case.

Cash Flow Hedge

Cash flow hedges protect against the risk that variable prices, costs, rates, or terms make future cash flows uncertain. In a cash flow hedge, the entity is exposed to a variable (i.e., price, cost, interest) and the derivative security protects the company by fixing that variable exposure. Some examples of cash flow hedges include,

1. The use of a futures contract to hedge against the fluctuations in the *expected* proceeds from the sale of inventory to be sold at the prevailing market price or the *expected* cost of inventory to be purchased at the prevailing market price.

2. The use of an interest rate swap to change nonprepayable variable interest payments into fixed-rate debt.

The difference in reported earnings between fair value and cash flow hedge accounting is one of timing. Changes in the fair values of *fair value hedges* are recognized currently in earnings (together with changes in the fair values of the assets or liabilities to which the derivatives relate). By contrast, changes in the fair values of the effective portion of *cash flow hedges* are *deferred* in Other Comprehensive Income (OCI) and recognized in net income when the hedged item impacts earnings (i.e., when the transaction occurs).

Foreign Currency Cash Flow Hedge Example

Hedge accounting can be used to reduce the effects of fluctuations in the *expected* proceeds from the sale of inventory to be sold at the prevailing market price of a foreign currency. To illustrate, we consider the accounting for a foreign currency cash flow hedge of an *expected* sale of inventory for €100,000 in the first week of January. We continue with the same assumptions that we use above and assume that current exchange rate ("spot rate") on the date the company anticipates the sale is $1.50:€1 and the company is concerned about the prospect of a weakening $US that will reduce the $US sale price (and cash inflow) in January. To hedge this risk, the company purchases a forward contract to sell €100,000 for $1.49:€1 (the current forward rate) on December 31, the closest date to the anticipated sale date. On December 31, the spot rate for the Euro is $1.30 as summarized in the following table:

Date	Spot Rate	Forward Exchange Rate to 12/31/01	Fair Value of Forward Contract
September 30............	$1.50:€1	$1.49:€1	$ —
December 31	$1.30:€1	$1.30:€1	19,000
			([$1.49:€1 − $1.30:€1] × €100,000 = $19,000)

We summarize the accounting for the derivative security (the forward contract) and the January sale as follows:

Forward Contract	At inception: No entry
	
	December 31:
	Forward contract receivable................................ 19,000
	    Other comprehensive income 19,000
	(to record the increase in fair value of the forward contract
	[$1.49:€1 − $1.30:€1] × €100,000 = $19,000)
	Cash.. 19,000
	    Forward contract receivable 19,000
	(to record the net settlement of the forward contract)

Sale	January:
	Cash.. 130,000
	    Sales 130,000
	(to record the sale at the spot rate [$1.30:€1] × €100,000 = $130,000)
	Accumulated other comprehensive income................... 19,000
	    Sales 19,000
	(to transfer the gain on the hedge activity from other comprehensive
	income to earnings when the forecasted transaction impacts earnings)

Notice that, under a cash flow hedge, the hedge (the forward contract) is reported at fair value and that changes to its fair value are deferred and recognized in *other comprehensive income* until the transaction to which the hedge relates (the sale) occurs.[18] The net effect is that the sale (and the related cash inflow) is recognized at the $1.49:€1 exchange rate locked in by the forward contract.

Hedge accounting allows companies to match changes in the fair value of the hedged item with changes in the fair values of the derivative security, thus lessening the earnings and balance sheet volatility arising from the risks the company seeks to mitigate. However, should these derivative securities be purchased for *speculative* purposes (or if the hedging criteria are not met), changes in the fair value of the derivative securities are recognized in earnings with no offsetting effects from the hedged item (since there isn't a hedged item). In that case, the company is merely purchasing an investment for speculative purposes and its financial statements will recognize the full effects of that investment.

PRACTICE INSIGHT

Accounting for Options.   An *option* is a contract which gives the buyer the right, but not the obligation, to buy or sell an underlying asset at a specified *strike price* on or before a specified date (the seller of the option has the corresponding obligation to sell or buy the asset if the buyer *exercises* the option). The buyer pays a premium to the seller for this right. An option that conveys to the owner the right to buy something at a specific price is referred to as a *call*; an option that conveys the right of the owner to sell something at a specific price is referred to as a *put*.

The accounting for options used as derivative securities is similar to that for the forward contract that we illustrate above, but with two significant differences:

1. The option is purchased. Consequently, there is an entry required at inception to debit the option security and credit cash, and
2. The effective portion of the option is typically measured by changes in the option's *intrinsic value* (with changes in fair value recognized in other comprehensive income), while the ineffective portion of the hedge is measured by changes in the option's *time value* (with changes in fair value recognized currently in earnings), where:
   a. **Intrinsic value** is the difference between the strike price and the current price, and
   b. **Time value** is the difference between the option's fair value and the intrinsic value (reflecting the value of the option to realize upside gain before the option expires—this time value declines to zero over the life of the option since there is no upside potential remaining after the expiration of the option).

We provide a detailed example of the accounting for options later in this chapter.

Qualification for Hedge Accounting
Hedge accounting treatment is only available for hedges that qualify for hedge accounting under FASB ASC 815-20-25. In order to qualify for hedge accounting, the following conditions must be satisfied:

■ **Nature of the hedging transaction**—The hedging transaction must be designated by the company as a fair value, cash flow, or foreign currency hedge. The risk management objective and strategy must be identified and documented, including identification of the hedging instrument, the hedged item (reported asset or liability) or transaction (firm commitment or forecasted transaction), the nature of the risk being hedged, and how the hedging instrument will be effective in hedging the identified exposure (i.e., for a fair value hedge, how changes in fair value of the hedged asset or liability could affect reported earnings, and for a cash flow hedge, how fluctuations in cash flows of a forecasted transaction could affect reported earnings).

■ **Assessment of hedge effectiveness**—The qualification for hedge accounting includes an expectation that the hedge will be highly effective. Highly effective means that changes in fair values or cash flows during the term of the hedge for the hedge instrument will be approximately equal to changes in fair values or cash flows during the term of the hedge for the risk being hedged

---

[18] We assume that the company assesses hedge effectiveness based on the entire change in fair value of the forward contract. Therefore, all changes in the fair value of the forward contact are reflected in other comprehensive income. Companies may choose to assess hedge effectiveness in a variety of ways (ASC 815-20-25-82). In general, the effective portion of the hedge effectiveness assessment is recognized in other comprehensive income and the ineffective portion of the hedge is recognized in current earnings.

(FASB ASC 815-20-25-75). In practice, highly effective generally means the correlation between the hedged item and the hedging instrument must be between 80 and 125%. Hedge effectiveness must be assessed at the time of hedge designation, and a conclusion must be supported that the hedging transaction is expected to be highly effective in offsetting changes in the fair value or cash flows attributable to the hedged risk at inception and throughout the term of the hedge.

- **Documentation and ongoing effectiveness assessment**—In order to qualify for the special hedge accounting, there must be formal documentation of the hedged item (or hedgeable risk), the hedging instrument, and how effectiveness will be assessed and how ineffectiveness will be measured. The formal documentation must be made with enough specificity and clarity that an independent third party could understand and identify the hedging relationship and re-perform the effectiveness tests and measurement of ineffectiveness. All documentation must be contemporaneous—that is the documentation must be completed at the time the hedge is created. The following items must be documented:

  ○ The risk management objective and strategy
    ❑ The nature of the risk being hedged
    ❑ How the hedging instrument (derivative) is expected to reduce the risk exposure

  ○ The hedging relationship
    ❑ Hedged risk, hedged item, and hedging instrument

  ○ How effectiveness will be assessed and the method to measure ineffectiveness

Exhibit 7.1 presents a graphical depiction of questions that must be answered in order for an investment in a financial derivative to be qualified for hedge accounting. If the conditions for hedge accounting are met, a derivative may be designated as a fair value hedge, a cash flow hedge, or a hedge of a foreign currency exposure and hedge accounting can be employed.[19] Note that application of hedge accounting does not change the fundamental requirement in ASC 815: All derivatives must always be measured and reported in the balance sheet at fair value at every interim and annual financial statement date. Instead, hedge accounting is a system of recognition and measurement that minimizes the net income volatility of mark-to-market accounting for derivatives. We now discuss the application of hedge accounting for derivatives.

EXHIBIT 7.1 Designation of a Financial Derivative for Hedge Accounting

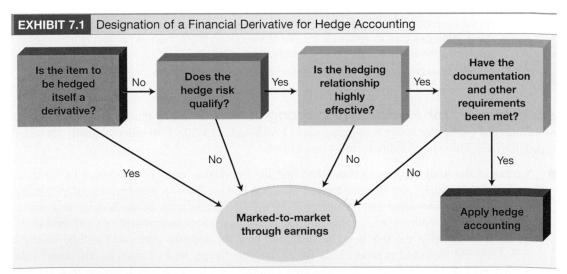

Source: *Guide to Accounting for Derivative Instruments and Hedging Activities, 2009* by PricewaterhouseCoopers, LLP

We conclude this section of the chapter with four examples that illustrate the accounting for typical transactions involving derivative financial instruments and we provide additional examples in Appendix 7B. We also provide a complete listing of required disclosures relating to the accounting for derivatives in Appendix 7A.

---

[19] FASB ASC 815-20-25-43 prohibits hedge accounting for the following (partial list): (1) an investment accounted for by the equity method, (2) an equity investment in a consolidated subsidiary, (3) a held-to-maturity security, (4) the risk of changes in its fair value attributable to interest rate risk, and (5) an asset or liability that is remeasured with the changes in fair value attributable to the hedged risk reported currently in earnings.

PRACTICE INSIGHT

Assessing the Effectiveness of Hedging Instruments

To qualify for hedge accounting, the hedging relationship, both at inception of the hedge and on an ongoing basis, shall be expected to be highly effective in achieving either of the following (FASB ASC 815-20-25-75):

a. Offsetting changes in fair value attributable to the hedged risk during the period that the hedge is designated (if a fair value hedge)

b. Offsetting cash flows attributable to the hedged risk during the term of the hedge (if a cash flow hedge).

All assessments of effectiveness shall be consistent with the originally documented risk management strategy for that particular hedging relationship. An entity shall use the effectiveness assessment method defined at hedge inception consistently throughout the hedge period to do both of the following (FASB ASC 815-20-25-80):

a. Assess at inception of the hedge and on an ongoing basis whether it expects the hedging relationship to be highly effective in achieving offset

b. Measure the ineffective part of the hedge.

The assessment of hedge effectiveness can be performed on either of the two following bases (FASB ASC 815-20-25-79):

a. **Prospective considerations.** The entity's expectation that the relationship will be highly effective over future periods in achieving offsetting changes in fair value or cash flows, which is forward-looking, can be based on regression or other statistical analysis of past changes in fair values or cash flows as well as on other relevant information.

b. **Retrospective evaluations.** An assessment of effectiveness shall be performed whenever financial statements or earnings are reported, and at least every three months.

This determination of hedge effectiveness is critical, as described in FASB ASC 815-20-35-2: If the hedge fails the effectiveness test at any time (that is, if the entity does not expect the hedge to be highly effective at achieving offsetting changes in fair values or cash flows), **the hedge ceases to qualify for hedge accounting**. At least quarterly, the hedging entity shall determine whether the hedging relationship has been highly effective in having achieved offsetting changes in fair value or cash flows through the date of the periodic assessment. That assessment can be based on regression or other statistical analysis of past changes in fair values or cash flows as well as on other relevant information.

The FASB does not explicitly define what *highly effective* is, but prevailing practice considers a hedge to be highly effective if the expected cumulative change in the value of the designated portion of the hedging instrument is between 80 to 125 percent of the inverse cumulative change in the fair value or cash flows of the hedged item. This begs the question, "why aren't all hedging instruments 100% effective?"

There can be a number of reasons why a hedging instrument will not be 100% effective. The following are common (FASB ASC 815-20-25-77):

1. **The basis of the hedging instrument can be different than that of the item being hedged.** For example, a company might seek to hedge fluctuations in interest rates from a variable-rate borrowing tied to the prime rate with a hedging instrument based off of LIBOR rates.

2. **The terms of the hedging instrument may not exactly match those of the hedged item.** These differences may result from available amounts in the hedging instrument (notional amounts, maturities, quantity, location, or delivery dates).

3. **A change in the counterparty's creditworthiness.** The market value of the hedging instrument can be affected by changes in the creditworthiness of the counterparty. Such changes in creditworthiness will, generally, not affect the market value of the hedged item.

There are several methods that companies can use to determine hedge effectiveness:

The shortcut method. Accounting standards allow a company to employ a shortcut method in certain circumstances to simplify the effectiveness assessment. This method allows a company to assume that there is no ineffectiveness present (i.e., without having to perform detailed effectiveness assessments) and to not record any ineffectiveness related to the hedging relationship. Because of the simplicity of this method and its obvious financial benefits, the FASB has set strict requirements for its use. These requirements are detailed in ASC 815-20-25-104 to 106 and include three core requirements:

continued next page

continued

   a. Interest rate risk must be the only risk identified as the hedged risk.

   b. The hedging instrument involves an interest rate swap.

   c. The hedge must involve a recognized interest-bearing financial asset or liability.

   The critical terms match approach. If the critical terms of the hedging instrument and of the entire hedged asset or liability or hedged forecasted transaction are the same, the entity could conclude that changes in fair value or cash flows attributable to the risk being hedged are expected to completely offset at inception and on an ongoing basis. Critical terms can be assumed to match if

   1) The forward contract is for purchase of the same quantity of the same commodity at the same time and location as the hedged forecasted purchase.

   2) The fair value of the forward contract at inception is zero.

   3) Either of the following criteria is met:
       a) The change in the discount or premium on the forward contract is excluded from the assessment of effectiveness and included directly in earnings
       b) The change in expected cash flows on the forecasted transaction is based on the forward price for the commodity. (FASB ASC 815-20-25-84)

   In this abbreviated method, the entity may forego performing a detailed effectiveness assessment in each period.

   The FASB provides a number of examples of the determination of hedge effectiveness in ASC 815-25-55 and 815-30-55.

PRACTICE INSIGHT

Counter-Party Risk   The purpose of derivative financial instruments is to transfer risk from one company to another. For example, a company might be concerned about the possible decline in the $US value of a foreign-currency-denominated account receivable. In order to hedge that risk, the company might execute a forward contract to sell the foreign currency and receive $US. That forward contract only has value, however, if the party on the other side of the transaction (the counter-party) ultimately purchases the foreign currency for $US when the contract matures. If the counter-party fails to honor its part of the agreement, the forward contract is of no value.

   The risk that the other party might not live up to its part of the bargain is known as *counter-party risk*. The only justification for recognizing a gain in a forward contract to offset the loss in a foreign-currency-denominated receivable is the expectation that the counter-party has the intention and ability to purchase the foreign currency in exchange for $US when the contract matures.

   Counter-party risk is very real. Many companies require counter-parties to back up their agreement with cash collateral or other acceptable forms of guarantees (like a bank letter of credit, for example). Disclosures relating to counter-parties are, generally, not adequate to assess the risk of non-performance. As a result, there is a hidden risk in companies' use of derivatives that is difficult to quantify.

Foreign Currency Hedge: Use of a Forward Contract to Hedge a Firm Commitment to Pay Foreign Currency[20]

On September 30, 2014, a U.S. company enters into a firm commitment to purchase equipment from a foreign supplier for €1,000,000.[21] The equipment is deliverable on March 31, 2015, and the €1,000,000 payment is due on June 30, 2015. The company expects the $US to weaken during this period of time. To hedge the commitment to pay €1,000,000, the company enters into a forward exchange contract on September 30, 2014, to receive €1,000,000 on June 30, 2015, at an exchange rate of €1:US$1.32. The

---

[20] Effective hedges of *forecasted* foreign-currency-denominated transactions (i.e., that are not firm commitments) can only be accounted for as cash flow hedges (FASB ASC 815-20-25-38). In contrast, recognized foreign-currency-denominated assets and liabilities and unrecognized foreign-currency-denominated firm commitments are afforded the choice of applying cash-flow hedge accounting or fair value hedge accounting (FASB ASC 815-20-25-12 and -38). This example illustrates fair value hedge treatment.

[21] Recall that an unrecognized firm commitment is an agreement for future performance that (1) specifies all significant terms, including the quantity to be exchanged, the fixed price, and the timing of the transaction and (2) includes a disincentive for nonperformance that is sufficiently large to make performance virtually assured.

net effect of this derivative contract and the original firm commitment is that the company has committed to pay a total of $1,320,000 on June 30, 2015. The current spot rate on September 30, 2014, is €1:US$1.25. To protect itself against a greater loss should the $US weaken more than expected, the company locked in a purchase price that is $0.07 higher than the spot rate. You can think of this commitment to pay additional $US as a type of insurance premium against even bigger losses.

The relevant spot and forward exchange rates during this time period are as follows:

Date	Spot Rates	Forward Rates for June 30, 2015 Settlement
September 30, 2014	€1.00 = US$1.25	€1.00 = US$1.32
December 31, 2014	€1.00 = US$1.26	€1.00 = US$1.31
March 31, 2015	€1.00 = US$1.29	€1.00 = US$1.31
June 30, 2015	€1.00 = US$1.30	N/A

Although companies have a choice of the hedge model to apply to a foreign currency exposure in an unrecognized firm commitment, fair value hedge accounting is preferred because it does not induce volatility in Other Comprehensive Income in the periods prior to settlement of the derivative. In applying fair value hedge accounting to an unrecognized firm commitment, (1) the forward contract is recognized as an asset or liability and marked to market through the income statement, and (2) an exactly offsetting gain or loss is recognized for the effective portion of the hedge and a firm commitment liability or asset is recognized. At the time that the equipment is received, a liability for the purchase price is recorded in the amount of the foreign currency payable multiplied by the current spot rate. The hedging relationship is terminated at that time. The liability is thereafter measured at the current spot exchange rate, with gains and losses reflected in earnings.

The equipment is recorded at the amount of the liability, net of the amount previously recorded for the firm commitment. The forward exchange contract remains on the accounting records as an effective hedge of the liability, since the gains and losses on both the liability (i.e., the hedged item) and the forward exchange contract (i.e., the hedging instrument) are recorded in current earnings and they naturally offset each other in the income statement.

Journal entries to reflect these transactions are as follows:

Date	Journal Entries		
September 30, 2014	No entry required		
December 31, 2014	Foreign exchange loss	10,000	
	Foreign currency forward contract (FV)		10,000
	(to recognize the fair value of the forward exchange contract = €1,000,000 × [$1.32 − $1.31]/€1)		
	Firm commitment	10,000	
	Foreign exchange gain		10,000
	(to recognize the fair value of the change in exchange rates underlying the firm commitment)		
March 31, 2015	Equipment	1,300,000	
	Firm commitment		10,000
	Accounts payable		1,290,000
	(to record the receipt of the equipment and the related payable at the March 31 spot rate)		
June 30, 2015	Foreign exchange loss	10,000	
	Foreign currency forward contract (FV)		10,000
	(to recognize the change in fair value of the forward exchange contract)		
	Foreign exchange loss	10,000	
	Accounts payable		10,000
	(to recognize the transaction loss on the foreign currency accounts payable)		
	Accounts payable	1,300,000	
	Foreign currency forward contract (FV)	20,000	
	Cash		1,320,000
	(to record the settlement of the forward contract receivable and accounts payable)		

Interest Rate Swap Example: Interest Rate Swap as a Hedge of a Fixed-Rate Instrument—Fair Value Hedge[22]

On June 30, 2014, our company borrows $10,000,000 of three-year 7.5% fixed-rate interest-only debt, and concurrently enters into a three-year interest-rate swap to synthetically convert the debt's fixed-rate interest payments to variable-rate payments. Under the terms of the swap, our company receives interest at a fixed rate of 7.5% and pays interest at a variable rate equal to the six-month LIBOR (London Inter-bank Offered Rate), based on a notional amount of $10,000,000. Both the debt and the swap require that payments be made or received on December 31 and June 30. The six-month U.S. LIBOR on each reset date determines the variable portion of the interest-rate swap for the following six-month period. Our company designates the swap as a fair value hedge of the fixed-rate debt. The specific risk being hedged is the change in the fair value of the debt that is caused by changes in market interest rates.

The six-month U.S. LIBOR rates and the swap and debt fair values are assumed to be as follows for the first year of the swap and debt agreements:

Date	Six-Month LIBOR	Swap Fair Value Asset (Liability)	Debt Fair Value
June 30, 2014.	6.00%	$ 0	$10,000,000
December 31, 2014	7.00%	(323,000)	9,677,000
June 30, 2015.	5.50%	55,000	10,055,000

For a fair value hedge, the swap is reported on the balance sheet as an asset or liability at fair value with changes in fair value reflected in the income statement each reporting period. The change in the fair value of the debt (that is, the gain or loss on the hedged item) attributable to changes in the benchmark interest rate (i.e., six-month LIBOR) is also reflected in earnings through adjustments to the debt's carrying amount.[23]

Following are the journal entries for this transaction:

Date	Journal Entries		
June 30, 2014	Cash	10,000,000	
	Note payable (3 year).		10,000,000
	(to record debt)		
December 31, 2014	Interest expense.	375,000	
	Cash		375,000
	(to record semiannual interest payment at 7.5%)		
	Cash	75,000	
	Interest expense		75,000
	(to record the settlement of the semiannual swap-amount receivable at 7.5%, less the amount payable at LIBOR, 6%, as an adjustment to interest)		
	Note payable (3 year) .	323,000	
	Gain on hedge.		323,000
	(to record the change in the debt's fair value that is attributable to changes in the benchmark interest rate (e.g., six-month LIBOR) at the end of the first reporting period)		
	Loss on hedge .	323,000	
	Swap contract.		323,000
	(to record the change in the fair value of the swap at the end of the first reporting period)		

---

[22] With respect to changes in market-wide interest rates, the fair value of variable-rate debt is equal to its face value while the fair value of fixed-rate debt changes in the opposite direction of interest rate changes. In contrast, changes in market interest rate has no effect on the cash interest payments on fixed-rate instruments while the amount of interest paid on variable-rate debt changes in the same direction as market interest rate changes. As a result, in relation to changes in market interest rates, fixed-rate instruments have fair value risk while variable-rate instruments have cash flow risk. Further, hedges of fixed-rate instruments are accounted for as fair value hedges and hedges of variable-rate instruments are accounted for as cash flow hedges.

[23] If the swap did not qualify as a hedge, the derivative would still be reported at fair value in the balance sheet, with the changes in fair value recognized in net income. However, the carrying value of the debt would be based on the amortized value of the original debt proceeds. Fair value reporting of the debt is only triggered if the swap qualifies as a fair value hedge.

Date	Journal Entries		
June 30, 2015	Interest expense..	375,000	
	Cash		375,000
	(to record the semiannual debt interest payment)		
	Cash	25,000	
	Interest expense		25,000
	(to record the receipt of the semiannual swap amount receivable at 7.5%, less the amount payable at LIBOR, 7%)		
	Loss on hedge	378,000	
	Note payable (3 year)...		378,000
	(to record the change in the debt's fair value that is attributable to changes in the benchmark interest rate (i.e., six-month LIBOR) at the end of the second reporting period)		
	Swap contract	378,000	
	Gain on hedge...		378,000
	(to record the change in the fair value of the swap at the end of the second reporting period)		

The debt is presented on the balance sheet at an amount that reflects the impact of changes in the benchmark interest rates (e.g., six-month LIBOR) on its fair value. The swap contract is presented on the balance sheet at its fair value. The changes in the fair value of (1) the debt that are attributable to the hedged interest rate risk and (2) the swap contract are recognized in current-period earnings. Net interest expense for the period reflects the debt's coupon rate adjusted for the swap's settlement for the period.

Fair Value Hedge of a Firm Foreign-Currency-Denominated Purchase Commitment with a Forward Contract

Our company's functional currency is the U.S. dollar. On October 1, 2014, we enter into a firm commitment to purchase equipment for delivery on March 31, 2015, in Euros (€). The price of the equipment is fixed at €1,000,000 with payment due on delivery. We are concerned that the $US may weaken vis-à-vis the Euro and, on the same date, we enter into a foreign currency forward contract to buy €1,000,000 on March 31, 2015. We will pay $2.10 per €1, which is the current forward rate as of March 31, 2015. We designate the foreign currency forward contract as a hedge of our risk of changes in the fair value of the firm commitment resulting from changes in the $/€ exchange rate. This hedging strategy will enable us to purchase the equipment for $2,100,000 (the forward price).

Assumptions

Spot rates, forward rates, and fair value of the foreign currency forward contract are as follows:

Date	Spot Rate	Forward Rates for March 31, 2015 Settlement	Fair Value Asset (Liability)	Change in Fair Value
October 1, 2014	€1 = $2.00	€1 = $2.10	$ —	$ —
December 31, 2014	€1 = $2.10	€1 = $2.12	$20,000[a]	$20,000
March 31, 2015	€1 = $2.15	—	$50,000	$30,000

[a] Determined using the change in forward rates.

The following journal entries will be made on October 1, December 31, and March 31:

Date	Journal Entries		
October 1, 2014	Memorandum entry made on documenting the existence of the hedging relationship		
December 31, 2014	Change in fair value of firm commitment (I/S)	20,000	
	Firm commitment (B/S)		20,000
	(to record the change in fair value of the foreign currency exposure of the firm commitment)		
	Forward contract (B/S).................................	20,000	
	Unrealized gain on forward contract (I/S)		20,000
	(to record the change in fair value of the foreign currency forward contract)		

continued next page

continued

Date	Journal Entries		
March 31, 2015	Change in fair value of firm commitment (I/S)	30,000	
	Firm commitment (B/S)		30,000
	(to record the change in fair value of the foreign currency exposure of the firm commitment)		
	Forward contract (B/S).....................................	30,000	
	Unrealized gain on forward contract (I/S)		30,000
	(to record the change in fair value of the foreign currency forward contract)		
	Cash (B/S)	50,000	
	Forward contract (B/S)		50,000
	(to record settlement of the foreign currency forward contract)		
	Plant and equipment (B/S)...............................	2,150,000	
	Cash (B/S)		2,150,000
	(to record the purchase of the equipment from the UK supplier at the March 31, 2015, spot rate)		
	Firm commitment (B/S)	50,000	
	Plant and equipment (B/S)...........................		50,000
	(to adjust plant and equipment to reflect the hedge of the firm commitment)		

Our hedging objective was to lock in the $US purchase price of the equipment. During the period the hedge was in place, the $US weakened vis-à-vis the Euro. With the hedge, we limited our net cash outflow to $2,100,000, a savings of $50,000 over the $2,150,000 (€1,000,000 at the spot exchange rate of €1:$2.15) that the equipment would have cost at the prevailing spot rate.

Cash Flow Hedge of a Foreign-Currency-Denominated Forecasted Sale with an Option Contract

Assume that on January 1, 2015, our company anticipates a sale to a Canadian customer of CAD700,000 in six months, and on January 1, when the spot rate was $1:CAD1.40 the company obtains an option to sell CAD700,000 on June 30, 2015, for $489,511 ($1:CAD1.43).[24] The cost and the fair value of this option agreement at inception is $16,000. The company is purchasing this option because it is concerned that the $US might strengthen (thus resulting in less $US for the sale). The option will be effective if the $US strengthens to a rate of $1:CAD1.43 or greater and will be ineffective if the dollar does not strengthen to that level, in which case the company will let the option expire and the $16,000 option cost will be offset, in whole or in part, by the increased cash received from the sale. The anticipated sale is ultimately consummated on June 30, 2015.

The following tables summarize the key data:

Date	Spot Rate	Fair Value of Option[a]	Intrinsic Value of Option	Time Value of Option[d]
1/1/2015.........	$1:CAD1.40	$16,000	$ 0	$16,000
3/31/2015........	$1:CAD1.45	$15,000	$ 6,752[b]	$ 8,248
6/30/2015........	$1:CAD1.50	$22,844[c]	$22,844[c]	$ 0

[a] Derived from an option pricing model such as the Black–Scholes model.
[b] (CAD700,000/1.43) – (CAD700,000/1.45)
[c] (CAD700,000/1.43) – (CAD700,000/1.50)
[d] Fair value – intrinsic value

We summarize the accounting for the derivative security (the option) and the June sale as follows:

[24] We are expressing the exchange rate in relation to $1 in this example—$1:CAD1.43 is equivalent to $0.699:CAD1 (dividing both sides by 1.43).

1/1/15	Purchased option	16,000	
	Cash		16,000
	(to record the purchase of the option)		
3/31/15	Loss on hedging activities	7,752	
	Other comprehensive income		6,752
	Purchased option		1,000
	(to recognize the change in the intrinsic value of the option as the effective portion of the hedge in other comprehensive income, the change in the time value of the option as the ineffective portion of the hedge in current earnings, and the change in the fair value of the option)		
6/30/15	Purchased option	7,844	
	Loss on hedging activities—excluded component	8,248	
	Other comprehensive income		16,092
	(to recognize the change in the intrinsic value of the option as the effective portion of the hedge in other comprehensive income, the change in the time value of the option as the ineffective portion of the hedge in current earnings and the change in the fair value of the option)		
	Cash	22,844	
	Purchased option		22,844
	(to recognize the cash received form the exercise of the option)		
	Accounts receivable	466,667	
	Sales		466,667
	(to record the sale transaction at the prevailing spot rate – CAD700,000 x [$1:CAD1.50] = $466,667)		
	Other comprehensive income	22,844	
	Sales		22,844
	(to reflect the reclassification of other comprehensive income to sales for the value of the option in the period that the sale is recognized)		

In this case, the company recognizes sales revenue of $489,511 ($466,667 + $22,844) at the exchange rate the company locked in at the inception of the option contract (CAD700,000 × [$1:CAD1.43] = $489,511). Had the company not hedged the foreign currency risk, it would have recognized sales of $466,667 at the prevailing spot rate of $1:CAD1.50. To mitigate this risk, the company incurred a cost of $16,000 to purchase the option, thus improving net cash flow by $6,844 ($489,511 − $466,667 − $16,000) and avoiding a more significant cash flow decline had the dollar strengthened to more than $1:CAD1.50.

PRACTICE INSIGHT

Embedded Derivatives

The FASB defines an embedded derivative as follows: "Implicit or explicit terms that affect some or all of the cash flows or the value of other exchanges required by a contract in a manner similar to a derivative instrument (FASB ASC 815-15 Glossary)."

An example of an embedded derivative is a loan under which interest payments are based on changes in an underlying index, like the S&P 500 Index. For this example, the computation of the interest payments relating to the S&P 500 Index is an embedded derivative, but the basic requirement to pay interest and principal when due is not an embedded derivative. In this case, the effect of embedding a derivative instrument in the loan contract is that some or all of the cash flows (i.e., interest payments) that otherwise would be required by the contract will be modified based on an *underlying* (the S&P index) that is applied to a notional amount (the interest computation in the loan)—see our definition of a derivative financial instrument on page 468 for a discussion of underlyings and notional amounts. Many debt, equity, lease, insurance and other executory contracts contain embedded derivatives in the form of payments that are computed with respect to interest rate, commodity and equity indexes.

Should a contract contain an embedded derivative, it must be accounted for separately if and only if all of the following criteria are met (FASB ASC 815-15-25-1):

a. The economic characteristics and risks of the embedded derivative are not clearly and closely related to the economic characteristics and risks of the host contract.

b. The hybrid instrument is not remeasured at fair value under otherwise applicable generally accepted accounting principles (GAAP) with changes in fair value reported in earnings as they occur.

c. A separate instrument with the same terms as the embedded derivative would . . . be a derivative instrument.

CHAPTER SUMMARY

Companies may generate receivables and payables that are denominated in currencies other than the $US and that must be translated into $US prior to the issuance of financial statements. This translation process results in gains and losses as the fair value of the $US strengthens and weakens vis-à-vis other world currencies as follows:

	Accounts Receivable Denominated in Foreign Currency	Accounts Payable Denominated in Foreign Currency
$US **Weakens**	Exchange gain	Exchange loss
$US **Strengthens**.	Exchange loss	Exchange gain

These exchange gains and losses affect reported earnings as the $US fair values of the foreign currency-denominated assets and liabilities fluctuate.

In order to reduce these effects on reported earnings, companies can purchase derivative financial instruments whose fair values are negatively correlated with those of the assets or liabilities to which they relate. Then, fluctuations in the fair values of the reported assets and liabilities are largely offset by opposite fluctuations in the fair values of the derivatives, thus lessening the effects currency fluctuations have on reported earnings.

Accounting standards group these exposures into two broad categories: fair value risks and cash flow risks. Companies often use derivatives to hedge their exposure to changes in the fair values of recognized assets and liabilities, generally seeking to protect against an exposure to loss of value of their receivables, investments (e.g., debt and equity securities or loans receivable), and inventories, or an increase in the fair value of their liabilities (accounts payable and debt related obligations). Cash flow hedges generally relate to the management of cash flow-related risk exposure with respect to recognized assets and liabilities, such as exposures to changes in variable-rate investment income and payments on variable-rate debt obligations, and to cash flow-related risks with respect to forecasted purchases or sales of recognized assets or liabilities, such as the forecasted purchase of a commodity or the forecasted sale of inventory.

The accounting for derivatives is codified in FASB ASC 815, and is largely based on an accounting model introduced in Statement of Financial Accounting Standards No. 133: Accounting for Derivative Instruments and Hedging Activities. The fundamental requirement in ASC 815 is simple: All derivatives must always be measured and reported in the balance sheet at fair value at every interim and annual financial statement date. Further, if certain conditions are met, companies are allowed to employ hedge accounting under which the assets and liabilities to which the derivatives relate are also marked to market.

If a derivative instrument qualifies as a fair value hedge, both the derivative and the asset (or liability) to which it relates are reported at fair value at each statement date. Gains or losses on the hedged net assets are offset (in whole or in part) by losses or gains in the derivative financial instrument. Consequently, the company's income statement is less volatile than it would otherwise have been as fluctuations in the fair values of reported hedged assets (liabilities) are offset (in whole or in part) by changes in the fair values of the derivative financial instruments.

If a derivative instrument qualifies as a cash flow hedge, the after-tax gain or loss on fair value remeasurement of the derivative is included as a component of Other Comprehensive Income (OCI). This means that these gains and losses do not affect net income during periods prior to the period during which the hedged cash flow is realized. The Accumulated Other Comprehensive Income (AOCI) effect of a given derivative is reversed in the period during which the hedged item affects net income. The effect of cash flow hedge accounting is to shield reported net income from derivatives-remeasurement volatility until the derivative and the hedged item can offset each other in reported earnings.

In Exhibit 7.2, we provide a summary of hedge accounting for derivatives, including the typical journal entries that are required for both the derivatives and the assets and liabilities to which they relate.

EXHIBIT 7.2	Summary of Hedge Accounting for Derivatives	

	Fair Value	**Cash Flow**
General examples	Hedge exposure to changes in fair value of 1. A recognized asset or liability 2. An unrecognized firm commitment	Hedge exposure to changes in cash flow of 1. A recognized asset or liability 2. A forecasted transaction
Firm commitment	Hedges the risk related to the fair value changes of the commitment. The firm commitment is recognized as an asset or liability if hedged.	Not applicable
Forecasted transaction	Not applicable	Hedges the cash flows related to a forecasted transaction. The forecasted transaction must be specifically identifiable, probable, and with a party external to the reporting entity.
Hedge accounting	Changes in its fair value will be recognized in earnings and offset by changes in the fair value of the hedged item attributable to the hedge risk.	Changes in its fair value will be deferred in other comprehensive income to the extent effective and later reclassified to earnings when the hedged item impacts earnings.
Benefits of hedge accounting	Reduction in the earnings volatility that would otherwise result from recording gains and losses relating to changes in fair value of the hedging instrument in a period different from the recognition of gains and losses relating to changes in the fair value of the hedged item.	
Gain or loss on hedged item	Included in net income[1]	Ineffective portion in net income Effective portion in other comprehensive income[2]
Gain or loss on hedging instrument	Included in net income[1]	Ineffective portion in net income Effective portion in other comprehensive income[2]
Types of risks that are hedged	■ Market price risk: The risk of a change in earnings due to either the market price movement of the entire hedged item or the overall cash flows stemming from changes in market conditions ■ Market interest rate risk: The risk that movements in market interest rates may affect either the right to receive (or obligation to pay or transfer) cash or other financial instruments in the future or the fair value of that right (or obligation) embodied in a financial asset or liability ■ Foreign exchange risk: The risk that changes in foreign exchange rates may affect the fair value of certain hedged items or the functional currency cash flows of the hedged transactions of an entity ■ Credit risk: The risk that a counterparty will fail to perform according to the terms of a financial asset or firm commitment contract. Credit risk affects the fair value of a financial asset, the financial component of a firm commitment, and the related cash flows	
Required documentation	■ The risk management objective and strategy for undertaking the hedge, including identification of the hedging instrument, the hedged item, the nature of the risk being hedged, and how the hedging instrument's effectiveness in offsetting the exposure to changes in the hedged item's fair value attributable to the hedged risk will be assessed. ■ Documentation of a reasonable method for recognizing in earnings the asset or liability representing the gain or loss on the hedged firm commitment. ■ Both at inception of the hedge and on an ongoing basis, the hedging relationship is expected to be highly effective in achieving offsetting changes in fair value attributable to the hedged risk during the period that the hedge is designated. An assessment of effectiveness is required whenever financial statements or earnings are reported, and at least every three months.	

[1] Gains and losses on a hedged asset/liability and the hedging instrument shall be recognized in current earnings. To the extent that the hedge is effective, the gains and losses will offset. To the extent the hedge is ineffective, the effect will show in current earnings as a gain or loss with no offset.

[2] The effective portion of the hedge is reported in other comprehensive income (check to make sure of linking of hedged asset/liability and hedging instrument; i.e., that value of both are valued from same index or rate). The ineffective portion is reported in earnings immediately.

EXHIBIT 7.2 (cont.) Summary of Hedge Accounting for Derivatives

Journal Entries for Hedges Assets and Losses
(Journal entries for liabilities and gains are reversed)

	Fair Value		**Cash Flow**	

At each balance sheet date

Fair Value

Forward contract:

Asset loss	XXX	
Asset		XXX
Fwd. Contr.	XXX	
Fwd. Contr. gain		XXX
(to record changes in fair value)		

Option contract:

Asset loss	XXX	
Asset		XXX
Option Contr.	XXX	
Option Contr. gain		XXX
(to record changes in fair value)		

Firm commitment:

Option/Fwd. Contr.	XXX	
Option/Fwd. Contr. gain		same
Loss on firm commitment	same	
Firm Commitment		XXX
(to record changes in fair value)		

Cash Flow

Forward contract:

Asset loss	same	
Asset		XXX
AOCI	XXX	
Fwd. Contr. gain		same
Fwd. Contr.	XXX	
AOCI		XXX
Discount exp.[1]	XXX	
AOCI		XXX
(to record changes in fair value)		

[1] Discount expense is the difference between forward and spot rates when contract is executed (amortized over life of forward contract)

Option contract:

Asset loss	same	
Asset		XXX
AOCI	XXX	
Option gain		same
Option Contr.	XXX	
AOCI		XXX
Option exp.[2]	XXX	
AOCI		XXX
(to record changes in fair value)		

[2] Option expense is the change in the time value of the option.

Forecasted transaction:

Option/Fwd. Contr.	XXX	
AOCI		XXX
Option/Disc. exp.	XXX	
AOCI		XXX
(to record changes in fair value)		

Expiration date

Accrue gains (losses) on asset and derivative as above

Forward contract:

Cash	XXX	
Fwd. Contr.		XXX
(to record receipt of cash and close-out of forward contract)		

Option contract:

Cash	XXX	
Option		XXX
(to record receipt of cash and close-out of option)		

Firm commitment:

Cash	XXX	
Fwd. Contr./Option		XXX
Firm commitment	XXX	
Adj. to income		XXX
(to record receipt of cash and close-out of forward contract or option)		

Accrue gains (losses) on asset and derivative as above

Forward contract:

Cash	XXX	
Fwd. Contr.		XXX
(to record receipt of cash and close-out of forward contract)		

Option contract:

Cash	XXX	
Option		XXX
(to record receipt of cash and close-out of option)		

Forecasted transaction:

Cash	XXX	
Fwd. Contr./Option		XXX
AOCI	XXX	
Adj. to income		XXX
(to record changes in fair value)		

COMPREHENSIVE REVIEW

On September 30, 2014, a U.S. company enters into a firm commitment to purchase equipment from a foreign supplier for €200,000. The equipment is deliverable on March 31, 2015, and the €200,000 payment is due on June 30, 2015. The company expects the $US to weaken during this period of time. To hedge the commitment to pay €200,000, the company enters into a forward exchange contract on September 30, 2014, to receive €200,000 on June 30, 2015, at an exchange rate of €1:US$1.42. The relevant spot and forward exchange rates during this time period are as follows:

Date	Spot Rates	Forward Rates for June 30, 2015 Settlement
September 30, 2014..............	€1.00:US$1.35	€1.00:US$1.42
December 31, 2014	€1.00:US$1.36	€1.00:US$1.41
March 31, 2015	€1.00:US$1.39	€1.00:US$1.41
June 30, 2015..................	€1.00:US$1.40	N/A

Required
Prepare the journal entries necessary to reflect the above transactions.

The solution to this review problem can be found on page 508.

APPENDIX 7A: Required Disclosures Relating to Derivatives

FASB ASC 815-10-50-1, 1A, and 4A require the following general disclosures relating to the use of derivatives:

a. How and why an entity uses derivative instruments (or such nonderivative instruments)
b. How derivative instruments (or such nonderivative instruments) and related hedged items are accounted for under Topic 815
c. How derivative instruments (or such nonderivative instruments) and related hedged items affect all of the following:
   1. An entity's financial position
   2. An entity's financial performance
   3. An entity's cash flows.
d. Its objectives for holding or issuing those instruments
e. The context needed to understand those objectives
f. Its strategies for achieving those objectives
g. Information that would enable users of its financial statements to understand the volume of its activity in those instruments
h. The location and fair value amounts of derivative instruments (and such nonderivative instruments) reported in the statement of financial position
i. The location and amount of the gains and losses on derivative instruments (and such nonderivative instruments) and related hedged items reported in any of the following:
   1. The statement of financial performance
   2. The statement of financial position (for example, gains and losses initially recognized in Other Comprehensive Income).

Specific disclosures are required for fair value derivatives under FASB ASC 815-25-50-1:

a. The net gain or loss recognized in earnings during the reporting period representing both of the following:
   1. The amount of the hedges' ineffectiveness
   2. The component of the derivative instruments' gain or loss, if any, excluded from the assessment of hedge effectiveness.
b. The amount of net gain or loss recognized in earnings when a hedged firm commitment no longer qualifies as a fair value hedge.

Specific disclosures are required for cash flow derivatives under FASB ASC 815-30-50-1:

a. A description of the transactions or other events that will result in the reclassification into earnings of gains and losses that are reported in Accumulated Other Comprehensive Income

b. The estimated net amount of the existing gains or losses that are reported in Accumulated Other Comprehensive Income at the reporting date that is expected to be reclassified into earnings within the next 12 months

c. The maximum length of time over which the entity is hedging its exposure to the variability in future cash flows for forecasted transactions excluding those forecasted transactions related to the payment of variable interest on existing financial instruments

d. The amount of gains and losses reclassified into earnings as a result of the discontinuance of cash flow hedges because it is probable that the original forecasted transactions will not occur by the end of the originally specified time period or within the additional period of time discussed in paragraphs 815-30-40-4 through 40-5.

APPENDIX 7B: Derivative Financial Instruments

Hedging Instruments

In general terms, the use of derivatives to mitigate fair value, cash flow, and foreign currency risks, like those described above, is called *hedging*. Companies routinely hedge recognized assets and liabilities, firm commitments, and forecasted transactions to reduce their exposure to variability in the fair value and cash flows associated with recognized assets and liabilities or future transactions, respectively. A company might, for example, hedge the market price risk associated with forecasted inventory purchases when changes in those prices cannot be quickly passed on to their customers. Or, a company might hedge the market price risk associated with forecasted inventory sales if its raw material or production costs are fixed and the pricing for the product is volatile.

Companies hedge these risks by employing a wide variety of financial instruments. All of these instruments can be purchased in the financial markets or from a derivatives broker. Derivatives are generally of three types: forward and futures contracts, option contracts, and swap contracts. We describe each of these instruments in this appendix.

Forward and Futures Contracts A **forward contract** ("forward") is a commitment to buy or sell a specified quantity of an asset or commodity at a specified price and future date. A forward gives the holder *the obligation* to buy or sell at a predetermined future date.[25] The buyer (assuming the *long position*) agrees to buy a particular item on a specified future date, and the seller (assuming the *short position*) agrees to sell that item on the specified future date at an agreed-upon price (the *delivery price* or *contract price*). The terms of the forward contract (e.g., settlement price) are privately negotiated between contracting parties, commonly with the assistance of financial intermediaries like derivatives brokers. While forwards historically originated as contractual commitments to actually deliver some specified quantity of underlying commodities at a predetermined price, today most negotiated forwards allow for net cash settlement of the contract.

One of the most common applications of forward contracts occurs in the foreign exchange markets. For example, consider our first example of our company purchasing product from Italy with a Euro-denominated payable of €150,000. In that example, we assumed that the $US weakened vis-à-vis the Euro and that the exchange rate fell from $1.30:1€ to $1.40:1€. In order to hedge this risk, our company might buy €150,000 forward to another company that exports from Italy and expects to receive €150,000 from its customers. The parties would agree to make the exchange of €150,000 on a specified future date (the *delivery date*) at a specified price (say $1.35:€1). Our company has, therefore, locked in the cost of obtaining €150,000 to settle the contract, thus insulating us from significant further weakness in the $US (of course, we are also giving up potential gain should the $US strengthen, but we are willing to do so as speculation on the $US is not our primary business and this is a risk that we do not want).

A **futures contract** ("futures") is a standardized, exchange-traded version of a forward. The contractual terms of futures are determined by the exchanges on which the futures trade. While all cash flows and transfers related to forwards occur on the settlement date, most futures exchanges require daily cash settlement of outstanding contracts. Although there are a number of structural differences between forwards and futures, we believe it is fairly safe to think of these contracts as almost the same for accounting purposes.

If a forward or futures contract is to be an effective hedge of a net asset (or future cash flows) position, then the net settlement value of the forward or futures will increase and decrease in value in the opposite direction to the fair value of the asset (or to the future cash flows) to which they relate. As a result, the buyer of these types of contracts is able to lock in the purchase or sale price for the asset and mitigate the risk of a fluctuation in fair value.

---

[25] Options give the holder *the right, but not the obligation* to buy or sell. We discuss options in greater detail later in this chapter.

To illustrate, assume that our company has an inventory of aluminum alloy that it will sell to a customer in 60 days. Assume that aluminum alloy is currently worth $0.85/lb. and the futures price indicates a decrease to $0.83. This forecast ultimately proves to be too low, however, as indicated in the following table of futures and market prices:

	Spot Price	60 Day Futures Price
Today	$0.85	$0.83
60 days later	$0.84	

Although the market anticipates a decrease in the price of aluminum alloy, we are concerned about the adverse effects of a possible greater decline in the market value of aluminum alloy (i.e., below $0.83), and want to lock in the price that we will be able to get for our product. Commodities prices can be highly volatile, and we don't want to take the chance that we will be forced to sell our aluminum alloy inventory when prices are too low to cover our costs.

We decide to purchase a 60-day futures contract on aluminum alloy at $0.83, and have, thereby, locked in a loss of $0.02/lb ($0.83/lb − $0.85/lb). We have mitigated the risk of a greater price decline (which was our original motivation to purchase the futures contract), but we have also (1) given up any upside potential if the price of aluminum alloy increases and (2) guaranteed that we will have a $0.02/lb loss when compared to the current spot rate. This may seem to be an irrational choice, but this certainty can allow managers to be more effective in their planning and control of the business. It is the same as paying an insurance company to protect against potential liability and losses from accidents, fires, and the like.

In the case of our aluminum alloy futures, on the settlement date, the price of aluminum alloy in the spot market is $0.84/lb, which is higher than the contractual amount per pound that we have a right to receive (i.e., $0.83). If the contract did not allow net settlement, then we would have to deliver the contractually specified quantity of aluminum alloy and we would receive $0.83/lb. However, the vast majority of futures contracts require net settlement, so we will have to pay the $0.01/lb difference between the forward rate and the current spot rate at the settlement date ($0.83/lb − $0.84/lb). Our original aluminum alloy inventory (i.e., the thing hedged) will be sold at the current spot rate (i.e., $0.84/lb), thereby netting us $0.83/lb (i.e., $0.84/lb − $0.01/lb) when combining the actual aluminum alloy sales and the net cash payment for the futures settlement.

Option Contract   An **option contract** gives a party the *right*, but not the *obligation*, to execute a transaction. A *call option* is a right to *buy* a specified quantity of an asset (e.g., security, commodity) at a specified price (the *strike price*) on or before the settlement date. A *put option* is an option to sell a specified quantity of a security (or commodity) at a specific price on or before the settlement date. Options are frequently used to mitigate risks associated with fluctuations in the market prices of securities or commodities. A company might, for example, purchase a call option to limit the price it will have to pay for a commodity, or it might purchase a put option to limit potential price declines in the value of a financial asset or commodity.[26]

Options are purchased by paying a relatively small premium for the right to control the large quantity of assets underlying the option (e.g., foreign currencies, oil, and fixed income securities). The price of the option consists of two components: an intrinsic value (i.e., what the option would be worth, if anything, if it were exercised immediately) and a time value (i.e., the additional value of an option due to the remaining time to maturity).

Intrinsic value is never less than zero because an option holder can just walk away from the deal. Nevertheless, even with zero intrinsic value an option can still be worth something because of its time value. The reason is that the time value of an option reflects the probability that the underlying asset's price will rise in the case of call options or fall in the case of put options. Therefore, an option's value normally increases with time to maturity because the holder has more time for underlying price to move advantageously.

The following example illustrates the use of options to protect the value of an account receivable denominated in Euros. Assume that on March 4 a company has a €125,000 account receivable due on June 2. Suppose further that on March 4 the exchange rate between the $US and the Euro is $1.56:€1.

To protect the $US value of its Euro-denominated receivable, the company purchases a put option on Euros, giving it the right, but not the obligation, to sell Euros and receive $US on June 2. On March 4, the premiums for put options expiring on June 2 are as follows:

---

[26] If an option can be exercised only at maturity, it is called a *European* option. If it can be exercised on or before maturity, it is called an *American* option.

Strike Price/€	Put Option Premium/€125,000
$1.60.	$7,287
$1.58.	$5,575
$1.56.	$4,125
$1.54.	$2,975
$1.52.	$2,100
$1.50.	$1,475

Our company could choose any of the strike (exercise) prices in this table, but the higher the strike price, the higher the premium.

Suppose our company decides to protect the $US value of its Euro-denominated account receivable by purchasing the June put (the right to sell Euros and receive $US) at $1.56 per Euro. It pays a total premium of $4,125. In doing so, it is purchasing an insurance policy, of sorts, guaranteeing that the $US value of the Euro will not decline significantly, causing it to suffer a foreign exchange loss. If the value of the Euro on June 2 falls below $1.56, the company will exercise its option and collect $1.56 for each Euro, thereby guaranteeing itself $195,000 (i.e., €125,000 × $1.56/€ = $195,000). But if the value of the Euro rises above $1.56, the company will walk away from the option and sell the €125,000 for whatever they were worth on the spot market on that date. For instance, if the Euro rises in value to $1.58, then the company will collect $197,500 (i.e., $1.58/€ × €125,000 = $197,500). The purchase of an option contract has, therefore, given the company downside protection while preserving upside potential.

Swap Contract A **swap contract** ("swap") is an arrangement between two or more parties to exchange future cash flows. It is a common arrangement for hedging interest rate and foreign currency risks. A company might use a swap contract to exchange a *fixed-for-floating* or a *floating-for-fixed interest rate* in order to increase or decrease the ratio of fixed and variable (floating) interest costs in its cost structure.

To illustrate, assume that on June 30 our company borrows $10 million of three-year 7.5% fixed-rate interest-only debt (principal due at maturity). Let's also assume that the company prefers variable-rate debt since its cash flows are positively correlated with the level of interest rates. As a result, the company enters into a three-year interest-rate swap with a bank to synthetically convert the debt's fixed rate to a variable rate. Under the terms of the swap, the company receives interest at a fixed rate of 7.5% and pays interest at a variable rate (say, equal to the six-month U.S. LIBOR), based on a notional amount of $10,000,000. Both the debt and the swap require that payments be made or received on December 31 and June 30 of each year. The six-month U.S. LIBOR rate on each reset date determines the variable portion of the interest-rate swap for the following six-month period.

The six-month U.S. LIBOR rates are assumed to be as follows for the first year of the swap and agreement:

Date	Six-Month U.S. LIBOR Rate
June 30.	6.00%
December 31	7.00%

For the period ending December 31 the company recognizes interest expense of $375,000 on the fixed-rate debt ($10 million × 7.5%/2), and receives a cash payment of $75,000 from the party agreeing to assume its fixed rate (7.5% − 6%, the variable rate for that time period). Its net interest expense is, therefore, 6% ($375,000 − $75,000 = $300,000; $300,000/$10,000,000 = 3.0%; 3.0% × 2 = 6.0%), the variable rate in effect during that period. And, for the period ending June 30 the company, again, recognizes interest expense of $375,000, and receives a payment of $25,000 (7.5% − 7%). Its net interest expense reflects the variable rate of 7% ($375,000 − $25,000 = $350,000; $350,000/$10,000,000 = 3.5%; 3.5% × 2 = 7.0%) during that period.

Interest rate swap agreements are typically arranged by banks that bring together the company desiring fixed-rate debt with another company desiring variable-rate debt. Companies can swap in either direction (i.e., fixed-for-variable or variable-for-fixed).

Fair Value Hedge Example: Use of Futures Contracts to Hedge Zinc Inventory

On October 1 a mining company has 10 million pounds of zinc inventory on hand at an average cost of $0.20 per pound. To protect the inventory from a possible decline in zinc prices, the company sells zinc futures contracts for 10 million pounds at $0.53 per pound for delivery in February of next year to coincide with its expected physical sale of its zinc inventory. The company designates the hedge as a fair value hedge (i.e., the company is hedging changes in the inventory's fair value, not changes in cash flows from anticipated sales). The zinc spot price on October 1 is $0.51 per pound.

On December 31, the Company's fiscal year-end, the February zinc futures price has fallen to $0.51 a pound, and the spot price has fallen to $0.49 a pound. On February 20 of next year the Company closes out its futures contract via net cash settlement. On the same date, the mining company sells 10 million pounds of zinc for $0.52 a pound, the spot rate on that date. Following are futures and spot prices, as well as the journal entries required to reflect the transactions for the relevant dates:

Date	Spot Rates	Futures Rates for Feb. 20 Settlement
October 1	$0.51	$0.53
December 31	$0.49	$0.51
February 20	$0.52	$0.52

Date	Journal Entries		
10/1	No entry is made to record the fair value of the futures contracts, because at the time of their inception their fair value is zero.		
12/31	Loss on inventory	200,000	
	Zinc inventory		200,000
	(to adjust the carrying amount of the inventory for changes in its fair value = 10 million lbs. × [$0.49 − $0.51])		
	Futures contract	200,000	
	Gain on hedge		200,000
	(to record the gain on futures contract—10 million lbs. × [$0.53 − $0.51])		
2/20	Cash	100,000	
	Loss on hedge	100,000	
	Futures contract		200,000
	(to close out futures contract and recognize the loss on the futures contract from 12/31 to 2/20 = 10 million lbs. × [$0.51 − $0.52])		
	Zinc inventory	300,000	
	Gain on inventory		300,000
	(to adjust the carrying amount of the inventory that is due to the increase in spot prices = 10 million lbs. × [$0.52 − $0.49])		
	Accounts receivable	5,200,000	
	Cost of goods sold*	2,100,000	
	Zinc sales		5,200,000
	Zinc inventory		2,100,000
	(to record the sale of 10,000,000 pounds of zinc inventory at $0.52 per pound)		

```
*   2,000,000    Avg. cost
     (200,000)   12/31 adj.
      300,000    2/20 adj.
    2,100,000
```

Cash Flow Example: Use of Options to Hedge an Anticipated Purchase of Inventory

A manufacturing company that utilizes gold in its products wants to hedge itself against an anticipated increase in the price of gold because the company believes it cannot pass that increase on to customers. The company purchases call options on gold futures as insurance. If gold prices increase, the profit on the purchased call options will approximately offset the higher price that the manufacturer must pay for the gold to be used in its manufacturing process. If gold prices decline, the manufacturer will lose the premium it paid for the call options, but can then buy gold at the lower price.

On January 5 the spot price of gold is $400 per ounce and the manufacturer anticipates the purchase of 200 ounces of gold in April. It purchases two call options to purchase gold for $400 per ounce for a premium of $7.50 an ounce. Each call option is for 100 ounces of gold and they both expire after April 15. Through

April 15 the spot price of gold rises by $25 an ounce to $425, and the April 15 call value is $25 an ounce ($425 spot price, less $400 strike price). The manufacturer settles its two call options on April 15 and buys from its suppliers 200 ounces of gold at the current spot rate.

The manufacturer's projected purchase of gold in April is considered a forecasted transaction. A derivative instrument that hedges the cash flows associated with forecasted purchases is considered a cash-flow hedge. Accordingly, the effective portion of the call options' gain or loss is reported in Other Comprehensive Income (OCI), and the ineffective portion is reported currently in earnings. Amounts accumulated in OCI are reclassified as earnings when the related inventory is sold or otherwise impacts earnings.

The manufacturer must record the fair value of the options on its balance sheet. Changes in the time value of the options are recorded currently in earnings. **Intrinsic value** is the excess of the spot price over the exercise price and **time value** is considered the excess of the fair value of the options over their intrinsic value. Changes in the options' intrinsic value, to the extent that they are effective as a hedge, are recorded in other comprehensive income. The balance in other comprehensive income is reclassified as earnings when the related inventory is sold.

Relevant prices for the call options and the spot price for gold are provided in the following table:

	Gold Spot Price	Time Value	Intrinsic Value	Total Value
January 5 . . .	$400	$1,500[a]		$1,500
April 15 . . .	425	0	$5,000[b]	5,000
Change . . .	$ 25[c]	−$1,500	$5,000	$3,500

[a] (200 × $7.50)
[b] (200 × [$400 − $425] strike price)
[c] (call value)

Journal entries to record the hedging transactions and the purchase of the gold are as follows.

Date	Journal Entries		
January 5	Purchased call options . . .	1,500	
	Cash . . .		1,500
	(to record the purchase of call options − 200 × $7.50)		
April 15	Option expense . . .	1,500	
	Purchased call options . . .		1,500
	(to record the change in the time value of the purchased call options [$1,500 less $0])		
	Purchased call options . . .	5,000	
	Other comprehensive income . . .		5,000
	(to record the change in the intrinsic value of the purchased call options—200 × ([$425 − $400] strike price)		
	Cash . . .	5,000	
	Purchased call options . . .		5,000
	(to record the cash settlement of the April call options— $25 × 200 ounces)		
	Gold inventory . . .	85,000	
	Cash . . .		85,000
	(to record the purchase of 200 ounces of gold at the purchase price of $425 per ounce)		

The purchase price for gold has increased by $25/oz. or $5,000 in total ($25 × 200). As of June 30, the company has deferred in other comprehensive income $5,000 of gains that have resulted from changes in the intrinsic value of the call option contracts. According to FASB ASC 815-30-35-39, the gains deferred in Other Comprehensive Income will be reclassified as earnings when the inventory is sold (i.e., when earnings are impacted). The company has, therefore, hedged the price increase in gold by the purchase of these call options, and that hedge results in no change in Cost of Goods Sold as a result of the price increase in gold.

Accounting for a Hedge of a Firm Commitment to Purchase Nickel with a Forward Contract

Our company has a contract to purchase 100,000 pounds of nickel from a supplier at $8.90 per pound this year on December 31. We are concerned with the fluctuations of the price of nickel during the commitment period, and we enter into a forward contract to sell 100,000 pounds of nickel at $8.90 per pound to hedge against the fluctuations in fair value of our firm commitment due to changes in the market price of nickel. The forward contract is designated as a fair value hedge of our firm commitment to purchase 100,000 pounds of nickel from our supplier in six months.

The spot price and forward price of nickel, and the fair value of the forward contract (ignoring discounting), are as follows:

Date	Spot Price	Forward Price for Dec. 31 Settlement	Fair Value Asset (Liability)
July 1	$9.00	$8.90	$ —
September 30.	8.85	8.80	10,000
December 31	9.10	—	(20,000)

The following journal entries are required to be made on July 1, September 30, and December 31.

Date	Journal Entries		
July 1	Memorandum entry only documenting the existence of this hedging relationship		
September 30	Forward contract (B/S).	10,000	
	Unrealized gain on forward contract (I/S)		10,000
	(to record the change in fair value of the forward contract attributable to the discounted change in the forward rate [i.e., the effective portion] ($8.90 − $8.80) × 100,000)		
	Unrealized loss on firm commitment (I/S)	10,000	
	Firm commitment (B/S)		10,000
	(to record the change in fair value of the firm commitment to purchase nickel ($10,000 − $0) = $10,000)		
December 31	Unrealized loss on forward contract (I/S).	30,000	
	Forward contract (B/S)		30,000
	(to record the change in fair value of the forward contract attributable to the discounted change in the forward rate [i.e., the effective portion of the hedge] ($9.10 − $8.80) × 100,000)		
	Firm commitment (B/S)	30,000	
	Unrealized gain on firm commitment (I/S).		30,000
	(to record the change in fair value of the firm commitment to purchase nickel $10,000 − ($20,000))		
	Forward contract (B/S).	20,000	
	Cash (B/S)		20,000
	(to record the settlement of the forward contract at December 31 ($9.10 − $8.90) × 100,000)		
	Nickel inventory (B/S).	910,000	
	Firm commitment (B/S)		20,000
	Cash (B/S)		890,000
	(to record the purchase of 100,000 pounds of nickel at $8.90 per pound)		

Since nickel prices increased, our company realized a gain of $20,000 on the firm commitment with our supplier, and this gain was offset by a loss of $20,000 on the forward contract. Therefore, even though our company paid $890,000 for the nickel inventory (i.e., the contract price), the inventory was recorded at the current market price of $910,000 (i.e., the purchase price plus the fair value of the firm commitment).

Hedge of an Available-for-Sale Security with a Put Option

Our company owns 500,000 shares of XYZ's publicly traded stock. As of January 1 these shares are trading at $50 per share and we have an unrealized gain relating to this investment of $1,000,000 in Accumulated Other Comprehensive Income (AOCI). We are concerned that the market price of the shares may decline and lock in our unrealized gain with the purchase of a put option on XYZ's stock from a bank for $100,000. This put option allows our company to sell our 500,000 shares of XYZ stock to the bank at $50 per share at December 31 of the current year.

The share price and fair value of our investment in XYZ were as follows:

Date	Share Price	Fair Value
January 1	$50	$25,000,000
March 31	60	30,000,000
June 30	45	22,500,000
September 30	40	20,000,000
December 31	30	15,000,000

The fair value (assumed and provided to us by our bank), intrinsic value, and time value of the put option are as follows:

Date	(A) Fair Value	(B) Intrinsic Value	(A) − (B) Time Value
January 1	$ 100,000	$ —	$100,000
March 31	90,000	—	90,000
June 30	2,575,000	2,500,000	75,000
September 30	5,025,000	5,000,000	25,000
December 31	10,000,000	10,000,000	—

The following journal entries will be made January 1, March 31, June 30, September 30, and December 31:

Date	Journal Entries		
January 1	Purchased put option (B/S)	100,000	
	Cash (B/S)		100,000
	(to record the purchased put option in the statement of financial position at fair value)		
March 31	Option expense – change in the time value of the put option (I/S)	10,000	
	Purchased put option (B/S)		10,000
	(to record the change in the time value portion of the put option ($90,000 − $100,000) = ($10,000))		
	Investment in XYZ (B/S)	5,000,000	
	OCI		5,000,000
	(to record the increase in fair value of the investment in XYZ in OCI; note that there was no change in the intrinsic value of the put option $30,000,000 − $25,000,000 = $5,000,000)		
June 30	Option expense – change in the time value of the put option (I/S)	15,000	
	Purchased put option (B/S)		15,000
	(to record the change in the time value portion of the put option $75,000 − $90,000 = ($15,000))		
	Purchased put option (B/S)	2,500,000	
	Unrealized gain on put option (I/S)		2,500,000
	(to record the change in the intrinsic value of the purchased put option)		
	OCI	5,000,000	
	Unrealized loss on investment in XYZ (I/S)	2,500,000	
	Investment in XYZ (B/S)		7,500,000
	(to record the change in fair value of the investment in XYZ. Note that the loss on this investment that is recognized in earnings is limited to the change in the put option's intrinsic value (i.e., the hedged risk). The remainder of the change in fair value is recorded in OCI. $22,500,000 − $30,000,000 = ($7,500,000))		

Date	Journal Entries		
September 30	Option expense – change in the time value of the put option (I/S)	50,000	
	Purchased put option (B/S)..		50,000
	(to record the change in the time value of the put option		
	$25,000 – $75,000 = ($50,000))		
	Purchased put option (B/S)	2,500,000	
	Unrealized gain on put option (I/S)		2,500,000
	(to record the change in the intrinsic value portion of the purchased put option $5,000,000		
	$2,500,000 = $2,500,000)		
	Unrealized loss on investment in XYZ (I/S).........................	2,500,000	
	Investment in XYZ (B/S)...		2,500,000
	(to record the change in fair value of the investment in XYZ		
	$20,000,000 – $22,500,000 = ($2,500,000))		
December 31	Option expense – change in the time value of the put option (I/S)	25,000	
	Purchased put option (B/S)..		25,000
	(to record the change in the time value portion of the put option		
	$0 – $25,000 = ($25,000))		
	Purchased put option (B/S)	5,000,000	
	Unrealized gain on put option (I/S)		5,000,000
	(to record the change in the intrinsic value of the purchased put option, this entry would be made		
	prior to the settlement of the put option $10,000,000 – $5,000,000 = $5,000,000)		
	Unrealized loss on investment in XYZ (I/S).........................	5,000,000	
	Investment in XYZ (B/S)...		5,000,000
	(to record the change in fair value of the investment in XYZ		
	$15,000,000 – $20,000,000 = ($5,000,000))		
	Cash (B/S)	25,000,000	
	Investment in XYZ (B/S)...		15,000,000
	Purchased put option (B/S)......................................		10,000,000
	(to record the settlement of the purchased put option through delivery of the shares of XYZ's stock		
	at a price of $50 per share to the bank)		
	AOCI (B/S)	1,000,000	
	Realized gain on investment in XYZ (I/S).........................		1,000,000
	(to reclassify the unrealized gain on XYZ's shares from AOCI to earnings on the sale of the shares		
	to the bank)		

Even though XYZ's share price fell to $30 per share, we were able to lock in a $50 share price as a result of entering into the put option. Thus, we were able to realize the gain of $1,000,000 that we originally wanted to protect (less the $100,000 premium paid for the option).

Superscript $^{A, (B)}$ **denotes assignments based on Appendix 7A (B).**

QUESTIONS

1. What is the definition of an "exchange rate" as the term is used in FASB ASC 830?
   (*Hint:* See the Glossary to FASB ASC 830.)

   > FASB ASC
   > Research

2. Briefly explain why the value of the $US fluctuates vis-à-vis other world currencies.

3. Explain why a weakening $US can result in a higher level of reported sales, expense and profit even if unit volumes remain constant.

4. Why is it necessary to translate foreign-currency-denominated income statement and balance sheet items into $US?
   (*Hint:* See FASB ASC 830-10-10.)

   > FASB ASC
   > Research

5. FASB ASC 830 requires the recognition in income of transaction gains and losses that result from fluctuations in the fair value of the $US vis-à-vis other world currencies. What is the rationale for the recognition of these gains and losses in income?
   (*Hint:* See FASB ASC 830-20-35-1.)

   > FASB ASC
   > Research

<table>
<tr><td>

FASB ASC
Research

</td><td>

6. Gains and losses related to fluctuations in the fair value of the $US vis-à-vis other world currencies may not be under the control of a company. Should these gains and losses, therefore, be considered as *extraordinary items* in the income statement?
(*Hint:* See FASB ASC 225-20-45-4(b).)

</td></tr>
</table>

<table>
<tr><td>

FASB ASC
Research

</td><td>

7. FASB ASC 830-20-35 requires the recognition of gains and losses relating to the change in exchange rates subsequent to the rate used in the initial measurement. If exchange rates change subsequent to the date of the financial statements, should the most recent financial statements be restated to reflect the change?
(*Hint:* See FASB ASC 830-20-35-8.)

</td></tr>
</table>

<table>
<tr><td>

FASB ASC
Research

</td><td>

8. Implementation of FASB ASC 830 might become quite cumbersome if companies are required to measure each transaction at the exchange rate in effect on the date of the transaction. Do accounting standards allow for the use of an average exchange rate for purposes of computing foreign currency translation gains and losses?
(*Hint:* See FASB ASC 830-10-55-10 and -11.)

</td></tr>
</table>

<table>
<tr><td>

FASB ASC
Research

</td><td>

9. In addition to the recognition of gains and losses that result from foreign-currency-denominated transactions, what additional information should management disclose in the MD&A?
(*Hint:* See FASB ASC 83-20-50-3.)

</td></tr>
</table>

<table>
<tr><td>

FASB ASC
Research

</td><td>

10. In what ways does a "firm commitment" differ from a "forecasted transaction" under FASB ASC 815?
(*Hint:* See Glossary to FASB ASC 815.)

</td></tr>
</table>

<table>
<tr><td>

FASB ASC
Research

</td><td>

11. FASB ASC 815-20-25-13 allows for the eligibility of a *forecasted transaction* for designation as a cash flow hedge. Can a transaction be considered to be a forecasted transaction based solely on management intent? Or, must other factors be considered?
(*Hint:* See FASB ASC 815-20-55-24.)

</td></tr>
</table>

Assignments with the 🔘 logo in the margin are available in BusinessCourse.
See the Preface of the book for details.

MULTIPLE CHOICE

<table>
<tr><td>

`LO1`

AICPA
Adapted

</td><td>

12. Recording accounts receivable denominated in a foreign currency
On June 19, Don Co., a U.S. company, sold and delivered merchandise on a 30-day account to Cologne GmbH, a German corporation, for 200,000 euros. On July 19, Cologne paid Don in full. Relevant currency rates were:

</td></tr>
</table>

	June 19	July 19
Spot rate.	$0.988	$0.995
30-day forward rate	0.990	1.000

What amount should Don record on June 19 as an account receivable for its sale to Cologne?

a. $197,600

b. $198,000

c. $199,000

d. $200,000

<table>
<tr><td>

LO2

AICPA
Adapted

</td><td>

13. Recognizing gains on derivative financial instruments
Neron Co. has two derivatives related to two different financial instruments, instrument A and instrument B, both of which are debt instruments. The derivative related to instrument A is a fair value hedge, and the derivative related to instrument B is a cash flow hedge. Neron experienced gains in the value of instruments A and B due to a change in interest rates. Which of the gains should be reported by Neron in its income statement?

</td></tr>
</table>

	Gain in Value of Debt Instrument A	Gain in Value of Debt Instrument B
a.	Yes	Yes
b.	Yes	No
c.	No	Yes
d.	No	No

14. Recognizing gains on derivative financial instruments

Toigo Co. purchased merchandise from a vendor in England on November 20 for 500,000 British pounds. Payment was due in British pounds on January 20.

The spot rates to purchase one pound were as follows:

November 20	$1.25
December 31	1.20
January 20	1.17

How should the foreign currency transaction gain be reported on Toigo's financial statements at December 31?

a. A gain of $40,000 as a separate component of stockholders' equity.

b. A gain of $40,000 in the income statement.

c. A gain of $25,000 as a separate component of stockholders' equity.

d. A gain of $25,000 in the income statement.

LO2

 AICPA Adapted

15. Definition of a derivative financial instrument

A derivative financial instrument is best described as

a. Evidence of an ownership interest in an entity such as shares of common stock.

b. A contract that has its settlement value tied to an underlying notional amount.

c. A contract that conveys to a second entity a right to receive cash from a first entity.

d. A contract that conveys to a second entity a right to future collections on accounts receivable from a first entity.

LO2

AICPA Adapted

16. Recognizing gains and losses on foreign-currency-denominated transactions

On October 1 of the current year, a U.S. company sold merchandise on account to a British company for 2,000 pounds (exchange rate, 1 pound = $1.43). At the company's December 31 fiscal year end, the exchange rate was 1 pound = $1.45. The exchange rate was 1 pound = $1.50 on collection in January of the subsequent year. What amount would the company recognize as a gain(loss) from foreign currency translation when the receivable is collected?

a. $0

b. $100

c. $140

d. ($140)

LO1

AICPA Adapted

17. Recognizing foreign currency exchange losses

On November 2, 2014, Platt Co. entered into a 90 day futures contract to purchase 50,000 Swiss francs when the contract quote was $0.70. The purchase was for speculation in price movement. The following exchange rates existed during the contract period:

	30 Day Futures	Spot Rate
November 2, 2014	$0.62	$0.63
December 31, 2014	0.65	0.64
January 31, 2015	0.65	0.68

What amount should Platt report as foreign currency exchange loss in its income statement for the year ended December 31, 2014?

a. $2,500

b. $3,000

c. $3,500

d. $4,000

LO1

 AICPA Adapted

LO1   **18. Recognizing foreign currency exchange losses**

On September 3, 2015, HH Corp. purchased merchandise for 10,000 units of the foreign company's local currency. On that date, the spot rate was $1.35. HH paid the bill in full on February 15, 2016, when the spot rate was $1.45. The spot rate was $1.40 on December 31, 2015. What amount should HH report as a foreign currency transaction gain (loss) in its income statement for the year ended December 31, 2016?

  a. $500
  b. $1,000
  c. ($500)
  d. ($1,000)

Use the following facts for Multiple Choice problems 19 through 20:

On November 3, the spot price for cotton was $0.81/lb., and the February futures price was $0.83/lb. On November 3, Levi Strauss sold 200 futures contracts on the commodity exchange at $0.83/lb. for delivery in February. Each contract was for 25,000 lbs. Levi Strauss designated these contracts as a cash flow hedge of 5 million lbs. of current inventory which it expected to sell in February. The average spot of this inventory when purchased was $0.58/lb. Levi Strauss properly documented the hedge and employed hedge accounting. On November 30, the company's fiscal year end, the February commodity exchange futures price was $0.85/lb.

LO2   **19. Recognition of assets and liabilities for futures contracts**

In the November 30 balance sheet, Levi Strauss should record the futures contracts as a

  a. $100,000 asset
  b. $100,000 liability
  c. $4,250,000 liability
  d. $4,250,000 asset

LO2   **20. Recognition of assets and liabilities for futures contracts**

If, on November 30, Levi Strauss concluded that the hedge was 100% effective, it should record the hedged cotton inventory in the November 30 balance sheet at

  a. $4,350,000
  b. $4,250,000
  c. $3,000,000
  d. $2,900,000

LO2   **21. Recognition of losses on derivatives in other comprehensive income**

The effective portion of a loss associated with a change in fair value of a derivative instrument should be reported as a component of other comprehensive income only if the derivative is appropriately designated as a

  a. Cash flow hedge of the foreign currency exposure of a forecasted transaction
  b. Fair value hedge of the foreign currency exposure of an unrecognized firm commitment
  c. Fair value hedge of the foreign currency exposure of a recognized asset or liability for which a foreign currency transaction gain or loss is recognized in earnings
  d. Speculation in a foreign currency

EXERCISES

LO1   **22. Journal entries for an account payable denominated in Mexican Pesos ($US weakens)**

Assume that your company purchases inventories from a Mexican supplier on December 15. The invoice specifies that payment is to be made on March 15 in Mexican Pesos (Peso) in the amount of 150,000 Pesos. Your company operates on a calendar year basis.

Assume the following exchange rates:

December 15	$0.040:1 Peso
December 31	$0.050:1 Peso
March 15	$0.060:1 Peso

Prepare the journal entries to record the purchase (assume perpetual inventory accounting), the required adjusting entry at December 31, and the payment on March 15.

23. **Journal entries for an account payable denominated in Canadian Dollars ($US strengthens)**   LO1

    Assume that your company purchases inventories from a Canadian supplier on November 3. The invoice specifies that payment is to be made on February 1 in Canadian dollars ($CAD) in the amount of $75,000 (CAD). Your company operates on a calendar year basis.

    Assume the following exchange rates:

November 3	$0.90:CA $1
December 31	$0.80:CA $1
February 1	$0.75:CA $1

    Prepare the journal entries to record the purchase (assume perpetual inventory accounting), the required adjusting entry at December 31, and the payment on Feb. 1.

24. **Journal entries for an account receivable denominated in Euros ($US weakens)**   LO1

    Assume that your company sells products to a customer located in France on October 15. The invoice specifies that payment is to be made on January 15 in Euros (€) in the amount of €350,000. Your company operates on a calendar year basis.

    Assume the following exchange rates:

October 15	$0.90:€1
December 31	$1.05:€1
January 15	$1.10:€1

    Prepare the journal entries to record the sale (ignore cost of goods sold), the required adjusting entry at December 31, and the receipt of payment January 15.

25. **Journal entries for an account receivable denominated in Swiss Francs ($US strengthens)**   LO1

    Assume that your company sells products to a customer located in Switzerland on November 20. The invoice specifies that payment is to be made on February 20 in Swiss Francs (CHF) in the amount of CHF 275,000. Your company operates on a calendar year basis.

    Assume the following exchange rates:

November 20	$1.15:1CHF
December 31	$1.10:1CHF
February 20	$1.05:1CHF

    Prepare the journal entries to record the sale (ignore cost of goods sold), the required adjusting entry at December 31, and the receipt of payment February 20.

26. **Economics of a fair value hedge**   LO2

    On September 30, our company executed a purchase order to buy 100,000 lbs. of copper on December 31 at a purchase price of $2.28/lb., the spot rate on the date the purchase order is signed. Also on September, 30, we execute a forward contract to sell 100,000 lbs. of copper for $0.92/lb., the forward price in effect on that date. Since this is a firm commitment, we classify this transaction as a fair value hedge and we can apply hedge accounting because we believe the hedge to be highly effective.

    The price of copper and the fair value of the forward contract on September 30 and December 31 are as follows:

	Copper	Forward Contract
September 30.	$2.28	$2.25
December 31	$2.21	$2.21

a. What does the relation between the sport and forward prices of copper tell you about the market's expectations for the price of copper through December?

b. What is the risk that we are trying to mitigate by the purchase of the forward contract?

c. At what price will the inventory be recognized when it is purchased on December 31 if the forecasts in the table above prove accurate?

d. What will be the net cash cost of the inventory if the forecasts in the table above prove accurate?

LO2   27. Journal entries for fair value hedge

Using the data in Exercise 26, prepare the required journal entries at September 30 and December 31.

LO2   28. Reported gain or loss on hedging transaction

On September 30, we enter into a futures contract to hedge the value of gold which we use on our manufacturing process and report on our balance sheet at $500,000. On December 31, the market value of gold had declined to $450,000. However, the futures contact that we had purchased increased in value by $45,000.

a. How much net profit or loss will be recognized?

b. Will this profit or loss be reflected in net income or other comprehensive income?

LO2   29. Cash flow hedge of anticipated purchase of inventory

We are a manufacturing company that uses gold in the production of our products. In January, we expect to acquire at least 200 ounces of gold in April and, to mitigate the risk of a price rise in the interim, we purchase two at-the-money spot April $291/oz. call options for a premium of $7.50 an ounce each since (each call option is for a notional amount of 100 ounces of gold). The relevant data are as follows:

Hedging Instrument and Commodity Price			
Date	Gold Spot Price	Option Strike Price	Option Premium
January.............	$291	$291	$7.50
April	$316		

a. Discuss the economic rationale for the purchase of the call options.

b. Compute the options' time value and intrinsic value at January and April.

c. Will we account for this hedge as a fair value hedge or a cash flow hedge?

d. Describe the accounting for the options' time value and intrinsic values.

e. Describe the accounting for unrealized gains or losses on the call option.

LO2   30. Cash flow hedge using foreign-currency options to hedge forecasted foreign sales

Our U.S. company anticipates sales to customers in New Zealand in six months on March 31 that will be denominated in the New Zealand Dollar (NZD). We purchase a foreign currency put option in the amount of the expected sales amount.

a. What is the risk that we are trying to mitigate by the purchase of the foreign currency put option?

b. Briefly describe how we will account for this transaction.

c. Assume that, on our statement date, the option's time value has decreased by $11,000 and the option's intrinsic value has increased by $238,095 as a result of the strengthening of the $US. Provide the required journal entry.

d. Assume that the deferred gain on the option is $652,174 on the date of the sale. Provide the required journal entry.

LO2   31. Accounting for fair value hedge of inventory (no ineffectiveness in the hedge)[27]

Our company reports commodities inventory on our balance sheet at $1 million. The inventory has a fair value of $1.1 million and we are concerned about a forecasted decline in the commodity price. We purchase a financial derivative in order to mitigate this risk. On the last day of the period, the fair value of the inventory has declined by $25,000 and the fair value of the derivative has increased by $25,000. All of the inventory is sold at its fair value and the derivative is settled on the last day of the period. Complete the following table of the required journal entries during the period:

---

[27] Adapted from ASC 815-25-55-36

	Debit (Credit)			
	Cash	Derivative	Inventory	Earnings
Recognize the change in the fair value of the derivative . . .				
Recognize the change in the fair value of the inventory . . .				
Recognize revenue from the sale.				
Recognize cost of goods sold relating to the sale.				
Recognize settlement of the derivative				
Total				

32. Accounting for fair value hedge of inventory (ineffectiveness in the hedge)[28]   LO2

Assume the same facts in exercise 31 except that the terms of the derivative security instrument do not perfectly match the inventory and its fair value has increased by $22,500 as compared with the decline in fair value of the inventory of $25,000. Complete the following table of the required journal entries during the period:

	Debit (Credit)			
	Cash	Derivative	Inventory	Earnings
Recognize the change in the fair value of the derivative . . .				
Recognize the change in the fair value of the inventory . . .				
Recognize revenue from the sale.				
Recognize cost of goods sold relating to the sale.				
Recognize settlement of the derivative				
Total				

33. Accounting for cash flow hedge of the forecasted sale of a commodity inventory[29]   LO2

Assume that our company decides to hedge the risk of changes in its cash flows relating to a forecasted sale of 100,000 bushels of wheat by entering into a derivative instrument. We expect to sell the 100,000 bushels of wheat on the last day of the period. On the first day of the period, we enter into derivative contract and designate it as a cash flow hedge of the forecasted sale (assume that we neither pay nor receive a premium on the derivative security and its fair value is zero at inception. Assume that the hedging relationship qualifies for cash flow hedge accounting and that we expect that there will be no ineffectiveness from the hedge.

At inception of the hedge, the expected sales price of 100,000 bushels of wheat is $1,100,000. On the last day of the period, the fair value of the derivative has increased by $25,000, and the expected sales price of 100,000 bushels of wheat has decreased by $25,000. Both the sale of 100,000 bushels of wheat and the settlement of the derivative contract occur on the last day of the period.

Complete the following table of the required journal entries during the period:

	Debit (Credit)			
	Cash	Derivative	Inventory	Earnings
Recognize the change in the fair value of the derivative . . .				
Recognize revenue from the sale.				
Recognize settlement of the derivative				
Reclassify the change in the fair value of the derivative instrument to earnings				
Total				

---

[28] Adapted from ASC 815-25-55-38.
[29] Adapted from ASC 815-30-55-20 to -22.

LO2 **34. Calculating the purchase cost of inventory in a fair value hedge of a firm commitment.**

Assume that our company enters into a firm commitment on July 15 to purchase 1,000 troy ounces of gold in December that will be used in our manufacturing process. The firm price commitment is required by our supplier. We expect the price of gold to decline over this period, however, and would, therefore, prefer to purchase it at the prevailing market price. Therefore, on July 15, we enter into a six-month forward contract to sell 1,000 troy ounces of gold on December 15 at the current forward rate of $310/troy ounce. Thus, the forward contract essentially "unlocks" the firm commitment. The forward contract requires net cash settlement on December 31, 20X1 and has a fair value of zero at inception. Assume that the spot price for gold declines to $285 on December 15. At what amount will the gold inventory be recorded when purchased?

LO2 **35. Interpreting footnote disclosure—Tiffany & Co.**

Tiffany & Co. reports the following table in the footnotes to its 2015 10-K:

(in thousands)	Years Ended January 31,			
	2015		2014	
	Pre-Tax Gain (Loss) Recognized in OCI (Effective Portion)	Pre-Tax Gain (Loss) Reclassified from Accumulated OCI into Earnings (Effective Portion)	Pre-Tax Gain (Loss) Recognized in OCI (Effective Portion)	Pre-Tax Gain (Loss) Reclassified from Accumulated OCI into Earnings (Effective Portion)
Derivatives in Cash Flow Hedging Relationships:				
Foreign exchange forward contracts[a]	$23,225	$18,717	$16,184	$17,660
Put option contracts[a]	—	—	1,241	2,201
Precious metal forward contracts[a]	(4,428)	(4,173)	(8,709)	(4,376)
Forward-starting interest rate swaps[b]	(4,177)	(1,517)	—	(1,535)
	$14,620	$13,027	$ 8,716	$13,950

[a] The gain or loss recognized in earnings is included within cost of sales.
[b] The gain or loss recognized in earnings is included within interest expense and financing costs.

Describe the difference in the impact on Tiffany's financial statements of the "Pre-Tax Gain (Loss) Recognized in OCI (Effective Portion)" and "Pre-Tax Gain (Loss) Reclassified from Accumulated OCI into Earnings (Effective Portion)."

PROMS

PROBLEMS

LO2 **36.[B] Use of futures contracts to hedge cotton inventory—fair value hedge**

On December 1, 2014, a cotton wholesaler purchases 7 million pounds of cotton inventory at an average cost of 75 cents per pound. To protect the inventory from a possible decline in cotton prices, the company sells cotton futures contracts for 7 million pounds at 66 cents a pound for delivery on June 1, 2015, to coincide with its expected physical sale of its cotton inventory. The company designates the hedge as a fair value hedge (i.e., the company is hedging changes in the inventory's fair value, not changes in cash flows from anticipated sales). The cotton spot price on December 1 is 74 cents per pound.

On December 31, 2014, the company's fiscal year-end, the June cotton futures price has fallen to 56 cents a pound, and the spot price has fallen to 65 cents a pound. On June 1, 2015, the company closes out its futures contracts by entering into an offsetting contract in which it agrees to buy June 2015 cotton futures contracts at 47 cents a pound, the spot rate on that date. Finally, the company sells its cotton for $0.47 per pound on June 1, 2015.

Following are futures and spot prices for the relevant dates:

Date	Spot	Futures
December 1, 2014	74¢	66¢
December 31, 2014	65¢	56¢
June 1, 2015	47¢	n/a

Prepare the journal entries to record the following:

a. Purchase of cotton

b. Sale of cotton futures contract

c. Adjusting entry at December 31

d. Sale of cotton on June 1

37.[B] **Use of futures contracts to hedge a forecasted transaction—cash flow hedge**

LO2

As of January, our company plans to purchase 200,000 lbs. of copper on May 31 at the prevailing spot rate. To hedge this forecasted transaction, we purchase May futures contracts in January for 200,000 lbs. of copper at the futures price of $1.58/lb. On May 31, we close out our futures contracts by entering into an offsetting contract in which we agree to buy 200,000 lbs. of May copper futures contracts at $1.84/lb., the spot rate on that date. We also purchase 200,000 lbs. of copper at $1.84/lb. on that date. Finally, we sell the inventory in June for $2.06/lb. Our company operates on a calendar year and issues financial statements quarterly.

Following are futures and spot prices for the relevant dates:

Date	Spot	Futures
January...................	$1.44	$1.58
March 31	$1.52	$1.67
May 31	$1.84	n/a

Prepare the journal entries to record the following:

a. Purchase of copper futures contract in January

b. Adjusting entry at March 31

c. Purchase of copper on May 31

d. Sale of copper on June 1

38. Use of variable-for-fixed swap agreement—fair value hedge

LO2

On June 30, our company borrows $25 million of 5-year 7.5% fixed-rate interest-only nonprepayable debt. We prefer variable-rate debt since our cash flows are positively correlated to the level of interest rates, and decide to enter into a fixed-for-variable interest rate swap. Under the terms of the swap, we receive interest at a fixed rate of 7.5% and pay interest at a variable rate equal to the six-month U.S. LIBOR, based on a notional amount of $25 million. Both the debt and the swap require that payments be made or received on December 31 and June 30. The six-month U.S. LIBOR rate on each reset date determines the variable portion of the interest-rate swap for the following six-month period. Our company designates the swap as a fair value hedge of the fixed-rate debt, with changes in the fair value that are due to changes in benchmark interest rates being the specific risk that is hedged.

The six-month U.S. LIBOR rates and the swap and debt fair values are assumed to be as follows for the first year of the swap and debt agreements:

Date	Six-Month U.S. LIBOR Rate	SWAP Fair Value	Debt Carrying Value
June 30 (date of borrowing).........................	6.00%	$ 0	$25,000,000
December 31	5.75%	68,750	25,068,750
June 30 (following year)	5.50%	137,500	25,137,500

Prepare the journal entries to record the following:

a. Borrowing on June 30 (year of borrowing)

b. Interest payment at December 31

c. Interest payment at June 30 (following year)

39.[B] **Use of futures contracts to hedge available-for-sale securities—fair value hedge**

LO2

On June 1, our company purchases $10 million book value of corporate bonds that we classify as available-for-sale (AFS). We intend to sell these securities on September 30 to meet planned funding needs. Since an increase in interest rates will cause the fair value of the securities to decrease, we decide to hedge against the risk of loss in the fair value of the debt securities that would result if the interest rates were to rise. As a result, we sell September Treasury-note futures contracts on June 1 in the amount of the debt securities.

We have determined that the hedging relationship between the futures contracts and the debt securities is highly effective (both at the inception of the relationship and on an ongoing basis) in achieving offsetting changes in the fair value that are due to changes in the benchmark interest rate. Accordingly, this transaction is designated as a fair value hedge.

Interest rates rise as we had predicted, and the prices of the corporate bonds (the hedged item) and the futures contracts (the hedging instrument), and the resulting gains and losses, are as follows:

Date	Securities Loss	Futures Gain	Net
August	$(100,000)	$75,000	$(25,000)
September	(50,000)	50,000	0
			$(25,000)

We sell the debt securities on September 30 at their fair value of $9,850,000.

Prepare the journal entries to record the following:

a. Purchase of the debt securities and futures contracts on June 1
b. Accrue changes in fair value of AFS debt securities and futures contract in August
c. Accrue changes in fair value of AFS debt securities and futures contract in September
d. Record sale of securities in September

LO2 40.ᴮ Use of option contracts to hedge available-for-sale securities—fair value hedge

Assume that our company purchased 100,000 shares of GE common stock at a cost of $50 per share on June 1. Since we did not plan to sell these securities in the near term, we classified the shares as "available for sale." The current market price is $65 per share, and we are concerned that the shares may be overvalued. In order to protect us from a decrease in the price of GE shares, on December 31, 2013, we purchase for a premium of $600,000 a put option, which gives us the right, but not the obligation, to sell 100,000 shares of GE at $65 per share, the current market price. The option expires on December 31, 2015 and qualifies as a fair value hedge.

The fair value of the GE shares and the option are as follows:

	12/31/2013	12/31/2014	12/31/2015
GE Price/Share	$ 65	$ 60	$ 57
Total	6,500,000	6,000,000	5,700,000
Put option:			
Time Value	600,000	350,000	0
Intrinsic value	0	500,000	800,000
Total	$ 600,000	$ 850,000	$ 800,000

Just prior to the option's expiration on December 31, 2015, we exercise the option (and deliver the GE shares to the option writer), since it is "in the money."

Prepare the journal entries to record the following:

a. Purchase of the GE securities on June 1
b. The change in the fair value of the shares as of December 31, 2013, and the purchase of the option (note: since the hedge is not purchased until December, the accrual of the increase in the share price must be to AOCI since the shares are classified as available-for-sale).
c. The change in the fair value of the GE shares and the put option as of December 31, 2014 (note: this is now accounted for as a derivative)
d. Record sale of securities on December 31, 2015

41. Use of a plain-vanilla interest-rate swap to hedge variable-rate debt—cash flow hedge   LO2

On June 30, our company borrows $10,000,000 of three-year, variable-rate interest-only, debt with interest payments indexed to the six-month U.S. LIBOR. It concurrently enters into a three-year interest-rate swap to convert the debt's variable rate to a fixed rate. Under the swap contract, we pay interest at a fixed rate of 7.5% and receive interest at a variable rate indexed to the six-month U.S. LIBOR, based on a notional amount of $10,000,000. Both the debt and the swap require that payments be made or received semiannually, on December 31 and June 30. The six-month U.S. LIBOR rate on each reset date of December 31 and June 30, determines the variable interest rate on the debt and the swap for the following six-month period. We designate the swap as a cash-flow hedge, which hedges the exposure to variability in the cash flows of the variable-rate debt.

The six-month U.S. LIBOR rates and the swap's fair values are assumed to be as follows for the first six months of the swap agreement:

Date	Six Month U.S. LIBOR Rate	Swap Fair Value
June 30. . . .	6.0%	$ 0
September 30. . . .	6.5%	150,000
December 31	7.0%	300,000

Our interest payments on the variable-rate debt and net payments (receipts) on the interest-rate swap are as follows for the first semiannual period:

	December 31
Variable-rate debt. . . .	$300,000
Interest-rate swap payment	75,000
	$375,000

Prepare the journal entries to record the following:

a. Borrowing on June 30

b. Accrual of interest at September 30

c. Interest payment at December 31

42.ᴮ Use of options to hedge an anticipated purchase of inventory   LO2

Our company uses gold as an input in the production process. Since the price of gold has been rising and our market prices cannot be increased in the short run, we believe that we are subject to the risk of gold price increases in the coming months. Therefore, we decide to purchase call options on gold futures (call options give us the option to purchase gold at the specified strike price). If gold prices increase, the profit on the purchased call options will approximately offset the higher price that we must pay for the gold to be used in our manufacturing process. And, if gold prices decline, our cost is the premium we paid for the call options (we can then buy gold at the lower price, however).

Since we will need the gold in May, 90 days from today (February), and our production plans call for 400 troy oz., we decide to purchase 4 option contracts (each option contract relates to 100 troy ounces of gold). The current market (spot) price for gold is $600/oz., and four June at-the-money options (i.e., for $600/oz.) calls are priced at a premium of $5 an ounce, for a total premium of $2,000 (4 × $5/oz. × 100 oz.).

Relevant data relating to the option and the underlying asset (gold) are as follows:

Option	Time Value	Intrinsic Value	Total Value
February. . . .	$2,000 (cost)	-0-	$ 2,000
March 31	$1,500 (assumed)	$ 6,000 ([615 − 600] × 400)	$ 7,500
May. . . .		$10,000 ([625 − 600] × 400)	$10,000

Gold	Spot Price
February	$600
March 31	$615
May	$625

Our projected purchase of gold is considered *forecasted* transaction, and the derivative is considered to be a cash-flow hedge.

Prepare the journal entries to record the following:

a. Purchase of the call options in February

b. Adjusting entries on March 31

c. Settlement of the options and purchase of gold in May

d. Reclassification of Other Comprehensive Income when the products using the gold are sold in June

LO2 **43. Use of futures contracts to hedge a receivable denominated in a foreign currency**

In May, our company sells $675,000 of inventory to a customer in France. The customer demands that the invoice be stated in Euros (€). The exchange rate on the date of sale is $1.35:€1. Accordingly, the invoice is written for €500,000, and payment is due in 90 days. Our company feels that the $US has been over-sold and is likely to rebound during the next 90 days, thus lowering the $US equivalent of the receivable. The current futures price for 90-day delivery of $1.30 reflects our view. Since we feel that the $US is likely to strengthen even more, we purchase a forward contract to sell Euros at $1.30 after 90 days. When the receivable is collected in 90 days, the exchange rate at that date is $1.27: €1.

Assume the following data relating to the spot and forward rates for the $US vis-à-vis the Euro:

	Spot Rate	Forward Rate
May	$1.35:€1	$1.30:€1
June 30	$1.30:€1	$1.28:€1
July	$1.27:€1	n/a

Prepare the journal entries to record the following:

a. Account receivable and sale (ignore cost of goods sold)

b. Adjusting entries on June 30

c. Collection of the account receivable in July

LO2 **44. Use of forward exchange contracts to hedge a firm commitment to pay foreign currency**

On September 30, our company has executed a purchase order for new equipment to be purchased from a supplier in Germany for a purchase price of €5 million. The terms of the purchase order meet the criteria of an unrecognized firm commitment. The equipment is deliverable on March 31 of next year. In order to hedge the commitment to pay €5 million, we enter into a forward exchange contract on September 30 to receive €5 million on March 31 at an exchange rate of $0.72:€1.

Assume the following exchange rates:

Date	Spot Rates	March 31 (next year)
September 30	$0.65:€1	$0.72:€1
December 31	$0.66:€1	$0.71:€1
March 31 (next year)	$0.69:€1	n/a

Prepare the journal entries to record the following:

a. Execution of the purchase order and forward contract

b. Adjusting entries at December 31

c. Receipt of equipment and payment to equipment supplier on March 31

LO2 **45.[B] Use of a forward-exchange contract to hedge the foreign-currency fair value risk of an available-for-sale security**

On September 30, our company purchases a foreign-currency-denominated debt security for €100,000. The security is classified as available-for-sale (AFS). We decide to hedge the risk of the currency fluctuations of this available-for-sale security over the next three months and enter into a forward contract to sell €100,000 on December 31, at an exchange contract rate of €1 = $1.49.

Assume the following exchange rates:

	Spot Exchange Rate	Forward Exchange Rate to December 31	Fair Value of AFS Security
September 30..............	€1 = U.S. $1.50	€1 = U.S. $1.49	€100,000
December 31	€1 = U.S. $1.30	€1 = U.S. $1.30	€110,000

This transaction is designated as a foreign currency fair value hedge. Changes in the fair value of the AFS securities that are attributable to the hedged foreign currency risk are recorded in earnings, along with the change in the fair value of the hedging instrument (i.e., the forward-exchange contract in this example). Changes in the fair value of the AFS securities that are due to unhedged risks (i.e., the $US equivalent of changes in market value) will continue to be recorded in Other Comprehensive Income as required by FAS 115.

Prepare journal entries to record the following:

a.   Purchase of the security on September 30

b.   Adjusting entries at December 31

46.ᴮ Use of options to hedge an anticipated purchase of inventory

LO2

We are a manufacturer that uses gold in our products and we want to mitigate the risk of future price increases as we will not be able to readily increase the selling price of our products. In order to mitigate this risk, we purchase New York COMEX call options on gold futures. If gold prices increase, the profit on the purchased call options will approximately offset the higher price that we will pay for the gold to be used in our manufacturing process. And, if gold prices decline, we will lose the premium we paid for the call options, but can then buy gold at the lower price.

In January, we purchase two at-the-money spot April $291/oz. call options for a premium of $7.50 an ounce each since we expect to acquire at least 200 ounces of gold in April (each call option is for a notional amount of 100 ounces of gold). In April, the spot price of gold rises to $316 an ounce, and the April call value is at $25 an ounce ($316 spot price, less $291 strike price). We settle our two April calls and buy 200 ounces of gold from our suppliers. This transaction is summarized as follows:

	Hedging Instrument and Commodity Price		
Date	Gold Spot Price	Option Strike price	Option Premium
January..............	$291	$291	$7.50
April	$316		

	Option Fair Value Analysis		
Date	Time Value	Intrinsic Value	Total Fair Value Prior to Exercise
January..............	$1,500*	$ 0**	$1,500
April	$ 0	$5,000***	$5,000

* 2 April calls = 200 × $7.50 = $1,500
** Intrinsic value is calculated as the difference between the spot price and the strike price. For April the intrinsic value is ($291 spot − $291 strike) × 200 = $0
*** ($316 − $291) × 200 = $5,000

Prepare the journal entries to record the following:

1.   Purchase of call options in January

2.   Adjusting entry to record the change in the time value of the purchased call options in April

3.   Adjusting entry to record the change in the intrinsic value of the purchased call options in April

4.   Journal entry to record the cash settlement of the purchased call options

5.   Journal entry to record the purchase of 200 oz. of gold at the spot price of $316/oz.

6. How will we account for the gains that we have deferred in accumulated other comprehensive income?

7. Provide an economic analysis of this transaction.

LO2 **47. Use of foreign-currency options to hedge forecasted foreign sales**

Our U.S. company anticipates sales to customers in New Zealand in six months on March 31 that will be denominated in the New Zealand Dollar (NZD) and are expected to amount to NZD 10,000,000 (these anticipated sales are not firm commitments at this date). We are concerned that the $US may strengthen vis-à-vis the NZD during the interim and, to hedge this exposure, we purchase a foreign currency put option with the following terms:

Contract amount	NZD 10,000,000
Trade date	September 30
Expiration date	March 31 (next year)
Strike price	NZD 2: $1
Spot rate on trade date	NZD 2: $1
Option premium	$20,000

The option is designated as a hedge of the company's forecasted sales, and we expect that at the hedge's inception and through the date of the forecasted sales, the hedge will be perfectly effective, since the critical terms of the option contract match those of the anticipated sales.

The spot and time value of the option over the next six months are as follows:

Date	Spot Rate (NZD:$US)	Time Value
September 30 (this year)	NZD 2.00 : $1	$20,000 (cost)
December 31 (this year)	NZD 2.10 : $1	$ 9,000 (assumed dealer quote)
March 31 (next year).	NZD 2.30 : $1	$ 0

a. Should we account for this transaction as a fair value hedge or a cash flow hedge? Why?

b. Briefly describe the accounting for this transaction.

c. Compute the option's intrinsic value and total value on September 30, December 31 and March 31.

d. Prepare journal entries for the following:

1. Purchase of the purchased option premium of $20,000 on March 31

2. The change in the time value and intrinsic value of the option on December 31

3. The change in the time value and intrinsic value of the option on March 31

4. Cash sales to foreign customer in the amount of NZD 10,000,000 at the spot rate of NZD 2.30:$1

5. Net cash settlement of the option at its maturity on March 31

6. Adjusting entry to transfer any deferred gains (losses) from AOCI into current earnings as of March 31

e. Summarize the economics of this transaction.

LO2 **48. Use of a forward contract to hedge a firm commitment (different dates for inventory purchase and forward contract settlement)**

In January 15, our company enters into an agreement to buy product from one of our Canadian suppliers that will be delivered at the end of March. The contract obligates us to pay CAD5,000,000 (Canadian dollars) on April 30. The contract meets the requirements of a firm commitment and our functional currency is the US dollar. In February, we believed that the $US would weaken vis-à-vis the CAD, thus increasing the $US value of the payable denominated in Canadian dollars (CAD), and we decided to hedge the foreign currency exposure by purchasing a forward contract to exchange $3,500,000 for CAD5,000,000 on April 30, 20X1 (forward rate of $0.70:CAD1). This forward contract was designated as a hedge of the firm commitment and effectiveness will be assessed based on the forward rates.

The relevant exchange rates over the period of this contract are as follows:

Date	Spot Rate ($US:CAD)	Forward Rate ($US:CAD)
January 15	$0.6897	
February 1	$0.7143	$0.7000
February 28	$0.7143	$0.7067
March 31	$0.7092	$0.7143
April 30	$0.7353	$0.7353

a. Compute the value of the forward contract as of the end of February, March and April.

b. Prepare appropriate journal entries as of the end of February, March and April.

c. Briefly describe the economics of this transaction.

TOPIC REVIEW

Solution

a.

November 2, 2014	Inventories	72,000	
	Accounts payable		72,000
	(6,000 units × €10/unit × $1.20:€1)		
December 31, 2014	Foreign currency transaction loss*	3,000	
	Accounts payable		3,000
	*(*6,000 units × €10/unit × $1.25:€1 - $72,000)*		
January 31, 2015	Accounts payable.	75,000	
	Foreign currency transaction loss	3,000	
	Cash*		78,000
	*(*6,000 units × €10/unit × $1.30:€1)*		

b.

November 2, 2014	Accounts receivable.	72,000	
	Sales		72,000
	(6,000 units × €10/unit × $1.20:€1)		
December 31, 2014	Accounts receivable.	3,000	
	Foreign currency transaction gain*		3,000
	*(*6,000 units × €10/unit × $1.25:€1 – $72,000)*		
January 31, 2015	Cash*	78,000	
	Foreign currency transaction gain.		3,000
	Accounts receivable*		75,000
	*(*6,000 units × €10/unit × $1.30:€1)*		

COMPREHENSIVE REVIEW SOLUTION

Date	Journal Entries		
September 30, 2014	No entry required		
December 31, 2014	Foreign exchange loss	2,000	
	Foreign currency forward contract (FV)		2,000
	(to recognize the fair value of the forward exchange contract = €200,000 × [$1.42 − $1.41]/€1)		
	Firm commitment	2,000	
	Foreign exchange gains		2,000
	(to recognize the fair value of the change in exchange rates underlying the firm commitment)		
March 31, 2015	Equipment	280,000	
	Firm commitment		2,000
	Accounts payable		278,000
	(to record the receipt of the equipment and the related payable at the March 31 spot rate = €200,000 × $1.39/€1 = $278,000)		
June 30, 2015	Foreign exchange loss	2,000	
	Foreign currency forward contract (FV)		2,000
	(to recognize the change in fair value of the forward exchange contract)		
	Foreign exchange loss	2,000	
	Accounts payable		2,000
	(to recognize the transaction loss on the foreign currency accounts payable)		
	Accounts payable.	280,000	
	Foreign currency forward contract (FV)	4,000	
	Cash		284,000
	(to record the settlement of the forward contract receivable and accounts payable = €200,000 × $1.42/€1)		

Consolidation of Foreign Subsidiaries

8

The **Coca-Cola Company** (Coca-Cola, Coke) is the world's largest beverage company. Finished beverage products bearing its trademarks are now sold in more than 200 countries.

Coke's consolidated financial statements include the Coca-Cola parent company and nearly 200 subsidiaries, most of which are incorporated outside of the United States. Many of these non-U.S. subsidiaries maintain their accounting records in currencies other than the $US. U.S. generally accepted accounting principles (GAAP) require companies to convert all of the accounts of subsidiaries' foreign-currency-denominated financial statements into the reporting currency (for Coke, it is the $US) before the consolidation process begins. The subsidiaries' income statements and balance sheets, now expressed in a single currency (i.e., the reporting currency), are then consolidated with the income statement and balance sheet of the parent company (nearly identical to the process we described in previous chapters).

COCA-COLA

For Coke, as the value of the $US falls relative to other world currencies, income statement accounts—that are initially recorded by foreign subsidiaries in local currencies—increase in $US value. Thus, Coke's sales expressed in $US appear higher simply because of relative shifts in the value of the $US vis-à-vis other currencies. The same effect occurs for expenses and profits (or losses).

In its 2014 10-K filing, Coke discloses that:

> *The unfavorable impact of foreign currency fluctuations decreased our consolidated net operating revenues by 2 percent. The unfavorable impact of changes in foreign currency exchange rates was primarily due to a stronger U.S. dollar compared to certain other foreign currencies, including the South African rand, Mexican peso, Brazilian real, Australian dollar and Japanese yen, which had an unfavorable impact on our Eurasia and Africa, Latin America, Asia Pacific and Bottling Investments operating segments.*

Assets and liabilities also appear greater as a result of the weakening $US and, assuming that the subsidiaries' assets exceed their liabilities, their Stockholders' Equity accounts grow as well. Depending on the "functional currency" of Coke's subsidiaries, the growth of the $US value of the subsidiaries' Stockholders' Equity is reflected either as (1) an increase in the equity account, Accumulated Other Comprehensive Income [i.e., via a process called "translation"], or (2) an increase in Retained Earnings via a gain recognized in net income [i.e., via a process called "remeasurement"].

We discuss the translation and remeasurement of the financial statements of foreign subsidiaries and their ultimate consolidation in this chapter.

Source: Coca-Cola, Inc., 2014 10-K.

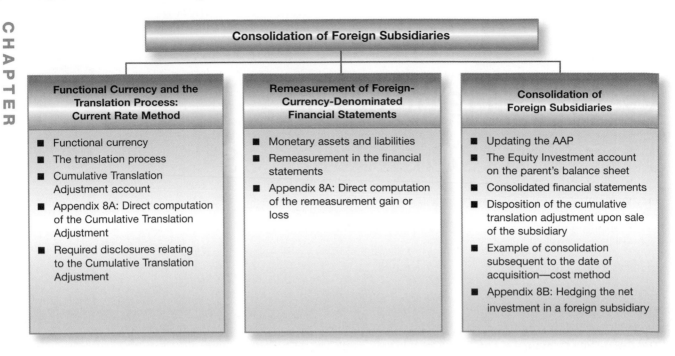

Many U.S.-based companies conduct operations in foreign countries, buying and selling goods and services with suppliers and customers located throughout the world. U.S. companies may transact business in foreign currencies and their subsidiaries may be headquartered, and conduct business in multiple currencies as well. Further, these subsidiary companies typically maintain their accounting records in currencies other than the $US *and produce financial statements that are denominated in those foreign currencies.* Ultimately, however, the U.S. parent company must produce consolidated financial statements that are expressed in $US. So, all of these foreign-currency-denominated transactions and financial statements must first be converted into $US before the consolidation process can begin.

The process by which this conversion is accomplished is codified in ASC 830, *Foreign Currency Matters,* which articulates the following two distinct processes to express all of a reporting entity's transactions and financial statements in a single reporting currency:

- **Foreign currency measurement**—This is the process by which a company expresses transactions, whose terms are denominated in a foreign currency, in its functional currency (the primary currency in which the company conducts its business as we discuss further below). Changes in functional currency amounts that result from fluctuations in exchange rates are called transaction gains or losses and transaction gains and losses are included in net income (these are the transaction gains and losses that companies may seek to hedge by the use of derivative financial instruments which we discuss in Chapter 7).

- **Foreign currency translation**—This is the process of expressing a subsidiary's foreign-currency-denominated financial statements in $US so that those financial statements can be consolidated with those of the parent company. Changes in reporting currency amounts that result from the translation process are called translation adjustments. Translation adjustments are included in the cumulative translation adjustment (CTA) account, which is a component of other comprehensive income (we describe the translation process in depth below).

In Chapter 7, we discuss foreign currency measurement of transactions, the impact of exchange rate fluctuations on profitability and the ways in which companies can mitigate earnings volatility. In this chapter, we continue to focus on foreign currency issues, but now direct our attention to the consolidation of subsidiaries for which financial statement information is denominated in foreign currencies.

Let's begin with a simple example of a parent company that maintains its accounting records in $US and its subsidiary that maintains its accounting records in Euros (€). If we attempt to consolidate the subsidiary's financial statements (without conversion into $US) with the parent's, we will be attempting to add units of $US to units of €. Because the units of measurement for the financial statements of our parent and subsidiary are not the same (i.e., mixing $ and €), we will arrive at summed quantities that are nonsensical; that is, we simply cannot add one unit of $US and one unit of € and arrive at two units of anything meaningful. To remedy this, we must include an intermediate step that converts the financial statements of our Euro-denominated subsidiary into $US before we include the subsidiary's information in our consolidation spreadsheet. That is, consolidations (and related consolidation spreadsheets) can only be completed if all of the companies' financial information is expressed in the same monetary unit. The conversion of subsidiaries' foreign-currency-denominated financial statements into the parent's reporting currency and the subsequent consolidation of the foreign subsidiary are the subjects of this chapter.

We begin with a discussion of the concept of a functional currency. We, then, discuss the mechanics by which its foreign-currency-denominated financial statements are converted into the reporting currency.

FUNCTIONAL CURRENCY

Each foreign subsidiary must determine its own *functional currency*.[1] This is the currency of the primary economic environment in which the subsidiary operates. Normally, that is the currency of the environment in which a subsidiary primarily generates and expends cash (FASB ASC 830-10-20 Glossary).

LO1 Describe the functional currency and the translation process.

If a subsidiary conducts its operations within a particular country, its functional currency will likely be the currency of that country. However, the determination of the functional currency of a subsidiary becomes more complex as it transacts its business in multiple currencies and the determination of the functional currency may require significant judgment. It is also not uncommon for the functional currency of a subsidiary to change over time as the nature and scope of its business changes.

ASC 830 identifies several general factors that may potentially influence the determination of the functional currency (we provide a full listing of the relevant indicators in the Practice Insight box on page 515):

- In which currencies does the subsidiary transact sales and ultimately generate its cash?

- In which currencies does the subsidiary purchase labor, materials, and other goods and services and ultimately expend cash?

- In which currencies does the subsidiary obtain its financing?

FASB ASC 830 does not provide specific guidance on the manner in which these factors should be considered or combined into an overall judgment. Usually, if the greatest proportion of sales and expenses is conducted in one currency, that currency would be selected as the functional currency.

When the functional currency for a foreign entity is determined, that functional currency should be used consistently unless significant changes in economic facts and circumstances indicate clearly that the functional currency has changed.[2]

Exhibit 8.1 illustrates the steps in the consolidation process for foreign subsidiaries. Before the subsidiary can be consolidated, its functional currency-denominated financial statements must be *translated* into the parent's reporting currency (the $US for U.S companies). And, if the financial statements of the subsidiary are initially expressed in a currency *other* than its functional currency, an additional step is required to first *remeasure* those financial statements into the functional currency. We discuss the remeasurement process later in the chapter and the circumstances for which it is required.

---

[1] Don't take our use of the word, "subsidiary," too literally. Indeed, a company (or subsidiary) might have more than one operating unit, such as multiple divisions or branches that conduct business in different countries. In that case, each operating unit may be considered a separate entity, each with its own functional currency (FASB ASC 830-10-45-6). In 2014, for example, Coca-Cola used 70 functional currencies in addition to the $US (Coca-Cola 2014 10-K).

[2] If the functional currency is changed, previously issued financial statements should not be restated into the new functional currency (FASB ASC 830-10-45-7).

EXHIBIT 8.1	Converting Foreign-Currency-Denominated Financial Statement Information

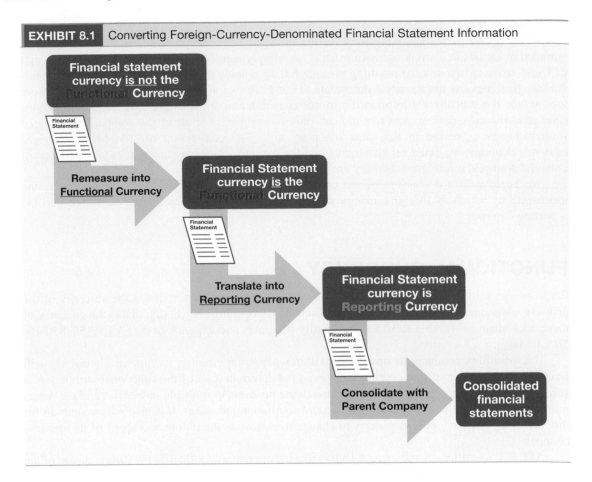

THE TRANSLATION PROCESS

The purpose of translation is to express the subsidiary's financial statements, expressed in its functional currency, in $US so that they can be consolidated with those of the parent company. This involves multiplying the foreign currency-denominated amount by a relevant exchange rate in order to yield the $US equivalent. For example, if the subsidiary's sales are express as €1,000 and the relevant exchange rate is $1.40:€1, the $US equivalent is equal to €1,000 × ($1.40/€1) = $1,400. After translation, the subsidiary's income statement would, therefore, report sales of $1,400.

The financial statements of the subsidiary should be translated using the following exchange rates (ASC 830-30-45-3):

■ The period-end exchange (spot) rate for assets and liabilities

■ The weighted average exchange rate for income statement accounts[3]

■ Historical exchange rates for equity accounts and dividends (except for Retained Earnings which is updated each period using the translated $US amounts for net income and dividends).

We provide a summary of the relevant exchange rates to use for the translation process in Exhibit 8.2 (for comparison, we also provide the relevant exchange rates for the remeasurement process that we describe later in the chapter).

---

[3] The translation approach technically requires the use of current exchange rates on the dates that each item of revenue and expense is recognized. As you can imagine, requiring companies to monitor exchange rates on the dates of all revenues, expenses, gains and losses can create an extremely burdensome record-keeping requirement for businesses. FASB ASC 830-10-55-10 acknowledges this difficulty and allows companies to "use averages and other methods of approximation" in the translation of income statement accounts. It states that "[a]verage rates used shall be appropriately weighted by the volume of functional currency transactions occurring during the accounting period. For example, to translate revenue and expense accounts for an annual period, individual revenue and expense accounts for each quarter or month may be translated at that quarter's or that month's average rate. The translated amounts for each quarter or month should then be combined for the annual totals."

PRACTICE INSIGHT

Determination of the functional currency   FASB ASC 830-10-55-5 provides the following guidance in the determination of the functional currency:

The following salient economic factors, and possibly others, should be considered both individually and collectively when determining the functional currency:

a. **Cash flow indicators**

   1. *Foreign currency.* Cash flows related to the foreign entity's individual assets and liabilities are primarily in the foreign currency and do not directly affect the parent entity's cash flows.

   2. *Parent's currency.* Cash flows related to the foreign entity's individual assets and liabilities directly affect the parent's cash flows currently and are readily available for remittance to the parent entity.

b. **Sales price indicators**

   1. *Foreign currency.* Sales prices for the foreign entity's products are not primarily responsive on a short-term basis to changes in exchange rates but are determined more by local competition or local government regulation.

   2. *Parent's currency.* Sales prices for the foreign entity's products are primarily responsive on a short-term basis to changes in exchange rates; for example, sales prices are determined more by worldwide competition or by international prices.

c. **Sales market indicators**

   1. *Foreign currency.* There is an active local sales market for the foreign entity's products, although there also might be significant amounts of exports.

   2. *Parent's currency.* The sales market is mostly in the parent's country or sales contracts are denominated in the parent's currency.

d. **Expense indicators**

   1. *Foreign currency.* Labor, materials, and other costs for the foreign entity's products or services are primarily local costs, even though there also might be imports from other countries.

   2. *Parent's currency.* Labor, materials, and other costs for the foreign entity's products or services continually are primarily costs for components obtained from the country in which the parent entity is located.

e. **Financing indicators**

   1. *Foreign currency.* Financing is primarily denominated in foreign currency, and funds generated by the foreign entity's operations are sufficient to service existing and normally expected debt obligations.

   2. *Parent's currency.* Financing is primarily from the parent or other dollar-denominated obligations, or funds generated by the foreign entity's operations are not sufficient to service existing and normally expected debt obligations without the infusion of additional funds from the parent entity. Infusion of additional funds from the parent entity for expansion is not a factor, provided funds generated by the foreign entity's expanded operations are expected to be sufficient to service that additional financing.

f. **Intra-entity transactions and arrangements indicators**

   1. *Foreign currency.* There is a low volume of intra-entity transactions and there is not an extensive interrelationship between the operations of the foreign entity and the parent entity. However, the foreign entity's operations may rely on the parent's or affiliates' competitive advantages, such as patents and trademarks.

   2. *Parent's currency.* There is a high volume of intra-entity transactions and there is an extensive interrelationship between the operations of the foreign entity and the parent entity. Additionally, the parent's currency generally would be the functional currency if the foreign entity is a device or shell corporation for holding investments, obligations, intangible assets, and so forth, that could readily be carried on the parent's or an affiliate's books.

EXHIBIT 8.2	Appropriate Exchange Rates to Use for Translation and Remeasurement	
Appropriate rates for:	**Translation**	**Remeasurement**
Balance Sheet Accounts:		
Cash, accounts receivable and other *monetary* assets	*Current*	*Current*
Prepaid expenses, inventory and other *nonmonetary* current assets	*Current*	*Historical*
Property, plant and equipment, intangible assets and other *nonmonetary* noncurrent assets	*Current*	*Historical*
Accounts payable, notes payable, bonds, deferred taxes and other *monetary* liabilities	*Current*	*Current*
Deferred revenues and other *nonmonetary* liabilities	*Current*	*Current*
Common stock and additional paid-in capital	*Historical*	*Historical*
Retained earnings (Note: regardless of method, you should think of RE as an accumulation of US-dollar-converted amounts. Components of NI conversion described below. Dividends converted at the declare-date rate)	(computed based on BOY balance + translated net income − translated dividends)	(computed based on BOY balance + remeasured net income − remeasured dividends)
Cumulative translation adjustment (*annual change* is part of other comprehensive income and the *accumulation* is a component of the "accumulated other comprehensive income" owners' equity account) . . .	(computed based on BOY carry-forward balance ± current period translation gain or loss **PLUG** that falls out of the trial balance)	(not applicable)
Income Statement Accounts:		
Revenues	*Weighted-average*	*Weighted-average*
Operating expenses	*Weighted-average*	*Weighted-average*
Depreciation expense	*Weighted-average*	*Historical*
Cost of goods sold	*Weighted-average*[†]	***Beg Inv at historical rates + Purchases at weighted-average rate − End Inv at purchase dates***
Remeasurement Gain (or Loss) each year's amount is included in determining net income	(not applicable)	(**PLUG** to balance the trial balance)

Current Rates: Exchange rate in effect as of the end of the period covered by the financial statements

Historical Rates: Exchange rates in effect when asset, liability or equity was initially acquired, incurred or recognized

Weighted Average Rates: Exchange rates averaged during the period covered by the financial statements, technically weighted by the volume of functional currency transactions

[†] Technically, ASC 830-10 requires remeasurement of inventories using the historical exchange rates (they are nonmonetary assets). Given the computation of inventory (BI + Purchases − EI = CGS), this means BI and EI would need to be calculated using the historical rates. However, ASC 830-10-55-10 allows for the following practicability exception: "Literal application of the standards in this Subtopic might require a degree of detail in record keeping and computations that could be burdensome as well as unnecessary to produce reasonable approximations of the results. Accordingly, it is acceptable to use averages or other methods of approximation. For example, because translation at the exchange rates at the dates the numerous revenues, expenses, gains, and losses are recognized is generally impractical, an appropriately weighted average exchange rate for the period may be used to translate those elements. Likewise, the use of other time-and-effort-saving methods to approximate the results of detailed calculations is permitted." Thus, we use weighted average rates for cost of sales.

In the translation process, all asset and liability accounts are translated at the current rate. Common Stock and Additional Paid-In Capital accounts are translated at the "historical" rate in effect on the date of acquisition of the subsidiary or the date at which stock is sold by the subsidiary subsequent to the acquisition. Income statement accounts are translated at the average exchange rate for the period. The ending balance in Retained Earnings is determined by starting with the beginning balance (the ending balance from the previous period stated in the reporting currency), adding translated net income and deducting translated dividends.

To illustrate the conversion of net asset and income statement accounts, assume that a parent company determines that the Euro (€) is the functional currency for its subsidiary for the year ended December 31, 2015. The exchange rate at December 31, 2015, is $1.48:€1 and the weighted-average exchange rate for the year ended December 31, 2015, is $1.45:€1. The translation process involves multiplying each of the subsidiary's Euro-demoninated asset and liability accounts by a factor of 1.48 and each of its Euro-demoninated income statement accounts by a factor of 1.45 to convert them into $US.[4]

---

[4] Our discussion has expressed exchange rates in terms of the $US relative to one unit of the foreign currency. The translation process can, then, be affected by multiplying the amount in the foreign currency by the exchange rate (i.e., €1000 × $1.48/€ = $1,480). Sometimes, exchange ratios are expressed in terms of the value of $1. For example, an exchange rate of $1.48:€1 can also be expressed as $1:€0.675. Should the exchange rate be expressed as $1:€0.675, you can either (1) first divide both sides by 0.675 to convert the ratio to $1.48:€1 before proceeding with the translation, or (2) simply use the $1:€0.675 rate and divide it into the Euro-denominated account balances.

After multiplying the various asset, liability, income statement, and equity accounts by a combination of current, weighted-average and historical rates as indicated in Exhibit 8.2, we virtually guarantee that the pre-consolidation trial balance will no longer have debits equal to credits (i.e., it won't balance). The debit or credit necessary to balance the translated trial balance is the amount of **Cumulative Translation Adjustment** (this amount can be positive or negative). The Cumulative Translation Adjustment is a component of Accumulated Other Comprehensive Income (AOCI), a stockholders' equity account.

In the first period of foreign currency translation, the entire amount of the Cumulative Translation Adjustment is included as current-period Other Comprehensive Income (OCI). In subsequent periods, the beginning amount of the Cumulative Translation Adjustment is included in the trial balance, with the incremental debit or credit necessary to balance the period-end trial balance included as current-period OCI. Together, the beginning Cumulative Translation Adjustment and the current-period Cumulative Translation Adjustment sum to the ending Cumulative Translation Adjustment which is presented in the balance sheet as a component of Accumulated Other Comprehensive Income (AOCI). The following example illustrates these translation procedures.

Translation Example—Year of Acquisition

To illustrate the translation of foreign-currency-denominated subsidiary financial statements, assume that a U.S.-based parent company purchases all of the outstanding common stock of subsidiary on January 1, 2015, when the exchange rate is $1.25:€1. The purchase price includes an Acquisition Accounting Premium (AAP) of €110,000, with a $US equivalent of $137,500 (€110,000 × $1.25/€). The AAP is related to undervalued PPE, which the parent is depreciating over an 11-year useful life.

We assume the following relevant exchange rates in the first year subsequent to the acquisition:

January 1, 2015 exchange rate	$1.25:€1
December 31, 2015 exchange rate	$1.39:€1
Weighted-average exchange rate for the year, 2015	$1.33:€1
Exchange rate when dividends are declared by subsidiary	$1.37:€1

At January 1, 2015, the $US value of the subsidiary's retained earnings is $803,250 (the BOY balance). For the year ending December 31, 2015, the subsidiary reports its financial statements in Euros. Exhibit 8.3 provides the subsidiary's Euros-based financial statements for the year ended December 31, 2015 (i.e., before conversion to $US).

EXHIBIT 8.3	Foreign Subsidiary's Pre-$US-Conversion Financial Statements for Year Ended December 31, 2015

Year Ending December 31, 2015	Subsidiary (in €)		Subsidiary (in €)
Income statement:		**Balance sheet:**	
Sales.	€1,250,000	Assets	
Cost of goods sold.	(750,000)	Cash.	€ 159,200
Gross profit.	500,000	Accounts receivable.	290,000
Operating expenses	(325,000)	Inventory.	372,500
Net income.	€ 175,000	Property, plant and equipment (PPE), net	896,800
		Total assets.	€1,718,500
Statement of retained earnings:			
BOY retained earnings	€ 630,000	Liabilities and stockholders' equity	
Net income.	175,000	Current liabilities.	€ 212,000
Dividends	(17,500)	Long-term liabilities	494,000
EOY retained earnings	€ 787,500	Common stock.	100,000
		APIC.	125,000
		Retained earnings	787,500
		Total liabilities and equity	€1,718,500

Using our assumptions regarding exchange rates and the financial statement information from Exhibit 8.3, the translation of the subsidiary's financial statements into $US is provided in the trial-balance-format conversion schedule in Exhibit 8.4.

EXHIBIT 8.4	Trial Balance Format for Translation of Foreign Subsidiary's Financial Statements (Year 2015)

	Subsidiary (in €)	Translation Rate	Subsidiary (in $)
Debits			
Cash.	€ 159,200	1.39	$ 221,288
Accounts receivable.	290,000	1.39	403,100
Inventory.	372,500	1.39	517,775
Property, plant and equipment (PPE), net	896,800	1.39	1,246,552
Cost of goods sold.	750,000	1.33	997,500
Operating expenses.	325,000	1.33	432,250
Dividends	17,500	1.37	23,975
Total debits.	€2,811,000		$3,842,440
Credits			
Current liabilities.	€ 212,000	1.39	$ 294,680
Long-term liabilities	494,000	1.39	686,660
Common stock.	100,000	1.25	125,000
APIC.	125,000	1.25	156,250
Retained earnings at BOY	630,000	a	803,250
Sales.	1,250,000	1.33	1,662,500
BOY cumulative translation adjustment.		a	0
Change in cumulative translation adjustment		b	114,100
Total credits	€2,811,000		$3,842,440

Notes:

a Represents the $US ending balance from the previous year. In this example, the January 1, 2015, Retained Earnings balance was given to you and there was no beginning Cumulative Translation Adjustment.

b Amount necessary to balance the $US-converted trial balance.

The translation of the subsidiary's trial balance into $US for the year ended December 31, 2015, involves the following steps:

1. **Translation using exchange rates**
   - The income statement is translated using the weighted-average exchange rate of $1.33:€1 for the year ended December 31, 2015.[5]
   - All net asset accounts (i.e., all balance sheet accounts other than Stockholders' Equity) are translated at the exchange rate in effect at December 31, 2015 ($1.39:€1).
   - Dividends are translated at the exchange rate in effect on the date of declaration ($1.37:€1).[6]

2. **$US beginning balances rolled forward from prior year $US ending balances**
   - The January 1, 2015, Retained Earnings balance is given to you in this example. For 2016, the beginning of year (BOY) Retained Earnings balance in $US will be $1,012,025, the December 31, 2015, end of year (EOY) Retained Earnings balance in $US (see Exhibit 8.5 for computation of the $1,012,025 ending balance).
   - The BOY Cumulative Translation Adjustment is rolled forward from the end of the prior year. Given that 2015 is the first year after acquisition, the balance of the BOY Cumulative Translation Adjustment at January 1, 2015, is zero.

[5] In practice, a quarterly average would likely be used to prepare the financial statements for each quarter. The annual amounts would be the sum of the four translated quarters.

[6] As mentioned previously, any change in the exchange rates between the date of dividend declaration and the date of dividend payment is recognized as foreign currency gain or loss in the income statement.

3. **Converted trial balance must balance**
   - ■ The current year change in the Cumulative Translation Adjustment is the amount needed to make debits equal credits in the trial balance. For the year ended 2015, current year change in the cumulative Translation Adjustment is $114,100. The EOY Cumulative Translation Adjustment is the net of the BOY balance at January 1, 2015 (i.e., zero) and the current year change in the cumulative Translation Adjustment (i.e., credit of $114,100). Thus, the EOY Cumulative Translation Adjustment at December 31, 2015, is an accumulated gain equal to $114,100.

Exhibit 8.5 provides the translated foreign subsidiary financial statements derived from the above conversion performed in Exhibit 8.4.

EXHIBIT 8.5	Translated Foreign Subsidiary's Financial Statements in $US (2015)		
	Subsidiary		**Subsidiary**
Income statement:		**Balance sheet:**	
Sales.	$1,662,500	Assets	
Cost of goods sold.	(997,500)	Cash.	$ 221,288
Gross profit.	665,000	Accounts receivable.	403,100
Operating expenses.	(432,250)	Inventory.	517,775
Net income.	$ 232,750	Property, plant and equipment (PPE), net	1,246,552
		Total assets.	$2,388,715
Statement of comprehensive income:			
Net Income	$ 232,750	Liabilities and stockholders' equity	
OCI: Current year translation adjustment gain (loss)	114,100	Current liabilities.	$ 294,680
Comprehensive income	$ 346,850	Long-term liabilities	686,660
		Common stock.	125,000
Statement of retained earnings:		APIC.	156,250
BOY retained earnings.	$ 803,250	Retained earnings	1,012,025
Net income.	232,750	Cumulative translation adjustment.	114,100
Dividends	(23,975)	Total liabilities and equity	$2,388,715
Ending retained earnings	$1,012,025		

The Cumulative Translation Adjustment is reported in Accumulated Other Comprehensive Income (AOCI) (FASB ASC 830-30-45-12), and is not included in paid-in capital. Further, *changes* in the Cumulative Translation Adjustment are reported in Other Comprehensive Income (OCI) in the determination of comprehensive income. Note that the change in the Cumulative Translation Adjustment is *not* a component of net income.[7]

Translation Example—Second Year After Acquisition

Now that you have some familiarity with the Cumulative Translation Adjustment account, we modify our example to cover a two-year period so that you can see how this account is updated from year to year. Exhibit 8.6 provides the subsidiary's Euro-based financial statements for the year ended December 31, 2016 (i.e., Year two and before conversion to $US).

---

[7] The FASB's reasoning for this treatment was expressed in Appendix C (i.e., the Basis for Conclusion) of the pre-codification standard as follows: "Translation adjustments do not exist in terms of functional currency cash flows. Translation adjustments are solely a result of the translation process and have no direct effect on reporting currency cash flows. Exchange rate changes have an indirect effect on the net investment that may be realized upon sale or liquidation, but that effect is related to the net investment and not to the operations of the investee. Prior to sale or liquidation, that effect is so uncertain and remote as to require that translation adjustments arising currently should not be reported as part of operating results" (SFAS 52, ¶111).

| **EXHIBIT 8.6** | Foreign Subsidiary's Pre-$US-Conversion Financial Statements for Year Ended December 31, 2016 |

Year Ending December 31, 2016	Subsidiary (in €)		Subsidiary (in €)
Income statement:		**Balance sheet:**	
Sales...	€1,500,000	Assets	
Cost of goods sold........................	(900,000)	Cash....................................	€ 426,900
Gross profit.................................	600,000	Accounts receivable.................	348,000
Operating expenses......................	(390,000)	Inventory..............................	447,000
Net income.................................	€ 210,000	Property, plant and equipment (PPE), net	826,800
		Total assets...........................	€2,048,700
Statement of retained earnings:			
BOY retained earnings..................	€ 787,500	Liabilities and stockholders' equity	
Net income.................................	210,000	Current liabilities.....................	€ 254,400
Dividends..................................	(21,000)	Long-term liabilities	592,800
EOY retained earnings..................	€ 976,500	Common stock........................	100,000
		APIC...................................	125,000
		Retained earnings	976,500
		Total liabilities and equity...........	€2,048,700

We assume the following relevant exchange rates (the exchange rates for the year ended December 31, 2015, are the same as in our previous example):

January 1, 2015 Exchange rate	$1.25:€1
December 31, 2015 Exchange rate	$1.39:€1
December 31, 2016 Exchange rate	$1.48:€1
Weighted-average exchange rate for the year, 2015	$1.33:€1
Weighted-average exchange rate for the year, 2016	$1.43:€1
Exchange rate when 2015 dividends declared subsidiary................................	$1.37:€1
Exchange rate when 2016 dividends declared subsidiary................................	$1.45:€1

Using the exchange rates presented above and financial statement information from Exhibit 8.6, we provide the translation of the subsidiary's financial statements into $US for the years ended December 31, 2015 and 2016 in Exhibit 8.7. (We also provide information from our previously performed translation for the year ended December 31, 2015, to assist you in the comparison of the two years.) Please note that, during the year, PPE, net, has decreased by €70,000, reflecting purchases of PPE assets in the amount of €137,800 and depreciation expense of €207,800. This information will become relevant when we prepare the Statement of Cash Flows in the next section.

The same basic steps conducted for the year ended December 31, 2015, were also conducted for the year ended December 31, 2016. The BOY Cumulative Translation Adjustment on December 31, 2015, is $114,100, as before. During the second year, the Cumulative Translation Adjustment account increases by $100,995, resulting in a Cumulative Translation Adjustment balance of $215,095 through December 31, 2016 (in Appendix 8A, we show you how to compute this Cumulative Translation Adjustment directly rather than as a plug figure). Each year, the Cumulative Translation Adjustment account is updated in this manner.

In our example, the $US weakened vis-à-vis the Euro and the Cumulative Translation Adjustment is positive, reflecting the growth in the net assets of the subsidiary. When the $US *strengthens* vis-à-vis the Euro during a given period, the change in the Cumulative Translation Adjustment for the period is negative. The Cumulative Translation Adjustment account can report a negative (i.e., debit) balance during periods of $US strengthening.

EXHIBIT 8.7	Trial Balance Format for Translation of Foreign Subsidiary's Financial Statements (Years 2015 and 2016)

	Year ended December 31, 2015			Year ended December 31, 2016		
	Subsidiary (in €)	Translation Rate	Subsidiary (in $)	Subsidiary (in €)	Translation Rate	Subsidiary (in $)
Debits						
Cash..........................	€ 159,200	1.39	$ 221,288	€ 426,900	1.48	$ 631,812
Accounts receivable..........................	290,000	1.39	403,100	348,000	1.48	515,040
Inventory.......................	372,500	1.39	517,775	447,000	1.48	661,560
Property, plant and equipment (PPE), net	896,800	1.39	1,246,552	826,800	1.48	1,223,664
Cost of goods sold........................	750,000	1.33	997,500	900,000	1.43	1,287,000
Operating expenses........................	325,000	1.33	432,250	390,000	1.43	557,700
Dividends	17,500	1.07	23,975	21,000	1.45	30,450
Current year translation adjustment − Loss			n/a			n/a
Total debits........................	€2,811,000		$3,842,440	€3,359,700		$4,907,226
Credits						
Current liabilities........................	€ 212,000	1.39	$ 294,680	€ 254,400	1.48	$ 376,512
Long-term liabilities	494,000	1.39	686,660	592,800	1.48	877,344
Common stock........................	100,000	1.25	125,000	100,000	1.25	125,000
APIC........................	125,000	1.25	156,250	125,000	1.25	156,250
Retained earnings at BOY	630,000	a	803,250	787,500	a	1,012,025
Sales........................	1,250,000	1.33	1,662,500	1,500,000	1.43	2,145,000
BOY cumulative translation adjustment..........		a	0		a	114,100
Change in cumulative adjustment		b	114,100		b	100,995
Total credits	€2,811,000		$3,842,440	€3,359,700		$4,907,226

Notes:

a Represents the $US ending balance from the previous year. In this example, the January 1, 2015, Retained Earnings balance was given to you and there was no January 1, 2015, Cumulative Translation Adjustment since the subsidiary was acquired on 1/1/15.

b Amount necessary to balance the $US-converted trial balance.

Exhibit 8.8 provides the translated foreign subsidiary financial statements derived from the above conversion performed in Exhibit 8.7.

EXHIBIT 8.8	Translated Foreign Subsidiary's Financial Statements in $US (2016)

	Subsidiary			Subsidiary
Income statement:		**Balance sheet:**		
Sales........................	$2,145,000	Assets		
Cost of goods sold........................	(1,287,000)	Cash........................		$ 631,812
Gross profit........................	858,000	Accounts receivable........................		515,040
Operating expenses........................	(557,700)	Inventory........................		661,560
Net income........................	$ 300,300	Property, plant and equipment (PPE), net		1,223,664
		Total assets........................		$3,032,076
Statement of comprehensive income:				
Net income	$ 300,300	Liabilities and stockholders' equity		
OCI: Current year translation adjustment gain (loss)	100,995	Current liabilities........................		$ 376,512
Comprehensive income	$ 401,295	Long-term liabilities		877,344
		Common stock........................		125,000
Statement of retained earnings:		APIC........................		156,250
BOY retained earnings........................	$1,012,025	Retained earnings		1,281,875
Net income........................	300,300	Cumulative translation adjustment..........		215,095
Dividends	(30,450)	Total liabilities and equity........................		$3,032,076
EOY retained earnings	$1,281,875			

Impact of F/X Fluctuations on Financial Statements   In the second year of our translation example, the CTA increased by $100,995 from the $114,100 balance reported in the first year. As the $US weakened vis-à-vis the Euro, Euro-denominated assets and liabilities of the subsidiary were translated into more $US and grew, thus increasing stockholders' equity via the CTA account. Although not as apparent, the income statement grew also as sales and expenses were translated into more $US and, because the company is profitable, it appeared more profitable as a result of the weakening $US.

Over time, the $US weakens and strengthens vis-à-vis other world currencies and, in the recent past, it has strengthened, resulting in lower $US equivalents for both balance sheet and income statement items. A strengthening $US negatively impacts sales and profits as witnessed in the 3Q earnings call discussion by Proctor & Gamble's, CFO, Jon Moeller (these transcripts are found in the Investor Relations section of the P&G web site):

> On a constant currency basis core earnings per share were up 10%, keeping us on track for double digit constant currency core earnings per share growth for the fiscal year. Including FX, which was an 18 percentage point drag on the quarter, core earnings per share were $0.92, down 8% versus the prior year. Foreign exchange hurts total $530 million after tax in the March quarter and $1.2 billion after tax fiscal year-to-date. They're forecast to be a $1.5 billion after tax hurt for the fiscal year. We're managing through the FX challenge with the combination of pricing, mixed enhancement and productivity cost savings and by pursuing opportunities on brands in countries and regions unaffected by FX.

The strengthening $US reduced P&G's earnings per share by 18 percentage points, from an increase of 10% to a decline of 8%, and the company projected the negative impact on net income for the year to be $(1.5) billion!

Analysts need to be aware of the impact of changing foreign currency exchange rates as they impact every line item in the income statement and balance sheet. F/X impact is, indeed, much more than the CTA as emphasized by Credit Suisse in its Equity Research report of July, 2015:

> Of course the culprit behind most of the FX related noise is the strong dollar. The U.S. dollar went on quite a run appreciating 22% against a basket of major currencies from June 30th 2014 through March 31, 2015 . . . and that had a big (generally negative) impact on reported results for U.S. companies. The last time we saw the dollar come close to strengthening like that over such a short period of time was back in 2009, when it was up nearly 20% over the nine months ending March 31, 2009.

Translation of the Statement of Cash Flows   The translation of the Statement of Cash Flows generally utilizes the weighted-average exchange rate for all line items, except for significant one-time transactions (e.g., purchases and sales of long-term assets, borrowings, and the payment of dividends). For these other items, exchange rate on the date of the transaction is utilized. Continuing the previous example for the year ending December 31, 2016, assume that the PPE asset is purchased when the exchange rate is $1.41:€1 and that the increase in long-term debt occurs toward the end of the year when the exchange rate is $1.47:€1. In addition, we assume that the exchange rate for dividends is the same on the date of declaration and the date of payment. The statement of cash flows (indirect method) is provided in Exhibit 8.9.

The underlying assumption is that the operating cash flows occur evenly throughout the year. As a result, they are translated at the *average* exchange rate of $1.43:€1. This is despite the fact that the specific accounts relating to these operating cash flows (current assets, other than cash, and liabilities) are translated at the EOY exchange rate of $1.48:€1 for the balance sheet.

The $21,425 Effect of Exchange Rate on Cash line item (highlighted in Exhibit 8.9) is a plug figure needed to yield the $410,524 ($631,812 − $221,288) increase in cash, based on the converted $US beginning and ending cash balances. This amount represents the increase in cash that is the result of changes in exchange rates and *not* from the generation of cash flow.

EXHIBIT 8.9	Statement of Cash Flows		
Net income	€ 210,000	a	$ 300,300
Depreciation expense	207,800	1.43	297,154
Change in accounts receivable	(58,000)	1.43	(82,940)
Change in inventories	(74,500)	1.43	(106,535)
Change in current liabilities	42,400	1.43	60,632
Net cash flows from operating activities	327,700		168,611
Purchases of property and equipment	(137,800)	1.41	(194,298)
Net cash flows from investing activities	(137,800)		(194,298)
Issuance of long-term debt	98,800	1.47	145,236
Dividends	(21,000)	1.45	(30,450)
Net cash flows from financing activities	77,800		114,786
Net change in cash	267,700		389,099
Effect of exchange rate on cash		b	21,425
Beginning cash	159,200	$1.39	221,288
Ending cash	€ 426,900	$1.48	$ 631,812

Notes:
[a] Computed in the income statement and carried forward
[b] Amount necessary to balance the computed $US-converted net change in cash against the difference between the $US-converted beginning and ending balances of cash.

Required Disclosures Relating to the Cumulative Translation Adjustment

FASB ASC 830-30-45-18 to -20 requires the following disclosures relating to the Cumulative Translation Adjustment in a separate financial statement, in notes to the financial statements, or as part of a statement of changes in equity:

a. Beginning and ending amount of Cumulative Translation Adjustment

b. The aggregate adjustment for the period resulting from the Cumulative Translation Adjustment and gains and losses from certain hedges and intra-entity balances

c. The amount of income taxes for the period allocated to the Cumulative Translation Adjustment

d. The amounts transferred from Cumulative Translation Adjustment and included in determining net income for the period as a result of the sale or complete or substantially complete liquidation of an investment in a foreign entity

In addition to these Cumulative Translation Adjustment-specific disclosures required under FASB ASC 830, Cumulative Translation Adjustment-related gains and losses must also meet the disclosure requirements for comprehensive income and its components, as required by FASB ASC 220. The primary requirement is that comprehensive income and its components must be reported "in a financial statement that is displayed with the same prominence as other financial statements that constitute a full set of financial statements" (FASB ASC 220-10-45-8). Most companies choose to report comprehensive income in the statement of equity, with a minority of companies reporting comprehensive income in a separate statement of performance. In Exhibits 8.5 and 8.8, we prepared a Statement of Comprehensive Income.

PRACTICE INSIGHT

Coca-Cola's Cumulative Translation Adjustment and AOCI A company's Stockholders' Equity can fluctuate dramatically as a result of changes in the relative strength of the $US vis-à-vis other world currencies. **Coca-Cola** provides a case in point. Following is the reconciliation of its Accumulated Other Comprehensive Income (Loss) account for 2013–2014:

AOCI attributable to shareowners of The Coca-Cola Company consisted of the following: (in millions)	2014	2013
Foreign currency translation adjustment	$(5,226)	$(2,849)
Accumulated derivative net gains (losses)	554	197
Unrealized net gains (losses) on available-for-sale securities	972	258
Adjustments to pension and other benefit liabilities	(2,077)	(1,038)
Accumulated other comprehensive income (loss)	$(5,777)	$(3,432)

Coke's Foreign currency translation adjustment component of AOCI became more negative by $2,377 billion from 2013 ($2,849) to 2014 ($5,226) as the $US strengthened vis-à-vis the currencies in which its subsidiaries maintain their financial statements. The Foreign currency translation adjustment component of AOCI typically fluctuates between positive and negative values as the $US weakens and strengthens vis-à-vis other world currencies.

TOPIC REVIEW 1

Translation Using the Current Rate Method

Assume that your company owns a subsidiary operating in Germany. The subsidiary conducts most of its business activities in the European Economic Union and maintains its books using the Euro as its functional currency. Following are the subsidiary's financial statements (in €) for the most recent year:

	Subsidiary (in €)
Income statement:	
Sales.	€1,095,000
Cost of goods sold.	(657,000)
Gross profit.	438,000
Operating expenses	(284,700)
Net income	€ 153,300
Statement of retained earnings:	
BOY retained earnings	€ 574,875
Net income	153,300
Dividends	(15,330)
Ending retained earnings	€ 712,845
Balance sheet:	
Assets	
Cash	€ 311,637
Accounts receivable	254,040
Inventory	326,310
PPE, net	603,564
Total assets.	€1,495,551
Liabilities and stockholders' equity:	
Current liabilities.	€ 185,712
Long-term liabilities	432,744
Common stock.	73,000
APIC	91,250
Retained earnings	712,845
Cumulative translation adjustment.	—
Total liabilities & equity	€1,495,551

	Subsidiary (in €)
Statement of cash flows:	
Net income.	€ 153,300
Change in accounts receivable	(42,340)
Change in inventories.	(54,385)
Change in current liabilities	30,952
Net cash flows from operating activities	87,527
Change in PPE, net	(56,064)
Net cash flows from investing activities.	(56,064)
Change in long-term debt	72,124
Dividends	(15,330)
Net cash flows from financing activities.	56,794
Net change in cash.	88,257
Effect of exchange rate on cash.	
Beginning cash	223,380
Ending cash	€ 311,637

The relevant exchange rates ($:€1) are as follows:	
BOY rate.	$0.95
EOY rate.	$1.04
Avg. rate	$1.01
PPE purchase date rate	$0.99
LTD borrowing date rate.	$1.03
Dividend rate	$1.02
Historical rate (Common stock and APIC)	$0.63

Required

Translate the subsidiary's income statement, statement of retained earnings, balance sheet, and statement of cash flows into $US using the current-rate method (assume that the BOY Retained Earnings is $437,543).

The solution to this review problem can be found on page 566.

THE REMEASUREMENT OF FOREIGN-CURRENCY-DENOMINATED FINANCIAL STATEMENTS

Exhibit 8.1 illustrates the translation process preceding consolidation. The first step considers the case in which the books of the subsidiary are not maintained in its functional currency. In that case, the financial records must first be *remeasured* into the functional currency before they can be translated into the reporting currency of the parent. We discuss the remeasurement process in this section.

LO2 Describe the remeasurement of foreign-currency-denominated financial statements.

Following are some of the more common situations that can require remeasurement of the financial statements:

■ **Subsidiary records not maintained in the functional currency**—A foreign entity may choose (or be required by law) to maintain its books and records in a local currency that is not its functional currency. If an entity's books of record are not maintained in its functional currency, remeasurement into the functional currency is required. That remeasurement is required before translation into the reporting currency (ASC 830-10-45-17).

■ **Subsidiary is not independent of the parent company**—In the second class are foreign operations that are primarily a direct and integral component or extension of the parent's operations. Significant assets may be acquired from the parent entity or otherwise by expending dollars and, similarly, the sale of assets may generate dollars that are available to the parent. Financing is primarily by the parent or otherwise from dollar sources. In other words, the day-to-day operations are dependent on the economic environment of the parent's currency, and the changes in the foreign entity's individual assets and liabilities impact directly on the cash flows of the parent entity in the parent's currency.

For this class, the $US is the functional currency and the subsidiary's financial records must be remeasured into the $US before translation into the reporting currency (ASC 830-10-45-4b).

■ **Subsidiary operates in a highly inflationary economy**—If a subsidiary operates in a highly inflationary economy, its financial statements must be remeasured into the reporting currency (i.e., the $US). A highly inflationary economy is one that has cumulative inflation of approximately 100 percent or more over a 3-year period (ASC830-10-45-11).

In the first case, remeasurement of the subsidiary's financial records into the subsidiary's functional currency results in financial records that can, then, be translated into the reporting currency of the parent prior to consolidation. In the last two cases, the financial records are remeasured into the $US and consolidation can, then, proceed without translation.

To remeasure the financial statements of our subsidiary, it is first necessary to classify the net asset accounts into two broad categories: monetary and nonmonetary:

Monetary Assets and Liabilities:	Monetary assets and liabilities are assets and liabilities whose amounts are fixed in terms of units of currency by contract or otherwise. Examples are cash, short- or long-term accounts and notes receivable in cash, and short- or long-term accounts and notes payable in cash. [APB 29, paragraph 3]
Nonmonetary Assets and Liabilities:	Nonmonetary assets and liabilities are assets and liabilities other than monetary ones. Examples are inventories; investments in common stocks; property, plant, and equipment; and liabilities for rent collected in advance.

After the net assets have been classified as being monetary and nonmonetary, the remeasurement process involves the following four steps, as detailed in the right-most column in Exhibit 8.2:

1. Nonmonetary assets and liabilities are restated at *historical* exchange rates (i.e., the exchange rates in effect when the nonmonetary assets and liabilities were initially recognized).

2. Revenues and expenses relating to those nonmonetary net assets (e.g., cost of goods sold, depreciation and amortization expense, deferred revenues) are also translated at the same *historical* exchange rates used for the asset to which they relate.[8]

3. Monetary assets and liabilities are restated at current exchange rates (i.e., the exchange rate in effect on the statement date).

4. The net gain or loss from the remeasurement process is reported in Net Income rather than in Other Comprehensive Income.

With its use of historical exchange rates for nonmonetary net assets (and related income statement accounts) and its effect on reported net income, remeasurement stands in stark contrast to the translation process that we discussed in the previous section. We now provide an example of remeasurement of a subsidiary's foreign-currency-denominated financial statements into the functional currency.

Remeasurement Example

To illustrate the remeasurement of subsidiary financial statements into a functional currency, we rely on the same facts from the translation example (discussed above). However, in this case, we make the following critical modification of the facts: instead of assuming that the Euro is the functional currency, we now assume that the $US is the functional currency. Given that the subsidiary's financial statements are

---

[8] Technically, ASC 830-10 requires remeasurement of inventories using the historical exchange rates (they are nonmonetary assets). Given the computation of inventory (BI + Purchases − EI = CGS), this means BI and EI would need to be calculated using the historical rates. However, ASC 830-10-55-10 allows for the following practicability exception: "Literal application of the standards in this Subtopic might require a degree of detail in record keeping and computations that could be burdensome as well as unnecessary to produce reasonable approximations of the results. Accordingly, it is acceptable to use averages or other methods of approximation. For example, because translation at the exchange rates at the dates the numerous revenues, expenses, gains, and losses are recognized is generally impractical, an appropriately weighted average exchange rate for the period may be used to translate those elements. Likewise, the use of other time- and effort-saving methods to approximate the results of detailed calculations is permitted."

recorded in Euros, we now must remeasure them into the $US. The following exchange rates include the same basic rates from the translation example, along with a few additional relevant rates:

January 1, 2015 Exchange rate	$1.25:€1
December 31, 2015 Exchange rate	$1.39:€1
December 31, 2016 Exchange rate	$1.48:€1
Weighted-average exchange rate for the year, 2015	$1.33:€1
Weighted-average exchange rate for the year, 2016	$1.43:€1
Exchange rate when 2015 dividends declared subsidiary.	$1.37:€1
Exchange rate when 2016 dividends declared subsidiary.	$1.45:€1
Exchange rate on dates of purchase of PPE assets:	
Land	$1.26:€1
Buildings.	$1.27:€1
Equipment.	$1.29:€1

As before, at January 1, 2015, the $US value of the subsidiary's Retained Earnings is $803,250. With respect to inventories, assume that the subsidiary uses the FIFO cost-flow assumption. In addition, ending inventories at December 31, 2015 and 2016 were entirely purchased on those dates, and all other inventory purchases occurred evenly throughout 2015 and 2016.

EXHIBIT 8.10 Financial Data of Foreign Subsidiary in Remeasurement Example

Year Ended December 31,	2015	2016	Year Ended December 31,	2015	2016
Beginning inventory	€ 310,417	€ 372,500	**Statement of retained earnings:**		
Purchases.	812,083	974,500	BOY retained earnings	€ 630,000	€ 787,500
Ending inventory.	(372,500)	(447,000)	Net income.	175,000	210,000
Cost of goods sold.	€ 750,000	€ 900,000	Dividends	(17,500)	(21,000)
			Ending retained earnings	€ 787,500	€ 976,500
Land	€ 326,800	€ 326,800			
Building	360,000	360,000			
Accum. deprec.—building	(30,000)	(60,000)			
Equipment	280,000	280,000	**Balance sheet:**		
Accum. deprec.—equipment	(40,000)	(80,000)	Assets		
Property, plant and equipment (PPE), net . . .	€ 896,800	€ 826,800	Cash.	€ 159,200	€ 426,900
			Accounts receivable.	290,000	348,000
			Inventory.	372,500	447,000
Depreciation expense—building	€ 30,000	€ 30,000	Property, plant and		
Depreciation expense—equipment	40,000	40,000	equipment (PPE), net	896,800	826,800
Depreciation expense.	€ 70,000	€ 70,000	Total assets.	€1,718,500	€2,048,700
Income statement:					
Sales.	€1,250,000	€1,500,000	Liabilities and stockholders' equity		
Cost of goods sold.	(750,000)	(900,000)	Current liabilities.	€ 212,000	€ 254,400
Gross profit.	500,000	600,000	Long-term liabilities	494,000	592,800
Operating expenses	(255,000)	(320,000)	Common stock.	100,000	100,000
Depreciation.	(70,000)	(70,000)	APIC	125,000	125,000
			Retained earnings	787,500	976,500
Net income.	€ 175,000	€ 210,000	Total liabilities and equity	€1,718,500	€2,048,700

Financial data for the subsidiary for the two most recent years (in Euros) is provided in Exhibit 8.10. The subsidiary's *net* monetary assets (i.e., monetary assets less monetary liabilities) at December 31, 2015 and 2016 are as follows:

Net Monetary Assets	Dec. 31, 2015	Dec. 31, 2016
Cash.	€ 159,200	€ 426,900
Accounts receivable.	290,000	348,000
Current liabilities.	(212,000)	(254,400)
Long-term liabilities	(494,000)	(592,800)
	€(256,800)	€ (72,300)

As is typical of many companies, while our subsidiary reports a *positive* net asset position (see earlier example), it also reports a *negative* net monetary position. This is because monetary liabilities are usually greater than monetary assets, primarily because of the inclusion of long-term debt as a monetary liability. As a result, when the $US weakens, as it does in this example, remeasurement *losses* result. This is analogous to the losses that result from a foreign-currency-denominated account payable or long-term debt when the $US weakens (see Chapter 7).

The remeasurement of our subsidiary from Euros to $US is provided in Exhibit 8.11. Remeasurement of our subsidiary's Euro-denominated financial statements into the $US functional currency for the years ended December 31, 2015 and 2016 involves the following steps. These steps are conceptually similar to the steps we applied in our translation example.

1. **Remeasurement using exchange rates:**
   - Monetary assets (cash and accounts receivable) and monetary liabilities (current liabilities and long-term debt) are remeasured at the EOY exchange rate.
   - Nonmonetary assets are remeasured at the exchange rates in effect when those assets were purchased.
   - Common Stock and APIC are remeasured at the exchange rate in effect when the stock was purchased by the parent.
   - Dividends are translated at the exchange rate in effect on the date of declaration.
   - Revenue and expense accounts—other than depreciation expense and cost of goods sold, as described below—are remeasured at the average exchange rates in each of the years. Accounting rules call for this treatment under the assumption that these non-property-related revenues and expenses occur evenly during each year.[9]
   - For each year in which cost of goods sold is computed, beginning inventory is remeasured at the BOY exchange rate (i.e., the rate in effect when the inventory was purchased, in this example). Purchases during the year are remeasured at the average exchange rate under the assumption that these occurred evenly throughout the year. Ending inventories are remeasured at the EOY exchange rate (i.e., the rate in effect when the inventory was purchased, in this example). Cost of goods sold, then, is computed using these remeasured amounts, as follows:

	2015			2016		
Beginning inventory	€310,417	× $1.25/€ =	$ 388,021	€372,500	× $1.39/€ =	$ 517,775
Purchases.	812,083	× $1.33/€ =	1,080,071	974,500	× $1.43/€ =	1,393,535
Ending inventory.	(372,500)	× $1.39/€ =	(517,775)	(447,000)	× $1.48/€ =	(661,560)
Cost of goods sold.	€750,000		$ 950,317	€900,000		$1,249,750

   - Land, buildings and equipment, together with the related accumulated depreciation, are remeasured using the exchange rates in effect when those assets were purchased. Depreciation expense relating to buildings and equipment is remeasured at the exchange rates used to remeasure those assets. The computations are as follows:

	Year Ended December 31, 2015			Year Ended December 31, 2016		
Land	€326,800	× $1.26/€ =	$ 411,768	€326,800	× $1.26 / € =	$ 411,768
Building	360,000	× $1.27/€ =	457,200	360,000	× $1.27 / € =	457,200
Accum. deprec.—building	(30,000)	× $1.27/€ =	(38,100)	(60,000)	× $1.27 / € =	(76,200)
Equipment	280,000	× $1.29/€ =	361,200	280,000	× $1.29 / € =	361,200
Accum. deprec.—equipment	(40,000)	× $1.29/€ =	(51,600)	(80,000)	× $1.29 / € =	(103,200)
Property, plant and equipment (PPE), net	€896,800		$1,140,468	€826,800		$1,050,768
Deprec. expense—building	€ 30,000	× $1.27/€ =	$ 38,100	€ 30,000	× $1.27 / € =	$ 38,100
Deprec. expense—equipment	40,000	× $1.29/€ =	51,600	40,000	× $1.29 / € =	51,600
Depreciation expense.	€ 70,000		$ 89,700	€ 70,000		$ 89,700

---

[9] As a practical matter, most real-world remeasurement disclosure indicates that all income statement accounts are remeasured using weighted-average rates. This is typically done because the weighted-average rates yield results that are immaterially different from strict adherence to the remeasurement procedures called for under FASB ASC 830.

2. **$US Beginning Balances Rolled Forward from Prior Year $US Ending Balances**
   - The January 1, 2015, Retained Earnings balance is given to you in this example. For 2016, the beginning of year (BOY) Retained Earnings balance in $US will be $1,020,041, the December 31, 2015, end of year (EOY) Retained Earnings balance in $US.
   - Note that remeasurement does not have a Cumulative Translation Adjustment. All remeasurement gains and losses are recognized in net income. Thus they are automatically rolled forward in the Retained Earnings balance.

3. **Converted Trial Balance Must Balance**
   - The remeasurement gain or loss can be inferred as the amount needed to cause debits to equal credits in the trial balance, after all of the preceding amounts are computed or entered (see highlighted line in Exhibit 8.11). If a debit is needed, then the remeasurement adjustment is a loss, and if a credit is needed, then the remeasurement adjustment is a gain. This gain or loss is recognized as part of net income. It is *not* reported as an extraordinary or unusual item in the income statement.

EXHIBIT 8.11	Trial Balance Format for Remeasurement of Foreign Subsidiary's Financial Statements (Years 2015 and 2016)

	Year Ended December 31, 2015			Year Ended December 31, 2016		
	Subsidiary (in €)	Translation Rate	Subsidiary (In $)	Subsidiary (in €)	Translation Rate	Subsidiary (in $)
Debits						
Cash.	€ 159,200	1.39	$ 221,288	€ 426,900	1.48	$ 631,812
Accounts receivable.	290,000	1.39	403,100	348,000	1.48	515,040
Inventory.	372,500	a	517,775	447,000	a	661,560
Property, plant and equipment (PPE), net	898,800	a	1,140,468	826,800	a	1,050,768
Cost of goods sold.	750,000	a	950,317	900,000	a	1,249,750
Operating expenses.	255,000	1.33	339,150	320,000	1.43	457,600
Depreciation.	70,000	a	89,700	70,000	a	89,700
Dividends	17,500	1.37	23,975	21,000	1.45	30,450
Remeasurement loss		c	42,567		c	13,467
Total debits.	€2,811,000		$3,728,340	€3,359,700		$4,700,147
Credits						
Current liabilities.	€ 212,000	1.39	$ 294,680	€ 254,400	1.48	$ 376,512
Long-term liabilities	494,000	1.39	686,660	592,800	1.48	877,344
Common stock.	100,000	1.25	125,000	100,000	1.25	125,000
APIC.	125,000	1.25	156,250	125,000	1.25	156,250
Retained earnings (BOY)	630,000	b	803,250	787,500	b	1,020,041
Sales.	1,250,000	1.33	1,662,500	1,500,000	1.43	2,145,000
Remeasurement gain		c	n/a		c	n/a
Total credits	€2,811,000		$3,728,340	€3,359,700		$4,700,147

Notes: a $US converted balance for inventory, cost of goods sold, PPE and depreciation expense computed in notes preceding this spreadsheet

b Represents the $US ending balance from the previous year. The January 1, 2015, balance was given to you.

c Amount necessary to balance the $US-converted trial balance. It is a loss because a debit was necessary to equalize trial balance. If a credit was needed, then plug would have been remeasurement gain instead of a loss.

Our subsidiary reports a remeasurement loss in both the prior year and the current year. This is the result of a net monetary liability (negative net monetary asset) position and a weakening $US. As the dollar weakens, the $US value of both assets and liabilities increase. And, since monetary liabilities are greater than monetary assets in this example (and typically), equity must decline and that decline is recorded as a remeasurement loss. The remeasurement loss reduces profitability in the current period. This remeasurement loss is a non-cash loss.

Notice that there is no Cumulative Translation Adjustment account when financial statements are remeasured. That is because the effects of currency fluctuations on the balance sheet are captured in the determination of Net Income and, thus, Retained Earnings. Exhibit 8.12 provides conventional financial statement presentation for the subsidiary's financial statements after they have been remeasured into the $US functional currency.

PRACTICE INSIGHT

Functional Currency in Highly Inflationary Economies: Venezuela At the December 2009 AICPA National Conference on Current SEC and PCAOB Developments in Washington, D.C., the SEC's Deputy Chief Accountant, Craig Olinger announced that the SEC determined that Venezuela is a highly inflationary economy, with greater than 100% inflation for the three-year period ending December 31, 2009. As a result, he stated that the SEC expected, beginning January 1, 2010, for all U.S. public companies with subsidiaries in Venezuela to designate the parents' reporting currency (i.e., most likely the $US) as the functional currency for the Venezuelan subsidiaries.

At first glance, the fact that an economy experienced 100% inflation over three years seems fairly cut-and-dry. However, in the months leading up to Mr. Olinger's speech, there was tremendous uncertainty about whether Venezuela surpassed the three-year 100% cumulative threshold. How could this be? According to Jack Ciesielski's *Analyst's Accounting Observer* ("A Currency Affair: Venezuelan Vagaries," 2010, Vol. 19, No. 3) there were two major factors that contributed to the Venezuelan confusion. First, there are two main price indices used to measure inflation in Venezuela: the Consumer Price Index (CPI) and the National Consumer Price Index (NCPI). The CPI is older and more established, but measured price levels only in the Caracas metropolitan area. The NCPI is a newer, nationwide index that started on January 1, 2008. Because the nationwide index has less than three years of data, companies applied inconsistent blends of the CPI and the NCPI during the past couple of years, and this led to some confusion about the "real" rate of inflation.

And, the second factor contributing to the Venezuelan confusion? Well, it turns out that there is more than one official exchange rate used in converting Venezuelan Bolivars (Bs) to $US. For "non-essential" goods and services, (e.g., automobile, chemicals, appliances, electronics, telecom, and, most importantly, repatriated dividends) the official exchange rate was 4.30 Bs/$US. For "essential" goods and services (e.g., food, medicine, heavy machinery, family remittances, and imports to the public sector related to schools, science and technology), the official exchange rate is 2.15 Bs/$US. On top of this two-rate system, companies could choose to participate in a parallel market for Bs, one that is not government sanctioned, has exchange-rate variability, and that is less favorable than the government rate. Which rate should a company use? SEC representatives declined to provide specific guidance and indicated that the appropriate rate depends on the facts and circumstances of each company and the transactions in which it engages.

EXHIBIT 8.12 Remeasured Foreign Subsidiary's Financial Statements in $US

Years Ended December 31,	2015	2016	Years Ended December 31,	2015	2016
Income statement:			**Balance sheet:**		
Sales.	$1,662,500	$2,145,000	Assets		
Cost of goods sold.	(950,317)	(1,249,750)	Cash	$ 221,288	$ 631,812
Gross profit.	712,183	895,250	Accounts receivable	403,100	515,040
Operating expenses	(339,150)	(457,600)	Inventory.	517,775	661,560
Depreciation	(89,700)	(89,700)	Property, plant and equipment (PPE), net. . . .	1,140,468	1,050,768
Remeasurement gain (loss) . .	(42,567)	(13,467)	Total Assets	$2,282,631	$2,859,180
Net income	$ 240,766	$ 334,483	Liabilities and stockholders' equity		
			Current liabilities	$ 294,680	$ 376,512
Statement of retained earnings:			Long-term liabilities	686,660	877,344
BOY retained earnings	$ 803,250	$1,020,041	Common stock	125,000	125,000
Net income	240,766	334,483	APIC	156,250	156,250
Dividends	(23,975)	(30,450)	Retained earnings.	1,020,041	1,324,074
Ending retained earnings	$1,020,041	$1,324,074	Total liabilities and equity	$2,282,631	$2,859,180

TOPIC REVIEW 2

Remeasurement

Assume that your company owns a subsidiary operating in New Zealand. The subsidiary has adopted the New Zealand Dollar (NZD) as its functional currency. Your parent company operates this subsidiary like a division or a branch office, making all of its operating decisions, including pricing of its products. You conclude, therefore, that the functional currency of this subsidiary is the $US and that its financial statements must be remeasured using the temporal method prior to consolidation. Following are the subsidiary's financial statements (in NZD) for the most recent year:

	In NZD
Beginning inventory	1,117,500
Purchases	2,923,500
Ending inventory	(1,341,000)
Cost of goods sold	2,700,000
Land	980,400
Building	1,800,000
Accum depreciation—building	(900,000)
Equipment	1,200,000
Accum depreciation—equipment	(600,000)
PPE, net	2,480,400
Depreciation expense—building	90,000
Depreciation expense—equipment	120,000
Depreciation expense	210,000

	Subsidiary (in NZD)
Income statement:	
Sales	4,500,000
Cost of goods sold	(2,700,000)
Gross profit	1,800,000
Operating expenses	(960,000)
Depreciation	(210,000)
Remeasurement gain or loss	
Net income	630,000

	Subsidiary (in NZD)
Statement of retained earnings:	
BOY retained earnings	2,362,500
Net income	630,000
Dividends	(63,000)
Ending retained earnings	2,929,500
Balance sheet:	
Assets	
Cash	1,280,700
Accounts receivable	1,044,000
Inventory	1,341,000
PPE, net	2,480,400
Total assets	6,146,100
Liabilities and stockholders' equity	
Current liabilities	763,200
Long-term liabilities	1,778,400
Common stock	300,000
APIC	375,000
Retained earnings	2,929,500
Total liabilities & equity	6,146,100

The relevant exchange rates for the $US value of the New Zealand Dollar (NZD) are as follows:

BOY rate	$0.76
EOY rate	$0.93
Average rate	$0.83
Dividend rate	$0.92
Historical rates	
Beginning inventory	$0.76
Land	$0.60
Building	$0.61
Equipment	$0.62
Historical rate (Common stock and APIC)	$0.48

Required

Remeasure the subsidiary's income statement, statement of retained earnings, and balance sheet into $US using the temporal method for the current year (assume that the BOY Retained Earnings is $1,578,336).

The solution to this review problem can be found on page 567.

LO3 Describe the consolidation of foreign subsidiaries when the parent uses the equity method to account for its Equity Investment.

CONSOLIDATION OF FOREIGN SUBSIDIARIES

After the financial statements of foreign subsidiaries are translated into the parent's reporting currency, the consolidation process proceeds in a manner that is similar to that which we describe in previous chapters. We illustrate the consolidation of our foreign subsidiary assuming that the parent uses the equity method to account for its investment in the subsidiary in the following example. We then perform the same consolidation assuming that the parent uses the cost method.

Example of Consolidation Subsequent to the Date of Acquisition—Equity Method

We continue with the facts from the previously discussed translation example for the year ended December 31, 2016. Before we review the consolidation spreadsheet, we discuss two issues that are particularly important for the consolidation of financial statements that are denominated in currencies other than the parent's reporting currency: accounting for an Acquisition Accounting Premium (AAP) and updating the Equity Investment account in the parent's financial statements.

Updating the AAP In the original facts for the translation example (provided at the beginning of this chapter), we stated that the purchase price on January 1, 2015, includes an AAP of €110,000, with a $US equivalent of $137,500 (€110,000 × $1.25/€). The AAP is related to undervalued PPE, which the *parent* is depreciating over an 11-year useful life. The AAP at December 31, 2016 (expressed in Euros), reflects the initial balance of €110,000 less two years of AAP amortization in the amount of €10,000, for an ending balance of €90,000. The updating of the AAP when expressed in $US is a bit more complicated and involves the following steps:

1. **BOY balance**—the beginning balance of the AAP (i.e., on January 1, 2016) is translated at the exchange rate in effect on that date ($1.39:€1). This beginning balance will be reflected in our **[A]** consolidation journal entry.

2. **AAP Depreciation**—the depreciation expense related to the AAP for the year ended December 31, 2016, is translated at the average exchange rate for the period ($1.43:€1), resulting in a converted amount of $14,300. This expense is recognized by the parent as a reduction of Equity Income (and a reduction of the Equity Investment account) and is reflected as operating expense in the consolidated income statement as a result of our **[D]** consolidation journal entry.

3. **Computed ending balance of the AAP**—the computed AAP ending balance at December 31, 2016 (expressed in $US) is $124,700 ($139,000 − $14,300).

4. **EOY AAP balance**—the ending balance of the AAP at December 31, 2016, must be translated at the current exchange rate of $1.48: €1, like all other assets. This results in a balance of $133,200 (€90,000 × $1.48/€) on December 31, 2016.

5. **AAP translation gain (loss)**—the difference between the EOY balance of the AAP (step #4) and the computed balance of the AAP (step #3) is the AAP translation gain (loss) for the year ended December 31, 2016. This translation gain (loss) is also reflected in our **[D]** consolidation journal entry.

In Exhibit 8.13, we provide a computation of the amounts that will be reported in our **[A]** and **[D]** consolidation journal entries for the year ended December 31, 2016.

EXHIBIT 8.13	Computation of Amounts That Will Be Reported in Our **[A]** and **[D]** Consolidation Journal Entries for the Year Ended December 31, 2016

AAP	€	Rate	$US	
@ Acquisition	€110,000	1.25	$137,500	
Amortization—2015	(10,000)			
BOY balance	100,000	1.39	139,000	**[A]**
Amortization—2016	(10,000)	1.43	(14,300)	**[D]**
Computed balance			124,700	
EOY balance @ 2016	90,000	1.48	133,200	
AAP translation gain (loss)			$ 8,500	**[D]**

One final observation: since the book value of the AAP assets reflects the accounting for those assets (depreciation, in this case) and the reported amount of those assets reflects fluctuations in exchange rates, it is possible that the reported amount of the AAP assets can *increase* in the face of a weakening $US even as their book values *decrease*.

Equity Investment Account on the Parent's Balance Sheet
In our example, the parent company owns 100% of its subsidiary. As a result, at every balance sheet date, the Equity Investment account must be equal to the Stockholders' Equity of the subsidiary plus the unamortized AAP. After the acquisition date, the parent makes its normal journal entries to the Equity Investment account to record Equity Income of $300,300, to record depreciation of the AAP in the amount of $14,300, and to record the reduction of the Equity Investment account to recognize the receipt of dividends in the amount of $30,450.

In addition, to maintain this equality of the Equity Investment account with the post-translation Stockholders' Equity of the subsidiary, the parent must also accrue the change of $100,995 in the Cumulative Translation Adjustment account for the year ended December 31, 2016, as follows (as computed in Exhibit 8.7):[10]

Equity investment	100,995	
Other comprehensive income		100,995
(to record the change in the Cumulative Translation Adjustment account for the year)		

In addition, because the Equity Investment account on the parent's balance sheet includes an AAP, the parent must make an *additional* journal entry to recognize the translation gain (loss) of $8,500 associated with the AAP. We computed this amount in Exhibit 8.13. This journal entry has the following form:

Equity investment	8,500	
Other comprehensive income		8,500
(to recognize the AAP translation gain for the year)		

This journal entry records change in the $US value of the AAP so that it is reported on the consolidated balance sheet in $US at the current exchange rate. The Cumulative Translation Adjustment account on the parent's balance sheet is, therefore, $8,500 higher than the Cumulative Translation Adjustment

[10] If the translation adjustment is negative, the Cumulative Translation Adjustment is debited and the Equity Investment account is credited.

account on the subsidiary's post-translation balance sheet, to reflect the Translation Adjustment relating to the AAP asset that is on the *parent's* (not the subsidiary's) balance sheet.

Given the subsidiary's financial statements at the end of Year 2 (in Exhibit 8.8), the ending balance of the Equity Investment account on the parent's balance sheet is $1,911,420 as follows:

		Equity Investment		
BOY	Common stock	125,000		
BOY	APIC	156,250		
BOY	Retained earnings	1,012,025		
BOY	Unamortized AAP	139,000		
BOY	Cumulative translation adjustment	114,100		
	Equity income	286,000	30,450	Dividends
	BV translation adjustment	100,995		
	AAP translation adjustment	8,500		
		1,941,870	30,450	
		1,911,420		

In Exhibit 8.14, we present the completed consolidation spreadsheet. In the first column, we provide the parent's financial statements for the year ended December 31, 2016. (The parent's financial statements were not previously provided in this chapter.) In the second column of the consolidation spreadsheet, we reproduce the subsidiary's financial statements for the year ended December 31, 2016 (from Exhibit 8.8).

Consolidation Journal Entries   Our C-E-A-D-I consolidation entries for Exhibit 8.14 are the following:

[C]	Equity investment income	286,000		Eliminates the change in the investment account during the year
	Cumulative translation adjustment			
	(current year portion).	109,495		
	Dividends (received by parent)		30,450	
	Equity investment		365,045	
[E]	Common stock (S) @ BOY	125,000		Eliminates the beginning balance in SE(S) by eliminating the BV portion of the beginning investment account
	APIC (S) @ BOY	156,250		
	Retained earnings (S) @ BOY.	1,012,025		
	BOY cumulative translation adjustment.	114,100		
	Equity investment @ BOY		1,407,375	
[A]	PPE, net @ BOY	139,000		Allocates beginning of year 100% AAP by eliminating the remaining investment account
	Equity investment @ BOY		139,000	
[D]	Amortization expense	14,300		Recognizes change in PPE AAP resulting from change in exchange rate during year
	Cumulative translation adjustment			
	(current year portion)		8,500	
	PPE, net @ BOY		5,800	
[I]	No intercompany transactions			

Our [C] and [E] consolidation journal entries now reflect the elimination of the portion of the Equity Investment account that relates to the BOY Cumulative Translation Adjustment and the current year Translation Adjustment (recall, the parent increases the Equity Investment account to reflect the Translation Adjustment for the year and, as a result, that account reflects the Cumulative Translation Adjustment at the beginning of the year). Our [D] consolidation journal entry is augmented to reflect the Cumulative Translation Adjustment relating to the AAP as we discuss above. The [A] consolidation journal entry is unaffected and there are no intercompany transactions to warrant an [I] consolidation journal entry.

EXHIBIT 8.14	Consolidation of a Foreign Subsidiary Spreadsheet, December 31, 2016

	Parent	Subsidiary	Consolidation Entries Dr	Consolidation Entries Cr	Consolidated
Income statement:					
Sales.	$5,000,000	$2,145,000			$ 7,145,000
Cost of goods sold.	(3,500,000)	(1,287,000)			(4,787,000)
Gross profit.	1,500,000	858,000			2,358,000
Equity income.	286,000		[C] $ 286,000		0
Operating expenses	(950,000)	(557,700)	[D] 14,300		(1,522,000)
Net income.	$ 836,000	$ 300,300			$ 836,000
Statement of retained earnings:					
BOY retained earnings	$4,251,500	$1,012,025	[E] 1,012,025		$ 4,251,500
Net income.	836,000	300,300			836,000
Dividends	(170,060)	(30,450)		[C] $ 30,450	(170,060)
Ending retained earnings	$4,917,440	$1,281,875			$ 4,917,440
Statement of accum. comp. income:					
BOY cumulative translation adjusment	$ 114,100	$ 114,100	[E] 114,100		$ 114,100
Translation gain (loss)	109,495	100,995	[C] 109,495	[D] 8,500	109,495
EOY cumulative translation adjustment	$ 223,595	$ 215,095			$ 223,595
Balance sheet:					
Assets					
Cash	$ 297,410	$ 631,812			$ 929,222
Accounts receivable	640,000	515,040			1,155,040
Inventory	970,000	661,560			1,631,560
Equity investment	1,911,420			[C] 365,045	0
				[E] 1,407,375	
				[A] 139,000	
Property, plant and equipment (PPE), net	5,166,000	1,223,664	[A] 139,000	[D] 5,800	6,522,864
	$8,984,830	$3,032,076			$10,238,686
Liabilities and stockholders' equity					
Current liabilities.	$ 400,500	$ 376,512			$ 777,012
Long-term liabilities	500,000	877,344			1,377,344
Common stock.	521,062	125,000	[E] 125,000		521,062
APIC	2,422,233	156,250	[E] 156,250		2,422,233
Retained earnings	4,917,440	1,281,875			4,917,440
Cumulative translation adjustment.	223,595	215,095			223,595
	$8,984,830	$3,032,076	$1,956,170	$1,956,170	$10,238,686

Disposition of the Cumulative Translation Adjustment Upon Sale of the Subsidiary

When the subsidiary is ultimately sold, the weak $US that gave rise to the positive Cumulative Translation Adjustment account in our example will result in increased *cash flow* as the proceeds from the sale will be worth more $US. This is a transaction gain that is similar to the gain we reported on an increased account receivable in Chapter 7. Consequently, FASB ASC 830 provides that, upon sale of the subsidiary, the Cumulative Translation Adjustment should be removed from the Stockholders' Equity of the parent company and reported as part of the gain or loss on sale (FASB ASC 830-30-40-1).

To illustrate, assume that the parent company in our ongoing translation example sells its foreign subsidiary for a cash sale price of $3,000,000 on December 31, 2016. The entry to record the sale is as follows (Exhibit 8.14 provides the balances of the Cumulative Translation Adjustment and the Equity Investment):

Cash	3,000,000	
Cumulative translation adjustment.	223,595	
Equity investment		1,911,420
Gain on sale.		1,312,175
(to record sale of foreign subsidiary)		

The positive Cumulative Translation Adjustment is eliminated from the parent's Stockholders' Equity and, thereby, increases the gain (or reduces the loss) on sale.

Example of Consolidation Subsequent to the Date of Acquisition—Cost Method

LO4 Describe the consolidation process when the parent uses the cost method to account for its Equity Investment.

In this section, we continue with our consolidation of the foreign sub in the second year after its acquisition, but now assume that the parent uses the cost method to account for its equity investment in the subsidiary. As we discussed in Chapter 3, the cost method consolidation begins with an adjustment to bring the Equity Investment account to the balance that the parent would have reported for that account had the parent used the equity method.

First, we compute the cost of the investment at acquisition. This will be the balance of the investment account at the beginning of the second year of the consolidation. Since the parent acquired 100% of the common stock of the subsidiary, the cost method investment account will have a balance equal to the balance of the common stock, APIC and Retained Earnings accounts of the subsidiary (i.e., its Stockholders' Equity on the acquisition date) plus the Acquisition Accounting Premium (AAP). The original cost of the investment (and its balance as of the beginning of the second year), assuming an exchange rate for the Euro of $1.25/€1 on the acquisition date, is computed as follows:

Subsidiary common stock	$ 125,000	(€100,000 × $1.25/€1 − Exhibit 8.3*)
Subsidiary APIC	156,250	(€125,000 × $1.25/€1 − Exhibit 8.3*)
Subsidiary retained earnings	803,250	(given − page 517)
AAP.	137,500	(€110,000 × $1.25/€ −page 517)
Investment @ cost	$1,222,000	

* This same amount is reported in the subsidiary Stockholders' Equity in Exhibit 8.14.

Had the parent used the equity method to account for its investment in the subsidiary, the Equity Investment account as of the beginning of 2016 would equal $1,546,375 (100% of the Stockholders' Equity of the subsidiary plus the remaining unamortized balance of the AAP), computed as follows (see Exhibit 8.14 and the top of page 534)[11]:

Common stock.	$ 125,000
APIC	156,250
Retained earnings	1,012,025
AAP.	139,000
CTA.	114,100
Equity investment.	$1,546,375

As we discussed in Chapter 3, the first step in the consolidation process when the parent uses the cost method to account for its equity investment in the subsidiary is to adjust the investment account

---

[11] Given the BOY Equity investment balance of $1,546,375, the EOY balance of $1,911,420 that is reported in Exhibit 8.14 is computed as follows:

Equity investment @ BOY 2016	$1,546,375
Equity income 2016	286,000
Dividends 2016.	(30,450)
Translation adjustment 2016	100,995
AAP translation adjustment	8,500
Equity investment.	$1,911,420

and the opening balance of Retained Earnings for the cumulative changes that would have been recognized had the parent used the equity method to account for its investment. The cumulative adjustment is equal to $324,375 (= $1,546,375 − $1,222,000) and the adjusting [ADJ] adjusting entry is as follows:

	Equity investment (P) @ BOY	324,375	
[ADJ]	Retained earnings (P) @ BOY		210,275
	Cumulative translation adjustment (CTA) @ BOY		114,100
	(to adjust the Equity Investment account, Retained Earnings and CTA from cost to equity method)		

Notice that the adjustment affects two equity accounts, rather than only Retained Earnings as was the case in Chapter 3. The credit to Retained Earnings reflects the increase in the Equity Investment account on the parent balance sheet at the beginning of 2016 equal to $210,275 ($232,750 subsidiary profit − $23,975 dividends paid to parent (see Exhibit 8.5) + $1,500 ($139,000 − $137,500) AAP adjustment), and the credit to the Cumulative translation adjustment reflects the BOY translation of $114,100 (see Exhibits 8.4 and 8.5). This credit to the CTA in the adjustment entry is only one of the differences that arise in the consolidation of foreign subsidiaries that is not present in the consolidation of domestic subsidiaries. The consolidation elimination entries below are similarly affected.

Given the adjustment to the opening balance of the Equity Investment and Retained Earnings accounts, the consolidation involves the following elimination entries:

[C]	Dividend income (P)	30,450		Eliminates the dividend income recognized by the parent's (cost) investment bookkeeping during the year
	Dividends (S)		30,450	
[E]	BOY Retained earnings (S).	1,012,025		Eliminate the BOY stockholders' equity of subsidiary and the BOY cumulative translation adjustment
	BOY Common stock (S).	125,000		
	BOY APIC (S)	156,250		
	Cumulative translation adjustment (CTA) @ BOY.	114,100		
	Equity investment (P) @ BOY		1,407,375	
[A]	PPE, net (S) @ BOY	139,000		Record BOY AAP related to building (Exhibit 8.13):
	Equity investment (P) @ BOY		139,000	Original amt. €110,000
				Amortization to 12/31/15 . . . . . . (10,000)
				BOY Book value. €100,000
				× $1.39/$1
				$139,000
[D]	Amortization expense (S)	14,300		Record 2016 depreciation related to AAP and the AAP translation gain (see Exhibit 8.13)
	Cumulative translation adjustment (CTA)		8,500	
	Building, net (S)		5,800	
[I]	No intercompany items in this example			

Exhibit 8.15 includes the completed consolidation spreadsheet, including the [ADJ] and C-E-A-D-I entries. Notice that the consolidated financial statements are the same as we report in Exhibit 8.14. The manner in which the parent company accounts for its investment in the subsidiary (i.e., equity method or cost method) has no effect on the consolidated financial statements as the equity investment and its related income are eliminated in the consolidation process.

EXHIBIT 8.15	Consolidation When Parent Uses the Cost Method to Account for the Pre-Consolidation Equity Investment

Parent Uses Cost Method	Parent	Subsidiary	Consolidation Entries Dr	Consolidation Entries Cr	Consolidated
Income Statement:					
Sales.	$5,000,000	$2,145,000			$ 7,145,000
Cost of goods sold.	(3,500,000)	(1,287,000)			(4,787,000)
Gross profit.	1,500,000	858,000			2,358,000
Dividend income.	30,450		[C] $ 30,450		0
Operating expenses	(950,000)	(557,700)	[D] 14,300		(1,522,000)
Net income.	$ 580,450	$ 300,300			$ 836,000
Statement of retained earnings:					
BOY retained earnings	$4,041,225	$1,012,025	[E] 1,012,025	[ADJ] $ 210,275	$ 4,251,500
Net income.	580,450	300,300			836,000
Dividends	(170,060)	(30,450)		[C] 30,450	(170,060)
Ending retained earnings	$4,451,615	$1,281,875			$ 4,917,440
Statement of accum. comp. income:					
BOY cumulative translation adjustment. . . .		$ 114,100	[E] 114,100	[ADJ] 114,100	$ 114,100
Current year translation gain (loss).		100,995		[D] 8,500	109,495
EOY cumulative translation adjustment. . . .		$ 215,095			$ 223,595
Balance sheet:					
Assets					
Cash.	$ 297,410	$ 631,812			$ 929,222
Accounts receivable.	640,000	515,040			1,155,040
Inventory	970,000	661,560			1,631,560
Equity investment—cost method	1,222,000		[ADJ] 324,375	[E] 1,407,375	0
				[A] 139,000	
PPE—net	5,166,000	1,223,664	[A] 139,000	[D] 5,800	6,522,864
	$8,295,410	$3,032,076			$10,238,686
Liabilities and stockholders' equity					
Current liabilities.	$ 400,500	$ 376,512			777,012
Long-term liabilities	500,000	$877,344			1,377,344
Common stock.	521,062	125,000	[E] 125,000		521,062
APIC	2,422,233	156,250	[E] 156,250		2,422,233
Retained earnings	4,451,615	1,281,875			4,917,440
Cumulative translation adjustment.		215,095			223,595
	$8,295,410	$3,032,076	$1,915,500	$1,915,500	$10,238,686

Cost Method

CHAPTER SUMMARY

Foreign subsidiaries may maintain their accounting records in currencies other than the $US. Each must define their functional currency, the currency of the primary economic environment in which the subsidiary operates. Normally, that is the currency of the environment in which a subsidiary primarily generates and expends cash. If the foreign-currency-denominated subsidiary financial statements are already in the functional currency, but not in the parent's currency, then the financial information must be "translated" into the parent's currency. If, however, the foreign-currency denominated subsidiary's financial statements are not already in the functional currency, then the financial information must, first, be "remeasured" into the functional currency.

Translation requires the use of current exchange rates, as follows:

a. Balance sheet accounts
   1. For assets and liabilities, the exchange rate at the balance sheet date shall be used.
   2. Equity accounts
      i. Common stock accounts are translated using the historical exchange rate from the date of the stock sale or repurchase.
      ii. Dividends are translated using the exchange rate in effect on the date the dividends are declared.
      iii. Retained earnings are updated each year for net income less dividends.

b. Income statement accounts
   1. Revenues and expenses are translated using the average exchange rate for the period.
   2. Gains and losses on transactions are translated using the exchange rate at the dates on which those elements are recognized shall be used.

Remeasurement is required if day-to-day operations of the subsidiary are dependent on the economic environment of the parent (and the parent's currency), and the changes in the foreign entity's individual assets and liabilities directly impact the cash flows of the parent entity in the parent's currency, or if the subsidiary operates in a highly-inflationary economy. Remeasurement involves the following four steps:

1. Nonmonetary assets and liabilities are restated at historical exchange rates (i.e., the exchange rates in effect when the nonmonetary assets and liabilities were initially recognized).

2. Revenues and expenses relating to those nonmonetary net assets (e.g., cost of goods sold, depreciation and amortization expense, deferred revenues) are also translated at the same historical exchange rates used for the asset to which they relate.

3. Monetary assets and liabilities are restated at current exchange rates (i.e., the exchange rate in effect on the statement date).

4. The net gain or loss from the remeasurement process is reported in net income rather than in other comprehensive income.

Once the subsidiary's financial statements have been translated into the $US, the consolidation process proceeds as usual. Following is a comprehensive example to illustrate these two approaches using the same fact set.

COMPREHENSIVE REVIEW

Our company formed a subsidiary company operating in Germany and capitalized it with 900,000 Euros (€) when the exchange rate to the $US was €1:$0.75. Since its inception, our subsidiary company has performed well, recording net income of €840,000 on sales of €6,000,000 in the most recent year. Cumulative retained earnings now stand at €3,906,000. Please find below the most recent financial information on our subsidiary. Relevant exchange rates are as follows:

BOY rate.	$1.22
EOY rate.	$1.31
Avg. rate.	$1.27
Dividend rate	$1.24
Historical rates:	
Land.	$0.83
Building	$0.83
Equipment	$0.83
Common stock and APIC.	$0.75

Required

Complete the table to translate and remeasure our subsidiary's financial statements. Assume a BOY Retained Earnings balance of $2,625,000 for the current rate method and $2,866,992 for remeasurement.

	Subsidiary (in €)	Current Rate		Remeasurement	
		Translation Rate	Subsidiary (in $)	Translation Rate	Subsidiary (in $)
Beginning inventory	1,490,000				
Purchases.	3,898,000				
Ending inventory.	(1,788,000)				
Cost of goods sold.	3,600,000				
Land	1,307,200				
Building	2,400,000				
Accum. depreciation—building	(1,200,000)				
Equipment	1,600,000				
Accum. depreciation—equipment	(800,000)				
PPE, net	3,307,200				
Depreciation expense—building	120,000				
Depreciation expense—equipment	160,000				
Depreciation expense.	280,000				
Income statement:					
Sales.	6,000,000				
Cost of goods sold.	(3,600,000)				
Gross profit.	2,400,000				
Operating expenses	(1,280,000)				
Depreciation	(280,000)				
Remeasurement gain or loss					
Net income.	840,000				
Statement of retained earnings:					
BOY retained earnings	3,150,000				
Net income.	840,000				
Dividends	(84,000)				
EOY retained earnings	3,906,000				
Balance sheet:					
Assets					
Cash	1,707,600				
Accounts receivable.	1,392,000				
Inventory	1,788,000				
PPE, net	3,307,200				
Total assets.	8,194,800				
Liabilities and stockholders' equity					
Current liabilities.	1,017,600				
Long-term liabilities	2,371,200				
Common stock.	400,000				
APIC	500,000				
Retained earnings	3,906,000				
Cumulative translation adjustment.					
Total liabilities & equity	8,194,800				

The solution to this review problem can be found on page 568.

APPENDIX 8A: Direct Computation of Translation Adjustment and Remeasurement Gain (Loss)

Direct Computation of the Translation Adjustment

In our chapter example beginning on page 518, we compute the Cumulative Translation Adjustment as the plug figure to balance our $US-converted pre-closing trial balance. The Cumulative Translation Adjustment can also be computed directly. Understanding this direct computation may help you to better understand the nature of this account.

The Cumulative Translation Adjustment represents the amount by which the parent's net investment in its subsidiary has increased or decreased as a result of fluctuations in the relative value of the $US. The parent's net investment in its subsidiary is the Equity Investment asset on its balance sheet (i.e., in this case the Equity Investment account is equal to the subsidiary's Stockholders' Equity because the parent owns 100% of the subsidiary).

The change in the Cumulative Translation Adjustment during a given year has the following components:

1. The increase or decrease in the $US value of the *BOY* net investment.

2. The increase in the $US value of the net investment related to earnings.

3. The decrease in the $US value of the net investment related to dividends.

To illustrate, in Exhibit 8.8, the corresponding computations are as follows:

1.	BOY Net assets × (EOY − BOY Exchange rates)	€1,012,500 [d]	× $0.09/€[a]	$ 91,125
2.	Net income × (EOY − Average Exchange rates).	€ 210,000 [d]	× $0.05/€[b]	10,500
3.	Dividends × (EOY − Dividend Exchange rates)	€ (21,000)[d]	× $0.03/€[c]	(630)
				100,995
	BOY Cumulative translation adjustment			114,100
	EOY Cumulative translation adjustment			$215,095

[a] The $US value of the Euro increased during the year from $1.39 to $1.48.
[b] The difference between the EOY ($1.48) and average ($1.43) exchange rates
[c] The difference between the EOY ($1.48) exchange rate and the exchange rate on the date dividends are declared ($1.45)
[d] Per Exhibit 8.6

A detailed explanation of each component of the computation follows:

1. The balance of the parent's net investment in the subsidiary at the beginning of the year is €1,012,500 (€787,500 + €100,000 + €125,000). That investment increased in value by $91,125 as the $US weakened from $1.39:€1 to $1.48:€1. Think of this like a foreign-currency-denominated asset (e.g., Account Receivable denominated in Euros) that increases in value as the $US weakens.

2. During the year, the net investment also increased as a result of profit earned by the subsidiary. We assume that this profit was earned ratably over the year. Consequently, the increase in the $US value of this additional investment of $10,500 is equal to the profit earned (€210,000) multiplied by the difference between the exchange rate at the end of the year ($1.48:€1) and the *average* exchange rate for the year ($1.43:€1).

3. During the year, the net investment decreased as a result of dividends paid to the parent. Consequently there was €21,000 *less* net investment to increase in $US value from the date of payment through the end of the year, resulting in a *decrease* of $630 which is equal to the €21,000 of dividends paid multiplied by the difference between the exchange rate at the end of the year ($1.48:€1) and the exchange rate in effect on the *date the dividends are declared* ($1.45:€1).[12]

The Cumulative Translation Adjustment for the year ended December 31, 2016, is $100,995. This adjustment represents the increase in the Cumulative Translation Adjustment from $114,100 at December 31, 2015, to $215,095 at December 31, 2016.

---

[12] Recall that any change in the exchange rates between the date of dividend declaration and the date of dividend payment is recognized as foreign currency gain or loss in the determination of net income (i.e., the preceding component in the reconciliation).

An alternate approach, yielding the same answer, is sometimes used:

BOY Net assets @ BOY Exchange rate	€1,012,500	× $1.39/€	$1,407,375
Net income	€ 210,000	× $1.43/€	300,300
Dividends	€ (21,000)	× $1.45/€	(30,450)
			1,677,225
EOY Net assets @ EOY Exchange rate	€1,201,500	× $1.48/€	1,778,220
Translation adjustment for the year			100,995
BOY Cumulative translation adjustment			114,100
EOY Cumulative translation adjustment			$ 215,095

Direct Computation of the Remeasurement Gain or Loss

In our remeasurement example on pages 525–530, we compute the remeasurement loss as the amount needed to make debits and credits equal in the $US-converted pre-closing trial balance. The remeasurement loss or gain can also be computed directly, similar to the approach we used to directly compute the translation gain or loss. The remeasurement loss in this example results from the following:

1. The increase or decrease in the $US value of the *BOY* net monetary asset (liability)
2. The increase in the $US value of net monetary assets related to earnings
3. The decrease in the $US value of net monetary assets related to dividends

To illustrate, in Exhibit 8.12, the corresponding computations are as follows:

1.	BOY Net monetary assets × (EOY − BOY Exchange rates)	€(256,800)[d]	× $0.09/€[a] =	$(23,112)
2.	Chg. Net monetary assets × (EOY − Avg. Exchange rates)	€ 205,500 [d]	× $0.05/€[b] =	10,275
3.	Dividends × (EOY − Div. Exchange rates)	€ (21,000)[d]	× $0.03/€[c] =	(630)
	Remeasurement loss			$(13,467)

[a] The increase in the $US value of the Euro increases during the year from $1.39 to $1.48 ($0.09).

[b] The difference between the EOY ($1.48) and average ($1.43) exchange rates

[c] The difference between the EOY ($1.48) exchange rate and the exchange rate on the date dividends are declared ($1.45)

[d] Per Exhibit 8.10 and/or the table of Net Monetary Assets, just below Exhibit 8.10.

The remeasurement loss for the year has three components:

1. The balance of the net monetary assets (a liability) at the beginning of the year is €(256,800) (computed in the previous section of this chapter). That liability increased in value by $23,112 as the $US weakened from $1.39:€1 to $1.48:€1, resulting in a loss. Given that this is a net monetary liability, think of this like an account payable liability that increases in value as the $US weakens and results in a loss.

2. During the year, the net monetary liability decreased as a result of cash flow generated by the subsidiary in the amount of €205,500 (see Exhibit 8.10):

Sales	€1,500,000
Purchases	(974,500)
Operating expenses	(320,000)
	€ 205,500

We assume that this cash flow (a monetary asset) was earned ratably over the year. Consequently, the increase in the $US value of this additional monetary asset of $10,275 is equal to the increase in net monetary assets (€205,500) multiplied by the difference between the exchange rate at the end of the year ($1.48:€1) and the *average* exchange rate for the year ($1.43:€1). The increase in the $US value of this monetary asset reduces the monetary loss for the year.

3. During the year, the net monetary liability increased (monetary asset decreased) as a result of dividends paid to the parent. The remeasurement loss is equal to the increase in the net monetary liability of

€21,000 multiplied by the difference between the exchange rate at the end of the year ($1:€1.48) and the exchange rate in effect on the *date the dividends are declared* ($1:€1.45).

Thus, the remeasurement loss for the year is $(13,467) and it reduces consolidated net income for the year.

An alternate approach, yielding the same answer, is sometimes used:

Change in net monetary assets:			
Beginning net monetary assets	(256,800)	× $1.39/€ =	$ (356,952)
Sales	1,500,000	× $1.43/€ =	2,145,000
Purchases	(974,500)	× $1.43/€ =	(1,393,535)
Operating expenses	(320,000)	× $1.43/€ =	(457,600)
Dividends	(21,000)	× $1.45/€ =	(30,450)
Ending net monetary assets	(72,300)		(93,537)
		× $1.48/€ =	(107,004)
Remeasurement loss			$ (13,467)

APPENDIX 8B: Hedging the Net Investment in a Foreign Subsidiary

A parent company's net investment in a foreign subsidiary fluctuates as a result of changes in the exchange rate of the $US relative to the functional currency of the subsidiary. Parent companies can hedge the fluctuations in the net investments in foreign subsidiaries by using financial derivative instruments, like those that we discuss in Chapter 7. In this section, we provide two examples of ways in which this hedge can be accomplished and the accounting for that hedging activity.

Example #1: Use of a Forward-Exchange Contract to Hedge a Net Investment in a Foreign Subsidiary

Our U.S.-based parent company has a net investment of £50 million in a British subsidiary. The functional currency for the British subsidiary is the British pound (£). On October 1, 2015, we enter into a six-month forward exchange contract to sell £50 million at £1 = $1.70, when the spot rate is £1 = $1.72, to hedge 100 percent of the beginning book value of our net investment in the subsidiary. All changes in the fair value of the forward contract will be reported in Cumulative Translation Adjustment since (a) the notional amounts of the forward contract and the hedged item match perfectly and (b) the underlying currency of the forward matches our subsidiary's functional currency. Assume the following:

Date	Exchange Rates Spot	Forward	Change in Fair Value of Forward Contract for the Period (ignore discounting)	Change in Fair Value of Net Investment in Foreign Subsidiary Attributable to Change in Spot Rates Gain (Loss)
October 1, 2015	£1 = $1.72	£1 = $1.70		
December 31, 2015	£1 = $1.65	£1 = $1.63	3,500,000*	(3,500,000)
March 31, 2016	£1 = $1.60	£1 = $1.60	1,500,000**	(2,500,000)
Cumulative total			5,000,000***	(6,000,000)

* $3,500,000 = [£50,000,000 × (1.70 − 1.63)]
**$1,500,000 = [£50,000,000 × (1.63 − 1.60)]
*** $5,000,000 = [£50,000,000 × (1.70 − 1.60)]

The effects of changes in exchange rates are reflected in the parent's Cumulative Translation Adjustment related to the subsidiary. As we discuss in Chapter 7, companies must always record derivatives at fair value at every balance sheet date; the forward contract in this example is no exception. The effective portion of the change in the fair value of the forward contract is recorded in Other Comprehensive Income in the same manner as the Translation Adjustment is recorded. Because it is a hedge, we would expect for the change in fair value of the derivative to offset (and reduce) the unhedged Cumulative Translation Adjustment.

Following are the required journal entries to reflect this hedge:

Date	Journal Entries		
October 1, 2015	(No entry is required, since the FC forward rate equals the contract rate)		
December 31, 2015	Forward contract receivable.	3,500,000	
	Cumulative translation adjustment		3,500,000
	(to record the change in the fair value of the forward contract in the Cumulative Translation Adjustment account)		
	Cumulative translation adjustment.	3,500,000	
	Net investment in foreign subsidiary		3,500,000
	(to record the translation of the company's net investment in the foreign subsidiary. The amount represents the net impact of translating the British subsidiary's assets and liabilities)		
March 31, 2016	Forward contract receivable.	1,500,000	
	Cumulative translation adjustment		1,500,000
	(to record the change in the fair value of the forward contract in the Cumulative Translation Adjustment account)		
March 31, 2016	Cumulative translation adjustment.	2,500,000	
	Net investment in foreign subsidiary		2,500,000
	(to record the translation of the company's net investment in the foreign subsidiary)		
	Cash	5,000,000	
	Forward contract receivable		5,000,000
	(to record the cash settlement of the gain on the forward contract)		

Example #2: Use of a Non-Derivative to Hedge a Net Investment in a Foreign Subsidiary

Our U.S.-based parent company has a net investment of R$50 million in a Brazilian subsidiary. The functional currency for the foreign subsidiary is the Brazilian real (R$). On January 1, 2015, we have a R$50 million foreign-currency-denominated loan payable that we wish to designate as a hedge of its net investment in the foreign subsidiary. Assume the following:

Date	Spot Rates
January 1, 2015	R$1: $0.625
December 31, 2015	R$1: $0.595

For simplicity's sake, also assume that the subsidiary has no income statement activity during the year.

The net assets of the Brazilian subsidiary are translated into U.S. dollars at the current exchange rate at each balance-sheet date. The effect of changes in exchange rates is reflected in the Cumulative Translation Adjustment, which is a component of Other Comprehensive Income. When a non-derivative instrument (e.g. the loan) is designated as a hedge of the foreign currency exposure of a net investment in a foreign operation, the change in the carrying value of the non-derivative attributable to the change in spot rates is recorded in Other Comprehensive Income in the same manner as the change in the Cumulative Translation Adjustment is recorded. As in this case, the notional amount of the loan payable is equal to the notional amount of the beginning balance of the net investment being designated, no ineffectiveness may be assumed and the entire change in fair value of the loan payable attributable to the change in spot rates will be recorded in the Cumulative Translation Adjustment for the reporting period.

The relevant journal entries to reflect the use of our loan to hedge our net investment in the foreign subsidiary are as follows:

Date	Journal Entries		
January	No entry required		
December	Loan payable	1,500,000	
	Cumulative translation adjustment		1,500,000
	(to record the change in carrying value attributed to		
	the foreign currency gain in the cumulative-translation-		
	adjustment account—(BRL 50,000,000 × [$0.625 − $0.595]) =		
	$1,500,000)		
	Cumulative translation adjustment.	1,500,000	
	Net investment in foreign subsidiary		1,500,000
	(to record the translation of the company's net investment in		
	the foreign subsidiary. The amount represents the net impact		
	of translating the foreign subsidiary's assets and liabilities)		

Superscript $^{A, (B)}$ denotes assignments based on Appendix 8A (B).

QUESTIONS

1. Define the term *foreign currency translation*. (*Hint:* See the Glossary to FASB ASC 830.)

   FASB ASC Research

2. Define the term *functional currency*. Can a company have more than one functional currency? (*Hint:* See the Glossary to FASB ASC 830.)

   FASB ASC Research

3. What are the general factors that we should consider in determining the functional currency of a foreign subsidiary? (*Hint:* See the Glossary to FASB ASC 830.)

   FASB ASC Research

4. Why does FASB ASC 830 allow for the use of average exchange rates in the translation of the income statement under the current rate approach and the remeasurement of revenues and expenses (other than those relating to assets remeasured at historical exchange rates) in the remeasurement process? (*Hint:* See FASB ASC 830-10-55-10.)

   FASB ASC Research

5. FASB ASC 830-10-45-7 requires consistency in the functional currency defined for a given entity, but does allow for a change in the defined functional currency if a change in circumstances warrants such a change. In the event of a change in the functional currency, is the company required to restate previously issued financial statements in terms of the new functional currency? (*Hint:* See FASB ASC 830-10-45-7.)

   FASB ASC Research

6. FASB ASC 830-10-45-17 and -18 discuss the recognition of gains and losses as a result of the remeasurement process. Are remeasurement gains and losses recognized for all assets and liabilities? If not, for what balance sheet accounts would remeasurement gains and losses be recognized?

   FASB ASC Research

7. Are remeasurement gains and losses considered to be *extraordinary items*? (*Hint:* See FASB ASC 830-10-45-19.)

   FASB ASC Research

8. If the parent company sells a foreign subsidiary, how is the Cumulative Translation Adjustment account relating to that subsidiary accounted for in recording the sale? (*Hint:* See FASB ASC 830-30-40-1.)

   FASB ASC Research

9. The translation of the financial statements of subsidiaries will typically result in translation adjustments. Are these translation adjustments reported in the determination of net income? (*Hint:* See FASB ASC 830-30-45-12.)

   FASB ASC Research

10. Is the balance of a noncontrolling interest equity account affected by translation adjustments for a less-than-wholly owned subsidiary? (*Hint:* See FASB ASC 830-230-45-17.)

11. Companies are required to provide a disclosure relating to the analysis of changes in the Cumulative Translation Adjustment account. What options are available to companies for the manner in which such disclosure can be provided? (*Hint:* See FASB ASC 830-30-45-18.)

Assignments with the 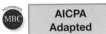 logo in the margin are available in BusinessCourse.
See the Preface of the book for details.

MULTIPLE CHOICE

LO1

**AICPA
Adapted**

12. Selection of appropriate exchange rate for translation
A foreign subsidiary's functional currency is its local currency, which has not experienced significant inflation. The weighted average exchange rate for the current year would be the appropriate exchange rate for translating:

	Salaries expense	Sales to external customers
a.	Yes	Yes
b.	Yes	No
c.	No	Yes
d.	No	No

LO1

**AICPA
Adapted**

13. Selection of appropriate exchange rate for translation
Gordon Ltd., a 100% owned British subsidiary of a U.S. parent company, reports its financial statements in local currency, the British pound. A local newspaper published the following U.S. exchange rates to the British pound at year end:

Current rate	$1.50
Historical rate (acquisition).	1.70
Average rate.	1.55
Inventory (FIFO)	1.60

Which currency rate should Gordon use to convert its income statement to U.S. dollars at year end?
a. $1.50
b. $1.55
c. $1.60
d. $1.70

LO1

**AICPA
Adapted**

14. Definition of functional currency
The functional currency is the currency:
a. Of the country in which the parent is located
b. Of the county in which the subsidiary is located
c. In which the subsidiary maintains its accounting records
d. Of the environment in which a subsidiary primarily generates and expends cash

LO2

**AICPA
Adapted**

15. Reporting of remeasurement gains and losses
Gains and losses from remeasuring a foreign subsidiary's financial statements should be reported:
a. In current income
b. In other comprehensive income
c. As an extraordinary item, net of income taxes
d. As a prior period adjustment

16. **Selection of appropriate exchange rate for remeasurement**
    An item that should be remeasured using the historical exchange rate is:

    a.   Accounts receivable
    b.   Long-term notes payable
    c.   Cash
    d.   Prepaid expenses

17. **Reporting of translation and remeasurement gains and losses**
    One of our subsidiary companies maintains its accounting records in Euros and designates the British Pound as its functional currency. Your computations yield a translation gain of $5,000 and a remeasurement loss of $7,000. What amount should you report as a gain or loss in your income statement?

    a. $0
    b. $5,000
    c.   ($7,000)
    d.   ($2,000)

18. **Effects of translation adjustments on income and cash flow**
    Assume that your subsidiary operated independently of the parent company. Which if the following is true?

	Translation adjustments have an immediate effect on cash flows	Translation adjustments should be reflected in earnings
a.	Yes	No
b.	Yes	Yes
c.	No	No
d.	No	Yes

19. **Cumulative translation adjustment account**
    During the translation process, the current year change to the cumulative translation adjustment is a function of which of the following relationships of the subsidiary?

    a.   Its operating cash flows
    b.   Its monetary assets minus monetary liabilities
    c.   Its current assets minus current liabilities
    d.   Its total assets minus total liabilities

20. **Reporting of translation gains and losses**
    If a subsidiary's financial statements are translated, the translation gain (loss) is related to changes in:

    a.   The subsidiary's operating profit
    b.   The subsidiary's net monetary assets
    c.   The subsidiary's stockholders' equity
    d.   The subsidiary's working capital

21. **Cumulative translation adjustment account**
    Which of the following statements is true regarding the cumulative translation adjustment?

    a.   Changes in the cumulative translation adjustment are reported in the income statement at each statement date.
    b.   The cumulative translation adjustment account affects the amount of gain or loss reported upon the sale of a foreign subsidiary.
    c.   The cumulative translation adjustment account is reported in accumulated other comprehensive income and is transferred into reported earnings when the transaction to which it relates affects reported earnings.
    d.   Changes in the cumulative translation adjustment account are added back in the computation of net cash flow from operating activities since they are non-cash income or expense.

EXERCISES

LO1 **22.** **Translation of financial statements**

Assume that your company owns a subsidiary operating in France. The subsidiary conducts most of its business activities in the European Economic Union and maintains its books in the Euro as its functional currency. Following are the subsidiary's financial statements (in €) for the most recent year:

Income statement:

Sales.............	€1,200,000
Cost of goods sold...	(720,000)
Gross profit........	480,000
Operating expenses..	(312,000)
Net income........	€ 168,000

Statement of retained earnings:

BOY ret. earnings....	€ 630,000
Net income........	168,000
Dividends	(16,800)
EOY ret. earnings....	€ 781,200

Balance sheet:

Assets

Cash..................	€ 341,520
Accounts receivable.......	278,400
Inventory................	357,600
Property, plant, and equipment (PPE), net	661,440
Total assets.............	€1,638,960

Liabilities and stockholders' equity

Curr. liabilities............	€ 203,520
L-T liabilities.............	474,240
Common stock...........	80,000
APIC..................	100,000
Ret. earnings	781,200
Total liabilities and equity ...	€1,638,960

Statement of cash flows:

Net income......................	€168,000
Change in accounts receivable	(46,400)
Change in inventories.............	(59,600)
Change in current liabilities	33,920
Net cash from operating activities ...	95,920
Change in PPE, net	(61,440)
Net cash from investing activities....	(61,440)
Change in long-term debt	79,040
Dividends	(16,800)
Net cash from financing activities ...	62,240
Net change in cash...............	96,720
Beginning cash..................	244,800
Ending cash	€341,520

The relevant exchange rates ($:€1) are as follows:

BOY rate...	$1.09
EOY rate...	$1.14
Avg. rate...	$1.11
PPE purchase date rate	$1.12
LTD borrowing date rate.......................................	$1.12
Dividend rate	$1.13
Historical rate (common stock and APIC)	$0.90

a. Translate the subsidiary's income statement, statement of retained earnings, balance sheet, and statement of cash flows into $US (assume that the BOY Retained Earnings is $492,099).

b.[A] Compute the ending Cumulative Translation Adjustment directly, assuming a BOY balance of $228,801.

23. Translation of financial statements

Assume that your company owns a subsidiary operating in Canada. The subsidiary maintains its books in the Canadian Dollar (CAD) as its functional currency. Following are the subsidiary's financial statements (in CAD) for the most recent year:

Income statement:	(in CAD)
Sales.................	1,350,000
Cost of goods sold........	(810,000)
Gross profit..............	540,000
Operating expenses.......	(351,000)
Net income..............	189,000

Statement of retained earnings:	
BOY retained earnings.....	708,750
Net income..............	189,000
Dividends	(18,900)
Ending retained earnings ...	878,850

Balance sheet:	(in CAD)
Assets	
Cash...................	384,210
Accounts receivable.......	313,200
Inventory................	402,300
Property, plant, and equipment (PPE), net	744,120
Total assets.............	1,843,830
Liabilities and stockholders' equity	
Current liabilities..........	228,960
Long-term liabilities	533,520
Common stock...........	90,000
APIC...................	112,500
Retained earnings	878,850
Total liabilities and equity ...	1,843,830

Statement of cash flows:	(in CAD)
Net income...........................	189,000
Change in accounts receivable	(52,500)
Change in inventories.................	(67,050)
Change in current liabilities	38,160
Net cash from operating activities	107,910
Change in PPE, net	(69,120)
Net cash from investing activities........	(69,120)
Change in long-term debt	88,920
Dividends	(18,900)
Net cash from financing activities	70,020
Net change in cash...................	108,810
Beginning cash......................	275,400
Ending cash	384,210

The relevant exchange rates ($:CAD) are as follows:

BOY rate...	$0.70
EOY rate...	$0.76
Avg. rate...	$0.73
PPE purchase date rate	$0.74
LTD borrowing date rate.......................................	$0.74
Dividend rate	$0.75
Historical rate (common stock and APIC)	$0.60

a. Translate the subsidiary's income statement, statement of retained earnings, balance sheet, and statement of cash flows into $US (assume that the BOY Retained Earnings is $553,612).

b.[A] Compute the ending Cumulative Translation Adjustment directly, assuming a BOY balance of $(37,237).

LO1 24. **Translation of financial statements**

Assume that your company owns a subsidiary operating in Brazil. The subsidiary maintains its books in the Brazilian real (BRL) as its functional currency. Following are the subsidiary's financial statements (in BRL) for the most recent year:

(in BRL)		(in BRL)		(in BRL)	
Income statement:		**Balance sheet:**		**Statement of cash flows:**	
Sales.	3,750,000	Assets		Net income.	525,000
Cost of goods sold.	(2,250,000)	Cash.	1,067,250	Change in accounts receivable	(145,000)
Gross profit.	1,500,000	Accounts receivable.	870,000	Change in inventories.	(186,250)
Operating expenses.	(975,000)	Inventory.	1,117,500	Change in current liabilities	106,000
Net income.	525,000	Property, plant, and		Net cash from operating activities	299,750
		equipment (PPE), net	2,067,000		
		Total assets.	5,121,750		
Statement of retained earnings:				Change in PPE, net	(192,000)
BOY retained earnings.	1,968,750	Liabilities and stockholders' equity		Net cash from investing activities.	(192,000)
Net income.	525,000	Current liabilities.	636,000		
Dividends.	(52,500)	Long-term liabilities	1,482,000	Change in long-term debt	247,000
EOY retained earnings.	2,441,250	Common stock.	250,000	Dividends.	(52,500)
		APIC.	312,500	Net cash from financing activities	194,500
		Retained earnings	2,441,250		
		Total liabilities and equity.	5,121,750	Net change in cash.	302,250
				Beginning cash.	765,000
				Ending cash	1,067,250

The relevant exchange rates for the $US value of the Brazilian real (BRL) are as follows:

BOY rate.	$0.22
EOY rate.	$0.29
Avg. rate.	$0.25
PPE purchase date rate	$0.26
LTD borrowing date rate.	$0.26
Dividend rate	$0.27
Historical rate (common stock and APIC)	$0.10

a. Translate the subsidiary's income statement, statement of retained earnings, balance sheet, and statement of cash flows into $US (assume that the BOY Retained Earnings is $1,537,810).

b.[A] Compute the ending Cumulative Translation Adjustment directly, assuming a BOY balance of $(1,037,185).

25. **Translation of financial statements**

    Assume that your company owns a subsidiary operating in Great Britain. The subsidiary maintains its books in the British pound (GBP) as its functional currency. Following are the subsidiary's financial statements (in GBP) for the most recent year:

	(in GBP)		**(in GBP)**		**(in GBP)**
Income statement:		**Balance sheet:**		**Statement of cash flows:**	
Sales...................	9,750,000	Assets		Net income......................	1,365,000
Cost of goods sold.........	(5,850,000)	Cash....................	2,774,850	Change in accounts receivable.......	(377,000)
Gross profit..............	3,900,000	Accounts receivable........	2,262,000	Change in inventories..............	(484,250)
Operating expenses........	(2,535,000)	Inventory.................	2,905,500	Change in current liabilities..........	275,600
Net income..............	1,365,000	Property, plant, and		Net cash from operating activities.....	779,350
		equipment (PPE), net	5,374,200		
		Total assets..............	13,316,550		
Statement of retained earnings:				Change in PPE, net	(499,200)
BOY retained earnings......	5,118,750	Liabilities and stockholders' equity		Net cash from investing activities......	(499,200)
Net income..............	1,365,000	Current liabilities...........	1,635,600		
Dividends	(136,500)	Long-term liabilities	3,853,200	Change in long-term debt	642,200
Ending retained earnings	6,347,250	Common stock............	650,000	Dividends	(136,500)
		APIC....................	812,500	Net cash from financing activities	505,700
		Retained earnings	6,347,250		
		Total liabilities and equity	13,316,550	Net change in cash................	785,850
				Beginning cash...................	1,989,000
				Ending cash	2,774,850

The relevant exchange rates for the $US value of the British pound (GBP) are as follows:

BOY rate.	$1.50
EOY rate.	$1.57
Avg. rate	$1.53
PPE purchase date rate	$1.54
LTD borrowing date rate.	$1.54
Dividend rate	$1.55
Historical rate (common stock and APIC)	$0.60

a. Translate the subsidiary's income statement, statement of retained earnings, balance sheet, and statement of cash flows into $US (assume that the BOY Retained Earnings is $3,998,306).

b.[A] Compute the ending Cumulative Translation Adjustment directly, assuming a BOY balance of $4,996,069.

LO1 **26. Translation of financial statements (2 years)**

Assume that your company owns a subsidiary operating in Australia. The subsidiary maintains its books in the Australian Dollar (AUD) as its functional currency. Following are the subsidiary's financial statements (in AUD) for the prior and most recent years:

	Prior Year (in AUD)	Current Year (in AUD)
Income statement:		
Sales.	7,875,000	9,450,000
Cost of goods sold.	(4,725,000)	(5,670,000)
Gross profit.	3,150,000	3,780,000
Operating expenses.	(2,047,500)	(2,457,000)
Net income.	1,102,500	1,323,000
Statement of retained earnings:		
BOY retained earnings.	3,969,000	4,961,250
Net income.	1,102,500	1,323,000
Dividends	(110,250)	(132,300)
Ending retained earnings	4,961,250	6,151,950
Balance sheet:		
Assets		
Cash.	1,002,960	2,689,470
Accounts receivable.	1,827,000	2,192,400
Inventory	2,346,750	2,816,100
Property, plant, and equipment (PPE), net.	5,649,840	5,208,840
Total assets.	10,826,550	12,906,810
Liabilities and stockholders' equity		
Current liabilities.	1,335,600	1,602,720
Long-term liabilities	3,112,200	3,734,640
Common stock.	630,000	630,000
APIC.	787,500	787,500
Retained earnings	4,961,250	6,151,950
Total liabilities and equity	10,826,550	12,906,810

	Current Year (in AUD)
Statement of cash flows:	
Net income.	1,323,000
Change in accounts receivable	(365,400)
Change in inventories.	(469,350)
Change in current liabilities	267,120
Net cash flows from operating activities	755,370
Change in PPE, net	441,000
Net cash flows from investing activities.	441,000
Change in long-term debt	622,440
Dividends	(132,300)
Net cash flows from financing activities.	490,140
Net change in cash.	1,686,510
Beginning cash.	1,002,960
Ending cash	2,689,470

The relevant exchange rates for the $US value of the Australian Dollar (AUD) are as follows:

	Prior Year	Current Year
BOY rate..	$0.97	$0.86
EOY rate..	$0.86	$0.73
Avg. rate..	$0.91	$0.79
PPE purchase date rate		$0.75
LTD borrowing date rate..............................		$0.75
Dividend rate	$0.87	$0.74
Historical rate (common stock and APIC)	$1.05	$1.05

a.   Translate the subsidiary's income statement, statement of retained earnings, balance sheet, and statement of cash flows into $US for both years (assume that the BOY Retained Earnings is $803,250 at the beginning of the *prior year*).

b.^A   Compute the ending Cumulative Translation Adjustment directly for the current year.

27. **Translation of financial statements (2 years)**

Assume that your company owns a subsidiary operating in Germany. The subsidiary conducts most of its business activities in the European Economic Union and maintains its books in the Euro as its functional currency. Following are the subsidiary's financial statements (in €) for the prior and most recent years:

	Prior Year	Current Year
Income statement:		
Sales..	€4,625,000	€5,550,000
Cost of goods sold..	(2,775,000)	(3,330,000)
Gross profit..	1,850,000	2,220,000
Operating expenses......................................	(1,202,500)	(1,443,000)
Net income...	€ 647,500	€ 777,000
Statement of retained earnings:		
BOY retained earnings...................................	€2,331,000	€2,913,750
Net income...	647,500	777,000
Dividends..	(64,750)	(77,700)
Ending retained earnings................................	€2,913,750	€3,613,050
Balance sheet:		
Assets		
Cash..	€ 589,040	€1,579,530
Accounts receivable......................................	1,073,000	1,287,600
Inventory	1,378,250	1,653,900
Property, plant, and equipment (PPE), net...........	3,318,160	3,059,160
Total assets..	€6,358,450	€7,580,190
Liabilities and stockholders' equity		
Current liabilities...	€ 784,400	€ 941,280
Long-term liabilities	1,827,800	2,193,360
Common stock...	370,000	370,000
APIC..	462,500	462,500
Retained earnings	2,913,750	3,613,050
Total liabilities and equity..............................	€6,358,450	€7,580,190

	Current Year
Statement of cash flows:	
Net income.	€ 777,000
Change in accounts receivable	(214,600)
Change in inventories.	(275,650)
Change in current liabilities	156,880
Net cash flows from operating activities	443,630
Change in PPE, net	259,000
Net cash flows from investing activities.	259,000
Change in long-term debt	365,560
Dividends	(77,700)
Net cash flows from financing activities. . . .	287,860
Net change in cash.	990,490
Beginning cash.	589,040
Ending cash	€1,579,530

The relevant exchange rates for the $US value of the Euro (€) are as follows:

	Prior Year	Current Year
BOY rate.	$1.23	$1.15
EOY rate.	$1.15	$1.09
Avg. rate	$1.19	$1.12
PPE purchase date rate		$1.11
LTD borrowing date rate.		$1.11
Dividend rate	$1.16	$1.10
Historical rate (common stock and APIC)	$1.35	$1.35

a. Translate the subsidiary's income statement, statement of retained earnings, balance sheet, and statement of cash flows into $US for both years (assume that the BOY Retained Earnings for the *prior year* is $803,250).

b.[A] Compute the ending Cumulative Translation Adjustment directly for the current year.

LO2   28. Remeasurement of financial statements

Assume that your company owns a subsidiary operating in Australia. The subsidiary has adopted the Australian Dollar (AUD) as its functional currency. Your parent company operates this subsidiary like a division or a branch office, making all of its operating decisions, including pricing of its products. You conclude, therefore, that the functional currency of this subsidiary is the $US and that its financial statements must be remeasured prior to consolidation. Following are the subsidiary's financial statements (in AUD) for the most recent year:

	(in AUD)
Beginning inventory	1,192,000
Purchases.	3,118,400
Ending inventory.	(1,430,400)
Cost of goods sold.	2,880,000
Land.	1,045,760
Building	1,920,000
Accum. deprec.—building	(960,000)
Equipment	1,280,000
Accum. deprec.—equipment	(640,000)
Property, plant, and equipment (PPE), net. . . .	2,645,760
Depreciation expense—building	96,000
Depreciation expense—equipment . . .	128,000
Depreciation expense.	224,000

	(in AUD)
Income statement:	
Sales.	4,800,000
Cost of goods sold.	(2,880,000)
Gross profit.	1,920,000
Operating expenses	(1,024,000)
Depreciation	(224,000)
Net income.	672,000
Statement of retained earnings:	
BOY retained earnings	2,520,000
Net income	672,000
Dividends	(67,200)
Ending retained earnings	3,124,800
Balance sheet:	
Assets	
Cash	1,366,080
Accounts receivable.	1,113,600
Inventory	1,430,400
Property, plant, and equipment (PPE), net	2,645,760
Total assets.	6,555,840
Liabilities and stockholders' equity	
Current liabilities.	814,080
Long-term liabilities	1,896,960
Common stock.	320,000
APIC	400,000
Retained earnings	3,124,800
Total liabilities and equity	6,555,840

The relevant exchange rates for the $US value of the Australian Dollar (AUD) are as follows:

BOY rate.	$0.86
EOY rate.	$0.73
Avg. rate	$0.79
Dividend rate	$0.74
Historical rates:	
Beginning inventory	$0.86
Land	$0.75
Building	$0.75
Equipment	$0.75
Historical rate (common stock and APIC)	$1.05

a. Remeasure the subsidiary's income statement, statement of retained earnings, and balance sheet into $US for the current year (assume that the BOY Retained Earnings is $1,714,726).

b.[A] Compute the remeasurement gain or loss directly assuming BOY net monetary assets of AUD(821,760), a net monetary liability.

LO2

29. Remeasurement of financial statements

Assume that your company owns a subsidiary operating in Great Britain. The subsidiary has adopted the British pound (GBP) as its functional currency. Your parent company operates this subsidiary like a division or a branch office, making all of its operating decisions, including pricing of its products. You conclude, therefore, that the functional currency of this subsidiary is the $US and that its financial statements must be remeasured prior to consolidation. Following are the subsidiary's financial statements (in GBP) for the most recent year:

	(in GBP)
Beginning inventory	670,500
Purchases	1,754,100
Ending inventory	(804,600)
Cost of goods sold	1,620,000
Land	588,240
Building	1,080,000
Accum. deprec.—building	(540,000)
Equipment	720,000
Accum. deprec.—equipment	(360,000)
Property, plant, and equipment (PPE), net	1,488,240
Depreciation expense—building	54,000
Depreciation expense—equipment	72,000
Depreciation expense	126,000

	(in GBP)
Income statement:	
Sales	2,700,000
Cost of goods sold	(1,620,000)
Gross profit	1,080,000
Operating expenses	(576,000)
Depreciation	(126,000)
Net income	378,000
Statement of retained earnings:	
BOY retained earnings	1,417,500
Net income	378,000
Dividends	(37,800)
Ending retained earnings	1,757,700
Balance sheet:	
Assets	
Cash	768,420
Accounts receivable	626,400
Inventory	804,600
Property, plant, and equipment (PPE), net	1,488,240
Total assets	3,687,660
Liabilities and stockholders' equity	
Current liabilities	457,920
Long-term liabilities	1,067,040
Common stock	180,000
APIC	225,000
Retained earnings	1,757,700
Total liabilities and equity	3,687,660

The relevant exchange rates for the $US value of the British pound (GBP) are as follows:

BOY rate.	$1.50
EOY rate.	$1.57
Avg. rate.	$1.53
Dividend rate	$1.54
Historical rates:	
Beginning inventory	$1.50
Land.	$1.54
Building	$1.54
Equipment	$0.54
Historical rate (common stock and APIC)	$0.60

a. Remeasure the subsidiary's income statement, statement of retained earnings, and balance sheet into $US for the current year (assume that the BOY Retained Earnings is $2,555,320).

b.[A] Compute the remeasurement gain or loss directly assuming BOY net monetary assets of GBP(462,240), a net monetary liability.

30. **Remeasurement of financial statements**

Assume that your company owns a subsidiary operating in Canada. The subsidiary has adopted the Canadian Dollar (CAD) as its functional currency. Your parent company operates this subsidiary like a division or a branch office, making all of its operating decisions, including pricing of its products. You conclude, therefore, that the functional currency of this subsidiary is the $US and that its financial statements must be remeasured prior to consolidation. Following are the subsidiary's financial statements (in CAD) for the most recent year:

	(in CAD)
Beginning inventory	2,346,750
Purchases.	6,139,350
Ending inventory.	(2,816,100)
Cost of goods sold.	5,670,000
Land.	2,058,840
Building	3,780,000
Accum. deprec.—building	(1,890,000)
Equipment	2,520,000
Accum. deprec.—equipment	(1,260,000)
Property, plant, and equipment (PPE), net.	5,208,840
Depreciation expense—building	189,000
Depreciation expense—equipment	252,000
Depreciation expense.	441,000

	(in CAD)
Income statement:	
Sales.	9,450,000
Cost of goods sold.	(5,670,000)
Gross profit.	3,780,000
Operating expenses.	(2,016,000)
Depreciation.	(441,000)
Net income.	1,323,000
Statement of retained earnings:	
BOY retained earnings.	4,961,250
Net income.	1,323,000
Dividends.	(132,300)
Ending retained earnings.	6,151,950

	(in CAD)
Balance sheet:	
Assets	
Cash	2,689,470
Accounts receivable	2,192,400
Inventory	2,816,100
Property, plant, and equipment (PPE), net	5,208,840
Total assets	12,906,810
Liabilities and stockholders' equity	
Current liabilities	1,602,720
Long-term liabilities	3,734,640
Common stock	630,000
APIC	787,500
Retained earnings	6,151,950
Total liabilities and equity	12,906,810

The relevant exchange rates for the $US value of the Canadian Dollar (CAD) are as follows:

BOY rate	$0.70
EOY rate	$0.76
Avg. rate	$0.73
Dividend rate	$0.75
Historical rates:	
Beginning inventory	$0.70
Land	$0.74
Building	$0.74
Equipment	$0.74
Historical rate (Common stock and APIC)	$0.60

a. Remeasure the subsidiary's income statement, statement of retained earnings, and balance sheet into $US for the current year (assume that the BOY Retained Earnings is $3,840,619).

b.[A] Compute the remeasurement gain or loss directly assuming BOY net monetary assets of CAD(1,617,840), a net monetary liability.

PROBLEMS

LO1, 3

31. Translation of financial statements and consolidation of a foreign subsidiary (no amortization of AAP)

Assume that your company owns a subsidiary operating in Great Britain. The subsidiary maintains its books in the British pound (GBP) as its functional currency. Following are the subsidiary's financial statements (in GBP) for the most recent year:

(in GBP)			(in GBP)			(in GBP)	
Income statement:			**Balance sheet:**			**Statement of cash flows:**	
Sales................	2,730,000		Assets			Net income...........	382,200
Cost of goods sold......	(1,638,000)		Cash.................	776,958		Change in accounts receivable	(105,560)
Gross profit...........	1,092,000		Accounts receivable........	633,360		Change in inventories..............	(135,590)
Operating expenses.....	(709,800)		Inventory................	813,540		Change in current liabilities	77,168
Net income...........	382,200		Property, plant, and			Net cash from operating activities	218,218
			equipment (PPE), net	1,504,776			
			Total assets...............	3,728,634			
Statement of retained earnings:						Change in PPE, net	(139,776)
BOY Ret. earnings	1,433,250		Liabilities and stockholders' equity			Net cash from investing activities......	(139,776)
Net income............	382,200		Current liabilities...........	463,008			
Dividends	(38,220)		Long-term liabilities	1,078,896		Change in long-term debt	179,816
EOY Ret. earnings	1,777,230		Common stock.............	182,000		Dividends	(38,220)
			APIC....................	227,500		Net cash from financing activities	141,596
			Retained earnings	1,777,230			
			Total liabilities and equity.....	3,728,634		Net change in cash................	220,038
						Beginning cash...................	556,920
						Ending cash	776,958

The relevant exchange rates for the $US value of the British pound (GBP) are as follows:

BOY rate..	$1.50
EOY rate..	$1.57
Avg. rate..	$1.53
PPE purchase date rate	$1.54
LTD borrowing date rate...	$1.54
Dividend rate	$1.55
Historical rate (Common stock and APIC)............................	$0.60

a.   Translate the subsidiary's income statement, statement of retained earnings, balance sheet, and statement of cash flows from British pounds (GBP) into $US (assume that the BOY Retained Earnings for the subsidiary is $2,535,897).

b.[A]   Compute the ending Cumulative Translation Adjustment directly, assuming a BOY balance of $(17,474). What journal entry did the parent company make as a result of this computation?

c.   Following are selected financial statement accounts for the parent:

Income statement:		**Balance sheet:**	
Sales......................................	$11,973,000	Assets	
Cost of goods sold........................	(8,381,100)	Cash.....................................	$ 1,255,795
Gross profit...............................	3,591,900	Accounts receivable........................	1,532,544
Equity income............................	584,766	Inventory.................................	2,322,762
Operating expenses.......................	(2,274,870)	Equity investment	3,747,165
Net income...............................	$1,901,796	Property, plant, and equipment (PPE), net......	12,370,504
			$21,228,770
Statement of retained earnings:		Liabilities and stockholders' equity	
BOY retained earnings.....................	$10,311,600	Current liabilities..........................	$ 959,037
Net income...............................	1,901,796	Long-term liabilities	650,000
Dividends	(412,464)		
Ending retained earnings	$11,800,932	Common stock............................	1,359,397
		APIC....................................	6,319,361
Statement of accum. comp. income:		Retained earnings	11,800,932
BOY cumulative translation adjustment	$ (17,474)	Cumulative translation adjustment...........	140,043
Current-year translation gain (loss)	157,517		$21,228,770
EOY cumulative translation adjustment..........	$ 140,043		

Assume the following information: The purchase price for the subsidiary included an AAP asset relating to Land that the parent estimated was worth GBP200,000 more than its book value on the subsidiary's balance sheet. Confirm the balance of the Equity Investment account of $3,747,165 on the parent's balance sheet.

d. Using your translated subsidiary financial statements from *Part a* and the parent's financial data provided in *Part c*, prepare the consolidation spreadsheet for the year.

LO1, 3

32. Translation of financial statements and consolidation of a foreign subsidiary (no amortization of AAP)

Assume that, ten years ago, your company acquired a subsidiary operating in Ireland. The subsidiary maintains its books in the Euro (€) as its functional currency. Following are the subsidiary's financial statements (in €) for the most recent year:

Income statement:

Sales	€4,410,000
Cost of goods sold	(2,646,000)
Gross profit	1,764,000
Operating expenses	(1,146,600)
Net income	€ 617,400

Statement of retained earnings:

BOY ret. earnings	€2,315,250
Net income	617,400
Dividends	(61,740)
EOY ret. earnings	€2,870,910

Balance sheet:

Assets
Cash	€1,255,086
Accounts receivable	1,023,120
Inventory	1,314,180
Property, plant, and equipment (PPE), net	2,430,792
Total assets	€6,023,178

Liabilities and stockholders' equity
Current liabilities	€ 747,936
Long-term liabilities	1,742,832
Common stock	294,000
APIC	367,500
Retained earnings	2,870,910
Total liabilities and equity	€6,023,178

Statement of cash flows:

Net income	€617,400
Change in accounts receivable	(170,520)
Change in inventories	(219,030)
Change in current liabilities	124,656
Net cash from operating activities	352,506
Change in PPE, net	(225,792)
Net cash from investing activities	(225,792)
Change in long-term debt	290,472
Dividends	(61,740)
Net cash from financing activities	228,732
Net change in cash	355,446
Beginning cash	899,640
Ending cash	€1,255,086

The relevant exchange rates for the $US value of the Euro (€) are as follows:

BOY rate	$1.09
EOY rate	$1.14
Avg. rate	$1.11
PPE purchase date rate	$1.12
LTD borrowing date rate	$1.12
Dividend rate	$1.13
Historical rate (Common stock and APIC)	$0.90

a. Translate the subsidiary's income statement, statement of retained earnings, balance sheet, and statement of cash flows into $US (assume that the BOY Retained Earnings is $4,096,449).

b.[A] Compute the ending Cumulative Translation Adjustment directly, assuming a BOY balance of $(1,447,141). What journal entry did the parent company make as a result of this computation?

c. Following are selected financial statement accounts for the parent:

Income statement:	
Sales.	$19,341,000
Cost of goods sold.	(13,538,700)
Gross profit.	5,802,300
Equity income.	685,314
Operating expenses	(3,674,790)
Net income.	$ 2,812,824

Statement of retained earnings:

BOY retained earnings	$16,657,200
Net income.	2,812,824
Dividends	(666,288)
Ending retained earnings	$18,803,736

Statement of accum. comp. income:

BOY cumulative translation adjustment.	$ (1,447,141)
Current-year translation gain (loss)	181,742
EOY cumulative translation adjustment.	$ (1,265,399)

Balance sheet:

Assets	
Cash	$ 1,961,828
Accounts receivable.	2,475,648
Inventory.	3,752,154
Equity investment.	4,368,948
Property, plant and equipment (PPE), net	19,983,121
	$32,541,699

Liabilities and stockholders' equity	
Current liabilities.	$ 1,549,214
Long-term liabilities	1,050,000
Common stock.	2,195,949
APIC	10,208,199
Retained earnings	18,803,736
Cumulative translation adjustment.	(1,265,399)
	$32,541,699

Assume the following information: The purchase price for the subsidiary included an [A] asset relating to land that the parent estimated was worth €300,000 more than its book value on the subsidiary's balance sheet. Compute the balance of the Equity Investment account of $4,368,948 on the parent's balance sheet.

d. Using your translated subsidiary financial statements from *Part a* and the parent's financial data provided in *Part c*, prepare the consolidation spreadsheet for the year.

33. **Translation of financial statements and consolidation of a foreign subsidiary (amortization of AAP)**

LO1, 3

Assume that your company owns a subsidiary operating in Brazil. The subsidiary maintains its books in the Brazilian real (BRL) as its functional currency. Following are the subsidiary's financial statements (in BRL) for the most recent year:

	(in BRL)		(in BRL)		(in BRL)
Income statement:		**Balance sheet:**		**Statement of cash flows:**	
Sales.	6,510,000	Assets		Net income.	911,400
Cost of goods sold.	(3,906,000)	Cash	1,852,746	Change in accounts receivable	(251,720)
Gross profit.	2,604,000	Accounts receivable	1,510,320	Change in inventories.	(323,330)
Operating expenses	(1,692,600)	Inventory.	1,939,980	Change in current liabilities	184,016
Net income.	911,400	Property, plant, and		Net cash from operating activities	520,366
		equipment (PPE), net	3,588,312		
		Total assets.	8,891,358		
Statement of retained earnings:				Change in PPE, net	(333,312)
BOY ret. earnings	3,417,750	Liabilities and stockholders' equity		Net cash from investing activities.	(333,312)
Net income.	911,400	Current liabilities.	1,104,096		
Dividends	(91,140)	Long-term liabilities	2,572,752	Change in long-term debt	428,792
EOY ret. earnings	4,238,010	Common stock.	434,000	Dividends	(91,140)
		APIC	542,500	Net cash from financing activities	337,652
		Retained earnings	4,238,010		
		Total liabilities and equity . . .	8,891,358	Net change in cash.	524,706
				Beginning cash.	1,328,040
				Ending cash	1,852,746

The relevant exchange rates for the $US value of the Brazilian real (BRL) are as follows:

BOY rate	$0.22
EOY rate	$0.29
Avg. rate	$0.25
PPE purchase date rate	$0.26
LTD borrowing date rate	$0.26
Dividend rate	$0.27
Historical rate (Common stock and APIC)	$0.10

a. Translate the subsidiary's income statement, statement of retained earnings, balance sheet, and statement of cash flows into $US (assume that the BOY Retained Earnings is $649,373).

b.[A] Compute the ending Cumulative Translation Adjustment directly, assuming a BOY balance of $219,711. What journal entry did the parent company make as a result of this computation?

c. Following are selected balance sheet accounts for the parent:

Income statement:

Sales	$26,846,000
Cost of goods sold	(18,792,200)
Gross profit	8,053,800
Equity income	220,350
Operating expenses	(5,100,740)
Net income	$ 3,173,410

Statement of retained earnings:

BOY retained earnings	$21,204,636
Net income	3,173,410
Dividends	(848,185)
Ending retained earnings	$23,529,861

Statement of accum. comp. income:

BOY cumulative translation adjustment	$ 219,711
Current-year translation gain (loss)	359,931
EOY cumulative translation adjustment	$ 579,642

Balance sheet:

Assets	
Cash	$ 6,320,609
Accounts receivable	3,436,288
Inventory	5,208,124
Equity investment	1,581,807
Property, plant, and equipment (PPE), net	27,737,287
	$44,284,115

Liabilities and stockholders' equity	
Current liabilities	$ 2,150,365
Long-term liabilities	7,750,000
Common stock	1,818,885
APIC	8,455,362
Retained earnings	23,529,861
Cumulative translation adjustment	579,642
	$44,284,115

Assume the following information: The purchase price for the subsidiary included an AAP asset relating to a Patent that the parent estimated was worth BRL300,000 more than its book value on the subsidiary's balance sheet. The Patent is being amortized at the rate of BRL30,000 per year and the BOY book value of the Patent is BRL270,000.

i. Compute the balance of the Equity Investment account of $1,581,807 on the parent's balance sheet.

ii. Compute the equity income of $220,350 reported by the parent in its income statement.

d. Using your translated subsidiary financial statements from *Part a* and the parent's financial data provided in *Part c*, prepare the consolidation spreadsheet for the year.

34. **Translation of financial statements and consolidation of a foreign subsidiary (amortization of AAP)**

LO1, 3

Assume that your company owns a subsidiary operating in Canada. The subsidiary maintains its books in the Canadian dollar (CAD) as its functional currency. Following are the subsidiary's financial statements (in CAD) for the most recent year:

(in CAD)		
Income statement:		
Sales.................	3,360,000	
Cost of goods sold.....	(2,016,000)	
Gross profit..........	1,344,000	
Operating expenses	(873,600)	
Net income..........	470,400	
Statement of retained earnings:		
BOY Ret earnings......	1,764,000	
Net income...........	470,400	
Dividends	(47,040)	
EOY Ret earnings......	2,187,360	

(in CAD)		
Balance sheet:		
Assets		
Cash.................		956,256
Accounts receivable.......		779,520
Inventory		1,001,280
Property, plant, and equipment (PPE), net		1,852,032
Total assets.............		4,589,088
Liabilities and stockholders' equity		
Current liabilities..........		569,856
Long-term liabilities		1,327,872
Common stock...........		224,000
APIC.................		280,000
Retained earnings		2,187,360
Total liabilities and equity ...		4,589,088

(in CAD)	
Statement of cash flows:	
Net income.....................	470,400
Change in accounts receivable	(129,920)
Change in Inventories.............	(166,880)
Change in current liabilities	94,976
Net cash from operating activities ...	268,576
Change in PPE, net	(172,032)
Net cash from investing activities....	(172,032)
Change in long-term debt	221,312
Dividends	(47,040)
Net cash from financing activities ...	174,272
Net change in cash..............	270,816
Beginning cash..................	685,440
Ending cash	956,256

The relevant exchange rates for the $US value of the Canadian dollar (CAD) are as follows.

BOY rate...	$0.70
EOY rate...	$0.76
Avg. rate...	$0.73
PPE purchase date rate	$0.74
LTD borrowing date rate..............................	$0.74
Dividend rate	$0.75
Historical rate (common stock and APIC)	$0.60

a. Translate the subsidiary's income statement, statement of retained earnings, balance sheet, and statement of cash flows into $US (assume that the BOY Retained Earnings is $1,181,880).

b.[A] Compute the ending Cumulative Translation Adjustment directly, assuming a BOY balance of $103,319. What journal entry did the parent company make as a result of this computation?

c. Following are financial statements for the parent:

Income statement:

Sales.	$13,856,000
Cost of goods sold.	(9,699,200)
Gross profit.	4,156,800
Equity income.	306,892
Operating expenses	(2,632,640)
Net income.	$ 1,831,052

Statement of retained earnings:

BOY retained earnings	$10,944,328
Net income.	1,831,052
Dividends	(437,773)
EOY retained earnings	$12,337,607

Statement of accum. comp. income:

BOY cumulative translation adjustment	$ 103,319
Current-year translation gain (loss)	175,222
EOY cumulative translation adjustment	$ 278,541

Balance sheet:

Assets

Cash	$ 1,901,767
Accounts receivable	1,773,568
Inventory	2,688,064
Equity investment	2,349,433
Property, plant, and equipment (PPE), net	14,316,019
	$23,028,851

Liabilities and stockholders' equity

Current liabilities	$ 1,109,866
Long-term liabilities	4,000,000
Common stock	938,779
APIC	4,364,058
Retained earnings	12,337,607
Cumulative translation adjustment	278,541
	$23,028,851

Assume the following information: The purchase price for the subsidiary included an AAP asset relating to a Patent that the parent estimated was worth CAD 500,000 more than its book value on the subsidiary's balance sheet. The parent is amortizing the AAP asset at a rate of CAD 50,000 per year and the BOY book value of the Patent is CAD 450,000.

    i.   Compute the balance of the Equity Investment account of $2,349,433 on the parent's balance sheet.

    ii.   Compute the equity income of $306,892 reported by the parent in its income statement.

  d. Using your translated subsidiary financial statements from *Part a* and the parent's financial data provided in *Part c*, prepare the consolidation spreadsheet for the year.

LO1, 3

35. Translation of financial statements and consolidation of a foreign subsidiary (amortization of AAP)
Assume that your company owns a subsidiary operating in Germany. The subsidiary maintains its books in the Euro (€) as its functional currency. Following are the subsidiary's financial statements (in €) for the most recent year:

	Subsidiary (in €)		Subsidiary (in €)		Subsidiary (in €)
Income statement:		**Balance sheet:**		**Statement of cash flows:**	
Sales.	5,670,000	Assets		Net income	793,800
Cost of goods sold	(3,402,000)	Cash	1,613,682	Change in accounts receivable . .	(219,240)
Gross profit.	2,268,000	Accounts receivable	1,315,440	Change in inventories.	(281,610)
Operating expenses	(1,474,200)	Inventory	1,689,660	Change in current liabilities	160,272
Net income.	793,800	PPE, net	3,125,304	Net cash flows from	
		Total assets.	7,744,086	operating activities	453,222
Statement of retained earnings:				Change in PPE, net	(290,304)
BOY retained earnings	2,976,750	Liabilities and stockholders' equity		Net cash flows from	
Net income.	793,800	Current liabilities.	961,632	investing activities.	(290,304)
Dividends	(79,380)	Long-term liabilities	2,240,784		
Ending retained earnings . . .	3,691,170	Common stock.	378,000	Change in long-term debt	373,464
		APIC	472,500	Dividends	(79,380)
		Retained earnings	3,691,170	Net cash flows from	
		Cumulative translation adjustment	—	financing activities	294,084
		Total liabilities & equity	7,744,086	Net change in cash.	457,002
				Effect of exchange rate on cash	
				Beginning cash.	1,156,680
				Ending cash	1,613,682

The relevant exchange rates for the $US value of the Euro (€) are as follows:

BOY rate.	$1.09
EOY rate.	$1.14
Average rate.	$1.11
PPE purchase date rate.	$1.12
LTD borrowing date rate.	$1.12
Dividend rate	$1.13
Historical rate.	$0.90

a. Translate the subsidiary's income statement, statement of retained earnings, balance sheet, and statement of cash flows into $US (assume that the BOY Retained Earnings is $3,155,355).

b.^A Compute the ending Cumulative Translation Adjustment directly, assuming a BOY balance of $250,898. What journal entry did the parent company make as a result of this computation?

c. Following are financial statements for the parent:

Income statement:

Sales.	$23,382,000
Cost of goods sold.	(16,367,400)
Gross profit.	7,014,600
Equity income.	792,318
Operating expenses.	(4,442,580)
Net income.	$ 3,364,338

Statement of retained earnings:

BOY retained earnings.	$18,468,554
Net income.	3,364,338
Dividends.	(738,742)
Ending retained earnings	$21,094,150

Statement of accumulated comprehensive income:

BOY cumulative translation adjustment.	$ 250,898
Current-year translation gain (loss)	231,982
EOY cumulative translation adjustment.	$ 482,880

Balance sheet:

Assets	
Cash.	$ 1,918,875
Accounts receivable.	2,992,896
Inventory.	4,536,108
Equity investment.	5,542,304
Property, plant, and equipment (PPE), net.	24,158,282
	$39,148,465

Liabilities and stockholders' equity	
Current liabilities.	$ 1,872,898
Long-term liabilities	6,750,000
Common stock.	1,584,190
APIC.	7,364,347
Retained earnings	21,094,150
Cumulative translation adjustment.	482,880
	$39,148,465

Assume the following information: The purchase price for the subsidiary included an AAP asset relating to a Patent that the parent estimated was worth €800,000 more than its book value on the subsidiary's balance sheet. The parent is amortizing the AAP asset at a rate of €80,000 per year and the BOY book value of the Patent is €400,000.

i. Compute the balance of the Equity Investment account of $5,542,304 on the parent's balance sheet.

ii. Compute the equity income of $792,318 reported by the parent in its income statement.

iii. Using your translated subsidiary financial statements from *Part a* and the parent's financial data provided in *Part c*, prepare the consolidation spreadsheet for the year.

TOPIC REVIEW

Solution 1

	Subsidiary (in €)	Translation Rate	Subsidiary (in $)
Income statement:			
Sales.................................	€1,095,000	$1.01	$1,105,950
Cost of goods sold......................	(657,000)	$1.01	(663,570)
Gross profit.............................	438,000		442,380
Operating expenses......................	(284,700)	$1.01	(287,547)
Net income.............................	€ 153,300		$ 154,833
Statement of retained earnings:			
BOY retained earnings...................	€ 574,875	given	$ 437,543
Net income.............................	153,300	above	154,833
Dividends..............................	(15,330)	$1.02	(15,637)
Ending retained earnings.................	€ 712,845	computed	$ 576,739
Balance sheet:			
Assets			
Cash...................................	€ 311,637	$1.04	$ 324,102
Accounts receivable.....................	254,040	$1.04	264,202
Inventory..............................	326,310	$1.04	339,362
PPE, net...............................	603,564	$1.04	627,707
Total assets............................	€1,495,551		$1,555,373
Liabilities and stockholders' equity:			
Current liabilities........................	€ 185,712	$1.04	$ 193,140
Long-term liabilities.....................	432,744	$1.04	450,054
Common stock..........................	73,000	$0.63	45,990
APIC..................................	91,250	$0.63	57,488
Retained earnings	712,845	above	576,739
Cumulative translation adjustment...........			231,962
Total liabilities & equity...................	€1,495,551		$1,555,373
Statement of cash flows:			
Net income.............................	€ 153,300	$1.01	$ 154,833
Change in accounts receivable	(42,340)	$1.01	(42,763)
Change in inventories.....................	(54,385)	$1.01	(54,929)
Change in current liabilities	30,952	$1.01	31,262
Net cash flows from operating activities	€ 87,527		$ 88,403
Change in PPE, net	€ (56,064)	$0.99	$ (55,503)
Net cash flows from investing activities........	€ (56,064)		$ (55,503)
Change in long-term debt	€ 72,124	$1.03	$ 74,288
Dividends..............................	(15,330)	$1.02	(15,637)
Net cash flows from financing activities........	€ 56,794		$ 58,651
Net change in cash.......................	€ 88,257		$ 91,551
Effect of exchange rate on cash.............		plug	20,340
Beginning cash..........................	223,380	$0.95	212,211
Ending cash	€ 311,637	$1.04	$ 324,102

Solution 2

	In NZD		In $US
Beginning inventory	1,117,500	$0.76	$ 849,300
Purchases	2,923,500	$0.83	2,426,505
Ending inventory	(1,341,000)	$0.93	(1,247,130)
Cost of goods sold	2,700,000		$2,028,675
Land	980,400	$0.60	$ 588,240
Building	1,800,000	$0.61	1,098,000
Accumulated depreciation—building	(900,000)	$0.61	(549,000)
Equipment	1,200,000	$0.62	744,000
Accumulated depreciation—equipment	(600,000)	$0.62	(372,000)
PPE, net	2,480,400		$1,509,240
Depreciation expense—building	90,000	$0.61	$ 54,900
Depreciation expense—equipment	120,000	$0.62	74,400
Depreciation expense	210,000		$ 129,300

	Subsidiary (in NZD)	Translation Rate	Subsidiary (in $)
Income statement:			
Sales	4,500,000	$0.83	$3,735,000
Cost of goods sold	(2,700,000)	computed	(2,028,675)
Gross profit	1,800,000		1,706,325
Operating expenses	(960,000)	$0.83	(796,800)
Depreciation	(210,000)	computed	(129,300)
Remeasurement gain or loss		plug #3	(69,948)
Net income	630,000		$ 710,277
Statement of retained earnings:			
BOY retained earnings	2,362,500	given	$1,578,336
Net income	630,000	plug #2	710,277
Dividends	(63,000)	$0.92	(57,960)
Ending retained earnings	2,929,500	computed	$2,230,653
Balance sheet:			
Assets			
Cash	1,280,700	$0.93	$1,191,051
Accounts receivable	1,044,000	$0.93	970,920
Inventory	1,341,000	computed	1,247,130
PPE, net	2,480,400	computed	1,509,240
Total assets	6,146,100		$4,918,341
Liabilities and stockholders' equity			
Current liabilities	763,200	$0.93	$ 709,776
Long-term liabilities	1,778,400	$0.93	1,653,912
Common stock	300,000	$0.48	144,000
APIC	375,000	$0.48	180,000
Retained earnings	2,929,500	plug #1	2,230,653
Total liabilities & equity	6,146,100		$4,918,341

COMPREHENSIVE REVIEW SOLUTION

The following table illustrates the translation and remeasurement of the subsidiary's financial statements using the Current Rate and Remeasurement approaches.

	Subsidiary (in €)	Current Rate Translation Rate	Current Rate Subsidiary (in $)	Remeasurement Translation Rate	Remeasurement Subsidiary (in $)
Beginning inventory	1,490,000			$1.22	$1,817,800
Purchases	3,898,000			$1.27	4,950,460
Ending inventory	(1,788,000)			$1.31	(2,342,280)
Cost of goods sold	3,600,000				$4,425,980
Land	1,307,200			$0.83	$1,084,976
Building	2,400,000			$0.83	1,992,000
Accum. deprec.—building	(1,200,000)			$0.83	(996,000)
Equipment	1,600,000			$0.83	1,328,000
Accum. deprec.—equipment	(800,000)			$0.83	(664,000)
PPE, net	3,307,200				$2,744,976
Depreciation expense—building	120,000			$0.83	$ 99,600
Depreciation expense—equipment	160,000			$0.83	132,800
Depreciation expense	280,000				$ 232,400

	Subsidiary (in €)	Current Rate Translation Rate	Current Rate Subsidiary (in $)	Remeasurement Translation Rate	Remeasurement Subsidiary (in $)
Income statement:					
Sales	6,000,000	$1.27	$ 7,620,000	$1.27	$7,620,000
Cost of goods sold	(3,600,000)	$1.27	(4,572,000)	computed	(4,425,980)
Gross profit	2,400,000		3,048,000		3,194,020
Operating expenses	(1,280,000)	$1.27	(1,625,600)	$1.27	(1,625,600)
Depreciation	(280,000)	$1.27	(355,600)	computed	(232,400)
Remeasurement gain or loss				plug #3	(65,448)
Net income	840,000		$ 1,066,800		$1,270,572
Statement of retained earnings:					
BOY retained earnings	3,150,000	given	$ 2,625,000	given	$2,866,992
Net income	840,000	above	1,066,800	plug #2	1,270,572
Dividends	(84,000)	$1.24	(104,160)	$1.24	(104,160)
EOY retained earnings	3,906,000	computed	$ 3,587,640	computed	$4,033,404
Balance sheet:					
Assets					
Cash	1,707,600	$1.31	$ 2,236,956	$1.31	$2,236,956
Accounts receivable	1,392,000	$1.31	1,823,520	$1.31	1,823,520
Inventory	1,788,000	$1.31	2,342,280	computed	2,342,280
PPE, net	3,307,200	$1.31	4,332,432	computed	2,744,976
Total assets	8,194,800		$10,735,188		$9,147,732
Liabilities and stockholders' equity					
Current liabilities	1,017,600	$1.31	$ 1,333,056	$1.31	$1,333,056
Long-term liabilities	2,371,200	$1.31	3,106,272	$1.31	3,106,272
Common stock	400,000	$0.75	300,000	$0.75	300,000
APIC	500,000	$0.75	375,000	$0.75	375,000
Retained earnings	3,906,000	above	3,587,640	plug #1	4,033,404
Cumulative translation adjustment			2,033,220		
Total liabilities & equity	8,194,800		$10,735,188		$9,147,732

LEARNING OBJECTIVES

1. Describe the appropriations and budgetary process. (p. 575)

2. Describe the types of funds employed in fund accounting. (p. 577)

3. Describe the measurement focus and basis of accounting. (p. 579)

4. Describe fund accounting journal entries. (p. 581)

5. Describe the preparation of fund financial statements. (p. 591)

Government Accounting: Fund-Based Financial Statements

Acton, Massachusetts, is located 25 miles northwest of Boston. The first colonial residents moved to Acton in 1639 and they established it as an independent town on July 3, 1735. At the beginning of the Revolutionary War, on April 19, 1775, a company of minutemen from Acton responded to the call to arms initiated by Paul Revere, William Dawes, and Samuel Prescott in their famous ride to warn the Colonists of the impending advance by British regulars, and they fought the British in one of the first two battles of the Revolutionary War at the North Bridge in Concord, Massachusetts, in the Battles of Lexington and Concord.

THE TOWN OF ACTON, MASSACHUSETTS

During the Battle of Concord, one of Acton's minutemen, Captain Isaac Davis, was killed. Davis was the first officer to die in the Revolutionary War. Each year on Patriot's Day (the third Monday in April), and in remembrance of their heroism, the Acton Minutemen lead a march from Acton Center to the Old North Bridge in Concord. This route is known as "The Isaac Davis Trail" and is listed on the National Register of Historic Places.

As is typical of New England towns, a Board of Selectmen oversee the Town government. All government initiatives, including its budget and appropriation process, are voted on at Town meetings. These meetings are open to all residents and occur at least annually. Anyone in attendance has the right to speak and to question any of the Selectmen or other Town officials. The Town meeting is an important part of the fabric of life in New England.

The outcome of these Town meetings is a series of motions (called warrants) that request appropriation of Town funds for a number of expenditures to benefit the community. These expenditures fund necessary governmental services like public safety, education, health and social services, recreation, and the like. Once approved, the anticipated expenditures must be funded, typically with taxes on real estate and personal property, fees for services, and grants from state and federal governments.

Acton Public Safety Building

(continued on next page)

(continued from previous page)

Management of and accounting for governmental activities is fundamentally different from the management of and accounting for a corporation. Governments are responsible to their constituents and must take every precaution to ensure that the monies they receive by taxing citizens are spent on the expenditures that the citizens approved in the budget. Governments are not allowed to use excess funds in one approved program to fund deficits in another.

In order to ensure that funds are properly spent, governments employ a particular type of accounting system that monitors each program separately. This system is called *fund accounting*, and its focus is on monitoring receipts and expenditures for the *current* year to make sure that cash inflows are only spent for approved programs and only up to the amount that the citizens approved when the budget was approved.

We discuss fund accounting for governments in this chapter.

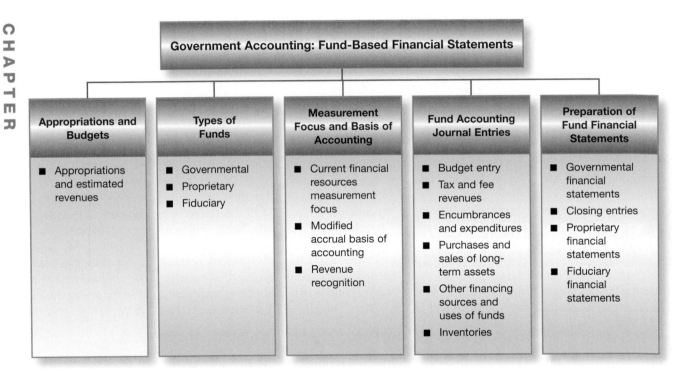

Government activities are fundamentally different from business activities. Governments receive cash from a number of sources such as taxes, fees, and borrowing, and spend those funds for the public good (public safety, education, health and social services, public works, and the like). Instead of focusing on issues related to profitability, like we do for businesses, some of the questions we have about the financial affairs of a government are the following:

1. Is it efficient in delivering the services that we expect?
2. Is it financially solvent?
3. Can we account for all of the funds that have been entrusted it?

There are a number of external parties that are interested in the answers to the questions we pose above:

- Citizens are concerned that services are provided in an *efficient* manner.
- Citizens demand assurance that all of the funds that have been entrusted to their governments can be *accounted* for.
- Regulators are concerned that governmental units maintain *compliance* with all applicable laws and regulations.
- Investors that purchase state and municipal bonds require financial information in order to determine the *risk* inherent in their investment.

The users of the financial reports of governmental bodies are much different from those of corporations and each of these groups has a legal right to access this information.

The Governmental Accounting Standards Board (GASB) is the primary standard-setting body for governmental accounting standards.[1] In 1987, the GASB issued its Concepts Statement 1, *Objectives of Financial Reporting* (GASB CS1), in which it identifies the groups we highlight above (citizenry, legislative, and oversight bodies, and investors and creditors) as the primary users of state and local governmental financial reports. Further, it confirms that these financial reports are used, primarily, "to compare actual financial results with the legally adopted budget; to assess financial condition and results of operations; to assist in determining compliance with finance-related laws, rules, and regulations; and to assist in evaluating efficiency and effectiveness" (GASB CS1, Summary).

PRACTICE INSIGHT

GAAP for Governments The Financial Accounting Foundation, which oversees the FASB, created the Governmental Accounting Standards Board (GASB) in 1984. The GASB is charged with the development of accounting and reporting standards for state and local governmental entities. GASB statements, together with those of a predecessor organization, the National Council on Governmental Accounting (NCGA), and the *AICPA Industry Audit Guide* (July 1984) that are still in effect, constitute generally accepted accounting standards for governments. In 1985, the GASB published its *Codification of Governmental Accounting and Financial Reporting Standards*, a summary of accounting standards that is "intended to provide authoritative accounting and financial reporting guidance for state and local governmental entities."

Following is a hierarchy of applicable standards for governments (GASB Statement 76):

a. Officially established accounting principles—Governmental Accounting Standards Board (GASB) Statements (Category A). All GASB Interpretations currently in effect also are considered as being included within Category A and are continued in force until altered, amended, supplemented, revoked, or superseded by subsequent GASB pronouncements.

b. GASB Technical Bulletins; GASB Implementation Guides; and literature of the AICPA cleared by the GASB (Category B).

If the accounting treatment for a transaction or other event is not specified by a pronouncement in Category A, a governmental entity should consider whether the accounting treatment is specified by a source in Category B.

Our references to governmental accounting standards include the following abbreviations:

GASB	GASB Statement
GASB CS	GASB Concept Statement
GASB ASC	GASB Codification
NCGAS	National Council on Governmental Accounting Standard
NCGAI	National Council on Governmental Accounting Interpretation

---

The philosophical cornerstone of governmental financial reporting is the concept of **accountability** which the GASB defines as follows: "Governmental accountability is based on the belief that the citizenry has a 'right to know,' a right to receive openly declared facts that may lead to public debate by the citizens and their elected representatives. Financial reporting plays a major role in fulfilling government's duty to be publicly accountable in a democratic society" (GASB CS1, ¶56).

It may surprise you to learn that governments are required to issue *two* types of financial reports:

1. **Fund financial statements**—governmental fund financial statements are prepared using a *modified accrual basis* of accounting and focus on the sources, uses, and balances of the resources that have been entrusted to governmental officials. A significant use of fund financial statements is to ensure that the resources entrusted to the government by its citizens have been used as approved and that the government has operated within the budget set for it by its citizenry.

2. **Government-wide financial statements**—these statements provide information about the government on an *accrual basis* and are similar to the types of financial reports we prepare for

---

[1] The Federal Accounting Standards Advisory Board (FASAB) sets accounting standards for the Federal Government.

corporations. These accrual basis statements allow users to better assess the financial condition of the government in order to make investment decisions.

For many years, governments were only required to issue fund financial statements and fund accounting still remains the primary accounting system by which governments are managed. Essentially, this type of accounting system organizes the government into discrete categories, called funds, each of which is accounted for separately. One of these funds is the General Fund that includes all of the activities you normally think of for a government: safety (fire and police departments), education (public schools), public works (streets and lights), health and social services, and the like. Governments can also establish funds for specific purposes, like a Capital Projects Fund relating to the construction of a new school or an Enterprise Fund relating to a municipal swimming pool that charges users a fee and operates like a business.

The primary purpose of fund accounting is to segregate the accounting for these activities so that they can be monitored. Why? Because governments raise funds primarily by taxing citizens and their use of those tax receipts is typically restricted by law. Government officials cannot spend more in a particular area than has been appropriated for that area in the budget, and they generally cannot move cash from one fund to another without legislative approval. Fund accounting is designed to provide the control mechanism necessary to ensure that cash is spent as appropriated in the budget.

So, why do we require the government-wide financial statements? The reason is this. Governmental fund accounting focuses primarily on cash inflows and outflows in the *current year*. Long-term assets (like infrastructure) and long-term liabilities (like bonds, leases and other long-term liabilities) are *not* reported on the governmental fund balance sheet. The absence of this information makes it difficult to effectively analyze the financial condition of the government from an investment perspective, say if you were interested in purchasing a municipal bond. In contrast, government-wide financial statements are prepared under accrual accounting and, as a result, include these long-term assets and liabilities. Consequently, we are better able to answer the first two questions we pose above about the governmental unit we are interested in:

1. Is it efficient in delivering the services that we expect?
2. Is it financially solvent?

Exhibit 9.1 illustrates the connection between the fund financial statements and the government-wide financial statements. The process begins with the entry for the approved budget (i.e., the warrants approved at the Town meeting that we discuss in our opening vignette relating to the Town of Acton), followed by the recording of transactions during the year, preparation of fund financial statements, and year-end closing entries. These are the topics for this chapter. In Chapter 10, we discuss the government-wide financial statements and we will show you the adjustments that are necessary to convert the fund financial statements to government-wide financial statements. You might think of these adjustments as being made in a spreadsheet similar to the consolidation entries we made earlier in the text, beginning with fund financial statements and ending with government-wide financial statements in the final column.

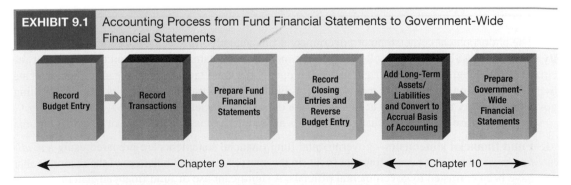

EXHIBIT 9.1 Accounting Process from Fund Financial Statements to Government-Wide Financial Statements

To illustrate the preparation of these financial statements, we use the Town of Acton, Massachusetts, a small New England town that is large enough to demonstrate the concepts we want to discuss, yet small enough so that we can clearly identify these concepts without the complexity of a larger state or municipal government. We begin our discussion of the accounting for governmental bodies with an overview of the budgeting process that establishes the level of spending for the upcoming fiscal year.

APPROPRIATIONS AND BUDGETS

The budgetary process is central to the effective functioning of a government. The GASB confirms the importance of a budget in its first Concept Statement: "[A budget] is a form of *control* usually having the force of law. A legally adopted budget provides both *authorizations of* and *limitations on* amounts that may be spent for particular purposes. Because budgetary authorizations result from competition for scarce resources and budgetary limitations generally cannot be exceeded without due process, the governmental entity needs to demonstrate that it is accountable from both the authorization and the limitation perspectives [emphasis the GASB]" (GASB CS 1, ¶19c).

LO1 Describe the appropriations and budgetary process.

The budgeting process establishes the types and levels of services that the government will provide to its citizens for the upcoming year. At the federal and state level, governments raise funds in the form of income or sales taxes (called *derived* taxes) and proposed spending levels must be set in relation to expected tax inflows. At the local level, cash inflows are primarily the result of taxes on real estate and personal property (called *imposed* taxes), and spending levels must be set in relation to the tax burden that citizens are willing to accept. Finally, purchases of capital assets (equipment, vehicles, etc.) and infrastructure (buildings, roads, bridges, etc.) are typically financed with bonds, and these projected inflows and expenditures must also be identified in the proposed budget.

Appropriations and Estimated Revenues

All governmental units present a budget to taxpayers that includes anticipated receipts and proposed expenditures. At the federal, state, and large municipal levels, that budget is presented to elected representatives. For smaller governments, like the Town of Acton, the budget is presented directly to its citizens. Although the process is essentially the same, examining the budgetary process at the level of a small town may provide a better illustration so that the accounting issues that we discuss later in the chapter will be easier to understand.

The budget for the Town of Acton must be approved by a vote of the Town residents in an annual Town meeting. That vote sets spending limits for the various governmental activities as well as the tax levy that will be required to fund those expenditures. Consequently, the establishment of spending and the tax revenues to support that spending are closely entwined.

The Town meeting *warrant* is the agenda for the meeting. It is drawn up by the Selectmen from various proposals made by the Selectmen, the School Committee, and other Boards, staff and citizens. The *warrant articles* are, in effect, motions relating to all of the significant financial decisions facing the Town for the upcoming fiscal year. The Town Moderator presides over the meeting and both the Board of Selectmen (which oversees the management of the Town) and the Finance Committee (which advises the Board of Selectmen) are in attendance to present the articles and to respond to questions and input from citizens.

Appropriations   In our discussions of the accounting for governmental units, we will refer to the word "appropriations." An **appropriation** is a sum of money that has been set aside for a specific use. For example, in a recent **Town of Acton** meeting, the Fire Department proposed the purchase of a new ladder truck and two other pieces of equipment for a total cost of $1,116,625. The motion to appropriate funds for the purchase of the fire truck was made by a member of the Board of Selectmen as follows:

Mr. Hunter moves that the Town appropriate $1,116,625 to be expended by the Town Manager for the purposes set forth in this Article including costs incidental and related thereto, and to raise such amount, $229,978, be transferred from the Ambulance Fees Revolving Fund and that the Treasurer, with the approval of the Selectmen, is authorized to borrow $886,647 under Massachusetts General Law, Chapter 44, Section 7, Paragraph 9, as amended, and that the Town appropriate $95,273 for the payment of interest costs on such borrowing in the current Fiscal Year and to raise such amount, $60,000 be transferred from the Ambulance Fees Revolving Fund Balance and $35,273 be raised from taxation, and that the Town Manager be authorized to sell, trade or dispose of vehicles and equipment being replaced and to expend any proceeds so received.

The appropriation provides for the expenditure of $1,116,625 for the purchase of a fire truck and authorizes the funding of that expenditure to be comprised of $886,647 of borrowing, with the remainder to be funded by various means, including the transfer of $229,978 from an ambulance fund. The warrant also appropriates $95,273 for the payment of interest for one year, to be raised by a $60,000 transfer from the ambulance fund and $35,273 from the municipal budget through taxation.

There are a number of items in this appropriation that are worth discussing at this point in the chapter:

1. Notice the use of the word, "expended." In governmental accounting, we will use the word "expenditure" in place of the word "expense" that we use in accrual accounting. An **expenditure** is a payment of money. Governmental accounting focuses on inflows and outflows of cash, not revenues and expenses determined on an accrual basis.

2. Governments account for their activities using a number of "funds." A **fund** is a separate accounting entity designed to keep track of all transactions and balances for a specific activity. As we will discuss later in the chapter, governments use these funds to keep track of assets and liabilities, as well as inflows and outflows of cash, which have been earmarked for a specific purpose.

3. Notice that the appropriation of cash for the payment of interest relates only to the **current fiscal year**. The time horizon for governmental budgets is one year. Interest and principal payments in future years will be appropriated in future budgets.

Estimated Revenues for the Governmental Fund

In addition to warrants relating to budgeted expenditures, like the purchase of a fire truck that we discuss above, governmental budgets must also include warrants relating to proposed taxes that will be levied upon its citizens to fund those expenditures. In contrast to federal and state governments which have access to income tax revenues, local governments are largely dependent upon real estate taxes and taxes on personal property for their funding. For the Town of Acton, nearly 90% of the cash inflows are derived from such taxes.

The development of budgets for estimated revenues from taxes, fees, and other sources and for proposed expenditures are not independent processes. Rather, they must be developed simultaneously in a negotiated process between the government and its citizens. It is the latter that decide the vision for the type of city or town in which they want to live and the level of taxes that they can afford and are willing to accept. It is not unusual for this budgetary process to go through several iterations of proposed expenditure levels and citizen response before both the total amount of the budget and the required tax levy are finally established.

Budgets for Enterprise Funds

Some of the initial articles presented at the Town meeting relate to budgets for Enterprise Funds. We will discuss Enterprise Funds in greater detail later in the chapter, but it is worthwhile to discuss them briefly here.

An **Enterprise Fund** is a government activity that is available to the public and is financed, in whole or in part, by fees charged to users of the enterprise. It is a business-like activity, and, because its funding does not require access to general tax revenues, its budget is presented separately from the general budget and together with other consent articles that are usually approved without much debate. Typical examples of Enterprise Funds include a municipal swimming pool that charges a membership or usage fee, and a waste disposal or sewage treatment facility that charges users based on their volume of waste or sewage.

The Town of Acton maintains a solid waste disposal and recycling facility that is funded by fees paid by the users of the facility. Following is the motion that was made for the solid waste disposal and recycling facility in the Acton Town meeting:

> *Move that the Town appropriate $977,534 for the purpose of solid waste disposal and recycling, and to raise such amount, $592,534 be raised from department receipts and $385,000 be transferred from retained earnings.*

The Solid Waste Enterprise Fund is one of many funds that the Town of Acton accounts for separately. Each of these funds has been created for a specific purpose and is accounted for as a separate entity so that its activities can be segregated for monitoring purposes.

FUND ACCOUNTING

Funds segregate the financial records of a government by activities.[2] These activities include ongoing activities (like public safety and education), special projects (like the construction of a bridge), business-like activities (such as a municipal swimming pool that charges users a fee), pension trusts to manage retirement plans for governmental employees, and many others. By segregating activities in this manner, governments can better monitor the inflows and outflows of resources for each activity to ensure that managers have not *overspent* the resources allotted to them in the budgetary process and to ensure that they have not *underspent* in an area that citizens deem to be important. In addition, government accountants must also ensure that funds allocated for a specified purpose, like a retirement plan for municipal employees, are not comingled with general purpose funds.

Fund accounting is different from accrual accounting that we use to prepare the financial statements for businesses. Its focus is on inflows and outflows of *current resources*, a much shorter time horizon than that which we use in accrual accounting. For example, PPE assets, which appear on accrual-based balance sheets, are *not* reported on fund-based balance sheets since they do not represent a current resource. Likewise, long-term debt is *not* reported on fund-based balance sheets since repayment will not be made from current resources.

Fund accounting provides an accounting system that allows us to effectively monitor the financial activities of a particular component of the government. This control mechanism is an important attribute of the fund accounting system. Governments operate by taxing citizens for specific purposes, and they must assure the citizenry that their taxes are used only for the activities that they have approved in the budgetary process.

We now turn to a discussion of the three types of funds that are maintained in the fund accounting system.

Types of Funds

LO2 Describe the types of funds employed in fund accounting.

Governments establish funds for any activity that must be specifically monitored by law or to achieve sound and expeditious financial administration and reporting. Funds are generally classified into three groups (GASB ASC 1300.103–114):

1. **Governmental Funds** relate to the type of activities that are customary for a government to perform, such as providing for public safety, education, and health and social welfare. They also include funds for special projects, such as the construction of a bridge or the issuance of a bond to fund a toll road. Governmental activities typically do not generate significant cash inflows and are funded by taxes (such as income and sales taxes, property taxes, and the like) together with federal and state aid to municipalities. Following are typical governmental activities:
   a. Collection of taxes and fees
   b. Provision of governmental services such as fire, public safety, education, and social services
   c. Construction of buildings, roads, lighting systems, bridges, and the like, together with the issuance of bonds or other forms of borrowing.

2. **Proprietary Funds** relate to business-like activities, such as a municipal swimming pool or solid waste disposal facilities that charge a fee for use. These fees for use are typically set at a level that is sufficient to cover the cost of the service provided, not to generate significant excess cash flows. The following proprietary activities are common:
   a. Providing public services such as public transportation and parking, garbage collection, hospitals, public colleges and universities, and recreational facilities
   b. Providing intergovernmental services, such as centralized information technology, photocopying, vehicles, supplies, and the like.

3. **Fiduciary Funds** are used to monitor resources that are required to be held in trust for others. They include funds for defined benefit pension plans, defined contribution plans, other post-employment

---

[2] The **formal definition of a fund** is as follows: "A fund is a fiscal and accounting entity with a self-balancing set of accounts recording cash and other financial resources, together with all related liabilities and residual equities or balances, and changes therein, which are segregated for the purpose of carrying on specific activities or attaining certain objectives in accordance with special regulations, restrictions, or limitations . . . Thus, from an accounting and financial management viewpoint, a governmental unit is a combination of several distinctly different fiscal and accounting entities, each having a separate set of accounts and functioning independently." (GASB ASC 1100.102 and 1300.101)

benefit plans, and the like. Fiduciary activities may also include the collection and disbursement of taxes, such as sales taxes, for another governmental entity.

We present a list of specific fund types in Exhibit 9.2 (GASB ASC 1300.103–114). There is only one requirement relating to the establishment of funds: there should be only one General Fund (GASB ASC 1300.116). Aside from that restriction, governments should establish and maintain those funds that are

---

EXHIBIT 9.2 | Types of Funds

1. **Governmental Funds**
   a) **General fund**—to account for all financial resources except those required to be reported in another fund.
   b) **Special revenue funds**—to account for the proceeds of specific revenue sources (other than trusts for individuals, private organizations, or other governments or for major capital projects) that are legally restricted to expenditures for specified purposes. Resources restricted to expenditures for purposes normally financed from the general fund may be accounted for through the general fund provided that applicable legal requirements can be appropriately satisfied; and use of special revenue funds is not required unless they are legally mandated. The general fund of a blended component unit should be reported as a special revenue fund.
   c) **Capital projects funds**—to account for financial resources to be used for the acquisition or construction of major capital facilities (other than those financed by proprietary funds or in trust funds for individuals, private organizations, or other governments). Capital outlays financed from general obligation bond proceeds should be accounted for through a capital projects fund.
   d) **Debt service funds**—to account for the accumulation of resources for, and the payment of, general long-term debt principal and interest. Debt service funds are required if they are legally mandated and/or if financial resources are being accumulated for principal and interest payments maturing in future years. The debt service transactions of a special assessment issue for which the government is not obligated in any manner should be reported in an agency fund (discussed below) rather than a debt service fund.
   e) **Permanent funds**—should be used to report resources that are legally restricted to the extent that only earnings, and not principal, may be used for purposes that support the reporting government's programs—that is, for the benefit of the government or its citizenry.

2. **Proprietary Funds**
   a) **Enterprise funds**—may be used to report any activity for which a fee is charged to external users for goods or services. These activities are typically those that are engaged in by businesses, and the objective is to charge fees to users that are sufficient to cover all of the costs incurred to provide the activity to its users. Activities are required to be reported as enterprise funds if any one of the following criteria is met. Governments should apply each of these criteria in the context of the activity's principal revenue sources.
      i) The activity is financed with debt that is secured solely by a pledge of the net revenues from fees and charges of the activity. Debt that is secured by a pledge of net revenues from fees and charges and the full faith and credit of a related primary government or component unit—even if that government is not expected to make any payments—is not payable solely from fees and charges of the activity. (Some debt may be secured, in part, by a portion of its own proceeds but should be considered as payable "solely" from the revenues of the activity.)
      ii) Laws or regulations require that the activity's costs of providing services, including capital costs (such as depreciation or debt service), be recovered with fees and charges, rather than with taxes or similar revenues.
      iii) The pricing policies of the activity establish fees and charges designed to recover its costs, including capital costs (such as depreciation or debt service).
   b) **Internal service funds**—may be used to report any activity that provides goods or services to other funds, departments, or agencies of the primary government and its component units, or to other governments, on a cost-reimbursement basis. Internal service funds should be used only if the reporting government is the predominant participant in the activity. Otherwise, the activity should be reported as an enterprise fund.

3. **Fiduciary Funds**
   a) **Pension (and other employee benefit) trust funds**—should be used to report resources that are required to be held in trust for the members and beneficiaries of defined benefit pension plans, defined contribution plans, other postemployment benefit plans, or other employee benefit plans.
   b) **Investment trust funds**—should be used to report the external portion of investment pools reported by the sponsoring government.
   c) **Private-purpose trust funds**—such as a fund used to report escheat property, should be used to report all other trust arrangements under which principal and income benefit individuals, private organizations, or other governments.
   d) **Agency funds**—should be used to report resources held by the reporting government in a purely custodial capacity (assets equal liabilities). Agency funds typically involve only the receipt, temporary investment, and remittance of fiduciary resources to individuals, private organizations, or other governments.

required by law and that are necessary for sound financial administration. Further, only the minimum number of funds consistent with legal and operating requirements should be established because unnecessary funds result in inflexibility, undue complexity, and inefficient financial administration (NCGAS 1,¶ 29).

Measurement Focus and Basis of Accounting for Governmental Funds

The financial statements for governmental funds are prepared using a different measurement focus and a different accounting basis than we use for the preparation of financial statements for a business, and the financial statements for proprietary funds and fiduciary funds. For governmental funds, we recognize revenues and expenditures using the *current financial resources measurement focus and the modified accrual basis of accounting* (NCGAS 1, ¶57):

LO3 Describe the measurement focus and basis of accounting.

- **Current financial resources measurement focus** refers to *what* is being reported. The words *current financial resources* mean resources that can be consumed in the near future. For assets, we include cash, prepaid items, investments, and receivables (PPE is not included in fund financial statements as it is consumed over a longer period of time). For liabilities, we include those obligations that we would expect to be liquidated with available financial resources, including such items as accounts payable and accruals (long-term liabilities are not reported in fund financial statements because their liquidation will require the use of *future* financial resources).

- **Modified accrual basis of accounting** refers to *when* the transaction is recognized.
  - **Revenues** are recognized in the accounting period in which they become both *measurable* and *available* to finance expenditures. "Available" means collectible within the current period or soon enough thereafter to be used to pay liabilities of the current period.
  - **Expenditures** should be recognized in the accounting period in which the fund liability is incurred.[3]

Governmental transactions are typically of two types: **exchange transactions** (such as sales of goods and services to outsiders in various business-like activities that are reported in Enterprise Funds), and **nonexchange transactions** (including income or sales taxes, real estate and personal property taxes, grants and private donations). Governments recognize revenues from *exchange transactions* when the transactions take place, and, for nonexchange transactions, when the resources are available to satisfy existing liabilities.[4]

We now discuss two special revenue recognition cases that are both important sources of revenue for governments and for which the revenue recognition principles are clearly established: revenue from property taxes and revenue from grants and other subsidies which are controlled by eligibility requirements.

Recognition of Revenues from Property Taxes   Property taxes are often a

significant source of revenues for local governments, and the method by which we recognize them can significantly impact reported financial results. Property taxes are levied pursuant to law as of a specific date, and, once levied, an enforceable legal claim attaches to the properties and/or taxpayers.

The property taxes due to a government, net of estimated uncollectibles, typically can be determined and recorded in the accounts when levied. Property taxes are typically levied (i.e., assessed) in one budgetary year and collected in the next. Under accrual accounting for businesses, the entire amount receivable would be recognized as revenue. Under governmental accounting, however, the tax revenues are recognized in the accounting period in which they become both *measurable* and *available* to finance expenditures. It is the second condition that concerns us. Property taxes are considered "available" in the year of assessment (and should, therefore, be recognized as revenue) if (1) their ultimate collectibility is reasonably assured (i.e., net of estimated uncollectible amounts), and (2) they are collectible soon enough in the subsequent period to finance *current*-period expenditures (NCGAS 1, ¶57).

---

[3] An exception is unmatured interest on general long-term debt and on special assessment indebtedness secured by interest bearing special assessment levies, which should be recognized when due.

[4] Resources received prior to the exchange transaction should be reported as deferred revenue and, subsequently, recorded as revenue once the revenue recognition requirements are met.

Collectible "soon enough in the subsequent period to finance current-period expenditures" is interpreted to mean within 60 days (NCGAI 3, ¶8). The 60-day rule implies that only the portion of the receivable that is expected to be collected within 60 days should be recognized as revenue in the year of assessment and the remaining amount (collectible after 60 days) should not be recognized as revenue until collected in the subsequent fiscal year. In this case, the taxes levied would be recognized as deferred revenue in the current year.

The entry to recognize property tax revenue for the portion that is expected to be collected within 60 days and to defer revenue recognition for the remaining amount is as follows:

Accounts receivable..	xxx	
Property tax revenues..		xxx
Deferred revenues...		xxx
(to recognize revenues for the portion of taxes receivable expected to be collected within 60 days from the end of the fiscal year and to defer revenue recognition for the remaining amount)		

Deferred revenues are recognized as revenue in the subsequent year when collected with a debit to Deferred Revenues and a credit to Property Tax Revenues for the amount of revenue recognized.

Revenue Recognition in the Presence of Eligibility Requirements for Grants and Other Subsidies

Local governments often receive aid from the state or federal government in the form of grants and other subsidies. These grants often contain conditions that must be met in order for the local government to use the funds. Following are typical conditions:

a. *Required characteristics of recipients.* The recipient has the characteristics specified by the provider (state grants to be used only in support of school districts would be an example).

b. *Time requirements.* Time requirements specified by enabling legislation or the provider have been met (such as the period during which the resources are required to be used).

c. *Reimbursements.* The provider offers resources on a reimbursement ("expenditure-driven") basis and the recipient has incurred allowable costs under the applicable program.

d. *Contingencies* (applies only to voluntary nonexchange transactions). The provider's offer of resources is contingent upon a specified action of the recipient and that action has occurred (for example, the recipient is required to raise a specific amount of resources from third parties or to dedicate its own resources for a specified purpose and has complied with those requirements).

Governments recognize receivables (or a decrease in liabilities) and revenues (net of estimated uncollectible amounts), when all applicable eligibility requirements, including time requirements, are met. Resources received before the eligibility requirements are met should be reported as deferred revenues (GASB ASC N50.117–.118).

Revenue and Expense Recognition for Proprietary and Fiduciary Funds

Proprietary (business-type activities) and Fiduciary (trust) Funds are accounted for differently from the Governmental Fund that we describe above. Revenues and expenses for Proprietary and Fiduciary Funds should be recognized on the *accrual basis* (i.e., revenues should be recognized in the accounting period in which they are earned and become measurable; expenses should be recognized in the period incurred, if measurable).[5] We discuss the measurement focus of Proprietary and Fiduciary Funds later in the chapter.

---

[5] The Statement of Net Position (for Proprietary Funds) and the Statement of Fiduciary Net Position (for Fiduciary Funds) are prepared using the *economic resources measurement focus.* "Economic resources" are broader than the "financial resources" measurement focus that we use in the preparation of the Governmental Funds financial statements. The economic resources measurement focus includes long-term assets and liabilities as well as current financial resources. We discuss the economic resources measurement focus in our discussion of Proprietary and Fiduciary Funds, later in this chapter, and in more depth in Chapter 10 in our discussion of government-wide financial statements.

Summary of Fund Types, Accounting Approaches, and Required Financial Statements

Exhibit 9.3 provides a summary of the types of Funds, the accounting approach utilized for each, and the required financial statements (GASB 34, Table B-2). We provide examples of each of these financial statements later in the chapter.

EXHIBIT 9.3	Summary of Fund Types, Accounting Approaches, and Required Financial Statements		
General Fund Type	**Specific Fund Types**	**Measurement Focus and Basis of Accounting**	**Basic Financial Statements**
Governmental	General Special revenue Capital projects Debt service Permanent	**Current financial resources** measurement focus **Modified accrual basis** of accounting	Balance sheet Statement of revenues, expenditures, and changes in fund balances
Proprietary	Enterprise Internal service	**Economic resources** measurement focus **Accrual basis** of accounting	Statement of net position Statement of revenues, expenses, and changes in fund net position Statement of cash flows
Fiduciary	Pension trust funds Investment trust funds Private-purpose trust funds Agency funds		Statement of fiduciary net position Statement of changes in fiduciary net position

We now turn to a discussion of the mechanics of fund accounting.

Fund Accounting Journal Entries

Fund accounting focuses on the sources and uses of *current* financial resources. Its primary objective is to ensure that managers do not overspend the monies that have been appropriated by the taxpayers, and its focus is on current financial resources. The focus on current financial resources means, for example, that we will record the purchase of PPE as an "expenditure" (essentially, cash-out) rather than as an asset like we would in the corporate world, and we will recognize the proceeds of long-term debt as Other Financing Sources (cash-in) rather than as a long-term liability. The omission of long-term assets and liabilities limits the usefulness of fund financial statements for the evaluation of the solvency of the governmental body and, thus, provides some of the impetus for the government-wide financial statements that we discuss in Chapter 10.

LO4 Describe fund accounting journal entries.

We begin our discussion of fund accounting with the initial journal entry to record the current year's budget, the first entry of the fiscal year.

Budget Entry In its FY2014 Town meeting, the **Town of Acton** residents approved total appropriations in the General Fund amounting to $84,106,764 (to simplify the exposition, we assume that budgeted amounts are equal to those reported in the town's financial statements that we reproduce later in the chapter). This dollar amount was the result of a long and, sometimes contentious, process of public hearings. The process began with an estimate of the total amount of funds that the Town would receive from the state and federal governments in the form of grants and subsidies, interest income and departmental income from fees. Then, Town administrators faced the daunting task of determining simultaneously how much would be spent on municipal services, like public safety and education, and how much would have to be raised in the form of taxes on Town residents. Although much of the municipal and education expenditures budget is fixed (e.g., salaries and benefits), discretionary expenditures are typically met with strong opposition from overburdened taxpayers.

The final budget appropriated $84,106,764 for municipal and education expenditures, employee benefits, debt service and capital outlays. To fund these projected outflows, the Town estimated that it would receive $71,536,337 in taxes on real estate, $2,700,000 in taxes on automobiles, $7,980,667 in grants from the State of Massachusetts, and miscellaneous other inflows of $1,339,000. These receipts, together with an estimated $490,660 in outflows from Other Financing Uses, would result in an estimated budget deficit of $1,041,420. This budgeted deficit would decrease the General Fund from a balance of $14,411,967 at the beginning of the year to $13,370,547 at year-end.

The approved budget is as follows:

	General
Revenues	
Property taxes.	$71,536,337
Excises.	2,700,000
Penalties and interest.	150,000
Licenses and permits.	199,000
Fees and other departmental.	686,000
Intergovernmental.	7,980,667
Charges for services.	27,000
Fines and forfeits.	119,000
Earnings on investments.	96,000
In lieu of taxes.	12,000
Miscellaneous.	50,000
Total revenues.	83,556,004
Expenditures	
General government.	7,236,779
Public safety.	6,915,317
Education.	54,107,577
Intergovernmental.	317,667
Highways and public works.	3,270,062
Human services.	1,785,233
Culture and recreation.	1,316,095
Employee benefits.	6,108,533
Debt service.	3,049,501
Total expenditures.	84,106,764
Excess of revenues over (under) expenditures.	(550,760)
Other financing uses.	(490,660)
Excess (deficiency) of revenues and other financing sources over expenditures and other financing (uses).	(1,041,420)
Fund balance beginning of year.	14,411,967
Fund balance end of year.	$13,370,547

In order to compute the tax bill for each parcel of real estate that yields the desired total amount of property tax revenue ($71,536,337 in this case), the Town's assessor estimates the total value of all real property subject to taxation. That estimate was about $3.72 billion in this year. Since the Town needed to raise $71.5 million in real estate tax, each parcel of real estate would be taxed at about 1.9% ($71.5 million/$3.72 billion) of its value. The real estate tax levy (i.e., the tax rate as a percentage of value) is, therefore, the computed percentage that yields the needed tax inflow.[6]

Once the budget is approved, it is entered into the Town's governmental fund accounting records with the following journal entry:[7,8]

---

[6] Sometimes tax rates are expressed in the form of $Tax per $1,000 of assessed valuation. This is known as a *mill rate*. For example, if the mill rate is $15 and the assessed valuation is $500,000, the assessed tax is $15 × $500 = $7,500 for the year, and the tax levy is typically paid in quarterly installments.

[7] Our convention in this text is to designate budgetary journal entries with all capital letters in order to distinguish them from journal entries relating to operating transactions.

[8] Governments typically use "control accounts" in the major journals, with subsidiary accounts recording the related detail (similar to the use of an Accounts Receivable control account that is supported by a subsidiary ledger containing the information relating to specific accounts). Our use of the term "CONTROL" signifies this type of account.

ESTIMATED REVENUES—TAX LEVY CONTROL........................	71,536,337	
ESTIMATED REVENUES—EXCISE TAX CONTROL......................	2,700,000	
ESTIMATED REVENUES—PENALTIES AND INTEREST CONTROL...........	150,000	
ESTIMATED REVENUES—LICENSES AND PERMITS CONTROL............	199,000	
ESTIMATED REVENUES—FEES AND OTHER DEPARTMENTAL CONTROL....	686,000	
ESTIMATED REVENUES—INTERGOVERNMENTAL CONTROL..............	7,980,667	
ESTIMATED REVENUES—CHARGES FOR SERVICES CONTROL...........	27,000	
ESTIMATED REVENUES—FINES AND FORFEITS CONTROL..............	119,000	
ESTIMATED REVENUES—EARNINGS ON INVESTMENTS CONTROL........	96,000	
ESTIMATED REVENUES—IN LIEU OF TAXES CONTROL..................	12,000	
ESTIMATED REVENUES—MISCELLANEOUS CONTROL..................	50,000	
BUDGETARY FUND BALANCE	1,041,420	
APPROPRIATIONS—GENERAL GOVERNMENT CONTROL		7,236,779
APPROPRIATIONS—PUBLIC SAFETY CONTROL...................		6,915,317
APPROPRIATIONS—EDUCATION CONTROL		54,107,577
APPROPRIATIONS—INTERGOVERNMENTAL CONTROL.............		317,667
APPROPRIATIONS—HIGHWAY AND PUBLIC WORKS CONTROL......		3,270,062
APPROPRIATIONS—HUMAN SERVICES ASSESSMENTS CONTROL ...		1,785,233
APPROPRIATIONS—CULTURE AND RECREATION CONTROL		1,316,095
APPROPRIATIONS—EMPLOYEE BENEFITS CONTROL.		6,108,533
APPROPRIATIONS—DEBT SERVICE CONTROL...................		3,049,501
ESTIMATED OTHER FINANCING USES		490,660
(to record budget)		

This entry allows Town administrators to regularly monitor actual vs. budget variances during the year in order to monitor expenditure levels. This monitoring process is critical since, unlike businesses, governments can only increase revenues through the legislative process and cannot move cash from one fund to another to make up for shortfalls. Consequently, Town managers must take elaborate steps to ensure that expenditures do not exceed appropriations. At the end of the accounting year, then, we will reverse this budget entry in the closing process, and one of our required disclosures is a schedule comparing actual expenditures with budgeted amounts. We discuss the closing process later in the chapter.

Budget Revisions   Sometimes, governments revise their budgets during the year to reflect changes in estimates. Usually, in the face of cost overruns, managers do not have the authority to move funds from one fund account to another, and the revision requires an additional appropriation that may require approval by the citizens.

To illustrate, assume that New England experiences a particularly harsh winter and that the costs for snow removal are higher than originally anticipated by $50,000. If the cost overrun requires an additional appropriation, the Town will make the following journal entry once the revised expenditure has been approved by citizens:

BUDGETARY FUND BALANCE	50,000	
APPROPRIATIONS—MUNICIPAL CONTROL..................		50,000
(to record the increased appropriation of $50,000 for snow removal)		

The budget comparison schedule we discuss above must also include a column relating to budget revisions in order to identify any changes from the original budget.

Tax and Fee Revenues   Taxes based on the assessed values (called *Ad Valorem* – Latin: by value) of real estate and personal property (autos, for example) are, typically, the largest sources of revenue for cities and towns. These taxes require an annual assessment of real and personal property values by the government, and the tax liability is usually set in the budgeting process as a percentage of assessed valuation as we discuss above.

Tax Levy Entry   When real estate taxes are assessed and the billings sent to residents, the Town makes the following journal entry to record the revenue and the associated receivable (the Town of Acton takes the position that the receivables are fully collectible since they are secured by a tax lien on the property that provides legal protection if the tax is not paid):[9]

Real estate taxes receivable.	71,536,337	
Revenues—property taxes		71,536,337
(to record the tax levy)		

Tax liens allow the Town to foreclose on the real estate similar to the protection afforded to mortgage lenders. If foreclosed, the real estate can be sold to raise funds for the payment of the lien. The Town is justified in taking the position that the receivable is fully collectible provided that it has experienced no losses as a result of the lien protection. Had the Town decided to reserve for uncollectible accounts in the amount of $3,000,000, for example, the journal entry would be adjusted as follows:

Real estate taxes receivable.	71,536,337	
Allowance for uncollectible taxes		3,000,000
Revenues—property taxes		68,536,337
(to record the tax levy)		

Should the Town subsequently decide to increase the Allowance for Uncollectible Taxes, the debit is to Revenues. Write-offs, if any, of uncollectible taxes are charged to the allowance account in the normal manner.

Assume that all of the taxes receivable are collected, except for $1,000,000 that are delinquent but estimated to be collectible. The Town makes the following journal entry to record the receipts and the reclassification of $1,000,000 of taxes receivable as delinquent:

1.	Cash	70,536,337	
	Real estate taxes receivable		70,536,337
	(to record collection of taxes receivable)		
2.	Real estate taxes receivable—delinquent	1,000,000	
	Real estate taxes receivable		1,000,000
	(to reclassify unpaid taxes receivable as delinquent)		

Journal entry #1 records the collection of the taxes. Journal entry #2 transfers the delinquent taxes into a receivable account that will be separately disclosed by the Town as delinquent so that readers of the financial statements will be aware of the proportion of receivables that have not been paid according to their terms. Again, the Town takes the position that these delinquent taxes are fully collectible and, therefore, no allowance for uncollectible accounts is required. That position should be reconsidered if experience indicates otherwise.

Personal Property (Excise) Tax Entry   Personal property taxes are assessed on specified items, like autos, as a percentage of assessed valuation. Each year, then, the personal property tax on a particular auto will decline with the reduction in its market value. When the personal property tax bills are mailed to residents, the Town makes the following entry to record the revenue and an (assumed) estimated allowance for uncollectible accounts in the amount of $200,000:[10]

---

[9] Notice that the full amount of the tax levy has been recognized as revenue. During the closing process for the year in which this tax is assessed, the amount expected to be collected after 60 days will be deferred. Assume that $50,000 is expected to be collected after 60 days. The required reversing entry is as follows:

Revenues—property taxes.	50,000	
Deferred revenues—property taxes.		50,000
(to defer the portion of the tax levy to be collected after 60 days from fiscal year-end)		

This Deferred Revenue will be recognized as Revenue in the following fiscal year.

[10] Again, the portion of the revenue that is not expected to be collected within 60 days will be deferred with a reversing entry in the closing process as we describe in footnote 8.

Personal property taxes receivable	2,700,000	
Allowance for uncollectible personal property taxes.		200,000
Revenues—personal property taxes		2,500,000
(to record excise taxes receivable less estimated uncollectible amounts of $200,000)		

Notice that the credit for the allowance for uncollectible accounts is not offset with a debit to an expense account as it is in the bad debt accrual for a business. Fund accounting is only concerned with inflows and outflows of current resources (cash). The allowance for uncollectible personal property taxes, therefore, only affects the amount of receivables that will ultimately be collected, hence, the reduction of the debit to the receivable account. If the allowance account is further adjusted, the offset will, again, be to the receivable account. And, if an account is written off, the write-off is made to the allowance account.

To illustrate, assume that the Town of Acton writes off a personal property tax receivable of $10,000. The entry to record the write-off is as follows:

Allowance for uncollectible personal property taxes	10,000	
Personal property tax taxes receivable		10,000
(to record the write-off of a $10,000 excise tax receivable)		

Encumbrances and Expenditures (Purchase Orders and Payment)

Accountability is the philosophical cornerstone of financial reporting in government. Accountability requires governments to justify the raising of public resources and the purposes for which they are used. The GASB summarizes the meaning of accountability and its applicability to financial reporting in the following statement in its Concepts Statement #1: "The Board believes that, at a minimum, demonstrating accountability through financial reporting includes providing information to assist in evaluating whether the government was operated within the legal constraints imposed by the citizenry" (GASB CS 1, ¶58). It is this belief that underlies the series of journal entries that relate to the generation of purchase orders for goods and services and their ultimate payment which we describe below.

As we discuss earlier in the chapter, purchases of capital assets (appropriations) must be approved in the budget process. When the purchase is ultimately made, the appropriation is used up, and the using up of an appropriation is called an **expenditure**.[11]

One of the objectives of fund accounting is to make sure that departments do not overspend the monies that have been appropriated to them in the budget process. We accomplish that objective by keeping track of both the amounts that have been expended to date as well as amounts that we have *committed to spend*. This latter amount is an encumbrance. An **encumbrance** is a purchase order or other contractual commitment that requires the payment of funds in the future relating to an existing appropriation.

To illustrate the accounting for encumbrances and subsequent expenditures, assume that the Town of Acton issues a purchase order in the amount of $50,000 for goods or services that have been previously appropriated. When the purchase order is signed, it becomes a claim against the appropriation that must be recognized in the related fund's balance sheet. Then, when the goods or services are received, the encumbrance restriction is reversed and the expenditure is recognized. The entries to reserve the fund balance and to record the receipt of the goods or services are as follows:

	Issuance of Purchase Order	Goods or Services Are Received
Budgetary accounts	ENCUMBRANCES . . . . 50,000 BUDGETARY FUND BALANCE —RESERVED FOR ENCUMBRANCES . . . 50,000 *(to record issuance of purchase order for goods or services)*	BUDGETARY FUND BALANCE —RESERVED FOR ENCUMBRANCES . . . . 50,000 ENCUMBRANCES . . . . 50,000 *(to reverse the previous encumbrance entry)*
Fund financial statement accounts	No entry	Expenditures . . . . 50,000 Cash or vouchers payable . . . . 50,000 *(to record purchase of goods or services)*

---

[11] The GASB codification formally defines **expenditures** as "decreases in (uses of) fund financial resources other than through interfund transfers" (GASB ASC Glossary 1800.114).

The use of encumbrance accounts is one of the most significant differences between fund accounting and accrual accounting. Under accrual accounting, a liability is not recognized until it is incurred, that is, when the goods or services are received and payment is required. It is at the point of receipt that a business would record the asset or expense and the related obligation to make payment to the vendor. Under fund accounting, however, an encumbrance is recorded when the purchase contract is signed.

The encumbrance is not a liability. It represents a restriction of the fund balance relating to a planned expenditure. The Town's funds have, thus, been restricted so that they cannot be spent for other purchases, thus assuring Town managers that they will not overspend their appropriated budgets. Later, when the goods or services are received, the encumbrance is removed and the expenditure is recorded. The removal of the encumbrance and the recognition of the expenditure are accomplished by two journal entries. The first journal entry reverses the temporary restriction placed on the fund by the encumbrance. The second entry records the expenditure for the actual amount paid or payable and the fund balance is reduced by the expenditure (the term vouchers payable is often used in a government and is similar to accounts payable in the business world).

Notice that the fund balance is reduced when the purchase invoice is issued, thus providing some measure of protection against the issuance of additional purchase orders that might result in total expenditures exceeding the amount appropriated for that expenditure. This control feature is illustrated in the following Practice Insight box.

Not all expenditure commitments need encumbrance control. Employee salaries that are fixed in nature may be recognized as expenditures when due without the need for a formal encumbrance. Finally, notice that the entry to record the encumbrance is a budgetary entry, not a journal entry in the fund accounts, and budget entries are reversed at year-end (we discuss the closing process later in this chapter).

PRACTICE INSIGHT

Use of Encumbrances to Monitor Expenditures The use of encumbrances provides the control necessary to ensure that mangers do not overspend the appropriation that has been approved by the citizens. The remaining authority to issue further appropriations of approved expenditures is given by the following formula:

$$\begin{array}{c}\text{Remaining authority to} \\ \text{authorize appropriations}\end{array} = \begin{array}{c}\text{BUDGETARY} \\ \text{APPROPRIATIONS}\end{array} - \left[\begin{array}{c}\text{ENCUMBRANCES} \\ \text{outstanding}\end{array} + \begin{array}{c}\text{Expenditures} \\ \text{to date}\end{array}\right]$$

At any time, therefore, government managers can assess their authority to issue additional appropriations.

Outstanding Encumbrances at Year-End It is possible that some orders that have been recorded as encumbrances during the year might not be filled by the end of the fiscal year. In order to preserve an orderly working relationship with suppliers, governments typically carry over prior year's commitments into the succeeding budget year. For some municipalities, however, the legal authority for government managers to honor these commitments might expire, thus necessitating a new appropriation for the expenditure in the succeeding budget year. Whether legal authority lapses or does not lapse (i.e., budgetary authority carries over to the new fiscal year), the government must remove the budgetary encumbrance and reserve its Fund Balance for the ongoing commitment. Other required journal entries differ depending on whether encumbrances formally lapse at the end of the fiscal year or whether they carry over to the subsequent year.

To illustrate, assume that the Town placed an order for the purchase of a truck in the amount of $50,000 that has not been received by the end of the fiscal year. The Town must make the following journal entries during the closing process:

BUDGETARY FUND BALANCE—RESERVED FOR ENCUMBRANCES..........	50,000	
ENCUMBRANCES..		50,000
Fund balance—unassigned..	50,000	
Fund balance—assigned......................................		50,000
(to reverse the budgetary encumbrance and reserve the fund balance for the outstanding encumbrance)		

Encumbrances at year-end will be reflected in the restricted, committed, or assigned categories of the fund balance depending on their character. In this case, the $50,000 encumbrance is recognized in the assigned fund category to reflect the outstanding purchase order.

Purchase and Sale of Long-Term Assets

The purchase of capital assets, like a truck, for governmental use (i.e., not for a business activity accounted for in an Enterprise Fund) highlights the *current financial resources measurement focus* that we discuss above. Our focus under this approach is only on "current financial resources," such as cash, investments, and receivables. Since we are only focusing on current financial resources, long-term resources, like PPE, are not recorded on the fund balance sheet.[12] Instead, purchases of capital assets are recorded as expenditures (a reduction of financial resources) and are not capitalized on the balance sheet as would be the case in the accounting for a business.

To illustrate the accounting for the purchase of a long-term asset, assume that the Town of Acton orders a machine to be used for general governmental purposes (i.e., not for a business-type activity). The order is placed for an estimated purchase cost of $40,000, and an encumbrance is recorded as follows:

ENCUMBRANCES	40,000	
BUDGETARY FUND BALANCE— RESERVED FOR ENCUMBRANCES		40,000
(to record issuance of purchase order for a machine)		

When the machine is finally received, assume that the actual cost is $42,500 due to additional features that were subsequently added by the Town to the machine order. The entry to record the receipt of the machine is as follows:

BUDGETARY FUND BALANCE—RESERVED FOR ENCUMBRANCES.	40,000	
ENCUMBRANCES.		40,000
Expenditures	42,500	
Cash or vouchers payable.		42,500
(to reverse the previous encumbrance entry and record purchase of machine)		

The machine is recorded as an expenditure in the Governmental Fund to recognize the reduction of current financial resources. It is not recorded on the fund balance sheet.

If the machine is subsequently sold, the inflow of current financial resources is recorded as Other Financing Sources. And, since the machine is not recorded on the balance sheet, no gain or loss on the sale is recognized. For example, assume that the machine is sold for $15,000 after it has been used for three years by the Town. The sale is recorded as follows:

Cash or accounts receivable	15,000	
Other financing sources*		15,000
(to record the sale of the machine)		

* The sale can also be recognized as Other Revenue if immaterial.

Since there is no asset in the balance sheet, no gain or loss on sale is recognized. Instead, the sale is recorded as an inflow of cash.

Other Financing Sources and Uses (Long-Term Debt and Leases, and Interfund Transfers)

Governments typically finance the purchase or construction of capital assets with long-term notes and bonds or by leasing. Since fund financial statements are prepared using the *current financial resources measurement focus*, these long-term liabilities are not recognized on the balance sheet. Instead, the proceeds of borrowing are recognized as Other Financing Sources, and the payment of principal and interest are recorded as Expenditures. In the following sections, we discuss three common financing transactions: borrowing with long-term debt, leasing, and interfund loans and transfers.

Long-Term Debt The proceeds from long-term debt are not recognized as revenue because the debt must be repaid, and the future payment amounts are not recognized on the balance sheet since they will require the use of future financial resources. Instead, the borrowing is reported as Other Financing

---

[12] Long-term assets for business-type uses are capitalized on the balance sheet of an Enterprise Fund just like they are for a business.

Sources. To illustrate, assume that the government sells a bond of $10,000,000 at par. The sale would be recorded as follows:

Cash	10,000,000	
Other financing sources—proceeds from bond issue............		10,000,000
(to record sale of a bond)		

Further assume that the bond is repaid together with interest of $500,000. The entry to record the repayment is as follows:

Expenditure—interest on bond	500,000	
Expenditure—repayment of bond	10,000,000	
Cash		10,500,000
(to record payment of interest and principal on bond issue)		

The principal and interest payments are recognized as expenditures when paid. Interest is not accrued like it is for businesses. Instead, it is recognized as an expenditure in the year in which it is due to be paid.

Capital Leases   Under fund accounting, leases are recorded like bonds: the present value of the minimum lease payments is recorded as Other Financing Sources.[13] And, the acquisition of the leased asset is recorded at the same amount as an expenditure. To illustrate, assume that the Town of Acton acquires an asset via a capital lease with a present value of the minimum lease payments equal to $40,000. The acquisition is recorded as follows:

Expenditure—capital outlay......................................	40,000	
Other financing sources—proceeds from capital lease		40,000
(to record the acquisition of a capital asset via lease)		

Assume further that the lease requires payment of $3,000, including $1,000 of interest and $2,000 to reduce the lease obligation. The payment is recorded as follows:

Expenditure—interest..	1,000	
Expenditure—lease obligation	2,000	
Cash		3,000
(to record the payment on a capital lease)		

In contrast to the accounting treatment for capital leases, operating leases are simply recorded as an expenditure when paid.[14] Neither the Expenditure nor Other Financing Sources are recognized.

Interfund Transactions   Fund accounting separates governmental activities into discrete accounting entities to allow managers to monitor spending to ensure compliance with budgetary and legal restrictions. Transfers of cash between funds must be monitored closely so that deficits in one fund cannot be masked by transfers into that fund from another fund. Consequently, GASB 34 requires any interfund transfers to be clearly identified unless they are merely reimbursements made for proper classification of the expenditure.

GASB ASC 1800.102 identifies four types of interfund activity and the proper accounting for each:

1. **Interfund loans**—amounts provided with a requirement for repayment. These loans are usually to be repaid within the fiscal year and are, thus, a temporary funding mechanism that will be eliminated by year-end.
   - ○ Interfund loans should be reported as interfund receivables in lender funds and interfund payables in borrower funds (not as other financing sources or uses in the fund financial statements).
2. **Interfund services provided and used**—sales and purchases of goods and services between funds for a price approximating their external exchange value. An example is an internal service fund such as a centralized motor pool for governmental vehicles or a centralized copy center that provides copy services to all branches of the government.

---

[13] Since Proprietary Funds utilize an economic resources measurement focus, both the leased asset and the lease obligation are recognized on the balance sheet of a Proprietary Fund.

[14] As of the writing of this text, the FASB and GASB are considering proposals that will eliminate the operating lease distinction.

○ Interfund services provided and used should be reported as revenues in seller funds and expenditures or expenses in purchaser funds.

3. **Interfund transfers**—flows of assets (such as cash or goods) without equivalent flows of assets in return and without a requirement for repayment. An example is the transfer of cash from the General Fund to a Debt Service Fund to provide cash for payment of debt obligations.

○ In governmental funds, transfers should be reported as Other Financing Uses in the funds making transfers and as Other Financing Sources in the funds receiving transfers.

○ In proprietary funds, transfers should be reported after nonoperating revenues and expenses.

4. **Interfund reimbursements**—repayments from the funds responsible for particular expenditures or expenses to the funds that initially paid for them. An example would include the General Fund making payment to the local utility for electricity and, subsequently, receiving reimbursement from other funds that are properly charged for the utility expenditure.

○ Reimbursements should be accounted for as a reduction of expenditure in the fund originally making payment.

Following is a summary of the general form of the journal entries required for interfund transactions:

Type of Interfund Transaction	Fund Paying Cash (X)		Fund Receiving Cash (Y)	
1. Loans	Due from Fund Y	xxx	Cash (from X)	xxx
	Cash (to Y)	xxx	Due to Fund X	xxx
2. Services	Expenditures*	xxx	Cash (from X)	xxx
	Cash (to Y)	xxx	Revenue	xxx
3. Transfers	Other financing uses	xxx	Cash (from X)	xxx
	Cash (to Y)	xxx	Other financing sources	xxx
4. Reimbursements	Expenditures	xxx	Cash	xxx
	Cash	xxx	Expenditures**	xxx

* If the fund purchasing services is a proprietary fund, *Expenses* is debited rather than Expenditures.
** The credit to Expenditures reverses the debit made when the goods or services were purchased. The result is the recognition of the Expenditure in Fund X, not in Fund Y.

Inventories Governments typically do not maintain large quantities of inventories. Consequently, purchases of inventories are usually recorded as expenditures either when the inventories are purchased (Purchases Method) or when used (Consumption Method). If the ending balance of inventories is considered to be material, the inventory should be reported in the balance sheet (GASB ASC 1600.127), and if the inventory is shown on the balance sheet, an amount equal to the inventory balance is shown as a reservation of the Fund Balance to signify that the fund is not available for expenditure.

To illustrate, assume that the Town of Acton purchases $3,000 of office supplies on account. Both the purchases and consumption methods begin by recording the inventory purchase as follows:

Expenditures 3,000
    Vouchers payable 3,000
(to record purchase of $3,000 of supplies inventory)

If the inventories are deemed to be material, the ending balance is recognized on the balance sheet using one of two acceptable approaches (the purchases method or the consumption method).

To illustrate, assume that the inventories are purchased close to the fiscal year-end and that $2,500 of the cost of the inventories remains unused at year-end. If this amount is material, the ending balance of the inventories under the purchases method and the consumption method is recognized as follows:

Purchases Method			Consumption Method		
Inventory—supplies	2,500		Inventory—supplies	2,500	
Fund balance—nonspendable		2,500	Expenditures		2,500
(to recognize the remaining balance of supplies inventory)			*(to recognize the remaining balance of supplies inventory)*		
			Fund balance—unassigned	2,500	
			Fund balance—nonspendable		2,500
			(to recognize the remaining balance of supplies inventory)		

Under both methods, inventories are reported on the balance sheet at the (unused) amount remaining of $2,500, and an equal amount of the Fund Balance is reserved to signify that it is not available for future expenditures. The balance sheet, therefore, is unaffected by the choice of the inventory reporting method. The only difference between the two methods lies in the Statement of Revenues, Expenditures, and Changes in Fund Balance:

- **Purchases method**—Expenditures equal the amount *purchased*
- **Consumption method**—Expenditures equal the amount *consumed*

Both methods are used in practice, and the choice depends on whether the budgeted appropriation is for expected purchases or expected consumption of inventories during the upcoming year.

TOPIC REVIEW 1

Prepare journal entries in the General Fund for each of the following events relating to the City of Lafayette (all amounts in $1,000s).

a. The citizens approve the following budget for the year:

ESTIMATED REVENUES	$41,041
ESTIMATED OTHER FINANCING SOURCES	2,000
APPROPRIATIONS	(40,182)
BUDGETARY FUND BALANCE	$ 2,859

b. The City records the following revenues (on account) and other financing sources (paid in cash) during the year:

Revenues—real estate and personal property taxes	$35,490
Revenues—intergovernmental	6,388
Other financing sources—bond proceeds	2,000

c. The City issues purchase invoices totaling $39,784 (record the issuance of invoices as a lump sum).

d. The City recognizes the following expenditures, all on account (these expenditures were previously reserved as budgetary encumbrances):

Expenditures—general government	$ 5,967
Expenditures—public safety	3,978
Expenditures—education	23,871
Expenditures—public works	1,989
Expenditures—human services	3,979

e. The City makes the following payments related to its outstanding debt:

Expenditures—debt principal payments	$700
Expenditures—debt interest payments	100

f. The City collects accounts receivable ($35,334 relating to property taxes and $6,069 relating to intergovernmental receivables) and pays outstanding accounts payable in the amount of $38,989 during the year.

g. The City recognizes an increase of $507 in Deferred Revenues as a year-end adjustment to yield a balance in that account of the total property taxes receivable that are not expected to be collected within 60 days.

The solution to this review problem can be found on page 619.

Fund Financial Statements

The pre-closing trial balance reflects all of the journal entries that we discuss above. We then use this to prepare the fund financial statements in the same way that we use the pre-closing trial balance to prepare the income statement and balance sheet for a corporation.

LO5 Describe the preparation of fund financial statements.

We prepare a different set of financial statements for each type of Fund (GASB ASC 2200.105b):

1. Governmental funds
   a. Balance sheet
   b. Statement of revenues, expenditures, and changes in fund balances
2. Proprietary funds
   a. Statement of net position
   b. Statement of revenues, expenses, and changes in fund net position
   c. Statement of cash flows
3. Fiduciary funds (and component units that are fiduciary in nature)
   a. Statement of fiduciary net position
   b. Statement of changes in fiduciary net position

In addition to differences in the required financial statements by fund category, it is also important to keep in mind that these financial statements are also prepared using a different measurement focus as we discuss above and in subsequent sections of this chapter:

- **Governmental Funds are prepared using the** *current financial resources measurement focus and the modified accrual basis of accounting,*

- **Proprietary and Fiduciary Funds are prepared using the** *economic resources measurement focus and the accrual basis of accounting.*

We now present and discuss the financial statements for each of the general fund types listed above.

Financial Statements for Governmental Funds

We present the fiscal year 2014 Balance Sheet for the Town of Acton in Exhibit 9.4. Fund financial statements should present the financial information of each major fund in a separate column. Non-major funds should be aggregated and displayed in a single column. The reporting government's main operating fund (i.e., the general fund) should always be reported as a major fund. Other funds are designated as major funds, and reported in separate columns in the fund financial statements, if the following requirements are met (GASB ASC 2200.159):

a. Total assets and deferred outflows of resources, liabilities and deferred inflows of resources, revenues, or expenditures/expenses are at least 10% of the corresponding total for all funds of the fund's type (i.e., a specific enterprise fund whose total assets are greater than 10% of the total assets of all enterprise funds), and

b. The same element(s) that met the 10 percent criterion in (*a*) is at least 5 percent of the corresponding element total for all governmental and enterprise funds combined.[15]

The Town of Acton reports two major funds: the General Fund and the Community Preservation Act Fund (a special revenue fund used to account for the accumulation of resources to purchase open space, provide affordable housing, or preservation of historical property under the guidelines of the Community Preservation Act of the Massachusetts General Laws). All other funds are aggregated in the Nonmajor Funds columns because they do not meet the size tests referenced above.

Receivables include taxes on real estate and personal property, together with penalties and interest on delinquent taxes. The Town takes the position that delinquent taxes are fully collectible since they are secured by liens on the related real estate and prior experience does not reveal collection losses.

---

[15] Governments may also report a fund as a major fund, even if it does not meet these financial thresholds, if the fund is deemed to be important because of public interest or consistency with prior fund financial statements.

The Town also reports nearly $8.6 million of grants and other aid receivable from the state and federal governments. This aid primarily relates to the Town's school system. Since collection of the receivables is not expected to occur within 60 days, the revenue related to these receivables is deferred in these financial statements.

EXHIBIT 9.4   Balance Sheet for the Town of Acton Governmental Funds

TOWN OF ACTON, MASSACHUSETTS
Balance Sheet
Governmental Funds
June 30, 2014

	General	Community Preservation Act	Nonmajor Governmental Funds	Total Governmental Funds
Assets:				
Cash and cash equivalents	$14,468,601	$4,823,556	$ 7,309,662	$26,601,819
Investments	1,373,342	—	3,844,622	5,217,964
Accounts receivable:				
Property taxes	665,968	6,598	—	672,566
Tax liens	1,189,600	6,366	—	1,195,966
Motor vehicle excise	197,241	—	—	197,241
User charges	—	—	107,596	107,596
Clause 41A property taxes	139,268	—	—	139,268
Special assessments	—	—	172,597	172,597
Departmental	4,001	—	96,702	100,703
Intergovernmental	8,599,761	—	930,124	9,529,885
Tax foreclosures	250,341	—	—	250,341
Due from other funds	289,909	—	—	289,909
Total assets	$27,178,032	$4,836,520	$12,461,303	$44,475,855
Liabilities:				
Warrants payable	$ 745,832	$ 4,365	$ 103,087	$ 853,284
Accrued payroll payable	193,560	131	35,037	228,728
Due to other fund	—	—	289,909	289,909
Unclaimed checks	22,055	—	—	22,055
Due to component unit	—	175,000	697,001	872,001
Total liabilities	961,447	179,496	1,125,034	2,265,977
Deferred inflows of resources[16]	—	—	—	—
Unavailable revenue	10,507,193	12,964	885,040	11,405,197
Total deferred inflows of resources	10,507,193	12,964	885,040	11,405,197
Fund equity:				
Fund balances:				
Nonspendable	—	—	1,990,737	1,990,737
Restricted	—	4,644,060	6,730,225	11,374,285
Committed	2,009,485	—	1,730,267	3,739,752
Assigned	1,596,387	—	—	1,596,387
Unassigned	12,103,520	—	—	12,103,520
Total fund balances	15,709,392	4,644,060	10,451,229	30,804,681
Total liabilities, deferred inflows of resources and fund balances	$27,178,032	$4,836,520	$12,461,303	$44,475,855

[16] Deferred Inflows of Resources are analogous to the deferred revenue liability in accrual accounting. For the Town of Acton, this represents the receipt of tax payments which cannot be recognized as current revenues under the current financial resources measurement focus.

There are two primary differences between the balance sheet for a governmental entity and that for a commercial business:

1. **No long-term asset and liability accounts.** Because the government balance sheet is prepared using the current financial resources measurement focus, long-term assets such as PPE and long-term liabilities are not recognized (recall, we record the purchase of PPE as an expenditure and the borrowing and repayment of long-term debt as other financing sources and uses), and

2. **Fund balances are reported for the excess of assets over liabilities.** These fund balances are grouped into the following five categories as defined in GASB (GASB ASC 2200.166–177) (our balance sheet for the Town of Acton reflects these categories):

   a. **Nonspendable**—amounts that cannot be spent because they are either (a) not in spendable form or (b) legally or contractually required to be maintained intact. The "not in spendable form" criterion includes items that are not expected to be converted to cash, for example, inventories and prepaid amounts. It also includes the long-term amount of loans and notes receivable, as well as property acquired for resale.

   b. **Restricted**—amounts that are restricted to specific purposes such as a. externally imposed by creditors (such as through debt covenants), grantors, contributors, or laws or regulations of other governments; or b. imposed by law through constitutional provisions or enabling legislation.

   c. **Committed**—amounts that can only be used for specific purposes pursuant to constraints imposed by formal action of the government's highest level of decision-making authority.

   d. **Assigned**—amounts that are constrained by the government's intent to be used for specific purposes, but are neither restricted nor committed.

   e. **Unassigned**—the residual classification for the general fund. This classification represents a fund balance that has not been assigned to other funds and that has not been restricted, committed, or assigned to specific purposes within the general fund.

The Town's financial condition is healthy. It reports over $14 million of cash at the end of the year and its receivables are collectible. It also reports significant financial flexibility with over $12 million of unassigned funds available for general use as directed by the Town managers.

We present the fiscal year 2014 Statement of Revenues, Expenditures and Changes in Fund Balances for the Town of Acton in Exhibit 9.5. The Statement of Revenues, Expenditures, and Changes in Fund Balances reports information about the inflows, outflows, and balances of current financial resources of each major governmental fund and for the nonmajor governmental funds in the aggregate. A total column should also be presented, and the statement should present the following information in the format and sequence indicated (GASB ASC 2200.165):

> Revenues (detailed)
> Expenditures (detailed)
>
>   Excess (deficiency) of revenues over expenditures
> Other financing sources and uses, including transfers (detailed)
> Special and extraordinary items (detailed)
>
>   Net change in fund balances
> Fund balances—beginning of period
>
> Fund balances—end of period

Items that should be reported as other financing sources and uses include the face amount of long-term debt, issuance premium or discount, certain payments to escrow agents for bond refundings, transfers, and sales of capital assets. Special and extraordinary items should be reported separately after "other financing sources and uses."

Revenues and Expenditures are reported both by line item and segregated into the funds to which they relate. The net amount is reported in an account called Net Change in Fund Balance for each of the fund categories. This amount is, then, added to the beginning balance of each fund to yield the ending balance that is reported on the Balance Sheet.

EXHIBIT 9.5	Statement of Revenues, Expenditures, and Changes in Fund Balances for the Town of Acton Governmental Funds

TOWN OF ACTON, MASSACHUSETTS
Statement of Revenues, Expenditures, and Changes in Fund Balances
Governmental Funds
Fiscal Year Ended June 30, 2014

	General	Community Preservation Act	Nonmajor Governmental Funds	Total Governmental Funds
Revenues:				
Property taxes..........................	$71,851,785	$ 838,496	$ —	$72,690,281
Tax liens	203,679	—	—	203,679
Excises	2,918,815	—	—	2,918,815
Penalties and interest	210,035	832	—	210,867
Licenses and permits	215,238	—	—	215,238
Fees and other departmental	1,042,001	—	—	1,042,001
Intergovernmental.......................	12,520,218	424,035	2,735,643	15,679,896
Charges for services....................	25,209	—	2,754,219	2,779,428
Fines and forfeits	90,672	—	—	90,672
Earnings on investments	158,450	21,469	196,841	376,760
In lieu of taxes..........................	15,233	—	—	15,233
Contributions	182,298	—	793,530	975,828
Miscellaneous..........................	—	50,000	—	50,000
Total revenues.......................	89,433,633	1,334,832	6,480,233	97,248,698
Expenditures:				
Current				
General government.....................	6,451,741	2,380,778	985,478	9,817,997
Public safety...........................	6,883,835	43	1,083,960	7,967,838
Education	59,066,027	—	2,900,925	61,966,952
Intergovernmental.......................	336,501	—	—	336,501
Highways and public works	3,326,826	—	632,112	3,958,938
Human services	1,987,499	19,673	580,046	2,587,218
Culture and recreation	1,306,039	353,608	614,110	2,273,757
Employee benefits and insurance...........	5,885,558	—	—	5,885,558
Debt service				
Principal	2,129,617	—	—	2,129,617
Interest	702,826	—	—	702,826
Debt issuance costs	127,521	—	—	127,521
Total expenditures....................	88,203,990	2,754,102	6,796,631	97,754,723
Excess of revenues over (under) expenditures ...	1,229,643	(1,419,270)	(316,398)	(506,025)
Other financing sources (uses):				
Operating transfers in....................	617,738	260,000	250,000	1,127,738
Operating transfers (out)..................	(1,133,660)	—	(617,738)	(1,751,398)
Issuance of refunding bonds	12,220,000	—	—	12,220,000
Premium of refunding bonds	768,190	—	—	768,190
Payment to refunded bonds escrow agent	(12,860,669)	—	—	(12,860,669)
Total other financing sources (uses)	(388,401)	260,000	(367,738)	(496,139)
Net change in fund balance	841,242	(1,159,270)	(684,136)	(1,002,164)
Fund balance, beginning	14,868,150	5,803,330	11,135,365	31,806,845
Fund balance, ending.....................	$15,709,392	$4,644,060	$10,451,229	$30,804,681

Closing Entries

Following the preparation of the financial statements, we perform the following closing activities:

1. Reverse the initial entry that recorded the approved budget for the year

2. Zero out actual revenues and expenditures recorded during the year and update the Fund Balance—Unassigned

3. Reserve the Fund Balance for encumbrances that are expected to be honored in the following year

To illustrate, we use the budgeted revenues and appropriations in the text and also assume that actual revenues and expenditures equal budgeted amounts. We also assume that outstanding encumbrances at the end of the year amount to $300,000 and lapse. Given these assumptions, our closing entries at the end of the year are as follows:

1.

APPROPRIATIONS—GENERAL GOVERNMENT CONTROL	7,236,779	
APPROPRIATIONS—PUBLIC SAFETY CONTROL	6,915,317	
APPROPRIATIONS—EDUCATION CONTROL	54,107,577	
APPROPRIATIONS—INTERGOVERNMENTAL CONTROL	317,667	
APPROPRIATIONS—HIGHWAY AND PUBLIC WORKS CONTROL	3,270,062	
APPROPRIATIONS—HUMAN SERVICES CONTROL	1,785,233	
APPROPRIATIONS—CULTURE AND RECREATION CONTROL	1,316,095	
APPROPRIATIONS—EMPLOYEE BENEFITS CONTROL	6,108,533	
APPROPRIATIONS—DEBT SERVICE CONTROL	3,049,501	
ESTIMATED OTHER FINANCING USES	490,660	
ESTIMATED REVENUES—TAX LEVY CONTROL		71,536,337
ESTIMATED REVENUES—EXCISE TAX CONTROL		2,700,000
ESTIMATED REVENUES—PENALTIES AND INTEREST CONTROL		150,000
ESTIMATED REVENUES—LICENSES AND PERMITS CONTROL		199,000
ESTIMATED REVENUES—FEES AND OTHER DEPARTMENTAL CONTROL		686,000
ESTIMATED REVENUES—INTERGOVERNMENTAL CONTROL		7,980,667
ESTIMATED REVENUES—CHARGES FOR SERVICES CONTROL		27,000
ESTIMATED REVENUES—FINES AND FORFEITS CONTROL		119,000
ESTIMATED REVENUES—EARNINGS ON INVESTMENTS CONTROL		96,000
ESTIMATED REVENUES—IN LIEU OF TAXES CONTROL		12,000
ESTIMATED REVENUES—MISCELLANEOUS CONTROL		50,000
BUDGETARY FUND BALANCE		1,041,420
(to close budgetary accounts established at the beginning of the year)		

2.

Revenues—tax levy	71,536,337	
Revenues—excise tax	2,700,000	
Revenues—penalties and interest	150,000	
Revenues—licenses and permits	199,000	
Revenues—fees and other departmental	686,000	
Revenues—intergovernmental	7,980,667	
Revenues—charges for services	27,000	
Revenues—fines and forfeits	119,000	
Revenues—earnings on investments	96,000	
Revenues—in lieu of taxes	12,000	
Revenues—miscellaneous	50,000	
Fund Balance—unassigned	1,041,420	
Expenditures—general government		7,236,779
Expenditures—public safety		6,915,317
Expenditures—education		54,107,577
Expenditures—intergovernmental		317,667
Expenditures—highway and public works		3,270,062
Expenditures—human services		1,785,233
Expenditures—culture and recreation		1,316,095
Expenditures—employee benefits		6,108,533
Expenditures—debt service		3,049,501
Other financing uses		490,660
(to close operating statement accounts)		

3.	BUDGETARY FUND BALANCE—RESERVED FOR ENCUMBRANCES.................	300,000	
	ENCUMBRANCES...		300,000
	Fund balance—unassigned...	300,000	
	Fund balance—assigned...		300,000

(to close remaining encumbrances and reserve fund balance for encumbrances that lapsed, but are expected to be honored in the following year)

TOPIC REVIEW 2

Continuing with our previous topic review, assume that the City of Lafayette generates the following trial balance that reflects the entries in Topic Review 1:

Trial Balance:	DR	CR
Cash..	$11,987	
Receivables:		
Real estate and personal property.....................................	936	
Intergovernmental..	9,679	
Payables...		$ 1,108
Deferred revenues		10,647
Fund balances:		
Assigned...		2,808
Unassigned...		5,252
Revenues—real estate taxes		34,983
Revenues—intergovernmental		6,388
Expenditures—general government....................................	5,967	
Expenditures—public safety	3,978	
Expenditures—education..	23,871	
Expenditures—public works	1,989	
Expenditures—human services	3,979	
Expenditures—debt principal payments	700	
Expenditures—debt interest payments	100	
Other financing sources—proceeds from bonds..........................		2,000
	$63,186	$63,186

Required

a. Prepare the Balance Sheet and the Statement of Revenues, Expenditures, and Changes in Fund Balances for the City of Lafayette.

b. Prepare the required closing entries to close out the budgetary and operating accounts. Assume that the City closes out $468 of remaining budgetary encumbrances outstanding and formally charges that balance to Fund Balance—unassigned since the outstanding invoices are expected to be honored in the next fiscal year.

The solution to this review problem can be found on pages 620–621.

Financial Statements for Proprietary Funds

Proprietary Funds include activities of the government that are similar to those of businesses. These include activities for which the government charges a fee to users that is sufficient to cover the costs to provide that activity. They are not designed as profit-making enterprises. Instead, the goal is to provide an activity that is valued by citizens and to charge a fee for that activity that is set to just cover the cost of providing the activity. An example is a municipal swimming pool that charges a fee for use that is sufficient to both recover construction costs over time and to cover the annual operating budget. This activity would be classified as a type of Proprietary Fund called an Enterprise Fund. Another example is an internal copying center that charges fees to other departments within the government. This type of activity would be classified as an Internal Service Fund, another category of Proprietary Funds.

The Town of Acton maintains three Enterprise Funds:

1. Sanitation—maintains a solid waste transfer station to collect solid waste and transport it to a landfill
2. Sewer—provides sewer treatment and charges a fee based upon gallons of water used by the household
3. Nursing—provides in-home nursing care to elderly residents of the Town and charges a fee per call.

The footnotes to the financial statements of the Town of Acton describe the Enterprise Funds as follows:

> ***Proprietary Funds.*** The Town of Acton, Massachusetts maintains three proprietary (enterprise) fund types. *Enterprise funds* are used to report the same functions presented as *business-type activities* in the government-wide financial statements. The Town of Acton, Massachusetts uses enterprise funds to account for its sanitation, nursing services and sewer operations.
>
> Proprietary funds provide the same type of information as the government-wide financial statements, only in more detail. The proprietary fund financial statements provide separate information for each enterprise fund. All three funds are considered to be major funds of the Town of Acton, Massachusetts.

Financial Statements for Proprietary Funds

The financial statements for Proprietary Funds include the following:

- Statement of Net Position
- Statement of Revenues, Expenses, and Changes in Fund Net Position[17]
- Statement of Cash Flows

These financial statements are similar to those for commercial enterprises in their use of accrual basis accounting and the presentation of a Statement of Cash Flows, and are similar to those prepared for governmental funds in their reference to net position. We present the financial statements for the Town of Acton's Proprietary Funds in Exhibits 9.6–9.8.

The Statement of Net Position reports assets in order of liquidity and liabilities in order of maturity like the balance sheet for a business. The Statement of Net Position should be presented in a classified format to distinguish between current and long-term assets and liabilities. Since a government does not have shareholders, we replace Stockholders' Equity with Net Position. This section is divided into Invested in Capital Assets, net of related debt, Restricted, and Unrestricted (GASB ASC 2200.172). We discuss these components in Chapter 10 as this is the reporting of Net Position that is required for the Government-Wide Statement of Net Position.

The operating statement for proprietary funds is the Statement of Revenues, Expenses, and Changes in Fund Net Position. Revenues should be reported by major source. This statement also should distinguish between operating and nonoperating revenues and expenses and should present a separate subtotal for operating revenues, operating expenses, and operating income. Nonoperating revenues and expenses should be reported after operating income. Revenues from capital contributions and additions to the principal of permanent and term endowments, special and extraordinary items, and transfers should be reported separately, after nonoperating revenues and expenses. The Statement of Revenues, Expenses, and Changes in Fund Net Position should be presented in the following sequence using the all-inclusive format (GASB ASC 2200.191):

---

[17] Notice the use of the word *expenses* in place of *expenditures* to reflect the use of accrual accounting.

Operating revenues (detailed)
Total operating revenues
Operating expenses (detailed)
Total operating expenses
Operating income (loss)
Non-operating revenues and expense (detailed)
Income before other revenues, expenses, gains, losses, and transfers
Capital contributions (grant, developer, and other), additions to permanent and term endowments, special and extraordinary items (detailed), and transfers
Increase (decrease) in net position
Net position—beginning of period
Net position—end of period

Governments should also present a statement of cash flows for proprietary funds. The **direct method** of presenting cash flows from operating activities should be used. In reporting cash flows from operating activities, governmental enterprises should report major classes of gross cash receipts and gross cash payments and their arithmetic sum—the net cash flow from operating activities (the direct method). The statement of cash flows for proprietary finds has four sections (GASB ASC 2450-112–123):

a. Operating—providing services and producing and delivering goods, and include all transactions and other events that are not defined as capital and related financing, noncapital financing, or investing activities,

b. Noncapital financing—borrowing money for purposes other than to acquire, construct, or improve capital assets and repaying those amounts borrowed,

c. Capital and related financing—acquiring and disposing of capital assets used in providing services or producing goods, borrowing money for acquiring, constructing, or improving capital assets and repaying the amounts borrowed, including interest, and paying for capital assets obtained from vendors on credit, or

d. Investing activities—making and collecting loans and acquiring and disposing of debt or equity instruments.

Finally, governmental enterprises should also provide a reconciliation of operating income to operating cash flows. The reconciliation should determine and report the same amount for net cash flow from operating activities, indirectly, by adjusting operating income to remove the effects of depreciation, amortization, and other deferred outflows of resources and deferred inflows of resources of past operating cash receipts and payments, such as changes during the period in inventory, liabilities, and the like, and all accruals of expected future operating cash receipts and payments, such as changes during the period in receivables and payables.

Accounting for Proprietary Funds The basis of accounting for Enterprise Funds is different from that used for Governmental Funds. The business-like activities of Proprietary Funds are accounted for using the *economic resources measurement focus and the accrual basis of accounting* (GASB ASC 1300.102b). "Economic resources" are broader than the "financial resources" measurement focus that we use in the preparation of the Governmental Funds financial statements. The economic resources measurement focus includes long-term assets and liabilities as well as current financial resources. And, under the accrual accounting that we use for Proprietary Funds, we recognize revenues when earned (and expenses when incurred), not just when they are available to finance current period expenditures, the criterion we use to recognize revenues for governmental fund financial statements.

We use the Town of Acton's Sewer Enterprise Fund to illustrate the typical journal entries for a Proprietary Fund (the entries correspond with the fund financial statements which we present in the next section).

1. **To record the sale of sewer services to residents and to other departments of the Town of Acton and other operating revenues.**

Accounts receivable...	892,959	
Revenues..		892,959

2. **To record general operating expenses and depreciation of the capital assets in the Sewer Fund.**

Expenses—general services	641,135	
Depreciation expense...	730,454	
Cash		641,135
Accumulated depreciation...................................		730,454

3. **To record grants from the State of Massachusetts, interest income on investments in the fund, and interest expense on the fund's liabilities.**

Cash	8,451	
Interest expense...	884,166	
Revenues—intergovernmental		726,074
Committed interest		147,333
Investment income		19,210

4. **Closing entry**

Revenues	892,959	
Revenues—intergovernmental...................................	726,074	
Committed interest...	147,333	
Investment income...	19,210	
Expenses—general services...............................		641,135
Depreciation expense		730,454
Interest expense ..../...................................		884,166
Net position—unrestricted.................................		470,179

An additional journal entry will be made to reallocate Net Position-Unrestricted to Invested in Capital Assets, Net of Related Debt, in order to record the change in the latter account during the year.

Financial Statements for Fiduciary Funds

Fiduciary Funds are used to monitor resources that are required to be held in trust for others. They include Pension Trust Funds (report resources that are required to be held in trust for the beneficiaries of defined benefit pension plans, defined contribution plans, or other employee benefit plans), Investment Trust Funds (report the external portion of investment pools reported by the government), Private Purpose Trust Funds (report trust arrangements under which principal and income benefit individuals, private organizations, or other governments), and Agency Funds (report resources held by the reporting government in a purely custodial capacity, such as State or Federal taxes collected by the local government) (GASB ASC 1300.111–114). Like those for Proprietary Funds, the financial statements of Fiduciary Funds should be reported using the economic resources measurement focus and the accrual basis of accounting.

Following is an excerpt from the Town of Acton's financial statements relating to its Fiduciary Funds:

> **Fiduciary Funds**—Fiduciary funds are used to account for resources held for the benefit of parties outside the government. Fiduciary funds are *not* reflected in the government-wide financial statements because the resources of those funds are *not* available to support the Town's own programs. The accounting used for fiduciary funds is much like that used for proprietary funds.

EXHIBIT 9.6	Statement of Net Position for the Town of Acton Proprietary Funds

TOWN OF ACTON, MASSACHUSETTS
Statement of Net Position
Proprietary Funds
June 30, 2014

	Sanitation	Sewer	Nursing	Total
Assets				
Current:				
Cash and cash investments	$2,929,918	$ 5,162,046	$226,213	$ 8,318,177
Accounts receivable, net of allowance for uncollectibles:				
User charges	—	92,860	169,113	261,973
Special assessments	—	719,820	—	719,820
Liens	—	71,681	—	71,681
Noncurrent:				
Accounts receivable:				
Special assessments	—	12,184,491	—	12,184,491
Other post employment benefit net asset	10,041	—	—	10,041
Assets not being depreciated	435,300	99,469	—	534,769
Assets being depreciated, net	393,757	16,988,009	—	17,381,766
Total assets	3,769,016	35,318,376	395,326	39,482,718
Liabilities				
Current:				
Warrants payable	23,886	20,615	24,684	69,185
Accrued wages payable	657	257	7,584	8,498
Accrued interest payable	—	111,002	—	111,002
Compensated absences	1,717	114	3,135	4,966
Bonds payable	—	803,800	—	803,800
Noncurrent:				
Compensated absences	6,866	454	12,541	19,861
Other post-employment benefit obligations	—	68,080	184,251	252,331
Bonds payable	—	16,000,200	—	16,000,200
Total liabilities	33,126	17,004,522	232,195	17,269,843
Net position				
Net investment in capital assets	829,057	283,478	—	1,112,535
Unrestricted	2,906,833	18,030,376	163,131	21,100,340
Total net position	$3,735,890	$18,313,854	$163,131	$22,212,875

Financial Statements for Fiduciary Funds

The financial statements for Fiduciary Funds include the following:

- Statement of Fiduciary Net Position
- Statement of Changes in Fiduciary Net Position

The Statement of Fiduciary Net Position reports the assets, deferred outflows of resources, liabilities, deferred inflows of resources, and net position by fund type. The Statement of Changes in Fiduciary Net Position is prepared using the accrual basis of accounting. The terms "Additions" and "Deductions" are used in place of revenues and expenses, and the activities of Agency Funds are not included in this statement.

EXHIBIT 9.7	Statement of Revenues, Expenses, and Changes in Net Position for the Town of Acton Proprietary Funds

TOWN OF ACTON, MASSACHUSETTS
Statement of Revenues, Expenses, and Changes in Net Position
Proprietary Funds
Fiscal Year Ended June 30, 2014

	Sanitation	Sewer	Nursing	Total
Operating revenues:				
Charges for services...	$ 668,705	$ 892,209	$315,630	$ 1,876,544
Other operating..	—	750	—	750
Total operating revenues.....................................	$ 668,705	$ 892,959	$315,630	$ 1,877,294
Operating expenditures:				
General services...	524,376	641,135	519,188	1,684,699
Depreciation...	123,118	730,454	—	853,572
Total operating expenditures...............................	647,494	1,371,589	519,188	2,538,271
Operating income (loss).....................................	21,211	(478,630)	(203,558)	(660,977)
Nonoperating revenues (expenses):				
Intergovernmental...	—	726,074	—	726,074
Committed interest..	—	147,333	—	147,333
Earnings on investments	11,268	19,210	996	31,474
Interest on debt...	—	(884,166)	—	(884,166)
Total nonoperating revenues (expenses).....................	11,268	8,451	996	20,715
Income (loss) before transfers.............................	32,479	(470,179)	(202,562)	(640,262)
Operating transfers in.......................................	—	—	135,000	135,000
Total transfers..	—	—	135,000	135,000
Change in net position	32,479	(470,179)	(67,562)	(505,262)
Total net position—beginning.................................	3,703,411	18,784,033	230,693	22,718,137
Total net position—ending	$3,735,890	$18,313,854	$163,131	$22,212,875

Accounting for Fiduciary Funds   The basis of accounting for Fiduciary Funds is the same as that used for Proprietary Funds (i.e., *economic resources measurement focus and the accrual basis of accounting*).

We use the Town of Acton's Private Purpose Trust Fund Charity to illustrate the typical journal entries for a Fiduciary Fund (the entries correspond with the fund financial statements which we present in the next section).

1. To record the gift and investment income.

Cash	14,233	
Additions—investment income		14,233

2. To record general payments relating to human services.

Deductions—human services	1,994	
Cash		1,994

3. Closing entry

Additions—investment income	14,233	
Deductions—human services		1,994
Net position..		12,230

EXHIBIT 9.8	Statement of Cash Flows for the Town of Acton Proprietary Funds

TOWN OF ACTON, MASSACHUSETTS
Statement of Cash Flows
Proprietary Funds
Fiscal Year Ended June 30, 2014

	Sanitation	Sewer	Nursing	Total
Cash flows from operating activities:				
Receipts from customers	$ 668,704	$894,123	$ 262,882	$1,825,709
Payments to employees	1,564	(3,511)	581	(1,366)
Payments to vendors	(500,862)	(632,403)	(485,940)	(1,619,205)
Net cash flows provided (used) by operating activities	169,406	258,209	(222,477)	205,138
Cash flows from noncapital related financing activities:				
Transfer from other funds	—	—	135,000	135,000
Net cash flows provided (used) by noncapital related financing activities	—	—	135,000	135,000
Cash flows from capital and related financing activities:				
Acquisition of capital assets	(25,712)	(36,078)	—	(61,790)
Special assessments	—	843,108	—	843,108
Committed interest on special assessments	—	147,333	—	147,333
Principal payments on bonds	—	(659,298)	—	(659,298)
Interest expense	—	(314,677)	—	(314,677)
Net cash flows provided (used) by capital and related financing activities	(25,712)	(19,612)	—	(45,324)
Cash flows from investing activities:				
Earnings on investments	11,268	19,210	996	31,474
Net cash flows provided (used) by investing activities	11,268	19,210	996	31,474
Net increase (decrease) in cash and cash equivalents	154,962	257,807	(86,481)	326,288
Cash and cash equivalents, July 1, 2013	2,774,956	4,904,239	312,694	7,991,889
Cash and cash equivalents, June 30, 2014	$2,929,918	$5,162,046	$ 226,213	$8,318,177
Reconciliation of net income to net cash provided (used) by operating activities:				
Operating income (loss)	$ 21,211	$ (478,630)	$(203,558)	$ (660,977)
Adjustments to reconcile operating income to net cash provided (used) by operating activities:				
Depreciation expense	123,118	730,454	—	853,572
(Increase) decrease in assets:				
Accounts receivable—customer	—	1,163	(52,748)	(51,585)
Other post employment benefits asset	580	—	—	580
Increase (decrease) in liabilities:				
Warrants, wages, absence and accounts payable	24,497	(69)	11,941	36,369
Other post employment benefits liability	—	5,291	21,888	27,179
Net cash provided by operating activities	$ 169,406	$ 258,209	$(222,477)	$ 205,138

Fiduciary Fund Financial Statements for the Town of Acton   The financial statements for the Town of Acton's Fiduciary Funds are presented in Exhibits 9.9 and 9.10.

EXHIBIT 9.9	Statement of Fiduciary Net Position for the Town of Acton Fiduciary Funds

TOWN OF ACTON, MASSACHUSETTS
Statement of Fiduciary Net Position
Fiduciary Funds
June 30, 2014

	Private Purpose Trust Fund Charity	Other Post Employment Benefits Trust	Agency Funds
Assets			
Cash and cash equivalents	$ —	$ —	$1,045,068
Investments	276,167	927,704	—
Total assets	$276,167	$927,704	$1,045,068
Liabilities			
Warrants payable	$ —	$ —	$ 9,711
Due to component unit	—	—	39,000
Other	—	—	996,357
Total liabilities	—	—	1,045,068
Net position			
Held in trust for OPEB benefits and other purposes	$276,167	$927,704	$ —

EXHIBIT 9.10	Statement of Changes in Fiduciary Net Position for the Town of Acton Fiduciary Funds

TOWN OF ACTON, MASSACHUSETTS
Statement of Changes in Fiduciary Net Position
Fiduciary Funds
Fiscal Year Ended June 30, 2014

	Private Purpose Trust Fund Charity	Other Post Employment Benefits Trust
Additions:		
Gift	$ 58	$ —
Interest, dividends, and other	$ 14,175	$129,044
Total additions	$ 14,233	$129,044
Deductions:		
Trust distributions	1,994	—
Change in net position before transfers	12,239	129,044
Transfers in (out):		
Operating transfers in (out)	—	488,660
Change in net position	12,239	617,704
Net position:		
Beginning of year	263,928	310,000
Ending of year	$276,167	$927,704

CHAPTER SUMMARY

Governments are required to issue two types of financial reports:

1. **Fund financial statements**—these financial statements are prepared using a *modified accrual basis* of accounting and focus on the sources, uses, and balances of the resources that have been entrusted to governmental officials.

2. **Government-wide financial statements**—these statements provide information about the government on an *accrual basis* and are similar to the types of financial reports we prepare for corporations.

We cover fund financial statements in Chapter 9 and government-wide financial statements in Chapter 10.

The primary purpose of fund accounting is to segregate the accounting for the government's activities so that transactions can be monitored. This monitoring is achieved by the use of formal budgets and the subsequent recording of expenditures in relation to budgeted amounts. The budgeting process includes the estimation of cash inflows and outflows. An **appropriation** is a sum of money that has been set aside in the budgeted amounts for a specific use. An **encumbrance** is a purchase order or other contractual commitment that requires the payment of funds in the future relating to an existing appropriation. **Expenditures** are decreases in (uses of) fund financial resources other than through interfund transfers.

Following is a listing of common fund types:

1. **Governmental Funds** relate to the type of activities that are customary for a government to perform, such as providing for public safety, education, and health and social welfare.
   a. **General fund**—to account for all financial resources except those required to be reported in another fund.
   b. **Special revenue funds**—to account for the proceeds of specific revenue sources that are legally restricted to expenditures for specified purposes.
   c. **Capital projects funds**—to account for financial resources to be used for the acquisition or construction of major capital facilities.
   d. **Debt service funds**—to account for the accumulation of resources for, and the payment of, general long-term debt principal and interest.
   e. **Permanent funds**—to report resources that are legally restricted to the extent that only earnings, and not principal, may be used for purposes that support the reporting government's programs.

2. **Proprietary Funds** relate to business-like activities.
   a. **Enterprise funds**—to report any activity for which a fee is charged to external users for goods or services.
   b. **Internal service funds**—to report any activity that provides goods or services to other funds, departments, or agencies of the primary government and its component units, or to other governments, on a cost-reimbursement basis.

3. **Fiduciary Funds** are used to monitor resources that are required to be held in trust for others.
   a. **Pension (and other employee benefit) trust funds**—to report resources that are required to be held in trust for the members and beneficiaries of defined benefit pension plans, defined contribution plans, other postemployment benefit plans, or other employee benefit plans.
   b. **Investment trust funds**—to report the external portion of investment pools reported by the sponsoring government.
   c. **Private-purpose trust funds**—to report all other trust arrangements under which principal and income benefit individuals, private organizations, or other governments.
   d. **Agency funds**—to report resources held by the reporting government in a purely custodial capacity.

Under governmental fund accounting, we recognize revenues and expenditures using the *current financial resources measurement focus* and *the modified accrual basis of accounting*

1. **Current financial resources measurement focus** refers to *what* is being reported. The words *current financial resources* mean resources that can be consumed in the near future.

2. **Modified accrual basis of accounting** refers to *when* the transaction is recognized.

a. **Revenues** are recognized in the accounting period in which they become both *measurable* and *available* to finance expenditures. "Available" means collectible within the current period or soon enough thereafter to be used to pay liabilities of the current period.

b. **Expenditures** should be recognized in the accounting period in which the fund liability is incurred.

We prepare a different set of financial statements for each type of Fund:

1. Governmental funds
   a. Balance sheet
   b. Statement of revenues, expenditures, and changes in fund balances
2. Proprietary funds
   a. Statement of net position
   b. Statement of revenues, expenses, and changes in fund net position
   c. Statement of cash flows
3. Fiduciary funds (and component units that are fiduciary in nature)
   a. Statement of fiduciary net position
   b. Statement of changes in fiduciary net position

■ **Governmental Funds are prepared using the** *current financial resources measurement focus and the modified accrual basis of accounting,*

■ **Proprietary and Fiduciary Funds are prepared using the** *economic resources measurement focus and the accrual basis of accounting.*

COMPREHENSIVE REVIEW

Part 1:

Prepare journal entries in the General Fund for each of the following events relating to the City of Santa Rosa (all amounts in $1,000s).

Required

a. The citizens approve the following budget for the year:

ESTIMATED REVENUES	$22,888
ESTIMATED OTHER FINANCING SOURCES	2,000
APPROPRIATIONS	(22,409)
BUDGETARY FUND BALANCE	$ 2,479

b. The City records the following revenues (on account) and other financing sources (paid in cash) during the year:

Revenues—real estate and personal property taxes	$19,793
Revenues—intergovernmental	3,563
Other financing sources—bond proceeds	2,000

c. The City issues purchase invoices totaling $22,187 (record the issuance of invoices as a lump sum).

d. The City recognizes the following expenditures, all on account (these expenditures were previously reserved as budgetary encumbrances):

Expenditures—general government	$ 3,327
Expenditures—public safety	2,219
Expenditures—education	13,313
Expenditures—public works	1,109
Expenditures—human services	2,219

e. The City makes the following payments related to its outstanding debt:

Expenditures—debt principal payments	$700
Expenditures—debt interest payments	100

f. The City collects accounts receivable ($19,706 relating to property taxes and $3,385 relating to intergovernmental receivables) and pays outstanding accounts payable in the amount of $21,744 during the year.

g. The City recognizes an increase of $283 in Deferred Revenues as a year-end adjustment to yield a balance in that account of the total property taxes receivable that are not expected to be collected within 60 days.

Part 2:

Assume that the City of Santa Rosa generates the following trial balance that reflects the entries above.

Trial Balance	DR	CR
Cash.	$ 7,217	
Receivables:		
Real estate and personal property	522	
Intergovernmental.	5,398	
Payables.		$ 618
Deferred revenues		5,938
Fund balances:		
Assigned.		1,566
Unassigned.		2,929
Revenues—real estate taxes		19,510
Intergovernmental revenues		3,563
Expenditures—general government.	3,327	
Expenditures—public safety	2,219	
Expenditures—education.	13,313	
Expenditures—public works	1,109	
Expenditures—human services	2,219	
Expenditures—debt principal payments	700	
Expenditures—debt interest payments	100	
Other financing sources—proceeds from bonds.		2,000
	$36,124	$36,124

Required

h. Prepare the Balance Sheet and the Statement of Revenues, Expenditures, and Changes in Fund Balances for the City of Santa Rosa.

i. Prepare the required closing entries to close out the budgetary and operating accounts. Assume that the City closes out $261 of remaining budgetary encumbrances outstanding and formally charges that balance to Fund Balance—unassigned since the outstanding invoices are expected to be honored in the next fiscal year.

The solution to this review problem can be found on pages 622–624.

APPENDIX 9A: Specialized Governmental Funds

Our discussion of fund accounting focuses on the General Fund. Governments may establish other types of governmental funds for specific purposes. These include Special Revenue Funds, Capital Projects Funds, Debt Service Funds, and Permanent Funds. We discuss these specialized funds in this appendix.

Special Revenue Funds

Special Revenue Funds account for the proceeds of specific revenue sources (other than trusts for individuals, private organizations, or other governments or for major capital projects) that are legally restricted to expenditure for specified purposes. These funds may be established as a result of legal requirements or donor restrictions that mandate the use of these revenues for a specific purpose and require separate reporting of the Fund's activities during the year, or because the government wishes to report a specialized activity separately from the activities of the general government.

The Town of Acton provides an example of a Special Revenue Fund that contains $4.8 million of cash that is restricted in its use as described in the following footnote disclosure:

> **Community Preservation Fund**—This special revenue fund is used to account for the activities prescribed by the Community Preservation Act of the Massachusetts General Laws. Expenditures are allowed for affordable housing, historic preservation and the purchase of open space.

This fund was created by the State of Massachusetts under the Community Preservation Act as described below:

> The Town adopted the Community Preservation Act, which allows for a 1.5% surcharge on real estate tax bills and a Commonwealth of Massachusetts match, in 2002. Since its passage, the Town has collected approximately $8.2 million from the 1.5% surcharge. Appropriations from this program continue to be approved annually at the Annual Town Meeting and they have provided funding for many projects in the areas of housing, recreation, open space, historic preservation, and other land acquisition.

Since the funds are restricted as to use, the Town of Acton must account for them using a Special Revenue Fund. The size of the fund mandates disclosure as a separate column on the balance sheet and the Net Position of the fund is reported as "Restricted" to highlight the fact that available cash cannot be used for general governmental purposes.

Special Revenue Funds are accounted for just like the General Fund we describe in the chapter. The current financial resources measurement focus and the modified accrual basis of accounting are used to account for transactions. Consequently, no long-term assets or liabilities are recognized on the Special Revenue Fund balance sheet.

Capital Projects Funds

Capital Projects Funds account for financial resources to be used for the acquisition or construction of major capital facilities (other than those financed by proprietary funds or in trust funds for individuals, private organizations, or other governments). These projects might include, for example, the construction of a school, a bridge, or streets and other infrastructure improvements. These Funds are established to account for a specific project, and typically relate only to one capital project. They commence with the appropriation and cease when the project is completed.

The current financial resources measurement focus and the modified accrual basis of accounting are used to account for transactions. Consequently, even though the Fund relates to the construction of a capital project, no long-term assets or liabilities are recognized on the Capital Projects Fund balance sheet. Instead, commitments under the construction contract with the builder are recognized as Encumbrances and payments under the construction contract are recorded as Expenditures.

To illustrate the accounting for a Capital Projects Fund, assume that the Town of Acton appropriates the sum of $5,000,000 for the construction of an addition to its high school. The construction is to be financed as follows:

Issuance of general obligation bond	$2,000,000
Grant from the State of Massachusetts	2,500,000
Transfer from the Town's Waste Disposal Enterprise Fund	500,000
Total	$5,000,000

The bond is to be repaid at $200,000 per year over a 10-year period plus interest at 4%, payable annually. The bond agreement requires the Town to establish a Debt Service Fund to account for the repayment of the bond.

Following are the journal entries related to the construction of the addition:[18]

1. To record the receivables from the Enterprise Fund and the State of Massachusetts:

Due from Enterprise Fund	500,000	
Due from the State of Massachusetts	2,500,000	
Other financing sources—transfers in		500,000
Revenues		2,500,000

2. To record the issuance of the bonds at par:

Cash	2,000,000	
Other financing sources—proceeds from bonds		2,000,000

3. To record the collection of the receivables:

Cash	3,000,000	
Due from Enterprise Fund		500,000
Due from the State of Massachusetts		2,500,000

4. To record the execution of the construction contract to be paid in two installments ($2,000,000 upon completion of initial site work and construction of the foundation, and the remainder upon completion of construction):

ENCUMBRANCES	5,000,000	
FUND BALANCE—RESERVED FOR ENCUMBRANCES		5,000,000

5. To record the first payment under the contract:

FUND BALANCE—RESERVED FOR ENCUMBRANCES	2,000,000	
ENCUMBRANCES		2,000,000
Expenditures—construction	2,000,000	
Cash		2,000,000

6. To record the final payment under the contract:

FUND BALANCE—RESERVED FOR ENCUMBRANCES	3,000,000	
ENCUMBRANCES		3,000,000
Expenditures—construction	3,000,000	
Cash		3,000,000

7. To close the Capital Projects Fund:

Revenues	2,500,000	
Other financing sources—transfers in	500,000	
Other financing sources—proceeds from bonds	2,000,000	
Expenditures—construction		5,000,000

Debt Service Funds

Debt Service Funds account for the accumulation of resources for, and the payment of, general long-term debt principal and interest. Funds for the repayment of the principal and interest on the debt are typically transferred into the Debt Service Fund from the General Fund. The current financial resources measurement focus and the modified accrual basis of accounting are used to account for transactions in the Debt Service Fund. Consequently, funds transferred into the Fund, as well as the bond payments out of the Fund, are accounted for as Other Financing Sources—Transfers In and Expenditures—Principal and Interest, respectively.

---

[18] If applicable law requires a budget entry for the project, the following entry would be recorded:

BONDS AUTHORIZED—UNISSUED	2,000,000	
ESTIMATED REVENUES—STATE OF MASS.	2,500,000	
ESTIMATED OTHER FINANCING SOURCES—		
TRANSFER FROM ENTERPRISE FUND	500,000	
APPROPRIATIONS		5,000,000

To illustrate, assume that the repayment of the bond issued for the capital project described above is to be made out of a Debt Service Fund with cash transferred in from the General Fund. The following journal entries account for these transactions:

8. The Town of Acton transfers $200,000 for the principal payment required under the bond issue plus $80,000 ($2,000,000 × 4%) interest:

Cash	280,000	
Other financing sources—transfers in......		280,000

9. To record the debt payment:[19]

Expenditures—bond principal	200,000	
Expenditures—bond interest	80,000	
Cash		280,000

10. To close the Debt Service Fund for the year:

Other financing sources—transfers in	280,000	
Expenditures—bond principal......		200,000
Expenditures—bond interest......		80,000

Permanent Funds

Permanent Funds report resources (typically from donations) that are legally restricted to the extent that only earnings, and not principal, may be used for purposes that support the reporting government's programs— that is, for the benefit of the government or its citizenry. The current financial resources measurement focus and the modified accrual basis of accounting are used to account for transactions in the Permanent Fund.

As an example, assume that an individual leaves the Town of Acton $500,000 in her will to be used for betterments to a park. Under the terms of the bequest, only the interest can be used for park betterments. The principal must be maintained in perpetuity.

1. To record the bequest:

Cash	500,000	
Revenues—additions to permanent endowments		500,000

2. To record purchase of investments with the donated funds:

Investments	500,000	
Cash		500,000

3. To record receipt of interest:

Cash......	25,000	
Revenues—investment income......		25,000

4. To record expenditure of for betterment of park:

Expenditures—park	10,000	
Cash		10,000

5. Closing entry:

Revenues—additions to permanent endowments......	500,000	
Revenues—investment income	25,000	
Expenditures—park......		10,000
Fund balance—assigned for park betterment......		515,000

---

[19] The debt payments are assumed to be made at the end of the fiscal year and are, therefore, recognized in the financial statements. Under the current financial resources measurement focus and the modified accrual basis of accounting, only the obligation to be paid from current resources is recorded and future debt payments are not accrued. Future debt payments are recognized, however, in the government-wide financial statements which are prepared using the accrual basis of accounting.

LO4

27. Property taxes

During the current year, Wythe County levied $2,000,000 property taxes, 1% of which is expected to be uncollectible. During the year, the county collected $1,800,000 and wrote off $15,000 as uncollectible. Wythe County expects to collect the remaining amounts owed within 60 days of the close of its fiscal year. What amount should Wythe County report as property tax revenue in its Statement of Revenues, Expenditures and Changes in Fund Balances for the current year?

a. $1,800,000
b. $1,980,000
c. $1,985,000
d. $2,000,000

LO2

28. Fund types

Harland County received a $2,000,000 capital grant to be equally distributed among its five municipalities. The grant is to finance the construction of capital assets. Harland had no administrative or direct financial involvement in the construction. In which fund should Harland record the receipt of cash?

a. Agency fund
b. General fund
c. Special revenue fund
d. Private purpose trust fund

LO1

29. Setting accounting standards

Which organization is responsible for setting accounting standards for state and local governments?

a. GASB
b. AICPA
c. FASB
d. FASAB
e. None of the above

LO3

30. Measurement focus and accrual basis of accounting

The economic resources measurement focus and the accrual basis of accounting are appropriate for which of the following funds:

a. Capital projects fund
b. Internal service fund
c. Debt service fund
d. Special revenue fund

LO1

31. Reporting objectives

Which of the following is *not* one of the GASB's reporting objectives?

a. Providing assurance that the governmental entity is solvent
b. Providing assurance that the governmental entity is in compliance with the approved budget
c. Providing information on the extent of the governmental entity's service efforts and accomplishments
d. Providing information relating to variances from the approved budget
e. All of the above are GASB objectives

LO3

32. Current financial resources measurement focus and modified accrual basis of accounting

Which of the following funds would be most appropriate for the use of the current financial recourses measurement focus and the modified accrual basis of accounting?

	Governmental	Proprietary	Fiduciary
a.	Yes	Yes	Yes
b.	No	Yes	Yes
c.	Yes	No	No
d.	No	No	Yes

33. **Fund types**   LO2

    The Town of Littleton collects special taxes from property owners to pay for the construction of a sewer many years ago. The town has no obligation for the bonds if property owners fail to pay their assessments. What type of fund should the Town use to account for the collection of these assessments?

    a. Capital projects
    b. Debt service
    c. General
    d. Agency

34. **Fund balance categories**   LO5

    Assume that the Town of Maynard reports a balance in a fund that is limited as to its use as a result of enabling legislation. The balance of the fund should be reported in which of the following categories?

    a. Assigned
    b. Nonspendable
    c. Restricted
    d. Committed

35. **Fund journal entry for taxes**   LO4

    Assume that the Town of Wellesley bills property owners for their 4th quarter real estate tax, but doesn't expect to collect a portion of the receivable until more than 60 days after the close of its fiscal year. The portion that it *does not* expect to collect should be accounted for with a credit to which account?

    a. A deferred outflow of resources
    b. A deferred inflow of resources
    c. An allowance for uncollectible accounts receivable
    d. Nonspendable fund balance

36. **Encumbrance accounting**   LO4

    The Town of Bolton recorded a reserve for encumbrances in the amount of $50,000 relating to the purchase of a truck. When the truck was received, the actual cost amounted to $49,000. What amount should the Town credit to the reserve for encumbrances when the truck is finally purchased?

    a. $50,000
    b. $49,000
    c. $1,000
    d. $(1,000)

37. **Debt service funds**   LO2

    Which of the following statements is *true* regarding debt service funds?

    a. Debt service funds can be used for any of the Governmental, Proprietary or Fiduciary funds
    b. Debt service funds can only be used for the Governmental and Proprietary funds
    c. Debt service funds can only be used for the Governmental fund
    d. Debt service funds can only be used for Fiduciary funds

38. **Depreciation expense**   LO4

    It is appropriate to record depreciation expense in all of the following funds except:

    a. An enterprise fund
    b. An internal service fund
    c. A fiduciary fund
    d. A capital projects fund

EXERCISES

LO4   **39. Journal entry to record the budget**

Assume that a city approves the following budget for the year:

ESTIMATED REVENUES	$50,000,000
ESTIMATED OTHER FINANCING SOURCES	10,000,000
APPROPRIATIONS.	(30,000,000)
ESTIMATED OTHER FINANCING USES	(25,000,000)
BUDGETARY IN FUND BALANCE	$ 5,000,000

Prepare the journal entry to record the budget.

LO5   **40. Preparation of fund balance section of the balance sheet**

The City of Boxborough general fund reports the following account information at year-end:
- $100,000 of unexpended funds from a State of Massachusetts for education costs
- $300,000 fund to be used for contingencies (unforeseen events)
- $200,000 for the remaining balance of a fund designated for construction of a new city park
- $15,000 of inventories
- $250,000 of remaining proceeds from a use tax required to be spent for emergency services
- $800,000 unassigned

Prepare the fund balance section of the balance sheet for the City of Boxborough.

LO4   **41. Journal entries related to encumbrances**

Assume that a town places an order for a truck with an estimated cost of $47,000. When the truck is delivered, the actual cost is $51,000. Prepare the journal entries to record the issuance of the purchase order and its payment when the truck is delivered.

LO4   **42. Journal entries to close encumbrances (encumbrances do *not* lapse)**

Assume that a city records $75,000 of encumbrances outstanding as of the end of the year. Prepare the journal entry to close the encumbrance account assuming that encumbrances do *not* lapse at year-end (i.e., budgetary authority continues into the succeeding year).

LO4   **43. Journal entries to close encumbrances (encumbrances *lapse* at year-end)**

Assume that a city records $45,000 of encumbrances outstanding as of the end of the year. Prepare the journal entry to close the encumbrance account assuming that encumbrances *lapse at year-end* (i.e., budgetary authority ceases and must be re-established in the succeeding year).

LO4   **44. Journal entry to record the sale of a truck**

Assume that a town sells a truck that it had originally purchased for $60,000 for a cash sale price of $25,000. Prepare the journal entry to record the sale.

LO4   **45. Journal entry to record the issuance and repayment of a bond**

Assume that a city issues a $5,000,000 bond at par. The city, subsequently, pays $250,000 in interest on the bond and $1,000,000 of the principal. Prepare the journal entries to record the issuance of the bond and the subsequent payments.

LO4   **46. Journal entry to record the lease of equipment and subsequent payment**

Assume that a town leases equipment on a capital lease. The present value of the leased equipment is $40,000. The city, subsequently, pays $3,000 on the lease, $1,000 of which is designated as interest and the remainder to a reduction of the lease obligation. Prepare the journal entries to record the acquisition of equipment via lease and the subsequent payment.

LO4   **47. Accounting for inventories (purchases method)**

Assume that a town purchases $4,000 of supplies on account toward the end of the year. A year-end audit reveals that $1,500 of the inventories remain unused. Prepare the journal entry for the purchase the inventories and the year-end adjusting entry assuming that the *purchases method* is used.

LO4   **48. Accounting for inventories (consumption method)**

Assume that a town purchases $4,000 of supplies on account toward the end of the year. A year-end audit reveals that $1,500 of the inventories remain unused. Prepare the journal entries for the purchase the inventories and the year-end adjusting entry assuming that the *consumption method* is used.

49. Preparation of journal entries for a number of transactions   **LO4**
Prepare journal entries for the following transactions for the City of Sparks, NV:

 a. The City Council approved its budget for the year for estimated revenues of $3,500,000 and appropriations of $3,400,000.

 b. Revenues received in cash amounted to $3,400,000 for the year.

 c. The City issues $500,000 of purchase orders.

 d. The City purchased goods and services under $450,000 of the purchase orders in *Part b* amounting to a cash payment of $445,000. The remaining $50,000 of purchase orders are still outstanding and unpaid at year-end.

 e. The City paid $2,000,000 of wages to City employees during the year. These wages were not evidenced by a formal encumbrance since they are recurring in nature.

50. Preparation of journal entries for a number of transactions   **LO4**
The Town of Bolton reports the following transaction during the month:

 1. Received a $200,000 grant from the State of Massachusetts that is unassigned

 2. Purchased a truck for $50,000 in cash

 3. Paid wages of $25,000 in cash

 4. Borrowed $50,000 from a bank to replenish funds used for the purchase of the truck

 5. Made an interest payment on the bank loan of $500 in cash

 a. Prepare journal entries in the general fund for these transactions.

 b. Prepare a Balance Sheet and a Statement of Revenues, Expenditures and Changes in Fund Balances for the general fund. Assume that the Town began the period with cash and an unassigned fund balance of $100,000.

PROBLEMS

51. Journal entries for a series of transactions   **LO4**
Prepare journal entries in the General Fund for each of the following events relating to the City of Bar Harbor (all amounts in $1,000s).

 a. The citizens approve the following budget for the year:

ESTIMATED REVENUES	$94,709
ESTIMATED OTHER FINANCING SOURCES	2,000
APPROPRIATIONS.	(92,728)
BUDGETARY FUND BALANCE	$ 3,981

 b. The City records the following revenues (on account) and other financing sources (paid in cash) during the year:

Revenues—real estate and personal property taxes	$81,900
Revenues—intergovernmental	14,742
Other financing sources—bond proceeds	2,000

 c. The City issues purchase invoices totaling $91,810 (record the issuance of invoices as a lump sum).

 d. The City recognizes the following expenditures, all on account (these expenditures were previously reserved as budgetary encumbrances):

Expenditures—general government.	$13,772
Expenditures—public safety	9,181
Expenditures—education.	55,086
Expenditures—public works	4,590
Expenditures—human services	9,181

e. The City makes the following payments related to its outstanding debt:

Expenditures—debt principal payments	$700
Expenditures—debt interest payments	100

f. The City collects accounts receivable ($81,540 relating to property taxes and $14,005 relating to intergovernmental receivables) and pays outstanding accounts payable in the amount of $89,974 during the year.

g. The City recognizes an increase of $1,170 in Deferred Revenues as a year-end adjustment to yield a balance in that account of the total property taxes receivable that are not expected to be collected within 60 days.

h. The City makes the required closing entries to close out the budgetary and operating accounts. In addition, the City closes out the remaining $1,080 balance of budgetary encumbrances outstanding and formally charges that balance to Fund Balance—assigned since the outstanding invoices are expected to be honored in the next fiscal year.

LO5 **52. Preparation of fund financial statements**

Assume that at the beginning of the fiscal year, the City of Bar Harbor reports the following balances in its accounts for the General Fund:

Beginning Balances:	DR	CR
Cash.	$19,320	
Receivables:		
Real estate and personal property	1,800	
Intergovernmental.	21,600	
Payables.		$ 720
Deferred revenues		23,400
Fund balances:		
Assigned.		5,400
Unassigned		13,200
	$42,720	$42,720

Using the journal entries you record for Problem 51,

a. Prepare the pre-closing trial balance for the General Fund.

b. From the pre-closing trial balance in *Part a*, prepare the City of Bar Harbor's Balance Sheet and the Statement of Revenues, Expenditures, and Changes in Fund Balances for the fiscal year for the General Fund.

LO4 **53. Journal entries for a series of transactions**

Prepare journal entries in the General Fund for each of the following events relating to the City of Jackson Hole (all amounts in $1,000s).

a. The citizens approve the following budget for the year:

ESTIMATED REVENUES	$181,526
ESTIMATED OTHER FINANCING SOURCES	4,600
APPROPRIATIONS.	(177,729)
BUDGETARY FUND BALANCE	$ 8,397

b. The City records the following revenues (on account) and other financing sources (paid in cash) during the year:

Revenues—real estate and personal property taxes	$156,975
Revenues—intergovernmental.	28,256
Other financing sources—bond proceeds	4,600

c. The City issues purchase invoices totaling $175,969 (record the issuance of invoices as a lump sum).

d. The City recognizes the following expenditures, all on account (these expenditures were previously reserved as budgetary encumbrances):

Expenditures—general government.	$ 26,396
Expenditures—public safety	17,597
Expenditures—education.	105,581
Expenditures—public works	8,798
Expenditures—human services	17,597

e. The City makes the following payments related to its outstanding debt:

Expenditures—debt principal payments	$690
Expenditures—debt interest payments	230

f. The City collects accounts receivable ($156,285 relating to property taxes and $26,843 relating to intergovernmental receivables) and pays outstanding accounts payable in the amount of $172,450 during the year.

g. The City recognizes an increase of $2,243 in Deferred Revenues as a year-end adjustment to yield a balance in that account of the total property taxes receivable that are not expected to be collected within 60 days.

h. The City makes the required closing entries to close out the budgetary and operating accounts. In addition, the City closes out the remaining $2,070 balance of budgetary encumbrances outstanding and formally charges that balance to Fund Balance—unassigned since the outstanding invoices are expected to be honored in the next fiscal year.

54. Preparation of fund financial statements   LO5

Assume that at the beginning of the fiscal year, the City of Jackson Hole reports the following balances in its accounts for the General Fund:

	General Fund	
	DR	**CR**
Beginning balances:		
Cash.	$37,030	
Receivables:		
Real estate and personal property	3,450	
Intergovernmental.	41,400	
Payables.		$ 1,380
Deferred revenues		44,850
Fund balances:		
Assigned.		10,350
Unassigned		25,300
	₵01,000	₵01,000

Using the journal entries you record for Problem 55,

a. Prepare the pre-closing trial balance for the General Fund.

b. From the pre-closing trial balance in *Part a*, prepare the City of Jackson Hole's Balance Sheet and the Statement of Revenues, Expenditures, and Changes in Fund Balances for the fiscal year for the General Fund.

LO5   **55. Preparation of financial statements from trial balance**

Following is the trial balance after all adjusting entries for the Village of Stapleton:

Trial Balance	DR	CR
Cash	$145,227	
Receivables:		
Real estate & personal property	11,700	
Intergovernmental	120,993	
Payables		$ 13,846
Deferred revenues		133,088
Fund balances:		
Assigned		35,100
Unassigned		65,650
Revenues—real estate taxes		437,288
Interegovernmental revenues		79,852
Expenditures—general government	74,597	
Expenditures—public safety	49,730	
Expenditures—education	298,382	
Expenditures—public works	24,865	
Expenditures—human services	49,730	
Expenditures—debt principal payments	1,950	
Expenditures—debt interest payments	650	
Other financing sources—proceeds from bonds		13,000
	$777,824	$777,824

Prepare the Balance Sheet and the Statement of Revenues, Expenditures and Changes in Fund Balances.

LO5   **56. Preparation of closing entries**

The Town of Red Tail reports the following trial balance after all entries have been made for the year:

Trial Balance	DR	CR
Cash	$ 192,147	
Receivables:		
Real estate & personal property	15,480	
Intergovernmental	160,083	
Payables		$ 18,319
Deferred revenues		176,085
Fund balances:		
Assigned		46,440
Unassigned		86,860
Revenues—real estate taxes		578,565
Interegovernmental revenues		105,651
Expenditures—general government	98,694	
Expenditures—public safety	65,797	
Expenditures—education	394,783	
Expenditures—public works	32,899	
Expenditures—human services	65,797	
Expenditures—debt principal payments	2,580	
Expenditures—debt interest payments	860	
Other financing sources—proceeds from bonds		17,200
	$1,029,120	$1,029,120

The Town's budget for the year, originally entered into the financial records, was as follows:

ESTIMATED REVENUES	$678,749
ESTIMATED OTHER FINANCING SOURCES	17,200
APPROPRIATIONS.	(664,551)
BUDGETARY FUND BALANCE	$ 31,398

In addition, the Town issued purchase orders for goods and services amounting to $7,740 that are outstanding at the end of the fiscal year. It intends to honor those purchase invoices.

Prepare the appropriate closing entries for the year.

TOPIC REVIEW

Solution 1

	General Fund		
a.	ESTIMATED REVENUES	41,041	
	ESTIMATED OTHER FINANCING SOURCES	2,000	
	APPROPRIATIONS		40,182
	BUDGETARY FUND BALANCE.		2,859
	(to record the budget)		
b.	Cash.	2,000	
	Receivables—real estate & personal property taxes	35,490	
	Receivables—intergovernmental revenues	6,388	
	Revenues—real estate & personal property taxes		35,490
	Revenues—intergovernmental		6,388
	Other financing sources—bond proceeds.		2,000
c.	ENCUMBRANCES	39,784	
	BUDGETARY FUND BALANCE—RESERVED FOR ENCUMBRANCES		39,784
	(to record the issuance of purchase invoices)		
d.	BUDGETARY FUND BALANCE—RESERVED FOR ENCUMBRANCES.	39,784	
	ENCUMBRANCES.		39,784
	(to reverse previous Encumbrance journal entry)		
	Expenditures—general government.	5,967	
	Expenditures—public safety	3,978	
	Expenditures—education.	23,871	
	Expenditures—public works	1,989	
	Expenditures—human services	3,979	
	Payables		39,784
	(to record expenditures)		
e.	Expenditures—debt principal payments	700	
	Expenditures—debt interest payments	100	
	Cash		800
	(to record debt payments)		
f.	Cash.	2,414	
	Payables.	38,989	
	Receivables—real estate & personal property taxes.		35,334
	Receivables—intergovernmental revenues		6,069
g.	Revenues	507	
	Deferred revenues		507
	(Deferral of revenues)		

Solution 2

a.

Balance Sheet	
Cash.	$11,987
Receivables:	
Real estate & personal property	936
Intergovernmental.	9,679
Total assets.	$22,602
Payables.	$ 1,108
Deferred revenues	10,647
Total liabilities.	11,755
Fund balances:	
Assigned.	2,808
Unassigned.	8,039
Total fund balances	10,847
Total liabilities and fund balances.	$22,602

Statement of Revenues, Expenditures, and Changes in Fund Balances	
Revenues	
Real estate taxes	$34,983
Intergovernmental	6,388
Total revenues	41,371
Expenditures	
General government.	5,967
Public safety	3,978
Education	23,871
Public works	1,989
Human services	3,979
Debt principal payments.	700
Debt interest payments.	100
Total expenditures	40,584
Excess (deficiency) of revenues over expenditures	787
Other financing sources (uses)	
Proceeds from bonds	2,000
Total other financing sources (uses).	2,000
Net change in fund balances	$ 2,787
Fund balances at beginning of year.	8,060
Fund balances at end of year.	$10,847

b.

APPROPRIATIONS.		40,182	
BUDGETARY FUND BALANCE		2,859	
ESTIMATED REVENUES			41,041
ESTIMATED OTHER FINANCING SOURCES			2,000

(to reverse budget entry)

Revenues—real estate & personal property taxes.		34,983	
Revenues—intergovernmental		6,388	
Other financing sources—bond proceeds		2,000	
Expenditures—general government			5,967
Expenditures—public safety			3,978
Expenditures—education			23,871
Expenditures—public works			1,989
Expenditures—human services.			3,979
Expenditures—debt principal payments.			700
Expenditures—debt interest payments.			100
Fund Balance—unassigned.			2,787

(to close out revenue and expenditure accounts)

BUDGETARY FUND BALANCE—RESERVED FOR ENCUMBRANCES.		468	
ENCUMBRANCES.			468
Fund Balance—unassigned		468	
Fund Balance—assigned.			468

(to close remaining encumbrances and reserve fund balance for encumbrances that lapsed, but are expected to be honored in the following year)

COMPREHENSIVE REVIEW SOLUTION

Part 1:

	General Fund		
a.	ESTIMATED REVENUES	22,888	
	ESTIMATED OTHER FINANCING SOURCES	2,000	
	APPROPRIATIONS		22,409
	BUDGETARY FUND BALANCE		2,479
	(to record the budget)		
b.	Cash	2,000	
	Receivables—real estate & personal property taxes	19,793	
	Receivables—intergovernmental revenues	3,563	
	Revenues—real estate & personal property taxes		19,793
	Revenues—intergovernmental		3,563
	Other financing sources—bond proceeds.		2,000
c.	ENCUMBRANCES	22,187	
	BUDGETARY FUND BALANCE—RESERVED FOR ENCUMBRANCES		22,187
	(to record the issuance of purchase invoices)		
d.	BUDGETARY FUND BALANCE—RESERVED FOR ENCUMBRANCES.	22,187	
	ENCUMBRANCES.		22,187
	(to reverse previous Encumbrance journal entry)		
	Expenditures—general government.	3,327	
	Expenditures—public safety	2,219	
	Expenditures—education.	13,313	
	Expenditures—public works	1,109	
	Expenditures—human services	2,219	
	Payables		22,187
	(to record expenditures)		
e.	Expenditures—debt principal payments	700	
	Expenditures—debt interest payments	100	
	Cash		800
	(to record debt payments)		
f.	Cash	1,347	
	Payables.	21,744	
	Receivables—real estate & personal property taxes		19,706
	Receivables—intergovernmental revenues		3,385
g.	Revenues	283	
	Deferred revenues		283
	(Deferral of revenues)		

Part 2:

h.

Balance Sheet	
Cash.	$ 7,217
Receivables:	
Real estate and personal property	522
Intergovernmental.	5,398
Total assets.	$13,137
Payables.	$ 618
Deferred revenues	5,938
Total liabilities.	6,556
Fund balances:	
Assigned.	1,566
Unassigned	5,015
Total fund balances	6,581
Total liabilities and fund balances.	$13,137

Statement of Revenues, Expenditures, and Changes in Fund Balances	
Revenues	
Real estate taxes	$19,510
Intergovernmental	3,563
Total revenues.	23,073
Expenditures	
General government.	3,327
Public safety.	2,219
Education	13,313
Public works.	1,109
Human services	2,219
Debt principal payments.	700
Debt interest payments.	100
Total expenditures	22,987
Excess (deficiency) of revenues over expenditures	86
Other financing sources (uses)	
Proceeds from bonds	2,000
Total other financing sources (uses).	2,000
Net change in fund balances	$ 2,086
Fund balances at beginning of year.	4,495
Fund balances at end of year.	$ 6,581

i. 1	APPROPRIATIONS...	22,409	
	BUDGETARY FUND BALANCE	2,479	
	ESTIMATED REVENUES.....................................		22,888
	ESTIMATED OTHER FINANCING SOURCES		2,000
	(to reverse budget entry)		
2	Revenues—real estate & personal property taxes........................	19,510	
	Revenues—intergovernmental...	3,563	
	Other financing sources—bond proceeds.............................	2,000	
	Expenditures—general government		3,327
	Expenditures—public safety		2,219
	Expenditures—education		13,313
	Expenditures—public works		1,109
	Expenditures—human services.................................		2,219
	Expenditures—debt principal payments		700
	Expenditures—debt interest payments...........................		100
	Fund balance—unassigned.....................................		2,086
	(to close out revenue and expenditure accounts)		
3	BUDGETARY FUND BALANCE—RESERVED FOR ENCUMBRANCES........	261	
	ENCUMBRANCES...		261
	Fund balance—unassigned	261	
	Fund balance—assigned.......................................		261
	(to close remaining encumbrances and reserve Fund Balance for encumbrances that lapsed, but are expected to be honored in the following year)		

LEARNING OBJECTIVES

1. Describe the Comprehensive Annual Financial Report (CAFR). (p. 629)

2. Describe government-wide financial statements. (p. 633)

Government Accounting: Government-Wide Financial Statements

To provide necessary public services to its citizens, the **Town of Acton** must develop infrastructure. It must construct roads and bridges; light its streets; purchase fire trucks and police cars; build public safety administrative facilities; construct elementary, middle, and high schools; build libraries; develop landfills or other waste disposal facilities; build administrative facilities

**THE TOWN OF ACTON,
**MASSACHUSETTS—
CONTINUED**

for Town services, parks, and other recreational facilities, and buildings to provide social services; and invest in numerous other capital projects that are necessary in order to provide the services and support that citizens expect.

Acton Public Safety Facility

These capital projects are typically financed with long-term borrowings that require the pledge of *future* tax revenues to provide the necessary funds to repay the debt. These borrowings are called municipal bonds (or *munis*) and the interest income to bond purchasers is typically exempt from federal tax In order to allow the debt to carry a lower interest rate and, therefore, to reduce the tax burden on citizens.

Buyers of these municipal bonds are typically pension funds and mutual funds that purchase the bonds for the benefit of their investors. So that the bonds can be accurately priced, they are usually rated just like corporate debt, and those debt ratings assess the relative probability of default using a number of credit ratios that measure projected cash inflows and outflows of the municipality.

The issue that concerns us in this chapter relates to the information that is required in order to accurately project cash inflows and outflows of the municipality. As you recall from our discussion in Chapter 9, fund-based financial statements report on a *current financial resources measurement focus* and use the *modified accrual basis of accounting*. The resulting financial statements are closer to cash basis accounting than they are to accrual accounting that we use to account for businesses.

(continued on next page)

(continued from previous page)

Long-term assets, such as Acton's public safety and high school buildings pictured on the previous page, are *not* reported on a governmental fund-based balance sheet. Neither is Acton's long-term debt that was issued to finance those infrastructure investments. These omissions make the financial statements less useful for the type of credit analysis that we discuss above.

In response, the GASB mandates the preparation of government-wide financial statements. These financial reports are prepared under accrual accounting and include infrastructure assets like PPE as well as long-term debt. Government-wide financial statements are prepared by adding accruals to the fund-based financial statements that we describe in Chapter 9. This requires municipalities to keep two sets of books: one to prepare fund-based financial statements and the other with the accruals necessary to prepare government-wide financial statements.

We describe the preparation of government-wide financial statements in this chapter.

Source: Town of Acton 2014 financial report

CHAPTER ORGANIZATION

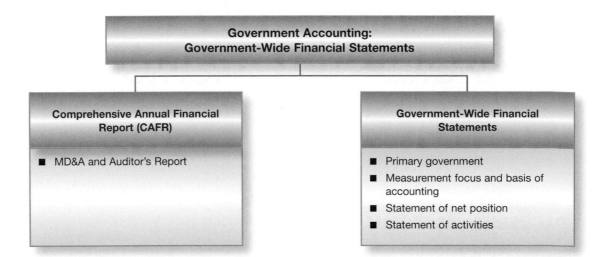

In our introduction to Chapter 9, we pose three questions that different user groups might ask concerning the operations of a government. One of these is whether a specific component of the government (the public safety department or the department of education, for example) has operated within its allotted budget. That question can be answered by the fund financial statements that we discuss in Chapter 9. Although fund financial statements provide useful information to assist leaders in managing their states or municipalities, they do not provide information that is useful in answering our two other questions relating to whether the government is operating *efficiently* or whether it is financially *solvent*. These questions require financial statements that include a broader definition of the resources available to governments and the future obligations that they must budget for. These broader financial statements are called government-wide financial statements.

Government-wide financial statements are mandated in GASB 34, "Basic Financial Statements—and Management's Discussion and Analysis—for State and Local Governments," (issued in 1999 and codified in GASB ASC 2200). These statements help users . . . (GASB 34, Preface)

a. Assess the finances of the government in its entirety, including the year's operating results

b. Determine whether the government's overall financial position improved or deteriorated

c. Evaluate whether the government's current-year revenues were sufficient to pay for current-year services

d. See the cost of providing services to its citizenry

e. See how the government finances its programs—through user fees and other program revenues versus general tax revenues

f. Understand the extent to which the government has invested in capital assets, including roads, bridges, and other infrastructure assets

g. Make better comparisons between governments.

GASB 34 mandates the issuance of a Comprehensive Annual Financial Report (CAFR) that includes both the fund financial statements that we discuss in Chapter 9 and the government-wide financial statements that we illustrate in this chapter, together with management's discussion and analysis (MD&A), supporting notes, and other required supplementary information.

Exhibit 10.1 illustrates the flow of accounting information from the fund-based financial statements which we discuss in Chapter 9 to the government-wide financial statements that we discuss in this chapter.

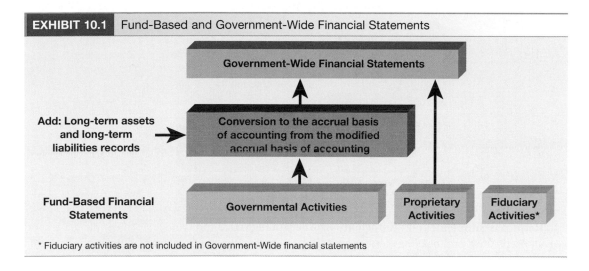

EXHIBIT 10.1 Fund-Based and Government-Wide Financial Statements

* Fiduciary activities are not included in Government-Wide financial statements

Once the fund financial statements are developed, long-term assets and liabilities, together with related accruals for accumulated depreciation, interest payable and others, are added to create the government-wide financial statements.

We begin our chapter with a discussion of the Comprehensive Annual Financial Report, the official annual report that all governments are required to issue.

COMPREHENSIVE ANNUAL FINANCIAL REPORT (CAFR)

The Comprehensive Annual Financial Report (CAFR) is the governmental entity's official annual report. It contains both fund financial statements and government-wide financial statements, as well as Management's Discussion and Analysis (MD&A), schedules necessary to demonstrate compliance with finance-related legal and contractual provisions that affect the government, and statistical data.

LO1 Describe the Comprehensive Annual Financial Report (CAFR).

The minimum requirements for basic financial statements and required supplementary information are presented in Exhibit 10.2 (GASB ASC 2200 Statement of Principle: Annual Financial Reporting ¶c, 102, and 103):

a. **Management's discussion and analysis.** The MD&A should introduce the basic financial statements and provide an analytical overview of the government's financial activities.

b. **Basic financial statements.** The basic financial statements should include:

1. **Government-wide financial statements.** The government-wide statements should display information about the reporting government as a whole, except for its fiduciary activities. The statements should include separate columns for the governmental and business-type activities of the primary government as well as for its component units. Government-wide financial statements should be prepared using the economic resources measurement focus and the accrual basis of accounting.

2. **Fund financial statements.** Fund financial statements for the primary government's governmental, proprietary, and fiduciary funds should be presented after the government-wide statements. Governmental fund financial statements should be prepared using the current financial resources measurement focus and the modified accrual basis of accounting (we discuss the accounting for funds in Chapter 9).

3. **Notes to the financial statements.** These footnotes should communicate information essential for the fair presentation of the financial statements that is not displayed on the face of the financial statements.

EXHIBIT 10.2 | Minimum Requirements for General Purpose External Financial Statements

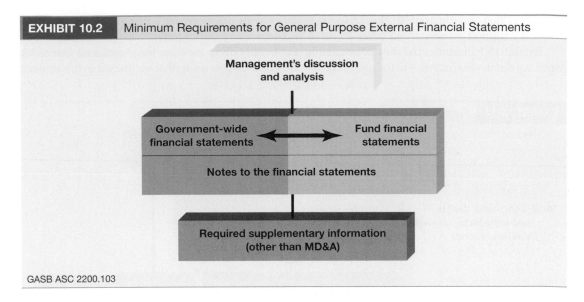

GASB ASC 2200.103

c. **Required supplementary information other than MD&A.** Included in the financial report and separate from the Notes to the Financial Statements, the required supplementary information consists of schedules, statistical data, and other information that the GASB has determined are an essential part of financial reporting and should be presented with, but are not part of, the basic financial statements of a governmental entity. In addition to those presentations, the RSI includes *budgetary comparisons* that include the originally adopted budget, the final budget (including any subsequent amendments), and the actual inflows and outflows and balances of net position. Governments are also encouraged, but not required, to provide a column indicating the variances between the final budget and the actual amounts.[1]

We first turn to a discussion of the MD&A and Auditor's Report, followed by a review of the government-wide financial statements. We conclude our discussion with a continuation of our Town of Acton example to illustrate the adjusting journal entries that are necessary to prepare the government-wide financial statements from the fund financial statements that we discuss in Chapter 9.

MD&A and Auditor's Report

The MD&A should include all of the following (GASB ASC 2200.109):

a. A brief discussion of the basic financial statements, including the relationships of the statements to each other, and the significant differences in the information they provide.

b. Condensed financial information derived from government-wide financial statements comparing the current year to the prior year.

c. An analysis of the government's overall financial position and results of operations to assist users in assessing whether financial position has improved or deteriorated as a result of the year's operations.

d. An analysis of balances and transactions of individual funds.

e. An analysis of significant variations between original and final budget amounts and between final budget amounts and actual budget results for the general fund (or its equivalent).

f. A description of significant capital asset and long-term debt activity during the year, including a discussion of commitments made for capital expenditures, changes in credit ratings, and debt limitations that may affect the financing of planned facilities or services.

g. A discussion by governments that use the modified approach to report some or all of their infrastructure assets including:

---

[1] The required statistical information has been further defined in GASB 2200 to include information about the modified approach for reporting infrastructure assets, and employee benefit related information.

1. Significant changes in the assessed condition of eligible infrastructure assets from previous condition assessments
2. How the current assessed condition compares with the condition level the government has established
3. Any significant differences from the estimated annual amount to maintain/preserve eligible infrastructure assets compared with the actual amounts spent during the current period.

h. A description of currently known facts, decisions, or conditions that are expected to have a significant effect on financial position or results of operations.

We provide excerpts from the MD&A for the Town of Acton in Exhibit 10.3. In addition to the discussion of financial highlights, the government-wide financial analysis, and the financial analysis of the government's funds, the Town also provides summary financial statements (we omit these at this point since we will present them in their entirety later in the chapter).

EXHIBIT 10.3	Excerpts from the MD&A for the Town of Acton's CAFR

Management's Discussion and Analysis

As management of the Town of Acton, Massachusetts, we offer readers of these financial statements this narrative overview and analysis of the financial activities of the Town of Acton, Massachusetts for the fiscal year ended June 30, 2014.

Financial Highlights—Primary Government

- The assets of the Town of Acton, Massachusetts exceeded its liabilities at the close of the most recent fiscal year by $164,277,936 *(net position)*.
- The government's total net position decreased by $2,201,517. The Governmental Activities decreased by $1,696,255 or 1.2%. The business type activities decreased by $505,262 or 2.2%.
- At the end of the current fiscal year, unassigned fund balance in the general fund was $12,103,520, or 13.7% of total general fund expenditures.
- The Town of Acton, Massachusetts' total general obligation bonds payable decreased by $2,663,830 or 6.8% during the current year. The change is attributed to a decrease in the Governmental Activities ($1,881,830 or 6.8%) and a decrease in the Business-type Activities ($782,000 or 4.4%). A considerable amount of the Business-type activity debt will be funded by betterment revenues.

Overview of the Financial Statements—Primary Government

The discussion and analysis is intended to serve as an introduction of the Town of Acton, Massachusetts' basic financial statements. The Town of Acton, Massachusetts' basic financial statements consist of the following: 1) government-wide financial statements, 2) fund financial statements, and 3) notes to the financial statements.

Government-wide financial statements.　The *government-wide financial statements* are designed to provide readers with a broad overview of the Town of Acton, Massachusetts' finances, in a manner similar to private-sector business.

The Government-wide financial statements include the Town of Acton, Massachusetts (the Primary Government) and the Acton Community Housing Trust (a component unit for which the town is financially accountable).

The *statement of net position* presents information on all of the Town of Acton, Massachusetts' assets/deferred outflows and liabilities/deferred inflows, with the difference reported as *net position*. Over time, increases or decreases in net position may serve as a useful indicator of whether the financial position of the Town of Acton, Massachusetts is improving or deteriorating.

The *statement of activities* presents information showing how the government's net position changed during the most recent fiscal year. All changes in net position are reported as soon as the underlying event giving rise of the change occurs, *regardless of the timing of related cash flows*. Thus, revenues and expenses are reported in this statement for some items that will only result in cash flows in future fiscal periods (e.g., uncollected taxes and earned but unused vacation leave).

The government-wide financial statements have separate columns for governmental activities and business-type activities. The Town's activities are classified as follows:

- **Governmental Activities**—Activities reported here include education, public safety, public works, library and general administration. Property taxes, motor vehicle excise taxes, state and other local revenues finance these activities.
- **Business-Type Activities**—Activities reported here are for sanitation, nursing services and sewer operations. User fees charged to the customers receiving services finance these activities.

continued

EXHIBIT 10.3 cont.	Excerpts from the MD&A for the Town of Acton's CAFR

Management's Discussion and Analysis

Fund financial statements. A *fund* is a grouping of related accounts that is used to maintain control over resources that have been segregated for specific activities or objectives. The Town of Acton, Massachusetts, like other state and local governments, uses fund accounting to ensure and demonstrate compliance with finance-related legal requirements. All of the funds of the Town of Acton, Massachusetts can be divided into three categories: governmental funds, proprietary funds and fiduciary funds.

Governmental funds. *Governmental funds* are used to account for essentially the same functions reported as *governmental activities* in the government-wide financial statements. However, unlike the government-wide financial statements, governmental fund financial statements focus on *near-term inflows and outflows of spendable resources*, as well as on *balances of spendable resources* available at the end of the fiscal year. Such information may be useful in evaluating a government's near-term financing requirements.

Because the focus of governmental funds is narrower than that of the government-wide financial statements, it is useful to compare the information presented for *governmental funds* with similar information presented for *governmental activities* in the government-wide financial statements. By doing so, readers may better understand the long-term impact of the government's near-term financing decisions. Both the governmental fund balance sheet and the governmental fund statement of revenues, expenditures and changes in fund balances provide a reconciliation to facilitate this comparison between *governmental funds* and *governmental activities*.

Proprietary funds. The Town of Acton, Massachusetts maintains three proprietary (enterprise) fund types. *Enterprise funds* are used to report the same functions presented as *business-type activities* in the government-wide financial statements. The Town of Acton, Massachusetts uses enterprise funds to account for its sanitation, nursing services and sewer operations.

Proprietary funds provide the same type of information as the government-wide financial statements, only in more detail. The proprietary fund financial statements provide separate information for each enterprise fund. All three funds are considered to be major funds of the Town of Acton, Massachusetts.

Fiduciary funds. Fiduciary funds are used to account for resources held for the benefit of parties outside the government. Fiduciary funds are *not* reflected in the government-wide financial statements because the resources of those funds are *not* available to support the Town's own programs. The accounting used for fiduciary funds is much like that used for proprietary funds. The Town maintains fiduciary funds to account for activities related to charitable trust funds and for its Other Post Employment Benefits (OPEB) trust fund. The OPEB Trust Fund is used to accumulate resources to provide funding for future OPEB liabilities.

The Town's financial statements are audited by **Giusti, Hingston and Company**. The audit opinion is presented in Exhibit 10.4.

EXHIBIT 10.4	Independent Auditor's Report for the Town of Acton

INDEPENDENT AUDITOR'S REPORT

Board of Selectmen
Town of Acton
472 Main Street
Acton, MA 01720

Report on the Financial Statements

We have audited the accompanying financial statements of the governmental activities, the business-type activities, the discretely presented component unit, each major fund and the aggregate remaining fund information of the Town of Acton, Massachusetts as of and for the year ended June 30, 2014, and the related notes to the financial statements, which collectively comprise the Town's basic financial statements as listed in the table of contents.

Management's Responsibility for the Financial Statements

Management is responsible for the preparation and fair presentation of these financial statements in accordance with principles generally accepted in the United States of America; This includes the design, implementation, and maintenance of internal control relevant to the preparation and fair presentation of financial statements that are free from material misstatement, whether due to fraud or error.

continued

EXHIBIT 10.4 cont.	Independent Auditor's Report for the Town of Acton

INDEPENDENT AUDITOR'S REPORT

Auditor's Responsibility

Our responsibility is to express opinions on these financial statements based on our audit. We conducted our audit in accordance with auditing standards generally accepted in the United States of America and the standards applicable to financial audits contained in *Governmental Auditing Standards*, issued by the Comptroller General of the United States. Those standards require that we plan and perform the audit to obtain reasonable assurance about whether the financial statements are free from material misstatement.

An audit involves performing procedures to obtain audit evidence, about the amounts and disclosures in the financial statements. The procedures selected depend on the auditor's judgment, including the assessment of the risks of material misstatement of the fianancial statements, whether due to fraud or error. In making those risk assessments, the auditor considers internal control relevant to the entity's preparation and fair presentation of the fianancial statements in order to design audit procedures that are appropriate in the circumstances, but not for the purpose of expressing an opinion on the effectiveness of the entity's internal control. Accordingly, we discuss no such opinion. An audit also includes evaluating the appropriateness of accounting policies used and the reasonableness of significant accounting estimates made by management, as well as evaluating the overall presentation of the fianancial statements.

We believe that the audit evidence we have obtained is sufficient and appropriate to provide a basis for our audit opinion.

Opinion

In our opinion, the financial statements referred to above present fairly, in all material respects, the respective financial position of the governmental activities, the business-type activities, the discretely presented component unit, each major fund and the aggregate remaining fund information of the Town of Acton, Massachusetts as of June 30, 2014 and the respective changes in financial position, and, where applicable, cash flows thereof for the year then ended in conformity with accounting principles generally accepted in the United States of America.

Giusti, Hingston and Company

Giusti, Hingston and Company
Certified Public Accountants
Georgetown, Massachusetts
December 8, 2014

GOVERNMENT-WIDE FINANCIAL STATEMENTS

LO2 Describe government-wide financial statements.

All state and local governments (states, cities, counties, towns, and villages) must issue government-wide financial statements (GASB ASC 2200.101). These financial statements consist of a *statement of net position* (similar to a balance sheet in the corporate world) and a *statement of activities* (the government equivalent of an income statement). GASB ASC 2200.110 requires that these statements:

a. Report information about the overall government without displaying individual funds or fund types

b. Exclude information about fiduciary activities, including component units that are fiduciary in nature (such as certain public employee retirement systems)

c. Distinguish between the primary government and its discretely presented component units

d. Distinguish between governmental activities and business-type activities of the primary government

e. Measure and report all assets (both financial and capital), liabilities, revenues, expenses, gains, and losses using the economic resources measurement focus and accrual basis of accounting.

Government-wide financial statements are prepared using the *accrual basis of accounting* that we use for businesses and present all of the assets and liabilities, revenues and expenses, of the governmental unit. They are designed to answer questions relating to whether the government is operating efficiently and whether it is solvent. These questions are, of course, similar to the questions we ask about businesses, and the government-wide financial statements that governments issue are similar to the corporate financial statements that we have reviewed thus far (with the notable exception of the reference to Net Position instead of Stockholders' Equity).

Primary Government

GASB 2200.112 states that "the focus of the government-wide financial statements should be on the primary government. . . . Separate rows and columns should be used to distinguish between the total primary government and its discretely presented component units."[2] The **primary government** is a governmental unit that,

a.   Has a **separately elected governing body**.

b.   Is **legally separate**.[3]

c.   Is **fiscally independent** of other state and local governments.[4]

(GASB ASC 2100.112)

The primary government is any state, city, county, town or village. Primary governments are separate legal entities, with governing bodies duly elected by the citizens to carry out the role of the government in meeting their needs, and with powers of taxation that make them fiscally independent so that they can set their own budgets and fund those budgets from tax inflows. The primary government is what we typically think of when we describe governmental activities.

In addition to the financial statements for the primary government, GASB ASC 2100 also requires separate presentation of financial statements for all of the primary government's component units. A **component unit** is a legally separate organization for which the elected officials of the primary government are *financially accountable* (GASB ASC 2100.102). A primary government is **financially accountable** for a component unit when

1. It can incur financial obligations (or derives financial benefits) from the component unit

2. It controls the appointment of a majority of the controlling board and can "impose its will" on the component's activities (GASB ASC 2100.120).

In addition, a component unit is a governmental unit whose exclusion from the government-wide financial statements would make them misleading in some sense, even if the primary government is not financially accountable for it.

Component units are usually reported using **discrete presentation** in which the financial statements of each component unit are presented in a column apart from those of the primary government and not included in the totals that are reported for the primary government. The discrete column(s) should be located to the right of the total column of the primary government, distinguishing between the financial data of the primary government (including its blended component units as we discuss below) and those of the discretely presented component units by providing descriptive column headings.

Some component units, despite being legally separate from the primary government, are so intertwined with the primary government that they are, in substance, the same as the primary government and should be reported as part of the primary government (see our Practice Insight: City of Boulder, Colorado, Blended Units for an example). This method of inclusion is known as **blending**. Because of the closeness of their relationships with the primary government, some component units should be blended as though they are part of the primary government; however, most component units should be discretely presented (GASB ASC 2600.105).

---

[2] Separate rows and columns also should be used to distinguish between the governmental and business-type activities of the primary government. Governmental activities generally are financed through taxes, intergovernmental revenues, and other nonexchange revenues. These activities are usually reported in governmental funds and internal service funds. Business-type activities are financed in whole or in part by fees charged to external parties for goods or services. These activities are usually reported in enterprise funds. (GASB ASC 2200.112)

[3] An organization has separate legal standing if it is created as a body corporate or a body corporate and politic, or if it otherwise possesses the corporate powers that would distinguish it as being legally separate from the primary government. Generally, corporate powers give an organization the capacity to have a name; the right to sue and be sued in its own name without recourse to a state or local governmental unit; and the right to buy, sell, lease, and mortgage property in its own name... A special-purpose government (or any other organization) that is *not* legally separate should be considered, for financial reporting purposes, part of the primary government that holds the corporate powers. (GASB ASC 2100.117)

[4] A government is fiscally *independent* if it can (a) determine its budget without another government having the substantive authority to approve and modify that budget, (b) levy taxes or set rates or charges without substantive approval by another government, and (c) issue bonded debt without substantive approval by another government. (GASB ASC 2100.115)

A component unit should be included in the reporting entity financial statements using the *blending method* in any of the following circumstances (GASB ASC 2600.113):

a. The component unit's governing body is substantively the same as the governing body of the primary government

b. The component unit provides services entirely, or almost entirely, to the primary government or otherwise exclusively, or almost exclusively, benefits the primary government even though it does not provide services directly to it.

c. The component unit's total debt outstanding, including leases, is expected to be repaid entirely or almost entirely with resources of the primary government.

In the following Practice Insight box, we present excerpts from the Denver, Colorado CAFR footnotes relating to its presentation of component units both as blended component units and discretely presented component units.

PRACTICE INSIGHT

City of Denver, Colorado, blended and discretely presented component units

Note A—Reporting Entity

The City and County of Denver (City) was incorporated in 1861 and became a Colorado Home Rule City on March 29, 1904... As required by U.S. GAAP, these financial statements present the City (primary government) and its component units. The component units discussed below are included in the City's reporting entity because of the significance of their operational or financial relationships with the City . . . Each component unit has a December 31st year end.

1. Blended Component Units.

Gateway Village General Improvement District and Denver 14th Street General Improvement District—The districts were created by the City as separate legal entities pursuant to state statute. Per statute, the City Council serves as ex officio Board of Directors for the districts. District Advisory Boards, appointed by the City Council, conduct and manage all affairs of the districts, which provide capital improvement and maintenance services entirely to the City, subject to overall approval and supervision of the ex officio Board of Directors. The districts are reported herein in the City's special revenue and debt service funds.

2. Discretely Presented Component Units.

9th Avenue, Cherry Creek North, Cherry Creek Subarea, Colfax, Downtown Denver, Old South Gaylord, West Colfax, Federal Boulevard, Bluebird, Fax-Mayfair, and Santa Fe Business Improvement Districts (BID)—Each BID was created by the City as a separate legal entity pursuant to state statute for the purpose of maintaining public improvements and planning development activities within each BID's geographic boundaries. The City appoints the governing boards of the BIDs and is able to impose its will through the approval of the BID's operating budgets. . . .

Denver Downtown Development Authority (DDDA)—The DDDA was created for the purpose of promoting public health, safety, prosperity, security, and general welfare in order to halt or prevent deterioration of property values or structures within the central business district and to assist in the development and redevelopment of the central business district, especially to benefit the property within the boundaries of the Authority. . . . The Board of Directors is appointed by the Mayor and confirmed by City Council, and City Council may remove any director at will. These appointments and the ability of the City to impose its will on the Authority make the City financially accountable for the Authority. . . .

Denver Preschool Program, Inc. (DPP)—DPP is a nonprofit corporation organized to administer the Denver Preschool Program that provides tuition credits for children of Denver families the year before the child is eligible for kindergarten. The City is legally obligated to provide financial support to DPP, as the program is funded by a sales and use tax increase of fifteen one-hundredths of one percent (0.15%) that was voter-approved through December 2026. The Mayor appoints six of the seven DPP board members and City Council appoints a council member as the other board member. The City appointments to the governing body and its financial obligations to DPP make the City financially accountable for the DPP. . . .

Measurement Focus and Basis of Accounting

Government-wide financial statements are prepared using the *economic resources measurement focus* and the *accrual basis of accounting* (GASB ASC 1600.103). **Economic resources** are broader than the "financial resources" measurement focus that we use in fund accounting. It includes long-term assets and liabilities as well as current financial resources, and is similar to the GAAP measurement focus that is used by businesses.

The **accrual basis of accounting** requires that

1. Revenues, expenses, gains, losses, assets, and liabilities resulting from *exchange and exchange-like transactions* should be recognized when the exchange takes place, with appropriate provision for uncollectible accounts (GASB ASC 1600.104).

2. Revenues, expenses, gains, losses, assets, and liabilities resulting from *nonexchange transactions* should be recognized as follows (GASB ASC N50):

   ○ **Derived Tax Revenue Transactions** (i.e., taxes on personal income, corporate income, and retail sales of goods and services)—Governments should recognize *assets* from derived tax revenue transactions in the period when the exchange transaction on which the tax is imposed occurs or when the resources are received, whichever occurs first. Governments should recognize *revenues*, net of estimated refunds and estimated uncollectible amounts, in the same period that the assets are recognized, provided that the underlying exchange transaction has occurred. Resources received in advance should be reported as deferred revenues (liabilities) until the period of the exchange (N50.113).

   ○ **Imposed Nonexchange Revenue Transactions** (i.e., property taxes; fines and penalties; and property forfeitures, such as seizures and escheats)—Governments should recognize *assets* from imposed nonexchange revenue transactions in the period when an enforceable legal claim to the assets arises or when the resources are received, whichever occurs first. Governments should recognize *revenues* from property taxes, net of estimated refunds and estimated uncollectible amounts, *in the period for which the taxes are levied,* even if the enforceable legal claim arises or the due date for payment occurs in a different period (N50.115).

   ○ **Government-Mandated Nonexchange Transactions and Voluntary Nonexchange Transactions** (i.e., federal programs that state or local governments are mandated to perform and state programs that local governments are mandated to perform, certain grants, certain entitlements, and donations by nongovernmental entities, including private donations by individuals)—Providers of resources in government-mandated or voluntary nonexchange transactions frequently establish eligibility requirements. Eligibility requirements are conditions established by enabling legislation or the provider that are required to be met before a transaction (other than the provision of cash or other assets in advance) can occur. That is, until those requirements are met, the provider does not have a liability, the recipient does not have a receivable, and the recognition of expenses or revenues for resources transmitted in advance should be deferred (N50.116).

Following is an excerpt from the Town of Acton's footnotes relating to the accounting principles used in the preparation of the government-wide financial statements:

> *The government-wide financial statements are reported using the economic resources measurement focus and the accrual basis of accounting, as are the fiduciary fund financial statements. Revenues are recorded when earned and expenses are recorded when a liability is incurred, regardless of the timing of the related cash flows. Property taxes are recognized as revenues in the year for which they are levied. Grants and similar items are recognized as revenue as soon as all eligibility requirements imposed by the provider have been met.*

The Town of Acton recognizes revenues on the accrual basis of accounting, that is, when earned. Likewise, expenses are recognized when incurred. Real estate and personal property taxes are a significant source of revenue for the Town. These are recognized when levied (i.e., when the assessment is made and tax billings are sent to Town residents). Finally, the Town receives funding from the State of Massachusetts and the federal government. This funding relates to support for education and building programs, and the funding typically carries a number of eligibility conditions. Revenues for grants and other subsidies are deferred and recognized only when all of the eligibility conditions have been met.

Statement of Net Position

The Statement of Net Position presents assets, deferred outflows of resources, liabilities, deferred inflows of resources, and net position. The difference between assets and liabilities must be labeled as *Net Position*, and cannot be labeled as equity, net fund balance, or other similar label (GASB ASC 2200.115). Separate rows and columns should be used to distinguish between the total primary government and its discretely presented component units, and a total column should be presented for the primary government. Separate rows and columns should also be used to distinguish between the governmental and business-type activities of the primary government.

Like financial statements for businesses, assets are presented in order of liquidity and liabilities in order of maturity. Liquidity for assets means how readily they are expected to be converted into cash. In the governmental setting, however, asset conversion to cash may be restricted by law or regulation which places additional limitations on the use of assets that may not be present in the business setting. The current and noncurrent segregation for assets and liabilities is also required for the statements of net position as it is for the financial statements of businesses.

The net position section of the statement should be displayed in three sections:

1. Net investment in capital assets
2. Restricted (distinguishing between major categories of restrictions), and
3. Unrestricted

We discuss the reporting for capital assets, including the net asset account, in the next section, followed by a discussion of restricted and unrestricted net position.

Capital Assets Capital assets are long-term assets, including land, land improvements, easements, buildings, building improvements, vehicles, equipment, works of art and historical treasures, and infrastructure assets (i.e., roads, bridges, tunnels, drainage systems, water and sewage systems, dams, and lighting systems). They are initially recorded at historical cost, including any costs that are directly attributable to asset acquisition—such as freight and transportation charges, site preparation costs, and professional fees. Sometimes governments receive donations from citizens. These *donated* assets are initially recorded at fair value (GASB ASC 1400.102).

Capital assets should be depreciated over their estimated useful lives unless they are indefinite lived assets (i.e., land) or are exempted from depreciation and reported using the modified approach that we discuss below (GASB ASC 1400.104). Any rational and systematic manner of depreciation can be used, including straight-line, accelerated, and composite depreciation methods.[5] If depreciated, capital assets should be reported net of accumulated depreciation.

Infrastructure assets that are part of a *network* (like a road or lighting system), are not required to be depreciated as long as two requirements are met (GASB ASC 1400.105):

---

[5] **Composite depreciation methods** refer to depreciating a grouping of similar assets (for example, interstate highways in a state) or dissimilar assets of the same class (for example, all the roads and bridges of a state) using the same depreciation rate. Initially, a depreciation rate for the composite is determined. Annually, the determined rate is multiplied by the cost of the grouping of assets to calculate depreciation expense.

A composite depreciation rate can be calculated in different ways. The rate could be calculated based on a weighted-average or on an unweighted-average estimate of useful lives of assets in the composite. For example, the composite depreciation rate of three interstate highways with estimated remaining useful lives of sixteen, twenty, and twenty-four years could be calculated using an unweighted average estimated as follows: $1/[(16 + 20 + 24)/3] = 5\%$ annual depreciation rate.

A composite depreciation rate may also be calculated based on an assessment of the useful lives of the grouping of assets. This assessment could be based on condition assessments or experience with the useful lives of the grouping of assets. For example, based on experience, engineers may determine that interstate highways generally have estimated remaining useful lives of approximately twenty years. In this case, the annual depreciation rate would be 5 percent. (GASB ASC 1400.176–179).

1. The government manages the infrastructure assets using an asset management system,[6] and

2. The government documents that the infrastructure assets are being preserved approximately at least at a condition level established and disclosed by the government.[7]

If the infrastructure assets meet these two requirements, they need not be depreciated and, instead, may be accounted for using the modified approach. The **modified approach** requires that, in lieu of depreciation expense, all maintenance expenditures made for those assets (i.e., except for additions and improvements) should be expensed in the period incurred (GASB ASC 1400.107).[8]

Works of Art and Historical Treasures

Purchased works of art and historical treasures should be recorded at their purchase price on the date of acquisition. Sometimes, governments receive donations of works of art and historical treasures. If donated, they should be recorded at fair value whether held as individual items or in a collection.

The capitalization of works of art and historical treasures is encouraged, but *is not required*, for collections that are:

1. Held for public exhibition, education, or research in furtherance of public service, rather than financial gain

2. Protected, kept unencumbered, cared for, and preserved,

3. Subject to an organizational body that requires the proceeds from sales of collection items to be used to acquire other items for collections (GASB ASC 1400.109).

Governments might prefer to expense rather than to capitalize works of art and historical treasures in order to avoid reporting the assets. An increase in net position might give citizens the impression that the resources of the government that are available to fund governmental activities have increased (thus decreasing the ability of the government to raise needed funds by taxation). And, since these works of art or historical treasures will not be converted to cash, that impression would be incorrect.

If the works of art or historical treasures are capitalized, whether as individual works of art and historical treasures or a collection of these items, they should be depreciated over their estimated useful lives unless the items are deemed to be "inexhaustible." In that case, depreciation is not required.

Net Investment in Capital Assets

Should the municipality incur liabilities that relate specifically to the acquisition, construction, or improvement of capital assets, those assets should be reported *net of the related debt* (in addition to the reduction for accumulated depreciation) in the statement of net position as follows (GASB ASC 2200.118):

	Capital assets (including restricted capital assets as discussed in the next section)
Less:	Accumulated depreciation
Less:	Outstanding balance of bonds, mortgages, notes, or other borrowings attributable to the acquisition, construction, or improvement of the capital assets
Equals	Net investment in capital assets

As we discuss above, the net position (i.e., the sum of all assets less all liabilities) should be displayed in three sections: Net Investment in Capital Assets, Restricted, and Unrestricted. The Net Investment in Capital Assets described above is one of the three components. Next, we describe the remaining two sections.

---

[6] An asset management system is defined as one that should: a. have an up-to-date inventory of eligible infrastructure assets, b. perform condition assessments on the infrastructure assets and summarize the results using a measurement scale, and c. estimate each year the annual amount to maintain and preserve the infrastructure asset at the condition level established and disclosed by the government (GASB ASC 1400.105).

[7] Maintenance of adequate documentary evidence requires the government to document that: a. complete condition assessments are performed in a consistent manner at least every three years, and b. the results of the three most recent complete assessments provide reasonable assurance that the infrastructure assets are being preserved approximately at least at the condition level established and disclosed by the government (GASB ASC 1400.106).

[8] Additions and improvements are defined as they are in the business world (i.e., expenditures that increase the capacity or efficiency of the asset rather than preserve its useful life). Additions and improvements should be capitalized (GASB ASC 1400.107).

EXHIBIT 10.5	Statement of Net Position for the Town of Acton, MA

TOWN OF ACTON, MASSACHUSETTS
Statement of Net Position
June 30, 2014

	Primary Government			Component Unit
	Governmental Activities	Business-Type Activities	Total	Acton Community Housing Trust
Assets				
Current:				
Cash and cash equivalents................	$ 26,601,819	$ 8,318,177	$ 34,919,996	$ 255,921
Investments	5,217,964	—	5,217,964	—
Accounts receivable:				
Property taxes	672,566	—	672,566	—
Tax liens	1,195,966	—	1,195,966	—
Motor vehicle excises	197,241	—	197,241	—
User charges	107,596	261,973	369,569	—
Special assessments..................	172,597	719,820	892,417	—
Departmental	100,703	—	100,703	—
Intergovernmental....................	2,148,503	—	2,148,503	—
Liens	—	71,681	71,681	—
Due from Town of Acton	—	—	—	911,001
Other...............................	—	—	—	18,000
Noncurrent:				
Accounts receivable:				
Intergovernmental	7,381,382	—	7,381,382	—
Clause 41 A property taxes.............	139,268	—	139,268	—
Special assessments not yet due	—	12,184,491	12,184,491	—
Other post employment benefit net asset	—	10,041	10,041	—
Capital assets:				
Assets not being depreciated	68,693,832	534,769	69,228,601	—
Assets being depreciated, net	69,402,423	17,381,766	86,784,189	—
Total assets	182,031,860	39,482,718	221,514,578	1,184,922
Liabilities				
Current:				
Warrants payable	853,284	69,185	922,469	—
Accrued salaries payable	228,728	8,498	237,226	—
Unclaimed checks	22,055	—	22,055	—
Accrued interest	223,012	111,002	334,014	—
Due to component unit..................	872,001	—	872,001	—
Compensated absences.................	183,019	4,966	187,985	—
Landfill closure/postclosure	2,500	—	2,500	—
Other................................	149,183	—	149,183	5,306
Bonds payable	2,221,724	803,800	3,025,524	—
Noncurrent:				
Compensated absences................	1,647,170	19,861	1,667,031	—
Landfill closure/postclosure	50,000	—	50,000	—
Other post employment benefit obligations ...	13,800,346	252,331	14,052,677	—
Other................................	2,464,027	—	2,464,027	—
Bonds payable	17,249,750	16,000,200	33,249,950	—
Total liabilities	39,966,799	17,269,843	57,236,642	5,306
Net position				
Net investment in capital assets	128,335,782	1,112,535	129,448,317	—
Restricted for:				
Special revenue	11,067,043	—	11,067,043	—
Perpetual funds:				
Expendable.........................	1,853,885	—	1,853,885	—
Nonexpendable.....................	1,990,737	—	1,990,737	—
Unrestricted	(1,182,386)	21,100,340	19,917,954	1,179,616
Total net position	$142,065,061	$22,212,875	$164,277,936	$1,179,616

Restricted and Unrestricted Net Position Net Position should be reported as *restricted* when governments are not free to use the asset as they wish. Such restrictions may be imposed by loan covenants, donor restrictions, laws or regulations. Restrictions may also be imposed as a result of constitutional provisions or enabling legislation (GASB ASC 2200.119).[9] The restricted designation informs users of the financial statements that all of the net position may not be available to meet the ongoing financial needs of the government. The remainder of the Net Position is classified as *unrestricted* (GASB ASC 2200.124). Unrestricted means that net position is available to meet the needs of the general operations of the government.

Statement of Net Position for the Town of Acton, MA We provide the Statement of Net Position for the Town of Acton, MA in Exhibit 10.5. The Statement of Net Position includes assets, liabilities, and the net position for the Town of Acton (the Primary Government) and the Acton Community Housing Trust (a component unit for which the town is financially accountable). Further, balances for the primary government (the Town) are categorized by Governmental and Business-Type Activities, defined as follows (GASB ASC 2200.113):

■ **Governmental Activities:** Generally financed through taxes, intergovernmental revenues, and other nonexchange revenues. These activities are usually reported in governmental funds and internal service funds in fund-based accounting (see Chapter 9).

■ **Business-Type Activities:** Financed in whole or in part by fees changed to external parties for goods or services.[10] These activities are reported in enterprise funds (see Chapter 9).

The Town of Acton provides the following explanation of the accounts reported in its statement of net position as discussed in its footnotes to the financial report:

■ **Cash and Investments.** Cash and short-term investments are considered to be cash on hand, demand deposits and short-term investments with original maturities of three months or less from the date of acquisition. Investments are reported at fair value.

■ **Accounts Receivable.**

 ○ **Real and Personal Property Taxes and Tax Liens.** By law, all taxable property in the State of Massachusetts must be assessed at 100% of fair market value. Once levied, which is required to be at least 30 days prior to the due date, these taxes are recorded as receivables in the fiscal year of levy. . . Real estate receivables are secured via the tax lien process and are considered 100% collectible. Accordingly, an allowance for uncollectible accounts is not reported.

 ○ **Motor Vehicle Excise Taxes.** Motor vehicle excise taxes are assessed annually for each vehicle registered in the Town and are recorded as receivables in the fiscal year of the levy... The allowance for uncollectible accounts is estimated based on historical trends and specific account analysis.

 ○ **User Charges** and **Clause 41 A Property Taxes.** Sewer charges and related liens are recorded as receivables in the fiscal year of the levy. Since the receivables are secured via the lien process, these accounts are considered 100% collectible and therefore do not report an allowance for uncollectible accounts.

 ○ **Special Assessments.** Municipalities often make improvements to their infrastructure, such as adding or repairing sidewalks, underground utilities and the like. The costs of these additions and improvements are often charged back to the property owners in the form of an assessment that is payable over time and represents a lien on the property until paid.

---

[9] *Enabling legislation* authorizes the government to obtain funds by taxation or charge and also requires the government to use the funds only for specific purposes.

[10] The Town of Acton has three business-type activities:
Nursing—Provides public health and visiting nurse services on a fee-for-service basis,
Sewer—Operates and maintains a sewer collection and treatment facility and charges users based on gallons of water used, and
Sanitation services—Operates and maintains a solid waste disposal and recycling facility and charges users an annual fee.

○ **Departmental.** Departmental receivables consist primarily of group insurance and cemetery receivables and are recorded as receivables in the fiscal year accrued. The allowance for uncollectible accounts is estimated based on historical trends and specific account analysis.

○ **Intergovernmental.** Various federal and state grants for operating and capital purposes are applied for and received annually. For non-expenditure-driven grants, receivables are recognized as soon as all eligibility requirements imposed by the provider have been met. For expenditure-driven grants, receivables are recognized when the qualifying expenditures are incurred and all other grant requirements are met. These receivables are considered 100% collectible and therefore do not report an allowance for uncollectible accounts.

■ **Capital Assets.** Capital assets, which include land, vehicles, buildings and improvements, capital improvements, machinery and equipment, infrastructure (e.g., sewer mains, roadways, and similar items), and construction in progress are reported in the applicable governmental or business-type activities column of the government-wide financial statements, and the proprietary fund financial statements. Capital assets are recorded at historical cost, or at estimated historical cost, if actual historical cost is not available. Donated capital assets are recorded at the estimated fair market value at the date of donation. Except for the capital assets of the governmental activities column in the government-wide financial statements, construction—period interest is capitalized on constructed capital assets if material. . . . Capital assets (excluding land and construction in progress) are depreciated on a straight-line basis. The estimated useful lives of capital assets are as follows:

Asset Class	Estimated Useful Life (in years)
Buildings and improvements	10–40
Improvements (other than buildings)	10–20
Infrastructure	40
Vehicles	5–15
Machinery and equipment	5–15

Notice that about half of the Town's capital assets are being depreciated, while half are not. This latter group recognizes all maintenance expenditures as expense in the period incurred.

■ **Interfund Receivables and Payables.** Transactions of a buyer/seller nature between and within governmental funds are eliminated from the governmental activities in the statement of position. Any residual balances outstanding between the governmental activities and business-type activities are reported in the statement of net position as "internal balances" (GASB ASC 1800.103).

■ **Intra-entity activity and balances.** Resource flows (except those that affect the statement of financial position only, such as loans, repayments, and deferred inflows of resources and deferred outflows of resources resulting from intra-entity transactions) between a primary government and its discretely presented component units should be reported as if they were external transactions—that is, as revenues and expenses. Amounts payable and receivable between the primary government and its discretely presented component units or between those components should be reported on a separate line.

■ **Deferred Inflows of Resources.** Deferred inflows of resources at the governmental fund financial statement level represents billed receivables that do not meet the available criterion in accordance with the current financial resources measurement focus and the modified accrual basis of accounting. Deferred inflows of resources is recognized as revenue in the conversion to the government-wide (full accrual) financial statements.

■ **Noncurrent Liabilities.** Long-term debt is reported as liabilities in the government-wide and proprietary fund statement of net position. Current and noncurrent liabilities also include the accrual for compensated absences (vacation and sick leave for Town employees) as well as Pension and Other Post-Employment Obligations.

- **Landfill Closure Liability.** The Town's estimated liability for closure and post-closure care costs for the landfill is $52,500 (current and noncurrent) as of June 30, 2014. The Town will be responsible for post-closure monitoring of the site for thirty years once the landfill is capped. The amount reported as landfill closure and post-closure liability at June 30, 2014, is based on what it would cost to perform all closure and post-closure care at June 30, 2014. Actual costs may be higher due to inflation, changes in technology or changes in regulations.

- **Net Position.** Net Position is classified into three components:
    - *a. Net investment in capital assets*—consists of capital assets net of accumulated depreciation and reduced by the outstanding balances of any bonds, mortgages, notes, or other borrowings that are attributable to the acquisition, construction, or improvement of those assets.
    - *b. Restricted*—Consists of resources with constraints placed on the use either by (1) external groups such as creditors, grantors, contributors, or laws or regulations of other governments; or (2) law through constitutional provisions or enabling legislation. Net position has been "restricted" for the following:
        - *Special revenue*—Special revenue funds are used to account for specific revenues that are legally restricted to expenditure for particular purposes.
        - *Permanent funds—expendable* represents amounts held in trust for which the expenditures are restricted by various trust agreements.
        - *Permanent funds—nonexpendable* represents amounts held in trust for which only investment earnings may be expended.
    - *c. Unrestricted*—All other resources that do not meet the definition of "*restricted*" or "*net investment in capital assets*".

Landfill Liability

Management of solid waste disposal is an important governmental activity. Typically, solid waste is transported to a disposal facility where it is buried. The municipality incurs labor and equipment costs to manage the facility while it is operational.[11] When the site is filled, the municipality, then, incurs costs to "cap" the landfill (i.e., to cover the landfill site and make it ready for its long-term post-closure use).

The Town of Acton reports a Landfill Closure Liability of $52,500 as of June 30, 2014 in its Statement of Net Position.[12] That estimated total current cost of landfill closure and post-closure care includes the following items (GASB ASC L10.103):

a. The cost of equipment expected to be installed and facilities expected to be constructed near or after the date that the landfill stops accepting solid waste and during the post-closure period. This may include gas monitoring and collection systems, stormwater management systems, groundwater monitoring wells, and, in some cases, leachate treatment facilities.

b. The cost of final cover (capping) expected to be applied near or after the date that the landfill stops accepting solid waste.

c. The cost of monitoring and maintaining the expected usable landfill area during the post-closure period. Post-closure care may include maintaining the final cover; monitoring groundwater; monitoring or collecting methane and other gases; collecting, treating, and transporting leachate; repairing or replacing equipment and facilities; and remedying or containing environmental hazards.

After the initial calculation of estimated total current cost of landfill closure and post-closure care, the liability should be adjusted each year for the effects of inflation or deflation, or when changes in the closure or post-closure care plan or landfill operating conditions increase or decrease estimated costs.

A portion of the estimated total current cost of landfill closure and post-closure care should be recognized as an expense and as a liability in each period that the landfill accepts solid waste. Recognition should begin on the date the landfill begins accepting solid waste, continue in each period that

---

[11] Capital assets that will be used exclusively for a landfill and that are excluded from the calculation of the estimated total current cost of closure and post-closure care should be fully depreciated by the date that the landfill stops accepting solid waste (GASB ASC L10.108).

[12] Notice that no such accrual is made in fund financial statements. The reason is that fund financial statements have a current financial resources measurement focus. This means that only the liabilities that will be satisfied by current financial resources are included as liabilities on the fund balance sheet. Since the landfill-related liability will be satisfied from *future* financial resources, it is not recognized on the fund balance sheet.

it accepts waste, and be completed by the time it stops accepting waste. Estimated total current cost should be assigned to periods based on landfill use (cubic yards, airspace, or other measure) rather than on the passage of time. Under this approach, the current-period amount should be based on the following formula (GASB L10.106):

$$\text{Current-period cost} = \left(\text{Total estimated cost} \times \frac{\text{Cumulative capacity used}}{\text{Total estimated capacity}} \right) - \text{Amount previously recognized}$$

Equipment and facilities included in the estimated total current cost of closure and post-closure care should not be reported as capital assets. Rather, their cost should be reported as a reduction of the accrued liability for landfill closure and post-closure care when they are acquired (GASB ASC L10.107).

Statement of Activities

The Statement of Activities presents the operations of the reporting government in two parts:

1. The net (expense) or revenue of each governmental function (i.e., general government, public safety, education, public works, and so on) and each business-type activity (the sanitation, sewer, and nursing enterprise funds discussed above),[13] and

2. General revenues (tax receipts, excise taxes, grants, investment income, etc.).

The difference between the net (expense) or revenue and the general revenues yields the change in net position for the year. This change when added to the beginning balance of net position (the ending net position balance from the prior year) yields the net position of the current year that is reported in the Statement of Net Position.

An objective of using the net (expense) revenue format is to report the relative financial burden of each of the reporting government's functions on its taxpayers. This format identifies the extent to which each function of the government draws from the general revenues of the government or is self-financing through fees and intergovernmental aid. At a minimum, the statement of activities should present:

a. Activities accounted for in governmental funds by function to coincide with the level of detail required in the governmental fund Statement of Revenues, Expenditures, and Changes in Fund Balances

b. Activities accounted for in enterprise funds by different identifiable activities

We present the Statement of Activities for the Town of Acton, MA in Exhibit 10.6. For the year ended June 30, 2014, the Governmental Activities report net (expense) of $(79,246,433), which is comprised of 8 individual functions. General Government, for example, reports expenses of $(8,593,144), Service income of $419,124 and Grants of $736,433 for net expense of $(7,437,587). The General Government, Public Safety and Education functions report combined net expense of $63,913,152 ($7,437,587 + $6,188,841 + $50,286,724) or 81% of the $79,246,433 of total net expense related to governmental activities. The three Business-Type Activities reported $(640,262)of net expense. In total, the Town of Acton's net expense is $(79,886,695). This is the amount that must be covered by General Revenues.

Presentation of the net expense of the individual functions of the Primary Government provides information about the relative financial burden of each of the reporting government's functions on its taxpayers. This format identifies the extent to which each function of the government draws from the general revenues of the government or is self-sustaining through fees and intergovernmental aid. Revenues are broken down into two categories:

---

[13] GASB ASC 2200.126 provides additional insight into the rationale for this format: "An objective of using the net (expense) revenue format is to report the relative financial burden of each of the reporting government's functions on its taxpayers. This format identifies the extent to which each function of the government draws from the general revenues of the government or is self-financing through fees and intergovernmental aid. . . . [T]his notion of burden on the reporting government's taxpayers is important in determining what is program or general revenue. General revenues, contributions to term and permanent endowments, contributions to permanent fund principal, special and extraordinary items, and transfers should be reported separately after the total net expenses of the government's functions, ultimately arriving at the "change in net position" for the period."

EXHIBIT 10.6 Statement of Activities for the Town of Acton, MA

TOWN OF ACTON, MASSACHUSETTS
Statement of Activities
Fiscal Year Ended June 30, 2014

Functions/Programs	Expenses	Program Revenues: Charges for Services	Program Revenues: Operating Grants and Contributions	Program Revenues: Capital Grants and Contributions	Net (Expenses) Revenues — Primary Government: Governmental Activities	Net (Expenses) Revenues — Primary Government: Business-Type Activities	Net (Expenses) Revenues — Primary Government: Total	Component Unit: Acton Community Housing Trust
Primary Government								
Governmental activities:								
General government	$ 8,593,144	$ 419,124	$ 736,433	$ —	$ (7,437,587)	$ —	$ (7,437,587)	$ —
Public safety	8,201,547	1,881,840	130,866	—	(6,188,841)	—	(6,188,841)	—
Education	62,551,163	1,029,595	11,234,844	—	(50,286,724)	—	(50,286,724)	—
Highways and public works	4,297,273	3,092	357,213	542,488	(3,394,480)	—	(3,394,480)	—
Human services	2,632,642	493,348	234,299	—	(1,904,995)	—	(1,904,995)	—
Culture and recreation	2,427,419	389,820	431,374	—	(1,606,225)	—	(1,606,225)	—
Employee benefits and insurance	7,563,997	—	—	—	(7,563,997)	—	(7,563,997)	—
Debt service	867,672	—	4,088	—	(863,584)	—	(863,584)	—
Total government activities	97,134,857	4,216,819	13,129,117	542,488	(79,246,433)	—	(79,246,433)	—
Business-type activities:								
Sanitation	647,494	668,705	11,268	—	—	32,479	32,479	—
Sewer	2,255,755	892,959	892,617	—	—	(470,179)	(470,179)	—
Nursing	519,188	315,630	996	—	—	(202,562)	(202,562)	—
Total business-type activities	3,422,437	1,877,294	904,881	—	—	(640,262)	(640,262)	—
Total primary government	$100,557,294	$6,094,113	$14,033,998	$542,488	$(79,246,433)	$ (640,262)	$(79,886,695)	—
Component units:								
Acton Community Housing Corporation	60,350	—	372,169	—			—	311,819
Total component unit	$ 60,350	$ —	$ 372,169	$ —			—	311,819
General revenues:								
Property taxes					72,978,287	—	72,978,287	—
Motor vehicle and other excise taxes					2,919,465	—	2,919,465	—
Penalties and interest on taxes					210,867	—	210,867	—
Other taxes, assessments and in lieu payments					15,233	—	15,233	—
Intergovernmental					1,302,663	—	1,302,663	—
Interest and investment income					87,867	—	87,867	—
Other revenue					182,296	—	182,296	—
Gain (loss) on disposal of assets					(11,500)	—	(11,500)	—
Transfer in (out)					(135,000)	135,000	—	—
Total general revenues, gains (losses) and transfers					77,550,178	135,000	77,685,178	—
Change in net position					(1,696,255)	(505,262)	(2,201,517)	311,819
Net position:								
Beginning of year					143,761,316	22,718,137	166,479,453	867,797
End of year					$142,065,061	$22,212,875	$164,277,936	$1,179,616

- **Program Revenues**—Program revenues derive directly from the program itself or from parties outside the reporting government's taxpayers or citizenry, as a whole. They reduce the net cost of the function to be financed from the government's general revenues. The following categories are included in the Program Revenues section:

  ○ **Charges for services** arise from customers who purchase, use, or directly benefit from the goods, services, or privileges provided. Revenues in this category include fees charged for specific services, such as water use or garbage collection; licenses and permits, such as dog licenses, liquor licenses, and building permits; operating special assessments, such as for street cleaning or special street lighting; and any other amounts charged to service recipients (GASB ASC 2200.137).

  ○ **Program-specific grants and contributions (operating and capital)** include revenues arising from mandatory and voluntary nonexchange transactions with other governments, organizations, or individuals that are restricted for use in a particular program. For example, a state may provide an operating grant to a county sheriff's department for a drug-awareness-and-enforcement program or a capital grant to finance construction of a new jail (GASB ASC 2200.138).

  ○ **Earnings on endowments** or permanent fund investments should be reported as program revenues if restricted to a program or programs specifically identified in the endowment or permanent fund agreement or contract. Earnings from endowments or permanent funds that finance "general fund programs" or "general operating expenses," for example, should not be reported as program revenue (GASB ASC 2200.139).

- **General Revenues**—All revenues are *general revenues* unless they are required to be reported as program revenues. All taxes, even those that are levied for a specific purpose, are general revenues and should be reported by type of tax—for example, sales tax, property tax, franchise tax, income tax. All other nontax revenues (including interest, grants, and contributions) that do not meet the criteria to be reported as program revenues should also be reported as general revenues. General revenues should be reported after total net expense of the government's functions (GASB ASC 2200.140).

Taxes (real estate and excise, including penalties, interest and liens) generate $72,978,287 or 94% of the total General Revenues for the Town of Acton. The remainder is comprised of Grants, Investment Income and Miscellaneous. Total General Revenues and Transfers (Grants) amount to $77,685,178.

Following is a reconciliation of Net Position for the year:

Net (expense) revenue of the primary government	$ (79,886,695)
Total general revenues and transfers	77,685,178
Change in net position	(2,201,517)
Net position (beginning-of-year)	166,479,453
Net position (end of year)	$164,277,936

The ending balance of Net Position equals the total Net Position balance reported on the Statement of Net Position.

TOPIC REVIEW

Preparation of the Statement of Activities

The City of Boxborough reports the following revenues for the fiscal year:

Real estate and personal property taxes	$17,992
Motor vehicle and other excise taxes	937
Grants and contributions not restricted	1,252

The City also reports the following revenues from fees it charges for services and operating grants and contributions it has received during the year as well as expenses it has incurred, categorized by governmental activity:

Functions/Programs	Charges for Services	Operating Grants and Contributions	Expenses
Primary government			
Governmental activities:			
General government.............................	$ 89	$ 147	$ 1,769
Public safety	298	78	2,091
Education	277	1,402	14,664
Public works..................................	22	50	879
Human services	216	35	511
Library..	17	24	328
Pension and benefits	—	831	1,404
Interest	—	—	324
Total governmental activities	$ 919	$2,567	$21,970

The City manages two business-type activities: a sanitation department which oversees solid and liquid waste disposal and a municipal pool. Both of these activities charge users a fee that is set at the beginning of the year at a level that is anticipated to cover the costs of providing the service. These fees cannot be changed during the year. As a result, these activities may produce a net profit or loss for the year, depending on the level of operating costs. The revenues and expenses for these services are provided in the following table:

Functions/Programs	Charges for Services	Expenses
Business-type activities:		
Sanitation	$1,172	$ 865
Municipal pool	133	188
	$1,305	$1,053

Required

Prepare the City of Boxborough Statement of Activities for the year (assume a beginning balance for Net Position of $44,585 for Governmental activities and $9,025 for Business-Type activities).

The solution to this review problem can be found on page 663.

Budgetary Comparison Schedule Budgetary comparisons should be presented for the general fund and for each major special revenue fund that has a legally adopted annual budget. The budgetary comparison schedule should present both (a) the original and (b) the final appropriated budgets for the reporting period as well as (c) actual inflows, outflows, and balances, stated on the government's budgetary basis. A separate column to report the variance between the final budget and actual amounts is encouraged but not required. Governments may also report the variance between original and final budget amounts (GASB ASC 2400.102).

Required Reconciliation to Government-Wide Statements Governments are required to present a summary reconciliation from the fund financial statements (Chapter 9) to the government-wide financial statements at the bottom of the fund financial statements or in an accompanying schedule (GASB ASC 2200.160). We present the reconciliation provided by the Town of Acton in Exhibit 10.7.

The reconciliation of the financial statements from Governmental Funds to Government-Wide reflects the difference between the *current financial resources measurement focus and the modified accrual basis of accounting* used in fund accounting and the *economic resources measurement focus and the accrual basis of accounting* used in the preparation of the Government-Wide financial statements. The Statement of Net Position and the Statement of Activities in the Government-Wide financial statements reflect the recognition of long-term assets and long-term liabilities and the recognition of revenue that is deferred in fund financial statements. These effects are summarized as follows:

EXHIBIT 10.7	Required Reconciliation to Government-Wide Statements

TOWN OF ACTON, MASSACHUSETTS
Reconciliation of the Balance Sheet—Governmental Funds
to the Government-wide Statement of Net Position
Fiscal Year Ended June 30, 2014

Total governmental fund balances...	$ 30,804,681
❶ Capital assets used in governmental activities are not financial resources and, therefore, are not reported in the funds	138,096,255
❷ Accounts receivable are not available to pay for current-period expenditures and, therefore, are deferred in the funds	11,154,856
❸ In the statement of activities, interest is accrued on outstanding long-term debt, whereas in governmental funds interest is not reported until due..	(223,012)
❸ Certain liabilities are not due and payable in the current period and, therefore, are not reported in the governmental funds	
Bonds payable	$(19,471,474)
⎰ Compensated absences..	(1,830,189)
❹ ⎨ Other liabilities	(2,613,210)
⎱ Landfill closure/postclosure costs	(52,500)
❸ Other post employment benefit obligations	(13,800,346)
Net position of governmental activities	$142,065,061

TOWN OF ACTON, MASSACHUSETTS
Reconciliation of the Statement of Revenues, Expenditures, and Changes In
Fund Balances of Governmental Funds to the Statement of Activities
Fiscal Year Ended June 30, 2014

Net change in fund balances—total governmental funds	$(1,002,164)
❶ Governmental funds report capital outlays as expenditures. However, in the statement of activities the cost of those assets is allocated over their estimated useful lives and reported as depreciation expense. This represents the amount by which difference between capital outlay and contributions exceeded depreciation in the current period................	44,946
❶ In the statement of activities, only the gain on the sale of capital assets is reported, whereas in the governmental funds, the entire proceeds of the sale are reported. This represents the difference in reporting the sale of capital assets.	(11,500)
❷ Revenues in the statement of activities that do not provide current financial resources are fully deferred in the statement of revenues, expenditures, and changes in fund balances. Therefore, the recognition of revenue for various types of accounts receivable (i.e. real estate and personal property, motor vehicle excise, etc.) differ between the two statements. This amount represents the net change in deferred inflows from the prior fiscal year..................	(1,663,596)
❸ The issuance of long-term debt (e.g., bonds and leases) provides current financial resources to governmental funds, while the repayment of the principal of long-term debt consumes the financial resources of governmental funds. Neither transaction, however, has any effect on net position. Also, governmental funds report the effect of premiums, discounts, and similar items when debt is first issued, whereas these amounts are amortized in the statement of activities. This amount reflects the net effect of these differences in the treatment of long-term debt and related items................	1,881,830
❹ Some expenses reported in the statement of activities, such as compensated absences, other post employment benefits payable and interest payable do not require the use of current financial resources and, therefore, are not reported as expenditures in the governmental funds. This amount represents the change in these accounts from the prior fiscal year.	(945,771)
Change in net position of governmental activities	$(1,696,255)

❶ Capital Assets: Government-Wide financial statements reflect long-term assets that are excluded in fund accounting under the *current financial resources measurement focus*, resulting in the following effects:
   a. Statement of Net Position—Capital Assets are recognized, thus increasing the Net Position ($138,096,255).
   b. Statement of Activities—
      i. Expenditures relating to the purchase of Capital Assets are eliminated and depreciation of the assets is recognized ($44,946).
      ii. Other financing sources relating to the sale of Capital Assets is eliminated and the gain or loss on sale is recognized ($−11,500).

❷ Accrued revenues: Government-Wide financial statements reflect the accrual of revenues that are expected to be received in cash beyond the 60 day horizon and are, therefore, not recognized in fund accounting, resulting in the following effects:

a. Statement of Net Position—Accounts receivable are recognized, thus increasing the Net Position ($11,154,856).

b. Statement of Activities—Current year revenues are recognized and prior year's revenues (which are currently recognized in the fund Statement of Revenues, Expenditures and Changes in Fund Balances) are eliminated. The negative amount reported in the current year reflects a reduction of deferred revenues over the two years ($-1,663,596).

❸ Long-term obligations: Government-Wide financial statements reflect the recognition of long-term obligations that are excluded in fund accounting, resulting in the following effects:

a. Statement of Net Position—Long-term debt, Pension and Other Post-Employment Obligations are recognized, thus decreasing the Net Position ($-223,012 + $-19,471,474 + $-13,800,346).

b. Statement of Activities ($1,881,830)
    i. Other Financial Sources relating to the issuance of debt are eliminated.
    ii. Interest expense is recognized.
    iii. Expenditures relating to the payment of principal and interest are eliminated.

❹ Accrued expenses

a. Statement of Net Position—accrued compensated absences are recognized, together with liabilities for landfill post-closure costs and other accrued liabilities ($-1,830,189 + $-2,613,210 + $-52,500).

b. Statement of Activities—accrued compensation expense, pension and OPEB expense, interest expense is recognized ($-945,771).

The effects relating to the differences between the *current financial resources measurement focus and the modified accrual basis of accounting* used in fund accounting and the *economic resources measurement focus and the accrual basis of accounting* used in the preparation of the Government-Wide financial statements are substantial. The increase in assets, net of the related increase in liabilities, resulted in the recognition of a Net Position of Governmental Activities that is $111 million greater than the Total Governmental Fund Balances reported under fund accounting. The Government-Wide Statements of Net Position and Activities provide a significant amount of additional information that is useful to help us evaluate the extent to which whether the government is operating efficiently or whether it is financially solvent.

CHAPTER SUMMARY

GASB 34 mandates the issuance of a **Comprehensive Annual Financial Report** (CAFR) that includes both the fund financial statements that we discuss in Chapter 9 and the government-wide financial statements that we illustrate in this chapter, together with management's discussion and analysis (MD&A), supporting notes, and other required supplementary information.

The minimum requirements for basic financial statements and required supplementary information are the following:

1. **Management's discussion and analysis.** The MD&A should introduce the basic financial statements and provide an analytical overview of the government's financial activities.

2. **Basic financial statements.** The basic financial statements should include:
   a. **Government-wide financial statements.** These financial statements consist of a *statement of net position* and a *statement of activities*. The government-wide statements should display information about the reporting government as a whole, except for its fiduciary activities. The statements should include separate columns for the governmental and business-type activities of the primary government as well as for its component units. Government-wide financial statements should be prepared using the economic resources measurement focus and the accrual basis of accounting.
   b. **Fund financial statements.** Fund financial statements for the primary government's governmental, proprietary, and fiduciary funds should be presented after the government-wide

statements. Fund financial statements should be prepared using the current financial resources measurement focus and the modified accrual basis of accounting (we discuss the accounting for funds in Chapter 9).

   c. **Notes to the financial statements.** These footnotes should communicate information essential for the fair presentation of the financial statements that is not displayed on the face of the financial statements.

3. **Required supplementary information other than MD&A.** Required supplementary information consists of schedules, statistical data, and other information that the GASB has determined are an essential part of financial reporting and should be presented with, but are not part of, the basic financial statements of a governmental entity. In addition to those presentations, the RSI includes *budgetary comparisons* that include the originally adopted budget, the final budget (including any subsequent amendments), and the actual inflows and outflows and balances of net position. Governments are also encouraged, but not required, to provide a column indicating the variances between the final budget and the actual amounts.

GASB 2200.112 states that "the focus of the government-wide financial statements should be on the primary government. . . . Separate rows and columns should be used to distinguish between the total primary government and its discretely presented component units." The **primary government** is a governmental unit that:

a. Has a separately elected governing body,

b. Is legally separate,

c. Is fiscally independent of other state and local governments.

   In addition to the financial statements for the primary government, GASB 34 also requires separate presentation of financial statements for all of the primary government's component units. A **component unit** is a unit of the primary government for which the primary government is *financially accountable*. A primary government is **financially accountable** for a component unit when:

1. It can incur financial obligations (or derives financial benefits) from the component unit.

2. It controls the appointment of a majority of the controlling board and can "impose its will" on the component's activities.

   A component unit should be included in the reporting entity financial statements using the blending method in either of these circumstances:

a. The component unit's governing body is substantively the same as the governing body of the primary government.

b. The component unit provides services entirely, or almost entirely, to the primary government or otherwise exclusively, or almost exclusively, benefits the primary government even though it does not provide services directly to it.

   Government-wide financial statements are prepared using the *economic resources measurement focus* and the *accrual basis of accounting*. **Economic resources** are broader than the "financial resources" measurement focus that we use in fund accounting. It includes long-term assets and liabilities as well as current financial resources, and is similar to the GAAP measurement focus that is used by businesses.

The **accrual basis of accounting** requires that

1. Revenues, expenses, gains, losses, assets, and liabilities resulting from *exchange and exchange like transactions* should be recognized when the exchange takes place.

2. Revenues, expenses, gains, losses, assets, and liabilities resulting from *nonexchange transactions* should be recognized as follows (GASB ASC N50):

   ■ **Derived Tax Revenue Transactions**—Governments should recognize assets from derived tax revenue transactions in the period when the exchange transaction on which the tax is imposed occurs or when the resources are received, whichever occurs first.

■ **Imposed Nonexchange Revenue Transactions**—Governments should recognize assets from imposed nonexchange revenue transactions in the period when an enforceable legal claim to the assets arises or when the resources are received, whichever occurs first.

■ **Government-Mandated Nonexchange Transactions and Voluntary Nonexchange Transactions**—Providers of resources in government-mandated or voluntary nonexchange transactions frequently establish eligibility requirements. Until those requirements are met, the provider does not have a liability, the recipient does not have a receivable, and the recognition of expenses or revenues for resources transmitted in advance should be deferred (N50.116).

The **Statement of Net Position** presents assets, liabilities, and net position. The difference between assets and liabilities must be labeled as *Net Position*, and cannot be labeled as equity, net fund balance, or other similar label. The **net position** section of the statement should be displayed in three sections:

1. Net investment in capital assets
2. Restricted (distinguishing between major categories of restrictions), and
3. Unrestricted

The **Statement of Activities** presents the operations of the reporting government in two parts:

1. The net (expense) or revenue of each governmental function and each business-type activity, and general revenues.
2. The difference between the net (expense) or revenue and the general revenues yields the change in net position for the year. This change when added to the beginning balance of net position yields the net position of the current year that is reported in the Statement of Net Position.

Governments are required to present a summary reconciliation from the fund financial statements (Chapter 9) to the government-wide financial statements at the bottom of the fund financial statements or in an accompanying schedule.

COMPREHENSIVE REVIEW

The City of Greenfield is preparing its government-wide financial statements for the year. Its accountant must prepare a number of journal entries to recognize assets and liabilities previously omitted from the fund financial statements and to recognize revenues and expenses for the year under accrual accounting that were not recognized under the current financial resources measurement focus and the modified accrual basis of accounting used to prepare the Statement of Revenues, Expenditures, and Changes in Fund Balances for its funds.

a. Prepare a list of the required reconciliations to recognize the following in the government-wide financial statements (all amounts in $1,000s):

1. Recognize Capital Assets of $32,752 as of the beginning of the year.
2. Record Depreciation Expense of $1,638 for the year and reverse Expenditures of $1,965 for Capital Outlays during the year.
3. Recognize $7,000 of Bonds Payable as of the beginning of the year.
4. Reverse Other Financing Sources of $2,000 and Expenditures – Debt Payments of $700 relating to increases and decreases in the bond liability during the year.
5. Reverse Deferred Revenue of $4,485 as of the beginning of the year.
6. Reverse $224 of Deferred Revenue recognized during the year.
7. Recognize Compensated Absences of $655 as of the beginning of the year and an increase in that liability of $33 during the year.
8. Recognize $20 of Accrued Interest Payable as of the beginning of the year and an increase in that liability of $33 during the year.
9. Recognize a liability of $901 relating to the City's landfill as of the beginning of the year. The estimate for this liability did not change during the year.

b. The City of Greenfield reports the following summary fund financial statements for its General Fund:

Balance Sheet		Statement of Revenues, Expenditures, and Changes in Fund Balances	
Cash.	$ 5,971	Revenues:	
Receivables:		Real estate taxes	$15,474
Real estate and personal property . . .	414	Intergovernmental	2,826
Intergovernmental.	4,281	Total revenues	18,300
Total assets.	$10,666	Expenditures:	
		General government.	2,640
Payables.	$ 490	Public safety.	1,760
Deferred revenues	4,709	Education	10,559
Total liabilities.	5,199	Public works.	880
Fund balances:		Human services	1,759
Assigned.	1,242	Debt principal payments.	700
Unassigned	4,225	Debt interest payments.	100
Total fund balances	5,467	Total expenditures	18,398
Total liabilities and fund balances.	$10,666	Excess (deficiency) of revenues over expenditures.	(98)
		Other financing sources (uses):	
		Proceeds from bonds	2,000
		Total other financing sources (uses).	2,000
		Net change in fund balances	$ 1,902
		Fund balances at beginning of year.	3,565
		Fund balances at end of year.	$ 5,467

Required

Given these fund financial statements and the reconciliations in *Part a*, prepare the government-wide Statement of Net Position and identify the Revenues, Expenses and Change in Net Position that should be reported in the Statement of Activities for the year.

The solution to this review problem can be found on page 664.

QUESTIONS

1. Government-wide financial statements are required under GASB 34. According to the GASB in the preface to GASB 34, in what ways do these additional financial statements help users?

2. What major assets and liabilities are included in the government-wide financial statements that are not included in the fund financial statements?

3. What is the Comprehensive Annual Financial Report (CAFR)?

4. GASB 34 states that "the focus of the government-wide financial statements should be on the primary government." How is the *primary government* defined?

5. In addition to the financial statements for the primary government, GASB 34 also requires separate presentation of financial statements for all of the primary government's *component units*. How is a component unit defined?

6. Describe the concept of *blending*.

7. What is the measurement focus and basis of accounting for government-wide financial statements?

8. Describe the format for the Statement of Net Position.

9. How do we account for capital assets in government-wide financial statements?

10. What are *composite depreciation methods*?

11. How do we account for works of art and historical treasures?

12. Solid waste disposal in a landfill is an important and costly activity for a local government. Describe the account for landfill liability in government-wide financial statements.

13. Describe the format for the Statement of Activities.

14. What is the difference between *program revenues* and *general revenues*?

Assignments with the logo in the margin are available in my BusinessCourse.
See the Preface of the book for details.

MULTIPLE CHOICE

15. Blended and discrete presentation

The Town of Carlisle's public school system is administered by a separately elected board of education which is not organized as a separate legal entity and does not have the ability to either issue bonds or assess taxes. The Town must approve the school system's budget. The Town should report the school system as follows:

	Blended	Discrete Presentation
a.	Yes	Yes
b.	Yes	No
c.	No	Yes
d.	No	No

16. Compensated absences expense

At the beginning of the current year, Paxx County's enterprise fund had a $125,000 balance for accrued compensated absences. At the end of the year, the balance was $150,000. During the year, Paxx paid $400,000 for compensated absences. What amount of compensated absences expense should Paxx County's enterprise fund report for the year?

a. $375,000

b. $400,000

c. $425,000

d. $550,000

17. Measurement focus for government-wide financial statements

What is the measurement focus and the basis of accounting for the government-wide financial statements?

	Measurement Focus	Basis of Accounting
a.	Current financial resources	Modified accrual
b.	Economic resources	Modified accrual
c.	Current financial resources	Accrual
d.	Economic resources	Accrual

18. Notes to the government-wide financial statements

All of the following statements regarding notes to the basic financial statements of governmental entities are true except:

a. The notes contain disclosures related to required supplementary information.

b. Some notes presented by governments are identical to notes presented in business financial statements.

c. Notes that are considered essential to the basic financial statements need to be presented.

d. It is acceptable to present notes in a very extensive format.

19. Types of taxes

Property taxes represent which of the following?

a. Mandated nonexchange transactions

b. Voluntary nonexchange transactions

c. Imposed tax revenues

d. Derived tax revenues

20. Governmental entities to include in government-wide financial statements

Which of the following should be included in the financial statements of the Town of Acton:

1. Primary government

    2.   Discretely presented component units

    3.   Blended component units

  a. 1 only

  b. 1 and 2 only

  c. 1, 2, and 3

  d. 2 and 3 only

21. Definition of primary government

Which of the following criteria are used to determine the Primary Government?

    1.   Separately elected governing body

    2.   Legally independent

    3.   Fiscally independent

  a. 1 only

  b. 1 and 2 only

  c. 1, 2, and 3

  d. 2 and 3 only

22. Accounting for works of art

The capitalization of works of art and historical treasures is encouraged, but is not required, for collections that are:

    1.   Held for public exhibition

    2.   Protected and preserved

    3.   Subject to an organizational body that requires the proceeds from sales of collection items to be used to acquire other items for collections.

  a. 1 only

  b. 1 and 2 only

  c. 1, 2, and 3

  d. 2 and 3 only

23. Component unit presentation

The Town of Maynard School System has a separately elected governing body that oversees its activities. The School system's budget must be approved by the Town of Maynard Board. The School system's financial results should be reported in the Town's financial statements in what manner?

  a. Discrete presentation

  b. Blending

  c. Inclusion as a footnote in the Town's CAFR

  d. Either blending or inclusion as a footnote

24. Component unit presentation

The Town of Littleton's Housing Authority provides loans to low income families within the Town. It is governed by a Board appointed by the Town of Littleton's Manager and its debt is guaranteed by the Town. In what manner should the Housing authority be reported?

  a. Discrete presentation

  b. Blending

  c. Inclusion as a footnote in the Town's CAFR

  d. Either blending or inclusion as a footnote

25. Accountability

The Statement of Activities is designed to provide information that allows readers to assess which of the following?

  a. Fiscal accountability

  b. Financial accountability

  c. Operational accountability

  d. Functional accountability

26. Management's discussion and analysis section of the CAFR

Which of the following should *not* be included in the management's discussion and analysis section of the CAFR?

    a. A forecast of revenues

    b. An explanation relating to changes in the City's fund balances

    c. A statement of condensed financial information contained in the government-wide financial statements

    d. A discussion of the condition of the City's infrastructure

LO1 27. **Required supplemental information in the CAFR**

Which of the following would *not* be reported as required supplementary information?

    a. Disclosures relating to pension actuarial valuations

    b. Discussion relating to the condition of the infrastructure

    c. Management's discussion and analysis

    d. A certificate of achievement

LO2 28. **Change in net position for governmental funds**

The town of Stow reports a net increase in its governmental funds of $15,000. During the year, it purchased a truck for $50,000 and recognized $2,000 for depreciation expense. Is the preparation of its Statement of Activities for the year, what amount should it report for the change in net position?

    a. $15,000

    b. $65,000

    c. $63,000

    d. $(37,000)

LO2 29. **Fiscal independence**

Which of the following is *not* a power that a municipality must possess in order to be considered fiscally independent?

    a. Ability to set its own budget

    b. Ability to issue bonds

    c. Ability to set and levy taxes

    d. Ability to set its own debt ceiling to control borrowings

LO1 30. **Budget vs. Actual disclosure**

Which of the following statements is *true* regarding the budget vs. actual comparison disclosure?

    a. Municipalities are encouraged but not required to present a comparison schedule of budget-to-actual amounts.

    b. The budget-to-actual comparison schedule is included in the footnotes to the CAFR.

    c. The budget-to-actual comparison schedule is included in the basic financial statements section of the CAFR.

    d. The budget-to-actual comparison schedule is included in the required supplementary information section of the CAFR.

EXERCISES

LO2 31. **Reconciliations to yield government-wide financial statements (capital assets)**

The City of Boxborough is preparing its government-wide financial statements from its fund financial statements.

    a. The City identifies Capital Assets with a book value of $500,000 (in $1,000s) at the beginning of the year that are depreciated at the rate of $25,000 per year. Its records also indicate that it spent $300,000 on new Capital Assets during the year. What two reconciliation entries must the City include in its government-wide financial statements relating to Capital Assets?

    b. Why must these reconciliation entries be included?

LO2 32. **Reconciliations to yield government-wide financial statements (bond liability)**

The Village of Viola is preparing its government-wide financial statements from its fund financial statements.

    a. The Village records an outstanding Bond Liability with a book value of $10,000 (in $1,000s) at the beginning of the year that requires a principal payment of $500 per year. Its records also indicate that it borrowed $2,000 on new Bonds during the year. What two reconciliation entries must the Village include in its government-wide financial statements relating to its Bond Liability?

    b. Why must these reconciliation entries be included?

33. **Reconciliations to yield government-wide financial statements (deferred revenues and compensated absences)**
    The City of Lexington is preparing its government-wide financial statements from its fund financial statements.

    a. The City records Deferred Revenue with a book value of $2,500 and Compensated Absences of $1,000 (in $1,000s) at the beginning of the year. During the year, these accounts increased by $500 and $150, respectively. What reconciliation entries must the City include in its government-wide financial statements relating to Deferred Revenues and Compensated Absences?

    b. Why must these reconciliation entries be included?

34. **Reconciliations to yield government-wide financial statements (landfill closure liability)**
    The City of Captiva is preparing its government-wide financial statements from its fund financial statements. The City maintains a landfill for solid waste disposal and estimates that its total capacity is 10 million tons. At the end of the prior year, the City estimated that it had used 3 million tons and reported a liability for closure and postclosure costs of $3 million. During the year, the City estimates that it used an additional 500,000 tons of capacity. Closure and postclosure costs are expected to be $10 million when the Landfill reaches capacity.

    a. What reconciliation entries must the City include in its government-wide financial statements relating to the Landfill Liability at the beginning of the year and as of the end of the year?

    b. Why must these reconciliations be included?

35. **Preparation of Government-Wide Statement of Net Position and Statement of Activities**
    Refer to Exercise 50 in Chapter 9. Prepare a Government-Wide Statement of Net Position and Statement of Activities for the Town of Bolton. Assume that the truck has a useful life of 5 years and that it was purchased at the mid-point of the Town's fiscal year.

PROBLEMS

36. **Preparation of the statement of activities**
    The City of Truro reports the following revenues for the fiscal year:

Real estate and personal property taxes	$70,876
Motor vehicle and other excise taxes	3,692
Grants and contributions not restricted	3,634

The City also reports the following revenues from fees it charges for services and operating grants and contributions it has received during the year as well as expenses it has incurred, categorized by governmental activity:

Functions/Programs	Charges for Services	Operating Grants and Contributions	Expenses
Primary government			
Governmental activities:			
General government	$ 351	$ 580	$ 6,969
Public safety	1,175	308	8,237
Education	1,092	5,524	57,768
Public works	87	195	3,465
Human services	850	138	2,012
Library	66	96	1,292
Pension and benefits	—	3,273	5,532
Interest	—	—	1,275
Total governmental activities	$3,621	$10,114	$86,550

The City manages two business-type activities: a sanitation department which oversees solid and liquid waste disposal and a municipal pool. Both of these activities charge users a fee that is set at the beginning of the year at a level that is anticipated to cover the costs of providing the service. These fees cannot be changed during the year. As a result, these activities may produce a net profit or loss for the year, depending on the level of operating costs. The revenues and expenses for these services are provided in the following table:

Functions/Programs	Charges for Services	Expenses
Business-type activities:		
Sanitation	$4,619	$3,407
Municipal pool	524	742
	$5,143	$4,149

Prepare the City of Truro Statement of Activities for the year (assume a beginning balance for Net Position of $175,638 for Governmental activities and $35,554 for Business-type activities).

LO2 37. **Preparation of the statement of activities**
The City of Ephraim reports the following revenues for the fiscal year:

Real estate and personal property taxes	$119,944
Motor vehicle and other excise taxes	6,248
Grants and contributions not restricted	6,149
Total general revenues and transfers	$132,341

The City also reports the following revenues from fees it charges for services and operating grants and contributions it has received during the year as well as expenses it has incurred, categorized by governmental activity:

Functions/Programs	Charges for Services	Operating Grants and Contributions	Expenses
Primary government			
Governmental activities:			
General government	$ 594	$ 981	$ 11,794
Public safety	1,989	521	13,939
Education	1,848	9,348	97,761
Public works	147	330	5,863
Human services	1,439	233	3,406
Library	112	163	2,187
Pension and benefits	—	5,540	9,361
Interest	—	—	2,158
Total governmental activities	$6,129	$17,116	$146,469

The City manages two business-type activities: a sanitation department which oversees solid and liquid waste disposal and a municipal pool. Both of these activities charge users a fee that is set at the beginning of the year at a level that is anticipated to cover the costs of providing the service. These fees cannot be changed during the year. As a result, these activities may produce a net profit or loss for the year, depending on the level of operating costs. The revenues and expenses for these services are provided in the following table:

Functions/Programs	Charges for Services	Expenses
Business-type activities:		
Sanitation	$7,817	$5,766
Municipal pool	887	1,256
	$8,704	$7,022

Prepare the City of Ephraim Statement of Activities for the year (assume a beginning balance for Net Position of $297,233 for Governmental activities and $60,168 for Business-type activities).

38. Reconciliations required to yield government-wide financial statements from fund financial statements and preparation of financial statements

The City of Bar Harbor is preparing its government-wide financial statements for the year. Its accountant must prepare a number of journal entries to recognize assets and liabilities previously omitted from the fund financial statements and to recognize revenues and expenses for the year under accrual accounting that were not recognized under the current financial resources measurement focus and the modified accrual basis of accounting used to prepare the Statement of Revenues, Expenditures, and Changes in Fund Balances for its funds.

a. Prepare the journal entries for the required reconciliations to recognize the following in the government-wide financial statements (all amounts in $1,000s):

1. Recognize Capital Assets of $199,360 as of the beginning of the year.
2. Record Depreciation Expense of $9,968 for the year and reverse Expenditures of $11,962 for Capital Outlays during the year.
3. Recognize $7,000 of Bonds Payable as of the beginning of the year.
4. Reverse Other Financing Sources of $2,000 and Expenditures – Debt Payments of $700 relating to increases and decreases in the bond liability during the year.
5. Reverse Deferred Revenue of $27,300 as of the beginning of the year.
6. Reverse $1,365 of Deferred Revenue recognized during the year.
7. Recognize Compensated Absences of $3,988 as of the beginning of the year and an increase in that liability of $199 during the year.
8. Recognize $20 of Accrued Interest Payable as of the beginning of the year and an increase in that liability of $33 during the year.
9. Recognize a liability of $5,482 relating to the City's landfill as of the beginning of the year. The estimate for this liability did not change during the year.

b. The City of Bar Harbor reports the following summary fund financial statements for its General Fund:

Balance Sheet	General Fund
Current:	
Cash	$ 30,240
Receivables:	
Real estate and personal property	2,520
Intergovernmental	26,060
Total assets	$ 58,820
Payables	$ 2,982
Deferred revenues	28,665
Total liabilities	31,647
Fund balance—unassigned	27,173
	$ 58,820
Statement of revenues, expenditures, and changes in fund balances:	
Total revenues—fund financial statements	$111,384
Total expenditures	107,912
Other financing sources and uses:	
Proceeds from bonds	2,000
Net change in fund balances	$ 5,472

Given these fund financial statements and the reconciliations in *Part a*, prepare the government-wide Statement of Net Position and identify the Revenues, Expenses and Change in Net Position that should be reported in the Statement of Activities for the year.

LO2   **39. Reconciliations required to yield government-wide financial statements from fund financial statements and preparation of financial statements**

The City of Jackson Hole is preparing its government-wide financial statements for the year. Its accountant must prepare a number of journal entries to recognize assets and liabilities previously omitted from the fund financial statements and to recognize revenues and expenses for the year under accrual accounting that were not recognized under the current financial resources measurement focus and the modified accrual basis of accounting used to prepare the Statement of Revenues, Expenditures, and Changes in Fund Balances for its funds.

a.   Prepare the journal entries for the required reconciliations to recognize the following in the government-wide financial statements (all amounts in $1,000s):

1.   Recognize Capital Assets of $968,320 as of the beginning of the year.
2.   Record Depreciation Expense of $48,416 for the year and reverse Expenditures of $58,099 for Capital Outlays during the year.
3.   Recognize $7,000 of Bonds Payable as of the beginning of the year.
4.   Reverse Other Financing Sources of $2,000 and Expenditures—Debt Payments of $700 relating to increases and decreases in the bond liability during the year.
5.   Reverse Deferred Revenue of $132,600 as of the beginning of the year.
6.   Reverse $6,630 of Deferred Revenue recognized during the year.
7.   Recognize Compensated Absences of $19,366 as of the beginning of the year and an increase in that liability of $968 during the year.
8.   Recognize $20 of Accrued Interest Payable as of the beginning of the year and an increase in that liability of $33 during the year.
9.   Recognize a liability of $26,629 relating to the City's landfill as of the beginning of the year. The estimate for this liability did not change during the year.

b.   The City of Jackson Hole reports the following summary fund financial statements for its General Fund:

Balance Sheet		Statement of Revenues, Expenditures, and Changes in Fund Balances	
Cash..........................	$142,250	Revenues:	
Receivables:		Real estate taxes	$457,470
Real estate and personal		Intergovernmental	83,538
property	12,240		
Intergovernmental..............	126,577	Total revenues...................	541,008
Total assets..................	$281,067		
		Expenditures:	
		General government..............	78,038
Payables......................	$ 14,485	Public safety....................	52,026
Deferred revenues	139,230	Education	312,154
		Public works....................	26,013
Total liabilities.................	153,715	Human services	52,026
Fund balances:		Debt principal payments...........	700
Assigned....................	36,270	Debt interest payments...........	100
Unassigned	91,082		
Total fund balances	127,352	Total expenditures	521,057
Total liabilities and fund balances....	$281,067	Excess (deficiency) of revenues over	
		expenditures...................	19,951
		Other financing sources (uses)	
		Proceeds from bonds	2,000
		Total other financing sources (uses)....	2,000
		Net change in fund balances.........	$ 21,951
		Fund balances at beginning of year....	105,401
		Fund balances at end of year........	$127,352

Given these fund financial statements and the reconciliations in *Part a*, prepare the government-wide Statement of Net Position and identify the Revenues, Expenses and Change in Net Position that should be reported in the Statement of Activities for the year.

40. Reconciliations required to yield government-wide financial statements from fund financial statements and preparation of financial statements

The Village of Lahinch is preparing its government-wide financial statements for the year. Its accountant must prepare a number of journal entries to recognize assets and liabilities previously omitted from the fund financial statements and to recognize revenues and expenses for the year under accrual accounting that were not recognized under the current financial resources measurement focus and the modified accrual basis of accounting used to prepare the Statement of Revenues, Expenditures, and Changes in Fund Balances for its funds.

a. Prepare the journal entries for the required reconciliations to recognize the following in the government-wide financial statements (all amounts in $1,000s):

1. Recognize Capital Assets of $2,848,000 as of the beginning of the year.
2. Record Depreciation Expense of $142,400 for the year and reverse Expenditures of $170,880 for Capital Outlays during the year.
3. Recognize $140,000 of Bonds Payable as of the beginning of the year.
4. Reverse Other Financing Sources of $40,000 and Expenditures—Debt Payments of $4,000 relating to increases and decreases in the bond liability during the year.
5. Reverse Deferred Revenue of $390,000 as of the beginning of the year.
6. Reverse $19,500 of Deferred Revenue recognized during the year.
7. Recognize Compensated Absences of $56,960 as of the beginning of the year and an increase in that liability of $2,848 during the year.
8. Recognize $400 of Accrued Interest Payable as of the beginning of the year and an increase in that liability of $667 during the year.
9. Recognize a liability of $78,320 relating to the Village's landfill as of the beginning of the year. The estimate for this liability did not change during the year.

b. The Village of Lahinch reports the following summary fund financial statements for its General Fund:

Balance Sheet		Statement of Revenues, Expenditures, and Changes in Fund Balances	
Cash..........................	$448,853	Revenues:	
Receivables:		Real estate taxes	$1,345,500
Real estate and personal		Intergovernmental	245,700
property	36,000		
Intergovernmental..............	372,285	Total revenues....................	1,591,200
Total assets...................	$857,138		
		Expenditures:	
		General government..............	229,525
Payables......................	$ 42,603	Public safety....................	153,017
Deferred revenues	409,500	Education	918,099
		Public works....................	76,508
Total liabilities.................	452,103	Human services	153,017
Fund balances:		Debt principal payments...........	4,000
Assigned.....................	108,000	Debt interest payments............	2,000
Unassigned	297,035		
		Total expenditures	$1,536,166
Total fund balances	405,035		
Total liabilities and fund balances....	$857,138	Excess (deficiency) of revenues over	
		expenditures....................	55,034
		Other financing sources (uses)	
		Proceeds from bonds	40,000
		Total other financing sources (uses)....	40,000
		Net change in fund balances	$ 95,034
		Fund balances at beginning of year....	310,001
		Fund balances at end of year........	$ 405,035

Given these fund financial statements and the reconciliations in *Part a,* prepare the government-wide Statement of Net Position and identify the Revenues, Expenses and Change in Net Position that should be reported in the Statement of Activities for the year.

LO2 41. **Interpretation of the reconciliations required to yield government-wide financial statements from fund financial statements and preparation of financial statements**
Following are the reconciliations from the Denver, CO 2014 CAFR. Briefly discuss the reasons for inclusion of each major section (capital assets, accrued revenues, accrued expenses and long-term obligations).

Reconciliation of the Balance Sheet—Governmental Funds to the Statement of Net Position
December 31, 2014 (dollars in thousands)

Amounts reported for governmental activities in the statement of net position are different because:

Total fund balance-governmental funds.	$ 854,206
Capital assets used in governmental activities, excluding internal service funds of $22,108 are not financial resources, and therefore, are not reported in the funds.	2,830,408
Accrued interest payable not included in the funds.	(21,106)
Deferred inflow of resources related to property taxes and long-term receivables are not available to pay for current-period expenditures, and therefore, are not recorded in the funds.	54,047
Deferred outflow of resources are not financial resources, and therefore are not reported in the funds and include:	
Accumulated decrease in fair value of hedging derivatives	34,773
Loss on refunding.	14,361
Interest rate swap liability.	(39,787)
Prepaid bond insurance, net of accumulated amortization.	735
Internal service funds are used by management to charge the cost of these funds to their primary users-governmental funds. The assets and liabilities of the internal service funds are included in governmental activities in the statement of net position.	20,904
Long-term liabilities, including bonds payable, are not due and payable in the current period and therefore are not reported in the governmental funds (this excludes internal service liabilities of $49,916).	(1,665,452)
Net position of governmental activities	$2,083,089

**Reconciliation of the Statement of Revenues, Expenditures and Changes in Fund Balances—
Governmental Funds to the Statement of Activities**
For the Year Ended December 31, 2014 (dollars in thousands)

Amounts reported for governmental activities in the statement of activities are different because:	
Net change in fund balances—total governmental funds	$80,501
Governmental funds report capital outlays as expenditures. However, in the statement of activities the cost of those assets is allocated over their estimated useful lives and reported as depreciation expense. This is the amount by which capital outlay exceeded depreciation expense in the current period:	
Capital outlay, including sale of assets.	122,282
Depreciation expense (excluding internal service)	(139,382)
Revenues in the statement of activities that do not provide current financial resources are not reported as revenue in the funds..	24,307
The issuance of long-term debt and other obligations (e.g., bonds, certificates of participation, and capital leases) provides current financial resources to governmental funds, while the repayment of the principal of long-term debt consumes the current financial resources of governmental funds. Neither transaction, however has any effect on change in net position. Also, governmental funds report the effect of premiums, discounts, and similar items when debt is first issued, whereas these amounts are amortized in the statement of activities. These differences in the treatment of long-term debt and related items consist of:	
General obligation bonds issued	(12,796)
Capital lease obligations	(19,905)
Principal retirement on bonds	71,987
Premium, discounts, and deferred gain (loss) on refunding.	7,249
Capital lease principal payments	26,072
Principal payments on note payable	400
Principal payments on intergovernmental agreement	560
Some expenses reported in the statement of activities do not require the use of current financial resources and, therefore, are not reported as expenditures in governmental funds:	
Compensated absences (excluding internal service)	(2,838)
Accrued interest payable	(14)
Legal liability	(2,572)
Pollution remediation	409
Net OPEB obligation.	(2,435)
Amortization of imputed debt-swap	515
Internal service funds are used by management to charge their cost to individual funds. The net expense of certain activities of internal service funds is reported within governmental activities.	(1,409)
Change in net position of governmental activities	$152,931

LO2 42. **Interpretation of the reconciliations required to yield government-wide financial statements from fund financial statements and preparation of financial statements.**

Following are the reconciliations from the Dallas, TX 2014 CAFR. Briefly discuss the reasons for inclusion of each major section (capital assets, accrued revenues, accrued expenses and long-term obligations).

DALLAS COUNTY, TEXAS

Reconciliation of the Balance Sheet—Governmental Funds to the Statement of Net Position For the Year Ended September 30, 2014

(in thousands of dollars)

Total fund balance-governmental funds.	$364,017
Amounts reported for governmental activities in the statement of net position are different because:	
Capital assets used in governmental activities are not financial resources and, therefore, are not reported in governmental funds.	582,966
Other long-term assets are not available to pay for current period expenditures and, therefore, are not reported in governmental funds.	16,392
Internal service funds are used by management to charge costs related to this fund. The assets and liabilities of the internal service fund are included in governmental activities in the statement of net position.	1,328
Certain liabilities, including bonds payable and related interest, are not due and payable in the current period and therefore are not included in governmental funds.	(427,920)
Net position of governmental activities	$536,783

DALLAS COUNTY, TEXAS

Reconciliation of the Statement of Revenues, Expenditures, and Changes in Fund Balances to the Statement of Activities

For the Year Ended September 30, 2014

(in thousands of dollars)

Amounts reported for governmental activities in the statement of activities are different because:	
Net change in fund balances total governmental funds.	$(32,787)
Governmental funds report all capital outlays as expenditures. However, in the statement of activities, the cost of some of the assets is allocated over their estimated useful lives and reported as depreciation expense. This is the amount by which capital outlays for County-owned assets exceeds depreciation in the current period.	40,604
The net effect of various transactions (e.g. sale of capital of assets).	(110)
Revenues in the Statement of Activities that do not provide current financial resources are not reported as revenues in the funds.	(1,657)
Some expenses reported in statement of activities are not fund expenditures (e.g. compensated absences that are liabilities not normally liquidated with current financial resources).	(41,979)
The issuance of long-term debt (e.g., bonds, tax notes) provides current financial resources to governmental funds, while the repayment of the principal of long-term debt consumes current financial resources of governmental funds. Neither transaction, however, has any effect on net position. Also, governmental funds report the effect of issuance costs, premiums, discounts, and similar items when debt is first issued, whereas these amounts are deferred and amortized in the statement of activities. This amount is the net effect of these differences in the treatment of long-term debt and related items.	27,247
Internal service funds are used by management to charge the costs to account for group medical self-insurance and workers compensation. The net revenue (loss) is reported with governmental activities.	(1,018)
Change in net position of governmental activities	$ (9,700)

TOPIC REVIEW

Solution

Functions/Programs	Expenses	Program Revenues		Net (Expense) Revenue
		Charges for Services	Operating Grants and Contributions	
Primary government				
Governmental activities:				
General government	$ 1,769	$ 89	$ 147	$ (1,533)
Public safety	2,091	298	78	(1,715)
Education	14,664	277	1,402	(12,985)
Public works	879	22	50	(807)
Human services	511	216	35	(260)
Library	328	17	24	(287)
Pension and benefits	1,404	—	831	(573)
Interest	324	—	—	(324)
Total governmental activities	$21,970	$ 919	$2,567	$(18,484)
Business-type activities:				
Sanitation	$ 865	$1,172	—	$ 307
Municipal pool	188	133	—	(55)
	$ 1,053	$1,305	$ 0	$ 252
Total primary government	$23,023	$2,224	$2,567	$(18,232)

	Governmental Activities	Business-Type Activities	Total
From above	$(18,484)	$ 252	$(18,232)
General revenues:			
Real estate and personal property taxes	$ 17,992	—	$ 17,992
Motor vehicle and other excise taxes	937	—	937
Grants and contributions not restricted	1,252	—	1,252
Total general revenues and transfers	$ 20,181	$ 0	$ 20,181
Change in net position	$ 1,697	$ 252	$ 1,949
Net position:			
Beginning of year	44,585	9,025	53,610
End of year	$ 46,282	$9,277	$ 55,559

COMPREHENSIVE REVIEW SOLUTION

Government-wide Financial Statements Spreadsheet	Governmental Activities	DR		CR		Governmental Activities
Balance Sheet						
Current:						
Cash	$ 5,971					$ 5,971
Receivables						
Real estate & personal property	414					414
Intergovernmental	4,281					4,281
Non-current:						
Receivables						
Capital assets, net of accumulated depreciation		1	32,752			33,079
		2	327			
Total assets	$10,666					$43,745
Payables	$490					$490
Accrued interest				8	53	53
Bond and notes payable				3	7,000	8,300
				4	1,300	
Compensated absences				7	688	688
Landfill closure and postclosure care costs				9	901	901
Deferred revenues	4,709	5	4,485			0
		6	224			
Total liabilities	5,199					10,432
Net position:						
Fund balance	5,467					5,467
Adjustments		3	7,000	1	32,752	28,661
		7	655	5	4,485	
		8	20			
		9	901			
Net income adjustments			below	(815)		(815)
						33,313
	$10,666					$43,745
Statement of Revenues, Expenditures, and Changes in Fund Balances						
Total revenues—fund financial statements	$18,300					$18,300
Adjustments:						
Deferred revenues				6	224	224
Total revenues—statement of activities						18,524
Total expenditures	18,398					18,398
Adjustments:						
Debt principal payments				4	700	(700)
Depreciation expense/capital outlay		2	1,638	2	1,965	(327)
Compensated absences		7	33			33
Interest expense		8	33			33
Total expenses—statement of activities						17,437
Misc. adjustments:						
Proceeds from bonds	2,000	4	2,000			0
Net change in fund balances/change in net position	$ 1,902		3,704		2,889	$ 1,087

LEARNING OBJECTIVES

1. Develop an understanding of the classification of net assets and preparation of the Statement of Financial Position. (p. 669)

2. Develop an understanding of the recognition of revenues and expenses and the preparation of the Statement of Activities. (p. 671)

3. Develop an understanding of functional expenses and the preparation of the Statement of Cash Flows. (p. 676)

Accounting for Not-for-Profit Organizations

11

The **American National Red Cross** was established by an Act of the United States Congress on January 5, 1905, for the primary purposes of furnishing volunteer aid to the sick and wounded of the armed forces in time of war and to carry on a system of national and international relief in time of peace to mitigate the suffering caused by fire, famine, floods, and other great natural calamities. Each year, victims of some 70,000 disasters turn to the more than half a million volunteers and 35,000 employees of the Red Cross.

THE AMERICAN RED CROSS

The mission of the Red Cross has since expanded to help people prevent, prepare for, and respond to emergencies. Today, in addition to domestic disaster relief, the American Red Cross offers services in five other areas: community services that help the needy; support and comfort for military members and their families; the collection, processing and distribution of lifesaving blood and blood products; educational programs that promote health and safety; and international relief and development programs. Through over 700 locally supported chapters, more than 15 million people gain the skills they need to prepare for and respond to emergencies in their homes, communities and world.

The American National Red Cross is a not-for-profit (NFP) organization and, as such, it is exempt from federal income taxes under Section 501(c)(3) of the Internal Revenue Code.[1] Tax-exempt status is conferred upon organizations that are not operated for the benefit of private interests, and no part of their net earnings may inure to the benefit of any private shareholder or individual, such as by the payment of dividends.

The financial statements of not-for-profit organizations have characteristics of the financial statements of both corporations and governments. Similar to corporations, NFPs employ accrual accounting and similar to the Government-Wide Statement of Net Position, the "equity" of NFPs is reported as "Net Assets." There are important differences, however. Some of the donations that the Red Cross and other NFPs receive are restricted as to usage by the donor, and NFPs have special rules for the recognition of revenue from restricted donations. Consequently, the Net Assets that result from these restricted donations must also be designated as restricted on the NFP's Statement of Net Position. We discuss the accounting for NFPs in this chapter.

In its annual report, the Red Cross highlights the fact that an average of 90 cents of every dollar the Red Cross spends is spent on humanitarian services. Prospective donors are quite interested in knowing the extent to which their donations reach intended recipients, as opposed to being spent on overhead. Accounting standards relating to voluntary health and welfare entities such as the Red Cross also mandate the issuance of reports that provide prospective donors with detailed information about the degree to which their donations are reaching their intended recipients. We discuss these reporting requirements in this chapter as well.

Sources: American National Red Cross website and 2014 annual report.

---

[1] The tax exemption does not apply to net income related to profit-making activities that are unrelated to its mission.

Not-for-profit (NFP) organizations are fundamentally different from for-profit business enterprises. They derive a significant portion of their resources in the form of contributions from individuals who do not expect a monetary payment in return; their operating purpose is to provide a social benefit, not to provide goods or services at a profit; and, they do not have ownership interests, such as shares of stock, and are, therefore, not "owned" like business enterprises. Despite the fact that they are not "owners," donors to NFPs and other interested parties are interested in financial information about the uses to which contributed funds are put, how efficiently services are delivered, expenses relating to the solicitation of donations, and the extent to which the not-for-profit's management have been effective stewards of the resources that have been entrusted to it.

Primary accounting guidance relating to not-for-profit organizations is contained in two accounting standards that the FASB issued in 1993: SFAS 116, "Accounting for Contributions Received and Contributions Made," and SFAS 117, "Financial Statements of Not-for-Profit Organizations." FASB ASC 958 currently codifies these standards, and requires not-for-profit organizations to issue three financial statements, together with appropriate footnotes (FASB ASC 958-205-05-5):

1. Statement of Financial Position (the NFP's balance sheet),
2. Statement of Activities (the NFP's income statement), and
3. Statement of Cash Flows.

In addition, health and welfare organizations, such as the Red Cross, are required to issue a Statement of Functional Expenses. This statement categorizes the expenses of the organization into a matrix with the expense label (salaries, wages, etc) in the rows and program and supporting services in the columns. This presentation allows the reader to assess the level of expenses not only by expense category (i.e., how much did we spend on wages in total?), but also by program or supporting service (i,e., how much did we spend on wages related to disaster relief or for fundraising?).

Not-for-profit organizations prepare their financial statements using accrual accounting, and they recognize revenue when it is earned. Revenue recognition in the NFP world is complicated, however, by the fact that some donations carry provisions limiting the types of activities for which the donation can be used (such as donations that can be used only for disaster relief), while other donations may be paid over a period of time, may be promises to donate in the future, or may stipulate that only the interest earned off of the donated funds can be used by the not-for-profit organization (the principal must be preserved in a segregated account). Consequently, we need additional guidance in order to properly account for the differing characteristics of these donations.

We address these accounting issues and many others in this chapter, and frame our discussion around the financial statements of our focus organization: The American Red Cross. We begin with the first of the three financial statements, the Statement of Financial Position.

STATEMENT OF FINANCIAL POSITION

The Statement of Financial Position reports the assets, liabilities and *net assets* of the not-for-profit (NFP). It provides information that focuses on the organization's liquidity, its ability to meet obligations and external financing requirements, and, in general, its ability to continue to provide needed services. As in the corporate world, NFPs report assets in order of liquidity and liabilities in order of maturity, together with subtotals for current assets and current liabilities. Footnote disclosures also provide additional information about the restrictions that donors have placed on the allowable uses of particular assets that can aid users in their evaluation of the liquidity and financial flexibility of the NFP and, ultimately, its ability to fulfill its mission.

LO1 Develop an understanding of the classification of net assets and preparation of the Statement of Financial Position.

When not-for-profit organizations receive donations, these contributions may, and typically do, contain restrictions on their use, such as

- restrictions on the types of activities for which the cash or other assets can be used,
- conditions that must be satisfied before the cash or other assets are available for use, and
- the portion of the donation that can be used currently and the portion that must be retained indefinitely.

These restrictions can significantly impact the liquidity of the organization and are so important that the FASB requires the reporting of the not-for-profit's net assets in three categories (FASB ASC 958-210-45-1 and Glossary):

1. **Permanently restricted net assets**—the part of the net assets of a not-for-profit organization resulting from contributions and other inflows of assets whose use by the organization is limited by donor-imposed stipulations that *neither* expire by passage of time nor can be fulfilled or otherwise removed by actions of the organization.[2] An example of a permanently restricted asset is the gift of an endowment which allows the not-for-profit to use the interest earned off of the endowment for unrestricted purposes, but prohibits the use of any of the original donation (the "principal").

2. **Temporarily restricted net assets**—the part of the net assets of a not-for-profit organization resulting from contributions and other inflows of assets whose use by the organization is limited by donor-imposed stipulations that *either* expire by passage of time or can be fulfilled by actions of the organization. An example of a temporary restriction is the donation of cash to the Red Cross that can only be used for relief efforts relating to a specific natural disaster, such as earthquake relief efforts.[3]

3. **Unrestricted net assets**—the part of net assets of a not-for-profit organization that is neither permanently restricted nor temporarily restricted by donor-imposed stipulations.[4]

Although any increase in net assets is welcomed, unrestricted donations are preferable to the NFP because they do not impose restrictions that might limit the liquidity and flexibility of the NFP to meet ongoing needs that are the focus of its mission.

Statement of Financial Position Example

We present the Statement of Financial Position for the Red Cross in Exhibit 11.1. Following are a number of observations on that statement to help you better understand the differences between the accounting for not-for-profits and the accounting for governments that we discuss in Chapters 9 and 10 (numbers correspond with the numbers in Exhibit 11.1):

❶ **Investments** are initially recorded at market value when purchased or received as donations, and are, subsequently, marked-to-market. If donated, the initial revenue from the donation as well as subsequent income (loss) is reported in the Statement of Activities and, if the donation contains donor-requested restrictions on their use, the increase in Net Assets is reported as Temporarily Restricted or Permanently Restricted on the Statement of Financial Position. Otherwise, the investments are reported in Net Assets as unrestricted.

---

[2] In addition, cash or other assets received with a donor imposed restriction that limits their use to long-term purposes should not be classified with cash or other assets that are unrestricted and available for current use (FASB ASC 958-210-45-6).

[3] Once the cash is used for the defined purpose, the NFP transfers the amount spent from *temporarily restricted* net assets to *unrestricted* net assets. We provide an illustration of temporarily restricted donations later in the chapter.

[4] Unrestricted net assets generally result from revenues from unrestricted contributions, but may also arise as a result of providing goods and services and receiving dividends or interest on investments (FASB ASC 958-210-20 Glossary).

EXHIBIT 11.1	Consolidated Statement of Financial Position for the Red Cross

THE AMERICAN NATIONAL RED CROSS
Consolidated Statement of Financial Position
June 30, 2014
(with comparative information as of June 30, 2013)

(In thousands)	2014	2013
Assets		
Current assets:		
Cash and cash equivalents.	$ 46,976	$ 82,721
❶ Investments	521,485	618,139
❷ Trade receivables, including grants, net of allowance for doubtful accounts of		
$4,463 in 2014 and $6,963 in 2013.	190,528	233,089
Contributions receivable, net	83,830	80,303
Inventories, net of allowance for obsolescence of $3,832 in 2014 and $4,714 in 2013.	108,979	112,950
Other current assets.	16,798	23,230
❸ Total current assets	968,596	1,150,432
Investments	1,553,756	1,466,762
❹ Contributions receivable, net.	11,981	12,205
❺ Land, buildings, and other property, net	995,695	1,018,454
Other assets.	261,615	250,982
Total assets.	$3,791,643	$3,898,835
Liabilities and Net Assets		
Current liabilities:		
Accounts payable and accrued expenses	$ 280,869	$ 325,810
Current portion of debt.	18,532	18,236
Postretirement benefits.	3,807	3,734
Other current liabilities	132,228	154,398
❸ Total current liabilities.	435,436	502,178
Debt	727,221	695,755
Pension and postretirement benefits	520,029	554,645
Other liabilities	148,199	156,200
Total liabilities.	1,830,885	1,908,778
❻ Net assets:		
Unrestricted net assets.	339,577	398,444
Temporarily restricted net assets	857,420	861,605
Permanently restricted net assets	763,761	730,008
Total net assets	1,960,758	1,990,057
Commitments and contingencies	—	—
Total liabilities and net assets.	$3,791,643	$3,898,835

❷ **Receivables** are reported net of the allowance for uncollectible accounts. We account for the allowance for uncollectible accounts in the same manner as we do for businesses (i.e., increases in the allowance account are expensed and reductions are debited to the allowance account with a corresponding credit to the receivable).

❸ **Current Assets and Current Liabilities** subtotals are reported for assets expected to be converted into cash, and liabilities expected to be paid, within one year.

❹ **Long-Term Contributions Receivable** are initially recognized at the present value of the future cash receipt and are, subsequently, accreted with a debit to the receivable and a credit to interest income until the contribution is paid.

❺ **Land, Buildings, and Other Property** are reported at historical cost, net of accumulated depreciation. Not-for-profits can use any reasonable method of depreciation.

❻ **Net Assets** are categorized as Unrestricted, Temporarily Restricted, and Permanently Restricted to provide the reader with information related to the Net Assets that are available to meet current needs.

TOPIC REVIEW 1

Preparation of Statement of Financial Position

Following is financial data for the Center for Dog Fitness, a not-for profit organization investigating the benefits of exercise for dogs.

Long-term liabilities	$157,550
Contributions receivable	148,350
Cash	2,530
Payables	108,100
Investments	579,600
PPE, net	285,200
Net assets—unrestricted	358,616
Net assets—temporarily restricted	278,024
Net assets—permanently restricted	113,390

Required

Given this information, prepare the Statement of Financial Position.

The solution to this review problem can be found on page 688.

STATEMENT OF ACTIVITIES

The Statement of Activities reports the not-for-profit's revenues, expenses, and change in net assets for the period. Its focus is to provide information to donors, creditors, and other interested parties to evaluate the organization's performance during a period, to assess an organization's service efforts and its ability to continue to provide services, and to evaluate the extent to which an organization's managers have discharged their stewardship responsibilities and other aspects of their performance (FASB ASC 958-225-05-3).

LO2 Develop an understanding of the recognition of revenues and expenses and the preparation of the Statement of Activities.

Format of the Statement of Activities

The general format of the Statement of Activities is as follows:

	Unrestricted	Temporarily Restricted	Permanently Restricted	Totals
Operating revenues:				
Contributions	xxx	xxx	xxx	xxx
Other	xxx	xxx	xxx	xxx
Net assets released from restrictions	xxx ←	(xxx)		
Total revenue and other	xxx	xxx	xxx	xxx
Operating expenses:				
Program Services				
Program A	xxx			xxx
Program B	xxx			xxx
Program C	xxx			xxx
⋮	⋮			⋮
Supporting services				
Fund raising	xxx			xxx
Management and general	xxx			xxx
Total operating expenses	xxx			xxx
Change in net assets	xxx	xxx	xxx	xxx
Net assets, beginning-of-year	xxx	xxx	xxx	xxx
Net assets, end-of-year	xxx	xxx	xxx	xxx

■ **Contributions**—Contributions from donors can be Unrestricted (i.e., can be used at the discretion of management) or may be Temporarily Restricted or Permanently Restricted. Contributions must be segregated into these categories (FASB ASC 958-225-45-2-8).

- **Other Revenues**—Other revenues includes such line items as fees from programs and services and investment income.

- **Net Assets Released from Restrictions**—Temporarily Restricted donations are those that contain restrictions relating to their use (i.e., donations specifically designated for Hurricane Sandy or Haitian relief efforts) or restrictions relating to the passage of time (i.e., a gift of a **term endowment** that is to be invested for five years before becoming available for general use). When the not-for-profit pays out cash in accordance with the donor's restriction, it records a decrease in Temporarily Restricted net assets and an increase in Unrestricted Net Assets in a line item called *net assets released from restrictions* in the operating revenues section of the Statement of Activities.

- **Operating Expenses**—*All* operating expenses are paid out of Unrestricted net assets (FASB ASC 958-225-45-7).

- **Change in Net Assets**—The net of revenues and expenses is the Change in Net Assets. This total is reported for each category of net assets (i.e., Unrestricted, Temporarily Restricted, and Permanently Restricted), and is added to the beginning balance of each category to yield the Net Assets at the end of the year that is reported in the Statement of Net Assets.

Accounting for Contributions

In the business world, revenues are recognized when *earned*, which generally means the point at which the business has done all that it is required to do under the agreement with its customer. In the not-for-profit world, the earning process is complicated by the fact that not-for-profits do not provide goods or services in exchange for the funds they receive. Instead, they accept funds from donors and distribute those funds in accordance with their charter and, possibly, under direction from the donor. The earning process is, therefore, more complicated, and we need additional guidance relating to the recognition of revenues from contributions.

Guidance relating to the accounting for contributions is provided in SFAS 116, "Accounting for Contributions Received and Contributions Made" and currently codified in FASB ASC 958-605. Before we proceed to our discussion of contributions, let's first define what a contribution is:

A **contribution** is an unconditional transfer of cash or other assets to an entity or a settlement or cancellation of its liabilities in a voluntary nonreciprocal transfer by another entity acting other than as an owner (FASB ASC 958-605 Glossary).[5]

Cash contributions with no restrictions on the use or availability of the funds are recognized as revenue when received. If the contribution is made in the form of a donor's promise to pay (i.e., a commitment to contribute funds at a future date), revenue is recognized and a receivable is recorded when the promise is made, provided that there is sufficient evidence in the form of verifiable documentation that a promise was made and received (FASB ASC 958-310-25-1). Execution of a written *unconditional* pledge would provide that kind of documentation (we discuss conditional pledges below). Further, when contributions are made in the form of future promises, they are recorded for the present value of the future contribution as *temporarily restricted revenues* (FASB ASC 958-605-45-3–7).

Gifts of long-lived assets received are also recognized as temporarily restricted revenues if the not-for-profit has an accounting policy to imply a time restriction relating to the donation that expires over the useful life of the donated assets, or as unrestricted revenues in the absence of such a policy (FASB ASC 958-605-45-6). In both cases, when the cash is received or the asset is used, the Temporarily Restricted Net Assets are released from the restriction and the release is recognized in the Statement of Net Assets as a reduction of Temporarily Restricted Net Assets and an increase in Unrestricted Net Assets (i.e., a transfer from Temporarily Restricted Net Assets to Unrestricted Net Assets).

---

[5] "Other assets" include, for example, securities, land, buildings, use of facilities or utilities, materials and supplies, intangible assets, services, and unconditional promises to give those items in the future (FASB ASC 958-605-15-11).

Conditional Promises   Conditional promises depend on the occurrence of a specified future and uncertain event to bind the promisor. A typical example of a conditional promise is the naming of a not-for-profit organization in the will of a donor. These bequests are conditional since wills can be amended and the bequest can be cancelled. Other examples include the promise of a matching gift by a company to match the contributions of its employees. Conditional promises are recognized as revenues when the conditions on which they depend are substantially met (i.e., when the conditional promise becomes unconditional) (FASB ASC 958-605-25-13).[6]

Contributions of Services   Donors sometimes contribute services rather than cash or other assets. These might include professional services, like accounting and legal, and the services of carpenters, electricians, and the like. Contributions of services are recognized only if the services require specialized skills, are provided by individuals possessing those skills, and would typically need to be purchased if not provided by donation. Contributions of services are reported at fair value (FASB ASC 958-605-25-16).

Contributions of Works of Art and Historical Treasures   Not-for-profits may receive gifts of collections of art, historical treasures, and other similar collectibles. These contributions, while valuable, may present problems for the receiving organization. The collections must be maintained and protected, often at a significant cost. Works of art, for example, may require periodic refurbishing, and usually must be exhibited in climate-controlled facilities with elaborate security systems. Before the not-for-profit accepts these donations, it must carefully consider these future costs as donors often seek to contribute only the works of art, and frequently do not also contribute the funds that will be required for their protection and preservation.

In addition, not-for-profits face the continual challenge of raising funds to support the programs that they are chartered to provide. To the extent that the donated collections are recognized as revenues, this might give future donors the false impression that the not-for-profit's revenue stream is strong and that donations are unnecessary. Desperately needed cash to support the not-for-profit's ongoing programs may be harder to solicit as a result of the revenues recognized from donated collections.

Even though the not-for-profit might be willing to accept the donation of the collection, it may not want to recognize the donation as revenue. Fortunately, GAAP provides a solution. An entity need not recognize contributions of works of art, historical treasures, and similar assets if the donated items are added to collections that meet all of the following conditions (FASB ASC 958-605-25-19 and Glossary):

a. Are held for public exhibition, education, or research in furtherance of public service rather than financial gain,

b. Are protected, kept unencumbered, cared for, and preserved, and

c. Are subject to an organizational policy that requires the proceeds from sales of collection items to be used to acquire other items for collections.

This means that the donated collection is neither recognized as an asset, nor is it recognized as revenue.

The Museum of Modern Art in New York provides an interesting example. Following is the asset section of its recent Statement of Financial Position:

---

[6] A conditional promise to give is considered unconditional if the possibility that the condition will not be met is remote. For example, a stipulation that an annual report must be provided by the donee to receive subsequent annual payments on a multi-year promise is not a condition if the possibility of not meeting that administrative requirement is remote. Further, if assets are transferred to the not-for-profit, but their use is conditioned upon a future event, the contribution is accounted for as a refundable advance until the conditions have been substantially met (FASB ASC 958-605-25-12).

THE MUSEUM OF MODERN ART
Consolidated Statements of Financial Position
June 30, 2014

(in thousands of dollars)	2014
Assets	
Cash and cash equivalents	$ 54,076
Receivables	
Accounts receivable and other	7,001
Contributions receivable, net	176,107
The Trust for Cultural Resources	35,395
Inventories	11,210
Prepaid expenses and other assets	12,046
Investments	
Accrued investment income and other receivables	4,186
Investments, at fair value	838,906
Investments held on behalf of others	—
Interest in net assets of International Council	6,427
Property, plant and equipment, net	502,310
Museum collections	—
Total assets	$1,647,664

The extensive art collection of The Museum of Modern Art in New York is reported on the Statement of Financial Position with no value. By not capitalizing donated art collections, The Museum of Modern Art does not have to report the donations as revenue.

Statement of Activities Example

We present the Statement of Activities for the Red Cross in Exhibit 11.2. Following are a number of observations on that statement to help you better understand its composition (numbers correspond with the numbers in Exhibit 11.2):

❶ Revenues are categorized (in columns) as Unrestricted, Temporarily Restricted, or Permanently Restricted (expenses are only recognized in the Unrestricted column). The Temporarily or Permanently Restricted categories include both the donation, if restricted, as well as any earnings from those restricted donations, such as investment income.

❷ Revenues are also categorized (in rows) as Revenues from Contributions and Revenues from Products or Services. In addition to receiving funds from contributors, not-for-profits may also sell products and services.[7]

❸ Not-for-profits report Investments at fair value on the statement date. Investment income includes interest and dividend income as well as realized and unrealized gains (losses). Contrary to the accounting for investments by businesses, not-for-profits do not have the available-for-sale or held-to-maturity classifications available to businesses under SFAS 115.[8]

❹ When Temporary Restrictions are released, say by the passage of time or by the use of funds as provided for in the restriction, the Net Assets so restricted are transferred from Temporarily Restricted to Unrestricted where they can be spent. This transfer is reflected in the "Net assets released from restrictions" row of the Statement of Activities.

---

[7] The Red Cross, for example, derives revenue from sales of whole blood and blood components and health services and from safety course fees. Blood sales are at prices that are sufficient to cover the Red Cross's research and development efforts to enhance the safety of the blood supply. Total costs relating to the acquisition and delivery of blood and R&D efforts are approximately equal to total revenues from blood sale (source: Red Cross annual report).

[8] SFAS 124 allows for an exception to this accounting for not-for-profits engaging in the same industry with businesses accounting for investments under SFAS 115: "Some investors, primarily health care organizations, indicated that because Statement 115 requires business entities to report changes in fair value of available-for-sale securities in a separate category of equity and to report held-to-maturity securities at amortized cost, users would be unable to make meaningful comparisons when not-for-profit organizations and business entities are engaged in the same industry. This Statement allows an organization with those comparability concerns to report in a manner similar to business entities by identifying securities as available-for-sale or held-to-maturity and excluding the unrealized gains and losses on those securities from an operating measure within the statement of activities (SFAS 124, footnote 3a).

EXHIBIT 11.2 Statement of Activities for the Red Cross

THE AMERICAN NATIONAL RED CROSS
Consolidated Statement of Activities
Year Ended June 30, 2014
(with summarized information for the year ended June 30, 2013)

(In thousands)	Unrestricted	❶ Temporarily Restricted	Permanently Restricted	Totals 2014	Totals 2013
❷ Operating revenues and gains:					
Contributions:					
Corporate, foundation and individual giving	$ 236,470	$273,629	$ —	$ 510,099	$ 830,998
United Way and other federated	25,857	77,882	—	103,739	95,530
Legacies and bequests	55,156	10,271	20,814	86,241	96,224
Services and materials	12,198	10,780	—	22,978	54,502
Products and services:					
Biomedical	1,889,790	—	—	1,889,790	2,037,732
Program materials	129,455	—	—	129,455	125,153
Contracts, including federal government	73,933	—	—	73,933	73,132
❸ Investment income	53,367	32,471	—	85,838	48,697
Other revenues	86,620	446	—	87,066	73,973
❹ Net assets released from restrictions	481,430	(481,430)	—	—	—
Total operating revenues and gains	3,044,276	(75,951)	20,814	2,989,139	3,435,941
❺ Operating expenses:					
Program services:					
Services to the Armed Forces	46,173	—	—	46,173	56,645
Biomedical services	1,979,894	—	—	1,979,894	2,164,815
Community services	49,458	—	—	49,458	57,200
Domestic disaster services	364,074	—	—	364,074	467,245
Health and safety services	196,125	—	—	196,125	216,222
International relief and development services	127,385	—	—	127,385	92,742
Total program services	2,763,109	—	—	2,763,109	3,054,869
❻ Supporting services:					
Fund raising	183,224	—	—	183,224	189,431
Management and general	115,899	—	—	115,899	136,283
Total supporting services	299,123	—	—	299,123	325,714
Total operating expenses	3,062,232	—	—	3,062,232	3,380,583
Change in net assets from operations	(17,956)	(75,951)	20,814	(73,093)	55,358
❼ Nonoperating gains (losses), net	12,235	71,766	12,939	96,940	92,181
Pension-related changes other than net periodic benefit cost	(53,146)	—	—	(53,146)	247,295
❽ Change in net assets	(58,867)	(4,185)	33,753	(29,299)	394,834
Net assets, beginning of year	398,444	861,605	730,008	1,990,057	1,595,223
Net assets, end of year	$ 339,577	$857,420	$763,761	$1,960,758	$1,990,057

❺ All operating expenses are reflected in the Unrestricted column (Temporarily Restricted Net Assets are first transferred into the Unrestricted category before they can be spent so long as the expenditure complies with the original restriction). The first category of operating expenses is Program Services. Program services are "The activities that result in goods and services being distributed to beneficiaries, customers, or members that fulfill the purposes or mission for which the not-for-profit entity (NFP) exists. Those services are the major purpose for and the major output of the NFP and often relate to several major programs." (FASB ASC 958-720 Glossary)

❻ The second category of expenses is Support Services. "Supporting activities are all activities of a not-for-profit organization other than program services. Generally, they include management and general, fund-raising, and membership-development activities" (SFAS ASC Master Glossary). This is an important category as it provides readers with information that is relevant to assess the proportion of each contribution dollar that is consumed by supporting activities and is, therefore, unavailable to be spent on the programs for which the not-for-profit has been created.

❼ The Red Cross categorizes the change in net assets as operating and nonoperating. Categorization in this manner is optional.[9]

❽ The difference between revenues and expenses is identified as the "change in net assets."[10] This change is computed for all three categories of Net Assets. When added to Net Assets at the beginning of the year, the sum yields Net Assets as of the end of the year.

TOPIC REVIEW 2

Preparation of Statement of Activities

Continuing with earlier topic review, following is additional financial data for the Center for Dog Fitness. Given this information, prepare the Statement of Activities.

Expenses—support	85,100
Net assets released from restriction.	46,000
Expenses—program.	598,000
Depreciation expense.	20,700

	Unrestricted	Temporarily Restricted	Permanently Restricted
Revenues—contributions.	$644,000	$ 64,400	$10,350
Revenues—investment	4,416	6,624	11,040
Net assets, beginning of year.	368,000	253,000	92,000

The solution to this review problem can be found on page 688.

STATEMENT OF CASH FLOWS

LO3 Develop an understanding of functional expenses and the preparation of the Statement of Cash Flows.

The primary purpose of a statement of cash flows is to provide information about the cash receipts and cash payments of an organization during a period. The Statement of Cash Flows for a not-for-profit is prepared in the same way as that for a business and the NFP may use either the direct or indirect method of computation.[11] It is divided into the usual Operating, Investing, and Financing categories whose sum yields the Net Change in Cash for the period.

---

[9] The FASB cites the following reasoning for this position: "The Board decided to neither require nor preclude a not-for-profit organization from classifying its revenues, expenses, gains, and losses as operating or nonoperating within its statement of activities. Present standards neither require nor preclude a business enterprise from classifying its revenues, expenses, gains, and losses in that way, and the Board found no compelling reason to prescribe more specific display standards for not-for-profit organizations (SFAS 117, ¶67).

[10] For Temporarily Restricted Net Assets, the difference is between revenues and "net assets released from restrictions."

[11] One exception is that "receipts of resources that by donor stipulation must be used for long-term purposes" be classified as a financing activity (FASB ASC 958-230-55-3).

We present the Statement of Cash Flows for the Red Cross in Exhibit 11.3.

EXHIBIT 11.3	Statement of Cash Flows for the Red Cross

THE AMERICAN NATIONAL RED CROSS
Consolidated Statement of Cash Flows
Year Ended June 30, 2014
(with comparative information for the year ended June 30, 2013)

(In thousands)	2014	2013
Cash flows from operating activities:		
Change in net assets	$ (29,299)	$394,834
Adjustments to reconcile change in net assets to net cash (used in) operating activities:		
Depreciation and amortization	65,637	63,205
Provision for doubtful accounts and contributions receivable	1,246	1,195
Provision (recovery) for obsolete inventory	(882)	610
Net gain on sales of property	(6,683)	(4,965)
Net investment and derivative gain.	(119,682)	(86,778)
Pension and postretirement related changes other than net periodic benefit costs	53,146	(247,295)
Permanently restricted contributions	(20,814)	(22,011)
Changes in operating assets and liabilities:		
Receivables	38,012	(24,234)
Inventories	4,853	316
Other assets	(4,201)	(106)
Accounts payable and accrued expenses	(44,941)	44,798
Other liabilities	(31,165)	(27,943)
Pension and postretirement benefits	(87,689)	(199,953)
Net cash used in operating activities	(182,462)	(108,327)
Cash flows from investing activities:		
Purchases of property	(53,305)	(39,035)
Proceeds from sales of property	17,110	13,134
Purchases of investments	(145,237)	(320,896)
Proceeds from sales of investments	275,573	302,296
Net cash provided by (used in) investing activities	94,141	(44,501)
Cash flows from financing activities:		
Permanently restricted contributions	20,814	22,011
Proceeds from borrowings	50,000	175,000
Repayments of debt	(18,238)	(14,367)
Net cash provided by financing activities	52,576	182,644
Net (decrease)/increase in cash and cash equivalents	(35,745)	29,816
Cash and cash equivalents, beginning of year	82,721	52,905
Cash and cash equivalents, end of year	$ 46,976	$ 82,721

PRACTICE INSIGHT

Proposed changes in the Not-For-Profit Financial Reporting Framework The FASB has proposed sweeping changes to the not-for-profit financial reporting model (*Presentation of Financial Statements of Not-for-Profit Entities*, issued April 22, 2015). The not-for-profit exposure draft reflects the influence of an earlier, more far-reaching financial statement presentation project that re-envisioned the entire U.S. financial reporting framework for business entities and proposed to redefine the notion of "operating" activities. Under the FASB's proposal,

- Financial information will be grouped into prescribed "operating," "investing," and "financing" categories, similar to the approach used in the statement of cash flows today. Operating activities will include transactions associated with assets and liabilities used in carrying out an entity's day-to-day business activities, including PPE assets.

- Not-for-profits will be required to use the direct method for cash flow reporting purposes. In addition, consistent with the operating treatment of PPE-related income items (depreciation, gains and losses on sale, etc.), acquisitions of property, plant and equipment would be included in cash flows from operations.

- "Operating excess (deficit)" would become a required GAAP operating performance metric for not-for-profits.

- Other proposed changes include reducing the three net asset classifications to two (with and without donor restrictions), and enhancing required liquidity disclosures.

The amendments, if approved, will be applied retrospectively.

STATEMENT OF FUNCTIONAL EXPENSES

FASB ASC 958 requires health and welfare organizations to provide a Statement of Functional Expenses "to help donors, creditors, and others in assessing an organization's service efforts, including the costs of its services and how it uses resources" (FASB ASC 958-205-45-6). This statement is presented in a matrix format: the columns categorize expenses by "functional classification," such as major classes of program services and supporting activities, and the rows report expenses by their "natural classification," such as salaries, rent, electricity, interest expense, depreciation, awards and grants to others, and professional fees. This format allows users to analyze the level and composition of the costs incurred to provide the various program services of the not-for-profit.

We produce the Statement of Functional Expenses for the Red Cross in Exhibit 11.4. The FY2014 Statement of Functional Expenses for the Red Cross reveals the following breakdown of total expenses for the year (in thousands):

Expense Category:		
Program services	$2,763,109	90.2%
Fund raising	183,224	6.0%
Management and general	115,899	3.8%
Total	$3,062,232	100.0%

In 2014, the Red Cross reported that over 90% of its expenses related directly to the programs and services it provides and less than 10% of its costs related to fundraising and overhead. This data is important for prospective donors to ensure that their contributions are being spent on the humanitarian efforts that they want to support. Additional information is provided relating to the types of services that the Red Cross provides and the proportion of its expenses relating to each.

| EXHIBIT 11.4 | Statement of Functional Expenses for the Red Cross |

THE AMERICAN NATIONAL RED CROSS
Statement of Functional Expenses
Year Ended June 30, 2014
(with summarized information for the year ended June 30, 2013)

Program Services

(In thousands)	Service to Armed Forces	Biomedical Services	Community Services	Domestic Disaster Services	Health and Safety Services	International Relief and Development Services	Total Program Services
Salaries and wages	$25,267	$ 886,080	$19,245	$ 98,119	$ 80,546	$ 20,891	$1,130,148
Employee benefits	6,267	219,777	4,773	24,337	19,978	5,182	280,314
Subtotal	31,534	1,105,857	24,018	122,456	100,524	26,073	1,410,462
Travel and maintenance	1,530	31,192	701	17,428	7,301	5,003	63,155
Equipment maintenance and rental	355	61,301	2,439	10,856	2,025	1,350	78,326
Supplies and materials	1,409	462,548	6,425	8,044	11,761	1,227	491,414
Contractual services	8,104	276,215	9,267	61,399	66,342	8,957	430,284
Financial and material assistance	2,224	2,990	4,698	132,466	2,565	84,110	229,053
Depreciation and amortization	1,017	39,791	1,910	11,425	5,607	665	60,415
Total expenses	$46,173	$1,979,894	$49,458	$364,074	$196,125	$127,385	$2,763,109

Supporting Services

	Fund Raising	Management and General	Total Supporting Services	Total Expenses 2014	Total Expenses 2013
Salaries and wages	$ 91,446	$ 46,115	$137,561	$1,267,709	$1,333,519
Employee benefits	22,682	11,438	34,120	314,434	443,467
Subtotal	114,128	57,553	171,681	1,582,143	1,776,986
Travel and maintenance	5,643	2,776	8,419	71,574	117,546
Equipment maintenance and rental	856	1,333	2,189	80,515	102,303
Supplies and materials	3,676	376	4,052	495,466	512,356
Contractual services	55,514	51,101	106,615	536,899	561,639
Financial and material assistance	646	299	945	229,998	246,548
Depreciation and amortization	2,761	2,461	5,222	65,637	63,205
Total expenses	$183,224	$115,899	$299,123	$3,062,232	$3,380,583

CHAPTER SUMMARY

Not-for-profit (NFP) organizations issue three financial statements, together with appropriate footnotes:

1. Statement of Financial Position (the NFP's balance sheet),
2. Statement of Activities (the NFP's income statement), and
3. Statement of Cash Flows.

The **Statement of Financial Position** reports the assets, liabilities and *net assets* of the not-for-profit (NFP). Donor restrictions can significantly impact the liquidity of the organization and are so important that the FASB requires the reporting of the not-for-profit's net assets in three categories:

1. **Permanently restricted net assets** the part of the net assets of a not-for-profit organization resulting from contributions and other inflows of assets whose use by the organization is limited by donor-imposed stipulations that *neither* expire by passage of time nor can be fulfilled or otherwise removed by actions of the organization.

2. **Temporarily restricted net assets**—the part of the net assets of a not-for-profit organization resulting from contributions and other inflows of assets whose use by the organization is limited by donor-imposed stipulations that *either* expire by passage of time or can be fulfilled by actions of the organization.

3. **Unrestricted net assets**—the part of net assets of a not-for-profit organization that is neither permanently restricted nor temporarily restricted by donor-imposed stipulations.

The **Statement of Activities** reports the not-for-profit's revenues, expenses, and change in net assets for the period. Guidance relating to the accounting for contributions is provided in SFAS 116, "Accounting for Contributions Received and Contributions Made" and currently codified in FASB ASC 958-605. A **contribution** is an unconditional transfer of cash or other assets to an entity or a settlement or cancellation of its liabilities in a voluntary nonreciprocal transfer by another entity acting other than as an owner.

Cash contributions with no restrictions on the use or availability of the funds are recognized as revenue when received. If the contribution is made in the form of a donor's promise to pay, revenue is recognized and a receivable is recorded when the promise is made, provided that there is sufficient evidence in the form of verifiable documentation that a promise was made and received. Further, when contributions are made in the form of future promises, they are recorded for the present value of the future contribution as *temporarily restricted revenues.*

Gifts of long-lived assets received are recognized as temporarily restricted revenues if the not-for-profit has an accounting policy to imply a time restriction relating to the donation that expires over the useful life of the donated assets, or as unrestricted revenues in the absence of such a policy. In both cases, when the cash is received or the asset is used, the Temporarily Restricted Net Assets are released from the restriction and the release is recognized in the Statement of Net Assets as a reduction of Temporarily Restricted Net Assets and an increase in Unrestricted Net Assets.

Conditional promises depend on the occurrence of a specified future and uncertain event to bind the promisor. Conditional promises are recognized as revenues when the conditions on which they depend are substantially met.

Donors sometimes contribute **services** rather than cash or other assets. Contributions of services are recognized only if the services require specialized skills, are provided by individuals possessing those skills, and would typically need to be purchased if not provided by donation. Contributions of services are reported at fair value.

An entity need not recognize contributions of **works of art**, historical treasures, and similar assets if the donated items are added to collections that meet all of the following conditions:

a. Are held for public exhibition, education, or research in furtherance of public service rather than financial gain,

b. Are protected, kept unencumbered, cared for, and preserved, and

c. Are subject to an organizational policy that requires the proceeds from sales of collection items to be used to acquire other items for collections.

The primary purpose of a **statement of cash flows** is to provide information about the cash receipts and cash payments of an organization during a period. The Statement of Cash Flows for a not-for-profit is prepared in the same way as that for a business and, unless changed by the proposed standards update, the NFP may use either the direct or indirect method of computation.

FASB ASC 958 requires health and welfare organizations to provide a **Statement of Functional Expenses** "to help donors, creditors, and others in assessing an organization's service efforts, including the costs of its services and how it uses resources." This statement is presented in a matrix format: the columns categorize expenses by "functional classification," such as major classes of program services and supporting activities, and the rows report expenses by their "natural classification," such as salaries, rent, electricity, interest expense, depreciation, awards and grants to others, and professional fees. This format allows users to analyze the level and composition of the costs incurred to provide the various program services of the not-for-profit.

COMPREHENSIVE REVIEW

Preparation of Financial Statements for Not-for-Profit

Following is financial data for Food 4 US, a not-for profit organization dedicated to providing food supplies in less developed countries.

Expenses—support	$136,900
PPE, net	458,800
Net assets released from restriction	74,000
Investments	932,400
Payables	173,900
Contributions receivable	238,650
Long-term liabilities	253,450
Expenses—program	962,000
Cash	4,070
Depreciation expense	33,300

Statement of Activities	Unrestricted	Temporarily Restricted	Permanently Restricted
Revenues—contributions	$1,036,000	$103,600	$ 16,650
Revenues—investment	7,104	10,656	17,760
Net assets, beginning of year	592,000	407,000	148,000

Required

Given this information, prepare the Statement of Activities and the Statement of Financial Position.

The solution to this review problem can be found on page 689.

QUESTIONS

1. Describe the differences between not-for-profit organizations and typical business enterprises.

2. What financial statements are not-for-profit organizations required to issue?

3. Describe two issues that relate to the recognition of revenues for not-for-profit organizations.

4. The Statement of Financial Position focuses attention on what issues relating to the not-for-profit organization?

5. Donations to not-for-profit organizations typically contain restrictions on their use, such as the activities for which the funds may be used or relating to the portion of the donation that may be spent for current use. How does the reporting of the Net Assets of the not-for-profit organization assist readers in understanding the effects of these restrictions on the organization's liquidity?

6. What is the purpose of the Statement of Activities?

7. Describe the differences in revenue recognition for:
   a. contributions received in cash with no restrictions on the use or availability of funds,
   b. contributions that relate to a promise to contribute cash in the future, and
   c. contributions of long-lived assets.

8. What are conditional promises? When are conditional promises recognized as revenue?

9. Describe the revenue recognition process for contributions of services.

10. Sometimes, not-for-profits receive contributions of works of art, historical treasures, and the like. In what ways can these contributions be problematic for the not-for-profit? Under what conditions can the not-for-profit avoid recognizing revenue for contributions of works of art, historical treasures, and the like?

MULTIPLE CHOICE

LO1

 AICPA Adapted

11. Restricted net assets

On January 1, Read, a nongovernmental not-for-profit organization, received $20,000 and an unconditional pledge of $20,000 for each of the next four calendar years to be paid on the first day of each year. The present value of an ordinary annuity for four years at a constant interest rate of 8% is 3.312. What amount of restricted net assets is reported in the year the pledge was received?

a. $66,240
b. $80,000
c. $86,240
d. $100,000

LO1

12. Required financial statements

Safe Paws, a humanitarian not-for-profit focusing on dog safety, is preparing its year-end financial statements. Which of the following financial statements is required?

a. Statement of revenue, expenses, and changes in fund balance
b. Statement of cash flows
c. Statement of changes in financial position
d. Statement of changes in fund balance

LO1

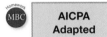 **AICPA Adapted**

13. Statement of financial position

Which of the following financial categories are used in a nongovernmental not-for-profit organization's statement of financial position?

a. Net assets, income, and expenses
b. Income, expenses, and unrestricted net assets
c. Assets, liabilities, and net assets
d. Changes in unrestricted, temporarily restricted, and permanently restricted net assets

LO1

 AICPA Adapted

14. Recording contribution

Belle, a nongovernmental not-for-profit organization, received funds during its annual campaign that were specifically pledged by the donor to another nongovernmental not-for-profit health organization. How should Belle record these funds?

a. Increase in assets and increase in liabilities
b. Increase in assets and increase in revenue
c. Increase in assets and increase in deferred revenue
d. Decrease in assets and decrease in fund balance

LO1

 AICPA Adapted

15. Recording contribution

Ragg Coalition, a nongovernmental not-for-profit organization, received a gift of treasury bills. The cost to the donor was $20,000, with an additional $500 for brokerage fees that were paid by the donor prior to the transfer of the treasury bills. The treasury bills had a fair value of $15,000 at the time of the transfer. At what amount should Ragg report the treasury bills in its statement of financial position?

a. $15,000
b. $15,500
c. $20,000
d. $20,500

LO1

 AICPA Adapted

16. Restricted net assets

In Year 2, the Nord Association, a nongovernmental not-for-profit organization, received a $100,000 contribution to fund scholarships for medical students. The donor stipulated that only the interest earned on the contribution be used for the scholarships. Interest earned in Year 2 of $15,000 was used to award scholarships in Year 3. What amount should Nord report as temporarily restricted net assets at the end of Year 2?

a. $115,000
b. $100,000
c. $15,000
d. $0

17. Classification of donated assets

The Veterinary College of Aurora received a new building from a benefactor with no restrictions as to its use. The Veterinary College does not have a policy implying a time restriction on donated assets. How should the donation be recognized?

LO2

a. Unrestricted
b. Temporarily restricted
c. Permanently restricted
d. Temporarily restricted or Permanently restricted

18. Statement of functional expenses

Fenn Museum, a nongovernmental not-for-profit organization, had the following balances in its statement of functional expenses:

LO3

AICPA Adapted

Education	$300,000
Fundraising	250,000
Management and general	200,000
Research	50,000

What amount should Fenn report as expenses for support services?

a. $350,000
b. $450,000
c. $500,000
d. $800,000

19. Temporarily restricted net assets

A nongovernmental not-for-profit organization received a $2 million gift from a donor who specified it be used to create an endowment fund that would be invested in perpetuity. The income from the fund is to be used to support a specific program in the second year and beyond. An investment purchased with the gift earned $40,000 during the first year. At the end of the first year, the fair value of the investment was $2,010,000. What is the net effect on temporarily restricted net assets at year end?

LO1

AICPA Adapted

a. $0
b. $10,000 increase
c. $40,000 increase
d. $50,000 increase

20. Statement of cash flows

Dog Whisperers, a not-for-profit organization, received unrestricted cash donations of $50,000 and $100,000 of contributions restricted solely for the purchase of land, buildings or equipment. In its statement of cash flows for the year, Dog Whisperers will report which of the following amounts:

LO3

	Operating Activities	Investing Activities	Financing Activities
a.	$150,000	$ 0	$ 0
b.	$ 50,000	$100,000	$ 0
c.	$ 50,000	$ 0	$100,000
d.	$ 0	$ 50,000	$100,000

21. Contributions revenue

A nongovernmental not-for-profit animal shelter receives contributed services from the following individuals valued at their normal billing rates:

LO2

AICPA Adapted

Veterinarian provides volunteer animal care	$8,000
Board members volunteer to prepare books for audit	4,500
Registered nurse volunteers as receptionist	3,000
Teacher provides volunteer dog walking	2,000

What amount should the shelter record as contribution revenue?

a. $8,000

b. $11,000

c. $12,500

d. $14,500

LO2 **22. Release from restrictions**

Terrier Town, a not-for-profit organization, received a grant in the amount of $200,000 that was restricted to fund dog protection activities during the upcoming year. Later in the year, Terrier Town recognized revenues of $500,000 and expenses of $450,000, including expenses relating to dog protection activities amounting to $150,000. What amount, if any, should Terrier Town report as net assets released form restriction during the year?

a. $0

b. $200,000

c. $150,000

d. $250,000

LO2 **23. Recording contribution**

Whitestone, a nongovernmental not-for-profit organization, received a contribution in December Year 1. The donor restricted use of the contribution until March Year 2. How should Whitestone record the contribution?

a. Footnote the contribution in Year 1 and record as income when it becomes available in Year 2

b. No entry required in Year 1 and record as income in Year 2 when it becomes available

c. Report as income in Year 1

d. Report as deferred income in Year 1

LO2 **24. Recording contribution**

Stapleton College received $200,000 from a donor that was restricted for student scholarships. During the year, the College awarded all of the scholarships to deserving students. How should the donation be recognized in the year-end statement of activities?

a. As both an increase and a decrease in unrestricted net assets

b. As a decrease in unrestricted net assets

c. With only a footnote reference

d. The transaction is not reported

EXERCISES

LO1, 2 **25. Preparation of financial statements for not-for-profit**

Following is financial data for the Center for Cardio Research, a not-for profit organization investigating the benefits of exercise for heart disease. Given this information, prepare the Statement of Activities and the Statement of Financial Position.

	Unrestricted	Temporarily Restricted	Permanently Restricted
Revenues—contributions.........................	$4,238,993	$ 427,332	$ 80,553
Revenues—investment	183,224	83,772	103,758
Net assets, beginning of year.....................	3,732,853	2,851,667	783,228

Long-term liabilities	$1,383,859
Contributions receivable	1,238,657
Expenses—support	882,937
Net assets released from restriction	337,833
Cash...	438,654
Payables...	827,938
Expenses—program...	3,658,933
Investments	984,688
Depreciation expense..	153,852
PPE, net...	7,339,456

26. **Preparation of financial statements for not-for-profit**

LO1, 2

Following is financial data for Opportunity Knocks, a not-for profit organization providing preschool care and education for children. Given this information, prepare the Statement of Activities and the Statement of Financial Position.

Long-term liabilities	$2,683,000
PPE, net	4,337,898
Expenses—support	993,227
Payables	1,837,222
Depreciation expense.	337,622
Investments	5,125,565
Net assets released from restriction.	621,337
Expenses—program.	7,938,665
Cash.	833,934
Contributions receivable.	2,437,938

	Unrestricted	Temporarily Restricted	Permanently Restricted
Revenues—contributions	$8,337,953	$ 827,334	$163,827
Revenues—investment	398,543	160,889	228,333
Net assets, beginning of year.	3,732,853	2,851,667	783,228

27. **Preparation of journal entries for not-for-profit**

LO1, 2

The Brewster Boosters is a not-for-profit organization that supports the Brewster White Caps baseball team in the summer Cape Cod League for college-aged baseball players. During the year, the organization recorded a number of financial activities. Prepare journal entries for each of the following activities:

a. The organization recognized the following revenues (the contributions are all on account and the investment returns are in cash):

Revenues—contributions (unrestricted).	$1,120,000
Revenues—contributions (temporarily restricted)	112,000
Revenues—contributions (permanently restricted)	18,000
Revenues—investment (unrestricted).	7,680
Revenues—investment (temporarily restricted)	11,520
Revenues—investment (permanently restricted)	19,200

b. Brewster Boosters recognized program expenses of $1,040,000 and expenses related to support activities of $148,000, both on account. Of the program expenses, $80,000 was paid from temporarily restricted funds and used in compliance with the donor's stipulations.

c. The organization acquired $52,000 of long-term assets during the year and recorded $36,000 of depreciation expense (record the net increase in long-term assets to the PPE, net account).

d. Brewster Boosters purchased $48,000 of investments during the year.

e. The organization collected $1,200,000 of contributions receivable and used the cash to pay $1,160,000 of accounts payable.

28. **Preparation of journal entries for not-for-profit**

LO1, 2

The Concord Historical Society is a not-for-profit organization whose mission is the preservation of Concord's historical treasures. During the year, the Society recorded a number of financial activities. Prepare journal entries for each of the following activities:

a. The Society recognized the following revenues (the contributions are all on account and the investment returns are in cash):

Revenues—contributions (unrestricted).	$16,800,000
Revenues—contributions (temporarily restricted)	1,680,000
Revenues—contributions (permanently restricted)	270,000
Revenues—investment (unrestricted).	115,200
Revenues—investment (temporarily restricted)	172,800
Revenues—Investment (permanently restricted)	288,000

b.   The Society recognized program expenses of $15,600,000 and expenses related to support activities of $2,220,000, both on account. Of the program expenses, $1,200,000 was paid from temporarily restricted funds and used in compliance with the donor's stipulations.

c.   The Society acquired $780,000 of long-term assets during the year and recorded $540,000 of depreciation expense (record the net increase in long-term assets to the PPE, net account).

d.   The Concord Historical Society purchased $360,000 of investments during the year.

e.   The Society collected $18,000,000 of Contributions Receivable and used the cash to pay $17,400,000 of accounts payable.

PROBLEMS

LO1, 2

29. Preparation of journal entries and financial statements for not-for-profit

Beagles Forever is a not-for-profit organization dedicated to the health, welfare, and promotion of beagles. One of its most famous is Uno, who won best in show at the prestigious Westminster Kennel Club Dog Show. Best-in-show judge Dr. J. Donald Jones of Marietta, Georgia, said that while the choice was difficult, the winner fit "the standard for perfection for the beagle," citing in particular the dog's attitude. "Everything he does is correct. And just look at his face," said Jones after awarding Uno his 33rd best-in-show title.

The organization reported the following post-closing trial balance at the end of last year:

Beginning Balances:	DR	CR
Cash.	$ 234,000	
Investments	3,120,000	
Contributions receivable.	676,000	
PPE, net	1,560,000	
Payables.		$ 520,000
Long-term liabilities		1,040,000
Net assets—unrestricted		2,080,000
Net assets—temporarily restricted.		1,430,000
Net assets—permanently restricted.		520,000
	$5,590,000	$5,590,000

The organization reported a cash return of 4% during the subsequent year, and the investments are allocated as follows:

Investment—Unrestricted =	20%
Investment—Temporarily Restricted =	30%
Investment—Permanently Restricted =	50%

In addition to the recognition of investment returns, the organization reported the following revenues and expenses, all on account:

Revenues—contributions (unrestricted).	$3,640,000
Revenues—contributions (temporarily restricted)	364,000
Revenues—contributions (permanently restricted)	58,500
Expenses—program.	3,380,000
Expenses—support	481,000

Of the total expenses, $260,000 relate to uses that are paid from temporarily restricted funds in accordance with the stipulations of the donors and are, therefore, released from restriction.

During the year, the organization collected $3,900,000 of receivables and paid $3,770,000 of accounts payable. In addition, it purchased long-term assets for cash in the amount of $169,000 and recognized depreciation expense of $117,000. The organization also purchased additional investments with excess cash in the amount of $156,000 and repaid $149,500 principal amount of long-term debt.

a.   Prepare journal entries for the organization's financial activities during the year.

b.   Prepare the year-end Statement of Activities and Statement of Financial Position.

30. Preparation of journal entries and financial statements for not-for-profit   LO1, 2

Youth Camps is a not-for-profit organization that owns a number of summer camps for inner-city children. At the end of last year, the organization reported the following trial balance:

	DR	CR
Cash.	$ 666,000	
Investments	8,880,000	
Contributions receivable.	1,924,000	
PPE, net	4,440,000	
Payables.		$ 1,480,000
Long-term liabilities		2,960,000
Net assets—unrestricted		5,920,000
Net assets—temporarily restricted.		4,070,000
Net assets—permanently restricted.		1,480,000
	$15,910,000	$15,010,000

The investments are allocated as follows: 42% are unrestricted, 37% are temporarily restricted (use of these funds is stipulated by the donors), and 21% are permanently restricted (only the interest income may be used to fund operating expenses if so directed by the organization's Board of Trustees, and no such designation was made for this year). Investment income (paid in cash) is 3% for the current year.

During the year, the organization received $10,360,000 in unrestricted donations and $1,036,000 in donations whose use is temporarily restricted as to use by donors. All of these donations are on account. In addition, it recognized program expenses of $9,620,000 and expenses relating to support of $1,369,000, both on account. Of the program expenses, $740,000 is spent using temporarily restricted funds for approved purposes, thus receiving the appropriate release from the donors' restrictions.

Youth Camps collected $11,100,000 of contributions receivable, paid $10,730,000 of payables and purchased additional land in the amount of $481,000 (depreciation expense of $333,000 is recognized related to the depreciable assets). Interest expense on the long-term debt is included in the expenses referenced above, and no repayment of the principal is recognized during the year.

a. Prepare journal entries for the organization's financial activities during the year.

b. Prepare the year-end Statement of Activities and Statement of Financial Position.

31. Preparation of journal entries and financial statements for not-for-profit   LO1, 2

Wings is a not-for-profit organization dedicated to the promotion of flying in youths. It owns a number of airplanes at various airports which it uses to provide introductory flights in order to encourage young adults to pursue flight training lessons and possible careers as commercial airline pilots. At the end of last year, Wings reported the following trial balance:

	DR	CR
Cash.	$ 144,000	
Investments	1,920,000	
Contributions receivable.	416,000	
PPE, net	960,000	
Payables.		$ 320,000
Long-term liabilities		640,000
Net assets—unrestricted		1,280,000
Net assets—temporarily restricted.		880,000
Net assets—permanently restricted.		320,000
	$3,440,000	$3,440,000

At year-end, the investments are allocated as follows:

> Investment—Unrestricted = 40%
> Investment—Temporarily Restricted = 35%
> Investment—Permanently Restricted = 25%

These investments earn a 3% cash return during the following year.

During the following year, Wings received $2,240,000 of unrestricted donations, $224,000 of donations whose use is temporarily restricted by donors as to use, and $36,000 of donations that are permanently restricted (i.e., only the interest can be used to cover program expenses if so approved by the Board of Trustees—no such approval was granted during the current year). All contributions are on account when made.

Program and support expenses for the current year are $2,080,000 and $296,000, respectively, both on account. Of the program expenses, $160,000 are funded from temporarily restricted funds as they are used for approved expenditures. During the year, Wings purchased an airplane for a cash purchase price of $232,000 and recorded depreciation expense on existing depreciable assets of $72,000. The organization purchased additional investments with excess cash in the amount of $96,000 and also repaid $92,000 principal amount of long-term debt. Finally, during the year, the organization collected $2,400,000 of contributions receivable and paid $2,320,000 of accounts payable.

a. Prepare journal entries for the organization's financial activities during the year.
b. Prepare the year-end Statement of Activities and Statement of Financial Position.

TOPIC REVIEW

Solution 1

Statement of Financial Position	
Cash.	$ 2,530
Investments	579,600
Contributions receivable.	148,350
Total current assets	730,480
PPE, net	285,200
Total assets.	$1,015,680
Payables.	$ 108,100
Total current liabilities.	108,100
Long-term liabilities	157,550
Total liabilities.	265,650
Net assets—unrestricted	358,616
Net assets—temporarily restricted.	278,024
Net assets—permanently restricted.	113,390
Total net assets	750,030
Total liabilities and net assets.	$1,015,680

Solution 2

Statement of Activities	Unrestricted	Temporarily Restricted	Permanently Restricted	Total
Revenues—contributions.	$644,000	$ 64,400	$ 10,350	$718,750
Revenues—investment	4,416	6,624	11,040	22,080
Net assets released from restriction.	46,000	(46,000)		
Total revenue and gains	694,416	25,024	21,390	740,830
Expenses—program.	598,000			598,000
Expenses—support	85,100			85,100
Depreciation expense.	20,700			20,700
Total operating expenses	703,800			703,800
Change in net assets	(9,384)	25,024	21,390	37,030
Net assets, beginning of year.	368,000	253,000	92,000	713,000
Net assets, end of year	$358,616	$278,024	$113,390	$750,030

COMPREHENSIVE REVIEW SOLUTION

Statement of Activities	Unrestricted	Temporarily Restricted	Permanently Restricted	Total
Revenues—contributions...................	$1,036,000	$103,600	$ 16,650	$1,156,250
Revenues—investment	7,104	10,656	17,760	35,520
Net assets released from restriction...........	74,000	(74,000)		
Total revenue and gains	1,117,104	40,256	34,410	1,191,770
Expenses—program......................	962,000			962,000
Expenses—support	136,900			136,900
Depreciation expense.....................	33,300			33,300
Total operating expenses	1,132,200			1,132,200
Change in net assets	(15,096)	40,256	34,410	59,570
Net assets, beginning of year...............	592,000	407,000	148,000	1,147,000
Net assets, end of year	$ 576,904	$447,256	$182,410	$1,206,570

Statement of Financial Position	
Cash...	$ 4,070
Investments	932,400
Contributions receivable...	238,650
Total current assets	1,175,120
PPE, net	458,800
Total assets...	$1,633,920
Payables..	$ 173,900
Total current liabilities..	173,900
Long-term liabilities	253,450
Total liabilities	427,350
Net assets—unrestricted	576,904
Net assets—temporarily restricted...................................	447,256
Net assets—permanently restricted..................................	182,410
Total net assets	1,206,570
Total liabilities and net assets.....................................	$1,633,920

LEARNING OBJECTIVES

1. Identify reportable operating segments. (p. 693)

2. Describe the accounting for interim financial reporting. (p. 701)

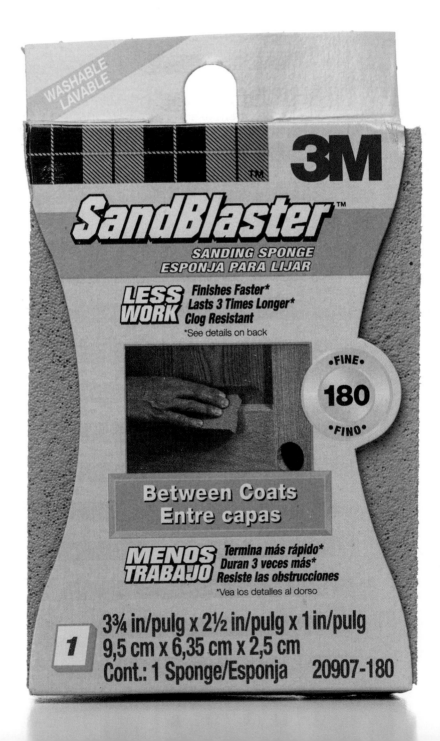

Segment Disclosures and Interim Financial Reporting

12

3M is a diversified technology company with a global presence in the following businesses: Industrial; Safety and Graphics; Electronics and Energy; Health Care; and Consumer. 3M is among the leading manufacturers of products for many of the markets it serves. Most 3M products involve expertise in product development, manufacturing and marketing, and are subject to competition from products manufactured and sold by other technologically oriented companies.

3M COMPANY

In a recent year 3M reported sales of over $31 billion, net income of nearly $5 billion, and total assets of over $31 billion. In our analysis of the company's operating results, it might be helpful to know which of these operating segments mentioned above are performing particularly well and which aren't. And, ultimately, an investor might have particular interest in knowing if the company's profitability is due to one operating segment. If so, future results might be significantly impacted by competition entering that space.

The operating performance of these business lines had traditionally been a closely guarded secret. Until the late 1960s, US-based companies were only required to provide limited disclosures about their international operations, and sometimes voluntarily provided disaggregated information about individual product lines and industries within the consolidated entity. The Securities and Exchange Commission (SEC) began requiring companies to provide "line-of-business" information in registration statements (1969), annual reports filed with the SEC (1970) and annual reports provided to stockholders and bondholders of companies filing with the SEC (1974).

In 1976, the Financial Accounting Standards Board issued Statement of Financial Accounting Standards (SFAS) No. 14: *Financial Reporting for Segments of a Business Enterprise*, requiring business enterprises to report segment information by industry and by geographic area. Although this standard was a step in the right direction, the basis for conclusions in SFAS No. 131: *Disclosures about Segments of an Enterprise and Related Information* (now codified in FASB ASC 280) states that "[m]any analysts said that they found [existing segment disclosures] helpful but inadequate." Analysts' complaints often focused on the fact that companies could define industry and geographic segments in highly aggregated and non-comparable ways. Current GAAP (i.e., SFAS No. 131, as codified in FASB ASC 280), takes the view that the reportable segments should be based on the same level of aggregation reviewed by top management in the organization.

In addition to the reporting of financial information on business segments, the SEC requires companies to report consolidated financial statements on a quarterly basis. This quarterly reporting presents some estimation and disclosure issues for accountants since all of the information that would normally be required for the preparation of year-end financial statements may not be available during each quarter. We discuss the issues involved in the preparation of interim financial statements in this chapter as well.

Source: 3M Company 2014 10-K

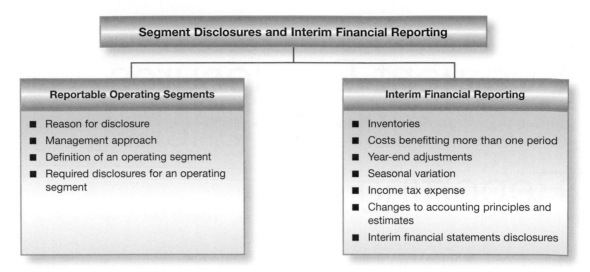

Users of financial statements have long argued for increased disclosure about the investment that companies make in their various businesses and the resulting profitability of those businesses. Companies, on the other hand, are reluctant to provide much transparency, citing the risks of increased competition and the resulting decline in profitability that such information might cause. In the late 1990s, US accounting standard setters decided that more useful information would be provided to investors and creditors if—as compared to poorly defined "industry segments" included in existing generally accepted accounting principles (GAAP)—segment reporting is based on the same business segments that are reviewed by the top decision makers of the reporting company.

Even after the passage of new disclosure requirements, the degree of transparency differs markedly across companies. **Apple Inc.**, for example, provides the following information about its various product lines in its 2014 10-K:

	2014	Change	2013	Change	2012
Net sales by product					
iPhone.	$101,991	12%	$ 91,279	16%	$ 78,692
iPad.	30,283	(5)%	31,980	3%	30,945
Mac.	24,079	12%	21,483	(7)%	23,221
iPod.	2,286	(48)%	4,411	(21)%	5,615
iTunes, software and services.	18,063	13%	16,051	25%	12,890
Accessories	6,093	7%	5,706	11%	5,145
Total net sales	$182,795	7%	$170,910	9%	$156,508
Unit sales by product					
iPhone.	169,219	13%	150,257	20%	125,046
iPad.	67,977	(4)%	71,033	22%	58,310
Mac.	18,906	16%	16,341	(10)%	18,158
iPod.	14,377	(45)%	26,379	(25)%	35,165

From this table, we are able to derive information about the importance of Apple's iPhone and iPad products as well as its Macintosh computers. Contrast this level of disclosure with that for **Coca-Cola** in the same year:

> As of December 31, 2014, our organizational structure consisted of the following operating segments: Eurasia and Africa; Europe; Latin America; North America; Asia Pacific; Bottling Investments; and Corporate . . .The business of our Company is nonalcoholic beverages . . . Management evaluates the performance of our operating segments separately to individually monitor the different factors affecting financial performance...Information about our Company's operations by operating segment for the year ended December 31, 2014 is as follows (in millions):

2014	Eurasia & Africa	Europe	Latin America	North America	Asia Pacific	Bottling Investments	Corporate	Eliminations	Consolidated
Net operating revenues:									
Third party...................	$2,730	$4,844	$4,597	$21,462	$5,257	$6,972	$ 136	$ —	$45,998
Intersegment.................	—	692	60	17	489	67	—	(1,325)	—
Total net revenues.............	2,730	5,536	4,657	21,479	5,746	7,039	136	(1,325)	45,998
Operating income (loss)..........	1,084	2,852	2,316	2,447	2,448	9	(1,448)	—	9,708
Interest income................	—	—	—	—	—	—	594	—	594
Interest expense...............	—	—	—	—	—	—	483	—	483
Depreciation and amortization......	47	75	56	1,195	96	315	192	—	1,976
Equity income (loss)—net.........	35	31	10	(16)	12	691	6	—	769
Income (loss) before income taxes...	1,125	2,892	2,319	1,633	2,464	715	(1,823)	—	9,325
Identifiable operating assets.......	1,298	3,358	2,426	33,066	1,793	6,975	29,482	—	78,398
Investments...................	1,081	90	757	48	157	8,781	2,711	—	13,625
Capital expenditures	30	54	55	1,293	76	628	270	—	2,406

The limited financial information that Coca-Cola choses to provide in that year stands in stark contrast to the product-level data which Apple provides. Both are in compliance with GAAP, however. In this chapter, we review the disclosure requirements relating to business segments. We also discuss those relating to interim financial reports.

REPORTABLE OPERATING SEGMENTS

Accounting guidance relating to required disclosures for operating segments is provided in SFAS 131, "Disclosures about Segments of an Enterprise and Related Information," which the FASB issued in 1997. That standard is now codified in FASB ASC 280. We begin with a discussion of the segment disclosure requirements, followed by an example.

LO1 Identify reportable operating segments.

Reason for Operating Segment Disclosures

There has long been a tension between companies and the users of their financial statements relating to the disclosure of details about the *components* of their business. Companies are justifiably concerned about the dissemination of information that might harm their competitive position (if we tell the market that a particular business line is very profitable, we will invite competition). Users of financial statements (the analyst community, in particular) argue that it is not sufficient merely to know that a company as a whole is profitable and is generating sufficient cash flow. In addition, we might want to know:

- **Is one component of the business carrying a number of losing components?** If so, increased competition in that market segment might have a negative impact on the company as a whole, much more so than if the company's financial performance was balanced across a number of business lines.

- **Is one component of the business generating a disproportionately large proportion of the company's free cash flow (generally defined as net cash flow from operating activities less capital expenditures)?** Again, if that is the case, the company might be particularly vulnerable to competitive pressure in that business line.

- **Are some of the company's business lines more capital intensive than others?** If so, growth in these components of the business might require significant future capital investment.

Disclosures relating to the components of a business have traditionally been sparse, relating to the geographical dispersion of the business rather than to its lines of business. In the mid-1990s, however, the pendulum shifted toward more disclosure, culminating with the issuance of SFAS 131 in 1997.

In its overview of the accounting standard, the FASB argues for increased disclosure as follows: "The objective of requiring disclosures about segments of a public entity and related information is to provide information about the different types of business activities in which a public entity engages and the different economic environments in which it operates to help users of financial statements do all of the following: a. Better understand the public entity's performance, b. Better assess its prospects for future net cash flows, and c. Make more informed judgments about the public entity as a whole" (FASB ASC 280-10-10-1).

Management Approach

Given the FASB's stated desire to increase the quantity and quality of information that a company must disclose about the components of its business, the logical starting point is, then, to define, generally, how we should decide what information to disclose. To make that determination, the standard prescribes the use of the "management approach."

The **management approach** requires disclosures for the same business units that are routinely reported to senior management. FASB ASC 280-10-05-3 and 05-4 describe this approach as follows:

The management approach is based on the way that management organizes the segments within the public entity for making operating decisions and assessing performance. Consequently, the segments are evident from the structure of the public entity's internal organization, and financial statement preparers should be able to provide the required information in a cost-effective and timely manner . . . The management approach facilitates consistent descriptions of a public entity in its annual report and various other published information. It focuses on financial information that a public entity's decision makers use to make decisions about the public entity's operating matters. The components that management establishes for that purpose are called operating segments.

Definition of an Operating Segment

The components of the business that are defined under the management approach are called operating segments. More specifically, FASB ASC 280-10-50-1 defines an **operating segment** as "a component of a public entity that has all of the following characteristics:

a. It engages in business activities from which it may earn revenues and incur expenses (including revenues and expenses relating to transactions with other components of the same public entity).

b. Its operating results are regularly reviewed by the public entity's chief operating decision maker to make decisions about resources to be allocated to the segment and assess its performance.

c. Its discrete financial information is available."

Not every component of the business is necessarily an operating segment. The corporate headquarters or certain functional departments, like R&D, may not earn revenues (they may be a cost center) and would not be designated as operating segments.

Quantitative Thresholds   Once an operating segment has been identified with the criteria presented above, it must be disclosed in the footnotes if it meets *any one* of the following three quantitative thresholds based on revenues, profit, and assets (FASB ASC 280-10-50-12):

a. Its reported revenue, including both sales to external customers and intersegment sales or transfers, is 10 percent or more of the combined revenue, internal and external, of all operating segments.

b. The absolute amount of its reported profit or loss is 10 percent or more of the greater, in absolute amount, of either:
   1. The combined reported profit of all operating segments that did not report a loss
   2. The combined reported loss of all operating segments that did report a loss.

c. Its assets are 10 percent or more of the combined assets of all operating segments.

PRACTICE INSIGHT

When Aggregation Is Not Beneficial   **Coca-Cola** is the world's largest beverage company. It owns or licenses more than 500 nonalcoholic beverage brands, primarily sparkling beverages but also a variety of still beverages such as waters, enhanced waters, juices and juice drinks, ready-to-drink teas and coffees, and energy and sports drinks. Coke owns and markets four of the world's top five nonalcoholic sparkling beverage brands: Coca-Cola, Diet Coke, Fanta, and Sprite. Finished beverage products bearing its trademarks, sold in the United States since 1886, are now sold in more than 200 countries.

In 2014, Coca-Cola generated nearly $46 billion in total revenues, reported over $7 billion in net income and generated over $10 billion in operating cash flow. Ever wondered which of its beverages is the most profitable? Well, Coke is mum about that. In its 2014 10-K, Coke discusses its operating segments as follows:

> #### Note 19—OPERATING SEGMENTS
>
> As of December 31, 2014, our organizational structure consisted of the following operating segments: Eurasia and Africa; Europe; Latin America; North America; Asia Pacific; Bottling Investments; and Corporate.

Bottom line, Coca-Cola deems all of its beverage lines to be similar as far as ASC 280 segment disclosures are concerned. So, when you look at the segment disclosure footnote in Coke's 10-K, you will find the normal categories of disclosure (revenues, operating profit, depreciation, capital expenditures, and assets) broken down into the operating segments listed above and you will be unable to learn which of its beverages is yielding the most sales, profit, and cash flow. Sometimes aggregation is not a good thing for users of financial statements.

Two or more operating segments may be aggregated into a single operating segment if the segments have similar economic characteristics, *and* if the segments are similar in each of the following areas (FASB ASC 280-10-50-11):

a. The nature of the products and services

b. The nature of the production processes

c. The type or class of customer for their products and services

d. The methods used to distribute their products or provide their services

e. If applicable, the nature of the regulatory environment, for example, banking, insurance, or public utilities.

This aggregation allows companies to group similar business units and may also allow them to reach the size requirements for a reportable segment listed above.

Once the operating segments have been identified and the data compiled, the final requirement is that the total external revenue reported by operating segments must constitute at least 75% of total consolidated revenue. If that threshold is not met, additional operating segments must be identified as reportable segments (even if they do not meet the quantitative thresholds) until at least 75% of total consolidated revenue is included in reportable segments (FASB ASC 280-10-50-14).[1]

Finally, FASB ASC 280 contains a "once in—always in" provision as follows:

■ If management judges an operating segment identified as a reportable segment in the immediately preceding period to be of continuing significance, information about that segment shall continue to be reported separately in the current period even if it no longer meets the criteria for reportability (FASB ASC 280-10-50-16).

■ If an operating segment is identified as a reportable segment in the current period due to the quantitative thresholds, prior-period segment data presented for comparative purposes shall be restated

---

[1] ASC 280 does not provide specific guidance on the maximum number of reportable segments, but suggests an upper limit of 10 (FASB ASC 280-10-50-18).

to reflect the newly reportable segment as a separate segment even if that segment did not satisfy the criteria for reportability . . . unless it is impracticable to do so (FASB ASC 280-10-50-17).

Required Disclosures for an Operating Segment

The company must disclose the following information for each operating segment and for all comparative years presented in the financial statements (FASB ASC 280-10-50-21 and 50-22):

1. General information:
   a. Factors used to identify the company's reportable segments, including the basis of organization (for example, whether management has chosen to organize the enterprise around differences in products and services, geographic areas, regulatory environments, or a combination of factors and whether operating segments have been aggregated)
   b. Types of products and services from which each reportable segment derives its revenues.
2. Required financial data:
   a. Profit or loss
   b. Total assets
   c. Additional financial data if the specified amounts are included in the measure of segment profit or loss reviewed by the chief operating decision maker or are otherwise regularly provided to the chief operating decision maker, even if not included in that measure of segment profit or loss:
      i. Revenues from external customers
      ii. Revenues from transactions with other operating segments of the same public entity
      iii. Interest revenue
      iv. Interest expense
      v. Depreciation, depletion, and amortization expense
      vi. Unusual items
      vii. Equity in the net income of investees accounted for by the equity method
      viii. Income tax expense or benefit
      ix. Significant noncash items other than depreciation, depletion, and amortization expense.

Generally, the amount of information that is disclosed for each financial item should be the same as that which is reported to the chief operating decision maker for purposes of making decisions about allocating resources to the business segments and assessing their performance.

Typical disclosures of segment financial data include the following as these accounts are usually reported to top management and, thus, are required under 2a–c above:

- Sales
- Income (net income or operating income)
- Depreciation and amortization expense
- Total assets
- Capital expenditures.

Notice the omission of the statement of cash flows.[2] This is not a required disclosure. Analysts can compute a crude estimate of free cash flows, however, given income, depreciation and capital expenditures (free cash flow = operating income + depreciation and amortization expense − capital expenditures). This estimate does not include cash generated or used as a result of changes in working capital accounts and, thus, is crude at best.

Reconciliation with Consolidated Totals   The segment disclosure must also include the following reconciliations of the segment totals to the consolidated financial statements (FASB ASC 280-10-50-30):

a. The total of the reportable segments' revenues to the public entity's consolidated revenues.

---

[2] Even though not a required disclosure, many companies voluntarily include a statement of cash flows in their interim reports.

b. The total of the reportable segments' measures of profit or loss to the public entity's consolidated income before income taxes, and discontinued operations. However, if a public entity allocates items such as income taxes to segments, the public entity may choose to reconcile the total of the segments' measures of profit or loss to consolidated income after those items.

c. The total of the reportable segments' assets to the public entity's consolidated assets.

d. The total of the reportable segments' amounts for every other significant item of information disclosed to the corresponding consolidated amount. For example, a public entity may choose to disclose liabilities for its reportable segments, in which case the public entity would reconcile the total of reportable segments' liabilities for each segment to the public entity's consolidated liabilities if the segment liabilities are significant.

The adjustments involved in the reconciliation to the consolidated totals typically relate to elimination entries (our **C-E-A-D-I** journal entries) and the financial data of business segments or components of the business that are not designated as operating segments and that are not, therefore, separately disclosed.

Disclosures Relating to Geographic Areas

In addition to the financial disclosures presented above, companies must also provide the following disclosures relating to the geographical concentration of revenues and assets in the U.S. and outside of the U.S. (FASB ASC 280-10-50-41):

a. Revenues from external customers attributed to the public entity's country of domicile and attributed to all foreign countries in total from which the public entity derives revenues. If revenues from external customers attributed to an individual foreign country are material, those revenues shall be disclosed separately. A public entity shall disclose the basis for attributing revenues from external customers to individual countries.

b. Long-lived assets other than financial instruments, long-term customer relationships of a financial institution, mortgage and other servicing rights, deferred policy acquisition costs, and deferred tax assets located in the public entity's country of domicile and located in all foreign countries in total in which the public entity holds assets. If assets in an individual foreign country are material, those assets shall be disclosed separately.

Disclosures Relating to Major Customers

Companies must disclose information about the extent of their reliance on major customers if revenues from transactions with a single external customer amount to 10% or more of the company's total revenues (FASB ASC 280-10-50-42). The company must disclose its reliance on significant customers, the total amount of revenues from each such customer, and the identity of the segment or segments reporting the revenues. The company does not need to disclose, however, the identity of a major customer or the amount of revenues that each segment reports from that customer.

Example—3M's Segment Disclosures

Following are the segment disclosures from 3M's 2014 annual report:

3M's businesses are organized, managed, and internally grouped into segments based on differences in markets, products, technologies, and services. 3M manages its operations in five operating business segments: Industrial; Safety and Graphics; Electronics and Energy; Health Care; and Consumer. 3M's five business segments bring together common or related 3M technologies, enhancing the development of innovative products and services and providing for efficient sharing of business resources. These segments have worldwide responsibility for virtually all 3M product lines. 3M is not dependent on any single product/service or market. Transactions among reportable segments are recorded at cost.

continued

Business Segment Products

Business Segment	Major Products
Industrial	Tapes, coated, nonwoven and bonded abrasives, adhesives, advanced ceramics, sealants, specialty materials, filtration products, closure systems for personal hygiene products, acoustic systems products, automotive components, abrasion-resistant films, structural adhesives and paint finishing and detailing products
Safety and Graphics	Personal protection products, traffic safety and security products, commercial graphics systems, commercial cleaning and protection products, floor matting, and roofing granules for asphalt shingles
Electronics and Energy	Optical films solutions for electronic displays, packaging and interconnection devices, insulating and splicing solutions for the electronics, telecommunications and electrical industries, touch screens and touch monitors, renewable energy component solutions, and infrastructure protection products
Health Care	Medical and surgical supplies, skin health and infection prevention products, drug delivery systems, dental and orthodontic products, health information systems and food safety products
Consumer	Sponges, scouring pads, high-performance cloths, consumer and office tapes, repositionable notes, indexing systems, construction and home improvement products, home care products, protective material products, and consumer and office tapes and adhesives

Business Segment Information

(Millions)	Net Sales			Operating Income		
	2014	2013	2012	2014	2013	2012
Industrial..................	$10,990	$10,657	$10,008	$2,389	$2,307	$2,244
Safety and Graphics.........	5,732	5,584	5,406	1,296	1,227	1,210
Electronics and Energy.......	5,604	5,393	5,458	1,115	954	1,026
Health Care...............	5,572	5,334	5,138	1,724	1,672	1,641
Consumer.................	4,523	4,435	4,386	995	945	943
Corporate and Unallocated ...	4	8	4	(251)	(321)	(472)
Elimination of Dual Credit.....	(604)	(540)	(496)	(133)	(118)	(109)
Total Company.............	$31,821	$30,871	$29,904	$7,135	$6,666	$6,483

(Millions)	Assets			Depreciation & Amortization			Capital Expenditures		
	2014	2013	2012	2014	2013	2012	2014	2013	2012
Industrial.................	$ 8,508	$ 8,833	$ 8,614	$ 383	$ 373	$ 324	$ 395	$ 511	$ 416
Safety and Graphics.........	4,939	5,122	5,085	234	255	237	221	207	189
Electronics and Energy.......	5,116	5,336	5,512	271	260	266	232	261	350
Health Care...............	4,344	4,329	4,296	181	171	169	169	120	113
Consumer.................	2,434	2,516	2,445	108	106	110	111	128	105
Corporate and Unallocated ...	5,928	7,414	7,924	231	206	182	365	438	311
Total Company.............	$31,269	$33,550	$33,876	$1,408	$1,371	$1,288	$1,493	$1,665	$1,484

3M discloses financial data relating to Sales, Operating Income, Assets, Depreciation and Amortization, and Capital Expenditures. These disclosure categories are typical. 3M also provides a reconciliation of the segment totals to the consolidated totals in the Corporate and Unallocated row in each category. The "Total Company" row equals the amounts reported in the consolidated financial statements.

Quantitative Thresholds   SFAS 131 requires disclosure for all segments that exceed *any* of the quantitative thresholds for revenues (sales), profit, and assets.

Revenues   All operating segments exceeding 10% of combined revenue, internal and external, of all operating segments must be separately disclosed. We do not have data on the internal revenues as these have been eliminated in the consolidation process. For external revenues, the threshold is 10% of $32,421 million ($31,821 million + $604 million − $4 million), or $3,242.1 million. All of the reported segments exceed that threshold as we would expect.

Profit   All operating segments for which the absolute value of segment profit or absolute value of segment loss exceeds 10 percent of the greater of the absolute value of aggregate segment profit (for profitable operating segments) or absolute value of aggregate segment losses (for unprofitable segments). All of 3M's segments are profitable, and the threshold is 10% of $7,519 million ($7,135 million + $133 million + $251 million), or $751.9 million. All of the reported segments exceed the profit threshold.

Assets   All operating segments with assets exceeding 10% of combined assets for all operating segments must be separately disclosed. All of 3M's segments, except Consumer, exceed the asset threshold of 10% of $25,341 million ($31,269 million − $5,928 million), or $2,534.1 million.

Other Disclosures   In addition to the financial data presented above, 3M also provides, by geographical area, the following required disclosure relating to its sales and long-lived assets, and voluntary disclosure related to its operating income:

(Millions)	Net Sales			Operating Income			Property, Plant and Equipment, Net	
	2014	**2013**	**2012**	**2014**	**2013**	**2012**	**2014**	**2013**
United States	$11,714	$11,151	$10,571	$2,540	$2,210	$1,938	$4,619	$4,478
Asia Pacific.	9,418	9,047	9,092	2,487	2,386	2,450	1,798	1,943
Europe, Middle East and Africa . . .	7,198	7,085	6,730	1,234	1,168	1,163	1,502	1,636
Latin America and Canada.	3,504	3,611	3,529	867	908	936	570	595
Other Unallocated	(13)	(23)	(18)	7	(6)	(4)	—	—
Total Company.	$31,821	$30,871	$29,904	$7,135	$6,666	$6,483	$8,489	$8,652

Corporate and unallocated operating income includes a variety of miscellaneous items, such as corporate investment gains and losses, certain derivative gains and losses, certain insurance-related gains and losses, certain litigation and environmental expenses, corporate restructuring charges, and certain under- or over-absorbed costs (e.g., pension, stock based compensation) that the company may choose not to allocate directly to its business segments. Because this category includes a variety of miscellaneous items, it is subject to fluctuation on a quarterly and annual basis.

FASB ASC 280-10-50-41 requires two disclosure categories: U.S. and outside of the U.S. (for public companies domiciled in the U.S.). 3M's disclosure of the U.S. and several geographic areas outside of the U.S. is typical.

Finally, companies are required to disclose significant concentrations of sales. 3M does not disclose that it has significant reliance on any one customer.

Analysis of Segment Disclosures   Prior to the issuance of SFAS 131, analysts complained that segment reporting was not as useful as it could be because segments were too highly aggregated and did not conform to the internal structure of companies. Analysts and other user groups lobbied the FASB to increase the amount of information contained in segment disclosures, and the current standard provides information that is similar to that which executives use to manage the business. This data can be helpful in understanding the factors that drive profits and cash flows.

From the segment disclosures presented above, we are able to break down 3M's sales and profit by operating segment:

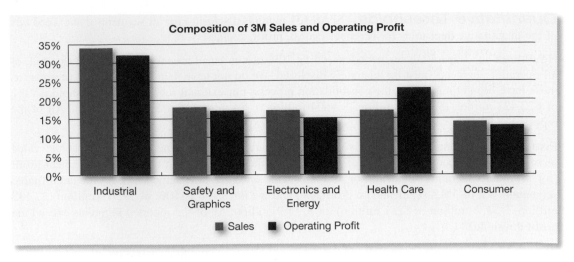

Each operating division contributes to 3M's profitability in approximate proportion to revenues, except for the Health Care segment which accounts for 23% of the company's profit and 17% of its sales. This appears to be an important business segment for the company.

SFAS 131 does not require disclosure of cash flows by segment. Given the data on profit, depreciation and amortization expense, and capital expenditures, however, we are able to compute a crude approximation to free cash flow as profit + depreciation and amortization expense − capital expenditures. The free cash flow by segment over the past three years, as computed with this crude formula, is as follows:

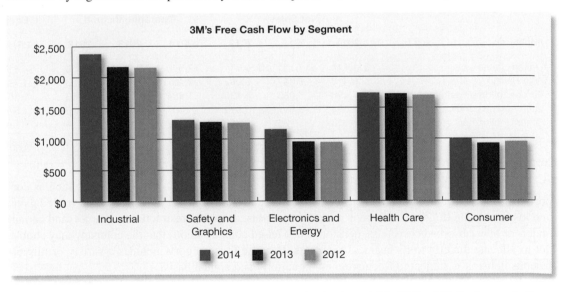

Again, the Health Care segment, while comprising 17% of sales, yields 23% of 3M's free cash flow. This is an important segment on this dimension as well.

Finally, given the sales, profit, and asset data, we can compute a crude DuPont disaggregation of return on assets for each operating segment:

	Profit Margin	Asset Turnover	Return on Assets
Industrial....................................	22%	1.29	28%
Safety and Graphics...........................	23%	1.16	26%
Electronics and Energy.......................	20%	1.10	22%
Health Care.................................	31%	1.28	40%
Consumer...................................	22%	1.86	41%

The return on assets (profit/assets) for the Health Care and Consumer segments are much greater than those of the other three segments. This is the result of high profit margins (profit/sales) and/or high asset turnover (sales/assets).

3M's sales, profit, and cash flows are relatively balanced, meaning that it does not depend to a disproportionate extent upon any one business segment for its financial performance. The Industrial segment, however, is clearly an important segment for the company. We would want to monitor its performance closely for any signs of weakness. In addition, we would be interested in management's strategy to improve the lower performing segments.

In summary, the segment disclosures under SFAS 131 are not as detailed as we would like, but are much better than they were prior to its issuance. Useful insights into the company's profitability and ability to generate cash flow can be gained from an analysis of the financial data contained in the required segment disclosures.

TOPIC REVIEW

Segment Disclosures

Assume that your company identifies the following business units that meet the core requirements to be categorized as business segments in your annual report:

($1,000s)	A	B	C	D	E
Sales.	$1,000	$5,000	$ 300	$ 800	$ 600
Profit.	500	1,000	(300)	(20)	100
Assets.	3,000	1,000	1,000	2,000	7,000

Required

a. Describe the core requirements for a business unit to be considered as a segment.
b. Which of the segments should be separately disclosed in the footnotes based on the quantitative thresholds?

The solution to this review problem can be found on page 716.

INTERIM FINANCIAL REPORTING

Interim financial reporting is essential in providing interested parties with timely financial information. Accounting guidance for interim financial reporting is provided in APB 28, "Interim Financial Reporting," issued in 1973 and currently referenced in FASB ASC 270.[3] The overriding philosophy of ASC 270 is that *each interim period should be viewed primarily as an integral part of an annual period* (FASB ASC 270-10-45-2). Further, companies should employ the same accounting principles for interim statements that they use for their annual reports. This means that, in general, revenues should be recognized when earned and expenses when incurred as they are usually recognized. In particular, since users of interim reports typically focus on the current quarter compared with the same quarter of the previous year, companies cannot adjust their revenue and expense recognition policy in order to achieve favorable year-over-year comparisons even though sales and net income for the year as a whole would not be affected.

There are a number of issues related to the preparation of interim financial statements that we discuss in the remainder of this chapter.

LO2 Describe the accounting for interim financial reporting.

Inventories

The accounting for inventories presents particular issues for interim financial statements. Several of these issues relate to the general concept that interim financial statements should be viewed as an integral part of an annual report.

---

[3] The SEC also requires publicly traded companies to file a Form 10-Q (quarterly report) that includes interim financial statements. These statements are somewhat limited, however, and need not be audited (Rule 10-01 of Regulation S-X). Further, Regulation S-X requires companies only to include major captions in their interim balance sheets, income statements and statements of cash flows, and allows them to omit most footnote disclosures. GAAP requirements for interim financial reports are much broader, but disclose less information than is contained in an annual report.

Estimated Gross Profit Companies may not take a physical inventory other than at year-end. ASC 270 permits companies to use estimated gross profit rates, or other reasonable methods, to determine the cost of goods sold during interim periods (FASB ASC 270-10-05-2). If they do, they are required to disclose the method used at the interim date and any significant adjustments that result from reconciliations with the annual physical inventory.

LIFO Liquidations, Lower of Cost or Market, and Standard Cost Systems **LIFO liquidations** arise when inventory quantities are reduced, resulting in the matching of lower-cost LIFO layers with current-period selling prices. Since each interim period should be viewed primarily as an integral part of an annual period, the LIFO liquidation should not be recognized if the company expects the inventory layer giving rise to the liquidation profit to be replaced. In that case, the cost of sales for the interim reporting period should include the expected cost of replacement of the liquidated LIFO base (FASB ASC 270-10-45-6b).

To illustrate, assume that we have two cost pools in our inventory:

	Units	Cost/Unit
Beginning of the quarter.	100	$50
Purchase #1	200	$60
	300	

At the beginning of the quarter (BOQ), we record 100 units on hand at a cost of $50 per unit. During the quarter, we purchase additional inventory (purchase #1) and we sell 250 units at $100/unit for cash. Our gross profit under LIFO is as follows:

Sales.	$25,000
Cost of goods sold (200@$60 + 50@$50)	(14,500)
Gross profit.	$10,500

We have realized an increase in gross profit by liquidating the older, lower-cost LIFO layer that existed at the beginning of the quarter (BOQ).

If, however, we expect to increase our quantities of inventories on hand by year-end by the purchase of inventories at a cost of $70, we should compute our gross profit for the interim reporting period as follows:

Sales.	$25,000
Cost of goods sold (200@$60 + 50@$70)	(15,500)
Gross profit.	$ 9,500

The revised gross profit assumes that the inventories will be replaced and, thus, no liquidation has occurred. Our journal entries to record the sale (assuming perpetual inventory accounting and assuming the anticipated replacement of the inventories) are as follows:

Cash.	25,000	
Sales		25,000
(to record the sale)		
Cost of goods sold.	15,500	
Inventory		14,500
Excess of replacement cost over LIFO cost		1,000
(to record Cost of Goods Sold in the interim income statement, assuming replacement of inventories at $70/unit)		

Cost of Goods Sold is $1,000 higher than we would have reported had we not anticipated replacement of the inventory by year-end.

The Excess of Replacement Cost over LIFO Cost account remains on the balance sheet as a deferred credit until year-end. If the 50 units of inventory are ultimately purchased (say, on account) at $70/unit, the journal entry to record the purchase will be as follows:

Inventory.	2,500	
Excess of replacement cost over LIFO cost	1,000	
Accounts payable		3,500
(to record the replacement of LIFO inventory liquidated at $70/unit)		

The Excess of Replacement Cost Over LIFO Cost account is eliminated because the LIFO liquidation did not occur due to the replacement of the lower cost LIFO layer.[4]

If the inventories are not replenished, however, Gross Profit is understated by the LIFO liquidation gain that we deferred. The Excess of Replacement Cost Over LIFO Cost account must, then, be written off to Cost of Goods Sold, thus increasing Gross Profit in the period that we know we will not be replenishing the inventory. This journal entry is as follows:

Excess of replacement cost over LIFO cost	1,000	
Cost of goods sold		1,000
(to remove the Excess of Replacement Cost over LIFO Cost account when the inventories are not replenished)		

Lower of Cost or Market

Our second issue relates to the reporting of inventories at the **lower of cost or market**. In the event of a decline in the market value of inventories, the resulting loss should normally be recognized in the interim period in which the loss occurs and subsequently recognized as gains (up to the amount of the loss recognized) in the later interim period if the market price recovers. If the decline in the market value of the inventory is expected to be *restored* by year-end, however, the decline is not recognized at the interim date since no loss is expected to be incurred in the fiscal year (FASB ASC 270-10-45-6c). This is another example of the treatment of an interim period as an integral part of the annual reporting period.

Standard Cost Accounting Systems

Companies often recognize purchase price variances or volume or capacity cost variances in the application of **standard cost accounting systems**. If those variances are planned and expected to be absorbed by the end of the annual period, the company should not recognize the cost of the variance in the interim reporting period. If the purchase price or volume variance is unplanned or unexpected, however, the cost should be reported in the interim period (FASB ASC 270-10-45-6d).

Costs Benefitting More than One Period

When a cost that is expensed for annual reporting purposes clearly benefits two or more interim periods, each interim period should be charged for an appropriate portion of the annual cost by the use of accruals or deferrals (FASB ASC 270-10-45-8). Following are three examples:

a. Companies often offer **quantity discounts** to customers based upon annual sales volume. The cost of those discounts should be recognized in the interim period, even if the annual purchase level has not yet been made if the company expects that the annual sales volume will be sufficient for the customer to receive the discount.

---

[4] If the inventories are, instead, replaced at $72/unit, the entry is changed to record the additional cost as an increase in Cost of Goods Sold:

Cost of goods sold	100	
Inventory.	2,500	
Excess of replacement cost over LIFO cost	1,000	
Accounts payable		3,600
(to record the replacement of LIFO inventory liquidated at $72/unit)		

The prior period's interim report is not restated.

To illustrate, assume that our customer purchases $50,000 of product from us this quarter and that we expect its annual purchases to be $200,000. Based on the anticipated annual purchases, our customer will be eligible for a 2% sales discount. We should accrue $1,000 ($50,000 × 2%) as a sales discount in our interim income statement for the quarter as follows (using the net method):

Sales.	1,000	
Accounts receivable		1,000
(to recognize sales discount for the quarter)		

b. **Property taxes** are often paid annually. Since the amount of taxes owed is a percentage of the assessed value of the property, tax payments do not change appreciably from year to year. The estimated annual cost, then, can be reliably estimated and should be apportioned equally to interim reporting periods.

Assume, for example, that property taxes are paid on June 30, and that we can reliably estimate the cost at $10,000 on a particular property. In the first quarter, we would accrue property tax expense as follows:

Property tax expense	2,500	
Property tax payable		2,500
(to accrue property tax expense for the quarter)		

On June 30, we record the payment as follows:

Prepaid property tax.	5,000	
Property tax expense	2,500	
Property tax payable	2,500	
Cash		10,000
(to record the payment of property tax and to recognize property tax expense for the quarter)		

And, on September 30 and December 31, we record property tax expense with the following entry:

Property tax expense	2,500	
Prepaid property tax		2,500
(to recognize property tax expense for the quarter)		

c. **Advertising costs** are paid to develop media that benefit the current and future periods. When paid, these costs are typically recorded as a prepaid asset. They are, subsequently, charged to expense when the prepaid asset is used up and the benefits of the advertising are realized. Even though the entire cost of the advertising may be recognized as an expense in the annual reporting period, that expense is allocated over the interim reporting periods that benefit from the expenditure.

To illustrate, assume that our company develops an advertising campaign for a product in February. The media will be aired in March and is expected to benefit sales of the product during the remainder of the year. The advertising cost would be reflected as expense in the second, third, and fourth quarters despite payment in the first quarter.

Year-End Adjustments

The amounts of certain costs and expenses are frequently subjected to year-end adjustments even though they can be reasonably approximated at interim dates. To the extent possible such adjustments should be estimated and the estimated costs and expenses assigned to interim periods so that the interim periods bear a reasonable portion of the anticipated annual amount. Examples of such items include inventory shrinkage, allowance for uncollectible accounts, allowance for quantity discounts, and discretionary year-end bonuses (FASB ASC 270-10-45-10).

For example, assume that our sales people are paid, in part, with a bonus commission of 5% of annual sales, provided that our total sales exceed $7.5 million for the year. In February, our sales people sell $1 million of product. Although we have not yet reached our $7.5 million in sales necessary to trigger the bonus commission, we expect that we will do so by year-end. As a result, we should accrue our bonus commission in this quarter. For the month of February, that accrual is as follows:

Bonus commission expense	50,000	
Bonus commission payable		50,000
(to accrue bonus commission expense for the month of February)		

Seasonal Variation

Revenues of certain businesses are subject to material seasonal variations. To avoid the possibility that interim results with material seasonal variations may be taken as fairly indicative of the estimated results for a full fiscal year, such businesses should disclose the seasonal nature of their activities, and consider supplementing their interim reports with information for twelve-month periods ended at the interim date for the current and preceding years (FASB ASC 270-10-45-11).

Tax preparation companies are typical of those that experience significant seasonal variation in sales and profit. For example, **Intuit, Inc.**, the developer and marketer of TurboTax tax preparation software, and Quicken (personal) and QuickBooks (business) financial software, makes the following disclosure in its 2014 10-K:

> **Seasonality**
>
> Historically, our QuickBooks, Consumer Tax, and Professional Tax offerings have been highly seasonal. Revenue from our QuickBooks desktop software products has tended to be highest during our second and third fiscal quarters. Sales of income tax preparation products and services are heavily concentrated from November through April. In our Consumer Tax business, a greater proportion of our revenue has shifted to later in this seasonal period due in part to the growth in sales of TurboTax Online, for which we recognize revenue when tax returns are printed or electronically filed... We typically report losses in our first quarter ending October 31 and fourth quarter ending July 31. During these quarters, revenue from our tax businesses is minimal while core operating expenses such as research and development continue at relatively consistent levels.

Income Tax Expense

Treating the interim period as an integral part of the annual reporting period also affects the accrual of tax expense in an interim period. Companies that experience seasonality in their sales, such as retailers that report a significant proportion of their sales in the fourth quarter or manufacturers that produce well in advance of a single selling season, may report lower levels of earnings, or even losses, in an interim period. The question arises whether to accrue estimated taxes at a lower rate to reflect the lower level of profit.

APB 28 requires companies to estimate the effective tax rate expected to be applicable for the *full fiscal year*, and to use that rate in providing for income taxes in an interim period (FASB ASC 740-270-25-2). Further, the effective tax rate should reflect anticipated investment tax credits, foreign tax rates, percentage depletion, capital gains rates, and other available tax planning alternatives, but should not take into account significant unusual items that will be separately reported or reported net of their related tax effect in reports for the interim period or for the fiscal year.[5,6]

To illustrate, assume that our company reports pretax income for the quarter of $100,000. This is typically a low-profit quarter for us, and we estimate that taxable income will be $800,000 for the year. We also expect to be eligible for tax credits of $50,000 that will reduce our required tax payment by

---

[5] The tax effects of losses that arise in the early portion of a fiscal year should be recognized only when the tax benefits are expected to be (a) realized during the year or (b) recognizable as a deferred tax asset at the end of the year in accordance with the provisions of SFAS 109, "Accounting for Income Taxes" (APB 28, ¶20).

[6] The tax effect of a valuation allowance expected to be necessary for a deferred tax asset at the end of the year for originating deductible temporary differences and carryforwards during the year should be included in the effective tax rate (APB 28, ¶21).

that amount. Our estimated tax liability for the year, based on a statutory federal corporate tax rate of 35% and average state tax rates (net of the federal tax credit) of 2.5%, is as follows:

Estimated annual taxable income	$800,000
Tax rate of 37.5% . . . . ×	0.375
	$300,000
Tax credit	50,000
Net tax liability	$250,000
÷ Taxable income . . . . ÷	$800,000
Percent of taxable income	31.25%

Based on our estimate of a 31.25% effective tax rate for the year, we should accrue $31,250 ($100,000 × 31.25%) of income tax expense for the quarter. The anticipated reduction of our effective tax rate, as a result of anticipated tax credits to be received in the fourth quarter, should be accrued during the year in our interim income statements.[7]

Changes to Accounting Principles and Estimates

In order to maintain comparability of the financial information across interim reporting periods, the FASB recommends that companies adopt any accounting changes during the first interim period of a fiscal year.

Whenever a change in accounting principles is made, SFAS 154, "Accounting Changes and Error Corrections," requires that the change be made retrospectively (i.e., financial statements for each individual prior period presented shall be adjusted to reflect the period-specific effects of applying the new accounting principle), with a cumulative adjustment to the beginning balance of assets and liabilities affected by the change in the earliest period reported, and an offsetting adjustment to Retained Earnings (FASB ASC 250-10-45-5). When a change in accounting principle is made in an interim period, the effect of the change on prior interim periods should be made retrospectively by adjusting each prior interim financial statement for the effects of the change (FASB ASC 250-10-45-14).[8]

Changes in accounting *estimates* are different from changes in accounting *principles*. These changes might include, for example, a change in the estimated balance of uncollected accounts receivable. The change in estimate is only accounted for prospectively (i.e., subsequent to the date of the change). No retrospective changes are made to previously issued interim or annual financial statements.

Interim Financial Statements Disclosures

As we discuss in the introduction to this section of the chapter, the SEC's reporting requirements for interim financial statements are sparse, only requiring major captions in the statements and omitting most footnote disclosures. The disclosure requirements for interim financial reports under APB 28,

---

[7] This also applies to losses reported in an interim period if profitability for the annual period is expected. FIN 18, "Accounting for Income Taxes in Interim Periods, an interpretation of APB Opinion No. 28," provides for the accrual of a tax *credit* to offset interim period losses, provided that it is "more likely than not" (i.e., greater than 50% probability) that the tax benefit will be received (FIN 18, ¶11). For example, if our company reports a pretax loss of $100,000, and we expect the company to be profitable for the year with an effective tax rate of 31.25%, we would report net income as follows:

Pretax loss	$(100,000)
Tax credit	31,250
Net loss	$ (68,750)

[8] When retrospective application to prior interim periods is impracticable, the desired change can only be made as of the beginning of a subsequent fiscal year (FASB ASC 250-10-45-14).

although greater than under Regulation S-X, are not as detailed as those for annual financial reports. Following are ASC 270-10-50-1 required disclosures for interim financial statements:

a. Income statement items:
1. Sales or gross revenues,
2. Provision for income taxes,
3. Net income,
4. Comprehensive income,
5. Basic and diluted earnings per share.

b. Footnote discussions of
1. Seasonal revenue, costs, or expenses
2. Significant changes in estimates or provisions for income taxes,
3. Disposal of a component of an entity and other unusual or infrequently occurring items,
4. Contingent items,
5. Changes in accounting principles or estimates, and
6. Significant changes in financial position.

c. The following information about reportable operating segments:
1. Revenues from external customers,
2. Intersegment revenues,
3. A measure of segment profit or loss,
4. Total assets for which there has been a material change from the amount disclosed in the last annual report,
5. A description of differences from the last annual report in the basis of segmentation or in the measurement of segment profit or loss, and
6. A reconciliation of the total of the reportable segments' measures of profit or loss to the company's consolidated income before income taxes and discontinued operations.

d. The following information about defined benefit pension plans and other defined benefit postretirement benefit plans:
1. The amount of net periodic benefit cost recognized, for each period for which a statement of income is presented, showing separately the service cost component, the interest cost component, the expected return on plan assets for the period, the gain or loss component, the prior service cost or credit component, the transition asset or obligation component, and the gain or loss recognized due to a settlement or curtailment, and
2. The total amount of the employer's contributions paid, and expected to be paid, during the current fiscal year.

e. The information about the use of fair value to measure assets and liabilities.

When summarized financial data are regularly reported on a quarterly basis, the foregoing information with respect to the current quarter and the current year-to-date or the last twelve months to date should be furnished together with comparable data for the preceding year.

Following is the 3M third quarter interim income statement for Q3 2014:

(in millions)	Three Months Ended September 30,		Nine Months Ended September 30,	
	2014	2013	2014	2013
Net sales...	$8,137	$7,916	$24,102	$23,302
Operating expenses				
Cost of sales....................................	4,205	4,148	12,420	12,130
Selling, general and administrative expenses	1,597	1,609	4,875	4,808
Research, development and related expenses	434	420	1,334	1,277
Total operating expenses	6,236	6,177	18,629	18,215
Operating income.................................	1,901	1,739	5,473	5,087
Interest expense and income				
Interest expense................................	28	33	110	113
Interest income.................................	(7)	(10)	(25)	(30)
Total interest expense—net.....................	21	23	85	83
Income before income taxes	1,880	1,716	5,388	5,004
Provision for income taxes.........................	569	471	1,569	1,399
Net income including noncontrolling interest.............	1,311	1,245	3,819	3,605
Less: Net income attributable to noncontrolling interest	8	15	42	49
Net income attributable to 3M	$1,303	$1,230	$ 3,777	$ 3,556

CHAPTER SUMMARY

The **management approach** for segment disclosures requires disclosures for the same business units that are routinely reported to senior management. The components of the business that are defined under the management approach are called **operating segments**: a component of a public entity that has all of the following characteristics:

a.   It engages in business activities from which it may earn revenues and incur expenses (including revenues and expenses relating to transactions with other components of the same public entity).

b.   Its operating results are regularly reviewed by the public entity's chief operating decision maker to make decisions about resources to be allocated to the segment and assess its performance.

c.   Its discrete financial information is available.

Once an operating segment has been identified with the criteria presented above, it must be disclosed in the footnotes if it meets *any one* of the following three quantitative thresholds based on revenues, profit, and assets:

a.   Its reported revenue, including both sales to external customers and intersegment sales or transfers, is 10 percent or more of the combined revenue, internal and external, of all operating segments.

b.   The absolute amount of its reported profit or loss is 10 percent or more of the greater, in absolute amount, of either:
    1.   The combined reported profit of all operating segments that did not report a loss.
    2.   The combined reported loss of all operating segments that did report a loss.

c.   Its assets are 10 percent or more of the combined assets of all operating segments.

The total external revenue reported by operating segments must constitute at least 75% of total consolidated revenue.

The company must disclose the following information for each operating segment and for all comparative years presented in the financial statements:

1. General information:
    a.   Factors used to identify the company's reportable segments
    b.   Types of products and services from which each reportable segment derives its revenues

2. Required financial data:
 a. Profit or loss
 b. Total assets

The segment disclosure must also include reconciliations of the segment totals to the consolidated financial statements. In addition to the financial disclosures presented above, companies must also provide the following disclosures relating to the geographical concentration of revenues and assets in the U.S. and outside of the U.S.:

a. Revenues from external customers

b. Long-lived assets other than financial instruments

Companies must also disclose information about the extent of their reliance on major customers if revenues from transactions with a single external customer amount to 10% or more of the company's total revenues.

Regarding interim financial reporting, the overriding philosophy of ASC 270 is that *each interim period should be viewed primarily as an integral part of an annual period.* Further, companies should employ the same accounting principles for interim statements that they use for their annual reports. And, since users of interim reports typically focus on the current quarter compared with the same quarter of the previous year, companies cannot adjust their revenue and expense recognition policy in order to achieve favorable year-over-year comparisons even though sales and net income for the year as a whole would not be affected.

Inventories

a. *Estimated Gross Profit*—ASC 270 permits companies to use estimated gross profit rates, or other reasonable methods, to determine the cost of goods sold during interim periods.

b. *LIFO Liquidations, Lower of Cost or Market, and Standard Cost Systems*—LIFO liquidation should <u>not</u> be recognized if the company expects the inventory layer giving rise to the liquidation profit to be replaced. In that case, the cost of sales for the interim reporting period should include the expected cost of replacement of the liquidated LIFO base.

c. *Lower of Cost or Market*—If the decline in the market value of the inventory is expected to be restored by year-end, the decline is not recognized at the interim date since no loss is expected to be incurred in the fiscal year.

d. *Standard Cost Accounting Systems*—If purchase price variances or volume or capacity cost variances are planned and expected to be absorbed by the end of the annual period, the company should not recognize the cost of the variance in the interim reporting period. If the purchase price or volume variance is unplanned or unexpected, however, the cost should be reported in the interim period.

Costs Benefitting More than One Period When a cost that is expensed for annual reporting purposes clearly benefits two or more interim periods, each interim period should be charged for an appropriate portion of the annual cost by the use of accruals or deferrals

Year-End Adjustments To the extent possible such adjustments should be estimated and the estimated costs and expenses assigned to interim periods so that the interim periods bear a reasonable portion of the anticipated annual amount.

Seasonal Variation Businesses should disclose the seasonal nature of their activities, and consider supplementing their interim reports with information for twelve-month periods ended at the interim date for the current and preceding years.

Income Tax Expense APB 28 requires companies to estimate the effective tax rate expected to be applicable for the *full fiscal year*, and to use that rate in providing for income taxes in an interim period.

Changes to Accounting Principles and Estimates Whenever a change in accounting principles is made, SFAS 154 requires that the change be made retrospectively, with a cumulative adjustment to the beginning balance of assets and liabilities affected by the change in the earliest period reported, and an offsetting adjustment to Retained Earnings. When a change in accounting principle is made in an interim period, the effect of the change on prior interim periods should be made retrospectively by adjusting each prior interim financial statement for the effects of the change.

COMPREHENSIVE REVIEW

Part 1: Our company has 5 business units that we classify as operating segments. Financial data for these units follows:

($1,000s)	A	B	C	D	E
Sales..............................	$ 5,000	$250	$1,500	$ 4,000	$3,000
Profit..............................	2,500	50	(1,500)	(100)	500
Assets.............................	15,000	500	5,000	10,000	2,500

Which of these operating segments should be disclosed in the footnotes to our financial statements?

Part 2: Describe the required accounting treatment for each of the following scenarios:

a. Based on the anticipated annual purchases, our customer will be eligible for a 2% sales discount, but its purchases in this quarter do not qualify for such a discount.
b. At the beginning of the year, we estimate that we will receive a property tax bill in the amount of $100,000 relating to our corporate headquarters.
c. During the quarter, we incur costs to develop an advertising campaign that we expect to be aired in the next quarter and benefit the next and following quarters.
d. We estimate that our sales people will achieve the annual level of sales needed to realize a 3% bonus commission, but they do not achieve that level of sales during the quarter or year-to-date.
e. This is typically a loss quarter for us, but we anticipate taxable income for the year and an expected effective tax rate of 30%.
f. We have experienced a decline in inventory quantities during the period that results in a LIFO liquidation gain.
g. We have changed the way we account for an item and don't know how that change should be reported.

The solution to this review problem can be found on page 717.

QUESTIONS

1. Why are analysts interested in segment disclosures?
2. Describe what is meant by the "management approach" to the disclosure of operating segments.
3. How is an operating segment defined?
4. Describe the quantitative thresholds that dictate whether an operating segment must be separately disclosed in the footnotes.
5. Under what conditions can two or more operating segments be aggregated for purposes of disclosure?
6. Describe the "once in—always in" provision of SFAS 131.
7. Describe, in general, the types of information that must be disclosed for each operating segment separately disclosed.
8. Describe the overriding philosophy for interim financial reporting.
9. Are companies allowed to estimate inventories and gross profit for interim financial statements?
10. Inventories are generally reported at the lower of cost or market. How is this rule implemented for interim financial statements?
11. Describe, in general, the way in which costs that benefit more than one interim reporting period should be handled.
12. Describe the accrual of income taxes for interim reporting periods.
13. Why does APB 18 require companies to disclose the seasonal nature of their business?
14. Describe how the changes to accounting principles are handled for interim reporting periods.
15. Describe, in general, the required disclosures for interim financial reports.

Assignments with the logo in the margin are available in BusinessCourse.
See the Preface of the book for details.

MULTIPLE CHOICE

16. Disclosure about external customers

Which of the following is a required disclosure regarding external customers?

a.   The name of the customer(s)

b.   The dollar amount of sales to the customer(s)

c.   The fact that transactions with the customer(s) constitute more than 10% of total revenues

d.   Information on major customers is not required in segment reporting

17. Reporting inventory losses in interim financial statements

Assume that your company determines that the value of its inventories have declined in the second quarter, but you assume that the market price will return to previous levels by the end of the year so that no loss will be recognized. At the end of the year, however, the market price reversal did not occur. When should the loss be reported in your company's interim income statements?

a.   Ratably over the second, third, and fourth quarters

b.   Ratably over the third and fourth quarters

c.   In the second quarter only

d.   In the fourth quarter only

18. Determination of reportable operating segments

Which of the following operating segments should be identified as a reportable segment given the information below?

Segment	Operating Profit (Loss)
A.......	$ 45,000
B.......	(50,000)
C.......	450,000
D.......	(200,000)

a.   C

b.   C and D

c.   B, C and D

d.   A, B, C, and D

19. Determination of reportable operating segments

Selected data for an operating segment of a business are to be separately reported when the revenue of the segment exceeds 10% of the:

a.   Combined net income of all segments reporting profits

b.   Total revenue from unaffiliated transactions

c.   Total revenue of all the entity's operating segments

d.   Separate tests for combined revenue from all segments reporting profits and losses

20. Determination of reportable operating segments

Which of the following is not one of the factors to consider in determining whether a business entity meets the definition of a reportable segment:

a.   It engages in business activities from which it may earn revenues and incur expenses.

b.   It engages in sales activities with unaffiliated entities.

c.   Its operating results are regularly reviewed by the entity's chief operating decision maker.

d.   Its discrete financial information is available.

21. Determination of reportable operating segments

Two or more operating segments may be aggregated into a single operating segment if the segments have similar economic characteristics, *and* if the segments are similar. Which of the following is not one of the factors used to determine similarity?

a.   Employment of many of the same people across the segments

b.   The nature of the products and services

c.   The nature of the production processes

d.   The type or class of customer for their products and services

LO2   22. **Accounting for inventories in interim financial statements**

Which of the following is *not true* regarding the treatment of inventories in interim financial statements:

     a.   Companies may not take a physical inventory other than at year-end.

     b.   LIFO liquidation should not be recognized if the company expects the inventory layer giving rise to the liquidation profit to be replaced.

     c.   Companies should always recognize the cost of the variances in the interim reporting period.

     d.   In the lower of cost or market test, if the decline in the market value of the inventory is expected to be *restored* by year-end, the decline is not recognized at the interim date.

LO2   23. **Accounting for costs that benefit more than one interim reporting period**

Which of the following is *not true* regarding the recognition of costs that benefit more than one interim reporting period?

     a.   Costs are generally recognized as expenses in the periods in which they are incurred.

     b.   The cost of quantity discounts should be recognized in the interim period, even if the annual purchase level has not yet been made if the company expects that the annual sales volume will be sufficient for the customer to receive the discount.

     c.   The estimated annual cost of property taxes that can be reliably estimated should be apportioned equally to interim reporting periods.

     d.   Even though the entire cost of advertising may be recognized as an expense in the annual reporting period, that expense is allocated over the interim reporting periods that benefit from the expenditure.

LO2   24. **Recording the effects of accounting changes**

Which of the following is *true* with respect to "accounting changes"?

     a.   Companies only record the effects of the change in accounting principles in the annual financial statements.

     b.   SFAS 154 requires that the change in accounting principles be made only in the most recent year presented in the comparative financial statements, with a cumulative adjustment to the beginning balance of assets and liabilities affected by the change in the earliest period reported, and an offsetting adjustment to Retained Earnings for that year.

     c.   The effects of changes in accounting principles are reflected only prospectively from the date of the change.

     d.   SFAS 154 requires that the change in accounting principles be made retrospectively, with a cumulative adjustment to the beginning balance of assets and liabilities affected by the change in the earliest period reported, and an offsetting adjustment to Retained Earnings.

EXERCISES

LO1   25. **Determination of an operating segment**

Our company has three business units, and you need to decide whether to classify them as operating segments that should be separately disclosed in the footnotes to your financial statements.

     a.   Our Research and Development unit is regularly reviewed by the CEO who reviews its costs on a regular basis. The unit has no revenues, however. It is only a cost center.

     b.   Our export company maintains a branch office in Paris, France. Our CEO regularly reviews the financial statements of the export company, including its revenues and expenses and its balance sheet, but the branch office is not reported separately.

     c.   Is the export company in part b an operating segment?

LO1   26. **Quantitative thresholds for classification as an operating segment**

Our company has 5 business units that we classify as operating segments. Financial data for these units follows:

($1,000s)	A	B	C	D	E
Sales.	$ 621	$ 853	$1,237	$2,832	$4,720
Profit.	103	(218)	832	1,337	(583)
Assets.	1,200	2,780	2,324	4,280	8,321

Which of these operating segments should be disclosed in the footnotes to our financial statements?

27. Quantitative thresholds for classification as an operating segment

Our company has 5 business units that we classify as operating segments. Financial data for these units follows:

($ millions)	A	B	C	D	E
Sales.................	$ 13,200	$241,300	$ 852,373	$1,538,317	$ 3,470,833
Profit.................	2,327	(5,738)	23,833	37,533	580,833
Assets.................	231,837	588,333	5,458,332	2,837,334	12,327,833

Which of these operating segments should be disclosed in the footnotes to our financial statements?

28. LIFO liquidation in an interim reporting period

Assume that our records include the following two LIFO inventory cost pools:

	Units	Cost/Unit
BOQ	600	$20
Purchase #1	800	$30
	1,400	

At the beginning of the quarter (BOQ), we report 600 units on hand at a cost of $20 per unit. During the quarter, we sell 1,000 units at $60/unit for cash. Assume that we expect to increase our quantities of inventories on hand by year-end by the purchase of inventories at a cost of $40.

  a. Compute the gross profit we should recognize on the sales during the quarter.

  b. Prepare the required journal entries to record the sales.

  c. What adjusting entry will be required at year-end if the planned replacement of the inventories does not occur?

29. Costs benefitting more than one interim reporting period

Describe the required accounting treatment for each of the following scenarios:

  a. Our customer purchases $500,000 of product from us this quarter and we expect its annual purchases to be $3,000,000. Based on the anticipated annual purchases, our customer will be eligible for a 2% sales discount.

  b. At the beginning of the year, we estimate that we will receive a property tax bill in the amount of $30,000 relating to our corporate headquarters.

  c. During the quarter, we incur costs to develop an advertising campaign that we expect to be aired in the next quarter and benefit the next and following quarters.

  d. We estimate that our sales people will achieve the annual level of sales needed to realize a 3% bonus commission. During the quarter, they report $1 million in sales.

30. Accrual of tax liability for an interim reporting period

Assume that our company reports pretax income for the quarter of $500,000. This is typically a low profit quarter for us, and we estimate that taxable income will be $4,000,000 for the year. We also expect to be eligible for tax credits of $180,000 that will reduce our required tax payment by that amount.

  a. Compute the estimated effective tax rate for the year assuming a statutory federal and state combined rate of 37.5%.

  b. Prepare the required journal entry to accrue tax liability for the interim period.

PROBLEMS

31. Analysis of segment disclosure footnote

The Walt Disney Company identifies five operating segments. Following are excerpts from the description provided in the company's 2014 10-K:

THE WALT
DISNEY
COMPANY

> The Walt Disney Company, together with its subsidiaries, is a diversified worldwide entertainment company with operations in five business segments: Media Networks, Parks and Resorts, Studio Entertainment, Consumer Products, and Interactive.

MEDIA NETWORKS The Media Networks segment includes broadcast and cable television networks, television production operations, television distribution, domestic television stations and radio networks and stations.

PARKS AND RESORTS The Company owns and operates the Walt Disney World Resort in Florida, the Disneyland Resort in California, Aulani, a Disney Resort & Spa in Hawaii, the Disney Vacation Club, the Disney Cruise Line and Adventures by Disney. The Company manages and has effective ownership interests . . . in Disneyland Paris, in Hong Kong Disneyland Resort and in Shanghai Disney Resort. The Company also licenses the operations of the Tokyo Disney Resort in Japan. The Company's Walt Disney Imagineering unit designs and develops new theme park concepts and attractions as well as resort properties.

STUDIO ENTERTAINMENT The Studio Entertainment segment produces and acquires live-action and animated motion pictures, direct-to-video content, musical recordings and live stage plays.

CONSUMER PRODUCTS The Consumer Products segment engages with licensees, publishers and retailers throughout the world to design, develop, publish, promote and sell a wide variety of products based on the Company's intellectual property through its Merchandise Licensing, Publishing and Retail businesses. In addition to using the Company's film and television properties, Consumer Products also develops its own intellectual property, which can be used across the Company's businesses.

INTERACTIVE The Interactive segment creates and delivers branded entertainment and lifestyle content across interactive media platforms. Interactive's primary operations include the production and global distribution of multi-platform games, the licensing of content for games and mobile devices, website management and design for other Company businesses and the development of branded online services.

The segment footnote in The Walt Disney Company 2014 annual report follows (in millions):

SEGMENT INFORMATION

The operating segments reported below are the segments of the Company for which separate financial information is available and for which segment results are evaluated regularly by the Chief Executive Officer in deciding how to allocate resources and in assessing performance.

	2014	2013	2012
Revenues			
Media Networks	$21,152	$20,356	$19,436
Parks and Resorts	15,099	14,087	12,920
Studio Entertainment			
Third parties	6,988	5,721	5,566
Intersegment	290	258	259
	7,278	5,979	5,825
Consumer Products			
Third parties	4,274	3,811	3,499
Intersegment	(289)	(256)	(247)
	3,985	3,555	3,252
Interactive			
Third parties	1,300	1,066	857
Intersegment	(1)	(2)	(12)
	1,299	1,064	845
Total consolidated revenues	$48,813	$45,041	$42,278

continued

	2014	2013	2012
Segment operating income (loss)			
Media Networks	$ 7,321	$ 6,818	$ 6,619
Parks and Resorts	2,663	2,220	1,902
Studio Entertainment	1,549	661	722
Consumer Products	1,356	1,112	937
Interactive	116	(87)	(216)
Total segment operating income	$13,005	$10,724	$ 9,964
Reconciliation of segment operating income to income before income taxes			
Segment operating income	$13,005	$10,724	$ 9,964
Corporate and unallocated shared expenses.	(611)	(531)	(474)
Restructuring and impairment charges	(140)	(214)	(100)
Other income/(expense), net	(31)	(69)	239
Interest income/(expense), net	23	(235)	(369)
Hulu equity redemption charge	—	(55)	—
Income before income taxes.	$12,246	$ 9,620	$ 9,260
Capital expenditures			
Media Networks			
Cable Networks.	$ 172	$ 176	$ 170
Broadcasting.	88	87	85
Parks and Resorts			
Domestic.	1,184	1,140	2,242
International	1,504	970	641
Studio Entertainment	63	78	79
Consumer Products	43	45	69
Interactive	5	13	27
Corporate	252	287	471
Total capital expenditures.	$ 3,311	$ 2,796	$ 3,784
Depreciation expense			
Media Networks	$ 238	$ 238	$ 241
Parks and Resorts			
Domestic.	1,117	1,041	927
International	353	327	314
Studio Entertainment	48	54	48
Consumer Products	59	57	55
Interactive	10	20	17
Corporate	239	220	182
Total depreciation expense	$ 2,064	$ 1,957	$ 1,784
Amortization of intangible assets			
Media Networks	$ 12	$ 13	$ 17
Parks and Resorts	2	2	—
Studio Entertainment	88	107	94
Consumer Products	109	89	60
Interactive	13	24	32
Corporate	—	—	—
Total amortization of intangible assets	$ 224	$ 235	$ 203
Identifiable assets			
Media Networks	$29,887	$28,627	
Parks and Resorts	23,335	22,056	
Studio Entertainment	15,155	14,750	
Consumer Products	7,526	7,506	
Interactive	2,259	2,311	
Corporate	6,024	5,991	
Total consolidated assets	$84,186	$81,241	

a. Confirm that each of Disney's segments exceeds one or more of the quantitative thresholds.

b. Using the breakdown of revenues and profit by segment, rank Disney's operating segments by the proportion of profit contributed in relation to its proportion of revenues.

c. Compute a rough DuPont analysis over the past three years of the operating segments (i.e., profit/ revenues, revenues/total assets, and return on assets as the product of the profit and turnover ratios). Discuss.

d. Compute the free cash flow for each operating segment over the three-year period using the following definition: free cash flow = operating profit + depreciation and amortization − capital expenditures. Discuss.

e. Summarize your conclusions about the financial performance of Disney's operating segments. What would you focus on in your analysis of future financial reports for the company?

TOPIC REVIEW

Solution

a. FASB ASC 280-10-50-1 defines an **operating segment** as "a component of a public entity that has all of the following characteristics:

- It engages in business activities from which it may earn revenues and incur expenses (including revenues and expenses relating to transactions with other components of the same public entity).
- Its operating results are regularly reviewed by the public entity's chief operating decision maker to make decisions about resources to be allocated to the segment and assess its performance.
- Its discrete financial information is available."

b. Our quantitative threshold tests indicate that *all* of the subsidiaries should be designated as reportable segments.

						Quantitative Thresholds		
Segment Test	**A**	**B**	**C**	**D**	**E**		**Profit**	**Loss**
Sales	Yes	Yes	No	Yes	No	$ 770		
Profit	Yes	Yes	Yes	No	No		$160	—*
Assets	Yes	No	No	Yes	Yes	$1,400		

*The threshold for the loss is not used since the absolute value of the profit threshold is higher.

The quantitative threshold for sales and assets is 10% of the total. For sales, the threshold is $770 ([$1,000 + $5,000 + $300 + $800 + $600] × 10%). Segments A, B, and D exceed the threshold based on sales. For assets, the threshold is $1,400 ([$3,000 + $1,000 + $1,000 + $2,000 + $7,000] × 10%). Segments A, D, and E exceed the threshold based on assets.

For the profit threshold, the segments must be divided into those reporting profits and those reporting losses. The threshold for the profitable segments is 10% of the sum of the profit for all profitable segments, or $160 ([$500 + $1,000 + $100] × 10%). The threshold for the loss segments is 10% of the sum of the losses for all loss segments, or $(32) ([$(300) + $(20)] × 10%). Since the absolute value of the profitable segments exceeds that of the loss segments, we use the profitable segment threshold of $160, and segments A, B and C exceed that threshold.

To be separately disclosed, a segment need pass only one of the quantitative thresholds. In this example, all five subsidiaries should be separately disclosed.

COMPREHENSIVE REVIEW SOLUTION

Part 1

Segment Test	A	B	C	D	E	Quantitative Thresholds Revenues	Profit	Loss	Assets
Sales...............	Yes	No	Yes	Yes	Yes	$1,375			
Profit...............	Yes	No	Yes	No	Yes		$305	—*	
Assets..............	Yes	No	Yes	Yes	No				$3,300

*The threshold for the loss is not used since the absolute value of the profit threshold is higher.

Segments A, C, D and E are reportable segments.

Part 2

a. The cost of those discounts should be recognized in the interim period, even if the annual purchase level has not yet been made if the company expects that the annual sales volume will be sufficient for the customer to receive the discount.

b. If the estimated annual property tax cost can be reliably estimated, it should be apportioned equally to interim reporting periods.

c. The advertising expense is allocated over the interim reporting periods that benefit from the expenditure.

d. The bonus expense should be accrued if it is likely that our sales people will realize a bonus for the year and the amount and be reliably estimated.

e. APB 28 requires companies to estimate the effective tax rate expected to be applicable for the full fiscal year, and to use that rate in providing for income taxes in an interim period (FASB ASC 740-270-25-2).

f. Since each interim period should be viewed primarily as an integral part of an annual period, the LIFO liquidation should not be recognized if the company expects the inventory layer giving rise to the liquidation profit to be replaced. In that case, the cost of sales for the interim reporting period should include the expected cost of replacement of the liquidated LIFO base (FASB ASC 330-10-55-2).

g. Whenever a change in accounting principles is made, SFAS 154, "Accounting Changes and Error Corrections," requires that the change be made retrospectively (i.e., financial statements for each individual prior period presented shall be adjusted to reflect the period-specific effects of applying the new accounting principle), with a cumulative adjustment to the beginning balance of assets and liabilities affected by the change in the earliest period reported, and an offsetting adjustment to Retained Earnings (FASB ASC 250-10-45-5).

Accounting for Partnerships

Boardwalk Pipeline Partners, LP, is a Delaware master limited partnership formed in 2005. It operates in the midstream portion of the natural gas and NGLs industry, providing transportation, storage, gathering, and processing services for those commodities. It owns approximately 14,625 miles of natural gas and NGLs pipelines, and underground storage caverns having aggregate capacity of approximately 208 billion cubic feet (Bcf) of working natural gas and 17.6 million barrels (MMBbls) of NGLs. Its pipeline systems originate in the Gulf Coast region, Oklahoma, and Arkansas and extend north and east to the midwestern states of Tennessee, Kentucky, Illinois, Indiana, and Ohio. The partnership's common units are traded under the symbol "BWP" on the New York Stock Exchange.

BOARDWALK PIPELINE PARTNERS, LP

Although the company is publicly traded, it is not a corporation. Its ownership interests are called *common units*. As of December 31, 2014, Boardwalk had 243.3 million common units outstanding. A master limited partnership (MLP) is a limited partnership that is publicly traded on an exchange. It combines the tax benefits of a limited partnership with the liquidity of publicly traded securities. There are two types of partners in this type of partnership: The limited partner is the person or group that provides the capital to the MLP and receives periodic income distributions from the MLP's cash flow, whereas the general partner is the party responsible for managing the MLP's affairs and receives compensation that is linked to the performance of the venture.

A partnership is a legal entity that is required to issue financial statements. Although Boardwalk's income statement is like others that you have seen, the equity section of its balance sheet, as of December 31, 2014, is quite different (in millions):

Partners' capital:	
Common units—243.3 million units issued and	
outstanding as of December 31, 2014 and 2013	$4,095.1
General partner	80.0
Accumulated other comprehensive loss	(72.8)
Total partners' capital	$4,102.3

Unlike the Stockholders' Equity of a corporation, Boardwalk Pipeline Partners reports Total Partners' Capital. This account represents the claim of the partners to the net assets of the partnership.

There are a number of similarities and differences between the accounting for partnerships and the accounting for corporations. Although many partnerships employ accrual accounting, if the partnership is not a public entity, it can adopt any accounting method that its owners choose to adopt, just like any other private entity. In this chapter, we discuss the partnership form of organization and the accounting for partnerships.

Source: Boardwalk Pipeline Partners, LP 2014 10-K

Partnerships are a popular form of organization, especially with service organizations like accounting firms and law firms. They allow numerous individuals to combine their efforts for a variety of business purposes in an organization that can last indefinitely and can survive the admission of new partners and the disassociation of existing partners as they retire.

From a tax standpoint, the taxing authorities view the partnership as a conduit to pass through income directly to the partners. The partnership thus avoids the problem of double taxation that is present with the corporate form of organization. Partnerships also pass through liabilities to the partners. Individual partners can manage their potential liability, however, by varying the structure of the partnership and with insurance.

Partnerships are a legal entity and, as such, they must issue financial statements. Unlike Boardwalk Pipeline Partners, LP (i.e., the partnership described at the beginning of the chapter), however, most partnerships are private organizations. As a result, they are not necessarily required to issue financial statements that are prepared in conformity with GAAP, provided (1) that the partners agree to the use of non-GAAP accounting policies and (2) the providers of non-partner capital to the partnership (e.g., banks) agree to accept non-GAAP-basis financial statements.[1] For private partnerships, some of the most prominent departures from GAAP include the use of cash basis and modified-cash basis of accounting and the revaluation of assets and creation of Goodwill upon the admission of a new partner if such accounting is permitted by the Partnership Agreement.

This chapter describes the accounting for partnerships. We begin with a general discussion of the partnership form of organization and its governance. Next, we consider the accounting issues involved in the formation of the partnership, the admission of new partners, and the ongoing operation of the partnership. Finally, we consider the accounting issues related to the winding up of the partnership.

---

[1] Another difference between publicly traded partnerships, like Boardwalk Pipeline Partners, LP and private partnerships is that publicly traded partnerships are required by the Securities and Exchange Commission to obtain independent audits of their annual financial statements. For example, the audit opinion dated February 20, 2015, and signed by the Houston, Texas, office of Deloitte & Touche LLP can be found on page 99 of the 2014 Boardwalk Pipeline Partners, LP annual report. In contrast, private partnerships generally are not statutorily required to obtain audits or reviews of their financial statements. However, the partners and/or non-partner capital providers might require the partnership to obtain some form of attestation related to the financial statements. Partnerships can be audited even if their accounting policies do not conform to GAAP, but they cannot receive an unqualified audit opinion unless their financial statements are prepared in conformity with GAAP.

THE PARTNERSHIP FORM OF ORGANIZATION AND ITS GOVERNANCE

The Uniform Partnership Act (1997), drafted by the National Conference of Commissioners on Uniform State Laws, provides a model for partnership governance that has been adopted by a majority of states.[2] It defines a **partnership** as an association of two or more individuals to co-own and operate a business (UPA, §101).

LO1 Describe the partnership form of organization.

The formation, ongoing operation, and ultimate dissolution of the partnership are governed by a Partnership Agreement. This agreement is a contract between the partners and, as such, it can generally reflect whatever the partners agree to. For our purposes, it is important to note that the partnership agreement describes the accounting policies that the partnership will use to account for all aspects of the partnership's operations, including the determination of profit and loss and how that profit and loss is to be allocated to the partners' Capital Accounts (their equity in the partnership).

As we note in the introduction, partnerships are *not* required to use GAAP. If a partnership is not publicly traded, it can adopt whatever accounting policies that the partners agree to use, including the use of accrual accounting, cash basis accounting, or some hybrid approach. When accounting for the partnership or auditing the partnership's financial records, you must first become thoroughly familiar with the partnership's accounting policies. These accounting policies will define all of the accounting topics we discuss in the remainder of this chapter.

Partnership agreements also typically contain the following general provisions:

a. **Partnership entity.** The partnership is a legal entity separate from its partners. As such, the partnership can buy and sell assets, enter into contracts, and borrow money. Assets purchased and liabilities incurred are assets and liabilities of the partnership and are not owned or owed by the partners themselves (UPA §§201,203).

b. **Partners as agents of the partnership.** Each partner can act for the partnership. The Partnership Agreement may, however, specifically identify those partners that are authorized to transact business on behalf of the partnership. These limitations of authority are typically evidenced by a Statement of Partnership Authority that is filed in the public domain.[3]

c. **Partnership is liable for actions of partners.** A partnership is liable for loss as a result of a wrongful act or omission of a partner acting in the ordinary course of business of the partnership or with authority of the partnership (UPA §305).

d. **Joint and several liability of partners.** All partners are jointly and severally liable for all obligations of the partnership. This means that every partner is liable for the obligations of the partnership (UPA §306).[4] For example, if the partnership does not have sufficient assets to pay its debts, creditors may collect the amounts due from any one of the partners, or from any and all of the partners in various amounts until the obligation is paid in full. In other words, if any of the partners do not have enough assets to pay an equal share of the award, the other partners must make up the difference.

e. **Partner Capital Accounts.** Each partner has a Capital Account to represent his or her interest in the partnership (i.e., the claim against the net assets of the partnership). That Capital Account is credited for the initial contribution to the partnership and is increased (decreased) for the partner's share of the partnership profits (losses) and is decreased by any amounts withdrawn from the partnership (called "drawings"). This Capital Account is similar to the Retained Earnings account for a corporation.

---

[2] You can download a copy of this document from the following URL:
http://www.uniformlaws.org/shared/docs/partnership/upa_final_97.pdf

[3] Although a partner may have no authority to act on behalf of the partnership under the Partnership Agreement, that prohibition is not effective against outside parties unless they are so notified by the Statement of Partnership Authority or have reason to believe that the partner has no such authority (UPA §301).

[4] A person admitted as a partner into an existing partnership is not personally liable for any partnership obligation incurred before the person's admission as a partner (UPA §306).

f. **Transfer of partnership interest.** Each partner has the right to sell his or her partnership interest (i.e., the right to receive distributions from the partnership). The purchaser of such an interest does not have the right to participate in the management of the partnership, however, without the consent of the remaining partners (UPA §503).

One of the most significant aspects of the partnership form of organization relates to the liability of the partners for the debts of the partnership. In the listing above, we cite the joint and several liability of the partners for the partnership debts. This potential liability is often of great concern to partners who may find themselves liable for obligations created as a result of the actions of other partners over which they have no control.

To address this potential liability, many professional service organizations, such as law firms and public accounting firms, are organized as **limited liability partnerships** (abbreviated as LLP). The LLP has elements of both partnerships and corporations. In an LLP, all partners have a form of *limited* liability, similar to that of the shareholders of a corporation.[5] However, unlike corporate shareholders, the partners have the right to manage the business directly rather than through a board of directors. In addition to structuring the partnership as an LLP, professional service organizations also typically maintain a significant amount of malpractice insurance as additional protection.

We now turn to accounting issues at four stages of the partnership life cycle: formation, operation, realignment, and liquidation. We use the term, "accounting issues," loosely, because partnership accounting has very little to do with the traditional issues that are central to accounting theory (e.g., recognition, measurement, or classification). Instead, partnership accounting is better described as issues related to bookkeeping for partners' individual Capital Accounts. Indeed, for each of the four areas (i.e., formation, operation, realignment, and liquidation) we discuss, the most critical question is whether we have appropriately determined and allocated contributions, income, and/or distributions to the individual partner Capital Accounts. Thus, we view partnership accounting as more closely resembling partner-capital bookkeeping than most of the accounting issues included in intermediate and advanced financial accounting texts.

ACCOUNTING FOR THE FORMATION OF THE PARTNERSHIP

LO2 Describe the accounting for the formation of the partnership.

When forming the partnership, partners contribute assets to the partnership (the partnership may also assume liabilities, such as a mortgage on a building contributed to the partnership), and their respective Capital Accounts are credited to represent their claim to the net assets of the partnership. Assets contributed and liabilities assumed are initially recorded at fair value based on valuations performed upon formation of the partnership.[6] Although the total credit to the Capital Accounts must equal the fair value of the assets contributed less liabilities assumed (to preserve the accounting equation), the Capital Account for an *individual* partner does not need to be equal to (or even proportional to) the value of the net assets he or she contributes. The initial values of the Capital Accounts are determined by the Partnership Agreement, and the partners can agree to any allocation they wish.

To illustrate, assume that Jack and Jill agree to form a partnership. Jack has operated a business as a sole proprietor for many years, and will contribute the net assets of his business to the partnership. Exhibit 13.1 presents the appraised value of the net assets of Jack's business.

---

[5] **Limited Partnerships (LPs)** have at least one general partner and a number of limited partners. The general partner is personally liable for the partnership's obligations and has management authority. The liability of the limited partners is limited to their capital contribution and they have no management authority. This form of organization addressed the liability issue and was popular until the rise of limited liability partnership (LLPs), which address the liability issue *and* also give the limited partners management authority. They are, thus, better suited for service organizations like accounting and law firms.

[6] Tangible assets can be valued using a variety of approaches, such as net realizable value for accounts receivables, market value for inventories, and appraised value for PPE. Current liabilities are typically recorded at book value. Intangible assets and long-term liabilities are valued at the present value of future cash receipts (payments).

EXHIBIT 13.1	Appraised Value of the Net Assets of Jack's Business		
Cash	$ 5,000	Accounts payable	$10,000
Receivables	10,000	Accrued liabilities	20,000
Inventories	25,000	Mortgage payable	30,000
Property, plant and equipment, (PPE)	80,000	Total liabilities	$60,000
Total assets	$120,000	Net assets	$60,000

Jill is contributing **$40,000** in cash to the partnership and her marketing expertise.

If Jack and Jill agree that their respective Capital Accounts should reflect the fair value of their contributions, the journal entry to record the contributions is as follows:

Cash	45,000	
Receivables	10,000	
Inventories	25,000	
Property, plant and equipment, (PPE)	80,000	
Accounts payable		10,000
Accrued liabilities		20,000
Mortgage payable		30,000
Jack capital		60,000
Jill capital		40,000
(to record initial capital contribution to the Jack and Jill Partnership)		

The debit to Cash reflects the total cash contributed ($5,000 from Jack's business and $40,000 by Jill), and the other assets and liabilities are recorded by the partnership at their appraised values. As we stated previously, however, the initial partner Capital Accounts need not be equal to (or even proportional to) the value of the net assets contributed by each partner. The partners can agree to any amount of net asset contribution by each partner, and can agree to any level of capital credit for the contribution.

In recording the formation of the partnership, when partners are assigned balances that do not equal their capital contributions, the partners must answer the following two questions:

1. Does the disproportionate capital contribution by one or more partners provide evidence that the newly formed partnership possesses an unrecognized intangible asset?

2. Then, if the answer to question 1 is "yes," do the partners wish to recognize the intangible asset on the books of the partnership?

If the answer to *either* of the foregoing questions is "no," then the partnership will apply the Bonus Method (described below) to allocate the total partnership capital into the partners' individual Capital Accounts. If the answers to *both* of the foregoing questions are "yes," then the partnership will apply the Goodwill Method (described below) to allocate the total partnership capital into the partners' individual Capital Accounts. While these two methods might appear to be different on the surface, they are actually quite similar.

The biggest difference between the Bonus and Goodwill Methods is that the Bonus Method only records the identifiable net assets contributed by the partners in the partnership's total net assets. In contrast, under the Goodwill Method, the total partnership net assets include the identifiable net assets contributed by the partners (i.e., same amount as the Bonus Method), *plus* an additional amount assigned to Goodwill (or some other implied intangible asset). Under both methods, however, the goal of the partnership formation process is to allocate the total partnership capital among the partners forming the partnership.

To illustrate this point, let's look at our initial partnership-formation example, with a few slight modifications. Specifically, assume that Jack places considerable value on Jill's marketing knowledge and the partners agree that Jill should receive a 50% (rather than 40%) capital interest upon formation of the partnership. We will also assume that either the partners don't believe that the disproportionate partnership interest awarded to Jill provides evidence of a partnership-specific intangible asset or they simply don't want to record the intangible asset that they believe Jill brings to the partnership.

Since the answer to *either* of the foregoing questions is "no," then the partnership applies the Bonus Method to allocate the total partnership capital into the partners' individual Capital Accounts. The partnership formation journal entry looks much like the previous entry, except for the amount credited to the partners' Capital Accounts:

Cash...	45,000	
Receivables	10,000	
Inventories	25,000	
Property, plant and equipment, (PPE)	80,000	
Accounts payable		10,000
Accrued liabilities.................................		20,000
Mortgage payable		30,000
Jack Capital......................................		50,000
Jill Capital		50,000

(to record initial capital contribution to the Jack and Jill Partnership, assuming that Jill receives a 50% capital interest and the partners apply the Bonus Method)

The reason this approach is called the **Bonus Method** is because Jill is effectively receiving compensation from Jack in exchange for Jill bringing her marketing knowledge to the partnership. That is, Jill contributed only $40,000 of the partnership's $100,000 of net assets, but is receiving capital credit equal to 50% (i.e., $50,000) of the net assets. Given that partnership agreements are enforceable legal contracts, a very real wealth exchange occurred on the date of formation. Jill now has a right to 50% of the undivided net assets of the partnership, and assuming that the net assets could all be liquidated for their book values, Jill has a right to a $50,000 liquidating payment if the partnership legally dissolved the moment after formation. In other words, Jill received a *de facto* bonus of $10,000 (i.e., $50,000 − $40,000) for joining the partnership.

In contrast, the **Goodwill Method** is based on the philosophy that Jill's disproportionate capital credit allocation could be viewed as evidence that the new Jack and Jill Partnership has a contributed intangible asset that is not included in the $100,000 of identifiable net assets. In particular, we can infer the value of the entire partnership entity (and the implied value of the intangible asset) if we believe the formation contributions by the two partners are independent, legitimate "arm's-length" transactions.[7] Given the foregoing facts, the overall value of the partnership can be estimated as $120,000 (i.e., $60,000 ÷ 50%) based on Jack's contribution.[8] And, the implied Goodwill asset in the partnership is computed to be $20,000 as follows:

Fair value of the Jack and Jill Partnership	$120,000
Less: Fair value of the identifiable net assets	(100,000)
Implied value of the Goodwill asset	$ 20,000

Given the appraised values of the identifiable assets and liabilities and the implied fair value of the Goodwill asset, the journal entry to record the formation of the partnership under the Goodwill Method follows:

---

[7] As with most financial accounting courses, we assume that all exchanges are the result of independent, legitimate "arm's-length" transactions, unless we explicitly indicate otherwise.

[8] We base the implied overall value on Jack's contribution for two reasons. First, the example's original facts indicate that Jill is bringing valuable skills to the partnership (i.e., marketing knowledge) and is being granted additional capital credit in lieu of contributing additional identifiable net assets. Second, as a practical matter, basing the overall entity value on Jill's contribution of identifiable net assets makes no sense. Based on Jill's contribution, the implied total partnership value is equal to $80,000 (i.e., $40,000 ÷ 50%). This amount is $20,000 lower than the contributed identifiable net assets of the partnership (i.e., $100,000). Thus, under the Goodwill Method, we typically assume that each of the partners receives a Capital Account credit that is at least equal to their identifiable net asset contributions.

Cash...	45,000	
Receivables..	10,000	
Inventories..	25,000	
Property, plant and equipment, (PPE)...................	80,000	
Goodwill...	20,000	
Accounts payable...............................		10,000
Accrued liabilities...............................		20,000
Mortgage payable..............................		30,000
Jack capital....................................		60,000
Jill capital.....................................		60,000

(to record initial capital contribution to the Jack and Jill Partnership, assuming that Jill receives a 50% capital interest and the partners apply the Goodwill Method)

Notice the addition of a new Goodwill asset to the partnership's balance sheet. In addition, the partners' Capital Accounts are increased proportionately.

If you are a bit uncomfortable with partners' ability to recognize this new Goodwill asset, that is understandable. However, you should realize that typical users of financial statements are not necessarily going to value the Goodwill asset in the same way that the partners do. For example, if the Jack and Jill Partnership attempted to apply for a loan using the balance sheet that results from the journal entry above, a bank will typically not consider this Goodwill asset in its evaluation of the partnership's ability to repay the loan. This means that the partnership likely won't be able to borrow more money just because it has more intangible assets on its books.

The application of the Bonus Method (versus the Goodwill Method) will not likely result in a disproportionate benefit accruing to one partner over the other. For example, if we were to assume that the partnership dissolved the moment after formation, Jack and Jill would still each have 50% interest in the net assets of the partnership under both methods. Even if we assumed that the partnership could liquidate its identifiable net assets for their recorded values, the Goodwill asset would likely need to be written off (i.e., it has no value separate from the business). Thus, after hypothetically writing off the Goodwill asset (and allocating the write-off to the two partners' Capital Accounts) and liquidating the remaining net assets, each partner would only receive $50,000. This is the same net realization each partner received under the hypothetical dissolution after applying the Bonus Method.

One final point, just as Jack and Jill can negotiate any division to the initial Capital Accounts, so can they also negotiate the division of partnership profit. For example, in our last example, the Capital Accounts are split 50% for Jack and 50% for Jill. The two partners can agree on a different allocation of profit, say 60/40, if they wish. T*he profit-sharing ratio does not need to conform to the proportion of capital that each partner owns.* We discuss profit-sharing ratios later in the chapter.

ACCOUNTING FOR CHANGES IN PARTNERSHIP OWNERSHIP (REALIGNMENT)

LO3 Describe the accounting for changes in partnership ownership.

After a partnership is formed, new partners can be added and existing partners can leave the partnership. The Partnership Agreement addresses specific conditions under which partners are admitted, the required capital contributions, accepted valuation timing and procedures for retiring partners, and other procedural matters. The resulting partnership-realignment accounting reflects the specific partner-admission or partner-retirement net asset transfers and the Capital Account changes to which the partners agreed. In addition, some of the practices and conventions do not necessarily conform to the GAAP traditionally applied to public companies and typical corporations.

For example, a common practice when admitting a new partner to a partnership is to *revalue* the partnership net assets to fair value. This practice provides the most transparency of the relative values contributed by the existing partners and the newly admitted partners. In addition, as we discuss above, the partnership can also look to the value of the arm's-length (i.e., independent) admission or retirement transaction to *infer* the fair value of the partnership as a whole, thus allowing the partnership to record previously unrecorded Goodwill. As you will see, this practice is very similar to the logic underlying the Goodwill Method in partnership formation.

In any partnership realignment, a critically important factor affecting the resulting accounting is whether the partnership entity is (1) paying or receiving cash or other net assets as part of the realignment transaction or (2) the new or retiring partners are engaging in transactions directly with individual partners (i.e., without involving the partnership entity in the exchange). For example, a new partner can enter a partnership by contributing net assets directly to the partnership entity or by buying some or all of the interest of an existing partner by paying cash directly to the existing partner. Because this latter type of transaction does not involve a direct transaction with the partnership entity, it sometimes confuses students and is more easily understood if one draws an analogy to shares of stock traded on the New York Stock Exchange. In these stock-exchange transactions, the ownership of major companies changes on a daily basis, without ever involving the company itself.

Important differences between the stock-exchange analogy and partnership accounting are (1) the partners must approve the transfer of any partnership interests to a new partner and (2) the fact that partnerships will sometimes look to the value of the exchanges involving incoming/outgoing individual partners and decide to record previously unrecorded intangible assets based on the exchange value. Of course, under current GAAP, corporations are not allowed to revalue their balance sheets based on exchanges of their shares.[9, 10]

In the sections that follow, we first consider revaluation of partnership net assets that occurs immediately before partnership realignment. Next, we discuss the simplest case of partnership realignment in which the new partner purchases an interest in the partnership that is proportional to the cash paid, either to an existing partner outside of the partnership or to the partnership itself. Then, we discuss two other scenarios that involve the recognition of a partner Capital Account that is disproportionate to the cash paid by the new partner.

Revaluation of Net Assets Prior to Partnership Realignment

When the ownership structure of partnerships changes, it is imperative that the net assets and partnership interests exchanged in the realignment transaction are measured at fair value. This not only includes the net assets contributed by a new, incoming partner(s), but also the net assets owned by the preexisting partners.[11] The reason for this practice is quite simple: if net assets are measured at fair value on both sides of the realignment transaction, then the parties to the realignment have the best possible chance of allocating partner Capital Accounts in a fair and unbiased manner.

When partnership net assets are revalued in anticipation of a realignment transaction, the resulting gains and losses accrue only to the partners who have an ownership interest in the entity during the period in which the net assets changed in value. The gains and losses that result from pre-realignment

---

[9] In transactions among individuals outside of the partnership entity, the partnership may choose to not record Goodwill implied by the disproportionate transaction values. This is because the same conditions for recording previously unrecorded intangible assets exist in partnership realignments as in partnership formation. (Recall that both of the following conditions must be met to record implied Goodwill in a partnership formation: (1) the disproportionate capital contribution by one or more partners provides evidence that the partnership possesses an unrecognized intangible asset and (2) the partners wish to recognize the intangible asset on the books of the partnership. These same conditions must be met in partnership realignments.) Thus, if the partnership decides to not record Goodwill, the only entry required for the partnership is to record the reduction of the Capital Account of the exiting partner(s) and to establish the Capital Account for the new partner(s).

[10] Partnership realignment transactions may also involve transfers of identifiable net assets into the partnership entity (i.e., in a partner admission) or out of the partnership entity (i.e., in a partner retirement). In these cases, the value of the transferred net assets might not equal the recorded value of the new or retiring partners' Capital Accounts. This is similar to the situation in partnership formation where the contributed net assets did not equal the initial balance in the partners' Capital Account. Similar to the case of partnership formation, the partnership in a realignment transaction can use the disproportionate contribution to the partnership or payment by the partnership to infer the overall value of the partnership entity. However, the partners are not required to record any resulting implied (previously unrecorded) intangible asset. At a minimum, the partnership must record (1) the net assets received or transferred in the realignment transaction (including implied Goodwill, if the partnership wishes to recognize it) and (2) the adjustment necessary to reflect the correct capital balance for the incoming or retiring partner. Any imbalance between (1) and (2) will result in transfers to or from the existing partners, and these transfers are typically allocated in proportion to the partners' profit-and-loss-sharing ratios.

[11] Pre-realignment revaluations can be done for changes in partnership interests other than the admission of a new partner, like partner retirements, for example. Unless otherwise indicated, for the remaining sections of this chapter, we will assume that the existing partners revalued the partnership net assets (i.e., to fair value) in anticipation of the described revaluation transactions.

revaluation are allocated to the existing partners' Capital Accounts in the revaluation profit-and-loss-sharing ratio designated in the Partnership Agreement.[12]

To illustrate, assume that the Jack and Jill Partnership has been operating for many years and that June now desires to join the partnership. The balance sheet of the Jack and Jill Partnership just prior to the admission of June is presented in Exhibit 13.2.

EXHIBIT 13.2	Balance Sheet of the Jack and Jill Partnership Immediately Prior to Revaluation Triggered by Planned Admission of June		
Cash..............................	$ 200,000	Accounts payable.................	$ 200,000
Receivables	300,000	Accrued liabilities.................	250,000
Inventories	100,000	Mortgage payable	350,000
Property, plant and equipment, (PPE) ...	500,000	Total liabilities...................	800,000
		Jack, capital.....................	75,000
		Jill, capital......................	225,000
		Total capital	300,000
Total assets......................	$1,100,000	Total liabilities and partner capital	$1,100,000

A valuation of the assets performed by Jack and Jill immediately prior to the admission of June reveals that inventories are **undervalued by $200,000** and property, plant and equipment is **undervalued by $400,000**. Assume that the Partnership Agreement provides that Jack and Jill share all profits and losses equally even though they do not report equal balances in their partner Capital Accounts (Jack "owns" $75,000 / $300,000 = 25% and Jill "owns" $225,000 / $300,000 = 75% of the partnership's net assets).

The journal entry to revalue the assets is as follows:

Inventories	200,000	
Property, plant and equipment, (PPE)	400,000	
Jack, capital		300,000
Jill, capital		300,000
(to revalue the inventories and PPE prior to the admission of June, revaluation "gain" shared equally)		

The balance sheet of the partnership following the realignment-related revaluation of the assets is presented in Exhibit 13.3.

EXHIBIT 13.3	Balance Sheet of the Jack and Jill Partnership Immediately After Revaluation Triggered by Planned Admission of June		
Cash..............................	$ 200,000	Accounts payable.................	$ 200,000
Receivables	300,000	Accrued liabilities.................	250,000
Inventories	300,000	Mortgage payable	350,000
Property, plant and equipment, (PPE) ...	900,000	Total liabilities...................	800,000
		Jack, capital.....................	375,000
		Jill, capital......................	525,000
		Total capital	900,000
Total assets......................	$1,700,000	Total liabilities and partner capital	$1,700,000

---

[12] If the Partnership Agreement does not include a special revaluation profit and loss sharing ratio, then the ordinary profit-and-loss-sharing ratio may be used. Under most states' laws, if the Partnership Agreement includes no mention of profit-and-loss-sharing, then all existing partners share the gains and losses equally.

Prior to the admission of June, the partnership's assets have been written up by $600,000 ($200,000 relating to inventories and $400,000 relating to PPE). The partners' Capital Accounts have also been increased by $600,000 ($300,000 for each partner).

The Jack and Jill Partnership balance sheet, just prior to June's admission as a new partner (but after revaluation of the partnership net assets), is presented in Exhibit 13.3. We now consider several ways in which June can become a new partner: purchasing a portion or all of the partnership interests from individual partners (i.e., without involving the partnership entity) and contributing cash or other net assets to the partnership in exchange for a partnership interest.

Admission of New Partner by Purchasing the Partnership Interest from One or Both Partners

We first assume that Jack and Jill each agree to sell one-third of their individual partnership interests to June for an aggregate total of $500,000, with Jack receiving $208,333 ($375,000/$900,000 × $500,000) and Jill receiving $291,667 ($525,000/$900,000 × $500,000). *This transaction is between Jack, Jill and June, acting as individuals, without transferring net assets into the partnership itself.* June's purchase of one-third of the total partnership capital for $500,000 implies a total value for the partnership of $1,500,000 ($500,000/$\frac{1}{3}$). The total capital, however, is only equal to $900,000 immediately before the partnership realignment (see Exhibit 13.3), and because this transaction is assumed to be "arm's length" (i.e., independent and unbiased), it can be considered evidence that the partnership includes a previously unrecognized intangible asset valued at $600,000.[13]

Similar to our observations when discussing partnership formation, two questions must be answered for a partnership to recognize previously unrecognized intangible assets during a partnership realignment:

1. Does the disproportionate capital contribution by one or more new partners provide evidence that the realigned partnership possesses an unrecognized intangible asset?

2. If the answer to question 1 is, "yes," do the partners wish to recognize the intangible asset on the books of the partnership?

If the answer to either of the foregoing questions is "no," then the partnership will simply reallocate (i.e., transfer) the selling partners' capital interest into the new partners' individual Capital Accounts (remember, even though we can infer the value of intangible assets valued at $600,000 in this case, the partners can decide not to recognize these assets). If the answers to *both* of the foregoing questions are "yes," then the partnership will apply the Goodwill Method to allocate the total partnership capital into the partners' individual Capital Accounts. We examine each of these possibilities in the following sections.

Reallocation of Capital Let's begin under the assumption that the answer to one or more of the questions that we pose above is "no." Since there is no transaction between June and the partnership itself (her payment is made directly to Jack and Jill), the partnership's net assets remain unchanged. Thus, the required journal entry records the reallocation of one-third of Jack's Capital Account balance and one-third of Jill's Capital Account balance into a newly created Capital Account for June:

Jack, capital	125,000[a]	
Jill, capital.	175,000[b]	
June, capital		300,000
(to record the purchase of one-third of Jack's and one-third of Jill's partnership interests by June)		

[a] $375,000 × $\frac{1}{3}$ = $125,000 [b] $525,000 × $\frac{1}{3}$ = $175,000

If the partners do not wish to record a previously unrecorded intangible asset, the amounts that June individually pays to Jack and Jill for their partnership interests do not affect the partnership except to

---

[13] Recall that we are assuming that the partnership revalues all identifiable net assets to their fair values. Thus, any remaining fair value in the entity is assumed to be unidentifiable Goodwill.

the extent that it must recognize Jack's and Jill's reduced ownership interests and June's admission to the partnership via an adjustment to their respective Capital Accounts.

Goodwill Method If, instead, we assume that the answer to both intangible-asset questions is "yes," then the partnership can use the arm's-length exchange to infer an overall value for the partnership entity. Based on this implied partnership value, the partnership can also determine the value of the previously unrecognized Goodwill. Based on the $500,000 aggregate total payment from June to Jack and Jill, the implied total value of the partnership is $1,500,000 (i.e., $500,000/$\frac{1}{3}$). This suggests that the partnership has a previously unrecorded Goodwill intangible asset in the amount of **$600,000** (i.e., $1,500,000 implied value − $900,000 balance of Jack and Jill Capital Accounts).

The partnership will record this intangible asset and allocate the resulting gain to the existing partners in proportion to their relative profit-and-loss-sharing ratios (i.e., we previously indicated that it was 50:50 for Jack and Jill, respectively). Thus, the recognition of Goodwill is recorded in the following journal entry:

Goodwill	600,000	
Jack, capital		300,000
Jill, capital		300,000
(to recognize previously unrecognized Goodwill upon admission of June to the partnership)		

Note that the partnership has recorded a new asset (Goodwill) in the amount of $600,000 as implied by the purchase price that June paid for a one-third interest in the partnership. Also, as a result of the recognition of this new asset, Jack's Capital Account balance has increased to **$675,000** (i.e., $375,000 + $300,000) and Jill's Capital Account balance has increased to **$825,000** (i.e., $525,000 + $300,000) immediately prior to June's admission (i.e., after recognizing the Goodwill asset).

Finally, to reflect the admission of June as a new partner, the partnership will record the following transfer of capital to reflect the transfer of one-third of the partnership capital from each existing partner (i.e., Jack and Jill) to June:

Jack, capital	225,000[a]	
Jill, capital	275,000[b]	
June, capital		500,000
(to record the purchase of one-third of Jack's and one-third of Jill's partnership interests by June after Goodwill is recognized)		

[a] **$675,000** × $\frac{1}{3}$ = $225,000   [b] **$825,000** × $\frac{1}{3}$ = $275,000

Realignment via Contribution of Cash or Other Net Assets to the Partnership—Base Case

In our previous example, June purchased her partnership interest with a payment directly to the partners who were acting as individuals. *We now assume that June buys her partnership interest by contributing cash or other assets to the partnership entity, itself.* In this case, we must record the receipt of cash or other net assets in addition to adjusting the Capital Accounts. In this section, we assume that the contribution to the partnership is proportional to the percentage of the book value of the capital that June purchases. We will later relax this assumption.

Let's assume that June contributes **$450,000** cash to the partnership in return for a one-third partnership interest. In this transaction, she is buying into the partnership at book value. Specifically, the total capital of the partnership after the contribution is $1,350,000 ($900,000 + $450,000), with June's partnership interest equaling exactly one-third of that total capital ($1,350,000 × $\frac{1}{3}$ = $450,000). The journal entry records the receipt of cash and the new partner's Capital Account:

Cash	450,000	
June, capital		450,000
(to record the capital contribution of June)		

In partnership realignments, just like in partnership formations, the parties are allowed to exchange any form of net assets as consideration. Recall that immediately preceding the realignment, the partnership entity will revalue (to fair value) the partnership net assets. The new partner(s) admitted to the partnership also value their contributed net assets at fair value. Thus, as long as the partnership agrees, the new partner(s) can, in principle, contribute *any* form of net assets upon admission to a partnership. Therefore, as an alternative to the preceding all-cash transaction, we could assume that June contributes cash in the amount of **$100,000** and a parcel of land with a fair value of **$350,000**. The entry to record the admission of June is as follows:

Cash..	100,000	
Land..	350,000	
June, capital		450,000
(to record the capital contribution of June)		

The land is initially recorded at its fair value on the date of the contribution, and June's Capital Account is $450,000, one-third of the total partnership capital, as before.

Realignment via Contribution of Cash or Other Net Assets to the Partnership—Bonus and Goodwill Methods

In our previous example, we assume that June bought a partnership interest that was proportional to the net book value of her contribution. New partners also commonly acquire their partnership interests at a premium (i.e., in excess of book value) to reflect the future earning potential of the partnership or some other previously unrecognized future economic benefit. Should the amount paid to a partnership in a partnership realignment transaction imply a premium, we need to, again, provide answers to the following two questions to determine the appropriate accounting:

1. Does the disproportionate capital contribution by one or more new partners to the partnership entity provide evidence that the realigned partnership possesses an unrecognized intangible asset?
2. If the answer to question 1 is, "yes," do the partners wish to recognize the intangible asset on the books of the partnership?

If the answer to either of the foregoing questions is "no," then the partnership will apply the Bonus Method of Capital Account reallocation. If the answers to *both* of the foregoing questions are "yes," then the partnership will apply the Goodwill Method of Capital Account reallocation.

Bonus Method   If we assume the answer to one of the questions that we pose above is "no," then the premium paid by the entering partners(s) is allocated to the Capital Accounts of the preexisting partners as a bonus. To illustrate, assume that June makes a cash contribution of **$450,000** to the partnership and will receive only a 20% interest in the partnership, with Jack and Jill owning the remaining 80%. Because the partnership is not recognizing previously unrecorded intangible assets as part of this transaction, the total net assets of the partnership will only increase by the $450,000 capital contribution. The total post-realignment partnership capital is **$1,350,000** ($900,000 + $450,000) and the calculation of the allocated bonus is presented in Exhibit 13.4:

EXHIBIT 13.4	Calculation of Bonus Following Admission of June with a 20% Interest	
June's capital contribution.................................		$450,000
June's capital credit:		
Total post-realignment capital.........................	$1,350,000	
× June's ownership percentage.........................	× 20%	
= June's capital credit		(270,000)
Bonus allocated to preexisting partners*...................		$180,000

* The bonus is allocated to the partners in the same ratio that profit (loss) is allocated to the partners' Capital Accounts.

June is paying a premium over book value in order to join the partnership (presumably reflecting the fact that she is buying into a profitable partnership) and the preexisting partners receive that premium as a bonus.

Since we are assuming in this example that the preexisting partners share profits and losses in a 50:50 proportion, the journal entry to record this transaction is as follows:

Cash...	450,000	
Jack, capital		90,000[a]
Jill, capital		90,000[a]
June, capital		270,000
(to record the purchase of a 20% partnership interest by June for $450,000)		

[a] **$180,000** × 50% = $90,000

Jack and Jill's Capital Accounts are now equal to $465,000 (i.e., $375,000 + $90,000) and $615,000 (i.e., $525,000 + $90,000), respectively, with the $1,080,000 (i.e., $465,000 + $615,000) total shared by Jack and Jill representing 80% of the total partner capital of $1,350,000.

Occasionally, existing partners may be willing to give up some of their ownership interest in the partnership in order to attract a new partner. In this case, the existing partners are selling their partnership interests at a discount, thus *paying a bonus to the new partner*. To illustrate, assume that June is contributing **$450,000** to the partnership as before, but now receives a 50% interest in the partnership. The calculation of the allocated bonus is presented in Exhibit 13.5:

EXHIBIT 13.5	Calculation of Bonus Following Admission of June with a 50% Interest

June's capital contribution..		$ 450,000
June's capital credit:		
Total post-realignment capital..	$1,350,000	
× June's ownership percentage	× 50%	
= June's capital credit		(675,000)
Bonus allocated to preexisting partners*		$(225,000)

* The bonus is allocated to the partners in the same ratio that profit (loss) is allocated to the partners' Capital Accounts.

Given the 50:50 profit-and-loss-sharing ratio of the preexisting partners, Jack and Jill are each transferring to June $112,500 (50% × **$225,000**) to attract her to the partnership. The journal entry to record this transaction is as follows:

Cash...	450,000	
Jack, capital..	112,500[a]	
Jill, capital...	112,500[a]	
June, capital		675,000
(to record the purchase of a 50% partnership interest by June for $450,000)		

[a] **$225,000** × 50% = $112,500

Jack and Jill's Capital Accounts are now equal to $262,500 (i.e., $375,000 − $112,500) and $412,500 (i.e., $525,000 − $112,500), respectively, with the $675,000 (i.e., $262,500 + $412,500) total shared by Jack and Jill representing 50% of the total partner capital of $1,350,000.

Goodwill Method

If we assume that the answers to both intangible-asset questions that we pose above are "yes," then the partnership can use the arm's-length contribution to the partnership to infer an overall value for the partnership entity. Based on this implied partnership value, the partnership can also determine the value of the previously unrecognized intangible assets. These intangible assets might include particular expertise, business contacts, and the like. In addition to recognizing the cash and other assets that the new partner contributes to the partnership, we can also recognize these intangible assets as Goodwill upon admission of a new partner.

To illustrate, we continue to assume that the Jack and Jill Partnership's balance sheet reflects total assets of $1,700,000, liabilities of $800,000, and partner capital of $900,000 immediately prior to the admission of June. Now, we will assume that June contributes **$450,000** for a 30% ownership position. Using the capital contribution as evidence of the overall value of the partnership entity, we determine that the partnership is worth a total of $1,500,000 (i.e., $450,000/30%).

Prior to the recognition of implied Goodwill, the identifiable net assets held by the partnership is equal to $1,350,000, which is comprised of the preexisting net assets of the partnership (i.e., $900,000) plus the identifiable net assets contributed by June (i.e., $450,000). Consequently, June is contributing an intangible asset with a fair value of **$150,000** ($1,500,000 − $1,350,000).

The partnership recognizes the cash contribution and the new intangible asset as Goodwill with the following journal entry:

Cash...	450,000	
Goodwill..	150,000	
Jack, capital		75,000[a]
Jill, capital		75,000[a]
June, capital		450,000
(to record the cash contribution and Goodwill asset and the related adjustments to the Capital Accounts)		

[a] $150,000 × 50% = $75,000

The journal entry to record the admission of June to the partnership increases total partnership net assets to $1,500,000 ($900,000 + $450,000 + $150,000) and June's initial capital balance of $450,000 represents a 30% interest in the total capital of the partnership. The capital accounts for Jack and Jill have been increased by $150,000 ($75,000 each) to reflect the implied value of Goodwill possessed by the partnership prior to the admission of June.

Summary There are a wide variety of approaches to the accounting for admission of partners to the partnership, whether for the initial capital contribution or the subsequent admission of new partners. We have described several of the most common methods, including the reallocation of capital among the partners and the creation of new partnership assets. It is important to keep in mind, however, that *the accounting for the admission of a partner is governed by the Partnership Agreement* and, because partnerships are private entities, the accounting policies need not conform to GAAP (e.g., revaluing partnership net assets immediately prior to realignment).

TOPIC REVIEW

a. Assume that Partners A and B each report a Capital Account of $100,000. Partner C wants to join the partnership. Because the partnership has been very profitable, Partners A and B require Partner C to contribute $200,000 in cash to the partnership in return for a 25% interest. Assume that Partners A and B share profits 60% and 40%, respectively, prior to the admission of Partner C. After admission of Partner C, Partners A and B retain their relative proportion of profit allocation after granting Partner C a 30% profit-allocation interest. Use the Bonus Method to record the journal entry on the books of the partnership to reflect the admission of Partner C.

b. Refer to the fact set in Part a. Assume that the partners believe that the payment by Partner C provides evidence of a previously unrecorded intangible asset in the partnership and the partners wish to record the intangible on the post-realignment partnership balance sheet. Use the Goodwill Method to record the journal entry on the books of the partnership to reflect the admission of Partner C.

The solution to this review problem can be found on page 754.

ALLOCATION OF PROFIT (LOSS), DRAWING ACCOUNTS AND THE CAPITAL ACCOUNT

LO4 Describe the allocation of profit (loss), drawing accounts, and the capital account.

In the previous section, we discuss the initial journal entry to the partner Capital Account upon formation of the partnership and admission of new partners in subsequent periods. Now, we discuss the increases and decreases to that account *during* the period. The partner Capital Account is updated in a manner that is similar to the way in which we update Retained Earnings for a corporation: the account is increased by profits and other credits to the partner and is decreased by withdrawals of capital from the partnership. We begin our discussion with the reconciliation of the Capital Account and conclude with an illustration of the types of income that a partner can earn and the manner in which profit is allocated to each partner.

Reconciliation of the Capital Account

The partners' Capital Accounts are reconciled in a manner that is similar to the reconciliation of Retained Earnings for a corporation. The general form of the reconciliation is presented in Exhibit 13.6.

EXHIBIT 13.6	General Form for the Reconciliation of Partner Capital Accounts		
	Beginning balance		)OO(
	Net investment:		
❶	Capital contributions.	xxx	
❷	Less: Drawings	(xxx)	xxx
	Income:		
	Salary (discussed below)	xxx	
	Interest on capital account (discussed below)	xxx	
❸	Allocation of partnership profit (loss)	xxx	xxx
	Ending balance.		xxx

The changes to the Capital Account include the following elements (numbers correspond to the table above):

❶ **Capital contributions**—partners may contribute additional capital to the partnership in the form of cash and other assets. After the initial capital contribution upon formation of the partnership or admittance of a new partner, subsequent capital contributions are usually made to offset declining liquidity and are frequently mandated for each partner (this is the so-called "capital call").

❷ **Drawings**—partners typically have the ability to withdraw funds from the partnership during the year. These withdrawals are called "drawings" and are usually recorded in a Drawing Account that is maintained for each partner and is closed to the partner's Capital Account at the end of the year.

❸ **Allocation of partnership profit (loss)**—the partnership income statement includes revenues and expenses other than salary paid to partners and interest on the Capital Accounts. The partnership profit, less deductions for salary and interest paid to partners, is allocated to the partners at the end of the year. The profit-sharing formula is specified in the Partnership Agreement and may or may not conform to the relative Capital Account balances. All profit must be allocated to partner Capital Accounts in some manner.

Allocation of Partnership Profit (Loss)

All partnerships must allocate profit (loss) to the partners' Capital Accounts. The allocation procedure is typically called the **sharing ratio** and it is defined in the Partnership Agreement.[14] Sharing ratios can be simple or complex and are different for each partnership. Consequently, accountants must read and understand the profit-sharing procedure carefully so that they can properly account for and audit the allocation of profit to the partners' Capital Accounts.

Partners derive income from the partnership in a variety of ways. In this section, we consider three of the most common: salaries, interest on the Capital Account, and allocation of partnership profit. None of these are typically reported as expenses in the partnership income statement. Rather, the income statement reports revenues and expenses, other than those related to distributions to the partners, to derive the income available for payment to partners.

---

[14] In the unlikely event that a sharing ratio is not defined in the Partnership Agreement, the allocation of profit to the partners' Capital Accounts is governed by state law. For those states which have adopted the Uniform Partnership Act of 1997, the allocation is defined as follows: "Each partner is entitled to an equal share of the partnership profits and is chargeable with a share of the partnership losses in proportion to the partner's share of the profits" (UPA, §401b).

Salaries   The Uniform Partnership Act of 1997 states that "a partner is not entitled to remuneration for services performed for the partnership" (UPA, §401h).[15] This position is based on the premise that work performed for the partnership is a form of investment by the partner, and that any payments to the partner performing such work should be treated as a distribution of profit.

Consistent with this notion, Partnership Agreements sometimes allow for a salary payment as part of the profit allocation process. Salary is computed as a fixed payment or as a variable rate based on some measure of output, such as hours worked, clients served, and so on. This salary payment is allocated to the partner and the net profit after this payment is allocated to the partners (including the partner receiving the salary) based on a profit-sharing ratio.

To illustrate, assume that the Jack, Jill, and June Partnership reports revenues in excess of expenses (other than a salary paid to June) of $150,000. June receives a salary of $30,000 relating to her work for the partnership, and we assume that the sharing ratio for the remaining income is 40%/40%/20% for Jack, Jill, and June, respectively.[16] The distribution of profit to the partners through the salary allocation is illustrated in Exhibit 13.7.

EXHIBIT 13.7	Partially Complete Allocation of Profit to Partners: Through Salary				
	Jack	**Jill**	**June**	**Allocation**	**Remaining**
Excess of revenues over expenses					$150,000
Salary			$30,000	$30,000	$120,000

The profit remaining after recognizing the salary to June is $120,000 ($150,000 − $30,000). This amount is allocated to the partners in the ratio 40%/40%/20% per the sharing ratio in the Partnership Agreement.

Interest on the Capital Account   Some Partnership Agreements also allow for the allocation of interest on the average Capital Accounts of the partners. This is not interest expense on debt that would be included in the partnership income statement. It is treated as a form of profit allocation like salary. The interest rate is specified in the Partnership Agreement. It may be a fixed rate or it may be tied to a published index, like the prime or LIBOR rates or a treasury rate. The Partnership Agreement also specifies the appropriate Capital Account balance to use in the computation of interest. This may be the beginning balance, ending balance, or a weighted-average balance using time as the weighting factor.

To illustrate, assume that the Jack, Jill, and June Partnership provides for an allocation based on interest earned on the weighted-average Capital Account balance during the year. The Capital Accounts for Jack and Jill are $450,000 as of the beginning of the year, and neither made a capital contribution during the year. Assume that June was admitted as a partner on April 30 with a capital contribution of $225,000. Finally, assume that the Partnership Agreement provides for an interest allocation of 5% based on the weighted-average Capital Account balance during the year. The average Capital Account balances and interest allocation for the three partners are computed as follows:

Partner	Weighted-Average Capital Account Balance	Interest Allocation	
Jack	$450,000 × 12/12 = $450,000	$450,000 × 5% =	$22,500
Jill	$450,000 × 12/12 = $450,000	$450,000 × 5% =	$22,500
June	($0 × 4/12) + ($225,000 × 8/12) = $150,000	$150,000 × 5% =	$ 7,500

The distribution of profit to the partners, including both salary and interest is illustrated in Exhibit 13.8.

---

[15] Partners are, however, permitted a reasonable salary in connection with work performed in the liquidation of a failed partnership (UPA, §401h). We discuss partnership liquidation later in this chapter.

[16] This sharing ratio can be expressed as percentages or in ratio form. The ratio form for this sharing ratio is 2:2:1 and each partner received his or her proportion of the total ratios. In this example, the ratios total to 5 (2+2+1). Jack and Jill receive 2/5=40% while June receives 1/5=20%.

EXHIBIT 13.8	Partially Complete Allocation of Profit to Partners: Through Salary and Interest				
	Jack	**Jill**	**June**	**Allocation**	**Remaining**
Excess of revenues over expenses					$150,000
Salary			$30,000	$30,000	120,000
Interest @ 5%	$22,500	$22,500	7,500	52,500	67,500

Both the salary paid to partners and the interest on their respective weighted-average Capital Account balances have been deducted from the net income of the partnership. The balance of $67,500 is now available for allocation to the partners based on the sharing ratio as specified in the Partnership Agreement.

Allocation of Remaining Profit

The allocation of remaining profit to the partners is based on a sharing ratio that is described in the Partnership Agreement. We will assume in our examples that the same sharing ratio applies to both profits and losses, but the Partnership Agreement could provide for different sharing ratios in the event of a loss. Further, the sharing ratio does not have to conform to the partners' respective Capital Account balances. The sharing ratio is negotiated among the partners and they can agree on any allocation formula.

To illustrate, let's assume that the remaining profit (after the salary and interest) is distributed to the partners in the ratio of 40%/40%/20% to Jack, Jill, and June, respectively. Continuing with our previous example, the allocation of profit to the partners is presented in Exhibit 13.9.

EXHIBIT 13.9	Full Allocation of Profit to Partners				
	Jack	**Jill**	**June**	**Total Allocation**	**Remaining**
Excess of revenues over expenses					$150,000
Salary			$30,000	$ 30,000	120,000
Interest @ 5%	$22,500	$22,500	7,500	52,500	67,500
Allocation of remaining profit	27,000	27,000	13,500	67,500	—
Total allocation	$49,500	$49,500	$51,000	$150,000	

The profit remaining after the salary and interest allocation is $67,500 ($150,000 − $30,000 − $52,500). Jack and Jill each receive 40% or **$27,000** ($67,500 × 40%) and June receives 20% or **$13,500** ($67,500 × 20%). Jack and Jill's Capital Accounts will be increased by $49,500 each, and June's will increase by $51,000.

Summary

It is important to remember that the allocation of profit is governed by the Partnership Agreement. That document will specify whether salary or interest is to be allocated to individual partners before the remaining profit is allocated to all partners. It will further indicate the sharing ratio, typically as a percent allocated to each partner or the ratio of allocation units. Finally, the Partnership Agreement can specify whether either salary or interest or both will be considered in the allocation, or whether neither will be included. In the latter case, the excess of revenues over expenses will be allocated to all partners based on the sharing ratio.

Statement of Capital Account Balances

The balance sheet for a partnership reports the ending balance of the partners' Capital Accounts. In our example, we provide a balance for each partner so that their respective equity in the partnership will be clearly stated on the face of the balance sheet. Often, however, the Capital Accounts will be aggregated into one line on the balance sheet: Partners' Capital. Regardless of the way in which the Capital Accounts are presented on the balance sheet, partnerships typically provide a separate statement that details the changes to the Capital Accounts during the year: the Statement of Partners' Capital.

The Statement of Partners' Capital for the Jack, Jill, and June Partnership is presented in Exhibit 13.10 (the numbers 1 and 2a,b relate to the journal entries in Exhibit 13.11).

EXHIBIT 13.10	Statement of Partners' Capital for the Jack, Jill, and June Partnership				
		Jack	**Jill**	**June**	**Total**
1	Capital account, beginning of year . . .	$450,000	$450,000	$ 0	$ 900,000
	Capital contributions	0	0	225,000	225,000
	Withdrawals	(20,000)	(20,000)	(10,000)	(50,000)
2b	Salary			30,000	30,000
	Interest @ 5%	22,500	22,500	7,500	52,500
	Allocation of remaining profit	27,000	27,000	13,500	67,500
	Capital account, end of year	$479,500	$479,500	$266,000	$1,225,000

(Braces indicate items for group 2b total $150,000)

The Statement of Partners' Capital begins with the Capital Accounts of the partners as of the beginning of the year. Jack and Jill both began the year with a Capital Account of $450,000. We assume for this example that June joined the partnership on April 30 (4 months into the partnership year) with a contribution of $225,000. We also assume that the partners drew funds out of the partnership for personal use. Those drawings were accounted for with the following journal entry:

Jack, drawing	20,000	
Jill, drawing	20,000	
June, drawing	10,000	
Cash		50,000
(to record drawing by partners)		

The Drawing Account for Jack and Jill reports a balance of $20,000 as of the end of the year, and the Drawing Account for June reports a balance of $10,000.

The partners' Capital Accounts increase by capital contributions and decrease by drawings, and increases to the Capital Accounts as a result of profit amount to $150,000. All of the profit is allocated to the partners in the form of salary, interest, and the allocation of profit using the sharing ratio. We assume for the following journal entries that the profit of $150,000 is comprised of revenues in the amount of $500,000 and expenses of $350,000.

Finally, at the end of the year, the journal entries to close the Drawing Accounts to partner Capital Accounts and to close revenue and expenses and allocate the profit to the partners' Capital Accounts per the schedule above are presented in Exhibit 13.11.

EXHIBIT 13.11	Journal Entries to Close the Drawing Accounts to Partner Capital Accounts and to Close Revenue and Expenses and Allocate the Profit to the Partners' Capital Accounts		
1	Jack, capital	20,000	
	Jill, capital	20,000	
	June, capital	10,000	
	Jack, drawing		20,000
	Jill, drawing		20,000
	June, drawing		10,000
	(to close the Drawing Accounts for the partners to their respective Capital Accounts)		
2a	Revenue	500,000	
	Expenses		350,000
	Income summary		150,000
	(to close revenue and expenses)		
2b	Income summary	150,000	
	Jack, capital		49,500
	Jill, capital		49,500
	June, capital		51,000
	(to close income summary and distribute the profit in accordance with the Partnership Agreement)		

The first journal entry closes out the Drawing Accounts with a reduction of partner capital to reflect the withdrawals. The second journal entry closes out revenue and expenses to Income Summary. This is similar to the closing entry made for a corporation. Finally, the last journal entry closes out Income Summary and allocates partnership profit to the partner Capital Accounts according to the sharing ratio.

PARTNERSHIP DISSOLUTION

When a partnership fails, it must be liquidated just like any other business. Assets are sold, and the resulting cash is used to repay moneys owed to creditors. Any remaining cash then is distributed to the partners. The process of winding up a partnership is typically described in detail in the Partnership Agreement.

LO5 Describe the accounting for the dissolution of a partnership.

The Uniform Partnership Act of 1997 provides a description of this process that serves as a useful overview. It describes the liquidation process as follows (UPA, §807):

a. The assets of the partnership must be converted to cash used to pay the obligations to creditors, including partners who are creditors, and any remaining cash must be distributed to the partners in accordance with the profit-sharing ratio.

b. Profits (losses) that result from the liquidation of the partnership assets must be credited (charged) to the partners' Capital Accounts.

c. If a partner's Capital Account becomes negative as a result of the sales of assets, the partner must make a cash contribution to the partnership in an amount sufficient to bring the Capital Account to a zero balance.

d. If a partner fails to contribute the full amount required, all of the other partners shall contribute (in their profit-sharing ratios) the additional amount necessary to satisfy the partnership obligations. In the event of such contribution, the partners shall have the right to sue the partner with the unfunded negative Capital Account for the amount owed to the partnership.

Bottom line: the partners are personally liable for the debts of the partnership if the assets are not sufficient to repay all of the obligations. It is this unlimited personal liability that led to the creation of the limited liability partnership we describe at the outset of this chapter and has also led to the use of significant amounts of malpractice insurance. Partners hope to lessen their personal liability with the legal structure of the partnership and the use of insurance. Of course, these efforts to reduce personal liability come at a cost. This is no different from any other cost that one incurs in order to transfer risk to another party.

Accounting for the Liquidation of a Partnership

The accounting for a liquidation of a partnership is a three-step process:

1. Sell the assets and record the gain (loss) as increases (decreases) to the partners' Capital Accounts in their profit-sharing ratio, and subtract any receivables due from partners from their respective Capital Accounts.

2. Eliminate any deficit Capital Account with a cash contribution from the partner (or by offsetting payables, if any, against the deficit balance). If the partner is insolvent, allocate the deficit to the remaining partners in their profit-sharing ratio (repeat this process if the allocation results in other Capital Accounts becoming negative).

3. Distribute the remaining cash to the partners for the remaining amount reported in their Capital Accounts.

Liquidation with Positive Capital Accounts
We begin our illustration of the liquidation process with an example in which all of the Capital Accounts remain positive throughout the liquidation process. Assume that the Jack, Jill, and June Partnership allocates profits (losses) in a sharing ratio of 30%/30%/40%, respectively, and reports the balance sheet in Exhibit 13.12 immediately prior to liquidation.

EXHIBIT 13.12	Balance Sheet of Jack, Jill, and June Partnership Immediately Prior to Liquidation

Cash..............................	$ 650,000	Total liabilities....................	$ 800,000
Property, plant and equipment, (PPE) ...	1,275,000	Jack, capital.....................	450,000
		Jill, capital......................	450,000
		June, capital....................	225,000
Total assets.......................	$1,925,000	Total liabilities and capital..........	$1,925,000

The partners desire to wind up the partnership, and the liquidation process involves the following three steps:

1. All of the noncash assets with a net book value of $1,275,000 are sold for an assumed sale price of $1,000,000. The loss on the sale of **$275,000** is allocated to the partners according to the sharing ratio of 30%/30%/40%.

2. The cash balance has now increased to $1,650,000 ($650,000 + $1,000,000) following the sale, and it is used to pay off all of the partnership's liabilities of $800,000, leaving a cash balance of $850,000.

3. The cash remaining after payment of creditors is distributed to the partners according to the balances in their respective Capital Accounts.

The liquidation schedule is summarized in Exhibit 13.13

EXHIBIT 13.13	Liquidation Schedule for the Jack, Jill, and June Partnership

				Partners' Capital		
Debit (Credit)	Cash	Noncash Assets	Liabilities	Jack	Jill	June
Capital account, prior to liquidation..........	$ 650,000	$1,275,000	$(800,000)	$(450,000)	$(450,000)	$(225,000)
1 Sale of noncash assets	1,000,000	(1,275,000)		82,500	82,500	110,000
	1,650,000	0	(800,000)	(367,500)	(367,500)	(115,000)
2 Payment of creditors	(800,000)		800,000			
	850,000	0	0	(367,500)	(367,500)	(115,000)
3 Distribution to partners....................	(850,000)			367,500	367,500	115,000
Post-liquidation balances..................	$ 0	$ 0	$ 0	$ 0	$ 0	$ 0

Notice that the cash balance remaining after all asset sales and payments of creditors of $850,000 is equal to the total balance in the partners' Capital Accounts. This will always be the case since any profit or loss on the sale of assets is allocated to the partner Capital Accounts.

The journal entries for the transactions illustrated above are presented in Exhibit 13.14 (the journal entry numbers correspond with the transaction numbers in Exhibit 13.13).

EXHIBIT 13.14	Journal Entries for the Liquidation of the Jack, Jill, and June Partnership

1	Cash...	1,000,000	
	Jack, capital...	82,500	
	Jill, capital..	82,500	
	June, capital..	110,000	
	Noncash assets.......................................		1,275,000
	(to record the sale of the noncash assets and allocate loss to partners pursuant to their sharing ratio)		
2	Liabilities...	800,000	
	Cash		800,000
	(to record payment of liabilities)		
3	Jack, capital..	367,500	
	Jill, capital..	367,500	
	June, capital..	115,000	
	Cash		850,000
	(to record distribution of cash to the partners)		

PRACTICE INSIGHT

Effect of Receivables from and Payables to a Partner on the Liquidation of a Partnership   The presence of receivables from and payables to a partner causes no particular problems for the liquidation of a partnership. Receivables from a partner are deducted from the partner's Capital Account prior to disbursement of cash. Payables to a partner are treated as other liabilities and should be paid prior to disbursement of the remaining cash.

To illustrate, assume that the Jack, Jill, and June Partnership reports the following balance sheet immediately prior to liquidation:

Cash............................	$1,550,000	Liabilities other than to partners...	525,000
Receivable—Jack..............	200,000	Note payable to Jill..............	100,000
		Jack, capital...................	450,000
		Jill, capital....................	450,000
		June, capital...................	225,000
Total assets....................	$1,750,000	Total liabilities and capital........	$1,750,000

The distribution proceeds as follows:

					Partners' Capital		
Debit (Credit)	Cash	Receivable from Jack	Liabilities	Payable to Jill	Jack	Jill	June
Capital account, prior to liquidation.........	$1,550,000	$200,000	$(525,000)	$(100,000)	$(450,000)	$(450,000)	$(225,000)
Net receivable against capital account.......		(200,000)			200,000		
	1,550,000	0	(525,000)	(100,000)	(250,000)	(450,000)	(225,000)
Payment of creditors............	(625,000)		525,000	100,000			
	925,000	0	0	0	(250,000)	(450,000)	(225,000)
Distribution to partners	(925,000)				250,000	450,000	225,000
Post-liquidation balances...........	$ 0	$ 0	$ 0	$ 0	$ 0	$ 0	$ 0

The receivable from Jack is netted against his Capital Account prior to distribution. The payable to Jill is treated like other liabilities and it is paid prior to distribution.

Liquidation with a Negative Capital Account and Cash Contribution

We now consider a case in which one of the partner's Capital Accounts becomes negative following the sale of noncash assets. Assume that June's Capital Account reports a balance of $80,000 rather than $225,000 immediately prior to the liquidation. This reduced Capital Account can arise, for example, if the partner withdraws a significant amount of funds for the partnership. The Jack, Jill, and June Partnership reports the balance sheet in Exhibit 13.15, immediately prior to liquidation.

EXHIBIT 13.15	Balance Sheet of the Jack, Jill, and June Partnership Immediately Prior to Liquidation

Cash...............................	$ 505,000	Total liabilities....................	$ 800,000
Property, plant and equipment, (PPE) ...	1,275,000		
		Jack, capital......................	450,000
		Jill, capital.......................	450,000
		June, capital......................	80,000
Total assets........................	$1,780,000	Total liabilities and capital..........	$1,780,000

The cash balance is $145,000 lower than it was in the previous example because June has withdrawn funds in that amount, resulting in a Capital Account that is $145,000 lower than in the previous example. The liquidation process now results in a negative Capital Account balance for June. We assume that June makes a capital contribution that is sufficient to bring her Capital Account to a zero balance prior to the distribution of cash to the remaining partners. The liquidation process involves the following steps:

1. All of the noncash assets with a net book value of $1,275,000 are sold for an assumed sale price of $1,000,000. The loss on the sale of **$275,000** is allocated to the partners according to the sharing ratio of 30%/30%/40%. This results in a negative balance in the Capital Account for June in the amount of $30,000.

2. We assume that June is solvent and makes a capital contribution of **$30,000** to the partnership which is allocated to the remaining partners in their sharing ratio which is now 50%/50% since Jack and Jill share in the profits and losses equally.

3. The balance in cash is now $1,535,000 following the sale of the noncash assets and the capital contribution by June, and it is used to pay off all of the partnership's liabilities of $800,000, leaving a cash balance of $735,000.

4. The cash remaining after payment of creditors is distributed to the remaining two partners according to the balances in their respective Capital Accounts.

The liquidation schedule is summarized in Exhibit 13.16

EXHIBIT 13.16	Liquidation of the Jack, Jill, and June Partnership

					Capital Accounts		
Debit (Credit)		Cash	Noncash Assets	Liabilities	Jack	Jill	June
Capital account, prior to liquidation..............		$ 505,000	$1,275,000	$(800,000)	$(450,000)	$(450,000)	$ (80,000)
1 Sale of noncash assets		1,000,000	(1,275,000)		82,500	82,500	110,000
		1,505,000	0	(800,000)	(367,500)	(367,500)	30,000
2 Capital contribution		30,000					(30,000)
		1,535,000	0	(800,000)	(367,500)	(367,500)	0
3 Payment of creditors		(800,000)		800,000			
		735,000	0	0	(367,500)	(367,500)	0
4 Distribution to partners........................		(735,000)			367,500	367,500	0
Post-liquidation balances.......................		$ 0	$ 0	$ 0	$ 0	$ 0	$ 0

The journal entries for the transactions listed above are summarized in Exhibit 13.17 (the journal entry numbers correspond with the transaction numbers in Exhibit 13.16).

EXHIBIT 13.17	Journal Entries for the Liquidation of the Jack, Jill, and June Partnership

1	Cash...	1,000,000	
	Jack, capital...	82,500	
	Jill, capital..	82,500	
	June, capital..	110,000	
	Noncash assets...		1,275,000
	(to record the sale of the noncash assets and allocate loss to partners pursuant to their sharing ratio)		
2	Cash...	30,000	
	June, capital		30,000
	(to record capital contribution of June)		
3	Liabilities..	800,000	
	Cash		800,000
	(to record payment of creditors)		
4	Jack, capital...	367,500	
	Jill, capital..	367,500	
	Cash		735,000
	(to record distribution of cash to the partners)		

Liquidation with a Negative Capital Account and No Cash Contribution (Insolvent Partner)

We next consider a case in which June's Capital Account becomes negative following the sale of noncash assets as before, but now we assume that June is *insolvent*, meaning that she cannot make a capital contribution to offset the negative balance in her Capital Account. In this case, the negative Capital Account balance is allocated to the remaining partners in their sharing ratio excluding the partner whose Capital Account has become negative.

We assume, as in the last example, that the Jack, Jill, and June Partnership reports the balance sheet in Exhibit 13.18 immediately prior to liquidation:

EXHIBIT 13.18	Balance Sheet of the Jack, Jill, and June Partnership Immediately Prior to Liquidation		
Cash..................................	$ 505,000	Total liabilities..................	$ 800,000
Property, plant and equipment, (PPE)	1,275,000		
		Jack, capital...................	450,000
		Jill, capital....................	450,000
		June, capital..................	80,000
Total assets.........................	$1,780,000	Total liabilities and capital.........	$1,780,000

The liquidation process results in a negative Capital Account balance for June as before, but we now assume that June cannot make a capital contribution that is sufficient to bring her Capital Account to a zero balance prior to the distribution of cash to the remaining partners. The liquidation process involves the following steps:

1. All of the noncash assets with a net book value of $1,275,000 are sold for an assumed sale price of $1,000,000. The loss on the sale of **$275,000** is allocated to the partners according to the sharing ratio of 30%/30%/40%. This results in a negative balance in the Capital Account for June in the amount of $30,000.

2. We now assume that June is insolvent and cannot make a capital contribution of **$30,000**. Her deficit Capital Account must be allocated to the remaining partners in their sharing ratio which is now 50%/50% since Jack and Jill share in the profits and losses equally.

3. The balance in cash is now $1,505,000 following the sale of the noncash assets. It is $30,000 lower than in the previous example since no capital contribution has been made by June. The remaining cash is used to pay off all of the partnership's liabilities of $800,000, leaving a cash balance of $705,000.

4. The cash remaining after payment of creditors is distributed to the remaining two partners according to the balances in their respective Capital Accounts.

The liquidation schedule is summarized in Exhibit 13.19.

EXHIBIT 13.19	Liquidation of the Jack, Jill, and June Partnership						
						Capital Accounts	
Debit (Credit)		**Cash**	**Noncash Assets**	**Liabilities**	**Jack**	**Jill**	**June**
	Capital account, prior to liquidation...............	$ 505,000	$1,275,000	$(800,000)	$(450,000)	$(450,000)	$ (80,000)
1	Sale of noncash assets	1,000,000	(1,275,000)		82,500	82,500	110,000
		1,505,000	0	(800,000)	(367,500)	(367,500)	30,000
2	Allocation of deficit.............................				15,000	15,000	(30,000)
		1,505,000	0	(800,000)	(352,500)	(352,500)	0
3	Payment of creditors	(800,000)		800,000			
		705,000	0	0	(352,500)	(352,500)	0
4	Distribution to partners.........................	(705,000)			352,500	352,500	0
	Post-liquidation balances.......................	$ 0	$ 0	$ 0	$ 0	$ 0	$ 0

The journal entries for the transactions listed above are presented in Exhibit 13.20 (the journal entry numbers correspond with the transaction numbers in Exhibit 13.19).

EXHIBIT 13.20	Journal Entries for the Liquidation of the Jack, Jill, and June Partnership

1	Cash..	1,000,000	
	Jack, capital..	82,500	
	Jill, capital..	82,500	
	June, capital..	110,000	
	Noncash assets......................................		1,275,000
	(to record the sale of the noncash assets and allocate loss to partners pursuant to their sharing ratio)		
2	Jack, capital...	15,000	
	Jill, capital..	15,000	
	June, capital		30,000
	(to allocate deficit Capital Account of insolvent partner, June)		
3	Liabilities...	800,000	
	Cash		800,000
	(to record payment of creditors)		
4	Jack, capital...	352,500	
	Jill, capital..	352,500	
	Cash		705,000
	(to record distribution of cash to the partners)		

Liquidation with Two Negative Capital Accounts and No Cash Contributions (Insolvent Partners)
We will now consider a case in which both Jack *and* June's Capital Accounts are lower as a result of excessive drawings. As a result, when June's Capital Account becomes negative following the sale of noncash assets and is allocated to the remaining partners in their sharing ratio, Jack's Capital Account also becomes negative. We assume in this example that he is also insolvent. As a result, his negative Capital Account must be allocated to the remaining partner, Jill.

The Jack, Jill, and June Partnership reports the balance sheet in Exhibit 13.21 immediately prior to liquidation:

EXHIBIT 13.21	Balance Sheet of the Jack, Jill, and June Partnership Immediately Prior to Liquidation

Cash..............................	$ 145,000	Total liabilities...................	$ 800,000
Property, plant and equipment, (PPE)	1,275,000		
		Jack, capital.....................	90,000
		Jill, capital......................	450,000
		June, capital....................	80,000
Total assets.........................	$1,420,000	Total liabilities and capital..........	$1,420,000

The liquidation process results in a negative Capital Account balance for June as before that is allocated to the remaining partners, resulting in a negative Capital Account balance for Jack as well. The liquidation process involves the following steps:

1. All of the noncash assets with a net book value of $1,275,000 are sold for an assumed sale price of $1,000,000. The loss on the sale of **$275,000** is allocated to the partners according to the sharing ratio of 30%/30%/40%. This results in a negative balance in the Capital Account for June in the amount of $30,000.

2. Since June is insolvent and cannot make a capital contribution of **$30,000**, her deficit Capital Account must be allocated to the remaining partners in their sharing ratio which is now 50%/50% since Jack and Jill share in the profits and losses equally. This allocation results in a negative Capital Account balance for Jack as well. And, since he is also insolvent, his negative Capital Account balance must be allocated to the remaining partner.

3. The balance in cash is now $1,145,000 following the sale of the noncash assets, and it is used to pay off all of the partnership's liabilities of $800,000, leaving a cash balance of $345,000.

4. The cash remaining after payment of creditors is distributed to the remaining partner, Jill, and is equal to her Capital Account balance.

The liquidation schedule is summarized in Exhibit 13.22.

EXHIBIT 13.22   Liquidation Schedule for the Jack, Jill, and June Partnership

	Debit (Credit)	Cash	Noncash Assets	Liabilities	Capital Accounts Jack	Jill	June
	Capital account, prior to liquidation.	$ 145,000	$1,275,000	$(800,000)	$(90,000)	$(450,000)	$ (80,000)
1	Sale of noncash assets	1,000,000	(1,275,000)		82,500	82,500	110,000
		1,145,000	0	(800,000)	(7,500)	(367,500)	30,000
2a	Allocation of deficit.				15,000	15,000	(30,000)
		1,145,000	0	(800,000)	7,500	(352,500)	0
2b	Allocation of deficit.				(7,500)	7,500	0
		1,145,000	0	(800,000)	0	(345,000)	0
3	Payment of creditors	(800,000)		800,000			
		345,000	0	0	0	(345,000)	0
4	Distribution to partners.	(345,000)			0	345,000	0
	Post-liquidation balances.	$ 0	$ 0	$ 0	$ 0	$ 0	$ 0

The journal entries for the transactions listed above are illustrated in Exhibit 13.23 (the journal entry numbers correspond with the transaction numbers in Exhibit 13.22).

EXHIBIT 13.23   Journal Entries for the Liquidation of the Jack, Jill, and June Partnership

1	Cash.	1,000,000	
	Jack, capital.	82,500	
	Jill, capital.	82,500	
	June, capital.	110,000	
	Noncash assets.		1,275,000
	(to record the sale of the noncash assets and allocate loss to partners pursuant to their sharing ratio)		
2a	Jack, capital.	15,000	
	Jill, capital.	15,000	
	June, capital		30,000
	(to allocate deficit Capital Account of insolvent partner, June)		
2b	Jill, capital.	7,500	
	Jack, capital		7,500
	(to allocate deficit Capital Account of insolvent partner, Jack)		
3	Liabilities.	800,000	
	Cash		800,000
	(to record payment of creditors)		
4	Jill, capital.	345,000	
	Cash		345,000
	(to record distribution of cash to the remaining partner)		

Installment Liquidations   The liquidation of a partnership usually takes some time to accomplish. In a protracted liquidation, partners in need of cash may petition the partnership to distribute funds before the liquidation has been completed. In that case, the administrator of the liquidation must decide what amount of funds can be distributed, if any, assuming that the Partnership Agreement allows for such interim distributions.

Since the administrator overseeing the liquidation has a fiduciary responsibility to protect the interests of all of the partners, no payment of funds to partners can be made if there is any possibility that the remaining cash balance will be insufficient to pay all of the partnership's creditors. Consequently, the individual overseeing the liquidation must be very conservative in estimating the sale price of the noncash assets as well as in estimating future liquidation expenses. It is not uncommon to assume that *no* cash will be realized from the sale of assets and that liquidation expenses will be high. Given these conservative assumptions, the probability of the partnership running out of cash before all debts are paid is minimal.

To illustrate this process, assume that the Jack, Jill, and June Partnership reports the balance sheet in Exhibit 13.24 immediately prior to its liquidation:

EXHIBIT 13.24	Balance Sheet of the Jack, Jill, and June Partnership Immediately Prior to Liquidation		
Cash..............................	$ 900,000	Total liabilities....................	$ 800,000
Property, plant and equipment, (PPE) ...	1,025,000		
		Jack, capital......................	450,000
		Jill, capital.......................	450,000
		June, capital.....................	225,000
Total assets........................	$1,925,000	Total liabilities and capital...........	$1,925,000

The partners have requested a distribution of cash prior to the sale of the noncash assets. The safest assumption is that the sale of the noncash assets will yield no cash inflow. Consequently, the excess of cash over total liabilities ($100,000) less estimated liquidation expenses may be safely distributed. If the administrator estimates $75,000 of liquidation expenses, only $25,000 can be safely distributed at this time. However, this does not address the amounts that can be paid to any individual partner, nor does it identify the partners to whom we can distribute the available $25,000.

We propose that the clearest way to determine the payment that can safely be made to each partner, without breaching the administrator's fiduciary duty, is to prepare a **Safe Payment Schedule**. As illustrated in Exhibit 13.25, this schedule starts with the partners' pre-distribution Capital Account balances. The reason we start with the Capital Accounts is because (1) these balances are the best *initial* estimates of the amounts the partners can demand as liquidation payments and (2) creditors are implicitly provided with priority over the partners because the results of this schedule will only pay out what is left after the creditors are assumed to receive their payments.

EXHIBIT 13.25	Safe Payment Schedule			
		Jack (30%)	Jill (30%)	June (40%)
Pre-distribution capital balances		$(450,000)	$(450,000)	$(225,000)
	Assumed Losses & Costs			
Loss of noncash assets	$(1,025,000)			
Liquidation costs and fees	(75,000)			
Distribution of potential losses and costs	$(1,100,000)	330,000	330,000	440,000
Potential liquidation distributions..............		(120,000)	(120,000)	215,000
Assume insolvency.........................		107,500	107,500	(215,000)
Liquidation distributions that can be safely paid ..		$ 12,500	$ 12,500	$ 0

After the pre-distribution capital balances, the Safe Payment Schedule collects and allocates assumed future losses and costs that could potentially reduce or eliminate future liquidation distributions to the partners. The word, "assumed," is extremely important. None of the losses and costs included in the schedule has actually happened, yet. In fact, they may not happen at all. The whole point of the schedule is to incorporate conservative estimates of the items that can adversely affect future cash payments to all claimants. In this Safe Payment Schedule, we listed two potential assumed losses and costs: the conservative assumption that all noncash assets will be written off (i.e., no cash realized on their disposal) and the additional estimate of the future (i.e., yet un-accrued) partnership liquidation costs.

The total assumed losses and costs equal $1,100,000 and must be allocated to the three partners in relative proportion to their profit-and-loss-sharing ratios. This results in the (assumed) allocation of a **$330,000** loss to Jack, a $330,000 loss to Jill, and a **$440,000** loss to June, and in potential liquidation distributions of $120,000 to Jack, $120,000 to Jill, and a deficit of $(215,000) to June. Given that we are simply attempting to determine the amount that can be safely paid (i.e., without overpayment), we must assume that June is insolvent and cannot repay the assumed deficit. *We make this assumption even if June has the ability to make a capital contribution that can eliminate this possible deficit.* Unless the amount is actually received by the partnership, there is the possibility that June would never pay that obligation, thereby exposing the liquidation administrator to undue fiduciary risk.

If we assume that June is insolvent, then we allocate June's residual deficit to Jack and Jill in proportion to their relative profit-and-loss-sharing ratios. According to the original profit and loss sharing agreement, Jack and Jill each gets a residual share of 30% of the profits, which means that, without June, they will each receive 50% (i.e., 30%/(30% + 30%) of June's assumed allocated deficit. After allocating **$107,500** of June's deficit to each of their accounts, Jack and Jill will each be entitled to a partnership distribution of **$12,500**. This total distribution of $25,000 (i.e., $12,500 × 2) equals the total amount we estimated that we could safely pay the partners in aggregate. The benefit of the Safe Payment Schedule is that it allows us to determine the individual amounts that we can pay each partner without breaching our fiduciary duty.

There are two potential complicating factors that may further limit the amount of cash that can be safely distributed in advance of the sale of the noncash assets:

1. It may be difficult to estimate the liquidation expenses. These potential expenses include sales commissions, advertising costs, and other costs of sale, legal, accounting and other professional fees, ongoing overhead costs of the PPE assets (utilities, taxes, maintenance, protection, insurance, and the like), and so on.

2. There may be unreported liabilities that were not properly accrued as of the balance sheet date. These liabilities may not have been known and might not have been foreseen as of the balance sheet date (a lawsuit, for example).

The liquidation administrator must be mindful of potential cash outflows and limit the cash distribution accordingly to ensure that all creditors are paid prior to the final distribution of cash to the partners.

CHAPTER SUMMARY

The Uniform Partnership Act (1997), drafted by the National Conference of Commissioners on Uniform State Laws, provides a model for partnership governance that has been adopted by a majority of states. It defines a **partnership** as an association of two or more individuals to co-own and operate a business. Partnership agreements also typically contain the following general provisions:

a. **Partnership entity.** The partnership is a legal entity separate from its partners.

b. **Partners as agents of the partnership.** Each partner can act for the partnership.

c. **Partnership is liable for actions of partners.** A partnership is liable for loss as a result of a wrongful act or omission of a partner acting in the ordinary course of business of the partnership or with authority of the partnership.

d. **Joint and several liability of partners.** All partners are jointly and severally liable for all obligations of the partnership.

e. **Partner Capital Accounts.** Each partner has a Capital Account to represent his or her interest in the partnership.

f. **Transfer of partnership interest.** Each partner has the right to sell his or her partnership interest. The purchaser of such an interest does not have the right to participate in the management of the partnership, however, without the consent of the remaining partners.

When accounting for the formation of a partnership, although the total credit to the Capital Accounts must equal the fair value of the assets contributed less liabilities assumed, the Capital Account for an *individual* partner does not need to be equal to (or even proportional to) the value of the net assets he or she contributes. The initial values of the Capital Accounts are determined by the Partnership Agreement, and the partners can agree to any allocation they wish.

In recording the formation of the partnership, when partners are assigned balances that do not equal their capital contributions, the partners must answer the following two questions:

1. Does the disproportionate capital contribution by one or more partners provide evidence that the newly formed partnership possesses an unrecognized intangible asset?

2. Then, if the answer to question 1 is "yes," do the partners wish to recognize the intangible asset on the books of the partnership?

If the answer to *either* of the foregoing questions is "no," then the partnership will apply the Bonus Method to allocate the total partnership capital into the partners' individual Capital Accounts. If the answers to *both* of the foregoing questions are "yes," then the partnership will apply the Goodwill Method to allocate the total partnership capital into the partners' individual Capital Accounts. The biggest difference between the Bonus and Goodwill Methods is that the **Bonus Method** only records the identifiable net assets contributed by the partners in the partnership's total net asset. In contrast, under the **Goodwill Method**, the total partnership net assets include the identifiable net assets contributed by the partners (i.e., same amount as the Bonus Method), *plus* an additional amount assigned to Goodwill (or some other implied intangible asset). Under both methods, however, the goal of the partnership formation process is to allocate the total partnership capital among the partners forming the partnership.

Regarding accounting for changes in partnership ownership (realignment), a common practice when admitting a new partner to a partnership is to revalue the partnership net assets to fair value. When partnership net assets are revalued in anticipation of a realignment transaction, the resulting gains and losses accrue only to the partners who have an ownership interest in the entity during the period in which the net assets changed in value.

The admission of a new partner by purchasing the partnership interest from one or both partners requires that two questions be answered for a partnership to recognize previously unrecognized intangible assets during a partnership realignment:

1. Does the disproportionate capital contribution by one or more new partners provide evidence that the realigned partnership possesses an unrecognized intangible asset?

2. If the answer to question 1 is, "yes," do the partners wish to recognize the intangible asset on the books of the partnership?

If the answer to either of the foregoing questions is "no," then the partnership will simply reallocate (i.e., transfer) the selling partners' capital interest into the new partners' individual Capital Accounts. If the answers to *both* of the foregoing questions are "yes," then the partnership will apply the Goodwill Method to allocate the total partnership capital into the partners' individual Capital Accounts.

With regard to allocation of profit (loss), drawing accounts, and the capital account, all partnerships must allocate profit (loss) to the partners' Capital Accounts. The allocation procedure is typically called the **sharing ratio** and it is defined in the Partnership Agreement.

Salaries   The Uniform Partnership Act of 1997 states that "a partner is not entitled to remuneration for services performed for the partnership" (UPA, §401h). Consistent with this notion, Partnership Agreements sometimes allow for a salary payment as part of the profit allocation process.

Interest on the Capital Account   Some Partnership Agreements also allow for the allocation of interest on the average Capital Accounts of the partners. It is treated as a form of profit allocation like salary.

Allocation of Remaining Profit   The allocation of remaining profit to the partners is based on a sharing ratio that is described in the Partnership Agreement.

Statement of Capital Account Balances   The Statement of Partners' Capital begins with the Capital Accounts of the partners as of the beginning of the year. The partners' Capital Accounts increase by capital contributions, decrease by drawings, and increase as a result of allocated profit.

When a partnership dissolves, or fails, it must be liquidated just like any other business. Assets are sold, and the resulting cash is used to repay moneys owed to creditors. Any remaining cash then is distributed to the partners. The process of winding up a partnership is typically described in detail in the Partnership Agreement.

The accounting for a liquidation of a partnership is a four-step process:

1. Sell the assets and record the gain (loss) as increases (decreases) to the partners' Capital Accounts in their profit-sharing ratio, and subtract any receivables due from partners from their respective Capital Accounts.
2. Pay in full the debts of the partnership.
3. Eliminate any deficit Capital Account with a cash contribution from the partner (or by offsetting payables, if any, against the deficit balance). If the partner is insolvent, allocate the deficit to the remaining partners in their profit-sharing ratio (repeat this process if the allocation results in other Capital Accounts becoming negative).
4. Distribute the remaining cash to the partners for the remaining amount reported in their Capital Accounts.

The clearest way to determine the payment that can safely be made to each partner, without breaching the administrator's fiduciary duty, is to prepare a **Safe Payment Schedule**. This schedule starts with the partners' pre-distribution Capital Account balances. After the pre-distribution capital balances, the Safe Payment Schedule collects and allocates assumed future losses and costs that could potentially reduce or eliminate future liquidation distributions to the partners.

COMPREHENSIVE REVIEW

a. Assume that two individuals agree to form a partnership. Partner A is contributing an operating business that reports the following balance sheet:

Cash.	$ 30,000	Accounts payable.	$ 90,000
Receivables	60,000	Accrued liabilities	60,000
Inventories	120,000	Total liabilities.	$150,000
Total assets.	$210,000	Net assets	$ 60,000

Partner B is contributing cash of $150,000. The partners agree that the initial capital of the partnership should be shared equally. Use the Bonus Method to prepare the journal entry to record the capital contributions of the partners.

b. Assume that Partners A and B each report a Capital Account of $900,000. Partner C wants to join the partnership as an equal one-third partner. Because the partnership has been very profitable, Partners A and B require Partner C to contribute $1,800,000 in cash to the partnership in return for a one-third interest. Assume that Partners A and B share profits 60% and 40%, respectively, prior to the admission of Partner C. After admission of Partner C, Partners A and B retain their relative proportion of profit allocation after granting Partner C a 30% profit-allocation interest. Use the Bonus Method to record the journal entry on the books of the partnership to reflect the admission of Partner C.

c. Refer to the fact set in Part b. Assume that the partners believe that the payment by Partner C provides evidence of a previously unrecorded intangible asset in the partnership and the partners wish to record the intangible on the post-realignment partnership balance sheet. Use the Goodwill Method to record the journal entry on the books of the partnership to reflect the admission of Partner C.

d. Assume that there are three partners in a partnership, A, B, and C. Partner C provides services to the partnership and is entitled to a salary of $20,000. Assume that the partnership revenues less expenses (other than salary to Partner C) amount is $100,000. Finally, assume that the Partnership Agreement provides for a sharing ratio of 40%/40%/20% for Partners A, B, and C, respectively. Prepare a schedule for the allocation of profit to the partners.

e. Assume that there are three partners in a partnership, A, B, and C. Partners A and B each began the year with a capital account of $250,000. Partner C was admitted to the partnership during the year with a capital contribution of $150,000. The Partnership Agreement provides for a salary to Partner C of $25,000 and interest on the respective Capital Accounts of $12,500/$12,500/$5,625, respectively. During the year, the partners withdrew $10,000/$10,000/$5,000 and the allocation of profit was $57,750/$57,750/$28,875, respectively. Prepare the Statement of Partners' Capital for the year.

f. The ABC Partnership reports the following condensed balance sheet:

Cash.........................	$126,250	Liabilities.......................	$200,000
Noncash assets	318,750	Partner A, capital	112,500
		Partner B, capital	112,500
		Partner C, capital	20,000
Total assets..................	$445,000	Total liabilities and partner capital ...	$445,000

The partners wish to liquidate the partnership. The noncash assets are sold for $250,000 with the loss distributed to the partners in the ratio of 30%/30%/40% to partner A, B, and C, respectively. The liabilities are paid in full. Assume that any partners with a negative balance in their respective Capital Accounts are insolvent and, therefore, do not make any capital contribution to the partnership (i.e., remaining partners must absorb the negative Capital Account according to their profit sharing formula). Prepare a schedule detailing the liquidation of the assets, repayment of the liabilities, and distribution of the remaining cash to the partners.

The solution to this review problem can be found on pages 754–756.

QUESTIONS

1. What is the definition of a partnership?
2. How are partnerships taxed?
3. Since partnerships are typically private organizations, they are not required to issue financial statements that are in conformity with GAAP. What are some of the more prominent departures from GAAP?
4. What does the "joint and several liability of partners" mean?
5. What is a limited liability partnership (LLP)?
6. What is the purpose of partner Capital Accounts? How does the Capital Account change during the accounting period?
7. What are drawings? How are drawings different from salary?

Assignments with the ⓂⒷⒸ logo in the margin are available in *my*BusinessCourse. See the Preface of the book for details.

MULTIPLE CHOICE

LO1

AICPA
Adapted

8. **Legal entities**
    Which of the following business forms are distinct legal entities separate from their owners?
    1. Sole Proprietorships
    2. Partnerships
    3. Corporations
    a. 1, 2, and 3
    b. 1 and 2
    c. 2 and 3
    d. 1 and 3

LO2

AICPA
Adapted

9. **Recording contributed capital**
    At what amount should noncash property that is contributed to a partnership be credited to the contributing partner's capital account?
    a. Original cost of the assets to the contributing partner.
    b. Assessed valuation of the contributing partner's assets for property tax purposes.
    c. Tax basis of the contributing partner assets.
    d. Fair value of the contributing partner assets.

10. **Partnership agreement**

    The partnership agreement does not include one of the following:

    LO1
    AICPA
    Adapted

    a. Language relating to the formation, ongoing operation, and ultimate dissolution of the partnership.
    b. A requirement that all financial statements will be prepared in accordance with GAAP.
    c. Language relating to the way in which profit and loss is to be allocated to the partners' Capital Accounts.
    d. Language relating to whether the partners wish to recognize the intangible asset on the books of the partnership upon formation of the partnership.

11. **Revaluation of net assets**

    Which of the following is true with respect to the revaluation of net assets prior to partnership realignment?

    LO3
    AICPA
    Adapted

    a. When partnership net assets are revalued in anticipation of a realignment transaction, the resulting gains and losses accrue only to the partners who have an ownership interest in the entity during the period in which the net assets changed in value.
    b. When partnership net assets are revalued in anticipation of a realignment transaction, only the resulting gains accrue to the partners who have an ownership interest in the entity during the period in which the net assets changed in value. Losses are allocated in proportion to the relative balances of the Capital Accounts.
    c. Partnership net assets cannot be revalued as a result of partnership realignment.
    d. Partnership net assets can only be written down to net realizable value and cannot be increased if market value exceeds their book value.

12. **Recording profit and loss**

    Which of the following is true with respect to the recognition of partnership profit or loss?

    LO4
    AICPA
    Adapted

    a. Capital contributions are treated as income to the partnership.
    b. Withdrawals of capital from the partnership are treated as expenses.
    c. Salary paid to a partner is not treated as an expense.
    d. The net of revenues less expenses is always allocated to the partners in proportion to their relative Partner Capital accounts.

13. **Partnership dissolution**

    Which of the following is not true with respect to the dissolution of a partnership?

    LO5
    AICPA
    Adapted

    a. The assets of the partnership must be converted to cash used to pay the obligations to creditors, including partners who are creditors, and any remaining cash must be distributed to the partners in accordance with the profit-sharing ratio.
    b. Profits (losses) that result from the liquidation of the partnership assets must be credited (charged) to the partners' Capital Accounts.
    c. If a partner's Capital Account becomes negative as a result of the sales of assets, the partner is relieved of all liability with respect to the partnership.
    d. If a partner's Capital Account becomes negative as a result of the sales of assets, the partner must make a cash contribution to the partnership in an amount sufficient to bring the Capital Account to a zero balance.

14. **Partnership liquidation**

    Which of the following is not true with respect to the liquidation of a partnership?

    LO5
    AICPA
    Adapted

    a. It may be difficult to estimate the liquidation expenses, thereby limiting the amount of cash that can be safely distributed.
    b. There may be unreported liabilities that were not properly accrued as of the balance sheet date. The liquidation administrator must, therefore, be conservative in estimating the amount of cash that can be safely disbursed.
    c. It is not uncommon to assume that no cash will be realized from the sale of assets.
    d. All of the above are true.

15. **Partner capital accounts upon formation of partnership—Bonus Method**

    Assume that two individuals agree to form a partnership. Partner A is contributing an operating business that reports net assets of $25,000. Partner B is contributing cash of $35,000. The partners agree that the initial capital of the partnership should be shared equally. What will be the initial balance of the Capital Accounts of the partners assuming that the partners wish to employ the Bonus Method?

    LO2
    AICPA
    Adapted

	Partner A	Partner B
a.	$0	$0
b.	$25,000	$35,000
c.	$30,000	$30,000
d.	$70,000	$70,000

LO2

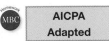

16. Partner capital accounts upon formation of partnership—Goodwill Method

Assume that two individuals agree to form a partnership. Partner A is contributing an operating business that reports net assets of $25,000. Partner B is contributing cash of $35,000. The partners agree that the initial capital of the partnership should be shared equally. What will be the initial balance of the Capital Accounts of the partners assuming that the partners wish to employ the Goodwill Method?

	Partner A	Partner B
a.	$25,000	$35,000
b.	$30,000	$30,000
c.	$35,000	$35,000
d.	$70,000	$70,000

LO4

17. Allocation of profit and loss

Assume that there are three partners in a partnership, A, B, and C. Partner C provides services to the partnership and is entitled to a salary of $60,000. Assume that the partnership revenues less expenses (other than salary to Partner C), amount is $300,000. Finally, assume that the Partnership Agreement provides for a sharing ratio of 40%/40%/20% for Partners A, B, and C, respectively. How much profit should be allocated to each partner?

	Partner A	Partner B	Partner C
a.	$100,000	$100,000	$100,000
b.	$120,000	$120,000	$60,000
c.	$120,000	$120,000	$120,000
d.	$96,000	$96,000	$108,000

LO3

18. Admission of new partner—Goodwill Method

Snickers and Opie are partners with capital balances of $90,000 and $50,000, respectively. They agree to admit Sparky as a partner with a 25% interest upon payment of $60,000. Assuming that the partners wish to recognize an intangible asset, what amount of goodwill should be reported?

a. $0

b. $10,000

c. $15,000

d. $40,000

LO3

19. Admission of new partner—Bonus Method

Assume the same fact set as in Multiple Choice question 18 and assume that the partners do not wish to recognize an intangible asset. What total amount should be recorded as a bonus to Snickers and Opie?

a. $0

b. $10,000

c. $15,000

d. $40,000

LO4

20. Allocation of profit and loss

Partners A and B report average capital balances of $320,000 and $200,000 for the year. The partnership agreement provides for interest at the rate of 10% on the average capital balance and an equal division of the remaining profit of $8,000 for the year. By what amount should B's capital account change for the year?

a. $4,000 decrease

b. $4,000 increase

c. $24,000 decrease

d. $24,000 increase

EXERCISES

21. Formation of partnership
LO2

Assume that two individuals agree to form a partnership. Partner A is contributing an operating business that reports the following balance sheet:

Cash..........................	$10,000	Accounts payable..................	$30,000
Receivables	20,000	Accrued liabilities	20,000
Inventories	40,000	Total liabilities....................	$50,000
Total assets.....................	$70,000	Net assets	$20,000

Partner B is contributing cash of $50,000. The partners agree that the initial capital of the partnership should be shared equally. Prepare the journal entry to record the capital contributions of the partners using both the Bonus Method and the Goodwill Method.

22. Change of partners
LO3

Assume that Partners A and B each report a Capital Account of $300,000. Partner A wants to retire and sell her partnership interest to Partner C for $400,000. Partner B agrees to the sale and admission of Partner C into the partnership at an equal ownership percentage. Record the journal entry on the books of the partnership to reflect the admission of Partner C using both the Bonus Method and the Goodwill Method.

23. Admission of new partner
LO3

Assume that Partners A and B each report a Capital Account of $300,000. Partner C wants to join the partnership as an equal one-third partner in consideration for a combined payment to Partners A and B of $200,000. Record the journal entry on the books of the partnership to reflect the admission of Partner C.

24. Admission of new partner
LO3

Assume that Partners A and B each report a Capital Account of $300,000. Partner C wants to join the partnership as an equal one-third partner in consideration for a payment to the partnership of $200,000 cash and a parcel of land valued at $100,000. Record the journal entry on the books of the partnership to reflect the admission of Partner C.

25. Admission of new partner—Bonus Method
LO3

Assume that Partners A and B each report a Capital Account of $300,000. Partner C wants to join the partnership as an equal one-third partner. Because the partnership has been very profitable, Partners A and B require Partner C to contribute $600,000 in cash to the partnership in return for a one-third interest. Assume that Partners A and B share profits 60% and 40%, respectively, prior to the admission of Partner C. After admission of Partner C, Partners A and B retain their relative proportion of profit allocation after granting Partner C a 30% profit-allocation interest. Use the Bonus Method to record the journal entry on the books of the partnership to reflect the admission of Partner C.

26. Admission of new partner—Goodwill Method
LO3

Refer to the fact set in Exercise 25. Assume that the partners believe that the payment by Partner C provides evidence of a previously unrecorded intangible asset in the partnership and the partners wish to record the intangible on the post-realignment partnership balance sheet. Use the Goodwill Method to record the journal entry on the books of the partnership to reflect the admission of Partner C.

27. Admission of new partner—Revaluation
LO3

Assume that Partners A and B have Capital Accounts equal to $400,000 and $200,000, respectively. Partner C wants to join the partnership as one-third partner. Partner C contributes $850,000 in cash to the partnership in return for a one-third interest. Prior to the admission of Partner C, Partners A and B wish to revalue the long-term assets of the partnership. They obtain an appraisal of the land and building that indicates a current value of $1 million. The land and building are currently reported on the partnership balance sheet at $200,000. Record the journal entry on the books of the partnership to reflect the revaluation of the land and building and the admission of Partner C with a capital contribution of $850,000. Assume that despite the evidence of a previously unrecognized intangible asset, the partners do not wish to record the intangible asset.

28. Admission of new partner—Goodwill Method
LO3

Assume that the partnership's balance sheet reflects Partner Capital of $200,000 and $300,000, respectively, for Partner A and Partner B immediately prior to the admission of Partner C. Partner C is contributing $400,000 for a one-third ownership interest. Prepare the journal entry to admit Partner C using the Goodwill Method.

LO4 **29. Allocation of profit to partners**

Assume that there are three partners in a partnership, A, B, and C. Partner C provides services to the partnership and is entitled to a salary of $200,000. Assume that the partnership revenues less expenses (other than salary to Partner C) amount is $500,000. Finally, assume that the Partnership Agreement provides for a sharing ratio of 40%/40%/20% for Partners A, B, and C, respectively. Prepare a schedule for the allocation of profit to the partners.

LO4 **30. Allocation of interest on capital accounts and profit to partners**

Assume that there are three partners in a partnership, A, B, and C. Partner C provides services to the partnership and is entitled to a salary of $50,000. In addition, assume that the Partnership Agreement provides for an interest allocation of 5% based on the weighted-average Capital Account balance during the year. There is a balance in each Capital Account for Partners A and B of $500,000 for the full year. Partner C, however, was admitted to the partnership for an initial capital contribution of $300,000 on March 31. Finally, assume that the partnership revenues less expenses (other than salary to Partner C and interest on capital balances) are $400,000, and that the Partnership Agreement provides for a sharing ratio of 40%/40%/20% for Partners A, B, and C, respectively. Prepare a schedule for the allocation of profit to the partners.

LO4 **31. Prepare statement of partners capital**

Assume that there are three partners in a partnership, A, B, and C. Partners A and B each began the year with a capital account of $500,000. Partner C was admitted to the partnership during the year with a capital contribution of $300,000. The Partnership Agreement provides for a salary to Partner C of $50,000 and interest on the respective Capital Accounts of $25,000/$25,000/$11,250, respectively. During the year, the partners withdrew $20,000/$20,000/$10,000 and the allocation of profit was $115,500/$115,500/$57,750, respectively. Prepare the Statement of Partners' Capital for the year.

PROBLEMS

LO5 **32. Liquidation schedule—positive capital accounts**

The ABC Partnership reports the following condensed balance sheet:

Cash	$200,000	Liabilities	$300,000
Noncash assets	600,000	Partner A, capital	125,000
		Partner B, capital	125,000
		Partner C, capital	250,000
Total assets	$800,000	Total liabilities and partner capital	$800,000

The partners wish to liquidate the partnership. The noncash assets are sold for $450,000 with the loss distributed to the partners in the ratio of 30%/30%/40% to partner A, B, and C, respectively. The liabilities are paid in full. Prepare a schedule detailing the liquidation of the assets, repayment of the liabilities, and distribution of the remaining cash to the partners.

LO5 **33. Liquidation schedule—one negative capital account with capital contribution**

The ABC Partnership reports the following condensed balance sheet:

Cash	$ 580,000	Liabilities	$ 800,000
Noncash assets	1,200,000	Partner A, capital	450,000
		Partner B, capital	450,000
		Partner C, capital	80,000
Total assets	$1,780,000	Total liabilities and partner capital	$1,780,000

The partners wish to liquidate the partnership. The noncash assets are sold for $900,000 with the loss distributed to the partners in the ratio of 30%/30%/40% to partner A, B, and C, respectively. The liabilities are paid in full. Partners make any capital contribution that is necessary to offset a negative balance in their respective Capital Accounts. Prepare a schedule detailing the liquidation of the assets, repayment of the liabilities, and distribution of the remaining cash to the partners.

34. Liquidation schedule—one negative capital account with *no* capital contribution

The ABC Partnership reports the following condensed balance sheet:

LO5

Cash.........................	$ 580,000	Liabilities.......................	$ 800,000
Noncash assets	1,200,000	Partner A, capital	450,000
		Partner B, capital	450,000
		Partner C, capital	80,000
Total assets.................	$1,780,000	Total liabilities and partner capital	$1,780,000

The partners wish to liquidate the partnership. The noncash assets are sold for $900,000 with the loss distributed to the partners in the ratio of 30%/30%/40% to partner A, B, and C, respectively. The liabilities are paid in full. Assume that any partners with a negative balance in their respective Capital Accounts are insolvent and, therefore, do *not* make any capital contribution to the partnership (i.e., remaining partners must absorb the negative Capital Account according to their profit sharing formula). Prepare a schedule detailing the liquidation of the assets, repayment of the liabilities, and distribution of the remaining cash to the partners.

35. Liquidation schedule—two negative capital accounts with *no* capital contribution

The ABC Partnership reports the following condensed balance sheet:

LO5

Cash.........................	$ 315,000	Liabilities.......................	$800,000
Noncash assets	900,000	Partner A, capital	65,000
		Partner B, capital	300,000
		Partner C, capital	50,000
Total assets.................	$1,215,000	Total liabilities and partner capital	$1,215,000

The partners wish to liquidate the partnership. The noncash assets are sold for $700,000 with the loss distributed to the partners in the ratio of 30%/30%/40% to partner A, B, and C, respectively. The liabilities are paid in full. Assume that any partners with a negative balance in their respective Capital Accounts are insolvent and, therefore, do *not* make any capital contribution to the partnership (i.e., remaining partners must absorb the negative Capital Account according to their profit sharing formula). Prepare a schedule detailing the liquidation of the assets, repayment of the liabilities and distribution of the remaining cash to the partners.

36. Liquidation schedule—safe payment schedule

On the date the partners in the ABCD Partnership decided to dissolve their partnership, the partners had the following pre-liquidation Capital Account balances:

LO5

Partner A, capital	$28,000
Partner B, capital	41,000
Partner C, capital	18,000
Partner D, capital	12,000

A, B, C and D share residual profits and losses in a 4:3:2:1 ratio. Accrued liabilities at the date of dissolution total $10,000 and noncash assets equal $105,000. During the first month of liquidation, assets having a book value of $55,000 were sold for $31,000. During the second month, assets having a book value of $32,000 were sold for $28,000. During the third month, the remaining unsold assets were determined to be worthless. The partners receive the maximum allowable payment at the end of each month. Prepare an installment liquidation schedule along with the necessary, supporting Safe Payment Schedules.

TOPIC REVIEW

Solution

a. Following the cash contribution, the total capital accounts (and total partnership net assets) are $400,000 (i.e., $100,000 + $100,000 + $200,000). The 25% capital interest means that Partner C will receive $100,000 of capital credit in exchange for the $200,000 contribution. Under the Bonus Method, we assume that Partner C is paying a $100,000 premium (i.e., $200,000 contribution by C, minus the $100,000 capital credit awarded to C) over book value in order to join the partnership, and the pre-existing partners receive that premium as a bonus. This $100,000 bonus is allocated according to the partners' profit-and-loss sharing ratio. This means Partner A will receive $60,000 (i.e., 60%) of capital credit for the bonus "paid" by Partner C, and Partner B will receive the remaining $40,000 (i.e., 40%). The journal entry to record this transaction is as follows:

Cash	200,000	
A, Capital		60,000
B, Capital		40,000
C, Capital		100,000
(to record the purchase of a 25% partnership interest by C for $200,000)		

b. Partner C contributed $200,000 in cash for a 25% capital interest, while the existing partners (i.e., Partners A and B, together) "contributed" $200,000 (i.e., $100,000 + $100,000) for a 75% post-realignment capital interest. If we believe these to be "arm's-length" transactions, then the total implied value of the new partnership is $800,000 (i.e., $200,000 contribution by Partner C ÷ 25%).

    The Goodwill implied by Partner C's capital contribution is equal to $400,000, which equals the total fair value of the partnership entity (i.e., $800,000) minus the fair value of the identifiable net assets of the partnership in the amount of $400,000 (equals the existing capital of $200,000 and the $200,000 of cash received by the partnership from Partner C). This Goodwill will be allocated to the existing partners in proportion to their relative profit and loss ratios.   The journal entry to record this transaction is as follows:

Cash	200,000	
Goodwill	400,000	
A, Capital		240,000
B, Capital		160,000
C, Capital		200,000
(to record the purchase of a 25% partnership interest by C for $200,000)		

COMPREHENSIVE REVIEW SOLUTION

a.	Cash	180,000	
	Receivables	60,000	
	Inventories	120,000	
	Accounts payable		90,000
	Accrued liabilities		60,000
	A, Capital		105,000
	B, Capital		105,000
	(to record initial capital contribution to the Partnership using the Bonus Method)		

b. Following the cash contribution, the total capital accounts (and total partnership net assets) are $3,600,000 (i.e., $900,000 + $900,000 + $1,800,000). The 1/3 capital interest means that Partner C will receive $1,200,000 of capital credit in exchange for the $1,800,000 contribution. Under the Bonus Method, we assume that Partner C is paying a $600,000 premium (i.e., $1,800,000 contribution by C, minus the $1,200,000 capital credit awarded to C) over book value in order to join the partnership, and the preexisting partners receive that premium as a bonus. This $600,000 bonus is allocated according to the partners' profit-and-loss sharing ratio. This means Partner A will receive $360,000 (i.e., 60%) of capital credit for the bonus "paid" by Partner C, and Partner B will receive the remaining $240,000 (i.e., 40%). The journal entry to record this transaction is as follows:

Cash	1,800,000	
A, Capital...		360,000
B, Capital...		240,000
C, Capital...		1,200,000
(to record the purchase of a 1/3 partnership interest by C for $1,800,000)		

c. Partner C contributed $1,800,000 in cash for a 1/3 capital interest, while the existing partners (i.e., Partners A and B, together) "contributed" $1,800,000 (i.e., $900,000 + $900,000) for a 2/3 post-realignment capital interest. If we believe these to be "arm's length" transactions, then the total implied value of the new partnership is $5,400,000 (i.e., $1,800,000 contribution by Partner C ÷ 1/3).

   The Goodwill implied by Partner C's capital contribution is equal to $1,800,000, which equals the total fair value of the partnership entity (i.e., $5,400,000) minus the fair value of the identifiable net assets of the partnership in the amount of $3,600,000 (equals the existing capital of $1,800,000 and the $1,800,000 of cash received by the partnership from Partner C). This Goodwill will be allocated to the existing partners in proportion to their relative profit and loss ratios. The journal entry to record this transaction is as follows:

Cash	1,800,000	
Goodwill	1,800,000	
A, Capital...		1,080,000
B, Capital...		720,000
C, Capital...		1,800,000
(to record the purchase of a 1/3 partnership interest by C for $1,800,000)		

d.

	A	B	C	Total Allocation	Remaining
Excess of revenues over expenses					$100,000
Salary..............................			$20,000	$ 20,000	80,000
Allocation of residual profit.............	$32,000	$32,000	16,000	80,000	—
Total allocation	$32,000	$32,000	$36,000	$100,000	

e.

	Partners			
	A	B	C	Total
Capital account, beginning of year	$250,000	$250,000	$ 0	$500,000
Capital contributions	0	0	150,000	150,000
Withdrawals	(10,000)	(10,000)	(5,000)	(25,000)
Salary			25,000	25,000
Interest	12,500	12,500	5,625	30,625
Allocation of remaining profit	57,750	57,750	28,875	144,375
Capital account, end of year	$310,250	$310,250	$204,500	$825,000

f.

Debit (Credit)	Cash	Noncash Assets	Liabilities	Partners' Capital Accounts 30% A	30% B	40% C
Balance prior to liquidation . . .	$126,250	$318,750	$(200,000)	$(112,500)	$(112,500)	$(20,000)
Sale of noncash assets	250,000	(318,750)		20,625	20,625	27,500
	376,250	0	(200,000)	(91,875)	(91,875)	7,500
Allocation of deficit				3,750	3,750	(7,500)
	376,250	0	(200,000)	(88,125)	(88,125)	0
Payment of creditors	(200,000)		200,000			
	176,250	0	0	(88,125)	(88,125)	0
Distribution to partners	(176,250)			88,125	88,125	0
Post-liquidation balances	$ 0	$ 0	$ 0	$ 0	$ 0	$ 0

Index

References to exhibits are followed by the letter "e", and footnote references include the letter "n".

757